FOR REFERENCE

Do Not Take From This Room

Ben Hodges

THEATRE WORLD®

VOLUME 65 / 2008–2009

John Willis, Editor Emeritus

THEATRE WORLD®
Volume 65
Copyright © 2009 by Ben Hodges

Published in 2009 by Applause Theatre & Cinema Books
An Imprint of Hal Leonard Corporation
7777 West Bluemound Road
Milwaukee, WI 53213

Trade Book Division Editorial Offices
19 West 21st Street, New York, NY 10010

Printed in the United States of America
Book design by Tony Meisel

ISBN 978–1-4234–7369–5
ISSN 1088–4564

www.applausepub.com

To John A. Willis, Editor Emeritus of *Theatre World*

Originally hired for .45 cents an hour, as a typist by *Theatre World* founders Daniel Blum and Norman McDonald, Mr. Willis assumed editorship of both *Theatre World* and *Screen World* upon the death of Mr. Blum in 1964. (Norman McDonald departed to Los Angeles and the Dorothy Chandler Pavilion some years earlier.)

Mr. Willis was editor in chief of both *Theatre World*, the definitive annual pictorial and statistical record of the American theatre, and its sister volume, *Screen World*, the definitive annual pictorial and statistical record of each domestic and international theatre season, for over forty years. He served as editor of *Dance World* from 1966-1979. He additionally served as an assistant editor to Daniel Blum on *A Pictorial History of Opera in America, A Pictorial History of the Silent Screen, A Pictorial History of the Talkies, A Pictorial History of Television, A Pictorial Treasury of Opera in America,* and *A Pictorial History of the American Theatre 1860-1960* (which editions thereof Mr. Willis himself updated in 1965, 1970, 1976, 1980, and 1985, respectively. With an unmatched record of scholarship of twentieth century theatre and film, as well as having accumulated a private archive without equal, Mr. Willis will be considered largely responsible for the record that will long exist of American theatre and international and domestic film in our time.

Mr. Willis additionally and personally administrated the Theatre World Awards for Outstanding Broadway and Off-Broadway Debuts for nearly forty years, overseeing the organization's full incorporation into a 501 (c) 3 nonprofit organization in 1997. Having been personally responsible for the recognition of performing talents that in many cases would gone otherwise unrecognized, Mr. Willis is without peer in his dedication and influence in the bolstering careers of performers for nearly a half-century.

With an unofficial record of having attending more New York theatrical productions than anyone alive or dead and having attended the theatre religiously between five and eight times a week, fifty weeks a year (with only two weeks off for vacation) for over forty years, Mr. Willis only falls short of a Guinness Book of World Records title for failing to keep the one respective souvenir that ironically he did not consider quite so important—ticket stubs.

On behalf of *Theatre World* and/or *Screen World*, Mr. Willis has received a Special 2001 Tony Honor for Excellence in the Theatre, a 2003 Broadway Theatre Institute Lifetime Achievement Award, a 1994 Special Drama Desk Award, a 1993 Outstanding Special Lucille Lortel Award, and the 1998 National Board of Review William K. Everson Award. He additionally has received awards from Marquis Who's Who Publications Board and Milligan College. He has also served on the nominating committees for the Tony Awards and the national board of the University of Tennessee Clarence Brown Theatre.

Originally from Morristown, Tennessee, he holds an undergraduate degree in English from Milligan College, and has done graduate work at Harvard University, Indiana University, and the University of Tennessee.

Retired from the New York Public School System with over twenty years of service as an English teacher, he is also a veteran of the U.S. Navy in the South Pacific during W.W. II., and has been a member of Actors Equity Association for over fifty years.

Now ninety-three years of age and enjoying a comfortable retirement at his home on Riverside Drive in New York City, Mr. Willis still enjoys clipping reviews and obituaries daily and attending the theatre from time to time.

Most especially, he treasures all 500 + Theatre World Award winners, all of whom he considers to be his "children."

Mr. Willis, you are a national treasure, and a very well kept one indeed.

PAST EDITORS	Daniel Blum (1945–1963)
	John Willis (1963–2007)
EDITOR EMERITUS	John Willis
EDITOR IN CHIEF	Ben Hodges (1998–present)
ASSOCIATE EDITOR	Scott Denny (2005-present)
ASSOCIATE REGIONAL EDITOR	Carol Delawder Dawson
CONTRIBUTING REGIONAL EDITOR	Nicole Estvanik Taylor
CONTRIBUTING OFF-OFF BROADWAY EDITOR	Shay Gines
ASSISTANT EDITORS	Amanda Flynn
	Rob Rokicki
STAFF PHOTOGRAPHERS	Rommel "Raj" Autencio, Henry Grossman, Walter McBride, Aubrey Rueben, Michael Riordan, Laura Viade, Michael Viade, Jack Williams

Theatre World would like to extend a very special thank you to all the New York and regional press agents, theatre marketing departments, and theatre photographers for their constant and steadfast support of this publication as well as for the endless resources that they provide to the editorial staff. Our gratitude is eternally extended to Joan Marcus, Carol Rosegg, Paul Kolnik, Richard Termine, Gerry Goodstein, Michael Daniel, Audrey Ross, John Barlow, Carol Fineman, Michael Hartman, Bethany Larson, Ryan Ratelle, Dennis Crowley, Kevin Roebak, Wayne Wolf, Leslie Baden, Matt Stapleton, Michelle Bergmann, Tom D'Ambrosio, Bill Evans, Jim Randolph, Chris Boneau, Jackie Green, Juliana Hannett, Allison Houseworth, Jessica Johnson, Shanna Marcus, Christine Olver, Joe Perrotta, Matt Polk, Matt Ross, Heath Schwartz, Susanne Tighe, Adrian Bryan-Brown, Jim Byck, Aaron Meier, Brett Singer, Bruce Cohen, Peter Cromarty, David Gersten, Ellen Jacobs, Karen Greco, Helene Davis, Irene Gandy, Jim Baldassare, Jonathan Slaff, Scott Klein, D.J. Martin, Bret Oberman, Keith Sherman, Glenna Freedman, Kevin McAnarney, Max Eisen, Beck Lee, Dan Fortune, Miller Wright, Marissa Altamura, Philip Carrubba, Jon Dimond, Richard Hillman, Rick Miramontez, Tony Origlio, Barbara Carroll, Philip Rinaldi, Timothy Haskell, Carrie Friedman, Richard Kornberg, Don Summa, Billy Zavelson, Howard Rubenstein, Robert Lasko, Sam Rudy, Bill Coyle, Adrianna Douzous, Jeremy Shaffer, Dan Demello, Shirley Herz, Ron Lasko, Gary Springer, Joe Trentacosta, Stephen Sunderlin, Susan L. Schulman, Judy Jacksina, Bridget Klapinski, Darron Molovinsky, Pete Sanders, Arlene Kriv, Sam Neuman, Candi Adams, Michael Borowski, Marc Thibodeau, Michael Portantiere, and Shayne Miller.

Thanks also to John Cerullo, executive vice president of Hal Leonard Corporation, Beth Allen, Epitacio Arganza; Jason Baruch and Sendroff and Baruch LLP; Seth Barrish, Lee Brock, Eric Paeper, and The Barrow Group Theater Company/The Barrow Group School; Jed Bernstein and the Commercial Theater Institute; Wayne Besen and Truth Wins Out; Nicole Boyd; Helen Guditis and the Broadway Theater Museum; Fred Cantor; Fred Caruso; Ann Cason and East Tennessee Life; Michael Che; Jason Cicci, Monday Morning Productions, and Summer Stage New York; Richard Cohen; Sue Cosson; Susan Cosson; Mart Crowley; Robert Dean Davis; Carol and Nick Dawson; Bob and Brenda Denny; Jamie deRoy; Tim Deak; Diane Dixon; Craig Dudley; Sherry Eaker; Ben Feldman and Beigelman, Feldman, and Associates PC, Emily Feldman; David Fritz; Christine and David Grimsby; the estates of the late Charles J. Grant Jr. and Zan Van Antwerp; Jason Hadzinikalov; Brad Hampton; Laura and Tommy Hanson; Richard M. Henderson Sr. and Patricia Lynn Henderson; Al and Sherry Hodges; Charlie and Phyllis Hurt; Leonard Jacobs; Gretchen, Aaron, Eli, and Max Kerr; Jane, Lynn, and Kris Kircher; Andrew Kirtzman, Louis Del Vecchio, and The Madison Fire Island Pines; David Lowry; Joaquin Matias; Barry Monush and Screen World; Howard Sherman and the American Theatre Wing; Jason Bowcutt, Shay Gines, Nick Micozzi, and the staff and respective voting committees of the New York Innovative Theatre Awards; Barbara O'Malley and John Ford; Petie Dodrill, Craig Johnson, Rob Johnson, Dennis Romer, Katie Robbins, Dean Jo Ann VanSant, Ed Vaughan, the late Dr. Charles O. Dodrill and the staff of Otterbein College/Otterbein College Department of Theatre and Dance, P.J. Owen; William Craver and Paradigm; Hugo Uys and the staff of Paris Commune; John Philip; David Plank; Angie and Drew Powell; Kay Radtke; Carolyn, David, Glenna, and Jonas Rapp; Ric Wanetik, David Hagans, Steve Gelston, Yvonne Ghareeb; Kim Jackson, Mollie Levin, and Ricochet LLC; Jetaun Dobbs, Sydney Davalos, Todd Haimes, and Roundabout Theatre Company; Kate Rushing; Bill Schaap; Emmanuel Serrano; Hannah Richman Slosberg and Jason Slosberg; Charlotte St. Martin and the League of American Theatres and Producers; Susan Stoller; Henry Grossman, Lucy Nathanson, Michael Riordan, John Sala, Mark Snyder, Martha Swope; Renée Isely Tobin and Bob, Kate, Eric, Laura, Anna, and Foster Tobin; Bob Ost and Theater Resources Unlimited Inc.; Laura Viade, Michael Viade, Zachary Kleinsmith, Katie Love, Rachel Werbel, and the staff of Theatre World and the John Willis Theatre World/Screen World Archive; Tom Lynch, Kati Meister, Erin Oestreich, Scott Denny, Barry Keating, Leigh Giroux, and the board of directors of The Theatre World Awards Inc.; Harry Haun, Howard Kissel, Matthew Murray, Frank Scheck, Michael Sommers, Doug Watt, Linda Winer, and the voting committee of The Theatre World Awards Inc.; Jack Williams, Barbara Dewey, and the staff of the University of Tennessee at Knoxville; Wilson Valentin; Kathie Packer and the estate of the late Frederic B. Vogel; Sarah Willis; George Wilson; Shane and Bill Wolters; and Doug Wright.

Contents

Theatre WORLD

1944-45 SEASON

The inside cover featuring Laurette Taylor as Amanda Wingfield in Tennessee Williams' The Glass Menagerie *from the first volume of* Theatre World 1944–1945

Introduction

Theatre World, under former editor John Willis, carried seasonal reviews of the Broadway season at the beginning of each publication, ceasing to do so in the mid-1990s. Beginning with this volume—the most current *Theatre World* publication ever released—we happily reinstitute this tradition. Seasonal introductions by our associate and contributing editors also appear at the beginning of each of the Off-Off-Broadway and regional theatre sections, respectively. It is our hope that the reintroduction of this element of the publication will continue to expand our reputation as the most complete annual pictorial and statistical record of the American theatre season, as well as place the voluminous amount of information collected within these pages in the appropriate and larger context within the respective areas of American theatre that are chronicled here.

To be clear, the editors of this publication are in the business of chronicling the entire season of American of theatre in all of its major venues. We are not critics, and these reviews are by design more overviews of highlights and explanations of the news in each respective area than critical commentary. Theatre criticism as it has been known throughout most of the twentieth century is—rightly or wrongly—losing relevance in the contemporary media age. And the landscape of the media of communication in the theatre industry, as well as all others, is changing faster than the ability of those dependent on it to keep up with it. The editors of this publication would not this point to wade into the pool of traditional theatre criticism which, if able to survive the media transition, will most likely do so with no noticeable resemblance to that of the past 100 years.

For our part, this publication has always been a labor of love by those involved with it, dependent on nothing more than a few enterprising people who love the theatre enough to chronicle all of it—the hits, the misses, and everything in between, each and every year. As such, it has survived and will continue to survive this media transition, and in whatever forms eventually come out on top, or are most relevant, because we are motivated in this endeavor only by our mission of maintaining the most complete annual pictorial and statistical record of the American theatre; *Theatre World* is a tool, reference, and record for students, historians, industry professionals, and theatre fans worldwide. We will continue to pursue that mission, whatever publishing or media challenges or opportunities lie ahead, without critical comment proper on the productions which we cover.

I would especially like to recognize the continued contribution of our estimable associate editor, Robert Scott Denny, who truthfully takes on the bulk of the onus of the day-to-day compilation of this publication. His enthusiasm is contagious and his thoroughness is admirable. In addition, we welcome several new contributing editors to this publication, including Off-Off-Broadway contributing editor Shay Gines, a founder and current executive director of the New York Innovative Theatre Awards, celebrating excellence Off-Off-Broadway. (There are,

of course, more productions produced Off-Off-Broadway than on Broadway and Off-Broadway combined.); regional theatre contributing editor Nivole Estvanik Taylor, current managing editor of *American Theatre;* and assistant editors, actress Amanda Flynn and actor/composer Robert Rokicki, who continue the tradition of artists who value this publication enough to take time from the pursuit of their artistic careers to help all of the editors, as needed, in every area of its compilation.

We all continue to try to work to expand the visibility and viability of this series, most notably with this volume being released sooner after the close of the theatre season than ever before in our sixty-five year history. It is our hope in so doing to continue to spread the word about the continued vibrancy of American theatre as well as our efforts to accurately and completely chronicle it. We continue to meticulously research the Off and Off-Off-Broadway theatre scene to make sure that productions are appropriately delineated by the appropriate classifications according to the Actors Equity classifications of either an Off or Off-Broadway contract—rather than the commonly held belief that this distinction is drawn simply by the size of the performance space. We continue to compile the most complete regional theatre season information from *all* theatres that submit to our publication, chronicling all of the respective theatres' productions during that season, with many accompanying photographs. We continue to compile the most complete theatrical awards section of the annual theatre season. We continue to highlight the Theatre World Awards, the oldest awards given for Broadway and Off-Broadway debut performances, once administrated solely by the editors of this publication and now a fully incorporated 501 (c) 3 nonprofit organization, but still and forever associated with *Theatre World*. We continue to compile our Broadway and Off-Broadway historical longest runs sections with accompanying photographs. And we continue to compile the most complete annual obituary entries of the annual theatre season, also with many accompanying photographs.

Finally, we continue to rely on our partners in this publication—the New York press agents and publicists, as well as New York and regional theatrical photographers, who continue to provide us gratis with the photographs and publicity information that enable us to provide this record. It is no small accomplishment to have amassed the most complete record of the American theatre of the past sixty-five years, as well as one of the most important collections of photographs and other theatre information from American theatre as exists anywhere on the planet. It is because of the dedication, appreciation, and permission of the New York theatre community, which understands the importance of our publication to the history of the theatre that we are allowed to continue this publication for posterity, and for this the editors all extend our eternal gratitude.

– Ben Hodges, Editor in Chief

Allie Trimm, Aaron Simon Gross and Graham Phillips in 13. *Opened at the Bernard B. Jacobs Theatre October 5, 2008 (photo by Joan Marcus)*

Will Ferrell in You're Welcome America. A Final Night with George W Bush. *Opened at the Cort Theatre February 5, 2009 (photo by Robert J. Saferstein)*

The Green Clowns of Slava's Snowshow. *Opened at the Helen Hayes Theatre December 7, 2008 (photo by Veronique Vial)*

Jennifer Mudge and Matthew Broderick in the Roundabout Theatre Company production of The Philanthropist. *Opened at the American Airlines Theatre April 26, 2009 (photo by Joan Marcus)*

Michael McCarty and Jan Maxwell in the Manhattan Theatre Club production of To Be or Not To Be. *Opened at the Samuel J. Friedman Theatre October 14, 2008 (photo by Joan Marcus)*

Haley Joel Osment and John Leguizamo in American Buffalo. *Opened at the Belasco Theatre November 17, 2008 (photo by Joan Marcus)*

BROADWAY
June 1, 2008–May 31, 2009

Top: *John Lithgow, Dianne Wiest, Patrick Wilson and Katie Holmes in* All My Sons. *Opened at the Gerald Schoenfeld Theatre October 16, 2008 (photo by Joan Marcus)*

Center: *Matthew Risch and Stockard Channing in the Roundabout Theatre Company production of* Pal Joey. *Opened at Studio 54 December 18, 2008 (photo by Joan Marcus)*

Bottom: *Thomas Sadoski and Marin Ireland in* reasons to be pretty. *Opened at the Lyceum Theatre April 2, 2009 (photo by Robert J. Saferstein)*

The cast of Cirque Dreams: Jungle Fantasy. *Opened at the Broadway Theatre June 26, 2008 (photo by Carol Rosegg)*

David Alvarez and Company in Billy Elliot The Musical. *Opened at the Imperial Theatre November 13, 2008 (photo by David Scheinmann)*

Joan Allen and Jeremy Irons in Impressionism. Opened at the Gerald Schoenfeld Theatre March 24, 2009 (photo by Joan Marcus)

Jeff Bowen and Hunter Bell in [title of show]. *Opened at the Lyceum Theatre July 17, 2008 (photo by Carol Rosegg)*

Frank Langella in the Roundabout Theatre Company production of A Man for All Seasons. *Opened at the American Airlines Theatre October 7, 2008 (photo by Joan Marcus)*

Meredith Patterson, Jeffry Denman and Company in Irving Berlin's White Christmas. *Opened at the Marquis Theatre November 23, 2008 (photo by Joan Marcus)*

The cast of A Tale of Two Cities. *Opened at the Al Hirschfeld Theatre September 18, 2008 (photo by Carol Rosegg)*

Raúl Esparza, Jeremy Piven and Elizabeth Moss in Speed-the-Plow. *Opened at the Barrymore Theatre October 23, 2008 (photo by Brigitte Lacombe)*

Peter Sarsgaard and Kristin Scott Thomas in The Seagull. *Opened at the Walter Kerr Theatre October 2, 2008 (photo by Joan Marcus)*

Daniel Radcliffe and Lorenzo Pisoni in Equus. *Opened at the Broadhurst Theatre September 25, 2008 (photo by Carol Rosegg)*

Brian d'Arcy James and Daniel Breaker in Shrek The Musical. *Opened at the Broadway Theatre December 14, 2008 (photo by Joan Marcus)*

Susan Sarandon, William Sadler, Geoffrey Rush, Brian Hutchison (background), Lauren Ambrose and Andrea Martin in Exit the King. *Opened at the Barrymore Theatre March 26, 2009 (photo by Joan Marcus)*

Marcia Gay Harden, Hope Davis, Jeff Daniels and James Gandolfini in God of Carnage. *Opened at the Bernard B. Jacobs Theatre March 22, 2009 (photo by Joan Marcus)*

Hallie Foote and Elizabeth Ashley in the Lincoln Center Theater production of Dividing the Estate. *Opened at the Booth Theatre November 20, 2008 (photo by Joan Marcus)*

Liza Minnelli in Liza's at the Palace...! *Opened at the Palace Theatre December 3, 2008 (photo by Eric Antoniou)*

The cast of Soul of Shaolin. *Opened at the Marquis Theatre January 15, 2009 (photo by Joan Marcus)*

Kieran Campion and Lily Rabe in the Manhattan Theatre Club production of The American Plan. *Opened at the Samuel J. Friedman Theatre January 22, 2009 (photo by Carol Rosegg)*

Malcolm Gets and Will Chase in The Story of My Life. *Opened at the Booth Theatre February 19, 2009 (Photo by Aaron Epstein)*

Michael Cerveris and Mary-Louise Parker in the Roundabout Theatre Company production of Hedda Gabler. *Opened at the American Airlines Theatre January 25, 2009 (photo by Nigel Parry / CPi)*

Lauren Graham in Guys and Dolls. *Opened at the Nederlander Theatre March 1, 2009 (photo by Carol Rosegg)*

Samantha Mathis, Colin Hanks and Jane Fonda in 33 Variations. *Opened at the Eugene O'Neill Theatre March 9, 2009 (photo by Joan Marcus)*

Above: *Karen Olivo, George Akram and the Company in* West Side Story. *Opened at the Palace Theatre March 19, 2009 (photo by Joan Marcus)*

Angela Lansbury, Susan Louise O'Connor and Rupert Everett (background) *in* Blithe Spirit. *Opened at the Shubert Theatre March 15, 2009 (photo by Robert J. Saferstein)*

Tovah Feldshuh in Irena's Vow. *Opened at the Walter Kerr Theatre March 29, 2009 (photo by Carol Rosegg)*

Constantine Maroulis and the Company in Rock of Ages. *Opened at the Brooks Atkinson Theatre April 7, 2009 (photo by Joan Marcus)*

Below: *The cast of* Hair. *Opened at the Al Hirschfeld Theatre March 31, 2009 (photo by Joan Marcus)*

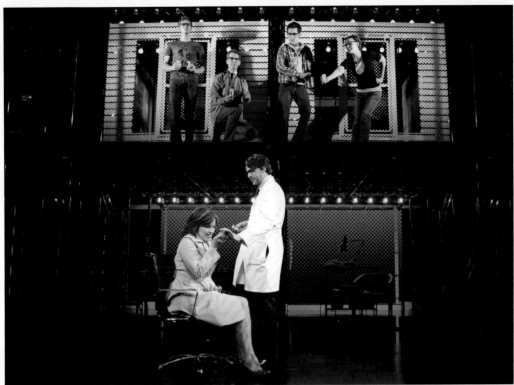

Alice Ripley and Louis Hobson (front) *with Aaron Tveit, J. Robert Spencer, Adam Chanler-Berat and Jennifer Damiano* (top) *in* Next to Normal. *Opened at the Booth Theatre April 15, 2009 (photo by Joan Marcus)*

Chad L. Coleman and Roger Robinson (front) *and the Company in the Lincoln Center Theater production of* Joe Turner's Come and Gone. *Opened at the Belasco Theatre April 16, 2009 (photo by T. Charles Erickson)*

Harriet Walter and Janet McTeer in Mary Stuart. *Opened at the Broadhurst Theatre April 19, 2009 (photo by Joan Marcus)*

Stephen Mangan (standing) *with* (clockwise) *Ben Miles, Amanda Root, Jessica Hynes, Amelia Bullmore, and Paul Ritter in* Table Manners, *part of* The Norman Conquests *trilogy. Opened at Circle in the Square April 23, 2009 (photo by Joan Marcus)*

Carla Gugino in Desire Under the Elms. *Opened at the St. James Theatre April 27, 2009 (photo by Liz Lauren)*

Mary Catherine Garrison and David Hyde Pierce in the Manhattan Theatre Club production of Accent on Youth. Opened at the Samuel J. Friedman Theatre April 29, 2009 (photo by Joan Marcus)

Nathan Lane and Bill Irwin in the Roundabout Theatre Company production of Waiting for Godot. Opened at Studio 54 April 30, 2009 (photo by Joan Marcus)

Megan Hilty, Allison Janney and Stephanie J. Block in 9 to 5: The Musical. Opened at the Marquis Theatre April 30, 2009 (photo by Joan Marcus)

Broadway and Beyond

Ben Hodges, Editor in Chief, *Theatre World*

Jane Fonda. Jeremy Irons. Marcia Gay Harden. Jeremy Piven getting sick on sushi. It was not an Academy Awards after-party; it was the 2008–2009 Broadway theatre season. And with as star-studded a season as any in recent memory, Broadway seemed strangely immune to the 2008–2009 economic recession which provided its New York backdrop. One explanation is that anticipation of, and fallout from, the fall 2007 Local One stagehands strike–the first in the union's history–may have pushed back the preparations for Broadway openings resulting in the crowded field during the 2008–2009 season. Another is that the high amount required to capitalize a Broadway show and the degree to which the capital needs to be raised in advance of opening may have resulted in plenty of Broadway shows already in the pipeline. Finally, the Writers Guild of America strike–commencing in November 2007 and which covered mainly movie and television writers–lasted over three months during the approaching summer 2008 hiatus and may have provided the opportunity for some name actors to focus on stage pursuits that they might not ordinarily have an opportunity to pursue.

The only tangible proof that many were aware of that Broadway struggled at all was the drama that played out in the tabloids over the capitalization of The Public Theater's 2008 summer hit *Hair* that was to transfer from the Delacorte Theater in Central Park to Broadway. Ultimately, Jeffrey Richards helped Elizabeth I. McCann close the gap in capitalization and the show went on to be a bona fide hit of the 2008–2009 season. But the true impact of the worst recession since the Great Depression will not be completely known until perhaps the 2009–2010 season or beyond and in any case well after the printing of this book.

In the summer of 2009 nonprofit theatres in New York and all across America were bracing for the full impact of the economic downturn to potentially hit during the 2009–2010 season, many having narrowly escaped financial hardship in 2008–2009 by the nature of theatre season subscriptions being sold in advance to audience members, thereby allowing the capitalization of a regional theatrical season much the way individual commercial productions are capitalized in New York and consequently potentially enabling the theatres to stave off any potential financial shortfall for at least another year. Or in the case of some theatres already struggling, prevent the coup de grâce. Some theatres worked creative solutions such as bringing on new board members charged with raising a quota of funds either from themselves or others in order to ensure that the show went on.

January 2009 saw a night of Broadway show closings that was nearly unprecedented, however, with existing shows feeling the brunt of a weakening economy (or getting out before they did). *Hairspray, Young Frankenstein, Boeing-Boeing, 13, Grease,* and *Spamalot* all closed their doors at the beginning of the new year. Still, many had had comparatively long runs, or at least had been critically lauded so that the economic news for Broadway still seemed better than that of the country as a whole, at least approaching what seemed to be the heart of the crisis in spring 2009.

However, offstage the changing media landscape continued to endanger even the most established of theatre professions. With the Internet and online publishing evolving faster than the ability of online newspapers to develop a business plan to keep up with it, print editions struggled even harder simply to stay in existence. And the job of the theatre critic, once as thoroughly ensconced as a Broadway theatre doorman, was itself on the way out. On October 31, 2008, Michael Reidel reported in the *New York Post* that Michael Sommers and Peter Filichia made exits a the *Star Ledger* in New Jersey and that Eric Grode had also left the *New York Sun,* in a trend that unfortunately as of this printing showed no signs of abating. The impact of the advent of online blogs and the new egalitarianism on letting the people decide, remains to be seen.

But perhaps one of the most uncommon economic indicators was the premiere of *IRT: A Tragedy in Three Stations,* a two-hour period play set in 1904 and telling the sometimes harrowing story of the construction of the New York City subway

system, written and directed by Jeff Stark and staged on subway platforms from Brooklyn to Manhattan. As actors and artists of all kinds find themselves commuting from further and further away to Manhattan in order to pursue their dreams, it was gratifying to know that there are still revolutionary means of producing new works right under our noses, even in one of the least expensive venues in one of the most expensive cities in the world in which to produce it.

* * *

One of the first offerings of the Broadway season, [title of show], was theatre's inside joke, and most agreed a pretty funny one. The musical itself was a musical about four actors/singers writing a musical–nurturing it from the New York festival circuit to Broadway. While The Producing Office teamed successfully with the Vineyard Theatre to capitalize on the dearth of new musicals traditionally opening during the summer months by opening their hit Tony Award-winning *Avenue Q* in the summer of 2003, the strategy did not work as well with [title of show], but it did last for nearly three months, long enough for most everyone in the theatre business–truly its most appreciative audience–to catch this sleeper. But although it did not entirely fill any anticipation of a long run, come awards time, Hunter Bell garnered a Tony nod for his extremely original book. Most importantly, the show was a springboard for the creative team of Jeff Bowen and Hunter Bell that all of Broadway–even those who did not catch the show–will be watching in the future.

What will certainly be remembered as the cinematic celebrity season officially began in September 2008 with the Broadway debut of Daniel Radcliffe, aka Harry Potter, as the troubled youth Alan Strang in the revival of Peter Shaffer's *Equus,* opposite 2006 Tony Award and Theatre World Award winner Richard Griffiths. And fellow Brit Kristin Scott Thomas led a cast that included Peter Sarsgaard of Chekov's *The Seagull* at the Walter Kerr Theatre in a new version by Christopher Hampton, transplanted from a successful run at the Royal Court Theatre in London and directed by Ian Rickson.

Frank Langella played Sir Thomas More in Robert Bolt's *A Man For All Seasons* in September 2008, opening simultaneously with *Frost/Nixon* on the large screen— a performance for which Langella had won a 2007 Tony Award for Best Actor in a Play onstage, and which would additionally garner him an Academy Award nomination on film. Langella's performance as Sir Thomas More was generally lauded and his reception was largely positive; he remains one of the more predictably recurrent performers on Broadway. A competent supporting cast included Maryann Plunkett as Alice More, who managed to play levity and heft with equal might.

The revival of *All My Sons* was the next offering that made more of a splash for the performers involved than for the production itself, as was disconcertingly typical during the first half of the 2008–2009 season, with John Lithgow, Dianne Weist, Patrick Wilson, and Katie Holmes bringing more buzz to Broadway than had author Arthur Miller graced the theatre himself on opening night.

Speed-the-Plow got more attention after the departure of star Jeremy Piven, citing complications of mercury poisoning, as well as for his being replaced by William H. Macy, than the production had upon opening. In fact, the play just seemed to get its legs just as it closed with the accomplished Macy, no stranger to Mamet's idiosyncratic dialogue, aptly taking over for Piven. The play remains best remembered, however, for thermometer jokes in the tabloid press and producer Jeffrey Richards' vigilance at taking Piven to task legally for his contractually premature departure, including Richards' filing a grievance with Actors Equity.

Sir Elton John scored again with the stage adaptation of *Billy Elliot,* while his previous hit *The Lion King* has been going strong on Broadway since 1997. And David Alvarez, Tret Kowalik, and Kiril Kulish managed a the triple triumph of the season, garnering not only a shared Theatre World Award for their simultaneous Broadway debuts in the role of Billy, but the Best Performance by a Leading Actor in a Musical Tony Award they all shared. Haydn Gwynne, in the role of dance instructor Mrs. Wilkinson, also secured a Theatre World Award for her Broadway debut.

Horton Foote's *Dividing the Estate* had played Primary Stages in the fall of 2007 and moved to Broadway for a run during the 2008–2009 season. Sadly, Foote would not live to see the best play Tony nomination his play would receive nor the performance of *The Orphans' Home Cycle*, which will premiere at Hartford Stage and New York's Signature Theatre Company during 2009–2010, Foote passed away in March 2009 at the age of ninety-two.

Irving Berlin's *White Christmas* had played nearly unprecedentedly at several regional theatres including the Denver Center Theatre Company and the Music Theatre of Wichita, before finally making its Broadway debut in November 2008.

Liza's at the Palace . . . marked another in a series of comebacks for Liza Minelli to Broadway, in a production that focused on Kay Thompson's influence on her, particularly following the death of her mother, Judy Garland, and the production garnered a Tony Award for Special Theatrical Event.

And while the revival of *Pal Joey*, by John O'Hara, Richard Rodgers, and Lorenz Hart also marked the return of another Broadway star—Stockard Channing—as Vera, a green monster (I mean ogre) made his debut in *Shrek The Musical!* nearby, marking another in the long line of films (this one by Dreamworks) that have made a successful transition from screen to stage.

Two thousand nine began with an old familiar face as former *Saturday Night Live* star Will Ferrell brought his most recognizable impersonation to Broadway, making his debut in *You're Welcome America. A Final Night with George W. Bush* in a sell out that seemed to set a record for the speed at which a Broadway could recoup its investment.

The most contested awards season in years began in earnest in March 2009 with one of the most celebrated cinematic stars of the past fifty years returning to Broadway after an absence of nearly that long. Seventy-one-year old Jane Fonda appeared in Moisés Kaufman's *33 Variations* and could be heard and seen nearly everywhere in the spring touting the show and declaring that she thoroughly enjoyed her return to the stage and New York, despite the obvious physical demands of the role. Colin Hanks collected a Theatre World Award for Outstanding Broadway Debut for his work in the play, which was presented to him by fellow cast member and previous Theatre World Award winner Susan Kellerman.

The parade of stars of stage and screens—small and large—continued right through the last string of shows to open during the 2008–2009 season with Angela Lansbury taking a supporting turn in Noël Coward's *Blithe Spirit*. Accompanied by screen favorite Rupert Everett and theatre perennial Christine Ebersole, Ms. Lansbury gave a performance as a medium that summoned, among other things, one of her most memorable performances in years. Susan Louise O'Connor turned in a performance that was out of this world enough to gain her a Theatre World Award for Outstanding Broadway Debut.

In a season rife with revivals, *West Side Story* was revived for a fourth time, this one somewhat controversially selectively weaving Spanish throughout the book and songs. Book writer Arthur Laurents, at age ninety, showed no signs of giving up, or giving up control, as he directed his version (read: vision) of *West Side Story*, following up his *Gypsy*, a standout from 2007–2008. Josefina Scaglione received a Theatre World Award for her Broadway debut in the role of Maria, a role she won after Laurents viewed an Internet YouTube clip of her performing Astor Piazzolla's composition of *Libertango*.

God of Carnage, by French author Yasmina Reza, brought the writer back to Broadway, first having triumphed there with *Art* in 1998. With a cast that boasted more established and accomplished performers than nearly any other of the season: Jeff Daniels, Hope Davis, James Gandolfini, of *The Sopranos* fame, and Marcia Gay Harden, the show proved that bad acting can be good for business and Reza took home the Tony Award for Best Play.

The revival of Eugene Ionesco's *Exit the King* featured a debut by Geoffrey Rush that saw him win a Theatre World Award for Outstanding Broadway Debut, as well as perform onstage with seasoned performers in any court—Susan Sarandon and Andrea Martin.

Four-time Tony nominee Tovah Feldshuh gave another tour de force in Dan Gordon's *Irena's Vow*, directed by Michael Parva, centering on the plight of twelve Jewish refugees during W.W. II and one woman's efforts to protect them from the Nazis.

The summer of 2009 would mark the fortieth anniversary of the Apollo 11 lunar landing as well as Woodstock, and the production of James Rado, Gerome Ragni, and Galt MacDermot's *Hair* that played the Delacorte in 2007 benefited upon its transfer in March 2009 from the resulting nostalgia and publicity surrounding 1969, as well as from a stellar cast including Gavin Creel (replacing Jonathan Groff from the Delacorte production) and Will Swenson, with direction by Diane Paulus. *Hair* transferred in March 2009 to Broadway, after an initial recession driven capitalization issue, to nearly unanimous rave reviews and captured the Tony Award for Best Revival of a Musical for the season.

Having been labeled a misanthrope by press in both the United States as well as Britain, Neil Labute and his *reasons to be pretty* did nothing this season to counter the monikor. With previous works including *In the Company of Men* and *Fat Pig*, Labute is one of America's foremost playwrights, specializing in naughty naturalism and people behaving badly. With just over 100 performances, *reasons to be pretty* closed, but Mr. Labute's reputation continues as one of the most stimulating writers of our time continues. Marin Ireland took home a Theatre World Award for Outstanding Broadway Debut for her work, which was anything but "regular."

Rock of Ages came along and reminded those of us in the theatre community that the decade of the 1980s is not too soon gone to prevent it from being recycled into a jukebox musical, and featured a standout performance by Wesley Taylor that won him a Theatre World Award for Outstanding Broadway Debut.

Brian Yorkey and Tom Kitt's *Next to Normal* turned out to be anything but with a much-lauded performance by Alice Ripley, in a musical centered on the unlikely subject matter of a woman with bipolar disorder and how the worsening illness affects her family. *Next to Normal* had played Off-Broadway at Second Stage in 2008, transferring to Broadway in April 2009. Ripley took home her first Tony Award for Best Actress in a Musical for her work.

August Wilson—America's most prolifically produced African-American male playwright—passed away in 2005, but his plays live on, this season with *Joe Turner's Come and Gone* in a production that was controversial for what it did not have—an African-American director. While widely reported that Wilson only allowed his productions to be directed by African Americans, the selection of Bartlett Sher, Intiman's Theatre's artistic director, (with the permission of Wilson's widow) as director did not seem to hurt the production one bit, and Chad L. Coleman took home a Theatre World Award for Outstanding Broadway Debut for his role as wanderer Herald Loomis.

Freidrich Schiller's *Mary Stuart* had first appeared on Broadway in 1900, and its latest revival with Janet McTeer and Harriet Walter transferred there following Sold Out engagements at the Donmar Warehouse and London's West End.

Alan Ayckbourn's *The Norman Conquests* was one of the bona fide hits of the season with an ensemble cast that was one of the most heralded in recent memory. And with the option of seeing each of the trilogy of plays individually, or alternately, strapping oneself in for the marathon "Trilogy Saturdays," there were as many opportunities to catch Alan Ayckbourn's play as laughs to be had once in attendance.

Eugene O'Neill's *Desire Under the Elms* under the direction of Goodman Theatre artistic director Robert Falls transferred from the Goodman where it had premiered during February 2009 with a cast that included Brian Dennehy as Ephraim, Carla Gugino as Abbie, and Pablo Schreiber as Eben.

Dolly Parton's *9 to 5* opened in April 2009, with still another noteworthy screen performer, Allison Janney, bounding across the boards. It came after a crowded field of Broadway shows had gobbled up the press, publicity, and public attention and seemed to suffer a bit from theatergoer fatigue come Tony time, although Parton received her first Tony Award nomination for her score.

Waiting for Godot kept us waiting for the last of the star turns with Nathan Lane, Bill Irwin, John Goodman, and John Glover teaming up for the Samuel Beckett revival—the last Broadway opening show of the 2008–2009 season.

Forty-three new Broadway productions opened this season, which was the most in more than twenty-five years. And while the full numbers for the Broadway season will not be released for 2009 until after close of the calendar year, Broadway's total grosses for the 2008 calendar year (which is measured from December 31, 2007 through December 28, 2008) were more than $940 million, with total paid attendance of more than 12.31 million. The same figures for 2008 were $938 million, and so between 2007 and 2008, at least, there was a $3 million increase in Broadway grosses.

* * *

Off-Broadway was not all *Ruined* by the fading economy or anything else as Lynn Nottage's masterwork about the plight of women in the Democratic Republic of Congo brought her approbation from all corners of the theatre world, as well as an Obie Award for Best New American Play, Outer Critics Circle Award for Best Off-Broadway Play, the New York Drama Critics' Circle Best Play Award, the Drama Desk Outstanding Play Award, and the 2009 Pulitzer Prize for Drama. Condola Rashad additionally was awarded a Theatre World Award for Outstanding Broadway Debut for her work as the tortured Sophie.

Perhaps the economy had a broader effect on Off-Broadways shows, with less lead time for capitalization, but simultaneously more risk, with Jack Heifner and David Kirshenbaum's musical version of *Vanities*—originally scheduled for a Broadway run, opted instead for a second chance at Second Stage. And the trend of one-person shows—that can survive on a leaner, meaner, budget, continued to grow, with those including Kahlil Ashanti's *Basic Training* at the Barrow Street Theatre; Mike Birbiglia's *Sleepwalk With Me*, at the Bleeker Street Theatre and directed by seasoned veteran and co-founder of the Barrow Group Theater Company, Seth Barrish; James Braly's *Life in a Marital Institution* at 59E59 Theatres, directed by Hal Books; Mike Daisey's *If you See Something, Say Something* at The Public Theater's Joe's Pub; Michael Laurence's *Krapp 39*, at the Soho Playhouse and directed by George Demas; *Humor Abuse* at MTC Stage 2 at City Center, created by Lorenzo Pisoni and Erica Schmidt, directed by Ms. Schmidt and featuring Mr. Pisoni; Don Reed's *East 14th: True Tales of a Reluctant Player* at New World Stages, Lisa Ramirez's *Exit Cuckoo*, directed by Colman Domingo, Alanna Ubach's *Patriotic Bitch*, directed by Ian McCrudden, and Suzanne Willet's *The Feminazi*, directed by Hillary Spector.

The stars struck Off-Broadway as well—if not in quantity, well, then, quality, with Cynthia Nixon appearing in Lisa Loomer's *Distracted* at the Roundabout Theatre Company and Christopher Durang continues to prove that if he can make it Off-Broadway he can make it anywhere, with his biggest hit in years—*Why Torture Is Wrong and the People Who Love Them*.

Off-Broadway proved that Broadway had no monopoly on screen adaptations and answered with *The Toxic Avenger*, with book and lyrics by Joe DiPietro and music and lyrics by David Bryan. This latest attempt at an adaptation of the mid-1980s cult film classic didn't have to worry about people staying away for fear or anything else.

Director David Cromer's visionary *Our Town*, by Thornton Wilder at the Barrow Street Theatre, in which he also plays the Stage Manager, took a show we all feel as though we've lived through and seen for a lifetime and made it fresh and new. Perhaps the transfer from Chicago (read: a little bit closer to Grover's Corners) made it ring true. Jennifer Grace was presented a Theatre World Award for Outstanding Off-Broadway Debut for her work as Emily.

Enter Laughing, The Musical, with a book by Joseph Stein and music and lyrics by Stan Daniels, and based on the book by Carl Reiner, was brought back by popular demand at the York Theatre, and Josh Grisetti received one of only three Theatre World Awards awarded for Off-Broadway productions.

The Signature Theatre Company, with a practice of producing a single playwright's works each season, decided to feature vintage works from the landmark Negro Ensemble Company this season, featuring Leslie Lee's *The First Breeze of Summer*, Samm-Art Williams' Home, and Charles Fuller's *Zooman and the Sign*.

Off-Broadway shows transferring to Broadway during the 2008–2009 season included *Hair, Irena's Vow, Rock of Ages*, and both *Finian's Rainbow*, by E.Y. Harburg, Fred Saidy, and Burton Lane, which debuted at City Center Encores! and with a cast including Cheyenne Jackson, Kate Baldwin, and Jim Norton, as well as *FELA!* featuring arrangements by Aaron Johnson and Antibalas and with choreography and direction by Bill T. Jones, are scheduled to transfer to Broadway during the 2009–2010 season. And while not transferring to Broadway, Stephen Sondheim debuted his first new New York show since 1994–*Road Show*–at The Public Theater, reworked again (formerly *Bounce!*, formerly *Wise Guys*) and with a book by John Weidman.

Finally, the Off-Broadway run of *I Love You, You're Perfect, Now Change* ended on July 27, 2008, after 5,003 performances and twenty previews, but only after becoming the second-longest-running musical in Off-Broadway history.

AWARDS SEASON

There were quite a few issues for the Tony Awards Administration Committee to determine during the 2008–2009 season, meeting five times in order to do so. Among the committee's most notable rulings were: the revival of David Mamet's *American Buffalo* was declared ineligible because it did not meet the performance requirement; the three boys in *Billy Elliot*, David Alvarez, Tret Kowalik, and Kiril Kulish were ruled eligible to be considered jointly in the category of Leading Actor in Musical; Horton Foote's *Dividing the Estate*, a reworked version of the play that had previously opened in 2007 was ruled eligible in the Best Play category; Angela Lansbury was ruled eligible in the Featured Actress in a Play category (which no doubt helped her secure the win later in the season); and Alan Ackybourn's *The Norman Conquests* was ruled eligible as a single play in the Best Revival of a Play category, and in such a crowded field, this ruling certainly did not hurt, and it took home the Tony at the 63rd annual Tony Awards on June 7, 2009.

Probably the most notable ruling by the Drama Desk Awards and/or Outer Critics was ruling *Next to Normal* ineligible for award consideration as it had played Off-Broadway at Second Stage during the 2007–2008 season. It was a designation that the New York Drama Critics' Circle did not agree with—that organization deciding that changes to the piece warranted it sufficiently enough a new musical to include it in competition with in the Best Musical category with *Billy Elliot*, which eventually emerged the victor (as it did from most every other awards presentation).

The New York Drama Critics also cited the cast of *The Norman Conquests* with a special honor, as did the Theatre World Awards for Outstanding Broadway and Off-Broadway Debuts, honoring a cast that included Amelia Bullmore, Jessica Hynes, Stephen Mangan, Ben Miles, Paul Ritter, and Amanda Root.

A thirty-year run Off-Broadway for Gerard Alessandrini's *Forbidden Broadway* brought accolades from all over town, including those of the Drama Desk Awards, which includes recognition of all professional New York theatre productions. Also among the Drama Desk honorees was the TADA! Youth Theater, as well as Atlantic Theater Company and artistic director Neil Pepe "for exceptional craftsmanship and, dedication to excellence and productions that engage, inspire, and enlighten."

Some awards committees, such as the Outer Critics Circle, solved the question of the Billys Elliot by bestowing special awards on the triumvirate. The Theatre World Awards included all three boys as one of its twelve awardees, the first time that three Broadway debuts—those of David Alvarez, Tret Kowalik, and Kiril Kulish—constituted one debut, and therefore the first time in its sixty-five year history that there were fourteen regular Theatre World Award winners. The full list of other awardees for Outstanding Broadway or Off-Broadway Debut were: Chad L. Coleman (*Joe Turner's Come and Gone*); Jennifer Grace (*Our Town*); Josh Grisetti (*Enter Laughing, The Musical*); Haydn Gwynne (*Billy Elliot, The Musical*); Colin Hanks (*33 Variations*); Marin Ireland (*reasons to be pretty*); Susan Louise O'Connor (*Blithe Spirit*); Condola Rashad (*Ruined*); Geoffrey Rush (*Exit the King*); Josefina Scaglione (*West Side Story*); and Wesley Taylor (*Rock of Ages*).

When the Tony Awards were broadcast on June 7, 2009, there was general applause over the selection of Neil Patrick Harris as host, an unlikely but ultimately inspired choice for the Tony Awards ceremony. It was an awards show–though chock full of just about everything Hollywood and/or Broadway could offer–the cavalcade of stars and musical numbers was a welcome respite from the parade of bad economic news that generally dominated the television during the spring of 2009. 7.43 million viewers agreed, which constituted in a 15 percent increase in viewership of the Tony Awards from 2008.

Billy Elliot tied *The Producers* in 2001 with the most nominations ever (fifteen), and took home ten Tonys, while *Next to Normal* and *God of Carnage* won three awards each. *Joe Turner's Come and Gone* received two Tony Awards, and *Liza's at the Palace* and *Hair* each won one.

While awards season itself presented no huge surprises, a few were in store after all of the statuettes had been awarded. Liza Minelli's latest swan song *Liza's at the Palace* . . . captured the American Theatre Wing Tony Award for Special Theatrical Event on the night of the Tony Awards, becoming the last official winner of the award, as the Tony Awards Administration and Management Committees decided a week later that the award would be retired. Created in 2001 to accommodate the growing landscape of nontraditional (read: controversial) productions such as *Contact* and *Blast!* the variety of perennial productions eligible in this category always made the announcement of its nominees of special interest. Then, in July 2009 the Tony Management Committee decided that members of the First Night Press List—journalists and others who receive tickets in order to publish reviews and other coverage—would not be eligible to vote on the Tony Awards, citing respective conflicts of interest. It was an announcement the effects of which on future winners of the coveted prize would not be known for some time.

Finally, The White House announced on Tuesday, May 12, 2009, that Rocco Landesman, who brought *Big River*, *Angels in America*, and *The Producers*, among other hits, to Broadway, had been nominated as the next chairperson of the National Endowment for the Arts. Landesman will no doubt bring a reputation for excellence and candor to his position and to the arena of politics that is quite possibly the only one more difficult to conquer than Broadway.

IN MEMORIAM

This editor has always taken particular pride in working on our obituary section. *Theatre World* has always been, aside from a reference for students, historians, and industry professionals worldwide, an actors' reference. Since I have been involved with editing of this book I became acutely aware of the fact that *Theatre World*'s obituaries are not only the most complete seasonal obituary records in print publication, but as we cover the entirety of the theatrical season from June 1 to May 31, we also are the last media outlet of any medium to publish actors' obituaries. As such, I have made it a priority of mine to make sure that our obituary records are as complete and accurate as any published in any medium. And, as always, we accompany our obituary records with photographs from our archives, made especially poignant by the fact that they were–almost without exception–submitted to our publication by the actors themselves during the past six decades for our former biography section. Theatre is an immediate art, and actors are trained by and large to live in the moment. I believe that as a result it is particularly important to stop and reflect upon the often remarkable careers of actors, directors, composers, lyricists, and production designers, among others, who have passed away each year, many of whom leave legacies of talent and accomplishments the likes of which are never be seen again.

The past year was a particularly harsh one for the loss of writers that was experienced in the twelve-month period that ended May 31, 2009: Eric Blau, creator of *Jacque Brel Is Alive and Well and Living in Paris*, which opened at the Village Gate in 1968 and, running for four years, became one of the longest-running shows in Off-Broadway history; Luther Davis, the writer of books for musicals including *Kismet*, *Timbuktu!* and *Grand Hotel;* Horton Foote, Pulitzer Prize-winning author of more than fifty plays, including *The Young Man From Atlanta*, *The Trip to Bountiful*, and *Dividing the Estate;* George Furth, writer of books with credits

including *Merrily We Roll Along*, *The Act*, and a Tony Award winner for *Company;* William Gibson, a Tony Award winner for his book of *The Miracle Worker*, he also penned *Golden Boy* and *Golda's Balcony;* Hugh Leonard, writers of the plays *Da*, *The au Pair Man*, and *A Life;* Harold Pinter, who challenged the intellects of actors and audiences alike, with plays including *The Homecoming*, *The Caretaker*, *The Birthday Party*, and *Betrayal;* and Dale Wasserman, book writer of *Man of La Mancha*, who also penned *One Flew Over the Cuckoo's Nest.*

The actor, producer, and philanthropist Paul Newman was not only one of the most successful and enigmatic actors of the twentieth century but also a special friend to this publication, as well as to the Theatre World Awards. A 1953 Theatre World Award winner for his Broadway debut in *Picnic*, Newman was a donor to the Awards for many years, even when he had to send his regrets (which he always did) if not being able to attend the annual ceremony.

Gerald Schoenfeld, chairman of The Shubert Organization and head of the nonprofit Shubert Foundation for over thirty years, was perhaps . . . no, simply *was*, more responsible for the revitalization of Times Square and midtown New York City than any mayor, or anyone else, over the past thirty years. A friend to my late friend, Frederic B. Vogel, the former head of the Commercial Theater Institute, they together worked as hard as any two people in the business to ensure that there were new productions and theatres in which they could play. Giants of their sort only come along a few times in a lifetime.

Finally, the first Theatre World Awards ceremony I ever attended was in 1993 as a volunteer recruited by Mr. Willis. It was a magical experience and I was as much a star-struck kid from East Tennessee via Ohio as any twenty-three year old Drama major fresh out of college. I was assigned as a greeter for that year's winners, and the first introduction I made was to Natasha Richardson, who walked into the Roundabout Theatre on the arm of her future husband, Liam Neeson. Nearly knocked down by her *je ne sais quoi*, Richardson was charming and gracious, but above all, a phenomenal talent—talent that had been so prominently on display that season with Neeson in *Anna Christie*, for which they both received a Theatre World Award. While the shock of her sudden and accidental death took the world by surprise, it was her passion for her work and life for which she will always be remembered.

1993 Theatre World Award *winners Natasha Richardson and Liam Neeson (for* Anna Christie*)*

Cirque Dreams: Jungle Fantasy

Broadway Theatre; First Preview: June 16, 2008; Opening Night: June 26, 2008; Closed August 24, 2008; 10 previews, 70 performances

Created and directed by Neil Goldberg, music and lyrics by Jill Winters; Produced by A+ Theatricals, Broadway Across America, Cirque Productions, Adam Troy Epstein, Fox Associates, New Space Entertainment, Albert Nocciolino, Providence Performing Arts Center, Theatre League; Choreography, Tara Jeanne Vallee; Costumes, Cirque Productions, Lenora Taylor, Santiago Rojo; Additional Music, David Scott, Keith Heffner, Billy Paul Williams, Tony Aliperti, Lance Conque, and Christopher Pati; Act Design, Neil Goldberg, Heather Hoffman, Iouri Klepatsky; Set, Jon Craine; Lighting, Kate Johnston; Sound, Craig Cassidy; Executive Producers, Alan Wasser, Allan Williams, James Geisler; Animal Sculpture Design, William Olson; Production Design, Betsy Herst; Marketing, Type A Marketing; Production Management, Juniper Street Productions; General Management, Alan Wasser Associates; Company Managers, Lane Marsh, Jake Hirzel; Stage Manager, Tricia Toliver; For Cirque Productions: Neil Goldberg (Founder/Artistic Director), Jim Geisler (Managing Director), Heather Hoffman (Assistant Artistic Director), Jill Diane Winters (Musical Director), Iouri Klepatsky (Acrobatic Coach), Gina Damato (Business Manager), Andee Cohen, Shirley Crane (Corporate Events & Sales Directors), Nicholas Mitsis, Bill Olson (Event Managers), Wendie Carper, Stacey Kelley (Directors Assistants), David Stauffer, Allison Goldberg (Marketing Coordinators), James Queen (Production Manager); Crew: Steve Gallo, Daniel Montes (production carpenters), Charles Rasmussen, Thomas Cole Jr., Declan McNeill (carpenters), Michael LoBue (production electrician), George Milne, Peter Becker, Dominick Intagliato (electricians), Christopher Pantuso (production properties supervisor), Richard Dalcortivo (production properties), Michael Orsillo, Tyler Ricci (properties), Tim Brannigan (head sound), Erin Brooke Roth (wardrobe supervisor), Dora Bonilla, Thomas Carlson, Holly Nissen, Aaron Simms, Dora Suarez (dressers); Advertising, Eliran Murphy Group; Press, The Publicity Office, Marc Thibodeau, Michael S. Borowski, Jeremy Shaffer

A scene from Cirque Dreams: Jungle Fantasy *(photos by Carol Rosegg)*

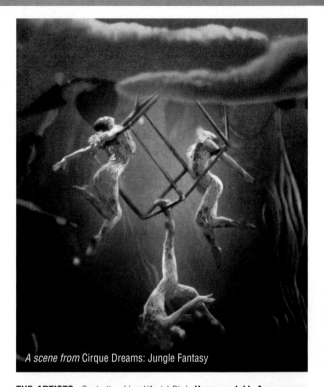

A scene from Cirque Dreams: Jungle Fantasy

THE ARTISTS Contorting Lizard/Aerial Bird **Uranmandakh Amarsanaa;** Adventurer **Marcello Balestracci;** Soultree Violinist **Jared Burnett;** Jungleboy **Zachary Carroll;** Mother Nature **Jill Diane;** Bee/Ensemble **Lauren Diblasi;** Bee/Ensemble **Iryna Dmytruk;** Frog Juggler **Ruslan Dmytruk;** Trapeze Owl **Ivan Dotsenko;** Balancing Giraffe/Snake Roller **Vladimir Dovgan;** Monkey Foot Manipulator **Nataliya Egorova;** Unicorn/Ensemble **Judah Frank;** Contorting Lizard/Aerial Bird **Buyankhishig Ganbaatar;** Contorting Lizard/Aerial Bird **Erdenesuvd Ganbaatar;** Blackbird Hairialist **Stefka Iordanova;** Vine Swinger **Denys Kucher;** Vine Swinger **Vitalii Lykov;** Percushroomist **Lee Miller;** Contorting Lizard/Aerial Bird **Odgerel Oyunbaatar;** Butterflyer/Jungle King **Sergey Parshin;** Jungle King/Ensemble **Pavel Pozdnyakov;** Jungleboy **Glenn Rogers;** Butterflyer/Ensemble **Naomi Sampson;** Emu/Ensemble **Konstantin Serov;** Trapeze Owl **Carly Sheridan;** Jungle King/Monkey Manipulator **Serguei Slavski;** Jungle King/Monkey Manipulator **Alexander Tolstikov;** Balancing Giraffe **Anatoliy Yeniy**

THE ADVENTURE Act 1 – *Jungle By Day:* A Bird is Born, Eyes Wide Open, Jungle Jumpin, Hop Stretch, Nature's Balance, Falling, Swinging Vines, You Can Grow Too, Frogging Monkey Business, Personality, Buttlerflying, Courage, Amazing; Act 2 –*Jungle By Night:* Coloring Dreams, Rollin' Around, Strange Things, Owls on a Perch, Take Credit, Jungle-ibrium, How Do You Feel, Roar, Stampede, Jungle Fantasy Finale

New York premiere of a theatrical, acrobatic and musical adventure presented in two acts. This production toured the U.S. prior to and following its Broadway engagement.

SYNOPSIS *Cirque Dreams Jungle Fantasy* is an exotic encounter inspired by nature's unpredictable creations that are brought to life by an international cast of soaring aerialists, spine-bending contortionists, acrobats, jugglers and musicians. The astounding feats performed are enhanced with over 150 costumes and set in a fantastical jungle ignited by striking visual effects. From the breathtaking aerial ballet of butterflies to the balancing giraffes, gigantic flowers and trees, this world-class explosion of athleticism, theatre and imagination is a Broadway first.

(clockwise from top left) Heidi Blickenstaff, Susan Blackwell, Hunter Bell and Jeff Bowen (photos by Carol Rosegg)

[title of show]

Lyceum Theatre; First Preview: July 5, 2007; Opening Night: July 17, 2007; Closed October 12, 2008; 13 previews, 102 performances

Music and lyrics by Jeff Bowen, book by Hunter Bell; Produced by Kevin McCollum, Jeffrey Seller, Roy Miller, Laura Camien, Kris Stewart, Vineyard Theatre; Director and Choreographer, Michael Berresse; Musical Direction and Arrangements, Larry Pressgrove; Set, Neil Patel; Costumes, Chase Tyler; Lighting, Ken Billington, Jason Kantrowitz; Sound, Acme Sound Partners; Casting, Telsey + Company; Technical Supervisor, Brian Lynch; Production Stage Manager, Martha Donaldson; Associate Producers, Rachel Helson, Sara Katz, Lams Entertainment, Jaimie Mayer, Heather Provost, Tom Smedes; Marketing, Scott A. Moore; Promotions, HHC Marketing; General Management, The Charlotte Wilcox Company; Company Manager, Alexandra Gushin Agosta; Stage Manager, Tom Reynolds; Assistant to the Director, Jennifer Ashley Tepper; Associate Design: David Barber (set), Craig Stelzenmuller (lighting), Nick Borisjuk (sound); Dance Captain, Benjamin Howes; Crew: Keith Buchanan (advance electrician), Carlos Parra (head spot), Colin DeVerna (second spot), McBrien Dunbar (advance carpenter), Adam Braunstein (head carpenter), Paul Brydon (automation flyman), Leah Nelson (head properties), Dan Robillard (advance sound), Brad Gyorgak (head sound), Kathleen Gallagher (wardrobe supervisor), Soomi Marano (dresser); Production Assistant, Zac Chandler; Management Intern, Morissa Gold; Intern, Leah Harris; For the Producing Office: John S. Corker, Debra Nir, Ryan Hill, Caitlyn Thomson; For Charlotte Wilcox: Seth Marquette, Matthew Krawiec, Dina Steinberg, David Roth, Steve Supeck, Margaret Wilcox; For the Vineyard Theatre: Douglas Aibel, (Artistic Director), Jennifer Garvey-Blackwell (Executive Director), Sarah Stern (Associate Artistic Director), Reed Ridgley (General Manager); Press, Sam Rudy Media Relations, Dale R. Heller, Robert Lasko, Charlie Siedenburg; Off-Broadway Cast recording: Sh-K-Boom/Ghostlight Records 4414

CAST Jeff **Jeff Bowen;** Hunter **Hunter Bell;** Heidi **Heidi Blickenstaff;** Susan **Susan Blackwell**

STANDBYS Courtney Balan (Heidi, Susan), Benjamin Howes (Jeff, Hunter)

PIANO Larry Pressgrove

MUSICAL NUMBERS Untitled Opening Number; Two Nobodies in New York; An Original Musical; Monkeys and Playbills; Part of It All; I Am Playing Me; What Kind of Girl Is She?; Die Vampire, Die; Filling Out the Form; Montage Part 1: September Song; Montage Part 2: Secondary Characters; Montage Part 3: Development Medley; Change It, Don't Change It/Awkward Photo Shoot; A Way Back to Then; Nine People's Favorite Thing; Finale

SETTING Place: [place]. Time: [time]. An original Broadway musical presented without intermission. The show began life at the first annual New York Musical Theatre Festival, September, 2004. The show was then workshopped at the Eugene O'Neill Theatre Center the following summer, and had a short engagement at Ars Nova September 11–27, 2005, presented by Bridge Club Productions. The show was produced Off-Broadway by the Vineyard Theatre from February 15–April 30, 2006 (see *Theatre World* Vol. 62, page 175), and encored at the Vineyard July 14 –October 1, 2006 (see *Theatre World* Vol. 63, page 129), playing 159 performances. The cast kept the show alive on the Internet by creating a series of short videos entitled "the *[title of show]* show" which captivated thousands of viewers who tuned in to see their adventures as they announced that *[title of show]* would be going to Broadway.

SYNOPSIS The ultimate "meta" musical, *[title of show]* takes a thoroughly unique and comical look at the pleasures and perils of the artistic process as two struggling writers and two struggling actresses take on the seemingly impossible task of creating a new musical about creating a new musical for a musical theatre festival, and subsequently an Off-Broadway production. Now with Broadway as their destination, the quartet's saga continues anew as they face mounting pressures and deadlines, and are nearly thrown off-track by disagreements, day jobs and insecurities in this funny and unforgettable look at the birth of a musical as it finally comes to life on the Great White Way.

Hunter Bell and Jeff Bowen

A Tale of Two Cities

Al Hirschfeld Theatre; First Preview: August 19, 2008; Opening Night: September 18, 2008; Closed November 9, 2008; 33 previews, 60 performances

Book, music and lyrics by Jill Santoriello, based on the novel by Charles Dickens; Produced by Barbra Russell, Ron Sharpe, Bernard Brogan, Sharon A. Fordham, Theater Associates, David Sonnenberg/Rami Evar, The Monagle Group, Joseph J. Grano, Fanok Entertainment, Mary E. Laminack, Nancy & Paul Audet, Jim Barry, Gasperino Entertainment, Vincent Russell, William M. Broderick, Alex Santoriello, in association with David Bryant, Spencer Brody, Harry Casey; Director and Choreography, Warren C. Carlyle; Music Supervision & Direction, Kevin Stites; Set, Tony Walton; Costumes, David Zinn; Lighting, Richard Pilbrow; Sound, Carl Casella, Dominic Sack; Hair, Tom Watson; Special Effects, Gregory Meeh; Orchestrations & Arrangements, Edward D. Kessel; Additional Arrangements, Bob Krogstad, Wendy Bobbitt Cavett, Kevin Stites; Music Coordinator, James Neglia; Casting, Barry Moss, Bob Kale; Fight Director, Michael Rossmy; Marketing, Sharon A. Fordham; Promotions, Margery Singer Company; Production Supervisor, Christopher C. Smith; Production Stage Manager, Kim Vernace; Associate Choreographer, Parker Esse; General Management, Town Square Productions (Don Frantz & Laurie Brown, Scott Bartelson, Lauren Breuning, Hillary Reeves); Executive Producers, Ron Sharpe & Barbara Russell; Company Manager, Robert Nolan; Stage Manager, Paul J. Smith; Assistant Stage Managers, Jason A. Quinn, Megan Schneid; Assistant Company Manager, Austin Nathanial; Dialect/Vocal Coach, Deborah Hecht; Makeup, Jon Carter; Stunt Coordinator, GZ Entertainment/Brian Schuley; Assistant Director, Michael Arden; Associate Design: Heather Wolensky (set), Jacob A. Climer (costumes), Michael Gottlieb (lighting), Robert Bell (lighting programmer), Wallace Ford (sound), Jeremy Chernick (special effects); Associate Production Supervision, Donald J. Oberpriller; Dramaturg, Tommy McArdle; Props Coordinator, David Towlun; Assistant Design: Amelia Dombrowski (costumes), Kathleen Dobbins, Graham Kindred, Jay Scott (lighting), Ashley Ryan (hair), James Milkey (special effects); Assistants: Adele Magnolia (producers), Molly Gachignard (author), Rebecca Lustig (set designer), Caitlin Hunt (costume designer), Rosemary Barker, Josh Green (orchestrator); Wrangler, Margaret Kath; Production: Erik Hanson (head carpenter), Russ Dobson (assistant carpenter/deck automation), James. W. Sturek (fly automation), Michael J. Ward (production/head electrician), Paul Ker (spotlight), Tom Burke Robert Miller, John Blixt (spot operators), Ty Lackie (sound operator), Dawn Makay (production/head props), Chris Makay (assistant props), Debbie Cheretun (wardrobe supervisor), Valerie Frith (assistant wardrobe supervisor), Barry Ernst (hair supervisor), Timothy Miller (assistant hair supervisor); Dance Captain, Randy Glass; Fight Captain, Jay Lusteck; Synthesizer Programmer, David Rosenthal, Adam Schneider (assistant); Music Preparation, Anixter Rice Music Service; Advertising, Serino-Coyne; Press, The Jacksina Company, Judy Jacksina, Jamie Morris, Kaitlyn Marie Berg; Concept recording: Castle Communications

James Barbour and Aaron Lazar

CAST Dr. Alexandre Manette **Gregg Edelman;** Little Lucie **Catherine Missal;** Marquis St. Evremonde **Les Minski;** Mr. Jarvis Lorry **Michael Hayward-Jones;** Miss Pross **Katherine McGrath;** Lucie Manette **Brandi Burkhardt;** Jerry Cruncher **Craig Bennett;** Madame Therese Defarge **Natalie Toro;** Ernest Lafarge **Kevin Earley;** Gaspard **Michael Halling;** Little Gaspard **Miles Kath;** Seamstress **Mackenzie Mauzey;** Gabelle **Kevin Greene;** Charles Darnay **Aaron Lazar;** John Barsad **Nick Wyman;** Sydney Carton **James Barbour;** Stryver **Fred Inkley;** Attorney General **William Thomas Evans;** English Judge **James Moye;** Cronies **Tim Hartman, Walter Winston Oneil;** French President **Raymond Jaramillo McLeod;** The Young Man **Drew Aber;** Turnkey **Jay Lusteck;** Number Keeper **Devin Richards;** Ensemble **Drew Aber, Catherine Brunell, Alison Cimmet, William Thomas Evans, Kevin Greene, Michael Halling, Tim Hartman, Fred Inkley, Georgi James, Jay Lusteck, Mackenzie Mauzy, Raymond Jaramillo McLeod, James Moye, Walter Winston Oneil, Dan Petrotta, Devin Richards, Rob Richardson, Rebecca Robbins, Jennifer Smith, Anne Tolpegin, Mollie Vogt-Welch, Alison Walla;** Swings **Jennifer Evans, Randy Glass, Eric Van Tielen**

UNDERSTUDIES Catherine Brunell (Lucie Manette), William Thomas Evans (Mr. Jaris Lorry), Randy Glass (Dr. Alexandre Manette, Marquis St. Evremonde), Michael Halling (Charles Darnay), Tim Hartman (Mr. Jarvis Lorry, John Barsad), Fred Inkley (Dr. Alexandre Manette, Jerry Cruncher, John Barsad), Georgi James (Little Lucie, Little Gaspard), Jay Lusteck (Jerry Cruncher, Ernest Defarge), James Moye (Marquis St. Evremonde, Ernest Defarge, Sydney Carton), Rob Richardson (Sydney Carton), Rebecca Robbins (Lucie Manette, Madame Therese Defarge), Jennifer Smith (Miss Pross), Anne Tolpegin (Madame Therese Defarge, Miss Pross), Eric Van Tielen (Charles Darnay)

ORCHESTRA Kevin Stites (Conductor); Paul Raiman (Associate Conductor/synthesizer); Nicholas Archer (Assistant Conductor/synthesizer); Martin Agee, Conrad Harris (violins), Debra Shufelt-Dine (viola); Laura Bontrager (cello); David Phillips (bass); Judith Mendenhall (flute/piccolo); Matthew Dine (oboe/English horn); Mark Thrasher (clarinet/bass clarinet/bassoon); Timothy Schadt, Terry Szor (trumpet); Anthony Cecere, William De Vos (French horns); Christopher Olness (tenor trombone/bass trombone/tuba); James Musto III (drums/percussion); Kory Grossman (timpani/percussion)

MUSICAL NUMBERS Prologue: The Shadows of the Night, The Way It Ought to Be, You'll Never Be Alone, Argument, Dover, The Way It Ought to Be (reprise 1), No Honest Way, The Trial, Round and Round, Reflection, The Way It Ought to Be (reprise 2), Letter From Uncle, The Promise, I Can't Recall, Now at Last, If Dreams Came True, Out of Sight Out of Mind, I Always Knew, Little One, Until Tomorrow, Everything Stays the Same, No Honest Way (reprise), The Tale, If Dreams Came True (reprise), Without a Word, The Bluff, Let Her Be a Child, The Letter, Lament, Finale: I Can't Recall

SETTING Paris and London during the late eighteenth century. New York premiere of a new musical presented in two acts. World premiere presented at the Asolo Repertory Theatre (Sarasota, Florida), directed by Producing Artistic Director Michael Donald Edwards (see *Theatre World* Vol. 64, page 289).

SYNOPSIS Set against the epic backdrop of the French Revolution and based on the classic Dickens novel, *A Tale of Two Cities* is a musical about injustice, vengeance and the redemptive power of love. When Dr. Manette is released from the French Bastille after 17 years, he is resurrected from the brink of madness by his daughter, Lucie. In England they meet two very different men: the exiled French aristocrat, Charles Darnay, whom Lucie marries, and the drunken cynic, Sydney Carton. Soon family secrets and political intrigue combine to draw Lucie and her family back to Paris. At the height of the Reign of Terror, the musical finds an unlikely hero in Sydney Carton.

The Company

Natalie Toro

The Company

Gregg Edelman
(photos by Carol Rosegg)

Drew Aber, Kevin Earley, Nick Wyman,
Miles Kath, Natalie Toro and Michael Halling

Equus

Broadhurst Theatre; First Preview: September 5, 2008; Opening Night: September 28, 2008; Closed February 8, 2009; 21 previews, 156 performances

Written by Peter Shaffer; Produced by The Shubert Organization, Elizabeth I. McCann, Roger Berlind, John Gore, Hirschfeld Productions, Bill Kenwright, Emily Fisher Landau, Arielle Tepper Madover, Peter May, Chase Mishkin, Spring Sirkin; Director, Thea Sharrock; Design, John Napier; Lighting, David Hersey; Sound, Gregory Clarke; Movement, Fin Walker; Casting, Telsey + Company; Production Stage Manager, Susie Cordon; General Manager, Joey Parnes, John Johnson, S.D. Wagner, Leslie Glassburn, Kit Ingui; Company Manager, Kim Sellon; Dialect & Vocal Coach, Deborah Hecht; Stage Manager, Allison Sommers; Assistant Stage Manager, Brian Rardin; Production Assistant, Cynthia Hennon; Associate Director, Rachel Russell; Assistant to the Director, Alicia Dhyana House; Assistant to the Movement Director/Dance Captain, Spencer Liff; Associate Design: Ray Huessy (set), Ted Mather (lighting), Chloe Chapin (costumes); Production: Larry Morley (carpenter), Steve Cochrane (electrician), Mike Smanko (prop supervisor), Beth Berkeley (sound engineer), Jeff Turner (head electrician), Rob Halliday (moving light programmer), Dave Olin Rogers (wardrobe supervisor), Sandy Binion, Geoffrey Polischuk (dressers); Advertising, Serino-Coyne; Press, Sam Rudy Media Relations, Jim Randolph, Dale R. Heller, Robert Lasko

CAST Martin Dysart **Richard Griffiths;** Alan Strang **Daniel Radcliffe;** Nurse **Sandra Shipley;** Hesther Saloman **Kate Mulgrew;** Frank Strang **T. Ryder Smith;** Dora Strang **Carolyn McCormick;** The Horseman & Nugget **Lorenzo Pisoni;** Harry Dalton **Graeme Malcolm;** Horses **Collin Baja, Tyrone A. Jackson, Spencer Liff, Adesola Osakalumi, Marc Spaulding;** Jill Mason **Anna Camp**

STANDBYS Bill Buell (Martin Dysart), Paul O'Brien (Martin Dysart, Frank Strang, Harry Dalton), Paul David Story (Alan Strang), Sandra Shipley (Hesther Saloman), Amanda Quaid (Jill Mason, Nurse), Susan Pellegrino (Dora Strang, Nurse), Spencer Liff (The Young Horseman/Nugget), Adesola Osakalumi (The Young Horseman/Nugget); Kevin Boseman (Horses)

2008–2009 AWARDS Tony Award: Best Sound Design of a Play (Gregory Clark); Drama Desk Award: Outstanding Lighting Design of a Play (David Hersey)

*Daniel Radcliffe and
Lorenzo Pisoni*

SETTING The main action takes place in Rokeby Psychiatric Hospital in southern England. Revival of a play presented in two acts. This production was originally presented in London at the Gielgud Theatre February 27–June 9, 2007, produced by David Pugh and Dafydd Rogers, and featuring Mr. Griffith and Mr. Radcliffe. The play was originally produced in London in 1973 at the National Theatre. The original Broadway production opened at the Plymouth Theatre (now the Schoenfeld Theatre) on October 24, 1974, transferred to the Helen Hayes October 5, 1976, and closed October 2, 1977, playing 1,209 performances (see *Theatre World* Vol. 31, page 16). The original production earned a Tony, Drama Desk, Outer Critics Circle, and New York Drama Critics Circle Awards for best play.

SYNOPSIS Alan Strang, a mild-mannered stable boy who has a pathological and sexual fascination with horses and whose home life is filled with bigotry and religious fervor, savagely blinds the six horses in his care. As psychiatrist Martin Dysart unravels the mysteries behind the boy's violent act, Dysart realizes he must confront demons of his own.

*Richard Griffiths
(photos by Carol Rosegg)*

*Richard Griffiths, Daniel Radcliffe
and the Horses*

Mackenzie Crook and Carey Mulligan
(photo by Johan Persson)

Art Malik and Zoe Kazan
(photo by Joan Marcus)

The Seagull

Walter Kerr Theatre; First Preview: September 16, 2008; Opening Night: October 2, 2008; Closed December 21, 2008; 18 previews, 93 performances

Written by Anton Chekhov, new version by Christopher Hampton; Originally presented by The Royal Court Theatre; Produced by Sonia Friedman Productions, Bob Boyett, Robert G. Bartner, Norman & Steven Tulchin, Fox Theatricals, Dena Hammerstein, Sharon Karamazin, Olympus Theatricals, Spring Sirkin, Tara Smith, Morton Swinsky, Karl Sydow, The Weinstein Company, Eric Falkenstein, Jamie deRoy, Jacki Barlia Florin, Larry Hirschhorn, Jay & Cindy Gutterman, Joe McGinnis; Director, Ian Rickson; Set/Costumes, Hildegard Bechtler; Lighting, Peter Mumford; Sound, Ian Dickinson; Composer, Stephen Warbeck; Production Stage Manager, Arthur Gaffin; U.K. Casting, Lisa Makin; U.S. Casting, Jim Carnahan; Production Management, Aurora Productions (Gene O'Donovan, W. Benjamin Heller II, Bethany Weinstein, Melissa Mazdra, Amy Merlino Coey, Laura Archer, Dana Hesch); Associate Producer for Robert Boyett Theatricals, Tim Levy; General Management, Stuart Thompson Productions/David Turner, Caroline Prugh, James Triner; U.K. General Management, Sonia Friedman Productions, Diane Benjamin, Pam Skinner, Matthew Gordon, Sharon Duckworth; Company Manager, Adam J. Miller; Stage Manager, Jamie Greathouse; U.K. Stage Manager, Maddy Grant; Associate Design: Luke Smith (U.K. set), Charlie Smith (U.S. set), Laura Hunt (U.K. costumes), Katie Irish (U.S. costumes), Steve Andrews (U.K. lighting), Dale Knoth (U.S. lighting), Joanna Lynne Staub (U.S. sound); Production: George Fullum (carpenter), Drayton Allison (electrician), Andy Meeker (head props), Bill Lewis (production sound), Kelly A. Saxon (wardrobe supervisor), Amelia Haywood (dresser for Ms. Scott Thomas), Mickey Abbate, Ron Fleming (dressers), Valerie Gladstone (hair supervisor); General Management Assistants, Megan Curren, Geo Karapetyan, Aaron Thompson; Advertising, SpotCo; Press, Boneau/Bryan-Brown, Jim Byk, Matt Ross

CAST Konstantin **Mackenzie Crook;** Yakov **Christopher Patrick Nolan;** Masha **Zoe Kazan;** Medvendenko **Pearce Quigley;** Sorin **Peter Wright;** Nina **Carey Wight;** Polina **Ann Dowd;** Dorn **Art Malik;** Shamrayev **Julian Gamble;** Arkadina **Kristin Scott Thomas;** Trigorin **Peter Sarsgaard;** A Housemaid **Mary Rose;** The Cook **Mark Montgomery**

UNDERSTUDIES Mary Rose (Masha, Polina), Mark Montgomery (Trigorin), Jarlath Conroy (Sorin, Shamrayev, Dorn), Jessica Cummings (Nina, Masha, A Housemaid), Lynnda Ferguson (Arkadina, Polina, The Cook), Jonathan Fielding (Konstantin, Yakov, Medvendenko)

SETTING The action takes place in the house and gardens of Sorin's estate. Two years pass between Acts Three and Four. Revival of the play in a new adaptation presented in four acts with one intermission. This production was originally produced at London's Royal Court Theatre (Ian Rickson, Previous Artistic Director; Dominic Cooke, Artistic Director; Kate Horton, Executive Director) January 18–March 17, 2007 with most of this cast. The play first appeared on Broadway in 1916, and has had six prior revivals. Tony Randall's National Actors Theatre at the Lyceum presented the most recent revival from November 29, 1992–January 10, 1993, featuring Tyne Daly, Ethan Hawke, Jon Voight, Laura Linney, Tony Roberts, and Maryann Plunkett (see *Theatre World* Vol. 49, page 14).

SYNOPSIS *The Seagull*, set during a turning point in Russian history, involves young Konstantin, who struggles to define himself as a writer. When his mother, the famous actress Arkadina and her lover Trigorin arrive to spend the summer at her family's country home, their appearance wreaks havoc on the rest of the family.

Left: *Peter Sarsgaard and Carey Mulligan*
(photo by Joan Marcus)

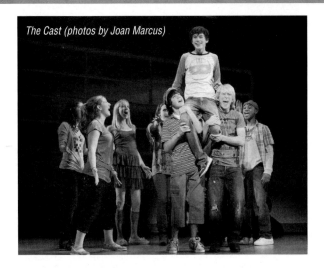

The Cast (photos by Joan Marcus)

13: A New Musical

Bernard B. Jacobs Theatre; First Preview: September 16, 2008; Opening Night: October 5, 2008; Closed January 4, 2009; 22 previews, 105 performances

Music and lyrics by Jason Robert Brown, book by Dan Elish and Robert Horn; Produced by Bob Boyett, Roger Berlind, Tim Levy, Ken Davenport, Ted Hartley, Stacey Mindich, Jane Bergère, Broadway Across America, Sharon Karmazin, Carl Mollenberg, Tom Miller, True Love Productions/Olympus Theatricals, Center Theatre Group; Director, Jeremy Sams; Choreography, Christopher Gattelli; Music Director, Tom Kitt; Arrangements and Orchestrations, Jason Robert Brown; Set and Costumes, David Farley; Lighting, Brian MacDevitt; Sound, Jon Weston; Casting, Mark Simon; Production Stage Manager, Rick Steiger; Technical Supervisor, Peter Fulbright; Executive Producer/General Management, 101 Productions Ltd., Wendy Orshan, Jeffrey M. Wilson, David Auster; Associate Producers, Shorenstein Hays Nederlander, The Araca Group; Associate Technical Supervisors, Mary Duffe, Colleen Houlehan; Company Manager, Sean Free; Vocal Coach, Liz Caplan; Stage Manager, Karen S. Armstrong; Assistant Stage Managers, Alex Libby, Lou Castro; Assistant Company Manager, Chris D'Angelo; Associate Director, Mark Schneider; Associate Music Director, Mat Eisenstein; Assistant to the Director, Anika Chapin; Associate Choreographer, Lou Castro; Assistant Choreographer, Pamela Remler; Fight Director, Tom Schall; Associate Design: Josh Zangen (set), MaryAnn D. Smith, Mary Fleming (costumes), Jennifer Schriever (lighting), Jason Strangfeld (sound); Assistant Design: Peter Hoerburger (lighting), Michael Eisenberg (sound); Assistants to Designers: Sydney Gallas (costumes), Zach Blane (lighting); Stylist Consultant, Maya Evans Judd; Moving Light Programmer, David Arch; Production: Paul Wimmer (carpenter), Scott "Gus" Poitras (assistant carpenter/automation), Michael Pitzer (electrician), Jeremy Wahlers (head electrician), Rob Presley (props supervisor), Jacob White (assistant props), Jason McKenna (sound supervisor), John T. Higgins (assistant sound), Linda Lee (wardrobe supervisor), Andrea Roberts (assistant wardrobe supervisor), Shana Albery, Andrea Gonzalez, John Webber (dressers), Jason Hayes (hair stylist); Dance Captain, Lou Castro; Music Preparation, John Blane; Keyboard Programmer, Randy Cohen; Advertising, Serino-Coyne; Press, Barlow · Hartman, Leslie Baden, Matt Shea; Cast recording: Sh-K-Boom/Ghostlight Records 4413

CAST Evan **Graham Phillips**; Evan (Sat. at 8 p.m.) **Corey J. Snide**; Patrice **Allie Trimm**; Brett **Eric M. Nelson**; Eddie **Al Calderon**; Malcolm **Malik Hammond**; Lucy **Elizabeth Egan Gillies**; Kendra **Delaney Moro**; Cassie **Brynn Williams**; Molly **Caitlin Gann**; Simon **Joey La Varco**; Richie **Eamon Foley**; Charlotte **Ariana Grande**; Archie **Aaron Simon Gross**

MUSICIANS Tom Kitt (Conductor/keyboard 1), Adam Michael Kaufman (keyboard II), Chris Raymond (guitar), Zach Poe (guitar), Zac Coe (percussion), Lexi Bodick (bass); Swings: Mat Eisenstein (keyboard), Charlie Rosen (bass, guitar, percussion)

UNDERSTUDIES Riley Costello (Archie, Eddie, Simon, Richie), Caitlin Gann (Kendra), Ariana Grande (Patrice), Eamon Foley (Malcolm), Henry Hodges (Evan, Archie, Simon, Richie), Joey La Varco (Brett, Eddie), Mary Claire Miskell (Patrice, Lucy, Molly, Cassie, Charlotte), Liana Ortiz (Lucy, Kendra, Molly, Cassie, Charlotte), Max Schneider (Brett, Malcolm, Simon, Richie)

MUSICAL NUMBERS 13/Becoming a Man, The Lamest Place in the World, Hey Kendra, Get Me What I Need, What It Means to Be a Friend, All Hail the Brain, Terminal Illness, Getting Ready, Any Minute, Good Enough, Bad Bad News, Tell Her, It Can't Be True, If That's What It Is, A Little More Homework, Brand New You

SETTING New York City and Indiana; the present. New York premiere of a new musical presented without intermission. Originally produced at Center Theatre Group, Los Angeles (Michael Ritchie, Artistic Director; Charles Dillingham, Managing Director) January 7–February 18, 2007 (see *Theatre World* Vol. 63, page 317); and subsequently produced by Goodspeed Musicals' Norma Terris Theatre in Chester, Connecticut (Michael P. Price, Artistic Director) May 9–June 8, 2008 (see Regional Theatre listings in this volume).

SYNOPSIS Performed by a cast and band of teenagers, *13* is a grown-up story about growing up. When his parents get divorced and he's forced to move from New York to a small town in Indiana, Evan Goldman just wants to make friends and survive the school year. The star quarterback is threatening to ruin his life and his only friend, Patrice, won't talk to him. The school freak sees an opportunity for blackmail and someone is spreading the nastiest rumors. This high-energy musical for all ages is about discovering that cool is where you find it, and sometimes where you least expect it.

Allie Trimm and Graham Phillips

A Man for All Seasons

American Airlines Theatre; First Preview: September 12, 2008; Opening Night: October 7, 2008; Closed December 14, 2008; 29 previews, 73 performances

Written by Robert Bolt; Produced by the Roundabout Theatre Company (Todd Haimes, Artistic Director; Harold Wolpert, Managing Director; Julia C. Levy, Executive Director); Director, Doug Hughes; Sets, Santo Loquasto; Costumes, Catherine Zuber; Lighting, David Lander; Original Music & Sound, David Van Tieghem; Hair & Wigs, Tom Watson; Production Stage Manager, James Fitzsimmons; Casting, Jim Carnahan & Carrie Gardner; General Manager, Rebecca Habel; Technical Supervisor, Steve Beers; Marketing/Sales Promotion, David B. Steffen; Development, Jeffory Lawson; Founding Director, Gene Feist; Associate Artistic Director, Scott Ellis; Company Manager, Carly DiFulvio; Stage Manager, Bryce McDonald; Assistant Director, David Ruttura; Roundabout General Manager, Sydney Beers; Director of Artistic Development and Casting, Jim Carnahan; Finance, Susan Neiman; Telesales, Daniel Weiss; Sales Operations, Charlie Garbowski Jr.; Associate Set Design, Jenny B. Sawyers; Set Designer's Assistant, Yoki Lai; First Costume Assistant, Nicole V. Moody; Costume Assistants, Lindsey Jones, David Newell; Assistant Lighting, Justin Partier; Lighting Designer's Assistant, Benjamin Farrar; Associate Sound, Jill BC DuBoff; Sound Designer Assistant, Brandon Wolcott; Production: Glenn Merwede (carpenter), Brain Maiuri (electrician), Andrew Forste (running properties), Dann Wojnar (sound operator), Christopher Mattingly (flyman), John Harrison (pyrotechnician), Kathy Fabian (props coordinator), Carrie Mossman (assistant props coordinator), Susan J. Fallon (wardrobe supervisor), Brittany Jones-Pugh, Kat Martin, Susan Kroeter, Vangeli Kaseluris (dressers), Manuela Laporte (hair and wig supervisor), Lauren Gallitelli (day wardrobe); Advertising, SpotCo; Press, Boneau/Bryan-Brown: Adrian Bryan-Brown, Matt Polk, Jessica Johnson, Amy Kass

CAST Sir Thomas More **Frank Langella;** Matthew, *his steward* **Peter Bradbury;** Richard Rich **Jeremy Strong;** Duke of Norfolk **Michael Gill;** Alice More **Maryann Plunkett;** Margaret More **Hannah Cabell;** Cardinal Wolsey **Dakin Matthews;** Thomas Cromwell **Zach Grenier;** Eustace Chapuys, *the Spanish* Ambassador **Triney Sandoval;** William Roper **Michael Esper;** King Henry VIII **Patrick Page;** Catherine Anger **Patricia Hodges;** The Jailer **Charles Borland;** Barmaid and others **Emily Dorsch;** Attendants **Curt Bouril, Alex Cole, Elizabeth Gilbert, Miguel Govea, Einar Gunn, Andy Lutz**

UNDERSTUDIES Charles Borland (Duke of Norfolk, King Henry VIII), Peter Bradbury (Richard Rich, Thomas Cromwell), Emily Dorsch (Margaret More, Catherine Anger), Patricia Hodges (Alice More), Ray Virta (Sir Thomas More, Cardinal Wolsey)

SETTING England. Act 1: 1529–1530. Act II: 1532–July 6, 1535. Revival of a play presented in two acts. Originally presented on Broadway at the ANTA Playhouse November 22, 1961–June 1, 1963, playing 637 performances (see *Theatre World* Vol. 18, page 50).

SYNOPSIS This legendary drama, receiving its first Broadway revival, is based on the fascinating, true story of English Chancellor Sir Thomas More and his moral objection to King Henry VIII's plan to leave the Catholic Church. When he is forced to decide whether to support or denounce the king, More chooses to take the most provocative action of all — to remain silent. An enduring exploration of politics, religion and power, *A Man for All Seasons* is a moving story about one man's fight for his beliefs and the price he must pay for his convictions.

Frank Langella (seated) *and Patrick Page*

Frank Langella and Zach Grenier *(photos by Joan Marcus)*

To Be or Not To Be

Samuel J. Friedman Theatre+; First Preview: September 16, 2008; Opening Night: October 14, 2008; Closed November 16, 2008; 32 previews, 40 performances

Written by Nick Whitby, based on the 1942 motion picture; Produced by Manhattan Theatre Club (Lynne Meadow, Artistic Director; Barry Grove, Executive Producer) by special arrangement with Bob Boyett, Roger Berlind, and Neal Street Productions; Director, Casey Nicholaw; Set, Anna Louizos; Costumes, Gregg Barnes; Lighting, Howell Binkley; Sound, Darron L. West; Projections, Wendall and Zak; Hair, Josh Marquette; Production Stage Manager, Charles Means; Casting, David Caparelliotis; General Manager, Florie Seery; Associate Artistic Director, Mandy Greenfield; Director of Artistic Development, Jerry Patch; Marketing, Debra Waxman-Pilla; Production Manager, Kurt Gardner; Director of Casting, Nancy Piccione; Development, Jill Turner Lloyd; Artistic Consultant, Daniel Sullivan; Artistic Administration/Assistant to Artistic Director, Amy Gilkes Loe; Literary Manager, Raphael Martin; Musical Development, Clifford Lee Johnson III; Finance, Jeffrey Bledsoe; Associate General Manager, Lindsey Brooks Sag; Subscriber Services, Robert Allenberg; Telesales, George Tetlow; Education, David Shookhoff; Associate Production Manager, Philip Naudé; Prop Supervisor, Scott Laule; Costume Supervisor, Erin Hennessy Dean; Company Manager, Seth Shepsle; Stage Manager, Elizabeth Moloney; Associate Director, Casey Hushion; Makeup Consultant, LaSonya Gunter; Dialect Coach, Thomas Schall; Associate Design: Dohyale Werle (set), Matthew Patchman (costumes), Ryan O'Gara (lighting), Matthew Hubbs (sound); Assistant to Projection Designers, Daniel Brodie; Hair Supervisor, Bert "Reo" Anderson; Production: Vaughn G. Preston (automation operator), John Fullum, Patrick Murray (flymen), Christopher Walters (assistant propertyman), Marc Polimeni (moving light programmer), Jane Masterson (conventional light programmer), Virginia Neininger, Suzanne Sponsler (dressers), Paige Grant (production assistant), Cassy Rush (child supervisor); Advertising, SpotCo; Press, Boneau/Bryan-Brown, Aaron Meier, Christine Olver, Matt Ross

CAST Rowicz **Peter Benson;** Grunberg **Robert Dorfman;** Sobinsky **Steve Kazee;** Dowasz **Peter Maloney;** Maria **Jan Maxwell;** Colonel Erhard **Michael McCarty;** Anna **Kristine Nielsen;** Young Grunberg **Brandon Perler;** Josef **David Rasche;** Silewski/Performer **Rocco Sisto;** Walowski/Major Schweinlich **Jimmy Smagula;** Eva **Marina Squerciati;** Officer **Mark J. Sullivan**

UNDERSTUDIES Dante Baldassin (Young Grunberg), Rufus Collins (Josef, Dowasz, Silewski/Performer, Officer), Angela Pierce (Maria, Ana, Eva), Jimmy Smagula (Colonel Erhardt, Grunberg), Mark J. Sullivan (Sobinsky, Rowicz, Walowski/Major Schweinlich)

Kristine Nielsen, Marina Squerciati and Jan Maxwell (photos by Joan Marcus)

SETTING Time: 1939. Place: Warsaw, Poland. World premiere of a new play presented without intermission.

SYNOPSIS At the Polski Theatre in 1939 Warsaw, Joseph and Maria Tura are about to open yet another smash with their theatrical troupe. As the German invasion gets underway, censors close the theatre, forcing the troupe to face desperate times. But when a handsome young bomber pilot enlists their help to catch a spy, what is a group of actors to do? This black comedy is a commentary on the World War II era and a tribute to the timeless joys of the theatre.

+Formerly the Biltmore Theatre, Manhattan Theatre Club renamed their Broadway home after the noted pioneer Broadway press agent, Samuel J. Friedman, during this production.

Robert Dorfman, Peter Benson, Marina Squerciati, Kristine Nielsen and David Rasche

Steve Kazee, Jan Maxwell and Kristine Nielsen

The back yard of the Keller Home at the outskirts of an American town.

The Company

All My Sons

Gerald Schoenfeld Theatre; First Preview: September 18, 2008; Opening Night: October 16, 2008; Closed January 11, 2009; 32 previews, 101 performances

Written by Arthur Miller; Produced by Eric Falkenstein, Ostar Productions, Barbara H. Freitag, Stephanie P. McClelland, Scott Delman/Blue Spruce Productions, Roy Furman, Ruth Hendel, in association with Hal Luftig, Jane Bergère, Jamie deRoy; Director, Simon McBurney; Set and Costumes, Tom Pye; Lighting, Paul Anderson; Sound, Christopher Shutt & Carolyn Downing; Projections, Finn Ross for Mesmer; Wigs, Paul Huntley; Associate Producer/Casting, Cindy Tolan; Production Stage Manager, Andrea "Spook" Testani; Technical Supervisor, Nick Schwartz-Hall; Associate Producers, Andrew Asnes/Adam Zotovich, Melanie Mills/Lauren Stevens, Scott Kluge/Nicholas Sopkin; Company Manager, Kimberly Kelley; General Management, Richards/Climan Inc.; Stage Managers, Alex Lyu Volckhausen, Dan Shaheen; Associate Director, Drew Barr; Associate Design: Frank McCullough, Lauren Alvarez (U.S. set), James Humphrey (U.K. set), Lauren Phillips (lighting), Amy Clark (costumes), Brian Beasley (projections); Fight Captain, Clark Johnson; Production: Don Robinson (carpenter), Cletus Karamon (electrician), Scott Laule (propertyman), Ned Hatton (sound operator), Peter Acken (projection programmer), Kay Grunder (wardrobe supervisor), Melissa Crawford, George Sheer (dressers), Erin Kennedy Lunsford (hair supervisor); Associate General Manager, John Gendron; General Management Associate, Jeromy Smith; General Management Assistant, Cesar Hawas; Director of Voice, Patsy Rodenburg; Production Assistants, Rachel Maier, Sarah Michele Penland; Casting Associate, Adam Caldwell; Child Wrangler, Katy Lathan; Advertising, SpotCo; Press, Boneau/Bryan-Brown, Jackie Green, Kelly Guiod

Patrick Wilson, Katie Holmes and Christian Camargo

CAST Joe Keller **John Lithgow**; Dr. Jim Bayliss **Damian Young**; Frank Lubey **Jordan Gelber**; Sue Bayliss **Becky Ann Baker**; Lydia Lubey **Danielle Ferland**; Chris Keller **Patrick Wilson**; Bert **Michael D'Addario**; Kate Keller **Dianne Wiest**; Ann Deever **Katie Holmes**; George Deever **Christian Camargo**; Neighbors **Sherman Howard, Clark Jackson, Lizbeth Mackay, Christopher Grey Misa, Danielle Skraastad**

UNDERSTUDIES Sherman Howard (Joe Keller, Dr. Jim Bayliss), Clark Jackson (Chris Keller, George Deever, Frank Lubey, Dr. Jim Bayliss), Lizbeth Mackay (Kate Keller, Sue Bayliss), Christopher Grey Misa (Bert), Danielle Skraastad (Ann Deever, Lydia Lubey)

SETTING The backyard of the Keller home on the outskirts of an American town; end of summer, 1946. Revival of the play presented in three acts with one intermission. Originally produced on Broadway at the Coronet Theatre January 29–November 8, 1947, playing 328 performances (see *Theatre World* Vol. 3, page 78.) The play was revived at the John Golden Theatre April 22–May 17, 1987 (see *Theatre World* Vol. 43, page 42).

SYNOPSIS *All My Sons* tells the story of a man who hastily sold defective airplane parts to the Army, which caused the crafts to crash, killing 21 men. His crime, which he long had deflected by blaming his business partner, comes back to light as his son plans to wed the partner's daughter.

Katie Holmes and Patrick Wilson

Katie Holmes and John Lithgow
(photos by Joan Marcus)

William H. Macy and Elizabeth Moss (photo by Robert J. Saferstein)

Raúl Esparza and William H. Macy (photo by Robert J. Saferstein)

Raúl Esparza and Jeremy Piven (photo by Brigitte Lacombe)

Speed-the-Plow

Barrymore Theatre; First Preview: October 3, 2008; Opening Night: October 23, 2008; Closed February 22, 2009; 24 previews, 140 performances

Written by David Mamet; Produced by Jeffrey Richards, Jerry Frankel, Jam Theatricals (Anry Granat, Jerry Mickelson, Steve Traxler), JK Productions (Judith Hansen & Kathleen Seidel), Ronald Frankel, Ostar Productions (Bill Haber), Peggy Hill, Bat-Berry Productions (Robert Masterson & Barry Weisbord), Ken Davenport, Scott Delman, Ergo Entertainment (Donny Epstein, Yeeshai Gross & Ellie Landau), Dede Harris, Alan D. Marks, Patty Ann McKinnon, Nicholas Quinn Rosenkranz, Adam Sansiveri, Jamie deRoy/Carl Mollenberg, in association with The Atlantic Theater Company; Director, Neil Pepe; Set, Scott Pask; Costumes, Laura Bauer; Lighting, Brian MacDevitt; Casting, Telsey + Company; Production Stage Manager, Matthew Silver; Technical Supervisor, Larry Morley; Fight Director, J. David Brimmer; Associate Producers, Rebecca Gold & Debbie Binso; Company Manager, Bruce Klinger; General Management, Richards/Climan Inc. (David R. Richards & Tamar Haimes); Stage Manager, David H. Lurie; Assistant Director, Jaime Castañeda; Associate Costumes, Bobby Tilley; Associate Lighting, Michael O'Connor, Caroline Chao; Assistant Set, Jeffrey Hinchee, Orit Jacoby Carroll, Lauren Alvarez; Associate General Manager, John Gendron; General Manager Associate, Jeromy Smith; Production Assistant, Jillian Oliver; Production Carpenter, Bill Craven; Production Electrician, Jimmy Maloney; Properties Coordinator, Kathy Fabian; Wardrobe Supervisor, Eileen Miller; Star Dressers, Laura Beattie, Kevin O'Brien; Assistant to Mr. Mamet, Pam Susemiehl; Assistants to Mr. Richards, Foster Kramer, Christopher Taggart; General Management Assistant, Cesar Hawas; Advertising, Serino-Coyne, Greg Corradetti, Tom Callahan, Robert Jones; Press, Jeffrey Richards Associates, Irene Gandy, Alana Karpoff, Elon Rutberg, Diana Rissetto

CAST Bobby Gould **Jeremy Piven** *; Charlie Fox **Raúl Esparza;** Karen **Elizabeth Moss**

*Succeeded by: Norbert Leo Butz (12/23/08), William H. Macy (1/13/09)

UNDERSTUDIES Jordan Lange (Gould & Fox), Eloise Mumford (Karen)

SETTING Time: 1980s. Place: Hollywood: Gould's office and his home. Revival of the play presented in three acts without intermission. Originally produced on Broadway by Lincoln Center Theater at the Royale Theatre May 3–December 31, 1988, playing 278 performances (see *Theatre World* Vol. 44, page 93).

SYNOPSIS *Speed-the-Plow* focuses on two high-powered Hollywood executives, Charlie Fox and Bobby Gould, who have come up from the mailroom together. Charlie brings Bobby a surefire hit with a major star attached. Bobby seems certain to give the green light, until his beautiful new secretary gets involved.

Jeremy Piven and Elizabeth Moss (photo by Brigitte Lacombe)

David Alvarez (photos by David Scheinmann)

Billy Elliot: The Musical

Imperial Theatre; First Preview: October 1, 2008; Opening Night: November 13, 2008; 40 previews, 228 performances as of May 31, 2009

Music by Elton John, book and lyrics by Lee Hall; based on the Universal Pictures/Studio Canal film *Billy Elliot* with screenplay by Lee Hall and direction by Stephen Daldry; Produced by Universal Pictures Stage Productions, Working Title Films, Old Vic Productions, in association with Weinstein Live Entertainment & Fidelity Investments; Director, Stephen Daldry; Choreography, Peter Darling; Associate Director, Julian Webber; Sets, Ian MacNeil; Costumes, Nicky Gillibrand; Lighting, Rick Fisher; Sound, Paul Arditti; Producers, Tim Bevan, Eric Fellner, Jon Fin, Sally Greene; Executive Producers, David Furnish, Angela Morrison; Musical Supervision and Orchestrations, Martin Koch; Music Director, David Chase; Associate Choreographer, Kathryn Dunn; Assistant Choreographer, Nikki Belsher; Hair/Wigs/Makeup, Campbell Young; U.K. Associate Design: Paul Atkinson (set), Claire Murphy (costumes), Vic Smerdon (lighting/programmer), John Owens (sound); Adult Casting, Tara Rubin; Children's Casting, Nora Brennan; Resident Director, B.T. McNicholl; Production Stage Manager, Bonnie L. Becker; Music Contractor, Michael Keller; Production Supervisors, Arthur Siccardi, Patrick Sullivan; General Management, Nina Lannan Associates/Devin Keudell; U.K. Casting, Pippa Ailion; Company Manager, Greg Arst; Associate Company Manager, Carol. M. Oune; Assistant Company Manager, Ashley Berman; Stage Manager, Charles Underhill; Assistant Stage Managers, Scott Rowen, Mary Kathryn Flynt; Supervising Dialect Coach (U.K.), William Conacher; Resident Dialect Coach, Ben Furey; Fight Director, David S. Leong; Dance Captains, Greg Graham & Cara Kjellman; Fight Captain, Grady McLeod Bowman; Choreographic Supervision, Ellen Kane; Staging and Dance Assistant, Lee Proud; Associate Music Director/Conductor, Shawn Gough; U.S. Associate Design: Brian Russman (costumes), Daniel Walker (lighting), Tony Smolenski IV (sound); Assistant Design: Jaimie Todd (sets), Rebecca Lustig (costumes), Kristina Kloss (lighting); Assistant to Ms. Gillibrand, Rachel Attridge; Moving Light Programmer (U.S), David Arch; Costume Shopper (U.K.), Bryony Fayers; Props Shoppers (U.K.), Kathy Anders, Lisa Buckley; Production Crew: Gerard Griffin (carpenter), Brian Hutchinson (flyman), Charles Heulitt III (automation carpenter), Jimmy Maloney Jr. (electrician), Kevin Barry (head electrician), Brad Robertson (assistant electrician), Joseph Harris Jr. (production props supervisor), David Bornstein (head propmaster), Reg Vessey (assistant propmaster), Bob Biasetti (production sound), Terri Purcell (wardrobe supervisor), Nanette Golia (associate wardrobe supervisor), Michael Berglund, Kenneth Brown, Charles Catanese, Lyssa Everett, Margiann Flanagan, Jay Gill, Joby Horrigan, Margo Lawless, Paul Ludick, Jeanine Naughton, Duduzile Ndlovu-Mitall, David Oliver, Lisa Preston, Jessica Scoblick, Pat Sullivan (dressers), Susan Corrado (hair/makeup supervisor), Monica Costea (assistant hair supervisor), Cory McCutcheon (hair dresser), Robert Wilson (head children's guardian), Annie L. Grappone (assistant head guardian), Elizabeth Daniels, John V. Fahey, John Funk, Amanda Grundy, Katherine Malak (guardians); Music Copying, Emily Grishman Music Preparation; Ballet Instructors, Finis Jhung, Francois Perron; Acrobat Instructor, Hector Salazar; Rehearsal Pianists, Joseph Joubert, Aron Accurso; Marketing, Allied Live/Laura Matalon, Tanya Grubich, Daya Wolterstorff, Sara Rosenzweig; Advertising, SpotCo (Drew Hodges, Jim Edwards, Tom Greenwald, Jim Aquino, Stacey Maya); General Management Associates, Adam Jackson, Steve Dow, Libby Fox; Press, Barlow · Hartman, John Barlow, Michael Hartman, Juliana Hannett, Michelle Bergmann; London Cast recording: Decca Broadway B0006 130-72

Left: *Gregory Jbara and Trent Kowalik*

CAST Billy **David Alvarez** or **Trent Kowalik** or **Kiril Kulish**; Mrs. Wilkinson **Haydn Gwynne**; Dad **Gregory Jbara**; Grandma **Carole Shelley**; Tony **Santino Fontana**; George **Joel Hatch**; Michael **David Bologna** or **Frank Dolce**; Debbie **Erin Whyland**; Small Boy **Mitchell Michaliszyn, Matthew Mindler**; Big Davey **Daniel Oreskes**; Lesley **Stephanie Kurtzuba**; Scab/Posh Dad **Donnie Kehr**; Mum **Leah Hocking**; Mr. Braithwaite **Thommie Retter**; Tracey Atkinson **Casey Whyland**; Older Billy/Scottish Dancer **Stephen Hanna**; Mr. Wilkerson **Kevin Bernard**; Pit Supervisor **Jeff Kready**; Tall Boy/Posh Boy **Keean Johnson**; Clipboard Woman **Jayne Patterson**; "Expressing Yourself" Dancers **Kevin Bernard, Grady McLeod Bowman, Jeff Kready, Stephanie Kurtzuba, David Larsen, Darrell Grand Moultrie, Jamie Torcellini, Grant Turner**; Ensemble **Kevin Bernard, Grady McLeod Bowman, Eric Gunhus, Stephen Hanna, Leah Hocking, Aaron Kaburick, Donnie Kehr, Jeff Kready, Stephanie Kurtzuba, David Larsen, Merle Louise, Darrell Grand Moultrie, Daniel Oreskes, Jayne Patterson, Tommie Retter, Jamie Torcellini, Grant Turner**; Ballet Girls **Juliette Allen Angelo, Heather Ann Burns, Eboni Edwards, Meg Guzulescu, Izzy Hanson-Johnston, Caroline London, Marina Micalizzi, Tessa Netting, Corrieanne Stein, Casey Whyland**; Swings **Maria Connelly, Samantha Czulada, Kyle DesChamps, Brianna Fragomeni, Greg Graham, Cara Kjellman, Kara Klein, David Koch, Liz Pearce**; Added: **David Eggers, Joshua Horner**

UNDERSTUDIES Tommy Batchelor* (Billy), Leah Hocking (Mrs. Wilkinson), Jayne Patterson (Mrs. Wilkinson), Donnie Kehr (Dad), Daniel Oreskes (Dad), Merle Louise (Grandma), Jeff Kready (Tony), David Larsen (Tony), Eric Gunhus (George), Jamie Torcellini (George), Keenan Johnson (Michael), Marie Connelly (Debbie)

*Tanner Pflueger replaced Tommy Batchelor 5/16/09-6/6/09 and alternated performances with the three original boys during that time.

ORCHESTRA David Chase (Conductor); Shawn Gough (Associate Conductor/keyboards); Ed Salkin, Rick Heckman, Mike Migliore, Jay Brandford (reeds); James Dela Garza, John Dent, Alex Holton (trumpets); Dick Clark, Jack Schatz (trombones); Roger Wendt, Eva Conti (French horns); Joseph Joubert (keyboards); JJ McGeehan (guitar); Randy Landau (bass); Gary Seligson (drums); Howard Jones (percussion)

MUSICAL NUMBERS The Stars Look Down, Shine, We'd Go Dancing, Solidarity, Expressing Yourself, Dear Billy (Mum's Letter), Born to Boogie, Angry Dance, Merry Christmas Maggie Thatcher, Deep Into the Ground, He Could Go and He Could Shine, Electricity, Once We Were Kings, Dear Billy (Billy's Reply), Company Celebration

2008–2009 AWARDS Tony Awards: Best Musical, Best Book of a Musical (Lee Hall), Best Direction of a Musical (Stephen Daldry), Best Choreography (Peter Darling), Best Leading Actor in a Musical (David Alvarez/Trent Kowalik/Kiril Kulish), Best Featured Actor in a Musical (Gregory Jbara), Best Orchestrations (Martin Koch) – tie with *Next to Normal*, Best Scenic Design of a Musical (Ian MacNeil), Best Lighting Design of a Musical (Rick Fisher), Best Sound Design of a Musical (Paul Arditti); Drama Desk Awards: Outstanding Musical, Outstanding Featured Actor in a Musical (Gregory Jbara), Outstanding Featured Actress in a Musical (Haydn Gwynne), Outstanding Direction of a Musical (Stephen Daldry), Outstanding Chroreography (Peter Darling), Outstanding Music (Elton John), Outstanding Book of a Musical (Lee Hall), Outstanding Orchestrations (Martin Koch), Outstanding Lighting Design of a Musical (Rick Fisher), Outstanding Sound Design (Paul Arditti); Outer Critics Circle Awards: Outstanding New Broadway Musical, Outstanding New Score, Outstanding Director of a Musical (Stephen Daldry), Outstanding Choreography (Peter Darling), Outstanding Featured Actor in a Musical (Gregory Jbara), Outstanding Featured Actress in a Musical (Haydn Gwynne), Outstanding Lighting (Rick Fisher), Special Achievement Award for David Alvarez, Trent Kowalik, Kiril Kulish; Drama Critics Circle Award: Best Musical; Drama League Award: Best Musical, Achievement in Musical Theatre (Elton John); **Theatre World Awards:** David Alvarez, Haydn Gwynne, Trent Kowalik, Kiril Kulish

SETTING A small mining town in County Durham, Northeast England, 1984–1985. Act 1: The eve of the Miner's Strike. Act 2: Six months later. American premiere of a musical presented in two acts. World premiere at the Victoria Palace Theatre (London), March 31, 2005 where it is still running.

SYNOPSIS Set behind the political backdrop of England's coal miner strike, *Billy Elliot The Musical* is a funny, heart-warming and feel-good celebration of one young boy's dream to break free from the expectations of his middle class roots. Based on the enormously popular film, this powerful new musical is the story of a boy who discovers he has a special talent for dance.

Carole Shelley

Trent Kowalik and the Ballet Girls

The Company

David Alvarez, Haydn Gwynne and the Company

Gregory Jbara and David Alvarez

Kiril Kulish and Stephen Hannah

Kiril Kulish and the Company

Cedric the Entertainer and John Leguizamo (photos by Joan Marcus)

American Buffalo

Belasco Theatre; First Preview: October 31, 2008; Opening Night: November 17, 2008; Closed November 23, 2008; 20 previews, 8 performances

Written by David Mamet; Produced by Elliot Martin, Ben Sprecher, Louise Forlenza, Bryan Bantry/Michael S. Rosenberg, Nica Burns/Max Weitzenhoffer, Wendy Federman, Bozeman Group LLC, Stewart F. Lane/Bonnie Comley, Karl Sydow, Jay Harris, William Franzblau, Oscar Joyner, Ken Wydro/Vy Higginsen, Ray Larsen, and Nelle Nugent, in association with Max Cooper and Norton Herrick; Director, Robert Falls; Sets & Costumes, Santo Loquasto; Lighting, Brian MacDevitt; Casting, Marjorie Martin; Fight Director, Rick Sordelet; Technical Supervisor, Larry Morley; Production Stage Manager, Robert Bennett; Associate Producers, Kenneth Treaton, Bob Reich, Sharon Carr, David O. Leiwant, David Jaroslawicz; Marketing, Marcia Pendelton/WTGP, Blanca Lasalle/Creativelink Inc., Leanne Schanzer Promotions; General Manager, Peter Bogyo; Company Manager, Lisa M. Poyer; Stage Manager, Denise Yaney; Rain Effects, Gregory Meeh/Jauchem and Meeh; Assistant Director, Stephanie Yankwitt; Associate Design: Jenny Sawyers (set), Mitchell Bloom (costumes), Jennifer Schriever (lighting); Assistant Set Design, Yoki Lai; Sound Consultant, Carl Casella; Associate Sound, Wallace Flores; Dialect Coach, Kate Wilson; Props Coordinator, Kathy Fabian/Propstar; Associate Props, Rose Howard; Prop Shoppers, Jennifer Breen, Carrie Mossman, Christina Gould; Flame Treatment, Turning Star; Assistant to the General Manager, Martin Giannini; Production Assistant, Aaron Gonzalez; Assistant to Mr. Martin, Kate Kenny; Assistants to Mr. Sprecher, Jennifer Wills & Kate Derby; Production: Michael Pitzer (electrician), Kathleen Gallagher (wardrobe supervisor), Kevin Andre Dickens (dresser); Advertising, Serino-Coyne; Press, Richard Kornberg & Associates, Don Summa, Billy Zavelson, Alyssa Hart

CAST Donny Dubrow **Cedric the Entertainer;** Bobby **Haley Joel Osment;** Walter Cole (Teacher) **John Leguizamo**

UNDERSTUDIES Michael Leon-Wooley (Donny Dubrow), Dane DeHaan (Bobby), Antonio Edwards Suarez (Walter Cole (Teacher)

SETTING Don's Resale Shop. A junkshop. One Friday. Revival of a play presented in two acts. Originally opened at Chicago's Goodman Theatre, and produced on Broadway at the Barrymore Theatre February 16–June 11, 1977 (see *Theatre World* Vol. 33, page 55). The play was revived at the Booth Theatre October 27, 1983–February 4, 1984 (see *Theatre World* Vol. 40, page 14), and Off-Broadway at the Atlantic Theater Company March 3–May 21, 2000 (see *Theatre World* Vol. 56, page 77).

SYNOPSIS *American Buffalo* follows three small-time crooks who wax philosophically about society while conspiring to steal a rare and valuable coin from a neighborhood collector. Volcanic and motor mouthed Teach schemes and spars with fatherly, street-smart junk shop owner Donny, enlisting Bobby, a slow-witted and desperate young delinquent, to carry out their misbegotten robbery.

Haley Joel Osment (kneeling) *and Cedric the Entertainer*

Right: *John Leguizamo, Haley Joel Osment and* (background) *Cedric the Entertainer*

Dividing the Estate

Booth Theatre; First Preview: October 23, 2008; Opening Night: November 20, 2008; Closed January 4, 2009; 31 previews, 50 performances

Written by Horton Foote; Produced by Lincoln Center Theater (André Bishop, Artistic Director; Bernard Gersten, Executive Producer) by arrangement with Primary Stages (Casey Childs, Founder and Executive Producer; Andrew Leynse, Artistic Director; Elliot Fox, Managing Director); Director, Michael Wilson; Sets, Jeff Cowie; Costumes, David C. Woolard; Lighting, Rui Rita; Original Music and Sound, John Gromada; Casting, Stephanie Klapper; Production Stage Manager, Roy Harris; Development, Hattie K. Jutagir; Marketing, Linda Mason Ross; General Manager, Adam Siegel; Production Manager, Jeff Hamlin; Wigs & Hair, Paul Huntley; Assistant Stage Manager, Cole P. Bonenberger; Company Manager, Matthew Markoff; Associate Director, Maxwell Williams; Assistant to the Director, Christy Pellegrini; Fight Director, B.H. Barry; Technical Supervision, William Nagle & Patrick Merryman; Associate Design: David Barber (sets), Kevin Brainerd (costumes), Ben Krall (lighting), Christopher Cronin (sound); Assistant to Mr. Rita, Carl Faber; Assistant Sound Design, Bridget O'Connor; Production: John Weingart (carpenter), Graeme McDonnell (electrician), Mark Dignam (propertyman), Jenny Montgomery (sound), Susan Barras (props), Moira MacGregor-Conrad (wardrobe supervisor), Catherine Dee & James W. Swift (dressers), Cindy Demand (hair supervisor); Casting Assistant, Jennifer Pardilla; Assistant to Casting Directors, Carrie Virginia Lee; Production Assistant, Marisa Levy; For Lincoln Center Theater: David S. Brown (Director of Finance), Kati Koerner (Director of Education), Jessica Niebanck (Associate General Manager), Paul Smithyman (Associate Production Manager), Rachel Norton (Associate Director of Development); For Primary Stages: Michelle Bossy (Associate Artistic Director), Jessica Sadowski Comas (Director of Development), Shanta Mali (Director of Marketing), Peter F. Feuchtwanger (Production Supervisor), Reuben Saunders (Business Manager); Advertising, Serino-Coyne; Poster Art, James McMullan; Press, Philip Rinaldi, Barbara Carroll

CAST Son **Devon Abner;** Lucille **Penny Fuller;** Stella **Elizabeth Ashley;** Mildred **Pat Bowie;** Doug **Arthur French;** Lewis **Gerald McRaney;** Cathleen **Keiana Richard;** Pauline **Maggie Lacey;** Mary Jo **Hallie Foote;** Emily **Jenny Dare Paulin;** Sissie **Nicole Lowrance;** Bob **James DeMarse;** Irene **Virginia Kull**

UNDERSTUDIES Kevin O'Rourke (Son, Bob), Stephen Bradbury (Bob, Lewis), Jill Tanner (Stella), Jennifer Harmon (Lucille, Mary Jo), Kelly Taffe (Mildred, Cathleen), Charles Turner (Doug), Annie Purcell (Pauline, Irene), Jennifer Joan Thompson (Emily, Sissie)

SETTING Time and Place: 1987; Harrison, Texas. Off-Broadway transfer of a new play presented in two acts. This production was previously produced at Primary Stages September 18–October 28, 2007 (see *Theatre World* Vol. 64, page 184) with most of this cast. A previous version of the play was presented at the McCarter Theatre Company in March 1989, and subsequently at the Great Lakes Theater Festival in October 1990 and the North Carolina School for the Arts in December 1991.

SYNOPSIS Set in Foote's fictional Harrison, Texas (a stand-in for his real-life hometown of Wharton), *Dividing the Estate* tells the often-hilarious story of an extended family that must confront its past as it prepares for its future as they encounter conflict over what should be done with their extensive property holdings.

Elizabeth Ashley, James DeMarse, Hallie Foote, Maggie Lacey and Devon Abner

The Company (photos by Joan Marcus)

Right: *Gerald McRaney, Elizabeth Ashley and Penny Fuller*

Irving Berlin's White Christmas

Marquis Theatre; First Preview: November 14, 2008; Opening Night: November 23, 2008; Closed January 4, 2009; 12 previews, 53 performances

Music and lyrics by Irving Berlin, book by David Ives and Paul Blake; based upon the Paramount Pictures film written for the screen by Norman Krasna, Norman Panama, and Melvin Frank; Produced by Kevin McCollum, John Gore, Tom McGrath, Paul Blake, The Producing Office (Kevin McCollum, Jeffrey Seller, John S. Corker, Debra Nir, Scott A. Moore, Caitlyn Thomson), Dan Markley, Sonny Everett, Broadway Across America, in association with Paramount Pictures; Director, Walter Bobbie; Choreography, Randy Skinner; Music Supervisor, Rob Berman; Sets, Anna Louizos; Costumes, Carrie Robbins; Lighting, Ken Billington; Sound, Acme Sound Partners; Orchestrations, Larry Blank; Vocal and Dance Arrangements, Bruce Pomahac; Music Coordinator, Seymour Red Press; Marketing, Scott A. Moore; Technical Supervisor, Brian Lynch; Production Stage Manager, Michael J. Passaro; Associate Choreographer, Kelli Barclay; Casting, Jay Binder, Nikole Vallins; General Management, John S. Corker, Barbara Crompton; Associate Director, Marc Bruni; Associate Producers, Richard A. Smith, Douglas L. Meyer, and James D. Stern; Company Manager, Barbara Crompton; Stage Manager, Jay McLeod; Associate Company Manager, Andrew Jones; Assistant Stage Manager, Jim Athens; Associate Music Director, David Gursky; Additional Orchestrations, Peter Myers; Assistant Director, David Ruttura; Directing Assistant, Ross Evans; Assistant Choreographer/Dance Captain, Sara Brians; Assistant Choreographer/Assistant Dance Captain, Mary Giattino; Principle Wigs, Paul Huntley; Ensemble Wigs, Howard Leonard; Associate Design: Todd Potter (sets), Ed McCarthy & Jim Milkey (lighting), Jason Badger (automated lighting programmer), Nick Borisjuk (sound); Production: Lehan Sullivan (production carpenter), Joe Valentino (head carpenter), Jeremy Palmer (flyman), Kenny Brock & Chris Doornbos (automation), Manuel Becker (production electrician), Jack Culver (head electrician), James Crayton & Chris Robinson (assistant electricians), Brad Gyorgak (sound engineer), Elizabeth Coleman (assistant sound engineer), George Wagner (production props master), David Speer (prop master), Lee Austin (production wardrobe supervisor), Jessica Worsnop (wardrobe supervisor), Ricky Yates (assistant wardrobe), Elisa Acevedo (hair supervisor); Producer and Management Assistants: Michael Bosner, Kim Marie Vasquez, Jen Collins, Samara Harand; Production Assistants, Thomas Recktenwald & Conwell Worthington III; Music Preparation, Chelsea Music Service/Paul Holderbaum; Synthesizer Programmer, Bruce Samuels; Rehearsal Pianists, Paul Masse & Matthew Perri; Advertising, SpotCo; Press, Boneau/Bryan-Brown, Joe Perrotta, Kelly Guiod; Show recording: Sh-K-Boom/Ghostlight Records 7915581225-2

CAST Bob Wallace **Stephen Bogardus;** Phil Davis **Jeffry Denman;** Ralph Sheldrake **Peter Reardon;** General Henry Waverly **Charles Dean;** Ed Sullivan Announcer **Sheffield Chastain;** Rita **Anne Horak;** Rhoda **Katherine Tokarz;** Tessie **Amy Justman;** Betty Haynes **Kerry O'Malley;** Judy Haynes **Meredith Patterson;** Jimmy **Jarran Muse;** Quintet **Cliff Bemis, Drew Humphrey, Wendy James, Amy Justman, Kevin Worley;** Mr. Snoring Man/Ezekiel Foster **Cliff Bemis;** Mrs. Snoring Man/ Sheldrake's Secretary **Wendy James;** Train Conductor **Drew Humphrey;** Martha Watson **Susan Mansur;** Susan Waverly **Melody Hollis;** Mike Nulty/Regency Room Announcer **Sheffield Chastain;** Regency Room Dancers **Stephen Carrasco, Chad Seib, Kevin Worley;** Ensemble **Phillip Attmore, Stephen Carrasco, Margot De La Barre, Anne Horak, Drew Humphrey, Wendy James, Amy Justman, Matthew Kirk, Sae La Chin, Jarran Muse, Alessa Neeck, Shannon O'Bryan; Con O'Shea-Creal, Kiira Schmidt, Chad Seib, Kelly Sheehan, Katherine Tokarz, Kevin Worley;** Swings **Jacob bin Widmar, Sara Brians, Mary Giattino, Richie Mastascusa**

Susan Mansur, Charles Dean, Kerry O'Malley, Stephen Bogardus, Jeffry Denman, Meredith Patterson, Peter Reardon, Melody Hollis and the Company

Stephen Bogardus and the Company (photos by Joan Marcus)

Jeffry Denman, Stephen Bogardus and the Company

UNDERSTUDIES Peter Reardon (Bob Wallace), Amy Justman (Betty Haynes), Kevin Worley (Phil Davis), Shannon O'Bryan (Judy Haynes), Cliff Bemis (General Waverly), Athena Ripka (Susan Waverly), Sheffield Chastain (Ralph Sheldrake), Wendy James (Martha Watson), Drew Humphrey (Mr. Snoring Man/Ezekiel Foster), Jacob bin Widmar (Mike McNulty/Ed Sullivan Announcer)

Meredith Patterson, Jeffry Denman and the Company

ORCHESTRA Rob Berman (Conductor); David Gursky (Associate Conductor/keyboards); Marilyn Reynolds, Paul Woodiel, Robin Zeh, Mary Whitaker, Susan French (violins); Chris Jaudes, Ronald Buttacavoli, Elaine Burt (trumpets); Micah Young (keyboards); Mairi Dorman, Danny Miller (celli); Steve Kenyon, Todd Groves, David Young, Allen Won, Mark Thrasher (woodwinds); Larry Farrell, Clint Sharman, Jeff Nelson (trombones); David Byrd-Marrow (French horn); Bill Hayes (percussion); Lou Bruno (bass); Rich Rosenzweig (drums)

MUSICAL NUMBERS Overture, Happy Holiday, White Christmas, Let Yourself Go, Love and the Weather, Sisters, The Best Things Happen While You're Dancing, Snow, What Can You Do With a General?, Let Me Sing and I'm Happy, Count Your Blessings Instead of Sheep, Blue Skies, Entr'acte, I Love a Piano, Falling Out of Love Can Be Fun, Sisters (reprise), Love You Didn't Do Right By Me/How Deep Is the Ocean, We'll Follow the Old Man, Let Me Sing and I'm Happy (reprise), How Deep Is the Ocean (reprise), We'll Follow the Old Man (reprise), White Christmas (reprise), Finale: I've Got My Love to Keep Me Warm

SETTING An army camp in Europe, Christmas Eve, 1944; New York City and the Columbia Inn in Vermont, December, 1954. New York premiere of a musical presented in two acts. World premiere at The Muny (St. Louis) in 2000. The Broadway production team launched this version of the show in San Francisco (Curran Theatre) in 2004. In the fall of 2005 three major productions opened simultaneously in Boston (Wang Theatre), Los Angeles (Pantages Theatre), and again in San Francisco (Orpheum Theatre). In 2006 the production was remounted at the Ordway Theatre in Minneapolis, and also played major engagements in Detroit and Toronto. In addition, the show was licensed and produced at numerous regional and dinner theatres in 2007, prior to the Broadway production.

SYNOPSIS Based on the holiday favorite classic 1954 film starring Bing Crosby, Danny Kaye, Rosemary Clooney, and Vera Ellen, *Irving Berlin's White Christmas* tells the story of two showbiz buddies who put on a show in a picturesque Vermont inn, and find their perfect mates — a sister act, no less — in the bargain. Featuring some of Berlin's most famous tunes, the Broadway production played a limited holiday engagement.

Stephen Bogardus, Kerry O'Malley, Jeffry Denman and Meredith Patterson

Liza's at the Palace… !

Palace Theatre; Opening Night: December 3, 2008; Closed January 4, 2009; 22 performances

Written by Liza Minnelli, additional material by David Zippel; Presented by John Scher and Metropolitan Talent Presents LLC and Jubilee Time Productions LLC; Director/Choreography, Ron Lewis; Set, Ray Klausen; Lighting/Production Stage Manager, Matt Berman; Sound Matt Kraus; Technical Supervisor, Fred Gallo; Musical Producer, Phil Ramone; Vocal Arrangements, Kay Thompson & Billy Stritch; Musical Supervisor, Billy Stritch; Conductor/Drummer, Michael Berkowitz; General Manager, Niko Companies Ltd.; Executive Producer/Ms. Minnelli's Manager, Gary Labriola; Musical Number Arrangements and Orchestrations, Ralph Burns, Ned Ginsburg, Marvin Hamlisch, Sonny Kompanek, Don Sebesky, Artie Schroek, Billy Stritch, and Torrie Zito; Musical Contractor, Ross Konikoff; Company Manager, Petrina Moritz; Assistant Choreography/Dance Captain, Tiger Martina; Assistant Stage Manager, Rocky Noel; Assistant Scenic Design, Robert F. Wolin; Assistant Sound Design, Bob Hanlon; Production: Peter Johnson (production carpenter), Jon Lawson (production electrician), Thomas Thoon (head front light), Brendon Boyd (lighting programmer), Ty Lackey (monitor engineer), Gary D. Labriola (teleprompter operator), Kathy Guida (wardrobe supervisor), Casey Paul (star dresser); Music Preparation, Chelsea Music (Donald Oliver and Paul Holderbaum); Photography, Rick Day, Daniela Frederici, Bill Westmoreland; Marketing, HHC Marketing (Hugh Hysell, Matt Sicoli, Nicole Pando); Personal Assistant to Ms. Minnelli, Lisa Day; Assistant to Ms. Minnelli, Phyllis Little; For Metropolitan Talent Presents: John Scher & Al Cafaro (Co-Chief Executive Officers), Errol Antzis (Chief Financial Officer), Ian Noble (Senior Producer), Jeanne Bohorquez (Associate Producer), Stacy Reader (Booking Coordinator), Brian O'Boyle (Marketing Director), Dana Wise (Marketing Manager), Howard Brooks (New Media Director), Nadine Dunn (New Media Coordinator), Scott Campbell (Ticketing Director), Diana Guthey (Assistant to Mr. Scher); Press, Cromarty & Company, Peter Cromarty, Alice Cromarty; Cast recording: Hybrid Recordings SNY200532

Liza Minnelli and
Cortes Alexander (seated),
Jim Caruso, Johnny Rodgers
and Tiger Martina (standing)
(photo by Bill Westmoreland)

Liza Minnelli (photo by Eric Antoniou)

STARRING Liza Minnelli; Featuring **Johnny Rodgers, Cortés Alexander, Jim Caruso, Tiger Martina**

ORCHESTRA Michael Berkowitz (Conductor/drums), Billy Stritch (piano), Rick Cutler (keyboards), David Nyberg (percussion), Dan Levine (trombone), Bill Washer (guitar), Chip Jackson (bass), Ross Konikoff & Dave Trigg (trumpet), Chuck Wilson (alto sax), Ed Xiques (baritone sax), Frank Perowsky (tenor sax)

MUSICAL NUMBERS *Act One:* Teach Me Tonight *(music by Gene DePaul, lyrics by Sammy Cahn)*; I Would Never Leave You *(music by Billy Stritch, Johnny Rodgers and Brian Lane Green)*; If You Hadn't, But You Did *(music by Jule Styne, lyrics by Betty Comden and Adolph Green)*; What Makes a Man a Man? *(music and lyrics by Charles Aznavour)*; My Own Best Friend *(music by John Kander, lyrics by Fred Ebb)*; Maybe This Time *(Kander/Ebb)*; He's Funny That Way *(music by Neil Moret, lyrics by Richard Whiting)*; Palace Medley *(new introduction by David Zippel, John Kander and Billy Stritch; original songs by Roger Edens;* "Shine on Harvest Moon" *by N. Bayes, J. Norworth, N. Graw,* "Some of These Days" *by S. Brooks;* "My Man" *by M. Yvain, A. Willemetz, J. Charles;* "I Don't Care" *by H. Sutton, R. Grant, J. Lennox)*; Cabaret *(Kander/Ebb)*; *Act Two:* But the World Goes 'Round *(Kander/Ebb)*; Hello, Hello *(music and lyrics by Kay Thompson)*; Jubilee Time *(Kay Thompson)*; Basin Street Blues *(music and lyrics by Spencer Williams, special verse by Kay Thompson)*; Clap Yo' Hands *(music by George Gershwin, lyrics by Ira Gershwin)*; Liza (All the Clouds'll Roll Away) *(music by George Gershwin, lyrics by Ira Gershwin/Gus Kahn)*; I Love a Violin *(Kay Thompson)*; Mammy *(music by Walter Donaldson, lyrics by Sam M. Lewis and Joe Young)*; Theme from *New York, New York (Kander/Ebb)*; I'll Be Seeing You *(music by Sammy Fain, lyrics by Irving Kahal)*

2008–2009 AWARDS Tony Award: Best Special Theatrical Event; Drama Desk Award: Special Award to Liza Minnelli

A theatrical concert and musical extravaganza presented in two acts.

SYNOPSIS Liza Minnelli brings her unmatchable magic to Broadway in her new show *Liza's At The Palace...* featuring an incomparable Minnelli songfest including many of her personal favorites and signature hits. And, for the first time onstage, Liza pays an affectionate salute to her godmother, the late Kay Thompson who was a legendary performer, author, as well a gifted vocal arranger and music director/vocal coach at MGM Studios, and who worked with stars such as Judy Garland, Frank Sinatra and Lena Horne. Supported by a quartet of dynamic singer/dancers (as "The Williams Brothers"), and a twelve-piece orchestra, Liza lovingly recreates Thompson's groundbreaking late-1940's nightclub act using Thompson's original vocal arrangements.

Slava's Snowshow

Helen Hayes Theatre; First Preview: November 8, 2008; Opening Night: December 14, 2008; Closed January 4, 2009; 7 previews, 35 performances

Created and staged by Slava Polunin by arrangement with SLAVA, Gwenael Allan, and Ross Mollison; Produced by David J. Foster, Jared Geller, Joseph Gordon-Levitt, Judith Marinoff Cohn, and John Pinckard; Sets/Costumes, Victor Plotkinov; Lighting, Alexander Pecherskiy; Sound, Rastyam Dubinnikov; Art Direction, Gary Cherniakhovskii; Russian Company Administrator, Natasha Tabachnikova; Associate Producers, Jay Kuo & Lorenzo Thione; General Manager, Foster Entertainment/Jennie Connery; Production Management, Juniper Street Productions (Hillary Blanken, Ana-Rose Greene, Kevin Broomell, Guy Kwan); Assistant Company Manager, Michael Altbaum; Marketing Director, Natasha Montero; Ensemble Members, Ivan Yaropolskiy & Vitaly Galich; Group Sales, Geoff Borman; Production: Dmitri Ushakov (technical supervisor), Doug Purcell (production carpenter), Joe Beck (production electrician), Roger Keller (production props), Robert Etter (production sound), Lorne MacDougall & Greg Fedigan (follow spots), Joe Moritz (assistant props), Olga Devyatisilnaya (wardrobe supervisor); Company Administrator (Europe), Anna Hannikaninen; Production Assistant, Sean Richardson; For Foster Entertainment: David Foster (Producer), Jared Geller (Producer/Director of Development), Jennie Connery (General Manager), David Reynolds (accounts), Malinda Sorci & Hannah Mason (associates), Lucy Foster and Edie Foster (interns); Advertising, Allied Live LLC; Press, Barlow · Hartman, John Barlow, Michael Hartman, Tom D'Ambrosio, Michelle Bergmann

CAST Yellow Clown (rotating) **Slava Polunin, Derek Scott, Robert Saralp;** Green Clowns (rotating) **Spencer Chandler, Christopher Lynam, Johnson, Fyodor Makarov, Tatiana Karamysheva, Ivan Polunin, Dmitri Khamzin, Elena Ushakova**

Broadway premiere of an Eastern European clown show presented in two acts. Originally presented Off-Broadway at the Union Square Theatre August 24, 2004–January 14, 2007 (see *Theatre World* Vol. 61, page 121).

SYNOPSIS Slava returns to New York for a limited Broadway engagement after a successful run downtown that closed two seasons prior, after playing over 1,000 performances. In *Slava's Snowshow*, Russia's greatest clowns (along with a few Americans) string together a series of breathtaking images performed to popular music. A giant cobweb stretches over the entire audience; a raging blizzard coats the audience in snow; the audience and cast keep giant helium-filled beach balls afloat. Lyrical, hilarious, poignant and brilliant, *Slava's Snowshow* has captivated audiences around the world.

Slava Polunin (photos by Veronique Vial)

Seven Green Clowns

A scene from Slava's Snowshow

A scene from Slava's Snowshow

Brian d'Arcy James and Daniel Breaker

Brian d'Arcy James and Sutton Foster

Christopher Sieber and the Company

Shrek The Musical

Broadway Theatre; First Preview: November 8, 2008; Opening Night: December 14, 2008; 37 previews, 193 performances as of May 31, 2009

Book and lyrics by David Lindsay-Abaire, music by Jeanine Tesori; based on the DreamWorks Animation motion picture and the book by William Steig; Produced by DreamWorks Theatricals and Neal Street Productions; Director, Jason Moore; Choreography, Josh Prince; Music Direction/Incidental Music Arrangements, Tim Weil; Orchestrations, Danny Troob; Sets/Costumes/Puppet Design, Tim Hatley; Lighting, Hugh Vanstone; Sound, Peter Hylenski; Hair/Wigs, David Brian-Brown; Makeup, Naomi Donne; Prosthetics, Michael Marino/Prosthetic Renaissance; Casting, Tara Rubin; Illusions Consultant, Marshall Magoon; Associate Director/Production Stage Manager, Peter Lawrence; Production Management, Aurora Productions; Dance Arrangements, Matthew Sklar; Vocal Arrangements, Jeanine Tesori & Tim Weil; Associate Orchestrator, John Clancy; Music Coordinator, Michael Keller; Marketing, Clint Bond Jr.; General Management, Stuart Thompson Productions, James Triner; Electronic Music Design, Andrew Barrett; Company Manager, Roeya Banuazizi; Stage Manager, Rachel A. Wolff; Assistant Stage Manager, Chad Lewis; Assistant Company Manager, Scott Armstrong; Assistant Director, Stephen Sposito; Associate Choreographer, Sloan Just; Dance Captain, Justin Greer; Puppet Captain, John Tartaglia; Assistants to Stage Managers, Stacey Zaloga & Bryan Rountree; Associate Design: Paul Weimer (set), Andrew Edwards (U.K. scenic), Tracy Christensen, Brian J. Bustos, Jack Galloway (costumes), Philip Rosenberg (lighting), Keith Caggiano (sound), Susan Corrado (hair/wigs), Dave Presto (prosthetics); Assistant Design: Derek Stenborg, Zhanna Gervich (U.S. set), Tim Blazdell (U.K. scenic), Ben Davies & Paul Tulley (U.K. model makers), Jessica Wegener, Sarah Laux (costumes), Anthony Pearson (lighting), Angela L. Johnson (makeup), Leon Dobkowski, Katie Irish, Roxana Ramseur (costume department); Moving Lights Programmer, Sharon Huizinga; Media Associate and Programmer, Laura Frank; Media Assistant, Joshua Fleitell; Production: Mike Martinez (production carpenter), Rick Styles (fly automation carpenter), James J. Fedigan, Randall Zaibek (production electricians), Mike Cornell (head electrician), Paul D.J. Davila (deck electrician), Andrew Dean (follow spot), Roy Franks (pyro/special effects electrician), Phil Lojo (production sound), David Dignazio (head sound engineer), Jerry Marshall (production props), Andrew Miller (assistant props), Michael Sancineto (wardrobe supervisor), Meghan Carsella (assistant wardrobe supervisor), Megan Bowers, Allesandro Ferdico, Dan Foss, Sara Foster, Tony Hoffman, Hiro Hosomizu, Pamela Hughes, Kurt Kielmann, Pamela Kurz, Emily Ockenfels, Julienne Schubert-Blechman (dressers), Jack Scott (Mr. James' dresser), Julien Havard (Ms. Foster's dresser), Carole Morales (production hair supervisor), Richard Orton (assistant hair supervisor), Joel Hawkins, Liz Mathews (hairdressers), Chelsea Roth (hair day worker), Angela L. Johnson (production makeup supervisor), Christina Grant (assistant makeup supervisor), Dave Presto ("Shrek" makeup artist); Dialect Coach, Stephen Gabis; Electronic Music Design Associate, Jeff Marder; Rehearsal Pianists, Jodie Moore, Matt Perri, John Deley; Rehearsal Percussionist, Warren Odze; Music Copying, Kaye-Houston Music (Anne Kaye & Doug Houston); Production Assistant, Jacqueline Prats; Music Department Assistant, Michael Gacetta; For Aurora Productions: Gene O'Donovan, W. Benjamin Heller II, Bethany Weinstein, Melissa Mazdra, Amy Merlino Coey, Laura Archer, Dana Hesch; For Stuart Thompson: David Turner, Caroline Prugh; For Tara Rubin: Eric Woodall, Laura Schutzel, Merri Sugarman, Rebecca Carfagna, Paige Blansfield, Dale Brown; For Renaissance Prosthetics: Hayes Vilandry, Roland Blancafor, Chris Kelly, Paul Komoda; Management Assistants, Megan Curren Geo Karapetyan, Quinn Corbin; Wrangler, Bridget Walders; Advertising, SpotCo; Press, Boneau/Bryan-Brown, Chris Boneau, Adrian Brian-Brown, Heath Schwartz; Matt Polk, Christine Olver; Cast recording: Decca Broadway B0012627-02

CAST Shrek **Brian d'Arcy James;** Princess Fiona **Sutton Foster;** Lord Farquaad **Christopher Sieber;** Donkey **Daniel Breaker;** Pinocchio **John Tartaglia;** Ensemble **Cameron Adams;** Sugar Plum Fairy/Gingy **Haven Burton;** Shoemaker's Elf/Duloc Performer/Blind Mouse **Jennifer Cody;** Sticks/Bishop **Bobby Daye;** Bricks **Ryan Duncan;** Ugly Duckling/Blind Mouse **Sarah Jane Everman;** Mama Bear **Aymee Garcia;** Young Fiona (Wed., Fri., Sun.) **Leah Greenhaus; Lisa Ho;** Baby Bear/Blind Mouse **Lisa Ho;** King Harold/Big Bad Wolf/Captain of the Guard **Chris Hoch;** Fairy Godmother/Magic Mirror Assistant/Bluebird **Danette Holden;** Ensemble **Marty Lawson;** Papa Ogre/Straw **Jacob Ming-Trent;** Teen Fiona **Marissa O'Donnell;** Peter Pan **Denny Paschall;** Young Fiona (Tues., Thurs., Sat.) **Rachel Resheff;** Gnome/Pied Piper **Greg Reuter;** Young Shrek/Dwarf **Adam Riegler;** White Rabbit **Noah Rivera;** Queen Lillian/Wicked Witch/Magic Mirror Assistant **Jennifer Simard;** Mama Ogre/Humpty Dumpty **Rachel Stern;** Barker/Papa Bear/Thelonius **Dennis Stowe;** Swings **Justin Greer, Carolyn Ockert-Haythe, Heather Jane Rolff, David F.M. Vaughn;** Standby for Shrek **Ben Crawford**

UNDERSTUDIES Jacob Ming-Trent (Shrek), Haven Burton and Sarah Jane Everman (Princess Fiona), Bobby Daye and Ryan Duncan (Donkey), Chris Hoch and Greg Reuter (Lord Farquaad), Denny Paschall and Noah Rivera (Pinocchio), Haven Burton (Teen Fiona), Leah Greenhaus and Rachel Resheff (Young Shrek)

ORCHESTRA Tim Weil (Conductor); Jason DeBord (Associate Conductor/keyboards); Antoine Silverman (Concertmaster); Jonathan Dinklage, Entcho Todorov, Sean Carney (violins); Jeanne LeBlanc, Anja Wood (celli); Bill Ellison (acoustic bass); Anders Bostrom (flutes); Charles Pillow, Jack Bashkow, Ron Jannelli (reeds); Anthony Kadleck, Bud Burridge (trumpets); Bruce Eidem, Morris Kainuma (trombones); Adam Krauthamer (French horn); John Delay (keyboards); Ken Brescia, Bob Baxmeyer (guitars); Luico Hopper (electric bass); Warren Odze (drums); Shane Shanahan (percussion)

MUSICAL NUMBERS Big Bright Beautiful World, Story of My Life, The Goodbye Song, Don't Let Me Go, I Know It's Today, What's Up, Duloc?, Travel Song, Donkey Pot Pie, This Is How a Dream Comes True, Who I'd Be, Morning Person, I Think I Got You Beat, The Ballad of Farquaad, Make a Move, When Words Fail, Morning Person (reprise), Build a Wall, Freak Flag, Big Bright Beautiful World (reprise), Finale

2008–2009 AWARDS Tony Award: Best Costume Design of a Musical (Tim Hatley); Drama Desk Awards: Outstanding Actor in a Musical (Brian d'Arcy James), Outstanding Set Design of a Musical (Tim Hatley), Outstanding Costume Design of a Musical (Tim Hatley); Outer Critics Circle Award: Outstanding Actor in a Musical (Brian d'Arcy James); Outstanding Actress in a Musical (Sutton Foster) – tie with Josefina Scaglione, Outstanding Scenic Design (Tim Hatley), Outstanding Costume Design (Tim Hatley)

New York premiere of a new musical presented in two acts. World Premiere at Seattle's 5th Avenue Theatre August 15, 2008, prior to its Broadway engagement (see Regional Theatre listings in this volume).

SYNOPSIS *Shrek The Musical* follows the adventures of Shrek, a lovable swamp-dwelling ogre, his wisecracking sidekick, Donkey, the lovely Princess Fiona, the vertically challenged Lord Farquaad, and a chorus of everybody's favorite fractured fairytale creatures. In order to regain his peaceful neighborhood, the fearsome ogre makes a deal with the wanna-be king to rescue his intended, a damsel in distress. But surprises are in store in this funny, fractured fairy tale. With more layers than ever and a completely original new score, *Shrek The Musical* proves that there's more to the story than meets the ears.

Brian d'Arcy James, Daniel Breaker and Sutton Foster

Right: *Leah Greenhaus, Sutton Foster and Marissa O'Donnell*

Pal Joey

Studio 54; First Preview: November 11, 2008; Opening Night: December 18, 2008; Closed March 1, 2009; 37 previews, 84 performances

Music by Richard Rodgers, lyrics by Lorenz Hart, new book by Richard Greenberg based on the original book by John O'Hara; Produced by the Roundabout Theatre Company (Todd Haimes, Artistic Director; Harold Wolpert, Managing Director; Julia C. Levy, Executive Director) in association with Marc Platt; Director, Joe Mantello; Musical Director, Paul Gemignani; Choreography, Graciela Daniele; Sets, Scott Pask; Costumes, William Ivey Long; Lighting, Paul Gallo; Sound, Tony Meola; Hair & Wigs, Paul Huntley; Makeup, Angelina Avellone; Production Stage Manager, Tripp Phillips; Orchestrations, Don Sebesky; Dance Arrangements, Eric Stern; Casting, Jim Carnahan & Bernard Telsey; Technical Supervisor, Steve Beers; Executive Producer/General Manager, Sydney Beers; Marketing/Sales Promotion, David B. Steffen; Founding Director, Gene Feist; Associate Artistic Director, Scott Ellis; Director of Artistic Development and Casting, Jim Carnahan; Education, Greg McCaslin; Finance, Susan Neiman; Telesales, Marco Frezza; Sales Operations, Charlie Garbowski Jr.; Company Manager, Denise Cooper; Stage Manager, Jason Hindelang; Associate Director, Dave Solomon; Associate Choreographer, Maddie Kelly; Associate Music Director, Annbritt duChateau; Dance Captain, Brian Barry; Properties, Kathy Fabian/Propstar; Associate Design: Orit Jacoby Carroll & Frank McCullough (sets), Tom Beall (costumes), Paul Toben (lighting), Zachary Williamson (sound), Giovanna Calabretta (wigs and hair); Assistant Design/Design Assistants: Lauren Alvarez & Jeff Hinchee (sets), Donald Sanders & Cathy Parrott (costumes), Sarah Jakubasz & Joel E. Silver (lighting), Jeremy Cunningham (Mr. Gallo); Associate Props Coordinators, Carrie Mossman & Scott Keclik; Propstar Artisans, Rose Howard, Christina Gould, Edward Morris; Prop Shoppers, Timothy Ferro, Tessa Dunning, Sarah Bird, Sid King, Jennifer Lutz; Production: Dan Hoffman (production carpenter), Paul Ashton (automation carpenter), Steve Jones (flyman), Peter Ruen (deck carpenter), Josh Weitzman (production electrician), John Wooding (assistant production electrician/follow spots), Timothy F. Rogers (automated lighting programmer), Sue Pelkoffer (conventional lighting programmer), Dorion Fuchs, Jocelyn Smith (follow spots), Aaron Straus (production sound engineer), John Bantay (deck sound), Lawrence Jennino (house properties), Dan Mendeloff & Jean Scheller (props run crew), Nadine Hettel (wardrobe supervisor), Ruth G. Carsch (hair/wig supervisor), Enrique Vega (hair assistant), Benedetta Celada (makeup assistant), Tara Delahunt, Joe Godwin, Victoria Grecki, Gina Gornick, Cristel Murdock, Mary Ann Oberpriller (dressers), John Bantay, Brian D. Gold, Alissa R. Zulvergold (production assistants); Rehearsal Pianist, Paul Ford; Rehearsal Drummer, Larry Lelli; Synthesizer Programmer, Randy Cohen; Music Preparation, Emily Grishman & Katherine Edmonds; Press, Boneau/Bryan-Brown, Adrian Bryan-Brown, Matt Polk, Jessica Johnson, Amy Kass

CAST Joey Evans **Matthew Risch***; Mike **Robert Clohessy;** Val **Nadine Isenegger;** Gladys Bumps **Martha Plimpton;** Diane **Kathryn Mowat Murphy;** Cookie **Lisa Gajda;** Linda English **Jenny Fellner;** Hank Armour **Brian Barry;** Seaver Swift **Timothy J. Alex;** Vera Simpson **Stockard Channing;** Ted/Tailor Shop Customer **Anthony Holds;** Drummer **Eric Sciotto;** Ernest **Steven Skybell;** Ludlow Lowell **Daniel Marcus;** The Kid **Hayley Podschun;** Workman **Mark Morettini;** Ensemble **Timothy J. Alex, Brian Barry, Bahiyah Sayyed Gaines, Lisa Gajda, Anthony Holds, Nadine Isenegger, Mark Morettini , Kathryn Mowat Murphy, Hayley Podschun, Krista Saab, Eric Sciotto;** Club Patrons **Meredith Forlenza, Quinn Mattfield, Nichole Orth-Pallavicini;** Swings **Kurt Froman, Abbey O'Brien**

*Matthew Risch permanently replaced Christian Hoff during previews (November 22) due to foot injury.

UNDERSTUDIES Eric Sciotto (Joey Evans), Nicole Orth-Pallavicini (Vera Simpson), Lisa Gajda (Gladys Bumps), Hayley Podschun (Linda English, Val), Mark Morettini (Mike, Ernest), Anthony Holds (Ludlow Lowell)

Matthew Risch and Stockard Channing
(photos by Joan Marcus)

ORCHESTRA Paul Gemignani (Conductor); Annbritt duChateau (Associate Conductor/keyboards); Larry Lelli (Assistant Conductor/drums/percussion); Sylvia D'Avanzo (Concertmistress/violin); Matthew Lehman (violin); Richard Brice (viola); Roger Shell (cello); Eric Weidman, Scott Shachter, Tom Christensen, Don McGeen (woodwinds); Dominic Derasse, Mike Ponella (trumpets); Robert Suttmann (trombone); Ron Sell (Music Contractor/French horn); John Beal (bass)

MUSICAL NUMBERS Chicago; You Mustn't Kick It Around; I Could Write a Book; Chicago (reprise); That Terrific Rainbow; What Is a Man?; Are You My Love?; Happy Hunting Horn; Bewitched, Bothered and Bewildered; Pal Joey (What Do I Care for a Dame?); Chez Joey; The Flower Garden in My Heart; In Our Little Den of Iniquity; Zip; Plant You Now, Dig You Later; Do It the Hard Way; Zip (reprise); I Still Believe in You; Bewitched, Bothered and Bewildered (reprise); Take Him; I'm Talkin' to My Pal; I Still Believe in You (reprise); I Could Write a Book (reprise)

SETTING Time: The late 1930s. Place: Chicago. Revival of the musical presented in two acts. Originally produced at the Barrymore Theatre (starring Gene Kelly, Vivienne Segal, and June Havoc) December 25, 1940–November 29, 1941, playing 374 performances. The show was revived at the Broadhurst Theatre (starring Harold Lang, Vivienne Segal, and Helen Gallagher) January 2, 1952–April 18, 1953, playing 540 performances (see *Theatre World* Vol. 8, page 81). The New York City Center Light Opera Company briefly revived the show May 29–June 9, 1963 (see *Theatre World* Vol. 19, page 117). The last Broadway revival was produced by Circle in the Square June 27–August 29, 1976 (see *Theatre World* Vol. 33, page 13), and City Center *Encores!* produced a staged concert of the show in their second season (starring Peter Gallagher, Patti LuPone, and Vicki Lewis) May 4–7, 1995 (see *Theatre World* Vol. 51, page 58).

SYNOPSIS Set in Chicago in the late 1930s, *Pal Joey* is the story of Joey Evans, a brash, scheming song and dance man with dreams of owning his own nightclub. Joey abandons his wholesome girlfriend Linda English, to charm a rich, married older woman, Vera Simpson, in the hope that she'll set him up in business.

Martha Plimpton and the Company

Soul of Shaolin

Marquis Theatre; First Preview: January 13, 2009; Opening Night: December 15, 2009; Closed January 31, 2009; 3 previews, 21 performances

Created and performed by the Shaolin Temple Wushu Training Center; Produced by Nederlander Worldwide Productions LLC and Eastern International Culture Film & Television Group (Fang Jun, Chairman; Li Zhixiang, General Manager; Fang Yongnian, Vice General Manager); Presented by China on Broadway (Inaugural Production; Robert Nederlander Jr., President & CEO; Don Frantz, COO; David Groelinger, CFO; Minhui Mark Ma, VP China); Director/Choreographer, Liu Tongbiao; Music, Zhou Chenglong; Stage Design, Xie Tongmiao; Costumes, Huang Gengying; Lighting, Song Tianjiao; Sound, Wu Feifei & Keith Caggiano; Martial Arts Directors, Jiang Dongxu & Zhu Huayin; Makeup, Chen Meiping; Shanghai Production Manager, Fang Yongnian; Shanghai Marketing Director, Wang Zaiping; General Management, Town Square Productions Inc. (Don Frantz & Laurie Brown); Marketing, Margery Singer Company; Asian Marketing, Wei Zhou; Shanghai General Manager, Li Zhixiang; Executive Director, Xue Weijun; Director & Stage Supervisor, Wang Zhenpeng; Shanghai Producer, Wang Jingbo; Chief Martial Arts Director, Jiao Hongbo; Creative and Directorial Consultant, Charles (Chase) Senge; Management Consultant, Robert Nolan; General Management Associate, Sue Abbott; Production Supervisor, Mike Ward; Associate Lighting, Joyce Liao; Moving Lights Programmer, Paul Sonnleitner; Production: Paul Ker (master electrician), John P. Lofgren (properties supervisor), I. Wang (wardrobe supervisor); Production Coordinator, Danielle Ruddess; Educator, Kelly Giles; China Broadway Partners Staff: Katherine Potter (VP of Finance & Marketing), Toby Simkin (VP Production), Melissa Caolo (Production Coordinator), Shawn Coutu (Director of Finance), Stanley Browne (Marketing), Yuanlei Leiley Zhang (Marketing Associate), Diana Glazer (Executive Assistant), Elizabeth Schwartz & Miranda Xu (Interns); Advertising, Eliran Murphy Group (Barbara Eliran, Jon Bierman, Frank Verlizzo, Sasha DeFazio); Press, Boneau/Bryan-Brown, Chris Boneau, Aaron Meir, Christine Olver

CAST Hui Guang (*young man*) **Yu Fei;** Hui Guang (*teenager*) **Dong Yingbo;** Hui Guang (*boy*) **Wang Sen;** Na Luo (*Master*) **Zhang Zhigang;** Abbot **Bai Guojun;** Hui Guang's Mother **Wang Yazhi;** Hui Guang's Mother (*special appearance*) **Li Lin;** Ensemble **Jia Honglei, Pan Fuynag, Li Guanghui, Dong Xingfeng, Lu Shilei, Zhang Xinbo, Xia Haojie, Li Panpan, Wang Yanshuang, Shi Zhendong, Liu Weidong, Cai Kehe, Yang Wei, Yang Xianyu, Sun Shengli, Dong Junpeng, An Pukang, Wang Xiaogang, Hou Yanjie, Tian Yinan, Wang Feihu, Liu Wancheng, Shang Yaofei**

SETTING Ancient China during a time of war. American premiere of a theatrical marital arts spectacle presented in two acts and six scenes.

SYNOPSIS Direct from appearances in Sydney, Macau, the People's Republic of China, and at the 2008 Beijing Olympics, *Soul of Shaolin* is a theatrical event that is unparalleled on Broadway. *Soul of Shaolin* tells the story of a boy named Hui Guang who is separated from his mother by war. Hui Guang is found and taken in by the legendary monks of the Shaolin temple and raised among them. As he becomes a man, Hui Gang becomes an accomplished master of Shaolin Kung Fu and embarks on a spectacular journey of self-discovery. *Soul of Shaolin* marks the first time a production from the People's Republic of China has appeared on Broadway.

The Company

Wang Yazhi
(photos by Joan Marcus)

A scene from Soul of Shaolin

*Kieran Campion and Lily Rabe
(photos by Carol Rosegg)*

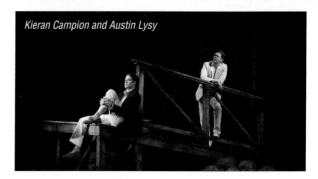

Kieran Campion and Austin Lysy

The American Plan

Samuel J. Friedman Theatre; First Preview: January 2, 2009 Opening Night: January 22, 2009; Closed March 22, 2009; 22 previews, 70 performances

Written by Richard Greenberg; Produced by Manhattan Theatre Club (Lynne Meadow, Artistic Director; Barry Grove, Executive Producer); Director, David Grindley; Set & Costumes, Jonathan Fensom; Lighting, Mark McCullough; Sound, Darron L. West & Bray Poor; Wigs, Josh Marquette; Production Stage Manager, Laurie Goldfeder; General Manager, Florie Seery; Associate Artistic Director, Mandy Greenfield; Artistic Development, Jerry Patch; Marketing, Debra Waxman-Pilla; Production Manager, Kurt Gardner; Casting, Nancy Piccione; Development, Jill Turner Lloyd; Artistic Consultant, Daniel Sullivan; Artistic Administration/ Assistant to Artistic Director, Amy Gilkes Loe; Musical Development, Clifford Lee Johnson III; Finance, Jeffrey Bledsoe; Associate General Manager, Lindsey Brooks Sag; Subscriber Services, Robert Allenberg; Telesales, George Tetlow; Education, David Shookhoff; Associate Production Manager, Philip Naudé; Prop Supervisor, Scott Laule; Costume Supervisor, Erin Hennessy Dean; Company Manager, Seth Shepsle; Stage Manager, Justin Scribner; Assistant Director, Rachel Slaven; Dialect Consultant, Kate Wilson; Fight Director, Thomas Schall; Associate Design: Jesse Poleshuck (set), Patrick Bevilacqua (costumes), Matthew Hubbs (sound); Assistant Design: Christine Peters (set), Bradley King (lighting); Hair/Makeup Supervisor, Kevin Phillips; Lightboard Programmer, Marc Polimeni; Assistant Production Manager, Kelsey Martinez; Assistant Props Supervisor, Julia Sandy; Props Carpenter, Peter Grimes; Theatre Manager, Russ Ramsey; Box Office Treasurer, David Dillon; Production: Vaughn G. Preston (automation operator), Chris Wiggins (head carpenter), Timothy Walters (head propertyman), Louis Shapiro (sound engineer), Jeff Dodson (master electrician), Angela Simpson (wardrobe supervisor); Virginia Neininger (dresser), Michael Alifanz (production assistant), Advertising, SpotCo; Press, Boneau/Bryan-Brown, Chris Boneau, Aaron Meier, Christine Olver

CAST Nick Lockridge **Kieran Campion;** Gil Harbison **Austin Lysy;** Olivia Shaw **Brenda Pressley;** Lili Adler **Lily Rabe;** Eva Adler **Mercedes Ruehl**

UNDERSTUDIES Kate Arrington (Lili Adler), Harriet D. Foy (Olivia Shaw), Patricia Hodges (Eva Adler), John Wernke (Nick Lockridge, Gil Harbison)

SETTING The Catskill Mountains during the summer of 1960, and ten years later in an apartment on the Upper West Side. Broadway premiere of a play presented in two acts. Manhattan Theatre Club produced the world premiere production Off-Broadway at City Center Stage II, January 23–February 18, 1990 (see *Theatre World* Vol. 46, page 83).

SYNOPSIS *The American Plan* tells the story Lili Adler and her mother Eva, who spend a summer in the Catskill Mountains, across the lake from a bustling resort hotel. When a handsome young stranger enters their world, the emotionally fragile Lili finds herself falling in love. But once her imperious mother learns of their relationship, lies are exposed, alliances are forged and Lili's one chance to escape Eva's control may be lost forever.

Kieran Campion and Austin Lysy

Hedda Gabler

American Airlines Theatre; First Preview: January 6, 2009 Opening Night: January 25, 2009; Closed March 29, 2009; 21 previews, 74 performances

Written by Henrik Ibsen, new adaptation by Christopher Shinn, literal translation by Anne-Charlotte Harvey; Produced by the Roundabout Theatre Company (Todd Haimes, Artistic Director; Harold Wolpert, Managing Director; Julia C. Levy, Executive Director); Director, Ian Rickson; Sets, Hildegard Bechtler; Costumes, Ann Roth; Lighting, Natasha Katz; Sound, John Gromada; Original Music, PJ Harvey; Makeup & Hair, Ivana Primorac; Wigs, Peter Owen; Production Stage Manager, James Fitzsimmons; Casting, Jim Carnahan & Stephen Kopel; General Manager, Rebecca Habel; Technical Supervisor, Steve Beers; Marketing/Sales Promotion, David B. Steffen; Founding Director, Gene Feist; Associate Artistic Director, Scott Ellis; Company Manager, Carly DiFulvio; Stage Manager, Bryce McDonald; Assistant Director, Sarah Cameron Sunde; Vocal Coach, Deborah Hecht; Director of Artistic Development and Casting, Jim Carnahan; Finance, Susan Neiman; Education, Greg McCaslin; General Manager, Sydney Beers; Telesales, Marco Frezza; Sales Operations, Charlie Garbowski Jr.; Associate Design: Josh Zangen (set), Michelle Matland (costumes), Aaron Spivey (lighting), Ryan Rummery (sound); Assistant Sound, Alex Neumann; Production: Denise Grillo (production properties), Constance Sherman (assistant to production properties), Glenn Merwede (production carpenter), Brain Maiuri (production electrician), Andrew Forste (running properties), Dann Wojnar (sound operator), Susan J. Fallon (wardrobe supervisor), Brittany Jones-Pugh, Kat Martin, (dressers), Manuela Laporte (hair and wig supervisor), Lauren Gallitelli (day wardrobe), Kate Baxter Davis (production assistant); Box Office Manager, Ted Osborne; House Manager, Steve Ryan; Advertising, SpotCo; Press, Boneau/Bryan-Brown, Adrian Bryan-Brown, Matt Polk, Jessica Johnson, Amy Kass

Above: *Mary-Louise Parker and Paul Sparks*

Left: *Mary-Louise Parker and Peter Stormare
(photos by Nigel Parry/CPi)*

CAST Miss Juliane Tesman (*Jørgen Tesman's Aunt*) **Helen Carey;** Berte (*the Tesman's maid*) **Lois Markle;** Jørgen Tesman **Michael Cerveris;** Mrs. Hedda Tesman (*his wife*) **Mary-Louise Parker;** Mrs. Thea Elvsted **Ana Reeder;** Judge Brack **Peter Stormare;** Ejlert Løvborg **Paul Sparks**

UNDERSTUDIES Opal Alladin (Mrs. Hedda Tesman, Mrs. Thea Elvsted), Peter Bradbury (Jørgen Tesman, Ejlert Løvborg), Lucy Martin (Miss Juliane Tesman, Berte), Ray Virta (Judge Brack)

SETTING The drawing room of the Tesman home in Christiana, Norway, 1890. Revival of the play with a new adaptation presented in two acts. This production marked the play's eighteenth Broadway revival. The Roundabout Theatre Company produced the sixteenth Broadway revival of the play (featuring Kelly McGillis and Laura Linney) June 1–August 7, 1994 at the Criterion Center Stage Right (see *Theatre World* Vol. 53, page 9). A previous revival directed by Nicholas Martin (featuring Kate Burton and Michael Emerson) played September 19, 2001–January 13, 2002 at the Ambassador Theatre (see *Theatre World* Vol. 58, page 25).

SYNOPSIS A woman of dangerous independence restrained by a conventional marriage, the newly married Hedda mourns the freedom and excitement of her former life by indulging in a cruel game, amusing herself with the misfortune she inflicts on those around her. As Hedda struggles to balance her wild desires against her chosen life, she sets into motion a manic chain of events that bring her story to a chilling end.

You're Welcome America.
A Final Night with George W. Bush

Cort Theatre; First Preview: January 20, 2009 Opening Night: February 5, 2009; Closed March 15, 2009; 18 previews, 56 performances

Written by Will Ferrell; Produced by Jeffrey Richards, Jerry Frankel, Steve Traxler, Home Box Office Inc., in association with Gary Sanchez Productions & Bat-Barry Productions, Ken Davenport, Ergo Entertainment, Ronald Frankel, Jon B. Platt, James D. Stern, The Weinstein Company, Tara Smith/b. Swibel, Dede Harris/Sharon Karmazin, and Arny Granat; Director, Adam McKay; Set, Eugene Lee; Costumes, Tom Broecker; Lighting, Brian MacDevitt; Sound, Peter Fitzgerald; Video, Lisa Cuscuna/Chris Cronin; Choreography, Matt Williams; Production Stage Manager, Charles Means; Flying Effects, Flying by Foy; Casting, Telsey + Company; Technical Supervision, Hudson Theatrical Associates (Neil Mazzella, Sam Ellis); General Management, Stuart Thompson Productions/David Turner, Caroline Prugh, James Turner; Executive Producer, Jessica Elbaum; Associate Producers, Michael Filerman & Seth Traxler; Company Manager, Cassidy J. Briggs; Wigs, Bettie Rogers; Stage Manager, Elizabeth Moloney; Associate Design: Edward Pierce (set), Eric Justian (costumes), Jennifer Schriever (lighting); Assistant Design: Jen Price (set), Megan Henninger (sound); Video Programmer, Chris Herman; Sound Production Assistant, Mallori Fitzgerald; Props, Kathy Fabian/Propstar; Props Associates, Carrie Mossman & Scott Keclik; Vocal Coach, Louis Colaianni; Production: Lyle Jones (wardrobe supervisor), Scott Cronick (star dresser), Yolanda Ramsay (hair supervisor), Edward Diaz (production carpenter), Scott DeVerna (production electrician), Lonnie Gaddy (production propertyman), Jens McVoy (production sound), Kevin Diaz (deck carpenter), Colin DeVerna (spot operator), Keith DeVerna (deck sound); Assistants: Betty Kay Overman (Mr. Ferrell), Lauryn Kahn (Mr. McKay), Jeremy Scott Blaustein (Associate to Mr. Richards), Christopher Taggart (Mr. Richards), Brandi Preston (Mr. Traxler), Terrie Lootens (Mr. Platt), Quinn M. Corbin, Megan E. Curren, Geo Karapetyan (Stuart Thompson Productions); Production Assistant, Raynelle Wright; Advertising, Serino Coyne Inc.; Press, Jeffrey Richards Associates, Irene Gandy, Alana Karpoff, Elon Rutberg, Diana Rissetto, Shane Marshall Brown

CAST George W Bush **Will Ferrell;** Secret Service Operative **Patrick Ferrell;** Dr. Scott Blumeth **Michael Delaney;** Condoleezza Rice **Pia Glenn;** Pilot **Adam Mucci**

UNDERSTUDIES Mindy Haywood (Condoleezza Rice/Pilot), Adam Mucci (Secret Service Operator/Dr. Scott Blumeth)

SETTING The Cort Theatre, the present. World premiere of a new play presented without intermission.

SYNOPSIS It's time for a change in America, but not without a few parting words from the 43rd President of the United States. Discover the man behind the myth, the truth behind the lies, and the logic behind the illogical. Will Ferrell, who often portrayed "W" during his tenure on *Saturday Night Live*, writes and stars in this new solo performance comedy (with the help of some friends) just as the new president enters the oval office.

Will Ferrell (photos by Robert J. Saferstein)

Will Ferrell

Will Ferrell

Malcolm Gets and Will Chase

The Story of My Life

Booth Theatre; First Preview: February 3, 2009 Opening Night: February 19, 2009; Closed February 22, 2009; 18 previews, 5 performances

Music and lyrics by Neil Bartram, book by Brian Hill; Produced by Chase Mishkin, Jack M. Dalgleish, Bud Martin, Carole L. Haber in association with Chunsoo Shin; Director, Richard Maltby Jr.; Set, Robert Brill; Costumes, Wade Laboissonniere; Lighting, Ken Billington & Paul Toben; Sound, Peter Fitzgerald & Carl Casella; Projections, Dustin O'Neill; Orchestrations, Jonathan Tunick; Music Direction, David Holcenberg; Music Coordinator, John Miller; Casting, Jay Binder/Sara Schatz; Production Stage Manager, Bess Marie Glorioso; Production Supervisor, Arthur Siccardi & Patrick Sullivan; Associate Director, Lisa Shriver; General Manager, Leonard Soloway; Company Manager, Judith Drasner; Stage Manager, Ana M. Garcia; Assistant to the Director, Joshua Wellman; Production Assistants, Meg Friedman & Melanie T. Morgan; Associate Lighting Designer, Cory Pattak; Assistant Scenic Designers, Dustin O'Neill & Angrette McCloskey; Assistant to the Costume Designer, Mary Ann Smith; Assistant to the Lighting Designer, Jim Milkey; Assistant to the Musical Contractor, Nichole Jennino; Production: Kenneth McDonough (carpenter), Mike Pilipski (properties), Susan Goulet (electrician), Brad M. Gyorgak (sound), Jesse Galvan (wardrobe supervisor), Vangeli Kaseluris (dresser); Music Preparation, Emily Grishman, Katherine Edmunds; Marketing, Type A Marketing; Advertising, Eliran Murphy Group (Barbara Eliran, Frank Verlizzo, Elizabeth Findley); Press, Keith Sherman & Associates, Glenna Freedman, Scott Klein, Brett Oberman, Matt Ross; Cast recording: PS Classics 981

CAST Thomas Weaver **Will Chase;** Alvin Kelby **Malcolm Gets;** Voice of Young Thomas **Alex Maizus;** Voice of Young Alvin **Austin McKinnis**

UNDERSTUDIES Bradley Dean (Thomas Weaver), Jim Stanek (Alvin Kelby)

MUSICIANS David Holcenberg (Conductor/piano), Sue Anschutz (Associate Conductor/keyboard), Bill Hayes (drums/percussion), Marc Schmied (bass), Elizabeth Lim-Dutton (violin), Ken Burward Hoy (viola), Sarah J. Seiver (cello), Les Scott (clarinet), Tom Sefcovic (bassoon), Timothy L. Schadt (trumpet)

MUSICAL NUMBERS Write What You Know, Mrs. Remington, The Greatest Gift, 1876, Normal, People Carry On, The Butterfly, Saying Goodbye (Part I), Here's Where It Begins, Saying Goodbye (Part 2), Independence Day, Saying Goodbye (Part 3), I Like It Here, You're Amazing Tom, Nothing There/Saying Goodbye (Part 4), I Didn't See Alvin, This Is It, Angels in the Snow

New York premiere of a new musical presented without intermission. World premiere at the Canadian Stage Company's Berkeley Street Theatre (Toronto, Canada) November 2, 2006. The American premiere was produced with this cast and production team at Goodspeed Musicals (Michael Price, Executive Director) October 10–November 2, 2008 (see Regional Theatre listings in this volume).

SYNOPSIS Thomas Weaver is a best-selling award-winning author. Alvin Kelby was his best friend for 30 years who stayed in his to hometown to the family bookstore. When Thomas returns after Alvin's death, he is unable to find the appropriate works to celebrate his friend's life. Time can test the bonds of a friendship, and when it does, Thomas calls on the only resource he has — his stories of Alvin — to learn where things went wrong. *The Story of My Life* is a soaring tribute to the power of friendship and the people who change our lives forever.

Left: *Malcolm Gets and Will Chase (photo by Aaron Epstein)*

Guys and Dolls: A Musical Fable of Broadway

Nederlander Theatre; First Preview: February 5, 2009 Opening Night: March 1, 2009; 28 previews, 105 performances as of May 31, 2009

Music and lyrics by Frank Loesser, book by Jo Swerling and Abe Burrows, based on the story and characters of Damon Runyon; Produced by Howard Panter for Ambassador Theatre Group, Robert G. Bartner/Norman & Steven Tulchin, Bill Kenwright, Northwater Entertainment, Darren Bagert, and Tom Gregory, with Nederlander Presentations Inc., David Mirvish, Michael Jenkins/Dallas Summer Musicals, Independent Presenters Network, Olympus Theatricals, and Sonia Friedman Productions; Director, Des McAnuff; Choreography, Sergio Trujillo; Music Director/Vocal Arrangements/Incidental Music, Ted Sperling; Sets, Robert Brill; Costumes, Paul Tazewell; Lighting, Howell Binkley; Sound, Steve Canyon Kennedy; Video, Dustin O'Neill; Hair & Wigs, Charles LaPointe; Fight Director, Steve Rankin; Casting, Tara Rubin; Orchestrations, Bruce Coughlin; Dance Arrangements, James Lynn Abbott; Conductor, Jeffrey Klitz; Music Coordinator, Michael Keller; Marketing, Type A Marketing/Anne Rippey; Technical Supervision, Don S. Gilmore; Production Stage Manager, Frank Hartenstein; General Management, Alchemy Production Group (Carl Pasbjerg & Frank Scardino); Associate Producers, Jill Lenhart & Peter Godfrey; Executive Producer, David Lazar; Company Manager, Jim Brandeberry; Makeup, Angelina Avallone; Video Content Production, The Oracle Group/Ari Novak; Associate General Manager, Chris Morey; Stage Manager, Kelly Martindale; Assistant Stage Manager, Alex Lyu Volckhausen; Assistant Company Manager, Sherra Johnston; Associate to the General Managers, Tegan Meyer; Dance Captain, Marcos Santana; Fight Captain, Graham Rowat; Dialect Coach, Stephen Gabis; Dramaturg, James Magruder; Assistant Director, Shelley Butler; Associate Design: Dustin O'Neill (sets), Nancy Palmatier (costumes), Mark Simpson (lighting), Andrew Keister (sound), Leah Loukas (hair); Assistant Set Design, Erica Hemminger, Steve Kemp, Caleb Levengood, Angrette McCloskey, Michael Locher, Daniel Meeker; Assistant Costumes Design, Michael Zecker, Courtney Watson, Maria Zamansky, Caitlin Hunt; Assistant Lighting, Christian DeAngelis; Moving Lights Programmer, David Arch; Video Programmer, Thomas Hague; Sound Programmer, Wallace Flores; Production: Fred Gallo (production carpenter), Todd Frank (head carpenter), Scott Poitras & David Cohen (assistant carpenters), James Fedigan (production electrician), Eric Norris (head electrician), Gary Fernandez & Lorne MacDougall (assistant electricians), Chris Pantuso (production property master), Jason Bowles (assistant property master), Julie Randolph (head sound engineer), Brett Bingman (assistant sound engineer), Stephanie Celustka (sound associate), Debbie Cheretun (wardrobe supervisor), Jim Hall (associate wardrobe supervisor), Michelle Rutter (hair supervisor), Mary Kay Yezerski-Bondoc (assistant hair supervisor), Rick Caroto (hair stylist), Don Bonilla, Fred Castner, Suzanne Delahunt, Maureen George, Betty Gillispie, Jim Hodun, Bob Kwiatkowski, Pamela Pierzina, Kyle Wesson (dressers); Music Copying, Emily Grishman, Katherine Edmonds; Keyboard Programmer, Randy Cohen; Assistant Keyboard Programmers, Jim Mironenik, Bryan Crook; Production Assistants, Jenny Slattery, Andrew Gottlieb, Alissa Zulvergold; Advertising, SpotCo (Drew Hodges, Jim Edwards); Press, Barlow · Hartman, John Barlow, Michael Hartman, Juliana Hannett, Michelle Bergmann

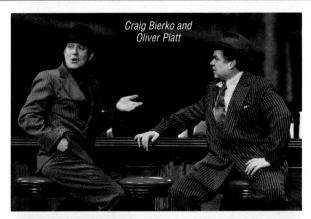
Craig Bierko and Oliver Platt

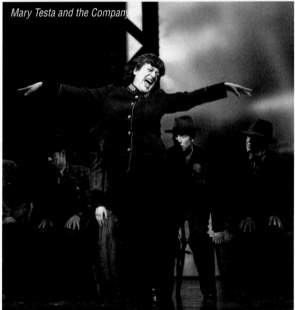
Mary Testa and the Company

Spencer Moses, Tituss Burgess and Steve Rosen

Craig Bierko and the Company

Lauren Graham and the Company

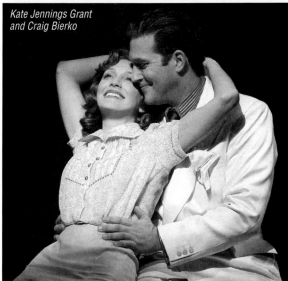

Kate Jennings Grant and Craig Bierko

CAST Nicely-Nicely Johnson **Tituss Burgess;** Benny Southstreet **Steve Rosen;** Rusty Charlie **Spencer Moses;** Sarah Brown **Kate Jennings Grant;** Agatha **Andrea Chamberlain;** Martha **Jessica Rush;** Calvin **William Ryall;** Arvide Abernathy **Jim Ortlieb;** Harry the Horse **Jim Walton;** Lt. Brannigan **Adam LeFevre;** Nathan Detroit **Oliver Platt;** Angie the Ox **Graham Rowat;** Society Max **James Harkness;** Liver Lips Louie **Nick Adams;** Damon **Raymond Del Barrio;** The Greek **Joseph Medeiros;** Brandy Bottle Bates **Ron Todorowski;** Scranton Slim **John Selya;** Sky Masterson **Craig Bierko;** Mimi **Lorin Latarro;** Joey Biltmore **Brian Shepard;** Adelaide **Lauren Graham;** General Cartwright **Mary Testa;** Big Jule **Glenn Fleshler;** Carmen **Kearran Giovanni;** Hot Box Girls **Kearran Giovanni, Lorin Latarro, Rhea Patterson, Jessica Rush, Jennifer Savelli, Brooke Wendle;** Ensemble **Nick Adams, Andrea Chamberlain, Raymond Del Barrio, Kearran Giovanni, James Harkness, Lorin Latarro, Joseph Medeiros, Spencer Moses, Rhea Patterson, Graham Rowat, Jessica Rush, Wiliam Ryall, Jennifer Savelli, John Selya, Brian Shepard, Ron Todorowski, Jim Walton, Brooke Wendle;** Swings **Melissa Fagan, Benjamin Magnuson, Marcos Santana**

UNDERSTUDIES Graham Rowat (Sky), Adam LeFevre (Nathan), Jim Walton (Nicely-Nicely, Lt. Brannigan), William Ryall (Arvide, Big Jule), Ben Magnuson (Benny), Jessica Rush (Sarah), Andrea Chamberlain (Adelaide, General Cartwright), Lorin Latarro (Adelaide)

ORCHESTRA Jeffrey Klitz (Conductor); Jeff Marder (Associate Conductor/keyboards); Cenovia Cummins (Concertmistress), Lori Miller, Ming Yeh (violins); Mairi Dorman-Phaneuf, Sarah Hewitt-Roth (celli); Don Downs, CJ Camerieri (trumpets); Mike Davis (trombone); Matt Ingman (bass trombone/tuba); Tom Murray, Ken Dubisz, Mark Thrasher (reeds); Greg Utzig (guitar/banjo); Mark Vanderpoel (bass); Steve Bartosik (drums); Javier Diaz (percussion)

MUSICAL NUMBERS Overture, Runyonland, Fugue for Tinhorns, Follow the Fold, The Oldest Established, Follow the Fold (reprise), I'll Know, A Bushel and a Peck, Adelaide's Lament, Guys and Dolls, Havana, If I Were a Bell, My Time of Day, I've Never Been in Love Before, Entr'acte, Take Back Your Mink, Adelaide's Lament (reprise), More I Cannot Wish You, The Crapshooter's Dance, Luck Be a Lady, Sue Me, Sit Down You're Rockin' the Boat, Follow the Fold (reprise), Marry the Man Today, Guys and Dolls (reprise)

SETTING New York City in the time of Damon Runyon. Revival of the musical presented in two acts. Originally produced on Broadway at the 46th Street Theatre (now the Richard Rodgers) November 24, 1950–November 28, 1953, playing 1,200 performances (see *Theatre World* Vol. 7, page 51). New York City Center Light Opera Company revived the show for brief 15 performance runs April 20–May 31, 1955 (see *Theatre World* Vol. 11, page 111), and ten years later April 28–May 9, 1965 (see *Theatre World* Vol. 21, page 143). An all African-American cast revival played the Broadway Theatre July 21, 1976–February 13, 1977 (see *Theatre World* Vol. 33, page 16). The last major revival (starring Nathan Lane, Faith Prince, Peter Gallagher, and Josi de Guzman) played the Martin Beck Theatre (now the Al Hirschfeld) April 14, 1992–January 8, 1995, playing 1,143 performances (see *Theatre World* Vol. 48, page 43).

SYNOPSIS One of Broadway's best-loved musicals returns in a new lavish production. Based on "The Idyll of Miss Sarah Brown" and "Blood Pressure" as well as characters and plot elements from other Damon Runyon stories, this musical fable of Broadway concerns a high-stakes gambler who unexpectedly falls for a mission doll, and a the operator of New York's oldest floating crap game who can't commit to marry his showgirl girlfriend after a fourteen-year engagement. McAnuff's production sets the story in the 1930s when the stories were actually written. The production also utilizes the character "Damon" as a framing device, the outside observer who weaves in and out of the stories as they unfold.

Left: *Kate Jennings Grant and Lauren Graham (photos by Carol Rosegg)*

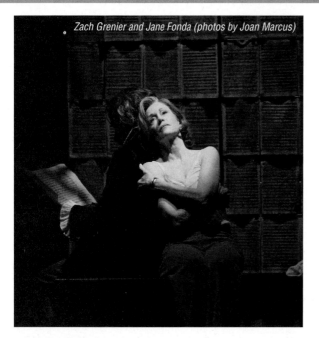

Zach Grenier and Jane Fonda (photos by Joan Marcus)

33 Variations

Eugene O'Neill Theatre; First Preview: February 9, 2009 Opening Night: March 9, 2009; Closed May 21, 2009; 31 previews, 85 performances

Written and directed by Moisés Kaufman, music by Ludwig van Beethoven; Presented by the Tectonic Theater Project (Moisés Kaufman, Artistic Director; Greg Reiner, Executive Director; Dominick Balletta, General Manager; Jeffrey LaHoste, Senior Producer); Produced by David Binder, Ruth Hendel, Barbara Whitman, Hal Goldberg, Marianne Mills, Latitude Link, Arielle Tepper Madover, Eric Schnall, and Jayne Baron Sherman; Sets, Derek McLane; Costumes, Janice Pytel; Lighting, David Lander; Sound, André J. Pluess; Projections, Jeff Sugg; Hair & Wigs, Charles LaPointe; Choreographer, Daniel Pelzig; Additional Costumes, David C. Woolard; Dramaturg, Mark Bly; Casting, James Calleri; Production Manager, Juniper Street Productions; Production Stage Manager, Linda Marvel; Marketing, Eric Schnall; General Management, 101 Productions Ltd. (Wendy Orshan, Jeffrey M. Wilson, David Auster, Elie Landau); Associate Producers, Arena Stage (Washington, D.C.), and La Jolla Playhouse (La Jolla, California); Company Manager, Heidi Neven; Stage Manager, Pat Sosnow; Assistant Stage Manager, Melissa M. Spangler; Assistant Director, Jimmy Maize; Music Consultant, Michael Friedman; Ms. Fonda's Wig Design, Martial Corneville; Ms. Fonda's Makeup Design, Angelina Avellone; Associate Design: Shoko Kambara (sets), Amelia Dombrowski (costumes), Justin Partier (lighting), Nick Borisjuk (sound/sound system design); Assistant Design: Grace Yoon (costumes), David Sanderson (sound), Adam Larsen (projections/animator), Jamie McElhinney (projections); Rehearsal Projection Assistant, Efren Delgadillo; Production: Tony Menditto (advance carpenter), Jack Anderson (head carpenter), Cletus Karamon (production electrician), Darin D. Stillman (sound engineer), Susan Barras (production properties coordinator), John H. Paull III (head properties supervisor), Jon Mark Davidson (assistant properties), Linda Lee (wardrobe supervisor), Andrea Roberts, John Webber, Lori Elwell (dressers), Heather Wright (hair supervisor), Joseph De-Luise, Ally Paull (technical production assistants), Libby Unsworth (production assistant), Andrew Raab (intern); Assistant to the Director, Luke Harlan; Assistant to Mr. Binder, Ryan Mackey; Advertising, Serino Coyne Inc.; Press, Boneau/Bryan-Brown, Chris Boneau, Matt Polk, Amy Kass

CAST Dr. Katherine Brandt **Jane Fonda;** Clara Brandt **Samantha Mathis;** Mike Clark **Colin Hanks;** Anton Diabelli **Don Amendolia;** Anton Schindler **Erik Steele;** Ludwig van Beethoven **Zach Greiner;** Dr. Gertrude Ladenburger **Susan Kellermann;** Ensemble **Scott Barrow, Emily Donahoe, Michael Winther;** Pianist/Musical Director **Diane Walsh**

UNDERSTUDIES Scott Barrow (Mike Clark, Anton Schindler), Emily Donahoe (Clara Brandt), Caitlin O'Connell (Standby for Dr. Katherine Brandt, u/s for Dr. Gertrude Ladenburger), Michael Winther (Ludwig van Beethoven, Anton Diabelli)

2008–2009 AWARDS Tony Award: Best Scenic Design of a Play (Derek McLane); **Theatre World Award:** Colin Hanks

SETTING Time: 1819, 1823, The Present. Place: New York, USA; Bonn, Germany; Vienna, Austria. New York premiere of a new drama with music presented in two acts. World premiere at Washington, D.C.'s Arena Stage (Molly Smith, Artistic Director; Guy Bergquist, Interim Managing Director) August 30, 2007 (see *Theatre World* Vol. 64, page 286). The West Coast premiere was presented at La Jolla Playhouse (Christopher Ashley, Artistic Director; Joan Cumming, Interim Managing Director) April 8–May 4, 2008 (see Regional Theatre listings in this volume).

SYNOPSIS 1819, fledgling publisher Anton Diabelli commissioned 50 composers to write a variation on a waltz he had created. Beethoven rejected the invitation, dismissing it as ordinary, but then obsessively created 33 variations on the theme. Modern day musicologist Katherine Brandt, a woman racing against time and Lou Gehrig's disease, travels to Bonn to solve the riddle of the composer's 200-year-old obsession, deciphering clues left behind in Beethoven's notebooks and letters. As she faces her own mortality, the complex relationship with her daughter, her past, her own obsession with genius, and Beethoven himself, she struggles to embrace the legacy of her own life. Combining true historical accounts and fictional characters, Kaufman's compositional journey merges past and present with the rich tapestry of Beethoven's finest compositions.

Susan Kellermann, Don Amendolia, Zach Grenier, Erik Steele, Jane Fonda, Samantha Mathis and Colin Hanks

Susan Kellermann and Jane Fonda

Blithe Spirit

Shubert Theatre; First Preview: February 26, 2009 Opening Night: March 15, 2009; 20 previews, 89 performances as of May 31, 2009

Written by Noël Coward; Produced by Jeffrey Richards, Jerry Frankel, Steve Traxler, Scott M. Delman, Bat-Barry Productions, Broadway Across America, Ken Davenport, Michael Filerman, Finn Scanlan Productions, Ronald Frankel, JK Productions, Kathleen K. Johnson, Patty Ann McKinnon, Judith Resnick, Terry Schnuck, Jamie deRoy/Alan D. Marks, Zev Buffman, Barbara & Buddy Freitag/Wendy Federman; Director, Michael Blakemore; Set, Peter J. Davison; Costumes, Martin Pakledinaz; Lighting, Brain MacDevitt; Sound, Peter Fitzgerald; Production Supervisor/Production Stage Manager, Steven Zweigbaum; Wigs & Hair, Paul Huntley; Casting, Telsey + Company; Production Manager, Aurora Productions (Gene O'Donovan, W. Benjamin Heller II, Bethany Weinstein, Melissa Mazdra, Amy Merlino Coey, Laura Archer, Dana Hesch); Company Manager, Bruce Klinger; General Manager, Richards/Climan Inc. (David R. Richards & Tamar Haimes); Stage Manager, Ara Marx; Associate Director, Kim Weild; Associate Design: Ted LeFevre (set), MaryAnn D. Smith (costumes), Caroline Chao (lighting); Makeup, Jason Hayes; Assistant Design: Peter Hoerburger (lighting), Megan Henninger (sound); Assistant to the Costume Designer, Noah Marin; Costume Intern, Sophia Anastasiou; Associate General Manager, John Gendron; General Manager Associate, Jeromy Smith; Production Assistant, Sarah Michele Penland; Production: Jim Kane (production carpenter), Dan Coey (production electrician), Peter Sarafin (production props), Laura McGarty (head props), Ed Chapman (production sound), Karen L. Eifert (wardrobe supervisor), Maeve Butler (Ms. Lansbury's dresser), Jill Frese & Geoffrey Polischuk (dressers), Erin Kennedy Lunsford (hair supervisor); Associate to Mr. Richards, Jeremy Scott Blaustein; Assistant to Mr. Richards, Christopher Taggart; Assistant to Mr. Traxler, Brandi Preston; General Management Assistant, Cesar Hawas; Advertising, Serino Coyne Inc; Press, Jeffrey Richards Associates, Irene Gandy, Elon Rutberg, Alana Karpoff, Shane Marshall Brown, Diana Rissetto

Angela Lansbury (photos by Robert J. Saferstein)

Christine Ebersole, Angela Lansbury, Rupert Everett and Jayne Atkinson

Deborah Rush, Rupert Everett, Angela Lansbury, Jayne Atkinson and Simon Jones

CAST Edith **Susan Louise O'Connor;** Ruth **Jayne Atkinson;** Charles **Rupert Everett;** Dr. Bradman **Simon Jones;** Mrs. Bradman **Deborah Rush;** Madame Arcati **Angela Lansbury;** Elvira **Christine Ebersole**

UNDERSTUDIES Mark Capri (Charles, Dr. Bradman), Elizabeth Norment (Elvira, Ruth, Edith), Sandra Shipley (Madame Arcati, Mrs. Bradman)

2008-2009 AWARDS Tony Award: Best Featured Actress in a Play (Angela Lansbury); Drama Desk Award: Outstanding Featured Actress in a Play (Angela Lansbury); Outer Critics Circle Award: Outstanding Featured Actress in Play (Angela Lansbury); Drama League Award: Best Revival of a Play; **Theatre World Award:** Susan Louise O'Connor

SETTING The living room of the Charles and Ruth Condomine's house in Kent, England; late 1930s. Revival of an improbable farce presented in seven scenes in three acts with one intermission. World premiere at the Piccadilly Theatre (London) July 2, 1941. American premiere at the Morosco Theatre November 5, 1941–January 5, 1943, playing 657 performances. The play had a brief return engagement at the Morosco September 6–October 2, 1943, and was revived at the Neil Simon Theatre (starring Blythe Danner, Judith Ivey, Geraldine Page, and Richard Chamberlain) March 10–June 28, 1987 (see *Theatre World* Vol. 43, page 36).

SYNOPSIS In *Blithe Spirit*, one of Coward's biggest successes, novelist Charles Condomine, living with his second wife, Ruth, invites a local medium, Madame Arcati, to his house. His intention is to do some research into the spirit world for his new book. But he gets more than he bargained for when Arcati conjures up the ghost of Elvira, his first wife. Caught between one live wife and one dead wife — both jealous of the other — Charles thinks matters couldn't be worse.

West Side Story

Palace Theatre; First Preview: February 23, 2009 Opening Night: March 19, 2009; 27 previews, 84 performances as of May 31, 2009

Book and direction by Arthur Laurents, music by Leonard Bernstein, lyrics by Stephen Sondheim; Conception and original direction and choreography by Jerome Robbins; Produced by Kevin McCollum, James L. Nederlander, Jeffrey Seller, Terry Allen Kramer, Sander Jacobs, Roy Furman/Jill Furman Willis, Freddy DeMann, Robyn Goodman/Walt Grossman, Hal Luftig, Roy Miller, The Weinstein Company, and Broadway Across America; Choreography Reproduction, Joey McKneely; Music Supervisor/Music Director, Patrick Vaccariello; Set, James Youmans; Costumes, David C. Woolard; Lighting, Howell Binkley; Sound, Dan Moses Schreier; Wigs & Hair, Mark Adam Rampmeyer; Makeup, Angelina Avallone; Casting, Stuart Howard, Amy Schecter, Paul Hardt; Associate Director, David Saint; Associate Choreographer, Lori Werner; Associate Producer, LAMS Productions; Translations, Lin-Manuel Miranda; Orchestrations, Leonard Bernstein with Sid Ramin and Irwin Kostal; Music Coordinator, Michael Keller; Production Stage Manager, Joshua Halperin; Original Broadway Production Co-Choreography, Peter Gennaro; Technical Supervisor, Brian Lynch; Marketing, Scott A. Moore; General Management, The Charlotte Wilcox Company (Seth Marquette, Matthew W. Krawiec, Dina S. Friedler, Margaret Wilcox); Company Manager, James Lawson; Assistant Company Manager, Erica Ezold; Stage Manager, Lisa Dawn Cave; Assistant Stage Manager, Jason Brouillard; Assistant to the Director, Isaac Klein; Assistant to Mr. McCollum and Mr. Seller, Caitlyn Thomson; Assistant to Mr. Nederlander; Ken Happel; Fight Director, Ron Piretti; Dance Captain, Marina Lazzaretto; Assistant Dance Captain, Michaeljon Slinger; Fight Captain, Joshua Buscher; Keyboard Programmer, Randy Cohen; Associate Design: Jerome Martin (set), Ryan O'Gara (lighting), David Bullard (sound); Assistant Design: Robert Martin, Daryl A. Stone, Maria Zamansky (costumes), Carrie Wood (lighting); Assistants to Designers: Sara James, Yuri Cataldo, Angela Harner (costume), Lazaro Arencibia (makeup); Moving Light Programmer, David Arch; Production: Chris Kluth (head carpenter/TheatreTech Associate), Cory Schmidt (production flyman), McBrien Dunbar & Robert M. Hentze (automation carpenters), Shaun Sites (advance automation carpenter), Keith Buchanan (head electrician), Chuck Fields (moving light technician), Patrick Harrington (spot operator), George Wagner (production properties supervisor), Chuck Dague (head properties), Lucas Indelicato (sound engineer), Scott Westervelt (wardrobe supervisor), Jessica Dermody (assistant wardrobe supervisor), Paula Schaffer (hair supervisor), Jennifer Bullock & Jeanette Harrington (assistant hair supervisors), Scotty Cain, Stephanie Fox, Kasey Graham, David Grevengoed, Sarah Hench, Hector Lugo, Dorothy Manning, Herb Oullette, Roy Seiler, Keith Shaw, Hilda Suli-Garcia (dressers); Assistant Keyboard Programmers, Bryan Cook, Jim Mironchik; Production Assistants, Rachel E. Miller, Zac Chandler; Advertising/Website, SpotCo/Drew Hodges, Jim Edwards, Tom Greenwald, Y. Darius Suyama, Pete Duffy; Press, Barlow · Hartman, John Barlow, Michael Hartman, Wayne Wolf, Matt Shea; Cast recording: Sony Masterworks 88697-52391-2

The Company

Karen Olivo and the Shark Girls

George Akram, Cody Green and the Company

CAST The Jets: Action **Curtis Holbrook;** Anybodys **Tro Shaw;** A-rab **Kyle Coffman;** Baby John **Ryan Steele;** Big Deal **Eric Hatch;** Diesel **Joshua Buscher;** Graziella **Pamela Otterson;** Hotsie **Marina Lazzaretto;** Kiddo (evenings and Sundays) **Nicholas Barasch;** Kiddo (Wed. & Sat. matinees) **Kyle Brenn;** Mugsy **Amy Ryerson;** Riff **Cody Green;** Snowboy **Mike Cannon;** Tony **Matt Cavenaugh;** Velma **Lindsay Dunn;** Zaza **Kaitlin Mesh;** 4H **Sam Rogers;** The Sharks: Alicia **Yanira Marin;** Anita **Karen Olivo;** Bebecita **Mileyka Mateo;** Bernardo **George Akram;** Bolo **Peter Chursin;** Chino **Joey Haro;** Consuela **Danielle Polanco;** Federico **Michael Rosen;** Fernanda **Kat Nejat;** Inca **Isaac Calpito;** Indio **Manuel Santos;** Lupe **Tanairi Sade Vazquez;** Maria **Josefina Scaglione;** Pepe **Manuel Herrera;** Rosalia **Jennifer Sanchez;** Tioi **Yurel Echezarreta;** The Adults: Doc **Greg Vinkler;** Glad Hand **Michael Mastro;** Krupke **Lee Sellars;** Lt. Schrank **Steve Bassett;** Swings **Haley Carlucci, Madeline Cintron, John Arthur Greene, Chase Madigan, Angelina Mullins, Christian Elán Ortiz, Michaeljon Slinger**

STANDBYS AND UNDERSTUDIES Standbys: Matthew Hydzik (Tony), Mark Zimmerman (Doc, Gladhand, Krupke, Lt. Schrank); Understudies: Joshua Buscher (Big Deal), Mike Cannon (Riff, Tony), Haley Carlucci (Fernanda, Maria), Lindsay Dunn (Graziella), John Arthur Greene (Action, Diesel, Riff), Eric Hatch (Action), Manuel Herrera (Bernardo), Chase Madigan (A-rab, Baby John, Snowboy), Yanira Marin (Anita, Consuela, Fernanda), Michael Mastro (Doc, Krupke, Lt. Schrank), Kaitlin Mesh (Anybodys), Kat Nejat (Anita, Maria), Pamela Otterson (Anybodys), Sam Rogers (A-rab, Baby John, Big Deal), Michael Rosen (Chino), Amy Ryerson (Graziella), Manuel Santos (Bernardo, Chino), Michaeljon Slinger (Diesel, Gladhand, Snowboy), Tanairi Sade Vazquez (Consuela)

ORCHESTRA Patrick Vaccariello (Conductor); Maggie Torre (Associate Conductor/piano); Martin Agee (Concertmaster/violin); Paul Woodiel, Robert Shaw, Victoria Paterson, Fritz Krakowski, Dana Ianculovici, Philip Payton (violins); Peter Prosser, Vivian Israel, Diane Barere, Jennifer Lang (celli); Bill Sloat (bass); Lawrence Feldman, Lino Gomez, Dan Willis, Adam Kolker, Gilbert DeJean (reeds); John Chudoba [lead], Trevor Neumann, Matthew Peterson (trumpets); Tim Albright (trombone); Jeff Nelson (bass trombone); Chris Komer, Theresa MacDonnell (French horns); Jim Laev (keyboard); Eric Poland (drums); Dan McMilla, Pablo Rieppi (percussion)

Cody Green and the Jets

The Company

*Josefina Scaglione
and Matt Cavenaugh*

MUSICAL NUMBERS Prologue; Jet Song; Something's Coming; Dance at the Gym; Maria; Tonight; America; Cool; One Hand, One Heart; Tonight (Quintet); The Rumble; Me Siento Hermosa (I Feel Pretty); Somewhere; Gee, Officer Krupke; Un Hombre Asi (A Boy Like That)/I Have a Love **2008–2009 AWARDS** Tony Award: Best Featured Actress in a Musical (Karen Olivo); Outer Critics Circle Award: Outstanding Actress in a Musical (Josefina Scaglione) – tie with Sutton Foster; **Theatre World Award:** Josefina Scaglione

SETTING Upper West Side of New York City during the last days of summer, 1957. Revival of the musical presented in 15 scenes in two acts. This production played a pre-Broadway engagement December 15, 2008–January 17, 2009 at Washington, DC's National Theatre, where the musical made its world premiere in 1957. Originally presented on Broadway at the Winter Garden Theatre September 26, 1957–June 27, 1959, playing 732 performances (see *Theatre World* Vol. 14, page 11). The show had a return engagement at the Winter Garden and then the Alvin (Neil Simon) Theatre April 24–December 10, 1960, playing 249 performances (see *Theatre World* Vol. 16, page 95). New York City Center Light Opera Company revived the show April 8–May 3, 1964 (see *Theatre World* Vol. 20, page 132). The last revival played the Minskoff Theatre February 7–November 30, 1980, playing 333 performances (see *Theatre World* Vol. 36, page 42).

SYNOPSIS *West Side Story* transports the achingly beautiful tale of Shakespeare's Romeo and Juliet to the turbulent streets of the Upper West Side in 1950s New York City. Two star-crossed lovers, Tony and Maria, find themselves caught between the rival street gangs of different ethnic backgrounds, the 'Jets' and the 'Sharks.' Their struggle to exist together in a world of violence, hate and prejudice is one of the most heart-breaking, relevant and innovative musical masterpieces of our time. This revival, directed by librettist Laurents, introduces an unprecedented element of selectively weaving Spanish (translated by Lin-Manuel Miranda) throughout the book and songs.

Cody Green and the Jets

*Manuel Herrera, George Akram and
Yurel Echezarreta (photos by Joan Marcus)*

Marcia Gay Harden, Hope Davis, Jeff Daniels and James Gandolfini

Marcia Gay Harden,
James Gandolfini,
Hope Davis
and Jeff Daniels
(photos by Joan Marcus)

Marcia Gay Harden and James Gandolfini

God of Carnage

Bernard B. Jacobs Theatre; First Preview: February 28, 2009 Opening Night: March 22, 2009; 24 previews, 81 performances as of May 31, 2009

Written by Yasmina Reza, translated by Christopher Hampton; Produced by Robert Fox, David Pugh & Dafydd Rogers, Stuart Thompson, Scott Rudin, Jon B. Platt, The Weinstein Company, and The Shubert Organization; Director, Matthew Warchus; Set and Costumes, Mark Thompson; Lighting, Hugh Vanstone; Music, Gary Yershon; Sound, Simon Baker/Christopher Cronin; Casting, Daniel Swee; Production Stage Manager, Jill Cordle; Production Management, Aurora Productions (Gene O'Donovan, W. Benjamin Heller II, Bethany Weinstein, Melissa Mazdra, Amy Merlino Coey, Laura Archer, Dana Hesch); General Management, Stuart Thompson Productions/David Turner; Company Manager, Chris Morey; Stage Manager, Kenneth J. McGee; Associate Director, Beatrice Terry; Associate Design: Nancy Thun (set), Daryl A. Stone (costumes), Ted Mather (lighting); Vocal Coach, Deborah Hecht; Makeup Consultant, Judy Chin; Production: Randall Zaibek (production electrician), Denise J. Grillo (production properties coordinator), Brien Brannigan (production sound), Kay Grunder (wardrobe supervisor), Derek Moreno (dresser); Casting Associate, Camille Hickman; General Managements Associates, James Triner, Dana Sherman, Caroline Prugh; Assistants: Nathan K. Claus (production), Zack Brown, Michael Megliola (to Mr. Vanstone), Quinn M. Corbin, Megan E. Curren, Geo Karapetyan (general management),Sarah Richardson (to Mr. Fox), Kevin Graham-Caso (to Mr. Rudin), Terrie Lootens (to Mr. Platt); RADA Trainee Assistant Director, Caroline Ranger; General Management Intern, Brittany Levasseur; Advertising, Serino Coyne Inc.; Press, Boneau/Bryan-Brown, Chris Boneau, Susanne Tighe, Christine Olver, Kelly Guiod

CAST Alan **Jeff Daniels;** Annette **Hope Davis;** Michael **James Gandolfini;** Veronica **Marcia Gay Harden**

STANDBYS Bruce McCarty (Alan, Michael), Charlotte Maier (Annette, Veronica)

2008–2009 AWARDS Tony Awards: Best Play, Best Direction of a Play (Matthew Warchus), Best Leading Actress in a Play (Marcia Gay Harden); Outer Critics Circle Award: Outstanding New Broadway Play, Outstanding Actress in a Play (Marcia Gay Harden); Drama League Award: Best Play

SETTING Michael and Veronica's living room; the present. American premiere of a new play presented without intermission. Mr. Warchus directed the English language premiere at the Gielgud Theatre (London) starring Janet McTeer and Ralph Fiennes March 25–June 14, 2008. The play received the 2009 Olivier Award for Best New Comedy. World premiere in Zurich, Switzerland December 8, 2006.

SYNOPSIS *God of Carnage* is a comedy of manners (without the manners) the deals with the aftermath of a playground altercation between two boys and what happens when their parents meet to talk about it. A calm and rational debate between grown-ups about the need to teach kids how to behave properly? Or a hysterical night of name-calling, tantrums and tears before bedtime? Boys will be boys... but the adults are usually worse... much worse...

Jeff Daniels and
Hope Davis

Impressionism

Gerald Schoenfeld Theatre; First Preview: February 28, 2009 Opening Night: March 24, 2009; Closed May 10, 2009; 23 previews, 56 performances

Written by Michael Jacobs; Produced by Ostar Productions, Roy Furman, Stephanie P. McClelland, Chase Mishkin, Jamie deRoy, Thomas Murphy, Broadway Across America, Michael Filerman, Eric Falkenstein, Morris Berchard, Matt Murphy/Suisman-Gasparian, Philip Geier/Donald R. Keough, Jennifer Manocherian/Wendy Federman, Randall L. Wreghitt, Barbara Freitag/ Ergo Entertainment, Max Onstage/Hugh Hysell/Richard Jordan; Director, Jack O'Brien; Sets, Scott Pask; Costumes, Catherine Zuber; Lighting, Natasha Katz; Projections, Elaine J. McCarthy; Sound, Leon Rothenberg; Hair & Wigs, Tom Watson; Original Music, Bob James; Casting, Laura Stanczyk; Production Manager, Juniper Street Productions; Production Stage Manager, Michael J. Passaro; Marketing, HHC Marketing; General Management, 101 Productions Ltd.; Company Manager, Steve Lukens; Stage Manager, Diane DeVita; Assistant to the Director, Christopher Schilder; Associate Design: Orit Jacoby Carroll (set), Aaron Spivey (lighting), Ashley Hanson (sound), Shawn E. Boyle, Austin Switser, Vita Tzykun (projections); Assistant Design: Lauren Alvarez & Frank McCullough (set), Patrick Bevilacqua, Nicole Moody & David Newell (costumes), Shawn Duan & Dan Ozminkowski (projections), Warren Stiles (assistant to Mr. Pask); Dialect Coach, Tim Monich; Production: David Fulton (production carpenter), Geoff Vaughn (advance carpenter), Michael Pitzer (production electrician), Shannon January (head electrician), Peter Sarafin (production props), David Levenberg (head props), Simon Matthews (production sound), Patrick Bevilacqua (wardrobe supervisor), Michael Growler, Del Miskie, Kimberly Mark Sirota, Mark Trezza & Libby Villanova (dressers), Katie Beatty (hair supervisor), T.J. Donoghue, Lars Pedersen & Tom Whipple (projection technicians); Technical Production Assistants, Ally Paull & Dee Wickert; Production Assistants, Ryan Durham, Joanne Mclerney; Associate Producer for Ostar Enterprises, Rachel Neuburger; Assistant to Mr. Haber, Theresa Pisanelli; Advertising, Serino Coyne Inc.; Press, Boneau/Bryan-Brown, Adrian Bryan-Brown, Jackie Green, Kelly Guiod

CAST Thomas Buckle **Jeremy Irons;** Katharine Keenan **Joan Allen;** Julia Davidson **Marsha Mason;** Young Katharine **Hadley Delany;** Douglas Finch **Michael T. Weiss;** Nicole Halladay **Margarita Levieva;** Chiambuane **André DeShields;** Ben Joplin **Aaron Lazar**

UNDERSTUDIES Stevie Ray Dallimore (Thomas Buckle, Douglas Finch), Henny Russell (Katharine Keenan, Julia Davidson), Caroline Rosenblum (Young Katharine), Elizabeth Olsen (Nicole Halladay), Harold Surratt (Chiambuane), Neal Bledsoe (Ben Joplin, Douglas Finch)

SETTING The Katharine Keenan Gallery, and places in Thomas' and Katharine's Memories; the present and the past. World premiere of a new play presented in eight scenes without intermission.

SYNOPSIS *Impressionism* tells the story of a world traveling photojournalist and a New York gallery owner who meet and find that there might be an art to help repair each other's broken lives.

André DeShields, Jeremy Irons, Joan Allen, Margarita Levieva and Aaron Lazar

Jeremy Irons and Joan Allen

Marsha Mason (photos by Joan Marcus)

Joan Allen and Jeremy Irons

Exit the King

Barrymore Theatre; First Preview: March 7, 2009 Opening Night: March 26, 2009; 21 previews, 77 performances as of May 31, 2009

Written by Eugene Ionesco, adapted by Neil Armfield and Geoffrey Rush; Produced by Stuart Thompson, Robert Fox, Howard Panter, Scott Rudin, Tulchin/Bartner, Jon B. Platt, John Frost, The Weinstein Company/Norton Herrick, Michael Edwards & Carole Winter, Daniel Sparrow/Mike Walsh, and The Shubert Organization; Director, Neil Armfield; Sets & Costumes, Dale Ferguson; Lighting, Damien Cooper; Sound, Russell Goldsmith; Composer, John Rodgers; Production Stage Manager, Evan Ensign; Casting, Daniel Swee; Production Management, Aurora Productions; General Management, Stuart Thompson Productions/Dana Sherman; Associate Producer, Ronnie Planalp; Company Manager, Adam J. Miller; Stage Manager, Jim Woolley; Associate Design: Ted LeFevre (set), Barry Doss (costumes), Dan Walker (lighting), Joanna Lynne Staub (sound); Wig Design Consultant, Paul Huntley; Production: Tony Menditto (production carpenter), Michael Hyman (production electrician), Dylan Foley (production props), Jason McKenna (production sound), Eileen Miller (wardrobe supervisor), Ruth Carsch (hair supervisor), Barry Berger (makeup supervisor), Barry Doss (dresser); Production Assistant, Bryan Rountree; General Management Associates, James Triner, David Turner, Caroline Prugh; Production Management Associates, Gene O'Donovan, W. Benjamin Heller II, Bethany Weinstein, Amy Merlino Coey, Melissa Mazdra, Laura Archer, Dana Hesch; General Management Assistants, Quinn Corbin, Megan Curren, Geo Karapetyan; Management Intern, Brittany Levasseur; Casting Associate, Camille Hickman; Musician Consultant, Michael Keller; Advertising, SpotCo (Drew Hodges, Jim Edwards, Tom Greenwald, Jim Aquino, Stacey Maya); For Company B: Louise Herron (Board Chair), Neil Armfield (Artistic Director), Brenna Hobson (General Manager); For Malthouse: Michael Kantor (Artistic Director), Stephen Armstrong (Executive Producer), Catherine Jones (Associate Producer & General Manager), Press, Boneau/Bryan-Brown, Chris Boneau, Susanne Tighe, Christine Olver

Susan Sarandon, William Sadler, Geoffrey Rush, Brian Hutchison (background), Lauren Ambrose and Andrea Martin

auren Ambrose, Geoffrey Rush and Susan Sarandon

Geoffrey Rush (photos by Joan Marcus)

CAST The Guard **Brian Hutchison**; King Berenger **Geoffrey Rush**; Queen Marguerite **Susan Sarandon**; Juliette **Andrea Martin**; The Doctor **William Sadler**; Queen Marie **Lauren Ambrose**; Trumpeter **Shane Endsley/Scott Harrell**

UNDERSTUDIES Michael Hammond (King Berenger, The Doctor), David Manis (King Berenger, The Guard), Erika Rolfsrud (Queen Marguerite, Queen Marie, Juliette)

2008-2009 AWARDS Tony Award: Best Leading Actor in a Play (Geoffrey Rush); Drama Desk Award: Outstanding Actor in a Play (Geoffrey Rush); Outer Critics Circle Award: Outstanding Actor in a Play (Geoffrey Rush); Drama League Award: Performance (Geoffrey Rush); **Theatre World Award:** Geoffrey Rush

SETTING Revival of an absurdist play presented in two acts. This production is based on the production produced by Melbourne, Australia's Company B (Belvoir St. Theatre) and Malthouse Theatres. Originally produced on Broadway by the Association of Producing Artists-Phoenix Repertory Company at the Lyceum Theatre January 9–June 22, 1968, in repertory with *The Cherry Orchard*, *Pantagleize*, and *The Show-Off* (see *Theatre World* Vol. 24, page 67).

SYNOPSIS *Exit the King* is a hilarious and poignant comedy about a megalomaniacal ruler, King Berenger, whose incompetence has left his country in near ruin. Despite the efforts of Queen Marguerite and the other members of the court to convince the King he has only 90 minutes left to live, he refuses to relinquish any control.

Tovah Feldshuh

Irena's Vow

Walter Kerr Theatre; First Preview: March 10, 2009 Opening Night: March 29, 2009; 21 previews, 73 performances as of May 31, 2009

Written by Dan Gordon; Presented by Invictus Theater Company and The Directors Company; Produced by Power Productions/Stan Raiff, Daryl Roth, Debra Black, James L. Nederlander/Terry Allen Kramer, and Peter Fine; Director, Michael Parva; Set, Kevin Judge; Costumes, Astrid Brucker; Lighting, David Castaneda; Projections, Alex Koch; Original Music and Sound, Quentin Chiappetta; Wigs and Hair, Leah J. Loukas; Production Stage Manager, Alan Fox; Technical Supervision, Arthur Siccardi, Patrick Sullivan; Marketing, HHC Marketing; Associate Producers, R. Erin Craig, Alexander Fraser, Roz Goldberg; General Manager, Leonard Soloway; Company Manager, Penelope Daulton; Additional Casting, Jim Carnahan; Stage Manager, Michael Joseph Ormond; Assistant Director, Katherine Heberling; Associate Lighting, Cory Pattak; Assistant Design: Jen Price (set), Josh Liebert (sound), Dragana Vucetic (costumes); Video Programmer, David Tirosh; Dialect Coach, Ralph Zito; Production: George E. Fullum (production carpenter), Vincent J. Valvo Jr. (production electrician), Timothy Bennett (production props), Michael Pilipski (prop supervisor), Penny Davis (wardrobe supervisor), Nathaniel Hathaway (hair supervisor), Ginny Hounsell & Kevin O'Brien (dressers); Marketing Team: Hugh Hysell, Matt Sicoli, Nicole Pando, Michael Redman, Todd Briscoe, Kayla Kuzbel, Paul Zahn; Assistants: Greg Raby (Ms. Roth), Kathleen Ragusa (Ms. Black), Ken Happel (Mr. Nederlander), Sara Shannon (Ms. Kramer), Veronika Crater (Mr. Fine), Sarah Koehler (production); Advertising, Eliran Murphy Group/ Barbara Eliran, Frank Verlizzo, Sasha DeFazio; Press, O+M Co., Rick Miramontez, Molly Barnett

CAST Irena Gut Opdyke **Tovah Feldshuh;** Major Rugemer **Thomas Ryan;** Schultz **Steven Hauck;** Ida Hallar **Maja C. Wampuszyc;** Lazar Hallar **Gene Silvers;** Fanka Silberman **Tracee Chimo;** Sturmbannführer Rokita **John Stanisci;** Helen/Rokita's Secretary **Sandi Carroll;** The Visitor/Polish Worker **Scott Klavan;** Mayor of Jerusalem/SS Officer **Peter Reznikoff**

STANDBYS AND UNDERSTUDIES Tina Benko (Standby for Irena Gut Opdyke), Heather Kenzie (Ida, Fanka, Helen/Rokita's Secretary), Paul O'Brien (Rugemer, Schultz, Mayor/Officer), Kevin O'Donnell (Rokita, Lazar, The Visitor/ Polish Worker)

SETTING An American high school, 1988; Occupied Poland, 1939–1945; Jerusalem, 1988. Transfer of the Off-Broadway play presented without intermission. Previously presented at Baruch Performing Arts Center – Rose Nagelberg Hall from September 7–November 25, 2008 (see Off-Broadway section in this volume).

SYNOPSIS *Irena's Vow* is the riveting, life-affirming story about one of the most courageous and unsung heroines of World War II. During the German occupation of Poland, Irena Gut Opdyke, a Polish Catholic, was forced to work as head housekeeper for a prominent German major. Over a two-year period of service, Irena would risk her own life in order to protect the lives of twelve Jewish refugees whom she secretly took under her care. *Irena's Vow* is the extraordinary true story of one woman's choice and the twelve lives that would ultimately be saved –or lost– by her decision.

Peter Reznikoff, John Stanisci (standing), Maja Wampuszyc, Gene Silvers (seated), Tracee Chimo, Tovah Feldshuh, Thomas Ryan, Scott Klavan and Sandi Carroll

Thomas Ryan, Tovah Feldshuh and John Stanisci (photos by Carol Rosegg)

Hair: The American Tribal Love-Rock Musical

Al Hirschfeld Theatre; First Preview: March 6, 2009 Opening Night: March 31, 2009; 29 previews, 71 performances as of May 31, 2009

Book and lyrics by Gerome Ragni & James Rado, music and orchestrations by Galt MacDermot; Produced by The Public Theater (Oskar Eustis, Artistic Director; Andrew D. Hamingson, Executive Director), Jeffrey Richards, Jerry Frankel, Gary Goddard Entertainment, Kathleen K. Johnson, Nederlander Productions Inc., Fran Kirmser Productions/Jed Bernstein, Marc Frankel, Broadway Across America, Barbara Manocherian/WenCarLar Productions, JK Productions/Terry Schnuck, Andy Sandberg, Jam Theatricals, The Weinstein Company/Norton Herrick, Jujamcyn Theaters, Joey Parnes, and by special arrangement with Elizabeth Ireland McCann; Director, Diane Paulis; Choreography, Karole Armitage; Music Director, Nadia Digiallonardo; Associate Producers, Arielle Tepper Madover, Debbie Bisno/Rebecca Gold, Christopher Hart, Apples and Oranges, Tony & Ruthe Ponturo, Joseph Traina; Sets, Scott Pask; Costumes, Michael McDonald; Lighting, Kevin Adams; Sound, Acme Sound Partners; Music Coordinator, Seymour Red Press; Casting, Jordan Thaler & Heidi Griffiths; Production Stage Manager, Nancy Harrington; Wigs, Gerard Kelly; Associate Producer (The Public Theater), Jenny Gersten; Marketing, Allied Live Inc.; Sponsorship, Rose Polidoro; General Management, Joey Parnes, John Johnson, S.D. Wagner; Company Manager, Kim Sellon; Stage Manager, Julie Baldauff; Assistant Stage Manager, Elizabeth Miller; Associate Company Manager, Leslie A. Glassburn; Assistant Company Manager, Kit Ingui; Assistant Directors, Allegra Libonati, Shira Milikowsky; Assistant Choreographer, Christine O'Grady; Dance Captain, Tommar Wilson; Associate Design: Orit Jacoby Carroll (set), Aaron Sporer (lighting), Lisa Zinni (costumes); Assistant Design: Jeffrey Hinchee & Lauren Alvarez (set), Joel Silver (lighting), Chloe Chapin (costumes), Alex Hawthorn (sound); Assistants to Designers: Warren Stiles (set), David Mendizabal (costumes); Costume Assistant, Sydney Ledger; Mural Illustration, Scott Pask with Amy Guip; Production: Larry Morley (production carpenter), Steve Cochrane/Richard Mortell (production electrician), Michael Smanko (production prop supervisor), Scott Sanders (production sound engineer), Brian Dawson (head electrician), Paul J. Sonnleitner (moving lights programmer), Jim Wilkinson (monitor mixer), John A. Robelen III (wardrobe supervisor), Gloria Burke (hair/wig supervisor), Cat Dee, Amelia Haywood, Shannon McDowell, Clarion Overmoyer, Gayle Palmieri (dressers), Danny Koye (hair dresser); Production Assistant, Johnny Milani; Music Consultant, Tom Kitt; Music Copyist, Rob Baumgardner; Associate to Mr. Richards, Jeremy Scott Blaustein; Assistant to Mr. Richards, Diana Rissetto, Christopher Taggart; Management Associate, Madeline Felix; Casting Assistant, Amber Wakefield; Marketing Team: Lara Matalon, Tanya Grubich, Victoria Cairl, Meghan Zaneski; Director of Communications (The Public Theater), Candi Adams; Director of Marketing (The Public Theater), Ilene Rosen; Advertising, SpotCo (Drew Hodges, Jim Edwards, Stephen Sosnowski, Tim Falotico, Tom Greenwald); Interactive Marketing, Situation Interactive (Damian Bazadona, Jessica Dachille, Jeremy Kraus, John Lanasa, Steve Rovery); Press, O+M Co., Rick Miramontez, Molly Barnett, Philip Carrubba, Elizabeth Wagner; Cast recording: Sh-K-Boom/Ghostlight Records 4467

CAST Dionne **Sasha Allen**; Berger **Will Swenson**; Woof **Bryce Ryness**; Hud **Darius Nichols**; Claude **Gavin Creel**; Sheila **Caissie Levy**; Jeanie **Kacie Sheik**; Crissy **Allison Case**; Mother/Buddahdalirama **Megan Lawrence**; Dad/Margaret Mead **Andrew Kober**; Hubert **Theo Stockman**; Abraham Lincoln **Saycon Sengbloh**; Tribe **Ato Blankson-Wood, Steel Burkhardt, Jackie Burns, Lauren Elder, Allison Guinn, Anthony Hollock, Kaitlin Kiyan, Nicole Lewis, John Moauro, Brandon Pearson, Megan Reinking, Paris Remillard, Saycon Sengbloh, Maya Sharpe, Theo Stockman, Tommar Wilson**; Tribe Swings **Briana Carlson-Goodman, Chasten Harmon, Jay Armstrong Johnson, Josh Lamon, Ryan Link, Michael James Scott**

Gavin Creel (center*) and the Tribe*

The Tribe

UNDERSTUDIES Steel Burkhardt (Berger), Jackie Burns (Jeanie, Sheila), Lauren Elder (Mother), Allison Guinn (Buddahdalirama), Chasten Harmon (Dionne), Jay Armstrong Johnson (Claude), Kaitlin Kiyan (Crissy), Josh Lamon (Dad, Margaret Mead), Ryan Link (Berger, Woof), Megan Reinking (Jeanie), Paris Remillard (Claude, Woof), Michael James Scott (Hud, Margaret Mead), Saycon Sengbloh (Dionne), Theo Stockman (Dad), Tommar Wilson (Hud)

MUSICIANS Nadia Digiallonardo (Conductor/keyboard), Lon Hoyt (Assistant Conductor/keyboard), Steve Bargonetti & Andrew Schwartz (guitar), Wilbur Bascomb (bass), Allen Won (woodwinds), Elaine Burt, Ronald Buttacavoli & Christian Jaudes (trumpets), Vincent MacDermot (trombone), Joe Cardello (percussion), Bernard Purdie (drums)

MUSICAL NUMBERS Aquarius, Donna, Hashish, Sodomy, Colored Spade, Manchester England, I'm Black, Ain't Got No, Sheila Franklin, I Believe in Love, Ain't Got No (reprise), Air, The Stone Age, I Got Life, Initials, Going Down, Hair, My Conviction, Easy to Be Hard, Don't Put It Down, Frank Mills, Hare Krishna, Where Do I Go, Electric Blues, Oh Great God of Power, Black Boys, White Boys, Walking in Space, Minuet, Yes I's Finished on Y'alls Farmlands, Four Score and Seven Years Ago/Abie Baby, Give Up All Desires, Three-Five-Zero-Zero, What a Piece of Work Is Man, How Dare They Try, Good Morning Starshine, Ain't Got No (reprise), The Flesh Failures, Eyes Look Your Last, Let the Sun Shine In

2008–2009 AWARDS Tony Award: Best Revival of a Musical; Drama Desk Award: Outstanding Revival of a Musical; Outer Critics Circle Award: Outstanding Revival of a Musical; Drama League Award: Outstanding Revival of a Musical

Will Swenson and the Tribe

The Tribe (photos by Joan Marcus)

Caissie Levy, Sashah Allen, Kacie Sheik, Allison Case and the Tribe

Gavin Creel, Will Swenson and the Tribe

SETTING New York City, the late 1960s. Revival of the rock musical presented in two acts. This production was previously presented at the Delacorte Theater as part of the Public Theater's Shakespeare in the Park July 22–September 14, 2008 (see listing in the Off-Broadway Company Series in this volume), which in turn was inspired by the three-performance run of the Diane Paulus directed fortieth anniversary concert version, presented as part of Joe's Pub in the Park at the Delacorte Theatre September 22-24, 2007, with many in this cast (see *Theatre World* Vol. 64, page 186). Originally produced Off-Broadway at the Public Theater October 17–December 10, 1967, the show reopened at the midtown discothèque Cheetah December 22, 1968–January 28, 1968. The production went through extensive rewrites and recasting, and transferred to Broadway at the Biltmore Theatre April 29, 1968, closing July 1, 1972 after 1,750 performances (see *Theatre World* Vol. 24, pages 59 and 11). The show had a brief revival at the Biltmore August 3–November 6, 1977 (see *Theatre World* Vol. 34, page 14). On September 20, 2004, The Actors Fund presented a one-night only benefit concert of the show featuring an all-star cast.

SYNOPSIS *Hair*, returning to Broadway for the first time in over thrity years, depicts the birth of a cultural movement in the '60s and '70s that changed America forever. The musical follows a group of hopeful, free-spirited young people who advocate a lifestyle of pacifism and free-love in a society riddled with intolerance and brutality during the Vietnam War. As they explore sexual identity, challenge racism, experiment with drugs and burn draft cards, the tribe in *Hair* creates an irresistible message of hope that continues to resonate with audiences 40 years later. Its groundbreaking rock score paved the way for some of the greatest musicals of our time. Now, the "Age of Aquarius" dawns again.

Tommar Wilson, Will Swenson and Bryce Ryness

Marin Ireland and Thomas Sadoski

Stephen Pasquale and Thomas Sadoski

Thomas Sadoski and Piper Perabo (photos by Robert J. Saferstein)

Right: *Thomas Sadoski and Marin Ireland*

reasons to be pretty

Lyceum Theatre; First Preview: March 13, 2009 Opening Night: April 2, 2009; 21 previews, 69 performances as of May 31, 2009

Written by Neil LaBute; Presented by Manhattan Class Company (MCC) Theater; Produced by Jeffrey Richards, Jerry Frankel, MCC Theater, Gary Goddard Entertainment, Ted Snowdon, Doug Nevin/Erica Lynn Schwartz, Ronald Frankel/Bat-Barry Productions, Kathleen Seidel, Kelpie Arts, Jam Theatricals and Rachel Helson/Heather Provost; Director, Terry Kinney; Set, David Gallo; Costumes, Sarah J. Holden; Lighting, David Weiner; Original Music and Sound, Rob Millburn & Michael Bodeen; Casting, Telsey + Company; Technical Supervisor, Hudson Theatrical Associates; Production Stage Manager, Christine Lemme; Fight Director, Manny Siverio; General Manager, Daniel Kuney, Christopher D'Angelo; Associate Technical Supervisor, B.D. White; Stage Manager, Matthew Farrell; Fight Captain, Michael D. Dempsey; Associate Design: Steven C. Kemp (set), Lauren Phillips (costumes), David Stollings (sound); Assistant Costume Design, Maggie Lee-Burdorff; Lighting Programmer, Marc Polimeni; Dramaturg, Stephen Williams; Vocal Coach, Deborah Hecht; Production: Adam Braunstein (head carpenter), Brian GF McGarity (electrician supervisor), Jonathan Cohen (head electrician), Jeremy Chernick (production props supervisor), Leah Nelson (head properties), Wallace Flores (sound supervisor), Sandy Binion (wardrobe supervisor), Susan Checklick (dresser), Alexis Qualis (production assistant); Advertising, SpotCo; Press, O+M Co, Rick Miramontez, Jon Dimond, Amanda Dekker

CAST Steph **Marin Ireland**; Kent **Steven Pasquale**; Carly **Piper Perabo**; Greg **Thomas Sadoski**

UNDERSTUDIES Ann Bowles (Carly, Steph), Michael D. Dempsey (Greg, Kent)

2008–2009 AWARDS Theatre World Award: Marin Ireland

SETTING The outlying suburbs. Not long ago. Transfer of the Off-Broadway comic drama presented in two acts. World premiere produced by MCC Theater (Robert LuPone, Bernard Telsey, Artistic Directors; William Cantler, Associate Artistic Director; Blake West, Executive Director) at the Lucille Lortel Theatre May 14–July 5, 2008 (opened June 2; see *Theatre World* Vol. 64, page 173).

SYNOPSIS America's obsession with physical beauty is confronted headlong in this brutal and exhilarating new play. In *reasons to be pretty*, Greg's tight-knit social circle is thrown into turmoil when his offhanded remarks about a female coworker's pretty face (and his girlfriend's lack thereof) get back to said girlfriend. But that's just the beginning. Greg's best buddy Kent, and Kent's wife Carly also enter into the picture and the emotional equation becomes exponentially more complicated. As their relationships crumble, the four friends are forced to confront a sea of deceit, infidelity and betrayed trust in their journey to answer that oh-so-American question: How much is pretty worth?

Rock of Ages

Brooks Atkinson Theatre; First Preview: March 20, 2009 Opening Night: April 7, 2009; 22 previews, 63 performances as of May 31, 2009

Book by Chris D'Arienzo; Produced by Matthew Weaver, Carl Levin, Barry Habib, Scott Prisand, Corner Store Fund, in association with Janet Billig Rich, Hillary Weaver, Toni Habib, Paula Davis, Simon & Stefany Bergson/Jennifer Maloney, Charles Rolecek, Susanne Brook, Israel Wolfson, Sara Katz/Jayson Raitt, Max Gottlieb/John Butler, David Kaufman/Jay Franks, Michael Wittlin, Prospect Pictures, Laura Smith/Bill Bodnar; Director, Kristin Hanggi; Choreography, Kelly Devine; Music Supervision, Arrangements & Orchestrations, Ethan Popp; Music Director, Henry Aronson; Music Coordinator, John Miller; Original Arrangements, David Gibbs; Set, Beowulf Boritt; Costumes, Gregory Gale; Lighting, Jason Lyons; Sound, Peter Hylenski; Projections, Zak Borovay; Hair & Wigs, Tom Watson; Makeup, Angelina Avallone; Casting, Telsey + Company; Production Stage Manager, Claudia Lynch; Vocal Coach, Liz Caplan Vocal Studios; Associate Choreographer, Robert Tatad; Associate Director/Stage Manager, Adam John Hunter; Associate Producer, David Gibbs; General Management, Frankel Green Theatrical Management (Richard Frankel, Laura Green, Joe Watson, Leslie Ledbetter); Technical Supervisor, Peter Fulbright/Tech Production Services Inc. (Colleen Houlehen, Mary Duffe, Miranda Wigginton); Company Management, Tracy Geltman (Manager), Susan Keappock (Assistant); Associate General Manager, Aliza Wassner; Assistant Stage Managers, Marisha Ploski & Matthew Dicarlo; Associate Design, Jo Winiarski (set), Karl Ruckdeschel (costumes), Austin Switser (projections & programming); Assistant Design: Julia Broer & Colleen Kesterson (costumes), Driscoll Otto (lighting), Barbara Samuels (assistant to lighting designer), Keith Caggiano (sound), Daniel Brodie (projections); Creative Advisor, Wendy Goldberg; Production: Brian Munroe (production carpenter), Ray Harold (assistant production carpenter), Mike LoBue (production electrician), Brent Oakley (head electrician), Phillip Lojo (production sound engineer), Jesse Stevens (assistant sound engineer), Mike Pilipski (production property master), Jacob White (head propman), Buist Bickly (propman), Robert Guy (wardrobe supervisor), Joshua Speed Schwartz (hair supervisor), Renee Borys, Michael Louis, Danny Mura, Arlene Watson, Susan Cook, Marisa Lerette (dressers); Production Assistant, Samantha Saltzman; Script Supervisor, Justin Mabardi; Synthesizer Programmer, Randy Cohen; Music Copying/Preparation, Firefly Music Service/Brian Hobbs; Rehearsal Pianist, Keith Cotton; Dance Captain, Bahiyah Sayyed Gaines; Advertising, Serino Coyne Inc.; Marketing Leanne Schanzer Promotions and The Pekoe Group; Internet Marketing, Art Meets Commerce; Press, Barlow · Hartman Public Relations, John Barlow, Michael Hartman, Leslie Baden, Matt Shea; Cast recording: New Line Records

CAST Lonny/Record Company Man **Mitchell Jarvis;** Justice/Mother **Michele Mais;** Dennis/Record Company Man **Adam Dannheisser;** Drew **Constantine Maroulis;** Sherrie **Amy Spanger;** Father/Stacee Jaxx **James Carpinello;** Regina/Candi **Lauren Molina;** Mayor/Ja'Keith Gill/Ensemble **André Ward;** Hertz **Paul Schoeffler;** Franz **Wesley Taylor;** Waitress/Ensemble **Savannah Wise;** Reporter/Ensemble **Katherine Tokarz**; Sleazy Producer/Joey Primo/Ensemble **Jeremy Woodard;** Young Groupie/Ensemble **Angel Reed;** Offstage Voices **Ericka Hunter, Tad Wilson;** Swings **Jeremy Jordan, Bahiyah Sayyed Gaines, Michael Minarik**

UNDERSTUDIES Ericka Hunter (Sherrie), Jeremy Jordan (Drew, Franz, Stacee Jaxx), Michael Minarik (Dennis, Hertz, Lonny, Stacee Jaxx), Bahiyah Sayyed Gaines (Justice), Katherine Tokarz (Justice, Regina), Tad Wilson (Dennis, Hertz, Lonny), Savannah Wise (Sherrie), Jeremy Woodard (Drew, Franz, Stacee Jaxx)

***ROCK OF AGES* BAND** Henry Aronson (Conductor/keyboard), Joel Hoekstra (guitar 1), David Gibbs (guitar 2), John Weber (drums), Winston Roye (bass)

MUSICAL NUMBERS We Built This City (Starship), Nothin' but a Good Time (Poison), Keep on Loving You (REO Speedwagon), Just Like Paradise (David Lee Roth), I Wanna Rock (Twisted Sister), Too Much Time on My Hands (Styx), Renegade (Styx), I Hate Myself for Loving You (Joan Jett & the Blackhearts),

Oh Sherrie (Steve Perry), Waiting for a Girl Like You (Foreigner), Shadows of the Night (Pat Benatar), Don't Stop Believing (Journey), Heaven (Warrant), The Search is Over (Survivor), We're Not Gonna Take It (Twisted Sister), High Enough (Damn Yankees), The Final Countdown (Europe), I Want to Know What Love Is (Foreigner), Harden My Heart (Quarterflash), Here I Go Again (Whitesnake), To Be With You (Mr. Big), Every Rose Has Its Thorn (Poison), Hit Me With Your Best Shot (Pat Benatar), Can't Fight This Feeling (REO Speedwagon), Wanted Dead or Alive (Bon Jovi), Cum on Feel the Noize (Slade/Quiet Riot), Any Way You Want It (Journey), Heat of the Moment (Asia), Sister Christian (Night Ranger), More Than Words (Extreme)

2008-2009 AWARDS Theatre World Award: Wesley Taylor

SETTING Los Angeles and Hollywood, 1987. Transfer of the Off-Broadway musical presented in two acts. Previously presented at New World Stages October 1, 2008–January 4, 2009 (see Off-Broadway section in this volume). World premiere at the Vanguard Hollywood January 26–February 18, 2006.

SYNOPSIS *Rock of Ages* is an explosive new musical with a heart as big as '80s rock hair. In 1987 on the Sunset Strip, as a legendary rock club faces its demise at the hands of eager developers, a young rocker hoping for his big break falls for a small town girl chasing big dreams of her own, and they fall in love to the greatest songs of the '80s. An arena-rock love story, *Rock of Ages* is told through the mind-blowing, face-melting hits of some of the era's greatest rockers including Journey, Bon Jovi, Styx, Reo Speedwagon, Pat Benatar, Twisted Sister, Poison, Asia and Whitesnake.

Amy Spanger (photos by Joan Marcus)

Constantine Maroulis

The Company

James Carpinello and Company

The Company

Constantine Maroulis and
Amy Spanger

Alice Ripley, Aaron Tveit and J. Robert Spencer

The Company

Next to Normal

Booth Theatre; First Preview: March 27, 2009 Opening Night: April 15, 2009; 20 previews, 54 performances as of May 31, 2009

Music by Tom Kitt, book and lyrics by Brian Yorkey; Produced by David Stone, James L. Nederlander, Barbara Whitman, Patrick Catullo, Second Stage (Carole Rothman, Artistic Director; Ellen Richard, Executive Director); Director, Michael Greif; Musical Staging, Sergio Trujillo; Set, Mark Wendland; Costumes, Jeff Mahshie; Lighting, Kevin Adams; Sound, Brian Ronan; Orchestrations, Michael Starobin & Tom Kitt; Vocal Arrangements, AnnMarie Milazzo; Music Director, Charlie Alterman; Music Coordinator, Michael Keller; Casting, Telsey + Company; Production Stage Manager, Judith Schoenfeld; Company Manager, Marc Borsak; Technical Supervisor, Larry Morley; General Management, 321 Theatrical Management (Nina Essman, Nancy Nagel Gibbs, Marcia Goldberg); Stage Manager, Martha Donaldson; Assistant Stage Manager, Sally E. Sibson; Assistant Director, Laura Pietropinto; Associate Choreographer, Dontee Kiehn; Assistant Music Director, Mat Eisenstein; Associate Design: Joel E. Silver (lighting), David Stollings (sound); Assistant Design: Rachel Nemec (set), Paul Toben, Aaron Sporer (lighting), Jon Collin & Shoko Kambara (scenic design assistants); Associate Technical Supervisor, Bradley Thompson; Dance Captain, Jessica Phillips; Writers' Assistant, Brandon Ivie; Production: Bill Craven (production carpenter), Richard Mortell (production electrician), Mike Farfalla (production electrician), Kenneth McDonough (carpenter), Ed White (flyman), Susan Goulet (electrician), James Keane (props), Chris Sloan (sound engineer), Elizabeth Berkeley (assistant sound engineer), Kyle LaColla (wardrobe supervisor), Sara Jane Darneille & Vangeli Kaseluris (dressers); Music Preparation, Emily Grishman; Drum and Percussion Arrangements, Damien Bassman; Additional Guitar Arrangements, Michael Aarons; Assistants: Aaron Glick (to Mr. Stone), Tara Geesaman, Jeanette Norton (to general managers), Stuart Shefter (production); Advertising, Serino Coyne Inc.; Press, Barlow · Hartman Public Relations, Michael Hartman, John Barlow, Tom D'Ambrosio, Michelle Bergmann; Cast recording: Sh-K-Boom/Ghostlight Records 4433

CAST Henry **Adam Chanler-Berat;** Natalie **Jennifer Damiano;** Dr. Madden/ Dr. Fine **Louis Hobson;** Diana **Alice Ripley;** Dan **J. Robert Spencer;** Gabe **Aaron Tveit**

UNDERSTUDIES Michael Berry (Dan, Dr. Madden/Dr. Fine), Meghann Fahy (Natalie), Jessica Phillips (Diana), Tim Young (Gabe, Henry)

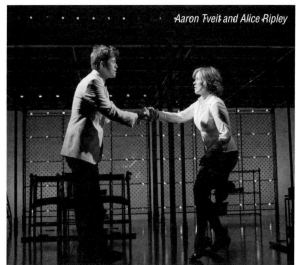

Aaron Tveit and Alice Ripley

Adam Chanler-Berat and Jennifer Damiano

J. Robert Spencer and Aaron Tveit

Alice Ripley and J. Robert Spencer

NEXT TO NORMAL BAND Charlie Alterman (Conductor/piano), Yuiko Kamakari (piano/violin), Benjamin Kalb (cello), Eric Davis (guitars), Michael Blanco (bass), Damien Bassman (drums/percussion)

MUSICAL NUMBERS Prelude, Just Another Day, Everything Else, Whos Crazy/ My Psychopharmacologist and I, Perfect for You, I Miss the Mountains, Its Gonna Be Good, He's Not Here, You Don't Know, I Am the One, Superboy and the Invisible Girl, I'm Alive, Make Up Your Mind/Catch Me I'm Falling, I Dreamed a Dance, There's a World, I've Been, Didn't I See This Movie?, A Light in the Dark, Wish I Were Here, Song of Forgetting, Hey #1, Seconds and Years, Better Than Before, Aftershocks, Hey #2, You Don't Know (reprise), How Could I Ever Forget?, It's Gonna Be Good (reprise), Why Stay?/A Promise, I'm Alive (reprise), The Break, Make Up Your Mind/Catch Me Im Falling (reprise), Maybe (Next to Normal), Hey #3/Perfect for You (reprise), So Anyway, I Am the One (reprise), Light

2008–2009 AWARDS Tony Awards: Best Original Score (Tom Kitt & Brian Yorkey), Best Actress in a Musical (Alice Ripley), Best Orchestrations (Tom Kitt & Michael Starobin) – tie with *Billy Elliot The Musical*

SETTING A suburban household; the present. A new musical presented in two acts. World premiere presented at Second Stage February 13–March 16, 2008 (see *Theatre World* Vol. 64, page 190) and subsequently presented this season at Arena Stage (Molly Smith, Artistic Director), November 21, 2008–January 18, 2009 with this cast (see Regional Theatre listings in this volume). Originally presented and workshopped (under the title *Feeling Electric*) at the New York Musical Theatre Festival, September 2005, and the Village Theatre (Issaquah Washington), June 21-23, 2005.

SYNOPSIS *Next to Normal* explores how one suburban household copes with its past and future. How does an almost average family navigate today's over-stimulated and over medicated world? This groundbreaking new musical takes a close look at contemporary mental illness and treatment as it shows how far two parents will go to keep themselves sane and their family's world intact.

*Alice Ripley and Louis Hobson
(photos by Joan Marcus)*

Joe Turner's Come and Gone

Belasco Theatre; First Preview: March 19, 2009 Opening Night: April 16, 2009; 31 previews, 53 performances as of May 31, 2009

Written by August Wilson; Produced by Lincoln Center Theater (André Bishop, Artistic Director; Bernard Gersten, Executive Producer); Director, Bartlett Sher; Sets, Michael Yeargan; Costumes, Catherine Zuber; Lighting, Brian MacDevitt; Sound, Scott Lehrer & Leon Rothenberg; Music, Taj Mahal; Stage Manager, Narda E. Alcorn; Casting, Daniel Swee; General Manager, Adam Siegel; Production Manager, Jeff Hamlin; Director of Development, Hattie K. Jutagir; Director of Marketing, Linda Mason Ross; Director of Finance, David S. Brown; Director of Education, Kati Koerner; Artistic Directors of Lincoln Center, Graciela Daniele, Nicholas Hytner, Jack O'Brien, Susan Stroman, Daniel Sullivan; Dramaturg/LCT Directors Lab, Anne Cattaneo; Musical Theatre Associate Producer, Ira Weitzman; Director of LCT3, Paige Evans; Associate General Manager, Jessica Niebanck; Associate Production Manager, Paul Smithyman; Company Manager, Matthew Markoff; Assistant Stage Manager, Michael P. Zaleski, Jon Carter; Hair & Makeup, Lou Zakarian; Vocal Coach, Deborah Hecht; Movement, Dianne McIntyre; Movement Assistant, Shireen Dickson; Props, Susan Barras; Associate Design: Mikiko Suzuki McAdams (set), Jennifer Schriever (lighting), David Thomas (sound); Assistant Design: Nicole Moody & David Newell (costumes), Rebecca Eichorn (lighting), Zach Blane (assistant to lighting designer), Ashley Hanson (sound); Production: John Weingart (production carpenter), Graeme McDonnell (production electrician), Mark Dignam (production propertyman), Wayne Smith (production soundman), Moira MacGregor-Conrad (wardrobe supervisor), Yolanda Ramsey (hair supervisor), Tina Marie Clifton, Kevin Andre Dickens (dressers); Assistant to Mr. Sher, Sarna Lapine; Production Assistant, Rosy Garner; Costume Shopper, Lindsey Jones; Guardian, Brooke Engen; Tutoring, On Location Education; Animal Training, William Berloni; Animal Handler, Monica Schaffer; Poster Art, James McMullan; Advertising, Serino Coyne Inc.; Press, Philip Rinaldi, Barbara Carroll

CAST Seth Holly, *owner of the boarding house* **Ernie Hudson;** Bertha Holly, *his wife* **LaTanya Richardson Jackson;** Bynum Walker, *a rootworker* **Roger Robinson;** Rutherford Selig, *a peddler* **Arliss Howard;** Jeremy Furlow, *a resident* **Andre Holland;** Herald Loomis, *a resident* **Chad L. Coleman;** Zonia Loomis, *his daughter* **Amari Rose Leigh;** Mattie Campbell, *a resident* **Marsha Stephanie Blake;** Reuben Scott, *a boy who lives next door* **Michael Cummings;** Molly Cunningham, *a resident* **Aunjanue Ellis;** Martha Pentecost **Danai Gurira**

UNDERSTUDIES Michael Rogers (Seth Holly, Bynum Walker), Brenda Thomas Denmark (Bertha Holly), Christopher McHale (Rutherford Selig), Nyambi Nyambi (Herald Loomis, Jeremy Furlow), Olivia Ford (Zonia Loomis), Afton C. Williamson (Mattie Campbell, Molly Cunningham, Martha Pentecost), Elon Van Buckley (Reuben Scott)

2008-2009 AWARDS Tony Awards: Best Featured Actor in a Play (Roger Robinson), Best Lighting Design of a Play (Brian MacDevitt); **Theatre World Award:** Chad L. Coleman

SETTING Time: August 1911. Place: A boardinghouse in Pittsburgh. Revival of a play presented in nine scenes in two acts. World premiere at the Eugene O'Neill Theater Center (Waterford, Connecticut) in 1984. The original Broadway production played the Barrymore Theatre March 27–June 26, 1988, playing 105 performances (see *Theatre World* Vol. 44, page 29).

SYNOPSIS The second play of August Wilson's ten-play Century Cycle, *Joe Turner's Come and Gone* tells the story of Herald Loomis who, after serving seven years hard labor, has journeyed North with his young daughter and arrives at a Pittsburgh boarding house filled with memorable characters who aid him in his search for his inner freedom. The play also examines the conflicts that faced many African-Americans as they struggled to find jobs and security in the years following the emancipation, as many of them migrated North.

Michael Cummings and Amari Rose Leigh

Roger Robinson, Aunjanue Ellis and Andre Holland

Marsha Stephanie Blake and Chad L. Coleman (photos by T. Charles Erickson)

Mary Stuart

Janet McTeer (photos by Joan Marcus)

Broadhurst Theatre; First Preview: March 30, 2009 Opening Night: April 19, 2009; 22 previews, 49 performances as of May 31, 2009

New version written by Peter Oswald, based on the original by Friedrich Schiller; Presented by the Donmar Warehouse (Michael Grandage, Artistic Director; James Bierman, Executive Director; Patrick Gracey, Acting General Manager); Produced by Arielle Tepper Madover, Debra Black, Neal Street Productions/ Matthew Byam Shaw, Scott M. Delman, Barbara Whitman, Jean Doumanian/ Ruth Hendel, David Binder/CarlWend Productions/Spring Sirkin, Daryl Roth/ James L. Nederlander/Chase Mishkin; Director, Phyllida Lloyd; Sets & Costumes, Anthony Ward; Lighting, Hugh Vanstone; Sound, Paul Arditti; Casting, Daniel Swee; U.K. Casting, Anne McNulty; Technical Supervisor, Aurora Productions; Production Stage Manager, Barclay Stiff; Marketing Director, Eric Schnall; General Management, 101 Productions Ltd. (Wendy Orshan, Jeffrey Wilson, David Auster, Ellie Landau); Company Manager, Sean Free; Hair, Campbell Young; Stage Manager, Brandon Kahn; Assistant Director, Seth Sklar-Heyn; Dialect Coach, Kate Wilson; Fight Director, Thomas Schall; Associate Design: Christine Peters (set), Daryl Stone (costumes), Philip Rosenberg & Jake DeGroot (lighting), Jeremy J. Lee (sound), Luc Verschueren (hair); U.K. Associate Costumes, Stephanie Arditti; Casting Associate, Camille Hickman; Aurora Productions: Gene O'Donovan, W. Benjamin Heller II, Bethany Weinstein, Amy Merlino Coey, Melissa Mazdra, Laura Archer, Dana Hesch; Production: Jon Lawson (production electrician), Mike Hill (moving lights programmer), William Lewis (production sound), Andrew Meeker (production props), Denise J. Grillo (prop shopper), Brian McGarty (house carpenter), Charlie DeVerna (house electrician), Brian Bullard (house flyman), Ron Vitelli (house properties), Kelly Saxon (wardrobe supervisor), Carmel Vargyas (hair supervisor), Mickey Abbate & Kristen Gardner (dressers); Production Assistant, Eileen Kelly; Assistant to Ms. Madover, Holly Ferguson; Advertising, SpotCo (Drew Hodges, Jim Edwards, Tom Greenwald, Y. Darius Suyama, Pete Duffy); Press, Boneau/Bryan-Brown, Adrian Bryan-Brown, Jim Byk, Rachel Strange

Harriet Walter

CAST Hanna Kennedy, *Mary's nurse* **Maria Tucci;** Sir Amias Paulet, *Mary's jailer* **Michael Countryman;** Mary Stuart, *Queen of Scotland* **Janet McTeer;** Mortimer, *Paulet's nephew* **Chandler Williams;** Lord Burleigh **Nicholas Woodeson;** Elizabeth, *Queen of England* **Harriet Walter;** Count Aubespine, *French Ambassador* **Michael Rudko;** Earl of Shrewsbury **Brian Murray;** Earl of Leicester **John Benjamin Hickey;** O'Kelly, *Mortimer's friend* **Adam Greer;** Sir William Davison **Robert Stanton;** Melvil, *Mary's house steward* **Michael Rudko;** Courtiers, Officers and others **Tony Carlin, Guy Paul, Adam Greer**

UNDERSTUDIES Tony Carlin (Aubespine, Melvil, Courtier, Officer, Earl of Leicester), Monique Fowler (Elizabeth, Hannah Kennedy), Adam Greer (Mortimer, Davison), Guy Paul (Lord Burleigh, Paulet), Michael Rudko (Earl of Shrewsbury), Jacqueline Antaramian (Mary, Hanna Kennedy)

SETTING Between Fotheringhay Castle and Elizabeth's Court at Westminster, 1587. Revival of a drama presented in two acts. This production was previously presented at the Donmar Warehouse (starring Ms. McTeer and Ms. Walter) July 14–September 3, 2005, and then transferred to the West End's Apollo Theatre October 7, 2005–January 14, 2006. The first major New York production opened at the Fifth Avenue Theatre on February 26, 1900. It was revived Off-Broadway at the Phoenix Theatre with Eve LeGallienne and Irene Worth, October 8–November 24, 1957 (see *Theatre World* Vol. 14, page 161). The Repertory Theatre of Lincoln Center revived the show at the Vivian Beaumont Theatre with Nancy Marchand and Salome Jens, October 30–December 18, 1971 (see *Theatre World* Vol. 28, page 70).

SYNOPSIS Seduction, greed and deception lie at the heart of the bitter rivalry between Mary, Queen of Scots, and her cousin, Elizabeth I of England. After being implicated in her husband's murder, Mary turns to Elizabeth for help but finds her cousin distrustful of her motives. Thus begins a bloody feud that will threaten not just their family bond, but the crown of England. *Mary Stuart*, in its first major revival in almost forty years, tells the story of two iconic women whose lust for power reveals one of the most thrilling displays of passion and politics the world has ever seen.

The Norman Conquests: Table Manners/ Living Together/Round and Round the Garden

Circle in the Square Theatre; First Preview: April 7, 2009 Opening Night: April 23, 2009; 18 previews, 44 performances as of May 31, 2009 (*Table Manners*: 7 previews, 17 performances; *Living Together*: 5 previews, 12 performances; *Round and Round the Garden*: 6 previews, 16 performances)

Written by Alan Ayckbourn; Presented by The Old Vic Theatre (Kevin Spacey, Artistic Director; Sally Greene, Chief Executive; John Richardson and Kate Pakenham, Producers); Produced by Sonia Friedman Productions, Steven Baruch, Marc Routh, Richard Frankel, Tom Viertel, Dede Harris, Tulchin/Bartner/Lauren Doll, Jamie deRoy, Eric Falkenstein, Harriet Newman Leve, Probo Productions, Douglas G. Smith, Michael Filerman/Jennifer Manocherian, Richard Winkler, in association with Dan Frishwasser, Pam Laudenslager/Remmel T. Dickinson, Jane Dublin/True Love Productions, Barbara Manocherian/Jennifer Isaacson; Director, Matthew Warchus; Set & Costumes, Rob Howell; Lighting, David Howe; Music, Gary Yershon; Sound, Simon Baker; Original Casting, Gabrielle Dawes; Production Stage Manager, Ira Mont; U.S. General Management, Frankel Green Theatrical Management (Richard Frankel, Laura Green, Joe Watson, Leslie Ledbetter); U.K. General Management, Diane Benjamin; Production Manager, Aurora Productions (Gene O'Donovan, Ben Heller, Bethany Weinstein); Company Manager, Kathy Lowe; Associate Company Manager, Townsend Teague; New York Casting, Jim Carnahan; Stage Manager, Julia P. Jones; Associate Director, Annabel Bolton; Assistant Director, Mark Schneider; Video Design, Duncan McLean; Dialect Consultant, Elizabeth A. Smith; Associate Design: Paul Weimer (set), Daryl Stone (costumes), Vivien Leone (lighting), Christopher Cronin (sound); Production Assistant, Nathan K. Claus; Wardrobe Supervisor, Sue Stepnik; Dressers, Bobby Clifton, Jessica Worsnop; Management Assistant, Andrew Michaelson; Circle in the Square Staff: Theodore Mann and Paul Libin (Directors), Susan Frankel (General Manager), Cheryl Dennis (house manager), Anthony Menditto (head carpenter), Stewart Wagner (head electrician), Owen E. Parmele (prop master), Jim Bay (sound engineer); Producer Assistants: Lucie Lovatt (Ms. Friedman), Katie Adams (Mr. Routh), Sonja Soper (Mr. Baruch), Tania Senewiratne (Mr. Viertel), Matthew Parent (Ms. Harris), Sarah Nashman (Mr. Bartner); Advertising, SpotCo (Drew Hodges, Tom Greenwald, Jim Edwards, Jim Aquino, Stacey Maya); Press, Boneau/Bryan-Brown, Adrian Bryan-Brown, Jim Byk, Aaron Meier, Rachel Strange

CAST Ruth **Amelia Bullmore;** Annie **Jessica Hynes;** Norman **Stephen Mangan;** Tom **Ben Miles;** Reg **Paul Ritter;** Sarah **Amanda Root**

UNDERSTUDIES Cassie Beck (Annie), Peter Bradbury (Norman), Angela Pierce (Ruth, Sarah), Tony Ward (Tom, Reg)

2008–2009 AWARDS Tony Award: Best Revival of a Play; Drama Desk Award: Outstanding Revival of a Play, Outstanding Ensemble Performance, Outstanding Director of a Play (Matthew Warchus); Outer Critics Circle Award: Outstanding Revival of a Play, Outstanding Director of a Play (Matthew Warchus), Outstanding Ensemble Performance; Drama Critics Circle Award: Special Citation to Matthew Warchus and the entire Cast; **Theatre World Award:** Special Award to the entire Cast

SETTING A Victorian house in England during a weekend in July; mid-1970s. *Table Manners*: the dining room (Act I Scene 1: Saturday, 6 p.m.; Act I Scene II: Sunday, 9 a.m.; Act II Scene I: Sunday, 8 p.m.; Act II Scene II: Monday, 8 a.m.); *Living Together*: the sitting room (Act I Scene 1: Saturday, 6:30 p.m.; Act I Scene II: Saturday, 8 p.m.; Act II Scene I: Sunday, 9 p.m.; Act II Scene II: Monday, 8 a.m.); *Round and Round the Garden*: the garden (Act I Scene 1: Saturday, 5:30 p.m.; Act I Scene II: Saturday, 9 p.m.; Act II Scene I: Sunday, 11 a.m.; Act II Scene II: Monday, 9 a.m.). Revival of three full-length plays presented in repertory, each play presented in 4 scenes in two acts. Prior to the Broadway engagement, the trilogy was produced by The Old Vic Theatre Company (London) September 11–December 20, 2008 (opened October 6) with this cast. The trilogy was first produced on Broadway at the Morosco Theatre December 5, 1975–June 19, 1976 (see *Theatre World* Vol. 32, page 28.)

SYNOPSIS *The Norman Conquests* comprises of three full-length plays—*Table Manners*, *Living Together*, and *Round and Round the Garden*. Each individual play offers a view of one comically catastrophic weekend, shared by six spouses and in-laws, at the family house in the country. And while each play is complete on its own terms, by viewing all three plays (in any order), the audience is able, detective-like, to piece together all of the hidden secrets and lies, the outrageous, hilarious and shocking interactions, which occurred over the weekend. Desperate lothario Norman, an assistant librarian, attempts to seduce his sister-in-law Annie, charm his brother-in-law's wife Sarah and woo his estranged wife Ruth, during a disastrously hilarious weekend of eating, drinking and misunderstanding.

Stephen Mangan in Table Manners

Amanda Root in Table Manners

Amelia Bullmore in Round and Round the Garden

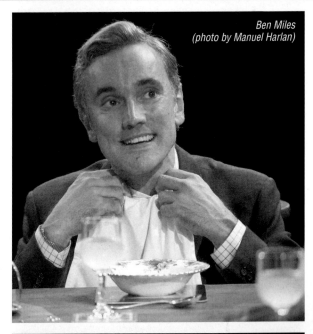

*Ben Miles
(photo by Manuel Harlan)*

(clockwise, around the table, from the left) *Jessica Hynes, Amelia Bullmore, and Paul Ritter, Stephen Mangan, Ben Miles, and Amanda Root in* Table Manners *(photo by Manuel Harlan)*

Stephen Mangan and Jessica Hynes (on the grass); Paul Ritter, Ben Miles and Amelia Bullmore in Round and Round the Garden

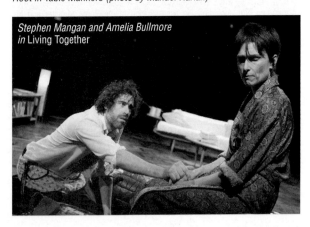

Stephen Mangan and Amelia Bullmore in Living Together

Jessica Hynes in Round and Round the Garden *(photos by Joan Marcus)*

Matthew Broderick and Jennifer Mudge (photos by Joan Marcus)

Anna Madeley and Matthew Broderick

RightL *Jonathan Cake, Matthew Broderick and Steven Weber*

The Philanthropist

American Airlines Theatre; First Preview: April 10, 2009 Opening Night: April 26, 2009; 19 previews, 41 performances as of May 31, 2009

Written by Christopher Hampton; Produced by the Roundabout Theatre Company (Todd Haimes, Artistic Director; Harold Wolpert, Managing Director; Julia C. Levy, Executive Director); Director, David Grindley; Set, Tim Shortall; Costumes, Tobin Ost; Lighting, Rick Fisher; Sound, Gregory Clarke; Dialects, Gillian Lane-Plescia; Production Stage Manager, Arthur Gaffin; Casting, Carrie Gardner; Production Management, Aurora Productions (Gene O'Donovan, W. Benjamin Heller II, Bethany Weinstein, Amy Merlino Coey, Laura Archer, Dana Hesch, Melissa Mazdra); General Manager, Rebecca Habel; Marketing/Sales Promotion, David B. Steffen; Founding Director, Gene Feist; Associate Artistic Director, Scott Ellis; Director of Artistic Development and Casting, Jim Carnahan; Finance, Susan Neiman; Education, Greg McCaslin; General Manager, Sydney Beers; Telesales, Marco Frezza; Sales Operations, Charlie Garbowski Jr.; Company Manager, Carly DiFulvio; Stage Manager, Jamie Greathouse; Assistant Director, Lori Wolter; Hair & Wigs, Ashley Ryan; Makeup, James Vincent; Associate Design: Tobin Ost (set), Daniel Walker (lighting); Assistant Design: Sean Tribble (costumes), Emma Belli, William Fricker, Jason Southgate (assistants to Mr. Shortall); Production Properties, Denise J. Grillo; U.K. Properties, Kate McDowell; Assistant to Production Properties, Constance Sherman; Production: Glenn Merwede (production carpenter), Brian Maiuri (production electrician), Andrew Forste (running properties), Dann Wojnar (sound operator), Susan J. Fallon (wardrobe supervisor), Manuela Laporte (hair & wig supervisor), Brittany Jones-Pugh, Kat Martin (dressers), Lauren Gallitelli (day wardrobe), Shelley Miles (production assistant); Advertising, SpotCo; Press, Boneau/Bryan-Brown, Adrian Bryan-Brown, Matt Polk, Jessica Johnson, Amy Kass

CAST John **Tate Ellington;** Philip **Matthew Broderick;** Donald **Steven Weber;** Celia **Anna Madeley;** Braham **Jonathan Cake;** Araminta **Jennifer Mudge;** Elizabeth **Samantha Soule**

UNDERSTUDIES Janie Brookshire (Celia, Elizabeth, Araminta), Matthieu Cornillon (John, Braham), Quentin Maré (Don, Philip)

SETTING The rooms of an English university professor in October 1970. Revival of a play presented in two acts. Originally presented on Broadway at the Barrymore Theatre March 11–May 15, 1971 (see *Theatre World* Vol. 27, page 39). The Donmar Warehouse (Michael Grandage, Artistic Director; James Bierman, Executive Producer) produced a production of the show in 2005, directed by Mr. Grindley, and featuring Ms. Madeley.

SYNOPSIS Written as a response to Moliére's classic play *The Misanthrope*, Christopher Hampton's biting bourgeois comedy *The Philanthropist* examines the empty, insular lives of university intellectuals. At the center of the story is Philip, a professor who seems almost absurdly removed from the political turmoil surrounding him, including the assassination of the Prime Minister and his cabinet.

Desire Under the Elms

St. James Theatre; First Preview: April 14, 2009 Opening Night: April 27, 2009; Closed May 24, 2009; 16 previews, 32 performances

Written by Eugene O'Neill; Presented by The Goodman Theatre (Chicago); Produced by Jeffrey Richards, Jerry Frankel, Steve Traxler, Bat-Berry Productions, Ronald Frankel, Norton Herrick, Judith Resnick, Daryl Roth, The Weinstein Company, Scott M. Delman/Alan D. Marks, Mort Swinsky/Michael Fuchs/Cindy & Jay Gutterman, Mark Johannes & Amy Danis/Jack Thomas, Morris Berchard/ Eric Falkenstein, Jujamcyn Theatres (Rocco Landesman, President; Paul Libin, Producing Director; Jack Viertel, Creative Director; Jordan Roth, Vice President), in association with Terri & Timothy Childs, Jam Theatricals, and Jamie deRoy; Director, Robert Falls; Set, Walt Spangler; Costumes, Ana Kuzmanic; Lighting, Michael Philippi; Original Music and Sound, Richard Woodbury; Production Stage Manager, Robert Bennett; Wigs, Charles G. LaPointe; Casting, Telsey + Company; Technical Supervisor, Larry Morley; Company Manager, Jolie Gabler; Associate Producer, Broadway Across America; General Manager, Richards/ Climan Inc. (David R. Richards & Tamar Haimes); Fight Director, Rick Sordelet; Dialect Coach, Patricia Fletcher; Stage Manager, Lois Griffing; Associate General Manager, John Gendron; General Management Assistant, Cesar Hawas; Fight Captain, Christian Conn; Assistant Design: Ann Bartek, Jisun Kim (set), Paul Hackenmueller (lighting), Amelia Dombrowski (costumes), Erich Bechtel, Nathaniel Hare (sound); Production: Todd Frank (production carpenter), Dan Coey (production electrician), Joanna Lynne Staub (production sound), Eric Castaldo (production props), Ron Martin (lighting programmer), Rob Bevenger (wardrobe supervisor), Justen Brosnan (hair supervisor), Kathleen Gallagher, David Marquez (dressers), Hagen Linss (hair assistant); Production Assistants, Conwell Worthington III, Kristen Parks; Associate to Mr. Richards, Jeremy Scott Blaustein; Assistant to Mr. Richards, Christopher Taggart; Assistant to Mr. Traxler, Brandi Preston; Advertising, SpotCo; Press, Jeffrey Richards Associates, Irene Gandy, Alana Karpoff, Elon Rutberg, Shane Marshall Brown, Diana Rissetto

Carla Gugino and Pablo Schreiber

Carla Gugino (photos by Liz Lauren)

Boris McGiver

CAST Eben Cabot **Pablo Schreiber;** Simeon Cabot **Daniel Stewart Sherman;** Peter Cabot **Boris McGiver;** Ephraim Cabot **Brian Dennehy;** Abbie Putnam **Carla Gugino**

UNDERSTUDIES Christian Conn (Eben), John Henry Cox (Ephraim), Kelly Hutchinson (Abbie), Michael Laurence (Simeon, Peter)

SETTING The Cabot farmhouse. New England. 1850. Revival of the play presented without intermission. This production was presented at the Goodman Theatre (Robert Falls, Artistic Director) January 17–March 1, 2009. Originally presented in New York at the Greenwich Village Theatre (transferring to the Earl Carroll Theatre, George M. Cohan's Theatre, and Daly's 63rd Street Theatre) playing November 11, 1924–October 17, 1925. The ANTA Playhouse revived the show January 16–February 23, 1952 (see *Theatre World* Vol. 8, page 83).

SYNOPSIS Master American playwright Eugene O'Neill conceived *Desire Under the Elms* as he slept one night, imbuing it with the emotional pitch of a fever dream. Ephraim Cabot returns to his remote New England farmhouse with his third wife—the alluring, headstrong young Abbie—launching his three grown sons into a bitter fight for their inheritance. When Ephraim's youngest son sets his sights on Abbie, the resulting tempest brings tragic consequences. Director Robert Falls streamlined the play to 100 minutes, cutting ten characters out of the play, to focus on the turbulent family drama at the core.

Rosie Benton and
David Hyde Pierce
(photos by Joan Marcus)

Accent on Youth

Samuel J. Friedman Theatre; First Preview: April 7, 2009 Opening Night: April 29, 2009; 24 previews, 39 performances as of May 31, 2009

Written by Samson Raphaelson; Produced by Manhattan Theatre Club (Lynne Meadow, Artistic Director; Barry Grove, Executive Producer) by special arrangement with Daryl Roth, Ostar Productions, Rebecca Gold/Debbie Bisno; Director, Daniel Sullivan; Set, John Lee Beatty; Costumes, Jane Greenwood; Lighting, Brian MacDevitt; Original Music & Sound, Obadiah Eaves; Hair & Wigs, Tom Watson; Production Stage Manager, Roy Harris; General Manager, Florie Seery; Associate Artistic Director, Mandy Greenfield; Director of Artistic Development, Jerry Patch; Marketing, Debra Waxman-Pilla; Production Manager, Kurt Gardner; Director of Casting, Nancy Piccione; Development, Jill Turner Lloyd; Artistic Consultant, Daniel Sullivan; Artistic Administration/Assistant to Artistic Director, Amy Gilkes Loe; Musical Development, Clifford Lee Johnson III; Finance, Jeffrey Bledsoe; Associate General Manager, Lindsey Brooks Sag; Subscriber Services, Robert Allenberg; Telesales, George Tetlow; Education, David Shookhoff; Associate Production Manager, Philip Naudé; Prop Supervisor, Scott Laule; Costume Supervisor, Erin Hennessy Dean; Company Manager, Seth Shepsle; Stage Manager, Denise Yaney; Assistant Director, Rachel Slaven; Makeup, Angelina Avellone; Mr. Pierce's Hair, Paul Huntley; Fight Director, Thomas Schall; Associate Design: Yoshinori Tanokura (set), Jennifer Moeller (costumes), Peter Hoerburger (lighting), Brandon Wolcott (sound); Assistant Design: Anya Klepicov (costumes), Grant Wilcoxen (assistant to Mr. MacDevitt); Production: Vaughn G. Preston (automation operator), Chris Wiggins (head carpenter), Timothy Walters (head propertyman), Marc Polimeni (moving light programmer), Louis Shapiro (sound engineer), Jeff Dodson (master electrician), Angela Simpson (wardrobe supervisor), Natasha Steinhagen (hair/makeup supervisor), Virginia Neininger (dresser), E'bess Greer (production assistant); Theatre Manager, Russ Ramsey; Box Office Treasurer, David Dillon; Advertising, SpotCo; Press, Boneau/Bryan-Brown, Aaron Meier, Christine Olver, Matt Ross

CAST Miss Darling **Lisa Banes;** Genevieve Lang **Rosie Benton;** Butch **Curt Bouril;** Dickie Reynolds **David Furr;** Linda Brown **Mary Catherine Garrison;** Frank Galloway **Byron Jennings;** Flogdell **Charles Kimbrough;** Steven Gale **David Hyde Pierce;** Chuck **John Wernke**

UNDERSTUDIES Ross Bickell (Frank Galloway, Flogdell), Curt Bouril (Chuck), Cynthia Darlow (Miss Darling), Jack Koenig (Steven Gaye, Butch), Karen Walsh (Genevieve Lang, Linda Brown), John Wernke (Dickie Reynolds)

SETTING The New York duplex of Steven Gaye over the course of a year; early 1930s. Revival of a comedy presented in three acts with one intermission. Originally presented on Broadway at the Plymouth Theatre (now the Schoenfeld) December 25, 1934–July 1935.

SYNOPSIS Samson Raphaelson's *Accent on Youth* is a rollicking salute to love's possibilities, both on stage and off. Successful playwright Stephen Gaye is about to abandon his latest script, when his young secretary offers him new inspiration. With her as his muse, he stages the show on Broadway, only to learn, to his dismay, that the show's young leading man is being inspired by her too.

David Hyde Pierce and Charles Kimbrough

9 to 5: The Musical

Marquis Theatre; First Preview: April 7, 2009 Opening Night: April 30, 2009; 24 previews, 36 performances as of May 31, 2009

Book by Patricia Resnick, music and lyrics by Dolly Parton; based on the motion picture produced by 20th Century Fox (screenplay by Patricia Resnick, screenplay and direction by Colin Higgins); Produced by Green State Productions, Richard Levi, John McColgan/Moya Doherty/Edgar Dobie, James L. Nederlander/Terry Allen Kramer, Independent Presenters Network, Jam Theatricals, Bud Martin, Michael Watt, The Weinstein Company/Sonia Friedman/Dede Harris, Norton Herrick/Matthew C. Blank/Joan Stein, Center Theatre Group (Michael Ritchie, Artistic Director; Charles Dillingham, Managing Director), Toni Dowgiallo, GFour Productions and Robert Greenblatt; Director, Joe Mantello; Choreography, Andy Blankenbuehler; Music Direction/Vocal Arrangements, Stephen Oremus; Sets, Scott Pask; Costumes, William Ivey Long; Lighting, Jules Fisher & Kenneth Posner; Sound, John H. Shivers; Casting, Telsey + Company; Imaging, Peter Nigrini & Peggy Eisenhauer; Hair, Paul Huntley & Edward J. Wilson; Makeup, Angelina Avellone; Technical Supervision, Neil A. Mazzella; Scenic Design Associate, Edward Pierce; Production Supervisor, William Joseph Barnes; Associate Director, Dave Solomon; Associate Choreographer, Rachel Bress; General Management, Nina Lannan Associates, Maggie Brohn; Marketing, Type A Marketing, Situation Interactive; Music Coordinator, Michael Keller; Orchestrator, Bruce Coughlin; Additional Orchestrations & Incidental Music Arrangements, Stephen Oremus & Alex Lacamoire; Dance Music Arrangements, Alex Lacamoire; Additional Music Arrangements, Kevin Stites & Charles duChateau; Company Manager, Kimberly Kelley; Associate Company Manager, Adam Jackson; Pre-Production Production Stage Manager, C. Randall White; Stage Manager, Timothy R. Semon; Assistant Stage Managers, Chris Zaccardi, Kathryn L. McKee; Assistant Producer, Brian Salb; Dance Captain, Mark Myars; Assistant Dance Captain, Jennifer Balagna; Associate Technical Supervisors, Irene Wang, Frank Illo; Associate Design: Nick Francone (set), Scott Traugott (costumes), Giovanna Calabretta (wigs and hair), Philip Rosenberg (lighting), David Patridge (sound); Assistant Design: Orit Jacoby Carroll, Frank McCullough, Lauren Alvarez (set), Robert J. Martin, Brenda Abbandandolo (costumes), Aaron Spivey, Carl Faber (lighting); Automated Lighting Programmer, David Arch; Imaging Associate, C. Andrew Bauer; Imaging Assistant, Dan Scully; LED Image Wall Programmer, Laura Frank/Luminous FX LLC; Additional Character & Castle Animation, Illum Productions (Jerry Chambless, Creative Director; Joseph Merideth, Animation Director); Production: Donald J. Oberpriller (production carpenter), Eric "Speed" Smith, Chad Hershey, Mark Diaz (carpenters), Gregory Husinko (production electrician), Eric Abbot (head electrician), Derek Healy (assistant electrician/Vari-Lite tech), Dan Tramontozzi (head sound), David Patridge (sound engineer), Dan Robillard (assistant sound), Timothy M. Abel (production properties), Michael Bernstein (head properties), Ken Keneally (assistant properties), Douglas Petitjean (wardrobe supervisor), Deirdre LaBarre (assistant wardrobe supervisor), Edward J. Wilson (hair supervisor), Steven Kirkham (assistant hair supervisor), Laura Beattie, Tracey Diebold, Adam Giradet, Kay Gowenlock, Timothy Greer, Barry Hoff, Maggie Horkey, Samantha Lawrence, John Rinaldi, Tree Sarvay, Kelly Smith, Ron Tagert (dressers), Charlene Belmond, Therese Ducey (hairdressers); Rehearsal Musicians, Jodie Moore, Sean McDaniel; Keyboard Programming, Randy Cohen; Music Copying, Emily Grishman Music Preparation, Katherine Edmonds; Music Assistant, Colleen Darnell; Production Assistants, Christopher Paul, Raynelle Wright, Stuart Shefter, McKenzie Murphy; Advertising, SpotCo; Press, Barlow · Hartman, Michael Hartman, John Barlow, Wayne Wolfe, Melissa Bixler; Cast recording: Dolly Records

CAST Violet Newstead **Allison Janney;** Doralee Rhodes **Megan Hilty;** Dwayne **Charlie Pollock;** Judy Bernly **Stephanie J. Block;** Roz Keith **Kathy Fitzgerald;** Kathy **Ann Harada;** Anita **Maia Nkenge Wilson;** Daphne **Tory Ross;** Franklin Hart Jr. **Marc Kudisch;** Missy **Lisa Howard;** Maria **Iona Alfonso;** Joe **Andy Karl;** Margaret **Karen Murphy;** Josh **Van Hughes;** Dick **Dan Cooney;** Bob Enright **Jeremy Davis;** Tinsworthy **Michael X. Martin;**

Ensemble **Ioana Alfonso, Timothy George Anderson, Justin Bohon, Paul Castree, Dan Cooney, Jeremy Davis, Autumn Guzzardi, Ann Harada, Neil Haskell, Lisa Howard, Van Hughes, Michael X. Martin, Michael Mindlin, Karen Murphy, Jessica Lea Patty, Charlie Pollock, Tory Ross, Wayne Schroder, Maia Nkenge Wilson, Brandi Wooten;** Swings **Jennifer Balagna, Mark Myars, Justin Patterson**

UNDERSTUDIES Ann Harada (Violet, Roz), Lisa Howard (Violet), Gaelen Gilliland (Judy, Doralee, Margaret, Missy), Jessica Lea Patty (Judy, Maria), Tory Ross (Judy, Roz, Kathy, Margaret), Autumn Guzzardi (Doralee), Michael X. Martin (Hart), Wayne Schroder (Hart, Dick, Tinsworthy), Karen Murphy (Roz), Paul Castree (Joe), Justin Patterson (Joe, Dwayne), Justin Bohon (Dwayne, Josh), Jeremy Davis (Dick), Michael Mindlin (Josh), Maia Nkenge Wilson (Kathy), Jennifer Balagna (Maria), Brandi Wooten (Missy), Dan Cooney (Tinsworthy)

ORCHESTRA Stephen Oremus (Conductor/keyboard 1); Matt Gallagher (Associate Conductor/keyboard 2); Jodie Moore (Assistant Conductor/keyboard 3); Michael Aarons, Jake Ezra Schwartz (guitars); John Putnam (guitars/pedal steel); Dave Phillips (bass); Dean McDaniel (drums); Dave Mancuso (percussion); Vincent Della Rocca, Aaron Heick, Dave Riekenberg (reeds); Bob Millikan, Brian Pareschi (trumpets); Keith O'Quinn, Jennifer Wharton (trombones); Suzy Perelmen, Chris Cardona, Amy Ralske (violins)

MUSICAL NUMBERS 9 to 5, Around Here, Here for You, I Just Might, Backwoods Barbie, The Dance of Death, Cowgirl's Revenge, Potion Notion, Joy to the Girls, Heart to Hart, Shine Like the Sun, Entr'acte, One of the Boys, 5 to 9, Always a Woman, Change It, Let Love Grow, Get Out and Stay Out, Finale: 9 to 5

2008–2009 AWARDS Drama Desk Award: Outstanding Actress in a Musical (Allison Janney)

SETTING Time: 1979. Place: In and around the offices of Consolidated. New York premiere of a new musical presented in two acts. World premiere at the Center Theatre Group's Ahmanson Theatre September 9–October 19, 2008 (see Regional Theatre listings in this volume).

SYNOPSIS When pushed to their boiling point by their boss, Franklin Hart Jr., Violet Newstead (the super-efficient office manager), Judy Bernly (a frazzled divorcee), Doralee Rhodes (the sexy executive secretary) turn the tables on him. The trio hatches a plan to get even with the sexist, egotistical, lying, hypocritical bigot, and that plan quickly spins wildly and hilariously out of control. Parton's original score includes more than 15 new songs as well as the Grammy Award winning, Academy Award nominated, and #1 Billboard title song from the 1980 motion picture upon which the musical is based.

Megan Hilty, Allison Janney and Stephanie J. Block

Marc Kudisch and Kathy Fitzgerald

Stephanie J. Block, Megan Hilty and Allison Janney

Stephanie J. Block and Marc Kudisch

The Company

Marc Kudisch and Megan Hilty

Allison Janney
(photos by Joan Marcus)

Nathan Lane, John Goodman and Bill Irwin

Nathan Lane and Bill Irwin (photos by Joan Marcus)

Waiting for Godot

Studio 54; First Preview: April 10, 2009 Opening Night: April 30, 2009; 32 previews, 36 performances as of May 31, 2009

Written by Samuel Beckett; Produced by the Roundabout Theatre Company (Todd Haimes, Artistic Director; Harold Wolpert, Managing Director; Julia C. Levy, Executive Director) by special arrangement with Elizabeth McCann; Director, Anthony Page; Sets, Santo Loquasto; Costumes, Jane Greenwood; Lighting, Peter Kaczorowski; Sound, Dan Moses Schreier; Hair & Wigs, Tom Watson; Fight Director, Thomas Schall; Production Stage Manager, Peter Hanson; Casting, Jim Carnahan, Kate Boka; Technical Supervisor, Steve Beers; Executive Producer/General Manager, Sydney Beers; Marketing/Sales Promotion, David B. Steffen; Founding Director, Gene Feist; Associate Artistic Director, Scott Ellis; Director of Artistic Development & Casting, Jim Carnahan; Education, Greg McCaslin; Finance, Susan Neiman; Telesales, Marco Frezza; Sales Operations, Charlie Garbowski Jr.; Company Manager, Denise Cooper; Stage Manager, Jon Krause; Assistant Director; Wes Grantom; Makeup, Angelina Avellone; Associate Design: Jenny Sawyers (set), MaryAnn D. Smith (costumes), David Bullard (sound); Assistant Design/Design Assistants: Anya Klepikov (Ms. Greenwood), Keri Thibodeau (lighting); Production: Dan Hoffman (production carpenter), Josh Weitzman (production electrician), John Wooding (assistant production electrician), Kathy Fabian (production properties), Carrie Mossman (assistant production properties), Lawrence Jennino (house properties), Dan Schultheis (Local One apprentice), David Gotwald (production sound engineer), Nadine Hettel (wardrobe supervisor), Joe Hickey (dresser), Elisa Acevedo (hair & wig supervisor), Rachel Bauder (production assistant), Jill Valentine (child wrangler), Chris Minnick (company manager intern); Advertising, SpotCo; Press, Boneau/Bryan-Brown, Adrian Bryan-Brown, Matt Polk, Jessica Johnson, Amy Kass

CAST Estragon **Nathan Lane;** Vladimir **Bill Irwin;** Pozzo **John Goodman;** Lucky **John Glover;** A Boy **Cameron Clifford** or **Matthew Schechter**

UNDERSTUDIES John Ahlin (Estragon, Pozzo), Anthony Newfield (Vladimir, Lucky)

SETTING Place: A country road. A tree. Time: Act I – Evening; Act II – Next day, same time. Revival of a play presented in two acts. Originally produced on Broadway at the John Golden Theatre April 19–June 9, 1956 (see *Theatre World* Vol. 12, page 107). The show had a brief revival at the Ethel Barrymore Theatre January 21-26, 1957.

SYNOPSIS *Waiting for Godot* remains Samuel Beckett's most magical and beautiful allegory. The story revolves around two seemingly homeless men waiting for someone – or something – named Godot. Vladimir and Estragon wait near a tree on a barren stretch of road, inhabiting a drama spun from their own consciousness. The result is a comical wordplay of poetry, dreamscapes and nonsense, which has been interpreted as a somber summation of mankind's inexhaustible search for meaning.

John Glover, Bill Irwin, Nathan Lane and John Goodman

Played Through / Closed this Season

Alfred Hitchcock's The 39 Steps

Cort Theatre+ First Previews: April 29, 2008; Opening Night: May 8, 2008; 23 previews, 515 performances as of May 31, 2009

Adapted by Patrick Barlow from the film by Alfred Hitchcock and the book by John Buchan; based on an original concept by Simon Corble and Nobby Dimon; Produced by the Roundabout Theatre Company (Todd Haimes, Artistic Director; Harold Wolpert, Managing Director; Julia C. Levy, Executive Director) in association with Bob Boyett, Harriet Newman Leve/Ron Nicynski, Stewart F. Lane/Bonnie Comley, Manocherian Golden Productions, Olympus Theatricals/Douglas Denoff, Marek J. Cantor/Pat Addiss, and the Huntington Theatre Company (Nicholas Martin, Artistic Director; Michael Maso, Managing Director), and Edward Snape for Fiery Angel Ltd.; Director, Maria Aitken; Set/Costumes, Peter McKintosh; Lighting, Kevin Adams; Sound, Mic Pool; Dialect Coach, Stephen Gabis; Original Movement, Toby Sedgewick; Additional Movement, Christopher Bays; Production Manager, Aurora Productions; Production Stage Manager, Nevin Hedley; Casting, Jay Binder, Jack Bowdan; General Manager, Rebecca Habel, Roy Gabay; Associate Producer/Roundabout General Manager, Sydney Beers; Marketing/Sales Promotion, David B. Steffen; Development, Jeffory Lawson; Founding Director, Gene Feist; Associate Artistic Director, Scott Ellis; Artistic Development/Casting, Jim Carnahan; Education, David A. Miller; Telesales, Daniel Weiss; Finance, Susan Neiman; Sales Operations, Charlie Garbowski Jr.; Executive Producer, 101 Productions Ltd.; Associate Producer, Marek J. Cantor; Company Manager, Daniel Kuney; ACM, Carly DiFulvio; Stage Manager, Janet Takami; Wigs, Jason Allen; Assistant Director, Kevin Bigger; Assistant Design: Josh Zangen (set), Aaron Sporer (lighting), Drew Levy (sound); Marketing, HHC Marketing; Advertising, Eliran Murphy Group; Press, Boneau/Bryan-Brown (Adrian Bryan-Brown, Jim Byk, Matt Polk, Jessica Johnson, Amy Kass)

Cliff Saunders and Sam Robards

Sam Robards, Arnie Burton, Cliff Saunders and Jennifer Ferrin (photos by Joan Marcus)

CAST Man #1 **Cliff Saunders**[*1]; Man #2 **Arnie Burton;** Richard Hannay **Charles Edwards**[*2]; Annabella Schmidt/Pamela/Margaret **Jennifer Ferrin**[*3]

UNDERSTUDIES Claire Brownell (Annabella Schmidt/Pamela/Margaret), Cameron Folmar (Man #1/Man #2), Mark Shanahan[*4] (Richard Hannay)

*Succeeded by: 1. Jeffrey Kuhn (10/28/08) 2. Sam Robards (7/8/08), Sean Mahon (1/21/09) 3. Francesca Faridany (10/28/08) 4. Rob Breckenridge

SETTING Scotland and London. New York premiere of a new comedy/thriller presented in two acts. Previously presented at the Tricycle Theatre in London in 2006, and at Boston's Huntington Theatre Company, September 14, 2007, prior to this engagement. The Broadway production originally played the American Airlines Theatre January 4–March 29, 2008 (12 previews and 87 performances which are included in the performance count above) before transferring to the Cort Theatre for a commercial run.

SYNOPSIS Four cast members play over 150 roles in this hilarious whodunit, part espionage thriller and part slapstick comedy. The story revolves around an innocent man who learns too much about a dangerous spy ring and is then pursued across Scotland and to London. *The 39 Steps* contains every legendary scene from the award-winning movie—the chase on the Flying Scotsman, the escape on the Forth Bridge, the first theatrical bi-plane crash ever staged, and the sensational death-defying finale in the London Palladium.

+ Closed January 5-20 to transfer to the Helen Hayes Theatre, resumed performances on January 21, 2009

Francesca Faridany and Sean Mahon

August: Osage County

Music Box Theatre+; First Preview: October 30, 2007; Opening Night: December 4, 2007; 18 previews, 616 performances as of May 31, 2009

Written by Tracy Letts; Originally produced by the Steppenwolf Theatre Company (Martha Lavey, Artistic Director; David Hawkanson, Executive Director); Produced by Jeffrey Richards, Jean Doumanian, Steve Traxler, Jerry Frankel, Ostar Productions, Jennifer Manocherian, The Weinstein Company, Debra Black/Daryl Roth, Ronald & Marc Frankel/Barbara Freitag, Rick Steiner/Staton Bell Group; Director, Anna D. Shapiro; Sets, Todd Rosenthal; Costumes, Ana Kuzmanic; Lighting, Ann G. Wrightson; Sound, Richard Woodbury; Original Music, David Singe; Dramaturg, Edward Sobel; Original Casting, Erica Daniels; New York Casting, Stuart Howard, Amy Schecter, Paul Hardt; Fight Choreography, Chuck Coyl; Dialect Coach, Cecilie O'Reilly; Production Stage Manager, Deb Styer; Production Supervisor, Jane Grey; Technical Supervisor, Theatersmith Inc./Smitty (Christopher C. Smith); Marketing Services, TMG–The Marketing Group; General Management, Richards/Climan Inc.; Assistant Producers, Mark Barber, Patrick Daly, Ben West; Company Manager, Mary Miller; Assistant Director, Henry Wishcamper; Design Assistants: Kevin Depinet, Matthew D. Jordan, Martin Andrew Orlowicz, Stephen T. Sorenson (sets), Amelia Dombrowski (costumes), Kathleen Dobbins, Kristina Kloss (lighting), Joanna Lynne Staub (sound), Management Associate, Jeromy Smith; Advertising, SpotCo; Press, Jeffrey Richards Associates, Irene Gandy, Judith Hansen, Diane, Elon Rutberg

CAST Beverly Weston **Michael McGuire**[*1]; Violet Weston **Deanna Dunagan**[*2]; Barbara Fordham **Amy Morton**[*3]; Bill Fordham **Jeff Perry**[*4]; Jean Fordham **Madeleine Martin**[*5]; Ivy Weston **Sally Murphy**[*6]; Karen Weston **Mariann Mayberry**[*7]; Mattie Fae Aiken **Rondi Reed**[*8]; Charlie Aiken **Francis Guinan**[*9]; Little Charles **Ian Barford**[*10]; Johnna Monevata **Kimberly Guerrero**[*11]; Steve Heidebrecht **Brian Kerwin**; Sheriff Deon Gilbeau **Troy West**[*12]

UNDERSTUDIES/STANDBYS Munson Hicks[*13] (Beverly Weston, Charlie Aiken), Susanne Marley (Mattie Fae Aiken, Violet Weston), Jay Patterson[*14] (Charlie Aiken, Bill Fordham, Sheriff Deon Gilbeau, Steve Heidebrecht), Dee Pelletier[*15] (Barbara Fordham, Ivy Weston, Karen Weston), Kristina Valada-Viars (Johnna Monevata, Ivy Weston, Karen Weston), Anne Berkowitz[*16] (Jean Fordham), Aaron Serotsky (Bill Fordham, Little Charles, Sheriff Deon Gilbeau, Steve Heidebrecht); Temporary: Jeff Still (Bill Fordham, Steve Heidebrecht, Sheriff Deon Gilbeau, Charles Aiken, Beverly Weston)

*Succeeded by: 1. John Cullum (9/16/08), Michael McGuire (9/23/08), John Cullum (11/11/09) 2. Estelle Parsons (6/17/08), Phylicia Rashad (5/26/09) 3. Johanna Day (10/14/08), Amy Morton (5/26/09) 4. Frank Wood (6/17/08) 5. Molly Ranson, Madeline Martin, Anne Berkowitz 6. Dee Pelletier (10/14/08), Sally Murphy (2/3/09) 7. Amy Warren (11/11/08), Mariann Mayberry (2/3/09) 8. Molly Regan (6/17/08), Elizabeth Ashley (2/3/09) 9. Robert Foxworth (6/17/08), Guy Boyd (12/16/08) 10. Jim True-Frost (6/17/08), Michael Milligan (10/14/08) 11. Samantha Ross (11/11/08), Kimberly Guerrero (2/3/09) 12. Scott Jaeck (10/14/08), Troy West (2/3/09) 13. Stephen Payne 14. Frank Deal 15. Drew Richardson, Dee Pelletier 16. Emily Watson

SETTING A large country home outside Pawhuska, Oklahoma, 60 miles northwest of Tulsa. New York premiere of a new play presented in three acts with two intermissions. World Premiere presented at the Steppenwolf Theatre Company June 28–August 26, 2007 with most of this cast. (see *Theatre World* Vol. 63, page 355).

SYNOPSIS When their patriarch vanishes, the Weston clan must return to their three-story home in rural Oklahoma to get to the heart of the matter. With rich insight and brilliant humor, Letts paints a vivid portrait of a Midwestern family at a turning point.

+ The show originally opened at the Imperial Theatre, temporarily closed April 20, 2008 and transferred to the Music Box Theatre April 29, 2008

Estelle Parsons (photo by Joan Marcus)

The original Company (photos by Joan Marcus)

Phylicia Rashad and Amy Morton (photo by Robert J. Saferstein)

Jennifer Barnhart, Trekkie Monster and Christian Anderson

Avenue Q

Golden Theatre; First Preview: July 10, 2003; Opening Night: July 31, 2003; 22 previews, 2,414 performances as of May 31, 2009

Music and lyrics by Robert Lopez and Jeff Marx, book by Jeff Whitty; Produced by Kevin McCollum, Robyn Goodman, Jeffrey Seller, Vineyard Theatre & The New Group; Director, Jason Moore; Choreography, Ken Roberson; Music Supervision/Orchestrations/Arrangements, Stephen Oremus; Puppets Conception/Design, Rick Lyon; Set, Anna Louizos; Costumes, Mirena Rada; Lighting, Howell Binkley; Sound, Acme Sound Partners; Animation, Robert Lopez; Music Director/Incidental Music, Gary Adler; Music Coordinator, Michael Keller; General Manager, John Corker; Technical Supervisor, Brian Lynch; Production Stage Manager, Beverly Jenkins; Casting, Cindy Tolan; Marketing, TMG–The Marketing Group; Associate Producers, Sonny Everett, Walter Grossman, Mort Swinsky; Stage Manager, Christine M. Daly; Company Manager, Nick Lugo; Resident Director, Evan Ensign; Associate Conductor, Mark Hartman; Assistant Director, Jen Bender; Assistant Stage Manager/Dance Captain, Sharon Wheatley; Associate Design: Todd Potter (set), Timothy F. Rogers (lighting); Music Copying, Emily Grishman and Alex Lacamoire; Animation and Video Production, Noodle Soup Production, Jeremy Rosenberg; Sound and Video Design Effects, Brett Jarvis; Advertising, SpotCo; Press, Sam Rudy Media Relations; Cast recording: RCA 82876-55923-2

CAST Princeton/Rod **Howie Michael Smith;** Brian **Nicholas Kohn;** Kate Monster/Lucy the Slut & others **Sarah Stiles**[*1]; Nicky/Trekkie Monster/Bad Idea Bear & others **Christian Anderson;** Christmas Eve **Ann Sanders;** Gary Coleman **Rashidra Scott**[*2]; Mrs. T./Bad Idea Bear & others **Jennifer Barnhart;** Ensemble **Sala Iwamatsu**[*3], **Jonathan Root;** Swings **Leo Daignault, Carmen Ruby Floyd, Matt Schreiber, Sharon Wheatley**

UNDERSTUDIES Jennifer Barnhart (Kate Monster/Lucy), Steven Booth (Ensemble, Princeton/Rod, Nicky/Trekkie/Bear), Minglie Chen (Christmas Eve, Kate Monster/Lucy, Mrs. T/Bear), Leo Daignault (Brian, Nicky/Trekkie/Bear), Carmen Ruby Floyd (Gary Coleman, Mrs. T./Bear), Sala Iwamatsu [3] (Christmas Eve, Mrs. T/Bear), Jonathan Root (Princeton/Rod, Brian, Nicky/Trekkie/Bear), Matt Schreiber (Brian, Nicky/Trekkie/Bear, Princeton/Rod), Sharon Wheatley (Kate Monster/Lucy, Mrs. T./Bear, Christmas Eve)

*Succeeded by: 1. Carey Anderson (7/8/08), Christy Carlson Romano (11/29/08), Carey Anderson (11/24/08) 2. Carla Renata (6/16/08), Tonya Dixon (1/15/09), Carla Renata (1/22/09) 3. Angela Ai

ORCHESTRA Gary Adler (Conductor/keyboard); Mark Hartman (Associate Conductor/keyboard); Maryann McSweeney (bass); Brian Koonin (guitar); Patience Higgins (reeds); Michael Croiter (drums)

MUSICAL NUMBERS Avenue Q Theme, What Do You Do With a BA in English?/It Sucks to be Me, If You Were Gay, Purpose, Everyone's a Little Bit Racist, The Internet Is for Porn, Mix Tape, I'm Not Wearing Underwear Today, Special, You Can Be as Loud as the Hell You Want (When You're Making Love), Fantasies Come True, My Girlfriend, Who Lives in Canada, There's a Fine, Fine Line, There Is Life Outside Your Apartment, The More You Ruv Someone, Schadenfreude, I Wish I Could Go Back to College, The Money Song, For Now

SETTING The present, an outer borough of New York City. A musical presented in two acts. For original production credits see *Theatre World* Vol. 60, page 25.

SYNOPSIS *Avenue Q* is about real life: finding a job, losing a job, learning about racism, getting an apartment, getting kicked out of your apartment, being different, falling in love, promiscuity, avoiding commitment, and internet porn. Twenty and thirty-something puppets and humans survive life in the big city and search for their purpose in this naughty but timely musical that features "full puppet nudity!"

(clockwise from left) *Princeton, Howie Michael Smith, Kate Monster and Carey Anderson (photos by Carol Rosegg)*

Paige Davis and Greg Germann

Missi Pyle and Mark Rylance
(photos by Joan Marcus)

Rebecca Gayheart and Greg Germann

Boeing-Boeing

Longacre Theatre; First Preview: April 19, 2008; Opening Night: May 4, 2008; Closed January 4, 2009; 17 previews, 280 performances

Written by Marc Camoletti, translated by Beverley Cross & Francis Evans; Produced by Sonia Friedman Productions, Bob Boyett, ACT Productions, Matthew Byam Shaw, Robert G. Bartner, The Weinstein Company, Susan Gallin/Mary Lu Roffe, Broadway Across American, Tulchin/Jenkins/DSM, and The Araca Group; Director, Matthew Warchus; Set and Costumes, Rob Howell; Lighting, Hugh Vanstone; Original Music, Claire Van Kampen; Sound, Simon Baker; Production Stage Manager, William Joseph Barnes; Curtain Call Choreography, Kathleen Marshall; U.S. Casting, Jim Carnahan; Dialect Coach, Deborah Hecht; Sales and Marketing, On the Rialto; Production Management, Aurora Productions (Gene O'Donovan, W. Benjamin Heller II, Bethany Weinstein, Melissa Mazdra, John Horsman, Asia Evans); Associate Producer for Boyett Theatricals, Tim Levy; U.K. General Management for Sonia Friedman, Diane Benjamin, Matthew Gordon; General Management, Stuart Thompson Productions (Caroline Prugh, James Triner, David Turner); Associate Producers, Jill Lenhart, Douglas G. Smith; Stage Manager, Robert Witherow; Associate Director, Mark Schneider; Hair, Larry R. Boyette; Company Manager, Cassidy J. Briggs; Literal Translation, Chris Campbell; Associate Design: Ted LeFevre (set), Brian Russman (costumes), Anthony Pearson (lighting), Christopher Cronin (sound); Production: Dan Coey (electrician), Wayne Smith (sound operator), Peter Sarafin (production props), Alan C. Edwards (props assistant), Kay Grunder (wardrobe supervisor), Elisa Acevedo (hair supervisor), Barry Doss, Kim Prentice (dressers), Caroline Anderson (production assistant); Casting Associate, Kate Schwabe; U.K. Costume Supervisor, Irene Bohan; Advertising, SpotCo; Press, Barlow · Hartman, Dennis Crowley, Michelle Bergmann

CAST Gloria **Kathryn Hahn**[*1]; Bernard **Bradley Whitford**[*2]; Berthe **Christine Baranski**; Robert **Mark Rylance**; Gabriella **Gina Gershon**[*3]; Gretchen **Mary McCormack**[*4]

*Succeeded by: 1. Paige Davis (10/7/08) 2. Greg Germann (9/9/08) 3. Rebecca Gayheart (10/7/08) 4. Missi Pyle (9/9/08)

UNDERSTUDIES Ray Virta (Bernard), Pippa Pearthree (Berthe), Roxanna Hope (Gabriella, Gretchen, Gloria)

SETTING Bernard's apartment in Paris, one Saturday in April; early 1960's. Revival of a play presented in two acts. Originally produced in London in 1962 (playing over 2,000 performances), the show premiered on Broadway at the Cort Theatre February 1-20, 1965, playing only 23 performances (see *Theatre World* Vol. 21, page 71). Matthew Warchus directed an Olivier nominated West End revival, featuring Mr. Rylance, which ran February 15, 2007–January 5, 2008.

SYNOPSIS Bernard is an English playboy in Paris with three girlfriends, who are all flight attendants. With the help of his housekeeper, Berthe, Bernard has organized a schedule to allow his three loves to each spend a night at his apartment whenever they are in Paris. This all works perfectly until the new double-speed Super Boeing arrives and changes the flight schedules.

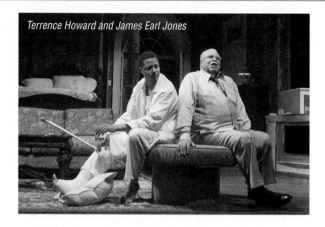
Terrence Howard and James Earl Jones

Cat on a Hot Tin Roof

Broadhurst Theatre; First Preview: February 12, 2008; Opening Night: March 6, 2008; Closed June 22, 2008; 25 previews, 124 performances

Written by Tennessee Williams; Produced by Front Row Productions and Stephen C. Byrd, in association with Alia M. Jones; Director, Debbie Allen; Set, Ray Klausen; Costumes, Jane Greenwood: Lighting, William H. Grant III; Sound, John Shivers; Hair, Charles LaPointe; Casting, Peter Wise & Associates; Production Supervisor, Theatresmith Inc.; Production Stage Manager, Gwendolyn M Gilliam; General Management, Nina Lannan Associates/Devin Keudell; Original Music, Andrew "Tex" Allen; Group Sales/Marketing, Marcia Pendelton/WTGP; Associate Producers, Clarence J. Chandran, Anthony Lacavera, Norm Nixon, Sheanna Pang, Beatrice L. Rangel, Jovan Vitagliano, Terrie Williams, Al Wilson; Assistant Stage Manager, Charles Underhill; Associate Design: Randall Parsons (set), MaryAnn D. Smith (costumes), Temishia Johnson (lighting), David Partridge (sound/sound mixer); Assistant to Ms. Greenwood, Christina Bullard; Dramaturg, Shauneille Perry; Dialects, Barbara Montgomery; Production: Gerry Griffin (carpenter), Jimmy Fedigan (electrician), Peter Donovan (head electrician), Philo Lojo (sound), Emiliano Pares, Laura MacGaritty (props), Kathy Guida (wardrobe supervisor), Michele Rutter (hair/makeup supervisor); Advertising, SpotCo; Marketing, Walk Tall Girl Productions/Marcia Pendelton; General Management Associate, Carol M. Oune; Saxophone Player, Gerald Hayes; Press, Springer Associates, Gary Springer, Joe Trentacosta, Shane Marshall Brown, D'Arcy Drollinger, Jennifer Blum, Ethnee Lea

CAST Maggie **Anika Noni Rose;** Brick **Terrence Howard;** Reverend Tooker **Lou Myers;** Doctor Baugh **Count Stovall;** Mae **Lisa Arrindell Anderson;** Sonny **Skye Jasmine Allen-McBean;** Big Mama **Phylicia Rashad;** Gooper **Giancarlo Esposito;** Sookey **Marja Harmon;** Dixie **Heaven Howard;** Trixie **Marissa Chisolm;** Lacey **Clark Jackson;** Big Daddy **James Earl Jones;** Servants **Bethany Butler, Robert Christopher Riley**

UNDERSTUDIES Count Stovall (Big Daddy), Robert Christopher Riley (Brick, Rev. Tooker, Lacey), Marja Harmon (Maggie, Mae), Bethany Butler (Maggie, Mae), Jane White (Big Mama), Clark Jackson (Gooper, Dr. Baugh, Rev. Tooker)

SETTING A summer evening gathering at the Pollitt family estate in Mississippi. Revival of the drama presented in three acts with two intermissions.

SYNOPSIS Winner of the 1955 Pulitzer Prize for Drama, the classic is revived with an Afro-American cast.

Will manipulative patriarch Big Daddy leave his plantation to his weasly son Gooper or his handsome alcoholic son Brick? And why doesn't Brick have a son of his own? Hot-blooded wife Maggie does her best to tempt Brick from his brooding and back into her bed.

Anika Noni Rose (photos by Joan Marcus)

Phylicia Rashad and Giancarlo Esposito

A Catered Affair

Tom Wopat, Faith Prince and Harvey Fierstein

Walter Kerr Theatre; First Preview: March 25, 2008; Opening Night: April 17, 2008; Closed July 27, 2008; 27 previews, 116 performances

Book by Harvey Fierstein, music and lyrics by John Bucchino; based on the Turner Entertainment motion picture distributed by Warner Brothers and written by Gore Vidal, and the original teleplay by Paddy Chayefsky; Produced by Jujamcyn Theatres, Jordan Roth, Harvey Entertainment/Ron Fierstein, Richie Jackson, Daryl Roth; John O'Boyle/Ricky Stevens/Davis-Tolentino, Barbara Russell/Ron Sharpe, in association with Frankel · Baruch · Viertel · Routh Group, Broadway Across America, True Love Productions, Rick Steiner/Mayerson-Bell-Stanton-Osher Group, and Jan Kallish; Director, John Doyle; Sets, David Gallo; Costumes, Ann Hould-Ward; Lighting, Brian MacDevitt; Sound, Dan Moses Schreier; Projections, Zachary Borovay; Hair, David Lawrence; Casting, Telsey + Company; Associate Director, Adam John Hunter; Music Director/Arrangements, Constantine Kitsopoulos; Orchestrations, Jonathan Tunick; Music Coordinator, John Miller; Associate Producers, Stacey Mindinch, Rhoda Mayerson; Marketing, Type A Marketing; Production Management, Juniper Street Productions; General Management, Alan Wasser, Allen Williams; Makeup, Angelina Avallone; Dialects/Vocal Coach, Deborah Hecht; Production Stage Manager, Adam John Hunter; Company Manager, Penelope Daulton; Stage Manager, Claudia Lynch; Assistant Stage Manager, Heather J. Weiss; Associate General Manager, Aaron Lustbader; Assistant General Manager, Jake Hirzel; ACM, Ashley Berman; Associate Design: Josh Zangen (sets), Sidney Shannon (costumes), Jennifer Schriever (lighting); David Bullard (sound), Austin Switser (projections); Assistant Design: Peter Hoerburger (lighting), Jeannette Harrington (hair); Automated Lighting, Timothy F. Rogers; Production: Tony Menditto (carpenter), Jack Anderson (head carpenter), Geoff Vaughn (automation), Michael S. LoBue (electrician), Drayton Allison (head electrician), Chris Pantuso (props supervisor), Eric Smith (assistant props supervisor), Penny Davis (wardrobe supervisor), Kevin O'Brien, Keith Shaw, Lolly Totero (dressers); Music Preparation, Kaye-Houston Music; Music Transcription, Mario Vaz De Mello; Advertising, Serino-Coyne; Press, O & M Company, Rick Miramontez, Jon Dimond, Molly Barnett, Jaron Caldwell; Cast recording: PS Classics 864

CAST Winston **Harvey Fierstein**; Dolores/Caterer **Heather Mac Rae**; Myra/Wedding Dress Saleswoman **Kristine Zbornik**; Pasha/Mrs. Halloran **Lori Wilner**; Janey **Leslie Kritzer**; Ralph **Matt Cavenaugh**; Sam/Mr. Halloran **Philip Hoffman**; Tom **Tom Wopat**; Aggie **Faith Prince**; Alice/Army Sergeant **Katie Klaus**; Swings **Jennifer Allen, Britta Ollmann**

UNDERSTUDIES Jennifer Allen (Aggie), Philip Hoffman (Tom), Katie Klaus (Janey), Britta Ollmann (Janey), Matthew Scott (Ralph), Lori Willner (Aggie), Mark Zimmerman (Winston, Sam/Mr. Halloran)

MUSICIANS Constantine Kitsopoulos (Conductor); Ethyl Will (Associate Conductor/piano); Dale Stuckenbruck (Concert Master); Liz Lim-Dutton (violin); Ken Burward-Hoy (viola); Susannah Chapman (cello); John Arbo (bass); Jim Ercole, Don McGeen (woodwinds); Neil Balm (trumpet/flugel); Dean Witten (percussion)

MUSICAL NUMBERS Partners, Ralph and Me, Married, Women Chatter, No Fuss, Your Children's Happiness, Immediate Family, Our Only Daughter, Women Chatter 2, One White Dress, Vision, Don't Ever Stop Saying 'I Love You', I Stayed, Married (reprise), Don't Ever Stop Saying 'I Love You' (reprise), Coney Island (reprise)

SETTING The Bronx, New York, the morning after Memorial Day and onward, 1953. A new musical presented without intermission. World premiere presented at the Old Globe Theatre, San Diego, California (Louis G. Spisto, Executive Producer) September 20–November 11, 2007.

Leslie Kritzer and Faith Prince (photos by Jim Cox)

SYNOPSIS A Catered Affair reveals relationships strained to their limits when a couple must decide whether to spend their life savings on a family business or to launch their only daughter's marriage with a lavish catered affair.

Chicago

Ambassador Theatre; First Preview: October 23, 1996; Opening Night: November 14, 1996; 25 previews, 5,204 performances as of May 31, 2009

Lyrics by Fred Ebb, music by John Kander, book by Fred Ebb and Bob Fosse; based on the play by Maurine Dallas Watkins; Production based on the 1996 City Center *Encores!* production; Original production directed and choreographed by Bob Fosse; Produced by Barry & Fran Weissler/Kardana/Hart Sharp Productions, in association with Live Nation; Director, Walter Bobbie; Choreography, Ann Reinking in the style of Bob Fosse; Supervising Music Director, Rob Fisher; Music Director, Leslie Stifelman; Set, John Lee Beatty; Costumes, William Ivey Long; Lighting, Ken Billington; Sound, Scott Lehrer; Orchestrations, Ralph Burns; Dance Arrangements, Peter Howard; Adaptation, David Thompson; Musical Coordinator, Seymour Red Press; Hair/Wigs, David Brian Brown; Casting, James Calleri/Duncan Stewart (current), Jay Binder (original); Technical Supervisor, Arthur P. Siccardi; Dance Supervisor, Gary Chryst; Production Stage Manager, David Hyslop; Associate Producer, Alecia Parker; General Manager, B.J. Holt; Company Manager, Jean Haring; Stage Managers, Terrence J. Witter, Mindy Farbrother; Assistant Choreographer, Debra McWaters; Dance Captains, Gregory Butler, Bernard Dotson, Gabriela Garcia; Associate General Manager, Hilary Hamilton; General Manager Associate, Stephen Spadaro; Assistant Director, Jonathan Bernstein; Press, The Publicity Office, Jeremy Shaffer; Cast recording: RCA 68727-2

CAST Velma Kelly **Nancy Lemenager**[*1]; Roxie Hart **Bianca Marroquin**[*2]; Amos Hart **Ray Bokhour**[*3]; Matron "Mama" Morton **Kecia Lewis-Evans**[*4]; Billy Flynn **Jeff McCarthy**[*5]; Mary Sunshine **D. Micciche**[*6]; Fred Casely **Gregory Butler**[*7]; Sergeant Fogarty **Adam Zotovitch**; Liz **Nicole Bridgewater**; Annie **Dylis Croman**; June **Donna Marie Asbury**; Hunyak **Jill Nicklaus**[*8]; Mona **Michelle DeJean**[*9]; Go-To-Hell-Kitty **Melissa Rae Mahon**; Harry/The Jury **Shawn Emanjomeh**; Aaron/"Me and My Baby"

Carol Woods (photos by Paul Kolnik)

Specialty **Eric Jordan Young**[*10]; Doctor/Judge **Bernard Dotson**[*11]; Martin Harrison/"Me and My Baby" Specialty **Michael Cusumano**; Bailiff/Court Clerk **Dan LoBuono**[*12]

UNDERSTUDIES Melissa Rae Mahon (Roxie/Velma), Jill Nicklaus (Roxie), Donna Marie Asbury (Velma, "Mama" Morton), Bernard Dotson (Billy), Eric Jordan Young (Billy, Amos), Adam Zotovich (Amos), Michelle M. Robinson ("Mama" Morton), David Kent/Denny Paschall/Brian Spitulnik (Fred Casely, "Me and My Baby"), J. Loeffelholtz (Mary Sunshine); Gabriela Garcia, David Kent, Sharon Moore, Brian Spitulnik (All other roles)

*Succeeded by: 1. Brenda Braxton (8/12/08), Tera MacLeod (10/27/08), Brenda Braxton (11/3/08), Amra-Faye Wright (2/2/09) 2. Michelle DeJean (6/2/08), Bianca Marroquin (9/15/08), Michelle DeJean (10/19/08), Charlotte d'Amboise (11/3/08), Melora Hardin (12/29/08), Charlotte d'Amboise (2/13/09), Bryn Dowling (2/23/09), Charlotte d'Amboise (3/9/09), Bryn Dowling (3/30/09), Charlotte d'Amboise (4/13/09) 3. Kevin Chamberlin (7/15/08), Raymond Bokhour (9/28/08), Scott Davidson (12/8/08), Raymond Bokhour (2/23/09) 4. Carol Woods (6/2/08), LaVon Fisher-Wilson (11/14/08), Carol Woods (1/5/09), LaVon Fisher-Wilson (3/30/09), Sofia Vergara (4/24/09) 5. Obba Babatundé (7/15/08), Tom Wopat (7/29/08), Jeff McCarthy (10/6/08), Tom Wopat (10/13/08), Tom Hewitt (11/3/08), Tom Wopat (2/16/09), Tom Hewitt (3/2/09), Tom Wopat (3/23/09), Tom Hewitt (4/20/09) 6. R. Lowe 7. Brian O'Brien 8. Nili Bassman 9. Jill Nicklaus (6/2/08) 10. James T. Lane 11. Jason Patrick Sands 12. Brian O'Brien, Dan LoBuono

ORCHESTRA Leslie Stifelman (Conductor); Scott Cady (Associate Conductor/piano); Seymour Red Press, Jack Stuckey, Richard Centalonza (woodwinds); John Frosk, Darryl Shaw (trumpets); Dave Bargeron, Bruce Bonvissuto (trombones); John Johnson (piano/accordion); Jay Berliner (banjo); Ronald Raffio (bass/tuba); Marshall Coid (violin); Ronald Zito (drums/percussion)

MUSICAL NUMBERS All That Jazz, Funny Honey, Cell Block Tango, When You're Good to Mama, Tap Dance, All I Care About, A Little Bit of Good, We Both Reached for the Gun, Roxie, I Can't Do It Alone, My Own Best Friend, Entr'acte, I Know a Girl, Me and My Baby, Mister Cellophane, When Velma Takes the Stand, Razzle Dazzle, Class, Nowadays, Hot Honey Rag, Finale

SETTING Chicago, Illinois. The late 1920s. A musical vaudeville presented in two acts. This production originally opened at the Richard Rodgers Theatre; transferred to the Shubert on February 12, 1997; and transferred to the Ambassador on January 29, 2003. For original production credits see *Theatre World* Vol. 53, page 14. The original Broadway production ran June 3, 1975–August 27, 1977 at the 46th Street Theatre (now the Richard Rodgers Theatre where this revival first played) playing 936 performances (see *Theatre World* Vol. 32, Page 8).

SYNOPSIS Murder, media circus, vaudeville, and celebrity meet in this 1920s tale of two of the Windy City's most celebrated felons and their rise to fame amidst a razzle dazzle trial.

Brenda Braxton and the Company

A Chorus Line

Gerald Schoenfeld Theatre; First Preview: September 18, 2006; Opening Night: October 5, 2006; Closed August 17, 2008; 18 previews, 759 performances

Conceived and originally choreographed and directed by Michael Bennett, book by James Kirkwood and Nicholas Dante, music by Marvin Hamlisch, lyrics by Edward Kleban; Originally co-choreographed by Bob Avian; Produced by Vienna Waits; Director, Bob Avian; Choreography restaged by Baayork Lee; Set, Robin Wagner; Costumes, Theoni V. Aldredge; Lighting, Tharon Musser, adapted by Natasha Katz; Sound, Acme Sound Partners; Music Direction and Supervision, Patrick Vaccariello; Orchestrations, Jonathan Tunick, Billy Byers, and Hershy Kay; Vocal Arrangements, Don Pippin; General Management, Alan Wasser Associates; Casting, Jay Binder; Production Manager, Arthur Siccardi; Production Stage Manager, William Joseph Barnes; Marketing, Apel; Company Manager, Susan Bell; Associate Company Manager, Adam J. Miller/Michael Altbaum; Stage Manager, Laurie Goldfeder; Assistant Stage Manager, Timothy Semon; Assistant Choreographer/Dance Captain, Michael Gorman; Assistant Dance Captain, Lyndy Franklin; Assistant Director, Peter Pileski; Associate Design: Suzy Benzinger

Mario Lopez and the Company

(costumes), Yael Lubetzky (lighting); Music Coordinator, Michael Keller; Synthesizer Programming, Bruce Samuels; Music Copying, Emily Grishman/ Katherine Edmonds; Advertising, Serino-Coyne; Marketing, TMG–The Marketing Group; Press, Barlow · Hartman, Wayne Wolfe; Cast recording: Sony BMG Music/ Masterworks Broadway 82876-89785-2

CAST Bobby **Will Taylor**; Don **Jason Patrick Sands**[1]; Tricia **Michelle Aravena**; Roy **David Baum**[2]; Zach **Mario Lopez**; Tom **Mike Cannon**[3]; Butch **E. Clayton Cornelious**[4]; Diana **Natalie Cortez**; Cassie **Charlotte d'Amboise**[5]; Maggie **Melissa Lone**; Val **Jessica Lee Goldyn**[6]; Sheila **Deidre Goodwin**; Larry **Nick Adams**; Lois **Nadine Isenegger**[7]; Richie **James T. Lane**; Vicki **Lorin Latarro**; Mark **Paul McGill**; Judy **Heather Parcells**; Greg **Tommy Berklund**; Bebe **Dena DiGiacinto**; Mike **Jeffrey Schecter**; Connie **J. Elaine Marcos**; Paul **Bryan Knowlton**; Frank **Grant Turner**; Kristine **Katherine Tokarz**; Al **Kevin B. Worley**[8]; Swings[9] **Joey Dudding, Lyndy Franklin, Jessica Lea Patty, Courtney Laine Mazza, Eric Sciotto, Deone Zanotto**

*Succeeded by: 1. Adam Perry 2. Todd Anderson 3. Kurt Domoney 4. Eric Dysart 5. Jessica Lea Patty (8/10/08), alternates: Nadine Isenegger (Thursdays), Jessica Lea Patty (Sundays) 6. Jenifer Foote (8/10/08) 7. Kim Shriver 8. Mike Cannon 9. Deanna Agulnega

ORCHESTRA Patrick Vaccariello (Conductor); Jim Laev (Associate Conductor/ keyboard 2); Ted Nash, Lino Gomez, David Young, Jacqueline Henderson (woodwinds); John Chudoba, Trevor Neumann, Scott Wenholt (trumpets); Michael Seltzer, Ben Herrington, Jack Schatz (trombones); Bill Sloat (bass); Greg Anthony/ Ann Gerschefski (keyboard 1); Maggie Torre (Assistant Conductor/keyboard 3); Dan McMillan (percussion); Brian Brake (drums)

MUSICAL NUMBERS I Hope I Get It, I Can Do That, And, At the Ballet, Sing!; Hello Twelve, Hello Thirteen, Hello Love; Nothing, Dance: Ten; Looks: Three, The Music and the Mirror, One, The Tap Combination, What I Did for Love, One: Reprise

SETTING An Audition. Time: 1975. Place: A Broadway Theatre. Revival of the musical presented without intermission.

SYNOPSIS Broadway gypsies lay their talents–and hearts–on the line at a unique chorus call audition for a Broadway musical. "This show is dedicated to anyone who has ever danced in a chorus or marched in step…anywhere."— Michael Bennett.

The Line (photos by Paul Kolnik)

The Country Girl

Bernard B. Jacobs Theatre; First Preview: April 3, 2008 Opening Night: April 27, 2008; Closed July 20, 2008; 25 previews, 97 performances

Written by Clifford Odets; Produced by Ostar Productions, Bob Boyett, The Shubert Organization, Eric Falkenstein, Roy Furman, Lawrence Horowitz, Jam Theatricals, Stephanie P. McClelland, Bill Rollnick/Nancy Ellison Rollnick, Daryl Roth/Debra Black, in association with Jon Avnet/Ralph Guild, Michael Coppel, Jamie deRoy/Michael Filerman, Philip Geier/Donald Keough, Max OnStage, Mary Lu Roffe; Director, Mike Nichols; Set, Tim Hatley; Costumes, Albert Wolsky; Lighting, Natasha Katz; Sound, Acme Sound Partners; Hair, David Brian Brown; Casting, Tara Rubin; Production Manager, Aurora Productions; Production Stage Manager, Barclay Stiff; General Management, 101 Productions Ltd; Associate Director, B.T. McNicholl; Company Management, Barbara Crompton, Steven Lukens; Stage Manager, Alexis Shorter; Makeup, Angelina Avallone; Mr. Nichols' Assistants, Colleen O'Donnell, Daniel Murray; Associate Design: Ted LeFevre (set), MaryAnn D. Smith (costumes), Yael Lubetzky (lighting), Jeffrey Yoshi Lee (sound); Assistant Costumes (L.A.), Susan Kowarsh Hall; Assistant to Mr. Wolsky, Marnie Russell; Production: David M. Cohen (carpenter), James Sturek (assistant carpenter), Michael Pitzer (electrician), Daryl Kral (sound), Peter Sarafin (props), Alan Edward (prop assistant), Andrew Meeker (head props), Kelly A. Saxon (wardrobe supervisor), Richard Orton (hair supervisor), Mickey Abbate, Sandy Binion, Franc Weinperl (dressers), Kyle Gates, Libby Unsworth (production assistants); Associate Producers, Rachel Neuburger (for Ostar), Tim Levy (for Boyett); Music Consultant, Suzana Peri ; Advertising, Serino-Coyne; Press, Boneau/Bryan-Brown, Jackie Green, Matt Ross

Joe Roland, Morgan Freeman, Peter Gallagher and Frances McDormand (photos by Brigitte Lacombe)

CAST Bernie Dodd **Peter Gallagher;** Larry **Lucas Caleb Rooney;** Phil Cook **Chip Zien;** Nancy Stoddard **Anna Camp;** Paul Unger **Remy Auberjonois;** Frank Elgin **Morgan Freeman;** Georgie Elgin **Frances McDormand;** Ralph **Joe Roland**

UNDERSTUDIES Joe Roland (Bernie, Larry), Amanda Leigh Cobb (Nancy), Peter Ratray (Frank), Angela Reed (Georgie)

SETTING 1950. The stage of a New York theatre, Frank's apartment, a dressing room in a Boston theatre, and a dressing room of a New York theatre. Revival of a play presented in eight scenes in two acts.

SYNOPSIS *The Country Girl* is a classic backstage story. The title character, Georgie, is married to actor Frank Elgin, once a great theatre star, now down on his luck. When Frank is offered a major role by hotshot director Bernie Dodd, he has the chance to make a major comeback.

Frances McDormand, Morgan Freeman and Peter Gallagher

Cry-Baby

Marquis Theatre; First Preview: March 15, 2008; Opening Night: April 24, 2008; Closed June 22, 2008; 45 previews, 68 performances

Book by Mark O'Donnell & Thomas Meehan, songs by David Javerbaum & Adam Schlesinger; based on the 1990 Universal Pictures film written and directed by John Waters; Produced by Adam Epstein, Allan S. Gordon, Élan V. McAllister, Brian Grazer, James P. MacGilvray, Universal Pictures Stage Productions, Anne Caruso, Adam S. Gordon, Latitude Link, The Pelican Group, in association with Philip Morgaman, Andrew Faber/Richard Mishaan; Director, Mark Brokaw; Choreography, Rob Ashford; Incidental Music/Arrangements/Music Director, Lynne Shankel; Creative Consultant, John Waters; Sets, Scott Pask; Costumes, Catherine Zuber; Lighting, Howell Binkley; Sound, Peter Hylenski; Hair, Tom Watson; Makeup, Randy Houston Mercer; Fight Director, Rick Sordelet; Orchestrator, Christopher Jahnke; Dance Arrangements, David Chase; Music Producer, Steven M. Gold; Music Coordinator, John Miller; Production Manager, Juniper Street Productions; Production Stage Manager, Rolt Smith; Associate Choreographer, Joey Pizzi; Marketing, HHC Marketing; Casting, Telsey + Company; General Management, Alan Wasser, Allan Williams; Company Manager, Kimberly Kelley; Associate Company Manager, Christopher D'Angelo; Stage Manager, Andrea O. Saraffian; Assistant Stage Manager, Jenny Slattery; Associate Director, Moritz von Stuelpnagel; Assistant Choreography/Dance Captain, Spencer Liff; Assistant Choreographer, Christopher Bailey; Assistant Dance Captain, Andrew C. Call; Baton Sequences, Pamela Remler; Associate Design: Orit Jacoby Carroll (set), Holly Cain (costumes), Ryan O'Gara (lighting), Keith Caggiano (sound), Assistant Design: Jeffrey A. Hinchee (set), Lynn Bowling, Court Watson (costumes), Carrie J. Wood (lighting); Music Preparation, Kaye-Houston Music; Synthesizer Programmer, Randy Cohen; Advertising, Serino-Coyne; Press; Richard Kornberg, Don Summa

CAST Mrs. Vernon-Williams **Harriet Harris;** Baldwin **Christopher J. Hanke;** Allison **Elizabeth Stanley;** Skippy Wagstaff **Ryan Silverman;** Pepper **Carly Jibson;** Wanda **Lacey Kohl;** Mona **Courtney Balan;** Dupree **Chester Gregory II;** Cry-Baby **James Snyder;** Lenora **Alli Mauzey;** Judge Stone **Richard Poe;** Ensemble **Cameron Adams, Ashley Amber,** Nick Blaemire, Michael Buchanan, Eric L. Christian, Colin Cunliffe, Stacey Todd Holt, Laura Jordan, Marty Lawson, Spencer Liff, Mayumi Miguel, Tory Ross; Eric Sciotto, Ryan Silverman, Peter Matthew Smith, Allison Spratt, Charlie Sutton; Swings **Lisa Gajda, Michael D. Jablonski, Brendan King, Courtney Laine Mazza**

UNDERSTUDIES Cameron Adams (Allison), Ashley Amber (Wanda), Michael Buchanan (Dupree), Eric L. Christian (Dupree), Colin Cunliffe (Baldwin), Lisa Gajda (Pepper, Mona), Stacey Todd Holt (Judge Stone), Laura Jordan (Mrs. Vernon-Williams), Courtney Laine Mazza (Wanda, Lenora), Tory Ross (Mrs. Vernon-Williams, Pepper, Mona), Eric Sciotto (Cry-Baby), Ryan Silverman (Cry-Baby), Peter Matthew Smith (Judge Stone, Baldwin), Allison Spratt (Allison, Lenora)

***CRY-BABY* MUSICIANS** Lynn Shankel (Conductor/keyboard 1); Henry Aronson (Associate Conductor/keyboard 2); John Benthal, Chris Biesterfeldt (guitars); Cenovia Cummins, Maxim Moston (violin/mandolin); Orlando Wells (violin/viola); Sarah Seiver (cello); Steve Count (bass); Frank Pagano (drums); Scott Kreitzer, Cliff Lyons, Roger Rosenberg (reeds); Brian O'Flaherty (trumpet); Dan Levine (trombone); Joe Mowatt (percussion)

MUSICAL NUMBERS The Anti-Polio Picnic; Watch Your Ass; I'm Infected; Squeaky Clean; Nobody Gets Me; Nobody Gets Me (reprise); Jukebox Jamboree; Screw Loose; Baby Baby Baby Baby Baby (Baby Baby); Girl, Can I Kiss You…?; I'm Infected (reprise), You Can't Beat the System; Misery, Agony, Helplessness, Hopelessness, Heartache and Woe; All in My Head; Jailyard Jubilee; A Little Upset; I Did Something Wrong…Once; Thanks for the Nifty Country!; This Amazing Offer; Do That Again; Nothing Bad's Ever Gonna Happen Again

SETTING Baltimore, 1954. New York premiere of a new musical presented in two acts.

SYNOPSIS Everyone likes Ike, nobody likes communism, and Wade "Cry-Baby" Walker is the coolest boy in town. He's a bad boy with a good cause – truth, justice, and the pursuit of rock 'n roll – and when he falls for a good girl who wants to be bad, her charm school world of bobby sox and barbershop quartets will never be the same. Wayward youth, juvenile delinquents, sexual repression, cool music, dirty lyrics, bizarre rejects…finally, the '50s come to life – for real this time!

Elizabeth Stanley, James Snyder, Christopher Hanke and the Company (photos by Joan Marcus)

James Snyder, Lacey Kohl, Courtney Balan, Carly Jibson, Chester Gregory II, Elizabeth Stanley & Spencer Liff and the Company

Curtains

Al Hirschfeld Theatre; First Preview: February 27, 2007; Opening Night: March 22, 2007; Closed June 29, 2008; 26 previews, 511 performances

Book and additional lyrics by Rupert Holmes, music & additional lyrics by John Kander, lyrics by Fred Ebb, original book & concept by Peter Stone; Produced by Roger Berlind, Roger Horchow, Daryl Roth, Jane Bergére, Ted Hartley, Center Theatre Group; Director, Scott Ellis; Choreography, Rob Ashford; Music Director/ Vocal Arrangements, David Loud; Orchestrations, William David Brohn; Sets, Anna Louizos; Costumes, William Ivey Long; Lighting, Peter Kaczorowski; Sound, Brian Ronan; Hair/Wigs, Paul Huntley; Dance Arrangements, David Chase; Fight Director, Rick Sordelet; Aerial Effects, Paul Rubin; Makeup, Angelina Avallone; Associate Choreographer, Joann M. Hunter; Casting, Jim Carnahan; Production Supervisor, Beverly Randolph; Technical Supervisor, Peter Fulbright; Music Coordinator, John Monaco; General Management, 101 Productions Ltd.; Marketing Services, TMG–The Marketing Group; Associate Producers, Barbara & Peter Fodor; Company Manager, Bruce Klinger; Stage Manager, Scott Taylor Rollison; Assistant Stage Manager, Kevin Bertolacci, Jerome Vivona; Associate Company Manager, Kevin Beebee; Dance Captain, David Eggers; Assistant Dance Captain, Ashley Amber; Assistant Director, Dave Solomon; Music Copying, Larry H. Abel, Music Preparation International; Advertising, Serino-Coyne; Press, Boneau/Bryan-Brown, Jim Byk, Juliana Hannett, Matt Ross; Cast recording: Manhattan Records/EMI Broadway Angel 92212 2

CAST Jessica Cranshaw/Connie Subbotin **Patty Goble;** Randy Dexter **Matt Wall;** Niki Harris **Erin Davie;** Bambi Bernét **Megan Sikora;** Bobby Pepper **Noah Racey;** Johnny Harmon **Michael X. Martin;** Georgia Hendricks **Karen Ziemba;** Aaron Fox **Jason Danieley;** Carmen Bernstein **Debra Monk;** Oscar Shapiro **Michael McCormick;** Christopher Belling **Edward Hibbert;** Lieutenant Frank Cioffi **David Hyde Pierce;** Mona Page **Shannon Lewis;** Harv Fremont **Aaron Ramey;** Roberta Wooster **Julie Tolivar;** Sidney Bernstein **Gerry Vichi;** Detective O'Farrell/Roy Stetson **Kevin Bernard;** Daryl Grady **John Bolton;** Sasha Iljinsky **David Loud;** Marjorie Cook **Jennifer Frankel;** Arlene Barruca **Nili Bassman;** Brick Hawvermale **Ward Billeisen;** Jan Setler **Jennifer Dunne;** Peg Prentice **Brittany Marcin;** Ronnie Driscoll **Joe Aaron Reid;** Russ Cochran **Christopher Spaulding;** Swings **Lorin Latarro, David Eggers, J. Austin Eyer, Stephanie Youell, Jerome Vivona**

ORCHESTRA David Loud (Conductor); Sam Davis (Associate Music Director/ piano-synthesizer); Steven Kenyon, Al Hunt, Owen Kotler, Mark Thrasher (woodwinds); R.J. Kelley, Angela Cordell (French horns); Don Downs, Matthew Peterson; Charles Gordon (House Contractor, trombone); Jennifer Wharton (bass trombone/tuba); Gregory Landes (percussion); Bruce Doctor (drums): Greg Utzig (guitars/banjo); Robert Renino (bass)

MUSICAL NUMBERS Wide Open Spaces, What Kind of Man?, Thinking of Him, The Woman's Dead, Show People, Coffee Shop Nights, In the Same Boat 1, I Miss the Music, Thataway!, He Did It, It's a Business, Kansasland, In the Same Boat 2, Thinking of Him (reprise), A Tough Act to Follow, In the Same Boat 3, A Tough Act to Follow (reprise)

SETTING 1959. Boston's Colonial Theatre during the out-of-town tryout of the new musical, *Robbin' Hood!* A new musical presented in two acts. American premiere produced at Center Theatre Group's Ahmanson Theatre by in Los Angeles, July 25–September 10, 2006, opening August 9.

SYNOPSIS When the hapless, talent-free star of a potential Broadway hit trying out in Boston dies on opening night during her curtain call, Lieutenant Frank Cioffi arrives on the scene to conduct an investigation. But the lure of the theatre proves irresistible. After an unexpected romance blooms for the stage-struck detective, he finds himself just as drawn toward making the show a hit, as he is in solving the murder.

Debra Monk and Gerry Vichi (photos by Joan Marcus)

Edward Hibbert, David Hyde Pierce and Erin Davie

Grease

Brooks Atkinson Theatre; First Preview: July 24, 2007; Opening Night: August 19, 2007; Closed January 4, 2009; 31 previews, 554 performances

Book, music and lyrics by Jim Jacobs and Warren Casey; additional songs by Barry Gibb, John Farrar, Louis St. Louis, Scott Simon; Produced by Paul Nicholas and David Ian, Nederlander Presentations Inc., Terry Allen Kramer, by special arrangement with Robert Stigwood; Director/Choreographer, Kathleen Marshall; Music Director, Kimberly Grigsby; Sets, Derek McLane; Costumes, Martin Pakledinaz; Lighting, Kenneth Posner; Sound, Brian Ronan; Wigs/Hair, Paul Huntley; Casting, Jay Binder, Jack Bowdan/Megan Larche; Associate Director, Marc Bruni; Associate Choreographer, Joyce Chittick; Orchestrations, Christopher Jahnke; Music Coordinator, Howard Jones; Production Supervisors, Arthur Siccardi, Patrick Sullivan; Production Stage Manager, David John O'Brien/John Bonanni; Executive Producer, Max Finbow; General Management, Charlotte Wilcox Company; Company Manager, James Lawson/Alexandra Gushin Agosta; Assistant Company Manager, Megan Trice/Michael Bolgar; Stage Manager, Beverly Jenkins/Stephen R. Gruse; Assistant Stage Manager, Colleen Danaher; Dance Captain, Amber Stone; Assistant to the Director, Jenny Hogan; Makeup, Joe Dulude II; Associate Design: Ted LeFevre (set), Matthew Pachtman (costumes), Aaron Spivey (lighting), Giovanna Calabretta (wigs and hair); Assistant Design: Anne Allen Goelz, Shoko Kambara (sets), Erica Hemminger, Court Watson (assistants to Mr. McLane), Sarah Sophia Turner (costumes), Tescia Seufferlein (assistant to Mr. Pakledinaz), Kathleen Dobbins (lighting), Michael Creason (sound); Moving Lights, David Arch; Assistant Dance Captain, Keven Quillon; Synthesizer Programmer, Randy Cohen; Advertising, Serino-Coyne; Press, Barlow · Hartman, Ryan Ratelle; Cast recording: Masterworks Broadway 88697-16398-2

CAST Danny Zuko **Max Crumm**[*1]; Sandy Dumbrowski **Laura Osnes**[*2]; Kenickie **Matthew Saldívar**[*3]; Sonny LaTierri **José Restrepo**[*4]; Roger **Daniel Everidge**[*5]; Doody **Ryan Patrick Binder**; Betty Rizzo **Jenny Powers**[*6]; Marty **Robyn Hurder**[*7]; Jan **Lindsay Mendez**; Frenchy **Kirsten Wyatt**; Patty Simcox **Allison Fischer**; Eugene Florczyk **Jamison Scott**; Miss Lynch **Susan Blommaert**; Vince Fontaine **Jeb Brown**[*8]; Cha-Cha DiGregorio **Natalie Hill**; Teen Angel **Stephen R. Buntrock**[*9]; Ensemble[*10] **Josh Franklin, Cody Green, Natalie Hill**[*9]**, Emily Padgett, Keven Quillon, Brian Sears, Christina Sivrich, Anna Aimee White**; Swings **Matthew Hydzik, Amber Stone**

UNDERSTUDIES Josh Franklin (Danny, Vince), Cody Green (Kenickie, Sonny), Natalie Hill (Rizzo, Marty), Matthew Hydzik (Danny, Teen Angel), Emily Padgett (Patty, Sandy), Keven Quillon (Roger, Sonny), Brian Sears (Doody, Eugene), Christina Sivrich (Frenchy, Jan, Miss Lynch), Amber Stone (Cha-Cha, Frenchy, Jan), Anna Aimee White (Marty, Patty, Sandy)

*Succeeded by 1. Derek Keeling (7/22/08) 2. Ashley Spencer (7/22/08) 3. Ace Young (9/9/08) 4. Xavier Cano 5. Will Blum, Todd Buonopane 6. Janine DeVita (6/26/08) 7. Helene York 8. Mike McGowan 9. Taylor Hicks (6/6/08), Stephen Buntrock (9/9/08) 10. Allie Schultz, Joe Komara, Joseph Medeiros, Josh Rouah, Jason Wooten, Christina Rose, Freddy Ramirez, Ashley Arcement

THE *GREASE* BAND Kimberly Grigsby/Henry Aronson (Conductor/synthesizer); Chris Fenwick/John Samorian (Associate Conductor/synthesizer/piano); John Clancy (drums); Michael Blanco (bass); Michael Aarons, Jim Hershman (guitars); John Scarpulla (tenor sax/woodwinds); Jack Bashkow (woodwinds)

MUSICAL NUMBERS Grease, Summer Nights, Those Magic Changes, Freddy My Love, Greased Lightnin', Rydell Fight Song, Mooning, Look at Me, I'm Sandra Dee, We Go Together, Shakin' at the High School Hop, It's Raining on Prom Night, Born to Hand-Jive, Hopelessly Devoted to You, Beauty School Dropout, Sandy, Rock 'n' Roll Party Queen, There Are Worse Things I Could Do, Look at Me, I'm Sandra Dee (reprise), You're the One That I Want, We Go Together (reprise)

Ashley Spencer, Derek Keeling (center) and the Company

SETTING 1959, in and around Rydell High School. Revival of the musical presented in thirteen scenes in two acts. Originally produced Off-Broadway at the Eden Theatre February 14, 1972 (see *Theatre World* Vol. 28, page 99); transferred to the Broadhurst Theatre June 7, 1972 (see *Theatre World* Vol. 29, page 8), running eight years and 3,388 performances. The show was revived at the Eugene O'Neill Theatre on May 11, 1994, running almost four years (see *Theatre World* Vol. 50, page 68).

SYNOPSIS The classic 1970s musical about the 1959 Rydell High School gang receives its second major revival, using songs written for the 1978 feature film. Max Crumm and Laura Osnes were cast from the reality television show "*Grease: You're The One That I Want*", a twelve week talent competition airing on NBC in the spring of 2007. After weekly eliminations, America voted Crumm and Osnes as their "Danny" and "Sandy", marking a unique casting method never before used in Broadway history. Coincidentally, their replacements, Derek Keeling and Ashley Spencer, were finalists in the reality competition.

Kristen Wyatt and Taylor Hicks (photos by Joan Marcus)

Gypsy

St. James Theatre; First Preview: March 3, 2008; Opening Night: March 27, 2008; Closed January 11, 2009; 27 previews, 332 performances

Boyd Gaines, Laura Benanti, and Patti LuPone

Book by Arthur Laurents, music by Jule Styne, lyrics by Stephen Sondheim; suggested by the memoirs of Gypsy Rose Lee; Produced by Roger Berlind, The Routh · Frankel · Baruch · Viertel Group, Roy Furman, Debra Black, Ted Hartley, Roger Horchow, David Ian, Scott Rudin, Jack Viertel; based on the City Center *Encores! Summer Stars* 2007 production; Director, Arthur Laurents; Choreography, Jerome Robbins (reproduced by Bonnie Walker); Music Director, Patrick Vaccariello; Sets, James Youmans; Costumes, Martin Pakledinaz; Lighting, Howell Binkley; Sound, Dan Moses Schreier; Casting, Jay Binder; Wigs/Hair, Paul Huntley; Makeup, Angelina Avallone; Production Stage Manager, Craig Jacobs; Orchestrations, Sid Ramin, Robert Ginzler; Dance Arrangements, John Kander; Music Coordinator, Seymour Red Press; General Management, Richard Frankel Productions, Laura Green; Technical Supervision, Juniper Street Productions; Company Manager, Sammy Ledbetter; Associate Company Manager, Townsend Teague; Stage Manager, Gary Mickelson; Assistant Stage Managers, Nancy Elizabeth Vest, Isaac Klein; Assistant Choreographer, Roger Preston Smith; Dance Captain, Bill Bateman; Associate Design: Jerome Martin (set), Martha Bromelmeier (costumes), Ryan O'Gara (lighting), David Bullard (sound), Giovanna Calabretta (wigs); Assistant Design: Adrienne Kapalko (set), Amanda Zieve (lighting), David Stollings (sound); Costumes Assistants, Sarah Cubbage, Tescia Seufferlein; Special Keyboard Arrangements, Danny Troob, Nathan Kelly; Synthesizer Programmer, Randy Cohen; Music Preparation; Anixter Rice Music Services; Advertising, Serino-Coyne; Press, Barlow · Hartman, Ryan Ratelle, Melissa Bixler; Cast recording: Time Life 80020-D

CAST Uncle Jocko/Pastey **Jim Bracchitta;** Georgie/Mr. Goldstone/Bougeron-Cochon **Bill Bateman;** Vladimir/Rich Boy **Kyrian Friedenberg;** Balloon Girl **Katie Micha*1;** Baby June **Sami Gayle;** Baby Louise **Emma Rowley*2;** Charlie/Tap Dancer **Matthew Lobenhofer;** Hopalong **Rider Quentin Stanton;** Rose **Patti LuPone;** Pop/Cigar **Bill Raymond;** Boy Scout **Andy Richardson*3;** Weber/Phil **Brian Reddy;** Herbie **Boyd Gaines;** Dainty June **Leigh Ann Larkin;** Louise **Laura Benanti;** Yonkers/Driver **Pearce Wegener;** L.A. **Steve Konopelski;** Tulsa **Tony Yazbeck;** Kansas **John Scacchetti;** Little Rock **Geo Seery;** East St. Louis **Matty Price;** Waitress/Renée **Jessica Rush;** Miss Cratchitt/Mazeppa **Lenora Nemitz;** Agnes **Nicole Mangi;** Marjorie May **Alicia Sable;** Geraldine **Mindy Dougherty;** Edna Mae **Nancy Renée Braun;** Carol Ann **Sarah Marie Hicks;** Betsy Ann Beckley Andrews; Tessie Tura **Alison Fraser;** Electra **Marilyn Caskey**

STANDBYS Lenora Nemitz/Linda Balgord (Rose), Jim Bracchitta (Herbie), Jessica Rush (Louise, Miss Cratchitt), Mindy Dougherty (Dainty June), Pearce Wegener (Tulsa, Pastey), Dorothy Stanley (Miss Cratchitt, Tessie Tura, Mazeppa,

Electra), Matt Gibson (Georgie, Pastey), John Scacchetti (Bougeron-Cochon), Andrew Boyer (Uncle Jocko, Cigar, Herbie), Katie Micha*1 (Baby Louise, Baby June), Alicia Sable (Balloon Girl, Agnes), Kyrian Friedenberg (Military Boys), Rider Quentin Stanton (Newsboys), Matty Price (Yonkers, L.A., Kansas, Tulsa, Uncle Jocko), Lisa Rohinsky (Louise, Balloon Girl, Renée, Waitress), Nancy Renée Braun (Waitress, Renée), Nicole Mangi (Baby Louise), Meg Guzulescu (Swing)

*Succeeded by: 1. Jaclyn Taylor Ruggiero 2. Katie Micha 3. Jacob Clemente

ORCHESTRA Patrick Vaccariello (Conductor); Jeffrey Harris (Associate Conductor-Musical Director/keyboard); Marilyn Reynolds, Fritz Krakowski Eric DeGioia, Dana Ianculovici (violins); Crystal Garner, Sally Shumway (violas); Peter Prosser, Vivian Israel (cello); Brian Cassier (bass); Edward Salkin, Adam Kolker, Dennis Anderson, Ralph Olsen, John Winder, Tom Murray (woodwinds); Tony Kadleck, James Delagarza, Kamau Adilifu, John Chudoba (trumpets); Bruce Eidem, Wayne Goodman, Robert Fournier (trombones); Nancy Billman (French horn); Susan Jolles (harp); Paul Pizzuti (drums); Thad Wheeler (percussion)

MUSICAL NUMBERS Overture, May We Entertain You, Some People, Some People (reprise), Small World, Baby June and Her Newsboys, Mr. Goldstone, Little Lamb, You'll Never Get Away From Me, Dainty June and Her Farmboys, If Momma Was Married, All I Need Is the Girl, Everything's Coming Up Roses; Madame Rose's Toreadorables, Together Wherever We Go, You Gotta Get a Gimmick, The Strip, Rose's Turn

SETTING Various cities throughout the U.S.; 1920s–1930s. Revival of the musical presented in two acts. Originally produced at the Broadway Theatre May 21, 1959, transferred to the Imperial Theatre and closed March 25, 1961 after 702 performances (see *Theatre World* Vol. 15, page 116). This production marked the fourth major revival: Winter Garden Theatre, September 23, 1974–January 4, 1975 (see *Theatre World* Vol. 31, page 8); St. James/Marquis Theatre, October 27, 1989–July 28, 1991, (see *Theatre World* Vol. 46, page 20); Shubert Theatre, March 31, 2003–May 30, 2004 (see *Theatre World* Vol. 59, page 58).

SYNOPSIS The musical fable, suggested by the memoirs of Gypsy Rose Lee, tells of the quintessential stage mother, Rose, as she embarks her daughters Louise and June across the vaudeville circuit in search of fame and success for them, only to find it in the halls of burlesque.

Laura Benanti (photos by Paul Kolnik)

Hairspray

Neil Simon Theatre; First Preview: July 18, 2002; Opening Night: August 15, 2002; Closed January 4, 2009; 31 previews, 2,641 performances

Book by Mark O'Donnell and Thomas Meehan, music by Marc Shaiman, lyrics by Marc Shaiman and Scott Wittman; based on the 1988 film written and directed by John Waters; Produced by Margo Lion, Adam Epstein, The Routh · Frankel · Baruch · Viertel Group, James D. Stern/Douglas L. Meyer, Rick Steiner/Frederic H. Mayerson, SEL & GFO, New Line Cinema, in association with Live Nation, Allan S. Gordon, Elan V. McAllister, Dede Harris, Morton Swinsky, John and Bonnie Osher; Director, Jack O'Brien, Choreography, Jerry Mitchell; Sets, David Rockwell; Costumes, William Ivey Long; Lighting, Kenneth Posner; Sound, Steve C. Kennedy; Casting, Telsey + Company; Wigs/Hair, Paul Huntley; Production Stage Manager, Lois L. Griffing; Associate Director, Matt Lenz; Associate Choreographer, Michele Lynch; Orchestrations, Harold Wheeler, Music Director, Lon Hoyt, Arrangements, Marc Shaiman; Music Coordinator, John Miller, General Management, Richard Frankel, Laura Green; Technical Supervisor, Tech Production Services Inc./Peter Fulbright; Associate Producers, Rhoda Mayerson, the Aspen Group, Daniel C. Staton; Company Managers, Bruce Kagel, Tracy Geltman; Stage Managers, Marisha Ploski, Thomas J. Gates; Makeup, Randy Houston Mercer; Music Copying, Emily Grishman, Katherine Edmonds; Dance Captains, Brooke Leigh Engen, Robbie Roby; Press, Richard Kornberg, Don Summa, Alyssa Hart; Cast recording: Sony SK 87708

CAST Tracy Turnblad **Marissa Perry**[*1]; Corny Collins **Clarke Thorell**; Amber Von Tussle **Ashley Spencer**[*2]; Brad **Kasey Marino**; Tammy **Brooke Leigh Engen**; Fender **Daniel Robinson**; Brenda **Leslie Goddard**; Sketch **Curt Hansen**; Shelley **Lori Eve Marinacci**; IQ **Todd Michel Smith**; Lou Ann **Kirsten Bracken**; Link Larkin **Ashley Parker Angel**[*3]; Prudy Pingleton/ Gym Teacher/Matron **Susan Mosher**; Edna Turnblad **George Wendt**[*4]; Penny Pingleton **Niki Scalera**; Velma Von Tussle **Karen Mason**; Harriman F. Spritzer/Principal/Mr. Pinky/Guard **Kevin Meany**; Wilbur Turnblad **Ken Marks**; Seaweed J. Stubbs **Tevin Campbell**; Duane **Travis Robertson**; Gilbert **Steven Cutts**; Lorraine **Terita R. Redd**; Thad **Dwayne Cooper**; The Dynamites **Carla Jay Hargrove, Judine Richard Somerville, Iris Burruss**; Little Inez **Carla Duren**[*5]; Motormouth Maybelle **Jenifer Lewis**[*6]; Denizens of Baltimore **Kirsten Bracken, Iris Burruss, Dwayne Cooper, Steven Cutts, Brooke Leigh Engen, Leslie Goddard, Curt Hansen, Carla Jay Hargrove, Tyrick Wiltez Jones, Lori Eve Marinacci, Kasey Marino, Kevin Meany, Susan Mosher, Terita R. Redd, Daniel Robinson, Todd Michel Smith, Judine Richard Somerville**; Swings/Understudies[*7] **Tracee Beazer, Ryan Christopher Chotto, Scott Davidson, Matthew S. Morgan, Jacqui Polk, Nicole Powell, Robbie Roby, Jason Snow, Willis White**

Marissa Jaret Winokur and Harvey Fierstein (photos by Paul Kolnik)

*Succeeded by: 1. Marissa Jaret Winokur (12/9/08) 2. Aubrey O'Day (7/18/08), Kate Loprest (9/19/08) 3. Constantine Rousouli (9/16/08) 4. Harvey Fierstein (11/11/08) 5. Melissa VanPelt 6. Charlotte Crossley (9/2/08) 7. Summer Broyhill, Lauren Kling, Annie Funke

ORCHESTRA Lon Hoyt (Conductor/keyboard); Keith Cotton (Associate Conductor/keyboard); Seth Farber (Assistant Conductor/keyboard), David Spinozza, Peter Calo (guitars); Francisco Centeno (electric bass); Clint de Ganon (drums); Walter "Wally" Usiatynski (percussion); David Mann, Dave Rickenberg (reeds); Bob Milliken (trumpet); Birch Johnson (trombone); Rob Shaw, Carol Pool (violins); Sarah Hewitt Roth (cello); Onstage Musicians: Ashley Parker Angel (guitar); Kevin Meany (glockenspiel); Niki Scalera (harmonica)

MUSICAL NUMBERS Good Morning Baltimore, The Nicest Kids in Town, Mama I'm a Big Girl Now, I Can Hear the Bells, The Legend of Miss Baltimore Crabs, The Madison, The Nicest Kids in Town (reprise), Welcome to the '60s, Run and Tell That, Big, Blond and Beautiful, The Big Dollhouse, Good Morning Baltimore, Timeless to Me, Without Love, I Know Where I've Been, Hairspray, Cooties, You Can't Stop the Beat

SETTING Time: 1962. Place: Baltimore. A musical presented in two acts. For original production credits see *Theatre World* Vol. 59, page 25. World premiere at the 5th Avenue Theatre (Seattle, Washington) June 2002.

SYNOPSIS It's 1962—the '50s are out and change is in the air. Baltimore's Tracy Turnblad, a big girl with big hair and an even bigger heart, has only one passion—to dance. She wins a spot on the local TV dance program, "The Corny Collins Show" and, overnight, is transformed from outsider to irrepressible teen celebrity. But can a plus-size trendsetter in dance and fashion vanquish the program's reigning princess, win the heart of heartthrob Link Larkin, and integrate a television show without denting her 'do? Only in *Hairspray!* Welcome to the '60s!

Harvey Fierstein, Marissa Jaret Winokur and the original cast

In the Heights

Richard Rodgers Theatre; First Preview: February 14, 2008; Opening Night: March 9, 2008; 29 previews, 512 performances as of May 31, 2009

Concept, music and lyrics by Lin-Manuel Miranda, book by Quiara Alegría Hudes; Produced by Kevin McCollum, Jeffrey Seller, Jill Furman, Sander Jacobs, Goodman/Grossman, Peter Fine, Everett/Skipper; Director, Thomas Kail; Choreographer, Andy Blankenbuehler; Music Director, Alex Lacamoire; Sets, Anna Louizos; Costumes, Paul Tazewell; Lighting, Howell Binkley; Sound, Acme Sound Partners; Arrangements and Orchestrations, Alex Lacamoire & Bill Sherman; Music Coordinator, Michael Keller; Casting, Telsey + Company; Marketing, Scott A. Moore; Company Manager, Brig Berney; General Manager, John S. Corker, Lizbeth Cone; Technical Supervisor, Brian Lynch; Production Stage Manager, J. Philip Bassett; Associate Producers, Ruth Hendel, Harold Newman; Wigs, Charles LaPointe; Assistant Director, Casey Hushion; Assistant Choreographer, Joey Dowling; Fight Director, Ron Piretti; Latin Assistant Choreographer, Luis Salgado; Fight/Dance Captain, Michael Balderrama; Stage Manager, Amber Wedin; Assistant Stage Manager, Heather Hogan; Associate Design: Donyale Werle, Todd Potter (set), Michael Zecker (costumes), Mark Simpson (lighting), Sten Severson (sound); Assistant Design: Hilary Noxon, Heather Dunbar (set), Caitlin Hunt (costumes), Greg Bloxham, Ryan O'Gara (lighting); Moving Lights, David Arch; Production: McBrien Dunbar (advance carpenter), Cheyenne Benson (advance flyman), Keith Buchanan (electrician), Dan Robillard (sound), George Wagner (Propmaster), Christopher Kurtz (spots), Brandon Rice (sound engineer), Rick Kelly (wardrobe supervisor), Jamie Stewart (hair supervisor), Gray Biangone, Jennifer Hohn, Moira MacGregor-Conrad (dressers); Music Copying, Emily Grishman; Rehearsal Pianist, Zachary Dietz; Keyboard Programming, Randy Cohen; Advertising, SpotCo; Press, Barlow · Harman, Wayne Wolfe, Melissa Bixler; Cast recording: Sh-K-Boom/Ghostlight Records 4428

CAST Graffiti Pete **Seth Stewart**; Usnavi **Lin-Manuel Miranda**[*1]; Piragua Guy **Eliseo Román**; Abuela Claudia **Olga Merediz**; Carla **Janet Dacal**; Daniela **Andréa Burns**; Kevin **Carlos Gomez**[*2]; Camila **Priscilla Lopez**; Sonny **Robin De Jesus**; Benny **Christopher Jackson**; Vanessa **Karen Olivo**[*3]; Nina **Mandy Gonzalez**; Ensemble **Tony Chiroldes, Rosie Lani Fiedelman, Joshua Henry**[*4], **Afra Hines, Nina LaFarga, Doreen Montalvo, Javier Muñoz**[*5], **Krysta Rodriguez**[*6], **Eliseo Román, Luis Salgado, Shaun Taylor-Corbett, Rickey Tripp**; Swings[*7] **Michael Balderrama, Blanca Camacho, Rogelio Douglas Jr., Stephanie Klemons**

Javier Muñoz and the Company

Rick Négron and Priscilla Lopez (photos by Joan Marcus)

UNDERSTUDIES Michael Balderrama (Graffiti Pete, Piragua Guy), Blanca Camacho (Abuela Claudia, Camila, Daniela), Tony Chiroldes (Kevin, Piragua Guy), Janet Dacal (Vanessa, Nina), Rogelio Douglas Jr. (Benny), Joshua Henry (Benny), Stephanie Klemons (Carla), Nina LaFarga (Nina), Doreen Montalvo (Abuela Claudia, Camila, Daniela), Javier Muñoz (Usnavi/Sonny/Graffiti Pete), Krysta Rodriguez (Nina, Carla, Vanessa), Eliseo Román (Kevin), Shaun Taylor-Corbett (Usnavi, Sonny, Piragua Guy), Rickey Tripp (Benny)

*Succeeded by: 1. Javier Muñoz (2/16/09) 2. Rick Negron (12/19/08) 3. Marcy Harriell (11/18/08) 4. Marcus Paul James 5. Dwayne Clark 6. Gabrielle Ruiz 7. Noemi Del Rio, Antuan Raimone, Jon Rua, Marcos Santana, Elise Santora, Alejandra Reyes

ORCHESTRA Alex Lacamoire (Conductor/keyboard 1); Zachary Dietz (Associate Conductor/keyboard 2); Raul Agraz (lead trumpet); Trevor Neumann (trumpet); Joe Fiedler, Ryan Keberle (trombones); Dave Richards, Kristy Norter (reeds); Andres Forero (drums); Doug Hinrichs, Wilson Torres (percussion); Irio O'Farrill (bass); Manny Moreira (guitars)

MUSICAL NUMBERS In the Heights, Breathe, Benny's Dispatch, It Won't Be Long Now, Inútil (Useless), No Me Diga, 96,000, Paciencia Y Fe (Patience and Faith), When You're Home, Piragua, Siempre (Always), The Club/Fireworks, Sunrise, Hundreds of Stories, Enough, Carnaval del Barrio, Atencíon, Alabanza, Everything I Know, No Me Diga (reprise), Champagne, When the Sun Goes Down, Finale

SETTING Washington Heights, Manhattan. Fourth of July weekend, the present. A new musical presented in two acts. Previously presented Off-Broadway at 37 Arts, February 8–July 15, 2007 (see *Theatre World* Vol. 63, page 162).

SYNOPSIS *In the Heights* follows two days in Washington Heights, a vibrant immigrant neighborhood at the top of Manhattan. From the vantage point of Usnavi's corner bodega, we experience the joys, heartbreaks and bonds of a Latino community struggling to redefine home. This original musical features a mix of hip-hop, salsa and meringue music.

Jersey Boys

August Wilson Theatre; First Preview: October 4, 2005; Opening Night: November 6, 2005; 38 previews, 1,467 performances as of May 31, 2009

Book by Marshall Brickman and Rick Elice, music by Bob Gaudio, lyrics by Bob Crewe; Produced by Dodger Theatricals (Michael David, Edward Strong, Rocco Landesman, Des McAnuff), Joseph J. Grano, Pelican Group, Tamara Kinsella and Kevin Kinsella, in association with Latitude Link, Rick Steiner and Osher/Staton/Bell/ Mayerson Group; Director, Des McAnuff; Choreography, Sergio Trujillo; Musical Director, Vocal Arrangements/Incidental Music, Ron Melrose; Sets, Klara Zieglerova; Costumes, Jess Goldstein; Lighting, Howell Binkley; Sound, Steve Canyon Kennedy; Projections, Michael Clark; Hair/Wigs, Charles LaPointe; Fight Director, Steve Rankin; Assistant Director, West Hyler; Production Supervisor, Richard Hester; Production Stage Manager, Michelle Bosch; Orchestrations, Steve Orich; Music Coordinator, John Miller; Technical Supervisor, Peter Fulbright; Casting, Tara Rubin (East), Sharon Bialy, Sherry Thomas (West); Company Manager, Sandra Carlson; Associate Company Manager, Tim Sulka; Associate Producers, Lauren Mitchell and Rhoda Mayerson; Executive Producer, Sally Campbell Morse; Promotions, HHC Marketing; Stage Manager, Michael T. Clarkston/Jason Brouillard/Michelle Reupert; Assistant Stage Manager, Rachel Wolff/Michelle Reupert/Brendan M. Fay; Dialect Coach, Stephen Gabis; Dance and Fight Captain, Peter Gregus; Music Technical Design, Deborah Hurwitz; Associate General Manager, Jennifer F. Vaughan; Marketing, Dodger Marketing; Advertising, Serino-Coyne; Press, Boneau/Bryan-Brown, Susanne Tighe, Heath Schwartz; Cast recording: Rhino R2 73271

CAST French Rap Star/Detective #1/Hal Miller/Barry Belson/Police Officer/Davis **Kris Coleman;** Stanley/Hank Majewski/Crewe's PA/Joe Long **Eric Gutman**[*1]; Bob Crewe/others **Peter Gregus;** Tommy DeVito **Christian Hoff**[*2]; Nick DeVito/Stosh/Billy Dixon/Norman Waxman/Charlie Calello/others **Donnie Kehr**[*3]; Joey/Recording Studio Engineer/others **Travis Cloer**[*4]; Gyp De Carlo/others **Mark Lotito;** Mary Delgado/Angel/others **Bridget Berger;** Church Lady/Miss Frankie Nolan/Bob's Party Girl/Angel/Lorraine/others **Heather Ferguson;** Bob Gaudio **Sebastian Arcelus**[*5]; Frankie's Mother/Nick's Date/Angel/Francine/others **Sara Schmidt;** Nick Massi **J. Robert Spencer**[*6]; Frankie Valli **Michael Longoria**[*7] (evenings) / **Cory Grant**[*8] (matinees); Thugs **Ken Dow, Joe Payne;** Swings **Michelle Knight, Rebecca Kupka**[*9], **John Leone**[*10], **Dominic Nolfi**[*11], **Eric Schneider**[*12]

UNDERSTUDIES Eric Gutman (Gaudio, Devito, Crewe, Massi), Donnie Kehr (Gyp, DeVito, Crewe), John Leone (Gyp, Massi, DeVito, Crewe), Russell Fischer (Valli), Dominic Nolfi (Gaudio, Devito), Matthew Scott (DeVito, Crewe, Gaudio), Eric Schneider (Valli), Travis Cloer (Valli), Miles Aubrey (Massi, Gyp), John Hickman (Gaudio, Massi, Gyp, Crewe), Taylor Sternberg, (Valli), Jake Speck (Gaudio, Massi, Devito)

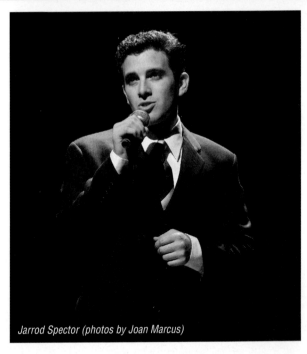

Jarrod Spector (photos by Joan Marcus)

*Succeeded by: 1. Matthew Scott (12/9/08) 2. Dominic Nolfi (9/30/08) 3. Miles Aubrey (7/20/08) 4. Russell Fischer (9/30/08) 5. Andrew Rannells (1/13/09) 6. Matt Bogart (9/30/08) 7. Jarrod Spector (9/30/08) 8. Dominic Scaglione Jr (9/24/08), Cory Grant (3/31/09) 9. Katie O'Toole (7/8/08) 10. Doug Crawford (9/16/08), John Hickman (11/11/08) 11. Jake Speck (9/30/08) 12. Taylor Sternberg (11/15/08)

MUSICIANS Adam Ben-David (Conductor/keyboards); Deborah Hurwitz (Associate Conductor/keyboards); Stephen "Hoops" Snyder (keyboards); Joe Payne (guitars); Ken Dow (bass); Kevin Dow (drums); Matt Hong, Ben Kono (reeds); David Spier (trumpet)

MUSICAL NUMBERS Ces Soirées-La (Oh What a Night), Silhouettes, You're the Apple of My Eye, I Can't Give You Anything But Love, Earth Angel, Sunday Kind of Love, My Mother's Eyes, I Go Ape, (Who Wears) Short Shorts, I'm in the Mood for Love/Moody's Mood for Love, Cry for Me, An Angel Cried, I Still Care, Trance, Sherry, Big Girls Don't Cry, Walk Like a Man, December, 1963 (Oh What a Night), My Boyfriend's Back, My Eyes Adored You, Dawn (Go Away), Walk Like a Man (reprise), Big Man in Town, Beggin', Stay, Let's Hang On (To What We've Got), Opus 17 (Don't You Worry 'Bout Me), Bye Bye Baby, C'mon Marianne, Can't Take My Eyes Off of You, Working My Way Back to You, Fallen Angel, Rag Doll, Who Loves You

SETTING New Jersey, New York, and across the U.S., 1950s–now. A new musical presented in two acts. For original production credits see *Theatre World* Vol. 62, page 34. World Premiere produced by La Jolla Playhouse, October 5, 2004.

SYNOPSIS "How did four blue-collar kids become one of the greatest successes in pop music history? You ask four guys, you get four different answers." *Jersey Boys* is the story of the legendary Four Seasons, blue-collar boys who formed a singing group and reached the heights of rock 'n' roll stardom.

Sebastian Arcelus, Jarrod Spector, Dominic Nolfi and Matt Bogart

Legally Blonde

Palace Theatre; First Preview: April 3, 2007; Opening Night: April 29, 2007; Closed October 19, 2008; 30 previews, 595 performances

Music and lyrics by Laurence O'Keefe and Nell Benjamin, book by Heather Hatch; based on the novel by Amanda Brown and the MGM motion picture; Produced by Hal Luftig, Fox Theatricals, Dori Berinstein, James L. Nederlander, Independent Presenters Network, Roy Furman, Amanda Lipitz, Broadway Asia, Barbara Whitman, FWPM Group, Ruth Hendel/Cheryl Wiesenfeld, Hal Golberg/David Binder, James D. Stern/Douglas L. Meyer, Robert Bartner-Michael A. Jenkins/Albert Nocciolino, Warner Trepp, in association with MGM ON STAGE, Darcie Denkert, Dean Stobler; Produced for Fox Theatricals by Kristin Caskey and Mike Isaacson; Director/Choreographer, Jerry Mitchell; Music Director/Conductor, James Sampliner; Orchestrations, Christopher Jahnke; Arrangements, Laurence O'Keefe & James Sampliner; Music Coordinator, Michael Keller; Sets, David Rockwell; Costumes, Gregg Barnes; Lighting, Kenneth Posner & Paul Miller; Sound, Acme Sound Partners; Casting, Telsey + Company; Hair, David Brian Brown; Associate Director, Marc Bruni; Associate Choreographer, Denis Jones; Technical Supervisor, Theatresmith Inc.; Animal Trainer, William Berloni; Production Stage Manager, Bonnie L. Becker; General Management, Nina Lannan Associates/Maggie Brohn; Marketing, TMG–The Marketing Group; Associate Producers, PMC Productions, Yasuhiro Kawana, Andrew Asnes/Adam Zotovich; Company Managers, Kimberly Kelley, Nathan Gehan; Stage Manager, Kimberly Russell; Assistant Stage Manager, Scott Rowen; Dance Captains, Rusty Mowery, Michelle Kittrell; Dialect Coach, Stephen Gabis; Fight Director, Thomas Schall; Makeup, Justen M. Brosnan; Additional Arrangements, Alex Lacamoire; Music Copyist, Emily Grishman; Synthesizer Programmer, Leland Music Company; Dog Handlers, William Berloni, Rob Cox; Advertising, Serino-Coyne; Press, Barlow · Hartman, Carol Fineman, Kevin Robak; Cast recording: Sh-K-Boom/Ghostlight Records 4423

Laura Bell Bundy, Bruiser and Christian Borle

Orfeh and the Company (photos by Paul Kolnik)

CAST Elle Woods **Laura Bell Bundy**[*1]; Warner Huntington III **Richard H. Blake**; Vivienne Kensington **Kate Shindle**; Emmett Forrest **Christian Borle**; Professor Callahan **Michael Rupert**; Paulette **Orfeh**; Serena **Tracy Jai Edwards**; Margot **Kate Rockwell**; Pilar **Asmeret Ghebremichael**; Shandi/Brooke Wyndam **Nicolette Hart**; Kate/Chutney **Stephanie Fittro**; Leilani **Becky Gulsvig**[*2]; Cece/DA Joyce Riley **Michelle Kittrell**[*3]; Kristine **April Berry**; Gabby **Beth Curry**[*4]; Veronica/Enid **Natalie Joy Johnson**[*5]; Judge **Amber Efé**; Mom/Whitney **Gaelen Gilliland**[*6]; Grandmaster Chad/Dewey/Kyle **Andy Karl**[*7]; Dad/Winthrop **Kevin Pariseau**; Carlos/Lowell **Matthew Risch**[*8]; Padamadan/Nikos **Manuel Herrera**; Aaron/Guard **Bryce Ryness**[*9]; Pforzhiemer **Jason Gillman**; Bruiser **Chico**; Rufus **Chloe**; Harvard Students, Marching Band, Cheerleaders, Inmates, Salespeople **Nathan Balser**[*10], **April Berry, Paul Canaan, Beth Curry, Tracy Jai Edwards, Amber Efé, Stephanie Fittro, Asmeret Ghebremichael, Gaelen Gilliland**[*6], **Jason Gillman, Becky Gulsvig**[*2], **Manuel Herrera, Natalie Joy Johnson**[*5], **Andy Karl**[*7], **Nick Kenkel, Michelle Kittrell**[*3], **Kevin Pariseau, Matthew Risch**[*8], **Kate Rockwell, Bryce Ryness**[*9]; Swings[*11] **Lindsay Nicole Chambers, Tiffany Engen, Rod Harrelson, Rusty Mowery, Dani Spieler, Casey Leigh Thompson**

*Succeeded by: 1. Bailey Hanks (7/23/08) 2. Autumn Hurlburt 3. Emily Padgett 4. Dani Spieler 5. Lucia Spina (7/23/08) 6. Cara Massey 7. Ven Daniel (7/23/08), Bryan West (9/10/08) 8. Kyle Brown 9. Barry Anderson 10. Josh Franklin 11. Jody Reynard, Eric Hatch

ORCHESTRA James Sampliner (Conductor/keyboard 1); Jason DeBord (Associate Conductor/keyboard 2); Antoine Silverman (violin/Concert Master); Jonathan Dinklage (viola); Peter Sachon (cello); Dave Trigg; Bud Burridge (trumpets); Keith O'Quinn (trombone); Vincent Della-Rocca, Dan Willis, Chad Smith (reeds); Roger Wendt (French horn); Greg Joseph (drums); Mark Vanderpoel (bass); Matt Gallagher (keyboard 3); John Putnam, Kenny Brescia (guitars); Pablo Rieppi (percussion)

MUSICAL NUMBERS Omigod You Guys, Serious, Daughter of Delta Nu, What You Want, The Harvard Variations, Blood in the Water, Positive, Ireland, Ireland (reprise), Serious (reprise), Chip on My Shoulder, So Much Better, Whipped Into Shape, Take It Like a Man, Bend and Snap, There! Right There!, Legally Blonde, Legally Blonde Remix, Omigod You Guys (reprise), Find My Way/Finale

SETTING The Delta Nu house in Southern California and Harvard Law campus in Cambridge, Massachusetts. New York premiere of a new musical presented in two acts. For original production credits see *Theatre World* Vol. 63, page 72.

SYNOPSIS Sorority star Elle Woods doesn't take "no" for an answer. When her boyfriend dumps her for someone more "serious," Elle puts down the credit card, hits the books and sets out to go where no Delta Nu has gone before: Harvard Law. Along the way, Elle proves that being true to herself never goes out of style.

Les Liaisons Dangereuses

American Airlines Theatre; First Preview: April 12, 2008; Opening Night: May 1, 2008; Closed July 6, 2008; 22 previews, 77 performances

Written by Christopher Hampton, based on the novel by Choderlos de Laclos; Produced by the Roundabout Theatre Company (Todd Haimes, Artistic Director; Harold Wolpert, Managing Director; Julia C. Levy, Executive Director); Director, Rufus Norris; Sets, Scott Pask; Costumes, Katrina Lindsay; Lighting, Donald Holder; Sound, Paul Arditti; Hair/Wigs, Paul Huntley; Voice & Speech Coach, Deborah Hecht; Fight Director, Rick Sordelet; Properties Coordinator, Kathy Fabian/Propstar; Production Stage Manager, Arthur Gaffin; Stage Manager, Jamie Greathouse; Casting, Jim Carnahan; General Manager, Sydney Beers; Technical Supervisor, Steve Beers; Marketing/Sales, David B. Steffen; Development, Jeffory Lawson; Founding Director, Gene Feist; Associate Artistic Director, Scott Ellis; Education Director, David A. Miller; Finance, Susan Neiman; Telesales, Daniel Weiss; Sales Operations, Charlie Garbowski Jr.; Company Manager, Nichole Jennino; Assistant Director, Wes Grantom; ACM, Carly DiFulvio; Associate Design: Jeff Hinchee (set), Mitchell Bloom (costumes), Caroline Chao (lighting), David Stephen Baker (sound); Assistant to Costume Designer, Daryl Stone; Production: Glenn Merwede (carpenter/automation), Brian Maiuri (electrician), Barb Bartel (deck electrician), Andrew Forste & Carmel Sheehan (properties), Chris Mattingly (flyman), Jill Anania (sound op), Susan J. Fallon (wardrobe supervisor); Brittany Jones-Pugh, Susan Kroeter, Luana Michaels (dressers); Rehearsal Pianist, Chris Fenwick; Press, Boneau/Bryan-Brown, Matt Polk, Jessica Johnson, Amy Kass

CAST La Marquise de Merteuil **Laura Linney;** Madame de Volanges **Kristine Nielsen;** Cécile Volanges **Mamie Gummer;** Major-domo **Tim McGeever;** La Vicomte de Valmont **Ben Daniels;** Azolan **Derek Cecil;** Madame de Rosemonde **Siân Phillips;** La Présidente de Tourvel **Jessica Collins;** Émilie **Rosie Benton;** Le Chevalier Danceny **Benjamin Walker;** Footman/Tenor **Kevin Duda;** Maid/Soprano **Jane Pfitsch;** Servants **Delphi Harrington, Nicole Orth-Pallavicini**

UNDERSTUDIES Nicole Orth-Pallavicini (Merteuil, Mme. de Volanges), Jane Pfitsch (Cécile, Émilie), Kevin Duda (Major-domo, Danceny), Tim McGeever (Valmont, Azolan), Delphi Harrington (Mme. de Rosemonde), Rosie Benton (Tourvel)

SETTING Various salons and bedrooms in a number of houses and châteaux in and around Paris, and in the Bois de Vincennes, one autumn and winter in the 1780's. Revival of a play presented in 18 scenes in two acts.

SYNOPSIS The battle of the sexes springs to life in this modern classic Olivier-winning play. For long-time friends and occasional lovers Vicomte de Valmont and Marquise de Merteuil love is simply a game of chess. But in a few false moves, they're about to find themselves locked in the ultimate checkmate. Filled with seduction, betrayal, and plenty of illicit passion, this dark comedy paints the pre-Revolutionary French aristocracy in all its cynicism and decadence.

Ben Daniels and Laura Linney (photos by Joan Marcus)

Ben Daniels and Mamie Gummer

Tshidi Manye and the Company

Blake Hammond and Danny Rutigliano (photos by Joan Marcus)

The Lion King

Minskoff Theatre; First Preview: October 15, 1997; Opening Night: November 13, 1997; 33 previews, 4,789 performances as of May 31, 2009

Music by Elton John, lyrics by Tim Rice, additional music and lyrics by Lebo M, Mark Mancina, Jay Rifkin, Julie Taymor, Hans Zimmer; book by Roger Allers and Irene Mecchi, adapted from screenplay by Ms. Mecchi, Jonathan Roberts and Linda Woolverton; Produced by Walt Disney Theatrical Productions (Peter Schneider, President; Thomas Schumacher, Executive VP); Director, Julie Taymor; Choreography, Garth Fagan; Orchestrations, Robert Elhai, David Metzger, Bruce Fowler; Music Director, Joseph Church; Sets, Richard Hudson; Costumes/Masks/Puppets, Julie Taymor; Lighting, Donald Holder; Masks/Puppets, Michael Curry; Sound, Tony Meola/Steve Canyon Kennedy; Hair/Makeup, Michael Ward; Projections, Geoff Puckett; Technical Director, David Benken; General Manager, Alan Levey; Project Manager, Nina Essman; Production Stage Manager, Ron Vodicka; Stage Manager, Antonia Gianino; Assistant Stage Managers, Victoria A. Epstein, Arabella Powell; Associate Director, Jeff Lee; Music Director/Supervisor, Colin Welford; Resident Director, Jen Bender; Resident Dance Supervisor, Ruthlyn Salomons; Associate Conductor, Karl Jurman; Executive Music Producer, Chris Montan; Vocal Arrangements, Lebo M; Company Manager, Steven Chaikelson; Associate Producer, Donald B. Frantz; Casting, Jay Binder; Original Press, Boneau/Bryan-Brown (to October); Current Press, Disney Theatricals, Dennis Crowley, Adriana Douzos, Lindsay Braverman; Cast recording: Walt Disney 60802-7

CAST Rafiki **Tshidi Manye;** Mufasa **Nathaniel Stampley;** Sarabi **Jean Michelle Grier;** Zazu **Jeff Binder;** Scar **Derek Smith;** Young Simba[*1] **Guy V. Barfield II** or **Shavar McIntosh;** Young Nala[*2] **Halle Vargas Sullivan** or **NicKayla Tucker;** Shenzi **Bonita J. Hamilton;** Banzai **James Brown-Orleans;** Ed **Enrique Segura;** Timon **Danny Rutigliano;** Pumbaa **Jim Ferris[*3];** Simba **Wallace Smith[*4];** Nala **Kissy Simmons[*5];** Ensemble[*6] Singers: **Alvin Crawford, Bongi Duma, Jean Michelle Grier, Michael Alexander Henry, Meena T. Jahi, Joel Karie, Ron Kunene, S'bu Ngema, Selloane Albertina Nkhela, Mpume Sikakane, L. Steven Taylor, Rema Webb, Kyle Wrentz, Kenny Redell Williams;** Dancers: **Kristina Michelle Bethel, Mucuy Bolles, Camille M. Brown, Michelle Brugal, Michelle Aguilar Camaya, Gabriel Croom, Alicia Fisher, Nicole Adell Johnson, Gregory A. King, Lisa Lewis, Brandon Louis Matthieus, Sheryl McCallum, Ray Mercer, Theresa Nguyen, Brandon Christopher O'Neal, Robin Payne, Natalie Ridley, Ryan Brooke Taylor, Phillip W. Turner;** Swings **Sean Bradford, Garland Days, Angelica Edwards, Tony James, Dennis Johnston, Sophia N. Stephens, Willa-Noel Montague;** Standbys **John E. Brady[*7]** (Timon, Pumbaa, Zazu), **Jack Koenig[*8]** (Scar, Pumbaa)

*Succeeded by: 1. Clifford Lee Dickson or Jeremy Gumbs 2. Chantylla Johnson or Cypress Eden Smith 3. Tom Alan Robbins 4. Dashaun Young 5. Ta'Rea Campbell 6. Charity De Loera, Lindiwe Dlamini, Christopher Freeman, Nicole Adell Johnson, LaQuet Sharnell 7. Jim Ferris 8. Thom Christopher Warren

MUSICAL NUMBERS Circle of Life, Morning Report, I Just Can't Wait to Be King, Chow Down, They Live in You, Be Prepared, Hakuna Matata, One by One, Madness of King Scar, Shadowland, Endless Night, Can You Feel the Love Tonight, King of Pride Rock/Finale

A musical presented in two acts. For original production credits see *Theatre World* Vol. 54, page 20. Originally opened at the New Amsterdam Theatre and transferred to the Minskoff Theatre June 13, 2006.

SYNOPSIS Based on the 1994 Disney animated feature film, *The Lion King* tells the story of the adventures of Simba, a young lion cub, as he struggles to accept the responsibilities of adulthood and his destined role as king.

The Little Mermaid

Lunt-Fontanne Theatre; First Preview: November 3, 2007; Opening Night: January 10, 2008; 50 previews, 581 performances as of May 31, 2009

Music by Alan Menken, lyrics by Howard Ashman and Glenn Slater, book by Doug Wright; based on the Hans Christian Anderson story and the Disney film produced by Howard Ashman & John Musker and written and directed by John Musker & Ron Clements; Director, Francesca Zambello; Choreography, Stephen Mear; Music Director/Incidental Music/Vocal Arrangements, Michael Kosarin; Orchestrations, Danny Troob; Sets, George Tsypin; Costumes, Tatiana Noginova; Lighting, Natasha Katz; Sound, John Shivers; Hair, David Brian Brown; Makeup, Angelina Avallone; Projections/Video, Sven Ortel; Dance Arrangements, David Chase; Music Coordinator, Michael Keller; Fight Director, Rick Sordelet; Casting, Tara Rubin; Associate Producer, Todd Lacy; Associate Director, Brian Hill; Associate Choreographer, Tara Young; Technical Director, David Benken; Production Stage Manager/Supervisor, Clifford Schwartz; Aerial Design, Pichón Baldinu; Dialogue/Vocal Coach, Deborah Hecht; Company Manager, Randy Meyer/Eduardo Castro; Assistant Company Manager, Margie Freeswick; Production Manager, Jane Abramson; Stage Manager, Theresa Bailey; Assistant Stage Managers, Kenneth J. McGee/Robert M. Armitage, Matthew Aaron Stern, Sarah Tschipke/Alexis Shorter; Dance Captain, Joanne Manning/Jason Snow; Fight Captain/Assistant Dance Captain, James Brown III; Associate Design: Peter Eastman (set), Tracy Christensen (costumes), Yael Lubetzky (lighting), David Patridge (sound), Jonathan Carter (hair), Peter Acken, Katy Tucker (projection), Angela Phillips (aerial); Magic/Illusion Design, Joe Eddie Fairchild; Sculptor, Arturs Virtmanis; Automated Lights, Aland Henderson, Joel Shier; Assistant Design: Gaetane Bertol, Larry Brown, Kelly Hanso, Niki Hernandez-Adams, Nathan Heverin, Rachel Short Janocko, Jee an Jung, Mimi Lien, Frank McCullough, Arnulfo Maldonado, Robert Pyzocha, Chisato Uno (set), Brian J. Bustos, Amy Clark (costumes), Craig Stelzenmuller, Richard Swan (lighting), Thomas Augustine (hair/hair supervisor); Additional Orchestrations, Larry Hochman, Michael Starobin; Electronic Music Design, Andrew Barrett; Music Preparation, Anixter Rice Music Service; Associate to Mr. Menken, Rick Kunis; Advertising, Serino-Coyne; Original Press, Boneau/Bryan-Brown (to October); Current Press, Disney Theatricals, Dennis Crowley, Adriana Douzos, Lindsay Braverman; Cast recording: Walt Disney Records D000108102

Eric LaJuan Summers, Faith Prince and Tyler Maynard
(photos by Joan Marcus)

Sean Palmer and Sierra Boggess

CAST Pilot **Merwin Foard**; Prince Eric **Sean Palmer**; Grimsby **Jonathan Freeman**; King Triton **Norm Lewis**; Sebastian **Tituss Burgess**[*1]; Ariel **Sierra Boggess**; Flounder **Trevor Braun** or **Brian D'Addario**; Scuttle **Eddie Korbich**; Gulls **Robert Creighton**[*2], **Tim Federle**[*3], **Arbender Robinson**[*4]; Ursula **Sherie Rene Scott**[*5]; Flotsam **Tyler Maynard**; Jetsam **Derrick Baskin**[*6]; Carlotta **Heidi Blickenstaff**[*7]; Chef Louis **John Treacy Egan**[*8]; Ensemble **Adrian Bailey**[*9], **Cathryn Basile**, **Heidi Blickenstaff**[*7], **Robert Creighton**[*2], **Cicily Daniels**, **John Treacy Egan**[*8], **Tim Federle**[*3], **Merwin Foard**, **Ben Hartley**, **Michelle Lookadoo**, **Alan Mingo Jr.**, **Zakiya Young Mizen**, **Arbender Robinson**[*4], **Bahiyah Sayyed Gaines**[*10], **Bret Shuford**, **Chelsea Morgan Stock**, **Kay Trinidad**, **Daniel J. Watts**[*11]; Swings[*12] **James Brown III**, **Meredith Inglesby**, **Joanne Manning**, **Betsy Morgan**, **Jason Snow**, **Price Waldman**

UNDERSTUDIES Adrian Bailey[*9] (King Triton), Derrick Baskin (Sebastian), Heidi Blickenstaff[*7] (Ursula), Robert Creighton[*2] (Scuttle), Cicily Daniels (Ursula), Tim Federle[*3] (Jetsam, Scuttle), Merwin Foard (Grimsby, King Triton), Alan Mingo Jr. (Sebastian), Betsy Morgan (Ariel), Arbender J. Robinson[*4] (Prince Eric), Bret Shuford (Flotsam, Prince Eric), J.J. Singleton/Cody Hanford (Flounder), Jason Snow (Flotsam, Grimsby, Jetsam), Chelsea Morgan Stock (Ariel), Price Waldman (Flotsam, Grimsby, Jetsam)

*Succeeded by: 1. Alan Mingo Jr (8/5/08), Tituss Burgess (10/28/08), Rogelio Douglas Jr (12/9/08) 2. Joe Abraham 3. Enrique Brown 4. Tyrone A. Jackson 5. Heidi Blickenstaff (1/29/09), Faith Prince (4/7/09) 6. Eric LaJuan Summers 7. Meredith Inglesby 8. Robert Creighton 9. J.C. Montgomery 10. Amy Hall 11. Ephraim M. Sykes, Rhett George 12. Julie Barnes, J. Austin Eyer, Lyndy Franklin, Courtney Laine Mazza, Michelle Pruiett

ORCHESTRA Michael Kosarin (Conductor); Greg Anthony (Associate Conductor/keyboard 2); Suzanne Ornstein (Concert Master); Mineko Yajima (violin); Roger Shell, Deborah Assael (celli); Nicholas Marchione, Frank Greene (trumpets); Gary Grimaldi (trombone); Jeff Caswell (bass trombone/tuba); Steven Kenyon, David Young, Marc Phaneuf (reeds); Zohar Schondorf (French horn); Aron Accurso (keyboard 1); Andrew Grobengieser (keyboard 3); Richard Sarpola (bass); John Redsecker (drums); Joe Passaro (percussion)

MUSICAL NUMBERS Overture, Fathoms Below, Daughters of Triton, The World Above, Human Stuff, I Want the Good Times Back, Part of Your World, Storm at Sea, Part of Your World (reprise), She's in Love, Her Voice, The World Above (reprise), Under the Sea, Sweet Child, Poor Unfortunate Souls, Entr'acte, Positoovity, Beyond My Wildest Dreams, Les Poissons, Les Poissons (reprise), One Step Closer, I Want the Good Times Back (reprise), Kiss the Girl, Sweet Child (reprise), If Only, The Contest, Poor Unfortunate Souls (reprise), If Only (reprise), Finale

World premiere of a new musical presented in two acts. The show had an out-of-town tryout in Denver, Colorado at the Denver Center, July 26, 2007.

SYNOPSIS Based on the 1989 Disney film and the Hans Christian Anderson fairy tale, *The Little Mermaid* is set in a magical kingdom beneath the sea, where a beautiful young mermaid named Ariel longs to leave her ocean home to live in the world above. But first, she'll have to defy her father, the king of the sea, escape the clutches of an evil sea witch and convince a prince that she's the girl with the perfect voice.

Mamma Mia!

Judy McLane, Carolee Carmello, Gina Ferrall

Winter Garden Theatre; First Preview: October 5, 2001: Opening Night: October 18, 2001; 14 previews, 3,152 performances as of May 31, 2009

Book by Catherine Johnson, music, lyrics, and orchestrations by Benny Andersson, Björn Ulvaeus, some songs with Stig Anderson; Produced by Judy Craymer, Richard East and Björn Ulvaeus for Littlestar Services Limited, in association with Universal; Director, Phyllida Lloyd; Sets and Costumes, Mark Thompson; Lighting, Howard Harrison; Sound, Andrew Bruce & Bobby Aitken; Wigs, Paul Huntley; Choreography, Anthony Van Laast; Musical Supervision/ Orchestrations, Martin Koch; Associate Musical Director, David Holcenberg; Musical Coordination, Michael Keller; Associate Director, Robert McQueen; Associate Choreographer, Nichola Treherne; Technical Supervisor, Arthur Siccardi; General Manager, Nina Lannan; Associate General Manager/Company Manager, Rina L. Saltzman; Production Stage Manager, Andrew Fenton; Stage Managers, Sherry Cohen, Dean R. Greer; Dance Captain, Janet Rothermel; Resident Director, Martha Banta; Casting, Tara Rubin; Music Coordinator, Michael Keller; Synthesizer Programmer, Nicholas Gilpin; Press, Boneau/Bryan-Brown; London Cast recording: Polydor 543 115 2

CAST Sophie Sheridan **Carey Anderson**[*1]; Ali **Veronica J. Kuehn**[*2]; Lisa **Samantha Eggers**; Tanya **Judy McLane**; Rosie **Gina Ferrall**; Donna Sheridan **Carolee Carmello**; Sky **Andy Kelso**[*3]; Pepper **Ben Gettinger**; Eddie **Raymond J. Lee**; Harry Bright **Ben Livingston**; Bill Austin **Pearce Bunting**[*4]; Sam Carmichael **Christopher Shyer**[*5]; Father Alexandrios **Bryan Scott Johnson**; Ensemble[*6] **Brent Black, Timothy Booth, Isaac Calpito, Allyson Carr, Meghann Dreyfuss, Lori Haley Fox, Frankie James Grande, Heidi Godt, Corey Greenan, Bryan Scott Johnson, Monica Kapoor, Corinne Melançon, Courtney Reed, Amina Robinson, Gerard Salvador, Traci Victoria, Leah Zepel**; Swings[*7] **Lanene Charters, Matthew Farver, Janet Rothermel, Ryan Sander, Collette Simmons**

UNDERSTUDIES Brent Black (Bill, Sam, Father Alexandrios), Timothy Booth (Harry, Bill, Sam), Isaac Calpito (Pepper), Lanene Charters (Lisa), Meghann Dreyfuss (Sophie), Samantha Eggers (Sophie), Matthew Farver (Eddie, Father Alexandrios), Lori Haley Fox (Tanya, Rosie, Donna), Frankie James Grande (Eddie), Heidi Godt (Donna, Tanya, Rosie), Corey Greenan (Sky), Bryan Scott Johnson (Harry, Bill), Monica Kapoor (Lisa), Veronica J. Kuehn[*2] (Sophie), Corinne Melançon (Donna, Tanya), Courtney Reed (Ali), Amina Robinson (Ali), Ryan Sander (Sky, Eddie), Gerard Salvador (Pepper), Leah Zepel (Ali)

*Succeeded by: 1. Carrie Manolakos (6/4/08), Alison Case (9/24/08), Brandi Burkhardt (1/27/09) 2. Amina Robinson (7/9/08) 3. Chris Peluso (9/24/08) 4. Michael Pemberton (8/13/08), Pearce Bunting (9/9/08) 5. Sean Allan Krill (9/24/08) 6. Meredith Akins, Ian Paget, Robin Levine, Tony Gonzales 7. Jon-Erik Goldberg, Joi Danielle Price, Britt Shubow

ORCHESTRA Wendy Bobbitt Cavett (Conductor/keyboard); Rob Preuss (Associate Conductor/keyboard 3); Steve Marzullo (keyboard 2); Myles Chase (keyboard 4); Doug Quinn, Jeff Campbell (guitars); Paul Adamy (bass); Gary Tillman (drums); David Nyberg (percussion)

MUSICAL NUMBERS Chiquitita; Dancing Queen; Does Your Mother Know?; Gimme! Gimmie! Gimmie!; Honey, Honey; I Do, I Do, I Do, I Do; I Have a Dream; Knowing Me Knowing You; Lay All Your Love on Me; Mamma Mia; Money Money Money; One of Us; Our Last Summer; Slipping Through My Fingers; S.O.S.; Super Trouper; Take a Chance on Me; Thank You For the Music; The Name of the Game; The Winner Takes All; Under Attack; Voulez-Vous

SETTING Time: A wedding weekend. Place: A tiny Greek island. A musical presented in two acts. For original production credits see *Theatre World* Vol. 58, Page 27.

SYNOPSIS *Mamma Mia!* collects a group of hit songs by the Swedish pop group ABBA and shapes them around the story of a single mother coping with her young daughter's marriage on a picturesque Greek isle. While the daughter plans her future with the love of her life, her mother is haunted by three different men who may or may not be her daughter's father.

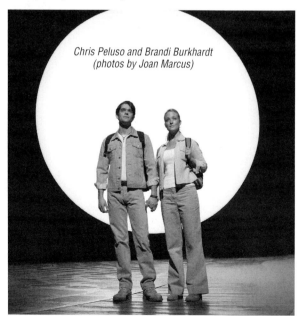
Chris Peluso and Brandi Burkhardt (photos by Joan Marcus)

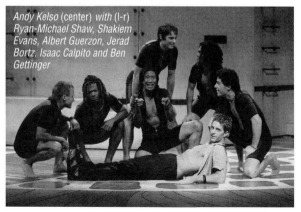
Andy Kelso (center) with (l-r) Ryan-Michael Shaw, Shakiem Evans, Albert Guerzon, Jerad Bortz, Isaac Calpito and Ben Gettinger

Mary Poppins

New Amsterdam Theatre; First Preview: October 14, 2006; Opening Night: November 16, 2006; 30 previews, 1,061 performances as of May 31, 2009

Rebecca Luker and Daniel Jenkins (photos by Joan Marcus)

Music and lyrics by Richard M. Sherman and Robert B. Sherman, book by Julian Fellowes, new songs and additional music/lyrics by George Stiles and Anthony Drewe; based on the stories of P.L. Travers and the 1964 Walt Disney Film; Produced and co-created by Cameron Mackintosh; Produced for Disney Theatrical Productions by Thomas Schumacher; Director, Richard Eyre; Co-Direction/Choreography, Matthew Bourne; Sets/Costumes, Bob Crowley; Lighting, Howard Harrison; Co-choreographer, Stephen Mear; Music Supervisor, David Caddick; Music Director, Brad Haak; Orchestrations, William David Brohn; Sound, Steve Canyon Kennedy; Dance/Vocal Arrangements, George Stiles; Associates: Anthony Lyn (director), Geoffrey Garratt (choreography) James Thane (producer); Makeup, Naomi Donne; Casting, Tara Rubin; Technical Director, David Benken; Production Stage Manager, Tom Capps; Resident Choreographer, Tom Kosis; Company Manager, Dave Ehle; Associate GM, Alan Wasser; Stage Management, Mark Dobrow, Valerie Lau-Kee Lai, Jason Trubitt, Michael Wilhoite; Dance Captain, Rommy Sandhu; Dialect/Vocal Coach, Deborah Hecht; Wigs, Angela Cobbin; Illusions, Jim Steinmeyer; Technical Director, David Benken; Production Supervisor, Patrick Eviston; Flying, Raymond King; Automation, Steve Stackle, David Helk; Properties, Victor Amerling, Tim Abel, Joe Bivone, John Saye; Keyboard Programming, Stuart Andrews; Music Contractor, David Lai; Advertising, Serino-Coyne; Music Copyist, Emily Grisham Music Preparation; Original Press, Boneau/Bryan-Brown (to October); Current Press, Disney Theatricals, Dennis Crowley, Adriana Douzos, Lindsay Braverman; London Cast recording: Disney Theatricals 61391-7

CAST Bert **Gavin Lee**[*1]; George Banks **Daniel Jenkins**; Winifred Banks **Rebecca Luker**; Jane Banks[*2] **Nichole Bocchi** or **Alexandra Berro** or **Lila Coogan**; Michael Banks[*3] **Matthew Gumley** or **Daniel Marconi** or **Jacob Levine**; Katie Nanna/Annie **Megan Osterhaus**; Policeman **Corey Skaggs**; Miss Lark **Ann Arvia**[*4]; Admiral Boom/Bank Chairman **Michael McCarty**[*5]; Mrs. Brill **Jane Carr**; Robertson Ay **Mark Price**; Mary Poppins **Ashley Brown**[*6]; Park Keeper **James Hindman**; Neleus **Brian Letendre**[*7]; Queen Victoria/Miss Smythe/Miss Andrew **Ruth Gottschall**; Von Hussler/Jack-In-A-Box **Sean McCourt**; Northbrook **Matt Loehr**[*8]; Bird Woman **Cass Morgan**[*9]; Mrs. Corry **Janelle Anne Robinson**; Fannie **Vasthy E. Mompoint**[*10]; Valentine **Dominic Roberts**[*11]; William **T. Oliver Reid**; Mr. Punch **James Hindman**; Glamorous Doll **Catherine Walker**; Ensemble[*12] **Ann Arvia**[*4], **Kristin Carbone, Case Dillard, Ruth Gottschall, Eric Hatch, James Hindman, Mark Ledbetter, Brian Letendre**[*7], **Matt**

Loehr[*8], **Melissa Lone, Michelle Lookadoo, Tony Mankser, Michael McCarty**[*5], **Jeff Metzler, Sean McCourt, Vasthy E. Mompoint**[*10], **Jesse Nager, Kathleen Nanni, Megan Osterhaus, Jayne Paterson, T. Oliver Reid, Dominic Roberts**[*11], **Janelle Anne Robinson, Nick Sanchez, Laura Shutter, Shekitra Starke, Catherine Walker, Kevin Samual Yee**; Swings[*13] **Pam Bradley, Chad Sieb, Nicholas Dromard, Suzanne Hylenski, Stephanie Kurtzuba, Rommy Sandhu, Sarah Solie**

*Succeeded by: 1. Adam Fiorentino (10/9/08) 2. Kelsey Fowler or Alison Jaye Horowitz or Cassady Leonard 3. Neil McCaffrey or Zach Rand or Marlon Sherman 4. Jessica Sheridan 5. Jeff Steitzer 6. Scarlett Strallen (10/9/08) 7. Nick Kepley 8. Sam Strasfeld 9. Ann Arvia 10. Amber Owens 11. Dennis Moench 12. Additional Ensemble replacements: Aaron J. Albano, Barrett Davis, Stephanie Stubbins. 13. Kathy Calahan, Brian Collier, Suzanne Hylenski, Jonathan Richard Sandler

MUSICIANS Brad Haak (Conductor); Kristen Blodgette (Associate Conductor/2nd keyboard); Milton Granger (Piano); Peter Donovan (bass); Dave Ratajczak (drums); Daniel Haskins (percussion), Nate Brown (guitar/banjo/E-Bow); Russ Rizner, Larry DiBello (horns); Jon Sheppard, Louis Hanzlik (trumpets); Marc Donatelle (trombone/euphonium); Randy Andos (bass trombone/tuba); Paul Garment (clarinet); Alexandra Knoll (oboe/English horn); Brian Miller (flutes); Stephanie Cummins (cello)

MUSICAL NUMBERS Chim Chim Cher-ee, Cherry Tree Lane (Part 1), The Perfect Nanny, Cherry Tree Lane (Part 2), Practically Perfect, Jolly Holiday, Cherry Tree Lane (reprise), Being Mrs. Banks, Jolly Holiday (reprise), A Spoonful of Sugar, Precision and Order, A Man Has Dreams, Feed the Birds, Supercalifragilisticexpialidocious, Temper, Temper, Chim, Chim, Cher-ee (reprise), Cherry Tree Lane (reprise), Brimstone and Treacle (Part 1), Let's Go Fly A Kite, Good For Nothing, Being Mrs. Banks (reprise), Brimstone and Treacle (Part 2), Practically Perfect (reprise), Chim Chim Cher-ee (reprise), Step in Time, A Man Has Dreams, A Spoonful of Sugar (reprise), Anything Can Happen, A Spoonful of Sugar (reprise), A Shooting Star

SETTING In and around the Banks' household somewhere in London at the turn of the last century. American premiere of a new musical presented in two acts. For original production credits, see *Theatre World* Vol. 63, page 41. Originally opened in London at the Prince Edward Theatre on December 15, 2004.

SYNOPSIS Based on the Walt Disney classic film and the novels by P.L. Travers, *Mary Poppins* is the story of the Banks family and how their lives change after the arrival of nanny Mary Poppins at their home at 17 Cherry Tree Lane in London.

Scarlett Strallen and Adam Fiorentino

Monty Python's Spamalot

Shubert Theatre; First Preview: February 14, 2004; Opening Night: March 17, 2005; Closed January 11, 2009; 35 previews, 1,574 performances

Book and lyrics by Eric Idle, music by John DuPrez and Eric Idle; based on the screenplay of *Monty Python and the Holy Grail* by Eric Idle, John Cleese, Terry Gilliam, Terry Jones, Michael Palin and Graham Chapman; Produced by Boyett Ostar Productions, The Shubert Organization, Arielle Tepper Madover, Stephanie McClelland, Lawrence Horowitz, Élan V. McAllister, Allan S. Gordon, Independent Presenters Network, Roy Furman, GRS Associates, Jam Theatricals, TGA Entertainment Ltd., Clear Channel Entertainment; Associate Producer, Randi Grossman, Tisch/Avnet Financial; Director, Mike Nichols; Choreography, Casey Nicholaw; Sets & Costumes, Tim Hatley; Lighting, Hugh Vanstone; Sound, Acme Sound Partners; Hair/Wigs, David Brian Brown; Special Effects, Gregory Meeh; Projections, Elaine J. McCarthy; Music Director/Vocal Arrangements, Todd Ellison; Orchestrations, Larry Hochman; Music Arrangements, Glen Kelly; Music Coordinator, Michael Keller; Casting, Tara Rubin; Associate Director, Peter Lawrence; Production Stage Manager, Frank Lombardi; Associate Choreography, Darlene Wilson; General Management, 101 Productions Ltd. Marketing, HHC Marketing; Company Management, Edward Nelson, Katharine Croke; Production Management, Aurora Productions/Gene O'Donovan; Fight Director, David DeBesse; Makeup, Joseph A. Campayno; Stage Management, Jim Woolley, Allison Lee, Kenneth J. McGee; Dance Captain, Pamela Remler/Callie Carter, Scott Taylor/Lee Wilkins; Fight Captain, Greg Reuter/Thomas Cannizzaro; Vocal Coach, Kate Wilson; Magic Consultant, Marshall Magoon; Puppetry Consultant, Michael Curry; Music Copying, Emily Grishman; Advertising, Serino-Coyne; Press, Boneau/Bryan-Brown, Adrian Bryan-Brown, Jackie Green, Aaron Meier, Christine Olver; Cast recording: Decca Broadway B0004265-02

Clay Aiken, Rick Holmes, Bradley Dean, Wally Dunn and Michael Siberry

CAST Historian/Not Dead Fred/French Guard,/Minstrel/Prince Herbert **Tom Deckman;** Mayor/Patsy/Guard 2 **David Hibbard**[*1]; King Arthur **Jonathan Hadary**[*2]; Sir Robin/Guard 1/Brother Maynard **Robert Petkoff**[*3]; Sir Lancelot/The French Taunter/Knight of Ni/Tim the Enchanter **Rick Holmes;** Sir Dennis Galahad/The Black Knight/Prince Herbert's Father **Bradley Dean;** Dennis' Mother/Sir Bedevere/Concorde **Steve Rosen**[*4]; The Lady of the Lake **Hannah Waddingham**[*5]; Sir Not Appearing/Monk **Kevin Covert**[*6]; Nun **Matthew Crowle;** God **John Cleese;** French Guards **Jonathan Brody**[*7], **Greg Reuter**[*8]; Minstrels **Emily Hsu, Brian J. Marcum, Greg Reuter**[*8]; Sir Bors **Brian J. Marcum;** Ensemble **Jonathan Brody**[*7], **Kevin Covert**[*6], **Matthew Crowle, Andrew Fitch, Jenny Hill, Emily Hsu, Brian J. Marcum, Abby O'Brien**[*9], **Ariel Reid**[*10], **Greg Reuter**[*8], **Vanessa Sonon, Brandy Wooten**[*11]; Standbys **Anthony Holds, Napiera Groves**[*12], **Michael O'Donnell;** Swings **Callie Carter**[*13], **Beth Johnson**[*14], **Pamela Remler, Rick Spaans, Lee A. Wilkins**[*15]

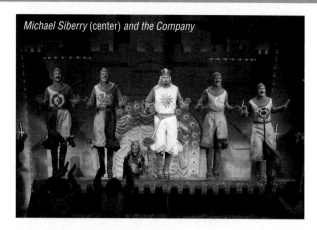

Michael Siberry (center) and the Company

*Succeeded by: 1. Drew Lachey (6/24/08), David Hibbard (9/16/08) 2. Stephen Collins (6/24/08), Michael Siberry (9/16/08) 3. Clay Aiken (9/19/08), Marin Moran (1/6/09) 4. Wally Dunn (6/17/08) 5. Marin Mazzie (6/17/08), Merle Dandridge (9/2/08) 6. Kevin Crewell 7. Thomas Cannizzaro 8. Gavin Lodge 9. Callie Carter 10. Nikki Della Penta 11.Stephanie Gibson 12. Mika Duncan 13. Kristie Kerwin 14. Piper Lindsay Arpan 15. Billy Sprague Jr.

ORCHESTRA Todd Ellison (Conductor); Antony Geralis (Associate Conductor/keyboards); Randy Cohen (Assistant Conductor/keyboards); Ann Labin (Concertmaster); Maura Giannini, Ming Yeh (violins); Richard Brice (viola); Diane Barere (cello); Ken Dybisz, Alden Banta (reeds); Craig Johnson, Anthony Gorruso (trumpets); Tim Albright (trombone); Theresa MacDonnell (French horn); Scott Kuney (guitars); Dave Kuhn (bass); Sean McDaniel (drums); Dave Mancuso (percussion)

MUSICAL NUMBERS Fisch Schlapping Song, King Arthur's Song, I Am Not Dead Yet, Come With Me, The Song That Goes Like This, All for One, Knights of the Round Table, The Song That Goes Like This (reprise), Find Your Grail, Run Away, Always Look on the Bright Side of Life, Brave Sir Robin, You Won't Succeed on Broadway, The Diva's Lament, Where Are You?, Here Are You, His Name Is Lancelot, I'm All Alone, The Song That Goes Like This (reprise), The Holy Grail, Find Your Grail Finale — Medley.

A new musical presented in two acts. For original production credits see *Theatre World* Vol. 61, page 55.

SYNOPSIS Telling the legendary tale of King Arthur and the Knights of the Round Table, and their quest for the Holy Grail, *Monty Python's Spamalot* features a chorus line of dancing divas and knights, flatulent Frenchmen, killer rabbits and one legless knight.

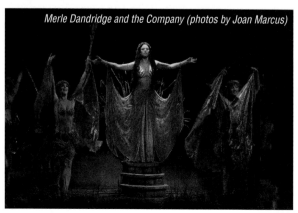

Merle Dandridge and the Company (photos by Joan Marcus)

Ethan Phillips, Dylan Baker

Laurie Metcalf (photos by Scott Landis)

November

Barrymore Theatre; First Preview: December 20, 2007; Opening Night: January 17, 2008; Closed July 13, 2008; 33 previews, 205 performances

Written by David Mamet; Produced by Jeffrey Richards, Jerry Frankel, Jam Theatricals, Bat-Barry Productions, Michael Cohl, Ergo Entertainment, Michael Filerman, Ronald Frankel, Barbara & Buddy Freitag, James Fuld Jr., Roy Furman, JK Productions, Harold A. Thau, Jamie deRoy/Ted Snowdon; Director, Joe Mantello; Set, Scott Pask; Costumes, Laura Bauer; Lighting, Paul Gallo; Casting, Telsey + Company; PSM, Jill Cordle; Technical Supervision, Hudson Theatrical Associates (Neil A. Mazzella, Sam Ellis, Irene Wang); General Management, Richards/Climan, Inc.(David R. Richards, Tamar Haimes, Laura Janik Cronin); Marketing Services, TMG; Company Manager, Bruce Klinger; Associate Producer/Assistant to Mr. Richards, Noah Himmelstein; Stage Manager, Neil Krasnow; Assistant Director, Stephanie Yankwitt; Associate Lighting, Phillip Rosenberg; Consultant, Darron L. West; Assistant to Mr. West, Matt Hubbs; Wigs, Paul Huntley, Martial Corneville; Assistant Set, Jeffrey Hinchee, Orit Carroll; Assistant Costumes, Bobby Tilley; General Management Associate, Jeromy Smith; Production: Nathan K. Claus (assistant), Frank Illo (carpenter), Jimmy Maloney (electrician), Denise J. Grillo (props), Kristine Bellerud (wardrobe supervisor), Erin Kennedy Lunsford (hair supervisor), Ken Brown (Mr. Lane's dresser), Rose Maire Cappelluti (dresser); Advertising, Serino Coyne; Press, Jeffrey Richards, Irene Gandy, Elon Rutberg

CAST Charles Smith **Nathan Lane;** Archer Brown **Dylan Baker;** A Representative of the National Association of Turkey By-Products Manufacturers **Ethan Phillips;** Clarice Bernstein **Laurie Metcalf;** Dwight Grackle **Michael Nichols**

STANDBYS Richard Kline (Charles Smith), Amy Hohn (Clarice Bernstein), Greg Stuhr (Archer Brown, Turkey Guy), Victor Talmadge (Dwight Grackle)

SETTING Morning, night, and morning; an office. World premiere of a new comedy presented in two acts.

SYNOPSIS Set just days before a major presidential election, *November* involves civil marriages, gambling casinos, lesbians, American Indians, presidential libraries, questionable pardons and campaign contributions.

Nathan Lane and Dylan Baker

Passing Strange

Belasco Theatre; First Preview: February 8, 2008; Opening Night: February 28, 2008; Closed July 20, 2008; 20 previews, 165 performances

Book and lyrics by Stew, music by Stew and Heidi Rodewald; Created in collaboration with Annie Dorsen; Produced by The Shubert Organization, Elizabeth Ireland McCann, Bill Kenwright, Chase Mishkin, Barbara & Buddy Freitag, Broadway Across America, Emily Fisher Landau, Peter May, Boyett Ostar, Ellie Hirschfeld/Jed Bernstein, Wendy Federman/Jacki B. Florin, Spring Sirkin/Ruth Hendel, Vasi Laurence/Pat Flicker Addiss, in association with The Public Theater (Oskar Eustis, Artistic Director; Mara Manus, Executive Director) and The Berkeley Repertory Theatre (Tony Taccone, Artistic Director; Susan Medak, Managing Director); Executive Producer/General Management, Joey Parnes; Director, Annie Dorsen; Choreography, Karole Armitage; Sets, David Korins; Costumes, Elizabeth Hope Clancy; Lighting, Kevin Adams; Sound, Tom Morse; Music Supervision/Orchestrations, Stew & Heidi Rodewald; Music Coordinator, Seymour Red Press; Casting, Jordan Thaler & Heidi Griffiths; Production Stage Manager, Tripp Phillips; Company Manager, Kim Sellon; Associate Producer, S.D. Wagner; Assistant Producer, John Johnson; Stage Manager, Jason Hindelang; Assistant Stage Manager, Cynthia Cahill; Management Associate, Kit Ingui; Assistant Director, Stephen P. Brackett; Assistant Choreographer, William Isaac; Dance Captain, David Ryan Smith; Light Wall Design, Kevin Adams, David Korins; Associate Set, Rod Lemmond; Design Assistants: Amanda Stephens, Nathan Koch (set), Aaron Sporer (lighting), Chloe Chapin (costumes), Kevin Brubaker (sound); Vocal Coach, Barbara Maier; Dialect Coach, Elizabeth Smith; Production: Larry Morley (carpenter), Steve Cochrane (electrician), Mike Smanko (prop supervisor), Tucker Howard (sound engineer), Bill Craven (head carpenter), Susan Goulet (head electrician), Dylan Foley (head props), Rich Mortel (moving light programmer), Dave Olin Rogers (wardrobe supervisor), Francine Buryiak, Julienne Shubert-Blechman (dressers), Thelma L. Pollard (hair consultant), John Bantay (assistant); Music Transcription, Matthew Henning; Music Copyist, Emily Grishman, Katharine Edmonds; Literary Manager, Gaydon Phillips; Management Assistant, Matt Farabee; Assistant to Stew, Mike James; Guitar Technician, Mike Fornatale; Guitar Instructor, Steve Bargunet; Advertising, Serino-Coyne; Press, Sam Rudy Media Relations, Dale R. Heller, Robert Lasko, Charlie Siedenburg; Cast recording: Sh-K-Boom/Ghostlight Records 4429

CAST Narrator **Stew;** Bass/Vocals **Heidi Rodewald;** Keyboard/Guitar/Backing Vocals **Jon Spurney;** Drums **Christian Cassan;** Guitar/Keyboard/Backing Vocals **Christian Gibbs;** Mother **Eisa Davis;** Youth **Daniel Breaker;** Terry/Christophe/Hugo **Chad Goodridge;** Sherry/Renata/Desi **Rebecca Naomi Jones;** Franklin/Joop/Mr. Venus **Colman Domingo;** Edwina/Marianna/Sudabey **de'Adre Aziza**

UNDERSTUDIES Billy Eugene Jones (Franklin/Joop/Mr. Venus), Kelly McCreary (Edwina Mariana/Sudabey, Sherry/Renata/Desi), Karen Pittman (Mother), David Ryan Smith (Narrator), Lawrence Stallings (Youth, Hugo/Christophe/Terry)

MUSICAL NUMBERS Prologue (We Might Play All Night), Baptist Fashion Show, Blues Revelation/Freight Train, Arlington Hill, Sole Brother, Must've Been High, Mom Song, Merci Beaucoup M. Godard, Amsterdam, Keys, We Just Had Sex, May Day, Surface, Damage, Identity, The Black One, Come Down Now, Work the Wound, Passing Phase, Love Like That

SETTING Los Angeles, Amsterdam, Berlin. The present. A new musical presented in two acts. Originally presented by Berkeley Repertory Theatre October 25–December 3, 2006, and The Public Theater, May 14–June 3, 2007 (see *Theatre World* Vol. 63, pages 313 and 223.)

SYNOPSIS Developed at the Stanford Institute for Creativity the Arts, Berkeley Repertory Theatre, and the Public Theater, *Passing Strange* takes audiences on an international journey from L.A. to Amsterdam, Berlin, and beyond as a young man from California searches for his identity. It features blues, rock and roll, gospel, and pop music written by Stew and Rodewald, who head the band The Negro Problem.

Daniel Breaker, Rebecca Naomi Jones, Colman Domingo, Chad Goodridge

Stew

Eisa Davis (background) and de'Adre Aziza (photos by Carol Rosegg)

David Cryer and George Lee Andrews

The Phantom of the Opera

Majestic Theatre; First Preview: January 9, 1988. Opening Night: January 26, 1988; 16 previews, 8,875 performances as of May 31, 2009

Music and book by Andrew Lloyd Webber, lyrics by Charles Hart; additional lyrics and book by Richard Stilgoe; based on the novel by Gaston Leroux; Produced by Cameron Mackintosh and The Really Useful Theatre Company; Director, Harold Prince; Musical Staging/Choreography, Gillian Lynne; Orchestrations, David Cullen, Mr. Lloyd Webber; Design, Maria Björnson; Lighting, Andrew Bridge; Sound, Martin Levan; Original Musical Director and Supervisor, David Caddick; Musical Director, David Lai; Production Supervisor, Peter von Mayrhauser; Casting, Tara Rubin; Original Casting, Johnson-Liff Associates; General Manager, Alan Wasser; Production Dance Supervisor, Denny Berry; Associate Musical Supervisor, Kristen Blodgette; Associate General Manager, Allan Williams; Technical Production Managers, John H. Paull III, Jake Bell; Company Manager, Steve Greer; Stage Managers, Craig Jacobs, Bethe Ward, Brendan Smith; Assistant Company Manager, Cathy Kwon; Press, The Publicity Office, Marc Thibodeau, Michael S. Borowski, Jeremy Shaffer; London Cast recording: Polydor 831273

CAST The Phantom of the Opera **John Cudio**[*1]; Christine Daae **Jennifer Hope Wills**[*2]; Christine Daae (alt.) **Elizabeth Loycano**; Raoul, Vicomte de Chagny **Tim Martin Gleason**[*3]; Carlotta Giudicelli **Patricia Phillips**; Monsieur André **George Lee Andrews**; Monsieur Firmin **David Cryer**; Madame Giry **Rebecca Judd**[*4]; Ubaldo Piangi **Evan Harrington**; Meg Giry **Polly Baird**[*5]; Monsieur Reyer/Hairdresser **Geoff Packard**[*6]; Auctioneer **John Kuether**; Jeweler (Il Muto) **Frank Mastrone**; Monsieur Lefevre/Firechief **Kenneth Kantor**; Joseph Buquet **Richard Poole**[*7]; Don Attilio **John Kuether**; Passarino **Jeremy Stolle**; Slave Master **Daniel Rychlec**[*8]; Solo Dancer/Flunky/Stagehand **Jack Hayes**; Page **Kris Koop**[*9]; Porter/Fireman **Chris Bohannon**[*10]; Spanish Lady **Sally Williams**[*11]; Wardrobe Mistress/ Confidante **Rayanne Gonzales**; Princess **Susan Owen**; Madame Firmin **Melodie Rubie**; Innkeeper's Wife **Wren Marie Harrington**[*12]; Marksman **Paul A. Schaefer**[*13]; Ballet Chorus of the Opera Populaire[*14] **Amanda Edge, Kara Klein, Gianna Loungway, Mabel Modrono, Jessica Radetsky, Carly Blake Sebouhian, Dianna Warren**; Ballet Swing **Laurie V. Langdon**; Swings[*15] **Scott Mikita, James Romick, Janet Saia**

*Succeeded by: 1. Howard McGillin (7/28/08) 2. Marni Raab (8/20/08) 3. Ryan Silverman (4/24/09) 4. Nancy Hess (2/9/09) Rebecca Judd (3/2/09) 5. Heather McFadden (5/5/09) 6. Kyle Barisch, Geoff Packard, Jim Weitzer, Geoff Packard 7. Scott Mikita, James Romick, Richard Poole 8. Joseph J. Simeone, Daniel Rychlec, Anton Harrison LaMon 9. Julie Schmidt, Kristie Dale Sanders, Satomi Hofmann 10. John Wasiniak, Chris Bohannon 11. Julie Schmidt, Sally Williams, Kristie Dale Sanders, Kimilee Bryant 12. Cristin J. Hubbard 13. Jim Weitzer 14. (variously) Dara Adler, Emily Adonna Janice Niggeling 15. (variously) Kyle Barisch, Julie Schmidt, Jim Weitzer

MUSICAL NUMBERS Think of Me, Angel of Music, Little Lotte/The Mirror, Phantom of the Opera, Music of the Night, I Remember/Stranger Than You Dreamt It, Magical Lasso, Notes/Prima Donna, Poor Fool He Makes Me Laugh, Why Have You Brought Me Here?/Raoul I've Been There, All I Ask of You, Masquerade/Why So Silent?, Twisted Every Way, Wishing You Were Somehow Here Again, Wandering Child/Bravo Bravo, Point of No Return, Down Once More/Track Down This Murderer, Finale

ORCHESTRA David Caddick, Kristen Blodgette, David Lai, Tim Stella, Norman Weiss (Conductors); Joyce Hammann (Concert Master), Alvin E. Rogers, Gayle Dixon, Kurt Coble, Jan Mullen, Karen Milne (violins); Stephanie Fricker, Veronica Salas (violas); Ted Ackerman, Karl Bennion (cellos); Melissa Slocum (bass); Henry Fanelli (harp); Sheryl Henze, Ed Matthew, Melanie Feld, Matthew Goodman, Atsuko Sato (woodwinds); Lowell Hershey, Francis Bonny (trumpets); William Whitaker (trombone); Daniel Culpepper, Peter Reit, David Smith (French horn); Eric Cohen, Jan Hagiwara (percussion); Tim Stella, Norman Weiss (keyboards)

SETTING In and around the Paris Opera House, 1881–1911. A musical presented in two acts with nineteen scenes and a prologue. For original production credits see *Theatre World* Vol. 44, page 20. The show became the longest running show in Broadway history on January 9, 2006.

SYNOPSIS A disfigured musical genius haunts the catacombs beneath the Paris Opera and exerts strange control over a lovely young soprano.

Howard McGillin and Marni Raab (photos by Joan Marcus)

Rent

Nederlander Theatre; First Preview: April 16, 1996; Opening Night: April 29, 1996; Closed September 7, 2008; 16 previews, 5,124 performances

Book, music, and lyrics by Jonathan Larson; Produced by Jeffrey Seller, Kevin McCollum, Allan S. Gordon, and New York Theatre Workshop; Director, Michael Greif; Arrangements, Steve Skinner; Musical Supervision/Additional Arrangements, Tim Weill; Choreography, Marlies Yearby; Original Concept/ Additional Lyrics, Billy Aronson; Sets, Paul Clay; Costumes, Angela Wendt; Lighting, Blake Burba; Sound, Kurt Fischer; Wigs/Hair/Makeup, David Santana; Film, Tony Gerber; General Management, Emanuel Azenberg, John Corker; Company Manager, Andrew Jones; Production Stage Manager, John Vivian; Resident Director, Evan Ensign; Stage Manager, Crystal Huntington; Dramaturg, Lynn M. Thompson, Production Coordinator, Susan White; Technical Supervision, Unitech Productions, Inc; Advertising, SpotCo; Press, Richard Kornberg, Don Summa; Cast recording: Dreamworks 50003

CAST Roger Davis **Will Chase;** Mark Cohen **Adam Kantor;** Tom Collins **Michael McElroy**[1]**;** Benjamin Coffin III **Rodney Hicks;** Joanne Jefferson **Merle Dandridge**[2]**;** Angel Schunard **Justin Johnson;** Mimi Marquez **Tamyra Gray**[3]**;** Maureen Johnson **Eden Espinoza;** Mark's Mom/Alison/ Others **Tracy McDowell;** Christmas Caroler/Mr. Jefferson/Pastor/Others **Marcus Paul James;** Mrs. Jefferson/Woman with Bags/Others **Maia Nkenge Wilson**[4]**;** Gordon/The Man/Mr. Grey/Others **Kyle Post**[5] Steve/Man with Squeegee/Waiter/Others **Telly Leung;** Paul/Cop/Others **Shaun Earl;** Alexi Darling/Roger's Mom/Others **Andrea Goss;** Swings **Karmine Alers, Owen Johnston II, Crystal Monée Hall, Trisha Jeffrey, Todd E. Pettiford, Destan Owens;** Standby for Mark: **Jay Wilkison**

UNDERSTUDIES Tracy McDowell (Maureen), Crystal Monée Hall (Joanne), Marcus Paul James (Bennie, Tom), Trisha Jeffrey (Joanne, Mimi), Owen Johnston II (Angel, Roger), Telly Leung (Angel), Kyle Post[5] (Mark, Roger), Maia Nkenge Wilson (Joanne Jefferson), Destan Owens (Bennie, Tom)

*Succeeded by: 1. Destan Owens (8/11/08), Michael McElroy (8/18/08) 2. Tracie Thoms (7/26/08) 3. Renée Elise Goldsberry (6/16/08) 4. Gwen Stewart (7/21/08) 5. Jay Wilkison

MUSICIANS Tim Weil (Conductor/keyboards), Steve Mack (bass), Kenny Brescia (guitar), Daniel A. Weiss (Associate Conductor/guitar), Jeffrey Potter (drums)

MUSICAL NUMBERS Tune Up, Voice Mail (#1–#5), Rent, You Okay Honey?, One Song Glory, Light My Candle, Today 4 U, You'll See, Tango: Maureen, Life Support, Out Tonight, Another Day, Will I?, On the Street, Santa Fe, We're Okay, I'll Cover You, Christmas Bells, Over the Moon, La Vie Boheme/I Should Tell You, Seasons of Love, Happy New Year, Take Me or Leave Me, Without You, Contact, Halloween, Goodbye Love, What You Own, Finale/Your Eyes

SETTING Time and place: New York City's East Village, 1990. A musical presented in two acts. For original production credits see *Theatre World* Vol. 52, Page 58. Originally presented Off-Broadway at the New York Theatre Workshop on February 13, 1996.

SYNOPSIS Based on Puccini's opera *La Boheme*, the musical centers on a group of impoverished young artists and musicians struggling to survive and create in New York's Alphabet City in the early 1990s, under the shadow of AIDS. Tragedy occurred when the 35-year-old author Jonathan Larson died of an aortic aneurysm after watching the final dress rehearsal of his show on January 24, 1996.

Tamyra Gray

The Company (photos by Joan Marcus)

South Pacific

Vivian Beaumont Theatre; First Preview: March 1, 2008; Opening Night: April 3, 2008; 37 previews, 485 performances as of May 31, 2009

Music by Richard Rodgers, lyrics and book by Oscar Hammerstein II, book and original staging by Joshua Logan, adapted from the novel "Tales of the South Pacific" by James A. Michener; Produced by Lincoln Center Theater (André Bishop, Artistic Director; Bernard Gersten, Executive Producer) in association with Bob Boyett; Director, Bartlett Sher; Musical Staging, Christopher Gattelli; Music Director, Ted Sperling; Sets, Michael Yeargan; Costumes, Catherine Zuber; Lighting, Donald Holder; Sound, Scott Lehrer; Orchestrations, Robert Russell Bennett; Dance & Incidental Music Arrangements, Trude Rittmann; Casting, Telsey + Company; Production Stage Manager, Michael Brunner; Musical Theatre Associate Producer, Ira Weitzman; General Manager, Adam Siegel; Production Manager, Jeff Hamlin; Development, Hattie K. Jutagir; Marketing, Linda Mason Ross; Finance, David S. Brown; Education, Kati Koerner; Dramaturg, Anne Cattaneo; Vocal Coach, Deborah Hecht; Company Manager, Matthew Markoff, Jessica Perlmeter Cochrane (9/23/08); Assistant Company Manager, Jessica Perlmeter Cochrane; Assistant Stage Managers, David Sugarman, Samantha Greene; Dance Captain, Wendy Bergamini; Assistant Dance Captain, Grady McLeod Bowman; Assistant Director, Sarna Lapine; Associate Choreographer, Joe Langworth; Associate Design: Lawrence King (sets), Karen Spahn (lighting), Leon Rothenberg (sound); Assistant Design: Mikiko Suzuki (sets), Holly Cain, David Newell, Court Watson (costumes), Caroline Chao (lighting); Rehearsal Pianist, Jonathan Rose; Wigs and Hair, Tom Watson; Makeup, Cookie Jordan; Properties Coordinator, Kathy Fabian; Music Coordinator, David Lai; Press, Philip Rinaldi, Barbara Carroll; Cast recording: Sony BMG – Masterworks Broadway 88697-30457-2

CAST Ensign Nellie Forbush **Kelli O'Hara**[*1]; Emile de Becque **Paulo Szot**[*2]; Ngana **Laurissa Romain;** Jerome **Luka Kain;** Henry **Helmar Augustus Cooper;** Bloody Mary **Loretta Ables Sayre;** Liat **Li Jun Li;** Bloody Mary's Assistants **Mary Ann Hu, Emily Morales**[*3]**, Kimber Monroe;** Luther Billis **Danny Burstein;** Stewpot **Victor Hawks**[*4]**;** Professor **Noah Weisberg**[*5]**;** Lt. Joseph Cable, USMC **Matthew Morrison**[*6]**;** Capt. George Bracket, USN **Skipp Sudduth**[*7]**;** Cmdr. William Harbison, USN **Sean Cullen;** Lt. Buzz Adams **George Merrick;** Yeoman Herbert Quale **Christian Delcroix;** Radio Operator Bob McCaffrey **Matt Caplan**[*8]**;** Seabee Morton Wise **Genson Blimline;** Seabee Richard West **Nick Mayo;** Seabee Johnny Noonan **Jeremy Davis**[*9]**;** Seabee Billy Whitmore **Robert Lenzi;** Sailor Tom O'Brien **Mike Evariste;** Sailor James Hayes **Jerold E. Solomon;** Sailor Kenneth Johnson **Christian Carter;** Petty Officer Hamilton Steeves **Charlie Brady**[*10]**;** Seaman Thomas Hassinger **Zachary James;** Shore Patrolman Lt. Eustis Carmichael **Andrew Samonsky**[*11]**;** Lead nurse Lt. Genevieve Marshall **Lisa Howard**[*12]**;** Ensign Dinah Murphy **Laura Marie Duncan;** Ensign Janet MacGregor **Laura Griffith**[*13]**;** Ensign Connie Walewska **Margot de la Barre**[*14]**;** Ensign Sue Yeager **Garrett Long;** Ensign Cora MacRae **Becca Ayers**[*15]**;** Islanders, Sailors, Seabees, Party Guests: **Becca Ayers**[*15]**, Genson Blimline, Charlie Brady**[*10]**, Matt Caplan**[*8]**, Christian Carter, Helmar Augustus Cooper, Jeremy Davis**[*9]**, Margot de la Barre**[*14]**, Mike Evariste, Laura Griffith**[*13]**, Lisa Howard**[*12]**, Maryann Hu, Zachary James, Robert Lenzi, Garrett Long, Nick Mayo, George Merrick, Kimber Monroe; Emily Morales**[*3]**, Andrew Samonsky**[*11]**, Jerold E. Solomon;** Swings **Wendi Bergamini**[*16]**, Grady McLeod Bowman**[*17]**, Darius Nichols**[*18]**, George Psomas**

*Succeeded by: 1. Laura Osnes (3/10/09) 2. David Pittsinger (12/2/09–1/12/09; 3/12/09–4/12/09) 3. Deborah Lew 4. Eric Anderson (1/6/09) 5. Matt Caplan (1/6/09) 6. Andrew Samonsky (1/6/09) 7. Murphy Guyer (9/2/08) 8. Peter Lockyer (1/6/09) 9. Michael Arnold (7/8/08) 10. Branch Fields (8/19/08), Charlie Brady, Craig Bennett (4/14/09) 11. Rob Gallagher (1/6/09) 12. Liz McCartney (6/24/08), Luca Spina (12/11/08–1/4/09), Liz McCartney (1/6/09) 13. Wendy

Paulo Szot and Kelli O'Hara (photos by Paul Kolnik)

Bergamini (11/4/08) 14. Ana Maria Andricain (vacation sub 10/14/09), Margot de la Barre (1/6/09) 15. Marla Mindelle (3/17/09) 16. Julie Foldesi (10/14/08) 17. Greg Roderick (6/24/09) 18. Eric L. Christian (6/26/08)

ORCHESTRA Ted Sperling (Conductor); Fred Lassen (Associate Conductor); Belinda Whitney (concertmistress), Antoine Silverman, Karl Kawahara, Katherine Livolsi-Landau, Lisa Matricardi, Jim Tsao, Michael Nicholas, Rena Isbin (violins); David Blinn, David Creswell (violas); Peter Sachon, Caryl Paisner (celli); Charles du Chateau (Assistant Conductor/cello); Lisa Stokes-Chin (bass); Liz Mann (flute/piccolo); Todd Palmer, Shari Hoffman (clarinet); Matt Dine/Kelly Perai (oboe/English horn); Damian Primis (bassoon): Robert Carlisle, Chris Komer, Shelagh Abate (French horns); Dominic Derasse, Gareth Flowers, Wayne Dumaine (trumpets); Mark Patterson, Mike Boschen (trombones); Marcus Rojas (tuba); Grace Paradise (harp); Bill Lanham (drums/percussion)

MUSICAL NUMBERS Overture, Dites-Moi, A Cockeyed Optimist, Twin Soliloquies, Some Enchanted Evening, Dites-Moi (reprise), Bloody Mary, There Is Nothin' Like a Dame, Bali Ha'i, My Girl Back Home, I'm Gonna Wash That Man Right Outa My Hair, Some Enchanted Evening (reprise), A Wonderful Guy, Bali Ha'i (reprise), Younger Than Springtime, Finale Act I, Entr'acte, Happy Talk, Honey Bun, You've Got to Be Carefully Taught; This Nearly Was Mine, Some Enchanted Evening (reprise), Finale Ultimo

SETTING The action takes place on two islands in the South Pacific during World War II. Revival of a musical presented in two acts.

SYNOPSIS Rodgers and Hammerstein's classic receives its first major New York revival, almost sixty years after its debut. The story centers on the romance between a southern nurse and a French planter who find love on a small tropical island amidst a backdrop of war and racism.

Spring Awakening

Eugene O'Neill Theatre; First Preview: November 16, 2006; Opening Night: December 10, 2006; Closed January 18, 2009; 28 previews, 859 performances

Book and lyrics by Steven Sater, music by Duncan Sheik, based on the play *The Awakening of Spring* by Frank Wedekind; Produced by Ira Pittelman, Tom Hulce, Jeffrey Richards, Jerry Frankel, Atlantic Theater Company, Jeffrey Sine, Freddy DeMann, Max Cooper, Mort Swinsky, Cindy & Jay Gutterman, Joe McGinnis, Judith Ann Abrams, ZenDog Productions, CarJac Productions, Aron Bergson Productions, Jennifer Manocherian, Ted Snowdon, Harold Thau, Terry Schnuck, Cold Spring Productions, Amanda Dubois, Elizabeth Eynon Wetherell, Jennifer Maloney, Tamara Tunie, Joe Cilibrasi, StyleFour Productions; Director, Michael Mayer; Choreography, Bill T. Jones; Musical Director, Kimberly Grigsby; Set, Christine Jones; Costumes, Susan Hilferty; Lighting, Kevin Adams; Sound, Brian Ronan; Orchestrations, Duncan Sheik; Arrangements, AnnMarie Milazzo, Simon Hale; Music Coordinator, Michael Keller; Casting, Jim Carnahan, Carrie Gardner; Fight Director, J. David Brimmer; Production Stage Manager, Heather Cousens; Associate Producers, Joan Cullman Productions, Patricia Flicker Addiss; Technical Supervision, Neil A. Mazzella, Sam Ellis; General Management, Abbie M. Strassler, Iron Mountain Productions; Company Manager, John E. Gendron; Marketing/Promotions, Situation Marketing, Damian Bazadona, Steve Tate; Stage Manager, Rick Steiger; Assistant Stage Manager, Bethany Russell; Assistant Company Manager, Scott Turowsky; Dance Captain, Lauren Pritchard; Fight Captain, Brian Charles Johnson; Consultants, Susan Blond, Simone Smalls, Liza Bychkov; Rubenstein Communications Inc., Amy Jacobs, Andy Shearer, Alice McGillion; Assistant Director, Beatrice Terry; Assistant Choreographer, Miguel Anaya Jr.; Associate Musical Director, Deborah Abramson; Music Copyist, Steven M. Alper; Press, Fifteen Minutes Public Relations, Pete Sanders; Cast recording: Decca Broadway B0008020-02

Hunter Parrish and Alexandra Socha

CAST Wendla **Alexandra Socha;** The Adult Women **Christine Estabrook;** Martha **Lilli Cooper**[1]; Ilse **Emma Hunton;** Anna **Phoebe Strole**[2]; Thea **Remy Zaken**[3]; The Adult Men **Glenn Fleshler;** Otto **Brian Charles Johnson**[4]; Hanschen **Matt Doyle;** Ernst **Blake Daniel;** Georg **Skylar Astin**[5]; Moritz **Blake Bashoff**[6]; Melchior **Kyle Riabko**[7]; Ensemble **Gerard Canonico**[8] **Eryn Murman, Matt Shingledecker**[9]**, Alice Lee;** Swings **Jesse Swenson, Frances Mercanti-Anthony, Jenna Ushkowitz**

*Succeeded by: 1. Amanda Castaños (7/21/08) 2. Emily Kinney (7/21/08) 3. Caitlin Kinnunen (7/21/08) 4. Gabriel Violett (7/21/08) 5. Andrew Durand (7/21/08) 6. Gerard Canonico (8/4/08) 7. Hunter Parrish (8/11/08) 8. Morgan Carr (7/21/08) 9. Zach Reiner-Harris

THE BAND Adam Ben-David (Conductor/keyboards); Thad DeBrock (guitars); George Farmer (bass); Trey Files (Associate Conductor/drums); Benjamin Kalb (cello); Oliver Manchon (violin/guitar); Hiroko Taguchi (violin)

MUSICAL NUMBERS Mama Who Bore Me, Mama Who Bore Me (reprise), All That's Known, The Bitch of Living, My Junk, Touch Me, The Word of Your Body, The Dark I Know Well, And Then There Were None, The Mirror-Blue Night, I Believe, The Guilty Ones, Don't Do Sadness, Blue Wind, Left Behind, Totally Fucked, The Word of Your Body (reprise), Whispering, Those You've Known, The Song of Purple Summer

SETTING A provincial German town in the 1890's. Transfer of the Off-Broadway musical presented in two acts. For original credits see *Theatre World* Vol. 63, page 56. Originally produced at the Atlantic Theatre Company May 19–August 5, 2006 (see *Theatre World* Vol. 62, page 152).

SYNOPSIS *Spring Awakening* is the contemporary musical adaptation of one of literature's most controversial plays. The musical boldly depicts a dozen young people and how they make their way through the complicated, confusing, and mysterious time of their sexual awakening. The story centers around a brilliant young student named Melchior, his troubled friend Moritz, and Wendla, a beautiful young girl on the verge of womanhood. Sheik and Sater's score features songs that illuminate the urgency of adolescent self-discovery, the burning intensity of teen friendships and the innate suspicion of the uncomprehending adult world.

Gerard Canonico (photos by Cass Bird)

Sunday in the Park with George

Studio 54; First Preview: January 18, 2008; Opening Night: February 21, 2008; Closed July 29, 2008; 32 previews, 149 performances

Allison Horowitz, Jessica Molaskey, Drew McVety, Brynn O'Malley, Jessica Grové, Daniel Evans, Michael Cumpsty, Jenna Russell

Music and lyrics by Stephen Sondheim, book by James Lapine; Originally presented by The Menier Chocolate Factory; Produced by the Roundabout Theatre Company (Todd Haimes, Artistic Director; Harold Wolpert, Managing Director; Julia C. Levy, Executive Director) in association with Bob Boyett, Debra Black, Jam Theatricals, Stephanie P. McClelland, Stewart F. Lane/Bonnie Comley, Barbara Manocherian/Jennifer Manocherian, and Ostar Productions; Presented in association with Caro Newling for Neal Street Productions and Mark Rubenstein; Director, Sam Buntrock; Musical Staging, Christopher Gattelli; Sets/Costumes, David Farley; Lighting, Ken Billington; Sound, Sebastian Frost; Projections, Timothy Bird & Knifedge: The Creative Network; Musical Supervisor, Caroline Humphris; Orchestrations, Jason Carr; Music Coordinator, John Miller; Production Stage Manager, Peter Hanson; Hair/Wigs, Tom Watson; Dialect Coach, Kate Wilson; Casting, Jim Carnahan; Technical Supervisor, Steve Beers; Executive Producer, Sydney Beers; Marketing/Sales, David B. Steffen; Development, Jeffory Lawson; Founding Director, Gene Feist; Associate Artistic Director, Scott Ellis; Education Director, David A. Miller; Finance, Susan Neiman; Sales Operations, Charlie Garbowski Jr.; Telesales, Daniel Weiss; Company Manager, Denise Cooper; Company Manager Assistant, Brent McCreary; Stage Manager, Jon Krause; Assistant Stage Manager, Rachel Zack; Assistant Director, Dave Solomon; Associate Director/Choreographer (U.K.), Tara Wilkinson; Assistant to the Choreographer, Lou Castro; Dance Captain, Hayley Podschun; Makeup, Angelina Avallone; Associate Design: Matthew Pachtman (costumes), Paul Toben (lighting), Nick Borisjuk (sound); U.K. Assistants to Mr. Farley, Julie Bowles, Sarah Cant, Machiko Hombu; Music Coordinator Assistant, Charles Butler; Music Preparation, Emily Grishman, Katherine Edmonds; Synthesizer Programmer, Bruce Samuels; For Knifedge: The Creative Network: Timothy Bird (Creative Director), Sam Hopkins & his Light Studio (revisualization & projection strategy), Nina Wilson (team leader/AFX Animator), Raf Anzovin (rigging), Ciara Fanning (content librarian), Shaun Freeman (character animator), John Keates (animator/technical director), Alex Laurent (matte artist), Andy McNamara (3D animator), Stephen Millingen (animator), Aaron Trinder (AFX animator), Sam Buntrock (additional animation), Amy Di Prima ("Putting It Together" effects producer), John Chimples ("Putting It Together" effects videographer), Advertising, SpotCo; Press, Boneau/Bryan-Brown, Matt Polk, Jessica Johnson, Amy Kass; London Cast recording: PS Classics 640

CAST George **Daniel Evans;** Dot/Marie **Jenna Russell;** An Old Lady/Blair Daniels **Mary Beth Piel;** Nurse/Mrs./Harriet Pawling **Anne L. Nathan;** Franz/Lee Randolph **David Turner;** Jules/Bob Greenburg **Michael Cumpsty;** Yvonne/Naomi Eisen **Jessica Molaskey;** A Boatman/Dennis **Alexander Gemignani;** Celeste #1/Elaine **Brynn O'Malley;** Celeste #2/Photographer **Jessica Grové;** Bather/Louis/Billy Webster **Drew McVety;** Louise/Bather **Kelsey Fowler** or **Alison Horowitz;** Frieda/Betty **Stacie Morgain Lewis;** Bather/A Soldier/Alex **Santino Fontana;** Mr./Charles Redmond **Ed Dixon**

ORCHESTRA Caroline Humphris (Conductor/piano); Thomas Murray (Associate Conductor/keyboard), Matthew Lehmann (violin/House Contractor), Mairi Dorman-Phaneuf (Cello), Todd Groves (Woodwinds)

MUSICAL NUMBERS Sunday in the Park With George, No Life, Color and Light, Gossip, The Day Off, Everybody Loves Louis, Finishing the Hat, We Do Not Belong Together, Beautiful, Sunday, It's Hot Up Here, Chromolume #7, Putting It Together, Children and Art, Lesson #8, Move On, Sunday

SETTING Act 1: A series of Sundays from 1884-1886 in a park on an island in the Seine just outside of Paris, and George's studio. Act 2: 1984, at an American art museum and on the island. Revival of the musical presented in two acts.

SYNOPSIS The Georges Seurat painting, "A Sunday Afternoon on the Island of La Grande Jatte," is the inspiration for this compelling musical fantasy which celebrates the art of creation and the creation of art. The first half of the show, set in 1884, sees the painting and its rich comic tapestry come to life in a world where, for George, art comes before love, before everything. In the second half, one hundred years later, we see the great grandson of George and his search for inspiration amongst the unfolding world of contemporary art.

Jenna Russell, Daniel Evans (photos by Joan Marcus)

Laurence Fishburne

Laurence Fishburne

Thurgood

Booth Theatre; First Preview: April 12, 2008; Opening Night: April 30, 2008; Closed August 17, 2008; 19 previews, 126 performances

Written by George Stevens Jr.; Produced by Vernon Jordan, The Shubert Organization, Bill Rollnick/Nancy Ellison Rollnick; Matt Murphy, Daryl Roth/Debra Black, Roy Furman, Jam Theatricals, Lawrence Horowitz, Eric Falkenstein, Max Onstage, James D'Orta, Jamie deRoy, Amy Nederlander, in association with Ostar Productions and The Westport Country Playhouse; Director, Leonard Foglia; Set, Allen Moyer; Costumes, Jane Greenwood; Lighting, Brian Nason; Projections, Elaine McCarthy; Sound, Ryan Rumery; Production Stage Manager, Marti McIntosh; Production Manager, Juniper Street Productions; General Management, Alan Wasser, Allan Williams; Company Manager, Dwayne Mann; Stage Manager, Bernita Robinson; Assistant Director, Cat Williams; Associate Set, Warren Karp; Associate Sound, Chris Cronin; Assistant Design: Christina Bullard (costumes), Michael Barczys (lighting), Shawn E. Boyle (projections); Dialect Coach, Suzanne Celeste Brown; Production: Ken McDonough (carpenter), Jon K. Lawson (electrician), Ronnie Burns (house electrician), Drew Scott (moving lights programmer), Randolph S. Briggs (projection programmer), Richard S. Briggs (projection research), Vita Tzykun (projection digital artist), Pete Sarafin (props), James Keane (house props), Bill Lewis (production sound), Valer Gladstone (wardrobe supervisor); Associate Producer, Rachel Neuburger for Ostar Enterprises; Assistant to Mr. Stevens, Dottie McCarthy; Research, Julie Goetz; Marketing, Type A Marketing; Assistant to Mr. Fishburne, Justin Cox; Press, Fifteen Minutes Public Relations, Pete Sanders

CAST Thurgood Marshall **Laurence Fishburne**

New York premiere of a new play presented without intermission. World premiere at Westport Country Playhouse in 2006 starring James Earl Jones.

SYNOPSIS *Thurgood* is a biographical portrait of Thurgood Marshall, which includes his childhood in Baltimore and his service as chief counsel of the NAACP, for which he argued the landmark Brown vs. Board of Education desegregation case in 1954. Marshall was appointed to the Supreme Court in 1967 and died in 1993.

Laurence Fishburne (photos by Carol Rosegg)

Top Girls

Biltmore Theatre; First Preview: April 12, 2007 Opening Night: May 3, 2007; Closed June 29, 2008; 24 previews, 63 performances

Written by Caryl Churchill; Produced by Manhattan Theatre Club (Lynne Meadow, Artistic Director; Barry Grove, Executive Producer; Daniel Sullivan, 07-08 Acting Artistic Director); Director, James Macdonald; Set, Tom Pye; Costumes, Laura Bauer; Lighting, Christopher Akerlind; Sound, Darron L West; Original Music, Matthew Herbert; Hair & Wigs, Paul Huntley; Dialect Consultant, Elizabeth Smith; Production Stage Manager, Martha Donaldson; General Manager, Florie Seery; Associate Artistic Director/Production, Mandy Greenfield; Marketing, Debra A. Waxman; Production Manager, Kurt Gardner; Casting, Nancy Piccione; Development, Jill Turner Lloyd; Artistic Administration/Assistant to Artistic Director, Amy Gilkes Loe; Literary Manager, Raphael Martin; Musical Development, Clifford Lee Johnson III; Finance, Jeffrey Bledsoe; Associate General Manager, Lindsey Brooks Sag; Subscriber Services, Robert Allenberg; Telesales, George Tetlow; Education, David Shookhoff; Associate Production Manager, Philip Naudé; Lighting/Sound Supervisor, Matthew T. Gross; Prop Supervisor, Scott Laule; Costume Supervisor, Erin Hennessy Dean; Company Manager, Seth Shepsle; Stage Manager, Amy McCraney; Assistant Director, Gene Taylor Upchruch; Associate Design: Frank McCullough (set), Bobby F. Tillery (costumes), Ben Krall (lighting), Matthew Hubbs (sound); Assistant Design: Bray Poor (sound); Hair/Makeup Supervisor, Jon Jordan; Assistant Hair/Makeup, La Sonya Gunter; Flymen, Patrick Murray, Leomar Susana; Assistant Propertyman, Sue Poulin; Lighting Programmer, Marc Polimeni; Dressers, Janet Anderson, Jackeva Hill; Production Assistant, Christina Elefante; Advertising, SpotCo; Press, Boneau/Bryan-Brown, Jim Byk, Aaron Meier, Heath Schwartz, Christine Olver

CAST Patient Griselda/Kit/Jeanine/Shona **Mary Catherine Garrison;** Waitress/Louise **Mary Beth Hurt;** Lady Nijo/Win **Jennifer Ikeda;** Marlene **Elizabeth Marvel;** Pope Joan/Angie **Martha Plimpton;** Dull Gret/Nell **Ana Reeder;** Isabella Bird/Joyce/Mrs. Kidd **Marisa Tomei**

UNDERSTUDIES Tina Benko (Marlene, Pope Joan/Angie), Angela Lin (Patient Griselda/Kit/Jeanine/Shona, Lady Nijo/Win), Anne Torsiglieri (Waitress/Louise, Dull Gret/Nell, Isabella Bird/Joyce/Mrs. Kidd)

SETTING Early 1980's; a restaurant in London, Joyce's back yard and kitchen in Suffolk, and Top Girls Employment Agency, London. Broadway premiere of a play presented in three acts with one intermission. Originally produced Off-Broadway at the Public Theater with a British cast December 28, 1982–January 30, 1983, playing 40 performances; reopened with an American cast February 24–May 29, 1983, playing 89 performances (see *Theatre World* Vol. 39, page 116).

Elizabeth Marvel and Marisa Tomei

SYNOPSIS Marlene has just been appointed head of the Top Girls Employment Agency. To celebrate, she throws a 'Mad Hatter' type dinner party for a fanciful array of mythical and historical women, including a Victorian-era Scottish traveler, a Japanese courtesan turned Buddhist nun, Pope Joan and Chaucer's Patient Griselda. Crossing cultures, generations and politics, the sparkling dinner conversation reveals the sacrifices made as well as the joys experienced by these extraordinary women. This bold, ingenious work offers an honest portrait of what it means to be a woman in the modern world.

Mary Catherine Garrison and Ana Reeder

Left: *Jennifer Ikeda and Mary Beth Hurt (photos by Joan Marcus)*

Wicked

Gershwin Theatre; First Preview: October 8, 2003; Opening Night: October 30, 2003; 25 previews, 2,310 performances as of May 31, 2009

Book by Winnie Holzman, music and lyrics by Stephen Schwartz; based on the novel by Gregory Maguire; Produced by Marc Platt, Universal Pictures, The Araca Group, Jon B. Platt and David Stone; Director, Joe Mantello; Musical Staging, Wayne Cilento; Music Supervisor, Stephen Oremus; Orchestrations, William David Brohn; Scenery, Eugene Lee; Costumes, Susan Hilferty; Lighting, Kenneth Posner; Sound, Tony Meola; Projections, Elanie J. McCarthy; Wigs/Hair, Tom Watson; Technical Supervisor, Jake Bell; Arrangements, Alex Lacamoire, Stephen Oremus; Dance Arrangements, James Lynn Abbott; Music Coordinator, Michael Keller; Special Effects, Chic Silber; Production Supervisor, Thom Widmann; Dance Supervisor, Mark Myars; Associate Director, Lisa Leguillou; Casting, Bernard Telsey; Production Stage Manager, Marybeth Abel; Stage Manager, Jennifer Marik; Assistant Stage Managers, Christy Ney, J. Jason Daunter; General Management, 321 Theatrical Management; Executive Producers, Marcia Goldberg and Nina Essman; Company Management, Susan Sampliner, Robert Brinkerhoff; Fight Director, Tom Schall; Flying, Paul Rubin/ZFX Inc.; Dressing/Properties, Kristie Thompson; Makeup, Joe Dulude II; Assistant Choreography, Corinne McFadden-Herrera; Music Preparation, Peter R. Miller; Synthesizer Programming, Andrew Barrett; Advertising, Serino-Coyne; Press, Barlow · Hartman; Cast recording: Decca B 0001 682-02

CAST Glinda Kendra Kassebaum[1]; Witch's Father/Ozian Official Michael DeVries; Witch's Mother Katie Webber[2]; Midwife Kathie Santen; Elphaba Stephanie J. Block[3]; Nessarose Cristy Candler[4]; Boq Ben Liebert[5]; Madame Morrible Miriam Margolyes[6]; Doctor Dillamond Stephen Skybell[7]; Fiyero David Burnham[8]; The Wonderful Wizard of Oz Lenny Wolpe[9]; Chistery Jonathan Warren[10]; Ensemble[11] Ioana Alfonso, Sonshine Allen, Brad Bass, Kathy Deitch, Michael DeVries, Lori Ann Ferreri, Lauren Gibbs, Todd Hanebrink, Kenway Hon Wai K. Kua, Reed Kelly, Chelsea Krombach, Lindsay K. Northen, Eddie Pendergraft, Alexander Quiroga, Noah Rivera, Michael Seelbach, Kathie Santen, Heather Spore, CJ Tyson, Jonathan Warren, Katie Webber; Standbys Julie Reiber[12] (Elphaba), Katie Adams[13] (Glinda); Swings[14] Clyde Alves, Kristina Fernandez, Anthony Galde, Kristen Leigh Gorski, Briana Yacavone, Ryan Weiss

*Succeeded by: 1. Alli Mauzey (11/11/08) 2. Kristen Leigh Gorski 3. Kerry Ellis (6/17/08), Marci Dodd (11/11/08), Nicole Parker (1/16/09) 4. Brynn O'Malley (11/11/08), Cristy Candler 5. Alex Brightman (11/4/08) 6. Jayne Houdyshell (6/17/08), Rondi Reed (3/17/09) 7. Timothy Britten Parker 8. Aaron Tveit (6/24/08), Kevin Kern (11/11/08), Aaron Tveit (1/21/09), Kevin Kern (3/10/09) 9. P.J. Benjamin (7/29/08) 10. Sam J. Cahn 11. Subsequent: Nova Bergeron, Sarah Bolt, Jerad Bortz, Sam J. Cahn, Maia Evvaraye-Griffin, Kristina Fernandez, Adam Fleming, Kristen Leigh Gorski, Kyle Dean Massey, Jonathan McGill, Rhea Patterson, Adam Perry, Charlie Sutton, Brian Wanee, Robin Wilner 12. Jennifer Dinoia 13. Laura Woyasz 14. Subsequent: Brenda Hamilton, Ryan Patrick Kelly, Lindsay Janisse, Amanda Rose, Jonathan Warren, Samantha Zack

ORCHESTRA Dominick Amendum (Conductor); David Evans (Associate Conductor/keyboards); Ben Cohn (Assistant Conductor/keyboards); Christian Hebel (Concertmaster); Victor Schultz (violin); Kevin Roy (viola); Dan Miller (cello); Konrad Adderly (bass); John Moses, John Campo, Tuck Lee, Helen Campo (woodwinds); Jon Owens, Tom Hoyt (trumpets); Dale Kirkland, Douglas Purviance (trombones); Theo Primis, Chad Yarbrough (French horn); Paul Loesel (keyboards); Ric Molina, Greg Skaff (guitars); Andy Jones (percussion); Matt VanderEnde (drums); Laura Sherman (harp)

MUSICAL NUMBERS No One Mourns the Wicked, Dear Old Shiz, The Wizard and I, What Is This Feeling?, Something Bad, Dancing Through Life, Popular, I'm Not That Girl, One Short Day, A Sentimental Man, Defying Gravity, No One Mourns the Wicked (Reprise), Thank Goodness, The Wicked Witch of the East, Wonderful, I'm Not That Girl (Reprise), As Long as You're Mine, No Good Deed, March of the Witch Hunters, For Good, Finale

SETTING The Land of Oz. A musical presented in two acts. World premiere presented in San Francisco at the Curran Theatre May 28–June 29, 2003. For original production credits see *Theatre World* Vol. 60, page 34.

SYNOPSIS *Wicked* explores the early life of the witches of Oz, Glinda and Elphaba, who meet at Shiz University. Glinda is madly popular and Elphaba is green. After an initial period of mutual loathing, the roommates begin to learn something about each other. Their life paths continue to intersect, and eventually their choices and convictions take them on widely different paths.

The Company (photos by Joan Marcus)

Left: *Marci Dodd and Alli Mauzey*

Marty Thomas, Kerry Butler, Curtis Holbrook (upstage center), André Ward, and Kenita Miller

Cheyenne Jackson

Xanadu

Helen Hayes Theatre; First Preview: May 23, 2007; Opening Night: July 10, 2007; Closed September 28, 2008; 49 previews, 510 performances

Book by Douglas Carter Beane, music and lyrics by Jeff Lynne & John Farrar, based on the Universal Pictures film screenplay by Richard Danus & Marc Rubel; Produced by Robert Ahrens, Dan Vickery, Sara Murchison/Dale Smith & Tara Smith/B. Swibel; Director, Christopher Ashley; Choreography, Dan Knechtges; Music Direction and Arrangements, Eric Stern; Sets, David Gallo; Lighting, Howell Binkley; Costumes, David Zinn; Sound, T. Richard Fitzgerald, Carl Casella; Projections, Zachary Borovay; Wigs/Hair, Charles LaPointe; Marketing, HHC Marketing; Technical Supervisor, Juniper Street Productions; Music Coordinator, John Miller; Casting, Cindy Tolan; Associate Producers, Allicat Productions, Marc Rubel & Cari Smulyan; Production Stage Manager, Arturo E. Porazzi; General Manager, Laura Heller; Company Manager, Jolie Gabler; Stage Manager, John M. Atherlay; Assistant Stage Manager, Peter Samuel; Associate to Mr. Ahrens, Eric Sanders; Associate Director, Dana Iris Harrel; Associate Choreographer, D.J. Gray; Dance Captain, Marty Thomas; Makeup, John Carter; Associate Design: Frank McCullough (set), Ryan O'Gara (lighting), Amelia Dombrowski, Sarah Laux (costumes), Austin Switser (projections); Casting Associate, Adam Caldwell; Assistant Choreographer, Allison Bibicoff; Skating Coach/Dance Assistant, David Tankersley; Skate Trainer/Supplier, Lezly Ziering; Music Copying, Kaye-Houston Music; Synthesizer Programmer, Karl Mansfiels; Advertising, Eliran Murphy Group; Press, Blue Current Public Relations, Pete Sanders, Andrew Snyder; Cast recording: PS Classics 858

CAST Sonny **Cheyenne Jackson**[1]; Thalia/Siren/Young Danny/80's Singer/Cyclops **Kyle Dean Massey**[2]; Euterpe/Siren/40's Singer/Thetis **Patti Murin;** Erato/Siren/40's Singer/Eros/Hera **Kenita Miller;** Melpomene/Medusa **Mary Testa;** Calliope/Aphrodite **Jackie Hoffman**[3]; Terpsicore/Siren/80's Singer/Hermes/Centaur **André Ward;** Clio/Kira **Kerry Butler;** Danny Maguire/Zeus **Tony Roberts;** Featured Skater **Marty Thomas;** Swings **Kate Loprest, Marty Thomas, Ryan Watkinson**[4]

UNDERSTUDIES Annie Golden (Calliope/Aphrodite, Melpomene/Medusa), Curtis Holbrook (Sonny), Patti Murin (Calliope/Aphrodite, Clio/Kira, Melpomene/Medusa), Kenita R. Miller (Clio/Kira), Kate Loprest (Clio/Kira), Peter Samuel (Danny Maguire, Zeus), André Ward (Calliope/Aphrodite, Melpomene/Medusa, Sonny)

*Succeeded by: 1. Curtis Holbrook (7/1/08), Cheyenne Jackson (7/29/08). 2 Curtis Holbrook (7/29/08). 3. Whoopi Goldberg (7/29/08), Jackie Hoffman (9/9/08) 4. Jacob ben Widmar

BAND Eric Stern (Music Director/synthesizers), Karl Mansfield (Associate Music Director/synthesizers), Chris Delis (guitar), Eric Halvorson (drums)

MUSICAL NUMBERS I'm Alive, Magic, Evil Woman, Suddenly, Whenever You're Away From Me, Dancin', Strange Magic, All Over the World, Don't Walk Away, Fool, The Fall, Suspended in Time, Have You Never Been Mellow?, Xanadu

SETTING Time: 1980. Place: Los Angeles and Mount Olympus. World premiere of a new musical presented without intermission.

SYNOPSIS *Xanadu,* based on the 1980 film, tells the story of one of the nine muses of ancient Greece who comes to earth to inspire the greatest of artistic achievements – a roller disco. Along the way she falls in love, bumps into an old acquaintance, and, for the first time, feels the desire to create herself.

(standing) *Mary Testa, Kerry Butler and Jackie Hoffman with* (kneeling l. to r.) *Curtis Holbrook, Anika Larsen, Kenita Miller and André Ward (photos by Paul Kolnik)*

Young Frankenstein
The New Mel Brooks Musical

Hilton Theatre; First Preview: November 11, 2007; Opening Night: November 8, 2007; Closed January 4, 2009; 30 previews, 484 performances

Book by Mel Brooks and Thomas Meehan, music and lyrics by Mel Brooks; based on the story and screenplay by Gene Wilder and Mel Brooks and on the motion picture by special arrangement with Twentieth Century Fox; "Puttin' on the Ritz" music and lyrics by Irving Berlin; Produced by Robert F.X. Sillerman and Mel Brooks, in association with The Routh · Frankel · Baruch · Viertel Group; Director & Choreography, Susan Stroman; Music Arrangements & Supervision, Glen Kelly; Sets, Robin Wagner, Costumes, William Ivey Long; Lighting, Peter Kaczorowski; Sound, Jonathan Deans; Special Effects, Marc Brickman; Wigs/Hair, Paul Huntley; Makeup, Angelina Avallone; Casting, Tara Rubin; Associate Director/Production Stage Manager, Steven Zweigbaum/Ira Mont; Associate Choreographer, Chris Peterson; Music Direction/Vocal Arrangements, Patrick S. Brady; Orchestrations, Doug Besterman; Music Coordinator, John Miller; General Management, Richard Frankel Productions, Laura Green; Technical Supervisors, Hudson Theatrical Associates/Neal Mazzella, Sam Ellis; Associate Producer, One Viking Productions, Carl Pasbjerg; Company Manager, Kathy Lowe; Associate Company Manager, Bobby Driggers; Stage Manager, Ira Mont/Ara Marx; Assistant Stage Manager, Ara Marx/Julia P. Jones; Assistant Director, Scott Bishop; Assistant Choreographer, Jeff Whiting; Dance Captains, James Gray, Courtney Young; Associate Design: David Peterson (set), Scott Traugott (costume), John Viesta (lighting); Animations, Joshua Frankel; Puppet Design, Michael Curry; Prosthetics, John Dods; Dialect Coach, Deborah Hecht, Additional Orchestrations, Michael Starobin; Synthesizer Programmer, Randy Cohen; Advertising, SpotCo; Press, Barlow · Hartman, Dennis Crowley, Michelle Bergmann; Cast recording: Decca Broadway B0010374-02

CAST Inspector Kemp/Hermit **Fred Applegate;** Dr. Frederick Frankenstein **Roger Bart;** Elizabeth **Megan Mullally**[*1]; Igor **Christopher Fitzgerald**[*2]; Inga **Sutton Foster**[*3]; Frau Blucher **Andrea Martin**[*4]; The Monster **Shuler Hensley;** Masha **Heather Ayers**[*5]; Ziggy/Shoeshine Man/Lawrence **Jim Borstelmann;** Herald/Bob/Transylvania Quartet **Paul Castree**[*6]; Mr. Hilltop/Transylvania Quartet **Jack Doyle;** Equine/Sasha/Ritz Specialty **Eric Jackson;** Medical Student/The Count **Matthew Labanca;** Medical Student/Victor/Transylvania Quartet **Kevin Ligon;** Tasha **Linda Mugleston;** Basha **Christina Marie Norrup;** Medical Student/Equine **Justin Patterson;** Telegraph Boy/Transylvania Quartet **Brian Shepard;** Ensemble **Heather Ayers**[*5], **Jim Borstelmann, Paul Castree**[*6], **Jennifer Lee Crowl, Jack Doyle, Renée Feder**[*7], **Amy Heggins**[*8], **Eric Jackson, Matthew Labanca, Kevin Ligon, Barrett Martin, Linda Mugleston, Christina Marie Norrup, Justin Patterson, Brian Shepard, Sarah Strimel**[*9]; Swings **James Gray, Kristin Marie Johnson, Craig Waletzko, Courtney Young**[*10]

*Succeeded by: 1. Michele Ragusa (8/5/08) 2. Cory English (11/25/08) 3. Beth Leavel (7/15/08) 4. Kelly Sullivan (7/8/08) 5. Linda Gabler 6. Aaron Ramey 7. Lara Seibert 8. Angie Schworer, Amy Heggins 9. Amanda Kloots-Larson 10. Beth Johnson Nicely

UNDERSTUDIES Heather Ayers (Elizabeth, Frau Blucher), Jim Borstelmann (Inspector Kemp/Hermit, The Monster), Paul Castree (Dr. Frederick Frankenstein), Renée Feder (Inga), James Gray (Igor), Matthew Labanca (Dr. Frederick Frankenstein), Kevin Ligon (Inspector Kemp/Hermit,), Linda Mugleston (Elizabeth, Frau Blucher), Christina Marie Norrup (Inga), Justin Patterson (The Monster), Brian Shepard (Igor)

ORCHESTRA Patrick S. Brady (Conductor/keyboard); Gregory J. Dlugos (Associate Conductor/keyboard 1); David Gursky/William Johnson (Assistant Conductor/keyboard 2); Vincent Della-Rocca, Steven J. Greenfield, Charles Pillow, Frank Santagata (woodwinds); Don Downs, Glenn Drewes, Scott Harrell (trumpets); Tim Sessions, Mike Christianson (trombones); Patrick Pridemore,

Judy Yin-Chi Lee (French horns); Rick Dolan–Concertmaster, Ashley D. Horne, Helen Kim/Una Tone (violins); Maxine Roach, Debra Shufelt-Dine (violas); Laura Bontrager, Chungsun Kim (cello); Bob Renino (bass); Perry Cavari (drums); Charles Descarfino (percussion)

MUSICAL NUMBERS The Happiest Town, The Brain, Please Don't Touch Me, Together Again, Roll in the Hay, Join the Family Business, He Vas My Boyfriend, The Law; Life, Life; Welcome to Transylvania, Transylvania Mania, He's Loose, Listen To Your Heart, Surprise, Please Send Me Someone, Man About Town, Puttin' on the Ritz, Deep Love, Frederick's Soliloquy, Deep Love (reprise), Finale Ultimo

SETTING Transylvania and New York City. World premiere of a new musical presented in two acts. Prior to its Broadway engagement, the show had an out-of-town tryout at the Paramount Theatre in Seattle, Washington, August 7–September 1, 2007.

SYNOPSIS Based on the hit 1974 film, *Young Frankenstein* is the wickedly inspired re-imagining of the Mary Shelley classic from the comic genius of Mel Brooks. When Frederick Frankenstein, an esteemed New York brain surgeon and professor, inherits a castle and laboratory in Transylvania from his deranged genius grandfather, he faces a dilemma: does he continue to run from his family's tortured past, or does he stay in Transylvania to carry on his grandfather's mad experiments reanimating the dead and, in the process, fall in love with his sexy lab assistant, Inga?

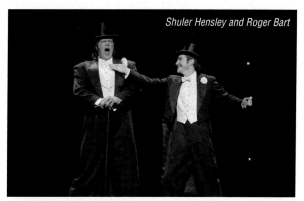
Shuler Hensley and Roger Bart

Beth Leavel (photos by Paul Kolnik)

Special Events

Broadway Bares 18: Wonderland

Roseland Ballroom; June 22, 2008

Produced by Broadway Cares/Equity Fights AIDS, Michael Graziano, Michael Clarkston, Scott Tucker; Presenting Sponsor, The M•A•C AIDS Fund; Executive Producer, Jerry Mitchell; Director, Denis Jones; Associate Director, Peter Gregus; Lighting, Paul Miller; Projections, Michael Clark, Brian Beasley, Leah Gelpe; Sound, Acme Sound Partners; Costume Coordinator, David Kaley; Hair Design/Coordination, Justen M. Brosnan, Kat Ventura; Makeup Design/Coordination, The M•A•C Pro Team; AntiGravity Artistic Director, Christopher Harrison; The Living Art of Armando Artistic Director, Armando Farfan Jr.; Scenic Design, Mary Houston; Props/Décor, David Masenheimer; Production Manager, Nathan Hurlin; Production Stage Manager, Timothy Eaker; Choreographers, Connor Gallagher, Nick Kenkel, Dontee Kiehn, Steve Konopelski, Lorin Latarro, Rhonda Miller, John Paolillo, Josh Rhodes, Shea Sullivan, Lee Wilkins; Rotation Masters, Christopher Sieber, Jennifer Cody; Associate Producer, Trisha Doss; Stage Managers, Michael Alifanz, Hilary Austin, Connie Baker, Andrea Jess Berkey, Jared T. Carey, Zac Chandler, Alix Claps, Casey Cook, Richard Costabile, Kimothy Cruse, Matthew DiCarlo, Chris Economakos, Theresa Flanagan, Bess Marie Glorioso, Marci Glotzer, Bradley Harder, Michail Haynes, Robyn Henry, Dan Holzberg, Samuel-Moses Jones, Laura Kayne, Gabe Kirshner, Terri Kohler, Talia Krispel, Ken McGee, Eric Montesa, Chris Munnell, Rob Piper, Andrew Polizzi, Thomas Recktenwald, Megan Schneid, Lisa Schwartz, Justin Scribner, Tim Semon, Jess W. Speaker III, David Sugarman, Carol A. Sullivan, Jason Trubitt, Sarah Tschirpke, Michael Willhoite, Deborah Wolfson; Opening Number ("Wonderland"): Music and lyrics by Jeff Bowen, book by Hunter Bell, music direction by Larry Pressgrove, choreography by Denis Jones; Press, Boneau/Bryan-Brown

John Carroll, Mary Birdsong, James Brown III and Michael Cunio (photo by Andrew Eccles)

THE COMPANY Mary Birdsong (Alice), Susan Mosher (Teacher), Tituss Burgess (White Rabbit), Matthew Morrison (Humpty Dumpty), Nathan Lane (Cheshire Cat), Andrea Martin (Mrs. Cheshire Cat), Tyler Maynard (Joan Crawford), Jennifer Cody (Christina Crawford), Julie White (Mock Turtle), Christopher Sieber (Knave of Hearts), Amber Efe (Dodo Bird), AntiGravity (Mad Hatter's Tea Party); Singers: Courtney Balan, Barrett Foa, Becky Gulsvig, Carla Hargrove, Skie Ocasio, Coco Sansoni, Dinah Steward, Tom Souhrada, Tory Ross; Ensemble: Nick Adams, Scott Ahearn, Dante Alan, John Alix, Sean S. Allison, Matthew Anctil, Beckley Andrews, Tommaso Antico, Michael Apuzzo, Dave August, Jolynn Baca, Sol Baird, Michael Balderrama, Sean Baptiste, Lori Barber, Brian Barry, Kiara Bennett, Tommy Berklund, John Berno, Michael Blatt, Amber Bloom, Shelly Bomb, Patrick Boyd, Thomas Bradfield, Sean Bradford, Steve Bratton, Nancy Renee Braun, Amy Brewer, James Brown III, Michelle Brugal, Tara Bruno, Michael Buchanan, Lawrence Bullock, Holly Ann Butler, Tym Byerz, Daniel Byrd, Michelle Camaya, Katie Cameron, Erin Carpenter, Allyson Carr, Callie Carter, Gage Cass, Camillo Castro, Alicia Charles, Andrew Cheng, Jennifer Cloer, Charlotte Cohn, Brian Collier, Rosie Colosi, Anna Cooke, Theresa Coombe, Joey Costella, Gabriel Croom, Jennifer Lee Crowl, Chris Crowthers, Holly Cruz, Michael Cunio, Colin Cunliffe, Nick Dalton, Marlowe Davis, Kayce Davis, Anthony DeCarlis, Kristin DeCesare, Vincent DePaul, Phillip Deyesso, Ashley deZeeuw, Michelle Dowdy, Janet Duran, Apolla Echino, Mark Stuart Eckstein, Trevor Efinger, Lynann Escatel, J. Autin Eyer, Armando Farfan, Rosie Lani Fiedelman, Jaime Fisher, Tony Falcon, Adam Fleming, Ramón Flowers, Eric Fogel, Mikala Freitas, Damian L. Furtch, Chris Galen, Spencer Gates, Asmeret Ghebremichael, Mark Gindick, Leslie Goddard, Shiloh Goodin, Frankie James Grande, Justin Greer, Latrice M. Gregory, Katy Grenfell, Jenny Gruby-Field, Erika Hamilton, Tim Hausmann, Luke Hawkins, Mair Heller, Dennis Henriquez, Erin Henry, Sarah Hicks, Afra Hines, Deirdre Hoetmer, William B. Hubert II, Rory Hughes, William S. Huntley III, Karen Hyland, Meredith Inglesby, Cheyenne Jackson, Ryan Jackson, Tony James, Heather Janneck, Kolina Janneck, Sarah Jenkins, Nicole Adell Johnson, Beth Johnson, Joey Johnson, Amy Karlein, Regan Kays, Nick Kenkel, Keway Kua, Michelle Kittrell, Stephanie Klemons, Amanda Kloots, Bryan Knowlton, Joe Komara, Keith Kuhl, Nina LaFarga, Leah Landau, Nikka Lanzarone, John Paul LaPorte, Lorin Latarro, Adam Lendermon, Spencer Liff, Emily Loftiss, Kate Loprest, Craig Lowry, Jermian M. Maestas, Erin Maguire, Christopher Mai, Timothy John Mandala, Tyler Marcum, Benjamin Martin, Chas McCallon, Christen McCollum, Ray Mercer, Jeff Metzler, Brant Michaels, Mayumi Miguel, Jacob Moody, Melissa MsTickle, Brian Patrick Murphy, Taela Naomi, NATEKid, Ron Nehass, Vince Nelson, Brian Newman, Katrina Newman, Brandon Christopher O'Neal, Shaun Ozminski, Jessica Pack, Liz Patek, Alison Paterson, Brandon Perayda, William Michael Peters, Hayley Podschun, Jacqui Polk, Eric Potter, Rachelle Rak, Johary Ramos, John Raterman, Ian Reece, Ariel Reid, Joe Aaron Reid, Jody Reynard, Kristian Richards, Paul Michael Riner, Amanda Ritchie, Josephine Rose Roberts, Travis Robertson, Arbender Robinson, Daniel Robinson, Robbie Roby, Miguel Romero, Matthew Rossoff, Constantine Rousouli, Ben Ryan, Amy Ryerson, Gerard Salvador, Sean Samuels, John San Juan, Kate Sarner, Kimberly Schafer, Amanda Schoppe, Ravi Sagar Seepersad, Jennifer Setzler, Ericka Shannon, LaQuet Sharnell, Robb Sherman, Kim Shriver, Brian Slaman, Dani Spieller, Shane Stitley, Chelsea Stock, Gregory D. Stockbridge, Lauren Strigari, Charlie Sutton, James Tabeek, Marty Thomas, Casey Leigh Thompson, Tigger!, Katherine Tokarz, Nicky Venditti, Kat Ventura, Luke Vexler, Josh Walden, Shonté Walker, Franklyn Warfield, Daniel J. Watts, Jesse Wildman, Jake Wilson, Sidney Erik Wright, Matthew Zimmerman

FUNDRAISING $874,372

SYNOPSIS A variety burlesque show presented without intermission. Since its inception in 1992, choreographer and director Jerry Mitchell – then in the ensemble of *The Will Rogers Follies* – put six of his fellow dancers up on the bar at an infamous "watering hole" in New York City's Chelsea district and raised $8,000 for Broadway Cares, the 18 editions of Broadway Bares have grown beyond all expectations, raising more than $5.7 million for Broadway Cares/Equity Fights AIDS.

Goodbye Yellow Brick Road

New Amsterdam Theatre; October 20, 2008

Written by Elton John and Bernie Taupin; Produced by Jeffrey Seller; Special Assistance, Scott Campbell, Michael T. Clarkston, Michael Graziano, Caitlyn Thomson, Tom Viola; Director/Choreographer, Andy Blanken Beuhler; Music Direction/Arrangements, Tom Kitt; Sound, Marie Renee Foucher; Lighting, Dan Walker; Production Stage Manager, Beverly Jenkins; General Manager, Lizbeth Cone; Production Manager/Stage Design, Nathan Hurlin; Stage Managers, Stephen Gruse, Heather Hogan, Nathan Hurlin, Samuel Moses Jones, Michael Palm, Alexis Pruassack, Amber Wedin; Special Material written by Dick Scanlon and Sherie Rene Scott; Keyboard Programmers, Randy Cohen & Jim Mironchik; Copyist, Colleen Darnall

CAST Elton John, Joey Arias, Ben Folds, Melissa Hough, Larry Keigwin, Jane Krakowski, Mary McBride, Lin-Manuel Miranda, John Cameron Mitchell, Kelli O'Hara, Sherie Rene Scott, Jake Shears, Shockwave, Stew, Rufus Wainwright, Patrick Wilson; The cast of *Hair* Ato Blankson-Wood, Steel Burkhardt, Allison Case, Lauren Elder, Jonathan Groff, Anthony Hollock, Kaitlyn Kiyan, Andrew Kober, Nicole Lewis, John Moauro, Darius Nichols, Brandon Pearson, Megan Reinking, Paris Remillard, Bryce Ryness, Saycon Sengbloh, Kacie Sheik, Theo Stockman, Tommar Wilson; The cast of *The Lion King* Kissy Simmons, Dashaun Young, Michelle Brugal, Gabriel Croom, Nicole Adell Johnson, Joel Karie, Ray Mercer, LaQuet Sharnell; The Broadway Inspirational Voices Gertie James, Mitzi Smith, Lucia Giannetta, Tasha Smith, La-Rita Gaskins, Danielle Greaves, Crystal Monee Hall, Lisa Mathis, Gavin Creel, Eliseo Román, Marcus Paul James, John Eric Parker; Dancers Joey Dowling, Neil Haskell, Spencer Liff, Cindy Salgado, Ron Todorowski, Ricky Tripp; The "Dirty Little Girls" Jenifer Foote, Asmeret Ghebremichael, Courtney Laine Mazza

THE TOM KITT BAND Tom Kitt (Conductor/piano), Damien Bassman (drums), Michael Arons & Alec Berlin (guitars), Randy Landau (bass), Dan Willis (reeds), Randy Cohen & Adam Ben David (keyboards); Back-up vocals: Gavin Creel, Crystal Monee Hall, Marcus Paul James, Mitzi Smith

MUSICAL NUMBERS Funeral for a Friend, Love Lies Bleeding, Candle in the Wind, Bennie and the Jets, Goodbye Yellow Brick Road, This Song Has No Title, Grey Seal, Jamaica Jerk-Off, I've Seen That Movie Too, Sweet Painted Lady, The Ballad of Danny Bailey, Dirty Little Girl, All the Girls Love Alice, Your Sister Can't Twist (But She Can Rock 'n' Roll), Saturday Night's Alright for Fighting, Roy Rogers, Social Disease, Harmony

SYNOPSIS A benefit concert presented without intermission. Celebrating the 35th anniversary of Elton John and Bernie Taupin's legendary double album *Goodbye Yellow Brick Road*, this one-night-only concert benefited Broadway Cares/Equity Fights AIDS, the Elton John AIDS Foundation and Friends In Deed.

Elton John and Bernie Taupin
(photo by Kevin Mazur/WireImage)

All About Eve

Eugene O'Neill Theatre; November 10, 2008

Screenplay by Joseph L. Mankiewicz based on Mary Orr's short story "The Wisdom of Eve," adapted for the staged reading by David Rambo; Presented by Tim Pinckney and The Actors Fund, courtesy of Twentieth Century Fox Film Corporation with special thanks to Duncan C. Weldon, Paul Elliot and Sonia Freedman; Director, John Erman; Line Producer, Patrick Weaver; Set Consultant, James Noone; Lighting Consultant, Kevin Adams; Costume Supervisor, Mary Ann Smith; Sound, Frances Elers; Casting, Jim Carnahan, Kate Boka; Production Stage Manager, Margie Howard; Program, Tina Royero; Press, Boneau/Bryan-Brown, Chris Boneau, Susanne Tighe, Christine Olver

CAST Addison deWitt **Brian Bedford;** Chief Prompter **Zoe Caldwell;** Karen Richards **Cynthia Nixon;** Eve Harrington **Keri Russell;** Margo Channing **Annette Bening;** Lloyd Richards **John Slattery;** Birdie Coonan **Angela Lansbury;** Bill Sampson **Peter Gallagher;** Miss Caswell **Jennifer Tilly;** Max Fabian **Joel Grey;** Pianist at the Party **Steve Ross;** Phoebe **Jessica Cummings;** Gus/Waiter/others **Victor Joel Ortiz;** A Girl **Maura Lisabeth Malloy**

SYNOPSIS A staged reading presented in two acts. In this benefit for The Actors Fund, the classic backstage drama based on the 1950 Twentieth Century Fox tells the story of a prominent yet aging Broadway star and the willingly helpful young fan who insinuates herself into the star's life and ultimately threatens the star's career and personal relationships.

The Actors Fund All About Eve *benefit reading: John Slattery, Angela Lansbury, Brian Bedford, Annette Bening, Keri Russell, Joel Grey and Zoe Caldwell (photo by Shevett Studios)*

Gypsy of the Year Competition

New Amsterdam Theatre; December 8 & 9, 2008

Written by Jody O'Neil; Presented by Broadway Cares/Equity Fights AIDS, Michael T. Clarkston, Michael Graziano, Scott Tucker; Director, Paul Smith; Associate Director, Schele Williams Kleinberger; Lighting, Philip Rosenberg; Sound, Kurt Fischer & Marie Renee Foucher; Production Manager, Nathan Hurlin; Production Stage Manager, Jason Trubitt; Stage Managers, Terry Alexander, Alix Clapps, Michael T. Clarkston, Casey Cook, Christopher Economakos, Bess Marie Glorioso, Alexis Prussack, Jennifer Rogers, Kim Russell, Nancy Wernick; Host: Seth Rudetsky with special guests Tyne Daly and Jonathan Hadary; Judges: Elizabeth Ashley, Dr. Harold Brody, Paige Davis, Howard McGillin, Kate Mulgrew, Patrick Page, Peter Sarsgaard, Marion Duckworth Smith, Kendall D. Ward; Judge Introductions: Seth Rudetsky, Gregory Jbara, Zack Jbara, Aidan Jbara; Awards Presentation: Christine Baranski, Harvey Fierstein, and John Lithgow (on-stage presentation and fundraising participants); Blake Daniel, Carey Mulligan, and Adam Fiorentino (fundraising-only participants); Sponsors, Continental Airlines, M•A•C AIDS Fund, and *The New York Times*; Press, Boneau/Bryan-Brown

HIGHLIGHTS Opening Number ("The Gypsy Robe") created by Ben Cohn & Nathan Tysen, directed and choreographed by Joshua Bergasse, featuring Harvey Evans, Tracee Beazer, Jeff Johnson-Doherty with Pascale Faye, Rommy Sandhu and Judine Somerville; Appearance by Don Richard and Jennifer Cody (as "Officer Lockstock" and "Little Sally" from *Urinetown*) performing "The Broadway Bailout"; Closing Number ("My First Time") written and performed by the cast of *[title of show]*: Hunter Bell, Jeff Bowen, Susan Blackwell, Heidi Blickenstaff, and Larry Pressgrove

COMPETITION Winner: *The Lion King* ("Guess Who's Coming to Dinner"); Runner-up: *Equus* ("The Love That Dare Not Speak Its Neigh"); Participants: The casts of *13* ("Under Eighteen!!"), *August: Osage County* ("The Backer's Audition"), *Grease* ("*Grease* Goes Red"), *Gypsy* ("*Gypsy* Top Ten"), *Hairspray* ("I Know Where I've Been"), *In the Heights*, *Mamma Mia!* ("*Mamma Mia* Presents '*Mamma Mia* Presents'"), *Naked Boys Singing* ("A Naked Boy's Mantra"), *Rock of Ages* ("Hillbilly Elliot"), *Monty Python's Spamalot* ("Forget Your Troubles"), *South Pacific* ("Terminator 5"), *The Little Mermaid* ("Key Westside Story"), *The Marvelous Wonderettes* ("Snowfall")

FUNDRAISING Total for 63 participating Broadway, Off-Broadway, and National Touring Companies: $3,061,148; Broadway Top Fundraiser: *Equus* ($203,746, the most raised by a Broadway play in *Gypsy of the Year Competition* history); First Runner-up: *Wicked* ($172,301); Second Runner-up: *South Pacific* ($140,552); Third Runner-up: *Hairspray* ($125,291); Off-Broadway Top Fundraiser: *The Marvelous Wonderettes* ($17,824); National Touring Shows Top Fundraiser: *Jersey Boys* – Chicago ($220,000); First Runner-up: *Wicked* – Chicago ($178,500); Second Runner-up: *Wicked* – Los Angeles ($161, 868); Total for 17 National Touring Companies: $1,210,868

Left: *Richard Griffiths and Daniel Radcliffe at the 20th Annual Gypsy of the Year Competition (photo by Peter James Zielinski)*

SYNOPSIS 20th annual talent and variety show presented without intermission. The *Gypsy of the Year Competition* is the culmination of a period of intensive fundraising where New York's most talented "gypsies," chorus members from Broadway and Off-Broadway shows, join in a competition variety show as six weeks of intensive fundraising by the community comes to a close. Since 1989, 20 editions of the *Gypsy of the Year* have raised a combined total of $35,730,000 for Broadway Cares/Equity Fights AIDS.

The Company of The Who's Tommy *Reunion Concert (photo by Peter James Zielinski)*

The Who's Tommy: 15th Anniversary Benefit Concert

August Wilson Theatre; December 15, 2008

Concept, music and lyrics by Pete Townsend, book by Pete Townsend and Des McAnuff, additional music and lyrics by John Entwistle and Keith Moon; Presented by Rockers on Broadway and the PATH Fund; Director, Donnie Kehr; Music Director/Vocal Arrangements, Joe Church; Projections, Wendall Harrington; Original Production Photos, Peter Cunningham; Lighting, Herrick Goldman; Sound, Lucas Corrubia; Production Manager, Mitch Keller; Stage Managers, Michael T. Clarkston and Matthew Melchiorre; Company Manager, Judith Drasner; Producer, Sandy Hicks; Executive Producers, Cori Gardner and Donnie Kehr; Assistant Directors, Ben Cameron, Gerry McIntyre; Stage Managers, Angela Allen, Christopher Economakos, Matthew Melchiore, Michael Palm, Rob Piper, Thomas Recktenwald, Jennifer Rogers; Associate Production Manager, Nathan Hurlin; Special Assistance, Michael T. Clarkston, Sandy Carlson, Michael Graziano, Nathan Hurlin, Mitch Keller, Bobby Maguire, Tom Viola; Sponsors, Base Entertainment, Jeff Davis, The Dodgers, The Frye Company, Joseph J. Grano Jr., Miller Coors, Kevin and Tamara Kinsella, Sony/BMG Masterworks, and Rothmann's Steakhouse; Special Presentation by Des McAnuff; Press, The Karpel Group

CAST Allied Soldier/Local Lad/Security Guard/Ensemble **Michael Arnold;** Cousin Kevin **Anthony Barrile;** Little Tommy **David Bologna;** Minister/Mr. Simpson/Ensemble **Bill Buell;** Kevin's Mother/Local Lass/Ensemble **Maria Calabrese;** Ensemble **Victoria Cave;** Tommy **Michael Cerveris;** Local Lass/Ensemble **Tracy Nicole Chapman;** Ensemble **Tracey Langran Corea;** Local Lad/Security Guard/Ensemble **Paul Dobie;** Mr. Walker **Jonathan Dokuchitz;** Judge/Kevin's Father/News Vendor/DJ/Ensemble **Tom Flynn;** The Gypsy **Cheryl Freeman;** Ensemble **Romaine Frugé;** Mrs. Walker **Marcia Mitzman Gaven;** Minister's Wife/Ensemble **Jody Gelb;** Local Lad/Security Guard/2nd Pinball Lad/Ensemble **Christian Hoff;** Ensemble **Todd Hunter;**

Uncle Ernie **Paul Kandel;** Local Lad/Security Guard/1ˢᵗ Pinball Lad/Ensemble **Donnie Kehr;** Local Lass/Mrs. Simpson/Ensemble **Pam Klinger;** Nurse/Local Lass/Ensemble **Lisa Leguillou;** Specialist/Ensemble **Norm Lewis;** Lover/Harmonica Player/Ensemble **Lee Morgan;** Local Lad/Security Guard/Hawker/Ensemble **Destan Owens;** Local Lass/Specialist Assistant/Ensemble **Alice Ripley;** Ensemble **Clarke Thorell;** Local Lass/Sally Simpson/Ensemble **Sherie Rene Scott;** Local Lad/Security Guard/Ensemble **Timothy Warmen**

BAND Joseph Church (Conductor/keyboard), Henry Aronson & Ted Baker (keyboards), Alan Childs (drums), Katie Dennis (French horn), Charles Descarfino (percussion), David Kuhn (bass), Kevin Kuhn & John Putnam (guitar)

MUSICAL NUMBERS Overture, Captain Walker, It's a Boy, We've Won, Twenty-One, Amazing Journey, Courtroom Scene, Sparks, Christmas, Do You Think It's Alright, Fiddle About, See Me Feel Me, Cousin Kevin, Sensation, Eyesight To the Blind, Acid Queen, Pinball Wizard, Underture, There's A Doctor I Found, Go To the Mirror, Listening To You, Tommy, Can You Hear Me?, I Believe My Own Eyes, Smash the Mirror, I'm Free, Miracle Cure, I'm Free/Pinball Wizard (reprise), Tommy's Holiday Camp, Sally Simpson, Welcome, Sally Simpson's Question, See Me Feel Me (reprise), Listening to You

SYNOPSIS Concert version of the musical presented in two acts. Originally produced on Broadway at the St. James Theatre April 22, 1993 (see *Theatre World* Vol. 50, page 81). This benefit concert (for Broadway Cares/Equity Fights AIDS, the Broadway Dreams Foundation and the Bachmann-Strauss Dystonia and Parkinson Foundation) reunited most of the original cast of the groundbreaking Broadway rock musical.

A Little Night Music

Studio 54; January 12, 2009

Music and lyrics by Stephen Sondheim, book by Hugh Wheeler, suggested by a film by Ingmar Bergman; Presented by the Roundabout Theatre Company (Todd Haimes, Artistic Director; Harold Wolpert, Managing Director; Julia C. Levy, Executive Director); Director, Scott Ellis; Music Director, Paul Gemignani; Orchestrations, Jonathan Tunick; Set Consultant, Derek McLane; Costume Consultant, Jeff Mahshie; Lighting, Kenneth Posner; Sound, Tony Meola & Zach Williamson; Projections, Wendall K. Harrington; Production Stage Manager, Lori M. Doyle; Associate Director, Dave Solomon; Casting, Jim Carnahan, Kate Boka; Technical Supervisor, Steve Beers; Executive Producer, Sydney Beers; Marketing & Sales, David B. Steffen; Founding Director, Gene Feist; Associate Artistic Director, Scott Ellis; Orchestra Contractor, Ronald Sell; Press, Boneau/Bryan-Brown

CAST Mr. Lindquist **Philip Cokorinos;** Mrs. Nordstom **Maija Lisa Currie;** Mrs. Anderssen **Julianne Borg;** Mr. Erlanson **Steven Goldstein;** Mrs. Segstrom **Leena Chopra;** Fredrika Armfeldt **Alexandra Socha;** Madame Armfeldt **Vanessa Redgrave;** Frid **Benjamin Walker;** Henrik Egerman **Steven Pasquale;** Anne Egerman **Jill Paice;** Fredrik Egerman **Victor Garber;** Petra **Kendra Kassebaum;** Desirée Armfeldt **Natasha Richardson;** Count Carl-Magnus Malcolm **Marc Kudisch;** Countess Charlotte Malcolm **Christine Baranski**

ORCHESTRA Paul Gemignani (Conductor); Sylvia D'Avanzo, C. Louise Owen, Kathleen Hannauer Genovia Cummins, Ming Yeh, Lisa Steinberg (violins); Richard Brice, Shelly Holland-Moritz (violas); Roger Shell, Deborah Assael (cello); John Beal (bass); Kathleen Nester (flute); Diane Lesser (oboe); Amy Zoloto (clarinet); Leno Gomez (bass clarinet); Marc Goldberg (bassoon); Russell Rizner, Chard Yarbrough, Ronald Sell (horns); Dominic Derasse, Carl Albach (trumpets); Dean Plank (bass trombone); Tony Gerales (piano); Thad Wheeler (percussion); Jennifer Hoult (harp)

MUSICAL NUMBERS Overture, Night Waltz, Now, Later, Soon, The Glamorous Life, Remember, You Must Meet My Wife, Liaisons, In Praise of Women, Every Day a Little Death, A Weekend in the Country, The Sun Won't Set, It Would Have Been Wonderful, Perpetual Anticipation, Send in the Clowns, The Miller's Son, Finale

SYNOPSIS A Gala Concert Reading of the musical presented in two acts. The original production was presented on Broadway at the Shubert Theatre February 25, 1973–August 3, 1974, playing 601 performances (see *Theatre World* Volume 29, page 56.) This concert was ultimately the last New York stage appearance for the beloved Natasha Richardson, whose tragic death shocked the theatre community and the world on March 19, 2009.

The Roundabout Theatre Company's A Little Night Music *Gala Concert reading: Stephen Pasquale, Jill Paice, Victor Garber, Natasha Richardson, Marc Kudisch, Christine Baranski, Benjamin Walker, Kendra Kassebaum and Vanessa Redgrave (photo by Walter McBride)*

Broadway Backwards 4

American Airlines Theatre; February 9, 2009

Created, written and directed by Robert Bartley, with special material written by Danny Whitman; Presented by The Lesbian, Gay, Bisexual & Transgender Community Center; Event Co-chairs, John Kander and Terrence McNally; Executive Producers, Tom Kirdahy and Jay Lesiger; Artistic Producer, Danny Whitman; Producer, Wilson Alexander Aguilar; Music Director, Paul Staroba; Associate Director & Choreographer, Penny Ayn Maas; Lighting, Paul Miller; Costumes, Lane Fragomeli; Sound, Michael Amabile, Stephen Gallagher, Jason E. Lutz; Arrangements/Orchestrations, Patrick Brady, Jeffrey Campos, Josh Clayton, Chris Kong, Ian Schugal, Paul Staroba, Jeffrey Thomson, Chris Tilley, Jesse Vargas; Production Stage Manager, Justin Scribner; Associate Producer, Amanda DeMeester; Stage Managers, Mary Kathryn Flynt, Jamie Greathouse, Melanie T. Morgan, Katherine Wallace, Richard Costabile; Assistant Stage Managers, Michael Alifanz, Susan Davison, Matthew DiCarlo, Andrea Jo Martin; Production Assistants, Hal Fickett, Lexie Pregosin, Sarah Sahin, Tiffany Tabatchnick; Sound Services, Rain Live Audio/Jaosn Lutz; Dance Captains, Kurt Domoney, Christine LaDuca; Music Assistant, Chris Kong; Assistant Costumes, Adam Giradet; Assistant Lighting, Joel Shier; Technical Consultant, Paul Davila; Voice of Goddess, Sue Gilad

CAST Host **Jim Caruso**; Starring **Nancy Anderson, Sandra Bernhard, Tituss Burgess, Mario Cantone, Len Cariou, Jenna Coker-Jones, Jenn Colella, Alan Cumming, Jenifer Foote, Gina Gershon, Whoopi Goldberg, Jessica Lee Goldyn, Deidre Goodwin, Florence Henderson, Cheyenne Jackson, Christopher Kale Jones, Aaron Lazar, Jose Llana, Rue McClanahan, Maureen McGovern, Sally Mayes, Becki Newton, Ron Palillo, Kate Reinders, Jai Rodriguez, Christopher Sieber, John Tartaglia, Marty Thomas, Michael Urie, Kirsten Wyatt, Tony Yazbeck**; With **Heather Adair, Frank Anderson, Tiffany Borelli, Bree Branker, Jason Michael Butler, Darryl Calmese Jr., Jessica Carter, Shaun Colledge, Richard Costa, Philip D'Amore, Katrina Rose Dideriksen, Veronica DiPerna, Kurt Domoney, Miguel Angel Falcon, Tony Falcon, Lyndy Franklin, Joseph Lee Gramm, Eric Gunhus, Aaron Kaburick, John-Charles Kelly, Stephanie Klemons, Christine LaDuca, Charis Leos, Lou Marino, Tim McGarrigal, Patrick O'Neill, Tess Paras, Adam Perry, Raegan Pierce, Antuan Raimone, Enrico Rodriguez, Chuck Saculla, Adam Shapiro, Kristen J. Smith, Steve Webber**

ORCHESTRA Paul Staroba (Conductor), Chris Kong (piano), James Mironchik (synthesizer), Sean McDaniel (drums), Jake Schwartz (guitar), Steve Gilewski (bass), Sylvia D'Avanzo & Mary Whitaker (violins), Anik Oulianine (cello), Josh Johnson & Christine MacDonnell (reeds), Dan Urness (trumpet), Eric Vierhaus (trombone)

SYNOPSIS Fourth annual benefit concert presented in two acts; dedicated to Kenny Ellinghaus. Conceived by Robert Bartley in 2006, *Broadway Backwards* features men singing women's songs, women singing men's songs, and same sex duets. *Broadway Backwards 4* highlights included Florence Henderson and a chorus of female dancers performing "There is Nothing Like a Dame," Jose Llana, Christopher Sieber and John Tartaglia singing "Matchmaker, Matchmaker," Len Cariou singing "Losing My Mind" from *Follies*, and Tituss Burgess' rendition of "Meadowlark" from *The Baker's Wife*.

Jenna Coker, Stephanie Klemons and Whoopi Goldberg performing "Gee, Officer Krupke" in Broadway Backwards 4 *(photo by Michael Portantiere/FollowSpotPhoto.com)*

Defying Inequality: The Broadway Concert

Gershwin Theatre; February 23, 2009

Written by Michael Slade and Mark Shanahan; Produced by 4good Productions (Anthony Galde, Di Ana Pisarri, Jen Waldman, Schele Williams); Directors, Anthony Galde and Schele Williams; Music Director/Arrangements/Orchestrations, James Sampliner; Production Supervisor, Chris Jamros; Associate Producers, Todd Miller, Briana Yacavone, b. swibel presents; Lighting, Philip S. Rosenberg; Assistant Lighting, Anthony Pearson; Production Stage Manager, Jason Trubitt; Stage Managers, Christy; Ney, Jason Daunter; Assistant Stage Managers, Cameron Holsinger, Tom Recktenwald, Tim Semon, Michael Wilhoite, Chris Zaccardi; VariLites, Craig Aves; Special Costumes, Michael Bottari and Ronald Case; Music Contractor, Michael Keller; Press, Fifteen Minutes Public Relations, Pete Sanders, Patrick Paris, Josh Ferri

CAST Host **Judy Gold** and **Carson Kressley**; Featuring **Matt Alber, Shoshana Bean, Douglas Carter Beane, P.J. Benjamin, Cubby Bernstein, Mike Birbiglia, Stephanie J. Block, Tamara Braun, Daniel Breaker, Lisa Brescia, Kerry Butler, Lynda Carter, Jim Caruso, Gavin Creel, Harvey Fierstein, Jane Fonda, John Gallagher Jr., Malcolm Gets, Jonathan Groff, Jayne Houdyshell, Mark Indelicato, Allison Janney, Capathia Jenkins, Nathan Lane, Leigh Ann Larkin, Cyndi Lauper, Adriane Lenox, Rue McClanahan, Bebe Neuwirth, Phyllis Newman, Kelli O'Hara, Keith Olbermann, Nicole Parker, David Hyde Pearce, Billy Porter, Nicole Power, Christine Quinn, Seth Rudetsky, Sherri Saum, Stephen Schwartz, Marc Shaiman, Al Sharpton, Carole Shelley, Christopher Sieber, Doug Spearman, Sally Struthers, Tamara Tunie, Michael Urie, Dyllun Von Ritter, Scott Whitman**; Video Messages **Tyne Daly, Elton John, David Furnish, Clinton Kelly, Stacy London**; Performances by cast members from *Billy Elliot The Musical, Don't Quit Your Night Job, Gypsy, Hair, Jersey Boys,* Laughing Pizza, *Mamma Mia!, Mary Poppins,* New York City Gay Men's Chorus, *Sesame Street, Spring Awakening,* The Broadway Boys, *The Color Purple, The Lion King, The Little Mermaid, Wicked*

MUSICIANS James Sampliner and Randy Cohen (keyboards), Andy Schwartz (guitar), Steve Count (bass), Joe Nero (drums)

SYNOPSIS A celebrity benefit for equal rights presented in two acts. The benefit proceeded Empire State Agenda, Equality California, Family Equality Council, Garden State Equality, and Vermont Freedom to Marry. The benefit included the New York stage debut of Marc Shaiman's Prop 8 – The Musical, which was originally produced as a star-studded short video on Will Ferrell and Adam McKay's FunnyOrDie.com.

Easter Bonnet Competition

Minskoff Theatre; April 27 & 28, 2009

Written by Jody O'Neil and Eric Kornfeld; Presented by Broadway Cares/Equity Fights AIDS; Executive Producer, Tom Viola; Producers, Michael T. Clarkson, Michael Graziano, Scott Tucker; Director, Kristin Newhouse; Sound, Alain Van Achte; Lighting, Philip Rosenberg; Production Manager, Nathan Hurlin; Production Stage Manager, Valerie Lau-Kee Lai; Stage Managers, Terry Alexander, Christine Daly, Thom Gates, Bess M. Glorioso, Bart Kahn, Jennifer Rodgers, David Sugarman, Jason Trubitt, Nancy Wernick; Associate Producer, Trisha Doss; Hosts: Joan Allen, Danny Burstein, André DeShields, Tovah Feldshuh, Gavin Creel, Johanna Day, Rebecca Luker, Karen Olivo, Laura Osnes, Javier Muñoz, Thomas Sadoski, Will Swenson, John Tartaglia; Judges: Laura Benanti, Brian d'Arcy James, Marsha Mason, Steven Pasquale, Alice Ripley, Jeff Daniels, Hope Davis, Marcia Gay Harden, James Gandolfini; Awards Announcers: Jane Fonda, Jeremy Irons, Susan Sarandon; Judge Introductions: Andrea Martin, Geoffrey Rush; Sponsors: *The New York Times* and Continental Airlines; Press, Boneau/Bryan-Brown

Alison Janney, David Hyde Pierce, Nathan Lane (center) and the Company in Marc Shaiman's "Prop 8 – The Musical, " featured in Defying Inequality: The Broadway Concert *(photo by Michael Portantiere/ FollowSpotPhoto.com*

HIGHLIGHTS Opening Number ("Broadway Don't You Bring Me No Bad News"): written and directed by Michael Lee Scott, choreographed by Tammy Colucci, musical directed by Jeffrey Biering, and featuring Norm Lewis, Aisha Da Haas, Susan Blackwell, Julia Murney, Heidi Blickenstaff, Seth Rudetsky, and Stephanie Gibson; Doris Eaton Travis (the 105-year-old original Ziegfeld Follies Girl with Gregory Jbara and the ballet girls of *Billy Elliot* dancing "Ballin' the Jack"), Don Richard and Jennifer Cody (as "Officer Lockstock" and "Little Sally" from *Urinetown*), Liza Minnelli (singing "New York, New York" during the opening number), Closing Number: Andrea Burns ("Help Is On the Way," the official anthem of BC/EFA) with the finale bonnet presentation

BONNET PRESENTATION Winner: *33 Variations* ("Voluntary Rehearsal"); First Runner-up: *Billy Elliot The Musical*; Second Runner-up: *Naked Boys Singing* ("Gravity"); Participants: The casts of *Mary Poppins* ("I Think We Need a Tap Number Here!"), *The Marvelous Wonderettes* ("The Marvelous Farmerettes"), *Chicago* ("The Chopping Block Tango"), *Avenue Q* ("You're Nothing Without Me"), *The Little Mermaid* ("A Tony Worthy Performance"), *Shrek* ("Stimulus Plan"), *Wicked* ("More"), *Mamma Mia!* ("The Rose"), *Guys and Dolls* ("Fugue for Easter Bonnet"), *The Lion King* ("Viva Las Lion King"), *The Phantom of the Opera* ("[sequel of show]"), *West Side Story*, *Hair* ("Broadwaymatch.com"), *Jersey Boys*, *Impressionism*, National Tour Bonnet ("Traveling Thru")

BONNET DESIGN AWARD *33 Variations* (Designed by David Masenheimer)

FUNDRAISING Total for 58 participating Broadway, Off-Broadway, and National Touring Companies: $3,402,147; Broadway Top Fundraiser: *33 Variations* ($183,546, the most money ever raised by a play in *Easter Bonnet Competition* history); First Runner-up: *Wicked* ($176,714); Second Runner-up: *Billy Elliot The Musical* ($155,103); Third Runner-up: *Shrek* ($139,304); Off-Broadway Top Fundraiser: *Distracted* ($31,389); National Touring Shows Top Fundraiser and Overall Top Fundraiser: *Rent* (352,060) First Runner-up: *Wicked* – San Francisco ($254,888); Second Runner-up: *Mamma Mia!* ($135,111); Third Runner-up: *Jersey Boys* – Chicago ($130,570)

The final fundraising numbers for the 23rd Annual Easter Bonnet Competition *(photo by Thomas Vrzala)*

SYNOPSIS 23rd annual talent and variety show presented without intermission. The *Easter Bonnet Competition* is the two-day Broadway spectacular that features the companies of more than 20 Broadway, Off-Broadway and touring productions singing, dancing, comedic sketches and donning hand-crafted original Easter bonnets. This annual Broadway tradition is the culmination of six intensive weeks of fundraising efforts by Broadway, Off-Broadway, and national touring productions. Since 1987, 23 editions of the *Easter Bonnet Competition* have raised a combined total of $39,000,000 for Broadway Cares/Equity Fights AIDS, which, in turn, has supported programs at the Actors Fund including the AIDS initiative, The Phyllis Newman Women's Health Initiative, as well as over 400 AIDS and family service organizations across the country.

Come to the Cabaret:
A Celebration of Kander and Ebb

Schoenfeld Theatre; May 4, 2009

Written and directed by John Doyle, music and lyrics by John Kander and Fred Ebb; Presented by the Acting Company (Margot Harley, Producing Artistic Director); Music Director, Mary Mitchell-Campbell; Assistant Director, Adam John Hunter; Lighting, Daniel Chapman; Sound, Lee Rothenberg; Production Stage Manager, Michael J. Passaro; Production Manager, Scot Brodsky; Press, Judy Katz

CAST **Raúl Esparza, David Hyde Pierce, Terrence McNally, Liza Minnelli, Debra Monk, Chita Rivera, Tom Wopat, Karen Ziemba;** Kit Kat Girls **Heather Laws, Kristin Olness, Christina Pawl, Leenya Rideout, Katrina Yaukey**

MUSICIANS Carmel Dean (piano), Jim Donica (bass), Michael Croiter (drums)

SYNOPSIS A concert presented without intermission. This evening of song and dance, benefiting the Acting Company (founded in 1972 by John Houseman and Margot Harley) paid tribute to the legendary songwriting team of John Kander and Fred Ebb, featuring artists who have been attached to their musicals.

Debra Monk and David Hyde Pierce in Come to the Cabaret: A Celebration of Kander and Ebb *(photo by Walter McBride)*

Top: *Sahr Ngaujah* (right) *and the cast of* Fela! A New Musical. *Opened at 37 Arts September 4, 2008 (photo by Monique Carboni)*

Center: *Melanie Boland, George Ashiotis, Nick Viselli, Pamela Sabaugh in the Theatre Breaking Through Barriers production of* The Cocktail Hour. *Opened at the Kirk Theatre on Theatre Row June 6, 2008 (photo by Carol Rosegg)*

Bottom: *The cast of* Rock of Ages. *Opened at New World Stages October 16, 2008 (photo by Joan Marcus)*

Phylis Somerville and Miguel Cervantes in Lincoln Center Theater's *Happiness at the Mitzi E. Newhouse Theater (photo by Paul Kolnik)*

John Gallagher, Jr. and Olivia Thirlby in Atlantic Theater Company's *Farragut North (photo by Jacqueline Mia Foster)*

Thomas Sadoski and Emily Bergl in Second Stage production of Becky Shaw *(photo by Joan Marcus)*

Cynthia Nixon and Josh Stamberg in Roundabout Theatre Company's Distracted *at the Laura Pels Theatre. (photo by Joan Marcus)*

Ethan Hawke in A Winter's Tale *at the Brooklyn Academy of Music's premiere season of The Bridge Project (photo by Joan Marcus)*

Yaya Da Costa (foreground) and Quincy Dunn-Baker in Signature Theatre Company's The First Breeze of Summer *(photo by Richard Termine)*

Jim Norton and Kate Baldwin in the City Center Encores! production of Finian's Rainbow *(photo by Joan Marcus)*

Josh Grisetti and Allison Spratt in the York Theatre Company production of Enter Laughing The Musical *(photo by Carol Rosegg)*

Manhattan Theatre Club's Ruined *with Quincy Tyler Bernstine, Saidah Arrika Ekulona, Chiké Johnson, and William Jackson Harper at New York City Center's Stage 1 (photo by Joan Marcus)*

Michael Countryman in Shipwrecked! An
Entertainment at Primary Stages
(photo by James Leynse)

Kristine Neilsen and Laura Benanti in The
Public Theater production of Why Torture
Is Wrong, and the People Who Love Them
(photo by Joan Marcus)

John Douglas Thompson in the Theatre for a New Audience production
of Othello at the Duke on 42nd Street (photo by Gerry Goodstein)

Michael Laurence in Krapp, 39 at the Soho Playhouse
(photo by Dixie Sheridan)

Mike Birbiglia in Sleepwalk With Me at the Bleecker Street Theatre
(photo by Joan Marcus)

Beth Malone, Victoria Matlock, Bets Malone and Farah Alvin in The Marvelous Wonderettes at the
Westside Theatre (photo by Carol Rosegg)

Michael West, Jared Bradshaw and Gina Kreiezmar in
Forbidden Broadway Goes to Rehab *at the 47th Street
Theatre (photo by Carol Rosegg)*

David Cromer in Our Town *at The Barrow Street Theatre
(photo by Carol Rosegg)*

First row: *Scott Klavan, Peter Reznikoff* (suit and tie), *Maja
Wampuszyc, Gene Silvers, Tracee Chimo, Tovah Feldshuh.*
Second row: *John Stanisci* (Nazi uniform), *Sandi Carroll, Stephen
Hauck* (white apron), *Thomas Ryan in* Irena's Vow *at the Baruch
Performing Arts Center (photo by Carol Rosegg)*

James Brandon in Corpus Christi *at the Rattlestick Playwrights Theater (photo by Mikki Willis)*

Nancy Opel in The Toxic Avenger *at New World Stages (photo by Carol Rosegg)*

Garden of Earthly Delights *at the Minetta Lane Theatre (photo by Richard Finkelstein)*

Dominic Fumusa, Noah Emmerich, Josh Lucas and Jennifer Mudge in Fault Lines *at the Cherry Lane Theatre (photo by Carol Rosegg)*

Deirdre O'Connell and J. Smith-Cameron In Looking for the Pony *at the McGinn/Cazale Theatre*

Sky Seals and Kelli Maguire in Sessions *at the Algonquin Theater (photo by Murray Head)*

feminazi

Players Theatre; First Preview: May 22, 2008; Opening Night: June 5, 2008; Closed August 2, 2008; 6 previews, 26 performances (Thursday through Saturday evenings)

Written by Suzanne Willett; Produced by Will It Productions in association with Louis S. Salamone & Lucky Penny Productions; Director, Hillary Spector; Set/Lighting/Technical Director, Jana Mattioli; Production Graphics, Tom Kramer; Press, Maya PR, Penny Landau

CAST Fran Schneider/Sarah Whitcomb/Virgin Mary/the Feminazi **Suzanne Willett**

Transfer of the Off-Off-Broadway play presented without intermission. Previously presented at the Players Theatre Loft March 27–May 4, 2008

SYNOPSIS *feminazi* is about strong women & the men they scare. The Feminazi, an authoritarian woman, dissects and ridicules a term used to shut up strong women; The Virgin Mary shares her angst about the way she raised Jesus; Sara, a middle-class white female, shares what it means to be a woman in a man's career; Fran, an older woman, refuses to be marginalized no matter how much society threatens her.

Suzanne Willett in feminazi *(photo by Tom Kramer)*

Patriotic Bitch

Clurman Theatre on Theatre Row; First Preview: May 29, 2008; Opening Night: June 5, 2008; Closed June 29, 2008; 6 previews, 21 performances

Written by Alanna Ubach; Produced by Rob Kolson and Chu-Chu Pictures; Director, Ian McCrudden; Choreography, Joseph Craeg; Set, Alexander G. Lyle; Lighting, Steve Shelley; Costumes, Tin Wornom; Music, Ina May Woo & Daniel A. Weiss; Photo/Art Work, Glen Wexler; Associate Producer, Christopher Nathaniel; Press, Pete Sanders

CAST Yolanda Rodriquez and others **Alanna Ubach**

New York premiere of a solo performance play presented without intermission.

SYNOPSIS A funny misfit finds where she belongs in this irreverent one-woman show in which Alanna Ubach portrays several women from different societies, countries and walks of life and their frustrations about how hard it is to catch a break in this world. They are all introduced by Yolanda Rodriguez, a humble Mexican bathroom attendant trying to survive in Los Angeles.

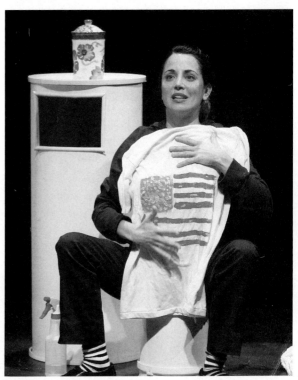

Alanna Ubach in Patriotic Bitch *(photo by Carol Rosegg)*

The Cocktail Hour

Kirk Theatre on Theatre Row; First Preview: May 24, 2008; Opening Night: June 6, 2008; Closed June 29, 2008; 10 previews, 22 performances

Written by A.R. Gurney; Presented by Theater Breaking Through Barriers (Ike Schambelan & George Ashiotis, Artistic Directors); Director, Ike Schambelan; Sets/Lighting, Bert Scott; Costumes, Chloe Chapin; Sound, Nicholas Viselli; PSM, Kimothy Cruse; ASM, Brooke Elsinghorst; Production Managers, David Chontos & Nicholas Lazzare; Marketing, Michelle Tabnick; Press, Shirley Herz & Associates

CAST Billy **George Ashiotis**; John **Nicholas Viselli**; Ann **Melanie Boland**; Nina **Pamela Sabaugh**

SETTING A city in upstate New York; an early evening in early fall. Revival of a play presented without intermission.

SYNOPSIS A writer returns home to ask permission of his parents to produce a show that he has written about them. Over cocktails, the family rehashes old slights and reopens old wounds but, with unflagging humor, they look toward the future.

Melanie Boland, George Ashiotis, Nick Viselli and Pamela Sabaugh in The Cocktail Hour *(photo by Carol Rosegg)*

Monsterface

Irish Arts Center Donaghy Theatre; First Preview: June 5, 2008; Opening Night: June 6, 2008; Closed June 28, 2008; 1 preview, 12 performances

Written by Daniel Roberts; Presented by Audax Theatre Group (Daniel Roberts & Daniel Tisman, Co-Founders); Director, Alex Lippard; Set, Michael Moore; Costumes, Kirche Zeile; Lighting, Graham Kindred; Sound, Paul Adams; Casting, Jenn Haltman; Stage Manager, Angela Allen; ASM, Michael Martin; Assistant Director, Brian Ziv; Press, Brett Singer and Associates

CAST Melanie Crane **Sarah Grace Wilson**; Anna Wood, Paul Crane **Ted Schneider**; Mr. Sanderson **Stuart Rudin**; Mickey **Jason Blaine**; Dr. Stovin **Davis Hall**; **Karen Lynn Gorney**

World premiere of a new play presented in two acts.

SYNOPSIS After Melanie Crane, a beautiful but middling actress suffers a mental breakdown, her husband Paul brings her to her childhood home of New Hope, PA to heal. On the night of a snowstorm and after an unspeakable secret is revealed, can the historical town of New Hope, where George Washington staged his famous Delaware crossing, help the Cranes save their marriage and their lives? Will it be Victory or Death for this troubled, modern couple?

Stuart Rudin and Jason Blaine in Monsterface *(photo by Monique Carboni)*

Three on a Couch

Soho Playhouse; First Preview: May 29, 2008; Opening Night: June 8, 2008; Closed June 22, 2008; 10 previews, 13 performances

Written by Carl Djerassi; Presented by Redshift Productions' Scientist's Studio (Max Evjen, Artistic and Executive Director; Megan Halpern, Artistic and Producing Director); Director, Elena Araoz; Set, Susan Zeeman Rogers; Costumes, Chloe Chapin; Lighting, Justin Townsend; Sound, Arielle Edwards & David Thomas; PSM, C.J. LaRoche; Press, Springer Associates, Joe Trentacosta

CAST Stephen Marx **Mark Pinter**; Miriam Marx **Lori Funk**; Theodore Hoffman **Brad Frazier**

U.S. premiere of a new play presented without intermission.

SYNOPSIS Commedia meets film noir in this comedy about art, ego, obsession ...and sticky fruit. A famous writer obsessed with reputation fakes his death in order to read his own obituaries. His shrink knows what's going on, but can't tell anyone, not even the writer's wife. But she's soon on his trail, as his 'death' ignites a chain of outrageous events.

A Dangerous Personality

Julia Miles Theatre; First Preview: June 4, 2008; Opening Night: June 11, 2008; Closed June 29, 2008; 7 previews, 18 performances

Written by Sallie Bingham; Presented by the Perry Street Theatre Company (David Elliott & Martin Platt, Co-Directors); Director, Martin Platt; Set, Bill Clarke; Lighting, Tom Sturge; Costumes, Martha Hally; Sound, Lindsay Jones; PSM, Allison Deutsch; Props, Troy Campbell; Graphics, Chris Rubino, Lauren Kosteski; Casting, Stephanie Klapper; Production Manager, Jason Adams; Production Supervisor, Paul Jones; ASM, Andrea Jo Martin; Assistant Lighting, Ethan Kaplan; Assistant Costumes, Erika Ingrid Lillienthal; Props, Beth Whitney; Press, David Gersten & Associates, Shane Marshall Brown, Kevin P. McAnarney, James Lopez

CAST Helena Petrovna Blavatsky **Jodie Lynne McClintock**; Colonel Henry Steel Olcott **Graeme Malcolm**; Little Dorritt **Nancy Anderson**; Countess Constance Wachtmeister **Lisa Bostnar**; Thomas Edison **Sheffield Chastain**; Reverend Hiram Bingham **Steve Brady**

SETTING The 'Lamasery', 302 W. 47th Street, NYC, 1878. A house in the Hindu Quarter of Bombay, India, 1879. World premiere of a new biographical play presented in two acts.

SYNOPSIS Russian-born spiritualist and philosopher Helena Blavatsky explored Tibet, fought with Garibaldi, rode across India on the back of an elephant, was friends with Thomas Edison – a terror to the establishment, and a nightmare to the British Raj.She lived everywhere from London to India to Hell's Kitchen – and was (and remains) one of the most controversial figures in world religion. With her colleague, Henry Steel Olcott, she created Theosophy – the science of religion, The Secret Doctrine – Christ without the Church. Her ideas are still as timely and thought provoking as then.

The Hired Man

59E59 Theater A; First Preview: June 5, 2008; Opening Night: June 11, 2008; Closed June 29, 2008; 7 previews, 23 performances

Book by Melvyn Bragg based on his novel, music & lyrics by Howard Goodall; Presented by New Perspectives Theatre Company (Daniel Buckroyd, Artistic Director; Chris Kirkwood, General Manager) as part of the Brits Off Broadway 2008 (Elizabeth Kleinhans, President & Artistic Director; Peter Tear, Executive Producer); Director, Daniel Buckroyd; Music Director, Richard Reeday; Design,

Juliet Shillingford; Lighting, Mark Dymock; Production Manager, Mandy Ivory-Castile; Choreography, Katie Howell; AEA Stage Manager, Amy Kaskeski; Consulting Director, Simon Green; Press, Sue Hyman Associates (London), Karen Greco (New York)

CAST John **Richard Colvin**; Joe/Harry **Lee Foster**; Sally/May **Katie Howell**; Jackson **Simon Pontin**; Seth **David Stothard**; Emily **Claire Sundin**; Isaac **Stuart Ward**; Pennington **Andrew Wheaton**

MUSICIANS Richard Reeday (piano), Jana Zielonka (keyboard)

MUSICAL NUMBERS Song of the Hired Men, Fill It to the Top, Now for the Time, Song of the Hired Men (reprise), Work, Who Will You Marry Then?, Get Up and Go Lad, I Wouldn't Be the First; Fade Away, Hear Your Voice, What a Fool I've Been, If I Could, Song of the Hired Men (reprise), You'll Never See the Sun, What Would You Say to Your Son?, Men of Stone, Farewell Song, War, Day Follows Day, Crossbridge Dance, No Choir of Angels, Hear Your Voice, Song of the Hired Men (reprise)

SETTING Rural Cumbria, U.K., at the turn of the twentieth century. American premiere of a musical presented in two acts. Originally produced in 1984 at the Nuffield Theatre in Southampton, and reprised at the Leicester Haymarket Theatre prior to a run in the West End.

SYNOPSIS *The Hired Man* tells the timeless, moving story of a young married couple and their struggle to carve a living from the land, just as the traditional rhythms of English country life are being interrupted by the gathering storm of war in Europe.

Simon Pontin and Claire Sundin in The Hired Man, *part of the Brits Off Broadway 2008 (photo by Tristram Kenton)*

Single Black Female

Duke on 42nd Street; First Preview: June 10, 2008; Opening Night: June 12, 2008; Closed June 29, 2008; 2 previews, 19 performances

Written by Lisa B. Thompson; Presented by New Professional Theatre (Sheila Davis, Artistic Director) and Black Spectrum Theatre (Carl Clay, Founder); Director, Colman Domingo; Set, Tim Mackabee; Costumes, Raul Aktanov; Lighting, Russell Phillip Drapkin; Sound, DJ Crystal Clear; Press, Sam Rudy Media Relations, Bob Lasko

CAST SBF1 **Soara-Joye Ross**; SBF 2 **Riddick Marie**

Revival of a play presented in two acts. Originally presented Off-Off Broadway with this cast at the Peter Jay Sharp Theatre at Playwrights Horizons June 15–25, 2006 (see *Theatre World* Vol. 63, page 280).

SYNOPSIS *Single Black Female* looks at the pleasures and perils of being a single middle class black woman who's got everything she wants and needs except more R-E-S-P-E-C-T -- and a man! The play mines topics such as dating (on the Internet and the old-fashioned way!), gynecology, family gatherings, shopping, racial bias, white folks and, poignantly, the odd sense of loss a black woman feels when she does find a man and leaves her single sisters behind.

Soara-Joye Ross and Riddick Marie in Single Black Female *(photo by Gerry Goodstein)*

Some Kind of Bliss

59E59 Theater C; First Preview: June 11, 2008; Opening Night: June 15, 2008; Closed June 29, 2008; 6 previews, 17 performances

Written by Samuel Adamson; Presented by Adam Knight as part of the Brits Off Broadway 2008 (Elizabeth Kleinhans, President & Artistic Director; Peter Tear, Executive Producer); Director, Toby Frow; Design, Lucy Osborne; Lighting, Stephen Holroyd; Composer/Sound, Richard Hammarton; Production Assistant, Karl Brown; Graphics/Photography, Matt Crockett; AEA Stage Manager, Cheryl D. Olszowka; Press, Ben Chamberlain (London), Karen Greco (New York)

CAST Rachel **Lucy Briers**

SETTING London, the present. American premiere of a new solo performance play presented without intermission. World premiere at Trafalgar Studios in the West End November 20, 2007.

SYNOPSIS Rachel, a small-time hack and seeker of minor adventure, sets off down the Thames Path to Greenwich to interview British pop legend Lulu for her tabloid's glossy supplement. But between London Bridge and Lulu's mirrored hallway lies a series of unpredicted and comic events

Lucy Briers in Some Kind of Bliss, *part of the Brits Off Broadway 2008 (photo by Alastair Muir)*

Vincent River

59E59 Theater B; First Preview: June 10, 2008; Opening Night: June 15, 2008; Closed June 29, 2008; 7 previews, 17 performances

Written by Philip Ridley; Presented by TFP–The Fish Partnership (Andrew Fishwick, Kate Mackonochie & Ros Povey, Producers; Ian Morris, Commercial Director; William Critzman, Associate Producer) in association with Old Vic New Voices as part of the Brits Off Broadway 2008 (Elizabeth Kleinhans, President & Artistic Director; Peter Tear, Executive Producer); Director/Sound, Steve Marmion; Lighting, Paul Miller; Assistant Director, Tobias Wright; AEA Stage Manager, Raynelle Wright; Press, Karen Greco

CAST Anita **Deborah Findlay**; Davey **Mark Field**

SETTING A run down apartment in Dagenham, East London; the present. American premiere of a new play presented without intermission. World premiere at the Hampstead Theatre in 2000, and revived by the Old Vic at Trafalgar Studios in October 2007.

SYNOPSIS *Vincent River* focuses on the meeting between a grief-stricken mother and a young boy who is in some way connected to the death of her son.

Mark Field and Deborah Findlay in Vincent River, *part of the Brits Off Broadway 2008 (photo by Carol Rosegg)*

Arias with a Twist

HERE Arts Center–Dorothy B. Williams Theatre; First Preview: June 12, 2008; Opening Night: June 18, 2008; Closed December 31, 2008; 181 performances

Created by Joey Arias & Basil Twist; Presented by HERE's Dream Music Puppetry Program and Tandem Otter Productions by Barbara Busackino in association with Johnnie Moore; Director, Basil Twist; Costume Design, Chris March; Original Songs, Alex Gilford; Musical Arrangements/Production, Eliot Douglas & Jean-Francois Houle; Video/Projections, Daniel Brodie; Lighting, Ayumu Saegusa; Sound, Greg Duffin; Artistic Advisor/Costume Concepts, Thierry M. Mugler; Stage Manager, Neelam Vaswani; Production Manager, Katy Cunningham; Puppetry Build Chief, Ceili Clemens; Wigs, Barry Hendrickson

CAST **Joey Arias**; Puppeteers **Oliver Dalzell, Randy Ginsberg, Kirsten Kammermeyer, Matt Leabo, Jessica Scott, Lindsay Abromaitis-Smith**

A solo performance play/exotic fantasy of song and puppetry presented without intermission.

SYNOPSIS Two national treasures unleash their epic imaginations to conjure a modern and intimate fantasy. Basil Twist's signature magic envelopes Joey Arias' legendary voice, transporting us to unpredictable worlds, channeling ecstatic desires, lavish nightmares and bizarre premonitions in a bejeweled cabinet of curiosities that could only be found in one of downtown's last enclaves for bohemian New York style. Playfully intended for mature audiences, not for children.

Joey Arias in Arias with a Twist *(photo by Steven Menendez)*

Voices of Swords

Urban Stages–Garment District Theatre; Opening Night: June 18, 2008; Closed June 22, 2008; 7 performances

Written by Kari Florin; Presented by Right Down Broadway Productions (Kari Florin, Artistic Director); Director, Spider Duncan Christopher; Set, Tamar Gadish; Costumes, Dana Murdock; Lighting, Zack Tinkelman; Sound, Zach Moore; PSM, Emileena Pedigo; ASM, Shai Trichter; Technical Director, Jean Paul Steinberg; Producing Associate, Larry Brandt; Graphics, Martha Sedgwick; Press, Charlie Seidenberg

CAST Alexis **Lauren Mufson**; Olivia **Rosemary Prinz**; Teddy **Gordon Joseph Weiss**; Mave **Mary Elaine Monti**; Matthew **Michael McKenzie**; Kosey **Robert M. Jiminez**

SETTING Greater New York City; late spring, the present. World premiere of a new play presented in two acts.

SYNOPSIS *Voices of Swords* tells the story of an indomitable woman, Olivia, who employs a personal organizer, Alexis, to win the battle with her wayward son. Unfortunately Alexis can't organize her own life, much less anyone else's. Fortunately Alexis shows Olivia that losing the battle can sometimes mean winning the war.

Rosemary Prinz and Robert Jimenez in Voices of Swords
(photo by Kristine Floren)

A Perfect Couple

DR2; First Preview: June 9, 2008; Opening Night: June 19, 2008; Closed July 12, 2008; 8 previews, 25 performances

Written by Brooke Berman; Presented by WET (Women's Expressive Theater) Productions (Sasha Eden and Victoria Pettibone, Executive Producers); Director, Maria Mileaf; Set, Neil Patel; Lighting, Matthew Richards; Sound, Bart Fasbender; Costumes, Jenny Mannis; Dramaturgy, Francine Volpe; Production Manager, Ralph Carhart; PSM, Larry K. Ash; ASM, Michael Block; Casting, Alaine Alldaffer; Technical Director, Dave Carrico; Associate Producers, Ami Ankin & Azizah Rowen; Assistant Producers, Ashley Eichhorn-Thompson & Danielle B. Tolley; Assistant Director, Tasha Gordon-Solmon; Art Directors, Silvia Minguzzi & Lisa Diehl; Makeup, Vincent Longo & Allison Elliott; Spin Cycle, Ron Lasko

CAST Emma **Annie McNamara**; Isaac **James Waterston**; Amy **Dana Eskelson**; Josh **Elan Moss-Bachrach**

SETTING An old family house during a summer weekend. World premiere of a new play presented without intermission

SYNOPSIS *A Perfect Couple* is a story about three best friends–Amy, Issac and Emma–and their young next door neighbor, Josh. After fifteen years of dating/living together/taking breaks and now, moving upstate, Amy and Isaac are finally tying the knot. Emma, their single best friend, has decided to get out of the city and join them for a summer weekend in the country. Over the long weekend, secrets are revealed and bonds are tested, forcing these friends to discover who they are now, versus who they thought they would become.

Dana Eskelson, James Waterston, Annie McNamara and Elan Moss-Bachrach in A Perfect Couple *(photo by Richard Mitchell)*

A Brush with Georgia O'Keeffe

St. Luke's Theatre; First Preview: June 14, 2008; Opening Night: June 21, 2008; Closed September 28, 2008; 3 previews, 44 performances (Saturday and Monday evening & Sunday matinee performances)

Written by Natalie Mosco; Director, Robert Kalfin; Presented by Briana Seferian for Earl Productions in association with Edmund Gaynes and Julia Beardsley; Set, Kevin Judge; Costumes, Gail Cooper Hecht; Lighting, Paul Hudson; Projections, Marilys Ernst; Original Composition/Sound, Margaret Pine; PSM, D.C. Rosenberg; ASM, Charlotte Volage; Intern, Elizabeth Schiavo; Associate Producer, Mitchell Sawyer; Casting, Irene Stockton; General Manager, Jessimeg Productions; Advertising, Epstein-O'Brien; Web, Jon Fenwick; Technical Director, Josh Iacovelli; Co-Artistic Director for St. Luke's, Pamela Hall; Press, Scotti Rhodes Publicity

CAST Georgia O'Keeffe **Natalie Mosco**; Alfred Stieglitz **David Lloyd Walters**; Dorothy Norman/others **Virginia Roncetti**

SETTING The Places Georgia O'Keefe lived and worked, during her life 1887-1986. Off-Broadway transfer of a new play presented without in two acts. Originally presented at the WorkShop Theatre Company March 20–April 5, 2008 (see *Theatre World* Vol. 64, page 272).

SYNOPSIS *A Brush with Georgia O'Keeffe* tells the story of the remarkable life of the celebrated American painter. One of the most important artists of the 20th Century, O'Keeffe was once torn between a career as an artist or musician and seemed to strike a balance between the two by infusing her painting with what she termed "visual music". As Alfred Stieglitz's model, muse and lover, she became the widely known subject for a long series of photographs that were part of his artistic legacy. But it was only after Stieglitz's death that O'Keeffe was finally free immerse herself in nature once again, the source that had truly defined her paintings and offered her 99 year old life its greatest meaning.

Natalie Mosco as Georgia O'Keeffe *(photo courtesy of Katvan Studios)*

BASH'd! A Gay Rap Opera

Zipper Factory Theatre; First Preview: June 12, 2008; Opening Night: June 23, 2008; Closed August 30, 2008

Written by Chris Craddock and Nathan Cuckow; Presented by Stephen Kocis, Carl D. White, Paul Boskind, and Michael Fillerman in association with David J. Gersten; Director, Ron Jenkins; Music, Aaron Macri; Costumes, Chase Tyler; Lighting, Bradley Clenents; Sound, Kris Pierce; Urban Consultant, Ken Ledbetter; PSM, Scott F. DelaCruz; Associate Producers, Louis Bluver, Scott Mallalieu, Proteus Spann; General Manager, Martian Entertainment & Aged in Wood, Carl D. White & Stephen Kocis; Press, David Gersten & Associates, Shane Marshall Brown

CAST T-Bag/Jack **Chris Craddock**; Feminem/Dillon **Nathan Cuckow**; Understudy **Dan Amboyer**

MUSICAL NUMBERS Cocksuckaz, Coming Out the Closet, Grab Some Ass, Love Theme/Baby I'm Your Man, Marriage Proposal/Debate, The Wedding Day, Bash'd, The Support Group Meeting, Straight Bash'd, Heaven, Reprise/R.I.P.

Off-Broadway premiere of a musical presented in one act. Originally produced in Edmonton, Canada and previously presented at the NY International Fringe Festival in 2007, where it won Outstanding Musical.

SYNOPSIS *BASH'd!* chronicles the tale of Jack and Dillon; two star-crossed lovers who must cope with the reality of hatred when one is brutally beaten. It is told entirely through rap, spoken word and poetry, turning the often-homophobic musical genre on its ear. Even though the topic is serious, the musical is high energy, irreverent, and provocative.

Palace of the End

Peter Jay Sharp Theater at Playwrights Horizons; First Preview: June 11, 2008; Opening Night: June 23, 2008; Closed July 13, 2008; 12 previews, 17 performances

Written by Judith Thompson, based on her monologue play *My Pyramids*; Presented by the Epic Theatre Ensemble (Zak Berman, Melissa Friedman, & Ron Russell, Founding Executive Directors); Director, Daniella Topol; Set, Mimi Lein; Costumes, Theresa Squire; Lighting, Justin Townsend; Original Music, Katie Down; Sound, Ron Russell; Projections, Leah Gelpe; PSM, Brenna St. George Jones; Production Manager, Jee S. Han; Casting, James Calleri; Press, O+M Company, Rick Miramontez, Jon Dimond, Molly Barnett

CAST Lynndie England **Teri Lamm**; Dr. David Kelly **Rocco Sisto**; Nehrjas Al Saffarh **Heather Raffo**

New York premiere of a play presented without intermission. Winner of the 2008 Susan Smith Blackburn Prize for playwrighting. *My Pyramids* was produced by Volcano at the Traverse Theatre in Edinburgh in August 2005; opened under the new title at the Canadian Stage Company in Toronto in February 2008.

SYNOPSIS *Palace of the End* is a triptych of monologues that intimately explores the experiences of three key figures of the Middle East crisis: Lynndie England, the U.S. soldier who was convicted of abusing detainees at Baghdad's Alu Gharib prison; David Kelly, the British weapons inspector who allegedly committed suicide after being involved in a government scandal; and Nehrjas Al Saffarh, a member of the Communist Party of Iraq who suffered under Saddham Hussein's regime and died when the Americans bombed her home during the initial Gulf War.

Teri Lamm in Palace of the End *(photo by Carol Rosegg)*

Stitching

The Wild Project; First Preview: June 17, 2008; Opening Night: June 25, 2008; Closed August 2, 2008

Written by Anthony Neilson; Presented by Adamanto Productions and Electric Pear Productions in association with Liebman Entertainment; Director, Timothy Haskell; Sets/Lighting, Garin Marschall; Costumes, Wendy Ang; Original Sound & Music, Daron Murphy; Props, Brooklyn Art Department (Justin Haskell and Aaron Haskell); PSM, Russell Marisak; Fight Choreographer, Maggie MacDonald; Media/Advertising, Art Meets Commerce; Press, Richard Kornberg & Associates, Billy Zavelson

CAST Abby **Meital Dohan**; Stu **Gian-Murray Gianino***

*Succeeded by John Ventimiglia (7/23/08)

American premiere of a new play presented without intermission.

SYNOPSIS Stu and Abby love each other so madly, they're driving each other crazy. *Stitching* follows the increasingly disturbing and inventive games the couple plays in order to connect. As they circle and test each other, they role-play with reality and fantasy to the point where even they don't seem sure what is real anymore. When Abby discovers she's pregnant, the choices they make will haunt them forever. The visceral poetry and physicality between the lovers creates a surprisingly tender, often humorous, brutal romance. *Stitching* challenges the notions of modern romance in an increasingly complex world.

Forbidden Broadway

DANCES WITH THE STARS / GOES TO REHAB!

47th Street Theatre; *Dances With the Stars*: First Preview: June 9, 2008; Opening Night: June 28, 2008; Closed August 31, 2008; 96 performances; *Goes to Rehab*: First Preview: September 1, 2008; Opening Night: September 18, 2008; Closed March 1, 2009; 208 perforamances

Written and created by Gerard Alessandrini; Produced by John Freedson, Harriet Yellin, and Jon B. Platt in association with Gary Hoffman, Jerry Kravat, and Masakazu Shibaoka; Directors, Gerard Alessandrini & Phillip George; Set, Megan K. Halpern; Costumes, Alvin Colt & David Moyer; Lighting, Mark T. Simpson; Sound, Sound Associates/Timothy Owen Mazur, Eric Bechtel; Musical Director, David Caldwell; PSM, Jim Griffith; Production Consultant, Pete Blue; Additional Costumes, David Moyer; Wigs/Hair, Carol Sherry; General Manager, Ellen Rusconi; Company Manager, Adam Levi; Group Sales/Marketing, SRO Marketing, Meri Krassner/Chris Presley; Advertising, Eliran Murphy Group; Press, Keith Sherman & Associates, Glenna Friedman; Cast recording: DRG Records 12633

CAST **Christina Bianco, Jared Bradshaw, Gina Kreiezmar, Michael West**; Pianist **David Caldwell**; Understudies **William Selby, Kristen Mengelkoch**

Newest editions of the longest continuing Off-Broadway revue presented in two acts.

SYNOPSIS Off-Broadway's longest continuing revue which parodies the current crop of Broadway shows and stars continues with a special summer edition and a new fall edition. This season's spoofs included: *[title of show]*, *A Tale of Two Cities*, *Gypsy*, *The Little Mermaid*, *Jersey Boys*, *Wicked*, *Sunday in the Park With George*, *South Pacific*, *Billy Elliot*, *Equus*, and Broadway stars such as Ethyl Merman, Harvey Fierstein, Liza Minnelli, and Patti LuPone are lovingly skewered by the genius pen of Alessandrini.

Christina Bianco and Jared Bradshaw in Forbidden Broadway Dances with the Stars *(photo by Carol Rosegg)*

Michael West and Gina Kreiezmar in Forbidden Broadway Goes to Rehab *(photo by Carol Rosegg)*

The Bacchae

Rose Theater at the Time Warner Center; First Preview: July 2, 2008; Opening Night: July 3, 2008; Closed July 13, 2008; 1 preview, 12 performances

Written by Euripides; New version by David Greig from a literal translation by Ian Ruffell; Presented by Lincoln Center Festival 2008, the National Theatre of Scotland, and the Edinburgh International Festival; Director, John Tiffany; Associate Director/Choreographer, Steve Hoggert; Composer/Music Director, Tim Sutton; Sets, Miriam Buether; Lighting, Colin Grenfell; Sound, Christopher Shutt; Associate to Sound, Colin Pink; Press, Sarah Needham

CAST Dionysus **Alan Cumming**; Pentheus **Cal MacAninch**; Cadmus **Ewan Hooper**; Tiresias **John Bett**; Agave **Paola Dionisotti**; Herdsman **Sharon Duncan-Brewster**; Messenger **Hazel Hlder**; Man **Jessika Williams**; The Bacchae **Sharon Duncan-Brewster, Hazel Holder, Melissa Keyes, Sally Amaka Okafor, Lisa Davina Philip, Sarah Quist, Ann-Marie Roberts, Jessika Williams, Emi Wokoma**

MUSICIANS Tim Sutton (Music Director/keyboards); Oliver Jackson (piano/keyboards); Mike Porter (drums/percussion)

American premiere of a new translation of a classic play presented without intermission. This production premiered at the King's Theatre in Edinburgh, Scotland on August 11, 2007.

SYNOPSIS Dionysus arrives at Thebes to claim godly recognition from a disbelieving, ascetic King Pentheus, opening the door to a sardonic, contemporary look at the battle between hedonism and repression. From the moment Scottish actor Alan Cumming's provocative Dionysus is lowered onstage from above, it is clear that playwright David Greig's interpretation takes the mask off one of the last great Athenian tragedies in his unique take on Euripides, making it a Bacchae for the 21st-century.

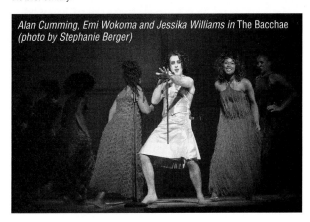

Alan Cumming, Emi Wokoma and Jessika Williams in The Bacchae *(photo by Stephanie Berger)*

Life in a Marital Institution

Soho Playhouse; First Preview: June 26, 2008; Opening Night: July 9, 2008; Closed August 31, 2008

Written by James Braly; Produced by The Deep End Productions and Little Johnny Koerber; Director, Hal Brooks; Producer, Anna Becker; Stage Manager, Lauren McArthur; Set, Michael V. Moore; Lighting, Colin D. Young; Press, Springer Associates, Joe Trentacosta

CAST James Braly

Revival of a solo performance play presented without intermission. Previously presented Off-Off Broadway at 59E59 Theater C February 19–March 16. 2008 (see *Theatre World* Vol. 64, page 208).

SYNOPSIS First comes love. Then comes marriage counseling. James Braly's show *Life in a Marital Institution (20 Years of Monogamy in One Terrifying Hour)* is a poignant, humorous tale of lust, love, betrayal, reproduction and redemption.

James Braly (photo by Andrew Schwartz)

East 14th: True Tales of a Reluctant Player

New World Stages–Stage 5; First Preview: May 22, 2008; Opening Night: July 10, 2008; Closed September 6, 2008

Written by Don Reed; Presented by Ridiculous Media and Michael Singer; Director, Don Reed; Sets/Costumes/Lighting, Matthew Allar; Music, John Taylor; Press, Keith Sherman & Associates

CAST Blinky/Tony/Darrell/Daddy **Don Reed**

A solo performance biographical play presented without intermission.

SYNOPSIS *East 14th: True Tales of a Reluctant Player* is a young man's coming-of-age in 1970s Oakland as he struggles to find out who he is in a world of religious fanatics, pimps, players, hustlers, and streetwalkers. In this autobiographical tale, Reed chronicles escaping an ultra strict upbringing, going out of his way to be something that he wasn't, and eventually, learning to keep it real.

Marie Antoinette: The Color of Flesh

St. Luke's Theatre; First Preview: June 26, 2008; Opening Night: July 10, 2008; Closed September 12, 2008; 3 previews, 29 performances (Thursday and Friday evening & Saturday matinee performances)

Written by Joel Gross; Produced by Earl Productions and Briana Seferian; Director, Robert Kalfin; Sets, Kevin Judge; Costumes, T. Michael Hall; Lighting, Paul Hudson; Sound, Merek Royce Press; PSM, D.C. Rosenberg; ASM, Charlotte Volage; Movement, Caitlin Heffernan; Projections, Karl Scholz; Assistant Producer, Mitchell Sawyer; Web, Jon Fenwick; Intern, Elizabeth Schiavo; Technical Director,

Josh Iacovelli; General Manager, Jessimeg Productions; Associate General Manager, Julia Beardsley; St. Luke's Co-Artistic Director, Pamela Hall; Press, Scotti Rhodes Publicity

CAST Elisabeth Louise Vigee le Brun **Samantha Ives**; Marie Antoinette **Amanda Jones**; Count Alexis de Ligne **Jonathan Kells Phillips**; Footman **Hugo Salazar Jr**,

SETTING Paris, Versailles, and Vienna; 1774-1793. Off-Broadway debut of a play presented in two acts. Originally presented by the New Jersey Repertory Theatre April 25–May 25, 2003. The show played Off-Off Broadway (produced by Earl Productions) at the 45th Street Theatre April 5–29, 2007 (see *Theatre World* Vol. 63, page 244).

SYNOPSIS *Marie Antoinette: The Color of Flesh* is a fictionalized love triangle between Queen Marie Antoinette, her portraitist, the renowned beauty Elisabeth Louise Vigee-Le Brun and Count Alexis de Ligne, an aristocrat and political radical. In the early years of their relationship with "Toinette" both the talented painter and the politically passionate Count use the naive young Queen to further their ambitions. Both learn to love the woman they are exploiting even as their actions encourage the revolution that takes her life.

Samantha Ives and Amanda Jones in Marie Antoinette: The Color of Flesh *(photo by Nicole Szalewski)*

The Strangerer

Barrow Street Theatre; First Preview: July 9, 2008; Opening Night: July 13, 2008; Closed August 7, 2008; 4 previews, 24 performances

Written by Mickle Maher; Presented by Theater Oobleck in association with the Barrow Street Theatre; Music/Sound, Chris Schoen; Sets, Mickle Maher; Piano, Abraham Levitan, Lighting, Martha Baynre; Production Manager, Jason Reuter; Stage Manager, Melissa Jernigan; Graphic Design, Colm O'Reilly; Photography, Kristin Basta; Advertising, Eliran Murphy Group; General Management, Two Step Productions (Cris Buchner, Kate Mott, Heather Levin); Press, O+M Company, Rick Miramontez, Jon Dimond

CAST George W. Bush **Guy Masey**; John Kerry **Mickle Maher**; Jim Lehrer **Colm O'Reilly**

SETTING The 2004 presidential election held at the University of Miami. New York premiere of a new play presented without intermission. World premiere at the Chopin Theatre (Chicago) in 2007.

SYNOPSIS One of the books on President Bush's 2006 vacation reading list was Albert Camus' absurdist tale of senseless murder, *The Stranger*. In hopes that the French philosopher might shed some light on the recent political clime–or vice versa–Maher's new play *The Strangerer* collides several of Camus' works with the first Bush/Kerry presidential debate in 2004. The formalities of the debate are overturned as Bush and Kerry struggle with the question not of if or why an innocent man should be killed (the man in question being moderator Jim Lehrer), but rather what is the proper manner in which to go about killing him. A fascinating and hilarious hybrid, *The Strangerer* is part political satire, part classical drama, part contemporary debate, and a murder mystery with the murderers in plain view.

Mickle Maher, Guy Massey and Colm O'Reilly in The Strangerer *(photo by Kristin Basta)*

Gate/Beckett

Gerald W. Lynch Theater; Opening Night: July 16, 2008; Closed July 27, 2008; *Eh Joe*: 2 previews, 6 performances; *I'll Go On*: 1 preview, 7 performances; *First Love*: 2 previews, 6 performances; *Beckett Poetry and Prose*: 2 performances

Three plays by Samuel Beckett; Presented by Lincoln Center Festival 2008 and the Gate Theatre (Michael Colgan, Artistic Director); Included: *Eh Joe*: Director, Atom Egoyan; Design, Eileen Diss; Lighting, James McConnell; *I'll Go On*: Texts selected by Gerry Dukes and Barry McGovern from the novels *Molloy, Malone Dies* and *The Unnamable*; Director, Colm O' Briain; Design, Robert Ballagh; Lighting, James McConnell; *First Love*: Director, Michael Colgan; Design, Eileen Diss; Lighting, James McConnell; *Beckett Poetry and Prose*: Director, Michael Colgan; Lighting, James McConnell; Press, Sarah Needham

CAST *Eh Joe*: Joe **Liam Neeson**; Woman's Voice **Penelope Wilton**; *I'll Go On*: **Barry McGovern**; *First Love*: **Ralph Fiennes**; *Beckett Poetry and Prose*: **Barry McGovern, Liam Neeson, Ralph Fiennes**

Three solo performance plays presented in repertory, each without intermission; two marathon performances presented July 26 & 27 with all 4 shows presented.

SYNOPSIS Dublin's renowned Gate Theatre performs three one-man dramas by Samuel Beckett as part of the Lincoln Center Festival, none of them originally written for the stage. These compelling works expose the intricate human condition that the Nobel Prize-winning author Beckett so deeply mined.

Stain

Kirk Theater on Theatre Row; First Preview: July 11, 2008; Opening Night: July 23, 2008; Closed August 23, 2008

Written by Tony Glazer; produced by Choice Theatricals LLC; Director, Scott C. Embler; Set, Eddy Trotter; Costumes, Cully Long; Lighting, Nick Kolin; Sound/Music, Andrew Eisele; Casting, Judy Bowman; Press, Springer Associates, Joe Trentacosta

CAST Carla **Karina Arroyave**; Theresa **Joanna Bayless**; George **Peter Brensinger**; Julia **Summer Crockett Moore**; Arthur **Jim O'Connor**; Thomas **Tobias Segal**

World premiere of a new play presented in two acts.

SYNOPSIS *Stain* is an edgy, dark comedy that centers on the quickly-crumbling life of 15-year-old Thomas and the complicated relationships he has with his father, mother, grandmother, best friend George, and his much-older girlfriend, Carmen. When dark family secrets are revealed, Thomas is confronted with a choice that will either save him or mark him forever.

Jim O'Connor and Tobias Segal in Stain *(photo by Orlando Behar)*

The Plant That Ate Dirty Socks

Lucille Lortel Theatre; First Preview: July 16, 2008; Opening Night: July 24, 2008; Closed August 22, 2008; 11 previews, 51 performances

Book, music, and lyrics by Joe Iconis; Based on the volume of the books by Nancy McArthur; Presented by Theatreworks USA (Barbara Pasternack, Artistic Director; Ken Arthur, Producing Director); Director, John Simpkins; Choreography, Jennifer Werner; Music Director, Jana Zielonka; Set, Michael Schweikardt; Costumes, Tracy Christensen; Lighting, Chris Dallos; Puppets, Eric Wright; Technical Coordinator, B.D. White; PSM, Jeff Davolt; Technical Director, Joseph Reddington; Props, Lake Simons; Production Assistant, Gabriel Kirshner; Development, Patrick Key; Marketing, Barbara Sandek; Education, Beth Prather; Production Manager, Bob Daley; Company Manager, Teresa Hagar; Casting, Robin D. Carus; Honorary Chair, Matt Lauer; Press, The Publicity Office, Jeremy Shaffer

CAST Michael **Jason Williams**; Jason/Mackenzie **Jeffrey Omura**; Patty Jenkins **Lauren Marcus**; Norman **Lance Rubin**; Dad **Kilty Reidy**; Mom **Lorinda Lisitza**; Fluffy **Michael Schupbach**

UNDERSTUDIES A.J. Shively (Michael, Jason, Norman, Dad), Liz Lark Brown (Patty Jenkins, Mom)

MUSICIANS Jana Zielonka (Conductor/piano), Jay Mack (percussion)

MUSICAL NUMBERS Welcome to My Room, If I Won the Science Fair, Plants Make Wonderful Pets, Robot and Gorilla and the Case of the Missing Socks, I Saw It Suck Up a Sock, Talk of the Town, If I Won the Science Fair, At the Science Fair, Sorta Kinda Not So Bad, Plants Make Wonderful Pets

World premiere of a musical for young audiences presented without intermission.

SYNOPSIS For ten-year-old neatnik Norman, sharing a room with his messy older brother Michael is a nightmare– with heaps of crumpled paper, clothes strewn about and piles of smelly, dirty socks everywhere. One day, Michael sends away for some "Amazing Beans," and before long, the boys are the proud owners of two giant plants. But as the plants grow taller and taller, the boys realize that their socks are mysteriously disappearing! As the plants' hunger for socks continue to grow, Norman and Michael must try to conceal their botanical secret from the rest of the kids on Levitt Lane, especially the frighteningly nosey cheerleader, Patty Jenkins.

Lance Rubin in The Plant That Ate Dirty Socks *(photo by Joan Marcus)*

Give 'Em Hell Harry!

St. Luke's Theatre; First Preview: July 20, 2008; Opening Night: July 27, 2008; Closed September 24, 2008; 3 previews, 27 performances (Tuesday and Sunday evening & Wednesday matinee performances)

Written by Samuel Gallu; Produced by Cindy Productions; Director, Stan Mazin; Lighting/Stage Manager, Josh Iacovelli; Sound, Doug Engalla; Assistant Program, Stephanie Ibanez; Press, Susan L. Schulman Publicity

CAST Harry S. Truman **Bix Barnaba**

SETTING The various milestones throughout Truman's life. New York premiere of a solo performance bio drama presented in two acts. Originally produced at the Lonny Chapman Group Repertory Theatre (North Hollywood, California).

SYNOPSIS In this one-man show about President Harry S. Truman, Bix Barnaba brings to life the politics and pressing issues that faced the thirty-third president with no mincing of words, including his legendary encounters with the press.

Bix Barnaba as Harry S. Truman in Give 'Em Hell, Harry! (photo by Doug Engalla)

Flamingo Court

New World Stages–Stage 2; First Preview: July 17, 2008; Opening Night: July 31, 2008; Closed September 28 2008; 17 previews, 68 performances

Written by Luigi Creatore; Presented by Theatre 21 and Carolyn Rossi Copeland; Director, Steven Yuhasz; Sets, James Youmans; Costumes, Carol Sherry; Sound, David A. Arnold; Lighting, Herrick Goldman; Projections, luckydave; Production Manager, Aduro Productions; PSM, Eileen F. Haggerty; Casting, Mark Simon; General Management, CRC Productions, Robert E. Schneider; Advertising, Eliran Murphy Group; Press, Keith Sherman & Associates

CAST Angelina/Clara/Chi Chi **Anita Gillette**; Dominic/Arthur/Harry Rossoff **Jamie Farr**; Marie/Charity Pipick **Lucy Martin**; Voice of Marian **Alex Bond**; Voice of Phillip **Tibor Feldman**; Mark Seagal **Herbert Rubens**; Walter Pipick **Joe Vincent**

SETTING A three-story apartment complex in South Florida, apartments 104, 204, and 304; the present. New York premiere of a three plays presented in two acts.

SYNOPSIS Ten characters, five actors, life in three condos, Flamingo Court follows the nosy and endearing residents of Flamingo Court, a South Florida apartment complex. Each apartment reveals a new story and a new lesson: Sex lives after sixty. Where there's a will, there's a relative. And love heals all wounds... at any age.

Anita Gillette and Jamie Farr in Flamingo Court (photo by Carol Rosegg)

Absinthe

Spiegeltent at South Street Seaport; Opening Night: August 6, 2008; Closed November 2, 2008; 103 performances

Created and produced by Spiegelworld, Ross Mollison, and Vallejo Gantner; Director, Wayne Harrison; Lighting, Martin Kinnane; PSM, Niluka Samaseker; Lighting, Chris Coyle; Sound, Art Williams, Rigger, Daryl Johns; Press, Richard Kornberg and Associates **CAST** Princess Anya **Anya Stankus**; Herself (Vocalist) **Kaye Tuckerman,** Herself (Artist) **Julie Atlas Muz**; Duo Sergio **Sergey Petrov & Sergey Dubovyk**; Duo Ssens **Geneviève Landry & Maxime Clabaut**; The Willers **Wanda & Jean-Pierre Poissonnet**; The Gazillionaire **Voki Kalfayan**; Penny **Anais Thomassian**; The Anastasinis **Fabio Anastasini & Giuliano Anastasini**; The Daredevil Chicken Club **Jonathan Taylor & Anne Goldman**; Herself (Acrobat) **Adil Rida**

Revised version of the cabaret/circus/variety-burlesque show presented in two acts, in repertory with Désir. Previously presented August 3–October 1, 2006 at the South Street Seaport (see Theatre World Vol. 63, page 131), and revived July 3–September 7, 2007 (see Theatre World Vol. 64, page 103).

SYNOPSIS Returning for its third year, Absinthe –Les Artistes de La Clique is a variety show on acid, a late-night saunter through the sultriest, strangest circus in town. Absinthe combines the traditions of vaudeville and music hall with Berliner Kabarett, Fairground attraction collides with sideshow burlesque to transform the elegant, sumptuous confines of the Spiegeltent into something just a little ... below the belt.

Désir

Spiegeltent at South Street Seaport; Opening Night: August 7, 2008; Closed November 2, 2008; 102 performances

Created and produced by Spiegelworld, Ross Mollison, and Vallejo Gantner; Director, Wayne Harrison; Sets, Josh Zangen; Costumes, David Quinn; Lighting, Martin Kinnane; Music Direction, Josh Abrahams; Choreography, John O'Connell; Press, Richard Kornberg & Associates

CAST Raphaelle Boitel, Annie-Kim Dehry, Marieve Hemond, Genevieve Morin, Olaf Triebel, Victoria Di Pace, Marawa Ibrahim, Evgeny Belyaev, Nikolay Titov, Anton Smirnov, Nikolay Shaposhnikov, Antoine Auger, Marco Noury

World premiere of a new circus/performance art theatrical piece presented without intermission, in repertory with *Absinthe*

SYNOPSIS Before Moulin Rouge, before Folies Bergere, there was Désir, the jewel of Paris. The producers of *Absinthe* and *La Vie* present a stunning new theatrical circus experience which takes you backstage at the greatest nightclub the world has ever seen. A meeting place for showgirls and soldiers, bejeweled courtesans and maharajahs, *Désir* is a carnival world devoted to the pursuit of beauty, clever seductions and breathtaking displays of acrobatic wonder. It is a sparkling merry-go-round where your last love affair is merely an entree to your next encounter.

Stephanie Barton-Farcas and Michael DiGioia in Elizabeth Rex *(photo by Erica Parise)*

Elizabeth Rex

Center Stage NY; First Preview: August 13, 2008; Opening Night: August 16, 2008; Closed September 28, 2008; 3 previews, 20 performances

Written by Timothy Findley; Presented by Nicu's Spoon (Stephanie Barton-Farcas, Artistic Director) in association with The Playwrights Guild of Canada; Director, Joanne Zipay; Stage Manager, Oksana Kalent; Assistant Stage Manager, Russell Waldman; Set, John Trevellini & Gabrielle Montgomery; Costumes, Rien Schlecht; Lighting, Steven Wolf; Sound & Original Music, Damon Law; Original Vocal Music, Michael DiGioia; Dialects, Molly Goforth; Movement, Elizabeth Mozer; Fight Director, Scott David Nogi; Stage Construction & Build Crew, John Trevellini & Larry Pease; Props and Light/Sound Running Crew, Oksana Kalent & Megan Hanley; Marketing/Press, Katie Rosin

CAST William Shakespeare **Scott Nogi**; Ned Lowenscroft **Michael DiGioia**; Jack Edmund **Andrew Hutcheson**; Percy Gower **Bill Galarno**; Matthew Welles **David Tully**; Harry Pearle **Erwin Falcon**; Tom Travis/Lord Robert Cecil **Tim Romero**; Kate Tardwell **Rebecca Challis**; Luddy Beddoes **Oliver Conant**; The Bear **Sammy Mena**; Lady Mary Stanley **Melanie Horton**; Lady Anne Countess of Henslowe **Ruth Kulerman**; Queen Elizabeth I **Stephanie Barton-Farcas**

SETTING Two barns in England; February 24, 1601, the night before the execution of the Earl of Essex. Off-Broadway transfer of a play presented in two acts. World premiere at Stratford Festival in 2000. Previously presented by Nicu's Spoon April 2–19, 2008 (see *Theatre World* Vol. 64, page 248).

SYNOPSIS In 1601, Queen Elizabeth I was forced by duty to condemn to death the Earl of Essex, widely believed to be her former lover. On the night before the execution, she demanded that William Shakespeare's acting troupe, The Lord Chamberlain's Men, perform a play to distract her from the heartbreak that would occur in the morning. This much is truth. Timothy Findley blends fiction with these historical facts and creates a powerhouse play about men, women, fantasy, death, and ultimately, love.

Masque of the Red Death & The Tell-Tale Heart & The Bells

St. Luke's Theatre; First Preview: August 27, 2008; Opening Night: September 3, 2008; Closed September 28, 2008; 4 previews, 16 performances

Tales and poems written by Edgar Allan Poe; Created and presented by Zombie Joe's Underground Theatre Group (North Hollywood, California) in association with Edmund Gaynes; Producer/Director, Zombie Joe; Original Score, Christopher Reiner; Assistant Director, Denise L. Devine; Costume Design & Fabrication, Jeri Batzdorff; Costume Assistance & Curtains, Jana Wimer; Sculpture, Brian "Skull" O'Connor; Production Flyer, John Falchi; Flyer Photo, Marti Matulis; Webmaster & PR, Randy "Kernel" Long; For West End Artists Company: Co-Artistic Director, Pamela Hall; General Manager, Jessimeg Productions; Associate General Manager, Julia Beardsley; Technical Director, Josh Iacovelli; Press, Susan L. Schulman

CAST *The Tell-Tale Heart & The Bells*: **Heike Brunner, Rich Wald, Denise L. Devine, Maria Olsen, Jonica Patella**; *Masque of the Red Death*: **Geoffrey Parrish, Billy Minogue, Mark Hein, Heike Brunner, Jana Wimer, Jonica Patella, Maria Olsen, Denise L. Devine, Jen Bendick**; Mistress of the Violin **Ann Marie Yoo**

New York premiere of dramatized versions of three short stories presented in two acts.

SYNOPSIS Zombie Joe's Underground Theatre Group makes its NYC debut with Edgar Allan Poe's *Masque of the Red Death & The Tell-Tale Heart & The Bells*. The company brings Poe's infamous tales of terror and intrigue to life with its 'tastefully macabre' theatrical style. The two-act mini-Poe Fest serves up torture and madness in its 'bloody-shoestring' style of stylized physicality and strange soundscapes—all in under two hours with intermission.

Denise L. Devine, Billy Minogue and Maria Olsen (photo by Zombie Joe)

Fela! A New Musical

37 Arts Theatre B; First Preview: August 5, 2008; Opening Night: September 4, 2008; Closed October 5, 2008

Music and lyrics by Fela Anikulapo Kuti, book, additional lyrics, & concept by Jim Lewis, book & concept by Bill T. Jones, co-conceived by Ruth & Steve Hendel; Presented by Ruth & Steve Hendel and Roy Gabay; Director/Choreographer, Bill T. Jones; Music Director, Aaron Johnson; Additional Music, Aaron Johnson and Jordan McLean; Sets/Costumes, Marina Draghici; Lighting, Robert Wierzel; Sound, Robert Kaplowitz; Video, Peter Nigrini; Arrangements, Aron Johnson &Antibalas; Additional Arrangements, Jordan McLean; Associate Director, Niegel Smith; Associate Choreographer, Maija Garcia; PSM, Jon Goldman; ASM, Hilary Austin; Original Mural/Scenic Art, IRLO, Omar and Nuclear Fairy; Casting, Mungioli Theatricals; Marketing, Walk Tall Girl Productions; Advertising/Media Services, Art Meets Commerce; General Manager, Roy Gabay; Press, Richard Kornberg & Associates

CAST Fela Anikulapo Kuti **Sahr Ngaujah**; Funmilayo **Abena Koomson**; Sandra **Sparlha Swa**; African Chanter/James Brown/Orisha **Ismael Kouyaté**; J.K. Brahman/Tap Dancer/Egungun **Calvin C. Booker**; Drummer/Mover **Talu Green**; Ensemble **Anne V. Andre, Corey Baker, Calvin C. Booker, Lauren De Veaux, Nicole Chantal De Weever, Rujeko Dumbutshena, Aimee Graham, Ismael Kouyaté, Maia McKinney, Daniel Soto, Jill M, Vallery, Iris Wilson**; Swings/Understudies **Karma Mayet Johnson, Marcus Phillips**

MUSICIANS Antibalas: Amayo (vocals & percussion), Victor Axelrod (organ/clavinet), Eric Biondo (trumpet), Stuart Bogie (Tenor Sax), Marcus Farrar (Shekere), Marcos Garcia (Guitar), Aaron Johnson (Conductor/trombone), Jordan McLean (trumpet), Nick Movshon (bass), Luke O'Malley (guitar), Martin Perna (baritone sax), Chris Vatalaro (drums)

MUSICAL NUMBERS Everything Scatter, Iba Orisa, Hymn, Medzi Medzi, Manteca, I Got the Feeling, The Clock/Originality, Yellow Fever/Ikoyi Blindness, Trouble Sleep, Teacher Don't Teach Me Nonsense, Lover, Upside Down, Expensive Shit, I.T.T./International Thief Thief, Kere Kay, Water No Get Enemy, Egbe Mio, Shuffering and Shmiling, Zombie, Trouble Sleep (reprise), Na Poi, Sorrow, Tears and Blood, Iba Orisa/Shakara, Sorrow, Tears and Blood/Shine, Coffin for Head of State, Kere Kay (reprise)

SETTING London, Nigeria, and Los Angeles. World premiere of a concert/dance/musical theatre piece presented in two acts.

SYNOPSIS In this new musical, audiences are welcomed into the extravagant, decadent and rebellious world of Afrobeat legend Fela Kuti. Using his pioneering music (a blend of jazz, funk and African rhythm and harmonies), *Fela!* explores Kuti's controversial life as artist, political activist and revolutionary musician. Featuring many of Fela Kuti's most captivating songs and Bill T. Jones's imaginative staging, this new show is a provocative hybrid of concert, dance and musical theater.

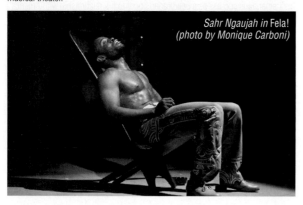

Sahr Ngaujah in Fela!
(photo by Monique Carboni)

King of Shadows

Theater for the New City; First Preview: September 2, 2008; Opening Night: September 7, 2008; Closed September 28, 2008; 6 previews, 22 performances

Written by Roberto Aguirre-Sacasa; Presented by the Working Theater (Connie Grappo, Artistic Director; Mark Plesent, Producing Director); Director, Connie Grappo; Set, Wilson Chin; Costumes, Emily Pepper; Lighting, Jack Mehler; Sound, M.L. Dogg; PSM, Annette Verga-Lagier; ASM, Nicholas Betito; Props, Joseph J. Egan; Casting, Stephanie L. Klapper; Production Manager, Ken Larson; Assistant Director, Joshua Brody; Press, Sam Rudy Media Relations

CAST Nihar **Satya Bhabha**; Jessica Denomy **Kat Foster**; Sarah Denomy **Sarah Lord**; Eric Saunders **Richard Short**

SETTING San Francisco; the present. World premiere of a new play presented in two acts.

SYNOPSIS *King of Shadows* centers around Nihar, a 15-year-old homeless runaway selling sex to survive, who claims he's being pursued by supernatural demons. When Jessica, a young social worker, takes him in, he forms a dangerous bond with her teenage sister that threatens everything she values. The famous fog of San Francisco mixes with a fog of fantasy and fear as each try to protect against a danger they don't understand. Who to trust? What to believe? Where are the boundaries? These remain unsolvable mysteries for two public servants and our society's most vulnerable.

Satya Bhabha and Sarah Lord in King of Shadows
(photo by Carel DiGrappa)

The Quarrel

DR2; First Preview: September 2, 2008; Opening Night: September 7, 2008; Closed September 28, 2008; 1 preview, 24 performances

Written by David Brandes & Joseph Telushkin, based on their film adapted from the short story "My Quarrel with Hersh Rasseyner" by Chaim Grade; Presented by DR2 and Gallant Arts (Danny Gallant) in association with Matt Okin & Melanie Sylvan; Director, Robert Walden; Stage Manager, Bernie Dove; Lighting, John Burkland; Assistant Director, Sarah Ries; Understudy Stage Manager, Laura Cafasso; DR2 Artistic Director, Daryl Roth; General Manager, T. Adam Hess; Associate General Manager, Steve Garcia; Technical Director, Ricardo Taylor

CAST Chaim Kolver **Sam Guncler**; Hersh Rasseyner **Reuven Russell**; Joshua **Federico Trigo**

SETTING Mount Royal Park, Montreal Canada. Early Fall, 1948; New York premiere of a new play presented without an intermission. World premiere at Playwrights Theatre of New Jersey (John Pietrowski, Artistic Director), and developed at The New Harmony Project.

SYNOPSIS Based on a PBS American Playhouse teleplay, the stage version of *The Quarrel* involves two estranged friends, torn apart by personal betrayal and uprooted by war, who meet after years of separation. One has become an Orthodox rabbi, the other a secular writer. Their accidental meeting sparks a battle of wits that tests the limits of friendship, faith and tolerance.

Reuven Russell and Sam Guncler in The Quarrel
(photo by Ira Machevsky)

The Marvelous Wonderettes

Westside Theatre – Upstairs; First Preview: August 26, 2008; Opening Night: September 14, 2008; Still playing as of May 31, 2009

Written and directed by Roger Bean; Presented by David Elzer, Peter Schneider and Marvelous NYC LLC; Choreography, Janet Miller; Sets, Michael Carnahan; Costumes, Bobby Pierce; Lighting, Jeremy Pivnick; Sound, Cricket S. Myers; Music Director/Orchestrations, Michael Borth; Music Supervisor/Vocal and Band Arrangements, Brian William Baker; Vocal Arrangements, Roger Bean; PSM, Anita Ross; ASM, Kelly Varley; Props, Kathy Fabian; Company Manager, Jennifer Pluff; Production Manager, Michael Casselli; General Manager, Roy Gabay; Associate Director/Dance Captain, Bets Malone; Associate Wigs, Robert-Charles Vallance; Marketing, HHC Marketing; Casting, Jay Binder & Jack Bowdan; Press, The Karpel Group, Bridget Klapinski, Adam Bricault; Cast recording: PS Classics 874
CAST Missy **Farah Alvin***; Betty Jean **Beth Malone**; Suzy **Bets Malone**; Cindy Lou **Victoria Matlock**

*Succeeded by Misty Cotton (3/6/09)

UNDERSTUDIES Leslie Spencer Smith (Suzy/Betty Jean/Cindy Lou); Kristen Beth Williams (Cindy Lou/Missy/Suzy)

MUSICIANS Michael Borth (Conductor/keyboards), Brandon Sturiale (keyboard 2), Danny Taylor (drums), Neal Johnson (guitar)

SETTING Springfield High School. Act 1: The 1958 Prom. Act 2: The 1968 ten-year reunion. New York premiere of a new musical with pop standards presented in two acts. World premiere at the Milwaukee Repertory Theatre (Joseph Hanreddy, Artistic Director; Timothy J. Shields, Managing Director),

SYNOPSIS *The Marvelous Wonderettes* is an effervescent musical blast from the past. Set at the Springfield High School prom and later their ten-year reunion, the Wonderettes (Betty Jean, Cindy Lou, Missy and Suzy–four young girls with hopes and dreams as big as their crinoline skirts and voices to match!) tell about their lives and loves, and perform such classic 50's and 60's songs as "Lollipop," "Dream Lover," "Stupid Cupid," "Lipstick on Your Collar," "Hold Me, Thrill Me, Kiss Me," "It's My Party," "It's In His Kiss (The Shoop Shoop Song)" and many more.

Victoria Matlock, Beth Malone, Farah Alvin and Bets Malone in
The Marvelous Wonderettes *(photo by Carol Rosegg)*

BABALU-CY! The Art of Desi Arnaz

Actors Temple Theatre; First Preview: August 23, 2008; Opening Night: September 17, 2008; Closed November 16, 2008; 12 previews, 44 performances

Written by Greg Purnhagen; Presented by Michael and Barbara Ross; Director/Choreographer, Gene Castle; Music Director/Arrangements, David Cook; Conductor, Roy Dunlap; Costumes, Cheryl McCarron; Lighting, Charles R. Gigantirllo; Sets/PSM, Jana Mattioli; ASM, Danielle Schetter; Graphics, David Simpson; Press, Penny M. Landau/Maya PR/Susan L. Schulman

CAST Desi **Greg Purnhagen**; Lucy **Emily Anne Smith**

MUSICIANS Roy Dunlap (Conductor), Ravi Best (trumpet), Johnny Durkin (percussion), James Hirschfeld (trombone), Chad Hochberg (drums), Kurt Stockdale (sax), Yoshi Waki (bass)

MUSICAL NUMBERS Overture, Babalu, Cuban Pete, Quizas Quizas, I'll See You In C-U-B-A, Tico Tico, Rainy Night In Rio, Yours, The Lady In Red, Cielito Lindo, She Could Shake the Maracas, You And The Night And The Music, The Straw Hat Song, By the Waters Of Te Minnetonka, I Love Lucy, I'm In Love With The Dragon's Dinner, We're Having a Baby, Man Smart, Woman Smarter, It Never Entered My Mind, El Cumbanchero

Off-Broadway premiere of a musical presented without intermission.

SYNOPSIS Greg Purnhagen's *BABALU-CY!* examines Desi Arnaz' career from his tremendous success as a bandleader/singer to his relationship with America's favorite red-head, Lucille Ball, complete with a seven-piece Latin band.

Taboos

Soho Playhouse; First Preview: September 10, 2008; Opening Night: September 19, 2008; Closed October 19, 2008

Written by Carl Djerassi; produced by Redshift Productions; Director, Melissa Maxwell; Set, Lauren Halpern; Lighting, Adrianna Durantt; Costumes, Chloe Chapin; Sound, Arielle Edwards; Projections, Katy Tucker; Press, Springer Associates, Joe Trentacosta

CAST Harriet **Helen Merino**; Cameron **John G. Preston**; Sally **Julie Leedes**; Priscilla **Jenn Schulte**; Max **Blake Delong**

American premiere of a new play presented in two acts.

SYNOPSIS What makes one a parent? Love, genetics, giving birth? This question lies at the center of Carl Djerassi's newest play *Taboos*. Retuning to his scientific roots, Djerassi explores the other side of planned parenthood. When a lesbian couple and an infertile fundamentalist Christian couple each look to have a child, more then biology gets in the way of the idea of the "perfect family." *Taboos* explores the unexpected, and often messy, results that arise when emotions and science collide.

Irena's Vow

Baruch College Performing Arts Center – Rose Nagelberg Theatre; First Preview: September 7, 2008; Opening Night: September 22, 2008; Closed November 25, 2008; 15 previews, 40 performances

Written by Dan Gordon; Presented by the Director's Company and the Invictus Theatre Company, Power Production NY (Stan Raiff) & the Polish Cultural Institute; Director, Michael Parva; Set, Kevin Judge; Lighting, David Castaneda; Sound, Astrid Brucker; Projections, Alex Koch; Original Music/Sound, Quentin Chiapetta; Wigs, Leah J. Loukas; Production Manager, Jeff Benish; PSM, Alan Fox; General Manager, Roy Gabay; Press, O&M Company, Rick Miramontez, Richard Hillman

CAST Irena Gut Opdyke **Tovah Feldshuh**; Major Rugemer **Thomas Ryan**; Schultz **Steven Hauck**; Ida Hallar **Maja C. Wampuszyc**; Lazar Hallar **Gene Silvers**; Fanka Silberman **Tracee Chimo**; Sturmbannführer Rokita **John Stanisci**; Helen/Rokita's Secretary **Sandi Carroll**; The Visitor/Polish Worker **Scott Klavan**; Mayor of Jerusalem/SS Officer **Peter Reznikoff**

SETTING An American high school, 1988; Occupied Poland, 1939–1945; Jerusalem, 1988. World premiere of a new play presented without intermission. Transferred to Broadway March 10, 2009 (see Broadway section in this volume).

SYNOPSIS *Irena's Vow* is the riveting, life-affirming story about one of the most courageous and unsung heroines of World War II. During the German occupation of Poland, Irena Gut Opdyke, a Polish Catholic, was forced to work as head housekeeper for a prominent German major. Over a two-year period of service, Irena would risk her own life in order to protect the lives of twelve Jewish refugees whom she secretly took under her care. *Irena's Vow* is the extraordinary true story of one woman's choice and the twelve lives that would ultimately be saved - or lost - by her decision.

Close Ties

Ensemble Studio Theatre; First Preview: September 7, 2008; Opening Night: September 25, 2008; Closed October 12, 2008

Written by Elizabeth Diggs; Presented by Ensemble Studio Theatre (William Carden, Artistic Director; Paul Alexander Slee, Executive Director); Director, Pamela Berlin; Set, Michael Schweikardt; Costumes, Suzanne Chesney; Lighting, Chris Dallos; Sound, David M. Lawson; Props, Mary Houston; PSM, Mary E. Leach; Press, David Gersten & Associates

CAST Josephine Whitaker **Judith Roberts**; Bess Whitaker Frye **Carole Monferdini**; Watson Frye **Jack Davidson**; Anna **Polly Lee**; Evelyn **Fiona Gallagher**; Connie **Julie Fitzpatrick**; Thayer **David Gelles Hurwitz**; Ira Bienstock **Tommy Schrider**

SETTING The Frye summer home in the Berkshires; August 1982. New York premiere of a play presented in two acts. Originally presented at the Long Wharf Theatre February 3, 1981.

SYNOPSIS *Close Ties* tells the story of three generations of the Frye family gathering at their vacation home in the Berkshires. The center for all of them has always been the willful matriarch, Josephine. The very fabric of a family is tested as they have to face the realization that this once indomitable center can no longer hold. *Close Ties* celebrates with humor and truth the mystery and very nature of family.

Fault Lines

Cherry Lane Theatre; First Preview: September 22, 2008; Opening Night: September 30, 2008; Closed November 9, 2008; 9 previews, 46 performances

Written by Stephen Belber; Presented by the Naked Angels (Geoffrey Nauffts, Brittany O'Neill & Julianne Hoffenberg); Produced by Dark Harbor Stories, Olympus Theatricals (Elizabeth Timperman, Dean Vanech), and The Araca Group (Matthew Rego, Michael Rego, Hank Unger, Amanda Watkins, Alyson Grossman) in association with New York Stage & Film (Johanna Pfaelzer, Mark Linn-Baker, Max Mayer, Leslie Urdang, Nathan Baynard, Liz Fox); Director, David Schwimmer; Set, Cameron Anderson; Costumes, Mattie Ulrich; Lighting, Jason Lyons; Sound, Bart Fasbender; PSM, Jon Goldman; Props, Matt Hodges; Casting, Howie Cherpakov; Advertising, Eliran Murphy Group; Press, O+M Company, Rick Miramontez, Amanda Dekker, Elizabeth Wagner

Thomas Ryan, Tovah Feldshuh and John Stanisci in Irena's Vow
(photo by Carol Rosegg)

Dominic Fumusa and Josh Lucas in Fault Lines
(photo by Carol Rosegg)

CAST Joe **Noah Emmerich**; Jim **Dominic Fumusa**; Bill **Josh Lucas**; Jess **Jennifer Mudge**

SETTING The back room of a bar. Off-Broadway premiere of a new play presented without intermission. Originally presented by New York Stage and Film and the Powerhouse Program at Vassar in August 2008.

SYNOPSIS Whole Foods, Edie Brickell and mini-hot dogs abound in this dark and twisted new comedy, in which a seemingly ordinary boys' night out turns sour for two friends when a stranger forces them to delineate the boundaries between loyalty, conviction and betrayal.

Outside Inn

59E59 Theater B; First Preview: October 1, 2008; Opening Night: October 5, 2008; Closed October 19, 2008; 4 previews, 13 performances

Written by Andreas Jungwirth, translated by Gabrielle Schafer; Presented by International Culture Lab (Melanie Dreyer and Gabriele Schafer, Co-Artistic Directors); Director, Melanie Dreyer; Set, Stephanie Mayer-Stanley; Costumes, Pei-Chi Su; Lighting, E.D. Intemann; Video Media, Austin Guest; Sound, Nicholas Crano; Stage Manager, Karin Anderson; Dramaturg/ASM, Nick Fracaro; Production Manager, Vadin Malinskiy; Producing Assistants, Theodora Loukas, Krista Parsons; Press, Karen Greco

CAST Chris **Roger Grunwald**; Paul **Markus Hirnigel**; Kathleen **Jenny Lee Mitchell**; Marina **Karen Sieber**

New York premiere of a play presented without intermission. World premiere at the Charity Randall Theatre in Pittsburgh September 12–15, 2007.

SYNOPSIS *Outside Inn* is a murder mystery that leaps across three continents, including present-day Germany, a small town near the Arizona-Mexican border and Namibia (the former German colony). Paul, a disillusioned German civic engineer unintentionally participates in the death of his boss, a Svengali-like tycoon. Rather than going to the police, Paul runs away to a small town in Arizona. With his mistress Marina by his side, he steals the identity of his former boss and flees across the Mexican border. The husband and wife Paul and Marina leave behind must face a future alone and a past that continues to haunt them.

Jenny Lee Mitchell and Karen Sieber in Outside Inn
(photo by Markus Hirnigel)

Two Rooms

Acorn Theatre on Theatre Row; First Preview: October 2, 2008; Opening Night: October 7, 2008; Closed October 19, 2008; 7 previews, 15 performances

Written by Lee Blessing; Presented by Platform Theatre Group (Greg Tully, Producer); Director, Peter Flynn; Set, Kevin Judge; Lighting, Thom Weaver; Costumes, Jennifer Caprio; Sound, Scott Stauffer; Production Manager, Travis Walker; PSM, Barbara Janice Kielhofer; Assistant Director, Stephen Amato; ASM, Marguerite Stimpson; General Manager, Seth A. Goldstein, The Splinter Group; Press, David Gersten & Associates

CAST Ellen **Adinah Alexander**; Walker **Patrick Boll**; Lainie **Angela Christian**; Michael Wells **Michael Laurence**

UNDERSTUDIES Female **Marguerite Stimpson**

Revival of a play presented in two acts.

SYNOPSIS *Two Rooms* tells the story of Lainie, a loving devoted wife, who is attempting to rescue her husband Michael from his kidnappers. As her husband's life hangs precariously in the balance, Lainie must deal with a story-hungry reporter and an emotionally detached bureaucrat while hoping to find a way to reconnect with her husband. *Two Rooms* is a tense psychodrama about the timeless story of two peoples' love and hope.

Black Watch

St. Ann's Warehouse; Opening Night: October 9, 2008; Closed December 21, 2008

Written by Gregory Burke; Presented by the National Theatre of Scotland (Vicky Featherstone, Artistic Director) and St. Ann's Warehouse (Susan Feldman, Artistic Director) in association with Affinity Company Theater; Director, John Tiffany; Associate Directors, Steven Hoggett (movement), Davey Anderson (music); Sets, Laura Hopkins; Costumes, Jessica Brettle; Lighting, Colin Grenfell; Video, Leo Warner and Mark Grimmer for Fifty Nine Prods.; Company Stage Manager, Carrie Hutcheon; Deputy Stage Manager, Sarah Alford-Smith; ASM, Fiona Kennedy; Casting, Anne Henderson; For St. Ann's: Finance, Alex Berg; External Affairs, Marilynn Donini; Marketing, Bill Updegraff; Development, Inga J. Glodowski; Production Manager, Owen Hughes; Company Manager, Keren-Or Reiss; Technical Director, Bill Kennedy; Production Coordinator, Aaron Rosenblum; Master Electrician, Christopher Heilman; Press, Blake Zidell & Associates

CAST Macca **David Colvin**; Stewarty **Ali Craig**; Fraz **Emun Elliott**; Kenzie **Ryan Fletcher**; Officer **Jack Fortune**; Writer/Sergeant **Paul Higgins**; Rossco **Henry Pettigrew**; Nabsy **Nabil Stuart**; Cammy **Paul Rattray**; Granty **Jordan Young**

Return engagement of a play presented without intermission. Previously presented at St. Ann's October 20–November 11, 2007 (see *Theatre World* Volume 64, page 118).

SYNOPSIS *Black Watch* follows the disassembling of Scotland's most esteemed regiment over the course of its final tour in Iraq, written from the personal testimonies of ten men on the ground. *Black Watch* reveals what it really means to be part of the War on Terror and what it means to make the journey home again. Lyrical and loaded with testosterone, the production makes powerful and inventive use of movement, music and song to create a visceral, complex and urgent piece of theater.

The cast of the National Theatre of Scotland's Black Watch
(photo by PA)

Urban Death

Players Theatre; First Preview: October 9, 2008; Opening Night: October 10, 2008; Closed November 22, 2008; 1 previews, 24 performances

Created and presented by Zombie Joe's Underground; Produced and directed by Zombie Joe; Original Score, Christopher Reiner; Dance Music, Stephen Cohn; Choreography, Denise L. Devine; Prosthetics, Tony Marsiglia; Webmaster/PR Manager, Randy "Kernel" Long; Flyer, Marti Matulis; Theatre Owner, Michael Sgouros; Theatre Managers, Carlo Rivieccio, Christy Benanti; Technical Director, Josh Iacovelli; Press, Susan L. Schulman

CAST Denise L. Devine, Amanda Dieli, Mark Hein, Russell Lewis, Brian Morgan, Geoff Parrish, Jonica Patella, Erikka Walsh, Lisa Wartenberg, Jana Wimer, Zombie Joe

New York premiere of an experimental theatrical piece presented without intermission.

SYNOPSIS Zombie Joe's Underground Theatre Group presents its new production of *Urban Death*. The show is a terrifying new production of inexplicable horrors, unfathomable monstrosities and the disturbed spirits that walk among us! The lights come up on a pile of grotesquely intertwined corpses in a mass grave. As the dead turn into zombies, you see over 30 horrifying vignettes in just under 60 minutes. Be warned: Blood will be spilled and guts will be a-flyin' in this R-rated scare-fest.

Spin

Cherry Lane Theatre; First Preview: October 3, 2008; Opening Night: October 11, 2008; Closed November 8, 2008; 7 previews, 25 performances

A collection of short plays presented by stageFARM (Carrie Shaltz, Founder / Executive Director and Alex Kilgore, Artistic Director); included: *America's Got Tragedy* by Gina Gionfriddo; Director, Alex Kilgore; *90 Days* by Elizabeth Meriwether; Director, Evan Cabnet; *Tone Unknown* by Adam Rapp; Director, Evan Cabnet; *Fun* by Mark Schultz; Director, Evan Cabnet; *Nail Biter* by Judith Thompson; Director, Alex Kilgore; Producer/Executive Director, Carrie Shaltz; PSM, Paige Van Den Berg; ASM, Amy Kajkeki; Sets, John McDermott; Lighting, Nicole Pearce; Sound, Ken Hypes; Projections, Jeff Sugg; Technical Director, Janio Marrero; Casting, Calleri Casting; Press, O+M Company, Amanda Dekker, Elizabeth Wagner

CAST *America's Got Tragedy*: Brian Seabreast **David Ross**; Dr. Elizabeth Charney **Rebecca Henderson**; Matt Stafford **Jesse Hooker**; Britney Spears **Drema Walker**; *90 Days*: Elliot **Patch Darragh**; Abby **Rebecca Henderson**; *Nail Biter*: David **Jesse Hooker**; *Fun*: Grady **Patch Darragh**; Jamie **Dreama Walker**; *Tone Unknown*: Victoria Houselight **Rebecca Henderson**; Ronan MC Cloud **Patch Darragh**; The Kid **David Ross**; Cerval Hyler **Jesse Hooker**

World premiere of five short plays with a theme presented without intermission.

SYNOPSIS After the success of last season's production of *Vengeance*, the stageFARM commissioned short plays from today's brightest playwrights as a barometer for what's happening now. *Spin* is this year's zeitgeist, it's the victory over substance.

Patch Darragh and Dreama Walker in Fun *(photo by Richard Termine)*

Basic Training

Barrow Street; First Preview: September 26, 2008; Opening Night: October 13, 2008; Closed December 1, 2008

Created by Kahlil Ashanti; Presented by Josephson Entertainment (Barry Josephson), VoiceChair Productions (Erich Jungwirth) and Richard Jordan Productions; Production Supervision, Hal Brooks; Lighting, Tyler Micoleau; Press, Keith Sherman & Associates

CAST Kahlil Ashanti

Off-Broadway premiere of a new comedy presented without intermission. Winner of the 2004 Montreal and Vancouver Fringe Festivals and the 2005 Edinburgh Fringe Festival Spirit of the Fringe and Scotsman Fringe First Award, BASIC TRAINING had its premiere in October 2004 in Los Angeles.

SYNOPSIS Kahlil Ashanti's comic tour-de-force *Basic Training* chronicles his enlistment in the U.S. Air Force as a member of the elite entertainment troupe Tops in Blue. Taking us on a theatrical journey of his time on tour as a comedian, actor, dancer and soldier, a life altering event forces his attention home to face the childhood he was trying so hard to forget. Twenty-three unforgettable characters guide you through this hilarious true tale of survival and redemption, all experienced through Ashanti's rapid fire talent.

*Kahlil Ashanti in
Basic Training
(photo by Julian Rad)*

*Steve Callahan as Judas and James Brandon as Joshua in
Corpus Christi (photo by Alek and Steph Photography)*

Judy and Me

St. Luke's Theatre; First Preview: October 1, 2008; Opening Night: October 14, 2008; Closed December 21, 2008; 15 previews, 67 performances

Written by Peter Mac; Produced by John Schaefer and Joseph John Macchia; Director, Charles Tolliver; Set, Tim McMath; Lighting, Josh Iacovelli; Costumes, Viviane Galloway; Assistant Costumes, Mira Veikley; Music Supervisor, David Shenton; Garland Historical Consultant, John Fricke; General Manager, Dr. John DJ Schaefer; Company Manager, Joseph Macchia; PSM, Dennis Petragnani; Marketing, Gary Shaffer & Associates; Press, grapeVine PR

CAST Stephanie Kapowski **Elyse Beyer**; Anthony Castalano **Christopher Brick**; Joanne Castalano **Jean Ann Kump**;

Judy Garland/Himself **Peter Mac**; Jimmy Bradford/Rick Spencer **Christopher McCabe**; Sal Castalano/Pussy Glamour **Basil Meola**; Understudies **Camille Fuoco** (Joanne), **Richard Guido** (Sal)

Off-Broadway premiere of an autobiographical new play presented without intermission. Previously presented Off-Off Broadway earlier this season. Camille Fuoco, the mother of playwright Peter Mac, finished the run as "Joanne," marking the first known time in history that someone has played her real life persona opposite her real life son on the stage.

SYNOPSIS *Judy and Me* addresses the issues of both homophobia and domestic abuse as it recounts the true story of sixteen-year old 'Anthony,' trapped in the narrow-minded suburb of Elmont, Long Island. An outcast at Sewankawa High School in Floral Park, Anthony is the daily target of verbal and physical torment from his classmates. His life at home is equally tenuous; his volatile, violent father is a constant source of pain to both Anthony and his mother. The teen finds his only escape in the music and entertainment of the legendary Judy Garland, who comes to life before his eyes and counsels him through his daily struggles.

Corpus Christi

Rattlestick Playwrights Theatre at 224 Waverly; Opening Night: October 13, 2008; Closed October 26, 2008; 15 performances

Written by Terrence McNally; Presented by 108 Productions (Los Angeles); Director, Nic Arnzen; Technical Director/Lighting, Jeremy Pivnick; Stage Manager, Elna Kordijan

CAST Peter **Nic Arnzen**; Simon **Amanda Axelrod**; Andrew **Jan Ambler**; Joshua **James Brandon**; Judas Iscariot **Steve Callahan**; John the Baptist **Melissa Caulfield**; Matthew **Elizabeth Cava**; James **Mark "Colby" Colbert**; Bartholomew **Steve Hasley**; Thomas **Molly O'Leary**; Philip **David Pevsner**; James the Less **Sheilagh Polk** (week 1), **Scott Presleyas** (week 2); Thaddeus **Suzanne Santos**

SETTING Corpus Christi, Texas; 1950's. Revival of a play presented in two acts. Originally presented by the Manhattan Theatre Club October 13, 1998 (see *Theatre World* Vol. 55, page 104). This revival was performed in honor of Matthew Shepard, whose brutal murder occurred just 24 hours prior to the play's world premiere in 1998. Proceeds from the show went to the Matthew Shepard Foundation, now also in its tenth anniversary, in support of their efforts to "Erase Hate" in today's society.

SYNOPSIS Terrence McNally's controversial *Corpus Christi* returns to New York. Retelling the Jesus story updated to 1950s Corpus Christi, Texas, the play originally opened ten years ago to intense protest and bomb threats, due to conservative Christian concerns about its depiction of a "gay Jesus."

Peter Mac as Judy Garland in Judy & Me (photo by Liz Ligouri)

Rock of Ages

New World Stages–Stage 1; First Preview: October 1, 2008; Opening Night: October 16, 2008; Closed January 4, 2009; 17 previews, 93 performances

Book by Chris D'Arienzo; Produced by Matthew Weaver, Carl Levin, Jeff Davis, and Corner Store Entertainment (Don Henig), in association with Scott Prisand, Janet Billig Rich, Hillary Weaver, Simon & Stefany Bergson, Charles Rolecek, Susanne Brook, Barry Habib, Israel Wolfson, Jennifer Maloney, and Prospect Pictures; Director, Kristin Hanggi; Choreography, Kelly Devine; Music Supervision, Arrangements & Orchestrations, Ethan Popp; Music Director, Matt Beck; Music Coordinator, John Miller; Original Arrangements/Associate Producer, David Gibbs; Set, Beowulf Boritt; Costumes, Gregory Gale; Lighting, Jason Lyons; Sound, Walter Trarbach; Projections, Zak Borovay; Hair & Wigs, Tom Watson; Makeup, Hagen Linss; Casting, Telsey + Company; PSM, Claudia Lynch; Richard Frankel Productions, Leslie Ledbetter; Production Manager, Peter Fulbright with Colleen Houlehen, Mary Duffe, Lyndsey Goode; Company Management, Tracy Geltman (Manager), Susan Keappock (Assistant); ASM, Jeff DaVolt; Associate Design, Jo Winiarski (set), Karl Ruckdeschel (costumes), Drew Levy (sound); Assistant Director, Daniel Horrigan; Assistant Choreographer, Robert Tatad; Creative Advisor, Wendy Goldberg; Dance Captain, Nova Bergeron; Advertising/Internet Marketing, Art Meets Commerce; Marketing, Leanne Schanzer Promotions; Music Copyist, Brian Allan Hobbs; Synthesizer Programmer, Randy Cohen; Press, The Karpel Group, Bridget Klapinski, Aïcha Dopp

The cast of Rock of Ages *(photo by Joan Marcus)*

CAST Lonny/Record Company Man **Mitchell Jarvis**; Justice/Mother **Michele Mais**; Dennis/Record Company Man **Adam Dannheisser**; Drew **Constantine Maroulis**; Sherrie **Kelli Barrett**; Father/Stacee Jaxx **Will Swenson**; Regina/Candi **Lauren Molina**; Mayor/Paul Gill/Ensemble **Brian Munn**; Hertz **Paul Schoeffler**; Franz **Wesley Taylor**; Waitress/Ensemble **Savannah Wise**; Reporter/Ensemble **Nova Bergeron**; Sleazy Producer/Joey Primo/Ensemble **Jeremy Woodward**; Ensemble **Angel Reed**; Offstage Singers/Swings **Jackie Burns, Tad Wilson**; Swings **Lara Janine, Christopher Spaulding**

UNDERSTUDIES Lara Janine (Sherrie, Regina), Savanna Wise (Sherrie), Christopher Spaulding & Jeremy Woodard (Drew, Franz, Stacee Jaxx), Tad Wilson (Lonny, Dennis, Hertz), Jackie Burns (Regina, Justice)

***ROCK OF AGES* BAND** Matt Beck (Conductor/keyboard), Joel Hoekstra (guitar 1), David Gibbs (guitar 2), John Weber (drums), Winston Roye (bass)

SETTING The Sunset Strip, Los Angeles. The late 1980s. New York premiere of a new musical with pop songs presented in two acts. Transferred to Broadway March 20, 2009 (see Broadway section in this volume).

SYNOPSIS It's the late 1980s and the final countdown is on for a legendary Hollywood rock club facing its demise at the hands of eager developers. When a young rocker hungry for his big break and a small town girl chasing her dreams land on the scene at this infamous venue, how far will ambition drive them? And will it be lights out for the club and all the regulars and rockers who have made it their home? *Rock of Ages* features a score by some of the best known rock and pop artists of the 1980s (see song listings in the Broadway section).

LaGuardia

Dicapo Opera Theatre; Opening Night: October 21, 2008; Closed December 13, 2008; 32 performances

Written by, Tony Lo Bianco; Adapted from the former play written by Paul Shyre; Presented by MNA Productions; Director, Tony Lo Bianco; Lighting, Paul Jones; Costumes, Patrizia Von Brandenstein; Press, James Sliman

CAST Fiorello LaGuardia **Tony Lo Bianco**

SETTING Fiorello LaGuardia's Gracie Mansion office, the last day of his third term; 1945. Revival of a solo performance play presented without intermission.

SYNOPSIS Tony Lo Bianco presents *LaGuardia*, a one-man show in which he portrays beloved mayor Fiorello LaGuardia. This courageous and colorful man was known for his honesty, and endeared himself to many with his fight against corruption in New York politics.

Tony LoBianco in LaGuardia *(photo courtesy of James Sliman)*

Capture Now

Bleecker Street Theatre; First Preview: October 10, 2008; Opening Night: October 22, 2008; Closed December 6, 2008

Written by Josh Jonas; Presented by Kurt Peterson and Jane Bergere; Director, Larry Moss; Set, Meghan Williams; Lighting, Matthew Richards; Sound, Shannon Slaton; General Manager, La Vie Productions; Press, Sam Rudy Media Relations

CAST Josh Jonas

World premiere of a solo performance play presented without intermission.

SYNOPSIS *Capture Now* is a unique coming-of-age story about two brothers: teenage Elijah and his little brother Ace who learn from each other what it means to be cool, who they would die for, and how rock 'n roll can uplift even the youngest of spirits. During this bittersweet and often funny tale, Elijah is both delighted and dazzled by his little brother's uncanny ability to teach him a thing or two about life ... from successful first date tips to negotiating his way through the cool crowd. *Capture Now* will do just that ... capture your attention, and hold it until the curtain falls.

Josh Jonas in Capture Now *(photo by Carol Rosegg)*

Peter Pan

Irondale Center for Theater Education and Outreach; Opening Night: October 22, 2008; Closed November 8, 2008

Written by J.M. Barrie, adapted by Jim Niesen and the Irondale Ensemble; Presented by the Irondale Ensemble Project; Director, Jim Neisen; Sets, Ken Rothchild; Lighting, Paul Hackenmueller; Costumes, Liz Prince; Stage Manager, Amy Von Vett; ASM, Jim Niesen; Executive Director, Terry Greiss; Managing Director, Maria Knapp; Development, Joseph McCarthy; Director of Education/Community and Youth Programs, Nicole Potter; Press, Art Meets Commerce, Tim Haskell

CAST Mrs. Darling/Tinkerbell/Curly **Ilana Niernberger**; Peter Pan **Jack Lush**; Wendy **Scarlet Rivera**; Mr. Darling/Nibs/Hook **Michael-David Gordon**; Barrie/Slightly **Damen Scranton**; Nana/Toodles/Starkey **Welland Hardwick**; Michael/First Twin/Smee **Nolan Kennedy**; John/Second Twin **Lindsay Vrab**

Revival of a play presented in two acts.

SYNOPSIS Brooklyn's Irondale Ensemble restages their critically acclaimed reinterpretation of J.M. Barrie's *Peter Pan*, the play he called a "terrible masterpiece." We all think we know it–but do we? Irondale probes this 1904 classic to discover why it continues to resonate as long as children are gay, and innocent and heartless.

Michael-David Gordon and Jack Lush (center) *in* Peter Pan *(photo by Gerry Goodstein)*

Break Out

Union Square Theatre; First Preview: September 18, 2008; Opening Night: October 23, 2008; Closed November 30, 2008; 7 previews, 90 performances

Written, choreographed and presented by SevenSense Inc. (Won-Kil Paek, Artistic Director; Director, Jun-Beom Juen; Kyung-Ah Han, Executive Producer; Tae-Hyung Kim, CEO); Produced by Show and Arts Inc.; Show Director, Jun-Beom Juen; Resident Director, Jung-Yul Yoon; Production Director for SevenSence, Hyun-Seung Seo; Composer, Sang-Ku Kang, Uk-Hyun Lee; Costumes, Hee-Ju Kim; Sets, Tae-Young Kim; Lighting, Yun-Young Koo; Sound, Yo-Chan Kim; Makeup, Mi-Suk Kim; Properties, Hee-Jung Lim; Stage Manager, Seo-Jin Lee; Local Coordinator, Min-Seob Kim; International Supervision, Song-Yee Han; Technical Director, John H. Paull; General Management, Roy Gaby; Advertising, Kyung-Ah Han; Press, O&M Company, Rick Miramontez, Molly Barnett, Amanda Dekkar

CAST Grey **Dae-Hyeok Lim**; Lump **Won-Jun Song**; Dandy **Jong-Wook Jeong**; Tricky **Chul-Hee Han**; Joker **Young-Nam Song**; Gundog **Jae-Hong Park**; SWAT **Seong-Jun Park**; Beauty 1 **Ji-Hee Jang**; Beauty 2 **Jin-Hee Kim**; Beauty 3 **Yoon-Hui Choi**

New York premiere of an extreme dance/comedy/acrobat theatrical piece presented without intermission

SYNOPSIS *Break Out*, an electrifying new show from the creative team behind last season's *Jump*, comes direct from London and Seoul. Hip-hop and break-dance meet cops-and-robbers comedy in this jaw-dropping, action-packed adventure, featuring a B-Boy crew that's simply dazzling. With a cast of nuns, nurses and break-dancing villains in the craziest jail break of all time, *Break Out* is a fun, madcap night out.

The Company of Break Out

The Files

59E59 Theater C; First Preview: October 22, 2008; Opening Night: October 24, 2008; Closed November 9, 2008; 2 previews, 18 performances

Text selection and adaptation by Ewa Wojciak & Katarzyna Madon-Mitzner, translated by Benjamin Johnston; Presented and realized by Theatre of the Eighth Day as part of the Made in Poland Festival 2008; Produced by 59E59 Theaters (Elysabeth Kleinhans, Artistic Director; Peter Tear, Executive Producer) and the Polish Cultural Institute; Director, The Ensemble; Design, Jacek Chmaj; Press, Karen Greco

CAST Adam Borowski, Tadeusz Janiszewski, Marcin Keszycki, Ewa Wojciak

American premiere of a new play presented without intermission.

SYNOPSIS Founded in 1964, Theatre of the Eighth Day unwittingly became Poland's foremost political theater of opposition under the Communist regime. Kept under surveillance by the Secret Police, plagued by the authorities, and accused of criminality, the theater managed to create some of the most important Polish performances of the 1970s. *The Files* is based on actual Secret Police reports on the Theatre's actors written during the period from 1975 to 1983 (reports that by definition also covered the actors' contacts, friendships, and meetings), juxtaposed with the actors' private letters at the time the reports were written, as well as parts of old performances to which the reports referred.

Pinkalicious, The Musical

Bleecker Street Theatre; Opening Day: November 1, 2008; Still playing as of May 31, 2009 (Saturday and Sunday performances)

Book and lyrics by Elizabeth Kann & Victoria Kann, music & lyrics by John Gregor; Produced by Vital Theatre Company (Stephen Sunderlin, Artistic Director; Linda Ames Key, Education Director; Mary Kate Burke, Associate Producer); Director, Teresa K. Pond; Original Director, Suzu McConnell-Wood; Choreography, Dax Valdes; Music Director, Jad Bernardo; Set, Mary Hamrick; Costumes, Colleen Kesterson & Randi Fowler; Props, Dan Jagendorf & Kerry McGuire; PSM, Kara M. Teolis; Stage Manager, Annie Deardorf; Casting, Bob Cline; Company Manager, Cadien Dumas; Press, Stephen Sunderlin

CAST Peter Pinkerton **Marc De La Concha**; Pinkalicious **Rori Nogee**; Dr. Wink **Molly Gilman**; Mr. Pinkerton **Nathaniel Timmerman**; Mrs. Pinkerton **Erin Wegner Brooks**

REPLACEMENTS/UNDERSTUDIES Lindsie Van Winkle, Jill Anthony Taylor, Dan Lawler, Colleen Fee, Kristin Parker, Bridget Riley, Jeff Barba, Rebecca Stavis, John Galas, Jace Nichols, Eric Restivo, Jonathan Bauchman, Rob Hinderliter

A musical for young audiences presented without intermission. Previously played at New World Stages January 12–May 25, 2008 (see *Theatre World* Vol. 64, page 268) and encored there August 2–September 21, 2008. Originally presented at the McGinn Cazale Theatre January 13–February 25, 2007, and extended at Soho Playhouse March 3–May 25, 2007 (see *Theatre World* Vol. 63, page 291).

SYNOPSIS Pinkalicious can't stop eating pink cupcakes despite warnings from her parents. Her pink indulgence lands her at the doctor's office with Pinkititis, an affliction that turns her pink from head to toe - a dream come true for this pink loving enthusiast. But when her hue goes too far, only Pinkalicious can figure out a way to get out of this predicament.

The cast of Pinkalicious (photo by Stephen Sunderlin)

The Middle Ages

Kirk Theatre on Theatre Row; First Preview: October 22, 2008; Opening Night: November 2, 2008; Closed November 23, 2008; 11 previews, 19 performances

Written by A.R. Gurney; Presented by Theater Breaking Through Barriers; Director, Ike Schambelan; Sets/Lighting, Bert Scott; Costumes, Chloe Chapin; Sound, Richard M. Rose; Hair & Wigs, Angelina Jerbasi; Fight Director, J. David Brimmer; PSM, Kimothy Cruse; ASM, Brooke Elsinghorst; Production Managers, David Chontos & Nicholas Lazzaro; Marketing, Michelle Tabnick; Press, Shirley Herz & Associates, Dan DeMello

CAST Barney **Terry Small**; Eleanor **Marilee Talkington**; Charles **George Ashiotis**; Myra **Melanie Boland**

SETTING The trophy room of a men's club, just after World War II through the late 1970s. Revival of a comedy presented in two acts. Originally presented by the Hartman Theatre Company January 5, 1978 (see *Theatre World* Vol. 34, page 199),

SYNOPSIS *The Middle Ages* tells the story of a family in conflict between long-standing traditions and the pressure for change. Son Barney needs to break free, but his father Charles, the president of a men's club, locks him in the trophy room when he misbehaves. On one such occasion, he meets the shy Eleanor, falls in love, and spends the next 30 years trying to win her over. Meanwhile, her mother, a social climber hungry for stability, strives to break into this rapidly failing world.

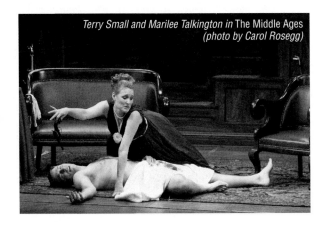

Terry Small and Marilee Talkington in The Middle Ages
(photo by Carol Rosegg)

The Tales of the Custard Dragon

DR2 Opening Night: November 2, 2008; Closed December 8, 2008; 12 performances

Music by Brad Ross, lyrics by Danny Whitman, adapted from Ogden Nash's story by Mary Hall Surface; Presented by Gallant Arts (Danny Gallant); Director, Robert Bartley; Music Director/Pianist, Brad Ross; Choreography, Danny Whitman; Set/Costumes, Greg Montgomery; PSM, Angela Allen

CAST Ink **Tiffan Borelli**; Belinda **Jen Faith Brown**; Mustard **Ethan Cadoff**; Pirate/Sir Garagoyle **Jeff Exxex**; Blink **Michael McGuirk**; Custard **Spencer Moses**

Off-Broadway transfer of a musical for young audiences presented without intermission. Originally produced at the Kennedy Center for the Performing Arts. Previously presented at the Algonquin Theatre February 16–March 8, 2008.

SYNOPSIS Based on the story by Ogden Nash, this new musical tells the story of Custard the Dragon and his friends Ink, Blink, and Mustard as they embark on a journey, in which Custard, a most unlikely hero, finds the courage to rescue his beloved Belinda from a menacing pirate and a wicked knight.

Jen Faith Brown, Spencer Moses and Jeff Essex in The Tales of the Custard Dragon (photo by Danny Whitman)

The Complete Performer

The Huron Club at Soho Playhouse; Opening Night: November 8, 2008; Closed December 27, 2008

Written and directed by Ted Greenberg; Presented by Darren Lee Cole and the Soho Playhouse

CAST Himself **Ted Greenberg**

Off-Broadway premiere of a solo performance comedy presented without intermission. Previously presented in the 2008 New York International Fringe Festival.

SYNOPSIS The Off-Broadway triumph with a halftime show and a taxi ride home! The Late Show with David Letterman's Emmy Award-winning writer, Ted Greenberg, and his crowd-rousing mascot combine stand-up, mindreading, magic, and full-frontal nudity in a quintessential New York theater experience—plus an after party with a live feed of the taxi ride home.

Bury the Dead

Connelly Theatre; First Preview: October 31, 2008; Opening Night: November 9, 2008; Closed November 23, 2008

Written by Irwin Shaw, pre-show material by Joe Carlarco; Presented by Transport Group; Director, Joe Calarco; Set, Sandra Goldmark; Costumes, Kathryn Rohe; Lighting, R. Lee Kennedy; Sound, Michael Rasbury; PSM, Wendy Patten; Stage Manager, Donald Butchko; Press, Richard Kornberg & Associates

CAST Our Host/Bess Schelling/Joan/Julia Blake/Katherine Driscoll/Mrs. Dean/Martha Webster **Donna Lynne Champlin**; A Townsperson/Third Soldier/Second General/Bevins/Private Webster **Jake Hart**; A Townsperson/A Sergeant/A Doctor/An Editor/Private Henry Levy **Fred Berman**; A Townsperson/Second Soldier/A Stenographer/A Reporter/Private James Dean **Mandell Butler**; A

Townsperson/First Soldier/A Whore/Private Walter Morgan **Matt Sincell**; A Townsperson/First General/Private Tom Driscoll **Jeff Pucillo**; A Townsperson/A Captain/Charlie/Private John Schelling **Jeremy Beck**

Revival of a play presented without intermission.

SYNOPSIS Shaw's harrowing 1936 classic *Bury the Dead* takes place during "the second year of the war that is to begin tomorrow night." While a military burial detail goes about its sad duties, the dead soldiers shockingly begin to rise up, pleading not to be buried. Word of their insurrection spreads rapidly: the dead will not yield so easily. In a series of touching scenes the dead men talk with their loved ones of the days of living, now lost forever.

Mindgame

Soho Playhouse; First Preview: October 28, 2008; Opening Night: November 9, 2008; Closed December 28, 2008

Written by Anthony Horiwitz; Presented by Monica Tidwell, Darren Lee Cole, Joseph Callari, and Michael Butler in association with Robert R. Blume, Mary Cossette, Pierre Cossette, Michael Baden, Linda Kenney Baden, Victor Lownes, and Rusty Holzer; Director, Ken Russell; Sets, Beowulf Boritt; Lighting, Jason Lyons; Costumes, Melissa Bruning; Sound, Bernard Fox; Fight Director, J. David Brimmer; Makeup/Hair, J. Jared Janas & Rob Greene; PSM, Dee Wicker; Assistant to the Director, Elize Russell; Casting, Lewis & Fox Casting, Kristine Lewis and Jamie Fox; General Manager, Darren Lee Cole and Faith A. Mulvhill; Production Manager, Peter Dean; Advertising/New Media Marketing/Website Design, Art Meets Commerce; Press, Keith Sherman & Associates

CAST Mark Styler **Lee Godart**; Dr. Farquhar **Keith Carradine**; Nurse Plimpton **Kathleen McNenny**

SETTING Hollywood-on-the-Thames, circa 1958. New York premiere of a new play presented in two acts. Originally produced in the West End at the Vaudeville Theatre in 2000.

SYNOPSIS When a writer of pulp crime novels gets an interview with a notorious serial killer he believes he has snared the coup of his career. But when he arrives at the asylum, he finds nothing can be trusted, not even his own eyes. Through a series of lies, manipulations and memories, dark secrets are revealed. Why is there a skeleton in the doctor's office? Where did the raw meat in the fridge come from? What is the nurse so afraid of? And most importantly, how does one get out?

Made in Poland

59E59 Theaters B; First Preview: October 29, 2008; Opening Night: November 9, 2008; Closed November 30, 2008

Written by Przemyslaw Wojcieszek, translated by Alissa Valles; Presented by The Play Company (Kate Loewald, Founding Producer; Lauren Weigel, Managing Producer) as part of the Made in Poland Festival 2008; Produced by 59E59 Theaters (Elysabeth Kleinhans, Artistic Director; Peter Tear, Executive Producer) and the Polish Cultural Institute; Director, Jackson Gay; Set, Ola Maslik; Costumes, Jessica Ford; Lighting, Matthew Richards; Sound, Bart Fasbender; PSM, Alaina Taylor; Fight Director, J. David Brimmer; Casting, Judy Henderson; Press, Karen Greco

CAST Bogus **Kit Williamson**; Father Edmund **Ed Vassallo**; Emil **Jonathan Clem**; Grzes **Ryan O'Nan**; Tekla/Helenka/Marianna **Eva Kaminsky**; Fazi **Jayce Bartok**; Irena **Karen Young**; Viktor **Rob Campbell**; Monika **Natalia Zvereva**

American premiere of a new play presented without intermission.

SYNOPSIS A rebellious young man demands guidance in post-communist Poland, challenging his priest, his teacher, his mother and even local gangsters to show him the way. In the end, love saves the day.

What's That Smell? The Music of JacobSterling

New World Stages–Stage 5; First Preview: November 1, 2008; Opening Night: November 9, 2008; Closed December 28, 2008; 11 previews, 54 performances

Book and lyrics by David Pittu, music by Randy Redd; Presented by Daryl Roth and the Atlantic Theater Company; Directors, Neil Pepe & David Pittu; Set, Takeshi Kata; Costumes, Martin Pakledinaz; Lighting, Matthew Richards; Sound, Jill BC Duboff; Projections, Dustin O'Neill; Music Director/Arrangements, Randy Redd; Wigs, Paul Huntley; Marketing, Allied Live; Associate Producer, Alexander Fraser; General Manager, Adam Hess; PSM, Alison DeSantis, Production Manager, Travis Walker; Stage Manager, Lauren Kurinskas; Company Manager, Tegan Meyer; Casting, MelCap Casting; Press, Boneau/Bryan-Brown, Joe Perrotta

CAST Leonard **Peter Bartlett**; Jacob **David Pittu**; Paisley **Chandra Lee Schwartz**; Eisenhower **Max Kumangai**; Jerod **Matt Schock**

Commercial transfer of a musical presented without intermission. The show previously played as part of the Atlantic Theater's season earlier (see listing in Company Series in this volume).
SYNOPSIS *What's That Smell* is described as a hilarious musical parody that charts the career of eternally up-and-coming (and fictitious) musical theater composer Jacob Sterling. A rare, up close and personal visit with an artist of questionable gifts who performs from his songbook and shares his human struggle to keep musical theater alive and well into the 21st century.

David Pittu and Peter Bartlett in What's That Smell: The Music of Jacob Sterling (photo by Doug Hamilton)

Sleepwalk With Me

Bleecker Street Theatre; First Preview: October 17, 2008; Opening Night: November 11, 2008; Closed June 7, 2009; 198 performances

Written by Mike Birbiglia; Presented by Eli Gonda, Ryan Scott Warren, Peter Saraf, Marc Turtletaub, and Nathan Lane; Director, Seth Barrish; Sets, Beowulf Boritt; Lighting, Jason Lyons; Sound, Jim Corona & Jody Elff; Board Operator, C.J. Thom; General Management, Richards/Climan Inc. (David Richards, Tamar Haimes, John Gendron); Associate Producers, Ellen Baker, Gina M. Duncan, Mike Lavoie; Executive Producers, Joseph Birbiglia, Dave Becky, Stephenie Davis; Company Manager, Chelsea Salyer; Assistant Producer, Arthur Chan; Technical Director, Josh Iacovelli; Advertising, Eliran Murphy Group; Press, Keith Sherman and Associates, Scott Klein, Brett Oberman, Glenna Friedman, Tamara Alfred

CAST Himself **Mike Birbiglia**

World premiere of a solo performance play presented without intermission **SYNOPSIS** In his theatrical debut, comedian Mike Birbiglia takes the audience on a hysterically funny and intensely personal journey through his struggles with sleepwalking and his reluctance to confront his fears of love, honesty and growing up. *Sleepwalk With Me* is the rare collision of comedy and theatre that touches your funny bone and tickles your heart.

Mike Birbiglia in Sleepwalk With Me *(photo by Joan Marcus)*

Waves

Duke on 42nd Street; First Preview: November 12, 2008; Opening Night: November 14, 2008; Closed November 22, 2008; 2 previews, 11 performances

A work devised by Katie Mitchell and the Company from the text of Virginia Woolf's novel; Presented by Lincoln Center Great Performers Series; Director, Katie Mitchell; Sets, Vicki Mortimer; Lighting, Paule Constable; Music, Paul Clark; Music Director/Arranger, Simon Allen; Video Design, Leo Warner/Fifty-Nine Productions Ltd; Sound, Gareth Fry; Company Voice Work, Kate Godfrey; Press, Eileen McMahon

CAST Kate Duchêne, Anastasia Hille, Kristin Hutchinson, Sean Jackson, Stephen Kennedy, Liz Kettle, Paul Ready, Jonah Russell

SETTING 1893–1933. American premiere of a new play presented in two acts.

SYNOPSIS *Waves* is based on Woolf's groundbreaking 1931 novel *The Waves*. Directed by renowned British director Katie Mitchell, associate director of the National, who conceived and created the work in collaboration with the company's actors and video artist Leo Warner of Fifty-Nine Productions, it had its London premiere in 2006. Virginia Woolf's stream-of-consciousness novel *The Waves* follows six people from childhood to old age. Almost plotless (short narrative sections advance the story), the book weaves together the characters interior monologues, in which their lives—problems, joys, regrets—unfold over the course of one day.

Waves (photo by Steve Cummiskey)

Catalpa

Irish Arts Center Donaghy Theatre; First Preview: November 12, 2008; Opening Night: November 16, 2008; Closed November 30, 2008; 4 previews, 25 performances

Written by Donal O'Kelly; Director, Bairbre Ni Chaoimh; Lighting and Sound, Ronan Fingleton; Music, Trevor Knight; Press, Karen Greco

CAST Donal O'Kelly

New York premiere of a solo performance play presented in two acts.

SYNOPSIS Based on the true story of the daring rescue of six Irish prisoners in 1875, Catalpa is an epic in the tradition of *Moby Dick, Gone with The Wind,* and *The Great Escape*, performed with virtuosity by Ireland's greatest playwright-performer. From the whaling town of New Bedford, Massachusetts, to the prison colony of Fremantle, Australia, to the scene of New York City's first ticker-tape parade, Donal O'Kelly takes us on a journey across the high seas aboard the whaling ship Catalpa. *Catalpa* has thrilled audiences and dazzled critics all over the world – Dublin, Melbourne, London, Chicago, Toronto, Paris, Copenhagen, Edinburgh, Glasgow, and Geneva.

Donal O'Kelly in Catalpa
(photo courtesy of Irish Arts Center))

The cast of Dear Edwina (photo by Sandra Coudert)

Dear Edwina

DR2; First Preview: November 14, 2009; Opening Night: November 16, 2008; Closed April 19, 2008; 197 performances

Book and lyrics by Marcy Heisler, Music by Zina Goldrich; Presented by Daryl Roth; Director, Timothy A. McDonald; Choreography, Steven G. Kennedy; Sets, Court Watson; Costumes, Theresa Squire; Lighting, Kathyrn Furst; Music Director, Mark Hartman; Orchestrator, Zina Goldrich, Michael Croiter; Marketing, Erin Auerbach; Casting, Dave Clemmons Casting; Press, Elizabeth Waldman Frazier; General Manager, Adam Hess; Production Manager, Greg Bellon; PSM, Cynthia Hennon; Company Manager, Kyle Provost; Press, Elizabeth Waldman Frazier

CAST Bobby Newsome **Tyler Adcock**; Edwina Spoonapple **Janice Mays**; Scott **Ernie Pruneda**; Billy Vanderploonk **Doug Thompson**; Annie Smith Meenhan Johnson **Shannon Tyo**; Keli Poshkonozovich **Katie Whetsell**; Swings **Gordon Maniskas, Morgan Rose**

MUSICIANS Joe Kinosian (Conductor/piano/Joe Spoonapple); Nicole Marcus (drummer/Myra Spoonapple)

MUSICAL NUMBERS Paw Paw Michigan; Up on the Fridge; Dear Edwina; Here Comes a Letter; Hephaestus; Say No Thank You; Another Letter!; Abigail; Frankenguest; Carrie; Fork, Knife, Spoon; Time for Intermission; Periwinkle; Hla, Lola; Ziggy; Put it in the Piggy; Thanks for Coming; Fridge Breakdown; Sing Your Own Song; Fridge Reprise; Hola, Lola Encore

SETTING The Spoonapple Family Garage, Paw Paw Michigan, U.S.A. The present. Off-Broadway debut of a new musical presented without intermission.

SYNOPSIS In the time-honored tradition of "Let's put on a show," Dear Edwina's plucky heroine, Edwina Spoonapple, decides that she and her pals will do just that. Edwina's special talent is giving advice, and she would do almost anything to be a part of the Kalamazoo Advice-a-palooza Festival. When a talent scout visits her hometown of Paw Paw, Michigan, Edwina, assisted by a host of quirky friends and neighbors, enthusiastically sings out her musical advice in hilarious and endearing songs about everything from party etiquette to the proper way to set a table.

Sandbox & The First Time

59E59 Theaters C; First Preview: November 13, 2008; Opening Night: November 16, 2008; Closed November 30, 2008; 5 previews, 11 performances

Written by Michal Walczak, translated by Benjamin Paloff; Presented by Immigrants' Theatre Project (Marcy Arlin, Founder) as part of the Made in Poland Festival 2008; Produced by 59E59 Theaters (Elysabeth Kleinhans, Artistic Director; Peter Tear, Executive Producer) and the Polish Cultural Institute; Directors, Piotr Kruszczcynski (Sandbox), Marcy Arlin (The First Time); Set, Robert Monaco; Lighting, Christopher Weston; Costumes, Grainne Coen (First Time) & Jola Lobasz (Sandbox); Sound, Elizabeth Rhodes; Music (Sandbox), Pawel Dampc; Assistand Director/Stage Manager/Props, Rasha Zamairi; Technical Director, Vadim Malinskiy; Props, Grainn Coen; ASM, Jahnu Stayton; Press, Karen Greco

CAST Sandbox: Alberic **Hristo Hugo**; Milla **Jelena Stupljanin**; The First Time: Maggie **Lisa Hugo**; Charles **Robert Baumgardner**

SETTING Sandbox: A playground in an apartment complex. The First Time: An apartment in an apartment complex. American premiere of two one-act plays presented with one intermission.

SYNOPSIS These two one-act comedies examine the ferocious, tragicomic, rough-and-tumble between the sexes. Both plays explore different stages of relationships, underlaid with a cynicism and absurdism often found in Eastern European theater. The battle of the sexes literally starts in the Sandbox, in this hilarious confrontation between a boy guarding his space and a girl who just wants to play. The First Time is an outrageous look at erotic interplay under absurd circumstances, when a woman demands from her eager boyfriend that their "first time" be perfect.

Hristo Hristov and Jelena Stupljanin in Sandbox,
part of the Made In Poland Festival (photo by Dixie Sheridan)

Perdita

Lion Theatre on Theatre Row; First Preview: November 13, 2008; Opening Night: November 18, 2008; Closed December 7, 2008

Written by Pierre-Marc Diennet; Presented by Matthew and Marine Putman; Director, Linsay Firman; Set, Nick Francone; Costumes, Blythe Quinlan; Lighting, Les Dickert; Sound and Original Music, Shane Rettig; Production Manager, Daniel R. Naish; Stage Manager, Annie Deardorff; Press, Kevin P. McAnarney

CAST Pierre-Marc Diennet

Off-Broadway premiere of a new solo performance play presented in two acts.

SYNOPSIS What is it like to be the son of a feminist hero? What is it like to be his mother? *Perdita* is the compelling story of two generations, two genders, two experiences of the same pioneering life. Perdita and her son travel to the four corners of the world and to the very edge of life to find out what it costs to be an inspiration. *Perdita* exposes the good works as well as the lovers, heartbreaks and the difficult balance of family life and career. The play is about the private side of a proud woman's public life and about what it cost her child to be with her while she lived it.

Garden of Earthly Delights

Minetta Lane Theatre; First Preview: November 8, 2008; Opening Night: November 19, 2008; Closed April 5, 2009

Written by Hieronymus Bosch, music by Richard Peaslee; Produced by Rhoda Herrick; Director, Martha Clarke; Music Director, Arthur Solari; Set, Christopher Akerlind; Costumes, Jane Greenwood; Lighting, Christopher Akerlind; Producing Associates, Barbara Foy and David Grausman; Assistant Director, Paola Styron; Choreographer, Martha Clarke; Assistant Set, Jeanette Yew; Assistant Lighting, Joyce Liao; Flying Design, Flying By Foy; General Manager, Two Step Productions; PSM, Jennifer Rae Moore; ASMs, Terri K. Kohler and Pamela Salling; Production Manager, Andrew Martini; Technical Director, Ben Zimmer; Consultant, David Hale; Press, Richard Kornberg & Associates;

A scene from Garden of Earthly Delights *(photo by Richard Finkelstein)*

CAST Sophie Bortolussi, Benjamin B. Bowman, Daniel Clifton, Francis Chiaverini, Elena Demyanenk, General McArthur Hambrick, Whitney V. Hunter, Gabrielle Malone, Matt Rivera, Andrew Robinson, Jenny Sandler, Isadora Wolfe, Understudies Miguel Anaya, Ann Chiaverini

MUSICIANS Egil Rostad (cello), Arthur Solari (percussion), Wayne Hankin (woodwinds)

Revival of a theatrical dance and performance art presented without intermission.

SYNOPSIS Visionary director Martha Clarke brings Hieronymus Bosch's provocative painting to life in *Garden of Earthly Delights*, exploring heaven, hell, and the beauty and sins in between. An inspired synthesis of visual and performing magic, this breathtaking flight of imaginative genius is sexy, evocative, and unlike anything you've ever seen on stage.

London Cries

Irondale Center for Theatre Education and Outreach; Opening Night: November 20, 2008; Closed December 20, 2008

Written by Di Trevis and Frank McGuinness, based on the book *London Labour & The London Poor* by Henry Mayhew, with songs from the Golden Age of the British Music Hall; Presented by Irondale Ensemble Project; Director, Di Trevis; Music, Dominic Muldowney; Stage Manager, Lindsay Vrab; Rehearsal Stage Manager, Zoe Lafferty; ASM, Patrena Murray; Sets, Ken Rothchild; Lighting, Carrie Yacono; Costumes, Liz Prince; Movement, Kim Jordon; Musical Director, John DiPinto; Voice/Dialects, Joe Windley; Assistants to Lighting, Scott Blackburn, Mac Kroneerg; Spot Operator, Amy VonVett; Artistic Director, Jim Niesen; Executive Director, Terry Greiss; Managing Director, Maria Knapp; Director of Development, Joseph McCarthy; Director of Education, Community and Youth Programs: Nicole Potter; Press, Art Meets Commerce, Tim Haskell

CAST Jenny **Jenny Galloway**; Tosher **Michael-David Gordon**; Nathanial **Michael Gabriel Goodfriend**; Archie **Welland Hardwick**; Lily **Sasha Higgins**; Bill **Nolan Kennedy**; Sadie **Ilana Niernberger**; Freddie Bishop **Richard Poe**; Mariah **Scarlet Maressa Rivera**; Polly **Nancy Rodriguez**; Samuel **Damen Scranton**

SETTING Victorian England. An old London theatre. World premiere of a new play presented in two acts.

SYNOPSIS From the crumbling walls and recesses of an old London theatre, the ghosts of yesteryear share their lives, their loves and the lilting melodies of a bygone Victorian era.

The cast of London Cries *(photo by Gerry Goodstein)*

Catch-22

Lucille Lortel Theatre; First Preview: November 14, 2008; Opening Night: November 23, 2008; Closed December 20, 2008

Written by Joseph Heller; adapted and directed by Peter Meineck; Presented by Aquila Theatre in association with the Lucille Lortel Foundation; Design, Peter Meineck; Movement, Desiree Sanchez; Sound, Mark Sanders; Production Manager, Nate Terracio; PSM, Cat Coffey; Press, David Gersten & Associates

CAST Yossarian **John Lavelle**; Ensemble **Mark Alhadeff, Teddy Alvaro, David Bishins, Chip Brookes, Emily Cardea, Christina Pumariega, Richard Sheridan Willis, Craig Wroe**,

SETTING A small island off the coast of Italy; 1944. World premiere of a play presented in two acts.

SYNOPSIS Yossarian is a bombardier on a B-25, based on a small island off the coast of Italy in 1944. He starts to question the futile and ridiculous administration of his air base and seeks a way to preserve his life when the whole world around him seems to be going mad. Like a modern-day Achilles, Yossarian protests with powerful and often hilarious results. *Catch-22* tackles huge things with rich metaphors, boldly drawn characters and near-impossible situations. It is a work of great theatricality with superb language and a sense of dark surrealism. Heller dares to examine the very philosophy of war and what it does to the humans that fight them. For a whole new generation of Americans, Yossarian Lives!

Mia Barron as Hillary Clinton and Darren Pettie as Bill Clinton in Hillary (photo by Jimbo)

Hillary: A Modern Greek Tragedy with a (Somewhat) Happy Ending

The Living Theatre; First Preview: November 22, 2008; Opening Night: November 24, 2008; Closed December 20, 2008; 3 previews, 21 performances

Written by Wendy Weiner; Presented by New Geroges (Susan Bernfeild, Artistic Director; Sarah Cameron Sunde, Associate Director); Director, Julie Kramer; Set, Lauren Helpern; Lights, Graham Kindred; Sound, Jill BC DuBoff & Joshua Higgason; Costumes, Amelia Dombrowski; Props, Eugenia Furneaux-Arends; Wigs/Makeup, Erin Kennedy Lunsford; PSM, Ryan Raduechel; ASM/Associate Production Manager, Laura Jane Collins; Assistant Director, Claire Moyer; Guy Friday/Box Office, Johnson Henshaw; Sound Operator, Eric Olson; Technical Director, Ben Weaver; Master Electrician, Evan True; Lighting Assistant, Dana Caputo; Costume Assistant, Stephanie Alexander; Casting, Paul Davis/Calleri Casting; Associate Producer, Rehana Mirza; Press, Jim Baldassare;

CAST Hillary **Mia Barron**; Bill **Darren Pettie**; Athena **Heidi Armbruster**; Aphrodite **Victoire Charles**; Chorus **Jorge Cordova, Charlie Hudson III, Jenny Mercein, Josie Whittlesey**

Off-Broadway premiere of a new play presented without intermission. New Georges first presented *Hillary* at The Public Theater last December in a two-performance workshop presentation. **SYNOPSIS** Athena, the Greek goddess of wisdom, and Aphrodite, the goddess of love, have been at war since time immemorial. When a young girl named Hillary Rodham devotes herself to Athena alone—spurning romance, makeup, and attractive hairstyles—Aphrodite takes revenge by having her fall in love with a man of mythical charm and appetites: Bill Clinton.

The Black Monk

Beckett Theatre on Theatre Row; First Preview: November 25, 2008; Opening Night: December 4, 2008; Closed January 4, 2009; 3 previews, 29 performances

Book, music and lyrics by Wendy Kesselman, based on a short story by Anton Chekhov; Presented by South Ark Stage (Rhoda Herrick, Producing Artistic Director); Director, Kevin Newbury; Musical Director/Arrangements/Pianist, Christopher Berg; Sets, Charlie Corcoran; Costumes, Jessica Jahn; Lighting, D.M. Wood; Properties, Jessica Provenzale; PSM, Kate McDoniel; Cello, Arthur Cook; Press, O+M Company, Rick Miramontez, Philip Carrubba

CAST Andrei **Elon Rutberg**; Tanya **Julie Craig**; Igor **Scott Robertson**; The Monk **Austin Pendleton**

SETTING A little house by the sea in Russia. World premiere of a musical presented without intermission.

SYNOPSIS A stunning new musical inspired by Anton Chekhov's story, *The Black Monk* follows the life of Andrei, a gifted young artist. After five years at school in Moscow, he returns home to his adopted father Igor and childhood love Tanya. As his artistic talent blossoms, will Andrei be able to hold on to love, family, and his sanity or will the power of the mysterious Black Monk drive him into the unknown.

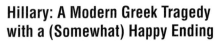

Elon Rutberg, Julie Craig, Austin Pendleton and Scott Robertson in The Black Monk (photo by Carol Rosegg)

Dust

Westside Theatre–Downstairs; First Preview: November 18, 2008; Opening Night: December 4, 2008; Closed January 18, 2009; 18 previews, 54 performances

Written by Billy Goda; Presented by Roger Alan Gindi and Cassidy Productions; Director; Scott Zigler; Sets, Caleb Wertenbaker; Costumes, Theresa Squire; Lighting, Charles Foster; Sound, Sharath Patel; Fight Director, Rick Sordelet; General Manager, Roger Alan Gindi; PSM, Pamela Edington; Stage Manager, April Ann Kline; Production Manager, Aduro Productions; Casting, Janet Foster; Marketing, HHC Marketing; Press, Keith Sherman & Associates

CAST Martin **Richard Masur**; Zeke **Hunter Foster**; Jenny **Laura E, Campbell**; Booby/Digs **Curtis McClarin**; Ralph/Man **John Schiappa**; Understudies **Elizabeth Olsen** (Jenny), **DeLance Minefee** (Bobby/Digs, Ralph/Man)

SETTING New York. A new thriller presented in two acts.

SYNOPSIS *Dust* is a power play. One man is an executive with money and a paunch. The other is an ex-con with street smarts and a minimum-wage position. What starts off as a battle of wills over who will do the dusting escalates into a war for respect, the upper hand and survival. Who will be standing when the dust settles?

Gimpel Tam

Jewish Community Center; First Preview: November 23, 2008; Opening Night: December 4, 2008; Closed December 28, 2008; 36 performances

Adapted and directed by Moshe Yassur, based on the short story "Gimpel and the Fool" by Isaac Bashevis Singer; Presented by The National Yiddish Theatre–Folksbiene; Composer, Radu Captari; Sets and Lighting, Roger Hanna; Costumes, Gail Cooper-Hecht; Sound, Don Jacobs; Choreography, Inka Justin; Music Director, Zalman Mlotek; Assistant Director, Motl Didner; Press, Beck Lee Media Blitz

CAST Gimpel **Adam Shapiro**; Dayan/Velvl **Jonathan Brody**; Berele/Borekh **Ilan Kwittken**; Surkele/Rabbi's daughter **Nicole Raphael**; Fayvl/Gezel **Ethan Sher**; Yeshive Bokher/Yankl **Richard Kass**; Zeyde/Der Rebbe **I.W. "Itzy" Firestone**; Shadkhn/Badkhn **Henry Peerce**; Elke **Daniella Rabbani**; Basye/Mamma **Amy Goldstein**; Rivke-Rokhl **Sheila Rubell**; Leyele **Lisa Fishman**; Der Shotn **Motl Didner**

MUSICIANS Joshua Camp, Louisa Strouse Boiman, Dmitri Slepovitch, Taylor Bergren-Chrisman

SETTING A shtetl of Frampol. American premiere of a new Yiddish musical play presented without intermission.

SYNOPSIS *Gimpel Tam* tells the morally complex story of Gimpel–often referred to as the quintessential schlemiel–an unlucky man who is beset by one misfortune after another. Gullible in the extreme, he believes even the most outlandish lies by his fellow townspeople. But when given a chance to exact revenge on those who have exploited him, Gimpel says no. Is he a fool? Folksbiene's bold, contemporary production of *Gimpel Tam* tries to reach beyond the folksy mysticism normally associated with Singer. This is a witty, freewheeling staging that will help cast the story of Gimpel in a new light, and reveal its very modern relevance.

Improbable Frequency

59E59 Theater B; First Preview: November 28, 2008; Opening Night: December 4, 2008; Closed January 4, 2009; 44 performances

Book and lyrics by Arthur Riordan, music by Bell Helicopter; Presented by A Rough Magic Theater Company; Director, Lynne Parker; Musical Director, Morgan Cooke; Sets, Alan Farquharson; Costumes, Kathy Strachan; Lighting, Sinead McKenna; Sound, Bell Helicopter; PSM, Paula Tierney; Production Manager, Gavin Harding; ASM, Justin Murphy; Sound Consultant, Ivan Birthistle; Production Electrician, Kevin Smith; Costume Supervisor, Breege Fahy; Hair and Makeup Val Sherlock; Publicist, Kathy Scott; Press, Karen Greco

CAST Philomena O'Shea **Sarah-Jane Drummey**; Tristram Faraday **Peter Hanly**; Myles na gCopaleencq/Muldoon **Darragh Kelly**; John Betjeman/O'Dromedary **Louis Lovett**; Erwin Schrödinger/The Colonel **Marty Rea**; Agent Green **Cathy White**;

SETTING Dublin; 1941. American premiere of a new musical presented in two acts.

SYNOPSIS While war rages across Europe, Dublin revels in its knife-edge neutrality as the fledgling Irish Free State tries to remain open for business. A hotbed of political and cultural bohemians, the city is host to a volatile mixture of exiled intellectuals, literary bar-lizards, British spies and Nazi sympathizers. When coded messages, broadcast during an Irish radio-requests show, draw the attention of the British, a young code breaker called Tristram Faraday is sent across the Irish Sea to investigate. His enquiries lead him into a series of deeply improbable encounters, where the truth is more improbable than anyone could have imagined.

Peter Hanly and Sarah-Jane Drummey in Improbable Frequency *(photo by Carol Rosegg)*

New House Under Construction

59E59 Theater A; First Preview: December 4, 2008; Opening Night: December 10, 2008; Closed January 4, 2009; 33 performances

Written by Alan Hruska; Presented by Victory Center with Rock and a Hard Place Productions and Red Horse Productions; Director, Alan Hruska; Set, Kenneth Foy; Costumes, Sarah J. Holden; Lighting, Jason Kantrowitz; Sound, Peter Fitzgerald; Original Music, Lisa Ralia Heffter; Pre-Show Music, Eric Hachikian; Casting, Barden-Schnee Casting, Allison Estrin; PSM, Bonnie Brady; ASM, Tiffany Tabatchnick; Technical Director, Vadim Malinsky; Props Jessica Levy; Press, Karen Greco

CAST Trevor **Anthony Crane**; Tony **Kevin Isola**; Sarah **Shannon Koob**; Judy **Nancy Lemenager**; Manny **Sam Coppola**

SETTING A new house, under construction. World premiere of new play presented without intermission.

SYNOPSIS After 15 years, 2 couples in their 40's are reunited during the construction of a new house. Old rivalries, secrets and choices made long ago come to the surface and the audience is brought into a story about love, lust and the "what-ifs" in life.

The cast of the musical ReWrite (photo by Alex Koch

SYNOPSIS A fun, quirky trio of mini-musicals by the young and talented Joe Iconis, *ReWrite*, is a musical comedy triple feature. *ReWrite* deals with time, with deadlines, with donuts. The deadlines one imposes on oneself and the deadlines that the universe imposes on us. It's about trying to live up to the expectations you created for yourself and trying to do it before your time runs out. It's about normal people, not the sort of people who get musicals written about them. Normal people dealing with little problems that seem huge and huge problems boiled down to something a bit more manageable.

Nancy Lemenager and Shannon Koob in New House Under Construction *(photo by Carol Rosegg)*

ReWrite

Urban Stages–Garment District Theatre; First Preview: December 6, 2008; Opening Night: December 10, 2008; Closed January 3, 2009

Book, music, and lyrics by Joe Iconis; Presented by Urban Stages (Frances Hill, Founder & Artistic Director; Lauren Schmiedel, Managing Director) in association with Sara Katz; Director, John Simpkins; Musical Director, Matt Hinkley; Set, Michael Schweikardt; Costumes, Michelle Eden Humphrey; Lighting, Chris Dallos; Sound, Craig Kaufman; Video/Projections, Alex Koch; PSM, Carol Sullivan; Stage Manager, Theresa Flanagan; Press, Springer Associates, Joe Trentacosta

CAST Nelson Drucker/The Slick Dude **Nick Blaemire**; Jenny Vecharelli/The Lady Customer **Lauren Marcus**; Ike McCauley/The Young Man **A.J. Shively**; The Woman **Lorinda Lisitza**; The Writer **Jason Williams**; The Girl Behind the Counter **Badia Farha**

World premiere of the new mini-musicals, *Nelson Rocks, Miss Marzipan, & The Process* presented in one act.

Women Beware Women

Theatre at St. Clements; First Preview: December 9, 2008; Opening Night: December 13, 2008; Closed January 18, 2009;

Written by Thomas Middleton; Presented by Red Bull Theater; Director/Adaptor, Jesse Berger; Set, David Barber; Costumes, Clint Ramos; Lighting, Peter West; Original Music, Scott Killian; Sound, Jessica Paz; Fight Director, Rick Sordelet; Choreography, Tracy Bersley; PSM, Nicole Bouclier; Casting, Stuart Howard; Press, David Gersten & Associates

CAST Mother/Hymen **Roberta Maxwell**; Leantio **Jacob Fishel**; Bianca **Jennifer Ikeda**; Guardiano **John Douglas Thompson**; Fabritio **Everett Quinton**; Livia **Kathryn Meisle**; Hippolito **Al Espinosa**; Isabella **Liv Rooth**; Ward **Alex Morf**; Sordido/Hebe **Jeff Biehl**; Cardinal **Jonathan Fried**; Duke **Geraint Wyn Davies**; Ensemble **Anthony Bagnetto, Darcie Champagne, Jodi Epstein, Lisa Helmi Johanson, Marc Levasseur, Alison Ostergaard, Shannon Wicks**

A new adaptation of a classic play presented in two acts.

SYNOPSIS Thomas Middleton's rarely performed masterwork of Jacobean juiciness, *Women Beware Women*, is a scathing social satire of sexual politics, with a spectacular tragicomic dénouement. The play speaks with a shockingly contemporary voice about sexual politics and women's rights, even as it is a playful parody of serious sexual games, ultimately showing a society imploding under the pressure of sexual manipulation, victimization and gender inequality.

Sessions

Algonquin Theatre–Kauffman Stage; First Preview: October 28, 2008; Official Opening Night: January 14, 2009; 64 previews, 140 performances as of May 31, 2009

Book, music and lyrics by Albert M. Tapper; Produced by Algonquin Theater Productions and Ten Grand Productions Inc.; Director, Thomas Coté; Choreography, Penny Ayn Mass; Additional Choreography, James Horvath; Music Director, Frank Minarik; Sets, John McDermott; Costumes, Michele Pasqua; Lighting, Brant Thomas Murray; Sound, Josh Liebert; Arrangements/Orchestrations/Music Supervisor, Steven Gross; PSM, Lara Maerz; Assistant Director, Cheyrl Lynn Swift; General Manager, Jason Hewitt, Joan Pelzer; Executive Producer, Tony Sportierllo; Casting, Ten Grand Productions; Production Manager, Chris Johnson; Press, Rogers Artist Media, Charlie Rogers

CAST Batxer/Voice **Al Bundonis**; Mary **Natalie Buster**; Leila **Maya Days**; George **Scott Richard Foster**; Dr. Peterson **John Hickok**; Mr. Murphy **Ken Jennings**; Mrs. Murphy **Liz Larsen**; Sunshine **Kelli Maguire**; Dylan **Sky Seals**; Understudy **Bertilla Baker**

MUSICIANS Fran Minarik (Conductor/keyboard), Sam Sadigursky (reed), Lisa Pike (horn), Peter Prosser (cello), Jonathan Gleich (percussion)

MUSICAL NUMBERS I'm Only Human, It's All on the Record, Wendy, Above the Clouds, Breathe, The Murphy's Squabble, I'm an Average Guy, Feels Like Home, If I Could Just Be Like Pete, I Saw the Rest of My Life, You Should Dance, This Is One River I Can't Cross, Living Out a Lie, I Never Spent Time with My Dad, I Just Want to Hold You, The Sun Shines In, This Is One River I Can't Cross (reprise), This Life of Mine, I Will Never Find Another You, Finale

SETTING The present. In Dr. Peterson's office and waiting room, and various locales in New York City. Revival of a new musical presented in two acts. Previously produced at the Peter Jay Sharp Theatre in June 2007 (see *Theatre World* Vol. 64, page 99).

SYNOPSIS Dr. Peter Peterson listens, advises and tests his patients. *Sessions* offers a humorous, poignant and relatable look into the familiar worlds of self-help, personal growth and those long hours that many have spent on a therapist's couch.

Oscar and the Pink Lady

Florence Gould Hall at the French Institute Alliance Française; Opening Night: January 16, 2009; Closed February 1, 2009; 12 performances

Written by Eric-Emmanuel Schmitt; Presented by The French Institute Alliance Française, in association with Eightyone Productions; Produced by the George Street Playhouse (David Saint, Artistic Director); Director, Franck Dunlop; Props, Michael Vaughn Sims; Lighting, Christopher J. Bailey; Costumes, Jane Greenwood; Sound, Lindsay Jones; Press, Jennifer Kutsher
CAST Granny Pink **Rosemary Harris**

SETTING A children's hospital. East Coast premiere of a new play presented without intermission. World premiere at the Old Globe, San Diego.

SYNOPSIS In *Oscar and the Pink Lady*, Rosemary Harris tackles an array of memorable characters, among them Oscar, a ten-year-old patient in the cancer ward of a hospital. She also brings to life his friends, his family, and of course Granny Pink, a candy-striper of sorts whose wit, compassion, and indomitable spirit transform the lives of those around her. Granny Pink's observations are by turns funny, touching, and profound, and Harris's luminous performance is ultimately a celebration of life. This mesmerizing adaptation of Schmitt's *Oscar et la dame rose* touches audiences both young and old.

Rosemary Harris in Oscar and the Pink Lady

Terre Haute

59E59 Theater B; First Preview: January 13, 2009; Opening Night: January 18, 2009; Closed February 15, 2009; 6 previews, 29 performances

Written by Edmund White; Presented by nabokov (Imogen Kinchin, Producer) and Karl Sydow; Director, George Perrin; Sets, Hannah Clark; Lighting, Mathew Eagland; Composer, Heather Fenoughty; PSM, Amy Kaskeski; Assistant Director, Emmy Frank; General Manager, A. Scott Falk; Production Manager, Ric Mountjoy; Producers, Igogen Kinchin, Karl Sydow; Casting, Stuart Howard Associates; Marketing Consultant, HHC Marketing/Hugh Husell; Press, Karen Greco

CAST James **Peter Eyre**; Harrison **Nick Westrate**

SETTING The Federal penitenly in Terre Haute, Indiana; late 1990s. New York premiere of a new play presented without intermission. Originally performed at The Assembly Rooms, Edinburgh, Scotland.

SYNOPSIS In *Terre Haute*, a famous author comes face-to-face with America's most notorious terrorist. As the clock ticks on death row, the bond between the two men grows. *Terre Haute* is inspired by Gore Vidal's famous essays on Oklahoma bomber Timothy McVeigh.

Nick Westrate in Terre Haute *(photo by Valentina Medda)*

Krapp, 39

Soho Playhouse; First Preview: January 13, 2009; Opening Night: January 22, 2009; Closed August 2, 2009

Written by Michael Laurence; Presented by Darren Lee Cole and the Soho Playhouse; Director, George Demas; Creative Collaborators, Jon Dichter & Alyssa Bresnahan; PSM, Dan da Silva; Lighting, Sonia Baidya; Sound, Bernard Fox; Sound Assistant, Ien DeNio; Production Manager, Jon Johnson; Graphics/Web Design, Jim Galub; Press, Springer Associates, Joe Trentacosta

CAST Michael Laurence

Off-Broadway premiere of a solo performance play presented without intermission. Originally by the Cliplight Theater in New York, and presented by the Present Company at the 2008 New York International Fringe Festival.

SYNOPSIS *Krapp, 39* is a voyeuristic prefiguring of Samuel Beckett's *Krapp's Last Tape*, and a deeply personal window on one man's last moment of youth. Reeling on his 39th birthday, an actor's obsessive identification with Beckett's famous character compels him to examine his own quixotic life and failures. His hilarious and heart breaking self-scrutiny plays out through intimate audio tapes, archival video, raw journal entries, haunted letters, racy confessions, and recorded conversations with the living and the lost.

Michael Laurence in Krapp, 39 *(photo by Dixie Sheridan)*

Blanche Survives Katrina in a FEMA Trailer Named Desire

Soho Playhouse; First Preview: January 15, 2009; Opening Night: January 25, 2009; Closed March 15, 2009

Written by Mark Sam Rosenthal; Presented by Kind Strangers and The Soho Playhouse (Darren Lee Cole, Producing Director; Faith A. Mulvhill, Executive Director); Director, Todd Parmley; Set, Kelly Tighe; Lighting, Sonia Baidya; Costumes, Angelina Margolis; Sound, Scott Rosenthal, Bernard Fox; PSM, Kate August; Props, David Yarritu; Wigs, J. Jared Janas & Rob Greene; Graphics, David Orton; General Manager, Darren Lee Cole; Press, Springer Associates, Joe Trentacosta

CAST Blanche DuBois **Mark Sam Rosenthal**

Off-Broadway premiere of a solo performance play presented without intermission. Previously presented at the 2008 New York International Fringe Festival.

SYNOPSIS Blanche Survives Katrina imagines that Tennessee Williams' tragic heroine, Blanche DuBois, has neither aged nor left New Orleans. She was there when Katrina hit; she was sent to the Superdome; she was evacuated to Shreveport and entangled in the heartless bureaucracy of FEMA. She gets involved with drugs, is adopted by an Arizona megachurch, and is 'job-placed' at a Popeye's cash register – having for good reason been permanently barred from teaching young schoolboys. Hers is a refugee story whose politics and pathos you have read but never experienced through the eyes of the desperately deliberately fragile, alcoholic, codependent, sex-addicted Blanche DuBois – America's most broken woman.

Mark Sam Rosenthal in Blanche Survives Katrina in a FEMA Trailer Named Desire *(photo courtesy of Kind Strangers)*

Looking for the Pony

McGinn/Cazale Theatre; First Preview: January 21, 2009; Opening Night: January 26, 2009; Closed February 8, 2009; 6 previews, 15 performances

Written by Andrea Lepcio; Presented by the Vital Theatre Company; Director, Stephan Golux; Sets, Adam Koch; Lighting, Aaron Copp; Costumes, Matthew Hemesath; Sound, Jessica Paz; Casting, Jack Doulin; PSM, Bernita Robinson; ASM, Annette Verga-Lagier; Assistant Lighting, Christina Watanabe; Technical Director, Dan Jagendorf; Master Electrician, John Anselmo; Line Producer, Pat McNamara; Props, Jospeh Egan; Press, Sun Productions, Stephen Sunderlin

CAST Eloisa **J. Smith-Cameron**; Lauren **Deirdre O'Connell**; Man **Debargo Sanyal**; Woman **Lori Funk**

Off-Broadway premiere of a new play presented without intermission. Originally developed and produced by Vital Theatre Company as part of its VITAL SIGNS New Works Festival in 2002.

SYNOPSIS Eloisa is finally ready to leave a lifeless career in finance to pursue a childhood dream when her sister Lauren is diagnosed with breast cancer. Lauren's perfect life and Eloisa's second chance collide as the sisters join forces to cure all that ails them. As funny as it is heart-breaking, *Looking For The Pony* is a rollercoaster ride through treatment, ambition, loss and acceptance.

Debargo Sanyal in Looking for the Pony *(photo by Ethan David Kent)*

Disfarmer

St. Ann's Warehouse; Opening Night: January 27, 2009; Closed February 8, 2009; 14 performances

Conceived, designed and directed by Dan Hurlin; Presented by St. Ann's Warehouse in association with MAPP International Productions and the Red Wing Performing Group; Created by the Ensemble; Text, Sally Oswald; Costumes, Anna Thomford; Lighting, Tyler Micoleau; Original Music, Dan Moses Schreier; Video, David Soll; Production Stage Manager, Aaron Rosenblum; Press, Blake Zidell

CAST Matt Acheson, Eric B. Davis, Chris M. Green, Dan Hurlin, Guy Klucevsek, Tom Lee, Darius Mannin, Eric Wright

World premiere of a new play presented in one act.

SYNOPSIS Avant-garde puppetry genius Dan Hurlin's newest work depicts the life of Mike Disfarmer, a portrait photographer in small-town Arkansas from the Great Depression to the 1950's who was discovered by the art world 20 years after his death. With *Disfarmer*, Hurlin has crafted a quiet meditation on the man who stood behind the camera. Carefully choreographed with an incredible attention to detail, *Disfarmer* is remarkable for the all-absorbing physicality of the five puppeteers as they create this magical, yet ordinary, world.

Emilie's Voltaire

Beckett Theatre at Theatre Row; First Preview: January 15, 2009; Opening Night: January 30, 2009; Closed February 7, 2009

Written by Arthur Giron; Presented by Living Image Arts Theatre Company (Mia Vaculik, Executive Director; Peter Marsh, Artistic Director); Director, Kevin Confoy; Set, Jito Lee; Lighting, Jake DeGroot; Costumes, Carol Pelletier; Sound, Geoffrey Roecker; Press, Judy Jacksina, Jamie Morris

CAST Voltaire **Michael Medeiros**; Emilie **Amy Lynn Stewart**

SETTING Paris, France; New Year's Eve, 1773. World premiere of a new play presented

SYNOPSIS Winner of the Galileo Prize in 2000, this innovative and uniquely rich, epic play plunges us into the tempestuous love affair of two great minds, the legendary scholar, Voltaire, scientist by day and actress by night, Emilie du Chatelet. In an era when intellect was a dangerous possession for a woman, two of the most intriguing and brilliant thinkers of their time, risked everything for a love affair that spanned decades.

White People

Atlantic Stage 2; First Preview: January 28, 2009; Opening Night: February 3, 2009; Closed March 1, 2009

Written by J.T. Rogers; Presented by Starry Night Entertainment and Craig Saavedra; Director, Gus Reyes; Set, John McDermott; Costumes, Michael Sharpe; Lighting, Les Dickert; Sound, Elizabeth Rhodes; PSM, Kate Hefel; Casting, Carrie Gardner; General Manager, Perry Street Theatricals (David Elliott & Martin Platt); Production Manager, Gabriel Evansohn; Press, Richard Kornberg & Associates

CAST Alan Harris **Michael Shulman**; Mara Lynn Doddson **Rebecca Brooksher**; Martin Bahmueller **John Dossett**

New York premiere of a new play presented without intermission.

SYNOPSIS Now—right now—what does it mean to be a white American? What does it mean for any American to live in a country that is not the one you were promised? *White People* is a controversial and darkly funny play about the lives of three ordinary Americans placed under the spot-light: Martin, a Brooklyn–born high powered attorney for a white-shoe law firm in St. Louis; Mara Lynn, a housewife and former home-coming queen in Fayetteville, North Carolina; and Alan, a young professor struggling to find his way in New York City. Through heart-wrenching confessions, they wrestle with guilt, prejudice, and the price they and their children must pay for their actions. *White People* is a candid, brutally honest meditation on race and language in our culture.

Rebecca Brooksher, Michael Shulman and John Dossett in White People *(photo by Joaquin Sedillo)*

Lansky

St. Luke's Theatre; First Preview: January 23, 2009; Opening Night: February 5, 2009; 2009; 16 previews, 90 performances

Written by Richard Krevolin and Joseph Bologna, inspired by the book "But He Was Good To His Mother: The Lives & Crimes of Jewish Gangsters" by Robert Rockaway; Presented by Kit Productions & Dan Israely; Director, Joseph Bologna; Sets, Josh Iacovelli; Costumes, Cyona Burstyn; Lighting, Graham Kindred; Projections, Christopher Ash; Sound, David Beaudry; Music, Grant Sturiale; General Manager, Jessimeg Productions, Edmund Gaynes, Julia Beardsley; Press, Beck Lee Media Blitz

CAST Meyer Lansky **Mike Burstyn**

SETTING 1971. Tel Aviv, Israel. New York premiere of a solo performance play presented without intermission.

SYNOPSIS *Lansky* concerns the efforts of the Jewish gangster and gambler, Meyer Lansky to become an Israeli citizen. The play uses Lansky's life story as a crucible to explore Jewish identity and the choices first generation Jewish Americans made in order to achieve wealth and success.

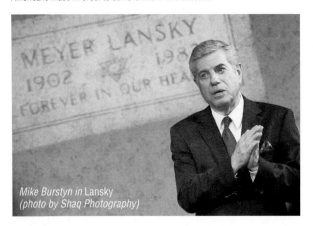

Mike Burstyn in Lansky
(photo by Shaq Photography)

Telephone

Cherry Lane Theatre; Opening Night: February 6, 2009; Closed February 28, 2009

Written by Ariana Reines, based on "The Telephone Book: Technology, Schizophrenia, Electric Speech" by Avital Ronell; Presented by Foundry Theatre (Melanie Joseph and Sunder Ganglani, Artistic Producers); Director, Ken Rus Schmoll; Set, Marsha Ginsberg; Lighting, Tyler Micoleau; Costumes, Carol Bailey; Sound, Matt Hubbs

CAST Thomas A. Watson **Matthew Dellapina**; Alexander Graham Bell **Gibson Frazier**; Miss St. **Birgit Huppuch**

World premiere of a new play in three acts presented without intermission.

SYNOPSIS *Telephone* is a nocturne about invention and love. Bell and Watson presented their invention to the public, and the first act finds them onstage again, but their task is more complicated. A biography of the phone and a meditation on the nature of the disembodied voice, *Telephone* operates like a switchboard connecting places and people across time and space. Miss St. (Jung's notorious schizophrenic madwoman) takes over in act two, she suffers the slander of invisible telephones and tells you all about it. In act three, people who love each other make phone-calls. *Telephone* is a delicate and tender yet ferociously poetic work that asks what it means to 'take a call' not knowing what or who might be on the other end.

East 10th Street: Self Portrait with Empty House

Axis Theatre; Opening Night: February 12, 2009; Closed February 28, 2009

Written by Edgar Oliver; Presented by the Axis Company (Randy Sharp, Artistic Director; Brian Barnhart, Producing Director; Jeffrey Resnick, Executive Producer); Director, Randy Sharp; Set/Production Manager, Ian Tooley; Lighting, David Zeffren; Sound, Steve Fontaine; Stage Manager, Marc Palmieri; Website & Graphics, Ethan Crenson; Press, Ron Lasko/Spin Cycle

CAST Himself **Edgar Oliver**

SETTING An East Village tenement apartment. Return engagement of a solo performance play presented without intermission. Previously presented at the Axis Theater November 6–22, 2008.

SYNOPSIS Long-standing, downtown theatre icon Edgar Oliver takes the audience on a fantastic voyage through the strange rooms of the apartment house where he has lived since his first years in New York. Inhabiting the dark, mysterious halls of an East Village tenement building are a dwarf Cabalist, a possible Nazi, the landlord's former wet nurse who apparently lives in a nest of rags, and many other memorable persons. Edgar leads the audience up to the final room, his own, at the top of the derelict stairs, wherein lie the secrets of his own family and the unbelievable odyssey that brought him there.

Mabou Mines DollHouse

St. Ann's Warehouse; Opening Night: February 12, 2009; Closed March 8, 2009; 23 performances

Adapted from *The Doll House* by Henrik Ibsen; Produced by Mabou Mines; Presented by St. Anne's Warehouse in association with Piece by Piece Productions; Director Lee Breuer; Sets, Narelle Sissons; Costumes, Meganne George; Lighting, Mary Louise Geiger; Sound, Edward Cosla; Puppetry, Jane Catherine Shaw, Choreography, Eamonn Farrell; Assistant Directors, Eamonn Farrell & Ilia Dodd Loomis; Tour Producer, Dovetail Productions, Sharon Levy; Music Collage Arrangements, Eve Beglarian; Press, Blake Zidell

CAST Nora Helmer **Maude Mitchell**; Torvald Helmer **Mark Povinelli**; Dr. Rank **Ricardo Gil**; Nils Krogstad **Kristopher Medina**; Kristine Linde **Honora Fergusson**; Helene **Margaret Lancaster**; Emmy Helmer **Hannah Kritzeck** (Emmy Helmer); Anna Maria **Jessica Weinstein**; Pianists **Ning Yu, Lisa Moore, Cristina Valdes**; Stage Hands **Eamonn Farrell, Ilia Dodd Loomis**; Understudy **Nic Novicki**

Revival of an avant-garde adaptation of the classic play presented in two acts. Premiered at St. Ann's Warehouse November 8, 2003. This production toured before closing at St. Ann's Warehouse.

SYNOPSIS Nora comes home with a Christmas present. It is a dollhouse so large that the children can play inside. All the period furniture, the crockery, the knick-knacks are the right size for the children, Emmy and Ivar, who are hardly more than three feet tall. Enter Torvald, Rank, and Krogstad. We find that the men are the same size as the children. Is this dollhouse the world of patriarchy, the world in which a woman never fits? Here Ibsen's feminism is metaphorically rendered as a parable of scale. The dollhouse is a man's world and only doll-like women, who allow their men to feel grand, can hope to live in it. Even the cod-Norwegian accents are miniaturized; like the accents in Disney's "It's A Small World". Nothing here is real except the pain. Both Torvald and Nora are trapped in a meta-narrative, playing out an illusion of male power. Both pay the price: the death of love.

Astronome: A Night at the Opera

Ontological Theater at St. Marks; First Preview: February 5, 2009; Opening Night: February 13, 2009; Closed April 5, 2009

Created by Richard Foreman and John Zorn; Presented by Ontological-Hysteric Theater; Director, Richard Foreman; Composer, John Zorn; Managing Director, Shannon Sindelar; Technical Director, Peter Ksander; Stage Manager, Brendan Regimbal; Sound Engineer, Travis Just; Props and Costumes Engineer, Meghan Buchanan; Lighting Engineer, Miranda Hardy; Assistant Director, Stephen Mosblech; Arts Management, Performing Artservices Inc; Press, Manny Igrejas

CAST Woman in All Black **Deborah Wallace**; Woman in Fez **Morgan von Prelle Pecelli**; Woman in White Blouse **Fulya Peker**; Man in Striped Hat **Karl Allen**, Man in Fez **Eric Magnus**; Man in White Blouse **Benjamin Forster**; Man in Green Face **Jamie Peterson**

World premiere of a new experimental play with music presented without intermission.

SYNOPSIS *Astronome: A Night At The Opera* is an opera about the initiation of five people into a world where ambiguous behavior alone leads to freedom—perhaps under the tutelage of the necessary 'false messiah.'

In Paradise & She Plundered Him

Cherry Lane Studio Theatre; First Preview: February 15, 2009; Opening Night: February 18, 2009; Closed March 7, 2009

Written by Eduardo Machado & Nick Norman; Presented by INTAR (Eduardo Machado, Artistic Director; John McCormack, Executive Director); Director, Billy Hopkins; Set/Lighting, Maruti Evans; Costumes, Brian Bevins; Sound, Betsy Rhodes; Press, David Gersten & Associates

CAST *In Paradise*: Marilyn **Leslie Lyles**; Carlos **Ed Vassallo**; *She Plundered Him*: Calder **Marl Elliot Wilson**; Keep **Leslie Lyles**; Anthony **James Chen**

World premiere of two short plays presented with intermission.

SYNOPSIS In Machado's *In Paradise* an estranged husband shows up on his wife's doorstep. Carlos left Marilyn seven years ago for another man, but both the conflicts and chemistry between them feels as fresh as if they were never apart. Deserted by his lover, Carlos has returned to Marilyn for answers and salvation. As they delve into the remains of their shared history, the power struggle between them plays out through recrimination, eroticism, anger, and love. In Norman's *She Plundered Him* the boundaries of familial relationships are tested in new and dangerous ways. Calder, already on a mental precipice, is convinced that he saw something unseemly pass between his wife, Keep, and son, Anthony...but did he? As Calder's obsessive jealousy spirals out of control and Keep and Anthony lie to him and one another, the family unit threatens to break irreparably.

Soul Samurai

HERE Arts Center; First Preview: February 14, 2009; Opening Night: February 19, 2009; Closed March 15, 2009; 5 previews, 24 performances

Written by Qui Nguyen; Presented by Ma-Yi Theater Company in association with Vampire Cowboys Theatre Company; Director, Robert Ross Parker; Costumes, Sarah Laux & Jessica Wagner; Sets/Lighting.Video, Nick Francone; Sound, Sharath Patel; Puppet Design, David Valentine; Fight Director, Qui Nguyen; Wigs/Hair, Ashley Ryan; PSM, Lyndsey Goode; ASM, Danielle Buccino; Producers, Abby Marcus, Suzette Porte; Production Manager, Gregg Bellon (Production Consolidated); Fight Captain, Jon Hoche; Press, Jim Baldassare

CAST Boss 2K/Fang/Marcus/Burnout/Master Leroy Green **Sheldon Best**; Grandmaster Mack/Masked Marcus/Hurt/Stranger/Pastor **Jon Hoche**; Dewdrop/Angela **Maureen Sebastian**; White Chocolate/Lady Snowflake/Sally December **Bonnie Sherman**; Cert/T-Bone/Avory/Online **Paco Tolson**

SETTING Present. Alternate reality New York City. World premiere of a new play presented without intermission.

SYNOPSIS *Soul Samurai* the story of Dewdrop and her fight through the mean streets of a post-apocalyptic Brooklyn. After avenging her lover's murder in the heart of Coney Island, Dewdrop now must make it back home to the Lower East Side before the shoguns of Kings County find her. In a play that mixes hip-hop culture, blaxploitation, and the martial arts, this production dials it back old school with this seventies-inspired samurai story. This is one slick slice with a sharp sword and a score to settle!

Paco Tolson, Maureen Sebastian and Jon Hoche in Soul Samurai *(photo by Jim Baldassare)*

Christine Jorgensen Reveals

Lion Theatre on Theatre Row; First Preview: February 19, 2009; Opening Night: February 26, 2009; Closed March 15, 2009

Written by Bradford Louryk; Presented by Greg Tully For The Platform Theatre Group; Director, Josh Hecht; Costumes, Mary Ping; Set, Wilson Chin; Lighting, Josh Bradford; Sound, Rob Kaplowitz; Projections, Kevin French; Props, Jung Griffin; Wigs, Jason P. Hayes

CAST Christine Jorgensen **Bradford Louryk**

SETTING 1958. A New York recording studio. Revival of a solo performance play presented without intermission.

SYNOPSIS In 1958, Christine Jorgensen the first American transsexual, walked into a recording studio in New York and allowed herself to be interviewed - for 51 minutes. Arguably the most revealing, truthful and riveting 51 minutes ever set down on vinyl. *Christine Jorgensen Reveals* is a one-man-tour-de-force-paintakingly-acurate-reincarnation of those searing and revolutionary 51 minutes.

Our Town

Barrow Street Theatre; First Preview: February 17, 2009; Opening Night: February 26, 2009; 10 previews, 109 performances as of May 31, 2009

Written by Thornton Wilder; Presented by Scott Morfee, Jean Doumanian, Tom Wirtshafter, Ted Snowdon, Eagle Productions, Dena Hammerstein/Pam Pariseau, The Weinstein Company, Burnt Umber Productions; Director, David Cromer; Sets, Michele Spadaro; Costumes, Alison Siple; Lighting, Heather Gilbert; Original Music/Music Director, Jonathan Mastro; Production Manager, B.D. White; PSM, Richard A. Hodge; ASM, Kate McDoniel; Associate Producers, Patrick Daly & Marc Biales; Assistant Director, Michael Page; General Management, Two Step Productions; Advertising, Eliran Murphy Group; Casting, Pat McCorkle, Joe Lopick, Assistant Director, Michael Page; Press, O+M Company

CAST Stage Manager **David Cromer***; Mrs. Gibbs **Lori Myers**; Mrs. Webb **Kati Brazda**; Dr. Gibbs **Jeff Still**; Joe Crowell Jr. **Adam Hinkle** Howe Newsome **Robert Beitzel**; George Gibbs **James McMenamin**; Rebecca Gibbs **Ronette Levenson**; Emily Webb **Jennifer Grace**; Wally Webb **Seamus Mulcahy**; Professor Willard **Wilbur Edwin Henry**; Mr. Webb **Ken Marks**; Simson Stimson **Jonathan Mastro**; Mrs. Soames **Donna Jay Fulks**; Constable Warren **George Demas**; Si Crowell **Jason Yachanin**; Joe Stoddard **Jay Russell**; Sam Craig **Jeremy Beiler**; Irma **Dana Jacks**; Citizen **Elizabeth Audley**; Farmer McCarty **Keith Perry**; Citizen **Kathleen Pierce**; Citizen **Mark Shock**

*Succeeded by Scott Parkinson (5/1/09)

UNDERSTUDIES Elizabeth Audley (Mrs. Soames), Jeremy Beiler (Simon Stimpson), Robert Beitzel (George), George Demas (Dr. Gibbs/Mr. Webb), Donna Jay Fulks (Mrs. Gibbs/Mrs. Webb), Adam Hinkle (Si Cromwell/Howie), Dana Jacks (Rebecca Gibbs/Emily Webb), Keith Perry (Constable Warren/Professor Willard/Joe Stoddard), Jay Russell (Stage Manager), Mark Shock (Sam Craig), Jason Yachanin (Joe Crowell, Jr./Wally)

AWARDS Theatre World Award: Jennifer Grace

SETTING 1901. Grover's Corners, New Hampshire. Revival of a play presented in three acts with two intermissions.

SYNOPSIS Director David Cromer takes on the role of the "Stage Manager" in this staging of Wilder's timeless play in which the action takes place in, among and around the audience, creating an intimacy between actors and audience and a powerful encounter with the play's searching questions about family, community and mortality.

David Cromer in
Our Town
(photo by Carol Rosegg)

Gates of Gold

59E59 Theater B; First Preview: February 19, 2009; Opening Night: March 1, 2009; Closed March 29, 2009

Written by Frank McGuinness; Presented by The Artists Theater Group Inc. in association with Warren Baker and & Sally Jacobs; Director, Kent Paul; Set, Michael Schweikardt; Lighting, Phil Monat; Costumes, Nanzi Adzima; Original Music, Robert C. Ress; Text/Dialogue Consultant, Robert Neff Williams; Hair, Leone Gagliardi; ASM, Byron F. Abens; Technical Director, Jason Adams; Properties, Sven Nelson; Casting, Barry Moss and Bob Kale; Stage Manager, E.G. Munroe; Press, Shirley Herz & Associates

CAST Gabriel **Martin Rayner**; Conrad **Charles Shaw Robinson**; Alma **Kathleen McNenny**; Kassie **Diane Ciesla**; Ryan **Seth Numrich**

American premiere of a new play presented without intermission.

SYNOPSIS *Gates of Gold* is an acerbic duel between two lovers, the fashionable and eloquent theatrical trailblazers who founded Dublin's Gate Theatre. *Gates of Gold* is witty and moving - a vibrant celebration of art, love, and finally, life itself.

Blood Type: RAGU

Actors' Playhouse; First Preview: February 20, 2009; Opening Night: March 1, 2009; Closed March 29, 2009; 14 previews, 30 performances

Written by Frank Ingrasciotta; Produced by Flying Machine Productions (Andrew Levine and Jon Baum); Director, Ted Sod; Lighting, Josh Bradford; Sound, Brandon Wolcott; Video, Joshua Higgason; PSM, Katherine Wallace; Co-Producer, Paul Borghese; Press, David Gersten & Associates

CAST Frank Ingrasciotta

Off-Broadway premiere of a solo performance play presented without intermission.

SYNOPSIS *Blood Type: RAGU* is a hilarious and poignant ride through the Italian immigrant experience based on the life of writer/performer Frank Ingrasciotta. This one-man show features more than 20 characters, who live, love and laugh as they struggle to thrive in a new culture. It's a fast paced coming of age story that is not just a comedy, not just a drama. It's family – and we all have one.

The Unseen

Cherry Lane Theatre; First Preview: March 5, 2009; Opening Night: March 8, 2009; Closed March 28, 2009

Written by Craig Wright; Produced by Baylor University and American Actors Company (Waco, Texas; Marion Castleberry, Founding Director; Stan Denman, Artistic Director; Director, Lisa Denman; Set, Sarah B. Brown; Lighting, Travis Watson; Costumes, Carl Booker; Sound, Dustin Chaffin; Dramaturg, DeAnna Toten Beard; Marketing, Sherry Jo Ward; Press/Marketing/Advertising, Art Meets Commerce

CAST Smash **Thomas Ward**; Wallace **Steven Pounders**; Valdez **Stan Denman**

SETTING A prison; three years between two scenes. New York premiere of a new play presented without intermission

SYNOPSIS *The Unseen* tells the story of two prisoners trying to crack the code of their imprisonment by a brutal, totalitarian regime. Known to each other through their voices alone, the two men help each other survive mentally and emotionally through an endless conversation. When a third prisoner is placed in the mix, more questions are asked than answered.

The New Hopeville Comics

American Theatre of Actors–Chernuchin Theatre; Opening Night: March 13, 2009; Closed March 28, 2009

Written by Sarah Hayes Donnell; Director, Jim Wren; Production Design, Steve Royal; Choreographer, Ashley Adamek; Art, Batton Lash; Lighting, David Sexton; Costumes, Denise Schumaker; General Manager, Amanda Azelrod of Lexador Productions LLC; Music Director, Tim Matson; Stage Manager, Aaron Heflich Shapiro; Production Manager, Kate Stratton; Composer, Nate Weida; Press, Ron Lasko

CAST Rockenroll **John Bennett**; Sex **Terren Wooten Clarke**; Delois **Carolyn Cole**; Perfect Man **Chris Critelli**; Flo **Shannon DeVido**; Molly **Sharah Hayes Donnell**; April **Christine Dwyer**; Doo-Doo Girl **Michelle Guadalupe**; Boy Scout **Wes Jetton**; Doo-Doo Girl **Shira Kobren**; Steve **Patrick Link**; Jill the Weather Boy **Terra Mackintosh**; Drugs **Carl Conway**; Pete Man on the Street **Jay Paranada**; Felix **Aaron Phillips**; Police Chief **J.T. Michael Taylor**; Boy Scout **John Wellington-Simon**; Mayor **Scott Lee Williams**; Ensemble **Heather Dudenbostel, Nick Gelona**;

MUSICIANS Justin Ansley (drums), Baby Copperhead & Nick Rowe (guitars), Martin Stam (bass), Nate Weida (keyboard)

SETTING Hopeville, U.S.A. Off-Broadway premiere of a new musical presented in two acts.

SYNOPSIS In Hopeville, U.S.A. your average superhero named Perfect Man protects the trusting and oblivious citizens against danger. His good deeds include grabbing a pair of scissors out of the hands of a running boy and rescuing the mayor's baby from falling out of a window. All is well until Perfect Man's girlfriend rejects him. He loses his confidence and his power. Soon Perfect Man meets his demise in the form of a villainous trio (Sex, Drugs and Rockenroll) who have been gleefully waiting for their opportunity to turn the unsuspecting town to chaos. Can the citizens wise-up, band together to fight villainy and put the hope back into Hopeville?

Schooling Giacomo

American Theatre of Actors–Sargent Theatre; First Preview: March 6, 2009; Opening Night: March 15, 2009; Closed April 26, 2009

Written by Richard Edwin Knipe, Jr; Presented by Robin Phillips; Director, Richard Edwin Knipe, Jr; Sets, Dana Kenn; Choreographer, Morgan Knipe; Lighting, Donald Kimmel, Lighting/Sound, Xena Petkanus

CAST Vukey Fanuchi **Kevin Trotta/Joe DeSpirito**; Giacomo (Young Jake) **Jordan Adelson/Justin Adelson**; Jake Montalto **Hugh Scully**; Abbey Montalto **Alanna Heraghty**; Young Abbey **Dominique Alvarado**; Dominic **Andrew Lionetti/Glenn John Arnowitz**; Charlie **George Petkanus**; Joe **Rick Apicella**; Irene **Robin Peck/Marian McCabe**; Pete Murphy **Kevin Nagle**

SETTING 1969–1970 and Present day. The Bronx, New York. Off-Broadway premiere of a new play presented in two acts.

SYNOPSIS *Schooling Giacomo* is a bittersweet comedy that travels back and forth in time between the summer of 1970 and today: set in The Bronx, the play captures the rich and flavorful history of an ethnically mixed child who was raised by three know-it-all Italian uncles, a neighborhood wise guy and a drunken Irish/German mother. Now a single father and school teacher, he realizes the true value of his education in the school of hard knocks for both him and his daughter.

ROOMS a rock romance

New World Stages–Stage 2; First Preview: February 27, 2009; Opening Night: March 16, 2009; Closed May 10, 2009; 20 previews, 64 performances

Music and lyrics by Paul Scott Goodman, book by Paul Scott Goodman and Miriam Gordon; Presented by Van Hill Entertainment and Red Griffith Media; Director, Scott Schwartz; Choreographer, Matt Williams; Sets, Adam Koch; Costumes, Alejo Vietti; Lighting, Herrick Goldman; Sound, Jon Weston; Music Supervisor/Arrangements/Orchestrations, Jesse Vargas; General Manager, Martian Entertainment LLC; PSM, Sara Jaramillo; Associate Producers, MetroStage, Small Pond Enterprises, HOP Theatricals LLC, Mass Street Productions, Wild Bird Productions, Fern R. Lopez, Rainerio J. Reyes, Jeffrey M. Raff; Marketing HHC Marketing; Casting, Cindy Rush; Production Manager, Scott DelaCruz; Company Manager, Lauren Yates; ASM, Jason Quinn; Dialect Coach, Doug Honorof; Associate Director, Nell Balaban; Copyist, Jaron Vesely; Co-Sound, Jason Strangeld; Associate Design, Amy Clark (costumes), Susan Nicholson (lighting); Press, David Gersten & Associates

CAST Monica P. Miller **Leslie Kritzer**; Ian Wallace **Doug Kreeger**

UNDERSTUDIES Celina Carvajal (Monica); Jason Wooten (Ian)

MUSICIANS Matt Hinkley (Conductor/guitars), Sean Driscol (Associate Conductor/guitars), Michael Pettry (keyboard), Steve Gilewski (bass), Jay Mack (drums), Randy Cohen (keyboard & V drum programming)

MUSICAL NUMBERS Room, Steps, The Music, Bring the Future Faster, Friday Night Dress, Scottish Jewish Princess, I Love You For All Time, Let's Go to London, All I Want is Everything, Let's Leave London, NYC Forever!, Little Bit of Love, Fear of Flying, Happiness, Clean, Rooms (reprise), My Choice, New Song for Scotland

SETTING Glasgow, London and New York City, 1977-1980. Off-Broadway premiere of a new musical presented without intermission

SYNOPSIS *ROOMS a rock romance* begins in late 1970's Glasgow where Monica, an ambitious singer/songwriter meets Ian, a reclusive rocker. The two quickly become entangled creatively and romantically. Their music takes them first to London and ultimately to New York City, where they discover the vibrant new music scene and create an intimate partnership, their love deepening while their personalities drive them apart. A five-piece rock band accompanies these two characters as they search for the balance between ambition and happiness.

The Cambria

Irish Arts Center; Opening Night: March 17, 2009; Closed March 22, 2009; 7 performances

Written by Donal O'Kelly; Presented by the Irish Arts Center in association with the Classical Theatre of Harlem; Director, Raymond Keane; Press, Karen Greco

CAST Donal O'Kelly, Sorcha Fox

New York premiere of a new play presented without intermission.

SYNOPSIS *The Cambria* was a trans-Atlantic paddle-steamer. On August 10, 1845, among the passengers on the Cambria's Boston-Cork route was an escaped slave called Frederick Douglass. His just-published life story had become a bestseller. He was forced to flee the US with a price on his head. He sought asylum in Ireland. Once Frederick Douglass' identity was revealed, he was thrown out of the first class deck, and a mob attempted to throw him overboard. *The Cambria* tells the story of how he went on to become what Abraham Lincoln called "the most impressive man I ever met".

La Didone

St. Ann's Warehouse; Opening Night: March 17, 2009; Closed April 26, 2009; 30 performances

Music by Francesco Cavalli, libretto by Giovan Francesco Busenello, additional text from Mario Bava's film "Terrore Nello Spazio" ("Planet of the Vampires"); Presented by St. Ann's Warehouse (Susan Feldman, Artistic Director); Produced by the Wooster Group and KunstenFestivaldesArts; Director, Elizabeth LeCompte; Director, Elizabeth LeCompte; Music Director, Bruce Odland; Sets, Ruud van den Akker; Lighting, Jennifer Tipton; Sound, Matt Schloss and Omar Zubair; Costumes, Antonia Belt; Video, Zbigniew Bzymek, Joby Emmons and Andrew Schneider; Assistant Director and Baroque Gesture Coach, Jennifer Griesbach; Technical Director, Aron Deyo; Cineturg, Dennis Dermody; Surtitle operators, Alessandro Magania and Fanny Frohnmeyer; Production Manager, Bozkurt Karasu; Stage Manager, Teresa Hartmann; Master Electrician, Robert Reese; Press, Blake Zidell

CAST Dido/Tiona **Hai-Ting Chinn**; Shadow of Aeneus/Cupid/Ghost of Sichaeus/Mark **Ari Fliakos**; Ghost of Sichaeus **Hank Heijink**; Neptune/Jarbas/Ilioneus/Jove/Ghost Chorus/Kir **Andrew Nolen**; Juno/Mercury/Anna/Voice of Cupid **Kamala Sankaram**; Shadow of Jarbas/Boar/Wess **Scott Shepherd**; Shadow of Dido/Old Man/Guard/Sanya **Kate Valk**; Acate/Dr. Karan/Burt/Brad **Judson Williams**; Aeneas/Ghost Chorus/Eldon **John Young**; Chorus **David Walker, Harvey Valdes**

MUSICIANS Jennifer Griesbach (keyboard), Hank Heijink (theorbo, baroque guitar), Andrew Nolen (bass singer) Kamala Sankaram (soprano singer, accordion), Scott Shepherd & Harvey Valdes (electric guitar, tenor voice), Kate Valk

American premiere of a theatrical opera presented without intermission.

SYNOPSIS The Wooster Group's *La Didone* is the seminal company's distinctive take on Francesco Cavalli's baroque opera. Aeneas, prince of Troy, lands on the shores of Africa after a violent sea storm. There he falls in love with Dido, queen of Carthage, and becomes entangled in a web of love, deception, power and madness. Leaping forward in time, Mario Bava's 1965 cult movie Terrore nello spazio crashes the spaceship Argos on the planet Aura, where its crew becomes locked in a desperate battle with zombies over the all-important "meteor rejector." The Wooster Group, in signature fashion, stirs these two Italian cultural artifacts together, dropping Aeneas' ships onto a forbidding planetary landscape, setting the lute alongside electric guitar, blending acoustic and electronic space, and finding an unexpected synergy between early baroque opera and pre-moonlanding sci-fi. The result is a 21st-century retelling of an ancient tale about the destructive (and redemptive) power of erotic passion and the sheer tenacity of human nature in the face of annihilation.

Hai-Ting Chinn and Andrew Nolen in the Wooster Group's production of La Didone (photo by Paula Court)

Shpiel! Shpiel! Shpiel!

Jewish Community Center; First Preview: March 15, 2009; Opening Night: March 19, 2009; Closed April 5, 2009

Three plays by Murray Schisgal; Produced by National Yiddish Theater–Folksbiene; Directors, Motl Didner (*The Pushcart Peddlers*), Gene Saks (*The Man Who Couldn't Stop Crying*), & Bob Dishy (*74 Georgia Avenue*); Translator, Moishe Rosenfeld; Musical Director, Zalmen Mlotek; Set, Vicki R. Davis; Costumes, Gail Cooper-Hecht; Lighting, Russel Phillip Drapkinl Sound, Don Jacobs, Serena Rockower; Supertitles, Matt Temkin; Press, Beck Lee Media Blitz

CAST *The Pushcart Peddlers*: Shimmel **Michael L. Harris**; Cornelius **Stuart Marshall**; Maggie **Dani Marcus**; *The Man Who Couldn't Stop Crying*: Benjamin **I.W. "Itzy" Firestone**; Judith **Suzanne Toren**; *74 Georgia Avenue*: Joseph **Tony Perry**; Marty **Harry Peerce**; Troubador **Lisa Fishman**

World premiere of three one-act plays presented with intermission.

SYNOPSIS Comprised of the comic plays, *Shpiel! Shpiel! Shpiel!* (*Play! Play! Play!*) chronicles the Jewish-American experience across three generations, in a sweeping panorama spanning early 20th century immigration through mid-century assimilation to the present day.

Enid Cortes, Gregory Konow, and Dustin Olson in 1984
(photo by Lucas Noonan)

1984

59E59 Theater C; First Preview: March 13, 2009; Opening Night: March 25, 2009; Closed April 26, 2009; 46 performances

Written by George Orwell, adapted by Alan Lyddiard; Presented by Godlight Theater Company (Joe Tantalo, Artistic Director); Director, Joe Tantalo; Design, Maruti Evans; Music and Sound, Andrew Recinos; Parole Song Vocals, Peg Recinos; Parole Song Lyrics, Andrew Recinos; Choreography, Hachi Yu; Fight Director, Rick Sordelet; Associate Set, Dominic Barone; Associate Lighting, Wilburn Bonnell; PSM, Christina Hurtado; ASM, Derek Shore; Consultant, Nick Tochell; Press, Karen Greco

CAST Winston Smith **Gregory Konow**; O'Brien **Dustin Olson**; Julia **Enid Cortes**; Syme **Aaron Paternoster**; Parsons **Nick Paglino**; Charrington **Michael Tranzilli**; Goldstein **Michael Shimkin**; Telescreens 1-4 **Deanna McGovern, Katherine Boynton, Sammy Tunis, Scarlett Thiele**

New York engagement of a play presented without intermission

SYNOPSIS *1984* is a chronicle of one man's struggle against the ubiquitous, menacing state power Big Brother that tries to dictate nearly every aspect of human life.

Jailbait

The Cherry Pit; First Preview: March 19, 2009; Opening Night: March 25, 2009; Closed April 25, 2009

Written by Deirdre O'Conner; Presented by the Cherry Lane Theatre (Angelina Fiordellisi, Artistic Director; James King, Managing Director; Mentor, Michael Weller; Director, Suzanne Agins; Set, Kina Park; Costumes, Rebecca Bernstein; Lighting, Pat Dignan; Sound, Daniel Kluger & Brandon Wolcott; PSM, Libby Unsworth; Press, Sam Rudy Media Relations

CAST Emmy **Wrenn Schmidt**; Claire **Natalia Payne**; Robert **Kelly AuCoin**; Mark **Peter O'Connor**

World premiere of a new play presented without intermission. Originally developed in Cherry Lane's 2008 Mentor Project. This production marked the inaugural production at The Cherry Pit, formerly known as the Bank Street Theatre

SYNOPSIS In *Jailbait, t*wo fifteen year old girls spend a night at a Boston club posing as college students. When the girls cross paths with two thirty-something men they must decide how far they are willing to go while playing at adulthood.

The Wizard of Oz

Theatre at Madison Square Garden; Opening Night: March 26, 2009; Closed April 5, 2009; 16 performances

Music and lyrics by Harold Arlen and E.Y. Harburg, adapted by John Kane from the book by L. Frank Baum, based on the Classic Motion Picture owned by Turner Entertainment Co. and Distributed by Warner Brothers; Presented by NETworks; Director, Nigel West; Choreographer, Leigh Constantine; Set/Costumes, Tim McQuillen-Wright; Lighting, Bob Bonniol, Rob Halliday; Sound, Shannon Slaton; Hair/Makeup, Bernie Ardia; Animals, William Berloni; Special Effects, J&M Special Effects; Projections, Second Home Productions; Aerographics, Flying by Foy; Projection Coordinator, Bob Bonniol, MODE Studios; Background Music, Herbert Stothart; Music Arranger, Peter Howard; Music Director/Conductor, Nate Patten; PSM, Ron Guarnieri; Production Manager, Justin Reiter; Company Manager, Joel T. Herbst; General Management, Gregory Vander Ploeg, Gentry & Associates; Casting, Dave Clemmons Casting; Tour Press/Marketing, Wendy Connor, True Marketing; Executive Producer, Seth C. Wenig

CAST Dorothy Gale **Cassie Okenka**; Hunk/Scarecrow **Noah Aberlin**; Hickory/Tinman **Chris Kind**; Zeke/Lion **Jason Simon**; Miss Gultch/Wicked Which of the West **Pat Sibley**; Professor Marvel/The Wizard of Oz **Robert John Bidermann**; Aunt Em/Glinda **Caitlin Maloney**; Uncle Henry/Emerald City Guard **Bruce Warren**; Toto **Snickers**; Ensemble **Brian Bailey, J. Ryan Carroll, Lauryn Ciardullo, David Geinosky, Beau Hutchings, K.C. Leiber; Tommy Martinez, Tommy Martinez, Timothy McNeill, Taylor Hilt Mitchell, Lauren Patton, Jessa Rose;Sara Ruzicka, Sarah Stevens**

MUSICIANS Nate Patten (Conductor); Joey Chancey (Assistant Conductor/keyboard); Ryan Claus, Brett Gregory, Terry Halvorson (reeds); Christopher Imhoff, Stephen Mark Morgan (trumpet); Clair Socci (trombone), Phil Coiro (drums)

Touring production of a musical presented in two acts.

SYNOPSIS Generations have loved the story of Dorothy's journey from Kansas to the magical land of Oz; experience it live on stage at the WaMu Theater at Madison Square Garden. This lavish live production of *the Wizard of Oz* pays tribute to MGM's classic 1939 film with dazzling sets and choreography, plus all the songs you know by heart.

Noah Aberlin, Cassie Okenka, Snickers, Jason Simon and Chris Kind in The Wizard of Oz (photo by Joan Marcus)

End Days

Ensemble Studio Theatre; First Preview: March 25, 2009; Opening Night: March 30, 2009; Closed April 19, 2009

Written by Deborah Zoe Laufer; Presented by Ensemble Studio Theatre (William Carden, Artistic Director; Paul Alexander Slee, Executive Director) and The Alfred P. Sloan Foundation (Doron Weber, Program Director); Director, Lisa Peterson; Set, Lee Savage; Sound & Composition, Ryan Rumery; Costumes, Suzanne Chesney; Lighting, Raquel Davis; PSM, Jeff Davolt; ASM, Michal V. Mendelson; Producer, Annie Trizna; EST/Sloan Program Director, Graeme Gillis; EST/Sloan Associate Program Director, Linsay Firman; Press, David Gersten & Associates

CAST Rachel **Molly Ephraim**; Nelson Steinberg **Dane DeHaan**; Arthur Stein **Peter Friedman**; Sylvia **Deidre O'Connell**; Jesus **Paco Tolson**

New York premiere of a new play presented in two acts.

SYNOPSIS Sixteen-year-old Rachel Stein is having a bad year. Her father hasn't changed out of his pajamas since 9/11. Her mother has begun a close, personal relationship with Jesus. Her new neighbor, a sixteen-year-old Elvis impersonator, has fallen for her, hard. And the Apocalypse is coming Wednesday. Her only hope is that Stephen Hawking will save them all.

Being Audrey

Connelly Theatre; First Preview: March 28, 2009; Opening Night: April 5, 2009; Closed April 26, 2009

Book by James Hindman, music and lyrics by Ellen Weiss, development by Jack Cummings III and Adam R. Perlman, additional book and lyrics by Cheryl Stern; Presented by the Transport Group; Produced by Sarah Ackerman, Yael & Nick Jekogian, and Amy Kincaid in association with Michelle Ackerman, Jamie deRoy, Marla Franzese, Ronald & Joanne Falcon, and Francesca James; Director, Jack Cummings III; Musical Direction/Arrangements/Orchestrations, Larry Meyers; Musical Staging/Choreography, Scott Rink; Set, Sandra Goldmark; Costumes, Kathryn Rohe; Lighting, R. Lee Kennedy; Sound, Michael Rasbury; PSM, Theresa Flanagan; Casting, Nora Brennan; Press, Richard Kornberg & Associates

CAST Claire Stark **Cheryl Stern**; "Fred" **Brian Sutherland**; Dr. Givenchy/others **Stephen Berger**; Dr. Leraby/others **Andrea Bianchi**; Nurse Trina/others **Valerie Fagan**; Dr. Williams/others **Mark Ledbetter**; Pablo/others **Michael Maricondi**; Dr. Think Pink/others **Blair Ross**; Narrator **Dominick Dunne**

SETTING New York City and a selection of Audrey Hepburn films. World premiere of a new musical presented without intermission.

SYNOPSIS When calamity strikes and her fairytale world threatens to collapse, Claire seeks refuge in her imagination, where she embarks on a hilarious, romantic adventure inspired by the films of her heroine, Audrey Hepburn. Claire's fantastical escape appears complete until she must confront the reality of what she stands to lose. *Being Audrey* celebrates the variety of life and the themes embodied by one of America's most beloved and enduring movie stars.

Cheryl Stern in Being Audrey *(photo by Carol Rosegg)*

Nick Cordero in The Toxic Avenger *(photo by Carol Rosegg)*

The Toxic Avenger

New World Stages–Stage 1; First Preview: March 18, 2009; Opening Night: April 6, 2009; 29 previews, 62 performances as of May 31, 2009

Book and lyrics by Joe DiPietro, Music and lyrics by David Bryan, based on Lloyd Kaufman's 1985 film *The Toxic Avenger*; Presented by Jean Cheever and Tom Polum; Director, John Rando; Choreographer, Wendy Seyb; Music Director, Doug Katsaros; Sets, Beowulf Boritt; Costumes, David C. Woolard; Lighting, Kenneth Posner; Sound; Kurt Fischer; Hair and Make-up, Mark Adam Rampmeyer; Prosthetics/Special Effects, John Dods; Fight Director, Rick Sordelet & David DeBese; PSM, Scott Taylor Rollison; Stage Manager, Kelly Hance; Production Manager, Robert G. Mahon III & Jeff Wild; Casting, McCorkle Casting; Company Manager, Megan Trice Orchestrations/Arrangements, David Bryan & Christopher Jahnke; General Management, Splinter Group Productions; Advertising & Marketing, Allied Live LLC; N.J. Marketing, Kelly Ryman; Dance Captain, Demond Green; Fight Captain, Nicholas Rodriguez; Assistant Director, Wes Grantom; Assistant Choreography, Keith Coughlin; Associate Set, Alexis Distler; Associate Lighting, Joel Shier; Properties, Karen Cahill; Press O+M Company, Rick Miramontez, Richard Hillman; Cast recording: Time Life 80140-D

CAST White Dude **Matthew Saldivar**; Black Dude **Demond Green**; Mayor Babs Belgoody/Ma Ferd/A Nun **Nancy Opel**; Melvin Ferd the Third **Nick Cordero**; Sarah **Sara Chase**

UNDERSTUDIES Nicholas Rodriguez (Melvin/Black Dude/White Dude), Erin Leigh Peck (Nun/Ma/Mayor/Sarah)

MUSICIANS Ian Herman (Conductor/keyboards), Alan Childs (drums), Chris Cicchino (guitars), Dan Grennes (bass)

MUSICAL NUMBERS Who Will Save New Jersey?, Jersey Girl, Get The Geek, Kick Your Ass, My Big French Boyfriend, Thank God She's Blind, Big Green Freak, Choose Me, Oprah, Hot Toxic Love, The Legend of the Toxic Avenger, Evil is Hot, Bitch/Slut/Liar/Whore, Everybody Dies, You Tore My Heart Out, All Men Are Freaks, The Chase, Hot Toxic Love (reprise), A Brand New Day in New Jersey

SETTING Present. Tromaville, Exit 13B on the New Jersey Turnpike. New York premiere of a new musical presented without intermission. World premiere presented by the George Street Playhouse October 10, 2008 (David Saint, Artistic Director; Todd Schmidt, Managing Director).

SYNOPSIS *The Toxic Avenger* is set in the mythical town of Tromaville, Exit 13B off the New Jersey Turnpike. An aspiring earth scientist, Melvin Ferd the Third, is determined to clean up the town's burgeoning toxic waste, until he is tossed into a vat of radioactive goo and emerges as a seven-foot mutant freak and New Jersey's first superhero. Armed with superhuman strength and a heart as big as Newark, he's out to save New Jersey, end global warming and woo Sarah, the prettiest, blindest librarian in town.

Angela's Mixtape

Ohio Theatre; First Preview: April 6, 2009; Opening Night: April 9, 2009; Closed May 2, 2009; 3 previews, 21 performances

Written by Eisa Davis; Presented by New Georges (Susan Bernfield, Artistic Director; Sarah Cameron Sunde (Associate Director) and Hip-Hop Theater Festival (Clyde Valentin, Executive Director); Director, Liesl Tommy; Set, Clint Ramos; Lighting, Sarah Sidman; Sound, Jane Shaw; Costumes, Jessica Jahn; PSM, Ryan Raduechel; ASM, Danielle Teague-Daniels; Props, Johnson Henshaw; Assistant Director, Colette Robert; Production Manager, Mark Sitko; Technical Director, Steve Lorick; Associate Producer, Anna Hayman; Casting, Paul Davis/Calleri Casting; Graphics, ALRdesign.com; Press, Jim Baldassare

CAST Mommy **Kim Brockington**; Grandma **Denise Bursel**; Eisa **Eisa Davis**; Cess **Ayesha Ngaujah**; Angela **Linda Powell**

SETTING 70s, 80s, and 90s. Birmingham, Alabama. World premiere of a new play presented without intermission. Joint world premiere with Synchronicity Performance Group, Atlanta. Developed at the Hip-Hop Theater Festival and the New York Theatre Workshop.

SYNOPSIS In *Angela's Mixtape*, Eisa uses the rhythms of music and memory to tell of a radical upbringing on the dividing line between Oakland and Berkeley, California, in a family that includes her aunt, professor and activist Angela Davis.

Eisa Davis in Angela's Mixtape *(photo by Jim Baldassare)*

Trinity 5:29

Axis Theatre; First Preview: April 2, 2009; Opening Night: April 9, 2009; Closed May 9, 2009

Written and produced by Axis Company (Randy Sharp, Artistic Director; Brian Barnhart, Production Director; Jeffrey Resnick, Executive Producer);; Director, Randy Sharp; Set, Kyle Chepulis; Lighting, David Zeffren; Costumes, Elisa Santiago; Sound, Steve Fontaine; Stage Manager, Edward Terhune; ASM, David Crabb; Production Manager, Ian Tooley; Assistant Lighting, Amy Harper, Alex Casagrande; Set Construction, Josh Higgason; Costume Construction, Aughra Moon; Sound Technician, David Balutanski; Website & Graphics, Ethan Crenson; Press, Ron Lasko, Spin Cycle

CAST Oppenheimer **Edgar Oliver**; Truman **Brian Barnhart**; Groves **Marc Palmieri**; Tatlock **Britt Genelin**; Various **David Crabb**

World premiere of a new play presented without intermission.

SYNOPSIS *Trinity 5:29* centers on J. Robert Oppenheimer, the father of the atomic bomb. When Trinity, the first atomic bomb, was tested at 5:29am on July 16, 1945, Oppenheimer whispered a quote from Hindu scripture, "I am become Death, the destroyer of worlds." Less than a month later, two 20-megaton bombs were dropped on Japan, killing almost a quarter of a million people. Trapped in a desert of complicated regret, guilt and justification, New Jersey native Oppenheimer spent the rest of his life trying to decipher his actions. Oppenheimer reflects on his journey as he remembers his girlfriend Jean Tatlock, the supposed Communist who committed suicide the year before; the arrogant, yet vulnerable General Groves, overseer of The Manhattan Project; and President Harry Truman, who pushed the button that started the end of the world.

Cirque du Soliel: KOOZA

Randall's Island; Opening Night: April 16, 2009; Closed June 21, 2009

Written and directed by David Shiner; Presented by iShares; Creation Director, Serge Roy; Sets, Stéphane Roy; Costumes, Marie-Chantale Vaillancourt; Guide, Guy Laliberté; Composer, Jean-François Côté; Choreographer, Clarence Ford; Lighting, Martin Labrecque; Sound, Jonathan Deans, Leon Rothenberg; Props, Rogé Francoeur; Acrbatic Equipment/Rigging, Danny Zen; Acrobatic Performance Designer, André Simard; Make-up, Forence Cornet; Press, The Publicity Office, Marc Thibodeau

CAST Fifty-three performing artists in the show, several have received awards from important circus arts competitions, notably in juggling and trapeze.

SYNOPSIS *KOOZA* tells the story of The Innocent, a melancholy loner in search of his place in the world. *KOOZA* is a return to the origins of Cirque du Soleil: It combines two circus traditions – acrobatic performance and the art of clowning. The show highlights the physical demands of human performance in all its splendor and fragility, presented in a colorful mélange that emphasizes bold slapstick humor.

Iliad: Book One

Lucille Lortel Theatre; First Preview: March 31, 2009; Opening Night: April 16, 2009; Closed April 25, 2009

Written by Homer; translated by Stanley Lombardo; Produced by the Aquila Theatre by special arrangement with the Lucille Lortel Foundation; Director, Peter Meineck; Production Design, Peter Meineck; Music, Anthony Cochrane; Movement, Desiree Sanchez; Production Manager, Nate Terracio; Photography, Richard Termine; Press, David Gersten & Associates

CAST Achilles/Ensemble **John Buxton**; Agamemnon/Ensemble **Nathan Flower**; Patroclus/Ensemble **Jeffrey Golde**; Chryses/Ensemble **Jay Painter**; Calchas/Ensemble **Natasha Piletich**; Chryseis/Ensemble **Vaishnavi Sharma**,

A new adaptation of a classic story presented without intermission.

SYNOPSIS Nine years after the start of the Trojan War, the Greeks are still unable to defeat their enemy. Agamemnon, the commander clashes with the best warrior, Achilles over the division of war-prizes and is forced to give back the girl Chryseis to her father after Apollo sends a terrible plague. Agamemnon claims Achilles' war-prize Briseis to save face and the furious Achilles withdraws from the fighting and asks the Gods to turn the war against the Greeks.

The cast of Iliad: Book One *(photo by Richard Termine)*

Kernel of Sanity

Abrons Arts Center–Recital Hall; First Preview: April 9, 2009; Opening Night: April 16, 2009; Closed April 25, 2009

Written by Kermit Frazier; Produced by New Federal Theatre; Director Petronia Paley; Set, Pavlo Vosyy; Costumes, Ali Truns; Lighting, Shirley Prendergast; Sound, Sean O'Halloran; Press, David Gersten & Associates

CAST Frank **Joel Nagle**; Rita **Madeline James**; Roger **Chaz Reuben**

SETTING A small Midwestern city; late 1970s. Off-Broadway premiere of a new play presented without intermission.

SYNOPSIS A young actor on his way from New York to California, takes a detour for a surprise visit to a crucial confrontation with a veteran actor: an actor he's worked with in only one play, but to whom he's found himself inexorably, if nearly unwittingly, attached. Three people– a black man, a white man, and a white woman–clash over their contradictory senses of marginalization and betrayal and their contrasting perceptions of illusion and reality.

King David

Promise Theatre (Playhouse 91); First Preview: April 9, 2009; Opening Night: April 16, 2009; Closed June 27, 2009; 6 previews, 64 performances

Script and score by David M. Sanborn and Ellen Sanborn; Presented by Sanborn Entertainment and Eastern Gate Entertainment (Felicia M. Lopes) in association with Dan and Margaret Drost and Joseph Callari; Director, Ellen Sanborn; Orchestrator/Associate Arranger, David Onn-San; Sound, Bernard Fox; Lighting, Matthew Miller; Costumes/Set, Elizabeth Richards; PSM, Melanie T. Morgan; Marketing, Leanne Schanzer; Graphic Design, Helen Dean Design; Press, Les Schecter, LS Public Relations

CAST David M. Sanborn

New York premiere of musical presented without intermission. Originally produced June 12, 1997 at the University of Nations in Hawaii. The show has been presented on five continents since then.

SYNOPSIS In the family friendly musical *King David*, this epic biblical tale comes alive as Sanborn, impersonates the voices of Arnold Schwarzenegger, Sean Connery, Jimmy Stewart, Billy Crystal, Robin Williams, Robert DeNiro, Antonio Banderas, Gene Kelly, Tom Hanks, Jim Carrey and others to depict key characters in this epic Biblical tale. The production is taken word-for-word from a translation of the Hebrew Scriptures.

David M. Sanborn in King David

Flamingo Court

New World Stages–Stage 5; Opening Night: April 18, 2009; Closed July 19, 2009; 47 performances

Written by Luigi Creatore; Presented by Theatre 21 and Carolyn Rossi Copeland; Director, Steven Yuhasz; Set, Steven Capone; Costumes, Carol Sherry; Lighting, Herrick Goldman; Sound, David A. Arnold; Projections, luckydave; PSM, Donald William Myers; Associate General Manager/Company Manager, Robert E. Schneider; ASM, Angela Allen; Original Casting, Mark Simon; Production Supervision, Peter R. Feuchtwanger/PRF Productions; Wigs/Hair, Jeanette Harrington; Associate Lighting, Susan Nicholson; Advertising, Eliran Murphy Group; Press, Springer Associates, Joe Trentacosta

CAST Angelina/Chi Chi **Diane J. Findlay**; Marie/Charity Pipick **Lucy Martin**; Dominic/Walter Pipick **Tim Jerome**; Voice of Marian/Clara **Alex Bond**; Voice of Phillip **Tibor Feldman**; Harry Rossoff **Herbert Rubens**, Arthur/Mark Seagal **Gordon Stanley**

SETTING A three-story apartment complex in South Florida, apartments 104, 204, and 304; the present. Revival of a three short plays presented without intermission. Originally presented earlier this season (see listing in this section).

SYNOPSIS Ten characters, five actors, life in three condos, Flamingo Court follows the nosy and endearing residents of Flamingo Court, a South Florida apartment complex. Each apartment reveals a new story and a new lesson: Sex lives after sixty. Where there's a will, there's a relative. And love heals all wounds...at any age.

World premiere of a play presented without intermission.

SYNOPSIS In *The Gingerbread House*, a dark comic satire about self seeking consumerism and greed, Brian and Stacey want a better life, the life they deserve. But what they're willing to do to get it will destroy their family, rip them apart...and finally get them into the Club.

Jason Butler Harner, Sarah Paulson and Bobby Cannavale in The Gingerbread House *(photo by Carol Rosegg)*

Exit Cuckoo

Clurman Theatre at Theatre Row; First Preview: April 17, 2009; Opening Night: April 23, 2009; Closed May 17, 2009; 6 previews, 25 performances

Written by Lisa Ramirez; Presented by the Working Theater (Connie Grappo, Artistic Director) in association with Eve Ensler; Director, Colman Domingo; Sets, Rachel Hauck; Lighting, Russel Phillip Drapkin; Costumes, Raul Aktanov; Sound, Matt O'Hare; Associate Director, Martin Damien Wilkens; Vocal Coach, Beth McGuire; PSM, Annette Verga-Lagier; Production Manager, B.D. White; Production Assistant, David Green; Press, Sam Rudy Media Relations, Bob Lasko

CAST Mrs. Sinclair/Lisa/Rosa/Mother/Fiona/Esther/Joshua/Val/Protester/Mrs. Johnson **Lisa Ramirez**

Off-Broadway premiere of a solo performance play presented without intermission. Previously presented in the 2008 Midtown International Theatre Festival, where it was awarded Best Overall Performance of a Solo Show.

SYNOPSIS *Exit Cuckoo*, based on Lisa Ramirez's experiences as a nanny, is about women, the choices they make, the competing pressures they are subject to, and the defining effect this has on how children are raised. The play is a hilarious and profoundly moving collage of mothers, nannies and caretakers, and the complex chemistry between them.

Tim Jerome and Diane J. Findlay in Flamingo Court *(photo by Carol Rosegg)*

The Gingerbread House

Rattlestick Theatre at 224 Waverly; First Preview: April 13, 2009; Opening Night: April 18, 2009; Closed May 10, 2009; 5 previews, 20 performances

Written by Mark Schultz; Presented by the stageFARM (Alex Kilgore, Artistic Director; Carrie Shaltz, Founder and Executive Director; Brittany O'Neill, Producer); Director, Evan Cabnet; Set, the stageFARM; Costumes, Jessica Wegener; Lighting, Ben Stanton; Sound, Zane Birdwell; Video/Projections, Richard DiBella; Fight Director, Drew Leary; Stage Manager, Katrina Renee Hermann; ASM, Trisha Henson; Casting, James Calleri; Associate Producer, Jen Driscoll; Press; O+M Company, Rick Miramontez, Amanda Dekker, Elizabeth Wagner

CAST Marco **Bobby Cannavale**; Brian **Jason Butler Harner**; Fran **Jackie Hoffman**; Stacey **Sarah Paulson**; Collin **Ben Rappaport**; Curtis and Maggie (Video) **L.J. Foley & Clare Foley**; Voice of Curtis **Charlie Kilgore**

A Nervous Smile

Kirk Theatre at Theatre Row; First Preview: April 17, 2009; Opening Night: April 26, 2009; Closed May 17, 2009; 9 previews, 19 performances

Written by John Belluso; Presented by Theatre Breaking Through Barriers (Ike Schambelan, Artistic Director); Director, Ike Schambelan; Sets and Lighting, Bert Scott; Sound, Alden Fulcomer; Wardrobe Stylist, Eugene; PSM, Kimothy Cruse; ASM, Brooke Elsinghorst; Production Managers, David Chontos & Nicholas Lazzaro; Marketing, Michelle Tabnick Tabnick; Assistant to the Director, Christina Roussos; Press, Shirley Herz Associates, Dan Demello

CAST Brian **Nicholas Viselli**; Eileen **Pamela Sabaugh**; Nic **Marilee Talkington**; Blanka **Melanie Boland**

SETTING Brian and Eileen's Upper West Side apartment in Manhattan; the present. New York premiere of a play presented without intermission. World premiere at the 2005 Humana Festival of New American Plays at Actors Theatre of Louisville.

SYNOPSIS The wealthy parents of a girl severely disabled with cerebral palsy are strained to the breaking point by the burden of caring for their daughter. With a friend whose son also has CP, they decide to leave the burden of their children and fly off to South America and Europe. *A Nervous Smile* is the final, most powerful play by John Belluso, a wonderful playwright with a disability who passed away more than two years ago.

Nicholas Viselli and Marilee Talkington in A Nervous Smile *(photo by Carol Rosegg)*

The Shanghai Gesture

Julia Miles Theatre; First Preview: April 21, 2009; Opening Night: April 30, 2009; Closed May 24, 2009; 5 previews, 28 performances

Written by John Colton, adapted by Marsha Sheiness; Presented by Mirror Repertory Company (Sabra Jones, Artistic Director); Director, Robert Kalfin; Sets, Michael Anania; Costumes, Gail Cooper Hecht; Music/Sound, Margaret Pine; Lighting, Paul Hudson; Fight Director, B.H. Barry; Stage Manager, Lisa McGinn; ASM, Angie Hesterman

CAST Cesar Hawkins **Richard B. Watson**; Lin Chi **Rob Yang**; Prince Oshima **Marcus Ho**; Poppy **Sabrina Veroczi**; Mother Goddamn **Tina Chen**; Creek Side Mary/Mme. Le Comtesse de Michot **Elena McGhee**; Ni Pau **Jacey Powers**; Koo Lot Foo **John Haggerty**; Sir Guy Charteris **Larry Pine**; Lady Blessington **Helen Coxe**; Lord Blessington **John FitzGibbon**; Mr. Dudley Gregory **Seth Powers**; Mrs. Dudley Gregory **Erin Krakow**; Mons. LeComte de Michot **Robert Lydiard**; Don Querebo D'Achuna **Allen Lewis Rickman**; Donna Querebo D'Achuna **Victoria Guthrie**; Tso Chi **Jo Yaang**; Tsa/Mime Show Father **Roger Wu**; Coolie #2/Boatman #4 **Nick Sakai**; Male Servant #1/Coolie #1/Chauffeur/Boatman #3 **Toshiji Takeshima**; Ensemble **Hyosun Choi, Nadia Gan**

SETTING Shanghai, China; Chinese New Year, 1926. Revival of a play presented in two acts.

SYNOPSIS Written in 1918 and last produced in New York on Broadway in 1926, *The Shanghai Gesture* is a 100-year-old historic American play that has always been controversial for its bold confrontation of still-relevant issues. The play confronts issues of women's rights, the sex trade, child abuse/slavery, and what happens when one country imposes its culture upon another.

The cast of The Shanghai Gesture *(photo by Carol Rosegg)*

Sophistry

Beckett Theatre on Theatre Row; First Preview: April 22, 2009; Opening Night: May 5, 2009; Closed May 24, 2009; 13 previews, 21 performances

Written by Jonathan Marc Sherman; Presented by South Ark Stage (Rhoda Herrick, Artistic/Producing Director); Director, James Warwick; Sets, Charles Corcoran; Costumes, Melissa Schlachtmeyer; Lighting, D.M. Wood; Sound, Graham Johnson; Properties, Meredith Ries; PSM, Christine Fisichella, ASM, Melissa Jernigan; Casting, Matthew Messinger; Press, O&M Company, Rick Miramontez, Philip Carrubba

CAST Whitey McCoy **Jonathan Hogan**; Willy **Maximillian Osinki**; Robin Smith **Natalie Knepp**; Debbie **Mahira Kakkar**; Igor Konigsberg **Ian Alda**; Xavier (Ex) Reynolds **Charlie Hewson**; Jack Kahn **Michael Carbonaro**; Quintana Matheson **Ellen Dolan**

SETTING May 1990–June 1991; the campus of a small New England College. Revival of a play presented without intermission. Originally presented at Playwrights Horizons October 12, 1993 (see *Theatre World* Vol. 50, page 142).

SYNOPSIS The subjective nature of truth within sexual relationships is the theme *Sophistry*, a play about college life in modern-day America. The self-absorbed lives of a group of students at a small New England college are disrupted when they're suddenly forced to deal with a crisis: Philosophy professor Whitey McCoy is accused of seducing a male student, Jack Kahn. Both Whitey and Jack tell the story, each from their conflicting memories, leaving everybody in doubt as to what is true.

Jonathan Hogan and Michael Carbonaro in Sophistry *(photo by Carol Rosegg)*

FOR LOVERS ONLY (Love Songs... Nothing But Love Songs)

New World Stages–Stage 5; First Preview: April 24, 2009; Opening Night: May 11, 2009; Closed August 3, 2009; 11 previews, 25 performances (Friday through Monday performances)

Written by Christopher Scott & Ken Lundie from a concept by Nancy Friday; Presented by Eric Krebs & Sara Lundie; Director/Choreographer, Mark Akens; Musical Director, Ken Lundie; Associate Musical Director, Mark Akens; Costumes, Bernard Grenier; Sets, Peter R. Feuchtwanger; Lighting, Ben Hagen; Sound, Eric M. Ballantine; PSM, Brian Westmoreland; Company Manager, Rebecca Josue; Associate Musical Director, Mark Akens; Casting, Barry Boss, Bob Kale; Press, David Gersten & Associates

CAST Glenn Seven Allen, Monica L. Patton, Dominique Plaisant, Trisha Rapier, Kevin Vortmann; Understudies **Kevin Green, Christine Hope**

Off-Broadway premiere of a new musical revue presented in two acts. Developed at AMAS Musical Theater Lab and workshopped in January 2009.

SYNOPSIS *FOR LOVERS ONLY (Love Songs... Nothing But Love Songs)* presents a cavalcade of love songs from pop to Puccini, from Broadway and around the world, interspersed through a fast-paced evening.

A More Perfect Union

East 13th Street Theatre (Classic Stage Company Space); First Preview: May 5, 2009; Opening Night: May 12, 2009; Closed June 7, 2009; 6 previews, 24 performances

Written by Vern Thiessen; Commissioned, Developed and Presented by the Epic Theater Ensemble (Zak Berman, Melissa Friedman, & Ron Russell, Founding Executive Directors); Director/Sound, Ron Russell; Sets, Troy Hourie; Costumes, Theresa Squire; Lighting, Tyler Micolean; PSM, Erin Koster; Production Manager, Jee S. Han; Casting, James Calleri; Press, O+M Company, Rick Miramontez, Jon Dimond, Molly Barnett

CAST Maddie **Melissa Friedman**; James **Godfrey L. Simmons Jr**,

SETTING A private library of the Supreme Court. World premiere of a new play presented without intermission.

SYSOPSIS *A More Perfect Union* is about two Law Clerks at the U.S. Supreme Court who have very different backgrounds and opposing political views. When they fall in love their relationship challenges their ethics and careers, as well as threatens to expose a dirty little secret about the Highest Court in our land. This serious comedy about justice, compromise, and what America wears underneath its fancy robes.

Godfrey L. Simmons, Jr. and Melissa Friedman in A More Perfect Union *(photo by Carol Rosegg)*

Danny and Sylvia: The Danny Kaye Musical

St. Luke's Theatre; First Preview: May 6, 2009; Opening Night: May 13, 2009; 5 previews, 16 performances as of May 31, 2009

Book and lyrics by Robert McElwaine, music by Bob Bain; Presented by Hy Juter and Edmund Gaynes; Director, Pamela Hall; Choreographer, Gene Castle; Sets, Josh Iacovelli; Lighting, Graham Kindred; Costumes, Elizabeth Flores; Music Director, David Fiorello; General Manager, Jessimeg Productions; PSM, Josh Iacovelli; Associate General Manager, Julia Beardsley; Props, Robert Pemberton; Press, Susan L. Schulman

CAST Danny Kaye **Brian Childers**; Sylvia Fine **Kimberly Faye Greenberg**

MUSICIANS David Fiorello (piano)

MUSICAL NUMBERS Another Summer, At Liberty, at the Club Versailles, At the London Palladium, Can't Get That Man Off My Mind, Danny Kaminsky, I Can't Live Without You, If I Knew Then, If I Needed a Guy, I'm a Star, Just one Girl, La Vie Paree, Now Look What You Made Me Do, Requiem for Danny Kaminsky, She's Got a Fine Head on My Shoulders, Sylvia's Song, Tummler, We've Closed On Opening Night, We Make a Wonderful Team, What Shall We Say, You Got A Problem With That, Anatole of Paris, The Maladjusted jester, Melody in 4F, One Life to Live, Tchaikovsky, Dinah, Minnie the Moocher, Ballin' the Jack, P.S. One Four Nine

SETTING 1936 to 1948 in New York, Hollywood and London. Off-Broadway premiere of a musical presented in two acts. Originally produced by the American Century Theater and later presented at the Chip Deffaa Invitational Theatre Festival of New York.

SYNOPSIS *Danny and Sylvia* the duo from the time the young undisciplined comic Danny Kaminsky meets aspiring songwriter Sylvia Fine at an audition in the 1930s. Under Sylvia's guidance as mentor, manager, and eventually, wife, Kaye rises from improvisational comic to international film star. The musical explores their inspired collaboration and the romance and conflict that made them such a volatile and successful couple.

Brian Childers and Kimberly Faye Greenberg in Danny and Sylvia: The Danny Kaye Musical (photo by Carol Rosegg)

The Dishwashers

59E59 Theater B; First Preview: May 8, 2009; Opening Night: May 13, 2009; Closed June 7, 2009; 5 previews, 27 performances

Written by Morris Panych; Presented by Shiloh Productions as part of Americas Off Broadway 2008 (Elizabeth Kleinhans, President & Artistic Director; Peter Tear, Executive Producer); Produced by the Chester Theatre Company; Director, Byam Stevens; Set, Charlie Corcoran; Lighting, Jill Nagle; Costumes, Arthur Oliver; Sound, Tom Shread; Stage Manager, April A. Kline; Press, Karen Greco

CAST Dressler **Tim Donoghue**; Moss **John Shuman**; Emmett **Jay Stratton**; Burroughs **Michael J. Fulvio**

New York premiere of a new play presented in two acts.

SYNOPSIS Dressler scrambles to keep the basement scullery of an upscale eatery functioning, marshaling his rag-tag team with a stream of hilarious rhetoric and old-fashioned working class pride. His fellow wage slaves, the ancient Moss and the downwardly mobile Emmett, just can't seem to grasp his inspirational style. Playwright Morris Panych walks a razor's edge between comedy and tragedy chronicling the plight of men working in the lower depths of a high end restaurant.

American Hwangap

The Wild Project; First Preview: May 9, 2009; Opening Night: May 17, 2009; Closed June 7, 2009; XX previews

Written by Lloyd Suh; Presented by The Play Company and Ma-Yi Theater; Director, Trip Cullman; Sets, Erik Flatmo; Costumes, Junghyun Georgia Lee; Lighting, Paul Whitaker; Sound, Fitz Patton; PSM, Jenn McNeil; Press, Sam Rudy Media Relations

CAST Esther Chun **Michi Barall**; Mary Chun **Mia Katigbak**; Ralph Chun **Peter Kim**; David Chun **Hoon Lee**; Min Suk Chun **James Saito**

SETTING A West Texas suburb; the present. New York premiere of a new play presented without intermission. World premiere presented at the Magic Theater April 4–May 3, 2009 (San Francisco)

SYNOPSIS Min Suk Chun is turning 60, and he's back in West Texas after leaving his family almost 15 years ago. As his ex-wife and three adult children wrestle with their broken past in preparing this American hwangap (a 60th birthday ritual celebrating the completion of the Eastern zodiac), an aging Korean would-be cowboy is back at the head of the table. But before the end of the night, he'll probably end up sitting in a tree without his pants on.

A Play on Words

59E59 Theater C; First Preview: May 12, 2009; Opening Night: May 17, 2009; Closed May 30, 2009; 5 previews, 13 performances

Written by Bryan Dykstra; Presented as part of Americas Off Broadway 2008 (Elizabeth Kleinhans, President & Artistic Director; Peter Tear, Executive Producer); Director, Margarett Perry; Set, Kelly Syring; Lighting, E.D. Intemann; Costumes, Hannah Kochman; Sound, Nate Richardson; Stage Manager, Trisha Henson; Press, Karen Greco

CAST Rusty **Mark Boyett**; Max **Bryan Dykstra**

New York premiere of a new play presented without intermission.

SYNOPSIS Seinfeld meets Waiting for Godot in this ferociously witty play on, about and exploding with language. Rusty and Max have been friends since grade school and they've been arguing almost the entire time. Today they're scheming up something big. Brian Dykstra's signature style crackles in this uproarious romp through backyard suburbia where two (slightly above) Average Joes spar in a relentlessly fanatical pursuit of what is said, what is intended, and what is.

Don't Leave It All to Your Children!

Actors Temple Theatre; First Preview: May 6, 2009; Opening Night: May 20, 2009; 9 previews, 12 performances as of May 31, 2009

Book, music and lyrics by Saul Ilson; Presented by Sausau Productions LLC; Director Saul Ilson; Staging, Rudy Tronto; Music Director, John Bell; Sets, Josh Iacovelli; Lighting, Graham Kindred; Stage Manager, Jana Llynn; General Mamager, Jessimed Productions; Photographer, Albert Hirson; Press, Susan L. Schulman

CAST Barbara Minkusl, Marcia Rodd, Steve Rossi, Ronnie Schell; Understudies Alix Elias, Rudy Tronto

MUSICAL NUMBERS The Best Medicine, You're a Boomer, The Golden Years, March in the Parade, Three of You, A Singles Cruise, Old Cronies, I Love You/Looking Back, My Grandchildren & Me, Where Did the Time Go?, It's the High Cost, A Man Named Mel, Age is Not a Factor, Ed Sullivan, What Do You Think About That?, Another Wrinkle, A Wonderful Life, Why Do We Do It, Don't Leave it All/Have a Good Time, Old Memories, The Best Medicine (reprise)

New York premiere of a musical revue presented without intermission

SYNOPSIS Don't Leave It All to Your Children! is a laugh-filled 90 minutes of music and comedy that celebrates the funny side of the Golden years.

The Success of Failure
(Or, The Failure of Success)

St. Ann's Warehouse; First Preview: May 22, 2009; Opening Night: May 26, 2009; Closed June 7, 2009; 3 previews, 12 performances

Written by Cynthia Hopkins; Produced by Accinosco in association with Joel Basin; Presented by St. Ann's Warehouse; Director, D.J. Mendel; Set/Video, Jim Findlay & Jeff Sugg; Sound, Jamie McElhinney; Lighting, Tyler Micoleau; Choreography, David Neumann & Annie B. Parson; Costumes, Tara Webb; Production Coordinator, Anthony Cerrato; Technical Director, Peter Warren; Press, Blake Zidell

CAST Ruom Yes Noremac **Cynthia Hopkins**; With **Jim Findlay, Jeff Sugg**

MUSICAL NUMBERS Song Before Love Songs, Evolution, Change the World, New in the World, Paradise, In the New Universe, New in the World (reprise), Amnesia is a Myth, Recurring Dreams, All Is Bliss, Blow Yo Horn, Pledge of Allegiance, Sunshine

New York premiere or a new musical/theatrical piece presented without intermission. World premiere at The Walker Center (Minneapolis, Minnesota).

SYNOPSIS An epic folk tale from the far distant future, The Success of Failure depicts the heroic saga of Ruom Yes Noremac's secret mission to save the world. During the course of her lonely journey through space, Ruom Yes Noremac realizes that only by failing to save the Earth can she succeed in saving "The Universe."

Pure Confidence

59E59 Theater A; First Preview: May 22, 2009; Opening Night: May 27, 2009; Closed July 3, 2009; 6 previews, 44 performances

Written by Carlyle Brown; Presented by the Mixed Blood Theatre Company (Jack Reuler, Artistic Director) as part of Americas Off Broadway 2008 (Elizabeth Kleinhans, President & Artistic Director; Peter Tear, Executive Producer); Director, Marion McClinton; Set, Joseph Stanley; Costumes, Christine A. Richardson; Lighting, Michael Wangen; Sound, C. Andrew Mayer; PSM, Julia Gallagher; Press, Karen Greco

CAST Simon Cato **Gavin Lawrence**; Colonel Wiley Johnson **Chris Mulkey**; Caroline **Christina Clark**; Mattie Johnson **Karen Landry**; Auctioneer/Tom Roland **Casey Greig**; George Dewitt/Clerk **Mark Sieve***

*Succeeded by Mark Rosenwinkel (6/09/09)

New York premiere of a new play presented in two acts. Previously presented at the Mixed Blood Theatre in Minneapolis with this cast.

SYNOPSIS On the eve of the Civil War, champion jockey Simon Cato is one of the most successful athletes of his day, dominating the sport of horse racing. But Simon is also a slave. Hired out regularly by his owner to Colonel Wiley Johnson, owner of the prize thoroughbred Pure Confidence, Simon wants the one thing the Colonel by law can't give him: his freedom.

Top to bottom, *Steve Rossi, Marcia Rodd, Ronnie Schell and Barbara Minkus in* Don't Leave It All to Your Children! *(photo by Albert Hirshon)*

PLAYED THROUGH / CLOSED THIS SEASON

Adding Machine

Minetta Lane Theatre; First Preview: February 7, 2008; Opening Night: February 25, 2008; Closed July 20, 2008; 16 previews, 149 performances

Original music by Joshua Schmidt, libretto by Jason Loewith & Joshua Schmidt, based on the play The Adding Machine by Elmer Rice; Produced by Scott Morfee, Tom Wirtshafter, Margaret Cotter; Director, David Cromer; Set, Takeshi Kata; Lighting, Keith Parham; Sound, Tony Smolenski IV; Costumes, Kristine Knanishu; Video, Peter Flaherty; Properties, Michele Spardaro; Music Director, J. Oconer Navarro; PSM, Richard A. Hodge; Production Management, Aurora Productions; Casting, Pat McCorkle/Joe Lopick; General Management, Two Step Productions; Advertising, Eliran Murphy Group; Company Manager, Kate Mott; ASM, Kate McDaniel; Assistant Director, Jessica Redish; Associate Sound, Drew Levy; Video Associate/Programmer, Dustin O'Neill; Original Sound, Jeff Dublinske & Josh Schmidt; Original Set, Matthew York; Recordings, Dan Gnader; Press, O&M Co., Rick Miramontez, Jon Dimond; Cast recording: PS Classics 865

CAST Mrs. Zero **Cyrilla Baer**; Mr. Zero **Joel Hatch**; Daisy **Amy Warren**; Mr. One **Daniel Marcus**; Mrs. One **Niffer Clarke**; Mr. Two **Roger E. DeWitt**; Mrs. Two **Adinah Alexander**; Boss **Jeff Still**; Shrdlu **Joe Farrell**

UNDERSTUDIES Adinah Alexander (Daisy), Randy Blair (Mr One/Mr. Two/Shrdlu), Niffer Clarke (Mrs. Zero), Roger E. DeWitt (Boss), Daniel Marcus (Mr. Zero), Ariela Morgenstern (Mrs. One, Mrs. Two)

MUSICIANS J. Oconer Navarro (Musical Director); Andy Boroson (piano/Assistant Music Director), Brad "Gorilla" Carbone (percussion), Timothy Splain (synthesizer/assistant to the Composer)

MUSICAL NUMBERS In Numbers, Office Reverie, In Numbers (reprise), I'd Rather Watch You, The Party, Zero's Confession, Once More, Ham and Eggs!, Didn't We?, The Gospel According to Shrdlu, Shrdlu's Blues, Daisy's Confession, I'd Rather Watch You (reprise), Freedom!, In Numbers (reprise), Freedom! (reprise), The Music of The Machine

SETTING Here and the afterlife, an American city in the 1920's. New York premiere of a new musical presented without intermission. Developed and world premiere at Chicago's Next Theatre Company (Jason Loewith, Artistic Director) on February 5, 2007.

SYNOPSIS Based on Rice's 1923 incendiary play, Adding Machine tells the story of Mr. Zero, a nameless cog in American business. After 25 years of exemplary work, he finds that his pencil and paper efforts have been replaced by a mechanical adding machine. In a vengeful rage, Mr. Zero murders his boss. He journeys through life, death and an afterlife in the Elysian Fields, where he is met with one last chance for romance and redemption.

Roger E. DeWitt, Joel Hatch and Daniel Marcus in Adding Machine (photo by Carol Rosegg)

Altar Boyz

New World Stages–Stage 4; First Preview: February 15, 2005; Opening Night: March 1, 2005; 1,776 performances as of May 31, 2009

Book by Kevin Del Aguila, music, lyrics, and vocal arrangements by Gary Adler and Michael Patrick Walker, conceived by Marc Kessler and Ken Davenport; Produced by Ken Davenport and Robyn Goodman, in association with Walt Grossman, Ruth Hendel, Sharon Karmazin, Matt Murphy, and Mark Shacket; Director, Stafford Arima; Choreography, Christopher Gattelli; Musical Director/Dance Music and Additional Arrangements, Lynne Shankel; Set, Anna Louizos; Costumes, Gail Brassard; Lighting, Natasha Katz; Sound, Simon Matthews; Orchestrations, Doug Katsaros, Lynne Shankel; Casting, David Caparelliotis; PSM, Sara Jaramillo; Hair, Josh Marquette; Production Manager, Andrew Cappelli; Associate Producer, Stephen Kocis; Press; David Gersten and Associates; General Manager, Martian Entertainment; Company Manager, Ryan Lympus; ASM, Alyssa Stone; Casting, David Petro; Associate Choreographer, Tammy Colucci; Music Programmer, Doug Katsaros; Cast recording: Sh-K-Boom Records 86050

A scene from Altar Boyz

CAST Matthew **Michael Kaden Craig**; Mark **Ryan J. Ratliff**[*1]; Luke **Neil Haskell**[*2]; Juan **Jay Garcia**[*3]; Abraham **Ryan Strand**[*4]; Voice of GOD **Shadoe Stevens**; Understudies **Austin Lesch**[5], **Joey Khoury**

*Succeeded by: 12. Travis Nesbitt (8/1/08) 2. Lee Markham (4/3/09) 3. Mauricio Perez (5/30/08) 4. Ravi Roth (10/13/08) 5. Mitch Dean (4/6/09)

ALTAR BOYZ BAND Jason Loffredo (Conductor/keyboard), Danny Percefull (keyboard), David Matos (guitar), Clayton Craddock (drums)

MUSICAL NUMBERS We Are the Altar Boyz, Rhythm in Me, Church Rulz, The Calling, The Miracle Song, Everybody Fits, Something About You, Body Mind & Soul, La Vida Eternal, Epiphany, Number 918, Finale: I Believe

SETTING Here and Now. A musical presented without intermission. Originally produced at the New York Musical Theatre Festival, September, 2004. For original production credits see (See *Theatre World* Volume 61, page 142)

SYNOPSIS A struggling Christian boy band (with one nice Jewish boy), trying to save the world one screaming fan at a time, perform their last tour date at the Dodger Stages. Their pious pop act worked wonders on the home state Ohio bingo-hall-and-pancake breakfast circuit, but will temptation for solo record deals threaten to split the Boyz as take a bite out of the forbidden Big Apple?

The Awesome 80s Prom

Webster Hall; First Performance: July 23, 2004 (Friday evenings only); Opening Night: September 10, 2004 (Fridays and Saturdays); 262 performances as of May 31, 2009 (Saturday evening performances only)

Written and produced by Ken Davenport; Co-Authored by The Class of '89 (Sheila Berzan, Alex Black, Adam Bloom, Anne Bobby, Courtney Balan, Mary Faber, Emily McNamara, Troy Metcalf, Jenna Pace, Amanda Ryan Paige, Mark Shunock, Josh Walden, Noah Weisberg, Brandon Williams, Simon Wong and Fletcher Young); Director, Ken Davenport; Choreography, Drew Geraci; Costumes, Randall E. Klein; Lighting, Martin Postma; Production Stage Manger, Carlos Maisonet; Associate Producers, Amanda Dubois, Jennifer Manocherian; Company Manager, Matt Kovich; ASM, Kathryn Galloway; Casting, Daryl Eisenberg; Press, David Gersten & Associates

CAST Johnny Hughes – The DJ **Dillon Porter**; Lloyd Parker – The Photographer **Daryl Embry**; Dickie Harrington – The Drama Queen **Bennett Leak**; Michael Jay – The Class President **Craig Jorczak**; Mr. Snelgrove – The Principal **Thomas Poarch**; Molly Parker – The Freshman **Lauren Schafler**; Inga Swanson – The Swedish Exchange Student **Emily McNamara**[*1]; Joshua "Beef" Beefarowski – A Football Player **Michael Barra**; Whitley Whitiker – The Head Cheerleader **Jessica West Regan**; Nick Fender – The Rebel **Michael Maloney**[*2]; Heather #1 – A Cheerleader **Allison Carter Thomas**; Heather #2 – The Other Cheerleader **Kate Wood Riley**; Kerrie Kowalski – The Spaz **Courtney Ell**[*3]; Melissa Ann Martin – Head of the Prom Committee **Angie Blocher**; Louis Fensterpock – The Nerd **Nick Austin**; Blake Williams – Captain of the Football Team **Major Dodge**[*4]; Mrs. Lascalzo – The Drama Teacher **Andrea Biggs**; Feung Schwey – The Asian Exchange Student **Anderson Lim**; The Mystery Guest **CP Lacey**

*Succeeded by: 1. Annie Ragsdale 2. Brandon Marotta 3. Missy Diaz 4.Jason Carden

SETTING Wanaget High's Senior Prom, 1989. An interactive theatrical experience presented without intermission

SYNOPSIS The Captain of the Football Team, the Asian Exchange Student, the Geek, and the Head Cheerleader are all competing for Prom King and Queen. The audience decides who wins while moonwalking to retro hits from the decade.

Blue Man Group

Astor Place Theatre; Opening Night: November 7, 1991; 9,440 performances as of May 31, 2009

Created and written by Matt Goldman, Phil Stanton, Chris Wink; Produced by Blue Man Productions; Director, Marlene Swartz and Blue Man Group; Artistic Directors, Caryl Glaab, Michael Quinn; Artistic/Musical Collaborators, Larry Heinemann, Ian Pai; Set, Kevin Joseph Roach; Costumes, Lydia Tanji, Patricia Murphy; Lighting, Brian Aldous, Matthew McCarthy; Sound, Raymond Schilke, Jon Weston; Computer Graphics, Kurisu-Chan; Video, Caryl Glaab, Dennis Diamond; PSM, Patti McCabe; Company Manager, Akia Squitieri; Stage Managers, Bernadette Castro, Jenny Lynch; Resident General Manager, Leslie Witthohn; General Manager of North American Productions, Alison Schwartz; Performing Director, Chris Bowen; Performing Directors, Chris Bowen, Michael Dahlen, Randall Jaynes, Jeffrey Doornbos, Brian Scott; Original Executive Producer, Maria Di Dia; Casting, Deb Burton; Press, Tahra Milan

CAST (rotating) **Shaneca Adams, Kalen Allmandinger, Gideon Banner, Wes Day, Josh Elrod, Isaac Gardner, Matt Goldman, John Hartzell, Colin Hurd, Michael Rahhal, Matt Ramsey, Pete Simpson, Phil Stanton, Steve White, Chris Wink**

MUSICIANS (rotating) Tom Shad, Geoff Gersh, Clem Waldmann, Dan Dobson, Dan Dobson, Jeff Lipstein, Byron Estep, Matt Hankle, Tommy Kessler, Jerry Kops, Josh Matthews, Jordan Perlson, Dave Corter

An evening of performance art presented without intermission. For original production credits see *Theatre World* Volume 48, Page 90.

SYNOPSIS The three-man new-vaudeville Blue Man Group combines comedy, music, art, and multimedia to produce a unique form of entertainment.

A scene from Blue Man Group *(photo courtesy of Blue Man Productions)*

The Castle

New World Stages–Stage 5; First Preview: March 30, 2008; Opening Night: April 27, 2008; Closed May 23, 2009; 8 previews, 57 performances (Saturdays only)

Conceived and directed by David Rothenberg, written in collaboration with the cast and Kenneth Harrigan; Produced by Eric Krebs and Chase Mishkin by arrangement with the Fortune Society; Press, O+M Company, Richard Hillman, Philip Carrubba

CAST Vilma Ortiz Donovan, Angel Ramos, Kenniet Harrigan, Casimiro Torres

Off-Broadway premiere of a unique theatrical event presented without intermission.

SYNOPSIS Four formerly imprisoned New Yorkers with a total of 70 years of incarceration relate their journeys of crime, privation, and redemption.

(Clockwise from left) *Angel Ramos, Casimiro Torres, Kenneth Harrington and Vilma Ortiz Donovan in* The Castle *(photo courtesy of Filip Kwiatkowski)*

The Fantasticks

Snapple Theater Center – Jerry Orbach Theater; First Preview: July 28, 2006; Opening Night: August 23, 2006; 27 previews, 1,055 performances as of May 31, 2009+

Book and lyrics by Tom Jones, music by Harvey Schmidt, suggested by the play *Les Romanesques* by Edmond Rostand; Produced by Terzetto LLC, Pat Flicker Addiss, and MARS Theatricals (Amy Danis/Mark Johannes); Director, Tom Jones; Original Staging, Word Baker; Sets and Costumes, Ed Wittstein; Lighting, Mary Jo Dondlinger; Sound, Dominic Sack; Casting, Terzetto LLC; Musical Director, Robert Felstein; Choreography/Musical Staging, Janet Watson; Production Stage Manager, Shanna Spinello; ASMs, Michael Krug, Brandon Kahn, Paul Blankenship; Associate Director, Kim Moore; Associate Producers, Carter-Parke Productions and Patrick Robustelli; Production Supervisor, Dan Shaheen; Press, John Capo–DBS Press; Cast recording: Sh-K-Boom/Ghostlight 84415

CAST The Narrator **Dennis Parlato**[*1]; The Boy (Matt) **Nick Spangler**[*2]; The Girl (Luisa) **Erica Piccininni**[*3]; The Boy's Father (Hucklebee) **Gene Jones**; The Girl's Father (Bellomy) **Steve Routman**; The Old Actor (Henry) **John Thomas Waite**; The Man Who Dies (Mortimer) **John Shuman**[*4]; The Mute **Jordan Nichols**[*5]; At the Piano **Robert Felstein**; At the Harp **Jacqueline Kerrod**

STANDBYS Tom Flagg (Hucklebee/Henry/Mortimer), Scott Willis (El Gallo/Hucklebee/Bellomy), Evy Ortiz (The Mute/Luisa), Jordan Nichols[*5] (Matt); Temporary: Richard Roland (El Gallo: 9/29/08–1/11/09)

*Succeeded by: 1. Lewis Cleale (9/15/08), Bradley Dean (3/30/09) 2. Jonathan Schwartz (3/30/09) 3. Margaret Anne Florence (7/21/08), Betsy Morgan (12/22/08), Ramona Mallory (3/30/09) 4. Michael Nostrand (7/7/08) 5. Douglas Ullman Jr. (3/7/09)

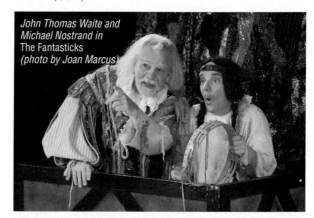

John Thomas Waite and Michael Nostrand in The Fantasticks *(photo by Joan Marcus)*

MUSICAL NUMBERS Overture, Try to Remember, Much More, Metaphor, Never Say No, It Depends on What You Pay, Soon It's Gonna Rain, Abduction Ballet, Happy Ending, This Plum is Too Ripe, I Can See It, Plant a Radish, Round and Round, They Were You, Try to Remember (reprise)

Revival of the musical presented in two acts. *The Fantasticks* is the world's longest running musical and the longest running Off-Broadway production ever. The original production opened at the Sullivan Street Playhouse on May 3, 1960 and closed January 13, 2002 playing over 17,000 performances (see *Theatre World* Volume 16 page 167 for original cast credits). May 3, 2009 kicked-off the beginning of the show's fiftieth anniversary year with a two day celebration, reuniting the authors and many former cast members from the original and revival productions. Mayor Bloomberg proclaimed May 4 "*Fantasticks* Day" and the celebration concluded with an after party with performances from Rita Gardner (the original "Louisa"), Daphne Rubin-Vega, Orfeh, Aaron Lazar, Groovelily, and Jill Paice.

SYNOPSIS *The Fantasticks* tells the story of a young boy and girl who fall madly in love at the hands of their meddling fathers, but soon grow restless and stray from one another. The audience uses its imagination to follow El Gallo as he creates a world of moonlight and magic, then pain and disillusionment, until the boy and girl find their way back to one another.

+The show was on hiatus from February 24–June 16, 2008 as new producers took over the production.

Fuerza Bruta: Look Up

Daryl Roth Theatre; First Preview: October 11, 2007; Opening Night: October 24, 2007; 14 previews, 637 performances as of May 31, 2009

Created and directed by Diqui James; Produced by Live Nation Artists Events Group, Fuerzabruta, Ozono, and David Binder; Composer/Musical Director, Gaby Kerpel; Lighting, Edi Pampin; Sound, Hernan Nupieri; Costumes, Andrea Mattio; Automation, Alberto Figueiras; General Coordinator, Fabio D'Aquila; Production, Agustina James; Technical Director, Alejandro Garcia; Marketing, Eric Schnall; Casting, James Calleri; Set-up Technical Supervisor, Bradley Thompson; General Manager, Laura Kirspel; PSM, Jeff Benish; Production Coordinator/ASM, E. Cameron Holsinger; Special Effects, Rick Sordelet; Press, The Karpel Group, Bridget Klapinski, Adam Bricault

CAST Freddy Bosche, Hallie Bulleit, Daniel Case, Dusty Giamanco, Michael Hollick, John Hartzell, Gwyneth Larsen, Joshua Kobak, Tamara Levinson, Rose Mallare, Brooke Miyasaki, Jon Morris, Marlyn Ortiz, Kepani Salgado-Ramos; Swings **Jason Novak, Kira Morris, Andy Pellick, Jeslyn Kelly, Ilia Castro**

U.S. premiere of a theatrical experience piece with music presented without intermission. Originally presented in Buenos Aries, and subsequently in Lisbon, London, and Bogata.

SYNOPSIS The creators of the long running hit *De La Guarda* push the boundaries of theatrical creativity, motivation and innovation in their new work featuring a non-stop collision of dynamic music, visceral emotion, and kinetic aerial imagery. *Fuerza Bruta: Look Up* breaks free from the confines of spoken language and theatrical convention as both performers and audience are immersed in an environment that floods the senses, evoking pure visceral emotion in a place where individual imagination soars.

A scene from Fuerza Bruta: Look Up *(photo courtesy of Fuerzabruta)*

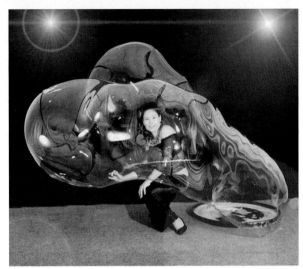

Ana Yang in The Gazillion Bubble Show
(photo by Nino Fernando Campagna)

The Gazillion Bubble Show

New World Stages–Stage 3; Previews: January 17–23, 2007; Opening Night: February 15, 2007; 944 performances as of May 31, 2009

Created and staged by Fan Yang; Produced and Set Design by Fan Yang and Neodus Company, Ltd.; Artistic Director, Jamie Jan; Show Director, Steve Lee; Lighting, Jin Ho Kim; Sound, Joon Lee; Gazilllion Bubbles FX, Special Effects, Alex Cheung; Theatrical Special Effects, CITC/Gary and Stephanie Crawford; Original Music, Workspace Co, Ltd.; Laser Design, Abhilash George; Lumalaser, Tim Ziegenbein; Lighting Effects, David Lau; Special Effects Inventor, Dragan Maricic; Production Stage Manager, Yeung Jin Son; Stage Manager, Min Song; Technical Director, Alan Kho; General Manager, New World Stages; Marketing, HHC Marketing; Marketing Director, Chermaine Cho; Press, Springer Associates, Joe Trentacosta, Gary Springer

Performed by **Ana Yang**

New York premiere of an interactive theatrical event presented without intermission. Fan Yang opened the Las Vegas production on February 2, 2008 and his wife performed the show in New York.

SYNOPSIS The first interactive stage production of its kind, complete with fantastic light effects and lasers, Fan Yang blends art and science to dazzle audiences with his jaw-dropping masterpieces of bubble artistry that defy gravity and logic as we know it. He holds Guinness World records for the biggest bubble ever blown, the largest bubble wall ever created (a staggering 156 feet!), most bubbles within a bubble, and in May 2006, was able to encapsulate 22 people inside a single soap bubble on live television.

I Love You, You're Perfect, Now Change

Westside Theatre – Upstairs; First Preview: July 15, 1996; Opening Night: August 1, 1996; Closed July 27, 2008; 20 previews, 5,003 performances

Music and Arrangements by Jimmy Roberts; lyrics and book, by Joe DiPietro; Produced by James Hammerstein, Bernie Kukoff, Jonathan Pollard; Director, Joel Bishoff; Musical Director, Kim Douglas Steiner; Set & Lighting, Neil Peter Jampolis; Costumes, Pamela Scofield; Original Costumes, Candice Donnelly; Sound, Duncan Edwards; Production Supervisor, Matthew G. Marholin; Stage Manager, William H. Lang; General Management, 321 Theatrical Management: Nancy Nagel Gibbs, Marcia Goldberg, Nina Essman; Associate Producer, Matt Garfield; Company Manager, Eric Cornell; Assistant Director/ASM, Wendy Loomis; Casting, Stuart Howard, Amy Schecter & Paul Hardt; Marketing, SRO Marketing; Press, Jim Randolph; Cast Recording, Varese Sarabande VSD-5771

CAST **Frank Vlastnik, Jonathan Rayson, Christy Faber, Anne Bobby**; Standbys **Will Erat, Karyn Quackenbush**; MUSICIANS **Kim Douglas Steiner** (Piano), **Patti Ditzel** (Violinist)

MUSICAL NUMBERS Cantata for a First Date, Stud and a Babe, Single Man Drought, Why? 'Cause I'm a Guy, Tear Jerk, I Will Be Loved Tonight, Hey There Single Guy/Gal, He Called Me, Wedding Vows, Always a Bridesmaid, Baby Song, Marriage Tango, On the Highway of Love, Waiting Trio, Shouldn't I Be Less in Love with You?, I Can Live with That, I Love You You're Perfect Now Change

A musical revue presented in two acts. For original production credits see *Theatre World* Volume 53, page 116. Originally produced by The American Stage Company (James N. Vagias, Executive Producer). Presented at The Long Wharf Theatre (Arvin Brown, Artistic Dirctor; M. Edgar Rosenblum Executive Director) May 9-June 9, 1996.

SYNOPSIS A musical comedy with everything you ever secretly thought about dating, romance, marriage, lovers, husbands, wives and in-laws, but were afraid to admit. After its amazing nearly twelve year run, the show concluded as the second longest running Off-Broadway musical in history.

Christy Faber, Anne Bobby, Frank Vlastnik and Jonathan Rayson: the closing company of I Love You, You're Perfect, Now Change *(photo by Carol Rosegg)*

Jackie Mason – The Ultimate Jew

New World Stages–Stage 1; Opening Night: March 18, 2008; Closed July 20, 2008; 120 performances

Written and directed by Jackie Mason; Produced by Jyll Rosenfeld, IAG & Allen Spivak/Adam Spivak/Larry Magrid; Set, Brian Webb; Lighting, Paul Miller; Sound, Ryan Powers; General Management, Theatre Production Group LLC; Associate Producers, Mickey Shapiro, Archie Gianunzio; PSM, Steve Sabaugh; Marketing, Keith Hurd; Technical Supervision, production glue, llc; Advertising, Endeavour; Assistant General Manager, Tegan Meyer; Personal Assistant, Melissa Flores; Technical Supervisor, Richard Cocchiara; Electrician, Michael Barczys; Master Electrician, John Paul Nardecchia; Production Sound, Joshua Redfearn; Press, David Gersten & Associates, Kevin P. McAnarney/James Lopez

Performed by **Jackie Mason**

A solo performance comedy show presented without intermission.

SYNOPSIS No election year would be complete without the irascible, irreplaceable and incomparable Jackie Mason, who brings his 8th and final one-man comedy tour de force, *Jackie Mason – The Ultimate Jew*, to New World Stages. Long passionate about politics, Mason is well known for his tough and outspoken position on a variety of issues. An elder statesman of the stand-up comedy world, he combines pungent political satire, insightful observations on the foibles of modern life, and impeccable timing to create material that leaves audiences laughing until they cry show after show.

Jackie Mason (photo courtesy of Bill Milne)

Jump

Union Square Theatre; First Preview: September 25, 2007; Opening Night: October 7, 2007; Closed July 20, 2008; 15 previews, 329 performances

Created by Yeagam Inc.; Produced by Cami Ventures LLC in association with Yegam Inc., Amuse Inc., New York Networks, Inc., and Hobijisu, LLC; Director, Chul-Ki Choi; Composer, Dong-Joon Lee; Choreography, Young-Sub Jin; Set, Tae-young Kim; Costumes, Dolsilnai Inc.; Original Lighting, Sung-Bin Lim; New York Lighting, Benjamin Pearcy; Sound, Soo-Yong Lee; Makeup, Pan Company; Comedy Director, Won-Kil Paek; Consulting Director, Jim Millan; Resident Director, Min-Seob Kim; Assistant Director, Jong-Ho Lee; General Manager, One Viking Productions/Carl Pasbjerg; International Supervision, Kyung-Ah Han; Technical Director, John H. Paull; Marketing, TMG–The Marketing Gourp; Korean Marketing, New York Networks Inc.; Executive Producer, Mark S. Maluso; Executive Producer/CEO, Yegam Inc., Kyung-Hun Kim; Martial Arts Choreography, Gye-Hwan Park; Production Supervisor, Matt Marholin; Music Consultant, Josh Heineman; Wigs and Makeup, Anna Hoffman; Stage Manager, Adam Norris; Associate Technical Director, Ron Nilson; Press, O+M Company, Rick Miramontez, Molly Barnett

CAST Old Man **Woon-Yong Lee** or **Joo-Sun Kim** or **Dong-Kyung Kim**; Grandfather **Cheol-Ho Lim** or **Han-Chang Lim** or **Sun-Gi Jung**; Father **Cheol-Ho Lim** or **Joo-Sun Kim**; Mother **Kyung-Ae Hong** or **Yeon-Jeong Park** or **Mi-Hwa Sung**; Uncle **Han-Chang Lim** or **Young-Jo Choi**; Daughter **Hee-Jeong Hwang** or **Kyung-Ae Hong** or **Yeon-Jeong Gong**; Son-in-Law **Hun-Young Jo** or **Dong-Kyun Kim**; Burglar 1 **Yun-Gab Hong** or **Hun-Young Jo** or **Young-Jo Choi**; Burglar 2 **Seung-Youl Lee** or **Tae-Sung Kim**

American premiere of a theatrical performance piece performed without intermission.

SYNOPSIS *Jump*, the high flying, internationally acclaimed new martial arts theater event, comes to New York following wildly successful engagements all around the world. The nonverbal Korean extravaganza brings the combination of slapstick comedy, acrobatics and martial arts to the stage, for the first time ever in live performance, in a highly unique theater spectacle that has been described as"Jackie Chan meets Charlie Chaplin."

Byung-Eun Yoo, Cheol-Ho Lim, Chang-Young Kim and Young-Jo Choi in Jump *(photo by Carol Rosegg)*

My First Time

New World Stages–Stage 5; First Preview: July 12, 2007; Opening Night: July 28, 2008; 181 performances as of May 31, 2009 (Friday and Saturday evenings)

Written by Ken Davenport and Real People Just Like You; Inspired by the website www.MyFirstTime.com created by Peter Foldy and Craig Stuart; Produced and directed by Ken Davenport; Production Design, Matthew A. Smith; Marketing, HHC Marketing; Casting, Daryl Eisenberg; Associate Producer/Press, David J. Gersten; General Management, DTE, Inc.; PSM, Kathryn Galloway; Associate General Manager, Matt Kovich; Associate to the Producer, Nicole Brodeur; Crew, Allison Hersh; Davenport Theatrical Enterprises: Jamie Lynn Ballard, Amanda Butcher, Matt Kovich; Press, David Gersten

CAST Dana Watkins, Marcel Simoneau[*], Kathy Searle, Cyndee Welburn

*Succeeded by Nathan Williams

World premiere of a new play presented without intermission.

SYNOPSIS *My First Time* is a new play in the style of *The Vagina Monologues*, featuring hysterical and heartbreaking stories about first sexual experiences written by real people, just like you. Four actors bring to life confessional monologues about the silly, sweet, absurd, funny, heterosexual, homosexual, awkward, shy, sexy and everything-in-between stories of first times submitted to the website. *My First Time*: I'll tell you mine if, you tell me yours.

Bill Dawes, Cydnee Welburn, Josh Heine and Kathy Searle in My First Time *(photo by Drew Geraci)*

My Mother's Italian, My Father's Jewish & I'm in Therapy

Westside Theatre – Downstairs; First Preview: November 3, 2006; Opening Night: December 8, 2006; Closed August 24, 2008; 40 previews, 684 performances

Written by Steve Solomon; Produced by Rodger Hess, Abby Koffler, Howard Rapp & Arnold Graham, Leah & Ed Frankel; Director, John Bowab; Sets, Ray Klausen; Lighting, Brian Nason; Sound, Carl Casella; Production Stage Manager, Jamie Rog; Production Management, Aurora Productions; General Manager, Richards/ Climan Inc; Associate Producer, Carol & Andy Caviar; Marketing, Leanne Schanzer Promotions; Press, Keith Sherman & Associates

Performed by **Paul Kreppel**[*]

*Steve Solomon returned from the touring production of the show to the Off-Broadway production from June 24–July 13, then was succeeded by Eddie Mekka on July 15.

New York premiere of a new solo performance play presented without intermission. Originally opened at Little Shubert Theatre starring Mr. Solomon; transferred to the Westside Theatre May 4, 2007.

SYNOPSIS In his biographical show, *Italian + Jewish = Therapy,* Steve Solomon combines comic voices, sound effects and astounding characters to bring alive a myriad of people from all walks of life. Billed as "one part lasagna, one part kreplach and two parts prozac," the show relates to the wacky side of the human condition.

Steve Solomon in My Mother's Italian, My Father's Jewish & I'm in Therapy *(photo courtesy of Charles Rapp Enterprises, Inc.)*

Naked Boys Singing

New World Stages–Stage 4; First Preview: July 2, 1999; Opening Night: July 22, 1999; 2,794 performances as of May 31, 2009 (Weekends only)

Written by Stephen Bates, Marie Cain, Perry Hart, Shelly Markham, Jim Morgan, David Pevsner, Rayme Sciaroni, Mark Savage, Ben Schaechter, Robert Schrock, Trance Thompson, Bruce Vilanch, Mark Winkler; Conceived and directed by Robert Schrock; Produced by Jamie Cesa, Carl D. White, Hugh Hayes, Tom Smedes, Jennifer Dumas; Choreography, Jeffry Denman; Music Director, Jeffrey Biering; Original Musical Director and Arrangements, Stephen Bates; Set/Costumes, Carl D. White; Lighting, Aaron Copp; Production Stage Manager, Heather Weiss/Scott DelaCruz; Assistant Stage Manager, Mike Kirsch/Dave August; Dance Captain, Craig Lowry; Press, David Gersten; Original Press, Peter Cromarty; L.A. Cast recording: Café Pacific Records

CAST Naked Maid **Gregory Stockbridge**; Radio **Eric Dean Davis**; Robert Mitchum **Marc Ginsburg**; Entertainer **Eric Potter**; Bris **Chris Layton**[1]; Porn Star **George Livengood**[2]; Muscle Addiction **Craig Lowry**[3]; Window **Timothy John Mandala**; Swings: **Spencer Gates**[4], **Dave August**; Piano: **Jeffrey Biering**

*Succeeded by: 1. Zachary Clause 2. Christopher deProphetis 3. Trevor Efinger 4. Craig Lowry

MUSICAL NUMBERS Gratuitous Nudity, Naked Maid, The Bliss of a Bris, Window to Window, Fight the Urge, Robert Mitchum, Jack's Song, Members Only, Perky Little Porn Star, Kris Look What You've Missed, Muscle Addiction, Nothin' But the Radio On, The Entertainer, Window to the Soul, Finale/Naked Boys Singing!

A musical revue presented in two acts. For original production credits see *Theatre World* Volume 56, page 114. Originally opened at The Actors' Playhouse; transferred to Theatre Four March 17, 2004; transferred to the John Houseman Theater September 17, 2004; transferred to the 47th Street Theatre November 12, 2004; transferred to the Julia Miles Theatre May 6, 2005; transferred to New World Stages October 14, 2005.

SYNOPSIS The title says it all! Caution and costumes are thrown to the wind in this all-new musical revue featuring an original score and a handful of hunks displaying their special charms as they celebrate the splendors of male nudity in comedy, song and dance.

The Cast of Naked Boys Singing *(photo by Joan Marcus)*

Perfect Crime

Snapple Theatre Center – 4th Floor; Opening Night: April 18, 1987; 9,034 performances as of May 31, 2009

By Warren Manzi; Presented by The Actors Collective in association with the Methuen Company; Director, Jeffrey Hyatt; Set, Jay Stone, Warren Manzi; Costumes, Nancy Bush; Lighting, Jeff Fontaine; Sound, David Lawson; PSM, Kim Moore; Stage Manager, Michael Danek; Press, John Capo–DBS Press

CAST Margaret Thorne Brent **Catherine Russell**; Inspector James Ascher **Richard Shoberg**; W. Harrison Brent **Patrick Ryan Sullivan**[*]; Lionel McAuley **Michael Brian Dunn**; David Breuer **Patrick Robustelli**; Understudies **Andrea Leigh, Don Noble**

*Succeeded by Robert Emmet Lunney (9/29/08)

SETTING Windsor Locks, Connecticut. A mystery presented in two acts. For original production credits see *Theatre World* Volume 43, page 96. Catherine Russell has only missed four performances since the show opened in 1987, and on April 18, 2009, she was inducted into the Guinness Book of Records for not missing a day of work in twenty-two years. The show originally opened at the Courtyard Playhouse (39 Grove Street); transferred to: Second Stage Uptown (now the McGinn-Cazale Theatre) August–October 1987; 47th Street Theatre: October–December 1987; Intar 53 Theater on 42nd Street (now demolished): January–April 1988; Harold Clurman Theatre (now demolished): May 1988–August 1990; 47th Street Theatre: August–December 1990; Theatre Four (now the Julia Miles Theatre): January 1991–September 1993; 47th Street Theatre: September 1993–January 1994; The Duffy Theatre at Broadway and 46th (now demolished): February 1994–May 2006; Snapple Theatre Center–Duffy Theatre: May 22, 2006–present. *Perfect Crime* played its 9,000th performance on May 2, 2009, and the show is the longest running play in the history of New York theatre.

SYNOPSIS Murder mystery about a psychiatrist who is accused of killing her husband by a detective who can't quite pin the murder on her. The complication is that the psychiatrist and the detective are in love.

Richard Shoberg and Catherine Russell in Perfect Crime
(photo by Fran Collin)

The Quantum Eye: Magic Deceptions

Snapple Theatre Center – Duffy Theatre+; Opening Night: February 9, 2007; 148 performances as of May 31, 2009

Created by Sam Eaton; Produced and directed by Samuel Rosenthal; Original Music, Scott O'Brien; Art Design, Fearless Design; Assistant Producer, Janet Oldenbrook; Artwork, Glenn Hidlago; House Manger, Janet Oldenbrook; Wardrobe, Larry the Tailer; Press, Timothy Haskell

Performed by **Sam Eaton**

Programme: A Gulity Conscience, One Card, Fourth Dimension, Two Words, Animal Instinct, Digimancy, Mental Sketch, Transmission, Mnemoncis, Strange News

A mentalist/magic show presented without intermission.

SYNOPSIS The spirit of Harry Houdini, and Victorian era New York are alive and none of your secrets are safe from *The Quantum Eye*.... Eaton takes audiences to the outer limits of human perception. His masterful use of prediction, supernormal mentalism, memorization and calculation will amaze and entertain audiences. It is an extraordinary blend of 21st Century mentalism and Victorian-era mystery. *The Quantum Eye* is proof that there is still magic in the air.

+The show originally opened at the WorkShop Theatre's Jewel Box Theatre and then transferred to Soho Playhouse's Huron Club on June 15, 2007, playing Friday nights. The show transferred to the Duffy Theatre on November 24, 2007 playing on Saturday twilights, and this season transferred to the Bleecker Street Theatre Downstairs on February 14, 2009, performing on Saturday twilights and Tuesday evenings.

Sam Eaton in The Quantum Eye: Magic Deceptions
(photo by Michael Kwiecinski)

Stomp

Orpheum Theatre; First Preview: February 18, 1994; Opening Night: February 27, 1994; 6,432 performances as of May 31, 2009

Created/Directed by Luke Cresswell and Steve McNicholas; Produced by Columbia Artists Management, Harriet Newman Leve, James D. Stern, Morton Wolkowitz, Schuster/Maxwell, Galin/Sandler, and Markley/Manocherian; Lighting, Mr. McNicholas, Neil Tiplady; Casting, Vince Liebhart/Scot Willingham; Executive Producers, Richard Frankel Productions/Marc Routh; Associate Producer, Fred Bracken; General Manager, Richard Frankel Productions/Joe Watson; PSM, Paul Botchis; ASM, Elizabeth Grunewald; Technical Director, Joseph Robinson; Company Manager, Tim Grassel; Assistant Company Manager, Maia Watson; Press, Chris Boneau/Adrian Bryan-Brown, Jackie Green, Joe Perrotta

CAST (rotating) **Camille Armstrong, Alan Asuncion, Jaclynn Bridges, Michelle Dorrance, Sean Edwards, Fritzlyn Hector, Brad Holland, Patrick Lovejoy, Stephanie Marshall, Keith Middleton, Jason Mills, Yako Miyamoto, Raymond Poitier, Joeseph Russomano, Marivaldo Dos Santos, Carlos Thomas, Jeremy Tracy, Dan Weiner, Nicholas V. Young, Elec Simon, Fiona Wilkes**

A percussive performance art piece presented with an intermission. For original production credits see *Theatre World* Volume 50, Page 113.

SYNOPSIS Stomp is a high-energy, percussive symphony, coupled with dance, played entirely on non-traditional instruments, such as garbage can lids, buckets, brooms and sticks.

Yako Miyamoto and Carlos "Peaches" Thomas in Stomp
(photo Steve McNicholas)

Scott Bielecky and Joli Tribuzio in Tony 'n Tina's Wedding
(photo courtesy of Dan Cochran)

Tony 'n' Tina's Wedding

Vinnie Black's Coliseum at Edison Hotel; Opening Night: February 6, 1988; 5,798 performances as of May 31, 2009 (Friday and Saturday evenings only)

Written by Artificial Intelligence; Conceived by Nancy Cassaro; Originally created by Thomas Allen, James Altuner, Mark Campbell, Nancy Cassaro, Patricia Cregan, Elizabeth Dennehy, Chris Fracchiolla, Jack Fris, Kevin Alexander, Mark Nassar, Larry Pellegrini, Susan Varon, Moira Wilson); Produced by Big Apple Entertainment, Raphael Berko, Jeff Gitlin; Director, Larry Pelligrini; Choreography, Hal Simons; Costumes/Hair/Makeup, Juan DeArmas; Stage Manager, Christy Benanti; ASM, Ryan Delorge; Wardrobe and Hair, Rebecca Gaston; Senior Production Coordinator, Drew Seltzer; Production Coordinator, Evan Weinstein; Marketing, Gary Shaffer; Promotions, DeMarcus Reed

CAST Valentina Lynne Vitale Nunzio **Joli Tribuzio**; Anthony Angelo Nunzio Jr. **Craig Thomas Rivela**; Connie Mocogni **Dina Rizzo**i; Barry Wheeler **Gregory Allen Bock**; Donna Marsala **Jessica Aquino**; Dominick Fabrizzi **Anthony Augello**; Marina Gulino **Dawn Luebbe**; Johnny Nunzio **Deno Vourderis**; Josephine Vitale **Anita Salvate**; Joseph Vitale **Rhett Kalman**; Sister Albert Maria **Daniela Genoble**; Anthony Angelo Nunzio, Sr. **John DiBenedetto**; Madeline Monore **Emily Rome Mudd**; Michael Just **Matthew Knowland**; Father Mark **Scott Voloshin**; Vinnie Black **Alan Tulin**[*]; Loretta Black **Cindi Kostello**; Sal Antonucci **Joe Leone**; Donny Dolce **Johnny Tammaro**; Celeste Romano **Sharon Kenny**; Carlo Cannoli **Anthony Ventura**; Rocco Caruso **Ray Grappone**

[*]Succeeded by Anthony Patellis (10/2/08)

SETTING Tony and Tina's wedding and reception. An interactive environmental theatre production. For original production credits see *Theatre World* Volume 44, page 63. Originally played at Washington Square Church and Carmelita's; transferred to St. John's Church (wedding ceremony) and Vinnie Black's Coliseum (reception) until August, 1988; transferred to St. Luke's Church and Vinnie Black's Vegas Room Coliseum in the Edison Hotel. The production closed May 18, 2003, then reopened on October 3, 2003. It closed again May 1, 2004, reopened under new co-producers (Raphael Berko and Jeff Gitlin) on May 15th, 2004.

SYNOPSIS Tony and Tina are getting hitched. Audience members become part of the exuberant Italian family—attending the ceremony, mingling with relatives and friends, eating, drinking and dancing to the band.

SPECIAL EVENTS

Rachel and Juliet

Kaye Playhouse at Hunter College; June 2, 2008; 1 performance

Written by Lynn Redgrave; Presented by the Shakespeare Society (Michael Sexton, Artistic Director)

CAST Lynn Redgrave

SYNOPSIS Lynn Redgrave performs her latest solo show, *Rachel and Juliet*, a tribute to her mother, the actress Rachel Kempson and her lifelong of the role of Juliet in *Romeo and Juliet*. Interweaving remembrance, anecdote, and passages from Shakespeare, Redgrave creates a companion piece to her unforgettable and highly acclaimed *Shakespeare for My Father*, which through Shakespeare's words examined her relationship with her father Michael Redgrave. Redgrave's other works about her acting family include *Mandrake Root* and *Nightingale*.

Broadway Barks 10

Shubert Alley; June 12, 2008

Script by Julie Halston & Richard Hester; Presented by Broadway Cares/Equity Fights AIDS; Produced by Richard Hester, Patty Saccente, Scott T. Stevens; Executive Producers & Hosts, Mary Tyler Moore, Bernadette Peters; Production Managers, Nathan Hurlin, Michael Palm; Stage Managers, Michelle Bosch, Monica Cuoco, Laura Koeneman Kaye, Sid King, Frank Lombardi, Jo McInerney, Ken McGee, Matthew Melchiorre, Kim Russel, Nancy Wernick, Jim Woolley; Sound, Ricco Corrubia; Press, Judy Katz

CAST Sebastian Arcelus, Christine Baranski, Laura Benanti, Kerry Butler, Victoria Clark, Glenn Close, Charlotte d'Amboise, Harvey Fierstein, Boyd Gains, Peter Gallagher, Schuler Hensley, Jackie Hoffman, Cheyenne Jackson, Andy Karl, Lacey Kohl, Nathan Lane, Li Jun Li, Michael Longoria, Mario Lopez, Priscilla Lopez, Heather MacRae, Andrea Martin, Nick Mayo, Judy McLane, Matthew Morrison, Michael Mulheren, Bebe Neuwirth, Orfeh, Faith Prince, Pamela Remler, Loretta Ables Sayre, Jennifer Smith

SYNOPSIS A star-studded dog and cat adopt-a-thon benefiting New York City animal shelters and adoption agencies. The event, produced by Broadway Cares/Equity Fights AIDS and sponsored by the ASPCA and PEDIGREE with additional sponsorship by the New York Times, helps many of New York City's shelter animals find permanent homes by informing New Yorkers about the plight of the thousands of homeless dogs and cats in the metropolitan area.

On Broadway! A Glittering Salute to the American Musical

New York City Center; October 27, 2008; 1 performance

Script by Deborah Grace Winer; Presented by Rolex; Produced and directed by Ann Marie DeAngelo; Host: Angela Lansbury; Honoring: Sono Osato, Brian Heidtke, Tommy Tune; PSM, Lori Rosecrans Wekselblatt; Lighting, Brad Fields; Musical Director, Jim Morgan; Executive Producer, Alexander J. Dubé; 23rd Anniversary Chairs, Anka K. Palitz & Allen Brill; Underwriters, Condé Naste and The Samuel I. Newhouse Foundation;

Mary Tyler Moore at Broadway Barks
(photo courtesy of Broadway Cares/Equity Fights AIDS)

CAST Big Apple Circus, Jane Krakowski, Donald Saddler, Mikhail Baryshnikov, Kelly Bishop, Bebe Neuwirth, Brooke Shields, Cheyenne Jackson, Noah Racey, Karen Ziemba, Ty Stevens, Randy Davis, Alexander Elisa, James T. Lane, Elena Zahlmann, Terence Duncan, Yukiko Kashiki, Carmella Lauer, Melissa Sadler, Rie Ogura, Mitchell Kilby, Derek Lauer, Joey Calveri, Stuart Capps, Leo Ash Evens, Stephanie Fittro, Shiloh Goodin, Ryan Jackson, Logan Keslar, Jamie Markovich, Kiira Schmidt, Matthew Steffens, Ryan Worsing, David Warren Gibson, Pam Sousa, David Baum, Jimmy Ray Bennett, Robert Bianca, Rachel Coloff, Mary Ann Lamb, Pamela Otterson, Adam Perry, Karine Plantadit, T. Oliver Reid, Jon Rua, Chandra Lee Schwartz, Mary MacLeod, Curtis Holbrook, Alex Sanchez, Herman Cornejo, Xiomara Reyes, An Nan, Zhu Zhengzhen, Anthony Bryant, Alexander Elisa, George de la Pena, Meredith Leda, Mark Baird, Randy Skinner, Jeremy Benton, Brandon Bieber, Sara Brians, James Gray, Billy Griffin, Jordan Grubb, Tiffany Howard, AJ Hughes, Angela Kahle, Robin Levine, Joseph Medeiros, Emily Morgan, Alison Paterson, Colin Pritchard, Katie Rooney, John Scacchetti, Erin West, Anna Aimee White, Ryan Worsing

SYNOPSIS A benefit concert presented without intermission. This gala benefited the Career Transition for Dancers, celebrating their 23rd Anniversary, and honored Sono Osato, Brian Heidtke, Tommy Tune for their contributions to the world of dance.

You're a Good Man, Charlie Brown

Gerald W. Lynch Theater; December 15, 2008; 1 performance

Music by Clark Gesner and Andrew Lippa, lyrics and book by Clark Gesner; Presented by Friends in Theater Company; Director, David Lefkowich; Music Director, Jonathan Rose; Producers, Phillip Accosso & Frances Mercanti-Anthony

CAST Linus **Matt Crowle**; Snoopy **Tom Deckman**; Lucy **Carmen Ruby Floyd**; Charlie Brown **Morgan Karr**; Schroeder **David Larsen**; Sally **Kenita R. Miller**

SYNOPSIS A concert version of the musical presented without intermission. The performance was a benefit for the Make-A-Wish Foundation. The Friends in Theater Company is celebrating its 10th Anniversary season. In that time FITC has raised over $75,000 for charities such as the Make-A-Wish Foundation, The American Cancer Society, and The World Trade Center Fund. After production costs 100% of the company's proceeds are donated to charity. Friends in Theater Company's mission is to bring the joy of theater to new audiences while providing hope to those who need it most

Striking 12

Zipper Factory Theatre; December 26–31, 2008; 7 performances

Book, music and lyrics by Brendan Millburn, Valerie Vigoda, and Rachel Sheinkin; Director, Ted Spurling; Cast recording: PS Classics 526

CAST The Man Who's Had Enough **Brendan Milburn**; SAD Light Seller and Others **Valerie Vigoda**; Party Host and others **Gene Lewin**

MUSICAL NUMBERS Snow Song (It's Coming Down), Last Day of the Year, Resolution, The Sales Pitch, Red and Green (And I'm Feeling Blue), Matches for Sale, Say What? Hey La La/Fine Fine Fine, Can't Go Home, Wonderful, Give the Drummer Some, Picture This, Caution to the Wind, It's Not All Right, Wonderful (reprise), Picture This/Snow Song (reprise), Closing

Limited return engagement of a musical performed without intermission. Originally presented by the Prince Music Theater, Philadelphia, and subsequently at The Old Globe, San Diego and Ars Nova in New York; Off-Broadway premiere at the Daryl Roth Theatre November 6–December 31, 2006 (see *Theatre World* Vol. 63, page 149).

SYNOPSIS Combining pop-rock, musical comedy and old-fashioned uplift with a healthy dose of 21st-century skepticism, *Striking 12* is the story of a Grumpy Guy who decides to avoid the hectic, loveless world on New Year's Eve, until he's visited by an incandescent salesgirl with the promise to chase away his winter doldrums. Performed by the members of the indie pop-rock band Groovelily, the show ignites the holiday spirit and connects lush musical textures and soaring vocals to make a new music that's all their own.

Broadway Bears XII

B.B. Kings; February 15, 2009

Hosted by Bryan Batt; Auctioneer: Lorna Kelly; Producer, Scott T. Stevens for Broadway Cares/Equity Fights AIDS; Production Manager, Michael Palm; Music Director, Michael Lavine; Opening Lyrics, Douglas Braverman; Stage Manager, Bess Marie Glorioso; Program/Poster, Carol A. Ingram; Press, Boneau/Bryan-Brown

TALENT Opening Number Singers **Bryan Batt, Christine Pedi, Christopher Sieber**; Bear Models **Catherine Hurlin, Mike McGowan, Jim Newman, Jennifer Smith**

HIGHEST BIDS *Sir Robin* from **Spamalot** ($16,000), created by JoAnna Cayot and signed by Clay Aiken; *Alan Strang and Nugget* [the horse from **Equus**] ($10,000), created by Nicolas Putvinski and signed by Daniel Radcliffe, Lorenzo Pisoni and Richard Griffiths; *Glinda* from **Wicked** ($7,000), created by John Henson and signed by Kristin Chenoweth and Kendra Kassebaum; *Growltigger* from **Cats** ($5,500), created by Therese Stadelmeier-Tresco and signed by Stephen Hanan and Betty Buckley; *Tommy Walker* from **The Who's Tommy** ($4,000), created by Andy Wallach and signed by Michael Cerveris; A set of *The Billys* from **Billy Elliot** ($4,000), including Boxing Billy, Dream Ballet Billy, Electricity Billy, and Finale Billy. This bear was created by Jessica Scoblilck and signed by David Alvarez; Tommy Batchelor; Kiril Kulish and Trent Kowalik; *Ashley* from Starlight Express ($3,800), created by Andy Wallach and signed by Andrea McArdle; *Betty Haynes* from **Irving Berlin's White Christmas** ($3,700), created by Carrie Robbins and signed by Kerry O'Malley, Stephen Bogardus, Jeffry Denman and Meredith Patterson; and, *Shrek* from **Shrek, the Musical** ($3,600) created by Tricorne & Lynne Mackey Studios and signed by Brian d'Arcy James

SYNOPSIS A Grand Auction of Broadway inspired teddy bears. A total of 45 teddy bears, donated by the North American Bear Company and transformed into uniquely costumed, handmade, one-of-a-kind, collectibles, raised $127,400 through online bids, telephone bids, and, of course, live bids. Proceeds went to Broadway Cares/Equity Fights AIDS.

ABC Daytime & SoapNet Salute to Broadway Cares

Town Hall; March 9, 2009; 1 performance

Produced by Michael T. Clarkston; Presented by ABC & SoapNet; Director, John Dietrich; Music Directors, Steven Freeman & Shawn Gough; Lighting, Jim French; Production Managers/Set, Nathan Hurlin; Sound, Sound Associates; Host: Cameron Mathison;

CAST *All My Children:* **Tamara Braun, Bobbie Eakes, Melissa Claire Egan, Ricky Paull Goldin, Susan Lucci, Biranne Moncrief, Eden Riegel, Cornelius Smith Jr,, Chrishell Stause, Aiden Turner, Denise Vasi, Walt Willey, Darnell Williams, Jacob Young**; *One Life to Live:* **Kristen Anderson, Melissa Archer, Camila Banus, BethAnn Bonner, Kathy Brier, John Brotherton, Brandon Buddy, Scott Clifton, Kassie DePaiva, Farah Fath, Crystal Hunt, Brian Kerwin, John-Paul Lavoisier, Mark Lawson, Hillary B. Smith, Jason Tam, Brittany Underwood**; *General Hospital:* **Bradford Anderson, Brandon Barash, Anthony Geary**; Special Guests: **David Alvarez, Trent Kowalik, Kiril Kulish**; Participating Auction Winners: **Valerie Medina, James J. Moran, Shpresa Nela, Lucille Russon**

SYNOPSIS Fifth annual evening of music, dance and sketches from the stars of ABC's daytime dramas. This benefit raised over $325,000 in ticket sales, auction bids, and online fundraising donations benefiting Broadway Cares/Equity Fights AIDS.

The Firebrand of Florence

Alice Tully Hall at Lincoln Center; March 16, 2009; 1 performance

Book by Edward Justus Mayer, lyrics by Ira Gershwin, music by Kurt Weill; Presented by Collegiate Chorale; Director, Roger Rees; Conductor, Ted Sperling; Coordinating Producer, Edward Barnes; Lighting, Frances Aronson; Projections, Michael Clark; PSM, Sanja Kabalin; Chorus, Collegiate Chorale

CAST Narrator **Roger Rees**; Hangman **Roosevelt Credit**; The Duchess **Victoria Clark**; Benvenuto Cellini **Nathan Gunn**; Angela **Anna Christy**; Duke of Florence **Terrence Mann**; Emilia **Kristy Swann**; Ottaviano di Medici **Patrick Goss**; Maffio/Ascanio/Pierre **David Pittu**; Ensemble **James Gamble, Andrew Flores, Wendy Baker, Heather Hill, Christine Sperry, Sarah Bleasdale, Lara Stevens, James Fredericks, Douglas Purcell, Tim Krol, Lawrence Long**

MUSICAL NUMBERS When the Bell of Doom is Clanging; Come to Florence; Life, Love, and Laughter; Our Master is Free Again; I Had Just Been Pardoned; You're Far Too Near Me; Alessandro the Wise; Sing Me Not a Ballad; When the Duchess is Away; The Nosy Cook; The Duchess's Letter; The Little Naked Boy; March of the Soldiers of the Duchy (Just in Case); A Rhyme for Angela; Hear Ye!; The World is Full of Villains; You Have to Do What You Do Do; How Wonderfully Fortunate!; Love Is My Enemy; Come to Paris

SYNOPSIS Concert version of an operetta presented in two acts. Written in 1945, the seldom produced *The Firebrand of Florence* revolves around Florentine artist Benvenuto Cellini whose death by hanging sentence is pardoned by the Duke so that he can complete a previously commissioned sculpture.

Legends!

Town Hall; March 23, 2009; 1 performance

Written by James Kirkwood, adapted by John Epperson; Produced by Robert McNamara & Michael C. Cohen for Friends In Deed; Director, Mark Waldrop; Set, Ray Klausen; Lighting/Sound/Stage Manager, Matt Berman; Costumes, Fabio Toblini; Choreography, Josh Rhodes; Costume Manufacturing, Eric Winterling, Eroco Costumes Inc, Studio Rogue, Tricorne Inc.; Hair, Katherine Carr & Gerrard Kelly; Makeup, Louis Braoun; Production Coordinators, Julia Johns & Thomas Recktenwald; ASM, Darrin Maurer; Press, The Publicity Office;

CAST Sylvia Glenn **Charles Busch**; Aretha **Whoopi Goldberg**; Leatrice Monsee **John Epperson (Lypsinka)**; Martin Klemmer **Bryan Batt**

SYNOPSIS A staged reading of Kirkwood's legendary play presented in two acts. A hilarious comedy about two glamorous, Hollywood has-beens and arch-rivals forced to consider working together on a new project to resuscitate their careers, *LEGENDS!* is one of the most notorious theatrical properties ever written – notably for what happened behind-the-scenes. This reading was a benefit for Friends In Deed, the crisis center for life-threatening illness.

Broadway for a New America

Peter Norton Symphony Space; April 13, 2009

Written & directed by Sarah Louise Lazarus; Presented by the Jewish Alliance for Change (Doni Remba, Executive Director); Produced by Kati Meister and Scott Denny; Music Director, Lawrence Yurman; Associate Producer, Jeremy Quinn; Production Manager, Mary K. Botosan; PSM, Kimothy Cruse; Lighting, Cory Pattak; Sound, David Schnirman; ASM, Alden Fulcomer & Michael Mele; Video, Andrew Stein; Assistant to the Director, Ben Bartolone; Stage Hands, Michael Lachance, Justin Roller; Volunteers, Sandy Cheitin, Oliver Garfunkel, Jordan

Gilbert, Jenny Paul, Dan Rousseau, Sami Saltzman, Amanda Stuart; Announcer, Robert Kalman; Press, Pete Sanders

CAST Host **Jim Dale**; Performers **Richard Belzer, Scott Blakeman, John Bucchino, Mike Burstyn, Melissa Errico, Tovah Feldshuh, Darrian Ford, Cheryl Freeman, Malcolm Gets, Peter Jöback, Shauna Hicks, Robert Klein, Linda Lavin, Nellie McKay, Ann Meara, Karla Mosley, Phyllis Newman, Christine Pedi, Alice Playten, Krysta Rodriguez, Seth Rudetsky, Jeremy Schonfeld, Lucas Steele, Billy Stritch, Noah Weisberg**; The Accidentals: **Emily Bindiger, Dennis Deal, Margaret Dorin, Bill Mitchell, Catherine Russell, Rosie Vallese, Jim Vincent**; The Broadway Boys: **Landon Beard, Danny Calvert, Jesse Nager, Michael James Scott, Lucas Steele, Marty Thomas**; The Broadway Tenors: **Matt Farnsworth, Brian Lane Green, Kevin Spiritas**; Featuring: T**he Circle Squared Chorus** and **The New York City Gay Men's Chorus**; Speakers **Wayne Besen (**Truth Wins Out**), Steven Goldstein** (Garden State Equality), **Gary Maffei** (Marriage Equality New York)**, Evan Wolfson** (Freedom to Marry), Cantor **David Berger** (Congregation Beth Simchat), Rabbi **J. Rolando Matalon** (Congregation B'nai Jeshurun)

MUSICIANS Larry Yurman (piano), Alex Rybeck (piano), Dick Sarpola (bass), Tim McLafferty (drums)

SYNOPSIS A benefit for marriage equality and a progressive agenda for change presented in two acts. The benefit and silent auction raised funds for the Jewish Alliance for Change to continue its work to promote the progressive agenda of the Obama administration and to raise awareness and support of gay marriage.

24 Hour Musicals

Grammercy Theatre; April 13, 2009; 1 performance

Presented by The Exchange; Included: *Multiphobia* Book and lyrics by Brian Crawley, music and lyrics by Gabriel Kahane; Director, Ted Sperling; *Rachel Said Sorry* Book by Gina Gionfriddo, music and lyrics by Lance Horne; Director, Maria Mileaf; *Dr. Williams* Book by Rinne Groff, music and lyrics by Justin Paul and Benj Pasek; Director, Trip Cullman; *Islands* Book by Jonathan Marc Sherman, music and lyrics by Robin Goldwasser and Julia Greenberg; Director, Sam Gold

CAST Richard Kind, Cady Huffman, Mandy Gonzalez, Nellie McKay, Dr, Joy Browne, Marnie Schulenburg, Capathia Jenkins, Scarlett Strallen, Gabriel Kahane, Robin Goldwasser, Tripp Cullman, Julia Greenberg, Benj Pasek, Justin Paul, Idina Menzel, Bebe Neuwirth, Cheyenne Jackson, Alicia Witt, Rachel Dratch, Mo Rocca, Tracie Thoms, Jonathan Marc Sherman, Ted Sperling, Jesse Tyler Ferguson, Tamara Tunie

SYNOPSIS The second annual *24 Hour Musicals* is a celebrity charity challenge where stars from theatre, film, TV and rock unite to create four brand new musicals in one day. The evening, presented by Exchange, benefits the Orchard Project.

Broadway Beauty Pageant

Symphony Space; April 20, 2009

Written and conceived by Jeffery Self; Produced by the Ali Forney Center; Director, Ryan J. Davis; Musical Director, Sonny Paladino; Producers, Ryan J. Davis, Jeffrey Self and Wil Fisher in association with Tim Hur; Host: Tovah Feldshuh; Judges: Ana Gasteyer, Beth Leavel, Charles Busch, Seth Rudetsky; Performances: Past pageant winners Marty Thomas (2008) & Frankie James Grande (2007); Special Guest: Miss New York Leigh-Taylor Smith; Press, O+M Company, Jaron Caldwell

CONTESTANTS James Brown III (Mr. *Little Mermaid*), Adam Fleming (Mr. *Wicked*), Anthony Hollock (Mr. *Hair*), Tony James (Mr. *Lion King*), David Larsen (Mr. *Billy Elliot*); Winner: **Anthony Hollock**

SYNOPSIS The Broadway Beauty Pageant, formerly titled Mr. Broadway, features male cast members representing their respective Broadway shows, competing for the title crown through talent, interview and swimsuit competitions. The contestants will go head to head in front of a panel of celebrity judges, but ultimately, the final vote is in the audience's hands. A benefit for the Ali Forney Center, the nation's largest and most comprehensive organization dedicated to LGBT youth.

David Larsen, Adam Fleming, Marty Thomas, 2009 Winner Anthony Hollock and current Miss NY Leigh-Taylor Smith at the Broadway Beauty Pageant *(photo by Peter James Zielinski)*

The Spy

Baruch College Performing Arts Center–Rose Nagelberg Theatre;; May 1–2, 2009; 2 performances

Written by Jeffrey Hatcher, based on the novel by James Fenimore Cooper; Presented by The Acting Company (Margot Harley, Producing Artistic Director); Director, Ian Belknap; Sets, Neil Patel; Costumes, Mathew J. LeFebvre; Lighting, Michael Chybowski; Music/Sound. Fitz Patton, Aaron Meicht; Fight Direction, J. David Brimmer; Hair/Wig/Makeup, Erin Kennedy Lunsford; Dialect Coach, Deborah Hecht; Dramaturg, Jo Holcomb; Casting, McCrkle Casting.; Production Manager, Joel Howell; PSM, Karen Parlato; ASM, Nick Tochelli

CAST Mr. Harper **Freddy Arsenault**; Sarah Evans **Carie Kawa**; Frances Wharton **Kelley Curran**; Mr. Wharton/Colonel Wellmer **Rick Ford**; Caesar Thompson **Willaim Sturdivant**; Harvey Birch **Robert Michael McClure**; Lieutenant Geoffrey Wharton **Sonny Valicenti**; Major Peyton Dunwoodie **Matthew Amendt**; Captian John Lawson **Andy Grotelueschen**; Corporal Singleton **Samuel Taylor**; Betty Flanagen/Katie Haynes **Georgia Cohen**; Skinner #1/Military Judge **Chris Thorn**; Captain's Man **Nick Tochelli**

UNDERSTUDIES Freddy Arsenault (Lt. Geoffrey Wharton), Matthew Amendt (Captain Lawson), Chris Thorn (Harvey Birch/Mr. Harper), Samuel Taylor (Major Dunwodie/Skinner #1/Military Judge), Ian Belknap (Caser Thompson/Corporal Singleton/Mr. Wharton/Colonel Wellmere), Kelley Curran (Katie Haynes), Carie kawa (Betty Flannagan), Georgia Cohen (Frances Wharton, Sarah Evans)

SETTING The American Revolutionary War (1778). Westchester County, New York. A new play presented in two acts.

SYNOPSIS Based on *The Spy*, the first espionage novel, we find ourselves in a territory that is ruled neither by the British army nor its Colonial rebels. Washington's army is in a fight to the death with the King's redcoats to determine who will control the wilderness north of the New York City. In this subtle and ambiguous wilderness, spies and counterspies play out their roles to achieve political goals and personal honor. No one in *The Spy*—man or woman—is who he or she appears to be. Lies are sometimes told by the best of them. And the truth—even a truth that could save a life or reputation—may never be known.

Leading Men IV

Birdland; May 11, 2009; 1 performance

Produced by Wayman Wong; Director, Alan Muraoka; Music Director, Seth Rudetsky; Host, John Tartaglia

CAST **Nick Adams, Tom Andersen, James Barbour, Jim Caruso, Michael Kadin Craig, Jack Donahue, Kevin Earley, Cody Green, Jonathan Groff, Norm Lewis, Graham Phillips, Tom Postilio, Zak Resnick, Nicholas Rodriguez, Tony Yazbeck**

SYNOPSIS Fourth annual benefit concert featuring Broadway's leading men. Presented as a benefit for Broadway Cares/Equity Fights AIDS

Top: *Michael Tucker, Josh Grisetti and Jill Eikenberry in the York Theatre Company production of* Enter Laughing The Musical. *Opened at the Theatre at St. Peter's Church September 10, 2008; Return Engagement Opened January 29, 2009 (photo by Carol Rosegg)*

Middle: *The Company of The Public Theater production of* Hair. *Opened at the Delacorte Theater in Central Park August 7, 2008 (photo by Michal Daniel)*

Bottom: *Saidah Arrika Ekulona and Condola Rashad in the Manhattan Theatre Club production of* Ruined. *Opened at City Center Stage I March 25, 2009 (photo by Joan Marcus)*

Abingdon Theatre Company

Sixteenth Season

Artistic Director, Jan Buttram; Managing Director, Samuel Bellinger; General Manager, Danny Martin; Associate Artistic Director/Literary Manager, Kim T. Sharp; Marketing, Doug DeVita; Development Associate, Sarah Rulfs; Play Development Advisor, Pamela Paul; Casting, William Schill; Facilities Manager, John Trevellini; Resident Production Manager, Ian Gurnes; Resident Dramaturg, Julie Hegner; Playwright Group Coordinator, Frank Tangredi; Production Manager, Ian Grunes; Press, Shirley Herz Associates; Cabaret Producer, David Flora; Playwright Group Coordinator, Frank Tangredi; Playwright Outreach Coordinator, Bara Swain

The English Channel by Robert Brustein; Director, Daniela Varon; Sets & Lighting, Mike Billings; Costumes, Laura Crow; Original Music & Sound, Scott Killian; PSM, Rebecca L. Hurlbert; Fight Choreography, Stafford Clark-Price; Cast: Sean Dugan (Christopher Marlowe), Stafford Clark-Price (William Shakespeare), Brian Robert Burns (Henry Wriothesley), Lori Gardner (Emilia Lanier)

Setting: The Mermaid Tavern in London; 1593. New York premiere of a new play presented without intermission; Dorothy Strelsin Theatre; September 14–October 5, 2008 (Opened September 21); 7 previews, 15 performances.

Beachwood Drive by Steven Leigh Morris; Director, Alan Mandell; Sets, Ken Larson; Costumes, Deborah J. Caney; Lighting, Matthew McCarthy; Sound, David Margolin; Video, Kymberly Mortenson; PSM, Genevieve Ortiz; Cast: Peter Brouwer (William Cromwell), David Medina (Rocky), Kat Powers (Katerina), Maria Silverman (Vera), Lena Starostina (Nadya), Brenda Thomas (Hansonia)

Setting: Los Angeles; the present. World premiere of a new play presented in two acts; June Havoc Theatre; October 17–November 16, 2008 (Opened October 29); 12 previews, 20 performances.

Freudian Slips by Marvin Lifschitz; Director, Tom Bloom; Sets, Lara Fabian; Costumes, Neville Bean & Nancy Nichols; Lighting, Travis McHale; Original Music & Sound, Margaret Pine; Dance Choreography, Warren Kelley; Fight Choreography, Joel Leffert; Production Manager, Aneta Feld; PSM, Laurie Rae Waugh; Cast: Sue Brady (Ensemble), Joel Leffert (Sigmund Freud), Warren Kelly (Thomas Buxton), Jason Marr (Sidney Layman), Allen Lewis Rickman (Otto Brotto), Margi Sharp (Madeline Shumsky), David Smilow (Hyman Shumsky)

Setting: London and Vienna; 1912. World premiere of a new play presented in two acts; Dorothy Strelsin Theatre; January 24–February 15, 2009 (Opened February 1); 8 previews, 15 performances.

Greek Holiday by Mayo Simon; Director, Stephen Hollis; Sets, Richard Turick; Costumes, Bettina P. Bierly; Lighting, Richard Currie; Original Music & Sound, Scott Killian; Fight Choreography, Rick Sordelet; PSM, Genevieve Ortiz; Cast: Sarah Knapp (Debra), Kathleen McElfresh (Janet), Tommy Schrider (Alex)

Setting: A Greek Isle; the present. New York premiere of a play presented in two acts; June Havoc Theatre; March 8–March 29, 2009 (Opened March 18); 12 previews, 13 performances.

Love Drunk by Romulus Linney; Director, Kelly Morgan; Sets, Jeff Pajer; Costumes, Deborah Caney; Lighting, Travis McHale; Sound, Kevin Lloyd; PSM, Caitlin Ferreria & Mark Wallace; Cast: Austin Pendleton (Wilbur Johnson), Kristina Valada-Viars (Karen Bannerman)

Setting: Wilbur's cabin in the Appalachians; the present. World premiere of a new play presented without intermission; Dorothy Strelsin Theatre; March 28–April 19, 2009 (Opened April 6); 8 previews, 15 performances.

Austin Pendleton and Kristina Valada-Viars in Love Drunk

Center: *Jason Marr, Margi Sharp and Joel Leffert in* Freudian Slips

Bottom: *Sean Dugan and Stafford Clark-Price in T*he English Channel *(photos by Kim T. Sharp)*

The Actors Company Theatre (TACT)

Sixteenth Season*

Co-Artistic Directors, Scott Alan Evans, Cynthia Harris, and Simon Jones; General Manager, Cathy Bencivenga; Consulting Development Manager, Erin Carney; Casting, Stephanie Klapper; Associate Producer, Jenn Thompson; Technical Director, Patrick Cecala; Master Electrician, John Anselmo; Wardrobe Supervisor, Sara McLoud; Press, Springer Associates, Joe Trentacosta (2008)/O+M Co., Richard Hilman (2009)

Bedroom Farce by Alan Ayckbourn; Director, Jenn Thompson; Set, Robin Vest; Costumes, Matha Hally; Lighting, Aaron Copp; Sound, Stephen Kunken; Props, Jennifer Blazek; Music, Amir Khosrowpour; PSM, Mel McCue; Fight Director, Ax Norman; ASM, E. Sara Barnes; Dialect Coach, Amelia White; Cast: Larry Keith (Ernest), Cynthia Harris (Delia), Scott Schaffer (Nick), Margaret Nichols (Jan), Sean Dougherty (Malcolm), Ashley West (Kate), Mark Alhadeff (Trevor), Susannah (Eve Bianco)

Setting: Suburban England, just a few years ago; Act 1: Three bedrooms, Saturday evening, 7 p.m.; Act 2: The same, a few moments later. Revival of a play presented in two acts; Beckett Theatre on Theatre Row; October 5–November 5, 2008 (Opened October 13); 8 previews, 27 performances. Originally produced on Broadway at the Brooks Atkinson Theatre March 29–November 24, 1979 (see *Theatre World* Vol. 35, page 37.)

Incident at Vichy by Arthur Miller; Director, Scott Alan Evans; Set, Scott Bradley; Costumes, David Toser; Lighting, Mary Louise Geiger; Sound, Jill BC DuBoff; Props, Nicole Gaignat; Music, Joseph Trapanese; PSM, Meredith Dixon; ASM, Christine Massoud; Assistant to the Director, Sarah Jadin; Dialect Coach, Markus Hirnigel; Cast: Mark Alhadeff (Lebeau), Ron McClary (Bayard), James Prendergast (Marchand), Michael Oberholtzer (Guard), Gregory Salata (Monceau), Leif Huckman (Gypsy), Richard Ferrone (Waiter), Russell Kahn (Boy), Jack Koenig* (Major), Dan Stowell (Detective), John Freimann (Old Jew), Christopher Burns (Leduc), Jamie Bennett (Police Captain), Todd Gearhart (Von Berg), Jeffrey C. Hawkins (Professor Hoffman), Dan Stowell (Ferrand); *Succeeded by: David Bishins

Setting: Vichy, France, 1942. A place of detention. Revival of a play presented without intermission; Beckett Theatre on Theatre Row; March 8–April 11, 2009 (Opened March 16); 8 previews, 27 performances. Orginally produced on Broadway at ATNA Washington Square Theatre December 3, 1964–May 7, 1965 (see *Theatre World* Vol. 21, page 128.)

SALON SERIES – STAGED READINGS AT TACT STUDIO

The Confidential Clerk by T.S. Eliot; Director, Drew Barr; PSM, E. Sara Barnes; Composer, Sung J. Hong; Cast: Nora Chester (Mrs. Guzzard), Delphi Harrington (Lady Elizabeth Mulhammer), James Murtaugh (Sir Claude Mulhammer), James Prendergast (Eggerson), Richard Thieriot (Colby Simpkins), Amy Lee Williams (Lucasta Angel), Jeffrey Hawkins (B. Hkagan); November 15–17, 2008

The Late George Apley by John Marquand & George S. Kaufman; Director, Christopher Hart; PSM, Christine Massoud; Composer, Amir Khosrowpour; Cast: Jamie Bennet (Howard Boulder), Nora Chester (Amelia Newcombe), Francesca Di Mauro (Lydia Leyton/Emily Southworth/Margaret), Richard Ferrone (Horatio Willing), Kelly Hutchinson (Eleanor Apley), Larry Keith (George Apley), Darrie Lawarence (Catherine Apley), James Prendergast (Wilson/Henry), Gregory Salata (Julian H. Dole), Sarah Jadin (Agnes Willing), Terry Layman (Roger Newcombe), Sherry Skinker (Jane Willing), Richard Thieriot (John Apley); December 13–15, 2008

Ladies in Retirement by Edward Percy & Reginald Denham; Director, Jenn Thompson; PSM, Kristen Vaphides; Music, Amir Khosrowpour; Cast: Mary Bacon (Lucy Gilham), Cynthia Harris (Leonora Fiske), Cynthia Darlow (Ellen Creed), Mark Alhadeff (Albert Feather), Francesca Di Mauro (Louisa Creed), Darrie

Cynthia Harris, Eve Bianco and Larry Keith in Bedroom Farce *(photos by Stephen Kunken)*

Lawrence (Emily Creed), Joan Shepard (Sister Theresa); January 10–12, 2009

Edward, My Son by Robert Morely & Noel Langley; Director, Harris Yulin; Composer, Wally Gunn; PSM, E. Sara Barnes; Cast: Larry Keith (Arnold Hold), Maia Danziger (Evelyn Holt), John Plumpis (Harry Soames), James Prendergast (Hanray), Lynn Wright, (Eileen Perry), Christopher Burns (Dr. Larry Parker), David Bishins (Mr. Waxman/Sumers), Mark Alhadeff (Cunningham/Mr. Prothero), Sarah Jadin (Phyliss Maxwell), Margot White (Betty Fowler); April 18–20, 2009

The Tavern by George M. Cohan; Director, Gregory Salata; PSM, E. Sara Barnes; Music, Amir Khosrowpour; Cast: Matt Fraley (Zach), Terry Layman (Freeman), Jamie Bennett (Willum), Mark Alhadeff (Vagabond), James Prendergast (Lamson, the Governor), Steve French (The Sheriff), Richard Ferrone (Ezra/Stevens), Emily Hagburg (Sally), Margaret Nichols (Violet), Nora Chester (Mrs. Lamson), Margot White (Virginia); May 16–18, 2009

"SWEET SIXTEEN" GALA

Honoring Angela Lansbury; Director, Scott Alan Evans; Music Director, Larry Goldberg; Master of Ceremonies, Simon Jones; Company Member Performers: Mary Bacon, Cynthia Darlow, Todd Gearhart, Larry Keith, Jack Koenig, Ron McClary, John Plumpis, Jenn Thompson; Guest Performers: Annaleigh Ashford, Catherine Brunell, Mara Davi, Aaron Lazar, Meredith Patterson, Ken Page, Faith Prince; Hudson Theatre; May 11, 2009

*This year marked the premiere season TACT performed under an Off-Broadway contract

(Left bench) Christopher Burns, Russell Kahn, Gregory Salata, Mark Alhadeff, Ron McClary, Richard Ferrone, (foreground) Dan Stowell, (rear bench) James Prendergast, Jeffrey C. Hawkins, Jamie Bennett and Jack Koenig in Incident at Vichy

Atlantic Theater Company

Twenty-third Season

Artistic Director, Neil Pepe; Executive Director, Andrew D. Hamingson/Jeffory Lawson; School Executive Director, Mary McCann; General Manager, Jamie Tyrol; Associate Artistic Director, Christian Parker; Development, Roni Ferretti; Development Associates, Catherine Williams, Jeremy Blocker, Cameron Shreve; Production Managers, Michael Wade & Gabriel Evansohn; Marketing, Jodi Sheeler (interim: Khalilah Ellott); Business Manager, Mara Ditchfield; Business Associate/Audience Services, Sara Montgomery; Operations, Ian Crawford; School Associate Directors, Steven Hawley & Kate Blumberg; Education, Frances Tarr; School Artistic Director, Geoff Berman; Casting, Telsey + Company; Press, Boneau/Bryan-Brown, Joe Perrotta, Kelly Guiod

What's That Smell: The Music of Jacob Sterling Book, lyrics, and co-direction by David Pittu, music, arrangements, and musical direction by Randy Redd; Co-Director, Neil Pepe; Sets, Takeshi Kata; Costumes, Martin Pakledinaz; Lighting, Matthew Richards; Sound, Jill BC DuBoff; Projections, Dustin O'Neill; PSM, Alison DeSantis; Company Manager, Juan Carlos Salinas; ASM, Lauren Kurinskas; Cast: Peter Bartlett (Leonard), David Pittu (Jacob), Brandon Goodman (Chorus), Matt Schock (Chorus), Heléne Yorke (Chorus)

World premiere of a new musical presented without intermission; Atlantic Stage 2; September 2–28, 2008 (Opened September 10); 13 previews, 23 performances. This production had a commercial transfer to New World Stages following its run at the Atlantic Theater Company (see page Off-Broadway Openings in this volume).

Farragut North by Beau Willimon; Produced by special arrangement with Stephen Pevner, Inc.; Director, Doug Hughes; Sets, David Korins; Costumes, Catherine Zuber; Lighting, Paul Gallo; Sound, Walter Trarbach & David Van Tieghem; Original Music, David Van Tieghem; Projection Art, Joshua White; PSM, Barclay Stiff; ASM, Brandon Kahn; Company Manager, Aaron Thompson; Assistant Director, David Ruttura; Associate Lighting, Paul Toben; Cast: John Gallagher Jr. (Stephen), Kate Blumberg (Ida), Chris Noth (Paul), Dan Bittner (Ben), Olivia Thirlby (Molly), Isiah Whitlock Jr (Tom), Otto Sanchez (Waiter/Frank)

Time/Place: Des Moines, Iowa; winter. World premiere of a new play presented in two acts; Linda Gross Theater; October 22–November 29, 2008 (Opened November 12); 24 previews, 23 performances.

Dan Bittner, John Gallagher Jr., Chris Noth and Kate Blumberg in Farragut North *(photo by Jacqueline Mia Foster)*

Peter Bartlett and David Pittu in What's That Smell? The Music of Jacob Sterling *(photo by Doug Hamilton)*

C.J. Wilson, Aya Cash, Daniel Ables and Joey Slotnick in "Peer Review," one of the three one-act plays in Offices *(photo by Doug Hamilton)*

The Cripple of Inishmaan by Martin McDonagh; Co-produced by Druid Theatre Company (Garry Hynes, Artistic Director; Tim Smith, General Manager); Director, Gary Hynes; Sets & Costumes, Francis O'Connor; Lighting, Davy Cunningham; Sound, John Leonard; Original Music, Colin Towns; U.S. Casting, Laura Stancyzk; Irish Casting, Maureen Hughes; Fight Director, J. David Brimmer; PSM, Freda Farrell; Company Manager, Aaron Thompson; ASM, Rebecca Spinac; Cast: Dearbhla Molloy (Eileen), Marie Mullen (Kate), David Pearse (JohnnyPateenMike), Aaron Monaghan (Billy), Laurence Kinlan (Bartley), Kerry Condon (Helen), Andrew Connolly (BabbyBobby), Patricia O'Connell (Mammy), John C. Vennema (Doctor); Understudies: Timothy Deenihan (JohnnyPateenMike, BabbyBobby, Doctor), Beth Dixon (Elieen, Kate, Mammy), Johnny Hopkins (Billy), Emily Landham (Helen)

Setting: 1934. The island of Inishmaan off the coast of Ireland. Revival of a play presented in two acts; Linda Gross Theater; December 9, 2008–March 15, 2009 (Opened December 21); 11 previews, 100 performances. World premiere at London's National Theatre (March 1997); New York premiere at The Public Theater March 17–May 1, 1998 (see *Theatre World* Vol. 54, page 96).

Offices by Ethan Cohen; Director, Neil Pepe; Sets, Riccardo Hernandez; Costumes, Laura Bauer; Lighting, David Weiner; Original Music & Sound, Obadiah Eaves; PSM, Alison DeSantis; ASM, Kyle Gates; Company Manager, Aaron Thompson; Wigs, Charles LaPointe; Fight Consultant, J. David Brimmer; Cast: *Peer Review*: Daniel Abeles (Mark), F. Murray Abraham (Cassady), Aya Cash (Laura), Joey Slotnick (Elliot), C. J. Wilson (Carl); *Homeland Security*: Daniel Abeles (Louie), Brennan Brown (Investigator), Aya Cash (Emma/Secretary), John Bedford Lloyd (Munro), Mary McCann (Judy), Greg Stuhr (Brad), C. J. Wilson (Wilten), Daniel Yelsky (Bobby); *Struggle Session*: F. Murray Abraham (Bum), John Bedford Lloyd (Lury), Daniel London (Beck), Greg Stuhr (Schilling), Joey Slotnick (Collegue #1), Brennan Brown (Collegue #2), C. J. Wilson (Colleague #3)

World premiere of a three one-act comedies presented without intermission; Linda Gross Theater; April 15–June 7, 2009 (Opened May 7); 25 previews, 38 performances.

Make Me by Leslie Ayvazian; Director, Christian Parker; Set, Anna Louizos; Costumes, Theresa Squire; Lighting, Josh Bradford; Music & Sound, Jill BC DuBoff; PSM, Robyn Henry; Casting, MelCap Casting; Fight Director, J. David Brimmer; ASM, Aaron Heflich Shapiro; Company Manager, Aaron Thompson; Cast: Anthony Arkin (Eddie), Candy Buckley (Mistress Lorraine), Jessica Hecht (Connie), J.R. Horne (Hank), Richard Masur (Phil), Ellen Parker (Sissy)

Jessica Hecht, Anthony Arkin and Candy Buckley (background) *in* Make Me *(photo by Doug Hamilton)*

World premiere of a new play presented without intermission; Atlantic Stage 2; May 20–June 14, 2009 (Opened May 31); 13 previews, 15 performances.

Aaron Monaghan and Kerry Condon in The Cripple of Inishmaan *(photo by Keith Pattison)*

Brooklyn Academy of Music

Founded in 1861

Alan H. Fishman, Chairman of the Board; Karen Brooks Hopkins, President; William I. Campbell, Vice Chairman of the Board; Joseph V. Melillo, Executive Producer

2008 NEXT WAVE FESTIVAL—26TH ANNUAL—THEATRE EVENTS

Sunken Red Adapted by Corien Baart, Guy Cassiers & Dirk Dirk Roofthooft from the novel by Jeroen Brouwers; Presented by Toneelhuis (Belgium) & ro theater (Rotterdam, Netherlands); Director, Guy Cassiers; Set/Video/Lighting, Peter Missotten; Sound, Diederik De Cock; Costumes, Katelijne Damen; Dramaturgy, Corien Baart & Erwin Jans; American Stage Manager, R. Michael Blanco; Cast: Dirk Roofthooft (Jeroen Brouwers)

U.S. premiere of a new multimedia play presented in without intermission; Harvey Theatre; October 7–11, 2006; 4 performances.

Woyzeck by Georg Büchner; Presented by Vesturport and The Reykjavik City Theatre; Director/Adaptor/Translation, Gísli Örn Gardarsson; English Translation, Ruth Little & Jón Atli Jónasson; Music, Nick Cave & Warren Ellis; Lyrics, Nick Cave; Design, Börkur Jónsson; Lighting, Lárus Björnsson; Costumes, Filippíá Elisdóttir; Sound, Olafur Örn Thoroddsen; Choir Arrangements, Pétur Pór Benediktsson; Voice/Text Coach, Ellen Newman; Stage Manager, Kristinn Karlsson; Movement, John-Paul Zaccarini; Producer, Rakel Gardarsdóttir; American Stage Manager, R. Michael Blanco; Co-Producers, the Young Vic, Bite:05, and Amsterdam het Muziek Theatre; Cast: Ingvar E. Sigurdsson (Woyzeck), Nína Dögg Filippusdóttir (Marie), Víkingur Kristjánsson (Captain), Harpa Arnardóttir (Doctor), Björn Hlynur Haraldsson (Drum Major), Ólafur Egill Egilsson (Andres), Árni Pétur Gudjónsson (Fiddler), Erlendur Eiríksson (Sergeant), Ólafur Darri Ólafsson (Entertainer), Jóhannes Níels Sigurdsson (The Swan/Doctor's Assistant); Choir: Atli Rafn Sigurdarson, Bjarni Bjarnason, Haraldur Björn Halldórsson, Ívar Örn Árnason, Karl Sigurdsson, Kristján Dereksson, Rúnar Freyr Gíslason, Sigurjón Brink

U.S. premiere of a new translation of the classic play presented without intermission; Howard Gilman Opera House; October 15–18, 2008; 3 performances.

Ingvar E. Sigurdsson in Woyzeck *(photo by Eddi)*

Meeting with Bodhisattva Presented by U Theatre (Taiwan); Director, Liu Ruo-Yu; Music Director, Huang Chih-Chun; Set & Lighting, Lin Keh-Hua; Costumes, Tim Yip; Stage Manager, Huang Nuo-Hsing; Technical Director, Su Chun-Hsueh; Company Manager, Yu Fei-Ling; Tour Manager, Lin Pei-Chun; Project Manager, June Huang Projects; Cast: Huang Chih-Chun, Huang Chih-Lin, Huang Kun-Ming, Chang Ya-Lun, Su Yin-Tsu, Huang Kuo-Chung, Yang Chin-Hsiung, Liu Shu-Chih, Liu Ping-Tsen, Ou Kui-Lan, Chang Ching-Yu

U.S. premiere of a martial arts, drumming, operatic dance and Buddhist chanting theatrical piece presented without intermission; Howard Gilman Opera House; October 29–November 1, 2008; 3 performances.

Le sept planches de la ruse (The Seven Boards of Skill) Conceived, designed and directed by Aurélien Bory; Presented by Compagnie 111 and Scènes de la Terre; Costumes, Sylvie Marcucci; Lighting, Arnaud Veyrat; Scenery, Pierre Dequivre & Arnaud Lucas; Sound, Stéphane Ley; Music, Raphaël Wisson; Additional Music, Arvo Pärt; Technical Directors, Arno Veyrat, Tristan Baudoin; Director/Translator Assistants, Evita De Ayguavives, Hugues Cohen; Producer, Jean Luc Larguier; Cast: Sun Ruichen, Yu Yingchun, Ding Hong, Jiang Huimin, An Liming, Chen Jianhui, Liu Yu, Qu Aiguo, Tan Zuoliang, Li Liang, Wang Wentao, Zhang Deqiang, Che Hu, Zhang Benchuan

U.S. premiere of a dance/cirus art/visual theatrical piece presented without intermission; Howard Gilman Opera House; November 5–8, 2008; 3 performances.

Arjuna's Dilemma Music by Douglas J. Cuomo, libretto adapted from the Hindu epic "Bhagavad Gita,"(translated by Dr. Ramananda Prasad) and the poetry of Kabir; Presented by Music-Theatre Group (Diane Wondisford, Producing Director); Director, Robin Guarino; Conductor/Music Director, Alan Johnson; Choreography, John Kelly; Set, Donald Eastman; Costumes, Gabriel Berry; Lighting, Robert Wierzel; Projections, William Cusick; Sound, David Meschter; Assistant Director, Amanda Consol; Production Manager, Paul Smithyman; PSM, Jason Kaiser; Stage Manager, Sara Bradley; Associate Producer, Younghee Kim-Wait; Cast: Tony Boutté (Arjuna), Humayun Khan (Voice of Krishna), John Kelly (Krishna); Women's Ensemble: Suzan Hanson, Anita Johnson, Barbara Rearick, Kirsten Sollek, Bora Yoon; Instrumental Ensemble: Bob Franceschini (saxophone), Badal Roy (tablas), Rex Benincasa (percussion), Jeffrey Carney (bass), Ann Cecil-Sterman (flute), Jennifer Choi (violin), Joyce Hammann (violin), Ron Lawrence (viola), Jim Pugliese (percussion), Andrew Sterman (woodwinds), Kathleen Supové (piano), Mary Wooten (cello)

World premiere of a chamber opera presented without intermission; Harvey Theatre; November 5–8, 2008; 3 performances.

Continuous City Co-conceived and directed by Marianne Weems, co-conceived and dramaturgy by James Gibbs, co-conceived and written by Harry Sinclair; Produced Claire Hallereau with The Builders Association; Set, Stewart Laing, James Gibbs, & Neal Wilkinson; Lighting, Jennifer Tipton; Video, Peter Flaherty; Sound and original Music, Dan Dobson; Production Manager, Neal Wilkinson; Technical Design, Joe Silovsky; Touring Technical Director, Josh Higgason; Costumes, Chantelle Norton; Video Associate, Austin Switser; Lighting Associate, Laura Mroczkowski; Technical Development, Tom Korder; Executive Producer, Kim Whitener; Lead Co-producer, Krannert Center for the Performing Arts (University of Illinois at Urbana-Champaign); Co-producers, Luminato Toronto Festival of Arts & Creativity, Carolina Performing Arts, University of California Berkeley Department of Theater, Dance and Performance Studies & Arts Research Center, and Walker Art Center; Deb's Blogs, Moe Angeles; Mirza Family Chats, Nabil Mirza, Rizwarz Mirza, & Ariba Sultan; Additional Design, dbox; Additional Dramaturgy, Jessica Chalmers; Cast: Moe Angelos (Deb), Rizwan Mirza (J.V.), Olivia Timothee (Sam), Harry Sinclair (Mike)

New York premiere of a multimedia theatrical piece presented without intermission; Harvey Theatre; November 18–22, 2008; 5 performances.

Opening Night by John Cassavetes, translated by Gerardjan Rijnders & Sam Bogaerts; Presented by Toneelgroep Amsterdam and NTGent (Belgium); Director/Adaptor, Ivo van Hove; Set & Lighting, Jan Versweyveld; Costumes, An d'Huys; Sound, Marc Meulemans; Video, Erik Lint; Camera, Judith Hofland, Menke Visser;

Dramaturg, Koen Tachelet; Cast: Elsie de Brauw (Myrtle), Jacob Derwig (Maurice), Oscar van Rompay (Gus), Lien De Graeve (Lena), Fedja van Huêt (Manny), Karina Smulders (Dorothee), Johan van Assche (David), Thomas Ryckewaert (Leo), Kristof van Boven (Kelly), Chris Nietvelt (Sarah), Hadewych Minis (Nancy)

U.S. premiere of a performance/video theatrical piece presented in Dutch with English titles without intermission; Harvey Theatre; December 2–6, 2008; 5 performances.

The Company of Opening Night *(photo by Jasper Vartjes)*

Lightning at our feet Music by Michael Gordon from the writing of Emily Dickenson; Presented by Michael Gordon and Ridge Theatre; Director, Bob McGrath; Films, Bill Morrison; Projections, Laurie Olinder; Dramaturgy, Daniel Zippi; Music Director, Ted Hearne; Set, Jim Findlay; Costumes, Ruth Pongstaphone; Lighting, John Ambrosone; Sound, Jamie McElhinney; Arrangements, Michael Gordon, Jennifer Charles, Leah Coloff, Ted Hearne, Courtney Orlando, Bora Yoon; Cast: Jennifer Charles (voice), Leah Coloff (cello/voice), Courtney Orlando (piano/violin/voice), Bora Yoon (guitar/viola/percussion/electronics/voice)

World premiere of a multimedia music and drama piece presented without intermission; Harvey Theatre; December 9–13, 2008; 4 performances

SPRING SEASON

The Bridge Project (Inaugural Season) Produced by BAM, The Old Vic and Neal Street Productions; Director, Sam Mendes; Sets, Anthony Ward; Costumes, Catherine Zuber; Lighting, Paul Pyant; Sound, Paul Arditt; Music, Mark Bennett; Casting, Nancy Piccione & Maggie Lunn; Music Director, Dan Lipton; Choreography, Josh Prince; Hair/Wigs, Tom Watson; PSM, Jane Pole; ASMs, Kevin Bertolacci & Cat Fiabane; Associate Director, Gaye Taylor Upchurch; Tour Producer, Claire Béjanin; Illusions, Peter Samelson; Dialects, Timothy Monich; Production Manager, Dominic Fraser; Associate Composer, Curtis Moore; Associate Design: Christine Peters (set), Dan Large (lighting), Tony Smolenski IV (sound); Props, Faye Armon; included: *The Cherry Orchard* by Anton Chekhov, translated by Tom Stoppard; Cast: Sinéad Cusack (Ranevskaya), Morven Christie (Anya), Rebecca Hall (Varya), Paul Jesson (Gaev), Simon Russell Beale (Lopakhin), Ethan Hawke (Trofimov), Dakin Matthews (Simeonov-Pishchik), Selina Cadell (Charlotta Ivanovna), Tobias Segal (Yepikhodov), Charlotte Parry (Dunyasha), Richard Easton (Firs), Josh Hamilton (Yasha), Gary Powell (Passer-by), Aaron Krohn (Post Office Clerk); Servants/Guests/Peasants: Michael Braun, Aaron Krohn, Mark Nelson, Jessica Pollert Smith, Gary Powell, Hannah Stokely; Musicians: Dan Lipton, Dana Lyn; Understudies: Michael Braun (Trofimov, Station

Master), Selina Cadell (Ranevskaya), Aaron Krohn (Yepikhodov, Yasha, Passer-by), Mark Nelson (Gaev, Pishchik), Jessica Pollert Smith (Anya, Dunyasha), Gary Powell (Lopakhin, Firs), Hannah Stokely (Charlotte, Varya); U.S. premiere of a revival of a play in a new translation presented in two acts; Harvey Theatre; January 3–March 8, 2009 (Opened January 14); 34 performances; *The Winter's Tale* by William Shakespeare; Cast: Simon Russell Beale (Leontes), Rebecca Hall (Hermione), Morven Christie (Mamillius), Paul Jesson (Camillo), Dakin Matthews (Antigonus/Shepherd), Sinéad Cusack (Paulina), Gary Powell (Cleomenes/Jailer/Gentleman/Bear/Shepherd), Michael Braun (Dion/Florizel), Mark Nelson (Lord of Sicilia/Gentleman/Mariner/Shepherd), Aaron Krohn (Servant of Sicilia/Gentleman/Servant of Bohemia/Musician), Hannah Stokely (Emilia/Shepherdess), Charlotte Parry (Lady-in-Waiting/Mopsa), Josh Hamilton (Polixenes), Morven Christie (Perdita), Richard Easton (Old Shepherd/Time), Tobias Segal (Young Shepherd), Ethan Hawke (Autolycus), Jessica Pollert Smith (Dorcas); Musicians: Dan Lipton, Dana Lyn; Understudies: Michael Braun (Autolycus, Jailer, Bear, Lord), Aaron Krohn (Florizel, Young Shepherd, Cleomenes, Mariner, Lord), Mark Nelson (Camillo, Antigonus, Old Shepherd, Time), Charlotte Parry (Hermione), Jessica Pollert Smith (Mamillius, Perdita, Emilia, Lady-in-Waiting), Gary Powell (Leontes, Polixenes, Servant of Bohemia, Lord), Tobias Segal (Servant of Sicilia, Dion), Hannah Stokely (Paulina, Mopsa, Dorcas); Revival of a play presented in two acts; Harvey Theatre; February 10–March 8, 2009 (Opened February 20); 29 performances.

Ethan Hawke, Sinéad Cusack, Paul Jesson in The Bridge Project production of The Cherry Orchard *(photo by Joan Marcus)*

The Company of The Bridge Project production of A Winter's Tale *(photo by Joan Marcus)*

Simon Russell Beale and Rebecca Hall in The Cherry Orchard
(photo by Joan Marcus)

The Merchant of Venice by William Shakespeare, adapted by Edward Hall and Roger Warren; Presented by Watermill Theatre (UK) and Propeller; Director, Edward Hall; Set, Michael Pavelka; Lighting, Ben Ormerod; Music, Propeller; Additional Music/Arrangements, Jon Trenchard; American Stage Manager, R. Michael Blanco; Relights on Tour, Richard Howell; Production Manager, Nick Ferguson; Company Stage Manager, Nick Chesterfield; Deputy Stage Manager, Claire Henders; ASMs, Dawon Maxfield & Bryony Rutter; Assistant Director, Paul Hart; Cast: Bob Barrett (Antonio), Sam Swainsbury (Salerio), Jack Tarlton (Bassanio), Richard Frame (Gratiano), Richard Dempsey (Lorenzo), Kelsey Brookfield (Portia), Chris Myles (Nerissa), Richard Clothier (Shylock), Jonathan Livingstone (Morocco), Thomas Padden (Tubal/Aragon), John Dougall (Lancelot Gobbo), Jon Trenchard (Jessica), Babou Ceesay (Duke of Venice), David Newman (Monsieur le Bon/Preacher): Understudies: Jonathan Livingstone, David Newman

Revival of a play presented in two acts; Harvey Theatre; May 6–17, 2009; 11 performances.

Richard III: An Arab Tragedy by William Shakespeare, adapted and directed by Sulaman Al-Bassam; Presented by Sabab/Sulayman Al-Bassam Theatre (Kuwait); Commissioned by the Royal Shakespeare Company; Design, Sam Collins; Original Music & Sound, Lewis Gibson; Lighting, Richard Williamson; Costumes, Abdullah Al Awadhi; Translation, Mehdi Al-Sayegh; Production Manager, Aude Albiges; Company Stage Manager, Faisal Al-Obaid; Deputy Stage Manager, Misha'al Al-Omar; ASM, Saad Samir; Surtitiles, Wafa'a Al-Fraheen; Technical Stage Coordinator, Corinna MacEwan; Press, Natasha Freedman; Cast: Carole Abboud (Queen Elizabeth), Bashar Abdullah (Emir Grey/Ratcliffe), Faisal Al Ameeri (Emir Rivers/Newscaster), Nigel Barrett (Mr Richmond), Nicolas Daniel (Minister of State Hastings/Lord Mayor), Monadhil Daood (King Edward IV/Catesby), Raymond El Hosny (Palace Advisor Buckingham), Nadine Joma'a (Lady Anne/Mistress Shore), Fayez Kazak (Emir Gloucester, later King Richard III), Jassim Al-Nabhan (Emir Clarence/Stanley), Amal Omran (Queen Margaret/Crown Prince Edward); Musicians: Sami Bilal, Ahmad Al Dabbous, Lewis Gibson, Faisal Khalaf, Sultan Al Meftah

Revival of a play in a new translation presented in Arabic with English titles without intermission; Harvey Theatre; June 9–12, 2009; 4 performances.

(Front, l. to r.) *Richard Clothier, Bob Barrett, Kelsey Brookfield and the Company of the Watermill Theatre/Propeller production of* The Merchant of Venice *(photo by Nobby Clark)*

Jassim al-Nabhan and Nicolas Daniel in Richard III: An Arab Tragedy
(photo by Rudd Jonkers)

City Center *Encores!*

Artistic Director, Jack Viertel; President/CEO of City Center, Arlene Shuler; Senior Vice President/Managing Director, Mark Litvin; General Manager, Stephanie Overton; Music Director, Rob Berman; Concert Adaptation, David Ives; Sets/Scenic Consultant, John Lee Beatty; Music Coordinator, Seymour Red Press; Company Manager, Michael Zande; Casting; Jay Binder, Jack Bowdan; Press, Helene Davis; Encores Artistic Associates: John Lee Beatty, Jay Binder, Walter Bobbie, David Ives, Kathleen Marshall

2009 SUMMER STARS (SECOND SEASON)

Damn Yankees Lyrics and music by Richard Adler and Jerry Ross, book by George Abbott and Douglass Wallop; based on the novel *The Year the Yankees Lost the Pennant* by Douglass Wallop; Director, John Rando; Choreography, Bob Fosse; Costumes, William Ivey Long; Lighting, Peter Kaczorowski; Sound, Scott Lehrer; Casting, Laura Stancyzk; PSM, Karen Moore; Wigs/Hair, Paul Huntley; Original Orchestrations, Don Walker; Choreography Reproduction, Mary MacLeod; Associate Music Director, David Gursky; Music Associate, Joshua Clayton; Stage Manager, Rachel S. McCutchen; ASM, Karen Evanouskas; Assistant Director, Anika Chapin; Assistant Choreographer, Greg Graham; Makeup, Angelina Avallone; Dance Captain, Shannon Lewis; Cast: P.J. Benjamin (Joe Boyd), Randy Graff (Meg Boyd), Sean Hayes (Applegate), Veanne Cox (Sister), Kathy Fitzgerald (Doris), Cheyenne Jackson (Joe Hardy), Baron Vaughn (Henry), Jimmy Ray Bennett (Sohovik), Robert Creighton (Smokey), T. Oliver Reid (Linville/Postmaster), Michael Mulheren (Benny Van Buren), Jimmy Smagula (Rocky), Megan Lawrence (Gloria Thorpe), Chandra Lee Schwartz (1st Teenage Girl), Pamela Otterson (2nd Teenage Girl), Jay Lusteck (Lynch/Commissioner), John Horton (Mr. Welch), Jane Krakowski (Lola), Rachel Coloff (Miss Weston), Stacey Sargeant (Assistant), Alexander Scheitinger (1st Boy), Cody Ryan Wise (2nd Boy), John Selya (Eddie/Mambo Dancer), David Garrison (Game Announcer); Ensemble: Nathan Balser, David Baum, Jimmy Ray Bennett, Rachel Coloff, Anderson Davis, Marya Grandy, Shannon Lewis, Jay Lusteck, Pamela Otterson, Adam Perry, Karine Plantadit, T. Oliver Reid, Jon Rua, Stacey Sargeant, Alexander Scheitinger, Chandra Lee Schwartz, Baron Vaughn, Cody Ryan Wise; Understudies: Jimmy Ray Bennett (Applegate), Shannon Lewis (Lola), Anderson Davis (Joe Hardy, Rocky), Jay Lusteck (Joe Boyd, Van Buren, Welch), Rachel Coloff (Doris, Sister), Marya Grandy (Meg, Gloria), T. Oliver Reid (Eddie/Mambo Dancer), David Baum (Smokey)

Sean Hayes in Damn Yankees *(photos by Joan Marcus)*

Musical Numbers: Overture; Six Months Out of Every Year; Goodbye, Old Girl; Heart; Shoeless Joe from Hannibal, MO; A Man Doesn't Know; A Little Brains, A Little Talent; A Man Doesn't Know (reprise); Whatever Lola Wants; Heart (reprise); Who's Got the Pain; Entr'acte; The Game; Near to You; Those Were the Good Old Days; Two Lost Souls; A Man Doesn't Know (reprise)

Setting: In and around Washington, D.C. during the waning months of the 1955 baseball season. Revival of the musical presented in two acts; July 5–27, 2008 (Opened July 10); 6 previews, 21 performances. Originally produced on Broadway at the 46th Street (Richard Rodgers) Theatre May 5, 1955 and played 1,019 performances (see *Theatre World* Vol. 11, page 100). The show was revived on Broadway at the Marquis Theatre March 3, 1994 (see *Theatre World* Vol. 50, page 46).

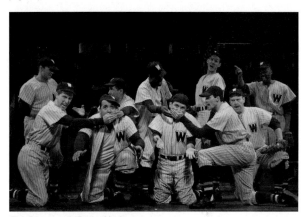

The Company in Damn Yankees

FALL AND SPRING SERIES (SIXTEENTH SEASON)

On the Town Music by Leonard Bernstein, book and lyrics by Betty Comden and Adolph Green; based on an idea by Jerome Robbins; Director, John Rando; Guest Musical Director, Todd Ellison; Original Choreography, Jerome Robbins; New Choreography, Warren Carlyle; Costume Consultant, Martin Pakledinaz; Lighting, Clifton Taylor; Sound, Tom Morse; Original Orchestrations, Leonard Bernstein, Hershy Kay, Don Walker, Elliott Jacoby & Ted Royal; PSM, Rolt Smith; Stage Manager, Andrea O. Saraffian; Associate Musical Director, Ethyl Will; Assistant Director, Anika Chapin; Assistant Choreography, Parker Esse, Melissa Rae Mahon; Robbins' Choreography Assisstant, Scott Wise; Projections, Mark Mongold; Additional Orchestrations, Bruce Coughlin; Music Associate, Josh Clayton; Cast: Geno Segers (First Workman/Quartet/S. Uperman), Michael Cusumano (Second Workman/First Sailor), Charlie Sutton (Third Workman/Third Sailor), Kevin Vortmann (Quartet/Announcer/Actor), Price Waldman (Quartet/Waldo Figment/Musician/Club Master of Ceremonies), J.D. Webster (Quartet/Musician), Christian Borle (Ozzie), Justin Bohon (Chip), Tony Yazbeck (Gabey), Ryan Jackson (Andy), Adam Perry (Tom/Second Sailor), Rachel Coloff (Flossie/Diana Dream/Dolores Dolores), Monica L. Patton (Flossie's Friend), Mary MacLeod (Subway Bill Poster), Jessica Lee Goldyn (Ivy Smith), Leslie Kritzer (Hildy Esterhazy), Jennifer Laura Thompson (Claire de Loone), Andrea Martin (Madame Maude P. Dilly), Michael Cumpsty (Judge Pitkin W. Bridgework), Julyana Soelistyo (Lucy Schmeeler); Ensemble: Lawrence Alexander, Andrea Beasom, Kristine Bendul, Tanya Birl, Angie Canuel, John Carroll, Rachel Coloff, Michael Cusumano, Susan Derry, Emilee Dupré, Autumn Hurlbert, Ryan Jackson, Mary MacLeod, Monica L. Patton, Adam Perry, Steve Schepis, Geno Segers, Charlie Sutton, Kevin Vortmann, Price Waldman, J.D. Webster, Ashley Yeater

Musical Numbers: I Feel Like I'm Not Out of Bed Yet; New York, New York; Gabey's Coming; Presentation of Miss Turnstiles; Come Up to My Place; Carried Away; Lonely Town; Carnegie Hall Pavane (Do, Re, Do), I Understand; Carried Away (reprise); I Can Cook Too; Lucky to Be Me; Times Square Ballet (Sailors On the Town); Entr'acte; So Long, Baby; I Wish I Was Dead; Conga Cabana; I Wish I Was Dead; Ya Got Me; Slam Bang Blues; I Understand (reprise); Imaginary Coney Island; Pas de deux; Some Other Time; The Real Coney Island; Finale Act II

Setting: One day in New York City. 1944. Wartime. Concert version of the musical presented in two acts; November 19–23, 2008; 6 performances. The original production opened at the Adelphi Theatre December 28, 1944 and played 462 performances (see *Theatre World* Vol. 1, page 60). The show was revived on Broadway at the Imperial Theatre October 31, 1971 (see *Theatre World* Vol. 18, page 18) and again at the Gershwin Theatre November 19, 1998 (see *Theatre World* Vol. 55, page 25).

Cristian Borle, Tony Yazbeck and Justin Bohon in On the Town

Music in the Air Music by Jerome Kern, book and lyrics by Oscar Hammerstein II; Director, Gary Griffin; Choreography, Michyael Lichtefeld; Costume Consultant, David C. Woolard; Sound, Scott Lehrer; Original Orchestrations, Robert Russell Bennett; PSM, Peter Hanson; Stage Manager, Jon Krause; Associate Music Director, James Lowe; Assistant Director, David S. Chapman; Associate Choreographer, Joe Bowerman; Wigs, Charles LaPointe; Music Associate, Josh Clayton; Cast: Tom Alan Robbins (Dr. Walther Lessing), Dawn Cantwell (Tila), Sierra Boggess (Sieglinde Lessing), Ryan Silverman (Karl Reder), Michael Marcotte (Town Crier), Stephen Carrasco (Herman), Gordon Stanley (Burgomaster), Rebecca Robbins (Frau Schreimann), Jack Doyle (Pflugfelder), Patty Goble (Frau Pflugfelder), Craig Bennett (Priest/Zookeeper), Walter Charles (Cornelius), David Schramm (Ernst Weber), Robert Sella (Uppmann), Anne L. Nathan (Marthe), Kristin Chenoweth (Frieda Hatzfeld), Douglas Sills (Bruno Mahler), Anne Horak (Hulde), Jonathan Gabriel Michie (Zoo Café Waiter/Assistant Stage Manager), Joy Hermalyn (Anna), Marni Nixon (Frau Direktor Lilli Kirschner), Dick Latessa (Herr Direcktor Kirschner); Ensemble: Craig Bennett, Dawn Cantwell, Stephen Carrasco, Jack Doyle, Patty Goble, Joy Hermalyn, Anne Horak, Amy Justman, Michael Marcotte, Jonathan Gabriel Michie, J. Maxwell Miller, Rebecca Robbins, Sarah Caldwell Smith, Gordon Stanley; Chorus: Paul Appleby, Erica Aubrey, Tony Capone, Carson Church, Leah Edwards, Colm Fitzmaurice, Kevin Grace, Mary Illes, Amanda Johnson, Jackie Thompson, Jamie Van Eyck, Mark Womack

Musical Numbers: Melodies of May, I've Told Every Little Star, Prayer, There's a Hill Beyond a Hill, And Love Was Born, I Am So Eager, Bubble Dance, I've Told Every Little Star (reprise), I'm Coming Home (Letter Song), I'm Alone, I Am So Eager (reprise), Finaletto, One More Dance, Night Flies By, I've Told Every Little Star (reprise 2), I'm Alone (reprise), When the Spring Is in the Air, In Egern on the Tegern See, The Song Is You, I'm Alone (reprise 2), The Song Is You (reprise), We Belong Together

Setting: Bavaria; 1930s. Concert version of the musical/operetta presented in two acts; February 5–8, 2009; 5 performances. The original production opened at the Alvin (Neil Simon) Theatre on November 8, 1932 and played 342 performances. The show was revived at the Ziegfeld Theatre October 8–November 24, 1951 (see *Theatre World* Vol. 8, page 30.)

Douglas Sills and Kristin Chenoweth in Music in the Air

Cheyenne Jackson and Jim Norton in Finian's Rainbow

Finian's Rainbow Music by Burton Lane, book by E.Y. Harburg and Fred Saidy, lyrics by E.Y. Harburg; Director/Choreography, Warren Carlyle; Costume Consultant, Toni-Leslie James; Lighting, Ken Billington; Sound, Scott Lehrer; Associate Director, Marc Bruni; PSM, Tripp Phillips; Original Orchestrations, Robert Russell Bennett & Don Walker; Choral Preparation, Ben Whiteley; Stage Manager, Jason Hindelang; Associate Choreographer, Parker Esse; Assistant Choreographer, Angie Canuel; Associate Music Director, Josh Clayton; Hair/Wigs, Wendy Parson; Dialect Coach, Deborah Hecht; Cast: Guy Davis (Sunny), William Youmans (Buzz Collins), Andrew Weems (Sheriff), Bernard Dotson (1st Sharecropper/1st Passion Pilgrim Gospeleer), Kevin Ligon (2nd Sharecropper/Mr. Robust), Tyrick Wiltez Jones (Henry), Leslie Donna Flesner (Diana), Alina Faye (Susan Mahoney), Jim Norton (Finian McLonergan), Kate Baldwin (Sharon McLonergan), Cheyenne Jackson (Woody Mahoney), Jeremy Bobb (Og, a Leprechaun), Joe Aaron Reid (Howard/2nd Passion Pilgrim Gospeleer), Philip Bosco (Senator Rawkins), J.D. Webster (Geologist/Preacher), Denis Lambert (Geologist), Ruben Santiago-Hudson (Billboard), Tim Hartman (Mr. Shears), Devin Richards (3rd Passion Pilgrim Gospeleer); Sharecroppers & Residents of Rainbow Valley: Tanya Biril, Bree Branker, Meggie Cansler, Bernard Dotson, Leslie Donna Flesner, Lisa Gajda, Tim Hartman, Mary Illes, Tyrick Wiltez Jones, Denis Lambert, Kevin Ligon, Monica L. Patton, Joe Aaron Reid, Devin Richards, Steve Schepis, Rashidra Scott, J.D. Webster, Terri White

Musical Numbers: Overture, This Time of Year, How Are Things in Glocca Morra?, Look to the Rainbow, Old Devil Moon, How Are Things in Glocca Morra? (reprise), Something Sort of Grandish, If This Isn't Love, Something Sort of Grandish (reprise), Necessity, That Great "Come-and-Get-It" Day, Entr'acte, When the Idle Poor Become the Idle Rich, Old Devil Moon (reprise), Dance of the Golden Crock, The Begat, Look to the Rainbow (reprise), When I'm Not Near the Girl I Love, How Are Things in Glocca Morra? (reprise 2)

Setting: Rainbow Valley, Missitucky. Concert version of the musical presented in two acts; March 26–29, 2009; 5 performances. The original production opened at the 46th Street (Richard Rodgers) Theatre January 10, 1947 and played 725 performances (see *Theatre World* Vol. 3, page 71). City Center Light Opera Company revived the show twice: May 18–29, 1955 (see *Theatre World* Vol. 11, page 113) and April 27–May 8, 1960 (see *Theatre World* Vol. 16, page 106). The second revival transferred briefly to the 46th Street Theatre May 23–June 1, 1960. This *Encores!* production was slated to transfer to Broadway in October 2009.

Terri White and the Company in Finian's Rainbow

Classic Stage Company

Forty-first Season

Artistic Director, Brian Kulick; Executive Director, Jessica R. Jenen; General Manager, Jeff Griffin; Development, Audrey Carmeli; Associate Artistic Director, Tony Speciale; Audience Services, John C. Hume; Assistant General Manager, Jen Soloway; Artistic Assistant, Steve Kaliski; Education, Jeffrey Feola; Casting, James Calleri; Production Manager, Travis Walker; Press, The Publicity Office, Michael Borowski, Marc Thibodeau

The Tempest by William Shakespeare; Director, Brian Kulick; Set, Jian Jung; Costumes, Oana Botez-Ban; Lighting, Brian Scott; Original Music & Sound, Christian Frederickson; PSM, Christina Lowe; ASM, Chandra LaViolette; Assistant Director, Tony Speciale; Technical Director, Peter Fry; Shakespeare Coach, Rachel Chavkin; Assistant Design: Abby Walton (costumes), Steve O'Shea (lighting); Properties, Sarah Bird; Cast: Craig Baldwin (Sebastian), Yusef Bulos (Gonzalo), Angel Desai (Ariel/Ariel as Ceres), Karl Kenzler (Antonio), Nana Mansah (Spirit/Spirit as Juno), Nyambi Nyambi (Caliban), Bhavesh Patel (Boatswain/Spirit/Adrian/Spirit as Isis), Mandy Patinkin (Prospero), Michael Potts (Alonso), Steven Rattazzi (Stefano), Stark Sands (Ferdinand), Tony Torn (Master of the Ship/Trinculo), Elisabeth Waterston (Miranda)

Revival of the play presented in two acts; East 13th Street Theatre; September 3–October 19, 2008 (Opened September 18); 55 performances.

Uncle Vanya by Anton Chekhov, translated by Carol Rocamora; Director, Austin Pendleton; Sets, Santo Loquasto; Costumes, Suzi Benzinger; Lighting, Jason Lyons; Music & Sound, Ryan Rumery; Sound, Daniel Baker; Hair, Paul Huntley; PSM, Jared T. Carey; ASM, Heather Davidson; Technical Director, Jack Blacketer; Associate Lighting, Peter Hoerburger; Assistant Director, Diana Basmajian; Assistant Costumes, Marco Piemontese; Properties, Mary Houston; Cast: Cyrilla Baer (Marina), Andrew Garman (The Watchman), Mamie Gummer (Sonya), Maggie Gyllenhaal (Yelena), Delphi Harrington (Maria Vasilyevna), George Morfogen (Serebryakov), Denis O'Hare (Vanya), Peter Sarsgaard (Astrov), Louis Zorich (Telegin); Understudies: Andrew Garman, Amanda Plant

Revival of a play presented in two acts; East 13th Street Theatre; January 17–March 8, 2009 (Opened February 12); 55 performances.

An Oresteia From the works of Aiskhylos, Sophokles, and Euripides, translated by Anne Carson; Directors, Brian Kulick & Gisela Cardenas (*Agamemnon & Elecktra*), Paul Lazar (*Orestes*); Associate Director/Choreography, Annie-B Parson; Set, Riccardo Hernandez; Costumes, Oana Botez-Ban; Lighting, Maruti Evans; Original Music & Sound, Christian Frederickson; PSM, Christina Lowe; Fight Director, Adam Rihacek; ASMs, April Ann Kline & Kara M. Teolis; Assistant Directors, Craig Bladwin, Sarah Kenney (dramaturg), & Jake Hooker; Wigs, Jon Carter; Dance Captain, David Neumann; Cast: *Agamemnon* by Aiskhylos: Christopher McCann (Watchman/Chorus Man 1), Yusef Bulos (Chorus Man 2), Dan Hurlin (Chorus Man 3), Michi Barrall (Chorus Woman 1), Annika Boras (Chorus Woman 2), Ching Valdes-Aran (Chorus Woman 3), Stephanie Roth Haberle (Klytaimestra), Mickey Solis (Herald), Steve Mellor (Agamemnon), Doan Ly (Kassandra), Craig Baldwin (Aigisthos), Eric Dyer (Guard); *Elektra* by Sophokles: Yusef Bulos (Paedagogus/Old Man), Jess Barbagallo (Phylades), Mickey Solis (Orestes), Annika Boras (Elektra), Craig Baldwin (Chorus Boy), Ching Valdes-Aran (Chorus Woman 1), Doan Ly (Chorus Woman 2), Michi Barrall (Chrysothemis), Stephanie Roth Haberle (Klytaimestra), Christopher McCann (Aigisthos), Eric Dyer (Guard); *Orestes* by Euripides: Mickey Solis (Orestes), Annika Boras (Elektra), David Neumann (Helen/Trojan Slave), Karinne Keithley (Hermione/Chorus), Dan Hurlin (Chorus), Steve Mellor (Menelaos), Christopher McCann (Tyndareos), Jess Barbagallo (Phlades), Eric Dyer (Messenger/Apollo)

Setting: Ancient Greece. World premiere of three classic plays in new adaptations presented in rotating repertory: Part One (*Agamemnon & Elektra*) presented with one intermission, Part Two (*Orestes*) presented without intermission (weekend marathon performances of both parts presented with two intermissions); East 13th Street Theatre; March 22–April 19, 2009 (Opened April 1); 25 performances (8 of Part One, 8 of Part Two, 9 Marathons).

ADDITIONAL EVENTS

First Look Festival: Brecht September 22–October 20, 2008; one-night-only staged reading and workshop series of the works of Bertolt Brecht; September 22: *The Caucasian Chalk Circle* directed by Javierantonio Gonzalez, featuring Steven Rattazzi and Elizabeth Waterston; September 29: *In the Jungle of Cities* directed by Rachel Chavkin, featuring Didi O'Connell and members of The TEAM; October 13: *The Good Person of Sezuan* adapted by Tony Kushner, directed by Tony Speciale, music by Christian Frederickson, featuring Maggie Gyllenhaal, Jeremy Strong, Jayne Houdyshell, Jason Butler Harner, Ben Shenkman, Ryder Smith, Mary Shultz, Roberta Maxwell and Judith Roberts; October 20: *Life of Galileo* directed by Brian Kulick, featuring Richard Easton

Monday Night Othello January 19–February 9, 2009; open rehearsal series of the play by William Shakespeare; January 19: directed by Michael Sexton, featuring Michael Cumpsty; January 26: directed by Brian Kulick, featuring Michael Potts and Alan Cumming; February 2: directed by Brian Kulich, featuring John Turturro and Alan Cumming; February 9: directed by Barry Edelstein, featuring Frances McDormand

The Young Company: Romeo and Juliet by William Shakespeare; Presented by the Graduate Acting Program of the Columbia University School for the Arts; Director, Tony Speciale; February 23–March 6, 2009; 15 performances.

The Proust Project March 23–April 13, 2009; inaugual adaptation series of staged readings based on Marcel Proust's *Remembrance of Things Past*; March 23 and April 13: *Swann in Love* by Pamela Hansford Johnson, featuring Michael Stuhlbarg; March 30: *Albertine Regained* by Pamela Hansford Johnson, featuring Michael Stuhlbarg; April 6: *Waste of Time* by Robert David McDonald

Denis O'Hare and Maggie Gyllenhaal in Uncle Vanya (photos by Joan Marcus)

Steve Mellor, Doan Ly (above) and Stephanie Roth Haberle, (on floor) in An Oresteia

Classical Theatre of Harlem

Tenth Season

Co-Founder/Artistic Director Alfred Preisser; Co-Founder/Executive Producer, Christopher McElroen; Producing/Development Associate, Jaime Carrillo; Producing Director, Susan Jonas; Artistic Associate, Karan Kendrick; Production Supervisor, Vincent J. DeMarco/Kelvin Productions, LLC; Press, Brett Singer and Associates/David Gersten and Associates

Three Sisters by Anton Chekhov; Co-presented by Harlem Stage; Director, Christopher McElroen; Ste, Troy Hourie; Costmes, Kimberly Glennon; Lighting, Aaron Black; Original Music, Alexander Sovronsky; PSM, Jenn McNeil; Cast: Roger Guenveur Smith (Vershinin), Earle Hyman (Ferapont), Carmen de Lavallade (Anfisa), Sabrina LeBeauf (Olga), Reg E. Cathey (Chebutykin), Amanda Mason Warren (Masha), Carmen Gill (Irina), Billy Eugene Jones (Andrey), Jonathan Earl Peck (Kulygin), Josh Tyson (Tuzenbach), Daphne Gaines (Nataliya Ivanovna), Phillip Christian (Solyony), Jonathan Ramey (Fedotik), Nathan Dame (Rodé)

Revival of a play presented without intermission; Harlem Stage Gatehouse; February 5–March 8, 2009 (Opened February 18); 9 previews, 25 performances.

Archbishop Supreme Tartuffe by Alfred Preisser and Randy Weiner, based on the play by Moliére; Director, Alfred Preisser; Set, Greg Mitchell; Costumes, Kimberly Glennon; Lighting, Aaron Black; Sound Bret Scheinfeld; PSM, Alexander Casanovas; Production Supervision, Michael Goodin, Roody Dorsainvil; Technical Director, Michael Cottom; Props, Morgan Eckert; Production Assistants, Allison J. Hamilton, Nicole Martinez, Nicholas Betito; Cast: André DeShields (Archbishop Supreme Tartuffe), Ted Lange (Orgon), Kim Brockington (Elmire), Lawrence Street (Cleante), Rejinald Woods (Big Jerome), Tyrone Davis Jr. (Little Jerome), Soneelea Nankani (Marianne), Jabari Brisport (Damis); Supreme Choir: Jennifer Akabue, Gina Marie Rivera, Charletta Rozzell, Kisa Willis; Understudy: Gerron Atkinson (Orgon, Big Jerome, Archbishop); Musicians: Kelvyn Bell (guitar), Chris Eddleton (drums), Larry Peoples (bass)

Off-Broadway premiere of a new adaptation of the classic play with music presented without intermission; Clurman Theatre on Theatre Row; June 12–July 19, 2009 (Opened June 25); 15 previews, 29 performances.

Additional Events

Future Classics Reading Series: "Changing the Face of American Theater" Presented at the Schomburg Center; October 15, 2008: *Saturday Night, Sunday Morning* by Katori Hall; Director, Lydia Fort; November 10, 2008: *Stepchild: Frederick Douglas & Abraham Lincoln* by David W. Blight and Peter Almond; Director, Alfred Preisser; Cast: Roger Guenveur Smith; November 19, 2008: *Halal Brothers* by Aladdin Ulla; Director, Christopher McElroen; January 21, 2009: *seed* by Radha Blank; Director, Niegel Smith; February 18, 2009: *Julius X* by Al Letson Jr; Director, Tracy Jack; March 18, 2009: *The Master Shepherd(s) of Hookyjook* by Yusef Miller; Director, Lydia Fort; April 15, 2009: *Prodigal Blood* by James Jorsling; Director, J. Kyle Manzay; May 20, 2009: *Diana Sands Project* by P.J. Gibson; Director, Reggie Life

Left: *Gina Marie Rivera, Tyrone Davis, Charletta Rozzell, André DeShields, Rejinald Woods and Jennifer Akabue in* Archbishop Supreme Tartuffe *(photo by Lia Chang)*

Below: *Sabrina LeBeauf, Phillip Christian (standing), Carmen Gill, Amanda Mason Warren and Josh Tyson (standing) in* Three Sisters *(photo by Troy Hourie)*

The Culture Project

Artistic Director, Allan Buchman; General Manager, David Friedman; Associate Producer, Olivia Greer; Producer, Manda Martin; Development, Roy Climenhaga, Amy Paul; Group Sales, Becky White; Assistant to the Artistic Director, Joi Sears; Communications, Melissa Hale Woodman; Programming, Jayashri Wyatt; Press, O&M Co., Rick Miramontez, Jon Dimond, Molly Barnett

Expatiate by Lenelle Moïse; Director, Tamilla Woodard; Choreography, Nathaniel Nicco Annan; Set/Costumes, Deb O; Lighting/Projections, Stephen Arnold; Music Director/Sound, Nick Moore; Stage Manager, Molly Minor Eustis; Cast: Lenelle Moïse (Claudie), Karla Mosley (Alphine)

Musical Numbers: Motherland, The Makings, Roller-Coaster, Baby Powder, Mourning, Aliens, Hyper-Empathy, Downer, Rebel

Off-Broadway premiere of a new play with music presented in two acts; 55 Mercer; July 7–August 3, 2008 (Opened July 16); 8 previews, 20 performances. Previously presented at the Culture Project's Women Center Stage Festival April 8, 2008 and at The Kitchen Theatre Company (Ithaca, New York) April 18–20, 2008.

In Conflict Adapted and directed by Douglas C. Wager; based on the book by Yvonne Latty; Presented in association with Temple University Theatres (Roberta Sloan, Executive Producer); Set, Anew Laine; Costumes, Marian Cooper; Lighting, J. Dominic Chacon; Sound, Christopher Cappello & Paul Winnick; Video, Warren Bass; Production Manager, PSM, Emily Ellen Roberts; Peter Dean; Stage Manager, James McCaffrey; Production Director, John Hoey; Assistant Director, Felipe Vergara; Assistant to the Director/Understudy, Laura Edoff; Voice/Dialect Coach, Diane Gaary; Music Advisor, Paul Winnick; Producing Associate, Scott Braun; Graphics, Brian Michael Thomas; Cast: Tim Chambers (John Ball Jr./Darrell Anderson), Ethan Haymes (Jon Stoltz), Amanda Holston (Kelly Dougherty), Suyeon Kim (Tammy Duckworth), Sean Lally (Ivan Medina/Robert Acosta), Joy Notoma (Tracy Ringo), Sam Paul (Sam White/Julius Tulley), Danielle Pinnock (Lisa Haynes), Tom Rader (Matthew Miller/Ty Simmons), Stan Demidoff (Alex Pressman/Dave Bischel), Damon Williams (Herold Noel/Jamel Daniels)

New York premiere of a new play presented without intermission in repertory with *The Atheist*; Barrow Street Theatre; September 18–November 16, 2008 (Opened September 24); 6 previews, 41 performances. Previously presented at Temple University October 4–13, 2007 with most of this cast.

Campbell Scott in The Atheist
(photo by T. Charles Erickson)

The Atheist by Ronan Noone; Co-Produced by Circle in the Square Theatre, Theodore Mann and Paul Libin; Director, Justin Waldman; Set, Cristina Todesco; Lighting, Ben Stanton; Costumes, Jessica Curtright; Sound, Alex Neumann; Stage Manager, Emily Ellen Roberts; Assistant Director, Hondo Weiss-Richmond; Production Manager/Creative Consultant, Peter Dean; Associate Production Manager, Daniel Naish; Cast: Campbell Scott (Augustine Early)

Revival of a solo-performance play presented without intermission in repertory with *In Conflict*; Barrow Street Theatre; October 6, 2008–January 4, 2009 (Opened October 12); 6 previews, 53 performances. A staged reading of the play starring Mr. Scott was previously presented as a benefit for the Culture Project on May 20, 2008 (see *Theatre World* Vol. 64, page 170), and the production was presented at Williamstown Theatre Festival June 25–July 26, 2008.

Lenelle Moïse and Karla Mosley in Expatriate *(photo by Vanessa Vargas)*

The Company of In Conflict *(photo by Ryan S. Brandenberg)*

Irish Repertory Theatre

Twenty-first Season

Artistic Director, Charlotte Moore; Producing Director, Ciarán O'Reilly; General Manager, Jeffrey Chrzczon; Development, Patrick A. Kelsey; Box Office Manager, Jeffrey Wingfield; Audience Services, Jared Dawson; Literary Manager, Kara Manning; Membership Manager, Abigail Lynn; Marketing, Melissa L. Pelkey; Dialect Coach, Stephen Gabis; Production Coordinator, Mac Smith; Casting, Deborah Brown; Press, Shirley Herz Associates, Dan Demello

Around the World in 80 Days by Mark Brown, based on the novel by Jules Verne; Presented in association with Cincinnati Playhouse in the Park; Director, Michael Evan Haney; Set, Joseph P. Tilford; Costumes, David Kay Mickelsen; Lighting, Betsy Adams; Sound, David Andrew Levy; PSM, Andrea L. Schell; Cast: Daniel Freedom Stewart (Phileas Fogg), Evan Zes (Passepartout/John Sullivan), John Keating (Detective Fix/others), Lauren Elise McCord (Aouda/others), Jay Russell (various characters), Mark Parenti (Musician/Foley Artist)

Setting: England, 1872. New York premiere of a new play presented in two acts; Francis J. Greenburger Mainstage; July 11–September 28, 2009 (Opened July 20); 11 previews, 81 performances. This production was the final show of the previous season.

Jay Russell John Keating and Daniel Stewart in Around the World in 80 Days (*photo by Sandy Underwood*)

The Master Builder by Henrik Ibsen, adapted by Frank McGuinness; Director, Ciarán O'Reilly; Set, Eugene Lee; Costumes, Linda Fisher; Lighting, Michael Gottlieb; Sound, Zachary Williamson; Hair/Wigs, Robert-Charles Vallance; Props Master, Rick Murray; Assistant Director, Helena Gleissner; PSM, Pamela Brusoski; ASM, Janice M. Brandine; Cast: Herb Foster (Knut Brovik), Daniel Talbott (Ragnar Brovik), Letitia Lange (Kaja), James Naughton (Halvard Solness), Kristin Griffith (Aline Solness), Doug Stender (Dr. Herdel), Charlotte Parry (Hilde), Janice M. Brandine (Townsperson)

Setting: The studio, study, and patio of Halvard Solness, Norway; September 1892. World premiere of a new adaptation of the classic play presented in two acts; Francis J. Greenburger Mainstage; October 10–November 30, 2008 (Opened October 23); 13 previews, 39 performances.

Confessions of an Irish Publican Adapted by Des Keogh from the writings of John B. Keane; Director, Charlotte Moore; Set, Murmod Inc.; Costumes, David Toser; Lighting, Mac Smith; Stage Manager, Sarah Tschirpke; Cast: Des Keogh (Martin McMeer and others)

World premiere of a solo performance play presented in two acts; W. Scott McLucas Studio Theatre; November 5–30, 2008 (Opened November 9); 5 previews, 22 performances.

James Naughton and Charlotte Parry in The Master Builder (*photo by Carol Rosegg*)

Des Keough in Confessions of an Irish Publican (*photo by Carol Rosegg*)

A Child's Christmas in Wales by Dylan Thomas, adapted, designed and directed by Charlotte Moore; Music Director, Mark Hartman; Lighting, Michael Gottlieb; Costumes, David Toser; PSM, Sarah Tschirpke; Stage Manager, Aaron Pratt; Cast: Edwin Cahill, Kerry Conte, Jon Fletcher, Victoria Mallory, Ashley Robinson

Revival of a one-act play with music presented without intermission; Francis J. Greenburger Mainstage; December 3, 2008–January 4, 2009 (Opened December 7); 5 previews, 29 performances. Previously presented in the Studio Theatre last season (see *Theatre World* Vol. 64, page 170).

Jon Fletcher, Victoria Mallory, Mark Hartman (at piano), Edwin Cahill, Kerry Conte and Ashley Robinson in A Child's Christmas in Wales *(photo courtesy of Irish Repertory Theatre)*

Aristocrats by Brian Friel; Director, Charlotte Moore; Set, James Morgan; Costumes, Linda Fisher; Lighting, Brian Nason; Sound, Zachary Williamson; Properties, Deirdre Brennan; PSM, Pamela Brusoski; ASM, Janice M. Brandine; Hair/Wigs, Robert-Charles Vallance; Assistant Costumes, Alice Garland; Assistant Sound, Reid Hall; Cast: Rufus Collins (Tom Hoffnung), Sean Gormley (Willie Driver), Geddeth Smith (Uncle George/Father), John Keating (Casimir), Lynn Hawley (Judith), Orlagh Cassidy (Alice), Laura Odeh (Claire), Ciarán O'Reilly (Eamon)

Setting: Ballybeg Hall, overlooking the village of Ballybeg, County Donegal, Ireland. Summer, mid-1970s. Revival of a play in three acts presented with one intermission; Francis J. Greenburger Mainstage; January 16–March 29, 2009 (Opened January 25); 10 previews, 64 performances. American premiere at Manhattan Theatre Club April 11–September 24, 1989 (see *Theatre World* Vol. 45, page 88).

Laura Odeh, Lynn Hawley, John Keating and Orlagh Cassidy in Aristocrats *(photo by Carol Rosegg)*

The Yeats Project Twenty-six plays by William Butler Yeats performed in repertory, with special evenings of dance, poetry, films and lectures; Presented in association with the W.B. Yeats Society of New York, The American Irish Historical Society, Glucksman Ireland House, and the Consulate General of Ireland New York (Niall Burgess, Consul General); Mainstage Directors, Charlotte Moore and Ciarán O'Reilly; Concert Readings Director, George C. Helsin; Sets, Charlie Corcoran; Costumes, David Toser; Lighting, Brian Nason; Sound, Zachary Williamson; Projections, Jan Hartley; Mask, Bob Flanagan; Properties, Deirdre Brennan; Original Music, Bill Whelan; Choreography, Barry McNabb; Stage Manager, Elis C. Arroyo, ASM, Leslie Grisdale; Mainstage Productions: (Cycle A) *The Countess Cathleen, The Cat And The Moon, On Baile's Strand*; (Cycle B) *The Land of Heart's Desire, The Pot of Broth, Purgatory, A Full Moon In March, Cathleen Ni Houlihan*; Studio Theatre Productions (concert readings): *At the Hawk's Well, Calvary, Deirdre, The Hour Glass, The King's Threshold, The Resurrection, The Shadowy Waters, The Words upon the Window Pane, The Green Helmet, The Only Jealousy of Emer, The Unicorn from the Stars, The Player Queen, The Dreaming of the Bones, Sophocles' Oedipus at Colonus, Sophocles' Oedipus Rex, The King of the Great Clock Tower, The Herne's Egg,* and *The Death of Cuchulain*; Mainstage Productions Cast: Kevin Collins, Peter Cormican, Terry Donnelly, Patrick Fitzgerald, Sean Gormley, Amanda Quaid, Amanda Sprecher, Justin Stoney, Fiana Toibin, William J. Ward

A festival of plays and special events; Francis J. Greenburger Mainstage Theatre and W. Scott McLucas Studio Theatre; April 8–May 3, 2009 (Opened April 15); Mainstage Productions: 8 previews, 20 performances (Cycle A: 5 previews, 9 performances; Cycle B: 3 previews, 11 performances); Studio Productions: 15 performances.

Peter Cormican, Mary Linda Rapelye and Christian Kauffmann in The Rivalry *(photo by Rick Teller)*

The Rivalry by Norman Corwin; Presented in association with the Vincent Dowling Theatre Company; Director, Vincent Dowling; Set, Eugene D. Warner; Costumes, Rosi Zingales; Lighting, Brian Nason; Sound, Zachary Williamson; Original Sound, Walter Mantani; PSM, Elis C. Arroyo; ASM, Pamela Brusoski; Cast: Mary Linda Rapelye (Adele Douglas), Peter Cormican (Stephen A. Douglas), Christian Kauffmann (Abraham Lincoln), Doug Stender (Republican Committeeman/Reporter)

Setting: Platforms and committee rooms in different Illinois towns, various hotels, the Douglas home, a railway station, and a moving train in summer and fall 1858. Revival of a play presented in two acts; Francis J. Greenburger Theatre; May 15–July 19, 2009 (Opened May 21); 7 previews, 61 performances. Originally produced on Broadway at the Bijou Theatre February 7–April 18, 1959 (see *Theatre World* Vol. 15, page 90).

After Luke and **When I Was God** by Cónal Creedon; Director, Tim Ruddy; Set, Lex Liang; Costumes, David Toser; Lighting, Brian Nason; Sound, Shannon Slaton; PSM, April A. Kline; ASM, Janice M. Brandine; Production Coordinator, Jake McGuire; Assistant to Set Designer, Stephanie Raines; Graphics, Melissa L. Pelkey; Cast: *After Luke*: Michael Mellamphy (Maneen/Mrs. Foley), Gary Gregg (Son), Colin Lane (Dadda); *When I Was God*: Gary Gregg (Father/Commentator), Michael Mellamphy (Referee/Young Dinny/Dino/Mother)

Setting: Cork, Ireland; Present Day. American premiere of two one-act plays presented with intermission; Francis J. Greenburger Mainstage Theatre; July 29–September 20, 2009 (Opened August 6); 8 previews, 47 performances.

Michael Mellamphy and Gary Gregg in When I Was God *(photo by Carol Rosegg)*

Gary Gregg and Colin Lane in After Luke *(photo by Carol Rosegg)*

The Keen Company

Ninth Season

Artistic Director, Carl Forsman; Executive Director, Wayne Kelton; Production Manager, Josh Bradford; Artistic Associate, Blake Lawrence; Audience Development Associate, Amanda Brandes; Resident Designers, Theresa Squire (Costumes), Josh Bradford (Lighting); Company Manager, Laura Braza; Resident Fight Director, Paul Molnar; Casting, Kelly Gillespie, McCorkle Casting; Press, Richard Kornberg & Associates, Billy Zavelson

The Fourposter by Jan de Hartog; Director, Blake Lawrence; Set, Sandra Goldmark; Sound, Jill BC DuBoff; PSM, Jess Johnston; ASM, Josh Yocom; Assistant Director, Brian Frederick; Technical Director, David Ogle; Assistant Design: Peiyi Wong (set), Kevin Thacker (costumes), Raquel Davis (lighting), Brandon Walcott (sound); Cast: Todd Weeks (Michael), Jessica Dickey (Agnes)

Setting: The bedroom of Michael and Agnes; Act One: 1890 and a year later; Act Two: 1901 and seven years later; Act Three: 1913 and twelve years later. Revival of the play in three acts in six scenes presented with two intermissions; Clurman Theatre on Theatre Row; October 7–November 22, 2008 (Opened October 19); 13 previews, 29 performances. Originally produced on Broadway at the Barrymore Theatre (and later the John Golden Theatre) with Hume Cronyn and Jessica Tandy October 24, 1951–May 2, 1953, playing 632 performances (see *Theatre World* Vol. 8, page 40.) Cronyn and Tandy also starred in a brief City Center revival January 5–16, 1955 (see *Theatre World* Vol. 11, page 108). The play is the basis for the 1966 musical, *I Do, I Do*.

Beasley's Christmas Party Adapted by C.W. Munger from the story by Booth Tarkington; Director, Carl Forsman; Sets, Beowulf Boritt; Sound, Will Pickens; Stage Manager, Emily Arnold; Assistant Director, Laura Braza; ASM, Josh Yocom; Production Manager, Josh Higgason; Movement, Tracy Bersley; Prop Master/Assistant Set Design, Buist Bickley; Associate Lighting, Peter Hoeburger; Assistant Costumes, Emily DeAngelis; Assistant Lighting, Lee Terry; Fiddle Player, John Cockman; Cast: Tony Ward (Booth), Joseph Collins (Beasley/Downey/Peck/others), Christa Scott-Reed (Anne/Widow/Grist/others)

Setting: Wainwright, a state capitol, around the the turn of the 20th Century. World premiere of a play presented without intermission; Clurman Theatre on Theatre Row; December 2, 2008–January 3, 2009 (Opened December 7); 6 previews, 24 performances.

Heroes by Gérald Sibleyras, translated by Tom Stoppard; Director, Carl Forsman; Set, Beowulf Boritt; Sound, Will Pickens; Stage Manager, Jess Johnston; Technical Director, Marshall Miller; Assistant Director, Laura Braza; ASM, Josh Yocom; Associate Lighting, Peter Hoerburger; Assistant Set/Props Maser, Buist Bickley; Assistant Costumes, Franny Bohar; Cast: John Cullum (Henri), Ron Holgate (Gustave), Jonathan Hogan (Philippe)

Setting: A veterans' home in France. 1959. New York premiere of a new play presented without intermission; Clurman Theatre on Theatre Row; February 24–April 11, 2008 (Opened March 8); 13 previews, 28 performances.

Keen Teens Three plays: *Firebirds* by Liz Flahive; Director, Blake Lawrence; *The Ghost of Enoch Charlton* by Cheri Magid; Director, Leah C. Gardiner; The Southride High School Forensics Team Presents *Assorted Tales of Robin Hood* by Jason Grote; Director, Heath Cullens; Clurman Theatre on Theatre Row; May 29–May 31, 2009.

Top: *Todd Weeks and Jessica Dickey in* The Fourposter (photo by Suzi Sadler)

Center: *Tony Ward, Joseph Collins and Christa Scott-Reed in* Beasley's Christmas Party *(photo by Suzi Sadler)*

Bottom: *Jonathan Hogan, Ron Holgate and John Cullum in* Heroes *(photo by Theresa Squire)*

Lincoln Center Theater

Twenty-fourth Season

Artistic Director, André Bishop; Executive Producer, Bernard Gersten; General Manager, Adam Siegel; Production Manager, Jeff Hamlin; Development, Hattie K. Jutagir; Finance, David S. Brown; Marketing, Linda Mason Ross; Education, Kati Koerner; Musical Theatre Associate Producer, Ira Weitzman; Dramaturg/LCT Directors Lab, Anne Cattaneo; Associate Directors, Graciela Danielle, Nicholas Hytner, Jack O'Brien, Susan Stroman, Daniel Sullivan; Resident Director, Bartlett Sher; Dramaturg and Director of Director of LCT Directors Lab, Anne Cattaneo; LCT3 Director, Paige Evans; Casting, Daniel Swee; Press, Philip Rinaldi, Barbara Carroll

Saturn Returns by Noah Handle; Director, Nicholas Martin; Sets, Ralph Funicello; Costumes, Robert Morgan; Lighting, Peter Kaczorowski; Original Music & Sound, Mark Bennett; Stage Manager, Robyn Henry; Company Manager, Jessica Perlmeter Cochrane; Assistant Company Manager, Daniel Hoyos; Assistant Director, Justin Waldman; Second Assistant Director, Portia Krieger; ASM, Rosy Garner; Cast: John McMartin (Gustin at 88), Rosie Benton (Suzanne/Zephyr/Loretta), James Rebhorn (Gustin at 58), Robert Eli (Gustin at 28); Understudies: Timothy Kiefer (Gustin at 28), Guy Paul (Gustin at 58), Donald Grody (Gustin at 88), Gretchen Hall (Suzanne/Zephyr/Loretta)

Setting: A living room in Grand Rapids, Michigan; 2008, 1978, 1948. New York premiere of a new play presented without intermission; Mitzi E. Newhouse Theatre; October 16, 2008–January 4, 2009 (Opened November 10); 29 previews, 64 performances.

Robert Eli, Rosie Benton and John McMartin in Saturn Returns *(photo by Joan Marcus)*

Happiness Book by John Weidman, music by Scott Frankel, lyrics by Michael Korie; Director and Choreography, Susan Stoman; Sets, Thomas Lynch; Costumes, William Ivey Long; Lighting, Donald Holder; Sound, Scott Lehrer; Orchestrations, Bruce Coughlin; Music Director, Eric Stern; Projections, Joshua Frankel; Casting, Tara Rubin; Associate Director/Choreographer, Joanne Manning; Stage Manager, Rolt Smith; Company Manager, Jessica Perlmeter Cochrane; Assistant Company Manager, Daniel Hoyos; Assistant Director/Choreographer, Jeff Whiting; Associate Set, Charlie Corcoran; Associate Sound, Drew Levy; Music Copying, Emily Grishman; Props, Kathy Fabian, Sarah Bird; Wigs/Hair, Paul Huntley; Dialect Coach, Deborah Hecht; Makeup, Angelina Avellone; ASM, Andrea O. Saraffian; Dance Captains, Holly Ann Butler, Eric Santagata; Associate

Hunter Foster, Sebastian Arcelus, Ken Page, Miguel Cervantes, Joanna Gleason, Jenny Powers, Pearl Sun and Robert Petkoff in Happiness *(photo by Paul Kolnik)*

Conductor, Paul Staroba; Music Coordinator, John Miller; Cast: Sebastian Arcelus (Zack), Miguel Cervantes (Miguel), Jenny Powers (Gina), Phyllis Somerville (Helen), Robert Petkoff (Neil), Pearl Sun (Cindy), Fred Applegate (Kevin), Ken Page (Maurice), Joanna Gleason (Arlene), Hunter Foster (Stanley); Ensemble: Ana Maria Andricain (Juanita/New Yorker), Patrick Cummings (Tommy Mathis/Jason Fitterman/New Yorker), Alan H. Green (USO Vocalist/Willie Mays/New Yorker), James Moye (Kevin's Father/Luther/New Yorker), Alessa Neeck (Pedi Cab Driver/Young Helen/Stewardess/Ginny/New Yorker), Robb Sapp (Mick Jagger/Marcello/New Yorker), Alexander Scheitinger (Young Kevin/New Yorker), Lina Silver (Yolanda/New Yorker), Idara Victor (Hyacinth/USO Vocalist/New Yorker); Swings: Holly Ann Butler, Janet Dickinson, Samantha Maza, Eric Santagata, Matt Wall; Orchestra: Eric Stern (Conductor), Paul Staroba (synth), Todd Groves & Roger Rosenberg (reeds), Dan Urness (trumpet), Steve Armour (trombone), Will DeVos (French horn), John Benthal (guitar), John Arbo (bass), Tim McLafferty (drums/percussion)

Hunter Foster and Sebastian Arcelus in Happiness *(photo by Paul Kolnik)*

Musical Numbers: Just Not Right Now, Blips, Flibberty Jibbers and Wobbly Knees, Best Seats in the Ballpark, Gstaad, The Boy Inside Your Eyes, Perfect Moments, Step Up the Ladder, Family Flashcards, The Tooth Fairy Song, Road to Nirvana, Gstaad (reprise), Happiness, Finale

Time: The Present. Place: New York City. World premiere of a new musical presented without intermission; Mitzi E. Newhouse Theatre; February 27–June 7, 2009 (Opened March 30); 31 previews, 69 performances.

John Lithgow: Stories by Heart Written and performed by John Lithgow; Stories included "Haircut" by Ring Lardner and "Uncle Fred Flits By" by P.G. Wodehouse, presented in rotating repertory; Director, Jack O'Brien; Stage Manager, Brandon Kahn; Set, Thomas Lynch; Lighting, Donald Holder; ASM, Zoë Chapin; Company Managers, Matthew Markoff, Jessica Perlmeter Cochrane; Assistant Company Manager, Daniel Hoyos; Lighting Operator, Josh Stein

Revival of a solo performance show presented without intermission; Mitzi E. Newhouse Theatre; Sunday and Monday evenings April 12–May 23, 2009; 14 performances. Lincoln Center previously presented the show last season (see *Theatre World* Vol. 64, page 173).

John Lithgow in Stories by Heart *(photo by Joan Marcus)*

LCT3 SERIES*

Clay by Matt Sax; Developed in collaboration with and directed by Eric Rosen; Presented by the Steinberg New Works Program; Additional Music, Jon Schmidt & Johnny Williams; Sets, Meghan Raham; Costumes, Emily Rebholz; Lighting, Jason Lyons; Sound/Orchestrations, Joshua Horvath; Stage Manager, Dennis J. Conners; ASM, Zoë Burke Chapin; Company Manager, Maia Sutton; Cast: Matt Sax (Clifford/Sir John/Father/Mother/etc); Music Tracks: Ava Marie Fain, Jorie Henton, Tina M. Howell, Travis Turner (vocals), Inger Carle (violin), Alison Chesley (cello), Joshua Horvath (guitar), Kevin O'Donnell (drums), Jason Sites (bass), Susan Voelz (violin)

New York premiere of a new hip-hop musical presented without intermission; Duke on 42nd Street; October 6–November 8, 2008 (Opened October 15); 11 previews, 29 performances. U.S. premiere September 2006 at About Face Theatre and Lookingglass Theatre Company, Chicago. Previously presented by Center Theatre Group at the Kirk Douglas Theatre September 2007 (see *Theatre World* Vol. 64, page 298).

Matt Sax in Clay *(photo by Don Ipock)*

Stunning by David Adjmi; Presented by the Steinberg New Works Program; Director, Anne Kauffman; Sets, David Korins; Costumes, Miranda Hoffman; Lighting, Japhy Weideman; Sound, Rob Kaplowitz; Fight Director, J. David Brimmer; Stage Manager, Megan Schwarz; ASM, Sara Cox Bradley; Company Manager, Josh Lowenthal; Assistant Director, Christy Denny; Associate Set, Amanda Stephens; Associate Lighting, Justin Partier; Props, Faye Armon; Dialect Coach, Shane Ann Younts; Assistant Fight Directors, John Robichau, Mike Yahn; Cast: Jeanine Serralles (Shelly Dweck), Cristin Milioti (Lily Schwecky), Sas Goldberg (Claudine Dushey), Charlayne Woodard (Blanche Nesbitt), Danny Mastrogiorgio (Ike Schwecky), Steven Rattazzi (Jojo Dweck)

Setting: Place: Midwood, Brooklyn. Time: Around now. New York premiere of a new play presented in two acts; Duke on 42nd Street; June 1–July 11 (Opened June 18); 12 previews, 36 performances. Originally produced by Woolly Mammoth Theatre Company, Washington, D.C. (Howard Shalwitz, Artistic Director; Jeffrey Herrmann, Managing Director) March 2008 (see *Theatre World* Vol. 64, page 339).

*Lincoln Center created this new programming initiative this season, devoted to producing the work of emerging playwrights, directors and designers.

Charlayne Woodard and Cristin Milioti in Stunning *(photo by Erin Baiano)*

MCC Theater (Manhattan Class Company)

Twenty-third Season

Artistic Directors, Robert LuPone & Bernard Telsey; Associate Artistic Director, William Cantler; Executive Director, Blake West; General Manager, Ted Rounsaville; Company Manager/Assistant General Manager, Kristina Bramhall; Literary Manager/Dramaturg, Stephen Willems; Literary Associate, Jamie Green; Development, Mara Richards; Development Associate, Jennifer Udden; Marketing, Ian Allen; Marketing Associate, Isabel Sinistore; Education/Outreach, John Michael DiResta; Youth Company, Stephen DiMenna; Production Manager, B.D. White; Resident Director, Doug Hughes; Resident Playwright, Neil LaBute; Technical Director, James Reddington; Producing Special Arrangements, The Lucille Lortel Theatre Foundation; Casting, Telsey & Company; Press, O&M Co., Rick Riramontez, Jon Dimond, Molly Barnett

Fifty Words by Michael Weller; Director, Austin Pendleton; Set, Neil Patel; Lighting, Michelle Habeck; Costumes, Mimi O'Donnell; Sound, Fitz Patton; Original Music, Josh Schmidt; PSM, Pamela Edington; Assistant Director, Diana Basamajian; Stage Manager, Jana Llynn; Properties, Michele Spadaro; Associate Scenic Design, Stephen Dobay & Lara Fabian; Cast: Norbert Leo Butz (Adam), Elizabeth Marvel (Jan)

World premiere of a new play presented without intermission; Lucille Lortel Theatre; September 10–November 8, 2008 (Opened October 1); 15 previews, 38 performances.

Elizabeth Marvel and Norbert Leo Butz in Fifty Words
(photos by Joan Marcus)

The Third Story by Charles Busch; Director, Carl Andress; Original Music, Lewis Flinn; Set, David Gallo; Costumes, Gregory Gale; Lighting, David Weiner; Sound, Chris Luessmann; Hair & Wigs, Tom Watson; Dialect Coach, Charlotte Fleck; Fight Director, Steve Rankin; PSM, Kelly Glasgow; Assistant Director, Sara Sahin; Properties, Michele Spadaro; Makeup, Pamela Stompoly-Ericson & Karl Giant; Associate Design: Stephen Dobay & Tom George (set), Justin Smiley (sound); Cast: Jonathan Walker (Drew/Steve Bartlett), Kathleen Turner (Peg/Dr. Rutenspitz), Charles Busch (Queenie Bartlett/Baba Yaga), Sarah Rafferty (Verna/Princess Vasalisa), Jennifer Van Dyk (Dr. Constance Hudson), Scott Parkinson (Zygote)

Charles Busch, Jonathan Walker and Kathleen Turner
in The Third Story

Setting: Omaha, Nebraska; 1940s. New York premiere of a new play presented in two acts; Lucille Lortel Theatre; January 14–March 15, 2008 (Opened February 2); 20 previews, 42 performances. World premiere produced by La Jolla Playhouse (Christopher Ashley, Artistic Director) September 16–October 21, 2008 (see Regional Theatre listings in this volume).

Coraline Music and lyrics by Stephin Merritt, book by David Greenspan; based on the novel by Neil Gaiman; Presented in association with True Love Productions; Director, Leigh Silverman; Choreography, Denis Jones; Music Director, Kimberly Grigsby; Set, Christine Jones; Costumes, Anita Yavich; Lighting, Ben Stanton; Pianist, Phyllis Chen; Dialect Coach, Deborah Hecht; Co-Production Manager, Adam Shive; PSM, David H. Lurie; Assistant Director, Pirronne Yousefzadeh; SSDC Observer, Isaac Butler; Stage Manager, Emily Ellen Roberts; Props, Kathy Fabian; Associate Scenic Design, Tim McMath; Props Associates, Jennifer Breen, Sarah Bird; Assistant Design: Nicole Smith (costumes), Lauren Phillips (lighting); Assistant Technical Director, Megan Caplan; Cast: Julian Fleisher (Cat), David Greenspan (Other Mother), Jayne Houdyshell (Coraline), Francis Jue (Father/Miss Forcible/Other Miss Forcible), January LaVoy (Mother/Miss Spink/Other Miss Spink), Elliot Villar (Mr. Bobo/Other Mr. Bobo), William Youmans (Other Father)

World premiere of a new musical presented without intermission; Lucille Lortel Theatre; May 8–July 5, 2009 (Opened June 1); 26 previews, 35 performances.

Jayne Houdyshell in Coraline

Manhattan Theatre Club

Thirty-seventh Season

Artistic Director, Lynne Meadow; Executive Producer, Barry Grove; General Manager, Florie Seery; Associate Artistic Director/Production, Mandy Greenfield; Director of Artistic Development, Jerry Patch; Artistic Consultant, Daniel Sullivan; Director of Artistic Administration/Assistant to the Artistic Director, Amy Gilkes Loe; Casting, Nancy Piccione; Director of Musical Theatre, Clifford Lee Johnson III; Development, Jill Turner Lloyd; Marketing, Debra A. Waxman; Finance, Jeffrey Bledsoe; Associate General Manager, Lindsey Brooks Sag; Subscriber Services, Robert Allenberg; Telesales, George Tetlow; Education, David Shookhoff; Production Manager, Kurt Gardner; Company Manager, Erin Moeller; Properties Supervisor, Scott Laule; Costume Supervisor, Erin Hennessy Dean; Press, Boneau/Bryan-Brown, Chris Boneau, Aaron Meier, Christine Olver

Romantic Poetry Book, lyrics and direction by John Patrick Shanley; music by Henry Krieger; Musical Staging, Devanand Janki; Music Director/Vocal Arrangements, Sam Davis; Orchestrations, August Eriksmoen; Music Coordinator, Howard Joines; Sets, David Korins; Costumes, Laura Bauer; Lighting, Donald Holder; Sound, Brian Ronan; PSM, Dawn Wagner; Additional Casting, David Caparelliotis; Stage Manager, Kelly Hance; Assistant Director, Rachel Slaven; Associate Music Director, Gregory M. Brown; Associate Conductor, Rick Bertone; Music Copying, Kaye-Houston Music; Associate Design: Rod Lemmond (set), Rebecca Makus (lighting); Associate Production Manager, Philip Naudé; Assistant Production Manager, Kelsey Martinez; Dance Captain, Paige Price; Cast: Jeb Brown (Red), Ivan Hernandez (Fred), Mark Linn-Baker (Carl), Jerry Dixon* (Frankie), Patina Renea Miller (Mary), Emily Swallow (Connie); Understudies: Todd Gearhart (Carl, Frankie, Fred, Red), Paige Price (Connie, Mary); Orchestra: Gregory M. Brown (Conductor/piano), Summer Bogtgess (cello), Jackie Henderson (clarinet/tenor sax/bari sax, bass clarinet), Justin Smith (violin/mandolin), Greg Thymius (flute/clarinet/tenor sax); *Succeeded by: Tom Lucca (11/18/08)

Musical Numbers: Romantic Poetry, Connie My Bride, Destiny, The Five Towns, I Have No Words, For a Third Time, Rumba Woman, Go Through the Motions, Trouble, Wait a Minute, What About Love?, Where Is Our Real Life?, While You Were in the Lobby, So I Got Married/He's Rich/I'm Bored, Crazy Lights, Is Anybody Home?/There's a Fire, Through the Night, The Curse, Do You Think It's Easy?, An Ordinary Man, You're My Only Guy, No One Listens to the Poor, Give Me Love or Let Me Wait, Beauty, Walking up the Stairs

New York premiere of a new musical presented without intermission; City Center Stage I; October 1–December 7, 2008 (Opened October 28); 29 previews, 48 performances. Originally presented by New York Stage and Film Company and the Powerhouse Theatre at Vassar in July 2007.

Patina Renea Miller, Jerry Dixon, Emily Swallow, Mark Linn-Baker, Jeb Brown and Ivan Hernandez in Romantic Poetry

Mark Linn-Baker and Jeb Brown in Romantic Poetry *(photos by Joan Marcus)*

Back Back Back by Itamar Moses; Director, Daniel Aukin; Sets & Costumes, David Zinn; Lighting, David Weiner; Sound, Ryan Rumery & Daniel Baker; PSM, Kasey Ostopchuck; Stage Manager, Kyle Gates; Assistant Director, Adam Knight; Associate Lighting, Jake DeGroot; Fight Director, Thomas Schall; Production Supervisor, Cast: Jeremy Davidson (Kent), James Martinez (Raul), Michael Mosley (Adam); Understudy: Maximilian Osinski

Setting: New York premiere of a play presented without intermission; City Center Stage II; October 30, 2008–January 4, 2009 (Opened November 18); 21 previews, 47 performances. World premiere at the The Old Globe (San Diego, California).

Ruined by Lynn Nottage; Co-produced by the Goodman Theatre (Robert Falls, Artistic Director; Roche Schulfer, Executive Director); Director, Kate Whoriskey; Set, Derek McLane; Costumes, Paul Tazewell; Lighting, Peter Kaczorowski; Sound, Rob Milburn & Michael Bodeen; Original Music, Dominic Kanza; Lyrics, Lynn Nottage; Movement Director, Randy Duncan; Casting Associate, Adam Belcuore; PSM, Donald Fried; Stage Manager, Amy McRaney; Hair/Wigs, Charles LaPointe; Dialect Coach, Charlotte Fleck; New York Fight Director, Thomas Schall; Chicago Fight Director; Nick Sandys; Guitarist, Simon Shabantu Kashama; Cast: Quincy Tyler Berenstine (Salima), Cherise Boothe (Josephine), Chris Chalk (Jerome Kisembe/Soldier), Saidah Arrika Ekulona* (Mama Nadi), William Jackson Harper (Simon/Soldier/Miner/Aid Worker), Chiké Johnson (Fortune/Soldier/Miner), Russell G. Jones (Christian), Kevin Mambo (Commander Osembenga/Soldier), Tom Mardirosian (Mr. Harari), Ron McBee (Pascal/Soldier), Condola Rashad (Sophie); Understudies: Axel Avin Jr (Osembenga, Simon, Soldiers), Byron Bronson (Harari, Jerome, Kisembe, Aid Worker, Soldier), Victoire Charles

James Martinez (seated) *and Jeremy Davidson in* Back Back Back

Quincy Tyler Bernstine, Saidah, Arrika Ekulona, Chiké Johnson and William Jackson Harper in Ruined

(Josephine, Mama Nadi), Carl Cofield (Christian, Fortune, Soldier, Miner), Susan Heyward (Salima, Sophie, Josephine); *Succeeded by: Portia (5/26/09)

Time: The recent past. Place: A bar in a small mining town in the Ituri Rainforest, Democratic Republic of Congo. World premiere co-production of a play presented in two acts; City Center Stage I; January 21–September 6, 2009 (Opened March 25); 22 previews, 238 performances. Prior to its New York run, *Ruined* played the Goodman Theatre November 7–December 8, 2008 (see Regional Theatre listings in this volume). *Ruined* was extended eight times from its original closing date, and was the most acclaimed new play of the season, garnering Drama Desk, Lucille Lortel, New York Drama Critics' Circle, Outer Critics' Circle awards for Outstanding New Play, as well as the 2009 Pulitzer Prize for Drama; **2009 Theatre World Award:** Condola Rashad

Humor Abuse Created and performed by Lorenzo Pisoni, co-created and directed by Erica Schmidt; Lighting, Ben Stanton; Sound, Bart Fasbender; PSM, Hannah Cohen; Scenic Consultant, John Lee Beatty; Casting, David Caparelliotis; Animation, Fear Not Films; Production Supervisor, Adam Lang; Props Runner, Brian Carfi; Understudy: Aidan O'Shea

World premiere of a solo performance play presented without intermission; City Center Stage II; February 19–April 19, 2009 (Opened March 10); 21 previews, 48 performances. Originally developed in residency at the Eugene O'Neill Theater Center.

Condola Rashad, Cherise Booth and Quincy Tyler Bernstine in Ruined

Lorenzo Pisoni in Humor Abuse

Robin Moseley, Gerry Bamman, Jeanine Serralles, Chad Hoeppner and Jack Wetherall in The Glass Cage *(photos by Richard Termine)*

Julia Coffey and Dalton Harrod in The Widowing of Mrs. Holroyd

Gerry Bamman, Saxon Palmer and Sandra Struthers-Clerc in The Glass Cage

Julia Coffey, Nick Cordileone, Randy Danson, Arthur Lazalde, James Warke, Allyn Burrows and Eric Martin Brown (on floor) in The Widowing of Mrs. Holroyd

Mint Theater Company

Seventeenth Season

Artistic Director, Jonathan Bank; General Manager, Sherri Kotimsky; Box Office Manager, Martha Graebner; Assistant to the Artistic Director, Hunter Kaczorowski; Development Consultant, Ellen Mittenthal; Dramaturg, Heather J. Violanti; Literary Associate, Kaitlin Stilwell; Casting, Stuart Howard, Amy Schecter & Paul Hardt; Press, David Gersten & Associates

The Glass Cage by J.B. Priestley; Director, Lou Jacob; Set, Roger Hanna; Costumes, Camille Assaf; Lighting, Marcus Doshi; Sound, Lindsay Jones; Properties, Deborah Gaouette; PSM, Brian Maschka; ASM, Andrea Jo Martin; Illustration, Stefano Imbert; Graphics, Hunter Kaczorowski; Cast: Gerry Bamman (David McBane), Jack Wetherall (Malcom McBane), Robin Moseley (Mildred McBane), Sandra Struthers-Clerc (Elspie McBane), Chad Hoeppner (John Harvey), Fiona Toibin (Bridget), Chet Carlin (Dr. Gratton), Jeanine Serralles (Jean McBane), Saxon Palmer (Angus McBane), Michael Crane (Douglas McBane)

Setting: The sitting room in the McBane house in Toronto; October, 1906. American premiere of a play presented in four scenes in two acts; September 4–November 8, 2008 (Opened September 21); 19 previews, 51 performances. Originally produced at the Crest Theatre (Toronto) in 1956.

The Widowing of Mrs. Holroyd by D.H. Lawrence; Director, Stuart Howard; Sets, Marion Williams; Costumes, Martha Hally; Lighting, Jeff Nellis; Sound, Jane Shaw; Dialects/Dramaturgy, Amy Stoller; Assistant Director, Quin Gordon; Fight Choreogarphy, Michael G. Chin; PSM, Allison Deutsch; ASM, Andrea Jo Martin; Illustration, Stefano Imbert; Graphics, Hunter Kaczorowski; Cast: Julia Coffey (Mrs. Holroyd), Eric Martin Brown (Holroyd), Nick Cordileone (Blackmore), Dalton Harrod or Lance Chantiles-Wertz (Jack Holroyd), Emma Kantor or Amanda Roberts (Minnie Holroyd), Randy Danson (Grandmother), James Warke (Rigley), Pilar Witherspoon (Clara), Sheila Strasack (Laura), Allyn Burrows (Manager), Arthur Lazalde (Miner); Understudies: James Warke (Holroyd, Blackmore), Sheila Stasack (Grandmother), Arthur Lazalde (Rigley)

Setting: In and around Holroyd's cottage in Bestwood, England; two evenings in the 1910s. New York premiere of a play presented in four scenes in three acts with one intermission; February 4–April 5, 2009 (Opened March 1); 27 previews, 37 performances. Written in 1910, the play was first produced for one-night-only at the Los Angeles Little Theatre in 1916. The play was not revived again until 1968 at London's Royal Court Theatre.

The New Group

Thirteenth Season

Artistic Director, Scott Elliott; Executive Director, Geoffrey Rich; Managing Producer, Barrack Evans; Managing Director/Development, Oliver Dow; Associate Artistic Director, Ian Morgan; Artistic Associate, James Gittins; Business Manager, Elisabeth Bayer; Marketing/Public Relations, Darren Molovinsky; Special Events/Individual Giving, Cristina Galeano; Marketing Assistant, Jenna Lauren Freed; Production Supervisor, Peter R. Feuchtwanger/PRF Productions; Casting, Judy Henderson; Press, The Karpel Group, Bridget Klapinski, Elizabeth Sorrell

Mouth to Mouth by Kevin Elyot; Director, Mark Brokaw; Sets, Riccardo Hernandez; Costumes, Michael Krass; Lighting, Mark McCullough; Sound and Original Music, David Van Tieghem; PSM, Valerie A. Peterson; Stage Manager, Fran Rubenstein; Assistant Director, Gahl Pratt; Choreography, John Caraffa; Dialect Coach, Deborah Hecht; Properties, Matt Hodges; Assistant Design: Maruti Evans (set), Jessica Pabst (costumes), Bradley King (lighting), Brandon Wolcott (sound); Casting Associate, Kimberly Graham; Production Assistant, Jenny Herron; Cast: Christopher Abbott (Phillip), David Cale (Frank), Lisa Emery (Laura), Darren Goldstein (Roger), Elizabeth Jasicki (Cornelia), Andrew Polk (Gompertz), Richard Topol (Dennis)

Setting: A house in a South London suburb and at a London restaurant. American premiere of a new play presented without intermission; Acorn Theatre on Theatre Row; October 22–December 6, 2008 (Opened November 6); 15 previews, 32 performances. World premiere at London's Royal Court Theatre in 2001.

Mourning Becomes Electra A trilogy by Eugene O'Neill; Director, Scott Elliott; Set, Derek McLane; Costumes, Susan Hilferty; Lighting, Jason Lyons; Sound, Shane Rettig; Score, Pat Metheny; PSM, Valerie A. Peterson; Assistant Director, Marie Masters; ASM, Stephanie Cali; Fight Director, David Anzuelo; Properties, Matt Hodges; Associate Costumes, Marina Reti; Assisant Design, Shoko Kambara (set), Grant Wilcoxsen (lighting), Jorge Cortes (sound); Casting Associate, Kimberly Graham; Company Manager, Jenna Lauren Freed; Cast: Carolyn Baeumler (Louisa Ames/Emma), Mark Blum (Brigadier-General Ezra Mannon), Joseph Cross (Orin Mannon), Susan Goodwillie (Minne Ames/Mrs. Hills), Mycah Hogan (Everett Hills, D. D./Joe Silva), Robert Hogan (Seth Beckwith), Jena Malone (Lavinia Mannon), Patrick Mapel (Captain Peter Niles), Sean Meehan (Amos Ames/Josiah Borden/Ira Macket), Anson Mount (Captain Adam Brant), Phoebe Strole (Hazel Niles), Lili Taylor (Christine Mannon), John Wojda (Dr. Joseph Blake/The Chantyman/Abner Small); Understudies: Susan Goodwillie (Lavinia, Hazel), Carolyn Baeumler (Christine), Sean Meehan (Brant), John Wojda (Ezra, Seth), Mycah Hogan (Orin, Peter), Geoffrey Bryant (Hills, Silva, Chantyman, Small, Macket, Blake, Ames, Borden), Therese Barbato (Mrs. Hills, Louise, Emma)

Setting: The Mannon house in New England; April 1865 and summer 1866. Revival of a trilogy of plays (*Homecoming, The Hunted,* and *The Haunted*) presented with two intermissions; Acorn Theatre on Theatre Row; January 27–March 1, 2009 (Opened February 19); 22 previews, 12 performances. Originally produced on Broadway at the Guild Theatre in October 1931.

Groundswell by Ian Bruce; Director, Scott Elliott; Sets, Derek McLane; Costumes, Eric Becker; Lighting, Jason Lyons; Sound, Sharon Rettig; PSM, Valerie A. Peterson; Dialect Coach, Stephen Gabis; Assistant Director, Marie Masters; ASM, Stephanie Cali; Properties, Matt Hodge; Assistant Set, Julia Noulin-Merat; Assistant Sound, Justin Smiley; Company Manager, Jenna Lauren Freed; Production Assistant, Katerina Madson; Cast: Larry Bryggman (Smith), David Lansbury (Johan), Souléymane Sy Savané (Thami)

tv Setting: The Garnet Guest Lodge, a beachfront guesthouse in a small port town on the South African West Coast on a foggy winter day. American premiere of a new play presented in without intermission; Acorn Theatre on Theatre Row; May 4–June 27, 2009 (Opened May 18); 13 previews, 44 performances.

Christopher Abbott, Lisa Emery and Richard Topol in Mouth to Mouth *(photos by Monique Carboni)*

Jena Malone and Lili Taylor in Mourning Becomes Electra

Larry Bryggman, David Lansbury and Souléymane Sy Savané in Groundswell

New Victory Theater

Thirteenth Season

President, Cora Cahan; Executive VP, Lisa Lawer Post; VP of Operations, Jarret M. Haynes; Curatorial Progamming, Mary Rose Lloyd; Development SVP, Cheryl Kohn; Education Programming, Edie Demas; Finance VP, Kim Dobbie Neuer; NVT Director of Theater Operations, Melinda Berk; Director of Production, David Jensen; NVT Technical Director, Robert Leach, NVT Production Coordinator, Colleen Davis; Public Relations, Laura Kaplow-Goldman; Marketing, Lauren P. Fitzgerald; Ticket Services, Robin Leeds; New 42nd Street Studios/The Duke on 42nd Street Director of Operations, Alma Malabanan-Mcgrath

The Green Sheep Based on the children's book *Where is the Green Sheep?* by Mem Fox; Presented by Seattle Children's Theatre; Director, Cate Fowler; Literary Advisor, Mem Fox; Music Advisor, Richard Gill; Dance Advisor, Jeff Meiners; Installation Designer, Roy Ananda; Composer, Fleur Green; Stage Manager, Sarah S. Mixson; Mentor, Wendy Schiller; Cast: Morgan M. Rowe, Connor Toms, Matt Johnston, Sarah S. Mixson

New York premiere of a strorytelling/puppetry show presented without intermission; New 42nd Street Studios; September 10–28, 2008; 20 performances.

A scene from The Green Sheep
(photo courtesy of Seattle Children's Theatre)

Rewind Created and presented by Knucklehead Zoo (Las Vegas); Director, Augustine Covert; Associate Directors, Abenamar Honrubia and Steve Corral; Choreography, Abenamar Honrubia; Management, Covert Operations Ltd.; Cast: Ricky Barraza, Justin Buenaventura, Steve Corral, Alfonso Echeverria, Christian Esccobedo, Leonardo Honrubia, Ronald Harris, Miguel Olague, Paul Thomas; Beatboxer: Adym Evans;

World premiere of a breakdance and hip-hop show presented without intermission New Victory Theatre; October 3–19, 2008; 15 performances.

Hunchback Conceived and designed by Jim Lasko, adapted and directed from the Victor Hugo novel by Leslie Bauxbaum Danzig; Presented by Redmoon Theatre (Chicago); Producer, Rebecca Hunter; Music, Michael Zerang; Text, Mickle Mahler; Costumes, Joel Klaff; Puppets, Laura Heit; Masks/Original Set, Shoshanna Utchenik; Cast: Calvin Dutton, Mary Winn Heider, Katie Rose McLaughlin, Alden Moore, Jeremy Sher, Samuel Taylor, Jay Torrence, Leah Urzendowski, Zeke Sulkes

A revised edition of puppet theatre show presented without intermission; New Victory Theatre; October 24–November 9, 2008; 14 performances. Previously presented by the Redmoon Theatre in 2007; an earlier version of the show was performed in New York in 2000 at the Henson International Festival of Puppet Theater.

Birdhouse Factory Created and directed by Chris Lashua; Presented by Circque Mechanics (Las Vegas); Co-director/Choreography/Costumes, Aloysia Gavre; Set/Ariel Rigging, Sean Riley; Machines/Circus Props, Chris Lashua, Chris Taylor, Tony Roan, Michael Redinger; Lighting, Heather Basarab; Additional Lighting, Blake Manship; Sound, Rex Camphuis; Original Music, Cody Westheimer & Julia Newman; Stage Manager, Claudette Waddle; Cast: Sagiv Ben Binyamim, Elisabeth Carpenter, Jesse Dryden, Aloysia Gavre, Thayr Harris, Wes Hatfield, Patrick Mcguire, Lindsay Orton-Hines, Micheal Redinger, Russ Stark, Khongorzul Tsevenoidov

New York premiere of a circus/acrobatic/physical comedy spectacular presented without intermission; New Victory Theatre; November 14–December 14, 2008; 28 performances.

Cirque Mechanics in Birdhouse Factory *(photo by Darin Basile)*

Holiday House Party by Dan Zanes and Friends; Produced by Festival Five Records and Pomegranate Arts; Tour Representation, Linda Brumach & Alisa Regas for Pomegranate Arts; Set/Lighting, Chad McCarver; Sound, David Schnirman; Management, Irene Cabrera; Cast: Dan Zanes; Musicians/Artists: Tareq Abboushi (bazuq); Colin Brooks (drums); Julian Crouch (vocals) Sonia de los Santos (guitar/vocals); John Foti (accordion/saxophone); Derick K. Grant, Kaleo Grant & Lulu Grant (tap dance); Saskia Sunshine Lane (bass); Elena Moon Park (fiddle/trumpet), Basya Schecter (vocals), Zafer Tawil (percussion), the Villa-Lobos Brothers with Claudia Valentina Montes (Mariachi band)

A theatrical concert presented without intermission; New Victory Theatre; December 19–January 4, 2009; 21 performances.

Cranked Created and presented by Green Thumb Theatre (Vancouver, Canada); Director, Patrick McDonald; Music/Beats, Kyprios and Stylust; Lyrics, Kyprios and Michael P. Northey; Cast: Kyle Cameron (Stan)

A solo performance play with hip-hop music presented without intermission; Duke on 42nd Street; January 9–25, 2009; 12 performances.

Jason and the Argonauts by Robert Forest; Presented by Visible Fictions (Glasgow, Scotland); Artistic Producer/Director, Douglas Irvine; Music, Daniel Padden; Set/Costumes, Robin Peoples; Stage Manager, Colin Sutherland; Production Manager, Andrew Coulton; Lighting, Paul Ancell; Cast: Simon Donaldson, Tim Settle

New York premiere of a new touring play presented without intermission; New Victory Theatre; January 23–February 1, 2009; 10 performances.

Taoub Created and directed by Aurélien Bory; Presented by Groupe Acrobatique de Tanger (Tangier, Morocco); Producers, Institut Francais Du Nord; Assistant Director, Pierre Rigal; Lighting, Arno Veyrat; Costumes, Mahmoud Tabit Ben Slimane; Production Managers, Joel Abriac & Cecile Herault; Cast: Jamila Abdellaqui, Abdeslam Brouzi, Adel Chaaban, Mohammed Achraf Chaaban, Abdelaziz El Haddad, Najib El Maimouni Idrissi, Amal Hammich, Mohammed Hammich, Younes Hammich, Samir Laaroussi, Yassine Srasi, Younes Yemlahi

An acrobat show presented without intermission; New Victory Theatre; February 6–22, 2009; 17 performances.

Henry V by William Shakespeare; Presented by The Acting Company (Margot Harley, Producing Director) and the Guthrie Theater (Joe Dowling, Director); Director, Davis McCallum; Set, Neil Patel; Costumes, Anita Yavich; Lighting, Michael Chybowski; Music Composition and Direction, Victor Zupanc; Fight Director, John Sipes; Voice & Text Consultants, Andrew Wade & Sara Phillips; Sound, Scott W. Edwards; Casting, McCorkle Casting; Text Preparation, Dakin Matthews; Production Manager, Joel Howell; PSM, Karen Parlato; ASM, Nick Tochelli; Wigs/Makeup, Erin Kennedy Lunsford; Staff Rep Director, Ian Belknap; Company Manager, Steven Varon; Supervisors: Daniel Chapman (lighting), Daphne Hayner (props), Brie Fuches (wardrobe), Tim Boyce (sound); Press, Judy Katz; Cast: Matthew Amendt–King Henry), Freddy Arsenault (Chorus #1–Scroop/Dauphin/Mac Morris/Bedford/Williams), Carie Kawa (Chorus #2–French Ambassador/Grey/Alice/Warwick), William Sturdivant (Chorus #3–Westmorland/Bourbon/Fluellen), Georgia Cohen (Chorus #4–Hostess/French Mayor/Herald/Queen), Robert Michael McClure (Chorus #5–Canterbury/Gower/Le Fer/Burgundy), Kelley Curran (Chorus #6–Boy/Katherine), Samuel Taylor (Chorus #7–Nym/Mountjoy/Court/Salisbury), Sonny Valicenti (Chorus #8–Gloucester/Constable/Jamy), Rick Ford (Chorus #9–Cambridge/French King/Erpingham),Chris Thorn (Chorus #10–Exeter/Pistol), Andy Grotelueschen (Chorus #11–Ely/Bardolph/Orleans/Bates/York)

Revival of the play presented in two acts; New Victory Theatre; February 27–March 8, 2009; 10 performances. This production toured the country prior to its New York engagement.

Black Violin Conceived and designed by Wilner Baptiste and Kevin Sylvester; Presented by Black Violin (Miami); Lighting, Ryan O'Gara; Sound, Dave Schnirman; Representation, Jeremiah Younossi; Stage Manager, Lindsay Stares; Cast: Wilner Baptiste, Kevin Sylvester, Dwayne Dayal, Jermaine McQueen

Matthew Amendt in The Acting Company's production of Henry V *(photo by Michal Daniel)*

A classical/jazz/hip-hop/R&B musical presentation performed without intermission; New Victory Theatre; March 13–22, 2009; 10 performances.

La Famiglia Dmitri Conceived and designed by Clown Dimitr; Presented by La Famiglia Dimitri (Verscio, Switzerland); Director, Masha Dimitri; Music, Oliviero Giovannoni and Julio Lavayen; Lighting, Lindsay Stares; Cast: Clown Dmitri, David Dmitri, Masha Dmitri, Nina Dmitri, Kai Leclerc

An acrobrat show with live music presented without intermission; New Victory Theatre; March 27–April 19, 2009; 24 performances.

Soledad Barrio and Noche Flamenca Presented by Noche Flamenca (Madrid, Spain); Director, Martin Santangelo; Choreography, Martin Santangelo, Soledad Barrio, Manuel Reyes; Lighting, S. Benjamin Farrar; Company Supervisor, Carlos Perez; Company Mnanager, Jeannine Baca; Dancers: Soledad Barrio, Manuel Reyes, Manuela Vargas; Singers: Manuel Gago, Emilio Florida; Guitarists: Salva de Maria & Eugenio Iglesias

A flamenco dance piece with music presented without intermission; New Victory Theatre; April 24–May 3, 2009; 11 performances.

The Queen of Colors Based on the children's book by Jutta Bauer; Presented by Erfreuliches TheatErfurt (Erfurt, Germany); Founders: Eva Noell, Paul Olbrich and Ronald Mernitz); Written, directed, and puppetry by Eva Noell and Paul Olbrich; Music, Oleksandr Voynov; Lighting and Sound, Ronald Mernitz; Cast: Ronald Mernitz, Eva Noell, Paul Olbrich, Oleksandr Voynov

A shadow puppet show presented without intermission; Duke on 42nd Street; May 1–17, 2009; 15 performances.

Rock 'n' Roll Penguin Presented by Gamar Jobat (Tokyo, Japan); Directed and performed by Ketch and Hiro-Pon; Lighting, Keiichi Koda; Stage Manager, Lindsay Stares; Sound, Maki Kinoshita

American premiere of a physical theatre piece presented without intermission; New Victory Theatre; May 8–24, 2009; 14 performances.

The Tom Tom Crew Conceived and directed by Scott Maidment; Presented by Aussie Acrobats and Daredevil Theater (Australia); Touring & Musical Director, Ben Walsh; Cast: Ben Walsh, Daniel Catlow, DJ Sampology, Tom Thum, Ben Lewis, Shane Witt, Karl Stock

An acrobatic theatre and rock concert "daredevil theater" piece presented New Victory Theatre; May 29–June 14, 2009; 15 performances.

New York Theatre Workshop

Twenty-sixth Season

Artistic Director, James C. Nicola; Managing Director, William Russo; Associate Artistic Director, Linda S. Chapman; Casting, Jack Doulin; Literary Associate, Geoffrey Scott; Artistic Administrator, Bryn Thorsson; Artistic Associates, Michael Greif, Michael Friedman, Ruben Polendo; Development, Alisa Schierman; Finance and Administration, George Cochran; Education, Caroline Reddick Lawson; Marketing, Cathy Popowytsch; General Manager, Harry J. McFadden; Production/Facilities Manager, Julie M. Mason; Technical Director, Brian Garber; Press, Richard Kornberg, Don Summa

Beast by Michael Weller; Presented in association with the National Actors Theatre Foundation; Director, Jo Bonney; Sets, Eugene Lee; Costumes, Colleen Werthmann; Lighting, David Lander; Original Music & Sound, David Van Tieghem; Video, Tal Yarden; Makeup and Effects, Nathan Johnson; Puppets, Bob Flanagan; Fight Director, Thomas Schall; PSM, Linda Marvel; Dialect Coach, Debroah Hecht; ASM, Sarah Bierenbaum; Assistant to the Playwright, Molly Rice; Assistant Director, Jonathan Solari; Assistant Design: Tristan Jeffers (set), Campbell Ringel (costumes), Ted Sullivan (lighting), Sam Doerr (sound); Props Master, Sean McArdle; Production Electrician, John Anselmo Jr.; Production Assistants, Joan Cappello, Emily Wilson; Cast: Raul Aranas (Mr. Aziz/Victor Leung), Jeremy Bobb (Schlynn/Smalldon/J.T.), Dan Butler (Captain Adler/GW), Lisa Joyce (Lieut/Sherine/Ann Voychevsky), Logan Marshall-Green (Jimmy Cato), Eileen Rivera (Lt. Mariana Sanchez/Camilla), Corey Stoll (Benjamin Voychevsky)

World premiere of a new play presented in six scenes in two acts; August 29–October 12, 2008 (Opened September 15); 19 previews, 32 performances.

The Grand Inquisitor Adapted by Marie-Hélène Estienne from *The Brothers Karamazov* by Fyodor Dostoyevsky; Produced by C.I.C.T/Théâtre des Bouffes du Nord; Co-presented by Theatre for a New Audience; Director, Peter Brook; Lighting, Philippe Vialatte; Production Manager, Caleb Wertenbaker; PSM, Christopher C. Dunlop; Executive Producer for U.S. Tour, Arktype/Thomas O. Kriegsmann; Production Electrician, John Anselmo Jr.; Cast: Bruce Myers (Narrator), Jake Smith (Christ)

American premiere of a play presented without intermission; October 22–November 30, 2008 (Opened October 29); 8 previews, 38 performances. Originally presented in Warwick, England in February 2006, and toured extensively throughout Europe, South America, and Australia, and had a sold out engagement at London's Barbican Theatre.

Things of Dry Hours by Naomi Wallace; Director, Ruben Santiago-Hudson; Sets, Richard Hoover; Costumes, Karen Perry; Lighting, Marcus Doshi; Sound & Original Music, David Van Tieghem; Fight Director/Dream Effects, David Leong; Composer, Bill Sims Jr.; Additional Music, Derek Wieland; PSM, Winnie Y. Lok; ASM, Emily Glinick; Assistant Director, Jade King Carroll; Production Electrician, John Anselmo Jr.; Prop Master, Sean McArdle; Assistant Design: Casey Smith (set), Darlene Jackson (costumes), Melissa Mizell (lighting), Brandon Wolcott (sound), Alexndra Morton (props); Hair, Valerie Gladston; Production Assistant, Danielle Buccino; Puppeteers/Crew, Crista Marie Jackson, Robert Westley; Cast: Garret Dillahunt (Corbin Teel), Delroy Lindo (Tice Hogan), Roslyn Ruff (Calli Hogan)

World premiere of a new adaptation of a new play presented in two acts; May 22–June 28, 2009 (Opened June 8); 19 previews, 24 performances. Originally produced by the Pittsburgh Public Theater (Ted Pappas, Producing Artistic Director) April 27–June 3, 2007 (see *Theatre World* Vol. 63, page 317).

Garret Dillahunt, Delroy Lindo and Roslyn Ruff in Things of Dry Hours *(photo by Joan Marcus)*

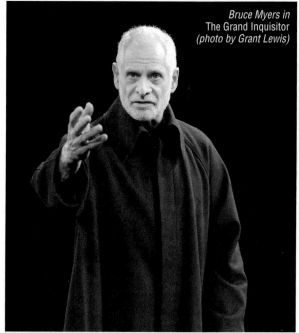

Bruce Myers in The Grand Inquisitor *(photo by Grant Lewis)*

Dan Butler, Jeremy Bobb, Corey Stoll and Logan Marshall-Green in Beast *(photos by Joan Marcus)*

Rosanne Ma, Emi F. Jones, Claro Austria and Shigeko Suga in Shogun Macbeth (photo by Corky Lee)

Glenn Kubota, Keoni Scott, Shigeko Suga, Nancy Eng and Bea Soong in The Secret of O-Sono (photo by Corky Lee)

Paola Irun in Ramona (photo by Dan Bretl)

Pan Asian Repertory Theatre

Thirty-second Season

Artistic Producing Director, Tisa Chang; Producing Associate, Abby Felder; Artistic Associate, Ron Nakahara; Marketing/Education Associate, Steven Osborn; Workshop Instructor, Ernest Abuba; Fight Coordinator, Michael G. Chin; Sound Coordinator, Andrew Phillips; Production Manager, Jay Janicki

Box Office, Emily Havlik; Lighting Assistant, Rocco Disanti; Set Execution, Tom Carroll; Web/Sound Assistant, Auric Abuba; Bookkeeper, Rosemary Khan; Photo Archivist, Corky Lee; Press, Keith Sherman and Associates

Shogun Macbeth Adapted by John R. Briggs from the play by William Shakespeare; Director, Ernest Abuba; Movement, Sachiyo Ito; Fight Choreography, Michael G. Chin; Set, Charlie Corcoran; Costumes, Carol A. Pelletier; Lighting, Victor En Yu Tan; Stage Manager, Elis C. Arroyo; ASM, Leslie A. Grisdale; Cast: Tom Matsusaka (Biwa Hoshi), Shigeko Suga (Yojo 1), Claro Austria (Yojo 2), Emi F. Jones (Yojo 3/Isha), Keoni Scott (Shogun Duncan/Old Siward), Marcus Ho (Malcolm), Claro de los Reyes (Donalbain), Ken Park (Shoko/Young Siward), Ron Nakahara (Angus), James Rana (Ross), Kaipo Schwab (Macbeth), Ariel Estrada (Banquo), Rosanne Ma (Fujin Macbeth), E. Calvin Ahn (MacDuff), Sacha Iskra (Fujin MacDuff), Yoko Hyun (Fleance/Tara Kaja/Tea Server/Shinsha), Nadia Gan (Boy MacDuff/Jiro Kaja)

Setting: 12th Century Japan. Revival of a play presented in two acts; Julia Miles Theater; November 4–December 7, 2008 (Opened November 12); 10 previews, 25 performances. Originally produced by Pan Asian Rep November 20, 1986 (see *Theatre World* Vol. 43, page 125).

December Staged Readings *Voices from Okinawa* by Jon Shirota; Director, Regge Life; Cast: Calvin Ahn, Claro Austria, Chris Doi, Nadi Gan, Akiko Hiroshima, Yoko Hyun, Karen Tsen Lee, Ken Park; Julia Miles Theatre; December 10, 2008; *Daphne Does Dim Sum (Mai Dan!)* by Eugenie Chan; Director, Ron Nakahara; Cast: Wai Ching Ho, Glenn Kubota, Bea Soong, Henry Yuk; Julia Miles Theatre; December 12, 2008.

Newworks 09 Four weeks of new works by diverse artists; Project Director, Ernest Abuba; Lighting, Rocco D'Santi; West End Theatre; March 16–April 19, 2009; included: World premiere productions: *Smart Ass* written and performed by Lan Tran; March 18–22; *The Secret of O-Sono* by Elsa Okon; Director, Ron Nakahara; Lighting, Rocco D'Santi; Set, Tom Lee; Movement Consultant, Sachiyo Ito; Original Music/Theramin, Shigeko Suga; Costumes, Carol A. Pelletier; Stage Manager, Karen E. Peck; Cast: Emi F. Jones (O-Sono), John Baray (Holy Man), Chris Doi (Shiro, the Poet), Nancy Eng (Aunt 2), Yoko Hyun (Yosuke), Glenn Kubota (Gensuke), Keoni Scott (Nagaraya), Bea Soong (Aunt 3), Shigeko Suga (Aunt 1); March 25–April 5; Monday Music Nights: March 16: *The Things I Love* a cabaret show by Christine Toy Johnson with Bruce Alan Johnson, and Robert Lee on piano; March 30: *Sung With Words* featuring jazz pianist Helen Sung with Melissa Stylianou (vocalist), Lonnie Plaxico (bass), Donald Edwards (drums); April 6: Andy Akiho (steel pans) with Asami Tamura (piano), Mariel Roberts (cello), Jeff Hanley (bass), Kenneth Salters (drums); Emerging Artist Shorts (March 31 & April 1): *Fish Dreams and Other Tales* and *Flight* performed by Mitsu Salmon, music by ryotaro; Lucas Kwong with Stephen Yu (violin) and Jeremy Siskind (piano); International Guest Artists: *Dinner* and *Ramona* written and performed by Paola Irún; Director, Kristina Smith; Original Music, Diego Serafini, Marco Todisco, and Rodrigo Ferreiro; April 7 & 8; *A Day After the Day* written and directed by Juyoung Hong; performed by Gyu-Bo Kim; April 9–11.

Pearl Theatre Company

Twenty-fifth Season`

Artistic Director, Shepard Sobel; Managing Director, Shira Beckerman; Associate Director, Joanne Camp; Development Manager/Press, Angi Taylor; Marketing/Press Director, Michael Page; Production and Facilities Manager, Gary Levinson; Dramaturg, Kate Farrington; Development Associate, Maggie-Kate Coleman; Marketing Associates, Christian Clayton, Alaina Feehan; Management Associate, Amy Dalba; Audience Services, Courtney Breslin; Assistant to the Artistic Director, Sarah Wozniak; Education, Carol Schultz; Costume Shop Manager, Niki Hernandez-Adams; Speech/Text Coach, Robert Neff Williams & Joanne Camp; Season Designers: Harry Feiner (set), Stephen Petrilli (lighting); Production Manager/Technical Director, Gary Levinson; Properties Manager, Kate Foster

The Oedipus Cycle by Sophocles, translated by Peter Constantine; Director, Shepard Sobel; Costumes, Devon Painter; Sound, M.L. Dogg; Stage Manager, Dassance Resler; Props, Kate Foster; Costume Artrisans, Karle Meyers & Kate Foster; Stage Management Assistants/Swings, Laura Bretherick, Emily Ewing, Elizabeth Salisch; Cast: *Oedipus the King*: Jolly Abraham (Jocasta/Chorus), Dominic Cuskern (Tiresias/Messenger from Corinth/Chorus), TJ Edwards (Priest/Shepherd), Susan Heyward (Tiresias' Guide/Second Messenger/Chorus), Jack Moran (Chorus), Joel Richards (Chorus); John Livingtonston Rolle (Creon/Chorus); Jay Straton (Oedipus); *Oedipus at Colonus*: Jolly Abraham (Antigone), Dominic Cuskern (Stranger), TJ Edwards (Oedipus), Susan Heyward (Ismene/Polynices), Jack Moran (Creon's Guard/Theseus'Attendant), Joel Richards (Creon's Guard/Theseus'Attendant); John Livingtonston Rolle (Creon/Chorus); Jay Straton (Theseus/Chorus); *Antigone*: Jolly Abraham (Antigone/Eurydice), Dominic Cuskern (Tiresias/Chorus), TJ Edwards (Guard), Susan Heyward (Ismene/Tiresias' Guide/Messenger), Jack Moran (Creon's Attendant), Joel Richards (Creon's Attendant); John Livingtonston Rolle (Creon); Jay Straton (Haemon); Understudies: Julie Ferres (Ms. Abraham), Kimberly DiPersia (Ms. Heyward), Dorien Makhloghi (Mr. Edwards), Jack Moran (Mr. Stratton), Joel Richards (Mr. Rolle), Raymond Wortel (Mr. Cuskern)

Setting: Ancient Greece, 5th Century B.C. World premiere translation of a revival of the trilogy of classic plays presented with two intermission; October 15–November 16, 2008 (Opened October 27); 13 previews, 22 performances.

Jack Moran, Dominic Cuskern, John Livingstone Rolle and Susan Heyward in The Oedipus Cycle *(photo by Bob Johnson)*

Nathan the Wise by Gotthold Lessing; Director, Richard Sewell; Costumes, Barbara A. Bell; Lighting, Deborah Constantine; Sound, Jane Shaw; Stage Manager, Wigs, Amanda Miller; Hats, Arnold Levine; Stage Manager, Lisa Ledwich; Assistant Lighting, Rebecca Cullars; Cast: Jolly Abraham (Sittah), Robin Leslie Brown (Daja), Robert M. Hefley (Nathan), Susan Heyward (Rachel), Robert Hock (Patriarch), Carman Lacivita (Kurt), John Livingstony Rolle (Al Hafi), Edward Seamon (Friar), Dathan B. Williams (Saladin); Understudies: Carol Schultz (Daja, Sittah), Stephanie Bratnick (Rachel), Joel Richards (Nathan, Patriarch), Ryan Metzger (Kurt, Al Hafi), Dorien Makloghi (Friar, Saladin); Swings: Laura Bretherick, Emily Ewing, Liz Salisch

Setting: Jerusalem, 1190. Revival of a play presented in two acts; December 9, 2008–January 4, 2009 (No previews); 28 performances.

Carman Lacivita, Robert Hock and Edward Seamon in Nathan the Wise *(photo by Luke Redmond)*

Sean McNall, Bradford Cover, Dominic Cuskern and TJ Edwards in Twelfth Night *(photo by Luke Redmond)*

Twelfth Night (or What You Will) by William Shakespeare; Director, J.R. Sulivan; Costumes, Liz Covey; Sound/Original Music, Amy Altadonna; Fight Director, Rod Kinter; Stage Manager, Dale Smallwood; ASMs, Laura Bretherick, Emily Ewing, Elizabeth Salisch; Costume Artisan, Anna Gerdes; Cast: Ali Ahn (Viola), TJ Edwards (Ship Captain), Michael Gabriel Goodfriend (Orsino), Kila Packett (Curio), Joseph Midyett (Valentine/Sebastian), Bradford Cover (Sir Toby Belch), Robin Leslie Brown (Maria), David L. Townsend (Sir Andrew Aguecheek), Sean McNall (Feste), Rachel Botchan (Olivia), Dominic Cuskern (Malvolio), TJ Edwards (Fabian), Jay Stratton (Antonio), Kila Packett (Priest)

Setting: The mythical land of Illyria, on the coast of the Adriatic Sea. Revival of a play in five acts presented with one intermission; January 20–February 22, 2009 (Opening Night February 2); 14 previews, 22 performances.

Tartuffe by Moliére, translated by Richard Wilbur; Director, Gus Kaikkonen; Costumes, Sam Fleming; Sound, M.L. Dogg; Stage Manager, Lisa Ledwich; Wigs, Martha Ruskai; Draper, Anna Gerdes; Cast:

TJ Edwards (Orgon), Rachel Botchan (Elmire), Carrie McCrossen (Mariane), Sean McNall (Damis), Robin Leslie Brown (Dorine), Carol Schultz (Mme. Pernelle), Dominic Cuskern (Cleante), John William Schiffbauer (Valere), Bradford Cover (Tartuffe), Kila Packett (Laurent), Julie Ferrell (Flipote), Kraig Swartz (M. Loyal/ An Officer)

Setting: The home of Orgon and Elmire in Paris, 1660s. Revival of a play presented in two acts; March 17–April 26, 2009 (Opened March 30); 14 previews, 29 performances.

John William Schiffbauer, Robin Leslie Brown and Carrie McCrossen in Tartuffe *(photo by Gregory Costanzo)*

Vieux Carré by Tennesse Williams; Director, Austin Pendelton; Costumes, Barbara A. Bell; Sound, Jane Shaw; Stage Manager, Dale Smallwood; Properties, Stephanie Tucci; Assistant Director, Patrick McNulty; Cast: Rachel Botchan (Jane), Sean McNall (The Writer), Carol Schultz (Mrs. Wire), Beth Dixon (Mary), Joseph Collins (Tye), George Morfogen (Nightingale), Pamela Payton-Wright (Carrie), Christian Pedersen (Sky), Claudia Robinson (Nursie)

Setting: A rooming house, 722 Toulouse Street in the French Quarter of New Orleans; winter 1938–spring 1939. Revival of a play presented in two acts; May 12–June 14, 2009 (Opened May 27); 16 previews, 20 performances.

* This was the final season that the Pearl Theatre Company resided at Theatre 80 at 80 St. Marks Place.

Rachel Botchan, TJ Edwards and Bradford Cover in Tartuffe *(photo by Gregory Costanzo)*

Above: *Sean McNall and Beth Dixon in* Vieux Carré *(photo by Gregory Costanzo)*

Left: *Sean McNall, Rachel Botchan and Joseph Collins in* Vieux Carré *(photo by Gregory Costanzo)*

Playwrights Horizons

Thirty-eighth Season

Artistic Director, Tim Sanford; Managing Director, Leslie Marcus; General Manager, Carol Fishman;

Director of Musical Theatre/Dramaturg, Christie Evangelisto/Kent Nicholson; Literary Manager, Adam Greenfield; Casting, Alaine Alldaffer; Production Manager, Christopher Boll; Development, Jill Garland; Controller, Anne Heibach; Marketing, Eric Winick; Director of Ticket Central, Emily Wilbur; School Director, Helen R. Cook; Dramaturg, Christie Evangelisto; Company Manager, Caroline Aquino; Associate Production Manager, Shannon Nicole Case; Technical Director, Brian Coleman; Press, The Publicity Office, Marc Thibodeau, Michael S. Borowski

Three Changes by Nicky Silver; Director, Milam Wilson; Set, Neil Patel; Costumes, Theresa Squire; Lighting, Ben Stanton; Sound, Bart Fasbender; PSM, William H. Lang; ASM, Kate Baxter Lang; Fight Director, J. David Brimmer; Cast: Maura Tierney (Laurel), Dylan McDermott* (Nate), Scott Cohen (Hal), Aya Cash (Steffi), Brian J. Smith (Gordon); * Suceeded by: Tim Hopper (September 30)

Setting: New York City's Upper West Side; Time: Act 1: Summer (Act 1) and ; Act 2: Eearly Aautumn (Act 2). Place. : New York City's Upper West Side. World premiere of a new play presented in two acts; Mainstage Theater; August 22–October 3, 2008 (Opened September 16); 27 previews, 21 performances.

Christopher Denham and Annette O'Toole in Kindness

Prayer for My Enemy by Craig Lucas; Director, Bartlett Sher; Set, John McDermott; Costumes, Catherine Zuber; Lighting, Stephen Strawbridge; Sound, Scott Lehrer; Music, Nico Muhly; PSM, Lisa Ann Chernoff; ASM, John Randolph Perry; Properties, Desirée Maurer; Cast: Cassie Beck (Marianne), Zachary Booth (Tad), Victoria Clark (Dolores), Jonathan Groff (Billy), Michele Pawk (Karen), Skipp Sudduth (Austin)

Setting: America and Iraq; 2003 and 2004. New York premiere of a new play presented without intermission; Mainstage Theatre; November 14–December 21, 2008 (Opened December 9); 29 previews, 15 performances. World premiere at the Intiman Theatre August 3, 2007 (see *Theatre World* Vol. 64, page 313).

Maura Tierney, Dylan McDermott and Scott Cohen in Three Changes *(photos by Joan Marcus)*

Kindness Written and directed by Adam Rapp; Set, Lauren Halpern; Costumes, Daphne Javitch; Lighting, Mary Louise Geiger; Sound, Eric Shim; Richard A. Hodge; ASM, Christina Elefante; Properties, Desiree Maurer; Video, Daniel Breton; Cast: Christopher Denham (Dennis), Annette O'Toole (Maryanne), Ray Anthony Thomas (Herman), Katherine Waterston (Frances)

Setting: The present; a hotel room in midtown Manhattan. World premiere of a new play presented in two acts; Peter Jay Sharp Theater; September 25–November 2, 2008 (Opened October 13); 21 previews, 24 performances.

Cassie Beck, Zachary Booth and Jonathan Groff in Prayer for My Enemy

Victoria Clark in Prayer for My Enemy

Kellie Overbey, Marylouise Burke and Dana Ivey in
The Savannah Disputation

The Savannah Disputation by Evan Smith; Director, Walter Bobbie; Set, John Lee Beatty; Costumes, David C. Woolard; Lighting, Kenneth Posner; Sound, Tony Meola; PSM, Robyn Henry; ASM, Nicole Bouclier; Cast: Dana Ivey (Mary), Kellie Overbey (Melissa), Marylouise Burke (Margaret), Reed Birney (Father Murphy)

New York premiere of a new play presented in one act with a brief intermission following scene three; Mainstage Theater; February 6–March 15, 2009 (Opened March 3); 29 previews, 15 performances. World premiere at Writers' Theatre (Glencoe, Illinois) September 26, 2007.

Inked Baby by Christina Anderson; Director, Kate Whoriskey; Set, Andromache Chalfant; Costumes, Kay Voyce; Lighting, Jason Lyons; Original Music & Sound, Rob Milburn & Michael Bodeen; PSM, Kasey Ostopchuck; ASM, Kate Baxter Davis; Movement Consultant, Warren Adams; Associate Lighting, Peter Hoerburger; Properties, Desirée Maurer; Cast: Che Ayende (Odlum), Michael Genet (Dr. Marion), Damon Gupton (Greer), LaChanze (Gloria), Angela Lewis (Lena), Nana Mensah (Medical Assistant), Nikkole Salter (Ky)

Setting: The present. World premiere of a new play presented without intermission; Peter Jay Sharp Theater; March 15–April 27, 2009 (Opened March 28); 21 previews, 16 performances.

Our House by Theresa Rebeck; Director, Michael Mayer; Set, Derek McLane; Costumes, Susan Hilferty; Lighting, Kenneth Posner; Sound, Darron L West; Associate Set, Shoko Kambara; PSM, James FitzSimmons; ASM, Cyrille Blackburn; Properties, Desirée Maurer; Effects, Séan McArdle; Cast: Morena Baccarin (Jennifer), Katie Kreisler (Alice), Stephen Kunken (Stu), Mandy Siegfried (Grigsby), Jeremy Strong (Merv), Haynes Thigpen (Vince), Christopher Evan Welch (Wes)

Setting: America. New York premiere of a new play presented in two acts; Mainstage Theater; May 15–June 21, 2009 (Opened June 9); 29 previews, 15 performances.

Damon Gupton, Angela Lewis and Michael Genet in Inked Baby

Stephen Kunken, Morena Baccarin, Christopher Evan Welch, Haynes Thigpen and Jeremy Strong in Our House

Primary Stages

Twenty-fourth Season

Founder and Executive Producer, Casey Childs; Artistic Director, Andrew Leynse; Managing Director, Elliot Fox; Associate Artistic Director, Michelle Bossy; Literary Manager, Tessa LaNeve; Development, Erica Raven/Jessica Sadowski Comas; Marketing, Shanta Mali; Business Manager, Reuben Saunders; Production Supervisor, Peter R. Feuchtwanger; Casting, Stephanie Klapper; Press, O&M Co., Rick Miramontez, Philip Carrubba

Buffalo Gal by A.R. Gurney; Presented in association with Jamie deRoy and Alan D. Marks; Director, Mark Lamos; Set, Andrew Jackness; Costumes, Candice Donnelly; Lighting, Mary Louise Geiger; Original Music & Sound, John Gromada; Original song "Say When" composed by Tom Cabaniss, lyrics by A.R. Gurney; PSM, Matthew Melchiorre; Props, Jay Duckworth; Assistant Director, Ian Belknap; ASM, Joanne E. Mclerney; Cast: James Waterston (Roy), Carmen M. Herlihy (Debbie), Jennifer Regan (Jackie), Susan Sullivan (Amanda), Dathan B. Williams (James), Mark Blum (Dan)

Setting: The present. Buffalo, New York. New York premiere of a new play presented without intermission; 59E59 Theater A; August 5–September 13, 2008 (Opened August 5); 13 previews, 27 performances. World premiere at the Williamstown Theatre Festival June 13, 2000.

Laura Odeh, Christine Lahti and Michael Cristofer in A Body of Water

Christine Lahti and Michael Cristofer in A Body of Water

A Body of Water by Lee Blessing; Director, Maria Mileaf; Set, Neil Patel; Costumes, Candice Donnelly; Lighting, Jeff Croiter; Sound, Bart Fasbender; PSM, Larry K. Ash; ASM, Jenn McNeil; Cast: Michale Cristofer (Moss), Christine Lahti (Avis), Laura Odeh (Wren)

Setting: Recently, a summer house. New York premiere of a new play presented in without intermission; 59E59 Theater A; September 30–November 16, 2008 (Opened October 14); 9 previews, 31 performances. World premiere produced at the Guthrie Theatre June 15, 2005.

Left above: *Jennifer Regan and Susan Sullivan in* Buffalo Gal *(photos by James Leynse)*

Left below: *James Waterston, Jennifer Regan, Carmen M. Herlihy, Dathan B. Williams, Susan Sullivan and Mark Blum in* Buffalo Gal

Love Child by Daniel Jenkins and Robert Stanton; Produced in association with Martin Hummel; Director, Carl Forsman; Choreography, Tracy Bersley; Set, Neil Patel; Costumes, Candace Donnelly; Lighting, Jeff Croiter; & Grant Yeager; PSM, Joanne E. Mclerney; Cast: Daniel Jenkins, Robert Stanton

New York premiere of a new play presented without intermission in rotating repertory with *A Body of Water*; 59E59 Theater A; October 12–November 19, 2008 (Opened October 26); 7 previews, 14 performances. Previously developed at New York Stage and Film.

Michael Countryman, Donnetta Lavinia Grays and Jeremy Bobb in Shipwrecked! An Entertainment

Daniel Jenkins and Robert Stanton in Love Child

Shipwrecked! An Entertainment— The Amazing Adventures of Louis de Rougemont (As Told by Himself) by Donald Margulies; Presented in association with Barbara and Alan D. Marks; Director, Lisa Peterson; Set, Neil Patel; Costumes, Michael Krass; Lighting, Stephen Strawbridge; Original Music and Sound, John Gromada; PSM, Matthew Melchiorre; ASM, Alison M. Roberts; Assistant Director, Brian Hanscom; Props Master, Jeremy Lydic; Dialect Coach, Samara Bay; Cast: Michael Countryman (Louis de Rougemont), Donnetta Lavinia Grays (Player 1), Jeremy Bobb (Player 2)

New York premiere of a new play presented without intermission; 59E59 Theater A; January 27–March 7, 2009 (Opened February 8); 13 previews, 29 performances. Originally commissioned and produced at South Coast Repertory September 23, 2007 (see *Theatre World* Vol. 64, page 331).

Chasing Manet by Tina Howe; Presented in association with Scott M. Delman, Alan D. Marks, Ted Snowdon, and Jamie deRoy; Director, Michael Wilson; Set, Tony Straiges; Costumes, David C. Woolard; Lighting, Howell Binkley; Original Music & Sound, John Gromada; Wigs and Hair, Mark Adam Rampmeyer; Associate Director, Maxwell Williams; PSM, Susie Cordon; ASM, Allison Sommers; Assistant Director, Brian Hanscom; Prop Master, Matt Hodges; Dramaturg, Rachel Ely; Cast: Jane Alexander (Catherine Sargent), Vanessa Aspillaga (Esperanza/Saviana/Angelica/Marie-Claire/Sybil), Lynn Cohen (Rennie Waltzer), Jack Gilpin (Royal Lowell/Sherwood/Marvin/Rob), Julie Halston (Iris/Rita/Charlotte), David Margulies (Henry/Maurice/Reginald Allen Pointer the III), Rob Riley (Charles/Gabe/Rémy Bonaparte)

Setting: Mount Airy Nursing Home; mid-1980s. World premiere of a new play presented in two acts: 59E59 Theater A; March 24–May 2, 2009 (Opened April 9); 16 previews, 41 performances.

Lynn Cohen and Jane Alexander in Chasing Manet

Rob Riley, Julie Halston, Lynn Cohen, David Margulies, Vanessa Aspillaga and Jack Gilpin in Chasing Manet

The Public Theater

Fifty-third Season

Artistic Director, Oskar Eustis; Executive Director, Mara Manus/Andrew Hamingson; General Manager, Nicki Genovese/Andrea Nellis; Associate Artistic Director, Mandy Hackett; Associate Producer, Jenny Gersten; Director of Musical Theatre Initiative, Ted Sperling; Under the Radar, Mark Russell; Casting, Jordan Thaler, Heidi Griffiths; Director of Production, Ruth E. Sternberg; Marketing, Ilene Rosen/Nella Vera; Capital Projects, Adrienne Dobsovits; Communications, Candi Adams; Development, Casey Reitz; Shakespeare Initiative, Barry Edelstein; Finance, Daniel C. Smith; Special Projects, Maria Goyanes; CFO, Andrea Nellis; Information Technology, Damon Hurd; Finance, Jack Feher; Ticket Services, Jimmy Goodsey; Joe's Pub, Shanta Thake; Press, Sam Neuman

Hamlet by William Shakespeare; Director, Oskar Eustis; Sets, David Korins; Costumes, Ann Hould-Ward; Lighting, Michael Chybowski; Composer, Mark Bennett; Sound, Acme Sound Partners; Fight Director, Thomas Schall; Puppetry, Basil Twist; PSM, Buzz Cohen; Stage Manager, Sean M. Thorne; Assistant Director, Rob Melrose; Vocal Consultant, Shane Ann Younts; Dramaturg, Barry Edelstein; Associate Set, Rod Lemmond; ASM, Ashley B. Delegal; Cast: Michael Stuhlbarg (Hamlet), Julio Monge (Francisco/Osric), Piter Marek (Barnardo/Fortinbras), Gilbert Owuor (Marcellus/Lucianus), Kevin Carroll (Horatio), André Braugher (King Claudius), Margaret Colin (Queen Gertrude), Sam Waterston (Polonius), Lauren Ambrose (Ophelia), David Harbour (Laertes), Paul O'Brien (Voltemand/Priest), W. Tré Davis (Cornelius/A Player/Ensemble), Jay O. Sanders (Ghost of Hamlet's Father/Player King/Gravedigger), Christopher Bonewitz (Reynaldo/Ensemble), Hoon Lee (Rosencrantz), Greg McFadden (Guildenstern), Stephen James King (Prologue/Ensemble), Miriam Silverman (Player Queen/Gentlewoman), Dana Lyn (Stenographer/Ensemble), Matt Carlson (Captain in the Norwegian Army/Ensemble); Musicians: Christopher Bonewitz (guitar), Matt Carlson (horn), Dana Lyn (violin); Puppeteers: Bruce Cannon, Emily DeCola, Erin Orr, Michael Schupbach

Revival of the play presented in two acts; Delacorte Theater; May 27–June 29, 2008 (Opened June 18); 19 previews, 11 performances.

Will Swenson and Jonathan Groff with the Tribe of Hair *(photo by Michal Daniel)*

Kacie Sheik and Darius Nichols in Hair *(photo by Michal Daniel)*

Margaret Colin, Michael Stuhlbarg (seated) and André Braugher in Hamlet *(photo by Michal Daniel)*

Hair Book and lyrics by James Rado and Gerome Ragni, music by Galt MacDermot; Director, Diane Paulus; Set, Scott Pask; Costumes, Michael McDonald; Lighting, Michael Chybowski; Sound, Acme Sound Partners; Psychedelic Art, The Joshua Light Show; Music Supervisor, Rob Fisher; Music Director/Conductor, Nadia DiGiallondardo; Music Coordinator, Seymour Red Press; Choreographer, Karloe Armitage; PSM, Nancy Harrington; Assistant Director, Dan Rigazzi; Assistant Choreographer, Brian Carey Chung; Associate Musical Director, Ted Baker; Stage Manager, Elizabeth Miller; Cast: Will Swenson (Berger), Bryce Ryness (Woof), Jonathan Groff [*] (Claude), Darius Nichols (Hud), Caren Lyn Manuel (Sheila), Patina Renea Miller (Dionne), Kacie Sheik (Jeanie), Allison Case (Crissy), Megan Lawrence/Dawn Falato [*] (Mother), Andrew Kober (Father/Margaret Mead), Nicole Lewis (White Boys Trio), Saycon Sengbloh (White Boys Trio), Jackie Burns (Black Boys Trio), Kaitlyn Kiyan (Black Boys Trio), Megan Reinking (Black Boys Trio); Tribe: Ato Blankson-Wood, Steel Burkhardt, Lauren Elder, Allison Guinn, Anthony Hollock, Kaitlin Kiyan, John M. Moauro, Brandon Pearson, Paris Remillard, Maya Sharpe, Theo Stockman, Tommar Wilson; Musicians: Nadia DiGiallondardo (Conductor/keyboard), Ted Baker (Assistant Conductor/Keyboard), Steve Bargonetti & Andrew Schwartz (guitar), Wilbur Bascomb (bass), Allen Won (woodwinds), Elaine Burt, Ronald Buttacavoli, Christian Jaudes (trumpet), Vincent Macdermot (trombone), Joseph Cardello (percussion), Bernard Purdie (drums); [*] Succeeded by: Christopher Hanke (8/17/08)

Revival of the musical presented in two acts; Delacorte Theater; July 22–September 14, 2008 (Opened August 7); 14 previews, 34 performances. This production transferred to Broadway later in the season with most of this cast and production team (see page 60 in this volume for more production information, including musical numbers). The original 1968 production of *Hair* was the first Off-Broadway musical to transfer to Broadway, and was the show that officially opened The Public Theater's long-time home on Lafayette Street.

If You See Something Say Something by Mike Daisey; Director, Jean-Michele Gregory; Lighting, K.J. Hardy; Joe's Pub General Manager, Kevin Abbott; Associate Lighting, Sabrina Braswell; Assistant Production Supervisor, Michelle Renkovski; Cast: Mike Daisey

New York premiere of a new solo performance monologue presented without intermission; Joe's Pub; October 15–November 30, 2008 (Opened October 27); 10 previews, 29 performances. World premiere at the Woolly Mammoth Theatre Company in July 2008.

Mike Daisey in If You See Something, Say Something *(photo by Kenneth Aaron)*

Alexander Gemignani and Michael Cerveris in Road Show *(photo by Joan Marcus)*

Road Show Music and lyrics by Stephen Sondheim, book by John Weidman; Director/Design, John Doyle; Costumes, Ann Hould-Ward; Lighting, Jane Cox; Sound, Dan Moses Schreier; Wigs/Hair, Paul Huntley; Music Director, Mary-Mitchell Campbell; Music Coordinator, Seymour Red Press; Orchestrations, Jonathan Tuick; PSM, James Latus; Stage Manager, Buzz Cohen; Music Copying, Emily Grishman & Katherine Edmonds; Associate Director, Adam John Hunter; Associate Design: Josh Zangen (set), David Bullard (sound); Assistant Design: Christopher Vergara (costumes), Melissa Mizell (lighting), Assistants: Alicia Quirk & Sean Thorne (production), Oran Elder (music director), Deanna Weiner (orchestra); Cast: Michael Cerveris (Wilson Mizner), Alma Cuervo (Mama Mizner), Aisha de Haas (Mrs. Trumbauer/others), Claybourne Elder (Hollis Bessemer), Colleen Fitzpatrick (Mary Monahan/others), Alexander Gemignani (Addison Mizner), Mylinda Hull (Boca Girl/others), Mel Johnson Jr (Plantation Owner/others), Orville Mendoza (Jockey/others), Anne L. Nathan (Aunt Eva/others), Tom Nelis (Plawright/others), William Parry (Papa Mizner), Matthew Stocke (Boxer/others), William Youmans (Prospector/others), Kristine Zbornik (Myra Yerkes/others); Understudies: Matthew Carlson (Bessemer, Ensemble Men), Colleen Fitzpatrick (Mama Mizner), David Garry (Wilson Mizner, Ensemble Men), Orville Mendoza (Addison Mizner), Tom Nelis (Papa Mizner), Katrina Yaukey (Ensemble Women); Musicians: Mary-Mitchell Campbell (Conductor/keyboard), Chris Fenwick (Assistant Musical Director), James Ercole, Steven Lyon Les Scott (reeds), Stu Satalof, Dave Gale (trumpets), Vincent Fanuele (trombone), Raymond Kilday (bass), Billy Miller (drums/percussion), Victor Heifets (violin), Deborah Sepe (cello); Cast recording: PS Classics 979/Nonesuch 518940

Musical Numbers: Waste, It's In Your Hands Now, Gold!, Brotherly Love, The Game, Addison's Trip, That Was a Year, Isn't He Something!, Land Boom, Talent, You, The Best Thing That Ever Has Happened, The Game (reprise), Addison's City, Boca Raton, Get Out, Go, Finale

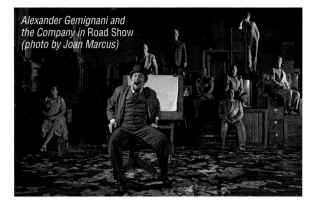

Alexander Gemignani and the Company in Road Show *(photo by Joan Marcus)*

Setting: America and elsewhere; 1896–1933. New York premiere of a musical presented without intermission; Newman Theater; October 28–December 28, 2008 (Opened November 18); 24 previews, 28 performances. An earlier version of the musical (entitled *Bounce*) was originally produced by the Goodman Theatre (Chicago) on June 30, 2003.

Taking Over by Danny Hoch; Co-presented by the Hip-Hop Theater Festival; Director, Tony Taccone; Set & Costumes, Annie Smart; Lighting & Projections, Alexander V. Nichols; Sound, Walter Trarbach; Composer, Asa Tacccone PSM, Barbara Reo; Vocal Coach, Deborah Hecht; Assistant Director, Jerry Ruiz; Assistant Design: Jedediah Ike (set), David Mendizabal (costumes), Jorge Arroryo (lighting), Drew Levy (sound); Production Assistant, Katrina Olson; Cast: Danny Hoch

New York premiere of a solo performance play presented without intermission; Anspacher Theater; November 7–December 21, 2008 (Opened November 23); 18 previews, 29 performances.

Danny Hoch in Taking Over *(photo by Joan Marcus)*

The Good Negro by Tracey Scott Wilson; Presented in association with Dallas Theater Center (Kevin Moriarty, Aristic Director; Mark Hadley, Managing Director); Director, Liesl Tommy; Sets & Costumes, Clint Ramos; LighitngLighting, Lap Chi Chu; Sound, Daniel Baker; Hair & Makeup, Jon Carter; PSM, Winnie Y. Lok; Stage Manager, Rachel Motz; Assistant Director, Colette Robert; Fight Director, Thomas Schall; Vocal Coach, Thom Jones; Assistant Design: Jonathan Collins (set), Jessica Pabst (costumes), Kathleen Dobbins (lighting), Daniel Kluger (sound); Cast: Curtis McClarin (James Lawrence), Joniece Abbott-Pratt (Claudette Sullivan), Erik Jensen (Gary Thomas Rowe Jr.), Brian Wallace (Policeman 1/Steeve Lane), Quincy Dunn-Baker (Policeman 2/Paul Moore), LeRoy McClain (Bill Rutherford), J. Bernard Calloway (Henry Evans), Rachel Nicks (Corinne Lawrence), Francois Battiste (Pelzie Sullivan)

Setting: The 1960s Deep South during the 1960s Civil Rights Movement. Off-Broadway premiere of a new play presented in two acts; LuEsther Hall; March 3–April 19, 2009 (Opened March 16); 15 previews, 40 performances. This show was originally developed for the inaugural "Public LAB" last season, and is the first show from that series to receive a full production from that series.

Curtis McClarin and Joniece Abbott-Pratt (foreground) with Quincy Dunn-Baker and Brian Wallace (background) in The Good Negro *(photo by Joan Marcus)*

Why Torture Is Wrong, and the People Who Love Them by Christopher Durang; Director, Nicholas Martin; Set, David Korins; Costumes, Gabriel Berry; Lighting, Ben Stanton; Composer, Mark Bennett; Sound, Drew Levy; PSM, Stephen M. Kaus; Stage Manager, Jillian M. Oliver; Fight Director, Thomas Schall; Wigs/Hair, Marilyn Jordan; Assistant Director, Erick Herrscher; Hooters Consultant, Brooks Ashmanskas; Assistant Director, Amanda Stephens; Associate Design: Amanda Stephens (set), Matthew Pachtman (costumes); Assistant Design: Rod Lemmond (set), Austin Smith (lighting), Will Pickens (sound); Associate Composer/Music Co-Arranger, Matthew Henning; Production Assistant, Johanna Thelin; Properties, Jessica M. Provenzale; Cast: Amir Arison (Zamir), Laura Benanti (Felicity), Kristine Nielsen (Luella), Richard Poe (Leonard), David Aaron Baker (Voice), John Pankow (Reverend Mike), Audrie Neena (Hildegarde)

World premiere of a new comedy presented in two acts; Newman Theatre; March 24–May 10, 2009 (Opened April 6); 15 previews, 40 performances.

The Singing Forest by Craig Lucas; Director, Mark Wing-Davey; Set, John McDermott; Costumes, Gabriel Berry; Lighting, Japhy Weideman; Original Music & Sound, John Gromada; PSM, Rick Steiger; Stage Manager, Zac Chandler; Fight Director, Thomas Schall; Dialect Coaches, Deborah Hecht, Sam Chwat; Assistant Director, Scott Illingworth; Associate Design: Matth Pachtman (costumes), Justing Partier (lighting); Assistant Design: Mikiko Suzuki MacAdams (set), Matthew Walsh (sound); Production Assistant, Deanna Weiner; Prop Master,

The Company in The Singing Forest *(photo by Carol Rosegg)*

Kristine Neilsen, Laura Benanti, Amir Arison and Richard Poe in Why Torture Is Wrong, and the People Who Love Them *(photo by Joan Marcus)*

Eric Reynolds; Cast: Mark Blum (Dr. Oliver Pfaff/Martin Rieman), Rob Campbell (Shar Unger/Max Schur), Louis Cancelmi (Jules Ahmad/Simon Hirsch), Olympia Dukakis (Loë Rieman), Pierre Epstein (Bill/Sigmund Freud), Jonathan Groff (Gray Korankyi/Walter Rieman), Randy Harrison (Laszlo Fickes/Gerhardt Zeitzler), Deborah Offner (Bertha Ahmad/ Anna Freud), Susan Pourfar (Beth Adler/Young Loë)

New York premiere of a new play presented in three acts with two intermissions; Martinson Hall; April 7–May 17, 2009 (Opened April 27); 22 previews, 24 performances. World premiere at the Intiman Theatre (Seattle) July 24, 2004 (see *Theatre World* Vol. 61, page 274).

Public LAB (Second Season)

Vital New Plays in Bare-Bones Productions Presented in Association with the LAByrinth Theater

Tales of an Urban Indian Written and performed by Darrell Dennis; Director, Herbie Barns; Set, Beowulf Boritt; Costumes, Fritz Masten; Lighting, Russell H. Champa; Sound, Matt Hubbs; PSM, Rebecca Goldstein-Glaze; Production Manager, Bethany Ford; Company Manager, Rebecca Sherman

Revival of a solo performance play presented without intermission; Shiva Theater; February 20–March 15, 2009 (Opened March 1); 29 performances. Previously presented at the Native Theater Festival at the Public last season; world premiere at the Native Earth Performing Arts Center (Toronto).

Bloody Bloody Andrew Jackson: The Concert Version Written and directed by Alex Timbers, music and lyrics by Michael Friedman; Presented in collaboration with Center Theatre Group in association with Les Freres Corbusier; Music Director, Justin Levine; Set, Donyale Werle; Costumes, Emily Rebholz; Lighting, Justin Townsend; Sound, Bart Fasbender; Arrangements/Orchestrations, Gabriel Kahane; Movement, Danny Mefford; Stage Violence, Jacob Grigolia-Rosenbaum; Dramaturgs, Anne Davison, Mike Sablone; PSM, Elizabeth Moreau; Stage Manager, Alaina Taylor; Production Manager, Bethany Ford; Assistant Directors, Adrienne Campbell-Holt, Marci Koltonuk; Cast: Benjamin Walker (Andrew Jackson), David Axelrod (Lyncoya), James Barry (Male Soloist), Darren Goldstein (John Calhoun), Greg Hildreth (Red Eagle), Jeff Hiller (John Quincy Adams), Lisa Joyce (Female Soloist), Lucas Near-Verbrugghe (Martin Van Buren), Bryce Pinkham (Henry Clay), Maria Elena Ramirez (Rachel), Kate Cullen Roberts (Elizabeth), Ben Steinfeld (James Monroe), Colleen Werthmann (The Storyteller); Musicians: Charlie Rosen (bass & piano), Kevin Garcia (drums), Justin Levine (piano & guitar)

World premiere of a new musical in development presented without intermission; Shiva Theater; May 5–24, 2009 (Opened May 17); 24 performances

Father Comes Home From the Wars (Part 1, 8 & 9) by Suzan-Lori Parks; Director, Jo Bonney; Set, Neil Patel; Costumes, Emilio Sosa; Lighting, Lap Chi Chu; Sound, Dan Moses Schreier; Video, Shawn Sagady; Song Music & Lyrics, Suzan-Lori Parks; Guitar Arrangements/Incidental Music, Lucas Papaelias; PSM, Christina Lowe; Stage Manager, Raynelle Wright; Production Manager, Andrew Kircher; Assistant Director, Colette Robert; Fight Director, David Anzuelo; Movement, Annie-B Parson; Dialects, Thom Jones; Cast: Part 1: The Union of My Confederate Parts: Nicole Beharie (Runaway Slave), Seth Gilliam (Homer), Patrice Johnson (Penny), James McDaniel (Hero), Joan MacIntosh (Odyssey Dog), Lucas Papaelias (Runaway Slave), Frederick Weller (Runaway Slave), Suzan-Lori Parks (Narrator), Kellie Overbey (Odyessey Dog Understudy); *Part 8: The Way We Live & Part 9: In Between the Wars*: Nicole Beharie (Penny), Seth Gilliam (Smith), Patrice Johnson (Nurse), Kellie Overbey (Ella), James McDaniel (Poet General), Lucas Papaelias (Soldier Chorus), Suzan-Lori Parks (Narrator), Frederick Weller (Soldier)

Setting: Part 1: 1865; Far West Texas, a slave cabin in the middle of nowhere; Part 8: Present day, in the Shiva @ The Public; Part 9: Present day, a country house, over the course of a weekend; World premiere of three parts of a new nine-play cycle in development presented with one intermission; Shiva Theater; June 5–28, 2009; 29 performances

ADDITIONAL EVENTS

Mandy Patinkin Back at the Public Three concerts in repertory ("Dress Casual," "Celebrating Sondheim," and "Mamaloshen") performed by Mandy Patinkin; Musical Director/Accompanist, Paul Ford

Revival of three concerts presented in repertory; Anspacher Theater; December 8–21, 2008; 11 performances.

Berlin/Wall Written and performed by David Hare; Director, Stephen Daldry; Lighting, Rick Fisher; Production Manager, Robert Saenz de Viteri; Stage Manager, Karen Armstrong; Video Systems, Sage Carter; Production Assistant, Raynelle Wright; Sound, Matt Gibney; Master Electrician, Nathan Watson; Light Board Programmer, Marc Schmittroth

American premiere of two monologues presented without intermission; Anspacher Theater; May 14–17, 2009; 5 performances.

LAByrinth Theater
In residence at The Public Theater

Seventeenth Season

Artistic Directors, John Ortiz, Philip Seymour Hoffman; Co-Artistic Director/ Executive Director, John Gould Rubin; Associate Producer, Marieke Gaboury; Associate Artistic Director, Florencia Lozano; Marketing, Trevor Brown; Development, Veronica R. Bainbridge; Company Manager, Kristina Poe; Literary Manager, Monique Carboni; Administrator, Nicola Hughes; Press, O&M Co., Rick Miramontez, Philip Carrubba

Sweet Storm by Scott Hudson; Presented in association with the Alchemy Theatre Company (Robert Saxner, Producing Artistic Director); Director, Padraic Lillis; Set & Costumes, Lee Umberger; Lighting, Sarah Sidman; Sound, Sarah Rhodes; Casting, Judy Bowman; Production Supervisor, La Vie Productions; PSM, Jessica J. Felix; Company Manager, Kristina Poe; Production Manager, James E. Cleveland; Fight Director, Qui Nguyen; Press, Kevin P. McAnarney; Cast: Jamie Dunn (Ruthie), Eric T. Miller (Bo)

Setting: Florida; 1960. A new play presented without intermission; Kirk Theatre on Theatre Row; June 11–August 16, 2009 (Opened June 17); 7 previews, 54 performances. Previously presented in the inaugural Public LAB June 29–30, 2008 (see *Theatre World* Vol. 64, page 234). 7 previews, 54 performances

Eric T. Miller and Jamie Dunn and in Sweet Storm
(photo by Monique Carboni)

PUBLIC LAB (SECOND SEASON)

Vital New Plays in Bare-Bones Productions Presented in Association with the Public Theater

Philip Roth in Khartoum by David Bar Katz; Director, John Gould Rubin; Set, Chris Barreca; Costumes, Daphne Javitch; Light, Japhy Weideman; Sound, Elizabeth Rhodes; Casting, Judy Bowman; PSM, Meredith Dixon; Cast: Amelia Campbell (Karen), Elizabeth Canavan (Allison), Alexander Chaplin (Andy), David Deblinger (Bruce), Jamie Klassel (Cindy), Michael Puzzo (Doug), Jenna Stern (Susan), Victor Williams (Carl)

World premiere of a new play in development presented in two acts; Shiva Theater; December 4–21, 2008; 17 performances.

Knives and Other Sharp Objects by Raúl Castillo; Director, Felix Solis; Set, Peter Ksander; Costumes, Ilona Somogyi; Lighting, Sarah Sidman; Sound, Bray Poor; PSM, Michael D. Domue; Stage Manager, Melissa Rae Miller; Production Manager, Bethany Ford; Assistant Director, Awoye Timpo; Cast: Noemi Del Rio (Beatrice), Joselin Reyes (Alex), Michael Ray Escamilla (Manuel), Amanda Perez (Loren), Ana Nogueira (Lucy), Candy Buckley (Lydia), Jaime Tirelli (Jaime), Ed Vassallo (Harvey), Angelo Rosso (Perry), David Anzuelo (Eddie)

World premiere of a new play in development presented in two acts; Shiva Theater; March 27–April 19, 2009; 29 performances

READING SERIES AND BENEFITS

Celebrity Charades 2008: We Will Rock You! Co-Hosts, Jackie Judd, Susan Kahn, Debbie Ohanian, Starkey Hearing Foundation; Dave Hoghe Award Recipient, Carole Shorenstein Hays; Charade Referee, Eric Bogosian; Live Auction Host, John Patrick Shanley; Players: John Ortiz, Philip Seymour Hoffman, Bob Balaban, Sam Rockwell, Yul Vazquez, Alan Cumming, Bobby Cannavale, Billy Crudup, Rachel Dratch, Edie Falco, Craing "muMs" Grant, Richard Kind, Aasif Mandvi, Christopher Meloni, Ana Ortiz, Joe Pantoliano, Judy Reyes, Cynthia Rowley, Justin Theroux, Yul Vázquez, David Zayas; sixth annual gala benefit for the LAByrinth Theater featuring an evening of charades; Terminal 5; October 20, 2008.

The Barn Series 2008 Ninth annual reading series; included: *Objects Are Closer Than They Appear* by Megan Mostyn-Brown; Director, Carolyn Cantor; *The April Hour* by Jonathan Smit; Director, Scott Illingworth; *Night Train* by Mel Nieves; Director, Felix Solis; *7 Captiva* Road by Andrea Ciannavei; Director, Michele Chivu; *Incendiary* by Adam Szymkowicz; Director, Damon Arrington; *A Life Time Burning* by Cusi Cram; *Bus Accident Play* by Raúl Castillo; Director, John Ortiz; *The Transparency of Val* by Stephen Belber; Director, John Ortiz; *Burning, Burning, Burning, Burning* by David Bar Katz; Director, John Gould Rubin; *Thinner Than Water* by Melissa Ross; Director, Mimi O'Donnell; *Face Cream* by Maggie Bofill; Director, Mimi O'Donnell; *The Motherf**ker with the Hat* by Stephen Adly Guirgis; Shiva Theater; October 23–November 15, 2008.

Live Nude Plays Third annual reading series; included: *Untitled* by Brett C. Leonard; *underneathmybed* by Florencia Lozano; Director, Pedro Pascal; *iso… (in search of)* by Justin Reinsilber, Ed Vassallo; Director, John Gould Rubin; *Minotaur: A Romance!* by David Anzuelo, music by Cristian Amigo; Director, Lou Moreno; Shiva Theater; November 16–19, 2008.

Bitter Honey II A collection of monologues written and performed by Eric Bogosian; A benefit for LAByrinth Theater Company; Anspacher Hall; June 2–3, 2009.

Donnie Keshawarz, Jeffrey DeMunn, Kevin O'Donnell and Jennifer Mudge in Geometry of Fire (photos by Sandra Coudert)

Danielle Slavick (kneeling center) and Lisa Joyce with (background) Annie McNamara, Joseph Gomez and Greg Keller in That Pretty Pretty; or, The Rape Play

Jessica Dickey in The Amish Project

Rattlestick Playwrights Theater

Fourteenth Season

Co-Founder/Artistic Director, David Van Asselt; Managing Director, Sandra Coudert; Finance, Brian Lon; Production Associate, Dan McClung; Box Office, Ira Lopez; Marketing, Corey Williams; Literary Associates, Denis Butkus, Julie Klein, Daniel Talbott; Casting, Jodi Bowman; Press, O&M Co.

Lady by Craig Wright; Co-presented by Barrow Street Theatre; Director, Dexter Bullard; Set, John McDermott; Costumes, Tif Bullard; Lighting, Nicole Pearce; Composer/Sound, Eric Shim; Stage Manager, Katrina Renee Herrmann; ASM, Alyssa Ritch; Assistant Director, Julie Kline; Fight Choreographer, Rick Sordelet; Cast: Michael Shannon (Kenny), Paul Sparks (Dyson), David Wilson Barnes (Graham)

New York premiere of a new play presented without intermission; Theatre 224 Waverly; August 28–October 11, 2008 (Opened September 8); 9 previews, 29 performances. Commissioned and originally presented by Northlight Theatre (Chicago, Illinois).

Geometry of Fire by Stephen Belber; Director, Lucie Tiberghien; Set, Robin Vest; Costumes, Anne Kennedy; Lighting, Peter West; Sound, Broken Chord Collective; Stage Manager, Katrina Renee Herrmann; ASM, Alyssa Ritch; Assistant Director, Alice Reagan; Fight Choreographer, Rick Sordelet; Technical Director, Brian Smallwood; Cast: Jeffrey DeMunn (Bob/Chuck), Donnie Keshawarz (Tariq), Jennifer Mudge (Cynthia and others), Kevin O'Donnell (Mel)

World premiere of a new play presented without intermission; Theatre 224 Waverly; November 15–December 21, 2008 (Opened November 24); 7 previews, 21 performances. Developmental production presented by New York Stage and Film Company and the Powerhouse Theatre at Vassar June 27, 2007.

That Pretty Pretty; or, The Rape Play by Sheila Callaghan; Director, Kip Fagan; Set, Narelle Sisson; Costumes, Jessica Pabst; Lighting, Matt Frey; Sound, Eric Shim; Hair/Maekup, Erin Kennedy Lunsford; Stage Manager, Katrina Renee Herrmann; ASM, Melissa Mae Gregus; Production Assistant, Ian Heitzman; Assistant Director, Emily Fishbaine; Fight Choreographer, Rick Sordelet; Assistant Hair/Makeup, Bridget Ritzinger; Technical Director, Brian Smallwood; Cast: Joseph Gomez (Rodney), Lisa Joyce (Agnes), Greg Keller (Owen), Annie McNamara (Jane Fonda), Danielle Slavick (Valerie)

World premiere of a new play presented in two acts; Theatre 224 Waverly; February 10–March 28, 2009 (Opened February 23); 11 previews, 25 performances.

The Amish Project by Jessica Dickey; Presented in association with Nora Productions; Director, Sarah Cameron Sunde; Set and Costumes, Lauren Helpern; Lighting, Nicole Pearce; Sound, Jill BC DuBoff; PSM, Kelly Shaffer; Assistant Director, Lillian Vince; Production Assistants, Johnson Henshaw & Morgan Gould; Cast: Jessica Dickey

Off-Broadway debut of a solo performance play presented without intermission; Theatre 224 Waverly; June 4–July 12, 2009 (Opened June 10); 5 previews, 29 performances. Originally presented in the 2008 NY Fringe Festival and further developed by Cherry Lane Theatre.

David Wilson Barnes, Michael Shannon and Paul Sparks in Lady

Roundabout Theatre Company

Forty-third Season

Artistic Director, Todd Haimes; Managing Director, Harold Wolpert; Executive Director, Julia C. Levy; Associate Artistic Director, Scott Ellis; Founding Director, Gene Feist; Artistic Development/Casting, Jim Carnahan; Education, Greg McCaslin; General Manager, Sydney Beers; General Manager Steinberg Center, Rachel E. Ayers; Finance, Susan Neiman; Marketing/Sales Promotion, David B. Steffen; Development, Jeffory Lawson; Sales, Charlie Garbowski Jr.; Production Manager, Kai Brothers; Associate Production Manager, Michael Wade; Company Manager, Nicholas Caccavo; Casting, Mele Nagler; Press, Boneau/Bryan-Brown, Jessica Johnson, Matt Polk, Amy Kass

Brad Fleischer and Ato Essandoh in Streamers
(photo by T. Charles Erickson)

Streamers by David Rabe; Presented in association with Huntington Theatre Company; Director, Scott Ellis; Set, Neil Patel; Costumes, Tom Broecker; Lighting, Jeff Croiter; Sound, John Gromada; Fight Director, Rick Sordelet; PSM, Stephen M. Kaus; Stage Manager, Eileen Ryan Kelly; Assistant Director, Cobey Mandarino; Associate Lighting, Grant Yeager; Cast: Hale Appleman (Richie), Charlie Hewson (Martin), Ato Essandoh (Carlyle), Brad Fleischer (Billy), J.D. Williams (Roger), John Sharian (Sgt. Rooney), Larry Clarke (Sgt. Cokes), Cobey Mandarino (M.P. Lieutenant), E.J. Cantu (PFC Hinson), Jason McDowell-Green (PFC Clark), Axel Avin Jr. (PFC); Understudies: Charlie Hewson (Billy), Jason McDowell-Green (M.P. Lieutenant, Martin), E.J. Cantu (Richie, Billy), Axel Avin Jr. (Roger)

Setting: An Army barracks in Virginia. 1965. Revival of a new play presented in two acts; Laura Pels Theatre; October 17, 2008–January 11, 2009 (Opened November 11); 29 previews, 72 performances. Originally presented by the Public Theater/ New York Shakespeare Festival at Lincoln Center's Mitzi Newhouse Theater April 21, 1976, playing 478 performances (see *Theatre World* Vol. 32, page 132). The Roundabout production was based on the 2007 Huntingting Theatre Company production.

Natalie Gold, Gio Perez and Maggie Burke in The Language of Trees

The Language of Trees by Stephen Levenson; Director, Alex Timbers; Set, Cameron Anderson; Costumes, Emily Rebholz; Lighting, David Weiner; Sound, M.L. Dogg; PSM, Erin Maureen Koster; Casting, Carrie Gardner; Production Manager, Michael Wade; ASM, Molly Minor Eustis; Assistant Production Manager, Elise Hanley; Props, Meghan Buchanan; Assistant Director, Adrienne Campbell-Holt; Cast: Natalie Gold (Loretta Trumble-Pinkerstone), Michael Hayden (Denton Pinkertone), Gio Perez (Eben Trumble-Pinkerstone), Maggie Burke (Kay Danley), Michael Warner (Bill Clinton)

Setting: The early spring and summer of 2003. World premiere of a new play presented without intermission; Roundabout Underground–Black Box Theatre; October 3–December 14, 2008 (Opened October 29); 25 previews, 55 performances.

Distracted by Lisa Loomer; Director, Mark Brokaw; Sets, Mark Wendland; Costumes, Michael Krass; Lighting, Jane Cox; Original Music & Sound, David Van Tieghem; Projections & Video, Tal Yarden; PSM, William H. Lang; Casting, Carrie Gardner; Stage Manager, Megan Smith; Assistant Director, Christopher M. Czyz; Cast: Cynthia Nixon (Mama), Matthew Gumley (Jesse), Josh Stamberg* (Dad), Aleta Mitchell (Dr. Waller/Mrs. Holly/Delivery Person/Nurse), Natalie Gold (Dr. Zavala/Waitress/Carolyn/Nurse), Mimi Lieber (Sherry), Shana Dowdeswell (Natalie), Lisa Emery (Vera), Peter Benson (Dr. Daniel Broder/Allergist/Dr. Jinks/Dr. Karnes); Understudies: Tom Galantich (Dad, Dr. Border/Dr. Karnes/Dr. Jinks), Susan Pellegrino (Dr. Waller/Mrs. Holly/Delivery Person/Nurse, Sherry), Susannah Schulman (Mama), Jenn Schulte (Dr. Zavala/Waitress/Carolyn/Nurse, Vera), Jake Schwencke (Jesse), Lindsay Teed (Natalie); *Succeeded by: Rick Holmes (4/7/09)

Setting: Now. The Suburbs. New York premiere of a new play presented in two acts; February 7–May 10, 2009 (Opened March 4); 29 previews, 86 performances. Originally produced by Center Theatre Group at the Mark Taper Forum, March 15–April 29, 2007 (*Theatre World* Vol. 64, page 317).

The Tin Pan Alley Rag by Mark Saltzman, music & lyrics by Irving Berlin & Scott Joplin, additional music and arrangements, Brad Ellis; Presented by special arrangement with Rodger Hess; Director, Stafford Arima; Choreography, Liza Gennaro; Music Director/Orchestrator/Arrangements, Michael Patrick Walker; Set, Beowulf Boritt; Costumes, Jess Goldstein; Lighting, Howell Binkley; Sound, Walter Trarbach; Hair/Wigs, Charles G. LaPointe; PSM, Tripp Philips; Dialects, Stephen Gabis; Casting, Stephen Kopel; Production Management, Aurora Productions; ASM, Cheryl D. Olszowka; Assistant Director, Todd L. Underwood; Assistant Choreographer, Drew Humphrey; Associate Design: Chloe Chapin (costumes), Ryan O'Gara (lighting), Drew Levy (sound); Master Technician, Nicholas Wolff Lyndon; Dance Captain, Randy Aaron; Additional Music and Lyrics, Reginald

Cynthia Nixon in Distracted *(photos by Joan Marcus)*

Cynthia Nixon, Peter Benson and Josh Stamberg *in* Distracted

DeKoven, Clement W. Scott, Ron Gutierrez, Maurice Abraham, Stephen C. Foster, Johannes Brahms; Cast: Michael Boatman (Scott Joplin), Michael Therriault (Irving Berlin), Randy Aaron (Willie/Gitlo/Joseph/Porter/others), Derrick Cobey (Rev. Alexander/Johnny/Williams/Ned/others), Jenny Fellner (Dorothy Goetz), Rosena M. Hill (Monisha/Miss Esther Lee/Librarian/others), James Judy (Jimmy Kelly/Alfred Ernst/John Stark/Turkey Plugger/others), Mark Ledbetter (Mooney Mulligan/Thaddeus/Hopeful Songwriter/others), Michael McCormick (Teddy Snyder), Erick Pinnick (Mr. Payton/Plugger/Havana MC/ E.M./others), Tia Speros (Sophie/Wedding Singer/Kate/Ida/others), Idara Victor (Freddie Alexander/ Treemonisha/Hattie Mae/others); Understudies: Derrick Cobey (Scott Joplin), Jeffrey Schecter (Irving Berlin and roles played by M. Ledbetter), Philip Hoffman (Teddy Snyder and roles played by J. Judy), Emily Shoolin (Dorothy Goetz & roles played by T. Speros), Joe Aaron Reid (roles played by R. Aaron, D. Cobey & E. Pinnick), Soara-Joye Ross (roles played by R. Hill & I. Victor); Musicians: Michael Patrick Walker (Piano 1/Conductor), Brian Cimmet (Piano 2)

Musical Numbers: Irving Berlin—I Love a Piano, Sweet Italian Love, Moishe (Abie) Sings an Irish Song, Yiddisha Nightingale, When the Midnight Choo Choo Leaves for Alabam', You'd Be Surprised, When I Lost You, Play a Simple Melody, Alexander's Ragtime Band; Scott Joplin—A Real Slow Drag, The Maple Leaf Rag, The Ragtime Dance, Solace, The Entertainer, Bethena, I Want to See My Child, Overture from *Treemonisha*, Finale: A Real Slow Drag; Additional Songs: Plugger Songs, Oh Promise Me, Queenie, Irish Colleen, Ring de Banjo, Hungarian Dance #5, American Symphony

New York premiere of a new musical presented in two acts; June 12–September 6, 2009 (Opened July 14); 36 previews, 62 performances. Originally produced at the Pasadena Playhouse in July 1997, and subsequently at the Goodspeed Opera House.

Above: *Michael Boatman and Michael Therriault in* The Tin Pan Alley Rag

Left: *Randy Aaron, Idara Victor, Derrick Cobey, Rosena M. Hill, Erick Pinnick, Mark Ledbetter, James Judy, Michael Therriault and Michael Boatman in* The Tin Pan Alley Rag

Second Stage Theatre

Thirtieth Season

Artistic Director, Carole Rothman; Executive Director, Ellen Richard; Associate Artistic Director, Christopher Burney; Finance, Janice B. Cwill; General Manager, Don-Scott Cooper; Development, Sarah Bordy; Sales, Noel Hattem; Marketing, Robert Marlin; Marketing Associate, Hector Coris; Ticket Services Manager, Greg Turner; Production Manager, Jeff Wild; Technical Director, Robert G. Mahon III; Literary Manager, Sara Bagley; House Manager, Joshua Schleifer; Advertising, Eliran Murphy Group; Press, Barlow · Hartman, Michael Hartman, Tom D'Ambrosio, Michelle Bergmann

Boys' Life by Howard Korder; Director, Michael Greif; Set, Mark Wendland; Costumes, Clint Ramos; Lighting, Kevin Adams; Sound, Fitz Patton; Casting, Telsey + Company; PSM, Amy McCraney; Stage Manager, Shanna Spinello; Assistant to the Director, Jennifer Ashley Tepper; Props Master, Susan Barras; Production Assistants, Alice Gordon-Hardy & Marcella Merkx; Production Manager, Robert G. Mahon III; Technical Director, Jeremy Palmer; Cast: Rhys Coiro (Jack), Peter Scanavino (Don), Jason Biggs (Phil), Michelle Federer (Karen), Dan Colman (Man), Stephanie March (Maggie), Betty Gilpin (Lisa), Laura-Leigh (Girl), Paloma Guzmán (Carla)

Setting: A Large City, 1988. Revival of a play presented without intermission; October 2–November 9, 2008 (Opened October 20); XX previews, XX performances. Originally produced by Lincoln Center Theater February 5, 1988 (see *Theatre World* Vol. 44, page 93). 21 previews, 34 performances

Jason Biggs, Rhys Coiro and Peter Scanavino in Boys' Life
(photo by Joan Marcus)

Becky Shaw by Gina Gionfriddo; Director, Peter DuBois; Set, Derek McLane; Costumes, Jeff Mahshie; Lighting, David Weiner; Sound, Walter Trarbach; Casting, Mele Nagler, David Caparelliotis; PSM, Lori Ann Zepp; Stage Manager, James W. Carringer; Associate Design: Shoko Kambara (set), Lauren Phillips (lighting), M.L. Dogg (sound); Props, Susan Barras; Wigs, Paul Huntley; Cast: Emily Bergl (Suzanna), David Wilson Barnes (Max), Kelly Bishop (Susan), Thomas Sadowski* (Andrew), Annie Parisse (Becky); Standbys: Mary Bacon (Suzanna, Becky), Benim Foster (Max, Andrew), Jane Summerhays (Susan); *Succeded by Dashiell Eaves (2/10/09)

New York premiere of a new play presented in two acts; January 16–March 16, 2009 (Opened February 13); XX previews, XX performances. World premiere at the 2008 Humana Festival at Actors Theatre of Louisville (see *Theatre World* Vol. 64, page 281). 25 previews, 77 performances

Kelly Bishop, David Wilson Barnes, Thomas Sadoski, Annie Parisse and Emily Bergl in Becky Shaw *(photo by Joan Marcus)*

Thomas Sadoski and Emily Bergl in Becky Shaw
(photo by Joan Marcus)

Everyday Rapture by Dick Scanlan and Sherie Rene Scott; Director, Michael Mayer; Choreography, Michele Lynch; Set, Christine Jones; Costumes, Tom Broecker; Lighting, Kevin Adams; Sound, Brian Ronan; Musical Director, Carmel Dean; Music Supervision/Orchestrations/Arrangements, Tom Kitt; Music Coordinator, Michael Keller; Casting, Mele Nagler, David Caparelliotis; PSM, Heather Cousens; Stage Manager, Bethany Russell; Associate Sound, Cody Spencer; Makeup, Tiffany Hicks; Magic Consultant, Steve Cuiffo; Dance Captain, Lindsay Mendez; Props, Susan Barras; Cast: Sherie Rene Scott, Lindsay Mendez, Betsy Wolfe, Eamon Foley; Musicians: Carmel Dean (piano/synthesizer), Jim Hershman (guitar), Gary Bristol (bass), Shannon Ford (drums), Hiroko Taguchi (violin)

Musical Numbers/Scenes: Both Sides Now, The Name of My Star, Beautiful Day, Like Magic, Reach Out and Touch, Four-Leaf Clover

World premiere of a new semi-autobiographical play with music/musical presented without intermission; April 7–June 14, 2009 (Opened May 3); XX previews, XX performances. A previous version of the show entitled *You May Worship Me Now* was presented March 31, 2008 as a benefit concert for the Actors Fund Phyllis Newman Women's Health Initiative. 31 previews, 43 performances

Sherie Rene Scott in Everyday Rapture *(photo by Carol Rosegg)*

Vanities, A New Musical Book by Jack Heifner (based on his play *Vanities*), music & lyrics by David Kirshenbaum; Presented in association with Junkyard Dog Productions, Demos/Bizar Entertainment, Robert G. Bartener, Michael Jenkins, Dancap Productions Inc., Kenny and Marleen Alhadeff, Jayson Raitt, Ambassador Theatre Group, Dallas Summer Musicals, Remmel T. Dickinson/Linda and Bill Potter, Sharon Rosen/The Raleigh Rally/Davelle, LLC; Director, Judith Ivey; Staging, Dan Knechtges; Set, Anna Louizos; Costumes, Joseph G. Aulisi; Lighting, Paul Miller; Sound, Tony Meola & Zach Williamson; Music Director/Additional Vocal Arrangements, Bryan Perri; Orchestrations/Additional Arrangements, Lynne Shankel; Music Coordinator, Howard Joines; Vocal Arrangements, Carmel Dean; Casting, Jay Binder/Sara Schatz; PSM, Scott Pegg; Stage Manager, Bethany Russell; Music Coypying, Kaye-Houston Music; Synthesizer Programmer, Randy Cohen; Associate Director, Richard Roland; Associate Choreographer, Penny Ayn Maas; Hair/Wigs, Josh Marquette; Associate Lighting, Jonathan Spencer; Props, Susan Barras; Cast: Lauren Kennedy (Mary), Sarah Stiles (Joanne), Anneliese van der Pol (Kathy); Standbys: Katie Adams (Joanne, Kathy), Julie Reiber (Mary, Kathy); Musicians: Bryan Perri (Conductor/key 1), Randy Cohen (Associate Conductor/key 2/organ), Peter Calo (guitar), Michael Pearce (bass), Joseph Mowatt (drums/percussion), Bryan Crook (reed 1), Scott Kreitzer (reed 2), Barry Danielian (trumpet)

Setting: A small town in Texas, fall 1963; A sorority house in Dallas, spring 1968; A penthouse terrace in Manhattan, summer 1974; a small town in Texas, winter, years later. New York premiere of a new musical presented in four scenes without intermission; June 30–August 9, 2009 (Opened July 16); XX previews, XX performances. World premiere presented by TheatreWorks (Palo Alto, California) and subsequently at the Pasadena Playhouse. The show had its initial showcase production in the 2006 National Alliance for Musical Theatre Festival of New Musicals. 19 previews, 26 performance

SECOND STAGE UPTOWN SERIES

10 Things to Do Before I Die by Zakiyyah Alexander; Director, Jackson Gay; Set, Wilson Chin; Costumes, Jenny Mannis; Lighting, Thomas Dunn; Sound & Music, Broken Chord Collective; PSM, Lori Ann Zepp; Stage Manager, Rachel Motz; Casting, Mele Nagler, David Caparelliotis; Management Associate, Nicholas Ward; Props, Susan Barras; Cast: Francois Battiste (Jason), Natalie Venetia Belcon (Vida), Kyle Beltran (Jose), Dion Graham (Andrew), Tracie Thoms (Nina)

World premiere of a new play presented in two acts McGinn/Cazale Theater; May 13–June 22, 2009 (Opened June 2); 19 previews, 18 performances.

Wildflower by Lila Rose Kaplan; Director, Giovanna Sardelli; Set, Steven C. Kemp; Costumes, Paloma Young; Lighting, Lap Chi Chu; Sound, Jill BC DuBoff; PSM, Lori Ann Zepp; Casting, Mele Nagler, David Caparelliotis; Stage Manager, Rachel Motz; Props, Meredith Ries; Cast: Nadia Bowers (Erica), Quincy Dunn-Baker (James), Ron Cephas Jones (Mitchell), Jake O'Connor (Randolph), Renée Felice Smith (Astor)

World premiere of a new play presented without intermission; McGinn/Cazale Theater; July 13–August 8, 2009 (Opened July 27); 14 previews, 16 performances.

Lauren Kennedy, Anneliese van der Pol and Sarah Stiles in Vanities *(photo by Craig Schwartz)*

Jake O'Connor and Renee Felice Smith in Wildflower

Signature Theatre Company

Eighteenth Season

Founding Artistic Director, James Houghton; Executive Director, Erika Mallin; Associate Artistic Director, Beth Whitaker; Associate Artist, Ruben Santiago-Hudson; General Manager, Adam Bernstein; Development, Katherine Jaeger-Thomas; Marketing, David Hatkoff; Production Manager, Paul Ziemer; Casting, Telsey + Company; Database, Dollye Evans; Box Office, Ben Schneider; Press, Boneau/Bryan-Brown, Juliana Hannett, Matt Ross, Jim Byk, Rachel Strange; Playwright-in-Residence, Negro Ensemble Company

The First Breeze of Summer by Leslie Lee; Director, Ruben Santiago-Hudson; Set, Michael Carnahan; Costumes, Karen Perry; Lighting, Marcus Doshi; Sound, David Margolin Lawson; Arrangements/Musical Direction, Bill Simms Jr.; Fight Director, Thomas Schall; Dialect Coach, Deborah Hecht; PSM, Winnie Y. Lok; ASM, Nathan K. Claus; Assistant Director, Nicole Watson; Wigs, Valerie Gladstone; Props, Sarah Bird, Dana Lewman; Assistant Design: Lucrecia Briceno (lighting), Steven Jones (sound); Cast: Harvy Blanks (Reverend Mosely), Yaya DaCosta (Lucretia), Sandra Daley (Gloria Townes), Crystal Anne Dickinson (Hope), Brandon Dirden (Nate Edwards), Jason Dirden (Lou Edwards), Quincy Dunn-Baker (Briton Woodward), Marva Hicks (Hattie), John Earl Jelks (Harper Edwards), Tuck Milligan (Joe Drake), Gilbert Owuor (Sam Green), Brenda Pressley (Aunt Edna), Keith Randolph Smith (Milton Edwards), Leslie Uggams (Gremmar Edwards)

The Company of The First Breeze of Summer
(photo by Richard Termine)

Setting: A small city in the Northeast on a Thursday afternoon through a Sunday night in June; mid-1970s. Revival of a play presented in two acts; Peter Norton Space; August 5–October 19, 2008 (Opened August 21); XX previews, XX performances. Originally produced by the Negro Ensemble Company at St. Mark's Playhouse March 2–April 27, 1975 (see *Theatre World* Vol. 31, page 117). The production transferred to Broadway at the Palace Theatre June 10–July 20, 1975 (see *Theatre World* Vol. 32, page 10). 16 previews, 64 performances

Home by Samm-Art Williams; Director, Ron OJ Parson; Set, Shaun Motley; Costumes, Ilona Somogyi; Lighting, William H. Grant III; Soundscape and Vocal Arrangements, Kathryn Bostic; PSM, Chandra LaViolette; ASM, Kara Aghabekian; Choreographer, Monica Bill Barnes; Assistant Director, Lileana Blain-Cruz; Dramaturg, Kirsten Bowen; Properties, Sarah Bird; Assistant Design: Ena Motley (set), Kate Cusack (costumes), Michael Jarrett (lighting); Sound Supervisor, Graham Johnson; Cast: Kevin T. Carroll (Cephus Miles); January LaVoy (Woman One/Pattie Mae Wells), Tracey Bonner (Woman 2)

Kevin T. Carroll (foreground),
January LaVoy and
Tracey Bonner in Home
(photo by Richard Termine)

Setting: Places: Cross Roads, North Carolina. A prison in Raleigh, North Carolina. And a very, very large American City. Time: Late 1950s to the present. Revival of a play presented without intermission; Peter Norton Space; November 11, 2008–January 22, 2009 (Opened December 7); XX previews, XX performances. Originally presented by the Negro Ensemble Company at St. Mark's Playhouse December 14, 1979–April 13, 1980. The show transferred to Broadway at the Cort Theatre in May 7, 1980–January 4, 1981 (see *Theatre World* Vol. 36, pages 65 and 145). 24 previews, 39 performances

Zooman and the Sign by Charles Fuller; Director, Stephen McKinley Henderson; Sets, Shaun Motley; Costumes, Katherine Roth; Lighting, Matthew Frey; Sound, Robert Kaplowitz; Fight Director, Rick Sordelet; PSM, Chandra LaViolette; ASM, Kara Aghabekian; Dramaturg, Kirsten Bowen; Assistant Director, Marisol Rosa-Shapiro; Assistant Design: Christopher Allison (set), Emily Rosenberg (costumes), Natalie Robin (lighting), Jessica Paz (sound); Cast: Ron Canada (Emmett Tate), Amari Cheatom (Zooman), Rosalyn Coleman (Rachel Tate), W. Tré Davis (Russell Adams), Peter Jay Fernandez (Donald Jackson), Lynda Gravatt (Ash Boswell), Jamal Mallory-McCree (Victor Tate), Evan Parke (Reuben Tate), Portia (Grace Georges)

Setting: The Tate home in Philadelphia; early 1980s. Revival of a play presented without intermission; Peter Norton Space; March 3–April 26, 2009 (Opened March 24); XX previews, XX performances. Originally produced by the Negro Ensemble Company at Theatre Four (now the Julia Miles Theatre) November 25, 1980–January 4, 1981 (see *Theatre World* Vol. 37, page 130). 22 previews, 35 performances

STAGED READING

Day of Absence Written and directed by Douglas Turner Ward; Cast: Peggy Alston, Norman Bush, Yaya DaCosta, Keith David, Brandon Dirden, Jason Dirden, Arthur French, January LaVoy, William Jay Marshall, Kathryn Meisle, Erica Peeples, Terrence Riggins, Heather Simms, Joyce Sylvester, Raphael Nash Thompson, Allie Woods; Peter Norton Space; February 1–2, 2009

Soho Rep

Thirty-third Season

Artistic Director, Sarah Benson; Executive Director, Tania Carmargo; Producer, Rob Marcato; Development Associate, Meghan Finn; Technical Director, Mark Stiko; Writer/Director Lab Co-Chairs, Maria Goyanes, Daniel Manley & Katherine Ryan; Development Consultant, Jennie Greer; Marketing Consultant, Melissa Ross; Marketing Associate, Barbara Sartore; Box Office, William Burke; Press, Sam Rudy Media Relations, Dale Heller

Blasted by Sarah Kane; Director, Sarah Benson; Sets, Louisa Thompson; Lighting, Tyler Micoleau; Sound, Matt Tierney; Costumes, Theresa Squire; Fight Director, J. David Brimmer; Props Master, Sarah Bird; Technical Director, Billy Burns; PSM, Danielle Monica Long; ASM, Dave Polato; Assistant Director, Meghan Finn; Dialect Coach, Charlotte Fleck; Casting, Jack Doulin; Assistant Design, Caleb Levengood (set), Natalie Robin (lighting), Emily Morgan DeAngelis (costumes), Hayley Morgan (props); Assistant Technical Director, Anthony Cerrato; Production Assistants, Erica Rippy, Whitney Edwards; Cast: Reed Birney (Ian), Marin Ireland (Cate), Louis Cancelmi (Soldier)

New York premiere of a new play presented without intermission; SoHo Rep at 46 Walker; October 2–December 21, 2008 (Opened October 9): 6 previews, 63 performances.

Sixty Miles to Silver Lake by Dan LeFranc; Co-produced by Page 73 Productions (Liz Jones & Asher Richelli, Executive Directors); Director, Anne Kauffman; Set & Costumes, Dane Laffrey; Lighting, Tyler Micoleau; Projections & Sound, Leah Gelpe; Production Manager, James E. Cleveland; Company Manager, Gretchen Margaroli; PSM, Rebecca Goldstein-Glaze; General Manager, La Vie Productions; Casting, James Calleri, Paul Davis; Assistant Director, Alice Reagan; Assistant Design: Hallie Stern (set & costumes), Lee Terry (lighting), Nick Gorczynski (projections/sound); Assistant Company Manager, Faiz Osman; Technical Director, Steve Lorick Jr.; Props, Mary Robinette Kowal; Voiceover, Michael D'Addario; Press for Page 73, Richard Kornberg & Associates, Don Summa; Cast: Joseph Adams (Ky), Dane DeHaan (Denny)

Setting: A car on a California highway. World premiere of a new play presented without intermission; SoHo Rep at 46 Walker; January 15–February 8, 2009 (Opened January 22); 7 previews, 19 performances.

Rambo Solo Conceived and directed by Pavol Liska and Kelly Cooper in conversation with Zachary Oberzan; Presented by Nature Theater of Oklahoma; Design & Video, Peter Nigrini; Production Managers, Robert Saenz de Viteri & Gabel Eiben; Company Manager, Elisabeth Conner; Production Assistants, Chris Borchardt, Elise Napoli, Toby Ring Thelin; Cast: Zachary Oberzan (Zack)

Setting: Zack's studio apartment in New York; the present. American premiere of a solo performance play presented without intermission; SoHo Rep at 46 Walker; March 19–April 19, 2009 (Opened March 21); 2 previews, 17 performances.

WORKSHOPS AND READINGS

Soho Rep Studio Workshops of new plays; included: *Black Cat Lost* by Erin Courtney (March 2009); *It Cannot Be Called Our Mothers But Our Graves* by The Theatre of a Two-Headed Calf (June 2009); *Job* by Thomas Bradshaw (July 2009).

Writer/Director Lab Reading Series Six writer/director pairs create new plays from scratch; included: *The Children's Employment Commission* by Jonathan Bernstein, directed by Katherine Kovner; *Sun Ran* by Sally Oswald, directed by Rafael Gallegos; *Him* by Katherine Ryan, directed by Stephen Brackett; *Mirage* by Susan Tenneriello, directed by Jerry Ruiz; *The Change* by Branden Jacobs-Jenkins, directed by Shoshona Currier; *Orange, Hat & Grace* by Gregory S. Moss, directed by Arin Arbus; May 19; Tuesdays April 13–May 19, 2009; 5 performances.

Reed Birney and Marin Ireland in Blasted *(photo by Simon Kane)*

Dane DeHaan and Joseph Adams in Sixty Miles to Silver Lake *(photo by Monique Carboni)*

Zachary Oberzan in Rambo Solo *(photo by Peter Nigrini)*

Stephanie Roth Haberle and Joan Macintosh in Chair
(photos by Gerry Goodstein)

John Douglas Thompson and Juliet Rylance in Othello

Christian Camargo and Jennifer Ikeda in Hamlet

Theatre for a New Audience

Thirtieth Season

Artistic Director, Jeffrey Horowitz; Managing Director, Dorothy Ryan; Chairman, Theodore Rogers; General Manager, Theresa von Klug; Development, Ernest A. Hood; Education, Joseph Giardina; Finance, Elizabeth Lees; Capital Campaign, Rachel Lovett; Associate Artistic Director, Arin Arbus; Associate General Manager, Sarah Elkashef; Grants Manager, David Pasteelnick; Development Associate, Daniel Bayer; Education Associate, Carie Donnelson; Finance Associate, Andrew Zimmerman; Capital Associate, Elizabeth Carena; Casting, Deborah Brown; Production Manager, Ken Larson; Technical Director, John Martinez/Jason Adams; Press, Bruce Cohen

The Grand Inquisitor by Marie-Hélène Estienne from *The Brothers Karamazov* by Fyodor Dostoyevsky; Produced by C.I.C.T/Théâtre des Bouffes du Nord; Co-presented by New York Theatre Workshop; October 22–November 30, 2008 (Opened October 29); 8 previews, 39 performances. (See complete listing under New York Theatre Workshop in this section).

Chair by Edward Bond; Director, Robert Woodruff; Sets & Costumes, David Zinn; Lighting, Mark Barton; Music & Sound, Michael Attias; Voice Coach, Andrew Wade; Dialect Consultant, Jane Gooderham; Fight Director, J. David Brimmer; Casting, Judy Bowman; PSM, Joanne E. McInerney; ASM, Ryan Durham; Lighting Syndicate, Doug Filomena; Properties Master, Meredith Ries; Assistant Director, James Dacre; Cast: Stephanie Roth Haberle (Alice), Will Rogers (Billy), Alfredo Narciso (Soldier), Annika Boras (Officer), Joan MacIntosh (Prisoner)

Setting: Alice's flat in London; 2077. Revival of a drama presented without intermission; Duke on 42nd Street; December 5–28, 2008; 6 previews, 21 performances.

Othello by William Shakespeare; Director, Arin Arbus; Sets, Peter Ksander; Costumes, Miranda Hoffman; Lighting, Marcus Doshi; Sound, Matt O'Hare; Compser, Sarah Pickett; Voice/Text Consultant, Robert Neff Williams; Dramaturg, Benjamin Nadler; Fight Director, B.H. Barry; Choreography, Doug Elkins; PSM, Renee Lutz; Properties, Tessa Dunning; Cast: John Douglas Thompson (Othello), Juliet Rylance (Desdemona), Denis Butkus (Roderigo), Ned Eisenberg (Iago), Graham Winton (Brabantio/Lodovico/Soldier), Lucas Hall (Cassio), Robert Langdon Lloyd (Duke of Venice/Senator/Gratiano), Christian Rummel (Montano/Senator), Alexander Sovronsky (Senator/Soldier/Cypriot Musician), Kate Forbes (Emilia), Elizabeth Meadows Rouse (Bianca)

Setting: Venice and Venetian occupied Cyprus; 1570. Revival of a play presented in five acts with one intermission; Duke on 42nd Street; February 14–March 7, 2009 (Opened February 22) with a return engagement April 15–24, 2009; 9 previews, 20 performances.

Hamlet by William Shakespeare; Director, David Esbjornson; Sets, Antje Ellerman; Costumes, Elizabeth Hope Clancy; Lighting, Marcus Doshi; Composer & Sound, Jane Shaw; Projections & Video, Sven Ortel; Voice & Text Consultant, Cicely Berry; Voice Coach, Andrew Wade; Dramaturg, Michael Feingold; Fight Director, B.H. Barry; PSM, Thomas J. Gates; ASM, Sid King; Properties, Tessa Dunning; Wigs & Makeup, Erin Lunsford; Cast: Casey Biggs (Claudius), Alyssa Bresnahan (Gertrude), Christian Camargo (Hamlet), Scott Drummond (Marcellus/Player/Captain), Alvin Epstein (Polonius), Jonathan Fried (Ghost of Hamlet's Father/Lucianus), Sean Haberle (Bernardo/Fortinbras), Graham Hamilton (Laertes), Tom Hammond (Horatio), Jennifer Ikeda (Ophelia), John Christopher Jones (Reynaldo/Gravedigger), Craig Pattison (Rosencrantz), Ryan Quinn (Osric/Player Queen), Robert Stattel (Priest/Player King), Richard Topol (Guildenstern)

Revival of the play presented in five acts with two intermissions; Duke on 42nd Street; March 19–April 12, 2009 (Opened March 29); 12 previews, 21 performances.

Vineyard Theatre

Twenty-eighth Season

Artistic Director, Douglas Aibel; Executive Director, Jennifer Garvey-Blackwell; General Manager, Reed Ridgley; Associate Artistic Director, Sarah Stern; Development, Scott Pyne; Marketing, Jonathan Waller; Education, Gad Guterman; Production Manager, Ben Morris; Assistant General Manager, Dennis Hruska; Marketing and Development Associate, Eric Emch; Casting, Henry Russell Bergstein; Press, Sam Rudy, Bob Lasko, Dale Heller

Wig Out! by Tarell Alvin McCraney; Director, Tina Landau; Set, James Schuette; Costumes, Toni-Leslie James; Lighting, Peter Kaczorowski; Sound, Robert Kaplowitz; Hair/Wig/Makeup, Wendy Parson; PSM, Barbara Reo; Associate Director, Kim Weild; Stage Manager, Katrina Lynn Olson; Properties/Assistant Set, Jessica Provenzale; Technical Director, David Nelson; Dialect Coach, Deborah Hecht; Assistant Director, Devorah Bondarin; Properties, Jay Duckworth; Music Consultant, Brent Frederick; Cast: Erik King (Lucian), Nathan Lee Graham (Rey-Rey), Clifton Oliver (Ms. Nina [Wilson]), Joshua Cruz (Venus), Glenn Davis (Deity), Rebecca Naomi Jones (Fay), Angela Grovey (Fate), McKenzie Frye (Faith), Daniel T. Booth (Serena), Sean Patrick Doyle (Loki), Andre Holland (Eric)

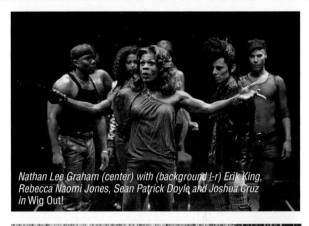

Nathan Lee Graham (center) with (background l-r) Erik King, Rebecca Naomi Jones, Sean Patrick Doyle and Joshua Cruz in Wig Out!

World premiere of a new play presented in two acts; Gertrude and Irving Dimson Theatre; September 10–November 16, 2008 (Opened September 30); 20 previews, 46 performances.

This Beautiful City Created by The Civilians, written by Steven Cosson and Jim Lewis, music and lyrics by Michael Friedman, from interviews by Emily Ackerman, Marsha Stephanie Blake, Brad Heberlee, Stephen Plunkett, Alison Weller, and the authors; Co-presented by Center Theatre Group; Director, Steven Cosson; Choreography, John Carrafa; Music Director, Erik James; Set, Neil Patel; Costumes, Alix Hester; Lighting, David Weiner; Sound, Ken Travis; Projections, Jason H. Thompson; PSM, Sarah Bierenbaum; ASM, Gregory T. Livoti; Properties, Jessica Provenzale; Assistant Director, Donya Washington; Cast: Emily Ackerman (Young Woman "God's Grace"/T-girl Christian), Brad Heberlee (New Life Associate Pastor/Fairness and Equality Worker), Marsha Stephanie Blake* (Emmanuel Choire Member/Ben Reynolds/New Pastor at Emmanuel), Brandon Miller (Alt Writer/Military Religious Freedom Activist/RHOP Leader), Stephen Plunkett (TAG Pastor/Priest/Marcus Haggard), Alison Weller (Fairness and Equality Leader/RHOP Member); Musicians: Erik James (keyboards/guitars/vocals), Chris Biesterfeldt (guitars/banjo/mandolin), Benjamin Campbell (bass), Richard Huntley (drums); * Succeeded by Rebecca Naomi Jones (3/7/09)

Nathan Lee Graham and Rebecca Naomi Jones in Wig Out!

Musical Numbers: Colorado, This Beautiful City, Whatever, An Email From Ted Haggard, End Times, Demons, Doubting Thomas, Take Me There, Freedom, Urban Planning, Another Email From Ted, Pikes Peak (A Model of Christian Charity)

Setting: Colorado Springs, Colorado; leading up to, and after, the 2006 election. New York premiere of a new musical presented in two acts; Gertrude and Irving Dimson Theatre; February 3–March 15, 2009 (Opened February 22); 20 previews, 21 performances. World premiere co-produced in the 2008 Humana Festival at Actors Theatre of Louisville and by the Studio Theatre (Washington, D.C.) as part of its 2008 Opening Our Doors Initiative (see *Theatre World* Vol. 64, page 281).

Developmental Lab Production

The Burnt Part Boys Book by Mariana Elder, lyrics by Nathan Tysen, music by Chris Miller; Director, Erica Schmidt; Cast: David Abeles, Skylar Astin, Al Calderon, Will Chase, Kevin Csolak, Andrew Durand, John Schippa, Timothy Warmen, Bubba Weiler

Setting: West Virginia; 1962. Developmental production of a new musical presented in two acts; Gertrude and Irving Dimson Theatre; May 26–June 6, 2006; 13 performances.

Alison Weller, Marsha Stephanie Blake, Stephen Plunkett, Emily Ackerman and Brad Heberlee in This Beautiful City *(photos by Carol Rosegg)*

Women's Project

Thirty-first Season

Producing Artistic Director, Julie Crosby, PhD.; Artistic Advisor, Liz Diamond; Associate Artistic Director, Megan E. Carter; Associate Producer, Allison Prouty; Marketing, Denise Ganjou; General Manager, Karron Karr; Grants, R. Justin Hunt, Alaina Feehan; Production Manager, Aduro Productions (Carolyn Kelson & Jason Janicki); Education, Johnmichael Rossi (interim); Facility Coordinator, Seth Morgan; Casting, Alaine Alldaffer; Consultants, Kat Williams, Bruce Cohen; Financial Services, Patricia Taylor; Press, Bruce Cohen

Aliens With Extraordinary Skills by Saviana Stanescu; Director, Tea Alagic; Set, Kris Stone; Costumes, Jennifer Moeller; Lighting, Gina Scherr; Sound & Original Music, Sarah Pickett; Dramaturgy, Megan E. Carter; PSM, Jack Gianino; Stage Manager, Jacqueline Prats; Dialect Coach, Charlotte Fleck; Associate Casting, Lisa Donadio; Projections/Slides, Emma Wilk; Assistant Director, Kate Gagnon; Assistant Design, Adriana Zollo & Patrick Rizzotti (set), Beth Goldenberg (costumes), Burke Brown (lighting); Production Assistant, Amber Chapel; Props, Stephanie Tucci; Wardrobe, Sam Ellingson; Electrician, Kia Rogers; Cast: Shirine Babb (INS Officer), Seth Fisher (Borat), Gian Murray Gianino (INS Officer), Kevin Isola (Bob), Natalia Payne (Nadia), Jessica Pimentel (Lupita)

World premiere of a new dark comedy presented in two acts; Julia Miles Theatre; September 22–October

26, 2008 (Opened September 30); 31 performances.

Freshwater by Virginia Woolf; Co-presented by SITI Company; Director, Anne Bogart; Set & Costumes, James Schuette; Lighting, Brian H. Scott; Sound, Darren L West; Hair & Wigs, Anne Ford-Coates; Dramaturgy, Megan E. Carter; Assistant Director, James Dacre; PSM, Elizabeth Moreau; Stage Manager, Jack Gianino; Associate Sound, Matt Hubbs; Assistant Costumes, Melissa Tim; Props Artisan, Stephanie Tucci; Assistant Sound, Asa Wember; Cast: Akiko Aizawa (Mary Magdalen), Gian Murray Gianino (Lt. John Craig), Ellen Lauren (Julia Margaret Cameron), Tom Nelis (Charles Hay Cameron), Barney O'Hanlon (George Frederick Watts), Stephen Duff Webber (Alfred Lord Tennyson), Kelly Maurer (Ellen Terry)

World premiere of an old play presented without intermission; Julia Miles Theatre; January 15–February 15, 2008 (Opened January 25); 34 performances.

Global Cooling: The Women Chill Co-presented by arts> World Financial Center under the direction of Debra Simon; Created by artists of Women's Project Lab; Lead Producers, Heather Cohn, Jennifer Conley Darling; Costumes, Brenda Abbandandolo; Properties, Stephanie Tucci; PSM, Ryan C. Durham; ASM, Ariana Schrier; Production Assistants, Lesley Brown, Safa Samiezade-Yazd, Charity Shubert; Media Installation, Andrea Thome; Media Installation Producer, Amanda Feldman; Art Installation, Annie Varnot; Art Installation Producer, Allegra Schorr; plays included: *Bear Market* by Kara Manning; Director, Wendy McClellan and Donya Washington; Producer, Diane Alianiello; *The Chorus of Lost Places* by Lynn Rosen; Director, Susanna Gellert; Music Director, Matt Castle; Producer, Marissa Rosenblum; *Call Your Mother Earth* by Bekah Brunstetter; Director, Meiyin Wang; Producer, Megan E. Carter; *Place Reimagined* by Alexis Clements; Choreographer, Elizabeth Montgomer; Producer, Diane Alianiello; *Moment of Zen* by Crystal Skillman; Director, Linsay Firman; Producer, Amanda Feldman; *Muddy the Waters* by Charity Henson-Ballard; Director, Heidi Carlsen; Producer, Aimee Davis; *The Finale* by Wendy McClellan & Donya Washington; Producer, Diane Alianiello; Cast: B. Brian Argotsinger, Casey Boyle, Addie Brownlee, Jorge Cordova, Kibibi Dillon, Danielle Famble, Richard Gallagher, Laura Gilbert, Rebecca Henderson, Sarah Hillmon, Beth Kirkpatrick, Julie Kline, Toby Knops, Russel Stuart Lilie, Rebecca Lingafelter, Byrony Lucas, Dominique Morisseau, Ned Noyes, Lance Olds, Allie Pfeffer, Haas Regen, Angel R. Rodriguez, Phoebe Rose Sandford, Myxolydia Tyler, Jasmin Walker

A festival of short plays and art/media installation; Various locations at World Financial Center; June 3–6, 2009; 9 performances.

Kevin Isola and Natalia Payne in Aliens with Extraordinary Skills *(photos by Carol Rosegg)*

Gian Murray Gianino, Kelly Maurer, Barney O'Hanlon, Tom Nelis and Ellen Lauren in Freshwater

Dominique Morisseau, Danielle Famble and Myxolydia Tyler in Global Cooling: The Women Chill

York Theatre Company

Fourtieth Season

Artistic Director, James Morgan; Chairman of the Board, W. David McCoy, Founding Director F. Janet Hayes Walker; Associate Artistic Director, Brian Blythe; General Manager, Elisa Spencer; External Relations, Bonnie J. Butkas (interim: Michael Perreca); Production Manager, Chris Robinson; Audience Services Manager, Bryan Guffey; Marketing Consultant, Michael Redman/HHC Marketing; Graphics/Administrative Assistant, Jeb Knight; Development/Box Office Assistant, Shahna Sherwood; Developmental Reading Series Coordinator, Jeff Landsman; Audience Development/Promotions, Jeff Duchen & Joe Aiello; Casting, Geoff Josselson; Press, David Gersten & Associates, Shane Marshall Brown, James Lopez

Enter Laughing The Musical Book by Joseph Stein, music and lyrics by Stan Daniels, based on the play *Enter Laughing* by Joseph Stein, from the novel by Carl Reiner; Director, Stuart Ross; Music Director/Arrangements/Orchestrations, Matt Castle; Set, James Morgan; Lighting, Chris Robinson; Costumes, David Toser; Properties, Deirdre Brennan; Original Orchestrations, Luther Henderson; Technical Director, Scott DelaCruz; PSM, Sarah Butke; ASM, Sarah Caddell (return engagement: Emily Durning); Assistant to the Director, Bradley Beahen; Wigs, The Broadway Wig Company; Cast: Josh Grisetti (David Kolowitz), Jill Eikenberry (Emma Kolowitz), Michael Tucker (Morris Kolowitz), Ray DeMattis (Mr. Foreman), Emily Shoolin (Wanda), Robb Sapp* (Marvin), Paul Binotto (Don Darwin/The Pope), Erick Devine (Pike/Barrymore), Jeanine LaManna* (Angela Marlowe), George S. Irving* (Harrison Marlowe), Gerry McIntyre (Don Baxter/Franklin/Peabody), Betsy DiLellio (Eleanor/Frenchie), Allison Spratt (Miss B), Matt Castle (Roger Hamburger); Musicians: Matt Castle (piano), Michael Pearce (bass), Brad "Gorilla" Carbone (percussion);* Return Engagement Cast Replacements: Lannon Killea (Marvin Kolowitz);,Bob Dishy (Harrison Marlowe), Marla Schaffel (Angela Marlowe); Return Engagement Understudies: Paul Binotto (Mr. Forman, Morris), Erick Devine (Harrison Marlowe), Betsy DiLellio (Wanda, Miss B), Lannon Killea (David Kolowitz), Bradley Beahen (Marvin), John Spalla (Pike/Barrymore, Roger Hamburger, Don Baxter/Franklin/Peabody, Don Darwin/The Pope), Rachel Coloff (Angela Marlowe, Emma Kolowitz, Elanor/Frenchie)

Musical Numbers: David Kolowitz, The Actor; Its Like; I'm Undressing Girls With My Eyes; You; The Man I Can Love; Say The Words; My Son, the Druggist; He Touched Her; Men; Boy, Oh Boy; Being With You; The Butler's Song; If You Want To Break Your Mothers Heart; Hot Cha Cha; So Long, 174th Street; David Kolowitz (reprise)

Josh Grisetti and the Company in Enter Laughing The Musical
(photos by Carol Rosegg)

Setting: New York, 1930s. Revised version of a musical presented in two acts; Theatre at St. Peter's Church; September 3–October 12, 2008 (Opening Night: September 10); 7 previews, 41 performances; Return Engagement January 21–March 20, 2009 (2nd Opening Night: January 29); 7 previews, 51 performances. Previously presented in the Musicals in Mufti last season (see *Theatre World* Vol. 64, page 200). The original version of the show, titled *So Long, 174th Street*, opened at the Harkness Theatre April 27, 1976 and closed after 16 performances. The production starred Robert Morse, and the cast included George S. Irving, who played the same role in the York Theatre production (see *Theatre World* Vol. 32, page 52). **2009 Theatre World Award:** Josh Grisetti

Janine LaManna, Josh Grisetti, and George S. Irving in
Enter Laughing The Musical

My Vaudeville Man! Book and lyrics by Jeff Hochhauser, music and lyrics by Bob Johnston, based on Jack Donahue's "Letters of a Hoofer to His Ma;" Co-producer, Melanie Herman; Director/Choreographer, Lynne Taylor-Corbett; Co-Choreographer, Shonn Wiley; Music Director/Orchestrations/Arrangements, Doug Oberhamer; Set, James Morgan; Costumes, David Toser; Lighting, Mary Jo Dondlinger; Co-Orchestrations, Bob Johnston; Casting, Carol Hanzel; General Manager, Martian Entertainment (Carl D. White, Lauren Yates, Scott DelaCruz, Steven DeLuca, Emily Pye, Carolyn Kuether); Props, Rich Murray; PSM, Sarah Butke; ASM, Bailie Slevin; Dialect Coach, Deborah Hecht; Assistant Director, Sam Underwood; Production Manager/Technical Director, Scott DelaCruz; Assistant to Ms. Herman, Lynn Rollins; Dummy Designer, Martin Izquierdo; Dance Consultant, Bob Fitch; Video Producer, Ryan McNally; Marketing, Leanne Schanzer Promotions; Cast: Karen Murphy (Mud Donahue), Shonn Wiley (Jack Donahue); Understudies: Susan Hoffman, Sam Underwood; Musicians: Doug Oberhamer (piano), Christine Riley (Associate Music Director), Dave Anthony (drums), Scott Thornton (bass); Cast recording: Jay Records

Musical Numbers: Vaudeville; The Shadow; Oh Bless Me Father #1; Picnic in the Kitchen; French Kiss; Oh Bless Me Father #2; Mud Donahue & Son; The Jack Donahue Almond Frappe; Oh Bless Me Father #3; A Sad Sad Life; My Son, I Know; I Was Wrong; The Tap Drunk; How Can I Put It Any Plainer; So The Old Dog Has Come Home; The Shadow (reprise); What If I'm Wrong?; O Bless Me Father #4; Vaudeville Man

Setting: Small time Vaudeville Theatres on the New England circuit, and in the Donhaue home in Charlestown, Massachusetts, during the spring of 1910. Off-Broadway premiere of a new musical presented in two acts; Theatre at St. Peter's Church; November 7, 2008–January 4, 2009 (Opened November 17); 11 previews, 30 performances. Developmental reading presented at the York Theatre; world premiere (under the title *Mud Donahue & Son*) presented at the 2007 New York Musical Theatre Festival (see *Theatre World* Vol. 64, page 247).

Shonn Wiley in My Vaudeville Man!

Shonn Wiley and Karen Murphy in My Vaudeville Man!

MUSICALS IN MUFTI—TWENTY-THIRD SERIES
MUSICAL THEATRE GEMS IN STAGED CONCERT PERFORMANCES

Minnie's Boys Book by Arthur Marx and Robert Fisher (based upon the lives of the Marx Brothers), music by Larry Grossman, lyrics by Hal Hackady; Originally produced on Broadway by Arthur Whitelaw, Max J. Brown and Byron Goldman; Director, Stuart Ross; Music Director/Piano, Matt Castle; Lighting, Chris Robinson; PSM, Sarah Butke; ASM, Bailie Slevin; Cast: Nancy McCall (Mrs. Krupnik/Burlesque Girl/Miss Whitehous), Beth Glover (Mrs. McNish/Mrs. Flanigan/Miss Eiffel Tower), Emily Shoolin (Miss Murdock/Mrs. Goldblatt/Burlesque Girl), Kelly Sullivan (Cindy Lou/Mrs. Fressen/Lotta Miles), Pamela Myers (Minnie Marx), Ryan Duncan (Leonard "Chico" Marx), Erik Liberman (Julius "Groucho" Marx), Nick Gaswirth (Adolph "Harpo" Marx), Dan Bogart (Herbie "Zeppo" Marx), Stuart Zagnit (Sam "Frenchie" Marx), Don Mayo (Mr. Hochmeister/Miss Maxie/ Mr. Albee), Jim Walton (Al Shean/Mr. Sidebark)

Musical Numbers: Five Growing Boys; Rich Is; More Precious Far; Four Nightingales; Underneath It All; Mama, a Rainbow; You Don't Have To Do It for Me; If You Wind Me Up; Where Was I When They Passed Out the Luck?; Hello, Big Time; You Remind Me of You; Minnie's Boys; Be Happy; Philadelphia; The Act; I'll Say She Is

Setting: Time: 1912–1927. Staged concert of a revival of a musical presented in two acts; Theatre at St. Peter's Church; May 29–June 1, 2008; 5 performances.

Grind Original book by Fay Kanin, music by Larry Grossman, lyrics by Ellen Fitzhugh, new book by Brad Rouse; Original Broadway Director, Harold Prince; Director, Annette Jolles; Music Director, Steven Marzullo; Lighting, Chris Robinson; PSM, Sarah Butke; ASM, Bailie Slevin; Cast: Bob Ari (Harry), Joe Cassidy (Doyle), Nikki Reneé Daniels (Satin), Brandon Victor Dixon (Leroy), Wendy Fox (Loretta), Chasten Harmon (Clementine), Linda Hart (Romaine), Larry Keith (Gus), Max Quinlan (Juggler), Michele Ragusa (Lizzie), Christopher Sergeeff (Juggler), Kelly Sullivan (Glyde/Katie), Jasmin Walker (Ruby); Musicians: Steven Marzullo (piano), David Nyberg (percussion)

Musical Numbers: This Must Be the Place; I Get Myself Out; A Sweet Thing Like Me; My Daddy Always Taught Me To Share; Cadava; Boys Will Be Boys; All Things To One Man; Katie, My Love; The Grind; Soups On; Rabbity Stew; We All George; Cadava (reprise); Never Put It In Writing; I Talk, You Talk; These Eyes of Mine; Timing; Down; New Man; A Century Of Progress; Finale

Setting: Harry Earle's Burlesque Theater, Chicago. Early March, 1933. Staged concert of a revival of a musical presented in two acts; Theatre at St. Peter's Church; June 13–15, 2008; 5 performances.

Goodtime Charley Book by Sidney Michaels, music by Larry Grossman, lyrics by Hal Hackady; Director, Michael Montel; Music Director/Piano, Lawrence Yurman; Lighting, Chris Robinson; PSM, Sarah Butke; ASM, Sarah Caddell; Cast: Scott Robertson (Charles), William Thomas Evans (Henry), Christianne Tisdale (Isabella), Ana Nogueira (Kate/False Joan), Michael Winther (Minguet), Alysha Umphress (Marie), Angela DeCicco (Yolande), Jonathan Hammond (Phillip), Bryn Dowling (Agnes), Stephen Mo Hanna (Archbishop), Nick Wyman (General), Matt McGrath (Charley), Jenn Colella (Joan of Arc)

Musical Numbers: History, Goodtime Charley, Voices & Vision, Bits and Pieces, To Make the Boy a Man, Why Can't We All Be Nice?, Born Lover, I Am Going to Love, Castles of the Loire, Coronation, You Still Have a Long Way to Go, Merci Bon Dieu, Confessional, One Little Year, I Leave the World

Setting: 15th Century France. Staged concert of a revival of a musical presented in two acts; Theatre at St. Peter's Church; June 27–29, 2009; 5 performances.

NEW2NY—PREMIERE SERIES
NEW YORK PREMIERES OF MUSICALS
IN STAGED CONCERT PERFORMANCES

Compose Yourself! The Music of Larry Grossman Music by Larry Grossman, text by Stuart Ross, lyrics by Hal Hackady, Ellen Fitzhugh, Betty Comden & Adolph Green, Fred Ebb, Amanda Green, Carol Hall, John Kane, Buzz Kohan, Michael Korie, Drey Shepperd; Director, Stuart Ross; Music Director, David Snyder; Lighting, Chris Robinson; PSM, Sarah Butke; ASM, Sarah Caddell; Cast: Nikki Renée Daniels, Jason Graae, Darius de Haas, Liz Larsen; Lorna Luft, Howard McGillin; Orchestra: David Snyder and Larry Grossman

Musical Numbers: Is This Anything?; Someday Baby; Nothing Is As Open As The Road; A Place Where You Belong; Welcome to Lulu's; Harmonica Player; A Heavy Load; Real Eel Electricity; Thirty-Eleven; Play It Again Sam; Love Connection; I'm the Other Woman; Stay With Me, Nora; Poor Sweet Baby; Mama, A Rainbow; Tomorrow's Good Old Days; Eight Little Notes; This Must Be The Place; Give 'Em What They Want; Don't Tell Me, Don't Be Anything Less; We All George; The Big Bow Wow; I Do What I Can With What I Got; The Animal In The Pit; I, Lover; Let Me Make Love To You; I'll Build Tomorrow; Gone Too Soon; Turns Out; Finale

Staged concert of a musical revue presented in two acts; Theatre at St. Peter's Church; July 11–13, 2008; 5 performances.

The Lady in Penthouse B Book and lyrics by Peter Napolitano, music by Matthew Ward; Director, Pamela Hunt; Music Director, Mark Hartman; Lighting, Chris Robinson; PSM, Sarah Butke; ASM, Sarah Caddell; Assistant to the Director, Jack Doyle; Cast: Gordon Stanley (George/Narrator/Bill/Tad Rubin), Stephen Bienskie (Frank Fortunato/Heavenly/Bob), Michael Cone (Aunt Maida/Assistant to Frank Fortunato), J.D. Webster (Michi/Binky/Burt/Assistant to Frank Fortunato), Nancy Dussault (Lady Susan), Sally Wilfert (Mel Mitchell)

Musical Numbers: The Lady in Penthouse B, Starting Over Sequence, The Lady in Penthouse B (reprise), Get It? Got It? Good!, Good Advice, Hold It In, A Quiet Evening at Home, Good Advice (reprise), Frank Fortunato, My Nightmare, A Quiet Evening at Home (reprise), A Party Tonight, The Lady in Penthouse B (reprise 2), I Know You, Get It? Got It? Good! (reprise), Looks Like Things/Living With Lady, You'll Never See It Again, Looks Like Things (reprise), Let's Have a Drink, Say Hello, The Lady in Penthouse B (reprise 3), I Know You (reprise)

Staged concert of a new musical presented in two acts; Theatre at St. Peter's Church; July 25–27, 2008; 5 performances.

In Transit by Kristen Anderson-Lopez, James-Allen Ford, Russell M. Kaplan, and Sara Wordsworth; Additional Material, Gregory T. Christopher and Karla Momberger; Director, Joe Calarco; Music Director, W. Brent Sawyer; Lighting, Chris Robinson; Sound, James Cleveland; Additional Casting, Alan Filderman; PSM, Sarah Butke; ASM, Sarah Caddell; Hanna Laird (Ali/various), Denise Summerford (Jane/various), Ann Sanders (Regina/various), Adam Overett (Trent/various), Graham Stevens (Nate/various), Ryan Thomas Dunn (Chris/Dave/various), Adam Matta (Boxman)

Musical Numbers: In Transit, No Dental, Four Days Home, Where are the Girls?, Saturday Night Obsession, Wingman, But Ya Know, Keep It Goin', A Little Friendly Advice, The Moving Song, Choosing Not to Know, Reunion, Getting There, In Transit (reprise), Funny That Way

Setting: New York City; Now. Staged concert of a new musical presented in two acts; August 8–10, 2008; 5 performances.

ADDITIONAL EVENTS

The Seven Year B*tch *The Songs of Dan Acquisto and Sammy Buck* Book and lyrics by Sammy Buck, music and percussion by Dan Aquisto; Presented as part of the NEO Spotlight Concert Series; Director, Carlos Armesto; Music Director & Onstage Therapist, Brian Cimmet; Lighting, Chris Robinson; Production Manager, Amy Sulds; Stage Manager, Bryan Blythe; Sound, Richard Kamerman; Cast: Becca Ayers, James Donegan, David Perlman, Amy Rutberg, Joanna Young, Sammy Buck, Dan Acquisto, Brian Cimmet

Musical Numbers: The Best Year Ever, Very Short *Like You Like It* Excerpts, Phil's Original Answer, It Could Totally Happen, Dangling the Carrot, Turn It Off, The Becca Ayers Song, Mama's Here, Not Her, We JEL, The Amy Rutberg Song, The Reversal Song, So Close So Far Away, I Wanna Know Why, I Never Knew, Aunt Evelyn's Inspirational Advice, Our Annual Lament, Free As a…, We Write

A musical revue presented without intermission; Theatre at St. Peter's Church; June 30, 2008. Previously presented at the Barrow Group Theatre October 1, 2007 as part of the New York Musical Theatre Festival and at the Laurie Beechman Theatre at the West Bank Café November 5, 2007.

A Tribute to George S. Irving A concert to honor Mr. Irving for receiving the seventeenth annual Oscar Hammerstein Award for Lifetime Achievement in Musical Theatre; Chairperson, Anita Jaffe; Director, Donald Sadler; Award Presenter, Alice Hammerstein Mathias; Cast: Joy Abbott, Loni Ackerman, Jim Dale, Jill Eikenberry, Anita Gillette, Josh Grisetti, Michael Tucker, Charlotte Rae, Michael Rupert, Maryann Plunkett; Players Club; December 8, 2008.

NEO5 A benefit concert celebrating new, emerging, outstanding music theatre writers; Music and lyrics by Craig Baldwin & Kathy Lombardi, Charles Bloom, Jonathan Brielle, Michael L. Cooper & Hyeyoung Kim, Patrick Dwyer, Steven Fisher & Joan Ross Sorkin, Daniel Green, Shoshana Greenberg & Jeffrey Dennis Smith, Brett Macias & Caroline Murphy, David Mallamud & Michael L. Cooper, Kristin Maloney & Robert Maggio, Dan Martin & Michael Biello, Julia Meinwald & Rachel Jett, Jeffrey Thomson & Jordan Mann, Peter Yarin & Justin Warner, Clay Zambo; Producer, Brian Blythe; Lighting, Chris Robinson; PSM, Sarah Butke; Cast: Todd Buonopane, Mike McGowan, Carolann Page, Sara Wordsworth Joe Cassidy, Matt Castle, Mandy Gonzalez, Marcie Henderson, Adam Kantor, Jodie Langel, Lorinda Lisitza, Julie Reyburn, Megan Sikora, Jim Stanek, Alysha Umphress, Lynne Wintersteller, Lauren Worsham, Jennifer Zimmerman, Nicholas Barnes, Jodie Bentley, J'nelle Bobb-Semple, Vivienne Cleary, Claybourne Elder, Frank Galgano, Nick Gaswirth, Gwen Hollander, Gayla Morgan, Doug Shapiro, Jason Michael Snow; Theatre at St. Peter's Church; April 27, 2009.

Joanna Young, Becca Ayers, David Perlman, Sammy Buck, Dan Acquisto, Amy Rutberg, James Donegan, Carlos Armesto (Director) and Brian Cimmet in The Seven Year B*tch *(photo by Scott Denny)*

Sarah Knapp and Tommy Schrider in Abingdon Theatre Company's production of Greek Holiday *(photo by Kim T. Sharp)*

Ethan Hawke in A Winter's Tale, *part of the inaugural Bridge Project presented at BAM (photo by Joan Marcus)*

Mandy Patinkin and Elizabeth Waterston in Classic Stage Company's production of The Tempest *(photo by Joan Marcus)*

David Greenspan in Manhattan Class Company's production of Coraline *(photo by Joan Marcus)*

Natalie Venetia Belcon and Tracie Thoms in Second Stage's production of 10 Things to Do Before I Die *(photo by Joan Marcus)*

Kevin T. Carroll (foreground), *January LaVoy and Tracey Bonner in Signature Theatre Company's production of* Home *(photo by Richard Termine)*

Top: *Hollis Scarborough, Trey Compton and Alison Luff in* Like You Like It *at the Gallery Players (photo by Jennifer Maufrais Kelly)*

Center: *Michele Pawk, Donna Bullock, Kevin Geer and Richard Kind in Artistic New Directions production of* Flyovers, *presented at the 78th Street Theatre (photo by Carol Rosegg)*

Bottom: *The Company of Vital Theatre Company's production of* The Frog and the Witch *(photo by Sun Productions/Stephen Sunderlin)*

Off-Off Broadway: of Art and Politics

Shay Gines, Founding Director,
New York Innovative Theatre Awards Foundation

With nearly 1,800 unique productions, the 2008-2009 season was an active year for Off-Off-Broadway (OOB). It was also a year of change and self-discovery that found the current generation of OOB practitioners grappling with community identity and efforts to unite disparate organizations and artists.

One of the most exciting aspects of OOB is the great variety and diversity that it provides to New York City. This community includes well-seasoned professionals who have dedicated themselves to this brand of non-commercial theatre for years, such as Judith Malina, Ellen Stewart, Penny Arcade, Richard Foreman, Israel Horovitz . . . the list goes on and on. It also provides opportunities for emerging artists to hone their skills and experiment with their craft. A variety of theatrical genres and styles can be found, from Shakespeare to performance art to classic American plays by renowned playwrights to premieres of new works by first time playwrights. Many define OOB based on the number of seats in the performance space (ninety-nine seats or less), but the reality is that OOB productions are performed in theatres of all sizes, in both indoor and outdoor venues, uptown and downtown, and throughout all five of New York City's boroughs. It offers New York City's theatregoers an abundance of choices.

However, this undefined array of theatre poses an interesting challenge for OOB practitioners because it is difficult to define what exactly constitutes OOB. Audiences are sometimes wary of productions in this sector because they are not quite sure what to expect. As a way of addressing this, there is a movement within the community to rebrand "Off-Off-Broadway" as "Independent" or "Indie" theatre. Community leaders are split on this issue. Defenders of the "indie theatre" brand cite the successful growth of the "indie film" and "indie music" industries due in part to the clear, strong branding of those sectors over the last decade. They believe that changing the nomenclature will allow audiences to rediscover this scene on their own terms. Others argue that changing the name is dismissive of a rich cultural history and heritage and may divide the community into splinter groups and factions, rather than strengthening it.

This debate is far from over and may continue for years. But in the meantime, this community can be characterized by a scrappy, tenacious nature, its inventive creative choices, and of course its shoestring budgets. Modest budgets are a hallmark of the community and can be both a curse and a blessing for OOB artists. While limited financing presents difficult challenges, especially in terms of finding affordable performance venues and production values, it also gives the artists a unique freedom to pursue their artistic vision, and allows them ownership of the work they create. This unfettered creativity is also a defining characteristic of the OOB community.

The recession of 2008-2009 found an already cash-strapped OOB scrambling for resources. Granting organizations reduced funding, and corporate sponsorships and personal donations dried up. In addition, a surprising number of OOB performance venues shuttered. The election of Barack Obama, a community organizer with a devotion to the arts and grassroots movements, excited a political interest within the community. These political and socioeconomic pressures had a significant influence on the activities of OOB and spurred a community wide political activism.

This activism was initiated at the Second Indie Theater Convocation held in July 2008. Hosted by the New York Theatre Experience www.nytheatre.com and the League of Independent Theater www.litny.org this meeting gathered members of the community to begin an ongoing discussion about the most important issues facing OOB and to create task forces to address these issues.

In September 2008 four theatres in the state-owned Archive Building were informed that their rents would be raised by as much at 500%, forcing these not-for-profits to evacuate the premises. This news acted as a sort of rallying cry for a community already poised for advocacy and activism. Thanks to the dedicated

work of Community Board 2 and the attention of concerned and outspoken members of the OOB community, this issue was brought to the attention of political leaders. City Council Speaker Christine Quinn noted that, "It is all too familiar a story in the Village to hear about longtime neighborhood fixtures being forced out because they can no longer afford to stay in the communities they made great." An agreement was eventually brokered between the landlord and the organizations that allowed these theatres to keep their spaces. This was a huge victory not only for the four theatres in jeopardy, and their neighborhood, but for OOB as a whole. It brought attention to a distressing trend affecting small theatres across New York City, and it demonstrated the effectiveness of an organized community effort.

This percolating political energy culminated in February 2009 when the Community Boards that serve Manhattan hosted a joint public forum addressing the state of small to mid-sized theatres in New York City. Hundreds of attendees crammed into The Players Club to show their support for the community and participate in the discussion. Speakers such as Manhattan Borough President Scott Stringer reaffirmed that theatre, and especially OOB, is an important part of what makes New York City vibrant. "The 45 million tourists are not coming here to see our big buildings," he said. "The reason they come is because they want to see our art and our talent." Other speakers such as Ben Cameron, program director of the Doris Duke Foundation, Virginia Louloudes of A.R.T./NY, Paul Nagle from Council Member Gerson's office, and Tamara Greenfield from Fourth Arts Block echoed this sentiment. They impressed upon the community board members and elected officials that small arts organizations are the foundation of NYC's cultural community.

This meeting resulted in a commitment from the community boards to make OOB a priority in their neighborhoods. Over the next few months, the community boards made good on their promise by backing legislation that supported local theatres and inviting members of the OOB community to attend and contribute to their meetings and resolutions.

One of the key issues identified during the public forum was the need for reliable statistics about the OOB community. While OOB is one of the largest arts communities in the country, with tens of thousands of artists and hundreds of theatre companies, there exists virtually no statistical data about it in the public realm. Two organizations are working to change that are, the Lower Manhattan Arts Leaders and the New York Innovative Theatre Foundation.

Eleven downtown arts organizations united to form a group called the Lower Manhattan Arts Leaders, which meets weekly to strategize and exchange ideas on how to best support one another and convince policy makers and funding organizations to invest in their arts, companies, and neighborhoods. They pooled their individual numbers: annual audience statistics, financial records, operating budgets, etc. The results showed that these eleven organizations had an aggregate operating budget of $15 million and served over 275,000 audience members each year. This collective effort set an example of how cells of organizations could join together to create compelling data on a neighborhood level. If this trend continues to grow, with these kinds of efforts being duplicated on a grass roots level across the community, the combined results could serve as an economic impact indicator for the OOB community.

The New York Innovative Theatre Foundation (www.nyitawards.org) launched a five-part research program to collect information about the OOB community and make it publically available. The first report, *Statistical Analysis of Off-Off-Broadway Budgets*, published in April 2008 examined how OOB producers were spending their production budgets. The study found that OOB spent approximately $31 million on productions alone. This number does not include administrative or operating budgets, incidental spending, or in-kind contributions. It is believed to be the first publically released examination of OOB production financials. A second report, *Study of Off-Off-Broadway Performance Venues* was released in December 2008 and tracked OOB theatres over a five-year period. This study showed that the OOB community had lost a significant number of theatres in Manhattan— over 25%- - to real estate development projects between 2003-2008. Three additional reports are forthcoming, including a demographic study of the OOB participants (to be released in August 2009), a study of OOB audiences, and ultimately a study of OOB's cultural and economic impact.

For decades the OOB community has been living by the motto of Reduce, Rreuse, Recycle [google this to see the more common structure as corrected]. Born from the necessity to stretch every dime as far as it can go, OOB designers and producers have become very adept at reimagining otherwise unwanted materials. It is a common practice to reuse sets, costumes, and props to find treasures in rubbish piles and to recycle bits and pieces of previously used materials into entirely new creations. While this is nothing new to OOB artists, it has suddenly become the height of fashion to Go Green. OOB theatre companies have therefore found support and camaraderie from environmentalists. The first eco-friendly theatre in New York was an OOB space: The Wild Project in Alphabet City. Other companies have found unexpected funding sources from environmental organizations not only for green renovations and capital projects, but also for artistic and organizational support of green business practices. There is green in going green, and many of these companies have garnered extra media coverage due to their environmental efforts. It is a win-win situation, and trends suggest that more OOB companies will be looking for ways to expand and promote their eco-friendly efforts.

Are the politics of the day reflected in the artistic work that we see on OOB stages? Yes, but in unanticipated ways:

The last few years has seen an increase in the number of OOB theatre festivals. These include: the New York International Fringe Festival, the FRIGID Festival, the Midtown International Theatre Festival, the Strawberry One-Act Festival, the Turnip Festival One-Act Play Competition, the undergroundzero festival, the New York Musical Theatre Festival, and the annual Brick Theatre Festival. There are in fact so many festivals that it is sometimes difficult to track them.

These events have jam-packed schedules presenting back-to-back performances late into the night. They are a smorgasbord of theatre, offering a variety of themes and theatrical disciplines for the audience to choose from. They provide the companies and artists involved a low-cost venue in which to present their work, albeit with limited production values (due to the shared space and incredibly quick transition time between productions—sometimes thirty minutes or less). They also provide built-in communal support from the festival's fellow artists. Festivals are a manifestation of the political efforts of the OOB scene: community building, maximizing the utilization of valuable facilities and sharing them, and making the most of every available resource.

On the flip side, the reduction in resources has resulted in fewer large-scale productions, specifically musicals. The song and dance nature of modern American musicals often requires proper venues for rehearsal and performance, with pianos and/or other expensive equipment. Musicals generally have larger casts, which means more costumes, props, and other production materials, which ultimately means larger budgets. Those musicals that have graced OOB stages this past season have been greatly scaled back, with smaller casts and a more intimate nature.

While reflecting on the early years of OOB and the Caffe Cino, playwright Robert Patrick recalled exploring "new directions, such as 'pop' shows using comic books as scripts." This trend of comic book theatre has resurfaced in recent years. Plays based on fanboy ideals have become a prominent trend in OOB. Companies such as the Vampire Cowboys, Nosedive Productions, Commander Squish Productions, Piper McKenzie Productions, Charles Battersby, and GeminiWorks have all produced works based on superheroes or comics. This has also been a common trend in popular film and television programs, and in the fall of 2009 Spider-Man the Musical will premiere on Broadway. These productions, often set in depressed worlds filled with injustice and corruption, explore how ordinary citizens pushed to the brink discover super abilities—powers they can use to change the world in which they live. These plays mirror an American psyche inundated with corrupt and dishonest politicians, engaged in an unpopular war, steeped in an unstable economic environment, and feeling helpless to change their circumstances. Comic -book theatre provides fantasy where we see ourselves as stronger and better equipped to face the challenges of uncertain times. However unlike the superheroes of the '50s and '60s, today's protagonists are darker and much more complicated; often saddled with unlikable character flaws, rejected by society, or given to egotistical tendencies that lead them into the very corruption they are fighting. This reflects a more skeptical mindset of modern artists who are distrustful of the pursuit of a perfect world and have witnessed the corruption of those with power.

2008 was a year of transition for the United States. An economic recession and rising unemployment rates saw consumers saving rather than spending. Home foreclosures left thousands of families and communities in shambles. Major American industries were brought to their knees as bedrocks of their communities were forced into bankruptcy. A heated presidential election asked voters if they were ready for change. The country was poised on a precipice between economic collapse and guarded recovery. It is not surprising that OOB's 2008 trajectory was so influenced by the economic and political environment.

The dramas and scandals of the headlines from the past year were significant and will inevitably work their way into the dramas and political satires played out on the stages of OOB. But perhaps even more significant was the way in which the community reacted to these pressures. While it took many hits from these external sources, the OOB community's impulse to band together and strengthen communal ties helped it weather the storm better than expected, once again proving the staying power of the artists and companies that make up the Off-Off-Broadway community.

Editor's Note: Due to the earliest publication deadline schedule than ever before of this, as well as what will be that of all future volumes of *Theatre World*, the editors regret the truncated submission deadline and any corresponding omission of productions or companies that have been previously contained within this section in previous volumes. While every effort is made to locate the contact information of record for all Off-Off-Broadway productions and companies in order to make timely requests for submission for production information, the nature of Off-Off-Broadway in many ways makes this process an extremely difficult one. In order to ensure the future inclusion of your company or production in our publication, please contact associate editor Scott Denny below in order to be provided instructions on how to do so: rskotd@gmail.com or 917.568.7444

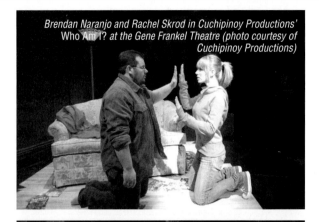

Brendan Naranjo and Rachel Skrod in Cuchipinoy Productions' Who Am I? at the Gene Frankel Theatre (photo courtesy of Cuchipinoy Productions)

Ivanna Cullinan, Suzanne Hayes, Tyrone Davis Jr., John Forkner, and Vanessa Morosco in The Rape of the Lock, presented by Judith Shakespeare Company at the Duo Theatre (photo by Anthony Ruiz)

Nicolle Rochelle in Blast From the Past Benefit Concert presented by AMAS (photo by Francois Bonneau and Sylvia Hoke)

Melaena Cadiz and Adam McLaughlin in Who You See Here at The Barrow Group (photo by Michael Thomas Holmes)

Trey Ziegler in the Roust Theatre Company production of Macbeth presented at the Mint Theatre Space (photo by Quinn Miller-Bedell)

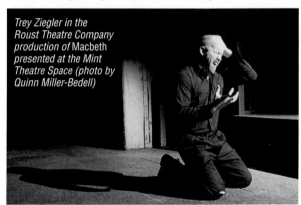

Bob Brader in Spitting in the Face of the Devil presented by John Montgomery Theatre Company at The Directors Studio (photo by Scott Wynn)

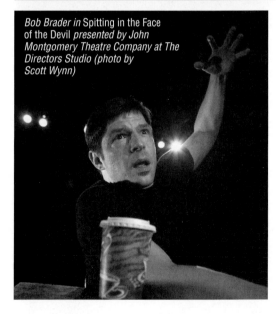

13th Street Repertory

Managing Artistic Director, Edith O'Hara; Producing Artistic Director, Sandra Nordgren

No More Waiting Book and lyrics by Chris Widney, music by David Christian Azarow; Director, Samantha Saltzman; Music Supervisor, Charles Czarnecki; Music Director, Michael James Roy; Stage Manager, Shannon O'Neil; Choreographer, Lynn Spector; Cast: Jenny Paul, Dustin J. Harder, Mark T. Evans, Brian C. Curl, Jeni Incontro, Benj Mirman; May 23–June 29

ANY 1 Man by George A. Peters II & Brandon F. Johnson; Cast: George A. Peters II; June 2–July 9

Jack Kerouac by Tom O'Neill; Director, Michael Flanagan; Stage Manager, Sarah Ludwinski; Cast: Mickey Pizzo, John William Schiffbauer, William Gozdziewski, Halleluyah Walcott, Adam Thomas Smith, Casandera M.J. Lollar; July 25–August 31

Cat and the Moon by Tom O'Neill; Director, Kim Davies; Stage Manager, Laura Schuman; Cast: Eugene Ashton-Gonzalez, Christopher Renni-Calliope, Shad Melvin, Justin Field; July 24–August 29

Platypi 10 Minute Play Festival Produced by Merit Theater and Film Group; included: *Puppet Love* by Stefanie Horowitz; Director, Jerry Lieblich; *A Fair Play* by Alexis Freitag; Director, Scott Rodrigue; *The Flower* by Sandra Nordgren; Director, Scott Rodrigue; *Atlantic City* by Jessica Aloe; Director, Tiffany Hogan; *A Portrait of the Artist as a Middle Aged Woman* by Jerry Lieblich; Director, Stefanie Horowitz; *Meet the Tetrominoes* by Matt Kern; Director, James Saad; *Greenlight* by James Saad; Director, Laura Schuman; *Hangman* by Kathryn Willingham; Director, Tiffany Hogan; *The Onion* by Scott Rodrigue; Director, Matt Kern; *Three Cheers for the UFO* by Juliana Thorstenn; Director, Malika Moro-Cohen; July 29–August 9

A Human Shield by Robert L. Kinast; Director, Robert Marra; Production Manager, Scott Rodrigue; Cast: Sam Antar, Mary Looram, Jessica Rhodes, Lauren Kelston, Jessica Lyn Morris; September 26–November 2

A Christmas Carol by Sandra Nordgren; Director, David Rosar Stearns; Music Director, Kezia Hirsey; Stage Manager, Chess Venice; Costumes/Set, Tom Harlan; Cast: Sam Antar, Shawn Belpanno, Kathryn N. Browne, Aimee Byers, Laura M Cleary, Angela T Collins, Lauren Cullum, Charlotte Durkee, Ken Eckert, Isabelle Goodman, Rose Goodman, Phoebe Groden, Colleen Jasinski, Ali Nicole Levinson, Coby Farnum Levinson, Mike Pirozzi, Sarah Sanders, Fred Stuart, Rachel Sugar, Nate Teron, Eric Tonken, Antony Toron; December 17–January 11

Spatz Donovan's Irish Cabaret by Spatz Donovan; January 5–March 26

Conversation with a Kleagle by Rudy Gray; Director, Kevin B. Ploth; Stage Manager, Hector Hicks; Cast, Shawn Belpanno, Toni Ann DeNoble, Shaun Patrick Flynn, Erroll W. Greaves, Mike Pirozzi, Reggie Resino, James P. Stephens, Aaron Walker, Tim Weinert; February 6–March 29

Beggars Rain by Robert Firpo-Cappiello; Director, Scott Rodrigue; Cast: Robert Firpo-Cappiello; March 26–August 27

Some Things Get Better with Age Book and lyrics by June-Rachelson-Ospa, music by Kezia Hirsey; Director, Christopher Scott; Stage Managers, Lillian Crystal Collazo & Rosanny Suazo; Cast: Donna Moore, Stephanie Hepburn, Susan McBrien; April 2–26

Finding the Rooster by Terence Patrick Hughes; Cast: Dave Benger, Kathryn Neville Browne, Kevin Hauver, Reggie Oldham, Jonathan Harper Schlieman; May 8–June 7

OPEN-ENDED PRODUCTIONS

Line by Israel Horovitz; Director, Edith O'Hare; Cast: Liche Ariza, Erroll W. Greaves, Gladys Murphy, Neil Feigeles, Kyle Hester; Opened in 1974; Thirty-fourth season

Wiseacre Farm by 13th Street Repertory playwrights; Director, Tom Harlan

Rumple Who? Book and lyrics by Will Bartlett; Director, Wendy Tonken

14th Street Theater

The Wedding Play by Brian MacInnis Smallwood; Presented by Two Guys and a Credit Card Productions; Director, Tim Errickson; Producers, Taylor Shann & Brian MacInnis Smallwood; Set, Elisha Schaefer; Costumes, Annie Simon; Fight Director, Maggie MacDonald; Stage Manager, Sarah Locke; ASM, Jenn Stimple; Cast: Joseph Mathers, Lindsay Wolf, Corey Ann Haydu, Ron Sanborn, Catherine Lynn Dowling, Janet Zarecor, Mark Souza, Cotton Wright, Steve Smith, Ryan Stevens, Derek Hiron, Neijah Djourachi, Michael Mraz, Troy Campbell; July 9–27

There or Here by Jennifer Maisel; Presented by the Hypothetical Theatre Company; Producing Artistic Director/Director, Amy Feinberg; Set, Mark Szymak; Lighting, Tim Kaufman; Sound, Tim Cramer; Costumes, Jessica Reed; Stage Manager, Suneeva Stapleton; ASM, Lauren Miller; Cast: Shalin Agarwal, Annie Meisels, Judy Rosenblatt, Alok Tewari, Deepti Gupta; September 6–28

How Many Licks? A theatrical dance suite presented by Racoco Productions (Rachel Cohen, Aritsic Director); October 3–11

Death of a Salesman by Arthur Miller; Presented by Theater Mitu; Director, Rubén Polendo; Music, Ellen Reid; Stage Manager, Hilary Austin; Set, Kate Ashton, Leighton Mitchell, Rubén Polendo; Costumes, Candida K. Nichols; Masks, Lori Petermann; Object Design, Sanaz Ghajarrahimi; Lighting, Kate Ashton, Sound, Alex Hawthorn, Dramaturgy, Chris Mills; Cast: Justin Nestor, Emily Davis, Dylan Dawson, Nathan Elam, Nikki Calonge; Voices: Bryce D. Howard, Jenni-Lynn Brick, Ryan West, Ben Fox, Aysan Celik, Nathan Baesel, Mark D. Schultz, Jason Lew, Adam Cochran, Jenny Donoghue; Band: Ellen Reid, Adam Cochran, Drew Vanderburg, Jes Levine, Harry Ezratty, Peter Orlanski; October 22–November 1

A Touch of the Poet by Eugene O'Neill; Presented by Friendly Fire (Alex Lippard, Artistic Director; Les Gutman, Producing Director); Director, Alex Lippard; Set, Michael V. Moore; Costumes, Amanda Bujak; Lighting, Miriam Crowe; Sound, Will Pickens; Cast: Daniel J. Travanti, Ellen Crawford, Steven Boyer, Richard Crawford, Richard B. Watson, Tessa Klein, Antoinette La Vecchia, Peter Rogan, Timothy Smallwood, Ian Stuart; December 2–20

Pope and Anti-Pope by Jeremy Goldstein; Presented and directed by Joe Gallagher; Cast: Adam Aguirre, Katherine Cox, Corey Ann Haydu, Jonathan Monk, Tiffany Redmon, Jennifer Rogers, Mark Souza; January 30–31

3-Legged Dog Theatre Company (3LD Art & Technology Center)

Art and Business Director, Kevin Cunningham; Managing Director, Victor Weinstock

The Only Tribe Story by Rebecca Bannor-Addae; Conceived and co-presented by Roland Gebhardt; Choreography, Peter Kyle; Music, Stephen Barber; Video, Reid Farrington; Lighting, Stephen Arnold; Cast: Christina Amendolia, Vincent McCloskey, Océane McCord, Rebecca Rainey, Ellenore Scott, Diego Vásquez, Emily Walsh, Matthew Westerby; December 3–20

Wickets Adapted & designed by Jenny Rogers; Choreography by Clove Galilee; Score, Jetliner & Adam Paskowitz; Cast: Katie Apicella, Lee Eddy, Jessica Jolly, Christianna Nelson, Maria Parra, Kristen Rozanski, Jona Tuck, Elizabeth Wakehouse, Lucas Steele; January 3–25

Rods and Cables Written & directed by Allison M. Keating; Executive Producer, Kevin Cunningham; Composer, Jason Sebastian; Set, Paul DiPietro; Costumes, Nellie Fleischner; Lighting, Kate Ashton; Sound, Marcelo Añez; Specialty Props/Effects, Gabe Barcia-Colombo; Video, Jeff Morey; PSM, Julia Funk; Assistant Design, Piama Habibullah; Animation/Special Vidoe, Aaron Harrow; Fight Director, Diego Villada; Gaffer, Matt McUsic; Special Lighting, David Tirosh; Cast: Lucille Duncan, Joshua Koehn, Jessie Paddock, Jason Lindner, Livia De Paolis, Cooper Grodin, Errickson Wilcox; Voice Overs: Julia Funk, Joshua Briggs, Jason Lindner, Marcelo Añez March 20–April 11

NON-RESIDENT PRODUCTIONS

Frequency Hopping Written & directed by Elyse Singer; Presented by the Hourglass Group; Score, Joshua Fried; Design, Elaine J. McCarthy; Costumes, Angela M. Kahler; Lighting, Tyler Micoleau; Sound, Marcelo Anez; Wigs/Makeup, J. Janas & R. Green; Dramaturg, Erika Rundle; Casting, Deborah Brown; Press, Ron Lasko; Assistant Director, Kathryn Hamilton; Cast: Erica Newhouse, Joseph Urla; June 8–29

Fire Throws Written and directed by Rachel Dickstein, Adapted from *Antigone* by Sophocles; Created in collaboration with the ensemble; Presented by Ripe Time; Score, Jewlia Eisenberg; Live Music, Charming Hostess; Set, Susan Zeeman Rogers; Costumes, Oana Botez-Ban; Lighting, Tyler Micholeau; Video Maya Ciarrocchi; Sound, Jane Shaw; Producer, Stephenie Duncan; Production Manager, Anthony Cerrato; Associate Director, Paula McGonagle; PSM, Joanna Leigh; Casting, Geoff Josselson; Press, Richard Kornberg & Associates; Cast: Erica Berg, Laura Butler, Kiebpoli Calnek, John Campion, Kimiye Corwin, Juliana Francis-Kelly, Kyle Leland, Paula McGonagle, Leajato Robinson, Jorge Rubio, Caesar Samayoa. February 18–March 28

In Security Written & performed by Anna Gutto; Presented by Unbound Collective; Director, Alexis Poledouris; Videos, Ann Oren; April 22–May 10

37 Arts

Ballerina Who Loves B-Boy Created & directed by Heeill Choi; Presented by COP NY & Show Born Productions; Producer, Sanghyun Lee; Executive Producer, Tae Six Oh & Ji-Youn Chang; Lighting, Jaewan Choi & Ji-Youn Chang; Set, Wilson Chin & Ji-Youn Chang; Video, See Youn Kwak; Music Director, Jim Sung An; Choreography, Jae Woo Kim; Press, Springer Associates; Cast: Hyosung An, Nyunghoon Baek, Da Heen Choi, Eunju Chu, Moonwoo Han, Youngkwang Joung, Chibae Kim, Chungki Kim, Daegeon Kim, Hongkwon Kim, Juho Kim, Junseok Kim, Kunhung Kim, Min Kung Kim, Minwoong Kim, Myounghun Kim, Soobin Kim, Bonglin Ko, Yongchan Lee, Sun Tae Lim, A. Rum Park, Eunjung Park, Eun Hae Yoo; October 1–December 21

45th Street Theatre

Epitaph for George Dillon by John Osborne; Director, Larry Moss; June 2–15

THE MEANING OF LIFE...and other useless pieces of information by Matte O'Brien; Presented by Rope Swing Entertainment; Set, Stephen K. Dobay; Costumes, Laurie Marman; Lighting, Brian Barnett; Sound, Kristyn R. Smith; Stage Manager, Allison Hersh; Cast: Shannon Michael Algeo, Seth Danner, Alex Herrald, Erin Kukla, Joe Tannenbaum, Shannon Tyo; July 9–19

Lights & Music by Patrick Letterii; Produced by John MacDonald & Maggie Maes; Director, Jeremy Quinn; Set, Eleanor Taylor Bye; Costumes/Props, Alex Argenti; Sound, Andrew Reynolds; PSM, Stephanie Suski; Cast: John MacDonald, Patrick C. Letterii, Haley Rawson, Lindsay Teed, Nick Bonnar; Guitar: Alex Kerpel, Bylie Burge; July 22–August 3

Man.gov and **Harm's Way** Two plays in repertory by Shern Bitterman; Presented by Circus Theatricals, Jack & Jeannine Shehlin; Director, Steve Zuckerman; Lighting, Derrick McDaniel; Original Music, Roger Bellon; Cast: (*Man.gov*): Robert Cicchini, Christopher Curry, Sarah Foret, Thomas Kopache, Jordan Lund, Britt Napier; (*Harm's Way*): Josh Allen, Ben Bowen, Sarah Foret, Wendy Makkena, Eric Pierpoint, Jack Stehlin; October 17–November 9

The Show Might Go On by Roger Bowen; Produced by Michael Horn & The Michael Chekhov Theatre Company; Director, Ann Bowen; Music, John Margolis; Cast: Jean Pierre Agostini, Tom Amici, Michelle Bialeck, Susan Capra, Alisha Racho-Jansen, Gary Lamadore, Bob McCartin, Max McGuire, Stew Miller, Tom Pavey, Lauren Piselli, Anna Pond, Max Stien, Kristina Tinoco; November 12–December 3

My Favorite Animal by Tom Sime; Presented by Joe & Sandi Black and The Modern Stage; Director, Phyllis Cicero; Cast: Matt Lyle, Catherine DuBord, Sylvia Luedtke, Nicholas Venceil, Ben Mayer; November 12–30

We All Fall Down by Nick Dujnic; Presented by Pop Megahit Theatre; Director, Kevin Diamond; Set, Aaron Gensler; Costumes, T.V. Alexander; Lighting, Allen Babcock; Sound, Christopher Rummel; PSM, Mel McCue; Cast: John Anderson, Paul Gagnon, Lucas Kavner, Stephen LaFerriere, Andrew Langton, Courtney Rost, Taylor Sele, Caitlin Thurnaue; December 5–20

Obama Drama: The Inaugural Celebration Plays by Nastaran Ahmadi, Zakiyyah Alexander, Sarita Covington, Marcus Gardley, Kimberly Megna, Harrison David Rivers, Matt Schatz, Tiffany Rachelle Stewart; Presented by Creative Destruction; January 15–17

Avow by Bill C. Davis; Presented by the Cardinal Group; Director, Jerry Less; Set/Props, Stephanie Tucci; Lighting, Christopher Weston; Stage Manager, Kayla Shriner-Cahn; Press, Kevin P. McAnarney; Cast: Elizabeth Bove, Jaron Farnham, Christopher Graham, Kate Middleton, Jeremiah Wiggins, Timothy Sekk, Joy Franz; February 20–March 8

59E59

East to Edinburgh Festival Included: *7 Sins* by James Judd; Director, Randall Rapstine; *Jeff Kreisler '08* Written & performed by Jeff Kreisler; *Dirt* by Robert Schneider; Director, David Robinson; *Jonathan Prager's Comedy Festical Encore* Written & performed by Jonathan Prager; *Mythellaneous* by Emily Davis; Director Bethany Burgess-Smith; Choreographer, Ally Daniels; *Queen of Wyoming* Written & performed by Maggie Simpson; Director, Laura Crook; *The Judgement of Paris* Adapted & directed by Austin McCorick; *I Lost My Laugh in the Revolution* Written & performed by Shameka Cunningham; Director, Ayan Cahrr; *Queen Rita's Blues Alley* Written & performed by Amontaine Aurore, music by Joseph "Macarldie" Dibbs & Amontaine Aurore, lyrics by Amontaine Aurore; Theater C; July 8–27

The Basketball Diaries by Jim Carroll, adapted by Matt Pelfrey; Presented by Godlight Theatre Company; Director, Joe Tantalo; Cast: Katherine Boynton, Deanna McGovern, Nick Paglino, Alex Pappas, Aaron Paternoster, John Porto, Mike Roche, Michael Shimkin, Arthur Solomon, Sam Whitten; Theater B; July 15–27

Do Not Disturb: An Evening of Five One-Act Plays by Carey Crim, Jeffrey James Keyes, Peter Macklin, Geoffrey Scheer, Benjamin J. Scott; Produced by Write Club NYC; Directors, Terry Berliner, Carey Crim, Chad Larabee, Geoffrey Scheer; Lighting, Cory Pattak; Cast: Kelley Curran, Noshir Dalan, Mark Emerson, Philip Guerette, Peter Macklin, Ryan Murphy, Derek Peith, David Sajadi, Timothy Sekk, Sarah Sokolovic, Carrie Yaeger; Theater C; July 29–August 10

Summer Shorts 2 Presented by John McCormack & J.J. Kandel; Set/Lighting, Maurti Evans; included: (Series A) *The Waters of March* by Leslie Lyles; Director, Billy Hopkins; *In Paradise* by Eduardo Machado; *On a Bench* by Neil Koenigsberg; Director, Merri Milwe; *Deep in the Hole* by Roger Hedden; Director, Billy Hopkins; (Series B) *Our Time is Up* by Keith Reddin; Director, Billy Hopkins; *Peoplespeak* by John Augustine; Director, Robert Saxner; *On Island* by Michael Domitrovich; Director, Mary Catherine Burke; *Plasir d'Amour* by Terrence McNally, music & lyrics by Skip Kennon; Director, Elizabeth Lucas; Theater B; July 31–August 28

The Seduction of Edgar Degas Written and directed by Le Wilhelm; Produced by Love Creek Productions in association with Rage Against Time; Sets, Viola Bradford; Lighting, Chris Johnson; Costumes, Cynthia Winstead; Cast: Jessica Mazo, Colleen Summa, Gabrielle Rosen, Lauren Ford, Tony White, Mark A. Kinch, Kirsten Walsh, Kristen Carter, Bob Manus, Alan Salsbury, Dustin C. Burrell, Valerie Austin, Jennifer Perrotta; Theater C; August 14–September 7

The Night Carter Was Bad by Ben Cikanek; Produced by Kids With Guns; Director, Mike Klar; Sets, Kevin Bain; Lighting, Paul Peyton Moffitt; Costumes, Heather Klar; Sound, Michael Wall; Cast: Tom Baran, Rachel Jordan Brown, Ginny Myers Lee, Kurt Rodeghiero; Theater C; October 1–18

Simon Green Sings Coward at Christmas Presented by The Yvonne Arnaud Theatre (Guidford, U.K); Music Director, David Shrubsole; Theater C; December 14–January 4

Ride by Jane Bodie; Director, Nick Flint; Produced by Outhouse Theatre Company; Set, James Hunting; Lighting, Cory Pattak; Cast: Jeremy Waters, Melissa Chambers; Theater C; January 15–February 8

Fresh Kills by Elyzabeth Gregory Wilder; Produced by Working Man's Clothes; Director, Isaac Byrne; Set, David Ogle; Lighting, Jake Platt; Costumes, Candice Thompson; Sound, Carl Wieman; Cast: Robert Funaro, Therese Plummer, Todd Flaherty, Jared Culverhouse; Theater C; February 12–March 1

78th Street Theatre Lab

Suite Atlanta by Frank Blocker; Presented by fn Productions; Director, Jon Michael Murphy; Cast: Tanesha M. Ford, Sydney Stone, Chris von Hoffmann, Frank Blocker; July 10–26

The Wasteland August 23

Break-Ups & Break-Downs Ibsen Celebration Presented by TheaterVision/Play Time; September 27–28

Evilution by Edward Musto; Director, Judd Silverman; Costumes, Catherine Fisher; Stage Manager, Nate Brauner; Cast: James Arden, Alison Crane, William Franke, Emily Edwards, Chelsea Holland, D.H. Johnson, David Lapkin; October 2–5

Dead Dogs by Greg Steinbruner; Presented by Underdog Productions; October 2–12

Cymbeline by William Shakespeare; Presented by Folding Chair Theatre; Director, Marcus Geduld; Cast: Lisa Blankenship, Gowan Campbell, Ian Gould, Paul Edward Hope, Karen Ogle, Josh Thelin; October 9–November 2

Tape by Stephen Belber; Director, Jeff Brelvi; Cast: Nicky Romaniello, Alex Maxwell, Cristina Marie; October 17–19

Oh, Whistle by M R James; Cast: Robert Lloyd Parry; October 22–November 8

The Secretaries by The Five Lesbian Brothers; Presented by Project: Theater; Director, Joe Jung; Stage Manager, Jacob Seelback; Cast: Karis Danish, Laura Dillman, Brian Frank, Tara Franklin, Jessi Blue Gormezano, Andrew McLeod, Jenny Schutzman; May 22–June 6

AL – A One Me Show Written and performed by Al Lubel; May 22–July 31

92nd Street Y – Lyrics & Lyricists Series

Artistic Director, Deborah Grace Wilner

Rodgers &...: Inside Five Collabortions Artistic Director/Host, Martin Charnin; Music Director/Piano, Dwight Beckmeyer; Cast: Shelly Burch, Michelle Liu Coughlin, Rich Gray, Hugh Panaro, Alton White; January 10–12

It Started With a Dream: David Zippel–Lyrics He Wrote–Lyrics He Wishes He Wrote Artistic Director/Host, David Zippel; Cast: Danny Gurwin, Deborah Grace Winer, Lillias White, David Zippel, Debbie Gravitte, Kate Baldwin, Kevin Earley; February 21–23

Sunny Side Up: Roaring Through the Twenties With DeSylva, Brown & Henderson Artistic Director, Robert Kimball; Host, Charles Osgood; Director/Choreographer, Randy Skinner; Music Director, Joe Thalken, Vince Giordano; Cast: Nancy Anderson, Jeffry Denman, Jason Graae, Randy Graff, Megan Sikora; April 4–6

The Man That Got Away: Ira After George Artistic Director/Host, Rex Reed; Director, Caitlin Carter; Music Director/Piano, Tedd Firth; Cast: Lucie Arnaz, Polly Bergen, Kurt Reichenbach, Tom Wopat; May 9–11

Sunday In New York: Mel Tormé In Words And Music Artistic Director/Piano, Billy Stritch; Director, Mark Waldrop; Cast: Billy Stritch, Marilyn Maye, La Tanya Hall, Hilary Kole, Johnny Rodgers; June 6–8

Amas Musical Theatre

Producing Artistic Director, Donna Trinkoff

Blast From the Past A benefit concert; Director/Choreographer, Maria Torres; Music Director, Doug Oberhamer; Production Supervisor, Peter Feuchtwanger; Sound, Ray Shilke; Stage Manager, Brian Westmoreland; Featuring music from past Amas productions: *Bubbling Brown Sugar, It's So Nice to Be Civilized, Opening Night, Barrio Babies, Zanna Don't!, SHOUT! The Mod Musical, 4 Guys Named Jose, Bobos, Starmites, Langston Hughes's Little Ham, Latin Heat, From My Hometown, Lone Star Love,* and *Wanda's World;* Cast: Adrian Bailey, Anton Briones, Erin Crosby, Janet Dacal, Ramon Del Barrio, Mark Stuart Eckstein, James Royce Edwards, Lauren Fijol, Harriet D. Foy, Kevin R. Free, Henry Gainza, Andre Garner, Georgia Hair, Beth Leavel, Adealani Malia, Michelle Marmolejo, Olga Merediz, Trisha Rapier, Sandra Reaves-Phillips, Vivian Reed, Nicolle Rochelle, Eliseo Roman, Sandie Rosa, Erica Shroeder, Corliss Taylor Dunn, Clarke Thorell, Kirk Torigoe and students from the Rosetta LeNoire Musical Theatre Academy; Honorees, Woodie King Jr., Dionne Warwick; Lighthouse International; March 30

Signs of Life: A Tale of Terezin Book by Peter Ullian, lyrics by Len Schiff, music by Joel Derfner; Director, Jeremy Dobrish; Music Director, Matt Castle; Cast: Sarah Davis, Leo Ash Evens, David Hibbard, William Parry, Noah Ruff, Nancy Ringham, Jason Michael Snow, Douglas Ullman Jr., Carl N. Wallnau; Amas Workshop Production; Actors Playhouse; April 28–30

No, No Nanette Music by Vincent Youmans, book by Otto Harbach & Frank Mandel, lyrics by Irving Caesar & Otto Harbach; Director, Christopher Scott; Choreographer, Monica Johnson; Set, Adam Koch; Costumes, Cheryl McCarron; Lighting, Seth Resier; Sound, Tom West; Music Director, Audra Bass; Rosetta LeNoire Musical Theatre Academy production; Hudson Guild Theatre; May 8–17

AMAS SIX O'CLOCK MUSICAL THEATRE LAB

Burly-Q! A Gay Burlesque by Peter Charles Morris, Phillip George, Ernie Lijoi, Tom Orr, and Hector Coris; Songs, Brad Ellis, Ethan Fein, Matt Eisenstein, Fred Barton, Matt Ward, Dick Gallagher; Director, Phillip George; Stage Manager, Brian Westmoreland; Actors Playhouse, October 22–23

Signs of Life: A Tale of Terezin Book by Peter Ullian, lyrics by Len Schiff, music by Joel Derfner; Director, Jeremy Dobrish; Metro Hospital; December 15

Keep on Walking Book by James Armstrong, lyrics by Joshua H. Cohen, music by Lavell Blackwell; Director, Christopher Catt; Music Director, James Sirois; Stage Manager, Nicole Libby; Actors Playhouse; January 21–22

Immigrant: The Story of Joe Hill by Sy Kahn; Director, David Glenn Armstrong; Judson Memorial Church; April 22

Road to Qatar by Stephen Cole & David Krane; Director, Marcia Milgram Dodge; Players Theatre Studios; May 28

Secrets of Songwriting by Randi Michaels Block & Michael Aman; Director, Michael Bush; Players Theatre Studios; June 23

American Globe Theatre

Artistic Director, John Basil; Executive Director, Elizabeth Keefe

20th Anniversary History Reading Cycle Featuring the history plays of William Shakespeare; *Richard II* directed by Stephen Davis; *Henry IV, Part I* directed by Allegra Schorr; *Henry IV, Part II* directed by Vincent Masterpaul; *Henry V* directed by John Basil; November 7–21

Henry V by William Shakespeare; Director, John Basil; Set, Vincent Masterpaul; Lighting, Mark Hankla; Composer, Scott O'Brien; Costumes/Fight Choreographer, Jim Parks; Stage Manager, Audrey Marshall; Cast: Geoffrey Barnes, Richard Fay, John Forkner, Christopher Guild, H. Dan Harkins, Melissa Hill, Seth James, Elizabeth Keefe, Julia Levo, Brandon McMillen, Christopher Newell, Malachy Orozco, Rainard Rachele, J.J. Reap, Adrien Saunders, James Savage, Kathryn Savannah, Joseph Small, Graham Stevens, Robbie Tann, Robert Lee Taylor, Dennis Turney; March 26–April 25

Romeo & Juliet by William Shakespeare; Director/Fight Choreographer, Stephen Davis; Costumes, Jim Parks; Cast: Alexis Black, Bjorn duPaty, Jon Hoche, Warren Jackson, Basil Rodericks, Erica Swindell, Amelia Workman; Presented as part of the *Shakespeare for Schools* Program; March 18–May 14

15th Annual Fifteen Minute Play Festival Set/Lighting, Mark Hankla; Stage Manager, Audrey Marshall; Thirty-five playwrights, directors and casts from all across the country; May 4–16

American Theatre of Actors

Heist by Paul Cohen; Presented by ElfQueen Productions, Tracy Weller & Michel Ranson; Director/Set, Kris Thor; Lighting, Lucrecia Briceno; Costumes, Michelle Koch; Dramaturg, Amy Rose Marsh; Cast: Amanda Bockelheide, Jeff Clarke, Rachel Jablin, Christopher Ryan Richards, Tracy Weller; Sargent Theatre; June 6–28

Merry Wives of Windsor by William Shakespeare; August 13–30

Night Maneuver by Howard Korder; Presented by Lighhouse Theatre Company; Director, Tom Bian; Lighting, Judy Merrick; Costumes, Brittany Holmes; Cast: Anthony Caronna, Alexander Smith; August 27–September 7

A Grave for Sister Agatha by Robert Crafford; Presented by Resilliance Productions; Director, Ken Bush; Producers, Ken Bush & Matthew A.J. Gregory; Design, Katie Lecoq; Costumes, Heather Tomlinson; Lighting, Justin Smiley; Stage Manager, John Nehlich; Cast: Sal Bardo, Jordan Feltner, Aaron Gaines, Avayar Kamari, Bill McAdams, Leslie C. Nemet, Christine Remus, Nate Rubin, Joy Shatz, Jermaine Small, Adam Smith, Elizabeth Woodard; September 10–21

Richard the Third by William Shakespeare; September 10–27

Ultimate Ryuji Sawa by Ryuji Sawa; Producer, Toshi Cappuccino; Design, Todd Neitring; Stage Manager, Shu Seo; Cast: Ryuji Sawa, Mutsumi Noda, Masaki Kiuchi, Koichi Hayashi, Takao Tokunaga, Yutaka Imaizumi, Shinya Iwashita, Sonoe Funabashi, Fumihiko Aoyama, Ozara Takami, Hiromi Takami; October 30–November 2

The Black Doctor by Ira Aldridge; Presented by Rebel Theater Company; Director, Nick Petrie; November 19–23

Art by Yasmina Reza; Cast: Blake Bradford, Steven Nelson, Michael Weems; Beckmann Theatre; January 23–25

Proof by David Auburn; Presented by Hudson Shakespeare Theatre; Director, Jon Ciccarelli; Producer, L. Robert Johnson; Cast: Noelle Fair, Devin Landin, Charles J. Roby, Jennifer L. Nasta; Beckmann Theatre; March 4–8

The Newlyweds Written, directed, & produced by Beverly Orozco; Presented by Aditi Pictures; Producer, Terrence Patterson; Stage Manager, Shawna Cathey; Cast: Ben Rivers, Giselle Rodriguez, Agueda Ramirez, Phil Smith, Leslie Frohberg, Christopher Williams, Latreesch Simmons, Shawnette Hamilton-Robertson; May 21–31

ArcLight Theater

Titus Andronicus by William Shakespeare; Director/Design, Jack Souza; Cast: Chris Moran, Frank Martinelli, Yancey Quinones, Thomas Yeager, Jack Souza, Beth Adler, David Duenias, Christopher Burke, Joseph Reese, Tara Kayton, Moti Margolin, Michael Piazza, Ryan Tramont, Clairin Kohl, Francesca Day, Misty Day; August 1–17

Lamppost Reuinion by Louis LaRusso; Produced by Vincent Pastore & Paul Borghese with Charlie Yanko; Director, Frank Licato; Cast: Vincent Pastore, Ricky Aiello, Frank Pellegrino, Robert Funaro, Anthony Ribustello; November 7–30

To Whom It May Concern by Aurin Squire; Presented by The Entertainment Agora; Director, David Gaard; Set, Bruce Eyster; Costumes, Michele Reisch; Lighting, Erich Loetterle; Cast: Matt Alford, Israel Gutierrez, Carmelo Ferro, Nicholas Reilly; March 19–April 19

The Oath *A Southern Gothic Tale* by Jacqueline Goldfinger; Presented by Maieutic Theatre Works (David Stallings, Artistic Director); Director, Cristina Alicea; Producer, Julie Griffith; Set, Blair Mienik; Costumes, Jessica Hooks; Lighting, Dan Gallagher; Sound, Martha Goode; Stage Manager, Raisa Noelle; Production Manager, Jarid Sumner; Dialects, Barrie Krenik; Hair/Makeup, Melanie Randolph; Cast: Sarah Cahney, Anthony Crep, Louise Flory, Robin Madel, Dianna Martin, Maureen O'Boyle; April 22–May 10

Artistic New Directions

Artistic Co-Directors, Janice L. Goldberg & Kristine Niven

Flyovers by Jeffrey Sweet; Co-presented by Jeff Landsman and the 78th Street Theatre Lab; Director, Sandy Shinner; Set/Lighting, Robin A. Paterson; Sound, Craig Lenti; Costumes, Caroline Berti; PSM, Jenna Dempesy; Press, Sam Rudy Media Relations; Cast: Kevin Geer, Richard Kind, Michele Pawk, Donna Bullock; 78th Street Theatre; January 29–February 15

Eclectic Evening of Shorts II, Boxers & Briefs included: (**Boxers**) *Doing Business* by Diana Hird; Director, Stephen Fried; *Unanticipated Guest* by Jeffrey Sweet; Director, Larry Rosen; *A Time Ripe and Rare* by Sue Bigelow & Carol Davis; Director Janice L. Godlberg; *Perforation* by David Lavine; Director, David Winitsky; *Expectation* by Arlene Hutton; Director, Alix Steel; *Episcus and Edendus* Book and lyrics by Greg Edwards, music by Ron Barnett; Director, Ethan Heard; Music Director, Nate Festinger; Cast: Crystal Finn, Christian Conn, Kristine Niven, Jennifer Wren, Carol Lempert, Jennifer Laine Williams, Dan Domingues, Brian Corrigan, Chris Campbell, Jeffrey Danneman, Ian Lowe, Eric Petersen, Megan Stern, Allison Goldberg, Felicia Ricci; (**Briefs**) *Beached* by Michelle Best; Director, Layne Racowski; *Dearly Beloved* Written & directed by Donald Steele; *Judgement of Paris* by Jeffrey Swan Jones; Director, Kathleen Brant; *Biggest Break* by Les Hunter; Director, Morgan Gould; *This Relationship* by Patrick Nash; Director, Kristine Niven; *Eli and Leah* Conceived by Douglas Manes; Dialogue/Director, Stephen Ringold; Cast: Michelle Best, Cooper Shaw, Ruth Sherman, Laughlin Rice, Paul Singleton, Trey Albright, Brian Gerard Murray, Amir Wachterman, Elena McGhee, James Nugent, Devin Moriarity, Elise Arsenault, Scotty Watson, David O. Marx, Douglas Manes, Donna Klimek; Shetler Studios; March 6–15

Atlantic Theater Company

ATLANTIC FOR KIDS

Holes by Louis Sachar, based on his book; Director, Josh Lewis; Set/Lighting, Gabriel Evansohn; Costumes, Jessica Pabst; Cast: Alex Coppola, Paul Corning, Matt Hanson, Jon Herman, Thomas Matthews, Brad Mielke, Eric Lockley, Benj Mirman, David Morris, Christian O'Brien, Dan Pfau, Torre Reigns, Amelia Rose, Suzi Sadler, Laryn Stout, Chloé Wepper, Sandra Williams; Linda Gross Theater; September 20–October 5

A Year With Frog & Toad Music by Robert Reale, book and lyrics by Willie Reale; based on the books by Arnold Lubel; Director, Jonathan Bernstein; Set/Lighting, Gabriel Evansohn; Cast: Saum Eskandani, Enzo Gentile, Julia Averill, Barbara Hollander, Hernando Uman; Linda Gross Theater; January 17–March 15

Axis Company

Executive Producer, Jeffrey Resnick; Artistic Director, Randy Sharp

Hospital 2008 A serial play by Axis Company; Music, lyrics, and direction by Randy Sharp; Set, Kyle Chepulis; Costumes, Matthew Simonelli; Lighting, David Zeffren; Sound, Steve Fontaine; Stage Manager, Edward Terhune; Cinematography, Ben Wolf; Film Editor, Laura Weinberg; Cast: Paul Marc Barnes, Brian Barnhart, Regina Betancourt, David Crabb, George Demas, Joe Fuer, Britt Geneli, Laurie Kilmartin, Lynn Mancinelli, Marc Palmieri, Edgar Oliver, Tom Pennacchini, Jim Sterling, Ian Tooley; June 5–July 19

Seven in One Blow, or The Brave Little Kid by the Brothers Grim, conceived by Axis Company; Director/Original Music, Randy Sharp; Lighting, David Zeffren; Costumes, Elisa Santiago; Sound, Steve Fontaine; Cinematography, Dan Hersey; Film Editor, Mike Huetz; Cast: Marc Palmieri, David Crabb, Margo Passalaqua, Jim Sterling, Brian Barnhart, George Demas, Lynn Mancinell, Britt Genelin, Edgar Oliver, Laurie Kilmartin, Regina Betancourt; Seventh annual presentation; December 5–21

Babel Theatre Project

Artistic Director, Geordie Broadwater; Producing Director, Jeremy Blocker

A Great Place To Be From by Norman Lasca; Director, Georgie Broadwater; Set, Tristan Jeffers; Costumes, Mike Floyd; Lighting, Eric Southern; Sound, Anthony Gabriele; Artistic Associate, Molly Kramer; General Manager, Aaron Thompson; Technical Director, Harry Kimball; Stage Manager, Caley Clocksin; Cast: Kim Martin Cotton, Matthew Johnson, Jacques Roy, Andrew Zimmerman; Kraine Theater; September 4–27

Groundwork Included: *The Hairy Dutchman* by Andy Bragen; *Book of Days* by Thomas Higgins; *Fingers* by Erica Lopez; *Brack's Last Bachelor Party* by Sam Marks; *Babs the Dodo* by Michael Mitnick; *Clear Cold Place* by Caroline Prugh; 78th Street Theatre Lab; January 24–25

Christmas is Miles Away by Chloe Moss; Director, Geordie Broadwater; Set, Daniel Zimmerman; Props, Eric Reynolds; Costumes, Becky Lasky; Lighting, Dan Scully; Sound, Anthony Gabriele; Stage Manager, Pisa Waikwandee; Assistant Director, Tom Costello; ASM, Emily Ann Strickland; Cast: Emily Landham, Roger Lirtsman, Alex Fast; Connelly Theatre; May 1–23

Bank Street Theatre*

Hanna Ichimomme by Ken Miyamoto; Presented by TKO Entertainment Inc.; Directors, Seiko Tano and Tetsuya a Chiba; Lighting, Rie Ono; Stage Manager, Shuhei Seo; Graphics, Todd Neitring; Press, Brett Singer; Cast: Seiko Tano; July 2–13

Two Spoons by Peter Mercurio; Presented by Other Side Productions; Director, Chuck Blasius; Set, Andrew Pape; Lighting, Rob Hilliard; Sound, Roger Anderson, Costumes, Jennifer Salta; Stage Manager, Debra Stunich; Costume Consultant, Ricky Lizalde; Choreography, Robin Carrigan; Set Construction, Josh Pugliese; Cast: Thomas Flannery Jr., Brian Gillespie, DeVon Jackson, Margo Singaliese, Grant James Varjas; September 5–28

*The Bank Street Theatre closed this season and was purchased by the Cherry Lane Theatre (renamed The Cherry Pit)

The Barrow Group (TBG Theatre)

Co-Artistic Director/Co-Founder, Seth Barrish; Co-Artistic Director, Lee Brock

ScoreFest by Steve Horowitz and the Code Ensemble; Director, Alix Steel; Conductor, Devin Maxwell; Cast: Amy Loughead, Alyson Schacherer, Drew Callander, John D. Ivy; September 9–11

Short Stuff V: Plays by Women including: Joan Ackermann, Tricia Alexandro, Kate Hoffower, Arlene Hutton, Barbara Lindsay, & Dee Ann Newkirk; Directors, Donna Jean Fogel, Shannon Patterson, Ron Piretti, Alix Steel; Lighting, Lauren Parrish; Stage Manager, Kate Erin Gibson; Cast: Tricia Alexandro, Chris Campbell, Cristala Carter, Jeffrey Danneman, Christina Denzinger, Becky Flaum, Eli Gelb, Renata Hinrichs, Jennifer Kaminsky, Colleen Murphy, Anne Richardson, Alyson Schacherer, Stephen Singer, Hope Singsen, Myra Thibault, Alison Wright; November 7–24

Who You See Here by Matt Hoverman; Co-produced by Man Underdog; Director, Stacy Shane; Production Supervisor, Porter Pickard; Stage Manager, Kate Erin Gibson; Costumes, Herb Ouellette; Lighting, Josh Bradford; Cast: Marika Becz, Melaena Cadiz, Joe Forbrich, Adam McLaughlin; March 6–23

The Monthly Nut Written & performed by James Braly; Director, Seth Barrish

The Tempermentals by Jon Marans; Co-produced by Man Underdog and Daryl Roth; Director, Jonathan Silverstein; Set/Costumes, Clint Ramos; Lighting, Josh Bradford; Sound, Daniel Kluger; Musical Consultant, Aaron Dai; Fight Director, Ron Piretti; Dialect Coach, Diego Daniel Pardo; PSM, Samone B. Weissman; Production Manager, Porter Pickard; Cast, Thomas Jay Ryan, Michael Urie, Tom Beckett, Matthew Schneck, Sam Breslin Wright; April 30–May 18

NON-RESIDENT PRODUCTIONS

Marko The Prince by Jovanka Bach; Produced by Immigrants' Theatre Project; June 16–July 14

The Painter by Reginald Oldham; Produced by The Barracuda Theater Club; Director, Jamey Isenor; Cast: Reginald Oldham, Hope Singsen, Ryan Stadler; September 20–October 6

Missa Solemnis or The Play About Henry by Roman Feeser; Director, Linda Nelson; October 27–November 23

Saving A Drowning Man by Scott Brooks; Produced by The Barracuda Theater Club; Director, Autumn Clark; Stage Manager, Apalonia Davalos; Cast: Tom Bartos, Lydnsay Becker, Curran Connor, Jamie Currier, Heather Dilley, Reginald Oldham, Jesse Wilson; January 30–February 2

The Network One-Act Festival Produced by Paul Michael; Associate Producer/Director, Patrick Woodall; March 2–22

Pvt. Wars by James McLure and **The Return of Odysseus** by Steven Gridley; Produced by Allison Taylor and the Apple Core Theater Company; April 3–19

Dying City by Christopher Shinn; Produced by Ocean Peak Productions; Cast: Emily Fletcher, Denis Lambert; Director, Lewis J. Stadlen; April 25–May 10

Grim, An Urban Fairytale by Jessica Litwak; May 11–18

Boomerang Theatre Company

Artistic Director, Tim Errickson; Managing Director, Francis Kuzler

As You Like It by William Shakespeare; Director, Matt Johnston; Stage Manager, Jessica Pecharsky; Costumes, Carolyn Pallister; Cast: Rebecca Comtois, Michael Criscuolo, Jessi Gotta, John Greenleaf, R. Paul Hamilton, Brian Moore, Eli Schneider, Maria Silverman, Alisha Spielmann, Christian Toth, Matthew Trumbull, Scott Williams; Central Park; July 19–August 10

Summer and Smoke by Tennessee Williams; Director, Cailin Heffernan; Stage Manager, Carol A. Sullivan; ASM, Marielle Duke; Costumes, Cheryl McCarron; Lighting, Christina Watanabe; Set, Nikki Black; Sound, Megan Henniger; Fight Director, Carrie Brewer; Dialect Coach, Amy Stoller; Cast: Taylor Adams, Mac Brydon, John Carey, Deborah Carlson, Jane Cortney, Kurt Elftmann, Corey Ann Haydu, Beth Ann Leone, John Mazurek, Mel Nieves, Jonathan Kells Phillips, Leigh Poulos, Zak Risinger; Center Stage NY; November 13–December 14

Native Speech by Eric Overmyer; Director, Christopher Thomasson; Stage Manager, Kristina Vnook; ASM, Jennifer McKnight; Set, Nikki Black; Costumes, Cheryl McCarron; Lighting, Christina Watanabe; Sound, Megan Henniger; Fight Director, Carrie Brewer; Cast: Jessica Angleskhan, Pierluca Arancio, Chris Chinn, Mel Nieves, Vinnie Penna, David Roberts, Michael R. Rosete, Stephanie Lyn Silver, Alisha Spielmann; Center Stage NY; November 20–December 21

Parking Lot Lonely Heart by Colin McKenna; Director, Philip Emeott; Stage Manager, Jack Lynch; Costumes, Cheryl McCarron; Lighting, Christina Watanabe; Set, Nikki Black; Sound, Megan Henniger; Fight Director, Carrie Brewer; Cast: John Greenleaf, Jamie Proctor, Craig Lee Thomas, Lillian Wright; Center Stage NY; November 15–December 20

First Flight 2009 Annual new play reading series; included: *American Pastime* by Mike Folie; Director, John Hurley; *Blooddrinker* Written & directed by Cailin Heffernan; *Krueger* by Zack Calhoon; Director, Sara Thigpen; *Stan Bradley's World of Dreams* by Isaac Rathbone; Director, Philip Emeott; *Fix Number Six* by Jerry Polner; Director, Michael Criscuolo; *Lies and Romance* by Tim Errickson; Director, Christopher Thomasson; ART/NY; March 26–29

The Brick Theater

Co-Founders, Robert Honeywell and Robert Gardner

The Film Festival: A Theater Festival Theatrical productions included: *Birthtaint* by Andrew Gilchrist; Director, Julie Rossman; *Bring Me the Head of John Ford* Written & directed by Casey Wimpee; *Code Alpha* directed by Judson Kniffen; *Crime Scene Cleaners, Inc. Eddie Eisenberg, Prop.* by Robert Saietta; *Death at Film Forum* Written & directed by Eric Bland; *Demons Five, Exorcists Nothing* by William Peter Blatty; Director, Jeff Lewonczyk; *I, Object!* by Adhesive Theater Project; *It's Gonna Be a Cold Night* Written & directed by Keith Biesack; *Kill Me Like You Mean It* by Kiran Rikhye; Director, Jon Stancato; *The Magnificent Ambersons by Orson Welles: A Reconstruction for the Stage* Adapted & directed by Ian W. Hill; *A Paranoid's Guide to History* presented by J. W. Regan; *Q&A: The Perception of Dawn* created by Danny Bowes and Gyda Arber; *The Stubborn Illusion of Time* created by Bone Orchard; *Suspicious Package* by Gyda Arber and Wendy Coyle; Director, Gyda Arber; *Tod & I* created by Piehole; *What I Took in My Hand* by The American Story Project; Director, Jess Chayes *You Bet Your Life LIVE: Film Trivia Edition* created by Lisa Levy; May 31–July 27

CollisionWorks 2008 Included: *Harry in Love: A Manic Vaudeville* by Richard Foreman; Director, Ian W. Hill; Cast: Walter Brandes, Josephine Cashman, Ian W. Hill, Tom Reid, Ken Simon, Darius Stone; *Spell* Written & directed by Ian W. Hill; Cast: Olivia Baseman, Fred Backus, Gavin Starr Kendall, Samantha Mason, Iracel Rivero, Alyssa Simon, Moira Stone, Liz Toft, Jeanie Tse, Rasmus Max Wirth, Rasha Zamamiri; *Everything Must Go (Invisible Republic #2)* Written & directed by Ian W. Hill; Cast: Gyda Arber, David Arthur Bachrach, Becky Byers, Patrick Cann, Maggie Cino, Tory Dube, Sarah Engelke, Ian W. Hill, Dina Rose, Ariana Seigel, Julia C. Sun; July 31–August 24

The New York Clown Theatre Festival Included: *2 Chairs, 2 Clowns/Chalk it Up* Presented and performed by ME YUMMIES Clown and Theatre Company; *12 Hours to High Rascalry* Created and developed Ensemble Adventures in Clown with director, Dodi DiSanto; *Big and Little* Co-created and performed by Galen Treuer & Noah Bremer; Director/Co-creator, Sara Richardson; *The BIG BANG and other small things* Written & directed by Mitchel Evans; *The Birdmann* Written and authorized by The Birdmann; *Brazilian Hulk Show* Created, directed, and performed by Pedro Muccioloco; *Bury My Heart at Dumbass Cowboy* Created by Jon Ferguson Theater; *The CanCan Dew* by Jenny Sargent & Aimee German; *C'est La Nuit Qu'il Faut Attraper La Lumiere* Created and written by Orianne Bernard & Giovanni Fusetti; *The Crow's Funeral* Written & performed by Kelly Nesbitt; *A Glass of Wine* Created and performed by Daniel Forlano; *Kill Me Loudly – A Clown Noir* by Deanna Fleysher, Jeff Seal, Chris Manley, Chris Roberti; Director, Eric Davis; *A Little Business at the Big Top* Created and performed by David Gaines; *El Magnifico!* Performed by Hilary Chaplain & David Engel; Director, Bob Berky; *The Maestrosities! Left Behind!* by The Maestrosities; *Manifesto!* Performed by Mark Jaster, Scott Burgess, Maia DeSanti, Sabrina Mandell; *The Nosdrahcir Sisters* Created and performed by Sara Richardson & Kimberly Richardson; *Number's Up!* Written & performed by John Leo; Directorial Consultant, Audrey Crabtree; *PANTS! – The Best Show Ever* Created and performed by Summer Shapiro & April Wagner; *Party of One* by Noel Williams & Sue Morrison; Director, Sue Morrison; *Running into Walls* Created and performed by Heather Pearl, Sarah Liane Foster, & Michael O'Neill; Director, Michael O'Neill; *The Russian Office A live installation* Created and performed by Denni Dennis; *The Soirée* Written & performed by Amanda Huotari; Director, Avner Eisenberg; *Ten West* Jon Monastero and Stephen Simon; Director, Bryan Coffee; September 5–28

Penny Dreadful Season 2 by Bryan Enk and Matt Gray; Presented in association with Third Lows Productions; Set, Timothy McCown Reynolds & Art Wallace; Costumes, Karen Flood; Lighting, Ian W. Hill & Berit Johnson; Sound, Christiaan Koop; Special Makeup Effects, Jane Rose; included: *Episode 6.5: The Future Ain't What It Used to Be* directed by Bryan Enk (September 15); *Episode 7: The Peril of Penny, a Damsel Lost in Time* directed by Mateo Moreno (October 18–19); *Episode 8: Caldwell and Viernik vs. the Creatures of the Night* directed by Bryan Enk, fight choreography by Qui Nguyen (November 15–16); *Episode 9: The Terrible Tale of the Black Dragon* directed by Matt Gray, movement by Natalie Thomas (December 13–14); *Episode 10: The Science and The Séance – Two Tales of Love and Horror* directed by Bryan Enk & Matt Gray, choreographed by Dina Rose Rivera & Matt Gray, fight choreography by Adam Swiderski (January 17–18); *Episode 11: The House Where Bad Things Happen* directed by Bryan Enk & Matt Gray (February 21–22); *Episode 12: The Last Century* directed by Brian Enk, Ian W. Hill, & Matt Gray (March 28–29)

Lord Oxford Brings You the Second American Revolution, Live! Written and composed by Robert Honeywell, developed with Sue Morrison; Director, Moira Stone; Orchestrations/Additional Music, Matt Van Brink; Design, Robert Eggers; Sound, Mick O'Brien; Lighting, Joe Levasseur; Costumes, Fab Shim; Cast: Gyda Arber, Lynn Berg, Audrey Crabtree, Toni Ann DeNoble, Rasheed Hinds, Robert Honeywell, Iracel Rivero, Marija Stajic Salvetti, Alyssa Simon, Lorenzo Scott; October 24–November 22

The Granduncle Quadrilogy by Jeff Lewonczyk; Director, Hope Cartelli; Costumes, Julianne Kroboth; Lighting, Ian W. Hill; Technical Advisor, Chris Connolly; Fight Director, Qui Nguyen; Sound, Mick O'Brien; Cast: Fred Backus, Ivanna Cullinan, Jessi Gotta, Richard Harrington, Gavin Starr Kendall, Melissa Roth; Choreographer, Jenny Schmermund; December 15–20

The Protestants Written and directed by Eric Blad; Art/Set, Abernathy Bland; Sound, David H. Turner; Lighting, Amanda Woodward; Cast: Siobhan Doherty, Scott Eckert, Gavin Starr Kendall, Maggie Marion, Victoria Tate, Hollis Witherspoon; January 22–February 14

TIMES 365:24:7 Developed and performed by Bone Orchard, conceived and directed by Anna G. Jones; Dramaturg, Roweena Mackay; Movement Director, Brian Farish; Vocal Coach, Maggie Surovell; Lighting, Jeanette Yew; Sound, Leslie Graves, Ted Pallas; Projections, Ted Pallas; Costumes, Lia Cinquegrano; Stage Manager, Kevin Swanland; Cast: Gardiner Comfort, Stephanie Bratnick, Laura Jensen, Brian Farish, Maggie Surovell, Ayesha Ngaujah, Fatih Genckal, Jason Fleitz, Perri Yaniv, Leslie Graves; March 14–April 11

The Nosemaker's Apprentice: Chronicles of a Medieval Plastic Surgeon by Nick Jones & Rachel Shukert; Director, Peter J. Cook; Costumes, Normandy Raven Sherwood; Set, Aaron Gensler; Lighting, Shaun Fillion; Sound, Jo Williamson; Stage Manager, Annalee Fannan; Cast: Rightor Doyle, Eric Gilde, Ian Lowe, Corey Sullivan, Molly Ward; May 1–23

The Colonists: A Puppet Show Story and direction by Nick Jones; Puppets, Robin Frohardt; Lighting/Video, Kris Anton; Musical and Pyromaniacal Consultant, Raja Azar; Cast: Matthew Brooks, Carole D'Agostino, Honey Goodenough, Katie McClenahan; May 3–24

Broken Watch Theatre Company

Aristic Director, Drew DeCorleto

The Framer by Edward Allan Baker; Director, Kevin Confoy; Set, Jito Lee; Costumes, Rebecca Bernstein; Sound, Daniel Kluger; PSM, Mel Ling Acevedo; Stage Manager, Jessica Felix; Press, Springer Associates; Cast: Craig Bockhorn, Suzanne DiDonna, David Fraioli, Lori Garrabrant, Matt Walton, Dared Wright; Michael Weller Theatre; June 5–22

Cherry Lane Theatre

Founder/Artistic Director, Angelina Fiordellisi; Managing Director, James King

The Amish Project Written & performed by Jessica Dickey; Director, Sarah Cameron Sunde; Staged as a work in progress; January 12–February 1, 2009

Housebreaking by Jakob Holder; Mentor, Charles Mee; Director, Daniella Topol; Set, Mimi Lien & Amy Rubin; Costumes, Theresa Squire; Lighting, Nicole Pearce; Cast: Saxon Palmer, Evan Thompson, Monique Vukovic; Mentor Project 2009; Studio Theatre; March 24–April 4

Tongues Reading Series January 2009; included: *The P Word* by Israel Horovitz; *The Motherf**ker with the Hat* by Stephen Adly Guirgis; *What a Way to Go* by David Bar Katz; *New Play* by Lynn Nottage; *Lady Macbeth's Lover* by Richard Vetere; *Foodies* Short plays about Foodies by Richard Vetere, Daniel Reitz, Neena Beber, Ellen Melaver, Michael Hollinger, Israel Horovitz, Richard Wesley, Nicole Burdette, Jonathan Marc Sherman, Seth Zvi Rosenfeld, David Bar Katz

NON-RESIDENT PRODUCTIONS

End of Summer by S.N. Behrman; Presented by Kaleidoscope Theatre Company (Marshall Mays, Artistic Director; Anthony Catanzaro, Managing Director; Irwin Kroot, Producing Director); Director, Marshall Mays; Set, Scott Aronow; Lighting, Pamela Kupper; Sound, Kyle Gordon; Costumes, Anthony Catanzaro; Stage Manager, Jared Forsythe; Cast: Andrea Alton, Dane A. Aska III, Varin Ayala, Samara Bay, Ron Bopst, Gavin Hoffman, Anton Koval, Andy Ridings, Jeremy Ritz, Celia Schaefer, Eva Schelbaum; Studio Theatre; May 31–June 7

The Fabulous Kane Sisters in BOX OFFICE POISON by Marc Geller

and Bill Roulet; Presented by Red Light District Theatre Company and Stephen Morfesis; Director, Marc Geller; Costumes, Jennifer Kirschman; Lighting, Frank DenDanto III; Stage Managers, Sara Turrone, Alan Stevens, Melissa Garno; Cast: Elizabeth Bove, Andrew Dawson, Brent Erdy, Marc Geller, Nicholas Gorham, Zach Kleinsmith, Christopher H. Matthews, Patrick McCarthy, Christian Pedersen, Marta Reiman, Bill Roulet, David A. Rudd, Sheila Stasack, Elizabeth West; Encore Replacements: Lucy McMichael, Suzannah Lawson Matalon; Presented as part of the NY Fringe Festival August 9–24; Fringe Encore at the Barrow Street Theatre September 4–14

Chocolate Factory Theater

Executive Director, Sheila Lewandowski; Artistic Director, Brian Rogers

1965UU by Mac Wellman; Director, Steve Mellor; Sets/Lighting, Kyle Chepulis; Sound, John Kilgore; Cast: Paul Lazar, Kate Marks, Heather Christian, Ed Jewett, Daniel Manley. September 11–October 4

Puncture by Nancy Bannon; Director/Choreographer, Nancy Bannon; Design, Brian MacDevitt; Sound, Darron L West; Costumes, Ilona Somogyi; Stage Manager, Cynthia Baker; Cast: Gabriel Baron, Sarah Rose Bodley, Megan Brunsvold,, Stephanie Liapis, Tricia Nelson, Ava Prince, Risa Steinberg, Lathrop Walker, A. Apostol; November 5–8

No Where Can Be Here Now by Judith M. Smith; Director/Choreographer, Judith M. Smith; Lighting, Jeannette Oi-Suk Yew; Visual Design, Keith Larson; Stage Manager, Lisa Haas; Cast: Laura Diffenderfer, Corinne Donly, Kobun Kaluza, Diana M., Konopka, Josh Rowe; November 12–15

redevelop (death valley) Conceived, directed and choreographed by Brian Rogers; Video, Madeline Best & Brian Rogers; Sets, Brad Kisicki; Costumes, Maggie Dick; Lighting, Chloe Z. Brown; Music, Chris Peck & Brian Rogers; Cast: Jennifer Lee Dudek, Sheila Lewandoski, Yoko Myoi, Mark Sitko; Februray 12–28

[   ] by Red Metal Mailbox; Writer/Director, Sarah Maxfield; Lighting, Chloe Z. Brown; Sets, Brad Kisicki; Costumes, Mary McKenzie; Sound, Jason Sebastian; Cast: Jillian Sweeney, Rachel Tiemann; March 25–28

A Family of Perhaps Three by Gertrude Stein; Produced by Target Margin Theater; Director, David Herskovits; Design, Lenore Doxsee; Stage Manager, Laura Wilson; Sound, Caroline Kaplan; Cast: Chinasa Ogbuagu, Allison Schubert, Indika Senanayake; May 17–June 6

Across The Road Created and performed by Colin Gee; Music, Erin Gee; June 17–20

Cuchipinoy Productions

Founding Co-Artistic Directors, Mario Corrales & Rodney E. Reyes; Production Manager, Anna Payumo

Who Am I Written and co-directed by Rodney E. Reyes; Co-Director, Mario Corrales; Sets, Mario Corrales; Lighting, Jerome Hoppe; Sound, Eric Johnson; Cast: Patrick Annelli, Dian Mills, Ginny Moore, Brendan Naranjo, Okierete Onaodowan, Anna Payumo, Rodney E. Reyes, Rachel Skrod; Gene Frankel Theatre; March 19–28

WORKSHOP READINGS

Who Am I by Rodney E. Reyes; October; *Anonymous* Written and directed by Rodney E. Reyes; February 12

DJM Productions

Artistic Director, Dave McCracken

Peep Show Male Written, directed and designed by Dave McCracken; Stage Manager, Miriam Hyfler; Lighting, Dave McCracken; Cast: Cedano, Dale Church, Jonah Dill-D'Ascoli, Tony Musco, Erin Roberts, Megan Simard, Doug Spagnola, Greg Thornsbury, Joelle Wayland-Lewis; The Dionysus Theatre's L'il Peach; October 8–November 15

An Evening with Eddie: Shadows of Poe by Randall O'Neill; Director/ Dramaturge, Karen Case Cook; Set/Costumes, Dave McCracken; Stage Manager/ Lighting, Bekah Hernandez; Cast: Randall O'Neill; The Dionysus Theatre's L'il Peach; April 16–April 25

The Drilling CompaNY

Producing Artistic Director, Hamilton Clancy; Associate Producer, Karen Kitz

Twelfth Night by Wiliam Shakespeare; Director, Kathy Curtiss; Cast: David Adams, Alessandro Colla, Kwaku Driskell, Adam Fujita, Bill Green, Michael Gnat, Karla Hendrick, David Marantz, Maria McConville, Iriemimen Ohiha, Will Schneider; Shakespeare in the Parking Lot; July 24–August 10

Henry the Fifth by William Shakespeare; Director, Laura Strausfeld; Cast: Ivory Aquino, Selene Beretta, Stephanie Carll, Don Carter, Hamilton Clancy, Patricia Chilsen, Sergio Diaz, James Davies, Courtney Esser, Dennis Gagomiros, John K. Heath, Jonathan Marballi, Camilla Rahbery, Joann Sacco, Aimee Whelan, Ray Wortel; Shakespeare in the Parking Lot; July 24–August 9

Healer by Stephen Bittrich; Director, Rob A. Wilson; Cast: William Apps, Jordan Feltner, Meghan McGeary, Lisa Peart, Dan Teachout; 78th Street Theatre Lab; January 6

Freedom by Scott Baker, Brian Dykstra, Trish Harnetiaux, Sean Lewis, Kate McCamy, Andrea Moon, Richard Mover, Eric Henry Sanders, Robert A. Wilson; Director, Hamilton Clancy, Tom Demenkoff, Jude Domski, Rebecca Hengstenberg, David Marantz, Richard Mover, Robert A. Wilson; Lighting, Miriam Nilofa Crow; Set, Jen Varbalow; Costumes, Lisa Renee Jordan; Sound, Chris Rummel; Stage Manager, Billie Davis; Cast: William Apps, Selene Beretta, Don Carter, Hamilton Clancy, Tom Demenkoff, Jordan Feltner, Dennis Gagomiros, Michael Gnat, Franklin Killian, Darren Lipari, Erin Mallon, Sajeev Pillai, Sonja Rzepski, Sean Patrick Reilly, Daisy Stone, Shaun Bennett Wilson; 78th Street Theater Lab; April 24–May 10

Mr. Bungle and the Incident on Lambdamoo by Trish Harnetiaux; Director, Eric Nightengale; Cast: Don Carter, Alessandro Colla, Neil Hellegers, Matt Korahias, Ruth Nightengale, Aimee Whelen; 78th Street Theatre; May 12

The Duplex

Booking Manager, Thomas Honeck; Technical Director, Lisa Moss

Monday Night New Voices Created and presented by Scott Alan; Third Mondays, monthly series

Mostly Sondheim Hosted by Kate Pazakis, Brian Nash, and Todd Buonopane; Guest hosts, Marty Thomas, Emily McNamara; Friday late-night, weekly series

Gashole: Hole-O-Matic Written & performed by Michael Holland and Karen Mack; Intern, Michael Anderson; Technical Director, Lisa Moss; Saturdays, Opened October 20, 2007, Saturday evenings, weekly series

New York Theatre Barn Monthy Cabaret Produced by David Rigler and Joe Barros; Opened January 14, 2007; Mondays, monthly series

Emerging Artists Theatre

Artistic Director, Paul Adams; Associate Artistic Director, Derek Jamison

EATfest Fall 2008 Thirteen short plays; included *The Sky is Falling* by Patrick Gabridge; Director, Amy Leland Hemphill; Cast: Amy Bizjak, Debra Lass, Erin Tito, Susan Wallack; *Stripping Eden* by Wayne Paul Mattingly; Director, Danielle Quisenberry; Cast: Eilis Cahill, Chris Henry; *Next* by Staci Swedeen; Director, Janelle Lannan; Cast: Andrea Alton, Joseph Callari, Jerry Alan Cole, Alexandra Zabriskie; *Jack Goes Up, Jack Goes Down* by Ted LoRusso; Director, Troy Miller, Cast: Jen Morris, Scott Raker; *Sharing the Pie* by Kathleen Warnock; Director, Peter Bloch; Cast: Sara Hatfield, Russell Jordan; *Hi Speed Disconnect* by Chris Widney; Director, Aimee Howard; Cast: Sarah Miriam Aziz, Dan Barnhill; *Furious* by Eric Appleton; Director, Marc Castle; Cast: Bill Farley, Jamie Heinlein; *Hot Line* by Lia Romeo; Director, Ned Thorne; Cast: Bryan Kaplan, Irene Longshore, Matt Stapleton; *Tranquil* by Andrew Rosendorf; Director, Dan Dinero; Cast: Enid Cortés, Jason Hare; *We Appear to Have Company* by Greg Freier; Director, John Hurley; Cast: Ed Schultz, Blanche Cholet, Kevin Brofsky; *Negotiating A Mindfield* by John A. Donnelly; Director, Rasa Allan Kazlas; Cast: Jane Altman, Shannon Marie Kerr, Jacqueline Sydney; *Weimar Hole* by Sara Jeanne Asselin; Director, Jonathan Warman; Cast: Deb Armelino, Moe Bertran, J. Stephen Brantley, Vinnie Costa, Maya Rosewood, Matthew Shawlin; *Old Flame* by Richard Ploetz; Director, Ian Streicher; Cast: Ron Bopst, Jerry Matz, Vivian Meisner, Jess Philips; Roy Arias Theatre Center; November 4–16

EATfest Spring 2009 Nine short plays; included: *Better Dresses* by Eugenia Woods; Director, Ron Bopst, Ryan Hilliard; Cast: Jerry Marsini, Sarah Miriam Aziz, Chelsea Rodriguez, Jacquelyn Poplar; *Gift of the Gun* by Alex Broun; Director, Molly Marinik; Cast: Tim Seib, Peter Levin; *Burying Mom* by Matt Fotis; Director, Deb Guston; Cast: Scott Raker, Janelle Lannan, Kelly Dynan, Hershey Miller, Alexandra Zabriskie, Deb Armelino, Jane Altman, Laura Beth Wells, Jacqueline Sydney; *Mrs. Jansen Isn't Here Now* by Steven Korbar; Director, Vivian Meisner; Cast: Dan Barnhill, Elizabeth A. Bell; *Moon Night* by Ted LoRusso; Director, Ian Streicher; Cast: Bernard Burlew, Chuck Saculla; *Five Worst Words* by Jason Matthews; Director, Dan Dinero; Cast: Tommy Day Care, Matt Boethin; *Family Comes First* by Jon Spano; Director, Dan Dinero; Cast: Lawrence M. Bullock, J. Stephen Brantley, Blake Walton, Adam Schneider, Vinnie Costa, Dusty Alvarado; *Memory River* by Vanda; Director, Troy Miller; Cast: Michele Fulves, Diane Tyler, Paul Caiola, Lian-Marie Holmes, Gary Cowling, Janelle Mims, Matt Hussong; *The Chiselers* by Mark Finley; Director, Melissa Attebery; Cast: Marie Wallace, Karen Stanion, Andrea Alton, Thomas Poarch, Nick Mathews; TADA! Youth Theater; February 23–March 8

Ensemble Studio Theatre

Artistic Director, William Carden; Executive Director, Paul Alexander Slee; Youngblood Artistic Directors, Graeme Gillis and R.J. Tolan

First Light 2009 Presented by EST/Alfred P. Sloan Foundation Science and Technology Project; Eleventh Annual; Program Director, Graeme Gillis; Workshops: *Posthumusical* Book, music and lyrics by Matt Schatz; Director, Jordan Young; *Lenin's Embalmers* by Vern Thiessen; Director, Geoff Brumlik; *Photograph 51* by Anne Ziegler; Director, Lynne Meadow; *Leave A Light On* by Anne Marie Healy; *Elaine's Brain* by David Ford; Director, Chris Smith; *Darwin's Challenge* by Jason Grote; *Beautiful Night* by Tommy Smith; Director, Evan Cabnet; Special Events: *Youngblood Presents E=mc brunch*; *Cabaret Scientifique*; January 4–23

EST Marathon 2009 31st Annual Festival of new one-act plays; Series A: *Trickle* by Kia Corthron; Director, Will Pomerantz; Cast: Geneva Carr, Shirine Babb, Tatiana Suarez-Pico, Nikki E. Walker, Jackie Chung; *For the Love of God, St. Teresa* by Christine Farrell; Director, Deborah Hedwall; Cast: Christine Farrell, Lucy DeVito, Brooke Fulton Myers; *Americana* by Garrett M. Brown; Director, Linsay Firman; Cast: Michael Cullen, Miles Bergner, Chris Ceraso, Ann Talman;

PTSD by Tommy Smith; Director, William Carden; Cast: Jay Patterson, Haskell King, Stephanie Janssen, Julie Fitzpatrick; *Face Cream* by Maggie Bofill; Director, Pamela Berlin; Cast: Bruce MacVittie, Paula Pizzi; Series B: *Carol & Jill* by Leslie Ayvazian; Director, Daniella Topol; Cast: Leslie Ayvazian, Janet Zarish; *Blood From A Stoner* by Jeanne Dorsey; Director, Maria Mileaf; Cast: David Margulies, Patricia Randell, Thomas Lyons; *Little Duck* by Billy Aronson; Director, Jamie Richards; Cast: Paul Bartholomew, Jane Pfitsch, Julie Leedes, Steven Boyer, Geneva Carr; *Daughter* by Cassandra Medley; Director, Petronia Paley; Cast: Gayle Samuels, Kaliswa Brewster, Lynne Matthew, Natalie Carter; *Sundance* by M.Z. Ribalow; Director, Matthew Penn; Cast, Richmond Hoxie, David Deblinger, Ean Sheehy, Rob Sedgwick, J.J. Kandel; May 22–June 27

YOUNGBLOOD COMPANY

Asking For Trouble 2008 Short plays by Zakiyyah Alexander, Lucy Alibar, Delaney Britt Brewer, Anna Monech, Qui Nguyen, Erica Saleh, Phil Schmiedl, Crystal Skillman, Maggie Smith, Lloyd Suh, Jesse Cameron Alick, Emily Conbere, Joshua Conkel, Amy Fox, Mira Gibson, Graeme Gillis, Ross Maxwell, Michael Sendrow, Lucy Thurber, Elyzabeth Gregory Wilder, Robert Askins, Eliza Clark, Sharon Eberhardt, Sam Forman, Edith Freni, Amy Herzog, Michael Lew, Patrick Link, Daria Polatin, Jeremy Soule, Daniel Talbott, Nikole Beckwith, Jihan Crowther, Ann Marie Healy, Mrinalini Kamath, Jon Kern, Courtney Brooke Lauria, Erin Murtaugh, Sharyn Rothstein, Matt Schatz, Emily Chadick Weiss; Directors, Isaac Butler, Shoshona Currier, Tamara Fisch, John Giampetro, Kel Haney, Kitt LaVoie, Jeff Lewonczyk, JV Mercanti, R.J. Tolan, Abigail Zealey Bess, Evan Cabnet, Andrew Grosso, Kel Haney, Jamie Richards, Erica Saleh, Marc Santa Maria, R.J. Tolan, Birgitta Victorson, Kim Weild, Sherri Eden Barber, Michole Biancosino, Isaac Butler, Steve Fried, John Giametro, Graeme Gillis, Michael Godfried, Alexa Polmer, Giovanna Sardelli, Tom Wotjtunik, Amanda Charlton, Adam Fitzgerald, Barrie Gelles, Melissa Kievman, Laura Konson, Larissa Lury, Sarah Malkin, Colette Robert, Debbie Saivetz, Jordan Young; October 21–25

Youngblood's Unfiltered Festival of new plays in studio productions; Series included: *Lake Water* by Delaney Britt Brewer; Director, Jordan Young; Cast: Steve Boyer, Quincy Confoy, Ann O'Sullivan, Audrey Lynn Weston; *Nodding Off* by Emily Chadick Weiss; Director, Abigail Zealey Bess; Cast: Chris Ceraso, Helen P. Coxe, Eunice Ha, William Oliver Watkins; *Princes of Waco* by Robert Askins; Director, Dylan McCullough; Cast: Evan Enderle, Christine Farrell, Scott Sowers, Megan Tusing; *Stockton* by Michael Lew; Director, Colette Robert; Cast: Julie Fitzpatrick, Ryan Karels, Julie Leedes, Diana Ruppe; February 5–March 7

The Flea Theater

Artistic Director, Jim Simpson; Managing Director, Todd Rosen; Producing Director, Carol Ostrow

Cato by Joseph Addison; Director, Jim Simpson; Set/Lighting, Zack Tinkleman; Costumes, Claudia Brown; Cast: André De Shields, Anthony Cochrane, Brian O'Neill, Christian Baskous, Jimmy Allen, Ben Beckley, Scott Rad Brown, Holly Chou, Ross Cowan, Jake Green, Eric Lockley, Craig Mungavin, Matthew Murumba, Carly Zien; October 10–November 1

The Footage by Joshua Scher; Director, Claudia Zelevansky; Set, Adrian Jones; Lighting, Ben Stanton; Costumes, Erin Murphy; Sound, Matt O'Hare; Cast: Elizabeth Alderfer, Celeste Arias, Blair Baker, Matthew Bretschneider, Jamie Effros, Nicolas Flower, Michael Guagno, Caroline Hurley, Rachel McPhee, Michael Micalizzi; Downstairs @ The Flea; October 23–November 30

Dawn by Thomas Bradshaw; Director, Jim Simpson; Sound, Brandon Wolcott; Lighting, Jeanette Lew; Costumes, Claudia Brown; Set, Michael Goldsheft; Cast: Gerry Bamman, Kate Benson, Laura Esterman, Drew Hildebrand, Jenny Seastone Stern, Jane Elliott, Alexis Macnab, Bobby Moreno, Jess Phly, Sarah Sakaan; November 9–December 6

A Light Lunch by A.R. Gurney; Director, Jim Simpson; Set, John McDermott; Lighting, Miranda Hardy; Costumes, Erin Murphy; Sound, Jill BC DuBoff; Cast: Havilah Brewster, Beth Hoyt, Tom Lipinski, John Russo; December 12–January 25

Love/Stories (or But You Will Get Used To It) by Itamar Moses; Director, Michelle Tattenbaum; Set, Jerad Schome; Lighting, Joe Chapman; Sound, Brandon Wolcott; Costumes, Jessica Pabst; Cast: Felipe Bonilla, Laurel Holland, Maren Langdon, Michael Micalizzi, John Russo; Downstairs @ The Flea; February 16–April 25

KASPAR HAUSER: a foundling's opera Composed and by Elizabeth Swados, Erin Courtney; Music Director, Kris Kukol; Movement Director, Mimi Quillin; Set, John McDermott; Lighting, Jeanette Lew; Costumes, Normandy Sherwood; Sound, Sam Goldman; Cast: Adrienne Deekman, Jennifer Fouché, Beth Griffith, Nicolas Greco, Joseph Dale Harris, Arlo Hill, Michael Hopewell, Amy Jackson, Erica Livingston, Chad Lindsey, Vella Lovell, Preston Martin, Kelly McCormack, Colin Mew, Jason Najjoum, Eliza Poehlman, Hannah Shankman, Marshall York, Carly Zien; February 13–March 28

Off the Main Road by William Inge; Director, Jim Simpson; Cast: Walter Bobbie, Rebecca Nelson, Jay O. Sanders, Rocco Sisto, Frances Sternhagen, Sigourney Weaver, Maren Langdon, Even Enderlee, Jamie Effros, Michael Mcalizzi; May 11

NON-RESIDENT PRODUCTIONS

Imperia Saves the World: Cause Baby, No Worry, No Funk, Time to be Sunshine Drunk Presented by Concrete Temple Theatre; June 10–15

The Amelia Project, Phase II Presented by Fly By Night Dance Theatre; June 19–22

Pinchbottom Declares War! by Porkpie; Presented by Collective: Unconscious; July 18–20

Linus and Alora by Andrew Irons; Presented by The Andhow! Theater Company; Director, Jessica Davis-Irons; Lighting, Owen Hughes; Sound/Original Music, Jill BC DuBoff; Set/Videos, Dustin O'Neill; Costumes, Becky Lasky; Choreographer, Jesse Hawley; September 4–27

The Economic Engine by Neil Rolnick; Presented by New York Art Ensemble; Music Director, Todd Reynolds; September 14

Flux Theatre Ensemble

Artistic Director, August Schulenburg; Managing & Development Director, Heather Cohn; Marketing & Executive Director, Kelly O'Donnell; Production Manager, Jason Pradine

A Midsummer Night's Dream by William Shakespeare; Director, August Schulenburg; Assistant Director: Angela Astle; Set, Will Lowry; Lighting, Jennifer Rathbone; Dramaturg, Ingrid Nordstrom; Cast: Jake Alexander, Kira Blaskovich, Tiffany Clementi, Michael Davis, Amy Fitts, Charlotte Graham, Maggie Hamilton, Candice Holdorf, Caitlin Kinsella, Nick Monroy, Matthew Murumba, Frederique Nahmani, Hannah Rose Peck, Brian Pracht, Christina Shipp, David Douglas Smith, Michael Swartz, Isaiah Tanenbaum, Nitya Vidyasager, Aaron Michael Zook; West End Theatre; June 5–22

Other Bodies by August Schulenburg; Director, Heather Cohn; Cast: Christina Shipp, Vince Nappo; Presented as part of the NY Fringe Festival; CSV Center–Flamboyan Theatre; August 8–24

The Angel Eaters Trilogy Three plays by Johnna Adams; Set, Caleb Levengood; Costumes, Emily DeAngelis; Lighting, Jennifer Rathbone; Sound, Asa Wembler; Dramaturg:, Kay Mitchell; Composer, Gerard Keenan; Props Coordinator, Angela Astle; Fight Directors, Autumn Horne and Shannon Michael Wamser; Stage Managers, Jodi Witherell, Autumn Horne, Emily Rae Johnson; ASM, DaVonne Bacchus; Puppeteer, Jake Alexander; Videographer, Thomas Monsees; *Angel Eaters* directed by Jessi Hill; Cast: Tiffany Clementi, Ken Glickfeld, Ian Heitzman,

Catherine Porter, Marnie Schulenburg, Isaiah Tanenbaum, Gregory Waller, Cotton Wright; *Rattlers* directed by Jerry Ruiz; Cast: Matthew Crosby, David Jackson, Becky Kelly, Jason Paradine, Amy Stewart, Jane Lincoln Taylor, Richard B. Watson; *8 Little Antichrists* directed by Kelly O'Donnell; Cast: Jake Alexander, Candice Holdorf, Felicia Hudson, Nora Hummel, Elise Link, Joe Mathers, Rebecca McHugh, Zack Robidas, August Schulenburg; Wings Theatre; November 3–22

Petty Theft by Adam Szymkowicz; Director, Angela Astle; Set, Heather Cohn; Costumes, Becky Kelly; Lighting, Andy Fritsch; Sound, Kevin Fuller; Choreography, Ashley Martinez; Props, Kelly O'Donnell & August Schulenberg; Production Manager, Jason Paradine; Stage Manager, Kate August; Cast: Todd D'Amour, Candice Holdorf, Lynn Kenny, Maria Portman, Brian Pracht, Zack Robidas, Marnie Schulenberg, Cotton Wright; Access Theater Gallery Space; April 23–May 17

Gallery Players

Executive Director, Neal J. Freeman; Artistic Director, Heather Siobhan Curran

The Reckoning of Kit & Little Boots by Nat Cassidy; Producer, Neal J. Freeman, Anna Olivia Moore for The Gallery Players; Director, Neal J. Freeman; Set, Hannah Shafran; Costumes, Ana Marie A. Salamat; Lighting, John Eckert; Stage Manager, Emily Ballou; Cast: Nat Cassidy, David Ian Lee, Alex Herrald, Keith Foster, Lara Stoby, Anna Olivia Moore, Andrew Firda; Presented at Manhattan Theatre Source; June 6–28

Hope's Arbor by Rich Espey; Producer, Neal J. Freeman, Anna Olivia Moore for The Gallery Players; Set, Hannah Shafran; Costumes, Ana Marie A. Salamat; Lighting, John Eckert; Stage Manager, G. Zhang; Cast: Lauren Marcus, Justine Campbell-Elliott, Justin Herfel, James Holloway, Emily Hagburg, Jessica Ko; June 6–28

The Underpants by Carl Sternheim, adapted by Steve Martin; Producer, Lara Terrell, Tom Wojtunik for The Gallery Players; Director, Seth Soloway; PSM, Jodi Witherell; Set, Stephen K. Dobay; Costumes, Danielle Schembre; Lighting, Tony Galaska; Sound, Ned Thorne; Cast: Catia Ojeda, Justin Herfel, Amy L. Smith, Nat Cassidy, Jason Schuchman, Peter Levine, Dennis Michael Keefe, DaVonne Bacchus; September 13–28

Like You Like It Book and lyrics by Sammy Buck, music by Daniel S. Acquisto; Producer, Heather Siobhan Curran for The Gallery Players; Director, Igor Goldin; Choreographer, Keith Andrews; Music Director, Jeffrey Campos; Set, Carl Tallent; Costumes, Hunter Kaczorowski; Lightis, Dan Jobbins; PSM, Kayla Shriner-Cahn; Props, Jaime Phelps; Cast: Alison Luff, Nathan Johnson, Hollis Scarborough, Jennifer Blood, Lance Olds, Clint Morris, Caitlin Kent, Trey Compton, Brynn Curry, Michael Lowney, Richard Connelly, Roy Flores, André Jordan, Jeff Barba, Lena Moy-Borgen, Elisabeth Ness, Rebecca Dealy, Carly Vernon; October 18–November 9

A Tuna Christmas by Ed Howard, Joe Sears, & Jaston Williams; Producer, Robin Mishik-Jett for The Gallery Players; Director, Andrew K. Russell; PSM, Erika Omundson; Set, Edward Morris; Lighting, Maureen Hanratty; Props, Nicole Gaignat; Costumes, Dawn Luna; Sound, David Roy; Cast: Justine Barnette, Brian Letchworth; December 6–21

Thoroughly Modern Millie Book by Richard Morris & Dick Scanlan, new music by Jeanine Tesori, new lyrics by Dick Scanlan; Producer, Brian Michael Flanagan for The Gallery Players; Director, Neal J. Freeman; Music Director, David Fletcher; Choreographer, Katharine Pettit; Set, Ann Bartek; Costumes, Megan Q. Dudley; Lighting, Ryan Bauer; PSM, Emily Rea; Cast: Alison Luff, Amy Grass, David Rossetti, Andy Planck, Justine Campbell-Elliott, Roy Flores, Jay Paranada, Debra Thais Evans, Megan Kane, Lorinne Lampert, Jill Sesso, Katie Kester, Ryan Finley, George Papas, Drew Pournelle, Frank Sansone, Rebecca Dealy, Kristin Donnelly, Angelyn Faust, Lauren Kay; January 31–February 22

Bus Stop by William Inge; Producer, Amanda White for The Gallery Players; Director, Heather Siobhan Curran; PSM, Trevor Regars; Set, Edward Morris; Costumes, Meredith Neal; Props, Nicole Gaignat; Lighting, Mike Billings; Sound, Neal J. Freeman; Cast: Rebecca Dealy, Annie Paul, Brad Thomason, Alisha Spielmann, John Blaylock, Justin Herfel, Shawn Parsons, Brad Lewandowski; March 14–29

The Who's Tommy Music and lyrics by Pete Townshend, book by Des McAnuff & Pete Townshend; Additional Music/Lyrics, John Entwistle, Keith Moon; Producer, Katie Adams for The Gallery Players; Director, Tom Wojtunik; Choreographer, Christine O'Grady; Music Director, Paul Seiz; PSM, Lara Terrell; Set, Michael Kramer; Lighting, Chris Walsh; Costumes, Hunter Kaczorowski; Sound, Kate Foretek; Projection, Ron Amato; Cast: Nathan Brisby, John Ashley Brown, Kennen Butler, Alexis DeDonato, Hayley Driscoll, Tommy Foster, Marcie Henderson, Tyson Jennette, Anna Lise Jensen, Daniel Henri Luttway, Blair Moore, Alex Pearlman, Jan-Peter Pedross, David Perlman, Anthony Pierini, Mia Romero, Chloe Sabin, Mitchell Scott Shapiro, Ryan Stone, Brett Travis; May 2–24

Gingold Theatrical Group: Project Shaw

Founder and Artistic Director/Producer/Director, David Staller; Grammercy Park South; montly public readings of the complete works of George Bernard Shaw at The Players Club; Associate Producers, Jerry Wade, Theresa Diamond, Anita Jaffe, Kate Ross, Bill Barbanes

Great Catherine and **Annjanska, the Wild Grand Duchess** Cast: Matthew Arkin, John Cullum, Tyne Daly, Alison Fraser, Nick Wyman, Tony Yazbeck; Host, Michael Reidel; June 23

Major Barbara Cast: Matt Cavenaugh, Nikki Coble, Michael Cumsty, Michael Esper, Adam Feldman, Annie Golden, Merwin Goldsmith, John Keating, Lianne Kressin, Megan Mullally, Ana Reeder, Scott Schafer, Alexis Soloski, Emily Young; Host, David Cote; July 21

Caesar and Cleopatra Cast: Tim Artz, Todd Gearhart, Anthony Holds, Simon Jones, Jack Koenig, Darrie Lawrence, Jon Levenson, Daniel Marconi, Madeleine Martin, Brian Murray, Daniel Reichard, Daphne Rubin-Vega, Seth Rudetsky; Host, Adam Felman; September 22

The Shewing-Up of Blanco Posnet Cast: Hannah Cabel, Mary Carver, Nora Chester, Ashley Wren Collins, Teddy Eck, Stephen Mo Hanan, Cheyenne Jackson, Lianne Kressin, Brian Scott Lipton, John Martello, Jeff McCarthy, Charlotte Moore, Nathaniel Shaw, Ronny Venable, Emily Young; Host, Michael Riedel; October 20

Jitta's Atonement Cast: Charles Busch, Annie Golden, George S. Irving, Jeanine Lamanna, Darrie Lawrence, Mary Beth Peil, Louis Zorich; Host, Michael Reidel; November 17

Saint Joan Cast: John Bolton, Teddy Eck, Alvin Epstein, Adam Feldman, Jack Gilpin, Jonathan Groff, Stephen Mo Hana, Timothy Jerome, Larry Keith, Somon Kendall, Jack Koenig, Marc Kudisch, Jon Levenson, James Ludwig, Daniel Marconi, Madeleine Martin, Marian Seldes, Victor Slezak, Daniel Truman, Nick Wyman; Host, Alexis Soloski; December 22

The Dark Lady of the Sonnets and **Shakes Vs. Shakes** Cast: Jayne Houdyshell, Daniel Jenkins, Liz Morton, Robert Stanton; Host, David Cote; January 19

Buoyant Billions Cast: Lori Ackerman, Emma Archid, Ezra Barnes, Bryan Batt, Ashley Wren Collins, Veanne Cox, William DeMerritt, Ed Dixon, Teddy Eck, Marshall Factora, George S. Irving, John Martello, Charlotte Moore, Graham Rowat; Host, David Sheward; February 16

O'Flaherty V.C. Cast: Michael Cerveris, George S. Irving, Brian Murray, Jane Powell, Marian Seldes, KT Sullivan; Host, Michael Riedel; March 16

The Inca of Perusalem & **Arthur and the Acetone** & **Interlude at the Playhouse** Cast: Gary Beach, Amanda Green, Simon Jones, Jay Rogers, Marla Schaffel, Mark Waldrop; Host, Mark Blankenship; April 20

The Man of Destiny & **The Glimpse of Reality** Cast: Kate Baldwin, Michael Cerveris, Bradford Cover, David Marguilies, Liz Morton; Host, David Rooney; May 18

Harlem Repertory Theater

Artistic Director, Keith Lee Grant

Ain't Misbehavin' Music by Fats Waller, based on an idea by Murray Horwitz and Richard Maltby, Jr.; Aaron Davis Hall; Director/Choreographer, Keith Lee Grant; Costumes, Natalia Peguero; Aaron Davis Hall; July 19–September 13

Tambourines To Glory by Langston Hughes, music by Burton Lane, book by E.Y. Harburg & Fred Saidy, lyrics by E.Y. Harburg; Director/Choreography, Keith Lee Grant; Cast: Lynette Braxton, Alexandra Bernard; Aaron Davis Hall; August 1–September 12

As You Like It by William Shakespeare; Aaron Davis Hall; September 4–14

HERE Arts Center

Artistic Director, Kristin Marting; Producing Director, Kim Whitener

MAINSTAGE RESIDENT PRODUCTIONS

Oph3lia Written and directed by Aya Ogawa, Sets/Costumes, Clint Ramos; Lighting/Video, Jeanette Oi-Suk Yew; Sound, Rich Kim; Music, Andy Gillis; Assistant Director, Joan Jubett; Stage Manager, Stacy Haggin; Cast: Laura Butler, Drae Campbell, Dawn Eshelman, Connie Hall, Ikuko Ikari, Hana Kalinski, Eunjee Lee, Mark Lindberg, Alanna Medlock, Jy Murphy, Jorge Alberto Rubio, Magin Schantz, Maureen Sebastian; June 11–July 2

The Young Ladies Of…/The Be(a)st of Taylor Mac Written & performed by Taylor Mac; Performed in repertory; Directors, Tracy Trevett (*Young Ladies*), David Drake (*The Be(a)st*), Set, David Evan Morris (*Young Ladies*), Lighting, Juliet Chia (*Young Ladies*); July 8–August 2

Oh What War by Jason Craig, conceived and directed by Mallory Catlett; Presented by Juggernaut Theatre; Music Director/Composer, Lisa Dove; Design, Peter Ksander; Video, Zbigniew Bzymek; Cast: Jason Craig, Jessica Jelliffe, Tom Lipinski, Kelli Rae Powell, Magin Schantz, Scott Sowers, G. Lucas Crane; September 10–October 4

837 Venice Boulevard Directed and Choreographed by Faye Driscoll with Michael Helland, Celia Rowlson-Hall, and Nikki Zialcita; November 13–22

Culturemart 2009 Festival of works-in-progress by resident artists; included: *Let's Watch!* by Kamala Sankaram; *The Venus Riff* by Johari Mayfield; *AmazingLand* by Geoff Sobelle, Trey Lyford, and Steve Cuiffo; *Border Towns* by Nick Brooke; *Don Cristobal* by Billy-Club Man, Erin Orr and Rima Fand; *Lucid Possession* by Toni Dove; *Alchemy of Light* by Ruth Sergel and Peter von Salis; *Sonnambula* by Michael Bodel; *Ego* by David Michael Friend; *Paris Syndrome* by Suzi Takahashi and Bertie Ferdman; *Aunt Leaf* by Jeffrey Mousseau and Barbara Weichmann; *Mosheh* by Yoav Gal; *Sounding* by Kristin Marting and Jennifer Gibbs; *Water (or the Secret Life of Objects)* by Sheila Callaghan; *Secret Rendezvous* by The South Wing; *Soul Leaves Her Body* by Peter Flaherty and Jennie Marytai Liu; Additional productions presented in collaboration with the UNDER THE RADAR Festival: *Removable Parts* by Corey Dargel; *Siren* by Ray Lee; Mainstage and Dorothy B. Williams Theater; January 3–February 4

Red Fly/Blue Bottle Music by Christina Campanella, words by Stephanie Fleischmann; Director, Mallory Catlett; Set, Jim Findlay, Lighting, Miranda K Hardy; Costumes, Olivera Gajic; Sound, Jeremy Wilson; Video, Peter Norrman; Live Video, Mirit Tal; Cast: Black-Eyed Susan, Jesse Hawley, Chris Lee, Sam Baker, Erich Shoen-Rene; April 8–May 2

NON-RESIDENT PRODUCTIONS

Lee/Gendary by Derek Nguyen; Director, Suzi Takahashi; Music, Jen Shyu; Additional Music and Sound, Adam Rogers; Video, Chris McClain; Stage Manager, Leta Tremblay; Lighting, Lucrecia Briceno; Costumes, Adam Corcoran; Cast: Soomi Kim, Shing Ka, Walker Lewis, Constance Parng, Ariel Shepley, Pai Wang; October 14–30

The Uncanny Appearance of Sherlock Holmes Created by the North American Cultural Laboratory (NACL); Director, Brad Krumholz; Lighting, Juliet Chia; Set, David Evans Morris; Cast: Glenn Hall, Sarah Dey Hirshan, Brett Keyser, Tannis Kowalchuk, Brad Krumholz, Liz Eckert, Ophra Wolf; December 2–21

Trio Molemo! Created and performed by Johnny Simons of Hip Pocket Theatre; with Lorca Simons and Lake Simons. February 6–8

Soul Samurai February 14–March 15 (see listing in Off-Broadway section of this volume)

Hot Mama Mahatma Two solo performance shows: *YO Mama* by Natalie Kim; Director, Matt Hoverman; *I Went to India To Get Enlightened and SO Did Not!* by Karen Fitzgerald; Director, Kenneth Heaton; March 20

Downtown Urban Theater Festival Seventh season; Presented by Creative Ammo Inc; Produced by Arcos Entertainment; included: *Life Could Be Un Sueño* by Lina Sarrello; *Man Up* by Carlos Andrés Gómez; *A Boy Called Noise* by Julia Steele Allen; *Alnernate Side Street Parking* by Dina Laura; *The King's Mistress* by Patricia Ione Lloyd; *Solo Man Watusi* by Mel Nieves; *Where My Girls At: A Comedic Look at Black Lesbians* by Micia Mosely; *America* by Kim Yaged; *T.A.B.* by Susan H. Pak; *Right to Return* by Pamela Sneed; *VIi Degrees* by Kash Goins; *Representa!* by Paul S. Flores & Julio Cardenas; May 6–16

DOROTHY B. WILLIAMS THEATER RESIDENT PRODUCTIONS

Arias with a Twist June 12–December 31 (see Off-Braodway listings in this volume)

Diva Created by the Sofie Krog Teater of Denmark Presented by HERE's Dream Music Puppetry Program and StartHERE: Innovative Theater for Young People; February 27–March 1

NON-RESIDENT PRODUCTIONS

S.H.A.V.E.D. Written & performed by Tara Ahmadinejad, Director, Willow Norton; September 9–October 9

Life After Bush Book and music, directed, and produced by Noah Diamond & Amanda Sisk; Music Director/Arrangements, DJ Thacker; Lighting, Christopher Brown; Sound, Matt Tennie; Production Manager, Blair Lampe; Cast: Tarik Davis, Noah Diamond, Brian Louis Hoffman, Sadrina Johnson, Kim Moscaritolo, Avi Phillips, Amanda Sisk; October 17–November 2

The 7th Annual Carnival of Samhain Presented by Drama Works; November 6–8

Love Cures Cancer– The Musical Written and directed by George L Chieffet, Music and lyrics by Paul Rajeckas, Performed by Paul Rajeckas, Lighting by Dayon Heard. January 23–February 20

Songs for Robots Created and performed by Michael Hearst from One Ring Zero, Ron Caswell from Slavic Soul Party, Ben Holmes from One Ring Zero, and Bryan Drye from The Four Bags; January 26–February 19

Finding Ways To Prove You're Not An Al-Quaeda Terrorist When You're Brown (And Other Stories of the Gindian) Written & performed by Snehal

Desai; Produced by Stephanie Ybarra; Director, Erik Pearson; Set, Timothy R. Mackabee; Lighting, Burke Brown; Costumes, Kate Cusak; Sound, Jana Hoglund; Dramaturg, Jason Fitzgerald; January 31–February 8

The Knockout Blow Written and directed by Tina Satter; Presented by Half-Straddle Performance Group; Music/Sound, Chris Giarmo; Set/Lighting, Zack Tinkelman, Cast: Jess Barbagallo, Eliza Bent, Julia Sirna-Frest; February 13–21

Fait Accompli Primer Created by Reggie Watts, Co-created and directed by Tommy Smith; February 14–22

Thirst: a spell for Christabel Written by Monika Bustamente; Produced by David Davoli; Director, Elena Araoz; Set, Susan Zeeman Rodgers; Costumes, Chloe Chapin; Lighting, Justin Townsend; Sound, Arielle Edwards; Props, Ian P Guzzone; Stage Manager, Rosie Goldman; Cast: Matthew Cowles, Lori Funk, Elizabeth Gross; March 10–April 12

Jeffrey and Cole: A Conversation About Annie Potts by Jeffry Self, Cole Escola; March 20

Puppet KafKa by B. Walker Sampson; Produced by Drama of Works; Director/Design, Gretchen Van Lente; Assistant Director, Rita Kompelmahker; Marionettes, Mirek Trejtnar; April 22–May 10

Horse Trade Theater Group

Managing Director, Erez Ziv; Associate Producer, Morgan Lindsey Tachco

KRAINE THEATER

Too Much Light Makes the Baby Go Blind created by Greg Allen; Presented by the Neo-Futurists; 30 plays in 60 minutes; Friday and Saturday evenings; open run

Too Much Pride Makes the Baby Go Gay Presented by the Neo-Futurists; Cast: Sarah Levy, Erica Livingston, Christopher Borg, Kevin R. Free, Joey Rizzolo, Jacquelyn Landgraf, Joe Basile, Cara Francis, Jill Beckman, Desiree Burch; June 27–29

Best of 2008 Cast: Alicia Harding, Cara Francis, Christopher Borg, Eevin Hartsough, Erica Livingston, Jacquelyn Landgraf, Jeffrey Cranor, Jill Beckman, Joey Rizzolo, Kevin R. Free, Rob Neill, Ryan Good, Sarah Levy, Joe Basile; December 12–20

2009 FRIGID New York Festival 3rd Annual; *Are We Freaks?* by Bricken Sparacino; Presented by Comedy Period; *The Black Jew Dialogues* by Larry Jay Tish, Ron Jones; Presented by The Black Jew Dialogues; *Camouflage* by Gail Roberts; Presented by Camouflage Productions; *The Expatriates* by Randy Harrison and Harrison Williams; Presented by The Beggers Group; *Jihad for Vent and Dummy* by Ronald E. Coulter; Presented by Coulter and Star Ventriloquists; *Live!...at the Cockpit: Will at Work with the Lord Chamberlain's Men* by Kobun Aloka Kaluza and T.D. White; *The Question House* by Una Aya Osato; Presented by Keep It Movin' Productions; *The Surprise* by Martin Dockery; Presented by Martin Dockery; February 25–March 8

RED ROOM

Excessecret: "Guess What It's About?" Presented by Theatre Reverb and Horse Trade Theater Group; Cast: Christopher Gilkey, Kristin Arneson; October 1–November 22

Watch Out (It's Go Time) Presented by Theatre Reverb and Horse Trade Theater Group; Cast: Christopher Gilkey, Kristin Arneson; October 1–November 22

(Not) Just A Day Like Any Other Cast/Writers: Eevin Hartsough, Christopher Borg, Kevin R. Free, Jeffrey Cranor; November 6–22

The Scandal by Kristen Kosmos; Presented by The Mangement; Director, Courtney Sale; Cast: Amy Patrice Gold; December 4–20

Ecstasy by Mike Leigh; Presented by Black Door Theatre Company and Horse Trade Theater Group; Director, Sara Laudonia; Set, Damon Pelletier; Sound, Christopher Rummel; Costumes, Lore Davis; Fight Chorepgrapher, Brandon McClusky; Stage Manager, Eliza Jane; Cast: Lore Davis, Stephen Heskett, Gina Lemoine, Josh Marcantel, Brandon McClusky, Mary Monahan; January 9–25

2009 FRIGID New York Festival 3rd Annual; *Brainstorming* by Rory Rave; Presented by Rory Raven; *Coffee Dad, Chicken Mom and the Fabulous Buddha Boy* by Nick Green; Presented by Mischief and Mayhem Theatre; *The Dysfunctional Guide to Home Perfection, Marital Bliss, and Passionate Hot Room* Presented by The Dysfunctional Theatre Company; *End of the Trail* by Sean Owens, Kenny Shults; Presented by EXIT Theatre; *The Giant's Causeways* by Nora S. McLaughlin; Presented by Nora S. McLaughlin; *THE HEFNER MONOLOGUES* by John Hefner; Presented by John Hefner; *How Does A Drug Deal Become a Decent 3rd Date?* by Kelly Aija Zemnickis; Presented by Green with Envy Productions; *Now, and at the Hour* by Christian Cagigal; Presented by EXIT Theatre; *Preparation Hex* Written & performed by Bob Brader, directed and developed by Suzanne Bachner; Presented by John Montgomery Theatre Company; *On Second Though* by Paul Hutcheson; Presented by Wog Productions; *Son of Man* by Lara Torgovnik & Anna Umansky; Presented by Melted Wax Productions; February 25–March 8**The Geographical History of America** by Lindsey Hope Pearlman, adapted from the novel by Gertrude Stein; Director, Randi Rivera; Set/Lighting, Jonathan Cottle; Costumes, Frances Pezik; Cast: Julia Crockett, Phil Gasper, Lindsey Hope Pearlman, Dylan Scott; May 14–23

UNDER ST. MARKS

The Chalk Boy Written and directed by Joshua Conkel; Presented by The Management and Horse Trade Theater Group; Stage Manager, Kelsi Welter; Sound, Adam Swiderski; Cast: Mary Catherine Donnelly, Marguerite French, Jennifer Harder, Kate Huisentruit; September 4–20

Woyzeck by George Buchner; Presented by Counting Squares Theater Company and Horse Trade Theater Group; Adapted/Director, Joshua Chase Gold; Cast: Stephen F. Arnoczy, Jared Baugh, Kendra Holton, Dan Kane, Aaron Kirkpatrick, Dena Kology, Madeleine Maby, Ryan Nicholoff, Deborah Radloff, Kristin Stewart; September 23–October 29

Brew of the Dead by Patrick Storck; Presented by The Dysfunctional Theatre and Horse Trade Theater Group; Director/Sound, Justin Plowman; Graphics, J.L. Soto; Cast: Eric Chase, Tom O'Connor, Amy Overman, Peter Schuyler, Amy Beth Sherman; October 3–November 1

Pumpkin Pie Show by Clay McLeod Chapman; Cast: Clay McLeod Chapman, Hannah Cheek; October 16–November 1

Vice Girl Confidential by Todd Michael; Presented by Grayce Productions; Director, Walter J. Hoffman; Cast: Jeff Auer, Emily King Brown, Thom Brown, Courtney Cook, Matthew F. Garner, Lawrence Lesher, Zach Lombardo, Jessica Luck, Todd Michael; November 5–16

Plucking Failures Like Ripe Fruits Presented by No Tea Productions and Horse Trade Theater Group; included: *Anything For You* by Cathy Celesia; *A Day For Surprises* by John Guare; *Breaking Even* by Dan Dietz; *4 a.m. (Open All Night)* by Bob Krakower; *Miss You* by David Auburn; *Please Have A Seat and Someone Will Be With You Shortly* by Garth Wingfield; *Sure Thing* by David Ives; *1-900-Desperate* by Christopher Durang; *Here We Are* by Dorothy Parker; *Request Stop* by Harold Pinter; *Cold* by David Mamet; Director, Lindsey Moore; Stage Manager, D. Robert Wolcheck; Light/Sound Design, Timothy Mather; Cast: Alicia Barnatchez, Brooke Eddey, Sabrina Farhi, Richard Lovejoy, Jeremy Mather, Jeff Sproul; November 20–December 6

Broken Dog Legs Written and directed by Emily Conbere; Presented by Amuse Collective and Horse Trade Theater Group; Cast: Penny Pollack; Presented with *The Container*; Director, Kel Haney; *Love Letter to Odysseus*; Director, Michael Rau; *I Need You*; Director, Larissa Lury; *Shaun Boyle*; January 23–31

2009 FRIGID New York Festival 3rd Annual; *95/turnpike/95: Chickens in Jersey* by Jeff Belander & Amanda Sage Comerfor; Presented by International BTC; *BAGS: Obsessions of a Hoardaholic* Written and presented by Lee Michael Buckman; *Dalton Trumbo's Johnny Got His Gun* by Bradley Rand Smith; Presented by Ricardo Perez-Gonzalez; *Freedom 85!* by Debra Hale; Presented by Hi-D Theatre; *habeas corpus* Presented by the real kim harmon; *Hysteri-KILLY! A One Freak Show* Written and presented by Kelly B. Dwyer; *Jet of Blood or the Ball of Glass* by Antonin Artaud; Presented by No. 11 Productions; *Melting in Madras* by Wilson Loria; Presnted by Wilson Loria; *Y* by Irene Glezos; Presented by Risk Exposure; February 25–March 8

The Cody Rivers Show Written & performed by Andrew Conner & Mike Mathieu; April 9–11

Caitlin and the Swan by Dorothy Fortenberry; Director, Joshua Conkel; Choreographer, Croft Vaughn; Music, Colin Wambsgans; Sound, Adam Swiderski; Costumes, Caite Hevner; Set, Timothy McCown Reynolds; Lighting, Kelsi Welter, Joshua Conkel; Graphics, Grace Kang, Jennifer Harder; Stage Manager, Kelsi Welter; Cast: Marguerite French, Shetal Shah, Teresa Stephenson, Brian Robert Burns, Jake Aron, Elliott T. Reiland; April 16–May 2

Bigger Than I Presented by Counting Squares Thater and Horse Trade Theater Group; Director, Nick Sprysenski; Contributing Writers, Michael Barringer, Jarred Baugh, Shannon Beeby, Edward Davis, Michelle Foytek, Joshua Chase Gold, Matt Greenbaum, Ben Hope, Kurt Jenkins, Aaron Kirkpatrick, Dena Kology, Melody Kology, Ryan Nicholoff, John O'Malley, Nick Sprysenski; Artistic Director, Ryan Nicholoff; Company Manager, Dena Kology; Production Manager, Joshua Chase Gold; Multimedia, Michael Barringer, Kanrarama Gahigiri, Lighting, Jessica Burgess; Sound, Joshua Chase Gold; Choreographer, John O'Malley; Cast: Edward Davis, Matt Greenbaum, Dena Kology, Ryan Nicholoff, Chris Worley; June 4–20

Impetuous Theater Group

Artistic Director, James David Jackson; Managing Director, Josh Sherman

P.S. 66: LaScare Academy A guided tour of disgustin one-acts; Co-presented by Small Pond Entertainment; Producer, Janet Zarecor; Production Manager, Brian MacInnis Smallwood; included: *Zombie Caller* Written and directed by John Hurley; Cast: Aaron Michael Zook, Michael Mraz, Maryann Peterson, Katie Hartke; *Demon in the Machine* by Brian MacInnis Smallwood; Director, James David Jackson; Cast: Anne Peterson, Chris Bell, Laura Gilreath, Will Schmincke, Andy Chelmko; *Guidance* by August Schulenburg; Director, Isaac Butler; Cast: Polly Lee, Alexander MacDonald, Carissa Cordes, Margaret Laney, Allison Friedman, My Ghoul O'Day, Jean Goto; *Let's All Say Asinine Things* by Bekah Brunstetter; Director, Jordana Williams; Cast: Danielle Cook, Erin Maya Darke; *Mushroom, Mushroom* by Andrew Chmelko; Director, Michael Rudez; Cast: Michael Mraz, Mark Souza, Stacey Maltin, Michael Lister, Tom Patterson, Chris Hale; *Mrs. Murray's Home Economic Class* by Janet Zarecor; Director, Sarah Ali; Cast: Kira Blaskovich, Neimah Djourabchi, Nick Monroy, Seth Austin, Joe Powell, Evelyn Alberty; LaSalle Academy @ 44 E 2nd Street; October 29–November 1

47:59 Festival Fifth annual; Produced by Marielle Duke & John Hurley; Stage Manager, Sarah Locke; included: *The Blame Game* by Corey Ann Haydu & August Schulenburg; Director, Nick Monroy; Cast: Kira Blaskovich, Anna Bridgforth, Andy Chmelko, Chris Hale; *The Leech* by Joe Matthers & Janet Zarecor; Director, Meghan Formwalt; Cast: Brian MacInnis Smallwood, Mark Souza, Lindsay Wolf; *America, Or God Shed His Grace on Thee (The Fabulous True Story of How Hud and Par Got America's Groove Back)* by August Schulenburg & Johnna Adams; Director, Averia Gaskin; Cast:Felicia Hudson, Jason Paradine; *The Last Son of Darkness* by Michael Mraz & Joseph Mathers; Director, C.L Weatherstone; Cast: Nathan Faudree, James David Jackson, Joe Powell; *Murder Mystery Book Club* by Janet Zarecor & Corey Ann Haydu; Director, Josh Sherman; Cast: Neimah Djourabchi, Alex MacDonald; *Moliere's "A School For Texas Chainsaw Massacre-*

ists" by Johanna Adams & Michael Mraz; Director, Taylor Shann; Cast: Chris Bell, Joe Gallagher, Steven Todd Smith, Callen Willis; Center Stage NY; February 28–March 1

After Darwin by Timberlake Wertenbaker; Director, John Hurley; Production Manager, Brian MacInnis Smallwood; Stage Manager, Sarah Locke; Set, Rachel Smallwood; Lighting, Shaun Fillion; Costumes, Jennifer Raskopf; Cast: Jonathan Tindle, Benjamin Ellis Fine, Heather Grayson, Tarantino Smith; Access Theater; May 7–24

Interborough Repertory Theater

Executive Director/Chief Curator, Kori Rushton; Associate Curator, Ben Vershbow; Development, Stacy Donovan

What To Do When You Hate All of Your Friends by Larry Kunofsky; Director, Jacob Krueger; June 10–13

Sandy the Dandy and Charlie McGee: A Case Study in Harsh Realities by Mat Sanders and Guerrin Gardner; Presented by TooMuchery Productions; Director, Nate Dushku; June 19–August 3; Encore: February 21–May 6

Paper Dolls by Patrick Huguenin; Presented by Lively Productions and Métropole Ink; Director, Lisa Siciliano; July 14–30

Southern Promises by Thomas Bradshaw; Director, Jose Zayas; August 5–31

Excavation by Kat Lissard; Director, Gregor Paslawsky; September 8–28

The Shipment Written and directed by Young Jean Lee; September 29–October 27; Encore: December 1–January 4

A TAG of Two Cities/NoLA Rising Director, Meryl Murman; Presented by SLIGHTLYaskew; November 14–16

Hamlet Solo with Raoul

Bhaneja; Director, Robert Ross Parker; January 9–11

Great Hymn of Thanksgiving/Conversation Storm by Rick Burkhardt; Presented by The Nonsense Company; February 4–15

Heartless by Eric Sanders; Director Pat Diamond; March 16–27

Sign-Arella Music by David J. Boyd, lyrics by David J. Boyd & Bob West, book by Kori Rushton, Bob West, David J. Boyd; Director Paul Urcioli; Associate Director/American Sign Language Master, Aaron Kubey; March 26–May 17

BARTLEBY by Herman Melville; Director, Ben Vershbow; May 29–30

Jewish Theatre of New York

Artistic Director, Tuvia Tenebom; Managing Director, Isi Tenenbom

Last Jew in Europe by Tuvia Tenenbom; Director, Louis Scarpati; Set, Mark Symczak; Costumes, Elgie C. Johnson; General Manager, Isi Tenenbom; Cast: Robert Tekavec, Melissa Klein, Max Brand; Triad Theater; June 1–September 14

Mountain Jews by Tuvia Tenenbom; Director, Tuvia Tenenbom; Set, Mark Symczak; Costumes, Elige C. Johnson; General Manager, Isi Tenenbom; Cast: Greg Engbrecht, Stacy LeVine, Robert Tekaver; Triad Theater; November 9–February 1

John Montgomery Theatre Company

Suzanne Bachner, Artistic Director; Bob Brader, Executive Director

Spitting in the Face of the Devil Written & performed by Bob Brader, directed and developed by Suzanne Bachner; Lighting/Tech Director, Douglas Shearer; The Directors Studio; March 9

Judith Shakespeare Company NYC

Artistic Director/Producer, Joanne Zipay; Associate Producer, Ginny Hack

The Rape of the Lock by Paul Hagen; Presented under RESURGENCE, a new play development program; Director, Jane Titus; Choreographer, Rob O'Neill; Composer, Benjamin Ickies; Costumes/Props, Rosalynd Darling; Set/Lighting, Michelangelo Alasá, Anthony Ruiz; Fight Director, Dan O'Driscoll; PSM, Aaron Diehl; Cast: Ivanna Cullinan, Tyrone Davis Jr., John Forkner, Suzanne Hayes, Leanne Littlestone, Vanessa Morosco, Matthew Fass; Duo Theatre; September 11–28

La MaMa Experimental Theatre Club (ETC)

Founder and Director, Ellen Stewart; Fourty-seventh Season

FIRST FLOOR THEATRE

Calling: An Opera of Forgiveness Written and directed by Wickham Boyle; Composer, Douglas Geers; Music Director, Edith Hirshtal; Conductor, Hiroya Miura; Choreographer, Edisa Weeks; Set, Marty Kapell; Lighting, Burke Brown; Cast: Roland Burks, Nique Haggerty, Jesse Murray; Musicians: Jay Hassler, Edith Hirshtal, Chihiro Shibayama, Maja Cerar, William Martina, Douglas Geers; September 12–28

Journeys Monologues of courageous women around the world: Hafsat Abiola (Nigeria) by Anna Deavere Smith; Farida Azizi (Afghanistan) by Ruth Margraff; Anabella de Leon (Guatemala) by Gail Kriegel; Inez McCormack (Northern Ireland) by Carol K Mack; Mukhtaran Mai (Pakistan) by Susan Yankowitz; Mu Sochua (Cambodia) by Catherine Filloux; Marina Pisklakova-Parker (Russia) by Paula Cizmar; Director, Evan Yionoulis; Lighting, Burke Brown; Sound, Sharath Patel; Production Coordinator, Linda Marvel; Cast: Betsy Aidem, Terry Donnelly, Mercedes Herrero, Rachael Holmes, Christine Toy Johnson, Alexandra Napier, Reena Shah; October 2–19

The Father by August Strindberg; Presented by Actors Without Borders; Translation, Tullan Holmqvist; Designer/Director, Zishan Ugurlu; Music, Givanni Spinelli; Dramaturg, Jeremiah Kipp; Costumes, Oana Botez-Ban; Lighting, Lucas Kreach; Cast: Lee Gundersheimer, Tullan Holmqvist, Chris Kapp, Fletcher Liegerot, Alissa Q. Newman, Jorge Rubio, Raïna von Waldenburg; Musicians: Valerie Kuehne, Carolanne Marcantonio, Helen Yee, Mina Yim; October 30–November 9

Lilliam Yuralia by Barbara Eda Young; Director, Austin Pendleton; Cast: Barbara Eda Young, Ben Hammer, John Magaro; November 13–30

Gang of Seven by Jim Neu; Director, Keith McDermott; Music, Harry Mann; Sets David Fritz; Costumes, Meg Zeder; Cast: Mary Shultz, Tony Nunziata, Chris Maresca, John Costelloe, Byron Thomas, Kristine Lee, Jim Neu; December 4–21

Yanagai! Yanagai! by Andrea James; Presented by the Australian Aboriginal Theatre Initiative; Director, Harold Dean James & Karen Oughtred; Music, Yuko Tsuji; Lighting, Tony Mulanix; Set, Harold Dean James; Costumes, Ramona Ponce; Puppets, Spica Wobbe; Cast: Elizabeth Clark, Rashidah Bernay Fowler, Tyree Giroux, Harold Dean James, Joy Kelly, Janet Miranda, Cezar Williams; January 8–25

The Love Project by Pearl Cleage, Zaron Burnett; Director, Harriet Schiffer

Scott; Cast: Rhodessa Jones, Idris Ackamoor; January 29–February 8

The Book of Lambert by Leslie Lee; Director, Cyndy A. Marion; Sets, Andis Gjoni; Lighting, Russel Phillip Drapkin; Costumes, David B. Thompson; Incidental Music, Joe Gianono; Stage Manager, Elliot Lanes; Cast: Clinton Faulkner, Joresa Blount, Sadrina Johnson, Heather Massie, Gloria Sauve, Arthur French, Howard L. Wieder, Omrae D. Smith; February 13–March 1

Shekinah by Charles Case; Director/Design, Peter S. Case; Music, Bruno Louchouarn; Cast: Tavia Trepte, Rick Zahn, Alex Emanuel, Steven Francisco; March 6–22

Er Toshtuk Created by Virlana Tkacz of Yara Arts and Kenzhegul Satybaldieva with Kyrgyz artists and Yara Arts Group; Director, Virlana Tkacz; March 27–April 12

Fools Mass Presented by Theatre Group Dzieci; Director, Matt Mitler; April 16–19

The System Written, directed, and set design by Nic Ularu; Presented by UniArt Theatre Co.; Lighting, James Hunter; Sound, Tim Schellembaum; PSM, K. Dale White, Paul Kaufman; Cast: Richard Jennings, John Patrick Driscoll, Chuck Whetzel, Andrew Reilly, Elisabeth "EG" Heard, Patrick Kelly, Paul Kaufmann; April 24–May 10

La Mama Moves Dance Festival Curated by Nicky Parraiso & Mia Yoo; May 5–31

Blue Day Written and directed by Alessandro Corazzi, translated by Celeste Moratti; May 28–June 14

THE ANNEX

Atomic City Conceived by Jens Backvall and Jon Morris; Presented by Terra Nova; Music, Tobias Sondén & Nis Bäckvall; Dramaturgs, Mette Guldborg Hansen, Anson Mount, Christoph Schletz; Lighting/Graphics, Felix Grimm; Costumes, Lejka Sievert; Set, Christian Wassman; Cast: Jens Bäckvall (Denmark), Nis Bäckvall (Sweden), Runa Kaiser (Denmark), Jon Morris (USA), Tobias Sondén (Sweden), Karl Sørensen (Denmark) and Sayda Trujillo (Guatemala); September 11–28

Alumnight Curated by Professor Dr. Zishan Ugurlu; Featuring: Laura Waldron, Phoebe Tyers, Claire Tyers, Cruz Turcott,, Lola Brown, LaTessa Davis, Lauren Munger, O.J. Morgan, Dan Jacobson, Eva Moore, Jean Rohe, Lauren Gabriela Mendez, Amy Holson-Schwartz, Nick Delaney, Meghan Kirk, Jessy Holterman; September 22–24

Room to Panic Created by Federico Restrepo & Denise Greber; Music, Elizabeth Swados; Director/Design/Choreography, Federico Restrepo; Costumes, Denise Greber; Music Director, Kris Kukul; Cast: Federico Restrepo, Denise Greber, Cary Gant, Allison Hiroto, Sara Galassini, Emily Vick, Linwood Young, Joah Gonzales, Kat Yew and Dmitry Chepovetsky; Musicians: Yukio Tsuji, Heather Paauwe, Jon Sapino; October 3–19

The Tibetan Book of the Dead by Jean Claude van Itallie; Presented by Shantigar in association with Pilgrim Theatre (Poland); Director, Kim Mancuso; Music, John VanEps & Steve Gorn; Costumes, Patricia Spees; Cast: Kermit Dunkelberg, Susan Thompson, Court Dorsey; October 27

APPAN Festival Asia-Pacific Performing Arts Network International Festival & Symposium; Artistic Director, SunOck Lee; November 8–9

Theatre of Death Screenings of and theatre of Tadeusz Kantor; November 10–16

Godot Written and performed by Sin Cha Hong; November 20–30

February Double-bill: *Little Island* Written & performed by Lee Sheer, and *One Day* by Lee Sher and Saar Harari, performed by Jye-Hwe Lin, Hsin-Yi Hsiang; Presented by LeeSaar The Company; Lighting, Joe Lavasseur; December 4–14

Mama, A Modern Folktale Created and choreographed by Mary Seidman; Composer, Cristina Spinei; Costumes, Karen Young; Set, Barbara Marks; Cast: Mary Seidman, Amy Pivar, Janis Brenner, Robin Becker, Amy Marshall, Elisa King,

Lisa Viola, Laura Bradley, Katie Dorn, Elinor Harrison, Tomomi Imai, Jolie Manza, Heidi Turzyn and Jessica Wontropski; December 18–21

Still the River Flows: Celebrations of Winter Ritual from the Carpatians Featuring artists from Kryvorivnia in the Carpathian Mountains of Eastern Europe; December 26–28

Vocal Migrations Composed by Tareke Ortiz, featuring artists from Mexico; January 2–11

Dust/Ceslestial Excursions/Made Out of Concrete Three operas written and directed by Robert Ashley; Set/Lighting, David Moodey; Sound, Cas Boumans; Cast: Robert Ashley, Sam Ashley, Thomas Buckner, Tom Hamilton, Jacqueline Humbert, Joan La Barbara, Joan Jonas, "Blue" Gene Tyranny; January 15–25

Hamlet by William Shakespeare; Director/Choreography, Kenji Kawarasaki; Presented by Company EAST (Japan); Lighting, Jin Nakayama; Video, Yoshiaki Takano; Production Manager, Yoshifumi Seo; Cast: Hiroshi Jin, Sho Tohno, Yoko Tomabechi, Yuji Koide, Barnardo, Mutsutaka Jin, Daisuke Kaji; January 29–February 8

Cotton Club Benefit Featuring Idris Ackamoor, Bemshi Shearer, Sheila Dabney, Keith David, André De Shields, Cary Gant, Joyce Griffin, Rhodessa Jones, Michael Lynch; February 3

Shadow: A Festival of Playreading Curated and directed by George Ferencz; included: *The Green Book* by Calvin Alexander Ramsey; Cast: Taeonna Ancrum, Spencer Cohen, Sheila Dabney, Cary Gant, Harry Mann, John–Andrew Morrison, Erwin E. A. Thomas; *Palmetto* by Holli Harms; Cast: Rance Luce Benson, Milan Conner, Helen Coxe, Maria Gabriele, Russell Jordan, Sharon McGruder, Valois Mickens, Nkosi Nkululeko, Alexis Slade, James Ware; *It Matters Where You're Buried* by Beth Campbell; Cast: ee Beebout,Sheila Dabney, Matthew Wrather; *The Hatians (How They Got That Way)* by Owa; Cast: Alex Alioto, Joane Cajuste, Cary Gant, John Andrew Morrison, Erwin E.A.Thomas, Jenne Vath, Chris Zorker; February 12–15

Coming, Aphrodite! Written and directed by Mary Fulham; Presented by Watson Arts Project; Sound, Tim Schellenbaum; Costumes, Ramona Ponce; Sets, Jim Boutin; Lighting, Alex Bartinieff; Choreographer, Heidi Latsky; Puppetry, Spica Wobbe; Lyrics, Paul Foglino; Stage Manager, Sarah Rae Murphy; Cast: Anne Gaynor, Greg Henits, Liz Kimball, Clayton Dean Smith; February 20–March 8

The Priest and the Clown by Sandro Gindro, adapted and directed by Daniela Morelli; Presented in association with the Italian Cultural Institute; Composer, Maurizio Camardi; Keyboards, Alfonso Santimone; Cast: David Sabasti; February 23

Baghdadi Bath by Jawad al-Assadi, translated by Robert Myers & Nada Saab; Director/Design, Zishan Ugurlu; Dramaturg, Jeremiah Kipp, Lighting, Garin Marschall; Sound, Tim Schellenbaum; Production Manager, Kaan Nazli; Stage Manager, Khodor Zaidan; Cast: Mohammad Jamil Dagman, Danny Boushebel, Charlotte Brathwaite, Abby French, Kate Hopkins; March 12–15

Haggadah Created and presented by Witness Relocation; Director/Choreography, Dan Safer; Set/Lighting Jay Ryan; Sound, Ryan Maeker; Video/Projections, Kaz Phillips; Costumes, Deb O.; Dramaturg, Yoni Oppenheim; Cast: Abigail Browde, Heather Christian, Sean Donovan, Mike Mikos, Wil Petre, Sam Pinkleton, Orion Taraban, Laura Berlin Stinger; March 20–29

Hear Me With The Eyes Created by Maria Elena Anaya & Jorge Chanona; April 2–12

La Mama Moves Dance Festival Curated by Nicky Parraiso & Mia Yoo; May 5–31

Asclepius Conceived, written, composed, and directed by Ellen Stewart; Co-presented by Great Jones Company; Additional Music, Michael Sirotta, Yukio Tsuji, Heather Paauwe; Choreography/Lighting, Federico Restrepo; Puppets, Theodora Skipitares; Cast: George Drance, Cary Gant, Denise Greber, Allison Hiroto, Onni Johnson, Michael Lynch, Benjamin Marcantoni, Matt Nasser, Prisca

Ouya, Eugene the Poogene, Frederico Restrepo, Valois, Meredith Wright, Perry Yung, Kat Yew May 28–June 14

Luzimbu Text, direction, costumes, and choreography by Prisca Ouya & Benjamin Marcantoni, music by Richard Cohen, Benjamin Marcantoni, Yukio Tsuji; Co-choreography, Gervais Tomadiatunga; Prince Dethmer Nzaba, Lungusu Malonga, Potri Ranka Manis; Cast: Nasiba Abdul-Karim, Tommy Agarwal, Nia Austin-Edwards, Inderia Carr, Sheila Dabney, Alexis Doster-Pennerman, Angela K. Harmon, Aïda Issaka, Lungusu Malonga, Benjamin Marcantoni, Valois Mickens, Allon Morgan, Rachida N'Gouamba, Deadra Renne Nelson Mason, Nayel Amira Nelson-Young, Prisca Ouya, Chaney Pollard, Tiffany Rose, Fitz Sam, Rohiatou Siby, N'tifafa Akoko Tete-Rosenthal, Jojo Tosin, Kat Yew; June 18–28

THE CLUB

Ko'olau Based on a true story of Kauai, Hawaii; Director/Design, Tom Lee; Music, Yukio Tsuji & Bill Ruyle; Costumes, Kanako Hiyama; Projections, Miranda Hardy & Tom Lee; Puppeteers: Matt Acheson, Marina Celander, Frankie Cordero, Takemi Kitamura, Yoko Myoi; September 18–October 5

Tongues and Hearts Written & performed by Woof Nova, Temple Crocker, Annie Kunjappy, Daniel Nelson, Curated by Morgan von Prelle Pecelli; October 10–19

The Doll Sisters (Ningyo Shimai) by Taeko Tomioka; Director/Designer, Setsu Asakura; Lighting, Ikuo Murobushi; Sound, Shoji Harashima; Choroegraphy/Assistant Director, Kikushiro Onoe; PSM, Jun Matsuno; Company Manager, Misa Hayashi; Stage Manager, Keiko Watanabe; Cast: Kazuko Yoshiyuki, Mieko Yuki, Jun Tanaka, Kikukata Onoe, Kikushiro Onoe; October 23–November 2

Ecstasy and the Ice Queen Written & performed by Justine Moore, developed and directed by Frederick Johntz; October 24–November 2

Neal Medlyn Rises Again!!! Conceived and performed by Neal Medlyn; With: Jim Andralis, Bridget Everett, Larry Krone, Kenny Mellman; October 27

ISBA Conceived and performed by Lanny Harrison; November 8–16

Ms. Green-Assisted Suicide Written & performed by Ryan Green; Director, Michael Cherry; Piano, Matthew Fetbrandt; November 14–15

Pink Bones Written & performed by Ulrich Fladl, Jose Sanchez, Guanani Cubana; November 21–23

New Indigenous Voices 2008: Indigenous Theatre from Aotearoa (New Zealand) Readings and discussions of plays by Makerita Urale and Victor Rodger; Presented gby Australian Aboriginal Theatre Initiative; Cast: Nancy Brunning, Robbie Magasiva, Anapela Polataivao; November 24–26

The Bad Hostess by Linda Simpson; Director, Julie Atlas Muz; Cast: Linda Simpson, Justin Christopher, Flloyd, Erin Markey, Chris Tanner; December 5–14

Christmas in Nickyland hosted and curated by Nicky Paraiso; Performances by Little Annie, Julie Atlas Muz, Joseph Keckler, The Venn Diagrams, Ellen Fisher, Chris Tanner & Lance Cruce, Rico Noguchi, Edgar Oliver, The Dyke Division of Theater of a Two-Headed Calf, Simon Miller, Split Britches (Peggy Shaw and Lois Weaver), Heather Christian with Chris Giarmo & Sasha Brown; December 19–21

Room for Cream Season One: The Box Set by Jess Barbagallo, Laryssa Husiak, Brooke O'Harra, Brendan Connelly, Laura Berlin Stinger; Presented in association with the Dyke Division of Theater of a Two-Headed Calf; Director, Brooke O'Harra; Eleven episodes of a dramatic serial play; January 22–February 8

Nostalgia Isn't What It Used To Be Presented in association with the Dyke Division of Theater of a Two-Headed Calf; Co-programmed by Brooke O'Harra & Sharon Hayes; Performances by: John Jesurun, Wu Ingrid Sang, The Nonsense Theater, Barabara Lanciers, Rachel Mason, Keegan Monaghan & Nik Gelormino, Ken Okiishi, Marcelle Meyer, Nick Mauss, Tara Mateik, Dropsy Dousman, Michael O'Neill, Novice Thoery, Lucy Sexton; 3 evenings of theatre and performance; February 13–15

Human Jukebox Written & performed by Josephe Keckler; Director, Elizabeth

Gimbel; February 20–March 8

Tonight: Lola Blau Written and composed by Georg Kreisler, English version by Don White; Director, Dick Top; Music Director, Joe Völker; Cast: Anna Krämer; March 13–22

Wilt Chamberlin's Kids Written & performed by Craig Blair, Maggie Champagne, Leslie Meisel, Freddy Sheffield; March 27–28

The Full Lucy Moon Show: A Night of April Fools Merriment Co-hosted by Lucy Sexton & Tom Murrin; Guests: Mike Iveson, Salley May, Gina Vetro, Edgar Oliver, Nature Theater of Oklahoma, Nick Woodeson; April 3–5

The Magic Show: The Story of the Barefoot Angels Written & performed by Abigail Nessen Bengson; Director, David Eppel; Live Music, Shaun McClain Bengson; April 10–19

White Elephant Written & directed by Lake Simons & John Dyer; Cast: Lake Simons, Erin Orr, Luis Tentindo, Yolo Myoi, John Dyer; April 24–May 3

La Mama Moves Dance Festival Curated by Nicky Parraiso & Mia Yoo; May 5–31

Beneath The Waves Presented by the Pan-Art Collective; May 8–10

The Poet and the Lamberjack Written and directed by Mike Gorman; June 17

The Living Theatre

Founder, Judith Malina

Eureka! by Judith Malina & Hanon Reznikov; Director, Judith Malina; Score, Patrick Grant; Set/Lighting, Gary Brackett; Choreography, Gene Ardor; Cast: Anthony Sisco, Silas Inches, Gene Ardor, Yasemin Ozumerzifon, Eric Olson, Maia Larraz, Erin Downhour, Natalie De Campo, Kennedy Yanko, Enoch Wu, Katherine Nook, Isaac Scranton, Eitan Brigantonelli; October 1–November 9

Looking Glass Theatre

Artistic Director, Justine Lambert; Managing Director, Jenn Boehm

Adventures of the Puppet Princess Written and directed by Jennifer Goodlander; October 18–November 23

The Spanish Wives by Max Giffith Pix, re-invented and directed by Aliza Shane; October 30–November 23

Plan B The Musical by Daniel Mitura, music by Rebecca Greenstein; Director, Natalie Glick; Cast: Haley Greenstein, Jeff Julian, Gloria Makino, Bryan Plofksy; January 23–February 7

Anna's Perfect Party and **The Amazing Magician's Marvelous Mistake** by Karin Diann Williams; Director, Nikki Rothenberg; Set, Peter Martino; Lighting, David Monroy; Costumes, Kate R. Mincer; Sound, Gregory Jacobs-Roseman; Cast: Kurt Bantilan, Diann Gogerty, Sara Guarnieri, Alex Headquist, Melissa Malone, Jamey Nicholas; February 21–April 5

NON-RESIDENT PRODUCTIONS

Just Shut Up and Smile Written & performed by Simona Berman; Director, Diana Basmajian; Costumes, Catherine Fisher; Stage Manager, Mikey Denis; Lighting, David Monroy; Press, Katie Rosin; March 16–April 3

Manhattan Repertory Theatre

Artistic Director, Ken Wolf

Summerfest 2008 Included: *Dove For Sale* by Kelly Diegnan; *Sharp Enough* by Chris Arnau; *Shy* by Ken Wolf; *Basic Training* by Daniel Landon; *Sweet Love, Sweet Lines, Sweet Life* by William Shakespeare; *The Dark Land of the Sun* by Paul Hufker; *The Misadventures of Julia Child* by Michelle Ramoni; *Chance* by Brian Patrick; *Pieces* by Angel Dillemuth; *Last Night* by Carolynne Gallo; *The Poop Show* by Margie Suvalle; *Holding Out* by Craig Durante; *Tinseltown Revue and Pump Up The Evil* by Elizabeth Gilliland; *The Callback* by Robert C. Buster Jr; *Love & Other Natural Disasters* by Karen B. Song; *The Housewarming* by Brody Lipton; *Loving Cassie* by Beth Derochea; *True or False: A Collage of the Subdivisions Within Love and Beauty* by Kat Ochsner; July 11–August 15

The Fall Play Festival 2008 Included: *birthday* by Helene Macaulay; *Something More Than This* by La'Chris Jordan; *The Threadbare Sex* by Naomi McDougall Jones & Mia Romero; *Everybody Dies* by Molly Rytzel; *Suicide Love* by Joseph Lizardi; *Charged: America, Land of the Pre-Approved* by Jennifer Ostrega; *Live Broadcast* by John William Schiffbauer; *Couples Counseling* by Carey Lovelace; *Good Sister Aeddy* by Aileen Kilburn; *Knowing Women* by Suzanne Logan; *Hell for the Company* by Michael Cusuanuko; *Unthymely* by Lynda Green; *36 24 36* by Naomi McDougal Jones, Candice Holdorf, Ann Malinowsky, Erin O'Connell, Danielle Tafeen, Stephanie Schweitzer, & James Sargent; *Jesus Freaks* by David Sirk; *Space* by Bekah Brunstetter; *The Bauble That Bought Manhattan* by Lise Johnson; *The 385-Pound Smoker* by Paul Cohen; *What Work Is* based on the poems of Philip Levine; September 10–December 12

Men by Ken Wolf; September 10–December 12

Romeo & Juliet by William Shakespeare; Presented in association with Bareshakespeare; Director, Angela Milton; December 6–14

Antigone by Jean Anouilh; Director, Rose Ginsberg; December 7–10

The People In My Hips Written and directed by Ken Wolf; January 17–February 7; Encored: April 4–18

Winterfest 2008 Included: *The People in My Hips* by Ken Wolf; *We Carry On* by Danny Mitarotondo; Director, Daniel Darwin; *The Spitting Image* by Sophie Klein; *The Hyenas Got It Down* Written & performed by Daniel Damiano; *Strange Bedfollows* by Lena Cigleris; *Chances Lose* by Alden Caple; *In Face* by E. Dale Smith; *DNA Dating* by David Sirk; *Spoiled Cherries* by Hollie Rosenberg; *By Love and Art Scarred* by John Lisbonwood; *Bad Fish* by Brianne Hogan; *Moony Mercury* by Tyler Ham Pong; *What Would Frankie S. Do?* by Dan Burkarth; *Yoga Nut* Written & performed by Jessica Bonnema; *One in Eight* by Peggy Baseman; *My Williamsburg Neighbor Downstairs* by Adam Harlan; *Mommy Made a Monster* by Josiah Indivisible; *Therapy R Us* by Adrienne Forah; *Craig the Unmusical* by Justin T. Klose; *The Uninvited Guest* by Victoria Kelleigh; *Joan 3:16* by Megan Sass; *Book* by Rudy Cecera; *Look After You* by Louise Flory; *The Odyssey of Teddy Einstein* by John Lisbon Wood; *The Confession* by Anthony M. Laura; *Bitter Crop* by Carston Turner; *Exile* by Lindsey Ferrentino; February 28–April 17

The New York Amazing Play Festival Included: *Blood* by Matt Williams; *King of the Mountain* by Tom Decker; *Through The Minds of Three* by Joseph Lizardi; *Hold Up At The Continental Garage* by Lori Marra; *Aesop Icarus* by Sean Kelly; *Monday* by Gloria Williams; *New Beulah* by Dan Moyer; *Crazy Girls* by Jennifer Bantelman; *The Nebula of Georgia* by Joe Nierle; *his name is edgar* by Amy E. Witting; April 22–June 1

Manhattan Theatre Source

The Seven Sins of a Body-Hating Food-Lover by Cassandra Hume; June 4–14

Sherlock and John by Nick Damici; June 4–14

Writers' Forum Readings Included (June 7): *"3pm,"* by Elizabeth Urello; *A Part/Belgian Waffling* by David Caudle; *First Communion* by Bill McMahon; *Donde Esta Pedro Mano?* by Montserrat Mendez; (June 14): *What We Planned For* by Jen Thatcher; *Empty Room* by John Watts; *Peace Be With You* by Wendy Allegaert; *Hush Little Baby* by Montserrat Mendez

O Happy Three Short plays, included: *Abkhazia God Bless You, Return of the King, & Tribes of Maronii* by Ed Malin; *Reunion* by Maria Micheles; *Cow City* by Peter Dizozza; PSM, Jane Shufer; Cast: Alaina Hammond, Mike Allen Hill, Elizabeth Ingber, John Andrew Morrison, Deborah T, Jenne Vath, Ted Williams, Chris Zorker; August 17–19

HomoGenius Festival by various authors; June 23–28

Guardians by Peter Morris; Director, Joseph Giardina; Stage Manager, Stephanie Giardina; Lighting, Alex Casagrande; Cast: Zack Abramowitz, Meryl Sykes. July 2–5

All the Rage by Keith Reddin; Director, Daryl Boling; Set, Travis McHale; Lighting, Kia Rogers; Costumes, Kathleen Leary; Sound, Andrew Bellware; Fight Choreographer, Carrie Brewer; Stage Manager, Ben Sulzbach; Cast: Greg Stuhr, Anne Bobby, Steve Deighan, Benjamin Jaeger-Thomas, Rich Fromm, Medina Senghore, Laura Schwenninger, Ryan Michael Jones, Jeffrey Plunkett, Peter Reznikoff; July 30–August 23

Writers' Forum Reading by L. Pontius, Vinnie Marano, Paul Jordan, Manny Igrejas; September 6

Estrogenius 2008 by various writers; October 1–November 1

In-Genius Festival works from the Writer's Forum; Written by various writers; January

Universal Robots by Mac Rogers; Director, Rosemary Andress; Set, Raul Abrego; Costumes, Nicky J. Smith; Lighting, Kia Rogers; Sound, len DeNio; Stage Manager, Dana Rossi; Cast: Esther Barlow, Jason Howard, David Ian Lee, David Lamberton, Michelle O'Connor, Ridley Parson, Nancy Sirianni, Tarantino Smith, Ben Sulzbach, Jennifer Gordon Thomas; February 12–March 7

Roses on the Rocks by Ellen Boscov; Director, Richard Caliban; Cast: Rachel Jones, Laura Montes, Scott Sowers, Fulvia Vergel, Edward T. Morris; Set, Carly Hirschberg; Costumes, Kia Rogers; Stage Manager, Paige van den Burg; June 6–27

PLAYGROUND DEVELOPMENT SERIES CO-PRODUCTIONS

Sleeper by David Ian Lee; Produced by Small Pond Entertainment; Stage Manager, Sandy Yaklin; Lighting Design, Ben Sulzbach; Cast: Micah Chartrand, David Dartley, Jason Griffith, Emily Hagburg, David Ian Lee, L. Jay Meyer, Karen Sternberg, Craig Lee Thomas, Kristen Vaughan; July 20–22, August 3–5

Nightingales by Lauren Johnson; Director, Francis Badia; Lighting/Sound, Anthony Galaska; Cast: Giancarlo D'Elia, Charlotte Hampden, Lauren Johnson, Dara Kramer, Kevin Maguire, Liza Mulvenna; August 10–12

Spontaneous Combustion by Blair Fell, Les Hunter, David Ian Lee, Ed Malin, Bill McMahon, Brian Otano, Mark J. Williams; Stage Manager, Montserrat Mendez; Cast: Jenee Bandler, James Edward Becton, Laura Cook, Cassandra Cruz, Nicolas Flower, Angela Funk, Helene Galek, Alaina Hammond, Dong-Eun Lee, Montserrat Mendez, Deniele Ramos-Cloutier, Eva Rosa, Lara Yaz; June 8–10

Mid-Twenites March 1–3

The Way Out by Timothy Nolan; Director, Vincent Marano; Cast: Shiek Mahmud-Bey; March 15–17

Yellow Wallpaper Adapted by Greg Oliver Bodine; Director, DeLisa M. White; Costumes, Jeanette Aultz Look; Lighting, Lauren Parrish; Stage Manager, Laura Schlachtmeyer; Cast: Annalisa Loeffler; March 23–24

BritBrits5: *Keeping Annabelle* by Rachel Welch; Director, Camilla Maxwell; *The Homecoming* by Denise de Bergerac; Director, Paula D'Alessandris; *The*

Last Thirteen Minutes of Your Life by Rachel Barnett; Director, Stephanie Staes; *I Heart Animals* by Camilla Maxwell; Director, Amir Arison; *Kitchen Sink Drama* by Andrew Bliss; Director, Jenny Sterlin; *Volcano* by Declan Feenan; Director, Paula D'Alessandris; *Daft in Death* by Kraig Smith; Director, Paula D'Alessandris; *The Well* by Richard Manton-Hollis; Director, Paula D'Alessandris; *Apple Pie* by Richard Gawthorne; Director, Paula D'Alessandris. April 26–May 5

Femme Feast: Butoh Dance Included: *Turn*; Choreographer, Stacey Lynn Smith; *Connecticut* by Bekah Brunstetter; Director, Michelle Bossy; *Senses* Written & directed by Lara Gold; *Truth or Dare* by Laconia Koerner; Director, Katie Carter; *Panda* by Lisa Ebersole; Director, Michelle Bossy; *Monster's Ball* by Laura Rohrman; Director, Michelle Pace; May 10–12

NON-RESIDENT PRODUCTIONS

The Reckoning of Kit & Little Boots by Nat Cassidy; **Hope's Arbor** by Rich Espey; Produced by Neal J. Freeman & Anna Olivia Moore for The Gallery Players/Engine37; June 17–21

Unexpressed: The Heart and Songs of John Bucchino Music and lyrics, John Bucchino; Produced by 11th Hour Theatre Co.; July 9–12

Sleeper by David Ian Lee; Produced by Small Pond Entertainment; Stage Manager, Sandy Yaklin; Lighting, Ben Sulzbac; Cast: Micah Chartrand, David Dartley, Jason Griffith, Emily Hagburg, David Ian Lee, L. Jay Meyer, Karen Sternberg, Craig Lee Thomas, Kristen Vaughan; July 20–22, August 3–5

La Vigilia by Vinne Marano; Produced by BOO Arts; September 3–20

Angels in the Architecture by Michelle Nordella, Benjamin Newman; Produced by Daring Boys Jump & Trial by Fire TheatreWorks; September 24–27

The Most Damaging Wound by Blair Singer; Produced by Australian American; November 6–29

How to Find Your Inner Asian by Nancy Kim; Produced by Rising Circle Theater Collective; December 3–6

It's a Wonderful (One Man Show) Life Written and produced by Sharon Fogarty; Cast, Jason Grossman; December 8–21

A Christmas Carol by Charels Dickens, adapted & produced by Greg Oliver Bodine; December 9–11

OFF-White Christmas Written and produced by Julie Perkins; Lighting, Alex Moore; Stage Manager, Montserrat Mendez; Choreographer, Liat Perelman; Cast: Lian Alweiss, Margaret Ann Brady, Matthew Johnson, Barbara Mundy, Julie Perkins, Deb Poppel, Mario Soto, Jennifer Valentine; December 13–21

St. Ignatius First Annual Hannukah Pageant Lyrics and direction by Jordana Williams, music by Sean Williams; Produced by Mac Rogers; Stage Manager, Montserrat Mendez; Choreographer, Jordana Williams, Sean Williams, Christopher F. Davis; Props, Sandy Yaklin; Cast: Amy Heidt, Robert Hoyt, Laura Liz Perloe, Seth Shelden, Byron St. Cyr; December 15–22

Witch Christmas! Written and produced by Sharon Fogarty December 17–28

On the Night of Anthony's 30th Birthday Party, Again by L. Pontius; Produced by Whirled Peas Productions; Director, Megan Demarest; Set, Jr. Jason Bolen; Costumes, Carly Hirschberg; Lighting, Drew Vanderburg; Sound, len DeNio; Stage Manager, Danielle Newell; Cast: Andrew Glaszek, Kate Grande, Tyler Hollinger, Stephanie Lovell, Synge Maher, Brandon Potter, Tom Everett Russell, Carsey Walker; March 11–28

Mrs. Warren's Profession by George Bernard Shaw; Director, Kathleen O'Neill; Costumes, David Withrow; Stage Manager, Dana Rossi; Set, Ben Schulzbach; Lighting, Dan Gallagher; Sound, Lisa len DeNio; Cast: Joy Franz, David Palmer Brown, Ashton Crosby, James Dutton, Joseph Franchini, Caralyn Kozolowski; April 1–18

Cathedral Written and directec by Joe Pintauro; Produced by Hudson Film Group; Stage Mangaer, Carol A. Sullivan; Lighting, Jason Jeunnette; Costumes,

Jenny D. Green; Props, Shayne Dutkiewicz; Sound, Ien DeNio; Cast: Jon Ecklund, Tom Godfrey, Vincent Marano, Kate Middleton, Cary Woodworth; April 22–May 16

My Expatriate Written and directed by Bill C. Davis; Produced by MAN underdog LLC.; Lighting, Josh Bradford; Sound, Daniel Kluger; Set, Craig Napoliello; Costumes, Herb Ouellette; Stage Manager, Ian Wehrle; Cast: Tandy Cronyn, Brad Fraizer, Jefferson Slinkard; May 20–May 30

The Medicine Show Theatre Ensemble

Artistic Director, Barbara Vann

Pleasures of Peace Conceived and directed by Barbara Van, writings by Louisa May Alcott, John Gruen, E.Y. "Yip" Harburg, Howard Pflanzer, David Nugent, Oscar Wilde and Susan Yankowitz; Music, Yael Acher, David Finkelstein, Lenny Hat, Rob Voisy; Set/Costumes, Uta Bekaia; Stage Manager, Richard Keyser; Cast: Molly C. Blau, Paul Daniel Cloeter, Mark J. Dempsey, Felix E. Gardon, Jason Alan Griffin, Beth Griffith, Ashley Anne Harrell, Nina Karacosta, Ward Nixon, Andrei Robakov, Peter Tedeschi, Alex Martinez Wallace, Ann Marie Yoo; June 12–28

Mr. Shakespeare & Mr. Porter, Vol. 1: Hamlet, MacBeth & A Midsummer Night's Dream Book by William Shakespeare, music by Cole Porter; Director/Concept, Barbara Vann; *Midsummer* Director, Alexis Hadsall; Music Director, Jake Lloyd; Arrangements, Yael Acher; Choreographer, Peter Schmitz; Costumes, Uta Bekaia; Set/Lighting, Jospeh T. Barna; Stage Manager, Richard Keyser, Sika Rautenberg; Cast: Robert Berliner, Molly C. Blau, Mercer Boffey, Oliver Conant, Mark Gering, Rachel Grundy, Cedric Jones, Richard Keyser, Eva Nicole, Vince Phillip, Sika Rautenberg, Celine Rosenthal, Charles J. Roby, Peter Tedeschi, Barbara Vann, Patrick Wickham, Lindsay Kitt Wiebe; November 13–December 5

Mr. Shakespeare & Mr. Porter, Vol. II: Richard III, Measure for Measure & A Midsummer Night's Dream Book by William Shakespeare, music by Cole Porter; Director/Concept, Barbara Vann; *Midsummer* Director, Alexis Hadsall; Music Director, Jake Lloyd; Arrangements, Yael Acher; Choreographer, Peter Schmitz; Costumes, Uta Bekaia; Set/Lighting, Jospeh T. Barna; Stage Manager, Richard Keyser, Sika Rautenberg; Cast: Robert Berliner, Molly C. Blau, Mercer Boffey, Oliver Conant, Mark Gering, Rachel Grundy, Cedric Jones, Richard Keyser, Eva Nicole, Vince Phillip, Sika Rautenberg, Celine Rosenthal, Charles J. Roby, Peter Tedeschi, Barbara Vann, Patrick Wickham, Lindsay Kitt Wiebe; December 6–21

Double Feature Two one-act plays by John Gruen: *I Want To Live* directed by Barbara Vann; Costumes/Set, Uta Bekaia; Choreographer, Jaime Galindo; Lighting, Richard Keyser; Cast: Peter Judd, Chavez Ravine, Alex Martinez Wallace, Vivien Landau, Ron Faber; *Mother Loves Her Boys* directed by Mark Canistraro; Set, Carl Tallent; Set Décor/Costumes, Uta Bekaia; Choreographer, Jaime Galindo; Lighting, Richard Keyser; Cast: Barbara Vann, Mark J. Dempsey, Fabio Taliercio, Peter Tedeschi, Daniela Amini, Alex Martinez Wallace, Renee Hermiz; March 21–April 29

Living With History: Camus, Sartre, De Beauvoir by Howard Pflanzer; Director, Barbara Vann; Cast, Mark Gering, Mike Lesser, Suzanne Lynch, Candice Fortin, Kip Potharas, Oliver Conant, Danielle Carter, Nina Karacosta, Richard Keyser; May 5–6

Mergatroyd Productions

Nancy G. McClernan, Founder and Director

Ten Minute Playfest Twenty 10-minute play readings by Ian August, Steven Bergman, Tom Bruett, Ann Farthing, Jonathan A. Goldberg, Claudia Haas, Janis Bulter Holm, Michael Jalbert, Sara Ilyse Jacobson, Jonathan Kravetz, N. G. McClernan, Sem Megson, Henry Meyerson, Milo Mowery, J.L. Osborne, Myra Slotnick, Walter Thinnes, Edward Versailles, Jonathan Wallace, Kathleen Warnock; Director, N.G. McClernan; Stage Manager, Debra Stunich; Cast: Jonathan Alexandratos, Lynsey Buckelew, Ann Farthing, Carl Conway Maguire, Halley Mayo, Mike Selkirk; Penny Templeton Studio; November 15–16

Stress and the City Eight short plays by N.G. McClernan; included: *Fox Force Five, Personal Jesus, Pooh Story, Stage Diving, The B Word, Mr. Black, Happily Married, The Helicopter*; Director, N. G. McClernan; Stage Manager, Jason Styres; Cast: Bruce Barton, Lynsey Buckelew, Ann Farthing, Nick Fondulis, Lori Kee, Mike Selkirk, Phoebe Summersquash; Penny Templeton Studio; January 24–February 8

Metropolitan Playhouse

Artistic Director, Alex Roe

East Village Chronicles, Volume 5 Eight short new plays; included: *Famine Church* by Michael Bettencourt, Elfin Vogel; *M21/Bellevue* by George Holets; *South Delancey* by David Parr; *The Pickle Lady* by Sharon Rothstein; *McGurk's "Suicide Hall" Saloon* by Dan Evans; *Tracking Gertrude Tredwell* by Jackob G. Hofmann; *East Sixth Street, between First and Second* by Debargo Sanyal; *All Good Cretins Go To Heaven* by Kathleen Warnock; Directors, Melissa Maxwell & Michael Hardart; Stage Manager, Brian Taylor; Lighting, Maryvel Bergen; Cast: Lyndsay Becker, William Cefalo, David Eiduks, Amy Fulgham, Scott Glascock, Chris Harcum, Paul Hufker, Carrie Heitman, Jenny Greeman, Bill Mootos, Joel Nagle, Anita Sabherwal, Brian Seibert; June 5–22

Alphabet City V Six solo-performance pieces Written & performed by Lisa Barnes, Katherine Renée Cortez, Tim Cusack, Sylvia Roldan Dohi, Jared Houseman, Jane O'Leary, Patrick James Lynch, Danielle Quisenberry, Abraham Sparrow; Director, Derek Jamison; August 13–24

Nowadays by George Middleton; Director, Alex Roe; Stage Manager, Tesfaye Hamanot; Costumes, Sidney Fortner; Lighting, Joyce Liao; Cast: Frank Anderson, Linda Blackstock, Jamie Dunn, Michael Hardart, Amanda Jones, Lisa Riegel, George Taylor, Matthew Trumbull. September 27–October 26

Anna Christie by Eugene O'Neill; Director, Robert Z. Kalfin; Stage Manager, Nathan Brauner; Sets, Michael Anania; Costumes, Rebecca J. Bernstein; Lighting, Paul Hudson; Composer/Sound, Margaret Pine; Cast: Joe Atack, Roger Clark, Nick Delany, Ian Campbell Dunn, Zachary Spicer, Rob Sulaver, Sam Tsoutsouvas, Jenne Vath, Karen Christie-Ward; November 14–December 14

Power by Arthur Arent; Director, Mark Harborth; Stage Manager, Valentine Amartey; Costumes, Sidney Fortner; Lighting, Maryvel Bergen; Cast: Eric C. Bailey, Scott Casper, Sidney Fortner, Alfred Gingold, Jenny Greeman, Michael Hardart, Rafael Jordan, Toya Nash, Jason Szamreta; March 14–April 12

It Pays to Advertise by Roi Cooper Megrue; Walter C. Hackett; Director, Michael Hardart; Stage Manager, Jack Lynch; Set, Heather Wolensky; Costumes, Rebecca Lustig; Lighting, Maryvel Bergen; Cast: Brian Cooper, Aaron Gaines, George C. Hosmer, Scott Kerns, Robert Leeds, Sarah Levine, Nalina Mann, Maire Rose-Pike; May 2–31

NON-RESIDENT PRODUCTIONS

Adventure Theater by Kenn Adams; Presented by Freestyle Repertory Theater; Cast: Laura Livingston, Will Cefalo; November 29–December 7

Melvillapalooza Ten new plays and readings hosted by Metropolitan Playhouse; included: *The Archangel* by Dan Evans; Presented by LuLu LoLo Productions; *Billy Budd* by Scott Barrow; *Ishmael and Ahab Mon Amour* by Michael Bettencourt; *Mr. Melville's Playhouse* by David Lally; *The Composition of Herman Melville (abridged)* by Rick Mitchell, Max Kinberg; *Cock-a Doodle-Doo!* by Danny Ashkenazi, presented by Frederick Byers; *Melvilliana, A Suite of Poems* Written & performed by Angela Alaimo O'Donnell; *The First Lowering* by Laura Livingston; *William Bell* by Alejandro Morales, presented by Packawallop Productions; Reading: *A Tanglewood Tale* by Juliane Hiam; January 12–January 25

Festival of the Vegetables Verse and music by Michael Kosch; Choreography, Rachael Kosch; Costumes, Rachael Kosch; Lighting, Maryvel Bergen; Cast: Alison Cook Beatty, Preston Burger, Diego Carvajal, Janna Diamond, Billy Dutton, Hope (Hao-Lun) Kuei, Alessandra Larson, Xisco "Coco" Monroe, Lily Eugenia Rudd, Joy Voelker; January 31–February 15

Cosmic Brew! Written and composed by Sylvie Degiez; Lighting, Morana Stipisic; Cast: Andrew Bell, Cathy Petignat; May 16–May 24

Midtown International Theatre Festival

Ninth annual; Founder and Executive Producer, John Chatterton; July 14–August 3, 2008; performances at the WorkShop Theatre Mainstage and Jewel Box; Where Eagles Dare Theatre and Studio

10-Speed Revolution by John Heimbuch; Director, Nathan Lemoine

A Perfect Specimen of Femininity Written & performed by Lisa Dominique; Director, Matt Hoverman

A Shot in the Dark Adapted by Harry Kurnitz from the play *L'Idiote* by Marcel Achard; Director, Rick Joyce

A Thousand Variations on a Lie Told Once by Stacey Lane; Director, Brad Fryman

As You Like It: The Big Fish by "The Dark Lady" Amelia Bassano Lanier (a.k.a. William Shakespeare); Director, Stephen Wisker

Bubby's Shadow by Andrew Rothkin; Director, Ramona Pula

By The Lighting of the Silvery Moon Written & performed by Sara Jeanne Asselin; Director, Melissa Firlit

Cherry Hill Written and directed by Matt Okin

Childhood Montana Written and directed by Mira Gibson

Cleopatra: A Life Unparalled by Cheryl E. Kearney; Director, Cheryl E. Kearney, Char Fromentin

Conduct of Life by Maria Irene Fornes; Director, Joshua Lee Ramos

Couldn't Say by Christopher Wall; Director, Lisa Rothe

Daguerreotypes by Elisa Abatsis; Directed by Karen Raphaeli

Dreamless Written & performed by Cheryl Smallman; Director, Cheryl King

Eighty-1 by Mary Stewart-David; Director, Mary Stewart-David; Choreographer, Kate Loprest

Entwine by Sean Michael Rice; Director, Eileen Trilli

Eugenio by Anthony Ernest Gallo; Director, Roland Branford Gomez

Exit Cuckoo by Lisa Ramirez; Director, May Adrales

Flagboy by Cornelius Jones, Jr.; Director, Joshua Ian

Flies in the Snuffbox by Anton Checkov; Director, Dustin Condren

Gerald's Method Written & directed by Daniel Gallant

Hilary and Monica: The Winter of Her Discontent Written and directed by Yvette Heyliger

How I Found an Affordable Apartment on the Upper Westside of Manhattan Without Really Trying Written & performed by Charles Gross

Interning by Nadia Owusu; Director, Rachel Egenes

Intimate Exchanges by Alan Ayckbourn; Director, Ann Garner

Jump Jim Crow by Henry Meyerson; Director, Tom Thornton

Kidnapping Laura Linney by Philip Mutz; Director, Nadia Mahhab

Love, Incorporated by Marc Castle; Director, Igor Goldin; Music Director, Phillip Kirchmab

Mother, May I? Written & performed by Joy Gabriel; Director, Bricken Sparacino

My Life as a Bald Soprano by Margaret H. Baker, Clint J. Borzoni; Director, Andrew T. Carter

Natalie Book by Mari Carras & Laurel Ollstein, lyrics by Mari Carras & Nick Kitsopoulos, music by Nicholas Carra & Nick Kitsopoulos; Director, Spiro Veloudos; Choreographer, Wendy Waring; Music Director, Micah Young

Out of Control by Bridget Harris; Director, Leah Bonvissuto

Penang by James L. Larocca; Director, Donya Washington

Prince Trevor Amongst the Elephants Written and directed by Duncan Pflaster

Quake by Melanie Marnich; Director, Miguel Rosales

Sacred is the New Profane by Cheryl Harnest; Director, Jeremy Bloom

Scandal in Manhattan Written and directed by Bobby Holder

Striptease Into the Trip to Bahia Blanca by Griselda Gambaro; Director, Oscar A. Mendoza

Sympathetic Division by Gia Marotta; Director, Maura Farver

The Director's Reality by Zach Udko, Matthew Jellison, Linda Giuliano, Erica Schreiber; Director, Michael Schwartz, Aaron Gonzalez, Laura Credido, Jessica McVea

The F Trip by Kim Schultz; Director, Avriel Hillman

The Ghost Dancers by Adam Hunault; Director, Nadine Friedman

The Higher Education of Khalis Amir by Monica Bauer; Director, Craig J. George

The Red Paintball Written and directed by Alyssa & Laura Waldron

The Wendy Complex Written and directed by Jeremy Bloom

They Walk Among Us Adapted by Maureen Van Trease; Director, Bricken Sparacino

Truth Is by Christopher Heath; Director, Lindy Rogers

Writer's Block by Shaun Gunning; Director, Michael Kimmel

Yom Kippur by Meri Wallace; Director, Halina Ujda

Zen and the Art of Doing Nothing Written and directed by Michael Wallach

Milk Can Theatre Company

Artistic Director, Julie Fei-Fan Balzer; Managing Director, Bethany Larsen

Galileo by Bertolt Brecht; Director, Julie Fei-Fan Balzer; Stage Manager, Lorraine Cink, Maureen Stanley; Set, Ann Bartek; Costumes, Erin Murphy; Lighting, Wilburn Bonnell; Cast: Matt Biagini, Natalie Caruncho, James Caulfield, Ryan Clardy, Robert A. Felbinger, Alex Herrald, Jed Peterson, Maria Silverman; April 30–May 16

The Science Plays Set, Ann Bartek; Lighting, Wilburn Bonnell; Costumes, Meredith Neal; Included: *The Sense of Genius* by Cheryl L. Davis; Director, Riv Massey; Cast: Craig Klein, Dan Evers, Amy Windle; *Gertrude & Alyce Will Serve Ye Soone* by Bethany Larsen; Director, Ryan Ratelle; Cast: Sarah Herklots, Cynthia Rice; *Newton's Genesis* by ML Kinney; Director, Bobbi Masters; Cast: Meg Mark, J.J. von Mehren, Nicholas Wilder; *Unraveled* by Riv Massey; Director, Bethany Larsen; Cast: Craig Klein, Misty Coy, Dan Evers, Susan Levin; *Drill* by Andy Snyder; Director, Kimberly VerSteeg; Cast: Matthew Campbell, Matthew Minor, Miriam Mintz; *Greener Grass* by Julie Fei-Fan Balzer; Director, Seth Gamble; Cast: Mary Cavett, Aryeh Lappin; May 2–17

The Milk Can, After Dark Written & performed by Katie Northlich; May 2–16 Scene Herd Uddered: Workshop Series

Heffertz by Hanoch Levin; Director, Riv Massey; Dramaturg, Bethany Larsen; Cast: Ellen Hada, Amanda Hopper, Adam Hyland, Chris Kloko, Lesley Miller, Collin Smith, Leal Vona, Amy Windle; October 20

Pretty by Sharon E. Cooper; Director, Kitt Lavoie; Cast: Josh Bywater, Chris Comfort, Arielle Gordon, Jenny Kirlin, Stephanie Parrott, Becky Sterling, Paul Young; November 17

10021: A Modern Tragedy by Bethany Larsen; Director, Julie Fei-Fan Balzer; Cast: Misty Coy, Maria Teresa Creasey, Dan Evers, Josh LaCasse, JJ vonMehren, Melanie F. Siegel, Collin Smith, Yesenia Tromp; December 15

Balance by ML Kinney; Director, Riv Massey; Cast: Stephanie Parrott, Amy Windle, Ellen Hada, ML Kinney, Kirsten Walsh; March 30

Moose Hall Theatre Company /Inwood Shakespeare Festival

Producing Artistic Director, Ted Minos

Romeo & Juliet by William Shakespeare; Director, Ted Minos; Technical Director/Costumes, Catherine Bruce; Fight Choreographer, Ray A. Rodriguez; Music, Luke St. Francis; Graphics, Lee Kaplan; Cast: Andrew Blair, Alvin Chan, Kimberly DiPersia, Dinh Q. Doan, Leo Giannopoulos, Matthew Hadley, Michael Hagins, Samuel Joseph, Roxann Kraemer, Jay Longan, Katherine McDonald, Ross Pivec, Kelslan Scarbrough, Adam Souza, Amar Srivastava, Frank Zilinyi, Robert Zilinyi; Inwood Hill Park Peninsula; June 4–21

La Bohéme by Giacomo Puccini; Director, E. Randahl Hoey; Conductor, Steven M. Crawford, Pianist, Keith Burton; Technical Director/Sound, Catherine Bruce; Lighting, Ryan Metzler; Graphics, Lee Kaplan; Producer, Ted Minos; Assistant Producer, Frank Zilinyi; Cast: Peter Buchi, Eleni Calenos, Douglin Murray Schmidt, Matthew Singer, Crystallia Spilianaki, Aaron Theno, Jason Thoms Chorus: David Bell, Raissa Dorff, Sequina DeBoise, Megan Keefe, David Hughey, César Rospigliosi, Menorah Winston; Inwood Hill Park Peninsula; Inwood Hill Park Peninsula; June 26–28

The Curse of Capistrano - ¡El Zorro! Adapted & directed by Ted Minos; Based on *The Curse of Capistrano* by Johnston McCulley; Technical Director/Costumes, Catherine Bruce; Fight Choreographer, Ray A. Rodriguez; Music, Luke St. Francis; Graphics, Lee Kaplan; Cast: Alex Coelho, Chris Cornwell, Michelle Foytek, Anne Gill, David M. Mead, Daya Méndez, Constance Parng, Corey Pierno,

Catherine Povinelli, Michelle Silvani, Tom Steinbach, Adam Souza, Jonathan Weber, Frank Zilinyi, Robert Zilinyi; Inwood Hill Park Peninsula; July 16–August 2

MultiStages

Artistic Director, Lorca Peress

Temple of the Souls by Anita Velez-Mitchell; Director, Lorca Peress; Teatro La Tea; October 30

Bad Lies, Wild Cries and Other Acts of Love by Adam Kraar; Director, Lorca Peress; Geraldine Page Salon; December 1

Shadows by David Sard; Director, Lorca Peress; Primary Stages; February 21

Musicals Tonight!

Producer and Artistic Director, Mel Miller

Irma la Douce Music by Marguerite Monnot, lyrics by Alexandre Breffort, English lyrics and book by Julian More, David Heneker & Monty Norman; Director, Thomas Sabella-Mills; Music Director, Rick Hip-Flores; Cast: Vanessa Lemonides, Selby Brown, Damian Buzzerio, John Coghlan, James Donegan, Eric Imhoff, Wade McCollum, Justin Sayre, Kevin Sims, Kit Treece, Christian Zaremba; McGinn/Cazale Theatre; October 14–26

Tovarich Book by David Shaw, music by Lee Pockriss, lyrics by Anne Croswell; based on the comedy by Jacques Deval & Robert E. Sherwood; Director, Thomas Sabella-Mills; Music Director, James Stenborg; Cast: Jackson Ross Best, Jeffrey Nauman, Barbara McCullough, Al Pagano, Laura Beth Wells, Paul Amodeo, Steve Ted Beckler, Shorey Walker, Dana Domenick, Ronald Hornsby, Lydia Gladstone, Amy Jackson, Robert Anthony Jones, Omer Shaish, Roger Rifkin; McGinn/Cazale Theatre; October 28–November 9

Cabaret Girl Book & lyrics by P.G. Wodehouse, music by Jerome Kern; Director, Thomas Sabella-Mills; Music Director, James Stenborg; Cast: Jackson Ross Best Jr., Marni Buckner, Ben Franklin, Scott Guthrie, Kate Marilley, Patricia Noonan, Natalie Puritz, Allen Lewis Rickman, Justin Sayre, Celia Tackaberry, Michael Wolland, Mark Woodard, Tia Zorne; McGinn/Cazale Theatre; March 3–15

Early to Bed Music by Fats Waller, book & lyrics by George Marion Jr.; Director, Thomas Sabella-Mills; Music Director, David Bishop; Cast: Oakley Boycott, Nicholas Davila, Vincent D'Elia, Jennifer Evans, Ali Ewoldt, Erik Hogan, Robert Anthony Jones, Jose Luaces, Jenny Neale, Eduardo Placer, Rtia Rehn, Justin Sayre, Allyson Tucker, Frank Viveros; McGinn/Cazale Theatre; March 17–29

You Never Know Music and lyrics by Cole Porter, additional music by Robert Katscher, book and additional lyrics by Rowland Leigh, adapted from the original by Seigfired Geyer and Karl Farkas, additional lyrics by Edwin Gilbert; Director, Thomas Sabella-Mills; Music Director, James Stenborg; Cast: Bill Coyne, Jennifer Evans, Todd Faulkner, Kevin Kraft, Kate Merrily, Christy Morton, James Zanelli; McGinn/Cazale Theatre; April 14–26

National Asian-American Theatre Company (NAATCO)

Founder/Artistic Producing Director, Mia Katigbak; Co-Founder, Richard Eng

Out Cry by Tennessee Williams; Director, Thom Sesma; Set, Czerton Lim; Lighting, Stephen Petrilli; Costumes, Candida K. Nichols; Sound, Jane Shaw; Stage Manager, Leta Tremblay; Cast: Mia Katigbak, Eduardo Machado; The Abingdon Theatre; November 29–December 1

Leah's Train by Karen Hartman; Director, Jean Randich; Set, Katheryn Monthei; Lighting, Stephen Petrilli; Costumes, Alixandra Gage Englund; Sound, Robert Murphy; Stage Manager, Leta Tremblay; Assistant Director, Krystal Banzon; Technical Director, Kevin Bartlett; Press, Sam Rudy Media Relations, Bob Lasko; Cast: Rafael Aranas, Louis Ozawa Changchin, Jennifer Ikeda, Mia Katigbak; Kristine Haruna Lee; TBG Theatre; February 6–28

New Federal Theatre

Artistic Director, Woodie King Jr.

3 One-Acts *The Toilet* by Amiri Baraka; Director, Hampton Clampton; *Salaam Huey Salaam* by Ed Bullins, Marvin X; Director, Mansoor Najee-ullah; *Amarie* by Hugh L. Fletcher; Director, Freedome Bradley; Abron Arts Center; October 23–November 16

Sundown Names and Night Gone Things by Leslie King; Director, Woodie King Jr.; Stage Manager, Elliot Lanes; Lighting, Shirley Prendergast; Set, John C. Schcffler; Costumes, David Thompson; Cast: Ralph McCain, Nathan Purdee, Marcus Naylor, Crystal Ann Dickinson, Stephen T. Williams, DeWanda Wise; The Castillo Theatre; May 14–June 7

New Georges

Artistic Director, Susan Bernfield; Associate Director, Sarah Cameron Sunde

Hillary: A Modern Greek Tragedy With a (Somewhat) Happy Ending by Wendy Weiner; Director, Julie Kramer; Set, Lauren Helpern; Costumes, Amelia Dombrowski; Lighting, Graham Kindred; Props, Eugenia Furneaux-Arends; Sound, Jill BC DuBoff & Joshua Higgason; PSM, Ryan Raduechel; Cast: Mia Barron, Darren Pettie, Heidi Armbruster, Victoire Charles, Jorge Cordova, Charlie Hudson III, Jenny Mercein, Josie Whittlesey; The Living Theater; November 22–December 20

Angela's Mix-Tape by Eisa Davis; April 9–May 2 (see Off-Broadway listings in this volume)

New York Classical Theatre

Artistic Director, Stephen Burdman

Cymbeline by William Shakespeare; Director, Louis Scheeder; Design, Amelia Dombrowski; Voice/Speech Coach, Barbara Adrian; Fight Chorography, Shad Ramsey; Stage Manager, Jennifer Marie Russo; Cast: Dan Domingues, Gian Murray Gianino, Erik Gratton, Adi Hanash, Patrick Jones, Ginny Myers Lee, David Marion, Michael Marion, Sherry Skinner, Clay Storseth; Central Park; May 29–June 22

The Tragedy of Macbeth by William Shakespeare; Director, Stephen Burdman; Design, Michelle Bohn; Fight Choreographer, Shad Ramsey; Stage Manager, Jennifer Marie Russo; Cast: Kersti Bryna, Erin Krakow, Jessica Barr, Stephen D'Ambrose, Cooper D'Ambrose, John-Patrick Driscoll, Sean Meehan, Bryant Mason, Shad Ramsey, Kim Stauffer, Josh Akin, Anthony Reimer, Joshua Decker, Jabari Brisport, Terence Stone; Battery Park; June 26–July 11

Misalliance by George Bernard Shaw; Director, Stephen Burdman; Design, Ciera Wells; Voice/Speech Coach, Joan Melton; Stage Manager, Marianne Broome; Cast: Kirsten D'Aurelio, Donald Grody, Sean Hagarty, Patrick Shibles Jones, Ginny Myers Lee, Jon Levenson, Rita Rehn, David Sedgewick, Nicholas Stannard; Central Park; July 31–August 24

New York International Fringe Festival

Twelfth annual; Producing Artistic Director, Elena K. Holy; August 8–24, 2008; performances at Schimmel Center & Schaberle Studio, Soho Playhouse, Theatre 80, The Deluxe at Spiegelworld, Cherry Lane Theatre, Players Theater, Connelly Theater, Theatres at 45 Bleecker Street, Barrow Street Theatre, and the CSV Cultural and Educational Center

III Written and directed by Joe Salvatore

2 By Sinner: Unburthen (To My Soul's Delight)/If Water Were Present It Would Be Called Drowning Written and directed by John Sinner

52 Man Pickup by Desiree Burch; Director, Isaac Byrne

The 70% Club by Mary McCallum; Director, John Wiggins

@lice in www.onderland Based on text by Lewis Carroll; Directors, Celeste Ballard, Maggie Burrows, Allegra Long; Choreographer, Celeste Ballard, Maggie Burrows, Allegra Long

The Alice Complex by Peter Barr Nickowitz; Director, Bill Oliver

All Hail the Great Serpent! by MURDERFIST; Director, Krobos the Eternal

America 20XX Written and directed by Cyriaque Lamar

The Amish Project by Jessica Dickey; Director, Sarah Cameron Sunde

Anaïs Nin Goes to Hell by David Stallings; Director, Cristina Alicea

Ariel View Compiled and directed by Andrea C. Graugnard, Daniel J. LeBlanc

Ascension by Cynthia G. Robinson; Director, Petronia Paley

Baby Cow by Christina Renee Miller; Developed with Matthew Hoverman

Be Brave, Anna! by Tara Schuster; Director, James Rutherford

beast: a parable Written and directed by J. Julian Christian

Becoming Britney by Molly Bell, Daya Curley; Director, Daya Curley; Choreographer, Mandy Bell, Molly Bell

Behold, the Bowery! Written and directed by Daniel Pfau

Big Beat/Back Flow Written, directed, and choreographed by Nichole Arvin, Asami Morita

Big Thick Road by Stanton Wood; Director, Edward Elefterion

Blanche Survives Katrina in a FEMA Trailer Named Destiny Written & performed by Mark Sam Rosenthal; Director, Todd Parmley

Boots by Giacondo Trevellini; Director, Michael Petranek

The Boss in the Satin Kimono by Blake Hackler; Director, Susanna Gellert

Bound in a Nutshell Based on texts of William Shakespeare's *Hamlet*; Adapted by Gregory Wolfe, Gregory Sherman; Director, Gregory Wolfe

The Boy in the Basement by Katharine Heller; Director, Nell Balaban

But For the Grace… Written and directed by David Eliet

Bye Bye Bombay by Cara Yeates; Director, Jonno Katz

Carl & Shelly, Best Friends Forever by Andrea Alton, Allen Warnock; Director, Jay Duffer

China-The Whole Enchilada by Mark Brown, music & lyrics by Mark Brown; Arrangements/Additional Music, Paul Mirkovich; Director, Jim Helsinger

Chandeleirva by Suzette Araujo; Director, Evan Tsitsias

Choke City Written and directed by Manny Liyes

Choose Your Own Play by Timmy Wood, Greg Hundemer, Caleb George, John Robert Hundemer, Paul Salazar; Director, Timmy Wood

The Chronicles of Steve: The Bossy Bottom by David LeBarron; Director, Gordon Vanderberg

CLONE by Christopher Loar; Director, Rafael Gallegos

The Complete Performer Written & performed by Ted Greenberg

Conjecture by Robin Rapoport; Director, Robin Rapoport

Control Jessica Hinds; Director, Lucia Peters

The Corn Maiden Written and directed by Jess McLeod; Adapted from the novel by Joyce Carol Oates

Creena Defoouie by Charlote Barton-Hoare; Director, James Hoare; Choreographer, Haruka Kuroda

Cruising to Croatia by Peter Mikochick; Director, Pamela Sabauth

Cycle: A Vaudeville Comedy by Rose Courtney; Music, Rachel Kaufman; Director, Craig Carlisle; Choreographer, Laure Sheehy

The Darling Children by Ivan Faute; Director, Stephen F. Murray

The Death of the Ball Turret Gunner Written and directed by Anna Moench

A December Eve's Visit with Frederick Demuth by Sylvia Ann Manning; Director, Gwynn MacDonald

The Deciders Book, music, & lyrics by Mitch Kess, additional lyrics by Carly Sheehan, additional music by Charles Bascombe; Director, J. Michaels; Music Director, David Fletcher

The Dershowitz Protocol by Robert Fotheril; Director, Anthony Frisina

Dingbat by Nancy Friedrich with artistic collaboraction & direction by James Whittington

The Disappearance of Jonah by Darragh Martin; Director, Dan Blank, Pitr Strait

Down Around Brown Town Written, directed, and choreographed by Frit & Frat Fulle

Doppelganger Joe Written and directed by Caroline Lesley

Dreadful Penny's Exquisite Horrors by Alexandra Herryman; Director, Glen Cullen, Parrish Morgan

The Dream~Casting Written, directed, and choreographed by Huilo Marvavilla

Eagle Squadron GO! by Garet Scott; Music, John Bauers; Director, Kevin Thompsen

Eggs and the Rebound Guy by LyaNisha R. Gonzalez; Director, Lisa-Erica James

Exodus by Daren Taylor; Director, Jessica McVea

Extraordinary Rendition Written and directed by James Balestrieri

The Fabulous Kane Sisters in BOX OFFICE POISON by Marc Geller, Bill Roulet; Director, Marc Geller

FACE (Every Good Boy Does Fine) by FACE; Director, Deanna Fleysher

Fancy Guts & Ghosts Written and directed by Amanda Raliegh, Karina Wolfe;

Fell by Harrison David Rivers; Director, Jess McLeod

A FIRE AS BRIGHT AS HEAVEN by Tim Collins

Fluency by Kimberly Patterson; Director, Jim Jichetti

FOR REASONS UNKNOWN by Andi Teron, Jeff Long; Director, Nathan Halvorson

Forteez Bluntz Chickenhedz 'N' Uva Necessateez by Bashi Rose; Director, Christopher McElreon

From The Inside, Out by Maggie Keenan-Bolger; Director, Erika Christensen

GALATEA by Frank Tangredi; Director, Alex Sol

Gargoyle Garden Book & lyrics by Jeff LaGreca, music by B. Allen Schultz; Director/Choreographer, Jeff LaGreca; Music Director, Silas N. Huff

A Gathering of Eagles by Charles Garo; Director, Dan Drew

The Gay No More Telethon Book & lyrics by Michael DiGaetano, music by Albin E. Konopko & Michael DiGaetano

GEM! A Truly Outrageous Parody by Amanda Allan; Music, Tyler Walker; Director, David Karl Lee; Choreographer, Robyn Sklaren

George the Fourth by Michael T. Middleton; Director, Dina Epshteyn

The Golden Aurora by Steven Fechter; Director, Ari Laura Kreith

Good Pictures by Ashlin Halfnight; Director, Domenic D'Andrea

Gratuitous Novelty: A Locked Away Cabaret Written, directed and choreographed by Rob Davidson

The Grecian Formula by Carter Anne McGowan; Director, Mary Jo Lodge

green eyes by Lizzie Leopold, Brian Mazzaferri, Jessica Rush, music & lyrics by Brian Mazzaferri; Director, Jessica Redish; Choreographer, Lizzie Leopold

Heaven Forbid(s)! Written and directed by Marco Antonio Rodriguez

Hidden Fees* by Victoria NikiForova; Director, Raphael Schklowsky

Hot Cripple by Hogan Gorman; Director, Isaac Klein

The Home for Wayward Girls and Fallen Women by Cyndi Freeman, Joseph Naftali

HOW TO FOLD A SHIRT Written and directed by Anthony Gelsomino

I Heart Hamas: And Other Things I'm Afraid To Tell You by Jennifer Jajeh; Director, W. Kamau Bell

I Love You, Petty, & Favre by David Scott; Director, John Buidon

The Johnny Book, music, lyrics, and direction by David L. Williams; Choreographer, Grady Bowman

JOHNNY LAW, Courtroom Crusader by Tim Ryan Meinelschmidt; Director, Christopher Fessenden

johnpaulgeorgeringo-an intimate experience with the fab four by Dave Jay & Bradley Calcaterra; Director, Bradley Calcaterra

Julius Caesar by William Shakespeare; Director, Jordan Reeves

KABOOM! by Michael W. Small; Director, BT McNicholl

Kansas City Or Along the Way by Robert Attenweiler; Director, Joe Stipek

Keep Your Eyes Open by 5th and 6th grade members of the PossEble Theater Lab

KNB The Musical Written and directed by Christopher Carter Sanderson; Choreographer, Erin Porvaznika

KNUCKLEBALL by William Whitehurst; Director, Jeremy Page

Krapp, 39 by Michael Laurence; Director, George Demas

La Vigilia (The Vigil) by Vincent Marano; Director, Kathleen O'Neill

THE LAST DANCE OF MARSHA KANE (Sugarcoating the Inevitable) by Rena Hundert; Director, Jeremy Taylor

Lecture, With Cello by Robert Moulthrop; Director, Kent Paul

The Legislative Process by Clarence Coo; Director, Mikhael Tara Garver

Life…Death…and Entertainment by Susan Damante; Director Sue Hamilton

The Longest Running Joke of the 20th Century by Stephen O'Rourke

Love is Dead: A NecRomantic Musical Comedy Book & lyrics by James Asmus & Andrew Hobgood, music by Julie Nichols; Director, Andrew Hobgood

Lucasville: The Untold Story of a Prison Uprising by Staughton Lynd, Gary L. Anderson, Christopher Fidram; Director, Brandon Martin

Lucila: a play for Gabriela Mistral by Sylvia Ann Manning; Director, Joe Franchini, Leecia Manning

Lydia's Funeral Video by Samantha Chanse; Director, Thomas Connors

Maladjusted. Misappropriated by Derek O'Connor; Director, Jack Halpin

Lydia's Funeral Video by Samantha Chanse; Director, Thomas Connors

A Man, A Magic, A Music Written & choreographed by Melvin Brown; Directors, Melvin Brown & Francesca Sansalone

Mare Cognitum by David McGee; Director, Jesse Edward Rossbrow

Meanwhile, Baghbad… by Joshua Cole; Director, Nick Leavens

Mirrors of Chartres Street: Faulkner in New Orleans/New Orleans in Faulkner by Rob Florence; Director, Perry Martin

Missing Man by Mary Scruggs; Director, Edward Thomas-Herrera

Monsters in the Wood by Brad Lawrence; Director, Maia Garrison

More Than Pants by Jennifer Subrin, Brigid Boyle

Mourn The Living Hector by Paul Cohen; Director, Shira Milikowsky, Julie Rossman

Murder of the Seas by Pierre-Marc Diennet; Director, Jason Schuler

My Salvation Has A First Name: A Weinermobile Journey by Robin Gelfenbien

The Naked Dead Elephant in the Middle of the Room Written and directed by Larson Rose

A Nasty Story by Sara Jeanne Asselin; Director, Melissa Firlit

Nightlife Jesus by Rich Ferguson, Paul Garrison; Choreographer, Kathleen Davidson

NOIR: a shot and a cellar by Joe Vonderhaar; Director, Tonika Todorova

NOT DARK YET by Timothy Nolan; Director, Susan W. Lovell

Now That She's Gone by Ellen Snortland; Director, John Mitchell; Choreographer, Leanne Fonteyn

Nudist in Love: A New Musical Music & lyrics by Nirmal Chandraratna, book by Shannon Thomason; Director, Sara Thigpen

O! Balleto by Lane Gifford, Neil Alexander; Director, Lane Gifford

Oatmeal and a Cigarette by George Sapio; Director, Melisaa Thompson

the October crisis (to laura) by Alejandro Morales; Director, Scott Ebersold

ON INSOMNIA AND MIDNIGHT by Edgar Chias; Director, Berioska Ipinza

One Seat in the Shade by John Reoli; Director, Bruce Ornstein

ONEWORD-an extended poetree by Gail Langstroth; Director, Bethany Caputo, Klaus Jensen; Choreographer, Gail Langstroth

Operation Adelmo Written & directed by Mike Wills; Arranger, Peter Saxe

Other Bodies by August Schulenburg; Director, Heather Cohn

Paper Dolls by Patrick Huguenin; Director, Gaye Taylor Upchurch

The Pantyhose Girl by Cynthia Frank; Director, Paul J. Michael

Panopticon by Steve Pardun; Director, Angela Astle

Parental Indiscretions by Steve Hayes, Tome Cayler

PennyBear Presented and performed by the Company; Director, James Whittington

Perez Hilton Saves The Universe (or at least the greater Los Angeles area): The Musical Book by Randy Blair & Timothy Michael Drucker, music by Zachary Redler, lyrics by Randy Blair; Director/Choreographer, Connor Gallagher

The Permanent Night by Kari Bentley-Quinn; Director, Heather Arnson

Piccola Cosi by Aja Nisenson

Pawnshop Accordions by Jonathan Wallace; Director, Aaron Gonzalez

Pieces on the Board Written and directed by Tim O'Leary

Prayer by Jonathan Kravetz; Director, Joseph Beuerlein

Psalms of a Questionable Nature by Marisa Wegrzyn; Director, Tracy Cameron Francis

R U Prime? by Lucas Roy Lehman; Director, Maura Kelley

RADIOTHEATRE Presents: The Mole People Written and directed by Dan Bianchi

Raised by Lesbians by Leah Ryan; Director, Dev Bondarin

Reasonable Doubt by Suzie Miller; Director, Lee Lewis

The Redheaded Man by Halley Bondy; Director, Jessica Fisch

The Refugee Girls Revue: A Musical Pardoy by Jena Friedman; Music, Boaz Reisman; Director, Scott Illingworth

Revolution on the Roof: A 60's Anti-War Musical by Aaron Latham; Director, Sergio Alvarado

Ripcords Book & lyrics by Anne Berlin, music by Andy Cohen; Director, Gregg Wiggins

Rosalee Was Here by Maura Campbell; Director, Toby Ring Thelin

Sad, Sad, Sad by Nigel O'Hearn, Duncan Coe; Director, Jeremy Sexton

A Sagacious Hunch Written & directed by John McDermott

Sailor Man by Scott Peteman, Ryan Iverson; Director, Peter Cook; Choreographer, Jacob Grigolia-Rosenbaum

Salt Lake, a New Ballet by Vicky Virgin; Director, Umit Celebi; Music Director, Michelle Kinney; Choreographer, Vicky Virgin

Sandy and Dandy and Charlie McGee: A Case Study in Harsh Realities by Guerrin Gardner, Mat Sanders; Music, Ryland Blackinton; Director, Stephen Brackett

Schoenberg Written & directed by John Fisher

Scratch by Aimee Gonzalez; Director, Meiyin Wang

Secrets of Lamp Lit Blinds: Three One Acts by Jason Williamson; Director, Michael Petrenek

See How Beautiful I Am: The Return of Jackie Susann by Paul Minx; Director, Paul Dubois

Self-Portrait as Schiele by Mark Lindberg; Director, Gerritt Turner

Sennentuntschi by Hansjorg Schneider; Director, Niklaus Talman

THE SEVEN LITTLE FOYS Written and directed by Chip Deffaa; Choreographer, Justin Boccitto

Sex, Cellulite and Large Farm Equipment: One Girls Guide To Living and Dying by River Huston; Director, Cheryl King

SHOTS: A LOVE STORY Written and directed by John Caswell Jr.

A Silly Silverstein Show by Shel Silverstein, adapted and directed by Jessica Marie Lorence; Music, Shel Silverstein & Pat Daley; Music Director, Luke Santy

The Sound of One Hanna Clapping by Hanna LoPatin; Director, Ana Gasteyer

SPITE by Tariq Hamami; Director, Mark Schneider

STARS IN A DARK SKY by R.E. Vickers; Director, Melanie Moyer Williams

STRANGE ATTRACTOR Written & directed by Marco Frezza

Symphony Pastorale/Fugue Series by Robert Barnett; Music, Brian Wilbur Grundstron; Director, Ed Wierzbicki

That Dorothy Parker by Carol Lempert; Director, Janice Goldberg

There Will Come Soft Rains by Stanislaw Lern, Bill Pronzini, Barry Malzberg; Adaptor/Director, Jon Levin

They Call Me Mister Fry by Jack Freiberger; Director, Jeff Michalski

The Third From The Left by Jean Colonomos; Director, Jon Lawrence Rivera

Thoroughly Stupid Things (or the Continuous Importance of Being Ernest) by Montserrat Mendez; Director, Megan Demarest; Choreographer, Jessica Linquata

Thumbelina: The Story of a Brave Little Girl by Liza Lentini

Tim Gunn's Podcast (a reality chamber opera) Based on Tim Gunn's actual podcast; Music/Book, Jeffrey Lependorf; Director, Linda Lehr

time, et. al.: a cautionary tale about love and time travel by Gil Varod, Jennifer Lynn Jordan; Director, Shannon Fillion

TINY FEATS OF COWARDICE by Susan Bernfield; Music, Rachel Peters; Director, Daniella Topol

TOO MUCH MEMORY by Keith Reddin, Meg Gibson; Director, Meg Gibson

Tough Guys Don't Shoot Blanks by Todd Michaels; Director, Noel Neeb

Traffic Jam by Jenniger Bogush; Director, Jennifer Sherron Stock

Trees Like Nails by Will Snider; Director, Deanna Weiner

Triumph of the Underdog by Mitch Montgomery, Morgan Allen; Director, Barbara Williams

Tune Up, Faulty Piston! Director, Andrew Scoville

Underwear: A Space Musical Book and lyrics by Heidi Ervin, music and lyrics by Brandon Gwinn; Director Joe Barros

UNEKA-ARNASA by the ensemble; Director, Kepa Ibarra

Untitled Masterpiece Written and directed by Patrick Flynn

The Umbrella Plays by Stephanie Janssen; Director, Daniel Talbott

Usher by Molly Fox, music by Sarah Hirsch; Director, Becca Wolf; Music Director, Brian Valencia

The Vajayjay Monologues by Lindsay Burns; Director, Vicki Stroich

Velvet Scratch Written & directed by Anastacia Revi

waiting: a play in phases by Gia Marotta; Director, Chloe Bass

WALLS by Aaron Ezra; Director, Markus Potter

The Warrior by Jack Gilhooley; Director, Kevin Murray

We Are The Lawmakers Written & directed by Marc Andreottola

We Three by Will Goldberg; Director, Erin Daley

Wildboy '74 by Eva Anderson; Director, Adrian A. Cruz

Wish You Were Here by Michael Philis

Woodhull: A Play About the Woman Who Ran for President by Liza Lentini; Director, Mary Geerlof

XY(T) by Kestryl Cael Lowrey

Zombie Adapted by Bill Connington; Director, Thomas Caruso

New York Musical Theatre Festival (NYMF)

Fifth annual; Executive Director and Producer, Isaac Robert Hurwitz; Founder, Kris Stewart; September 15–October 5, 2008; performances at TBG Theatre, American Theatre of Actors (Chernuchin), 45th Street Theatre, 37 Arts, Manhattan Movement and Arts Center, Nuyorican Poet's Café, Zipper Factory Theatre

FULL PRODUCTIONS

About Face Book & lyrics by David Arthur, music by Jeffrey Lodin; Director, Nick Corley

Bedbugs!!! Book & lyrics by Fred Sauter, music by Paul Leschen; Director, Samuel Buggeln

Bonnie & Clyde: A Folktale Book by Hunter Foster, music & lyrics by Rick Crom; Director, Mark Waldrop

The Bubble Book & lyrics by Karen Paull, music & lyrics by David Pack; Director/Choreographer, Terry Berliner

Castronauts Book by Bobby Houston & Patricio Bisso, lyrics by Bobby Houston, music by Randy Courts; Director, Will Pomerantz

COLLEGE The Musical Book, music, & lyrics by Drew Fornarola, Scott Elmegreen; Director, Jeremy Dobrish

Cyclone (and the Pig-Faced Lady) Book & lyrics by Dana Leslie Goldstein, music by Rima Ford; Director, Elysa Marden

The Fancy Boy Follies Book & lyrics by David Pevsner, music by Stephen Bates, Jamie Forsyth, Mark Hummel, Chris Lavely, Michael Orland, Jeff Rizzo, Michael Skloff, David Pevsner, additional material by Bruce Vilanch

The Hatpin Book & lyrics by James Miller, music by Peter Rutherford; Director, Kim Hardwick

Heaven in Your Pocket Book by Mark Houston, Francis J. Cullinan, Dianne Sposito, music & lyrics by Mark Houston; Director, Alan Souza

I Come For Love Book, music, & lyrics by Terrence Atkins, Jeffery Lyle-Segal; Director, Michael Berry

Idaho! Book & lyrics by Buddy Sheffield, music by Buddy Sheffield & Keith Thompson; Director, Matt Lenz

Jason & Ben Book, music, & lyrics by Matthew Loren Cohen; Director, James Beaudry

The Jerusalem Syndrome Book & lyrics by Laurence Holzman & Felicia Needleman, music by Kyle Rosen; Director, Annette Jolles

Love Jerry Book, music, & lyrics by Megan Gogerty; Director, Hilary Adams

Max and the Truffle Pig Book by Suzanne Bradbeer, music by Bert Draesel, lyrics by Nancy Leeds; Director, Erica Gould

Play It Cool Book by Martin Casella & Larry Dean Harris, lyrics by Mark Winkler, music by Philip Swan; Additional Music, Jim Andron, Michael Cruz, Marilyn Harris, Robert Kraft, Emilio Palame, Joe Pasquale, Dan Siegel, Larry Steelman; Director, Sharon Rosen

The Road To Ruin Book, music, & lyrics by William Zeffiro; Director, Mary Catherine Burke

She Can't Believe She Said That! Book, music, & lyrics by Matt Prager; Director, Josh Hecht

That Other Woman's Child Book, music, lyrics, and direction Sherry Landrum

To Paint The Earth Book & lyrics by Daniel F. Levin, music by Jonathan Portera; Director, Michael Bush

Twilight in Manchego Book, music, and lyrics by Matt Gould; Director, Billy Porter

Villa Diodati Book by Collette Inez & Mira J. Spektor, music & lyrics by Mira J. Spektor, lyrics by Collette Inez; Additional Lyrics, Lord Byron, Pery Bysshe Shelley; Director, Rob Urbanati

Wood Book & lyrics by Dan Collins, music by Julianne Wick Davis; Director, Thomas Caruso

DANCE SERIES *The Hourglass and the Poisoned Pen* Co-created by Mark Yonally, Andrew Pepoy, Chicago Tap Theatre; *Sophia's Fall* Book & lyrics by Rob

Seitleman, music & lyrics by Benjamin Birney; Director/Choreographer, Jason Summers; *Ward 9* by Gregory Victor & Matt Williams, music by Ludwig Van Beethoven; Choreographer, Matt Williams; Directors, Mark Robinson & Matt Williams; *Wild About Harry* Book by Susan DiLallo, music by Dan Acquisto; Director, Elizabeth Lucas; Choreographers, Joshua Bergasse, Daryl Gray, Maurice Brandon Curry, Jeff Shade, Shea Sullivan

DEVELOPMENTAL SERIES *BLACKfootNotes* by Rajendra Ramoon Maharaj; Director, Nick Petrie;

Fairy Tale Book by Joshua Robinson, music & lyrics by John D. Bronston II; Director, Rob McIntosh;

I Love You, Madame President Book by Pyhllis Lynd & Martha Kerns, music & lyrics by Phyllis Lynd; Director, Matthew Hamel; *Lines* Book, music, & lyrics by Timothy Huang; Director, Maurice Brandon Curry; *Robin Hood* Book, music, & lyrics by Timothy Frey; Director, Rusty Curcio; *Ubu* Book by Bradley Aufil, Tony Mayes, & Monty Holamon, music & lyrics by Monty Holamon; Director, Brantley Aufill; *Wrapped* Book by Dennis Nehaman, music & lyrics by Craig Nehamen

CONCERTS Benj Pasek and Justin Paul in Concert; *The Gay Agenda* starring Micah Bucey and Nicholas Williams; *Party Worth Crashing: The Cast of Godspell Sings Kerrigan-Lowdermilk* Music and lyrics by Brian Lowdermilk and Kait Kerrigan; Prospect Theater Company 10th Anniversary Concert featuring the music of Jim Bauer, Randy Courts & Mark St. Germain, Rick Hip-Flores, Gihieh Lee & Tim Nevits, Peter Mills & Stephen Weiner, Maryrose Wood & Andrew Gerle; Host: Stephen Bogardus; Director, Cara Reichel; *Prozak and the Platypus* CD Release Party Book & lyrics by Elise Thoron, music by Jill Sobule

SPECIAL EVENTS *Chocolate Soup* Book by Jill Jaysen, music & lyrics by Matt Corriel; *Freshly Tossed* created and curated by Wendy Seyb & Mark Lonergan; *Giant Killer Shark: The Musical* created by Sam Sutherland; *A Puppet Music Thing* curated by Alissa Hunnicutt

NYMF @ NITE–Parties and Nightlife NYMF Broadway Prom; NYMF Opening Night Celebration; NYMF's Next Broadway Sensation

EDUCATIONAL EVENTS & SEMINARS ASCAP Foundation Educational Series moderated by Peter Filichia; Guests: Chad Beguelin & Matthew Sklar, Mark Hollmnan, Nell Benjamin, Zina Goldrich, Bobby Lopez, Matt Prager

PARTNER EVENTS "Musicals on Television" Series; *10 Minutes of Happiness* by Roi "Bubi" Escudero; *8 Women: A Karaoke Murder Mystery* Adapted by Robert Thomas, Leigh Hile, and Sarah Levine from the screenplay by Fracois Ozon; Director, Leigh Hile; *Generations* Music & lyrics by Avi Kunstler, story, music, lyrics & direction by Matt Okin; *Midnight Madness* Book, lyrics, and direction by Cynthia Meryl, music by Jack Bender; *Souls Searching* Music & lyrics by Avi Kunstler, story, additional music & lyrics, and direction by Matt Okin; *You Can Take The Girl Outta Brooklyn* Written & performed by Susan Collins

Nicu's Spoon

Founder and Artistic Director, Stephanie Barton-Farcas

No Niggers, No Jews, No Dogs by John Henry Redwood; Director, Stephanie Barton-Farcas; Set, Gabrielle Montgomery; Cast: Pamela Mitchell, Aaliyah Miller, Russell Waldman, Rachel Handshaw, Patrick Mitchell, Dana Jones, Skai Konyha, Marvin Telp; Spoon Theatre; July 12–27

Kite Cut Loose in the Middle of the Sky by David Greenberg; Director, Russell Waldman; Lighting, Tamora Wilson; Stage Manager, Bonnie Hilton; Cast: Rebecca Challis, Leo Otero, Margaret Baker, Mark Armstrong, David Tully, Tim Romero, Rachel Handshaw; Spoon Theatre; October 8–26

Tibet Does Not Exist by Don Thompson; Director, Pamela Butler; Set, John Trevellini; Costumes/Sound, Stephanie Barton-Farcas; Lighting, Steven Wolf; Stage Manager, Alvero Sena; Press, Katie Rosin; Cast: Oliver Conant, Katie

Labahn, Susannah McLeod, Sammy Mena, Scott David Nogi, Tim Romero, Sara Thigpen, Peter Quinones; Spoon Theatre; April 10–26

Ohio Theatre

Summerworks 2008 Thirteenth annual festival of new plays presented by Clubbed Thumb; included: *Gentleman Caller* by Ann Marie Healy; Director, Brooke O'Hara; Design, Peter Ksander; Costumes, Tara Webb; Sound, Ian Antonio & Russell Greenberg; Production Manager, Mark Sitko; Stage Manager, Donald Butchko; Associate Design, Andreea Mincic; Cast: Hannah Cabell, Beth Hoyt, Meg MacCary, Hubert Point-Du-Jour; June 8–14; *Vendetta Chrome* by Sally Oswald; Director, Alexis Poledouris; Set, Jason Simms; Costumes, Jessica Pabst; Lighting, Gina Scherr; Sound, Joe Varca; Choreography, Tracy Bersley; Production Manager, Julie Rossman; Stage Manager, Theresa Flanagan; Cast: Jeanine Serralles, Tracee Chimo, Lisa Rafaela Clair, Rebecca Hart, Caroline Tamas, Ariana Venturi, Sam Breslin Wright, Jenny Seastone Stern, Ginger Eckert; June 15–21; *Slavery* by Sigrid Gilmer; Director, Robert O'Hara; Sets, Caleb Levengood; Lighting, Raquel Davis; Costumes, Clint Ramos; Sound, Daniel Odham; Production Manager, Mark Sitko; Stage Manager, Chelsea Usherwood; Cast: Spencer Scott Barros, Glenn Cruz, Amanda Duarte, Tim Frank, Hasani Issa, Jocelyn Kuritsky, Edward Nattenberg, Maria-Christina Oliveras, Gita Reddy, Paco Tolson; June 22–28

Ice Factory '08 Fifteenth annual festival presented by Soho Think Tank (Robert Lyons, Artistic Director); included: *Don Not Do This Ever Again* by Karinne Keithley; Director, Maria Goyanes; July 9–12; *TRACES/fades* Written and directed by Lenora Champagne, music by Daniel Levi; July 16–19; Neil Young's *Greendale (a rock opera)* by Neil Young, adapted by Bruce DuBose; Presented by Undermain Theatre (Texas); Director, Katherine Owen; July 23–26; *Heistman* by Matthew Maher; Presented by El Gato Teatro; Director, Gabriella Barnstone; Cast: Steven Rattazzi; July 30–August 2; *Red-Haired Thomas* by Robert Lyons; Director, Oliver Butler; August 6–9; *W.M.D.* Created and presented by Sponsored by Nobody; Director, Kevin Doyle; August 13–16; *Victory at the Dirt Place* Written and directed by Adriano Shaplin; Presented by Riot Group; August 20–23

The Invitation by Brian Parks; Presented by Wordmonger Productions; Director, John Clancy; Set/Costumes, Rose A.C. Howard; Lighting, Eric Southern; Cast: David Calvitto, Leslie Farrell, Katie Honaker, Paul Urcioli, Eva van Dok; September 10–27

Chekhov Lizardbrain by Robert Quillen Camp and the Ensemble; Presented by Soho Think Tank and Pig Iron Theatre Company; Director, Dan Rothenberg; Sound, Nick Kourtides; Costumes, Olivera Gajic; Sets, Anna Kiraly; Lighting, James Clofelter; Stage Manager, Katie Driscoll; Cast: Gabriel Quinn Bauriedel, Geoff Sobelle, James Sugg, Dito van Reigersberg; October 9–19

Surrender Written and directed by Josh Fox & Jason Christopher Hartley; Presented by International WOW Company; Lighting, Charles Foster, Scott Needham; Set, Nicolas Locke; Sound, Josh Fox; Video, Liquid Lux Works; October 29–November 16

Dance Dance Revolution Presented by Les Freres Corbusier; Director, Alex Timbers; Choreographer, Danny Mefford; Music, Gary Adler & Phoebe Krutz; Set, Donyale Werle; Costumes, Emily Rebholz; Lighting, Justin Townsend; Sound, Jeremy Lee; Stage Manager, Andrea Wales; December 3–20

10 Blocks on the Camino Real by Tennessee Williams; Presented by Target Margin; Director, David Herskovitz; Set/Lighting, Lenore Doxsee; Costumes, Ásta Bennie Hostetter; Music Director, David Rosenmeyer; Stage Manager, Jacqueline Prats; Cast: Purva Bedi, Satya Bhabha, Curt Hostetter, McKenna Kerrigan, Dara Seitzman, Raphael Nash Thompson; January 18–30

Red Haired Thomas by Robert Lyons; Director, Oliver Butler; Presented by Soho Think Tank; Lighting, Mike Riggs; Sound, Nathan Leigh; Costumes, Sydney Maresca; Set, Tom Gleeson; Stage Manager, Bailie Slevin; Cast: Danny Beiruti, Danielle Skraastad, Peter Sprague, Alan Benditt, Nicole Raphael; March 9–28

I Have Been to Hiroshima Mon Amour by Chiori Miyagawa; Presented by Voice and Vision and Crossing Jamaica Avenue Theatre Company; Director, Jean Wagner; Cast: Joel de la Fuente, Juliana Francis-Kelly, Sue Jean Kim; May 14–30

Ontological-Hysteric Theater

Founder and Artistic Director, Richard Foreman; Managing Director, Shannon Sindelar

Vicious Dogs on Premesis Text by Saviana Stanescu; Presented by Witness Relocation; Director/Choreographer, Dan Safer; Set/Lighting, Jay Ryan; Video, Kaz Phillips; Sound, Ryan Maeker; Costumes, Pandora Andrea Gastelum; Press, Jonathan Slaff; Cast/Co-Choreographers: Heather Christian, Sean Donovan, Mike Mikos, Laura Berlin Stinger; The Incubator; May 29–June 14

Lasanta Co-presented by Sintroca; Directors/Design, Madeleine Bernatchez & Efran Delgadillo Jr.; Choreography, Shannon Gillen; Music, Lady Lucille; Costumes, Kadie Midlam; Lighting, Laura Mroczkowski; Video, Michael Casselli; Stage Manager, Julie Watson; Cast: Ali Ahn, Marjuan Canady, Elsa Carette, Faryn Einhorn, Hazuki Homma, Tom Lipinski, Emma Ramos, Juan Villa, Samantha Yonack; The Incubator; June 26–July 5

Yellow Electras Presented by Red Handle; July 11–19

mythic figurations: a power triptych Written and directed by Samara Naeymi; Co-presented by Title:Point Productions; Set, Peter Ksander; Lighting, Miranda Hardy; Costumes, Solace Naeymi; Stage Manager, Brendan Regimbal; Graphics, Fil Vocasek; Cast: Theresa Buchheister, Vonia Arslanian, Ilan Bachrach; The Incubator; July 31–August 9

The Knockout Blow Written and directed by Tina Satter; Music, Chris Giarmo; Design/Lighting, Zack Tinkelman; Cast: Jess Barbagallo, Eliza Bent, Julia Sima-Frest; The Incubator; August 13–16

What We Should Judge When We Judge…Written, directed, and performed by Jake Hooker; Design, Tlaloc Lopez-Waterman; Video, Brian Rogers; August 20–23

Heavenly Robe, Carmonk and Blackhole Written and directed by Yuto Kurosaka; Choreography, Yoshito Sakuraba; Music, Shogo Samata; Costumes, Kui Konno; Musicians, Takeshi Suzuki & Shusuke Inaba; Cast: Xander X, Chloe Bourguignon, Feliziano Flores, Isis King, Meg Hahn, Ritsuko Mano, Hiromi Shimada, Suzzanne Ponomarenko; August 27–30

The Accursed Items by J. Robert Lennon, adapted and choreographed by Andrew Dinwiddie; September 3–6

The Two Sisters; or Douglas Mery, Next to Nothing by Anthony Cerrato & Matt Cosper; Co-presented by Brainum Bros. and Sons Theatrical Ooutfit; Director, Anthony Cerrato; Set, Kaitlyn Mulligan; Costumes, Annie Simon; Lighting, Stephen Arnold; Sound, Jason Sebatian; Technical Consultant, Paul di Pietro; Stage Manager, Julie Watson; Cast: Tara Macmullen, Melissa Miller, Aaron White; The Incubator; September 10–27

SINTESI/dogpile Mini-festival hosted by the Incubator; Performances by Target Margin, Juliana Francis-Kelly, Theater of a Two-Headed Calf, Jake Hooker and Noel Allain, Hoi Polloi (Alec Duffy), Cherry Red Productions, Anthony Cerrato, Maria Chavez, Object Collection, DJ Mendel; October 2–4

Untitled neo 10 point 2 project Presented by New York Neo-Futurists; Cast: Justin Tolley, Rob Neill, Connor Kalista; October 9–11

Radio Festival NYC 2008 Co-presented by free103point9; Radio Theater (October 16) included: *The Assembler Dilator* Created and presented by 31 Down radio theater; Director, Shannon Sindelar; Cast: Caitlin McDonough Thayer & Mike Sharpie; Music of Japanther and Killer Dreamer; Radio Poetics (October 17) included: Curator, Danny Snelson; Performances by Joe Milutis, Kareem Estefan, Alexis Bhagat, Danny Snelson; Radio Talks (October 18) included: Judy Dunaway presents Sex Workers' Internet Radio Lounge; the works of Laura Vitale; Radio

Noise (October 18) included: Neg-Fi, Noveller, Tom Roe, Twisty Cat (Ed Bear, Lea Bertucci, Tianna Kennedy)

The less we talk Created and presented by Hoi Polloi; Director, Alec Duffy; Set, Mimi Lien; Lighting, Miranda Hardy; Costumes, Jessica Pabst; April 16–May 2

Caleb Hammond's 1000 Wolves Written, directed, & performed by Caleb Hammond; October 23–November 1

Sine Waves Goodbye Written and directed by Jamie Peterson; Presented by The Paper Industry; Set/Lighting, Peter Ksander; Costumes, Megan Buchanan; Stage Manager, Brendan Regimbal; Cast: Adam Lerman, Brian Smolin, Ilan Bachrach, Megan Tusing, Stephanie Austin Green; May 14–23

Opening Doors Theatre Company

Artistic/Managing Director, Suzanne Adams; Associate Artistic Director/Marketing, Hector Coris

The Best Little Whorehouse Goes Public Book by Larry L. King & Peter Masterson, music & lyrics by Carol Hall; Director, Hector Coris; Music Director, Michael Lavine; Choreography, Dana Boll; Stage Manager, Brian Busby; Cast: Dana Baràthy, Bryce Bermingham, Rebecca Greenberg, Brooke Jacob, Justin Jones, Brian Tom O'Connor, Brett Rigby, Jason B. Schmidt, Rachel Louise Thomas, Lexi Windsor; Duplex Cabaret Theatre; June 22–July 1

Goldilocks Music by Leroy Anderson, book & lyrics by Jean Kerr & Walter Kerr, additional lyrics by Joan Ford; Director, Daniel Haley; Music Director, Jessica Stewart; Stage Manager, Billie Di Stefano; Cast: Lee Cavellier, Clare Chihambakwe, Ryan Hallert, Rachael Lee, Jean McCormick, Andy McLeavey, Billy Sharpe, Jennifer Teska, Rachel Louise Thomas; Duplex Cabaret Theatre; September 12–14

Fade Out, Fade In Music by Jule Styne, book & lyrics by Betty Comden & Adolph Green; Director, Suzanne Adams; Music Director, Jessica Stewart; Choreography, Christine Schwalenberg; Production Manager, Billie Di Steffano; Cast: Sarah Cooney, Hector Coris, Brian DeCaluwe, Warren Freeman, Sarah Lilley, Jean McCormick, Patrick John Moran, Lawrence Street, Rob Ventre, Lexi Windsor; Duplex Cabaret Theatre; February 27–March 10

I Love My Wife Music by Cy Coleman, book & lyrics by Michael Stewart; Director/Choreography, Marc Tumminelli; Music Director, Ted Kociolek; Co-choreography, Stephanie Fittro; Production Manager, Billie Di Stefano; Cast: Billy Ernst, Christy Faber, Dennis Michael Keefe, Ted Kociolek, Nicholas Marinucci, Jean McCormick, Gregory Jon Phelps, Lou Steele; Duplex Cabaret Theatre; May 29–June 9

Origin Theatre Company

Artistic Director, George C. Heslin

1st Irish 2008 First annual festival of Irish playwrights; included: *End of Lines* Five premiere short plays by Gary Duggan, Pat Kinevane, Morna Regan, Ursula Rani Sarma, Abbie Spallen; Director, Julia Gibson, George C. Heslin, Slyse Rothman, David Sullivan, Fiana Toibin; 59E59 Theater B; *The Selfish Giant* by Oscar Wilde, adapted by Brenda Bell; Director, Ian Bjourkland; The Players Theatre; *Yellow* by Amanda Coogan; Curator, Marina Abramovic; Artistic Space Gallery; *Rum and Vodka* by Conor McPherson; Director, John Brant; Manhattan Theatre Source; *Great White American Teeth* Written & performed by Fiona Walsh; Director, Virginia Scott; Manhattan Theatre Source; *When I Was God* by Cónal Creedon; Director, Tim Ruddy; Manhattan Theatre Source; *Disco Pigs* by Edna Walsh; Director, Dan Brick, Linda Murray; 59E59 Theater B; *Bleeding Poets* by Daniel Reardon; Director, M. Burke Walker; The American Irish Historical Society; *Mojo Mickybo* by Owen McCafferty; Director, Stephen Russell; 59E59 Theater B; *Love Peace and Robbery* by Liam Heylin; Director, Kerry Waters Lucas; September 6–28

Leaves of Glass by Philip Ridley; Co-presented by Stiff Upper Lip; Director, Ludovica Villar-Hauser; Set, Mark Symczak; Lighting, Doug Filomena; Costumes, Christopher Lone; Sound, Jill BC DuBoff; Fight Director, Carlo Rivieccio; Stage Manager, Katrina Lynn Olson; Cast: Euan Morton, Xanthe Elbrick, Victor Villar-Hauser, Alexa Kelly; Peter Jay Sharp Theatre at Playwrights Horizons; January 14–February 8

Performance Space 122 (P.S. 122)

Artistic Director, Vallejo Gantner; Executive Director, Steve Warnick

Right Here. Right Now Presented by Young Dance Collective; June 5–8

Blind Spot Presented by Palissimo; Director/Choreographer, Pavel Zustiak; Lighting, Joe Levasseur; Costumes, Nick Vaughan; Set/Sound, Pavel Zustiak; Cast: Gina Bashour, Yoel Cassell, Ashleigh Leite, Anthony Whitehurst; June 11–15

5th Annual SoloNOVA Arts Festival June 18–July 2

The Mephisto Project (or a Date with the Devil) Conceived and staged by Jean-Philippe Clarac & Olivier Deloeuil; Presented by Opera Francais de New York; Cast: Daniel Mobbs, Keith Miller, Jennifer Rivera, Benedicte Jourdois, Marjorie Folkman; June 19–20

Pure Presented by Readymade Dance Theater Company; Director/Choreographer, Zsolt Palcza; July 17–20

Whisper Written and directed by Peter S. Petralia; Presented by Proto-type Theater; Music/Sound, Philip Reeder; Lighting, Rebecca M.K. Makus; Cast: Alice Booth, Giligan Lees, Andrew Westerside; July 9–13

Neal Medlyn's Unpronounceable Symbol Written & performed by Neal Medlyn; Additional material by Kenny Mellman, Carmine Covelli, Adrienne Truscott, David Neumann, Murray Hill, Bridget Everett, Michael Patrick King, Farris Craddock; July 9–20

A Day in Dig Nation by Michael McQuilken & Tommy Smith; Presented by The Flying Carpet Theater; Director, Adam Koplan; Animation, Gene Lange; Projections/Sound, Michael McQuilken; Cast: Michael McQuilken; August 13–23

Impulse to Suck Conceived, designed, and performed by Karen Finley; August 14

Camp Summer Camp Conceived by Eileen Goddard, Alex Reeves, & Nick Bixby; Cast: Amy Overman, King Aswad, Ojay Morgan, Lauren Cavanaugh, Tim Bungeroth, TV, Annabelle Meunier, Caitlin Mehner, Jessica Delfino; August 21–30

Southern Promises by Thomas Bradshaw; Director, Jose Zayas; Set, Ryan Elliot Kravetz; Lighting, Evan Purcell; Sound, David M. Lawson, Costumes, Carla Bellisio; Dialects, Maggie Surovell; Cast: Hugh Sinclair, Lia Aprile, Erwin Thomas, Jeff Biehl, Peter Mccabe, Sadrina Johnson, Derrick Sanders, Matt Huffman; September 7–27

The Passion Project Created, directed, and presented by Reid Farrington; Costumes, Sara Jeanne Asselin; Set, Janet D. Clancy; Dramaturg/Technical Assistance, Stephen O'Connell & Austin Guest; Cast: Shelley Kay; September 10–20 (Developed at 3LD Art & Technology Center June 19–July 19)

louder Created and presented by Verdensteatret (Norway); Concept, Design, and Direction, Asle Nilsen, Lisbeth J. Bodd, Håkon Lindbäck, Piotr Pajchel, Ali Djabbary, Marius Kjos, Mara Oldenburg, Petter Steen, Christian Blom, Bergmund Waal Skaslien, Elisabeth Gmeiner, Hai Nguyen Dinh, Christina Peios, Rune Madsen, Trond Lossius Pajchel; September 25–28

Diptyque: A Standing Boy and **With My Own Hands** Double bill co-presented by French Institute Alliance Française as part of Crossing The Line; Produced by L'A; Co-producer, Theatre 2 Gennevilliers; *A Standing Boy* Created by Rachid Ouramdane, performed and directed by Pascal Rambert; Music, Alexandre Meyer; Lighting, Yves Godin; *With My Own Hands* Text, direction, and installation by Pascal Rambert, performed by Kate Moran; Sound, Alexandre Meyer; Lighting, Pierre Leblanc; Costumes, Maison Martin Margiela; October 3–4

Waves of Mu Conceived, created, performed by Amy Caron; Co-presented with the P.S. 122 Gallery as part of Room; Neuroscientific Collaborators, Vittorio Gallese, M.D., PhD, Lindsay Oberman, PhD, V.S. Ramachandran, M.D., PhD; Audio, Matt Mateus & Koffi Sessi; Video, Alexander Johnstone & Brian Ray; Costumes, Heather Mathiesen & Jennifer McGrew; Installation Artists/Collaborators, Amy Caron, Courtney Colvin, Trish Empey, Josh Gray, Millar Kelley, Mattson MacFarland, Elmer Presslee, Stefanie Slade, Kelly Schaefer, Margaret Willis; Cast: Amy Caron, Margaret Willis, Sara Kuhn, Peter Sciscioli, Stephanie Sleeper, Annie Bradley, Andrew Lyman-Clarke; October 10 - 19

BLIND.NESS by Simona Semeni in collaboration with the cast; Presented by WaxFactory; Co-produced by Cankarjev Dom; Director, Ivan Talijancic; Set, Minimart; Video, Antonio Giacomin; Surround Sound, Random Logic; Costumes, Haans Nicholas Mott; Lighting, Solomon Weisbard; Technical Directors, Igor Remeta & Mark Sitko; Executive; Producers, Ivan Talijancic for WaxFactory (New York) & Simona Semeni for Integrali (Ljubljana) Cast: Melody Bates, Gillian Chadsey, Erika Latta, Breeda Wool; October 12–November 1

The Society Direction, script, choreography, & set by Jo Strømgren; Presented by Jo Strømgren Kompani; Co-producers, Abrons Arts Center, Norwegian National Theatre, Bergen International Festival, & BIT Teatergarasjen; Sound, Lars Årdal; Lighting, Stephen Rolfe; Costumes, Peter Löchstöer; Props, Tina Peios; Music, Charles Aznavour, Guo Song, Cai Dan Zhuo Ma, Hu Song Hua, The East is Red Choir, & The Doors; Photographer, Knut Bry; General Managers, Ann-Christin Danhammer, Inger Margrethe Stoveland; Cast: Bartek Kaminski, John Fjelnseth Brungot, Trond Fausa Aurvåg; October 15–19

Death Written, choreographed, & performed by Sara Juli; Director, Chris Ajemian; Lighting, Owen Hughes; Costumes, Maggie Dick; October 24–November 2

Screen Test Created and directed by Rob Roth, text by Romy Ashby & Rob Roth; Co-presented by the Abrons Arts Center Costumes, Todd Thomas; Music: Theo Kogan & "Theo and the Skyscrapers"; Music Director, Sean Pierce; Choreographer, Vangeline; Cast: Theo Kogan; Dancers: Maki Shinagawa, Mandy Caughey, Pamela Herron, Stacy Lynn Smith, George Graham; Originally created at P.S. 122 in 2006; October 30–November 3

The Lastmaker Created and presented by Goat Island (Chicago); Co-commissioned by the Chicago Cultural Center, Nuffield Theatre (Lancaster U.K.), Chelsea Theatre (London), Alfred ve Dvore Theatre (Prague); Director, Lin Hixson; Cast: Karen Christopher, Matthew Goulish, Mark Jeffery, Bryan Saner, Litó Walkey; November 6–16

Jester of Tonga Written & performed by Joe Silovsky with Voices of Stanley; Video, Joseph Silovsky & Jesse Dean; Web Design, Maggie Tronic Hoffman; Graphic Artist, Boxcar Billy Burns; Fish Exploder, Eric Dyer; Music, Jesse Dean; Other sounds & Tonga live recordings,Voices of Stanley, Jesse Dean, & Todd Griffin; November 13–23

Cape Disappointment written by Hannah Bos & Paul Thureen, directed and developed by Oliver Butler; Presented by The Debate Society; Set, Karl Allen; Lighting, Mike Riggs; Costumes, Sydney Maresca; Sound, Nathan Leigh; Animation, Tony Candelaria & Stef Choi; Cast: Hanna Bos, Paul Thureen, Oliver Butler, Michael Cyril Creighton, Pamela Payton-Wright; November 22–December 7

LEWIS FOREVER: Freak the Room Created and performed by George Lewis Jr., Isabel Lewis, Ligia Manuel Lewis, Sarah Lewis, and Eric Green; Set, Joanna Joy Seitz; Lighting, Megan Byrne; Dramaturgy, Branden Jacobs-Jenkins; Muisc, Lewis Forever, Sun Ra, and Nina Simone; November 30–December 14

Point Blank Concept, text, & direction by Edit Kaldor; Presented by Filter (Antwerp), Productiehuis Rotterdam, Kata (Amsterdam); Photographs, Frank

Theys; Made in collaboration with Nada Gambier, Frank Theys, Nicola Unger, Io Tillett Wright, Monika Rinck, & Ugo Dehaes; Software, Marc Boon; Technique, Hans Meijer, Etienne Guilloteau;Cast: Edit Kaldor, Nada Gambirer; December 11–14

Meow to the World! Created and performed by Meow Meow; Music Director, Lance Horne; Co-presented by David Binder & Josh Wood at The Highline Ballroom; December 17–22

COIL Festival 2009 Included: *The Crumb Trail* (see listing below); *Jester of Tonga* by Joseph Silovsky; *LEWIS FOREVER: Freak the Room* by Lewis Forever; *Pent Up: A Revenge Dance* (see listing below); *Eight* (see listing below); *Welcome to Nowhere (bullet hole road)* by Temporary Distortion; *Trash Warfare* by The Shalimar; *Geisha* by LeeSaar The Company; *Holiday House* by The BodyCartography Project; *Blind Spot* by Palissimo; *The Passion Project* by Reid Farrington; *Architecting* (see listing below); January 6–17

Eight Written and directed by Ella Hickson; Presented by Tantrum Productions; Cast: Alice Bonifacio, Simon Ginty, Ishbel McFarlane, Holly McLay, Solomon Mousley, Henry Peters, Gwennie Von Einseidel, Michael Whitham; Presented in associateion with The Carol Tambor Best of Edinburgh as part of the COIL Festival January 6–13; extended January 14–25

The Crumb Trail by Gina Moxley; Presented by Peter Pan Theater (Ireland); Director, Gavin Quinn; Design, Aedin Cosgrove; Cast: Bush Moukarzel, Aoife Duffin, Gina Moxley, Arthur Riordan; Presented at P.S. 122 as part of the COIL Festival and the Public Theater's UNDER THE RADAR January 7–12; extended January 15–17

Architecting Created and presented by The TEAM (Theater for the Emerging American Movement), written in collaboration with Davey Anderson, Dave Polato, Lucy Kendrick Smith, Nathan Wright; Co-presented by the National Theater of Scotland; Director, Rachel Chavkin (Artistic Director); Set/Costumes, Nick Vaughan; Video, Brian Scott; Sound, Matt Hubbs; Lighting, Jake Heinrichs; Cast: Kristen Sieh, Jessica Almasy, Frank Boyd, Jill Frutkin, Libby King, Jake Margolin; Developed at the BAC, the 2007 CUNY Prelude Festival, 3LD Art & Technology Center, the Orchard Project. Architecting (Part One) world premiere at the 2008 Edinburgh Fringe Festival; Presented as part of the COIL Festival (and also as part of the Public Theater's UNDER THE RADAR) January 9–18; extended at P.S. 122 January 22–February 15

Pent Up: A Revenge Dance by Okwui Okpokwasili, developed, designed, and directed by Peter Born; Cast: Okwui Okpolwasili, Gloria Huwiler; Developed at 651 ARTS and presented as a work-in-progress in 2006 as part of 651's annual Salon 651 series; Presented as part of the COIL Festival January 11; extended February 8–22

CHAUTAUQUA! Written by James P. Stanley and Normandy Raven Sherwood, created and developed by the National Theater of the United States of America (Ryan Bronz, Mark Doskow, Yehuda Duenyas, Jesse Hawley, Jonathan Jacobs, Normandy Sherwood, James Stanley); Director, Yehuda Duenyas; Guest Choreographer, Faye Driscoll; Lighting, Ben Kato; Sound, Yehuda Duenyas; Costumes, Normandy Raven Sherwood; Original Songs, Jesse Hawley; Associate Designer, Nate Lemoine; Technical Director, Billy Burns; Video, Sarah Demoen; Cast: Ilan Bachrach, Jesse Hawley, Matt Kalman, Ean Sheehy, Normandy Raven Sherwood, James P. Stanley; Keynote Speakers: Mark Russell, Edgar Oliver, Dalton Helms, Robert Zuckerman, Samantha Hunt, Rollo Royce, Jonathan Lethem, Zoe Rosenfeld, Greta Byrum, Juliana Francis Kelly, Vallejo Gantner, Kathie Russo; Guest Artists: Bill Burns, Barbara Allen, Brian Patchett, Steve Cuiffo, Michlel Carlo, H.R. Britton, Rich Maxwell; Musicians: Maria Illic, Tom Chiu, Noah Lindquist; Dancers: Emily Sears, Belinda He, Laura Nicoll, Cassandra Starr, Annabelle Meunier, Jill Guidera, Sara Pauley, Jeso O'Neill, Stephane Magloire, Jeremy X. Halpern, Erin Jennings, Lauren Barri Holstein, Paige Collette, Chris Masullo, Yve Laris Cohen; February 21–March 15

Venice Saved: A Seminar Createed by David Levine & CiNE; Adapted by Gordon Dahlquist; Cast: Jeff Biehl, James Hannaham, Jon Krupp, Gideon Lewis-Kraus, Christianna Nelson, Colleen Werthmann, David Levine; March 21–April 5

Yessified! Text by Bruce Andrews; Choreography, Sally Silvers; Cast: Javier Cardona, Alan Good, Sara Beth Higgins, Takemi Kitamura, Alejandra Martorell, Miriam Parker, Julia Panine-Troiani, Keith Sabado, Sally Silvers; March 22–29

Beowulf: A Thousand Years of Baggage–a Banana Bag & Bodice SongPlay by Jason Craing; Produced and presented by the Shotgun Players; Co-Presented by and at Abrons Arts Center; Director, Rob Hipskind; Music, Dave Malloy; Set, Banana Bag & Bodice; Lighting, Miranda Hardy; Sound, Brendan West; Original Costumes, Kaibrina Buck; Dramaturgy, Mallory Catlett; Choreography, Anna Ishida & Shaye Troha; Stage Manager Catherine Coffey; Sound Engineer, Micah Sapp; Cast: Jason Craig, Anna Ishida, Jessica Jelliffe, Christopher Kuckenbaker, Dave Malloy, Shaye Troha, Beth Wilmurt; Musicians/Chorus: Jen Baker, Dan Bruno, Ezra Gale, Benjamin Geller, Mario Maggio, Dave Malloy, Andre Nigoghossian, Andy Strain; March 13–April 18

Cinderella Toe Jam II: Royal Pink Presented by the Mei-Be WHATever Dance Ensemble; April 2–5

Problem Radical(s) Written and directed by Kara Feely; Presented by Object Collective; Music, Travis Just; Installation, Hannah Dougherty; Video, Daniel Kotter; Costumes, Peter Ksander; Lighting, Miranda Hardy; Stage Manager, Sarah Nerboso; Cast: Karl Allen, Sarah Dahlen, Francesco Gagliardi, Caitlin McDonough Thayer; April 24–May 10

Cracked Ice or Jewels of the Forbidden Skates Written & directed by Jennifer Miller, additional text by Deb Margolin; Music, Kenny Mellman; Design, Jonathon Berger; Choreographer, Faye Driscoll; Cast: Jennifer Miller, Carlton Ward, Ahsley Brockington, Rae C. Wright, Sally May, Adrienne Truscott, Tanya Gagne; April 25–May 10

Avant-Garde-Arama Goes Askew by Polly Frost, Stan Richardson, & William Huffman; Hosts, Bianca Leigh & Everett Quinton; Cast: Bianca Leigh, Karen Grenke, Theatre Askew company members, Irene Ruiz-Riveros, BLISS Dance-Theatre, GERALDCASELDANCE, Isengart, The Din; May 15–May 16

...within us Choreographed by Megan V. Sprenger; Presented by mvworks; Lighting, Joe Lavasseur; Sound, Jason Sebastian, Set, Brad Kisicki; Costumes, Mary McKenzie; Cast: Tara O'Con, Maria Parshina, Alli Ruszkowski, Richert Schonorr; May 17–24

Near-Death Experiences and Other Live Acts Works by Corey Dargel, Nathan Davis, Mario Diaz de Leon, Stephen Lehman; Presented by the International Contemporary Ensemble; May 22–23

Jimmy Written, directed, & performed by Marie Brassard; Produced by Infarouge & Festival TransAmériques; Co-presented by Conseil des arts et des lettres Quebec; Set/Props, Simon Guilbault; Assistant Set, Catherine Chagnon; Lighting, Eric Fauque; Sound, Michael F. Côté; May 27–June 14

Real Dancing with the Real Stars Performance Space 122's annual Spring Benefit honoring Ishmael Houston-Jones & C.Carr; Benefit Producer, Lucy Sexton; Performances by Phillipe Petit, Bill T. Jones' *Fela!*, Liam Mower, Elizabeth Streb, Yvonne Meier, Adrienne Truscott, & Regina Rocke; Hosts, Isaac Mizrahi & Richard Move; Judges, Stephen Daldry, Bebe Neuwirth, Justin Bond; Presentations by Claire Danes, DANCENOISE, Charles L. Kerr, Martha Wilson; Video Work by Charles Atlas; Pre-show performance installation by The Butoh Rockettes; DJ, Andrew Andrew; Stage Manager, Lori E. Seid; Abrons Arts Center; May 27

III A trio of one-woman shows; Presented by Human Company; Lighting, Jay Scott; Set, Heather Wolensky; Technical Supervision, Joshua Redfearn; included: *Is It True What They Say About Dixie* Developed and directed by Kelly Hanson, co-developed and performed by Beth Bradford; *Fugue States: The 7 Successful Secrets to Cultivating and Unshakeable Character* Co-developed and directed by Connor Kalista, co-developed and performed by Cara Francis, co-developed by Susanna Gellert; *Forceps Delivery* Co-developed and directed by Royd Climenhaga, co-developed and performed by Danielle Fink; May 28–May 31

Personal Space Theatrics

Artistic Director, Nicholas Cotz; Managing Director, Kaia Lay Rafoos; Production Director, Mel Wadle

The Safari Party by Tim Firth; Director, Nicholas Cotz; Set/Props, David Esler; Costumes, Kathleen Leary; Lighting, Michael Riotto & Anjeanette Stokes; Sound, Chris Rummel; Props, C. Alexander Smith; Cast: Janet Prince, Ed Schiff, Erika Sheffer, Patrick Shibles Jones, Rebecca Street, Stuart Williams; Kaufmann Theatre at The Algonquin; September 20–October 11

Peter Jay Sharp Theatre at Playwrights Horizons

Samuel French Short Play Festival 33rd annual; July 15–20; Judges: Thomas Bradshaw, Kathleen Clark, Israel Horovitz, Shirley Lauro, Eduardo Machado, Jane Milmore; included (* indicates winning plays to be published by Samuel French): *(W)hole* by Lane Bernes; *40 Stat. 76* by Arlene Hutton; *A Chicken Goes to Broadway* by Kate Louise Sugarcane Marks; *A Dark Wood* by Rob Cardazone; *A New Shade of Red* by Jessica Hinds; *Ayravana Flies or A Pretty Dish* by Sheila Callaghan*; *Balls* by George Cameron Grant; *Blind Date* by Don Creedon; *Checkpoint* by Jason Platt; *DNA* by Christina Gorman; *Evenstar Ellesar* by Forrest Stone; *Falutin* by C.S. Hanson; Friendly Fire by T.E. Abrams; *F**king Art* by Bekah Brunstetter*; *Good Enough* by Kitt Lavoie; *Harborside* by Tom Matthew Wolfe; *Juniper; Jubilee* by Janine Nabers*; *Kiss and Tell* by Steven Yockey; *Kissing Will* by Virginia Reynolds; Marginalia by Kendall Rileigh; Marked by Cassandra Lewis; *Molly Finn RIP we love you* by Cary Gitter; *Muffin* by Jennifer Brown; *Pi Yao and the Farmers' Daughters* by Maurice Martin; Seal Song by Jennifer Fell Hayes; Sex and Money and Money and Sex by Jack Karp; *The Adventures of…* by Kathleen Warnock; *The Art Lady*, by Justin Deabler; *The Cherry Sisters* by Sean O'Donnell; *The Club* by James Christy; *The Dying Breed* by Thomas Higgins*; *The Grave* by Gabe McKinley*; *The Queen is Dead* by Casey Wimpee; *The Thread Men* by Thomas Dunn*; *The Visit* by Delorah Whitney; *Twilight's Child* by Mark Borkowski; *Underneath it All* by Tom Rushen; *When Rodney Met the Vikings* by Pamela Robbins; *Wild Follows* the Queen by Matthew Paul Olmos; *Yog Sothoth* by Lia Romeo

Phare Play Productions

Artistic Director, Blake Bradford; Executive Director, Christine Vinh Weems

Inside Spragg's Shorts Six one-act plays by Jennifer Spragg; included: *Not So Calm, But Still Totally Dead* directed by Christopher Simon; Cast: Adeel Ahmed, Scott Morales, Erin Roberts, Aref Syed; *Wombsgiving* directed by Blake Bradford; Cast: Mary Brown, Emily Ehlinger, Deborah Johnston, Oliver Thrun, Roland Uruci, Nora Vetter; *Apocalypse Earlier* directed by Tanya Fazal; Cast: Adeel Ahmed, Megan Delay, Mary Jane Gocher, Christine Grenier, Faith O'Gorman, Jere Williams; *Ladies and Gentlemen, the 2,746th President of the United States* directed by Glenn English; Cast: Tanya Fazal, Chelsea Holland, Adam Kuruvilla Lelyveld, Scott Morales, Nick Santasier; *Big Bang Teary* directed by Christopher Burris; Cast: Shura Alexandra, Graeme Humphrey, David Law, Aref Syed; *Daddy Issues* directed by Christopher Simon; Cast: Erin E. Sullivan, Al Miro, Erin Roberts; Wings Theatre; June 14–18

The House of Bernarda Alba by Frederico Garcia Lorca, adapted by Blake Bradord; Director, Kymm Zuckert; Cast: Jade Halley Bartlett, Kyla Druckman, Mary Jane Gocher, Susanne Gottesman-Traub, Anne Hammond, Deborah Johnstone, Kimberly Lantz, Meaghan Reilly, Rebecca Servon, Kymm Zuckert; Wings Theatre; July 12–23

The Importance of Being Ernest by Oscar Wilde; Director, Christine Vinh Weems; Cast: Derek Calibre, Derrick Marshall, Michael McKeogh, Carol Neiman, Faye Rex, Kevin Sebastian, Rebecca Servon, Roland Uruci; The Off-Off Broadway Playhouse at Roy Arias Studios; November 5–16

Pants on Fire by Bill Svande; Directors, Blake Bradford & Brooklyn Scalzo; Cast: Mary Jane Gocher, Edward Monterosso, Bill Purdy, Alan Altschuler, Jim Heaphy, Peggy Queener; The Off-Off Broadway Playhouse at Roy Arias Studios; November 8–16

Quisisana by Bill Svande; Director, Blake Bradford; Cast: Joan Darling, Kendall Zwillman, Michael Citrinitti, Henry Packer, Mitch Giannunzio, James Cassano, Patrick Cooley, Natasha Malinsky; American Theatre of Actors–Sargent Theatre; November 28–December 14

Trader Jack and the Stinger by Bill Svande; Director, Blake Bradford; Cast: Steven Ungar, Roland Uruci, Peggy Queener, Jade Halley Bartlett, Sylvia Roldan Dohi; American Theatre of Actors–Sargent Theatre; November 29–December 14

Mind Bleach by Jennifer Spragg, Matt Klan, Michael Weems, & Blake Bradford; Host, Lindy Loo; Directors, Blake Bradford & Christine Vinh Weems; Cast: Blake Bradford, Jackie Byrne, Alex Hill, Dominique Jones, Matt Klan, Eric Loscheider, Jennifer Spragg, Michael Weems, Marian Brock, Tamara Cacchione, Graeme Humphrey, Gina Labozetta, Klemen Novak, Brooklyn Scalzo, Christine Vinh Weems; Broadway Comedy Club; January 26, February 9 & 23, March 9

Tape and **Waiting Life** Two plays by Stephen Belber; Director, Christine Vinh Weems; Cast: Matt Klane, Michael Weems, Sara Towber, Emily Ehlinger, Jade Rothman; Matthew Corozine Studio Theatre; February 27–March 1

I, Undertow by Blake Bradford; Cast: Michael Weems, Sara Ierner, Carol Neiman, Bill Purdy, Laurence Waltman, Peggy Queener, Emily Fitzpatrick, Susanne Gottesman-Traub, Molly Church; American Theatre of Actors–Beckman Theatre; March 26–April 5

Call Waiting Written and directed by Nora Vetter; Cast: Katee Brown, Gretchen Ferris, Sean Gallagher, Adam Files, Shawn Dempewolff, Libby Tatum; American Theatre of Actors–Beckman Theatre; March 28–April 5

A Comedy of Errors by William Shakespeare, adapted and directed by Michael Hagins; Cast: Lino Del Core, Abraham Adams, Alec A. Head, Blaine Pennington, Aubrie Therrien, Catherine Leong, Kattee Brown, Adam Files, Peter Kilcommons, Marian Brock, Aryanna Celenda, Ann Breitbach, Christopher Boerger; American Theatre of Actors–Beckman Theatre; May 14–24

Bludgeon the Lime by Michael Weems; Director, Brooklyn Scalzo; Cast: Jim Heaphy, Kendall Zwillman, Meaghan Reilly, Meagan Robar, Jade Rothman, Leticia Diaz, Rocio Mendez; American Theatre of Actors–Beckman Theatre; May 16–24

Phoenix Theatre Ensemble

Artistic Directors, Craig Smith, Elise Stone, Michael Surabian, Amy Wagner

An Enemy of the People by Henrik Ibsen, translated by Rolf Fjelde; Director, Amy Wagner; Set/Lighting, Maruti Evans; Costumes, Suzanne Chesney; Sound, Elizabeth Rhodes; Composer, David Nelson; Stage Manager, Amanda Kadrmas; Cast: John Lenartz, Joseph J. Menino, Laura Piquado, Kelli Holsopple, Tom Escovar, Michael Surabian, Angus Hepburn, Josh Tyson, Brian A. Costello, Dmitri Friedenberg, Jack Tartaglia; Connelly Theatre; September 3–20

Indiscretions (Les Parents Terribles) by Jean Cocteau, translated by Jeremy Sams; Director, Jonathan Silverstein; Set, Michael V. Moore; Costumes, Brent Barkhaus; Lighting, Lucrecia Briceno; Sound, Elizabeth Rhodes; Stage Manager, Samone B. Weissman; Cast: Gayton Scott, Jan Leslie Harding, Dan Cordle, William Connell, Melissa Miller; Connelly Theatre; February 20–March 14

Phoenix For The Family Saturday Morning Series presented by Grimms-n-Giggles; included: *Aesop's Fables* Adapted & directed by Kathy Menino, music by

Donna DiCerto; Cast: Michael Donaldson, Jessica Bailey, Michael Edmund, Laura DiCerto, Jeremy Sarver, Sarah P. Kerr, Kacy Lissenden; September 6–20; *Puss in Boots* Adapted & directed by Kathy Menino, music & lyric, musical direction, and sound by Ellen Mandel; Choreography, Jessica Colotta; Set, Jeff Duer & Erin Duer; Lighting, Amy Wagner; Cast: Bill Knepper, Steve Freitas, Alexis Powell, Thomas Tyburski, Florence Pape, Frank Magnasco; Connelly Theatre; February 28–March 14

Ping Chong & Company

Artistic Director, Ping Chong; Managing Director, Bruce Allardice

Inside/Out: Voices From The Disability Community Written and directed by Ping Chong, Sara Michelle Zatz; Lighting, & Brant Thomas Murray; Stage Manager, Courtney Golden; Sign Language Interpreters, Lynnette Taylor, Bill Moody; Audio Describer, Andrea Miskow; Cast: Josh Hecht, Monique Holt, Christopher Imbrosciano, Vivian Cary Jenkins, Matthew S Joffe, Zazel-Chavah O'Garra, Blair Wing; New York Times Center; March 20–21

Prospect Theater Company

Producing Artistic Director, Cara Reichel; Managing Director, Melissa Huber; Dark Nights Curator/Producer, Dev Bonderin

Illyria Book, music, lyrics & adaptation by Peter Mills & Cara Reichel; Based on *Twelfth Night* by William Shakespeare; Director, Cara Reichel; Music Director/Orchestrations, Daniel Feyer; Sets, Erica Beck Hemminger; Costumes, Naomi Wolff; Lighting, Ji-youn Chang; Sound, Kris Pierce; Choreography, Christine O'Grady; PSM, Kat West; Associate Producer, Kyle Provost; Casting, Diana Glazer; General Manager, Ryan C. Durham; Production Manager, Mary E. Leach; ASM, Andrea Hayward; Assistant Director, Christopher Diercksen, MaryBeth Smith; Dance Captain, Lauren Adams; Fight Captain, Kat West; Properties, John Sundling; Press, Corinne Zadick; Cast: Brandon Andrus, Jimmy Ray Bennett, Mitch Dean, Ryan Dietz, Jessica Grové, Andrew Miramontes, Jim Poulos, Dan Sharkey, Laura Shoop, Tina Stafford, Lauren Adams, John Mervini, Jed Peterson, Megan Stern; Band: Daniel Feyer, Jason Andert, Thomas Piercy, Yury Shubov, Allison Seidner, Brian Grochowski, Bruce Doctor; Hudson Guild Theatre; October 18–November 16

The Dome by Deborah Abramson, Michael L. Cooper, Rinne Groff, Jason Grote, Hyeyoung Kim, Norman Lasca, Laura Marks, Marisa Michelson, David A. Miller; Director, May Adrales, David Miller, Stefanie Sertich; Sets, Meredith Ries; Costumes, Emily Deangelis; Lighting, Evan Purcell; Video, Richard Dibella; Cast: Travis Allen, Dorothy Abrahams, Dino Antoniou, Sarah Bowles, Kelechi Ezie, John Gardner, Kathryn Holtkamp, Jesse Kearney, Whitney Lee, Britt Lower, Danijela Popovic, Sarah Statler, Kyle Williams, Andrew Zimmerman; West End Theatre; January 31–March 1

Golden Boy of the Blue Ridge Music, lyrics & adaptation by Peter Mills, book, lyrics, adaptation & direction by Cara Reichel; Based on J.M. Synge's *The Playboy of the Western World*, Music Director, Eli Zoller; Fight Choreography, Jacob Grigolia-Rosenbaum; Sets/Props/Technical Director, Tate R. Burmeister; Costumes, Sidney Shannon; Lighting, Evan Purcell; Sound, Daniel Erdberg; Stage Manager, Kat West; Assistant Director, Rachel Dart; Associate Producer, Aidan Levy; General Manager, Nick Robertson; Press, Corinne Zadik; Casting, Diana Glazer; ASM, Kristine Ayers; Cast: Melody Allegra Berger, Matthew Dure, Jeff Edgerton, Carol Hickey, Victoria Huston-Elem, Dennis Michael Keefe, Mark Mozingo, Mike Rosengarten, Dan Sharkey, Scott Wakefield; 59E59 Theater B; April 4–May 3

DARK NIGHTS SERIES

Solo Conceived and directed by Gretchen Cryer; Hudson Guild Theatre; included: *If You Want Me, You Can Have Me – Right Now* Written & performed by Elizabeth Rose (October 25); *Red Flags* Written & performed by Susan Gordon-Clark (October 25); *An Ode to Anna* Written & performed by Malachy Cleary (October 26); *The Sex Education of My Mother* Written & performed by Carol Hall (October 26); *Things Better Left Done* Written & performed by Fred Nelson; *Life in ¾ Time* Written & performed by Susan Laubach (October 26); *Alice & Elizabeth's One Woman Show* Written & performed b Alice Barden (October 27); *Why Do I Choose These Men?* Written & performed b Jacqueline Santiago (October 28); *Confessions of a Mormon Family* Written & performed by Emmett Foster (October 29); *Short Story* written & performed by Betsy Parrish (November 5); *Guido Girl* written & performed by Marianne Ferrari (November 12)
30 ideas, 3 of them good by The Artful Conspirators (David A. Miller, Artistic Director) November 1–4

One-Sixteenth by Rachel Schwartz & **Love Dr. Mueller** Adapted from the writings of Cookie Mueller; Director, Kareem Fahmy; Hudson Guild Theatre; November 8–11

S.O.N.G TEAM Presented and performed by Prospect Theater Company members; West End Theatre; February 4, 9–11, 14–15

Piano Forte! Featuring David Abeles & Scott Pearson; West End Theatre; February 7–8

Red Rover by A. Rey Pamatmat; Music, Matt Park; Director, Dominic D'Andrea; February 16–17

Transit Conceived by Dev Bondarin, Belinda Mello, & Cara Reichel; West End Theatre; February 21–23

Hidden Sky Music & lyrics by Peter Foley, book by Kate Chisholm; Based on the short story "The Masters" by Ursula Le Guin; February 24 & 28

Onward by Katie Kring, music by J. Oconer Navarro; Director, Diana Glazer; Producer, Tate Theatricals; 59E59 Theater B; April 2–4

Recess Created and performed by Una Aya Osato; 59E59 Theater B; April 7

SYMPOSIUM: A Conversation Conceived and performed by David Chernicoff & Kobi Libii; 59E59 Theater B; April 9

Hoaxocaust by Barry Levey; Director, Jeremy Gold Kronenberg; 59E59 Theater B; April 18–19

Map Quest Ten minute musicals created by Bix Bettwy & Eric Kubo, Oron Eldor & Adam Mathias, Sean Hartley, Allison Hubbard & Kim Oler, Heidi Heilig & Michael Pettry, John Herin & Alden Terry, Dan Ho & Chris Wade, Gordon Leary & Julia Meinwald; Director, Dev Bondarin; Producer, Donald Butchko; 59E59 Theater B; April 25–28

Public Theater

Artistic Director, Oskar Eustis; Managing Director, Andrew Hamingson

Native Theater Festival Second annual; Curator, Sheila Tousey; included: *Martha Redbone* at Joe's Pub; *The Conversion of Ka'Ahumanu* by Victoria Nalani Kneubuhl; *Chasing Honey* by Laura Shamas; Director, Alanis King; *Re-Creation Story* by Eric Gansworth; Director, Leigh Silverman November 12–15

UNDER THE RADAR Events at The Public included: *3 Years, 8 Months, 20 Days* presented by Amrita Performing Arts; *Architecting* presented by The TEAM and the National Theatre of Scotland; *COUNTY OF KINGS: the beautiful struggle* Written & performed by Lemon Anderson; *First Love* by Samuel Beckett; performed by Conor Lovett of Gare St. Lazare Players Ireland; *Into The Dark Unknown: The Hope Chest* created by Holcombe Waller; *LIGA, 50% reward & 50% punishment* a multimedia piece by Netherlands troupe, Kassys; *Sight is the sense that dying* *people tend to lose first* Written & directed by Tim Etchells; performed by Jim Fletcher; *Transition* by Reggie Watts and Tommy Smith's; *Woyzeck* performed by Sadari Movement Laboratory in association with AsiaNow; January 7–18

Pulse Ensemble Theatre

Artistic Director, Alexa Kelly; Company Manager, Brian Richardson; Literary Manager, Nina Da Vinci Nichols

Twelfth Night by William Shakespeare; Director, Alexa Kelly; Set, John McDermott; Lighting, Steve O'Shea; Costumes, Kristine Koury; Sound, Brian Richardson; Stage Manager, Shelly VanVliet; Cast: Loren Fenton, Nick Fleming, R.J. Foster, Sean Fredricks, Mick Hilgers, Camille Mazurek, David McLellan, Justin M. Carter, Annie Paul, Raushanah Simmons, Brian Richardson, Richard Vernon; Riverbank State Park Ampitheatre; August 7–24

Queens Players

Founder and Artistic Director, Richard Mazda

Vampire Lesbians of Sodom and **Sleeping Beauty or Coma** Two plays by Charles Busch; Director, Ken Hailey; Cast: Alexander Santiago-Jirau, Erin Frances Robder, Adam Cooley, Michael Miller, Tim McDonough, Elizabeth Claire Taylor, Nathaniel Kressen; The Secret Theatre; June 18–28

Comedy in Queens by V.E. Kimberlain, Ira Sargent, Jack Karp, Edward Musto, Judd Silverman, Steven Wojtas, Susan Gross, Isaac Rathbone, J Snodgrass, & Stefanie Zadravec; Featuring *Hamster Trance; One Night Stand; Jump; Recurring; If You Are My Soulmate, Why Are You Such An Asshole?; Conquering the Fear; Smash and Grab; Leaving; All The Comforts of Home; Aquasaga; It's A Wonderful Play; Death & Motor Vehicles;* The Secret Theatre; July 16–August 2

Mrs. Warren's Profession by Geroge Bernard Shaw; Director, Ken Hailey; Costumes, Tom Kleinert; Stage Manager, Teresa Cajigas; Cast: Katie Braden, Savannah Mazda, Benjamin Weaver, Gary Lizardo, Daniel Wolfe, Alan Altschuler; The Secret Theatre; September 10–27

Theatre of Fear *The System* by Andre De Lorde; Director, Tim Sullivan; *Double Crossed* by Richard Mazda; *The Good Death* by Richard Mazda; Director, Greg Cicchino; *Tell Tale Heart* by Edgar Allen Poe; Director, Richard Mazda; The Secret Theatre; October 16–November 1

Everyman by Anonymous; Director, Rich Ferraioli; Cast: Kirsten Anderson, Dara Jade Tiller, Robin Cannon, Shelleen Kostabi, Karina Bazelyuk, Alicia Blasingame, Melina Paez, Nancy Crawford; The Secret Theatre; November 6–22

Act Four: One Act Fourth annual Long Island City One-Act Festival; included: *Who's Next* by Kirsten Anderson; *Duet* by Sue Yokum; *A Bed Story* by Scott Gerschwer; *For Amy Our Daughter* by Alaina Hammond; *Moment of Death* by Chuck Spoler; *Barbed Wire Oak* by Trystin S. Bailey; *The Garden of Eden* by Sue YoKum; *Surprise* by Paul Gibney; *Man's Best Friend* by Trystin S. Bailey; *Bumps in the Sand* by Scott Gerschwer; Director, Rich Ferraioli, Kyle Haggerty, Greg Cicchino, Richard Mazda; Cast: Justin Randolph, Rachel Pearl, Brandon Ferraro, Rachel Nau, Dara Tiller, Kate Villanova, Aaron Sharff, Amanda Adili, Tyler Etheridge, Gary Lizardo, Rony Goffer, Tiffany D. Turner, Katie Braden, Kyle Haggerty, Julie Nelson, Kirsten Anderson, Robin Cannon, Kwasi Osei, Amy Cerullo, Margaret Ying Drake, Kilvin Johnson Jr, Thomas Michael Quinn, Vincent Ingrisano, Crista Marie Jackson, Jason Michael Miller, Joe Cummings, David Doumeng; The Secret Theatre; January 14–31

Dr. Faustus by Christopher Marlowe; Director, Richard Mazda; Cast: Daniel Smith, Adam Feingold, Meryl Williams, Sarah Sakaan, Whitney Stone, Margaret Ying Drake, Vincent Ingrisano, Henry Packer, Ross Pivec, Leah Reddy, Tyler Etheridge, Kat Gang; The Secret Theatre; February 12–28

Antigone by Sophicles; Director, Greg Cicchino; Cast: Dara Tiller, Katie Braden, Ira Sargent, Amanda Adili, Tiffany Turner, David Doumeng, Chris Duncan, Kelly McCabe; The Secret Theatre; March 12–28

Hamlet by William Shakespeare; Director, Rich Ferraioli; Set/Lighting, R. Allen Babcock; Sound, Graham Stone; Cast: Rony Lee Goffer, Shelleen Kostabi, Daniel Smith, Claire Morrison, Kirsten Anderson, TJ Clark, Kirk Gostkowski, Alyssa Van Gorder, Tony Scheinman, Henry Packer, John Michael Marrs, Ross Pivec, John Curtis, Michael Eisenstein, Lindsay Mack; The Secret Theatre; April 16–May 1

The Imaginary Invalid by Moliére; Director, Matthew A.J. Gregory; Cast: Robert Sherrane, Cate Battiglione, Taryn Turner, Anthony Martinez, Sheila Jones, Hailey McCarty, Tiffany Denise Turner, Christen Gee, Paul Pricer, Kirsten Anderson, Kyle Haggerty, Fernando Gambaroni; The Secret Theatre; May 14–31

RADIOTHEATRE

Creator, Dan Bianchi; Executive Producer, Cynthia Bianchi

King Kong by Dan Bianchi; Director/Sound Designer/Composer, Dan Bianchi; Sound Engineer, Wes Shippee; Lighting, Matt Everett; Cast, Frank Zilinyi, Jerry Lazar, Mike Borak,Zach Lombardo, Cash Tilton, Serrah McCall; Players Theatre; June 1–July 8

H.G. Wells' The Island of Dr. Moreau by Dan Bianchi; Director/Sound Designer/Composer, Dan Bianchi; Sound Engineer, Wes Shippee; Lighting, Matt Everett; Cast: Frank Zilinyi, Jerry Lazar, Mike Borak, Zach Lombardo, Cash Tilton, Serrah McCall; Players Theatre; June 1–July 8

The Mole People by Dan Bianchi; Director/Sound Designer/Composer, Dan Bianchi; Sound Engineer, Wes Shippee; Lighting, Matt Everett; Cast: Jerry Lazar; Players Theatre; August 9–20

Dracula by Dan Bianchi; Director/Sound Designer/Composer, Dan Bianchi; Sound Engineer, Wes Shippee; Lighting, Matt Everett; Cast: Frank Zilinyi, Anthony Crep, Joe Fellman, Chris Riquinha, R.Patrick Alberty, Alexandra Loren, Shelleen Kostabi; Players Theatre; November 11–December 30

Sundays with Poe Twenty of E.A. Poe's stories in repertory adapted by Dan Bianchi; included: *The Pit And The Pendulum; The Tell Tale Heart; The Fall Of The House Of Usher; Ligeia; The Cask Of Amontillado; The Sphinx; Hop Frog; Berenice; The Masque Of The Red Death; The Oval Portrait; The Black Cat; William Wilson; The Oblong Box; The Case of M.Valdemar; Morella; The Premature Burial; The System Of Dr.Tarr and Prof.Fether; The Imp Of The Perverse*; Director/Sound Engineer/Composer, Dan Bianchi; Sound Engineer/Lighting, Wes Shippee; Co-Producer, Horse Trade Theater Group; Cast: Frank Zilinyi, Joe Fellman, Cash Tilton, Shelleen Kostabi, Cheryl Zilinyi, Serrah McCall; UNDER St. Marks Theatre; January 25–December 27, 2009

Repertorio Español

La Vida es Sueño (Life is a Dream) by Calderón de La Barca; Director, René Buch; Sets, Robert Weber Federico; Cast: Luis Carlos de La Lombana, Francisco Rivela; Gramercy Arts Theatre; November 7–December 21

Cartas a una Madre (Letters to a Mother) by Marcelo Rodríguez Venezuela; English Translation, Heather McKay; Director, José Zayas; Cast: Miriam Cruz, Rosie Berrido, Ernesto de villa Bejjani, Mariangélica Ayala, Barbara Jiménez; Gramercy Arts Theatre; December 11–May 5

La Casa de los Espíritus (The House of the Spirits) by Isabel Allende & Caridad Svich; Director, José Zayas; Cast: Nelson Landrieu, Denise Quiñones, Rosie Berrido; Gramercy Arts Theatre, Opened February 18; open run

Retro Productions

Producing Artistic Director, Heather E. Cunningham

The Tender Trap by Max Shulman & Robert Paul Smith; Director, David Storck; Set, Jack Cunningham & Rebecca Cunningham; Costumes, Ben Philipp; Lighting, Kerrie Lovercheck; Sound, Bobby McGinnis; Props, Heather E. Cunningham; PSM, Jeanne Travis; Stage Manager, Daniel Mirsky; Production Assistant, Michelle Guan; Cast: Ric Sechrest, Matilda Szydagis, Jim Kilkenny, Heather E. Cunningham, Elise Rovinsky, Casandera M. J. Lollar, Alex Herrald, C.K. Allen; The Spoon Theater; November 6–22

When You Comin' Back, Red Ryder? by Mark Medoff: Director, Ric Sechrest; Set, Jack Cunningham & Rebecca Cunningham; Costumes, Kathryn Squitieri; Lighting, Kerrie Lovercheck; Special Electrics, Justin Sturges; Sound, Jeanne Travis; Props, Heather E. Cunningham; Stage Manager, Jeanne Travis; Fight Director, Ian Marshall; Cast: Ben Schnickel, Heather E. Cunningham, Richard Waddingham, Dave T. Koenig, Matidla Szydagis, David Blais, Christopher Patrick Mullen, Casandera M. J. Lollar; The Spoon Theater; May 7–23

Rising Phoenix Repertory

Artistic Director, Daniel Talbott; Associates, Denis Butkus, Addie Johnson Talbott, Julie Kline, Brian Roff, Samantha Soule

Don't Pet the Zookeeper by Napoleon Ellsworth; Director, Jessica Bauman; Cast: Denis Butkus, Julie Kline, Jacob Murphy, Daniel Talbott; Seventh Street Small Stage; July 23–August 1

Too Much Memory by Keith Reddin & Meg Gibson; Presented with Piece by Piece Productions as a project of the New York Theatre Workshop's Jonathan Larson Lab; Director, Meg Gibson; Sets, Ola Maslik; Lighting, Joel Moritz; Fights, Joseph Travers; Costumes, Clint Ramos; Sound, Eric Shim & Brandon Epperson; Video, Joe Tekippe; Cast: Aria Alpert, MacLeod Andrews, Peter Jay Fernandez, Laura Heisler, Martin Moran, Seth Numrich, Jamel Rodriguez, Ray Anthony Thomas, Wendy vanden Heuvel; New York Theatre Workshop Fourth Street Theatre; December 9–22

Nobody by Crystal Skillman; Director, Daniel Talbott; Cast: MacLeod Andrews, Jessica Dickey, Kathryn Kates, Polly Lee, Haynes Thigpen, Molly Ward; Seventh Street Small Stage; February 19–28

Birthday by Crystal Skillman; Director, Daniel Talbott; Cast: Denis Butkus and Julie Kline; Seventh Street Small Stage; April 2–10

Roust Theatre Company

Artistic Director, James Phillip Gates; Producing Director, Tracy Hostmyer; Associate Producer, Kristin Barnett

Macbeth by William Shakespeare; Director, James Philip Gates; Set, Casey Smith; Lighting, Travis Sawyer; Costumes, Heather Klar; Sound, John Kemp; PSM, Christine Massoud; Fight Director, Ben Curns; Cast: Kristin Barnett, Melissa Center, Tracy Hostmyer, Emily Hubelbank, Duane Boutte, Craig Braun, Nick Lawson, Tom Macy, Hugh Martin, Tyler, Moss, Michael Peterson, Andrew Pifko, Isaac Woofter, Trey Ziegler; Mint Theatre Space; November 13–December 6

(un)SUSPECT(ed) by Kevin McHatton; Director, James Phillip Gates; Cast: Tracy Hostmyer; Joe Osheroff, Kimani Shillingford, James Phillip Gates; Studio 107; May 21

Ryan Repertory Company

Artistic Director, John Sannuto; Executive Director, Barbara Parisi; Technical Director, Michael Pasternack; Multi-Media Director, Rick Pulos

The Cry of Crows by James Lee Bray; Director, Ely Aina Rapoza; Design, Barbara Parisi; Cast: Jess Beveridge, Elisabeth Toft, Erin Wilhelm, Greg Mocker, Eno Edet, Norrell Moore; Harry Warren Theatre; October 16–November 12

The Empty Chair by Tim Kelly; Director, Marie Ingrisano, Ran Isner; Design, Barbara Parisi; Cast: Lizzie Bell, Ananias J. Dixon, Marie Ingrisano, Paul Ingrisano, Ran Isner, Manuel de la Portilla, Chelsea Roe, Samantha Jane Tilton, Jin-Xiang (JX) Yu; Harry Warren Theatre; April 17–26

It's a ...Baby? Written & performed by Cara Restaino; Director, Barbara Parisi; Design, Basil Horn, John Sannuto, Cara Restaino; Lighting, Barbara Parisi; Media, Cara Restaino, Lindsay Limauro; Harry Warren Theatre; May 13–24

In Conclusive Woman Written & performed by JulieRae (Pratt) Mollenkamp; Associate Director, Taylor Gozia; Stage Manager/Media Operator, Joshua Minnis; Sound, Matt Anderson; Technical Director, Rick Pulos; Production Design Concept, ICW & RRC; Harry Warren Theatre; June 14–28

ShakespeareNYC

Founder/Artistic Director, Beverly Bullock; Managing Director, Peter Herrick

Henry IV Part 1 and **Part 2** by William Shakespeare; Director, Beverly Bullock; Fight Director, Al Foote III; Lighting, Maryvel Bergen; Sound, John D. Ivy; Stage Manager, Steve Barrett; Cast: Benjamin Curns, Steven Eng, Peter Galman, Peter Herrick, Brian Morvant, Joseph Mitchell Parks, Joseph Small, Nicholas Stannard, Josh Vink; Clurman Theatre on Theatre Row; September 11–27

Shetler Theatre 54

Spain by Michael Rubenfeld; Presented by the Bridge Theatre Company (Artistic Directors, Esther Barlow and Dustin Olson); Director, Shana Gold; Cast: Todd D'Amour, Esther Barlow, Michael Rubenfeld; Shetler Studios; December 4–14

Silent Heroes by Linda Escalera Baggs; Presented by Roundtable Ensemble; Director, Rosemary Andress; Producer, Joshua P. Weiss; Set/Lighting, Nick Francone; Costumes, Kevin Hucke; Sound/Music, Jonathan Sanborn; Stage Manager, Henry Cheng; Press, Jim Baldassare; Cast: Dionne Audain, Julie Jesneck, Kelly Ann Moore, Sarah Saunders, Rosalie Tenseth, Lisa Velten Smith; January 8–24

Sonnet Repertory Theatre

Co-Artistic Directors, Todd Loyd & Tiffany Little Canfield; Founding Artistic Director/Executive Director, Robyn Parrish; Co-Founder/Director Press and Marketing, Katrina Kent

The Collaborative Series *Don't Call It A Comeback* by Sean Kent; Director, Robyn Parrish; *The Bank Teller* by Jim Knable; Director, Michael Lluberes; *I Like You, You're Hot* by Greta Gerwig; Director, Jeremiah Maestas; Cast: Luke Robertson, Leah Walsh, Alequw Reid, Zoey Martinson, Laura Espisito, Julie Sharbutt, Ben Yannette, Kristopher Alexander, Maechi Aharanwa, Matt Harrington, Anthony Wofford; JCC; Summer 2008

A Midsummer Night's Dream by William Shakespeare; Director, Tiffany Little Canfield; Cast: Ross Beshear, Eriv Martin Brown, Jeff Burchfield, Chance Carroll, Lauren Culpepper, Michael Lluberes, Jack R. Marks, Candice McKoy, Ian Merrigan, Glenn Peters, John Halbach, Sarah Price, Kit Williamson, Emerald Angel Young, Aleyna Bartnick, Charlotte Beede, Lily Pilblad, Talli Weiss; Bank Street Theatre; July 18–27

Sonnet Sings The Bard Cast: Alan Menken, Heidi Blickenstaff, Jeff Bowen, Celia Keenan-Bolger, Stephen Flaherty, Matt Cavenaugh, Bobby Lopez, Rick Lyon, Rebecca Naomi Jones, Paul David Story, Henry Krieger, Paris Remillard, Kaitlin Kayan, Susan Blackwell; Birdland; November 17

Stone Soup Theatre Arts

Artistic Director, Nadine Friedman; Managing Director, Leigh Goldenberg; Artistic Associate, D.R. Mann Hanson

The Living by Anthony Clarvoe; Director, Elyzabeth Gorman; Set, Jonathan Cottle; Costumes, David Moyer; Lighting, Evan Purcell; Sound, Martha Goode; Stage Manager, Alexandra Duerr; Cast: Musa Bacon, Brian Byus, Eric Eisenbrey, Rachel Handshaw, Al Patrick Jo, Abe Koogler, Gregory Lay, Kevin Mitchell, Joy Notoma, Sarah Todes; Richmond Shepard Theatre; April 18–May 3

What Happens to Women Here by Ben Trawick-Smith; Director, Amy Kaissar; Associate Director, Mike Petranek; Set, Jonathan Cottle; Costumes, Jessica Lustig, Laura Taber Bacon; Lighting, Evan Purcell; Sound, William Neal; Stage Manager, Cory Kane. Cast: Jennifer Boehm, Ellen DiStasi, DR Mann Hanson, Darly Lathon, Morgan Nichols, Kirsta Peterson, Eric Rice, Erika Robel, Maria Schirmer; Richmond Shepard Theatre; April 18–May 3

Summer Play Festival (SPF)

Fifth annual; Founder and Executive Producer, Arielle Tepper Madover; Managing Director, Thom Clay; Programming, Sam Levy; Development, Jackie Leitzez; Marketing, Jennifer Taylor; July 1–27, 2008; performances at the Public Theater

The Black Suits Book, music, & lyrics by Joe Iconis, book co-written by Robert Maddock; Director, John Simpkins; Cast: Nick Blaemire, Sarah Glendening, Annie Golden, Krysta Rodriguez, Lance Rubin, Jason Tam, Jason Williams

Esther Demsack by Billy Finnegan; Director, Stafford Arima; Cast: Elzbieta Czyzewska, Paul Fitzgerald, Noah Galvin, Marin Hinkle, Claudia Shear

Future Me by Stephen Brown; Director, Joanna Settle; Cast: Michael Braun, Aaron Lohr, Chris McCann, Chris McKinney, Linda Powell

Green Girl by Sarah Hammond; Director, Wendy McClellan; Cast: Campion Hall, Erik Jensen, Julie Jesneck, Keira Keeley, Will Rogers, Jessica Wortham

Neighborhood 3: Requisition of Doom by Jennifer Haley; Director, Kerry Whigham; Cast: David Aaron Baker, Reyna de Courcy, Brian Gerard Murray, Sally Wheeler

The Ones That Flutter by Sylvia Reed; Director, Stephen Brackett; Cast: Chris Chalk, Struan Erlenborn, Julia Gibson, Dan Lauria, Danielle Skraastad

Tell Out My Soul by Jacquelyn Honess-Martin; Director, Evan Cabnet; Cast: Cynthia Darlow, Sherman Howard, Jenny Ikeda, Laura Leigh, Annie Parisse

Tio Pepe by Matthew Lopez; Director, Caitlin Moon; Cast: Vaniek Echeverria, Barrett Foa, Nathaniel Mendez, April Ortiz, Benita Robledo

Teatro IATI

Executive Director, Vivian Deangelo; Associate Artistic Director, Winston Estevez; Production Manager, German A. Baruffi, Production Manager

Performing Arts Marathon 2008 Annual festival featuring theater, dance, and music productions; included: *The Ecuador Project* Collected, written and adapted by Leslie Fields; Director, Jesse Baxter; Cast: Jeremy Feldman, Rachel

Martsolf, Lydia Pérez-Carpenter, Mary K. Redington; *Good Sex, Good Day* Written and directed by Yolanda Garcia Serrano; Set, Yanko Bakulic; Lighting, Jason Sturm; Sound, Marcelo Añez; Cast: Carla Gil, Noelle Mauri, Liana Velasquez; *San Salvador after the Eclipse* by Carlos Velis; Director, Elmer Salmeron; Cast: Adriana Hernandez, Karen J. Robles, Ricardo J. Salazar, Jose M. Guardado; *On Becoming* Concept, compositions, and performances by Sasha Bogdanowitsch & Sabrina Lastman; *Tango Jazz Duo* Voice and compositions by Sabrina Lastman; Piano, Fernando Otero; *The Latin Choreographers Festival* Founder/Curator, Ursula Verduzco; Stage Manager/Lighting, Benjamin Briones; Production Assistant, Lucia Campoy; Choreographers, Benjamin Breiones, Javier Dzul, Anabella Gonzalez, Karina Lesco, Yesid Lopez, Jaciel Neri, Frances Ortiz, Ursula Verduzco; July 9–26

El Huésped Vacío (The Guest and the Void) by Ricardo Prieto; Director, Jorge Merced; Lighting, Jason Sturm; Set, Yanko Bakulic; Costumes, Jose Luis Morales; Graphics, Patricia Becker; Cast: George Bass, Vivian Deangelo, Gerardo Gudiño, Patricia Becker, German Baruffi; October 2–19

Por si alguien llega (In Case Someone Arrives) A reading of poems written and read by Yrene Santos; Director, Jose M. de la Rosa; Lighting, Jason Sturm; Music, William González Castañeda; January 30–31

El Corazón de Antígona (Antigone's Heart) by Pati Doménech; Director, Jorge Lopez, Pati Doménech; Set, Sara Huete, Costumes, Paula Roca; Puppets/Masks, Cristina Laso; Choreographer, Regina Navarro; Cast: Maria Vidal; February 5–8

El Huésped Vacío (The Guest and the Void) by Ricardo Prieto; Director, Jorge Merced; Lighting, Jason Sturm; Set, Yanko Bakulic; Costumes, Jose Luis Morales; Graphics, Patricia Becker; Cast: George Bass, Vivian Deangelo, Gerardo Gudiño, Patricia Becker, German Baruffi; April 16–26

Vital Vox: A Vocal Festival Artisic Directors, Sabrina Lastman & Sasha Bogdanowitsch; performances included: (((PHONATION))) performed by Bora Yoon; *VEUS* performed by Sofia Koutsovitis; *VOICE & CELLO* performed by Leah Coloff; *THE MUSIC OF MONK AND BOGDANOWITSCH* performed by Sasha Bogdanowitsch, Emily Eagen, Toby Newman, Peter Sciscioli, Sabrina Lastman, Jeremy Lydic; *DRUM N FACE* by Adam Matta; *BOOK OF ANGELS* by John Zorn Vocal Project (Ayelet Rose Gottlieb, Basya Schechter, Sofia Rei Koutsovitis, Malika Zarra); *VOICE & BODY PERCUSSION* by Gino Sitson; *ON BECOMING* by Sasha Bogdanowitsch, Sabrina Lastman; May 1–2

terraNOVA Collective

Artistic Director, Jennifer Conley Darling; Associate Artistic Director, James Carter

Blue Before Morning by Kate McGovern; Director, Gia Forakis; Scenic Consultant, Derek McLane; Sound & Music: Katie Down; Lighting, Bruce Steinberg; Costumes, Suzanne Chesney; Video & Projections, S. Katy Tucker; Cast: Kether Donohue, Phyllis Johnson, Jenny Maguire, Chris McKinney, Flaco Navaja, Jennifer Dorr White; DR2 Theatre; October 17–November 8

soloNOVA Arts Festival Sixth annual festival of solo performers and visual artists; included: *The Surprise* Written & performed by Martin Dockery; Director, Jean Michele Gregroy; *Fun Design with Svelte [Can You Believe How Fun This Is?!]* Created and performed by Preston Martin; *Cozi Sa Wala* Written & performed by Abena Koomson; Director, Keith Oncale; *Mann Seeking Man: Jesus-Lovin' Schoolgirl Seeks Soulmate* Written & performed by Ryan Migge; Director, Suzanne Agins; *Traces* Conceived and performed by Leigh Evans; *Where My Girls At?* Written & performed by Micia Mosley; Director, Tamilla Woodard; *Face* Written & performed by Haerry Kim; *Creating Illusion* Written & performed by Jeff Grow; Director, Jessi D. Hill; *The Magic Show: The Story of the Barefoot Angels* Written & performed by Abigail Nesson Bengson; Director, David Eppel; *Piccola Cosi* Written & performed by Aja Nisenson; Director, Brian Dilg; Visual Artists:

Kenneth LeRiche and Amy Kalyn Sims; Late Night Music Performances: Amy Soucy, Brendan O'Hara, Brent Shuttleworth, Corn Mo and DJ Reganomics; Late Night Spoken Word Performances: Darian Dauchan, Kelly Zen-Yie Tsai, Vanessa Hidary, Patrick Rosal and DJ Ruzzel D; Late Night Comedy: Livia Scott, Joseph Keckler, Ophira Eisenberg, Red Bastard; DR2 Theatre and D-Lounge; May 6–30

Theater for The New City

Executive Director, Crystal Field

JOYCE AND SEWARD JOHNSON THEATER

It's The Economy Stupid Written and directed by Crystal Field; Music, David Tice; Music Director, Mark York; Costumes, Susan Gittens, Myrna Duarte; Sound, Joy Linscheid, David Nolan; Flats, Walter Gurbo; Cranky, Mary Blanchard; Cast: Lenin Alevante, Ashleigh Awusie, Alexander Bartenieff, Briana Bartenieff, Celestina Bradsher-Layne, John Buckley, Bridget Dowret, Crystal Field, Jasmin Gonzalez, Michael-David Gordon, Sana Haque, Ben Harburg, Nikki Jenkins, Kubbi, Zen Mansley, Mark Marcante, Philip Martinez, Richard Mays, Cat Migliaccio, Iveliz Negron, Alison Nolan, Gabriela Nunic, Allison Patrick, Willa Pittman, Primy Rivera, Justin Rodriguez, Helen Sanders, Alexander Simmons, Oliver Thrun, Ramon Torres, Christine Vega, Calvin Williams, Dor Zemet; August 2–September 14

Cobu Japanese Drumming and Tap Dance; Director, Yuki Yamamori; August 14–17

Village Halloween Costume Ball Various performers and performances; October 31

Dancing in the Dark by Robert Kornfeld; Director, Tom Thornton; Set, Mark Marcante; Lighting, Alexander Bartenieff; Costumes, Susan Gittens; Cast: Susan Izatt, Kristen Wiles, Michael Gnat, Elaine Barrow; November 12–30

The Sourdough Philosophy Circus and Pageant Presented by Bread and Puppet Theater; December 4–21

Times Square Angel Written & performed by Charles Busch; Director, Carl Andress; December 15

Freedoms Ring: Dreams for a New Era A pre-inaugural celebration featuring various performers and performances; January 19

Thunderbird American Indian Dancers Annual dance concert and pow-wow; January 30–February 8

The Two Cents Opera Written, composed, and directed by Elodie Lauten; Cast: Gregg Lauterbach, Karmen Kluge, Jennifer Greene, Mary Hurlbut, Ulysses Borgia, Khoi Bao Le; March 12–29

The #7 Train by Eun-Hee Kim; Choreographer, Hey-Jeong Yoon; April 9–12

The Mechanical Written and directed by Michael McGuigan; Devised and Produced by Bond Street Theater; Lighting, Benjamin Tevelow; Costumes, Carla Bellisio; Cast: Brian Foley, Meghan Frank, Richard Newman, Joanna Sherman, Joshua Wynter, Anna Zastrow; April 16–May 10

14th Annual Lower East Side Festival of the Arts Various performers and performances; May 22–24

In The Silence of the Heart Written and directed by Joanna Chan; Presented by Yangtze Repertory Theater of America; Songs, Kenyatta Hughes; Raps, Jermaine Archer & Clarence Maclin; Set, Pavlo Bosyy; Lighting, Joyce Liao; Costumes/Choreography, David Chien-Hui Sein; Live Music, Su Sheng; Cast: Tamala Baldwin, Carl Hendrick Louis, Hector L. Hicks, Bruce Le and David Brandon, also includes Corey Campbell, Conrado De La Rose, Rachel Filsoof, Mimi Jefferson, Dennis Johnson, Michael A. Jones, Ming Kwai, Victor Landol, Saoko Okano, Annie Q, Sen Yang; May 28–June 14

CINO THEATER

Ceremonies 17 Written and directed by Eugenia Macer-Story; Choreographer, Von Jacobs; Stage Manager, Adrian Gallard; Cast: Kyle Cheng, Jonah Dill-D Ascoli, Thane Floreth, Roxanne Garcia, Megumi Haggerty, Joseph Lymous, Jane Montosi, Jen Oda, Val Ponciano, Chinatsu Uehara, Eva Visco; August 28–September 14

A Village of Fools Written and directed by Stephen Ringold, stories by Isaac Bashevis Singer; Presented by The Grand Faloons; Music, Elizabeth Swados, Ilene Weiss, Kevin Schmidt; October 16–26

Lysistrata's Children Written and directed by Philip Suraci; Set, Caroline Abella; Puppets/Masks, Spica Wobbe; Cast: Monica Bell, Mercer Borris, Josh Feiger, Max Fishelson, Natasha Fishelson, Alex James, Ava Kuslansky, Sinead Larkin, Jacob Lowenherz, Will Mairs, Emily Margolis, Delfin Meehan, Maghnus Mareneck, Philippe Noisy, Annie Saenger, Isabella Shoji, Dyulani Thomas, Clay Walsh; November 6–23

Nutcracker: Rated R Choreographed by Angela Harriell; Stage Manager, Tashika Futch; Production Coordinator, Adrian Gallard; Cast: Jennifer Carlson, Jesus Chapa-Malacara, Hyosun Choi, Sarah Conrad, Gregory Dubin, Christopher Dunston, Angela Harriell, Christina Johnson, Kate Lawrence, Rachel Ma, Michael MacLaren, Kimberly Prosa, Joseph Schles, David F. Slone, Juliana Smith, Clare Tobin; December 17–January 4

Who Murdered Love? by Lissa Moira; Music, Richard West; Director, Lissa Moira; March 5–22

Walking from Rumania Written and directed by Barbara Kahn; Music, Allison Tartalia; Set, Mark Marcante; Lighting, Richard Reta; Costumes, Alice J. Garland; Cast: Zina Anaplioti, Michelle Cohen, Robert Gonzales Jr., Jenny Grace, Andrew Langton, Sylvia Milo, Natalie Reder, Nate Rubin, Kevyn Settle, Steph Van Vlack, Amanda Yachechak; March 26–April 19

All Aboard the Marriage Hearse Written and directed by Matt Morillo; Cast: Nick Coleman, Jessica Moreno; April 23–May 17

Belle of the Ball Bearings by Elizabeth Battersby; Director, Caroline Murphy; Set, Mark Marcante; Lighting, Alexander Bartenieff; Sound, Richard Reta; Stage Manager, Tashika Futch; Cast: Elizabeth Battersby; June 4–27

CABARET THEATER

Adam of the Apes by Oliver Thrun; Director, Nora Vetter; Cast: Ashley Awusie, Bill Bira, Jonathan Craig, Matt Gerathy, David Mansley, Al Miro, Dani Suder, Aimee Todoroff, Oliver Thrun, Nora Vetter; August 8–9

Eksua Itsi: Behind the Mirror Directed and choreographed by Vangeline and Diego Pinon; Stage Manager, Scott Pisticelli; Emcee, Katherine Adamenko; Lighting, Alexander Bartenieff; Cast: Diego Pinon, Pamela Herron, Mandy Caughey, Maki Shinagawa; September 18–October 5

The Sorceres's Butterfly by Daniela Altieri; November 13–23

Stay Over by Matt Morillo, Maria Micheles; Director, Matt Morillo; Cast: JessAnn Smith, Tom Pilutik, Lori Faiella; January 8–February 1

Laugh, Damn Ya, Laugh! by Walter Corwin; Director, Jonathan Weber; Lighting, Mark Marcante; Set, Joy Linscheid; Music, Arthur Abrams; Cast: Jessica Day, Tony King, Samantha Mason, Dani Suder, Oliver Thrun; February 5–22

Vangeline Theater in Tropic of Cancer Choreographer, Vangeline; Cast: Mandy Caughey, Maki Shinagawa, Pamela Herron, Azumi Oe, Katherine Adamenko, Fernamdo Batista, Marghuerita Tisato, Stacy Lynn Smith; February 27–28

The Love of Brothers by Mario Golden; Director, Andreas Robertz; March 5–29

The Mind of a Child Written and directed by Michael Vazquez; and **Indiosyncracy** Written & performed by Indio Melendez; Director, Veronica Caciedo; April 9–26

Anonymous Written & performed by Anna Lisa McClelland; Director, Alex Marino; June 4–6

Tomando Cafe by Rosateresa Castro-Vargas; Director, Joanie Fritz Zosike; Stage Manager, Nicky Roe; Sets, Dara Wishingrad; Cast: Rosateresa Castro-Vargas, Priscilla Flores; June 11–28

COMMUNITY SPACE THEATER

No Applause, Just Throw Money Written and directed by Trav S.D.; Cast: Maggie Cino, Leela Corman, Gyda Arber, Danny Bowes, Michael Criscuolo, Roger Nasser, Mike Rutkoski, Scott Stiffler, Art Wallace; September 18–October 5

The Very Sad Story of Ethel and Julius Written and directed by Vit; Set, Tom Lee; Lighting, Federico Restrepo; Cast: Debbie Beshaw, Michelle Beshaw, Brian P. Glover, Alan NetheronTheresa Linnihan, Valois Mickens, Stephen Ryan, Ronny Wasserman; November 28–December 14

Here Comes the Change Written and directed by Bina Sharif; Lighting, Alexander Bartenieff; Cast: Raul Jennings, Omar Robinson, Sonia Torres, Jonathan Weber, Kevin Martin, Bina Sharif, Oliver Thrun, Jordan Gallagher; December 18–January 4

Strangely Wonderful Written by Jack Tynan; Director, Mark Marcante; January 13–February 1

Paso Del Norte by Juan Rulfo; Director, German Jaramillo; Music, Pablo Mayor; Lighting, Miguel Angel Valderrama; Cast: Ramiro Sandoval, Jorge Luis Vera, Juanita Lara, Anita Guzman, Giovanna Moreno, Pedro Espinoza, Antionio Herreros, Saul Perez; February 12–27

The Lonely Soldier Monologues by Helen Benedict; Director, William Electric Black; Choreographer, Jeremy Lardieri; Sound, Jim Mussen; Costumes, Tilly Grimes; Lighting, Federico Restrepo; Cast: Allisonn Troesch, Athena Colon, Cara Liander, Julia Grob, Kim Weston-Moran, Macah Coates, Verna Hampton; March 5–22

Paula Written and directed by Eduardo Machado; Stage Manager, Hannah Woodward; Costumes, Michael Bevins; Sound, Betsy Rhodes; Cast: Nikki Calonge, Lori Fischer, Catherine Curtin, Crystal Field, Liam Torres; April 9–26

Lincoln on Hester Street by Lu Hauser; Director, George Ferencz; Stage Manager, Robie Varga; Costumes, Sally Lesser; Lighting, Alexander Bartenieff; Set, Mark Marcante; Cast: Britt Bachmann, Jenne Vath, Michael Selkirk, Anthony Sisco, Florence Marcisak; April 30–May 17

Out of Whack: The All Kids Rock Musical Workshop Written and directed by Matt Okin; Cast: Daniel Chelemer, Nicole DeLuca, Jacky Gold, Jessica Lieberman, Heather Levinson, Sara Ravid, Chloe Roe, Rebecca Sichel, Yuval Talby; June 14–17

Tamur Lenk Written and directed by Eugenia Macer-Story; Cast: Richard Craven, Jackie Margolis, Pamela Mayo, Stefanie Tara, Nate Steinwachs, Francesse Maingrette, Doug Stone, Eva Visco, Cathie Boruch, Zen Mansley; June 25–July 12

Theater Ten Ten

Producing Artistic Director, Judith Jarosz

The Tempest by William Shakespeare; Director, Judith Jarosz; PSM, Emily Gasser; Costumes, Viviane Galloway; Sets, Giles Hogya, David Fuller; Lighting, Sherrice Kelly; Sound/Video, Aaron Diehl; Cast: Matt Bernhard, Richard Brundage, Sybille Bruun, Ka-Ling Cheung, Greg Foro, David Fuller, Anne Gill, Catherine Handy, Scott Michael Morales, Kendall Rileigh, David Weinheimer; October 17–November 16

The Philanderrerby George Bernard Shaw; Director, Leah Bonvissuto; Sets, David Fuller; Costumes, Mira Veikley; Lighting, Sherrice Kelly; Cast: Julian Stetkevych, Anne Gill, Tatiana Gomberg, Duncan Hazard, Greg Horton, Shauna Horn, Mickey Ryan, Barrie Kreinik; February 13–March 15

Ruddigore by Gilbert & Sullivan; Adaptor/Director, David Fuller; Music Direction, Jason Wynn; PSM, Erienne Wredt; Sets/Lighting, Giles Hogya; Choreography, Brittney Jensen; Costumes, Mira Veikley; Cast: Natalie Charle Ellis, Greg Horton, Judith Jarosz, Amy Mahoney, Michael McGregor Mahoney, Kristopher Monroe, Sierra Rein, David Tillistrand, Jason Wynn, Adam Yankowy, Cristiane Young; April 24–May 24

Theatre Row Theatres

BECKETT THEATRE

The Time of Mendel's Trouble Book, music, lyrics, & direction by Jermiah Ginsberg, book co-written by Wendy Ginsberg; Choreography, Carolyn Ancey Paddock, General Manager, Peter Bogyo; Set, Kelly Tighe; Costumes, Tescia Seufferlein; Lighting, Paul Miller; Sound, Andy Leviss; Orchestrations/Vocal Arrangements/Musical Director, Peter P. Fuchs; Casting, Cindi Rush; PSM, Elle Aghabala; Press, Shirley Herz; Cast: David Demato, Ira Denmark, Adrienne Doucette, SuEllen Estey, David, Everett, Veronica Fuchs, Ryan Hilliard, Tyrick Wiltez Jones, Josh Lamon, Matt Landers, Desiree Lulay, Grace Mills, Chris Reber, Tom Richter, Tovah Rose, Sheila Wormer; July 18–August 2

Noon Day Sun by Cassandra Medley; Presented by Diverse City Theater Company; Director, Gregory Simmons; Set & Lighting, Maruti Evans; Sound, Elizabeth Rhodes; Costumes, Arnulfo Maldonago; Creative Director, David Derr; PSM, Kathryn Hayzer; Cast: Victor Lirio, Gin Hammond, Ron Cephas Jones, Melanie Nicholls-King, Michael McGlone, David Newer, Penelope Darcel; August 14–August 30

A Number by Caryl Churchill; Presented by The Clockwork Theatre; Director, Beverly Brumm; Set, Larry Laslo; Lighting, Benjamin C. Tevelow; Costumes, Jocelyn Melechinsky; Technical Director, Vincent Vigilante; Casting, Todd Thaler; PSM, Stephanie Cali; Cast: Sean Marrinan, Jay Rohloff; September 6–26

Much Ado About Nothing by William Shakespeare; Presented by Oberon Theatre Ensemble; Director, Mark Karafin; Cast: Gabe Bettio, Walter Brandes, Jordan Brown, Mac Brydon, Don Castro, John Dewey, Brad Fryman, Jennifer Gawlik, Bill Green, Derric Harris, Lara Ianni, Jake Lacy, Adam Petherbridge, Lorenzo Scott, Philip Watt, Cotton Wright, Elizabeth Zins; February 12–February 28

American Rapture Short plays by Alex Dinelaris (*Spin Cycle, Blind Date, Rain, Judging Jacqueline,* and *Forgiven*) presented with *Hello Out There* by William Saroyan; Presented by Oberon Theatre Ensemble; Director, Alex Dinelaris; Set, Kathryn Veillette; Lighting, Jessica Hinkle; Costumes, Kathleen McAllister; Stage Manager, Dee Dee Katchen; Cast: Gabe Bettio, Jane Cortney, Max Darwin, Brad Fryman, Vince Gatton, William Laney, Diánna Martin, Donovan Patton, Laura Siner, Christine Verleny, Stewart Walker; February 12–March 1

CLURMAN THEATRE

Perfect Harmony Written and directed by Andrew Grosso, developed and presented by The Essentials (David Barlow, Jeffrey Binder, Drew Cortese, Meg DeFoe, Autumn Dornfeld, Alec Duffy, Cameron Folmar, Santino Fontana, Jordan Gelber, Vayu O'Donnell, Thomas Piper, Scott Janes, Nicole Lowrance, Maria Elena Ramirez, Jeanine Serralles, Margie Stokley, Marina Squerciati, Noah Weisberg, Margot White, Blake Whyte, Marshall York); Set, Eliza Brown; Costumes, Becky Lasky; Lighting, Brian Jones; PSM, Carlos Maisonet; Music Director, Ray Bailey; Casting, Geoff Josselson; Line Producer, La Vie Productions/Erin Craig; Press, Jim Baldassare; Cast: Dana Acheson, Clayton Apgar, Sean Dugan, Benjamin Huber, Vayu O'Donnell, Scott Janes, Amy Rutberg, Kathy Searle, Margie Stokley, Nisi Sturgis; July 5–August 9

Summer and Smoke by Tennessee Williams; Presented by Blue Sky Theatre Company; Director, Tlaloc Rivas; Set, Jonathan Collins; Lighting, Kate Ashton; Costumes, Tilly Grimes; Music/Sound, Brian McCorkle; PSM, Cherie B. Tay; Production Associate, Claudia Acosta; Cast: Samuel Adams, Jessica Angleskhan, Mia Bankston, Harry Barandes, Michael Frederic, Rachael Hip-Flores, Lena Hurt, Clyde Kelley, Jorge Montenegro, Stu Richel, Mary Sheridan, Melodie Wolford; August 21–31

Caesar and Cleopatra by George Bernard Shaw, adapted by Eric Overmeyer; Presented by Resonance Theatre Ensemble in repertory with *23 Knives*; Director, Kent Paul; Original Music, Robert C. Rees; Set, Sarah B. Brown; Costumes, Michelle Eden Humphrey; Lighting, Pamela Kupper; Sound, Nick Moore; Cast: Pun Bandhu, Alberto Bonilla, Chris Ceraso, Michael Chmiel, Rand Guerrero, Christopher Hayes, Rafael Jordan, Geraldine Librandi, Joe MacDougall, Sophie Maerowitz, Brad Makarowski, Jessica Myhr, Brian Tom O'Connor, Krosby J. Roza, Wrenn Schmidt, Sarah Stockton, Grant James Varjas, Maxwell Zener; January 11–February 7

23 Knives by Christopher Boal; Presented by Resonance Theatre Ensemble in repertory with *Caesar and Cleopatra*; Director, Eric Parness; Set, Sarah B. Brown; Costumes, Sidney Shannon; Lighting, Pamela Kupper; Original Music/ Sound, Nick Moore; Cast: Todd Alan Crain, Demetri Martin, Rafael Jordan, Patrick Melville, Ryan Tramont; January 11–February 7

KIRK THEATRE

Pandora's Box Series of 10 dramatized monologues; Presented by Sister Outsider Entertainment; included: *Be All You Can Be* by Deya Garcia, Sofia Quintero; *Chewy-n-Jocelyn 4 Evah* by Lissette J. Norman; *Ciora* by Sandra Alvarez, Aurora Guerrero; *Confidentiality* by Jasmin Colon; *Don't Knock it 'til You Try It* by Desi Moreno-Penson; *ID, Please!* by Tine Bartolome; *Passing* by Janis Astor del Valle; *Patria* by Janis Astor del Valle; *The Border Made me Gay* by Frenanda Coppel; *Twenty-Four* by Aurora Guerrero; Director, Elisha Miranda; Film Director, Aurora Guerrero; July 2–July 6

Kidstuff by Edith Freni; Presented by Partial Comfort Productions; Director, Erica Gould; Set, Caleb Livengood; Lighting, Jason Jeunnette; Costumes, Whitney Locher; Sound, John Ivey; Stage Manager, Becca Doyle; Cast: Sarah Nina Hayon, Justin Blanchard, Sharon Freedman, Vincent Madero, Peter O'Connor, Cynthia Silver, Chris Van Djik; September 3–September 27

Caligula by Albert Camus; Presented by Horizon Theatre Repertory (Rafael De Mussa, Artistic Director; Andrew Cohen, Managing Director) Director, Rafael De Mussa; Lighting, Jeff Croiter; Sets, Peter R. Feuchtwanger; Sound, Barbara Vlahides; Costumes, Jennifer Nweke; Fight Choreography, Rick Sordelet; Dance Choreography, Bruce Heath; Stage Manager, Susan Manikas; Cast: Gustav Bodor, Jeff Campanella, Rafael De Mussa, Ben Gougeon, Israel Gutierrez, Quester D. Hannah, Tabetha Lorina-Baker, Romy Nordlinger, Chris Triana, Jordan Turchin, Miles Warner, Brandon Wood; December 4–December 30

Twelfth Night by William Shakespeare; Presented by NY Neo-Classical Ensemble (Stephen Stout, Artistic Director; Bill Griffin, Managing Director); Director, Stephen Stout; Set, Eli Kaplan-Wildmann; Costumes, Jessica Pabst; Lighting, Carl Wiemann; Sound, Duncan Cutler; Choreography, Traci Thomas; Score, Matthew Roi Berger; Stage Manager, Andrew Zachary Cohen; Cast: Matthew Roi Berger, Corinne Donly, Richard Douglass, Bill Griffin, Daliya Karnofsky, Cale Krise, Melissa Lusk, Grace McLean, Hubert Point-DuJour Jr., Matt Sadewitz, Robbie Collier Sublett, Brandon Uranowitz; January 8–January 24

Cherry Smoke by James McManus; Presented by Clockwork Theatre; Director, Jade King Carroll; Set, Jay Rohloff & Vincent Vigilante; Lighting, Taryn Kennedy; Costumes, Olga Mill; Sound, Iaeden Hovorka; Technical Director, Michael Zimmerman; PSM, Owen M. Smith; Cast: Marianna McClellan, Doug Nyman, Kate Rogal, Jay Rohloff; February 21–March 14

Gaugleprixtown by Andrew Muir; Presented by Studio 42 (Bradford Louryk, Artistic Director); Director, David F. Chapman; Set, Martin Andrew; Costumes, Bobby Frederick Tilley; Lighting, Peter Hoerburger; Sound, Sharath Patel; Production Manager, David Ogle; Press, Judy Jacksina; PSM, Christy Thede; Cast: Devon Berkshire, Tony Roach, Kurt Uy; March 19–April 4

LION THEATRE

Coming Home Three one-acts; Presented by Living Image Arts; Set, Sarah B. Brown; Costumes, Sarah James; Lighting, Scott Hay; Sound, Keith Rubenstein; included: *Counting* by Maria Gabriele; Director, Christine Farrell; Cast: Maria Elizabeth Ryan, Maria Gabriele; *Sparrow* by Linda Faigao-Hall; Director, Ian Morgan; Cast: Luz Lor, Banaue Miclat; *Last Call on Bourbon Street* by William K. Powers; Director, Alexa Polmer; Cast: Tyler Bunch, Stu Richel, Todd Davis, Andrew Eisenman, Amanda Bruton, Raushanah Simmons; May 29–June 14

The Complete Works of William Shakespeare (Abridged) by Adam Long, Daniel Singer, & Jess Winfield; Director, Melissa Clearly Pearson; June 10–June 13

Rich Boyfriend by Evan Smith; Presented by The New Group as part of the (naked) series; Director, Ian Morgan; Cast: William Jackson Harper, Zach Wegner, Wayne Wilcox; June 18–June 28

What to do When You Hate All of Your Friends by Larry Kunofsky; Presented by Four Chairs Theatre; Director, Jacob Krueger; Set, Niluka Hotaling; Costumes, Melissa Trn; Lighting, Gina Scherr; Sound, Ryan Maeker; Choreography, Josie Bra; PSM, Louise Ochart; Production Manager, Sally Jane Kerschen-Sheppard; Casting, Judy Bowman; Press, David Gibbs; Assistant Director, Markus Paminger; Cast: Todd D'Amour, Carrie Keranen, Susan Louise O'Connor, Josh Lefkowitz, Amy Staats; July 19–August 23

Duet for One by Tom Kempinski; Presented by Lamb Pond Productions in association with Pamela Frost; Director, Rae Ritke; Cast: Anna Pond, David Lamberton; September 4–September 7

Refuge of Lies by Ron Reed; Presented by Firebone Theatre; Director, Steve Day; Set, Rebecca Ferguson; Score/Sound, Josh Liebert; Lighting, Michael Jarrett; Costumes, Marina Reti; Cast: Drew Dix, Joanne Josephe, John Knauss, Richard Mawe, Arthur Pellman, Lorraine Serabian, Libby Skala; September 12–September 28

The Rise and Fall of Annie Hall by Henry Blume; Presented by Stage 13; Director, Sam Gold; Set/Costumes, Dane Laffrey; Lighting, Ben Stanton; Sound, Jane Shaw; PSM, Rebecca Goldstein-Glaze; Producer; Lisa Dozier; Cast: Noah Bean, Dan Fogler, Kate Gersten, Erica Newhouse, Charles Socarides; October 24–November 9

Artists Rising A showcase of composers and lyricists; Presented by kef productions; Director, Adam Fitzgerald; Music Director, Michael Pesce; Pianist, Matt Vinson; Lighting, Kati Fitzgerald; Composers/Lyricists, Brad Alexander, Janet Allard, David H. Bell, Rob Broadhurst, Nathan Christensen, Julianne Wick Davis, Carmel Dean, Jeremy Desmon, Ed Dixon, Kyle Ewalt, Vadim Feichtner, Kevin Fisher, Anna K. Jacobs, Rachel Jett, Steven Lutvak, Michael Mahler, Adam Mathias, Chris Miller, Dianne Adams McDowell, Scott Murphy, Matte O'Brien, Gena Oppenheim, Mac Rogers, Todd Schroeder, Niko Tsakalakos, Nathan Tysen, Matt Vinson, Michael Walker, Jordana Williams, Sean Williams; Cast: Tracy Bersley, Justin Brill, Kristy Cates, Alexis Fishman, Demond Green, David Gurland, Simotra Houston, Erin Kukla, Rob Maitner, Carrie Manolakos, Michael Pesce, Will Reynolds, Niko Tsakalakos, Michael-August Turley, Sally Wilfert, Cassie Wooley; December 12–December 13

Brazil Created and presented by Todd Pate and CASES Insights Project; Director, Daniel Stageman; December 16–December 18

Dammerung by Peretz Hirshbein, English adaptation by Ellen Perecman, Marc Geller and Clay McLeod Chapman; Presented by New Worlds Theatre Project; Director, Marc Geller; Lighting, Sabrina Braswell; Costumes/Sets, Marc Geller; Stage Manager, Margot Fitzsimmons; Cast: Andrew Dawson, Alison Frederick, Jeremy Gender, Nicholas Gorham, Michael Mott, Cally Robertson, Augustus Truhn; January 8–25

Belles by Mark Dunn; Presented by Heiress Productions; Director, Marisa Viola; Set, Jonathan W. Collins; Costumes, Emily DeAngelis; Lighting, Jessica Greenberg; Sound, Chris Rummel; Cast: Laura Faith, Ashton Heyl, Rebecca Lovett, Kristi McCarson, Christina Shipp, Kelly Strandemo; March 19–April 12

¡ AMERICANIZE ! A Survival Guide to Life in America Four one-act plays; Presented by Living Image Arts in repertory with *God, Sex and Blue Water*, included: *Anger and the Doughnut* by Robert Askins; Director, Alexa Polmer; *Charles Winn Speaks* by C.S. Hanson; Director, Lynn M. Thomson; *Dirt* by Tony Zertuche; Director, Claudia Acosta; *Graceful Living* by Maria Gabriele; Director, Holli Harms; Cast: Katya Campbell, Julie Fitzpatrick, Nancy Franklin, Kelli Lynn Harrison, Christopher Kipiniak, Robb Martinez, Ryan Lee, Elka Rodriguez, J.J. Perez, Tatiana Suarez-Pico, Jelena Stupljanin; April 16–May 9

God, Sex, and Blue Water by Linda Faigao-Hall; Presented by Living Image Arts in repertory with *¡ AMERICANIZE !*; Director, Nelson T. Eusebio III; Set, Michael Locher; Lighting, Catherine Tate; Costumes, Christina Bullard; Sound, Geoffrey Roecker; Stage Manager, Stefania Schramm; ASMs, Brian Barnett, Emily Gasser, Julio Perez; Producers, Peter Marsh & Mia Vaculik; Cast: Leanne Cabrera, Andrew Eisenman, Lydia Gaston, Ryan McCarthy; April 18–May 9

Reflections An evening of short plays: *Catastrophe* by Samuel Beckett; *Swan Song* by Anton Chekhov; *Their Town* by Alvin Eng; *What Happened Then* by Michael Feingold; *Compromise* by Ian Strasfogel; Presented by Resonance Ensemble; Director, Eric Parness; Lighting, Pamela Kupper; Set, Sarah B. Brown; Costumes, Colleen Kesterson; Original Music/Sound, Nick Moore; Stage Manager, Jenna Lazar; ASM, Kris Roberts; Production Manager, Joe Duran; Cast: David Arthur Bachrach, Todd Butera, Bill Fairbairn, Nicole Gordino, Grant James Varjas, Christine Verleny; May 16–June 6

STUDIO THEATRE

Stripper Created and presented by Supernova Theatre Company; Producer/Director, Blair Wing; Lighting, Sonia Baiyda; Sound, Curtis Brown; Cast: Morgan de Beetham, Ashlee Mundy, Diana Bae; June 16–22

Good Theater for People who Love Bad Theater An evening of one-act guilty pleasures; Presented by Barlow Theater Group; included: *Night Motherfucker* by Jonathan Wallace; Director, Jeremy Wechter; *Juxtaposed* Written & directed by Mike Kouri; *The New Flame* Written & directed by Douglas Treem; *The Good Life* by Matt Hoverman; Director, Derrick Hawkins; *Good Drugs for People Who Love Bad Drugs* by Craig McNulty; Director, Guil Parreiras; Cast: Michelle Ciarrocca, Laura Cone, Mike Kouri, Jessica Page, Brad Rosenberg, Cheryl Santiago, Mike Sorrentino, John Squires; June 25–29

Dog Day Afternoon Written and directed by Francisco Solorzano; Presented by Barefoot Theatre Company; Set, Adam Rodriguez; Lighting, Eric Nightengale; Costumes, Victoria Malvagno; Sound, Tasha Guevara; Stage Manager, Joanna Leigh Jacobsen; Cast: Jeremy Brena, Charles Casano, John Gazzale, Lydia Gladstone, John Harlacher, Betty Hudson, Kendra Leigh Landon, Ruben Luque, Victoria Malvagno, Amanda Plant, Lorriane Rodriguez, Gil Ro, Francisco Solorzano, Anika Solveig, Joli Tribuzio, Steven R. Weinblatt; June 16–August 16

Down for the Count by Tyriq Mustaqiym; Presented by Black Legacy Productions; Director, Spurgeon H. Allmond; Cast: J. Ernest Glenn, Dameon Hart, Candice Hassell, April L. Simpson, Hadaya Turner, Dustin Wallace Jr.; November 1–8

Bird's Eyeview Created and presented by CASES Insight Project; Director, Todd Pate; July 28–December 18

Five Seconds to Air Written and directed by Evan Storey & Laura Dickinson, additional material by Jess Oppenheimer, Madelyn Pugh, Bob Carroll Jr, & Charlotte M. Russell; Presented by Evan Storey in association with Dwight Allen O'Neal & Nathan "Seven" Scott; Cast: Joel Malazita, Nitzan Halperin, Christina Cataldo, Cain Perry, Anthony Marino, Stephon O'Neal Pettway, Myles Jordan; September 4–14

Three Movements by Martin Zimmerman; Presented by Heiress Productions; Director, Maura Farver; Choreography, Avichai Scher; Set, Josh Zangen; Costumes, Melinda C. Basaca; Lighting, Joel E. Silver; Sound, Sharath Patel; Cast: Erin Fogarty, Maria Portman Kelly, Mike Timoney; October 17–October 26

Empire's New Clothes Created and presented by Synaesthetic Theatre; Directors, Suchan Vodoor & Tina West; Cast: Kym Bernazky, Alexandra Gray, Ted Hannan, M.A. Makowski, Margaret O'Sullivan, Heather Lee Rogers, Carla Stangenberg; November 21–23

Tartuffe by Moliére; Presented by Beyond the Wall Productions; Director, Danya Nardi; December 5–20

Falling in Love with Love Presented by Isle of Shoals Productions Inc.; Director, Lance Hewett; Music Director, Bryan Williams; February 12–15

Zombie Written & perfomed by Bill Connington, based on the novella by Joyce Carol Oates; Presented by Razors Edge Productions; Director, Thomas Caruso; Set, Josh Zangen; Lighting, Joel E. Silver; Sound/Graphics, Deirdre Broderick; Production Assistant, Naomi Ahorn; Press, David Gibbs; February 18–May 16

An Infinite Ache by David Schulner; Director, Quin Gordon, Sean O'Halloran, Linda Trinh; April 2–April 4

Pound Written & directed by William Roetzheim; Presented by American International Theatre (Alix Steel, Artistic Director); Lighting, Barbara Samuels; Stage Manager, Kate Gibson; Cast: Jeff Berg; May 27–June 19

The Town Hall

Artistic/Executive Director, Lawrence C. Zucker

Summer Broadway Festival Written and hosted by Scott Siegel; included: *A Night At The Operetta*: Director, Dan Foster; Music Director, Fred Barton; Cast: John Easterlin, Alexander Gemignani, Jason Graae, Lisa Howard, Milla Illieva, Mark Kudisch, William Michals, Raymond Jaramillo McLeod, Karen Murphy, Brian Charles Rooney, Jennifer Hope Willis, Christine Andreas, Bill Daugherty (July 14); *Broadway's Rising Stars*: Director, Emily Skinner, Scott Coulter; Choreographer, Vibecka Dahle; Music Director, John Fischer; Cast: Mark Cajigao, Dawn Cantwell, Jenna Dallacco, Jon Fletcher, Kyu-Jeong Han, F. Michael Haynie, Lucy Horton, Joshua Isaacs, Greg Kenna, Jennifer LaMonica, Elena Mindlina, Karen Myatt, Seth A. Peterson, Danielle Simone Roundtree, Ryan Scoble, Sara Sheperd, Joy Suprano, Malia Tippets, Stephanie Torns, Shanyn Trammell (July 21); *All Singin'! All Dancin'!*: Director, Scott Siegel; Choreographer, Josh Rhodes; Music Director, Bruce Barnes, Fred Barton, Tracy Stark; Cast: Marie-France Arcilla, Michael Balderrana, David Eggers, Lisa Gadja, Eric Hatch, Cady Huffman, Kendrick Jones, Lorin Lattaro, Sabra Lewis, Melissa Rae Mahon, Brittany Marcin, Mayumi Miguel, Alli Mauzey, Liz McCartney, Tim McGarrigal, William Michals, Jody Reynard, Megan Sikora, Brian Spitulnik, Melinda Sullivan, Natasha Yvette Williams (July 28)

Broadway Cabaret Festival Fourth annual festival created, written, and hosted by Scott Siegel; included: *A Tribute To Lerner & Lowe*: Director, Jeffry Denman; Music Director, Ross Patterson; Cast: Ron Bohmer, Jim Caruso, Robert Cuccioli, Erin Denman, Alexander Gemignani, Douglas Ladnier, Lorin Latarro, Sarah Jane McMahon, Julia Murney, Marni Nixon, Daniel Reichard, Kevin Worley (October 17); Colm Wilkinson's *Broadway & Beyond*: Director, Dan Foster; Music Director, Jon Fischer; Cast: Colm Wilkinson, Susan Gilmore, Alana Bridgewater (October 18); *Broadway Originals*: Director, Dan Foster; Music Director, Jon Fisher; Cast: Michael Arden, Lucie Arnaz, D'Jamin Bartlet, Gary Beach, Kerry Butler, Liz Callaway, Alan Campbell, Joan Copeland, Chuck Cooper, Robert Cuccioli, Cheryl Freeman, Rita Gardner, Stephen Mo Hanan, Alli Mauzey, Karen Morrow, Pam Myers, Alice Ripley, Bobby Steggert, Terri White (October 19)

Broadway By The Year Series created, written, and hosted by Scott Siegel; Advisor, Barbara Siegel; Music Director/Arranger, Ross Patterson; Sheet Music

Consultant, Michael Lavine; *Broadway By The Year 1924*: Director/Choreographer, Jeffry Denman; Cast: James Barbour, Erin Denman, Jason Graae, Kendrick Jones, Marc Kudisch, Sarah Jane McMahon, Kerry O'Malley, Ryan Silverman, Melinda Sullivan, Kevin Worley; Special Guest: Howard Fishman Quartet (February 23); *Broadway By The Year 1931*: Director, Brad Oscar; Choreographer, Jeffry Denman; Cast: F. Murray Abraham, Mara Davi, Jeffry Denman, Kendrick Jones, Kerry O'Malley, Brad Oscar, David Pittu, Melinda Sullivan, Tony Yazbeck, Chip Zien; Special Guests: Karen Akers, Barb Jungr (March 30); *Broadway By The Year 1944*: Director/Choreographer, Jeffry Denman; Cast, Kate Baldwin, Jeffry Denman, Stephen DeRosa, Kendrick Jones, Shannon Lewis, Sarah Jane McMahon, William Michals, Melinda Sullivan, Tony Yazbeck (May 11); *Broadway By The Year 1970*: Director/Choreographer, Jeffry Denman; Cast: Scott Coulter, Darius de Haas, Jeffry Denman, Stephen DeRosa, Melissa Errico, Cheryl Freeman, Kendrick Jones, Sahr Ngaujah, Christiane Noll, Meredith Patterson, Martin Vidnovic, Max Von Essen; Special Guests: Tovah Feldshuh, Ute Lemper, Walter Willison (June 15)

Vampire Cowboys Theatre Company

Artistic Directors, Qui Nguyen and Robert Ross Parker; Managing Director, Abby Marcus

The Saturday Night Saloon: Season 2 Included: *VCS Radio Monster Theatre Presents* by Robert Ross Parker; *Cynthia and the Dreadful Kite* by Webb Wilcoxen; *Assymetric* by Mac Rogers; *Speed Demons* by James Comtois; *Red Rover* by Rey Pamatmat; *Kill Your Mess* by Megan Mostyn-Brown; Directors, Pete Boisvert, Dominic D'Andrea, Jill DeArmon, Abe Goldfarb, Josh Hecht, Matt Johnston, Meredith McDonough, Robert Ross Parker, Patrick Shearer, Jordana Williams; Cast: Alexis Black, Elizabeth Canavan, TJ Clark, James Comtois, J. Eric Cook, Stephanie Cox-Williams, Andrea Day, Jaden DeArmon, Danelle Eliav, William Jackson Harper, Jon Hoche, Jinn S. Kim, Jamie Klassel, Joshua Koehn, Michael Kohn, Daryl Lathon, Leah Lees, Jason Lindner, Mick Micozzi, Qui Nguyen, Kelley O'Donnell, Matt Park, Robert Ross Parker, Margo Brooke Pellmar, Jocelyn Pierce, Justin Reinsiber, Mac Rogers, David Spangler, Paco Tolson, Christian Toth, Aaron Roman Weiner, Scott Williams, Sean Williams, Sidney Williams, Max Woertendyke, Christopher Yustin; The Battle Ranch; Monthly on Saturdays, September 12–January 3

Revamped: Seventies Soul by Raul Castillo, Carla Ching, Matthew Freeman, Graeme Gillis, Jeff Lewonczyk, Rob Neil, Lloyd Suh; Director, Kyle Ancowitz; Carla Ching, Dominic D'Andrea, Ashton Giuame, Michael Lew, Jeff Lewonczyk, RJ Tolan; Cast: Oscar Avila, Jill Beckman, Alexis Black, Jackie Chung, David Delgrosso, Chris Diercksen, Cara Francis, Graeme Gilis, Jenny Gomez, Ryan Good, John K. Hart, Jon Hoche, Jeff Lewonczyk, Jason Liebman, Toya Lillard, Jodi Lin, Kellie Montanio, Gregg Mozgala, Rob Newill, Denyse Owens, JJ Perez, Robert Pinnock, Kevin Prowse, Johnny Pruitt, David Spangler, Matthew Trumball; HERE Arts Center Mainstage; November 17

Soul Samurai: First Bite by Qui Nguyen; Director, Robert Ross Parker; Cast: Jon Hoche, Maureen Sebastian, Bonnie Sherman, Paco Tolson, Temar Underwood; The Battle Ranch; October 26–27

Soul Samurai by Qui Nguyen; HERE Arts Center; February 14–March 15 (see Off-Broadway Listings in this volume)

Vital Theatre Company

Producing Artistic Director, Stephen Sunderlin; Education Director,Linda Ames Key; General Manager, Kerry McGuire; Eleventh Season

MAINSTAGE

My Left Breast Written & performed by Susan Miller; Director, Nela Wagman; McGinn/Cazale Theatre; October 3–5

Looking for the Pony by Andrea Lepcio; Director, Stephan Golux; January 21–February 8 (see listing in Off-Broadway section)

VITAL FAMILY PROGRAMMING

The Bully Music & lyrics by John Gregor, book by David L. Williams; PSM, Kara Teolis; Stage Manager, Shani Colleen Murfin; Set, Mary Hamrick; Lighting, Christina Watanabe; Cast: Scott Lilly, Jay Paranada, Stephen Stocking, Kyle Minshew, Abigail Taylor, John Magalhaes, Peter Waugh, Monique Beasley, Colleen Lis, Thom Caska, George E. Salazar, Ashley Hannon; McGinn/Cazale Theatre; September 13–October 1

Daisy in Disguise Book & lyrics by Stacie Lents, music by Simon Gray; Director, David Hilder; PSM, Kara Teolis; Stage Manager, Shani Colleen Murfin; Music Director, Simon Gray; Costumes, Elisabeth Vastola; Lighting, Christina Watanabe; Sets, David Geinosky; Cast: Rebecca Lieb, Norman Payne, Stephanie Torns, Bethany James, Angie Perez, Ross Hewitt; McGinn/Cazale Theatre; October 11–November 16

Pinkalicious, The Musical Book and lyrics, Elizabeth Kann & Victoria Kann, music & lyrics, John Gregor; Bleecker Street Theatre; Opened November 1, open run (see Off-Broadway listings in this volume)

The Klezmer Nutcracker Book by Ellen Kushner based on her novel *The Golden Dreydl*, music by The Shirim Klezmer Orchestra; Director, Linda Ames Key; Choreographer, Dax Valdes; PSM, Kara M. Teolis; Stage Manager, Leah McVeigh; Costumes, Hunter Keczorowski; Lighting, Christina Watanabe; Sets, Adam Koch; Sound, Simon Gray; Cast: Danielle Strauss, Julie McKay, Dan J. Gordon, Jonathan Bauchman, Toni Ann DeNoble, Lindsey Levine, Alan House, Melana L. Lloyd, Christopher Michael Lacey, Ellen Kushner, Bethany White; McGinn/Cazale Theatre; December 6–January 3

Princess of Riverside Drive Book by Lindsay Joelle, music & lyrics by Justin S. Fletcher; Director, Teresa K. Pond; Stage Manager, Kristin Orlando; Set, Adam Koch; Lighting, Christina Watanabe; Costumes, Elisabeth Vastola; Choreographer, Jessica Redish; Cast: Bridget Riley, Brittany Kiernan, Jessica DiSalvo, Julie McKay, John Galas, David Ballard; McGinn/Cazale Theatre; January 10–March 1

The Frog and the Witch Book & lyrics by Sammy Buck, music by Dan Acquisto; Director, Elizabeth Lucas; Choreographer, Shea Sullivan; Music Director, Jad Bernardo; Stage Manager, Kristin Orlando; Set, Adam Koch; Costumes, Cherie Cunningham; Lighting, Christina Watanabe; Cast: Jeff Barba, Monique Beasley, Angela Dirksen, Caitlin Mesiano, George E. Salazar, Rebecca Stavis; McGinn/Cazale Theatre; March 14–April 26

The Wild Project

This is Way Beyond My Remote Control by Megan Bienstock; Produced by Great Scott Films Inc.; Director, Mahayana Landowne; Set, Yoki Lai; Lighting, Natlaie Robin; Sound, Jason Sebastian; Costumes, Charlotte Gaspard; Video, Shaun Duan; Stage Manager, Aaron Heflich Shaporo; Cast: Claire Byrne, Tyler Hollinger, Katrina Foy, Desiree Matthews, Jason Altman, Laura Carbonell; October 16–November 2

The Sexual Neuroses of Our Parents by Lukas Barfuss, translated by Neil Blackadder; Director, Kristjan Thor; Set, Moza Saracho; Music Sound, Joel Bravo; Cast: Grace Gummer, Laura Heidinger, Kathryn Kates, Max Lodge, Charlie Mitchell, Luis Moreno, Jim Noonan, Peter O'Connor; November 6–22

The Secret Agenda of Trees by Colin McKenna; Presented by J. Edward Cecala and Push Productions in association with The Wild Project; Director,

Michael Kimmel; Sets/Lighting, Ben Kato; Costumes, Jessica Gaffney; Production Manager, Elizabeth Nielson; Technical Director, Patrick Cecala; Associate Producer, Erin Porvanik; PSM, Syche Hamilton; Original Music, Brian Reilly; Press, Sam Rudy Media Relations; Cast: Lillian Wright, Michael Tisdale, Reyna de Courcy, Christian Navarro, Brian Reilly; March 15–April 11

Artifacts of Consequence by Ashlin Halfnight; Presented by Electric Pear Productions (Melanie Sylvan, Executive Producer; Ashlin Halfnight, Artistic Director); Director, Kristjan Thor; Set, Jennifer de Fouchier; Lighting, Kathleen Dobbins; Costumes, Amelia Dombrowski; Composer/Sound, Mark Valadez; Stage Manager, Andrea Wales; Props, Aaron Haskell & Justin Haskell; Cast: Sara Buffamanti, Tobias Burns, Hanna Cheek, Marty Keiser, Rebecca Lingafelter, Jayd McCarty, Amy Newhall; April 16–May 2

Wings Theatre Company

Artistic Director, Jeffrey Corrick; Managing Director, Robert Mooney

Dance at Bataan Written and directed by Blake Bradford; Stage Manager, Bridget Halloran; Lighting, Michael Megliola;Costumes, Carrie Colden;Sound, Kymm Zuckert; Fight Choreography, Matt Klan; Cast: Tamara Cacchione, Sarah Hankins, Jim Heaphy, Patrick McGhee, Annie Pesch, Jade Rothman, Christopher Simon, Christine Vinh, Michael Weems; June 28–July 26

Chuck and Ginger: Thawed for Your Pleasure by Melissa Cruz & Michael Leedy; Director, Michael Davis; Musical Director, Aya Kato; Cast: Chuck Babcock, Ginger Babcock, Chie Mizuno; September 7–October 12

Caprice Music, lyrics, and book by Robert Lux, additional lyrics by Jim Keeler; Director/Choreographer, Fred C.L. Mann; Musical Diector, David Hancock Turner; Costumes, Kurt A. Smith; Sets Justin Couchara; Lighting, Joyce Liao; Stage Manager, Chelsea Underwood; Cast: LinDel Sandlin, Joey Kovach, Jimmy Glidden III, Frank Galgano, Jared Joplin, Sue Berch, Melissa Zimmerman, Vanessa Wendt, Mary Anne Prevost, Cooper Cerulo, Anthony Fusco; September 17–October 5

Pig Tale by Chris Weikel; Presented by TOSOS, Barry Child & Chester LaRue; Director/Sound, Mark Finley; Set, Ray Klausen; Costumes, Steve Epstein; Lighting, Ahmed Tigani; Stage Manager, Jennifer Marie Russo; Assistant Director, Tracy Calhoun; Technical Director, Michael Muccio; Cast: Moe Bertran, Tim Dietrich, Jesse May, Patrick Porter; December 5–January 3

Down the Rabbit Hole Written & performed by Erin Jividen; Presented by EJ Rocks; January 16–31

Gay Slave Handbook Written and directed by Blake Bradford; Cast: Jackie Byrne, Peter Carrier, Justin Maruri; February 26–March 14

WorkShop Theater Company

Artistic Directors, Timothy Scott Harris and Elysa Marden; Executive Director, Riley Jones-Cohen

MAINSTAGE

A Perfect Ganesh by Terrence McNally; Director, Peter Sylvester; Stage Manager, Michael Palmer; Set, Aaron P. Mastin; Costumes, Cynthia D. Johnson; Sound, Peter Carpenter; Tech Director, John Sisson; Cast: CK Allen, Ellen Barry, Charlotte Hampden, Gary Mahmoud; August 27–September 13

Moonlight and Love Songs by Scott c. Sickles; Director, David Gautschy; Lighting/Set, Duane Pagano; Sound, David Schulder; Stage Manager, Michael Palmer; Cast: David Palmer Brown, Anne Fizzard, David M. Mead, Jeff Paul, Nicole Taylor, Ryan Tresser, Jeff Woodman; November 6–22

A Memory Play by Bob Stewart; Director, Gary Levinson; Cast: Trey Albright, Susan Izatt, Artie Ray; December 3–20

She Said, She Said by Kathryn Chetkovitch; Director, Peter Sylvester; Set, Mark Symczak; Lighting, Duane Pagano; Sound, Peter Carpenter; Costumes, Cynthia Johnson; PSM, Michael Palmer; Press, Jim Baldassare; Cast: Ashley Anderson, Tom Berdik, Julianne Carpenter, Dee Dee Friedman, Mark Hofmaiser, Shelley McPherson; March 12–April 3

PLAYS IN PROCESS AT THE JEWEL BOX THEATER

Crazy Little Thing Called Love: Our 2008 Summer Festival of One-Act Plays Included: *The Domestic Life of Franz Joseph Haydn* by David Schmitt; Director, David Gautschy; *Knowing You* by Kathryn Chetkovich; Director, Marc Geller; *The Pain in the Poetry* by Glenn Alterman; Director, Allison Smith; *The Perfect Plan* by John McKinney; Director, Lisa Milinazzo; *Turtles & Bulldogs* by Scott C. Sickles; Director, Katie Braden; Cast: Ashley Anderson, Susan Barrett, Joel Brady, Ken Glickfeld, Michael Gnat, Charlotte Hampden, Nelson Lugo, Ben Masur, Clare Patterson, Sara Turrone, Fred Velde, Christine Verleny, David Wirth; June 5–10

Weird by Ben Alexander; Director, Richard Kent Green; Sound, David Schulder; Stage Manager, Stefania Diana Schramm; Cast: Alexandra Devin, Sauda Jackson, Nelson Lugo, Clare Peterson, Fred Velde, Christine Verleny; Septembe 24–October 4

American Cake by Jonathan Pereira; Director, Kristen Williams-Smith; Lighting, Duane Pagano, Stage Manager, Alexandra Devin; Cast: Jonathan Pereira; October 29–November 1

NON-RESIDENT PRODUCTIONS

Learn Me My Need by Elizabeth Irwin; Presented by Sublime One Productions; Director, Damon Dunay; Cast: Emil Mequita, Elizabeth Irwin, Yadira Martinez, Ronald Washington, Raphael Bollea, Melissa Wood, Nelson Ruiz; June 20–28

Small Craft Warning by Tennessee Williams; Presented by Whitehorse Theater Company; Director, Cyndy A. Marion; Sets, John C. Scheffler; Costumes, David B. Thompson; Lighting, Debra Leigh Siegel; Music, Joe Gianono; Dramaturg, Vanessa R. Bombardieri; Fight Director, Michael G. Chin; Stage Manager, Ellior Lanes; Cast: Graham Anderson, Patrick Terance McGowan; Andrea Maulella, Rod Sweitzer, Linda S. Nelson, Peter Bush, Christopher Johnson, Tommy Heleringer, Mark Ransom; September 19–October 5

Ages of Man by John Gielgud; Cast: George Innes; January 19–27

Jonathan Weber and Corey Pierno in The Curse of Capistrano - ¡El Zorro! presented by Moose Hall Theater Company/Inwood Shakespeare Festival (photo by Ted Minos)

Talli Weiss and Aleyna Bartnick in Sonnet Repertory's production of A Midsummer Night's Dream (photo by Jason Woodruff)

Jason Tam and Krysta Rodriguez in The Black Suits, part of the Summer Play Festival (photo by Carol Rosegg)

Dan Lauria in The Ones That Flutter, part of the Summer Play Festival (photo by Carol Rosegg)

(front) *Andrew Dawson,* (back l to r) *Michael Mott, Jeremy Gender and Nicholas Gorham in the New Worlds Theatre Project production of* Dammerung, *presented at the Lion Theatre on Theatre Row (photo by Marc Geller)*

Jennifer Ikeda and Louis Ozawa Changchien in the National Asian American Theatre Company (NAATCO) production of Leah's Train, *presented at TBG Theatre (photo by William P. Steele)*

Lillian Wright and Michael Tisdale in The Secret Agenda of Trees *at The Wild Project (photo by Ian Carmody)*

Right: *Brian Gillespie, Thomas Flannery Jr., Grant James Varjas, DeVon Jackson and Margo Singaliese in Other Side Productions'* Two Spoons at the Bank Street Theatre *(photo by Sarah Donovan)*

*The Company of the RADIOTHEATRE
production of* Dracula *at the Players
Theatre (photo by Dan Bianchi)*

Bruce Barton in Pooh Story, *a short play in* Stress and the City,
*presented by Mergatroyd Productions at the Penny Templeton Studio
(photo by N. G. McClernan)*

Bill Roulet and Marc Geller in The Fabulous Kane Sisters *in* Box Office
Poison, *presented as part of the 2008 New York International Fringe
Festival at the Cherry Lane and Barrow Street Theatres
(photo courtesy of Marc Geller)*

Top: *Christopher Fitzgerald and Company in the world premiere musical* Minsky's. *Opened at Center Theatre Group's Ahmanson Theatre (Los Angeles, California) February 6, 2009 (photo by Craig Schwartz)*

Center: *Angela K. Thomas, Joe Wilson Jr., Barbara Meek, Nigel Richards, and Lynnette R. Freeman in* A Raisin in the Sun. *Opened at Trinity Repertory Theatre (Providence, Rhode Island) January 30, 2009 (photo by Mark Turek)*

Bottom: *Steve Blanchard, Melissa Gilbert and Kara Lindsay in the world premiere musical* Little House on the Prairie. *Opened at the Guthrie Theater (Minneapolis, Minnesota) July 26, 2008 (photo by Michal Daniel)*

The Regional Theatre World

Nicole Estvanik Taylor, Managing Editor, *American Theatre* magazine

When times are tough, an obvious strategy for theatre companies pressed to cut payroll is to pick shows with smaller casts. So it's no surprise that the stock of certain solo plays and two-handers held strong in the 2008–09 season: David Sedaris' *Santaland Diaries* (a snarky, solo alternative to the evergreen *A Christmas Carol*) and Stephen Temperley's *Souvenir* (a duet for a pianist and an earnest, tone-deaf soprano) played across the country at theatres big and small. *The Lady With All the Answers*, the Ann Landers bio-play by David Rambo that premiered in 2005, also continued its popularity this season as a solo vehicle for several actresses, including Nancy Dussault at Arizona Theatre Company, Helena Ruoti at Pittsburgh Public Theater, and Mimi Kennedy at Cleveland Play House and Pasadena Playhouse. And after an impressive span of months touring in her own one-woman public-school tapestry *No Child . . .* Nilaja Sun stepped back this season to let other performers have a go—including Rachael Holmes (at Ithaca, New York's Hangar Theatre), Nina Domingue (at Cleveland Public Theatre), and Lela Elam (at GableStage in Coral Gables, Florida).

Fewer actors, trimmed budgets . . . the end? Luckily for actors and audiences alike, small-cast shows were just a small part of the story this season. At TheaterWorks in Hartford, Connecticut, director Rob Ruggiero elected to give the multi-character *No Child . . .* a try as an ensemble piece. Donald Margulies' *Shipwrecked! An Entertainment: The Amazing Adventures of Louis de Rougemont (as told by himself)*—which debuted last season and is fast getting picked up throughout the nation—was written for a multi-tasking trio, but it has room to expand, as evidenced by a production at Actors Theatre of Louisville in Kentucky that beefed up its cast with several puppeteers and sound-effects performers. And at the opposite end of the spectrum, Atlanta's Alliance Theatre premiered a gospel version of *Jesus Christ Superstar* with a cast of fifty. Directed by Alliance artistic director Susan V. Booth, it was conceived, arranged, and carried to fruition over the course of more than six years by *Smokey Joe's Cafe* composer Louis St. Louis. The production's wide appeal was reflected not only in the exuberant reviews it received but in its marketing: Visitors to the theatre's website were able to send "Gospel Grams" (audio e-cards, essentially) in which the production's soulful choir exhorted the recipient to take out the trash, run to the conference room to snag the last bagel, or simply to have a nice day, in the same rousing harmonies that could be heard on the Alliance's stage hailing the coming of Christ.

In truth, many of the plays on this year's roster were notable not for their mini or maxi casts but for the names that popped up again and again. Playwright Sarah Ruhl added a new script to her résumé this year—Berkeley Rep's premiere of *In the Next Room (or the vibrator play)*. Like the hit musical *Spring Awakening*, Ruhl's play turned to the late nineteenth century to explore the budding of sexual self-awareness within a close-lipped, buttoned-up society. The play goes to Lincoln Center this fall, but it's too soon to tell whether it will be embraced around the nation the way her *The Clean House*, *Eurydice*, and *Dead Man's Cell Phone* have been. Five-year-old *Eurydice*, in particular, gained momentum this season, its quirky and heartbreaking expression of loss seen on stages including Houston's Alley Theatre and Undermain Theatre in Dallas, Milwaukee Repertory Theater, Victory Gardens Theater of Chicago, Maryland's Round House Theatre, New Repertory Theatre of Massachusetts, Know Theatre of Cincinnati, Curious Theatre Company in Denver, Florida's Hippodrome State Theatre, and Artists Repertory Theatre in Oregon, among others. David Lindsay-Abaire's more earth-bound exploration of grief, *Rabbit Hole*—along with two other plays that made big NYC splashes not long ago, John Patrick Shanley's *Doubt* (like *Rabbit Hole*, a Pulitzer Prize–winner), and Conor McPherson's *The Seafarer*—also figured prominently on theatre schedules nationwide, proving that although audiences may still flock to a raucous staging of *Noises Off*, they haven't lost their taste for serious subject matter.

A number of new productions swinging the spotlight on American involvement in the Middle East are further proof of this. At Center Theatre Group in Los Angeles,

Moisés Kaufman helmed Rajiv Joseph's new play *Bengal Tiger at the Baghdad Zoo*. One critic, Charles McNulty, was not shy in predicting an exciting future for Joseph and his play: "Attending the opening," he wrote in the *Los Angeles Times*, "gave me a sense of what it must have been like to be in London when Caryl Churchill burst on the scene at the Royal Court in the 1970s." The playwright has received tangible votes of confidence from such sources as the National Endowment of the Arts (which named *Bengal Tiger* one of two Outstanding New American Plays in 2008) and the 2009 Kesselring Fellowship. Meanwhile, Oregon Shakespeare Festival in Ashland premiered a play examining the war in Iraq from the perspective of the returning soldier, Julie Marie Myatt's *Welcome Home, Jenny Sutter*. And George Packer's *Betrayed*, based on his *New Yorker* article about the hazards faced by Iraqi interpreters, followed up last season's Off-Broadway success with West Coast runs at L.A. Theatre Works (an audio theatre producer) and the Bay Area's Aurora Theatre Company, as well as a southeastern outing at GableStage.

Interest in the Middle East—a region whose fate, Americans have come increasingly to realize, is tied up with their own—was not limited to Iraq. *Jihad Jones and the Kalishnikov Babes*, by Yussef El Guindi, dealt with Arab-American stereotypes from a Hollywood-satire perspective. *Jihad* was one of several projects to snag the commitment of a "rolling world premiere" at multiple theatres, under the umbrella of the twenty-six-member National New Play Network; it began its journey at San Francisco's Golden Thread Productions in summer 2008 and moved on during the ensuing season to InterAct Theatre Company in Philadelphia and Kitchen Dog Theater in Dallas. Golden Thread also partnered with Chicago's Silk Road Theatre Project and New York's Lark Play Development Center to create a Middle East America initiative supporting plays by and about Americans with Middle Eastern backgrounds. Adriana Sevan was given the project's first $10,000 commission for a script about the Armenian genocide. In Philadelphia, the Wilma Theater mounted the second U.S. production of Linda Gaboriau's English translation of *Incendies (Scorched)*, by Lebanese-born, Canada-based playwright Wajdi Mouawad, which sends characters to an unnamed Middle Eastern country to unravel a family mystery. And on the heels of a film version, Khaled Hosseini's best-selling novel of Afghanistan, *The Kite Runner*, made its way to the stage at San Jose Repertory Theatre in an adaptation by Matthew Spangler.

There were other notable page-to-stage projects in the past season—take Word for Word Performing Arts Company in San Francisco, which specializes in that genre. Six years after its successful collaboration with short-fiction master Tobias Wolff, it staged *More Stories by Tobias Wolff*, garnering a mention on the *San Francisco Chronicle* "Best of 2008" list. Another San Francisco troupe known for working with top authors, Campo Santo, developed *Fukú Americanus*, developed from the Pulitzer Prize–winning novel *The Brief Wondrous Life of Oscar Wao* by Junot Díaz, and *Angry Black White Boy*, adapted by actor/writer/rapper Dan Wolf from a novel by local author Adam Mansbach. At Steppenwolf Theatre Company in Chicago, meanwhile, Frank Galati, the man whose 1988 *Grapes of Wrath* arguably raised the bar for literary adaptations, directed his own version of Haruki Murakami's *Kafka on the Shore*. At Cleveland Play House, Lee Blessing adapted *Heaven's My Destination*, a novel by Thornton Wilder. And composer Michael John LaChiusa premiered big Texas tuner *Giant*, written with Sybille Pearson and based on the novel by Algonquin Round Table regular Edna Ferber, at Signature Theatre in Arlington, Virginia. Signature was this year's winner of the regional theatre Tony Award, and *Giant* is the first fruit of its major American Musical Voices commissioning project.

Fleshing out the theatrical syllabus were several classic tomes that most audience members either read in school, or pretended to. (Incidentally, as with Shakespeare productions, the Great Books tended to spur theatres to invest in much larger casts.) Christopher Sergel's 1988 adaptation of *To Kill a Mockingbird* put another dozen or so professional productions under its belt in 2008–09, including one at Hartford Stage in Connecticut, directed by Michael Wilson, that featured Matthew Modine in the heroic Gregory Peck role. Jon Jory's adaptation of *Pride and Prejudice* arrived, three years after its premiere, at the theatre he steered for three decades before his recent retirement, Actors Theatre of Louisville. Meanwhile, at Milwaukee Rep, artistic director Joseph Hanreddy and director J.R.

Sullivan penned their own version of the Austen favorite, and their script is poised to play in 2010 at both Oregon Shakespeare Festival and Utah Shakespearean Festival (where Sullivan is on staff). Paul Gordon's 2007 musical version of another Austen tale, *Emma*, visited both Cincinnati Playhouse in the Park and the Repertory Theatre of St. Louis in a fall 2008 co-production. Marilyn Campbell and Curt Columbus' 2003 adaptation of *Crime and Punishment* got several major productions this year—in Cleveland, Indianapolis, Berkeley, Minneapolis, and Pittsburgh—while New Haven, Connecticut's Yale Repertory Theatre premiered a new adaptation of another Dostoevsky work, *Notes from Underground*, written by its director and star, Robert Woodruff and Bill Camp. In the same city, Long Wharf Theatre produced a new version of Hemingway's *The Old Man and the Sea*, adapted by Eric Ting and Craig Siebels and directed by Ting.

Less highbrow, perhaps, but no less familiar are the *Little House on the Prairie* books, musicalized in fall 2008 at Minneapolis's Guthrie Theater under the watchful eye of Francesca Zambello. As catnip for the nostalgic young female demographic (with whom she may already have scored some points for helming Broadway's *Little Mermaid*) veteran opera director Zambello even cast Melissa Gilbert, famous for her childhood portrayal of Laura Ingalls Wilder on the *Little House* TV series, in the role of the Wilder matriarch. Boasting a book by Rachel Sheinkin (Tony-winner for *The 25th Annual Putnam County Spelling Bee*), music by Rachel Portman (Oscar-winning composer for the film *Emma*) and lyrics by Donna DiNovelli, the production will kick off a major nationwide tour in the 2009–10 season with a month-long berth at Paper Mill Playhouse of New Jersey.

Theatre for young audiences has long relied on popular children's books as fodder, and that was certainly true this season, with Newbery-winning author Lois Lowry adapting her *Gossamer* for Oregon Children's Theatre and First Stage Children's Theatre of Milwaukee. (OCT is where another of her books, *The Giver*, was first brought to life four seasons ago, but this was Lowry's first crack at transforming her own work for the stage.) Another kids' classic came to life in D.C., when the Kennedy Center for the Performing Arts staged a concert version of *The Trumpet of the Swan: A Novel Symphony* in December. The starry setting of E.B. White's story by playwright/librettist Marsha Norman and composer Jason Robert Brown featured such actors as Kathy Bates, Richard Thomas, and Fred Willard, plus trumpeter Christopher Michael Venditti and a thirty-five-piece orchestra—but was a special engagement that ran only for three performances.

Beloved children's books aside, arguably the most illustrious marquee of any literary production this season was the coming of Voltaire to Philadelphia's Arden Theatre Company: a refurbishing of the 1956 Leonard Bernstein operetta *Candide*. In 1999, for England's Royal National Theatre, John Caird gamely polished up a libretto that had benefited from initial and later contributions by Richard Wilbur, Hugh Wheeler, Lillian Hellman, Dorothy Parker, Stephen Sondheim, and John Latouche. Terrence J. Nolan's staging at Arden marks the U.S. regional theatre debut of the Caird version, which shows a renewed faithfulness to the source material.

What a difference a vowel makes: composer Josh Schmidt's much-anticipated follow-up to his musical *Adding Machine* was not based on Voltaire's *Candide*, but on George Bernard Shaw's *Candida*. His *A Minister's Wife* premiered at Writers' Theatre in Glencoe, Illinois. And Shaw was hardly the only canonized dramatist to be scrutinized through a new lens. In the case of William Inge and Tennessee Williams, never-before-seen-works came under the stage lights this year. Premieres of a few unknown short plays by Inge were staged at the festival in Independence, Kansas, that bears his name. And Williams' *The Enemy: Time*, which can be viewed as an early study for his *Sweet Bird of Youth*, was staged for the first time by Jef Hall-Flavin in Minneapolis at Gremlin Theatre and then in Provincetown, Massachusetts, at a festival bearing *that* playwright's name.

Living legend Tony Kushner received his own festival of sorts. More than 90,000 people attended Kushner-centric events at the Guthrie from April to June 2009, including a new staging of his and Jeanine Tesori's musical, *Caroline, or Change*; *Tiny Kushner*, a collection of short works; and his new full-length play, written for the occasion: *The Intelligent Homosexual's Guide to Capitalism and Socialism with a Key to the Scriptures*. Directed by Michael Greif, the play centers on a

Brooklyn patriarch who can't reconcile his philosophies, developed over a lifetime working on the docks, with the realities of the twenty-first century. It was a big year for Kushner, who also received the first biennial Steinberg Distinguished Playwright Award (or "Mimi," for one of the namesakes of the Harold and Mimi Steinberg Charitable Trust, which funds the generous $200,000 prize).

Eugene O'Neill also got his three months in the spotlight, at Chicago's Goodman Theatre, where visiting productions from the likes of Toneelgroep Amsterdam, the Wooster Group, and hometown companies the Hypocrites and Neo-Futurists played alongside Goodman artistic director Robert Falls' own contribution, a *Desire Under the Elms* starring Brian Dennehy and Carla Gugino, which transferred to Broadway. Another major American playwright, Horton Foote, died in March 2009; his legacy is still sinking in. Foote left behind a just-completed set of nine plays called *The Orphans' Home Cycle*, three of which are brand-new. The cycle will be premiered in its entirety at Hartford Stage and New York's Signature Theatre Company this coming season. To whet his audience's appetite, Hartford Stage head Michael Wilson brought home his staging of Foote's *Dividing the Estate*, which he'd first directed in New York.

Other major play cycles that were completed or advanced this year include the NEA's second Outstanding New American Play winner, Tarell Alvin McCraney's *The Brother/Sister Plays*. The completed trio of Louisiana-set works by this fast-rising scribe was given back-to-back staging at New Jersey's McCarter Theatre, directed by Tina Landau and Robert O'Hara, in spring 2009. In April, New York's SITI Company continued its association with the Humana Festival of New American Plays at Actors Theatre of Louisville by debuting piece three of its Museum Plays quartet, *Under Construction*. At Portland Center Stage in Oregon over the winter, writer/director Nancy Keystone presented in full her ambitious three-part *Apollo*, eight years in the making, which ties together the U.S. space program, Nazi scientists, and the Civil Rights Movement. Ping Chong premiered *Inside/Out . . . voices from the disability community*, the latest in his *Undesirable Elements* oral history series, commissioned by VSA arts. And intergalactic explorer Cynthia Hopkins unveiled *The Success of Failure (or, The Failure of Success)*, capping off her *Accidental Trilogy*, at Minneapolis's Walker Art Center in April before bringing it to Brooklyn's St. Ann's Warehouse.

In addition to *Desire Under the Elms*, several highlights of the Manhattan season originated in other cities—including the latest Pulitzer winner for drama, *Ruined*, which Lynn Nottage based on her interviews with brutalized women in Africa, and which transports the audience to a bar and brothel in the war-torn Congo. The play originated at the Goodman before transferring to Manhattan Theatre Club. Similarly, Arena Stage in Washington, D.C., gave the musical *Next to Normal* a production following last season's Off-Broadway run, preparing it for its Broadway opening; L.A.'s Center Theatre Group birthed *9 to 5: The Musical;* and in southern California, La Jolla Playhouse was the last of many developmental stops for Moisés Kaufman's Beethoven mystery *33 Variations* before it landed on the Great White Way.

Another musical, *Memphis*, about racial tensions in the 1950s music industry, received a co-production at La Jolla and Seattle's 5th Avenue Theatre. Written by Joe DiPietro and David Bryan (a founding member of the band Bon Jovi), the La Jolla production followed up on a joint world premiere in the 2003–04 season by the now defunct North Shore Music Theatre in Massachusetts and California's TheatreWorks. Christopher Ashley chose to direct it as his first production in the La Jolla artistic director position; *Memphis* is scheduled to open on Broadway in fall 2009 with co-stars who have been with it through several incarnations, Montego Glover and Chad Kimball. Also in California: Bob Martin (*The Drowsy Chaperone*'s co-writer and original Man in Chair), with composer/lyricist team Charles Strouse and Susan Birkenhead, premiered a new Broadway-geared show at Center Theatre Group, *Minsky's Book*. *Chaperone*'s director/choreographer Casey Nicholaw was in the driver's seat, and *Saturday Night Live* comedienne Rachel Dratch made a rare live-theatre appearance.

Other noteworthy productions that appear in the following pages include Steppenwolf's *Up*, by Bridget Carpenter, which bore the same burden/advantage as MCC Theater of New York's *Coraline*: premiering almost simultaneously with a major animated film of the same title. (Carpenter's play, though sharing some concepts with the Pixar movie *Up*, does not tell the same story.) Steppenwolf company member Tracy Letts, whose national profile recently shot sky-high with his explosive Pulitzer-anointed drama *August: Osage County*, premiered his next show, *Superior Donuts*, there in June 2008—his first script to be set in Chicago. Another hot name from *August*, its director Anna Shapiro, was spotted in spring 2009 at the Goodman directing new work by Regina Taylor, whose 2002 hat-homage *Crowns* reigns as one of the most produced musicals in the country. Taylor's *Magnolia* is set in 1960s Atlanta and—like previous Taylor play *Drowning Crow*—reinvents a Chekhov play (*The Cherry Orchard*, in this case). Veteran stager of myths Mary Zimmerman returned to material she first explored in the 1990s with *Arabian Nights*, which had an extended run at Berkeley Rep, Chicago's Lookingglass Theatre Company, and Kansas City Repertory Theatre. Esteemed South African dramatist Athol Fugard premiered his latest, *Coming Home*, at Long Wharf, with which he's had a long association. Paula Vogel, newly a New Haven resident after switching from running Brown University's playwriting program to overseeing the one at Yale, premiered her *Civil War Christmas* at Long Wharf. And Anna Deavere Smith's newest interview-based piece *Let Me Down Easy*, which debuted at Long Wharf last season, moved to Cambridge's American Repertory Theatre this past fall, then to Austin's ZACH Theatre in the spring, and is scheduled to land in Manhattan come October 2009.

Sadly, the shuttering of North Shore Music Theatre noted above was part of a larger wave of permanently lowered curtains in the 2008–09 season. With funding scarce, box-office returns less certain, debt more difficult to navigate—and, in such an environment, leadership succession issues knottier than ever—the not-for-profit professional theatre field bid farewell to Theatre de la Jeune Lune in Minneapolis, Mum Puppettheatre in Philadelphia, Milwaukee Shakespeare, Stamford Theatre Works in Connecticut, American Musical Theatre of San Jose, Foothills Theatre Company of Worcester, Massachusetts, Mill Mountain Theatre in Roanoke, Virginia, and Madison Repertory Theatre in Wisconsin. (Another group of theatres, including Chicago's About Face, San Francisco's Magic Theatre, Shakespeare Santa Cruz, and Kentucky Repertory Theatre, launched emergency campaigns with urgent deadlines to keep their operations going, garnering enough support to move forward.)

A special RIP goes out to Madison Rep, which may have been on to something in its last full season. It commissioned a play about Green Bay Packers coach Vince Lombardi (ESPN's "Coach of the Century") from Eric Simonson titled *Lombardi/ The Only Thing*, which has promisingly moved on to a second production at Milwaukee's Next Act Theatre. Meanwhile, Alabama Shakespeare Festival hit on its highest-grossing play in the twenty-four-year history of its Octagon Theatre venue—*Bear Country*, by Michael Vigilant—running it at 98 percent audience capacity for nearly seven weeks and transferring in August 2009 for another run at Birmingham's Virginia Samford Theatre. Its subject? Football coaching hero Paul "Bear" Bryant. Consider too that in spring 2008, Indiana's Theatre at the Center tapped into another midwestern football legend in *Knute Rockne: All American*. Can the Bill Parcells (or Lance Armstrong) musical be far behind? Sports play a huge role in many Americans' lives; there's intrinsic drama in a championship game or a record-breaking athletic career; and sports, like theatre, are local at their core—so it makes sense to carve out space for them on the American stage.

Despite periodic clouds of discouraging news that darkened the theatre field's landscape during the 2008–09 season, numerous companies found occasions to celebrate their histories *and* their futures. Dallas Theater Center welcomed new artistic director Kevin Moriarty, who is preparing the company to move into swell new digs at the new Dallas Center for the Performing Arts. He chose to open his career as DTC artistic director by helming an updated, Americanized *The Who's Tommy*, casting local actor Cedric Neal in the title role and turning to local band Oso Closo for instrumentation. (Rockers, take note of Dallas: a more recent concept album, Neil "Heart of Gold" Young's *Greendale*, also got a staging in that city this year at Undermain Theatre.) In New Jersey, Crossroads Theatre Company, which won the regional Tony ten years ago, marked its thirtieth anniversary by hiring director Rajendra Ramoon Maharaj to revisit George C. Wolfe's daring satire *The Colored Museum*, which premiered there in 1986. In Washington, D.C., Ford's Theatre, which had been closed for eighteen months for renovations to the historic performance space where Lincoln was shot, reopened in time for Lincoln's 200th birthday. And the Walnut Theatre in Philadelphia, not to be outdone by Honest Abe, celebrated its own bicentennial by producing *A Streetcar Named Desire*, which got its sultry start six decades ago on the Walnut's storied boards.

Editor's Note: Due to the earliest publication deadline schedule than ever before of this, as well as what will be that of all future volumes of *Theatre World*, the editors regret the truncated submission deadline and any corresponding omission of productions or companies that have been previously contained within this section in previous volumes. While every effort is made to locate the contact information of record for all League of Resident Theatres in America in order to make timely requests for submission for production information, the nature of turnover in all areas of the arts (and particularly interns who may have been assigned the task of compiling much of this information) in many ways makes this process an extremely difficult one. The editors also recognize that there are many professional theatres in the United States that do not happen to have a LORT designation. And while it is impossible for our staff to attempt to track annually the evolution of those many theatres outside of the LORT designation, in order to ensure the future inclusion of your professional theatre company in our publication regardless of designation, please contact associate editor Scott Denny below in order to be provided instructions on how to do so: rskotd@gmail.com or 917.568.7444

ACT–American Conservatory Theatre

San Francisco, California
Forty-second Season
Artistic Director, Carey Perloff; Executive Director, Heather Kitchen

Rock 'n' Roll by Tom Stoppard; a co-production with Huntington Theatre Company; Director, Carey Perloff; Set, Douglas W. Schmidt; Costumes, Alex Jaeger; Lighting, Robert Wierzel; Sound, Jake Rodriguez; Dramaturg, Michael Paller; Stage Manager, Kimberly Mark Webb; Assistant Stage Manager, Danielle Callaghan; Cast: René Augesen (Eleanor, Older Esme), James Carpenter (Milan, Waiter), Manoel Felciano (Jan), Anthony Fusco (Interrogator, Nigel), Natalie Hegg (Gillian, Magda, Pupil), Delia MacDougall (Lenka), Nicholas Pelczar (The Piper, Stephen), Marcia Pizzo (Candida), Summer Serafin (Esme, Alice), Jud Williford (Ferdinand), Jack Willis (Max); West Coast Premiere; September 11–October 12, 2008

The Quality of Life by Jane Anderson; a co-production with the Geffen Playhouse and Jonathan Reinis Productions; Director, Jane Anderson; Set, Donald Eastman; Costumes, Lydia Tanji; Lighting, Kent Dorsey; Sound, Richard Woodbury; Dramaturg, Michael Paller; Stage Manager, Elisa Guthertz; Assistant Stage Manager, Heath Belden; Cast: Laurie Metcalf (Jeannette), Dennis Boutsikaris (Neil), Steven Culp (Bill), JoBeth Williams (Dinah), October 24–November 23, 2008

A Christmas Carol by Charles Dickens; Adapted by Carey Perloff and Paul Walsh; Music, Karl Lundeberg; Director, Domenique Lozano (Original Director, Carey Perloff); Choreography, Val Caniparoli; Set, John Arnone; Costumes, Beaver Bauer; Lighting, Nancy Schertler; Sound, Jake Rodriguez; Musical Director, Laura Burton; Répétiteur, Nancy Dickson; Dramaturg, Michael Paller; Stage Manager, Karen Szpaller; Assistant Stage Manager, Danielle Callaghan; Cast: Megan Apple, Isabella Ateshian, James Bigelow, Britannie Bond, Allison Brennan, Nik Brocchini, James Carpenter, Ella Ruth Francis, Nick Gabriel, Cindy Goldfield, B.W. Gonzalez, Kathryn Hasson, Natalie Hegg, William Halladey Lanier, Sharon Lockwood, Megumi Nakamura, Philip Martinson, Nicholas Pelczar, Kai Nau, Rondrell McCormick, Jarion Monroe, Amara Radetsky, Lloyd Roberson II, Patrick Russell, Joshua Rechtschaffen, Tobiah Richkind, Ken Ruta, Lauren Safier, J. Peter Scattini, Rachel Share-Sapolsky, Liz Sklar, Noah Pawl Silverman St. John, Christopher Tocco, Samuel Breakstone Tunick, Stephen Barker Turner, Mfoniso Udofia, Kelsey Venter, Ilya Verzhbinsky, Cat Walleck, Erin Michelle Washington, Phyllis Wattis, Weston Wilson, Sarah Withers, Kira Yaffe; December 4–December 27, 2008

Rich and Famous by John Guare; Director, John Rando; Musical Director/Performance Pianist, Laura Burton; Set, Scott Bradley; Costumes, Gregory Gale; Lighting, Alexander V. Nichols; Sound, Jeremy J. Lee; Dramaturg, Michael Paller; Stage Manager, Elisa Guthertz; Assistant Stage Manager, Heath Belden; Cast: Brooks Ashmanskas (Bing Ringling), Mary Birdsong (Leanara/Veronica Gulpp-Vestige/Allison/Mom), Stephen DeRosa (Stage Manager/Anatol/Torah/Dad/Tybalt Dunleavy), Gregory Wallace (Aphro/Hare Krishna); January 8–February 8, 2009

Souvenir, A Fantasia on the Life of Florence Foster Jenkins by Stephen Temperley; Director, Vivian Matalon; Set, R. Michael Miller; Costumes, Tracy Christensen; Lighting, Ann G. Wrightson; Sound, David Budries; Stage Manager, Jack Gianino; Assistant Stage Manager, Danielle Callaghan; Cast: Donald Corren (Cosme McMoon), Judy Kaye (Florence Foster Jenkins); February 13–March 15, 2009

War Music by Christopher Logue; Adapted by Lillian Groag; Director, Lillian Groag; Composer, John Glover; Choreography, Daniel Pelzig; Set, Daniel Ostling; Costumes, Beaver Bauer; Lighting, Russell H. Champa; Sound, Jeff Mockus; Dramaturg, Michael Paller; Cast: René Augesen, Charles Dean, Lee Ernst, Anthony Fusco, Sharon Lockwood, David A. Moss, Andy Murray, Nicholas Pelczar, Christopher Tocco, Gregory Wallace, Erin Michelle Washington, Jud Williford, Jack Willis; March 26–April 26, 2009

Boleros for the Disenchanted by José Rivera; Director, Carey Perloff; Set, Ralph Funicello; Costumes, Sandra Woodall; Lighting, Nancy Schertier; Original Music/Sound, Fabian Obispo; Assistant Director, Steven Anthony Jones; Cast: Robert Beltran (Don Fermin/Older Eusebio), Drew Cortese (Eusebio/Priest), Lela Loren (Flora/Eve), Rachel Ticotin (Dona Milla/Older Flora), Michele Vazquez (Petra/Monica); May 7–May 31, 2009

At Home at the Zoo by Edward Albee; Director, Rebecca Bayla Taichman; Set, Robert Brill; Costumes, David F. Draper; Lighting, Stephen Strawbridge; Sound, Jake Rodriguez; Dramaturg, Michael Paller; Stage Manager, Joseph Smelser; Assistant Stage Manager, Stephanie Schliemann; Cast: René Augesen (Ann), Anthony Fusco (Peter), Manoel Felciano (Jerry); June 5–July 5, 2009

Actors Theatre of Louisville

Louisville, Kentucky
Forty-fifth Season
Artistic Director, Marc Masterson; Managing Director, Jennifer Bielstein

The Ensemble Project by Matthew Baldiga, Catherine Bandenko, Julia Bentz, David Michael Brown, Steven Christopher, Alison Clayton, Michael Dalto, Eric Eteuati, Ami Jhaveri, Anna Kull, Aaron Matteson, Katherine Moeller, Chris Moore, Allison Moy, Claudine Mboligikpelani Nako, Andy Nogasky, Nancy Noto, LaKeisha Randle, Daniel Reyes, Jon Riddleberger, Anne Veal, Jacob Wilhelmi; Stage Manager, Cadi Thomas; Props, Jessie Combest; Assistant, Amy Attaway; Assistant, Nathan Green; Assistant, Michael Legg; Assistant, Rachel Lerner-Ley; Assistant, Lila Neugebauer; Assistant, Brendan Pelsue; Cast: Matthew Baldiga, Catherine Bandenko, Julia Bentz, David Michael Brown, Steven Christopher, Alison Clayton, Michael Dalto, Eric Eteuati, Ami Jhaveri, Anna Kull, Aaron Matteson, Katherine Moeller, Chris Moore, Allison Moy, Claudine Mboligikpelani Nako, Andy Nogasky, Nancy Noto, LaKeisha Randle, Daniel Reyes, Jon Riddleberger, Anne Veal, Jacob Wilhelmi; Alexander Speer Arts & Commerce Building; September 3 and 5, 2008

Glengarry Glen Ross by David Mamet; Director, Marc Masterson; Set, Paul Owen; Costumes, Lorraine Venberg; Lighting, Brian J. Lilienthal; Sound, Matt Callahan; Properties Designer, Mark Walston; Stage Manager, Debra Anne Gasper; Dramaturg, Amy Wegener; Production Assistant, Erica Sartini; Cast: Larry John Meyers (Levene), Stephen Duff Webber (Williamson), Charles Weldon (Moss), Richard Bekins (Aaronow), William Mapother (Roma), John Leonard Thompson (Lingk), Phillip Cherry (Baylen); Pamela Brown Auditorium; August 26–September 20, 2008

43 Plays for 43 Presidents by Andy Bayiates, Sean Benjamin, Genevra Gallo, Chloë Johnston, and Karen Weinberg; Director, Sean Daniels; Set, Paul Owen; Costumes, Emily Ganfield; Lighting, Brian J. Lilienthal; Sound, Matt Callahan; Properties Designer, Doc Manning; Video Designer, Scott Goodman; Fight Supervisor, Lee Look; Movement Coordinator, Pablo!; Stage Manager, Kathy Preher; Production Assistant, Mary Spadoni; Dramaturg, Julie Felise Dubiner; Cast: Cassie Beck, Nick Cordileone, Abigail Bailey Maupin, Gregory Maupin, Aaron Munoz; Victor Jory Theatre; September 9–28, 2008

Dracula originally dramatized by Hamilton Deane and John L. Balderston from Bram Stoker's novel; Adapted by William McNulty; Director, William McNulty; Set, Paul Owen; Costumes, Lorraine Venberg; Lighting, Tony Penna; Sound, Benjamin Marcum; Original Music, Benjamin Marcum; Properties Designer, William Griffith; Properties Designer, Doc Manning; Dialect Coach, Rinda Frye; SAFD Fight Director, k. Jenny Jones; Fight Captain, David Ian Lee; Stage Manager, Michael D. Domue; Production Assistant, Sara Kmack; Dramaturg, Julie Felise

Dubiner; Cast: Marc Bovino (Renfield), Randolph Curtis Rand (Count Dracula), Katherine Moeller (Ms. Sullivan), William McNulty (Van Helsing), Jeffrey Withers (Dr. Seward), Chris Moore (Mr. Briggs), Kim Stauffer (Lucy), David Ian Lee (Jonathan Harker), Helen Lister (Undead Ensemble), Claudine Mboligikpelani Nako (Undead Ensemble), Nancy Noto (Undead Ensemble), Daniel Reyes (Undead Ensemble), Hannah Shelby (Undead Ensemble), Bingham Theatre; September 19–November 1, 2008

Pride and Prejudice by Jane Austen; Adapted by Jon Jory; Director, Jon Jory; Choreography, Karma Camp; Original Music, Peter Ekstrom; Set, Paul Owen; Costumes, Marcia Dixcy Jory; Lighting, Brian J. Lilienthal; Sound, Matt Callahan; Properties Designer, Mark Walston; Dialect Coach, Don Wadsworth; Production Stage Manager, Paul Mills Holmes; Assistant Stage Manager, Debra Anne Gasper; Dramaturg, Sarah Lunnie; Casting, Harriet Bass; Cast: V.C. Heidenreich (Mr. Bennet), Lada Vishtak (Lydia Bennet/Georgiana), Alexandra Tavares (Elizabeth Bennet), Katherine McLeod (Mary Bennet/Charlotte Lucas), Emily Cedergreen (Jane Bennet), Allison Moy, (Kitty Bennet), Peggity Price (Mrs. Bennet), Thomas Matthew Kelley (Mr. Bingley/Fitzwilliam), Anthony Marble (Mr. Darcy), Joel Van Liew (Mr. Lucas/Gardiner/Collins), Julie Evan Smith (Miss Bingley/Mrs. Gardiner), Drew Cortese (Lt. Wickham), Pat Nesbit (Lady Catherine de Bourgh/Housekeeper), Michael Dalto (Dancer/Officer/Manservant), Pamela Brown Auditorium; September 30–November 2, 2008

A Tuna Christmas by Jaston Williams, Joe Sears, and Ed Howard; Director, Drew Fracher; Original Producer, Charles H. Duggan; Set, Paul Owen; Costumes, Emily Ganfield; Lighting, Tony Penna; Sound, Benjamin Marcum; Properties Designer, Joe Cunningham; Stage Manager, Stephen Horton; Production Assistant, Melissa Blair; Casting, Zan Sawyer-Dailey; Cast: Warren Kelley (Thurston Wheelis, Elmer Watkins, Bertha Bumiller, R.R. Snavely, Aunt Pearl Burras, Sheriff Givens, Ike Thompson, Inita Goodwin, Leonard Childers, Phoebe Burkhalter, Joe Bob Lipsey), Brad DePlanche (Arles Struvie, Didi Snavely, Petey Fisk, Jody Bumiller, Charlene Bumiller, Stanley Bumiller, Vera Carp, Dixie Deberry, Helen Bedd, Farley Burkhalter, Garland Poteet), Victor Jory Theatre; October 30, 2008–January 4, 2009

A Raisin in the Sun by Lorraine Hansberry; Director, Israel Hicks; Set, Paul Owen; Costumes, Lorraine Venberg; Lighting, Brian J. Lilienthal; Sound, Benjamin Marcum; Properties Designer, Doc Manning; Stage Manager, Debra Anne Gasper; Production Assistant, Mary Spadoni; Dramaturg, Adrien-Alice Hansel; Casting, Zan Sawyer-Dailey; Cast: Joy DeMichelle Moore (Ruth Younger), Pierre LaFran Priest, Jr. (Travis Younger), Terrence Riggins (Walter Lee Younger), Nicole Gant (Beneatha Younger), Marlene Warfield (Lena Younger), Gilbert Owuor (Joseph Asagai), Justice Pratt (George Murchison), Willis Burks II (Bobo), Mick Weber (Karl Lindner), Robert Greene (Moving Men), Clyde Tyrone Harper (Moving Men), Bingham Theatre; November 11–December 13, 2008

 A Christmas Carol by Charles Dickens; Adapted by Barbara Fields; Director, Sean Daniels; Set, Paul Owen; Costumes, Lorraine Venberg; Lighting, Deb Sullivan; Sound, Matt Callahan; Properties Designer, Doc Manning; Properties Designer, Mark Walston; Music Supervisor, David Keeton; Dialect Coach, Rinda Frye; Movement Coordinator, Delilah Smyth; Production Stage Manager, Paul Mills Holmes; Assistant Stage Manager, Kathy Preher; Dramaturg, Julie Felise Dubiner; Casting, Emily Ruddock; Cast: William McNulty (Ebenezer Scrooge), J. Bernard Calloway (Bob Cratchit), Trent Blanton (Fred, Mr. Fezziwig), Nick Cordileone (Marley, Young Marley, Undertaker), David Keeton (Grasper, Townsperson), Ann Hodapp (Mrs. Grigsby, Cook), Daphne Gaines (Ghost of Christmas Past, Mrs. Blakely), Isaac J. Kresse (Boy Scrooge, Simon, Tom Cratchit), Fred Major (Schoolmaster, Old Joe), Matthew Baldiga (Young Ebenezer, Snarkers), Stephanie Weeks (Belle, Mrs. Fred), Jacob Wilhemi (Fezziwig Guest, Topper), Catherine Bandenko (Fan, Martha Cratchit), Navida Stein (Mrs. Fezziwig, Mrs. Dilber), Claudine Mboligikpelani Nako (Marigold Fezziwig, Dorothea), Katherine Moeller

(Petunia Fezziwig, Sophia), Alexandra Chand (Marjoram Fezziwig, Belinda Cratchit, Want), Chris Moore (Ghost of Christmas Future, Fezziwig Guest), David Ryan Smith (Ghost of Christmas Present, Forrest), Heidi Schreck (Mrs. Cratchit), Hero Isabella Cordileone (Tiny Tim, Ignorance, Basil Fezziwig), Hunter Mayfield (Peter Cratchit, Billy), Steven Rausch (Dick Wilkins, Cecil), David Michael Brown (Townspeople, Party Guests, Carolers, Children), Eric Eteuati (Townspeople, Party Guests, Carolers, Children), Ami Jhaveri (Townspeople, Party Guests, Carolers, Children), Clare Rose Kresse (Townspeople, Party Guests, Carolers, Children), Allison Moy (Townspeople, Party Guests, Carolers, Children), Pamela Brown Auditorium; November 26–December 23, 2008

THE LATE SEATING AT ACTORS

The Kronauer Cream Adventure, Suspense, Mystery, Cowboy, Indian Hour by Sean Daniels; Director, Mike Brooks; Sound, Matt Callahan; Music, Chris Bryant; Foley Effects, Stowe Nelson; Lighting, Alexandra Manuel; Sound, Matt Callahan; Sound, Mareth Griffith; Sound Engineer, Jacob Rosene; Stage Manager, Kelsey Daye Lutz; Assistant Stage Manager, Cadi Thomas; Producer, Katherine Bilby; Producer, Mike Brooks; Producer, Cathy Colliver; Producer, Matt Dobson; Producer, Emily Ruddock; Cast: Chris Bryant, Matt Callahan, Chris Hartman, Leah Roberts; Bingham Theatre; October 17, 2008

Five Minutes with...Keith Age, Louisville Ghost Hunters Society Lighting, Alexandra Manuel; Sound, Matt Callahan; Sound, Mareth Griffith; Sound Engineer, Jacob Rosene; Stage Manager, Kelsey Daye Lutz; Assistant Stage Manager, Cadi Thomas; Producer, Katherine Bilby; Producer, Mike Brooks; Producer, Cathy Colliver; Producer, Matt Dobson; Producer, Emily Ruddock; Bingham Theatre; October 17, 2008

Specific Gravity Ensemble, Ghosts and Empty Sockets by Christie Baugher; Director, Christie Baugher; Sound, Mareth Griffith; Lighting, Alexandra Manuel; Sound, Matt Callahan; Sound, Sound Engineer, Jacob Rosene; Stage Manager, Kelsey Daye Lutz; Assistant Stage Manager, Cadi Thomas; Producer, Katherine Bilby; Producer, Mike Brooks; Producer, Cathy Colliver; Producer, Matt Dobson; Producer, Emily Ruddock; Cast: Katherine Summerfield (The Girl), Sarah Feldman, (Sheila), Parker Bowles (Gate Attendant), Bingham Theatre; October 17, 2008

Five Minutes With...Ashley Cecil, The Painting Activist Lighting, Alexandra Manuel; Sound, Matt Callahan; Sound, Mareth Griffith; Sound Engineer, Jacob Rosene; Stage Manager, Kelsey Daye Lutz; Assistant Stage Manager, Cadi Thomas; Producer, Katherine Bilby; Producer, Mike Brooks; Producer, Cathy Colliver; Producer, Matt Dobson; Producer, Emily Ruddock; Bingham Theatre; October 17, 2008

Music Music, Dangerbird; Lighting, Alexandra Manuel; Sound, Matt Callahan; Sound, Mareth Griffith; Sound Engineer, Jacob Rosene; Stage Manager, Kelsey Daye Lutz; Assistant Stage Manager, Cadi Thomas; Producer, Katherine Bilby; Producer, Mike Brooks; Producer, Cathy Colliver; Producer, Matt Dobson; Producer, Emily Ruddock; Bingham Theatre, October 17, 2008

SOLO MIO FESTIVAL

Identified by Ami Jhaveri; Director, Kim Stauffer; Dramaturg, Brendan Pelsue; Cast: Ami Jhaveri; Alexander Speer Arts & Commerce Building; October 24, 2008

This is Why it Matters by Steven Christopher; Director, David Ian Lee; Dramaturg, Sarah Lunnie; Cast: Steven Christopher; Alexander Speer Arts & Commerce Building; October 24, 2008

Perfect by Catherine Bandenko; Director, Amy Attaway; Dramaturg, Amy Wegener; Cast: Catherine Bandenko; Alexander Speer Arts & Commerce Building; October 24, 2008

My Parents are in the Audience. No, Seriously, They Are. Thanks Mom & Pop by Jacob Wilhelmi; Director, Nathan Green; Dramaturg, Rachel Lerner-Ley; Cast: Jacob Wilhelmi; Alexander Speer Arts & Commerce Building; October 24, 2008

Tales to Tell Our Children by Anne Veal; Director, Lila Neugebauer; Dramaturg, Sarah Lunnie; Cast: Anne Veal; Alexander Speer Arts & Commerce Building; October 24, 2008

The Most Important Thing by Matthew Baldiga; Director, Michael Legg; Dramaturg, Rachel Lerner-Ley; Cast: Matthew Baldiga; Alexander Speer Arts & Commerce Building; October 24, 2008

Aloha! by Eric Eteuati; Director, Gregory Maupin; Dramaturg, Brendan Pelsue; Cast: Eric Eteuati; Alexander Speer Arts & Commerce Building; October 24, 2008

Isaiah 23:16 by LaKeisha Randle; Director, Joy DeMichelle Moore; Dramaturg, Rachel Lerner-Ley; Cast: LaKeisha Randle; Alexander Speer Arts & Commerce Building; November 21, 2008

Deborah DuBois by Alison Clayton; Director, Lila Neugebauer; Dramaturg, Julie Felise Dubiner; Cast: Alison Clayton; Alexander Speer Arts & Commerce Building; November 21, 2008

The Hamlet Complex by Aaron Matteson; Director, Marc Masterson; Dramaturg, Brendan Pelsue; Cast: Aaron Matteson; Alexander Speer Arts & Commerce Building; November 21, 2008

"And those who were seen dancing were thought insane by those who couldn't hear the music." by David Michael Brown; Director, Nathan Green; Dramaturg, Sarah Lunnie; Cast: David Michael Brown; Alexander Speer Arts & Commerce Building; November 21, 2008

Freud's Next Top Lady by Anna Kull; Director, Julie Felise Dubiner; Dramaturg, Sarah Lunnie; Cast: Anna Kull; Alexander Speer Arts & Commerce Building; November 21, 2008

Sex, Drugs and TMNT by Michael Dalto; Director, Gil Reyes; Dramaturg, Rachel Lerner-Ley; Cast: Michael Dalto; Alexander Speer Arts & Commerce Building; November 21, 2008

Upside Down Plain Face by Allison Moy; Director, Amy Attaway; Dramaturg, Brendan Pelsue; Cast: Allison Moy; Alexander Speer Arts & Commerce Building; November 21, 2008

Bant by Jon Riddleberger; Director, Amy Attaway; Dramaturg, Brendan Pelsue; Composer, Kristine Lee; Sound, Stowe Nelson; Cast: Jon Riddleberger; Alexander Speer Arts & Commerce Building; December 19, 2008

Abuela's House by Daniel Reyes; Director, Michael Legg; Dramaturg, Brendan Pelsue; Sound, Stowe Nelson; Cast: Daniel Reyes; Alexander Speer Arts & Commerce Building; December 19, 2008

December 19, 2008-Eschete by Chris Moore; Director, Nick Cordileone; Dramaturg, Brendan Pelsue; Sound, Stowe Nelson; Cast: Chris Moore; Alexander Speer Arts & Commerce Building; December 19, 2008

Beautiful by Claudine Mboligikpelani Nako; Director, Gil Reyes; Dramaturg, Sarah Lunnie; Sound, Stowe Nelson; Cast: Claudine Mboligikpelani Nako; Alexander Speer Arts & Commerce Building; December 19, 2008

Worth Your Salt by Julia Bentz; Director, Emily Ruddock; Dramaturg, Rachel Lerner-Ley; Sound, Stowe Nelson; Cast: Julia Bentz; Alexander Speer Arts & Commerce Building; December 19, 2008

Game for Fools by Andy Nogasky; Director, Nathan Green; Dramaturg, Sarah Lunnie; Sound, Stowe Nelson; Cast: Andy Nogasky; Alexander Speer Arts & Commerce Building; December 19, 2008

Seasons for Eva B by Katherine Moeller; Director, Heidi Schreck; Dramaturg, Adrien-Alice Hansel; Sound, Stowe Nelson; Cast: Katherine Moeller; Alexander Speer Arts & Commerce Building; December 19, 2008

The Only Way to Say... by Nancy Noto; Director, Lila Neugebauer; Dramaturg, Rachel Lerner-Ley; Sound, Stowe Nelson; Cast: Nancy Noto; Alexander Speer Arts & Commerce Building; December 19, 2008

Match Games by Wayne S. Rawley, David Ives, Mark Harvey Levine, D.W. Gregory, Robert D. Kemnitz, Jennifer McMaster, Julie Marie Myatt, Jacquelyn Reingold, Courtney Baron, Martin Russell, Michael Bigelow Dixon, and Val Smith; Curator, Amy Wegener; Curator, Michael Bigelow Dixon; Director, Michael Bigelow Dixon; Set, Paul Owen; Costumes, Lorraine Venberg; Lighting, Jeff Nellis; Sound, Benjamin Marcum; Properties Designer, Mark Walston; Dance Supervisor, Bravo Dance Studio; Dance Supervisor, Alex Loukhnel; Stage Manager, Kimberly J. First; Production Assistant, Mary Spadoni; Dramaturg, Amy Wegener; Casting, Emily Ruddock; Casting, Zan Sawyer-Dailey; Cast: Adinah Alexander (Ensemble), Sue Cremin (Ensemble), Brandon Morris, (Ensemble), Douglas Rees (Ensemble), Meredith Zinner (Ensemble), Bingham Theatre; January 6–February 7, 2009

Rock & Roll: The Reunion Tour created by Matt Callahan, Sean Daniels, Julie Felise Dubiner, and David Hanbury; Director, Sean Daniels; Set, Michael B. Raiford; Costumes, Emily Ganfield; Lighting, Brian J. Lilienthal; Sound, Matt Callahan; Properties Designer, Mark Walston; Musical Director, Jon Spurney; Stage Manager, Kathy Preher; Production Assistant, Melissa Blair; Dramaturg, Julie Felise Dubiner; Cast: Jeremy Lee Cudd (Terrance/Drums), David Hanbury (Johnny/Guitar), Rebecca Hart (Estro/Bass and Guitar), Ami Jhaveri (Narrator/Bass), Jon Spurney (Teacher/Guitar), Victor Jory Theatre; January 22–February 8, 2009

Shipwrecked! An Entertainment: The Amazing Adventures of Louis de Rougemont (As Told By Himself) by Donald Margulies; Director, Marc Masterson; Set, Michael B. Raiford; Costumes, Sonya Berlovitz; Lighting, Brian J. Lilienthal; Sound, Darron L. West; Properties Designer, Doc Manning; Puppet Designer, Jason von Hinezmeyer; Puppetry Consultant, Jon Ludwig; Dialect Coach, Rocco Dal Vera; Production Stage Manager, Paul Mills Holmes; Production Assistant, Sara Kmack; Dramaturg, Adrien-Alice Hansel; Cast: Richard McMillan (Louis de Rougemont), Melody Butiu (Player 1), Eric Bondoc (Player 2), Eric Eteuati (Puppeteer), Allison Moy (Puppeteer), Jon Riddleberger (Puppeteer), Jacob Wilhelmi (Puppeteer), Michael Dalto (Sound Effects), Katherine Moeller (Sound Effects), Steven Rausch (Sound Effects), Pamela Brown Auditorium; February 3–28, 2009

The Lincoln Project: Louisville: My Childhood Home by Craig Brauner, Antonio D. Burroughs, Cara Chang, Jade Grant, Kirsten Knighten, Mitchell E. Martin, Terrance E.J. McCraney, Mary Nitzken, Collin Sage, and Sheila Wilson; Director, Jess Jung; Stage Manager, Kelsey Daye; Lighting, Derek Miller; Sound, Stowe Nelson; Cast: Craig Brauner, Antonio D. Burroughs, Cara Chang, Jade Grant, Kirsten Knighten, Mitchell E. Martin, Terrance E.J. McCraney, Mary Nitzken, Collin Sage, Sheila Wilson; Pamela Brown Auditorium; February 12, 2009

The Lincoln Project: Prestonburg: The Angels of Our Nature by Rachel Hazelett, Ashley Kendrick, Tanner Sammons, Skyler Slone, Abigail Stanley, Tyler Thacker, and Miranda Thompson; Stage Manager, Kelsey Daye; Lighting, Derek Miller; Sound, Stowe Nelson; Cast: Rachel Hazelett, Ashley Kendrick, Tanner Sammons, Skyler Slone, Abigail Stanley, Tyler Thacker, Miranda Thompson; Pamela Brown Auditorium; February 12, 2009

The Lincoln Project: Bowling Green: In a Larger Sense by Malissa Bryant, Katie Cohron, Alison Itzkowitz, Kelly Johnson, Ben Luna, Indyea Nixon, Katie Schuck, and Keitan Stacks; Director, Jacob Stoebel; Manager, Kelsey Daye; Lighting, Derek Miller; Sound, Stowe Nelson; Cast: Malissa Bryant, Katie Cohron,

Alison Itzkowitz, Kelly Johnson, Ben Luna, Indyea Nixon, Katie Schuck, Keitan Stacks; Pamela Brown Auditorium; February 12, 2009

THE TENS (APPRENTICE COMPANY TEN-MINUTE PLAY SHOWCASE)

3:59 am: a drag race for two actors by Marco Ramirez; Director, Amy Attaway; Set, Brenda Ellis; Costumes, Lindsay Chamberlin; Lighting, Alex Manuel; Sound, Jacob Rosene; Sound, Mareth Griffith; Sound, Stowe Nelson; Properties Designer, Jessie Combest; Properties Designer, Elliot Cornett; Properties Designer, Taj Whitesell; Master Electrician, Rob Broderson; Media Technologist, Philip Allegier; Stage Manager, Kelsey Daye Lutz; Assistant Stage Manager, Cadi Thomas; Assistant Stage Manager, Leslie Cobb; Dramaturg, Adrien-Alice Hansel; Dramaturg, Rachel Lerner-Ley; Dramaturg, Sarah Lunnie; Dramaturg, Brendan Pelsue; Dramaturg, Amy Wegener; Cast: Matthew Baldiga (Hector), Daniel Reyes (Laz), Pamela Brown Auditorium; January 19, 2009

Every Day is Tuesday by Jill Snow; Director, Sean Daniels; Set, Brenda Ellis; Costumes, Lindsay Chamberlin; Lighting, Alex Manuel; Sound, Jacob Rosene; Sound, Mareth Griffith; Sound, Stowe Nelson; Properties Designer, Jessie Combest; Properties Designer, Elliot Cornett; Properties Designer, Taj Whitesell; Master Electrician, Rob Broderson; Media Technologist, Philip Allegier; Stage Manager, Kelsey Daye Lutz; Assistant Stage Manager, Cadi Thomas; Assistant Stage Manager, Leslie Cobb; Dramaturg, Adrien-Alice Hansel; Dramaturg, Rachel Lerner-Ley; Dramaturg, Sarah Lunnie; Dramaturg, Brendan Pelsue; Dramaturg, Amy Wegener; Cast: Claudine Mboligikpelani Nako (Jane), LaKeisha Randle (Katherine), Catherine Bandenko (Layla), Alison Clayton (Margaret), Pamela Brown Auditorium; January 19, 2009

508 by Amy Herzog; Director, Jeff Rodgers; Set, Brenda Ellis; Costumes, Lindsay Chamberlin; Lighting, Alex Manuel; Sound, Jacob Rosene; Sound, Mareth Griffith; Sound, Stowe Nelson; Properties Designer, Jessie Combest; Properties Designer, Elliot Cornett; Properties Designer, Taj Whitesell; Master Electrician, Rob Broderson; Media Technologist, Philip Allegier; Stage Manager, Kelsey Daye Lutz; Assistant Stage Manager, Cadi Thomas; Assistant Stage Manager, Leslie Cobb; Dramaturg, Adrien-Alice Hansel; Dramaturg, Rachel Lerner-Ley; Dramaturg, Sarah Lunnie; Dramaturg, Brendan Pelsue; Dramaturg, Amy Wegener; Cast: Michael Dalto (Shelly), Anna Kull (Shelli), Chris Moore (Voiceover), Pamela Brown Auditorium; January 19, 2009

Roanoke by Michael Lew; Director, Paul Mills Holmes; Music and Lyrics, Matt Schaltz; Set, Brenda Ellis; Costumes, Lindsay Chamberlin; Lighting, Alex Manuel; Sound, Jacob Rosene; Sound, Mareth Griffith; Sound, Stowe Nelson; Properties Designer, Jessie Combest; Properties Designer, Elliot Cornett; Properties Designer, Taj Whitesell; Master Electrician, Rob Broderson; Media Technologist, Philip Allegier; Stage Manager, Kelsey Daye Lutz; Assistant Stage Manager, Cadi Thomas; Assistant Stage Manager, Leslie Cobb; Dramaturg, Adrien-Alice Hansel; Dramaturg, Rachel Lerner-Ley; Dramaturg, Sarah Lunnie; Dramaturg, Amy Wegener; Cast: Steven Rausch (Steve), Ami Jhaveri (Florencia), Nancy Noto (Melanie), Andy Nogasky (Matt); Pamela Brown Auditorium; January 19, 2009

The Curse of the Horned Babby by Lisa Dillman; Director, Gregory Maupin; Set, Brenda Ellis; Costumes, Lindsay Chamberlin; Lighting, Alex Manuel; Sound, Jacob Rosene; Sound, Mareth Griffith; Sound, Stowe Nelson; Properties Designer, Jessie Combest; Properties Designer, Elliot Cornett; Properties Designer, Taj Whitesell; Master Electrician, Rob Broderson; Media Technologist, Philip Allegier; Stage Manager, Kelsey Daye Lutz; Assistant Stage Manager, Cadi Thomas; Assistant Stage Manager, Leslie Cobb; Dramaturg, Adrien-Alice Hansel; Dramaturg, Rachel Lerner-Ley; Dramaturg, Sarah Lunnie; Dramaturg, Brendan Pelsue; Dramaturg, Amy Wegener; Cast: Anne Veal (Cobbler's Wife), Anna Kull (Baker's Wife), Nancy Noto (A Crone), Eric Eteuati (A Wandering Minstrel); Pamela Brown Auditorium; January 19, 2009

27 Ways I Didn't Say "Hi" to Laurence Fishburne by Jonathan Josephson; Director, Lila Neugebauer; Set, Brenda Ellis; Costumes, Lindsay Chamberlin; Lighting, Alex Manuel; Sound, Jacob Rosene; Sound, Mareth Griffith; Sound, Stowe Nelson; Properties Designer, Jessie Combest; Properties Designer, Elliot Cornett; Properties Designer, Taj Whitesell; Master Electrician, Rob Broderson; Media Technologist, Philip Allegier; Stage Manager, Kelsey Daye Lutz; Assistant Stage Manager, Cadi Thomas; Assistant Stage Manager, Leslie Cobb; Dramaturg, Adrien-Alice Hansel; Dramaturg, Rachel Lerner-Ley; Dramaturg, Sarah Lunnie; Dramaturg, Brendan Pelsue; Dramaturg, Amy Wegener; Cast: LaKeisha Randle (Laurence Fisburne), Jon Riddleberger (Jon), David Michael Brown (Jon); Pamela Brown Auditorium; January 19, 2009

What Makes a Man by Rachel Lerner-Ley; Director, Amy Attaway; Set, Brenda Ellis; Costumes, Lindsay Chamberlin; Lighting, Alex Manuel; Sound, Jacob Rosene; Sound, Mareth Griffith; Sound, Stowe Nelson; Properties Designer, Jessie Combest; Properties Designer, Elliot Cornett; Properties Designer, Taj Whitesell; Master Electrician, Rob Broderson; Media Technologist, Philip Allegier; Stage Manager, Kelsey Daye Lutz; Assistant Stage Manager, Cadi Thomas; Assistant Stage Manager, Leslie Cobb; Dramaturg, Adrien-Alice Hansel; Dramaturg, Rachel Lerner-Ley; Dramaturg, Sarah Lunnie; Dramaturg, Brendan Pelsue; Dramaturg, Amy Wegener; Cast: Katherine Moeller (Amanda), Jacob Wilhelmi (Ben); Pamela Brown Auditorium; January 19, 2009

Good Girl by Julia Brownell; Director, Mike Brooks; Set, Brenda Ellis; Costumes, Lindsay Chamberlin; Lighting, Alex Manuel; Sound, Jacob Rosene; Sound, Mareth Griffith; Sound, Stowe Nelson; Properties Designer, Jessie Combest; Properties Designer, Elliot Cornett; Properties Designer, Taj Whitesell; Master Electrician, Rob Broderson; Media Technologist, Philip Allegier; Stage Manager, Kelsey Daye Lutz; Assistant Stage Manager, Cadi Thomas; Assistant Stage Manager, Leslie Cobb; Dramaturg, Adrien-Alice Hansel; Dramaturg, Rachel Lerner-Ley; Dramaturg, Sarah Lunnie; Dramaturg, Brendan Pelsue; Dramaturg, Amy Wegener; Cast: Aaron Matteson (James), Julia Bentz (Jenna), Alison Clayton (Rosalind), Ami Jhaveri (Celia), Pamela Brown Auditorium; January 19, 2009

Craigslist: Last Posts\Last Days by Eric Czuleger; Director, Michael Legg; Set, Brenda Ellis; Costumes, Lindsay Chamberlin; Lighting, Alex Manuel; Sound, Jacob Rosene; Sound, Mareth Griffith; Sound, Stowe Nelson; Properties Designer, Jessie Combest; Properties Designer, Elliot Cornett; Properties Designer, Taj Whitesell; Master Electrician, Rob Broderson; Media Technologist, Philip Allegier; Stage Manager, Kelsey Daye Lutz; Assistant Stage Manager, Cadi Thomas; Assistant Stage Manager, Leslie Cobb; Dramaturg, Adrien-Alice Hansel; Dramaturg, Rachel Lerner-Ley; Dramaturg, Sarah Lunnie; Dramaturg, Brendan Pelsue; Dramaturg, Amy Wegener; Cast: Andy Nogasky, Steven Rausch, Jacob Wilhelmi, David Michael Brown, Eric Eteuati, Michael Dalto, Matthew Baldiga, Julia Bentz, Daniel Reyes, Catherine Bandenko, Jon Riddleberger, Anne Veal, Chris Moore; Pamela Brown Auditorium; January 19, 2009

33ʳᵈ ANNUAL HUMANA FESTIVAL OF NEW AMERICAN PLAYS

Ameriville by Universes (Gamal Abdel Chasten, Mildred Ruiz, William Ruiz a.k.a. Ninja, and Steven Sapp), Director, Chay Yew; Set, Paul Owen; Costumes, Lorraine Venberg; Lighting, Russell Champa; Sound, Benjamin Marcum; Properties Designer, Alice Baldwin; Movement Supervisor, Millicent Johnnie; Video Designer, Jason Czaja; Stage Manager, Megan Schwarz; Dramaturg, Morgan Jenness; Cast: Gamal Abden Chasten, Mildred Ruiz, William Ruiz a.k.a. Ninja, Steven Sapp; Bingham Theatre; March 1–April 5, 2009 Slasher by Allison Moore; Director, Josh Hecht; Set, Paul Owen; Costumes, Jennifer Caprio; Lighting, Russel Champa; Sound, Matt Callahan; Properties Designer, Doc Manning; Dialect Coach, Rinda Frye; Fight Director, k. Jenny Jones; Stage Manager, Robin Grady; Production Assistant, Melissa Blair; Dramaturg, Amy Wegener; Casting, Alaine Alldaffer Casting; Cast: Lusia Strus

(Frances McKinney), Christy McIntosh (Christi Garcia and others), Mark Setlock (Marc Hunter), Nicole Rodenburg (Sheena McKinney), Katharine Moeller (Hildy McKinney), Lucas Papaelias (Jody Joshi); Bingham Theatre; March 6–April 5, 2009

Absalom by Zoe Kazan; Director, Giovanna Sardelli; Set, Paul Owen; Costumes, Lorraine Venberg; Lighting, Brian J. Lilienthal; Sound, Benjamin Marcum; Properties Designer, Mark Walston; Fight Director, k. Jenny Jones; Stage Manager, Debra Anne Gasper; Assistant Stage Manager, Paul Mills Holmes; Dramaturg, Amy Wegener; Casting, David Caparelliotis; Casting, Mel Cap Casting; Cast: Todd Weeks (Adam Weber), Ben Huber (Teddy Weber), Katie Kreisler (Sophia Weber), Stephanie Janssen (Julia Grimes Weber), Peter Michael Goetz (Saul Weber), J. Anthony Crane (Cole Maddox); Pamela Brown Auditorium; March 10-April 11, 2009

The Hard Weather Boating Party by Naomi Wallace; Director, Jo Bonney; Set, Paul Owen; Costumes, Jennifer Caprio; Lighting, Russell Champa; Sound, Matt Callahan; Properties Designer, Doc Manning; Movement Consultant, Delilah Smyth; Fight Director, k. Jenny Jones; Stage Manager, Kathy Preher; Production Assistant, Mary Spadoni; Dramaturg, Adrien-Alice Hansel; Casting, Vince Liebhart Casting; Cast: Michael Cullen (Staddon Vance), Jesse J. Perez (Lex Nadal), Kevin Jackson (Coyle Forrester), Bingham Theatre; March 14–April 4, 2009

Under Construction by Charles L. Mee; Director, Anne Bogart; Created and performed by the SITI Company; Set, Neil Patel; Costumes, James Schuette; Lighting, Brian H. Scott; Video Designer, Brian H. Scott; Sound, Darron L. West; Properties Designer, Mark Walston; Musical Arranger, Rachel Grimes; Stage Manager, Elizabeth Moreau; Production Assistant, Dave Sleswick; Dramaturg, Sarah Lunnie; SITI Executive Director, Megan Wanlass Szalla; Cast: Akiko Aizawa, J. Ed Araiza, Leon Ingulsrud, Ellen Lauren, Tom Nelis, Barney O'Hanlon, Makela Spielman, Samuel Stricklen, Stephen Duff Webber

Wild Blessings: A Celebration of Wendell Berry Adapted for the stage by Marc Masterson and Adrien-Alice Hansel; Director, Marc Masterson; Original Music & Music Direction, Malcolm Dalgish; Set, Michael B. Raiford; Costumes, Lorraine Venberg; Lighting, Brian J. Lilienthal; Sound, Matt Callahan; Properties Designer, Doc Manning; Video Designer, Donna L. Lawrence; Production Stage Manager, Paul Mills Holmes; Production Assistant, Sara Kmack; Dramaturg, Adrien-Alice Hansel; Cast: Helen-Jean Arthur, Malcolm Daglish, Tracy Conyer Lee, Larry John Meyers, Phil Pickens; Pamela Brown Auditorium; March 1–April 11, 2009

Brink! by Lydia R. Diamond, Kristoffer Diaz, Greg Kotis, Deborah Joe Laufer, Peter Sinn Nachtrieb, and Deborah Stein; Director, Sean Daniels; Set, Paul Owen; Costumes, Emily Ganfield; Lighting, Brian J. Lilienthal; Sound, Benjamin Marcum; Properties Designer, Alice Baldwin; Orchestrations, David Keeton; Vocal Arranger, David Keeton; Music Supervisor, Margret Fenske; Movement Director, Delilah Smyth; Fight Director, Lee Look; Stage Manager, Mary Spadoni; Dramaturg; Julie Elise Dubiner; Cast: 2008-2009 Acting Apprentice Company; Bingham Theatre; March 27, 29 & April 3 –5, 2009

On the Porch One Crisp Spring Morning by Alex Dremann; Director, Sean Daniels; Set, Paul Owen; Costumes, Emily Ganfield; Costumes, Lindsey Chamberlain; Lighting, Nick Dent; Sound, Benjamin Marcum; Properties Designer, Mark Walston; Production Stage Manager, Paul Mills Holmes; Dramaturg, Julie Felise Dubiner; Cast: Katie Kreisler (Mother), Nancy Noto (Daughter), Pamela Brown Auditorium; April 4–5, 2009

3:59 am: a drag race for two actors by Marco Ramirez; Director, Amy Attaway; Set, Paul Owen; Costumes, Emily Ganfield; Costumes, Lindsey Chamberlain; Lighting, Nick Dent; Sound, Benjamin Marcum; Properties Designer, Mark Walston; Production Stage Manager, Paul Mills Holmes; Dramaturg, Julie Felise Dubiner; Cast: Daniel Reyes (Laz), Matthew Baldiga (Hector), Pamela Brown Auditorium; April 4–5, 2009

Roanoke by Michael Lew; Director, Steven Rahe; Music/Lyrics by Matt Schatz; Set, Paul Owen; Costumes, Emily Ganfield; Costumes, Lindsey Chamberlain; Lighting, Nick Dent; Sound, Benjamin Marcum; Properties Designer, Mark Walston; Production Stage Manager, Paul Mills Holmes; Dramaturg, Julie Felise Dubiner; Cast: Anna Kull (Florencia), Steven Rausch (Steve), Katie Kreisler (Melanie), Andy Nogasky (Sir Walter Raleigh); Pamela Brown Auditorium; April 4–5, 2009

NEW VOICES PLAY FESTIVAL

Picture Perfect by Audrey Simpson; Director, Steven Rahe; Set, Brenda Ellis; Costumes, Lindsay Chamberlin; Lighting, Derek Miller; Sound, Stowe Nelson; Properties Designer, Joe Cunningham; Stage Manager, Cadi Thomas; Assistant Stage Manager, Kelsey Daye; Assistant Stage Manager, Leslie Cobb; Fight Choreographer, Lee Look; Dramaturg, Adrien-Alice Hansel; Dramaturg, Rachel Lerner-Ley; Dramaturg, Sarah Lunnie; Dramaturg, Julie Mercurio; Dramaturg, Jeffrey Mosser; Dramaturg, Steven Rahe; Dramaturg, Jacob Stoebel; Cast: Jacob Wilhelmi (Adam), Daniel Reyes (Jeremy), Nancy Noto (Lavern), Ami Jhaveri (Mrs. Napalm), Anna Kull (Andrea); Bingham Theatre; April 19–20, 2009

Vanilla by Jordan Golding; Director, Lila Neugebauer; Set, Brenda Ellis; Costumes, Lindsay Chamberlin; Lighting, Derek Miller; Sound, Stowe Nelson; Properties Designer, Joe Cunningham; Stage Manager, Cadi Thomas; Assistant Stage Manager, Kelsey Daye; Assistant Stage Manager, Leslie Cobb; Fight Choreographer, Lee Look; Dramaturg, Adrien-Alice Hansel; Dramaturg, Rachel Lerner-Ley; Dramaturg, Sarah Lunnie; Dramaturg, Julie Mercurio; Dramaturg, Jeffrey Mosser; Dramaturg, Steven Rahe; Dramaturg, Jacob Stoebel; Cast: Andy Nogasky (John), Michael Dalto (Walter), Eric Eteuati (Ice Cream Man), Claudine Mboligikpelani Nako (Mary); Bingham Theatre; April 19–20, 2009

The Never Before Seen Interview of Norman McClellan by Max Abner; Director, Anna Kull; Set, Brenda Ellis; Costumes, Lindsay Chamberlin; Lighting, Derek Miller; Sound, Stowe Nelson; Properties Designer, Joe Cunningham; Stage Manager, Cadi Thomas; Assistant Stage Manager, Kelsey Daye; Assistant Stage Manager, Leslie Cobb; Fight Choreographer, Lee Look; Dramaturg, Adrien-Alice Hansel; Dramaturg, Rachel Lerner-Ley; Dramaturg, Sarah Lunnie; Dramaturg, Julie Mercurio; Dramaturg, Jeffrey Mosser; Dramaturg, Steven Rahe; Dramaturg, Jacob Stoebel; Cast: Chris Moore (Interviewer), Jon Riddleberger (Norman),;Bingham Theatre; April 19–20, 2009

Imagination by Annabelle Horton; Director, Jeffrey Mosser; Set, Brenda Ellis; Costumes, Lindsay Chamberlin; Lighting, Derek Miller; Sound, Stowe Nelson; Properties Designer, Joe Cunningham; Stage Manager, Cadi Thomas; Assistant Stage Manager, Kelsey Daye; Assistant Stage Manager, Leslie Cobb; Fight Choreographer, Lee Look; Dramaturg, Adrien-Alice Hansel; Dramaturg, Rachel Lerner-Ley; Dramaturg, Sarah Lunnie; Dramaturg, Julie Mercurio; Dramaturg, Jeffrey Mosser; Dramaturg, Steven Rahe; Dramaturg, Jacob Stoebel; Cast: Eric Eteuati (Alex), Nancy Noto (Mom), David Michael Brown (Man), Steven Rausch (Knight), Jacob Wilhelmi (23), Claudine Mboligikpelani Nako (12), Claudine Mboligikpelani Nako (Voiceover); Bingham Theatre; April 19–20, 2009

Sugarless by Brittany Henderson; Director, Amy Attaway; Set, Brenda Ellis; Costumes, Lindsay Chamberlin; Lighting, Derek Miller; Sound, Stowe Nelson; Properties Designer, Joe Cunningham; Stage Manager, Cadi Thomas; Assistant Stage Manager, Kelsey Daye; Assistant Stage Manager, Leslie Cobb; Fight Choreographer, Lee Look; Dramaturg, Adrien-Alice Hansel; Dramaturg, Rachel Lerner-Ley; Dramaturg, Sarah Lunnie; Dramaturg, Julie Mercurio; Dramaturg, Jeffrey Mosser; Dramaturg, Steven Rahe; Dramaturg, Jacob Stoebel; Cast: Allison Moy (Lauren), Katherine Moeller, (Katie), Aaron Matteson (Hans), Jon Riddleberger (Rick); Bingham Theatre; April 19–20, 2009

Shrink by Craig Brauner; Director, Jacob Stoebel; Set, Brenda Ellis; Costumes, Lindsay Chamberlin; Lighting, Derek Miller; Sound, Stowe Nelson; Properties Designer, Joe Cunningham; Stage Manager, Cadi Thomas; Assistant Stage Manager, Kelsey Daye; Assistant Stage Manager, Leslie Cobb; Fight Choreographer, Lee Look; Dramaturg, Adrien-Alice Hansel; Dramaturg, Rachel Lerner-Ley; Dramaturg, Sarah Lunnie; Dramaturg, Julie Mercurio; Dramaturg, Jeffrey Mosser; Dramaturg, Steven Rahe; Dramaturg, Jacob Stoebel; Cast: David Michael Brown (Andrew), Julia Bentz (Mrs. Delacour), Ami Jhaveri (Mom), Matthew Baldiga (Bully), Chris Moore (Dad); Bingham Theatre; April 19–20, 2009

The Spy Who Never Loved Me by Peytone Lightfoot; Director, Julie Mercurio; Set, Brenda Ellis; Costumes, Lindsay Chamberlin; Lighting, Derek Miller; Sound, Stowe Nelson; Properties Designer, Joe Cunningham; Stage Manager, Cadi Thomas; Assistant Stage Manager, Kelsey Daye; Assistant Stage Manager, Leslie Cobb; Fight Choreographer, Lee Look; Dramaturg, Adrien-Alice Hansel; Dramaturg, Rachel Lerner-Ley; Dramaturg, Sarah Lunnie; Dramaturg, Julie Mercurio; Dramaturg, Jeffrey Mosser; Dramaturg, Steven Rahe; Dramaturg, Jacob Stoebel; Cast: Aaron Matteson (Bond), Anne Veal (Mina), LaKeisha Randle (Scarlett); Bingham Theatre; April 19–20, 2009

What is Normal? by Patrick O'Rourke; Director, Brendan Pelsue; Set, Brenda Ellis; Costumes, Lindsay Chamberlin; Lighting, Derek Miller; Sound, Stowe Nelson; Properties Designer, Joe Cunningham; Stage Manager, Cadi Thomas; Assistant Stage Manager, Kelsey Daye; Assistant Stage Manager, Leslie Cobb; Fight Choreographer, Lee Look; Dramaturg, Adrien-Alice Hansel; Dramaturg, Rachel Lerner-Ley; Dramaturg, Sarah Lunnie; Dramaturg, Julie Mercurio; Dramaturg, Jeffrey Mosser; Dramaturg, Steven Rahe; Dramaturg, Jacob Stoebel; Cast: Andy Nogasky (Superman), Matthew Baldiga (Aquaman), Michael Dalto (Batman), Daniel Reyes (Green Lantern), Steven Rausch (Flash), Alison Clayton (Wonder Woman); Bingham Theatre; April 19–20, 2009

Alabama Shakespeare Festival

Montgomery, Alabama
Thirty-seventh Season
Producing Artistic Director, Geoffrey Sherman; Chief Operating Instructor, Michael Vigilant

Three Mo' Divas by Marion J. Caffey; Director/Choreography, Marion J. Caffey; Assistant Director, Melanie Gaskins; Executive Assistant, Diane R. Dispo; Orchestrator, Joseph Joubert; Music Director, Annastasia Victory; Associate Music Director, John Coffey; Set, Dale F. Jordan; Costumes, Toni-Leslie James; Lighting, Richard Winkler; Hair and Wigs, Bettie O. Rogers; Sound, Byron Hurst; Stage Manager, Scott Peg; Production Assistant, Heather Newman; Cast: Laurice Lanier (Diva), Nova Y. Payton (Diva), Jamet Pittman (Diva), Understudies: Kearstin Piper Brown, Yvette Gonzalez-Nacer; Band: Annastasia Victory (Piano), John Coffey (Keyboard 2), Etienne Lytle, (Keyboard 3), Sipho Kunene (Drums), Markeith Black (Guitar), John Toney (Bass); Festival Stage; September 26–October 5, 2008

Charlotte's Web book by E. B. White; Dramatized by Joseph Robinette; Director, Nancy Rominger; Set, Peter Hicks; Costumes, Jennifer Ables; Lighting, Curtis Hodge; Sound, Andrew Brockman; Movement, Denise Gabriel; Dramaturg, Susan Willis; Stage Manager, Crystal McCall; Assistant Director, Kristi Jacobs; Assistant Stage Manager, Bronwen Herandez; Cast: Peter Gray (Wilbur), Amanda Catania (Charlotte/Mrs. Arable, Baby Spider), Amanda McCallum (Fern/Goose/Spectator 1), Johnson Chong (Arable/Templeton/ Lurvy), Adam Souza (Homer/Sheep/Spectator 2/Avery), David Stewart Hudson (Narrator/Gander/Reporter/Uncle/President of the Fair), Patrick Vest (Announcer at the Fair), Chris Roe (Uncle's Owner); Octagon Theatre; October 11–November 23, 2008

A Christmas Carol: The Musical Based on the Story by Charles Dickens; Music by Alan Menken; Lyrics by Lyn Ahrens; Book by Mike Ockrent and Lynn Ahrens; Director, Geoffrey Sherman; Choreography, Karen Azenberg; Music Director, Tom Griffin; Set, Paul Wonsek; Costumes, Elizabeth Novak; Lighting, Phil Monat; Sound, Richelle Thompson; Assistant Musical Director, Carolyn Violi; Stage Manager, Tanya J. Searle; Assistant Stage Manager, Scott Pegg; Production Assistant, Heather Newman; Dance Captain, Nikol Wolf; Cast: Graham Allen (Caroler/Charity Man/Scrooge's Father/Undertaker/Fezziwig Guest), Ashley Anthony (Scrooge at 8/Ignorance), Jessica Azenberg (Caroler/Fruit Seller/Ghost/Fezziwig Guest/Creditor/Charity Girl/Monk), Jessica Blair (Woman 1/Ghost/Fezziwig Guest/Charity Girl/Monk), James Bowen (Sandwichboard Man/Ghost of Christmas Present), Rodney Clark (Ebenezer Scrooge), Cory Coleman (Blind Old Hag/Fezziwig Guest), Hailey Covington (Grace Smythe/Girl Worker/Fezziwig Guest/Belinda Cratchit), Sandy Draper (Caroler/Martha Cratchit/Fan), Liz Eckert (Caroler/Londoner/Ghost/Fezziwig Guest/Creditor/Charity Girl/Monk), Emma Grant (Girl Worker/Want), Paul Hopper (Beadle/Mr. Fezziwig), Naden Kreitz (Jonathon/Boy Worker/Fezziwig Guest/Fred's son), Matt Leisy (Chestnut Seller/Scrooge at 18/Drunk Londoner), Adam Lendermon (Banker/Ghost/Fezziwig Guest/Creditor/Sailor), Ellyn Marie Marsh (Lamplighter/Ghost of Christmas Past/Charity Girl), Lauren Martin (Caroler/Harry's Wife/Scrooge's Mother/Fezziwig Guest/Fred's Guest), Jackson Massey (Nikolas/Scrooge at 12/Peter Cratchit), Ivory McKay (Charity Man/Ghost/Fezziwig Guest/Gravedigger), Seth Meriwether (Jonathon/Boy Worker/Fezziwig Guest/Fred's son), Meegan Midkiff (Londoner/Emily/Sally Anderson), Mary Cate Norris (Tiny Tim), Patti Perkins (Charwoman/Mrs. Mops/Mrs. Fezziwig), Hayden Pruett (Girl Worker/Want), Michael Ramey (Banker/Ghost/Fezziwig Guest/Sailor), Will Ray (Fred Anderson/Fezziwig Guest), Matt Renskers (Poulterer/Gaoler/Fezziwig Guest/Ghost of Christmas Future), Rebecca Rich (Charwoman/Mrs. Cratchit/Fezziwig Guest), Ashley Rivers (Caroler/Londoner/Pantomime Girl/Ghost Swing/Fezziwig Guest/Charity Girl/Monk), Chris Roe (Mr. Smythe/Gaoler/Fezziwig Guest/Fred's Guest), Matthew Sailors (Nikolas/Scrooge at 12/Peter Cratchit), Billy Sharpe (Bob Cratchit), Crispin South (Tiny Tim), Greg Spradlin (Fishmonger/Mr. Hawkins/Fezziwig Guest/Fred's Guest), Eric Theilman (Pie Seller/Ghost/Fezziwig Guest/Gravedigger), Mary Allison Tyner (Caroler/Martha Cratchit/Fan), Danny Vaccaro (Harry/Ghost/Fezziwig Guest/Drunk Londoner/Gravedigger), Patrick Vest (Undertaker/Judge/Fezziwig Guest), Sam Walker (Scrooge at 8/Ignorance), Victoria Webb (Grace Smythe/Girl Worker/Fezziwig Guest/Belinda Cratchit), Nikol Wolf (Londoner/Pantomime Girl/Ghost/Fezziwig Guest/Creditor/Charity Girl/Monk) Mark Woodard (Old Joe/Marley's Ghost), Jarrod Yuskauskas (Caroler/Charity Man/Ghost/Fezziwig Guest/Young Marley), Festival Stage; November 7–December 24, 2008

Bear Country by Michael Vigilant; Director, Tim Rhoze; Set, Katherine Ross; Costumes, Elizabeth Novak; Lighting, AnnMarie Duggan; Sound, Brett Rominger; Dramaturg, Marlon Bailey; Stage Manager, Michael Andrew-Rodgers; Production Assistant, Crystal McCall; Cast: Rodney Clark (Coach Bryant), Gregory Jones (Young Bryant/ Young Coach Bryant), John Patrick Hayden (Uncle/Coach Cowan/Coach Hank/Football Player/Reporter/Technician/Television Announcer/Attorney/Racist), Yaegel T. Welch (Radio Announcer/Friend/Floor Manager/Grandpa/Student Protestor), World Premiere; Octagon Theatre; January 9–February 15, 2009

The Furniture of Home by Elyzabeth Gregory Wilder; Director, Nancy Rominger; Set, Peter Hicks; Costumes, Susan Branch Towne; Lighting, Curtis Hodge; Sound, Brett Rominger; Dramaturg, Susan Willis; Stage Manager, Luisa Ann Torress; Production Assistant, Crystal McCall; Cast: Anne Letscher (Kendall), Greta Lambert (Dottie), Phillip Clark (Butch), Alexis Camins (Boone), World Premiere; Octagon Theatre; March 6–March 29, 2009

The Three Musketeers Adapted by Charles Morey; Director, Geoffrey Sherman; Composer, James Prigmore; Set, Paul Wonsek; Costumes, Patrick Holt; Lighting, Phil Monat; Sound, Joe Payne; Fight Director, Dale Girard; Movement Consultant, Denise Gabriel; Dramaturg, Susan Willis; Assistant Fight Director, Joe Isenberg; Stage Manager, Tanya J. Searle; Assistant Stage Manager, Scott Pegg; Production Assistant, Heather Newan, Crystal McCall; Cast: Esau Pritchett (Dumas), Jeffrey de Picciotto (D'Artagnan), Rodney Clark (Rochefort), Chris Roe (Athos), Nathan M. Hosner (Porthos), Michael Daniel Anderson (Aramis), Ray Chambers (Richelieu), Cory Coleman (Constance Bonacieux), Caroline Strong

(Milady de Winter), Lauren Anne Martin (Anne of Austria), Patrick Vest (Planchet), Matt Renskers (Louis XIII/Felton/Musketeer #1), Joseph Reed (Bonacieux/Harbor Master/Huguenot), Blake Kubena (Buckingham/Musketeer #2), Matt D'Amico (Jussac/Ambusher/Huguenot), Gregory Spradlin (Bicarat/ Ambusher/Huguenot), Jarrod Yuskauskas (Cook/ Innkeepers/ Godeau/ Antoine/ Huguenot), Graham Allen (Musketeer #3/ Cardinal's Guard/ Surly Fellow #1/ Disreputable Type/ Fancy Man/ Huguenot), Peter Gray (Musketeer #4/Cardinal's Guard/Ambusher/ Fancy Man/ Huguenot), David Stewart Hudson (Cardinal's Guard/ Ambusher/ Huguenot), Adam Souza (Cardinal's Guard/ Surly Fellow #2/ Disreputable Type/ Huguenot), Johnson Chung (Townsperson Boy/ King's Servant/ Ambusher/ Fancy Boy/ Huguenot/ Buckingham's Guard), Amanda McCallum (Townsperson Boy/ King's Servant/ Ambusher/ Fancy Boy/ Huguenot/ Buckingham's Guard), Kaytie Morris (Madame de Lannoy/ Nun/Inkeeper's Wife/ Tavern Wench), Amanda Catania (Kitty/ Nun/ Tavern Wench/ Lady at Court); Festival Stage; April 24–June 7, 2009

Othello by William Shakespeare; Director, Geoffrey Sherman; Composer, James Conely; Set, Robert F. Wolin; Costumes, Elizabeth Novak; Lighting, Phil Monat; Sound, Richelle Thompson; Fights, Jason Armit; Movement, Denise Gabriel; Dramaturg, Susan Willis; Stage Manager, Scott Pegg; Assistant Stage Manager, Tanya J. Searle; Production Assistant, Heather Newman; Cast: Esau Pritchett (Othello), Rodney Clark (Brabantio), Blake Kubena (Cassio), Matt D'Amico (Iago), Nathan M. Hosner (Roderigo), Patrick Vest (Duke of Venice), Matt Renskers (Senator/Soldier), Jarrod Yuskauskas (Senators/Soldiers), Joseph Reed (Montano), Graham Allen (Gentleman of Cyprus), Chris Roe (Gentleman of Cyprus), Adam Souza (Gentleman of Cyprus), Gregory Spradlin (Gentleman of Cyprus), Michael Daniel Anderson (Lodovico), Jeffrey de Picciotto (Gratiano), Kaytie Morris (Desdemona), Caroline Strong (Emilia), Cory Coleman (Bianca), Amanda Catania (Messenger/Lady), Johnson Chong (Herald), Peter Gray (Officer), Lauren Anne Martin (Lady), Amanda McCallum (Lady); Festival Stage; May 1–June 6, 2009

The Comedy of Errors by William Shakespeare, Director, Diana Van Fossen; Composer, James Conely; Set, Robert F. Wolin; Costumes, Brenda Van der Wiel; Lighting, Phil Monat; Sound, Richelle Thompson; Fight Director, Jason Armit; Movement Consultant, Denise Gabriel; Dramaturg, Susan Willis; Stage Manager, Tanya J. Searle; Assistant Stage Manager, Scott Pegg; Production Assistant, Heather Newman; Cast: Esau Pritchett (Solinus), Joseph Reed (Egeon), Michael Daniel Anderson (Antipholus of Ephesus), Blake Kubena (Antipholus of Syracuse), Jeffrey de Picciotto (Dromio of Ephesus), Chris Roe (Dromio of Syracuse), Jarrod Yuskauskas (Balthasar), Patrick Vest (Angelo), Matt Renskers (Doctor Pinch), Gregory Spradlin (First Merchant), Nathan M. Hosner (Second Merchant), Graham Allen (Officer), Johnson Chong (Jailer), Peter Gray (Messenger), Caroline Strong (Abbess), Kaytie Morris (Adriana), Amanda McCallum (Luciana), Lauren Anne Martin (Luce), Cory Coleman (Courtesan), Amanda Catania (Pirate), Peter Gray (Pirate), David Stewart Hudson (Pirate), Adam Souza (Pirate), Festival Stage; May 8–June 7, 2009

Misalliance by George Bernard Shaw, Director, Wendy McClellan; Set, Peter Hicks; Costumes, Katrina Cahalan-Wilhite; Lighting, Tom Rodman; Sound, Richelle Thompson; Dramaturg, Susan Willis; Speech and Dialect Coach, Mary Irwin; Stage Manager, Heather Newman; Assistant Stage Manager, Crystal McCall; Cast: Chris Roe (Johnny), Matt Renskers (Bentley), Cory Monroe Coleman (Hypatia), Greta Lambert (Mrs. Tarleton), Patrick Vest (Lord Summerhays), Jarrod Yuskauskas (Mr. Tarleton), Graham Allen (Joey Percival), Lauren Anne Martin (Lina), Greg Spradlin (Gunner); Octagon Theatre; June 26–July 4, 2009

Beehive by Larry Gallagher, Director, Larry Gallagher; Choreography, Karen Azenberg; Musical Director, Joel Jones; Set, Peter Hicks; Costumes, Elizabeth Novak; Lighting, Paul Wonsek; Sound, Richelle Thompson; Stage Manager, Tanya J. Searle; Production Assistant, Melissa Van Swol; Sound Consultant, Joe Payne; Cast: Ginger Bess, Anna Eilnsfeld, Brooke Jacob, Robyn Payne, Terita Redd, Sasha Sloan; Band: Joel Jones (Piano), Mike Duncan (Guitar), Joe Cosgrove (Bass), Greg Jackson (Drums), Brett Rominger (Saxaphone), Carly Johnson (Trumpet), James Zingara (Trumpet); Festival Stage; June 10–August 2, 2009

Alley Theatre

Houston, Texas
Sixty-second Season
Artistic Director, Gregory Boyd; Managing Director, Dean Gladden

Agatha Christie's The Unexpected Guest by Agatha Christie; Director, James Black; Set, Kevin Rigdon; Costumes, Alejo Vietti; Lighting, Kevin Rigdon; Sound, Joe Pino; Stage Managers, Elizabeth M. Berther & Terry Cranshaw; Cast: Raymond Postgate (Richard Warwick), Elizabeth Heflin (Laura Warwick), James Black (Michael Starkwedder), Anne Quackenbush (Miss Bennett), Brandon Hearnsberger (Jan Warwick), Melissa Hart (Mrs. Warwick), Todd Waite (Henry Angell), Jeffrey Bean (Sergeant Cadwallader), John Tyson (Inspector Thomas), Paul Hope (Julian Farrar); Hubbard Stage; July 10–August 3, 2008

Cyrano de Bergerac by Edmond Rostand, Adapted by Brian Hooker; Director, Gregory Boyd; Set, Hugh Landwehr; Costumes, Alejo Vietti; Lighting, Rui Rita; Sound, Rob Milburn & Michael Bodeen; Fight Director, Brian Byrnes; Stage Managers, Elizabeth M. Berther & Terry Cranshaw; ASM, Rebecca R.D. Hamlin; Cast: Jeffrey Bean (Cyrano de Bergerac), James Belcher (Ligniere/The Capuchin), James Black (Le Bret), Elizabeth Bunch (Orange Girl/Baker/Musician/ Sister Marthe), Brian Byrnes (Brissaille/Cadet), Josie de Guzman (Duenna), Justin Doran (Christian), Bettye Fitzpatrick (Doorkeeper/Mother Marguerite), Brandon Hearnsberger (Marquis 1/Cadet), Elizabeth Heflin (Roxane), Paul Hope (Montfleury/Baker), Chris Hutchison (Valvert/Cadet), Philip Lehl (Marquis 2/ Cadet/Spaniard), Emily Neves (Prostitute/Musician/Sister Claire), Melissa Pritchett (Prostitute/Lise/Nun), David Rainey (Cuigy/Cadet/Spaniard), John Tyson (Ragueneau), Todd Waite (Comte de Guiche); Ensemble: Matt Redden, Spencer Plachy, Caleb George, Luis Gonzalez, Kalob Martinez, Rivka Noskeau, Elissa Levitt, Noe Mendoze III; Hubbard Stage; October 3–November 2, 2008

Jeffrey Bean and Elizabeth Bunch in Cyrano de Bergerac
(photo by Michael Daniel)

Secret Order by Bob Clyman; Director Charles Towers; Set, Bill Clarke; Costumes, Martha Hally; Lighting, Kevin Rigdon; Sound, Pierre Dupree; Stage Manager, Sara Elida Mills; Cast: Dylan Chalfy (William Shumway), Larry Pine (Robert Brock), Melissa Miller (Alice Curiton), Kenneth Tigar (Saul Roth); Neuhaus Stage; October 24–November 23, 2008

A Christmas Carol–A Ghost Story of Christmas by Charles Dickens; Director James Black; Set, Tony Straiges; Costumes, Alejo Vietti; Lighting, Rui Rita; Sound, John Gromada; Choreography, Hope Clarke; Music Director, Deborah Lewis; Stage Manager, Terry Cranshaw; ASM, Rebecca R.D. Hamlin; Cast: Natalie Arneson (Restoration Apparition/Fred's Sister-In-Law), Jeffrey Bean

(Ebenezer Scrooge), James Black (Mrs.Dilber/Jacob Marley), Justin Doran (Mr. Marvel), Bettye Fitzpatrick (Mary Pidgeon/Spirit of Christmas Past), Paul Hope (Second Solicitor/Mr.Fezziwig), Chris Hutchison (Bob Cratchit), John Johnston (18th Century Apparition/Mr. Topper), Charles Krohn (Undertaker/Old Joe), Philip Lehl (First Solicitor/Fiddler), Emily Neves (Belle/Fred's Wife), Melissa Pritchett (Mary Stuart Apparition/Rich Lady/Dance Captain), David Rainey (Bert/Spirit of Christmas Present); Understudies: James Belcher, Josie de Guzman, Patrick Mitchel; Hubbard Stage; November 21–December 28, 2008

The Santaland Diaries by David Sedaris; Adapted for the stage by Joe Mantello; Director, David Cromer; Set, Karin Rabe; Costumes, Blair Gulledge; Lighting, Kevin Rigdon; Sound, Pierre Dupree; Stage Manager, Sara Elida Mills; Cast: Todd Waite (Crumpet); Neuhaus Stage; December 2–December 28, 2008

Mrs. Warren's Profession by Bernard Shaw; Director Anders Cato; Set, Hugh Landwehr, Costumes, David Murin; Lighting, Clifton Taylor; Sound, Scott Killian; Stage Manager, Elizabeth M. Berther; ASM, Sara Elida Mills; Cast: Jane Pfitsch (Vivie), John Tyson (Praed), Elizabeth Heflin (Mrs. Warren), Todd Waite (Sir George Crofts), Brandon Hearnsberger (Frank Gardner), Alison Coriell (Factory Woman), Traci Hines (Factory Woman), Laura Kaldis (Factory Woman), Elissa Levitt (Factory Woman), Rivka Noskeau (Factory Woman), Lyndsay Sweeney (Factory Woman); Hubbard Stage; January 9–February 1, 2009

Eurydice by Sarah Ruhl; Director, Gregory Boyd; Set, Hugh Landwehr; Costumes, Alejo Vietti; Lighting, Rui Rita; Sound, Josh Schmidt; Choreography, Krissy Richmond; Stage Manager, Terry Cranshaw; Cast: Mary Rasmussen (Eurydice), Jay Sullivan (Orpheus), John Feltch (Father), David Rainey (Nasty Interesting Man/Lord of the Underworld), Melissa Pritchett (Little Stone), Philip Lehl (Loud Stone), Justin Doran (Big Stone); Neuhaus Stage; January 30–March 1, 2009

The Man Who Came to Dinner by Moss Hart and George S. Kaufman; Director, John Rando; Set, Alexander Dodge; Costumes, Gregory Gale; Lighting, Pat Collins; Sound, Pierre Dupree; Stage Manager, Elizabeth M. Berther; ASM, Rebecca R.D. Hamlin; Cast: Jeffrey Bean (John), James Belcher (Mr. Stanley), James Black (Sheridan Whiteside), Marjorie Carroll (Mrs. Dexter), Josie de Guzman (Maggie Cutler), Bettye Fitzpatrick (Mrs. McCutcheon), Elizabeth Heflin (Lorraine Sheldon), Paul Hope (Beverly Carlton), Chris Hutchison (Sandy/A Luncheon Guest), Kimberly King (Harriet Stanley), Charles Krohn (Dr. Bradley), Christianne Mays (Mrs. Ernest W. Stanley), Emily Neves (June Stanley), Spencer Plachy (Richard Stanly), Anne Quackenbush (Miss Preen), John Tyson (Professor Metz/Banjo), Todd Waite (Bert Jefferson); Hubbard Stage; February 20–March 22, 2009

Todd Waite, John Tyson and James Black in
The Man Who Came to Dinner *(photo by T. Charles Erickson)*

Mauritius by Theresa Rebeck; Director, Scott Schwartz; Set & Lighting, Kevin Rigdon; Costumes, Alejo Vietti; Sound, Josh Schmidt; Fight Director, Brian Byrnes; Stage Manager, Terry Cranshaw; ASM, Rebecca R.D. Hamlin; Cast: Elizabeth Bunch (Jackie), Jeffrey Bean (Philip), Chris Hutchison (Dennis), David Rainey (Sterling), Kelly McAndrew (Mary); Hubbard Stage; April 10–May 3, 2009

Rock 'n' Roll by Tom Stoppard; Director, Gregory Boyd; Set, Hugh Landwehr; Costumes, Alejo Vietti; Lighting, Pat Collins; Sound, Rob Milburn & Michael Bodeen; Hair, David H. Lawrence; Projections, Clint Allen; Dialects, Stephen Gabis; Stage Manager, Elizabeth M. Berther; Cast: Spencer Plachy (The Piper/Policeman), Emily Neves (Esme/Deirdre), Todd Waite (Jan), James Black (Max Morrow), Josie de Guzman (Eleanor), Melissa Pritchett (Gillian/ Magda), Philip Lehl (Interrogator), Justin Doran (Ferdinand), James Belcher (Milan/Waiter), Sara Gaston (Candida); Neuhaus Stage; April 24–May 24, 2009

The Farnsworth Invention by Aaron Sorkin; Director, David Cromer; Set, Takeshi Kata; Costumes, Janice Pytel; Lighting, Keith Parham; Sound, Josh Schmidt; Projections, Clint Allen; Stage Manager, Terry Cranshaw; ASM, Rebecca R.D. Hamlin; Cast: Jeffrey Bean (David Sarnoff), Brandon Hearnsberger (Philo T. Farnsworth), James Belcher (Leslie Gorrell/Ensemble), James Black (Atkins/Walter Gifford/Douglas Fairbanks/Lippincott/Ensemble), Elizabeth Bunch (Lizette Sarnoff/Mary Pickford/Ensemble), Justin Doran (Wachtel/Ensemble), Sara Gaston (Betty/Ensemble), John Paul Green (Young David Sarnoff/Stan Willis/Ensemble), Elizabeth Heflin (Mina Edison), Paul Hope (William Crocker/Ensemble), Chris Hutchison (Pem's Father/Cliff Gardner/Ensemble), Charles Krohn (Justin Tolman/Ensemble), Philip Lehl (Sarnoff's Father/Jim Harbord/Joseph Schenck/Ensemble), Emily Neves (Pem Farnsworth/Ensemble), Justin O'Brien (Wilkins/Analyst/Ensemble), Melissa Pritchett (Sarnoff's Mother/Pem's Mother/Agnes Farnsworth/Ensemble), David Rainey (Harlan Honn/Lennox/Ensemble), John Tyson (George Everson/Ensemble), Todd Waite (Simms/Vladimir Zworykin/Ensemble) Ty Doran or Sean Hardin (Young Philo T. Farnsworth); Hubbard Stage; June 5–June 28, 2009

Alliance Theatre

Atlanta, Georgia
Fortieth Season
Artistic Director, Susan V. Booth; Managing Director, Thomas Pechar

Gem of the Ocean by August Wilson; Director, Kenny Leon; Set, Edward E. Haynes, Jr.; Costumes, Meriann Verheyen; Lighting, Annie Wrightson; Sound, Clay Benning; Original Sound, Dan Moses Schreier; Original Music, Kathryn Bostic; Assistant Director, Eugene Lee; Repertory Stage Manager, Lark Hackshaw; Dramaturg, Jade Lambert Smith; Casting, Jody Feldman and Harriet Bass; Cast: Chad L. Colman (Caesar Wilks), Donald Griffin (Eli), Tonia M. Jackson (Black Mary), Larry Larson (Rutherford Selig), E. Roger Mitchell (Citizen Barlow), Afemo Omilami (Solly Two Kings), Michele Shay (Aunt Ester), Understudies: David Koté (Caesar Wilks/Eli/Solly Two Kings), Eric J. Little (Citizen Barlow), Yvonne Singh (Aunt Ester/Black Mary); Alliance Stage; August 30–September 28, 2008

Radio Golf by August Wilson; Director, Kent Gash; Set, Edward E. Haynes, Jr.; Costumes, Meriann Verheyen; Lighting, Annie Wrightson; Sound, Clay Benning; Original Sound, Dan Moses Schreier; Original Music, Kathryn Bostic; Assistant Director, Eugene Lee; Repertory Stage Manager, Lark Hackshaw; Dramaturg, Jade Lambert Smith; Casting, Jody Feldman and Harriet Bass; Cast: Chad L. Colman (Harmond Wilks), Donald Griffin (Sterling Johnson), Tonia M. Jackson (Mame Wilks), E. Roger Mitchell (Roosevelt Hicks), Afemo Omilami (Elder Joseph Barlow), Understudies: David Koté (Elder Joseph Barlow/Sterling Johnson), Eric J. Little (Harmond Wilks/Roosevelt Hicks), Yvonne Singh (Mame Wilks); Alliance Stage; August 39–September 28, 2008

The Second City: Too Busy to Hate… Too Hard to Commute Written and Created by the cast of The Second City; Additional Material by Ed Furman and TJ Shanoff; Director, Matt Hovde; Musical Director, Lisa McQueen; Stage Manager, Lee Brackett; Dramaturg, Jade Lambert Smith; Casting, Beth Kleigerman and Marc Warzecha and Jody Feldman; Cast: Anthony Irons (Ensemble), Michael Lehrer (Ensemble), Robyn Norris (Ensemble), Amy Roeder (Ensemble), Tim Stoltenberg (Ensemble), Rick Walker (Ensemble), Musicians, Lisa McQueen; Hertz Stage; September 19–November 2, 2008

Managing Maxine by Janice Shaffer; Director, Susan V. Booth; Set, Joseph Tilford; Costumes, Linda Roethke; Lighting, Deb Sullivan; Sound, Clay Benning; Music, Haddon Kime; Stage Manager, Pat A. Flora; Dramaturg, Celise Kalke; Casting, Jody Feldman and Harriet Bass; Cast: Ross Bickell (Arthur), Courtenay Collins (Emmie), Howard Elfman (Louis), Larry Larson (Larry), Judy Leavell (Joanne), Courtney Patterson (Ivy), Jana Robbins (Maxine), Understudies: Howard Elfman (Arthur), Jo Howarth (Joanne), Judy Leavell (Maxine), Tafee Patterson (Emmie/Ivy), David Skoke (Louis/Larry); Alliance Stage; October 8—November 2, 2008

Goodnight Moon Adapted by Margaret Wise Brown and Clement Hurd; Book, Music and Lyrics, Chad Henry; Director, Rosemary Newcott; Set, Kat Conley; Costumes, Katherine Aurora Callahan; Lighting, Deb Sullivan; Sound, Clay Benning; Music Direction and Sound Composition, Clint Thornton; Choreography, Hylan Scott; Stage Manager, Liz Campbell; Dramaturg, Celise Kalke; Casting, Jody Feldman; Cast: Amber Iman (Old Woman/Mama Bear/Puppeteer), Jmichael (Piano Player/Moon), Sharon Litzky (Mouse/Dog/Baby Bear/Puppeteer), Derek Manson (Little Bunny), Brandon O'Dell (Tooth Fairy/Papa Bear/The Cat/Telephone/Puppeteer), Understudies: Sindu Giedd (Old Woman/Mama Bear/Mouse/Dog/Baby Bear/Puppeteer), Mark W. Schroeder (Piano Player/Moon/Little Bunny/ Tooth Fairy/Papa Bear/The Cat/Telephone/Puppeteer); Alliance Stage; November 3–November 16, 2008

A Christmas Carol by Charles Dickens; Adapted by David H. Bell; Director, Rosemary Newcott; Set, D. Martyn Bookwalter; Costumes, Mariann Verheyen; Lighting, Diane Ferry Williams; Sound, Clay Benning; Musical Direction, Michael Fauss; Stage Manager, Pat A. Flora and Robert Allen Wright; Dramaturg, Celise Kalke; Casting, Jody Feldman; Cast: Christy Baggett (Ensemble), Elizabeth Wells Berkes (Belle/Ensemble), Tabitha Christopher (Mrs. Dilber/Mrs. Fezziwig/Ensemble beginning Dec. 9), Ritchie Crownfield (Ensemble beginning Dec. 9), Je Nie Flemming (Mrs. Cratchit/Ensemble), Neal A. Ghant (Bob Cratchit), Bart Hansard (Mr. Fezziwig/Christmas Present/Ensemble), David Howard (Topper/Ensemble), Jamiah Hudson (Belinda/Ensemble), Chris Kayser (Ebenezer Scrooge), Jahi Kearse (Dick Wilkins/Ensemble), Royce Mann (Tiny Tim/Ensemble), Tendal Mann (Richard/Ignorance/Ensemble), Derek Manson (Peter/Ensemble), Daniel Thomas May (Marley/Ensemble), Bernadine Mitchell (Mrs. Dilber/Mrs. Fezziwig/Ensemble until Dec. 7), Tess Lene Palisoc (Melinda/Want/Ensemble), Courtney Patterson (Christmas Past/Peg/Ensemble), Thomas Piper (Young Scrooge/Ensemble), Glenn Rainey (Ensemble until Dec. 7), Brydan Rogers (Daniel/Turkey Boy/Ensemble), Brad Sherill (Fred/Ensemble), Hanley Smith (Fan/Martha/Ensemble), James Washburn III (Wyatt/Ensemble), Minka Wiltz (Bess/Ensemble), Understudies: Christy Baggett (Mrs. Fezziwig), Elizabeth Wells Berkes (Christmas Past/Peg), Tabitha Christopher (Mrs. Dilber/Mrs. Fezziwig/Ensemble until Dec. 7), Ritchie Crownfield (Topper beginning Dec. 9), Joshua Donahue (Dick Wilkins/Peter/Ensemble), Je Nie Flemming (Mrs. Dilber), Neal A. Ghant (Marley/Ensemble), David Howard (Christmas Present/Mr. Fezziwig), Jamiah Hudson (Want/Ignorance/Melinda), Jahi Kearse (Bob Cratchit), Sims Lamason (Bess/Fan/Martha/Ensemble), Tendal Mann (Tiny Tim), Derek Manason (Fred/Young Scrooge), Tess Lene Palisoc (Belinda), Glenn Rainey (Topper until Dec. 7), Brydan Rogers (Wyatt), Brad Sherill (Ebenezer Scrooge), Hanley Smith (Belle/Ensemble), James Washburn III (Wyatt/Ensemble), Minka Wiltz (Mrs. Cratchit), Musicians: Michael Fauss (Music Director and Conductor/Keyboards), Diedre

Henson Agustin (Harp), Butch Sievers (Percussion); Alliance Stage; November 28–December 24, 2008

Jesus Christ Superstar GOSPEL Lyrics by Tim Rice; Music by Andrew Lloyd Webber; Conceived and Arranged by Louis St. Louis; Director, Susan V. Booth; Set, Michael Yeargan; Costumes, Paul Tazewell; Lighting, Robert Wierzel; Sound, Jon Weston; Gospel Vocal Arrangements, Darryl Jovan Williams; Orchestrations, Dave Pierce; Dance Arrangements, Louis St. Louis; Music Copying, Anne Kaye; Musical Director, Michael Mitchell; Stage Manager, Pat A. Flora; Dramaturg, Jade Lambert Smith; Casting, Jody Feldman and Alan Filderman; Choreography, Hope Clarke; Cast: Keith Adams (Simon/Ensemble), Stephanie Battle (Herod Backup/Dance Ensemble), Rodney Boydkin (Priest/Guard/Ensemble), Phillip Boykin (Caiaphas/Ensemble), Jaime Cepero (Ensemble), Chandra Currelley (Judas Backup/Herod Backup/Ensemble), Darius de Haas (Jesus), Jesse Jones (Dance Ensemble), Arian Keddell (Dance Ensemble), Nicole Long (Mary Magdalene), Philip Dorian McAdoo (Peter/Ensemble), Bernardine Mitchell (Judas Backup/Ensemble), Destan Owens (Pilate/Ensemble), CJay Hardy Philip (Judas Backup/Herod Backup/Ensemble), Glenn Rainey (Ensemble), Eugene H. Russell, IV (Priest/Guard/Ensemble), Brett Sturgis (Dance Ensemble), Charles E. Wallace (Dance Ensemble), J.D. Webster (Annas/Ensemble), Darryl Jovan Williams (Judas), Hollie E. Wright (Dance Ensemble), Eric Jordan Young (Herod/Ensemble), Choir: Adam McKnight (Choir Leader), Charlene Anderson, Christy Clark, Jae Franklin, Latarsha Horne, Cynthia Jackson, Jenifer Jordan, Jamie Katz, Naomi Lavette, Paul Lockett, Demond Mason, Cassandra McCullough, Arle Michel, Eric Moore, Jennifer Myles, Latrice Pace, Valerie Payton, Steven Roberts, Jeremy Sage, Tameka Scotten, Jonathan Smith, Tim Stylez, Alecia Terry, Paul Vincent, Cory Washington, Raena White, BurgAndy Williams, Yolanda Williams; Understudies: Keith Adams (Jesus), Jaime Cepero (Simon), Christy Clark (Herod Backup/Judas Backup/Ensemble), Adam McKnight (Annas/Herod), Eric Moore (Peter), Latrice Pace 9Herod backup/Judas Backup/Ensemble), Glenn Rainey (Pilate), Steven Roberts (Priest/Guard/Ensemble), Eugene H. Russell (Caiaphas), Jonathan Smith (Ensemble), Tim Stylez (Judas), Raena White (Mary Magdalene), Alliance Stage; January 14–February 22, 2009

Darius de Haas in Jesus Christ Superstar *(photos by Greg Mooney)*

Smart Cookie by Julia Brownell; Director, Jeremy B. Cohen; Set, Lee Savage; Costumes, Miranda Hoffman; Lighting, Jaymi Lee Smith; Sound Design and Music Composition, Lindsay Jones; Stage Manager, Lark Hackshaw; Dramaturgs, Celise Kalke and Sarah Slight; Casting, Jody Feldman and Harriett Bass; Cast: Rebecca Blumhagen (Ana), Courtenay Collins (Cookie), Dori Garziano (Danielle and Others), Blake Lowell (Spencer), Larry Larson (Kevin), Nancy Lemenager (Bitsy), Understudies: Dori Garziano (Bitsy), Kate Graham (Ana/Danielle and

Others), Mira Hirsch (Cookie), James Sutton (Kevin), William Webber (Spencer), Hertz Stage; January 30–February 22, 2009

Class of 3000 LIVE by André Benjamin and Tommy Lynch; Adapted by Rosemary Newcott; Director, Rosemary Newcott; Set, Kat Conley; Costumes, Sydney Roberts; Lighting, Pete Shinn; Sound, Clay Benning; Music Direction, Justin Ellington; Stage Manager, Liz Campbell; Dramaturg, Neely Gossett; Casting, Jody Feldman; Choreography, Iris Goode; Cast: Jonathan Davis (Kam), Bernard Jones (Li'l D), Wendy Melkonian (Madison/Bianca), Brandon O'Dell (Phil), Sinatra Onyewuchi (Sunny Bridges), Zany Pohlel (Kim), Justin Tanner (Eddie), Scott Warren (Bus Driver/Manager/Principal Luna/Mr. Baylor/Puppeteer), Sharisa Whatley (Tamika), Understudies: Brandon Chubbs (Li'l D/Sunny Bridges), Doug Graham (Phil/Eddie/Kam), Randall Havens (Bus Driver/Manager/Principal Luna/Mr. Baylor/Puppeteer), Kayla Sklar (Kim/Tamika/Madison/Bianca); Alliance Stage; March 6–March 29, 2009

Brandon O'Dell, Sharisa Whatley, Sinatra Onyewuchi, Wendy Melkonian and Jonathan Davis in Class of 3000 LIVE

26 miles by Quiara Alegría Hudes; Director, Kent Gash; Set, Kat Conley; Costumes, English Benning; Lighting, William H. Grant, III; Sound, Clay Benning; Projections, Adam Larson; Stage Manager, Lark Hackshaw; Dramaturg, Celise Kalke; Casting, Jody Feldman and Alan Filderman, CSA; Cast: Bethany Anne Lind (Olivia), Jason Macdonald (Aaron), Triney Sandoval (Manuel), Socorro Santiago (Beatriz), Understudies: Rose Bianco (Beatriz), Dowd Keith (Olivia), Khalid Robinson (Aaron/Manuel); Hertz Stage; March 20–April 12, 2009

Jacques Brel is Alive and Well and Living in Paris Conception, English Lyrics and Additional Material by Eric Blau and Mort Shuman; Based on Lyrics and Commentary by Jacques Brel; Music by Jacques Brel; Director, Susan V. Booth; Set, Leslie Taylor; Costumes, Mariann Verheyen; Lighting, Pete Shinn; Sound, Clay Benning; Music Direction, Robert Strickland; Original Music Direction, Michael Fauss; Stage Manager, Pat A. Flora; Dramaturg, Michael Evenden; Casting, Jody Feldman and Harriett Bass; Musical Staging, Craig A. Meyer; Cast: Courtenay Collins (Actress 1), Joseph Dellger (Actor 1), Steffi Garrard (Actress 2), Craig A. Meyer (Actor 2), Understudies: Shawn Megorden (Actress 1/Actress 2), Bradley Renner (Actor 1/Actor 2), Musicians: Robert Strickland (Music Director and Piano/Conductor), S. Renee Clark (Asst. Music Director and Piano/Conductor performing Apr. 21-26), Ramon Pooser (Bass), Lyn Deramus (Bass performing Apr. 16), Butch Sievers (Drums), William Hatcher (Guitar); Alliance Stage; April 15–May 10, 2009

American Repertory Theatre

Cambridge, Massachusetts
Thirtieth Season
Diane Paulus, Artistic Director; Gideon Lester, Director; Robert J. Orchard, Executive Director

Let Me Down Easy Conceived, Written, and Performed by Anna Deavere Smith; Director, Eric Ting; Set, David Rockwell; Costumes, Ann Hould-Ward; Lighting, Michael Chybowski; Original Musical Elements, Joshua Redman; Sound, David Remedios; Projection, Jan Hartley; Movement, Elizabeth Roxas-Dobrish; Dialect Coach, Amy Stoller; Stage Manager, Shannon Richey; Loeb Drama Center, October 18–November 9, 2008

The Communist Dracula Pageant by Americans, for Americans, a Play about the Romanian Revolution of 1989 with Hallucinations, Phosphorescence, and Bears; by Anne Washburn; Director, Annie Kauffman; Set, Mimi Lien; Costumes, Christal Weatherly; Lighting, Tyler Micoleau; Sound, David Remedios; Music, Michael Friedman; Choreography, Doug Elkins; Stage Manager, Katherine Shea; Cast: Thomas Derrah (Nicolaeo Ceausescu), Karen MacDonald (Elena Ceaucescu/Pageant Elena), Will LeBow (Vlad Tepes/Functionary), Ensemble: Remo Airaldi, Kaaron Briscoe, Sheila Carrasco, Shawn Cody, John Kuntz, Matthew Maher, James Senti, Josh Stamell, Roger K. Stewart; Pageanteers: Adam Eli Clem, John M. Costa, Wayne Fritsche, Carrie Ann Quinn; World Premiere; Zero Arrow Theatre, October 18–November 9, 2009

Aurelia's Oratorio Writer and Director, Victoria Thierrée Chaplin; Technical Direction/Sound, Monika Schumm; Stage Manager, Gerd Walter; Lighting, Thomas Dobruszkès; Backstage Support, Aurélie Guin, Antonia Paradiso, Monika Schwarzl; Lighting, Laura de Bernadis, Philippe Lacombe; Sound, Victoria Thierrée Chaplin, Paolo Barcucchi; Set, Victoria Thierrée Chaplin; Costumes, Victoria Thierrée Chaplin, Jacques Perdiguez, Veronique Grand, Monika Schwarzl; Company Management/Administration, Didier Bendel; Photography, Richard Haughton; Collaboration with La Compagnie du Hanneton; Co-Produced by Theatre "L'Avant-Scene", La Ferme du Buisson, Cognac, René Marion, Director, Executive Producer, US Tour, ArKtype/Thomas O. Kriegsmann; Loeb Drama Center; November 28–January 3, 2009

The Seagull by Anton Chekhov; Translator, Paul Schmidt; Director, János Szász; Set, Riccardo Hernandez; Costumes, David Zinn; Lighting, Christopher Akerlind; Sound, David Remedios; Production Stage Manager, Chris De Camillis; Dramaturgs, Ryan McKittrick, Lynde Rosario; Vocal Coach, Nancy Houfek; Cast: Karen MacDonald (Irina Nikolayevna Arkadina), Mickey Solis (Konstantin Gavrilovich Treplev), Jeremy Geidt (Pyotr Nikolayevich Sorin), Molly Ward (Nina Mikhailovna Zarechnaya), Remo Airaldi (Ilya Afanasyevich Shamrayev), Cheryl D. Singleton(Paulina Andreyevna), Nina Kassa (Masha), Brian Dykstra (Boris Alexeyevich Trigorin), Thomas Derrah (Yevgeny Sergeyevich Dorn), Shawn Cody (Medvedenko), Dan Pecci (Yakov), Assistant Stage Manager, Katherine Shea; Assistant Dramaturgs, Paul Stacey and Brendan Shea; Assistant Vocal Coach, Jane Guyer; Dance Instructor, Cheryl Turski; Loeb Drama Center; January 10–February 1, 2009

Endgame by Samuel Beckett; Director, Marcus Stern; Set, Andromache Chalfant; Costumes, Clint Ramos; Lighting, Scott Zielinski; Sound, David Remedios; PSM, Katherine Shea; Dramaturgs, Ryan McKittrick, Heidi Nelson; Vocal Coach, Nancy Houfek; Cast: Will LeBow (Hamm), Thomas Derrah (Clov), Remo Airaldi (Nagg), Karen MacDonald (Nell), ASM, Amanda Robbins-Butcher; Assistant Dramaturg, Whitney Eggers; Assistant Vocal Coach, Julie Foh; Loeb Drama Center; February 14–March 21, 2009

Trojan Barbie by Christine Evans; Director, Carmel O' Reilly; Set and Costumes, David Reynoso; Lighting, Justin Townsend; Sound, David Remedios; Stage Manager, Chris De Camillis; Dramaturgs, Gideon Lester and Katie Mallinson; Vocal Coach, Nancy Houfek; Cast: The Trojans: Paula Langton (Hecuba), Kaaron Briscoe (Polly X), Nina Kassa (Cassandra), Skye Nöel

(Andromache), Emily Alpren (Clea), Lisette Silva (Esme), The Others: Careena Melia (Helen), Karen MacDonald (Lotte), Renzo Ampuero (Mica), Carl Foreman (Talthybius/Max), Jim Senti (Menelaus/Jorge/Clive/Officer in Blue), ASM, Katherine Shea; Production Associate, Kyle Carlson; Production Associate, Emily Page; Movement Director, Cheryl Turski; Assistant Director, Pirronne Yousefzadeh; Assistant Vocal Coach, Jane Guyer; Loeb Drama Center; March 28–April 23, 2009

Romance by David Mamet; Director, Scott Zigler; Set, J. Michael Griggs; Costumes, Miranda Hoffman; Lighting, D.M. Wood; Sound, David Remedios; Stage Manager, Katherine Shea; Dramaturg, Sean Bartley; Vocal Coach, Jane Guyer; Cast: Thomas Derrah (The Prosecutor), Remo Airaldi (The Defendant), Jim True-Frost (The Defense Attorney), Will LeBow (The Judge), Jim Senti (The Bailiff), Cari Foreman (Bernard), Doug Chapman (The Doctor), Assistant Stage Manager, Amanda Robbins-Butcher; Loeb Drama Center, May 9–June 7, 2009

David Mamet Double Bill: The Duck Variations by David Mamet; Director, Marcus Stern; Lighting, Jeff Adelberg; Sound, David Remedios; Stage Manager, Chris De Camillis; Production Assistant, Graydon Gund; Cast: Thomas Derrah (Emil Varec), Will LeBow(George S. Aronovitz),

Sexual Perversity In Chicago by David Mamet; Director, Paul Stacey; Costumes, Mallory Freers; Lighting, Jeff Adelberg; Sound, David Remedios; Stage Manager, Kyle Carlson; Production Assistant, Graydon Gund; Cast: Tim Eliot (Bernard), Scott Lyman (Dan), Susannah Hoffman (Deborah), Laura Parker (Joan), an A.R.T. Institute for Advanced Theater Training Production; Zero Arrow Theatre, June 11–28, 2009

Scott Lyman and Susannah Hoffman in Sexual Perversity in Chicago
(photo by Kati Mitchell)

Arden Theatre Company

Philadelphia, Pennsylvania
Twenty-first Season
Artistic Director, Terrence J. Nolen; Managing Director, Amy Murphy

Candide The Royal National Theatre Version; Music by Leonard Bernstein; Book adapted from Voltaire by Hugh Wheeler; In a New Version by John Caird; Lyrics by Richard Wilbur, Additional Lyrics by Stephen Sondheim, John Latouche, Lillian Hellman, Dorothy Parker and Leonard Bernstein; Director, Terrence J. Nolen; Costumes, Rosemarie McKelvey; Stage Manager, Katherine Hanley; Cast: Joel T. Bauer (Maximillian), Ben Dibble (Candide), Erin Driscoll (Paquette), Liz Filios (Cunegonde), Nick Gaswirth (Vanderdendur), Soctt Greer (Voltaire/Dr. Pangloss), Mary Martello (The Old Woman), Christopher Patrick Mullen (Martin), Richard Ruiz (Cacambo), Ensemble: Mat Burrow, Jeffrey Coon, Matthew Ferraro, Jessica Gruver, Darren Michael Hengst, Gabrielle Hurtt, Melissa Kolczynski, Kristin Purcell, Marian Sunnergren, Sorab Wadia; F. Otto Haas Stage; September 11–October 19, 2008

Gee's Bend by Elyzabeth Gregory Wilder; Director, Eleanor Holdridge; Set, Marjorie Bradley Kellogg; Costumes, Alison Roberts; Lighting, Les Dickert; Sound, Christopher Colucci; Stage Manager, Stephanie Cook; Cast: Kala Moses Baxter (Nella), Edwina Findley (Sadie), Marjorie Johnson (Alice/Asia), Kes Khemnu (Macon); Arcadia Stage; October 9–December 7, 2008

James and the Giant Peach by David Wood; Book by Roald Dahl; Director, Whit MacLaughlin; Set, Matt Saunders; Costumes, Christal Weatherly; Lighting, Brian J. Lilienthal; Sound, Jorge Cousineau; Stage Manager, Elana Wolf; Cast: Oberon Adjepong (Grasshopper), Frederick Andersen (Earthworm), Stephanie English (Aunt Sponge), James Ijames (James), Brian Osborne (Centipede), Ceal Phelan (Spider), Amanda Schoonover (Ladybird), Harum "RJ" Ulmer (Aunt Spiker); F. Otto Haas Stage; December 10, 2008–February 8, 2009

My Name Is Asher Lev by Aaron Posner; Book by Chaim Potok; Director, Aaron Posner; Set, Dan Conway; Costumes, Alison Roberts; Lighting, Thom Weaver; Sound, James Sugg; Stage Manager, Alec Ferrell; Cast: Adam Heller (Man), Karl Miller (Asher), Gabra Zackman (Woman); Arcadia Stage; January 8 – March 15–2009

A Year with Frog and Toad Music by Robert Reale; Book and Lyrics by Willie Reale; Based on the Books by Arnold Lobel; Director, Whit MacLaughlin; Set, Donald Eastman; Costumes, Richard St. Clair; Lighting, Drew Billiau; Sound, Jorge Cousineau; Stage Manager, John Flak; Cast: Jeffrey Coon (Frog), Ben Dibble (Toad), Erin Driscoll (Bird/Turtle), Nick Gaswirth (Snail/Bird), Danielle G. Herbert (Mouse/Bird); F. Otto Haas Stage; March 4–April 19, 2009

Something Intangible by Bruce Graham; Director, Terrence J. Nolen; Set, James Kronzer; Costumes, Rosemarie McKelvey; Lighting, Mitch Dana; Sound, Jorge Cousineau; Stage Manager, Stephanie Cook; Cast: Scott Greer (Dale Wiston), Sally Mercer (Sonia Feldman), Ian Merrill Peakes (Tony Wiston), Walter Charles (Doc Bartelli/Gustav Von Meyerhoff), Doug Hara (Leo Baxter); Arcadia Stage; April 9 – June 7, 2009

The Seafarer by Conor McPherson; Director, David O'Connor; Set, David P. Gordon; Costumes, Alison Roberts; Lighting, John Stephen Hoey; Sound, Jeff Lorenz; Stage Manager, Katherine M. Hanley; Cast: Joe Hickey (Nicky Giblin), Anthony Lawton (Ivan Curry), Brian Russell (Richard Harkin), Greg Wood (Mr. Lockhart), William Zielinski (James "Sharky" Harkin); F. Otto Haas Stage; May 14–June 14, 2009

Arena Stage

Washington, DC and Arlington, Virginia
Fifty-eighth Season
Artistic Director, Molly Smith; Managing Director, Edgar Dobie

Resurrection by Daniel Beaty; Music by Daniel Bernard Roumain; Director, Oz Scott; Costumes, Karen Perry; Lighting, Victor En Yu Tan; Sound, Timothy Thompson; Set, G.W. Mercier; Stage Manager, Kurt Hall; Cast: Thuliso Dingwall (10/Eric), Turron Kofi Alleyene (20/'Twon), Che Ayende (30/Dre), Alvin Keith (40/Isaac), Michael Genet (50/Mr. Rogers), Jeffery V. Thompson (60/The Bishop); World Premiere; Crystal City; August 29–October 5, 2008

Michael Genet, Che Ayende, Alvin Keith, Thuliso Dingwall, Jeffrey V. Thompson and Turron Kofi Alleyne in Resurrection

Wishful Drinking Created and Performed by Carrie Fisher; Director, Tony Taccone; Set/Lighting/Projections, Alexander V. Nichols; Stage Manager, Daniel Kells; General Manager, CESA Entertainment, INC.; Lincoln Theatre; September 5–September 28, 2008

Citizen Josh Written and Performed by Josh Kornbluth; Director, David Dower; Stage Manager, Darl Andrew Packard; Crystal City; October 9–October 26, 2008

Next to Normal Music by Tom Kitt, Book by Brian Yorkey; Director, Michael Greif; Music Director, Charlie Alterman; Costumes, Jeff Mahshie; Lighting, Kevin Adams; Stage Manager, Judith Schoenfeld; Cast: Adam Chanler-Berat (Henry), Jennifer Damiano (Natalie), Louis Hobson (Dr. Madden/Dr. Fine), Alice Ripley (Diana), J. Robert Spencer (Dan), Aaron Tveit (Gabe); Crystal City; November 21, 2008–January 18, 2009

I Love A Piano Music and Lyrics by Irving Berlin, Conceived and Written by Ray Roderick and Michael Berkeley; Director/Choreography, Ray Roderick; Costumes, Sam Flemming; Lighting, Stacey Boggs; Set, J Branson; Sound, Demetrius Grandel; Cast: Ryan Lammer (Jim), Emily Mattheson (Sadie), Alix Paige (Eileen), Michael Turay (George), Jason Weitkamp (Alex), Tom Bruett (Swing), Talia Corren (Swing); Lincoln Theatre; January 2–February 15, 2009

A Delicate Balance by Edward Albee; Director, Pam MacKinnon; Costumes, Ilona Somogyi; Lighting, Allen Lee Hughes; Set, Todd Rosenthal; Sound, Timothy Thompson; Stage Manager, Martha Knight; Cast: Kathleen Chalfant (Agnes), Terry Beaver (Tobias), Ellen McLaughlin (Claire), Helen Hedman (Edna), James Slaughter (Harry), Carla Harting (Julia); Crystal City; February 6–March 15, 2009

A Long and Winding Road by Philip Himberg and Maureen McGovern; Director, Philip Himberg; Musical Director, Jeffrey D. Harris; Costume Director, Joseph P. Salasovich; Costumes, Gayle Susan Baizer; Production Manager, Carey Lawless; Performer, Maureen McGovern; Crystal City; March 27–April 12, 2009

Crowns by Regina Taylor; Book by Michael Cunningham and Craig Marberry; Director/Choreography, Kenneth Lee Roberson; Costumes, Austin K. Sanderson; Lighting, Nancy Schertler; Sound, Timothy Thompson; Stage Manager, Amber Dickerson; Cast: Mary Millben (Wanda), Kara-Tameika Watkins (Jeanette), Marva Hicks (Velma), Zurin Villanueva (Yolanda), E. Faye Butler (Mother Shaw), NaTasha Yvette Williams (Mabel), Phillip Boykin (Man), Betty Carter (Swing-Mother Shaw/Velma/Mabel), Lulu Fall (Swing-Jeanette/ Yolanda/Wanda), Stephawn P. Stephens (Swing-Man); Lincoln Theatre; March 27–April 26, 2009

Legacy of Light by Karen Zacarías; Director, Molly Smith; Costumes, Linda Cho; Lighting, Michael Gilliam; Sound/Original Music, André J. Pluess; Stage Manager, Susan R. White; Cast: Lise Bruneau (Émilie du Châtelet), Stephen Schnetzer (Voltaire), David Covington (Saint-Lambert/Lewis), Carla Harting (Olivia/Wet Nurse), Lindsey Kyler (Millie/Pauline), Michael Russotto (Peter/Marquis du Châtelet), Jennifer Mendenhall (Swing-Olivia/Wet Nurse), World Premiere; Crystal City; May 8–June 14, 2009

Looped by Matthew Lombardo; Director, Rob Ruggiero; Costumes, William Ivey Long; Lighting, Michael Gilliam; Sound, Michael Hooker; Stage Manger, Amber Dickerson; Production Manager, Carey Lawless; Cast: Valerie Harper (Tallulah Bankhead), Jay Goede (Danny Miller), Michael Karl Orenstein (Steve); Lincoln Theater; May 29—June 28, 2009

Valerie Harper in Looped

Arizona Theatre Company

Tucson and Phoenix, Arizona
Forty-second Season
Artistic Director, David Ira Goldstein; Executive Director, Jessica L. Andrews; Managing Director, Kevin E. Moore

Enchanted April by Matthew Barber, Novel by Elizabeth von Arnim; Director, Timothy Near; Set, Kent Dorsey; Costumes, Maggie Morgan; Lighting, David Lee Cuthbert; Composer, Roberta Carlson; Sound, Brian Jerome Peterson; Dialect Coach, Lynne Soffer; Associate Lighting, T. Greg Squires; Stage Manager, Glenn Bruner; Cast: Al Espinosa (Frederick Arnott), Patricia Kilgarriff (Mrs. Graves), Monette Magrath (Caroline Bramble), Kathryn Meisle (Rose Arnott), Matthew Floyd Miller (Mellersh Wilton), Tony Roach (Antony Wilding), Lynn Soffer (Costanza), Finnerty Steeves (Lotty Wilton), Temple of Music and Art (Tucson), September 13–October 4, 2008; Herberger Theater Center (Phoenix), October 9–October 26, 2008

The Lady with All the Answers by David Rambo; Director, Samantha K. Wyer; Set, Tom Burch; Costumes, Sam Fleming; Lighting, Jennifer Setlow; Sound, Brian

Jerome Peterson; Dialect Coach, Dianne J. Winslow; Dramaturg, Jennifer Bazzell; Associate Lighting, T. Greg Squires; Stage Manager, Timothy Toothman; Cast: Nancy Dussault (Ann Landers), Temple of Music and Art (Tucson), October 18–November 8, 2008; Herberger Theatre Center (Phoenix), November 13–November 30, 2008

Hair Book and Lyrics by Gerome Ragni and James Rado; Music by Galt MacDermot; Director, David Ira Goldstein; Choreography, Patricia Wilcox; Musical Director/Conductor, Christopher McGovern; Costumes, Kish Finnegan; Lighting, Michael Gilliam; Sound, Abe Jacob; Dramaturg, Carrie J. Cole; Associate Lighting, T. Greg Squires; Stage Manager, Glenn Bruner; Cast: Melvin Bell, III (Tribe), Stefanie Brown (Tribe), Michael Buchanan (Woof), Joey Calveri (Berger), Matt DeAngelis (Tribe), Kyle Harris (Claude), Morgan James (Sheila), Miles A. Johnson (Tribe), Tamika Lawrence (Tribe), Lauren Lebowitz (Jeanie), Meghan Murphy (Tribe), Kyle Taylor Parker (Hud), Jacqueline Rez (Tribe), Sal Sabella (Tribe), Rashidra Scott (Dionne), Alexis Sims (Tribe), Rebecca Spigelman (Tribe), Erica Sweany (Crissy), Stephen Turner (Tribe), Jake Wilson (Tribe), Orchestra: Christopher McGovern (Keyboards), Jim Wall (Drums), Jay Johnson (Percussion), Eric Scott Anthony (Guitar), Christopher A. Kent (Guitar), Eric Massimino (Bass), Greg Armstrong (Reeds), Michael Harrison (Trumpet) Bill Theurer, Jr. (Trumpet), Temple of Music and Art (Tucson), November 29–December 23, 2008; Herberger Theater Center (Phoenix), December 31, 2008–January 18, 2009

The Company in Hair *(photos by Tim Fuller)*

It's a Wonderful Life: A Live Radio Play Adapted by Joe Landry; Director, Samantha K. Wyer; Set, Gary Wissmann; Costumes, Maggie McFarland; Lighting, Jennifer Setlow; Sound, Brian Jerome Peterson; Stage Manager, Erica McKibben; Cast: Paul Gibson (Sound Effects), Roberto Guajardo (Freddie Filmore), Maren Maclean (Lana Sherwood), Kerry McCue (Sally Applewhite), Bob Sorenson (Harry "Jazzbo" Heywood), Kyle Sorrell (Jake Laurents); Herberger Theater Center; December 4–December 7, 2008

A Raisin in the Sun by Lorraine Hansberry; Director, Lou Bellamy; Set, Vicki Smith; Costumes, Matthew LeFebvre; Lighting, Michelle Habeck; Sound, James C. Swonger; Assistant Director, Dominic Taylor; Associate Lighting, T. Greg Squires; Stage Manager, John Kingsbury; Cast: Adeoye (Joseph Asagai), Lorin Akers (Moving Man), David Alan Anderson (Walter Lee Younger), Damron Russell Armstrong (Bobo), Victor Bowleg (Moving Man), Franchelle Stewart Dorn (Lena Younger), Aric Generette Floyd (Travis Younger), Kyle Haden (George Murchison), Bakesta King (Beneatha Younger), Erika LaVonn (Ruth Younger), Patrick Thomas O'Brien (Karl Lindner), Joseph Rodgers (Moving Man), David Tinsley (Moving Man), Temple of Music and Art (Tucson), January 10–January 31, 2009; Herberger Theater Center (Phoenix), February 5–February 22, 2009

Somebody/Nobody by Jane Martin; Director, Jon Jory; Set, Matthew Smucker; Costumes, Marcia Dixcy Jory; Lighting, Michael Philippi; Sound, Brian Jerome Peterson; Assistant Director, Desdemona Chiang; Fight Choreography, Ken Merckx; Dramaturg, Jennifer Bazzell; Associate Lighting, T. Greg Squires; Stage Manager, Bruno Ingram; Cast: Claire Buchignani (Stalker), Elizabeth Gilbert (Galaxy), Jeremy Stiles Holm (Joe Don), Jessica Martin (Loli), Alexandra Tavares (Sheena), Amy Kim Waschke (Beverly), Temple of Music and Art (Tucson), March 7–March 28, 2009; Herberger Theater Center (Phoenix), April 2–April 19, 2009

Bakesta King, Franchelle Stewart Dorn, David Alan Anderson, Erika LaVonn and Aric Generette Floyd in A Raisin in the Sun

Hershey Felder in Beethoven, As I Knew Him The Music of Ludwig van Beethoven; Text by Hershey Felder; Director, Joel Zwick; Set, Françoise-Pierre Couture; Lighting, Richard Norwood; Sound, Erik Carstensen; Projections, Andrew Wilder and Christopher Ash; Assistant Lighting, Tamora Wilson; Production Manager, Matt Marsden; Consultant, Jeffrey Kallberg, PhD; Associate Lighting, T. Greg Squires; Stage Manager, Gigi Garcia, Cast: Hershey Felder (Gerhard von Breuning/Ludwig van Beethoven), Temple of Music and Art (Tucson) April 8–April 27, 2009; Herberger Theater Center (Phoenix), May 7–May 24, 2009

Hershey Felder in Concert: The American Songbook Sing-Along Projections, Christopher Ash; Assistant Lighting, Tamora Wilson; Production Manager, Matt Marsden; Associate Lighting, T. Greg Squires; Stage Manager, Gigi Garcia, Cast: Hershey Felder; Temple of Music and Art (Tucson), April 30–May 3, 2009; Herberger Theater Center (Phoenix), May 29–May 31, 2009

Arkansas Repertory Theatre

Little Rock, Arkansas
Thirty-third Season
Producing Artistic Director, Robert Hupp; Managing Director, Michael McCurdy

Les Misérables by Alain Boublil and Claude-Michel Schonberg; Concept by Victor Hugo; Music & Lyrics by Claude-Michel Schonberg & Herbert Kretzmer; Director, Robert Hupp; Set, Robert Andrew Kovach; Costumes/Production Manager, Rafael Colon Castanera; Lighting, Michael Eddy; Sound, M. Jason Pruzin; Stage Manager, Christine Lomaka; Choreography, Robert Kolby Harper; Music Director, Eric K. Johnston; Cast: Jeanine Pacheco (Cosette); Evan Shyer (Eniolras); Nina Sturtz (Eponine); Maria Couch (Fantine); Shelby Kirby (Gayroche); Christopher Carl (Javert); Douglas Webster (Jean Valjean); Catherine Smitko (Madame Thérnadier); Chris Newell (Marius); Michael Accardo (Thenardier); Gracie Stover, Molly Russ, Julia Landfair (Young Cosette/Young Eponine); The Rep and the Stella Boyle Smith Trust, in co-production with the Phoenix Theatre Company; September 12–October 12, 2008

It's a Wonderful Life: A Radio Play by Joe Landry; Director, Robert Hupp; Set, Mike Nichols; Costumes, Margaret A. McKowen; Production Manager, Rafael Colon Castanera; Lighting, Katharine Lowery; Sound, M. Jason Pruzin; Stage Manager, Tara Kelly; Cast: Josh Thelin (Actor #1), Larry Daggett (Actor #2), A. Bryan Humphrey (Actor #3), Amy Hutchins (Actor $4), Alanna Hammill Newton (Actor #5); December 5, 2008–December 28, 2008

Looking Over The President's Shoulder by James Still; Director, Gilbert McCauley; Set, Mike Nichols; Costumes, Shelly Hall; Production Manager, Rafael Colon Castanera; Lighting, William Marshall; Sound, M. Jason Pruzin; Stage Manager, Tara Kelly; Cast: Lawrence Hamilton (Alonzo Fields); January 30, 2009–February 15, 2009

The Foreigner by Larry Shue Director, Nicole Capri Bauer; Set, Mike Nichols; Costumes, Trish Clark; Production Manager, Rafael Colon Castanera; Lighting, Matthew Webb; Sound, M. Jason Pruzin; Cast: Candyce B. Hinkle (Betty Meeks), Caitlin Kinsella (Catherine Simms), Paul Tigue (Charlie Baker), Scott McLean Harrison (Ellard Simms), Michael Accardo (Froggy LeSueur), Liam Joynt (Owen Musser), Loren Dunn (Reverend David Marshall Lee); March 13, 2009–April 5, 2009

The Elephant Man by Bernard Pomerance; Director, Cliff Fannin Baker; Set, Mike Nichols; Costumes, Marianne Custer; Production Manager, Rafael Colon Castanera; Lighting, Matthew Webb; Sound, M. Jason Pruzin; Stage Manager, Stephen Horton; Cast: Matt Walker (Carr Gomm, Conductor), Joseph Graves (Frederick Treves/Belgium Policeman), Steve Wilkerson (John Merrick), Nathan Klau (Pin Head Manager/Policeman/Porter/Lord John), Val Landrum (Pin Head/Mrs. Kendal/Countess), Alanna Hammill Newton (Pin Head, Nurse Sandwich, Princess Alexandria), Wesley Mann (Ross/Bishop Walsham How/Snork); April 24, 2009–May 10, 2009

The Who's Tommy by Des McAnuff and Pete Townshend; Concept by Des McAnuff and Pete Townshend; Music & Lyrics by Pete Townshend; Additional Music and Lyrics by John Entwistle and Keith Moon; Director, Lynne Kurdziel Formato; Set, Mike Nichols; Costumes, Emily Strickland; Production Manager, Rafael Colon Castanera; Lighting, Michael Eddy; Sound, M. Jason Pruzin; Stage Manager, Christine Lomaka; Choreography, Lynne Kurdziel Formato; Music Director, Eric Alsford; Cast: Ethan Paulini (Cousin Kevin), Julia Nightengale Landfair (Four-Year-Old Tommy), Matthew D. Brooks (Hawker), Brad Little (Mr. Walker), Amy Halldin (Mrs. Walker), Brian Hissong (Narrator/Tommy), Katie Emerson (Sally Simpson), Henry Melborn (Ten-Year-Old Tommy), Christina Saoius (The Gypsy), Vincent D'Elia (Uncle Ernie), June 5, 2009–June 28, 2009

Barter Theatre

Abingdon, Virginia
Seventy-sixth Season
Producing Artistic Director, Richard Rose; Director of Production, Nicholas Piper; Director of Advancement, Jayne Duehring; Managing Director, Jeremy Wright

Joseph and the Amazing Technicolor® Dreamcoat by Tim Rice and Andrew Lloyd Webber; Director, Richard Rose; Music Director, Tim Robertson; Children's Choir Director, Jane D. Morrison; Dance Captain, Sean Campos; Set, Cheri Prough DeVol; Costumes, Amanda Aldridge; Wigs and Makeup, Ryan Fisher; Lighting, Lucas Benjaminh Krech; Sound, Bobby Beck; Stage Manager, Cindi A. Raebel; Assistant Stage Manager, Holley Housewright; Cast: Hannah Ingram (Narrator), Ben Mackel (Joseph), Eugene Wolf (Jacob), Michael Poisson (Reuben), Jasper McGruder (Simeon), Rick McVey (Levi), Mike Ostroski (Napthali), Nicholas Piper (Isaachar), Mary Lucy Bivins (Asher), Amy Baldwin (Dan), Ezra Colón (Zebulun), Sean Campos (Gad), Gwen Edwards (Judah), Ashley Campos (Benjamin), East Tennessee Children's Choir (Youth Choir); Barter Theatre; February 5–April 18, 2009

Adjoining Trances by Randy Buck; Director, Evalyn Baron; Set, Ashleigh Burns; Costumes, Colleen Alexis Metzger; Wigs and Makeup, Ryan Fisher; Lighting, Greg Potter; Sound, Bobby Beck; Music, Peter Yonka; Stage Manager, Jessica Borda; Cast: Michael Poisson (Tennessee Williams), Amy Baldwin (Carson McCullers); Barter Stage II; February 24–March 21, 2009

The Company of Joseph and the Amazing Technicolor Dream Coat

Of Mice and Men by John Steinbeck; Director, Katy Brown; Set, Cheri Prough DeVol; Costumes, Amanda Aldridge; Wigs and Makeup, Ryan Fisher; Lighting, Lucas Benjaminh Krech; Sound, Bobby Beck; Music, Ben Mackel and Peter Yonka; Fight Choreography, Mike Ostroski; Fight Captain, Ezra Colón; Stage Manager, Cindi A. Raebel; Assistant Stage Manager, Holley Housewright; Cast: John Hardy (George), Mike Ostroski (Lennie), Eugene Wolf (Candy), Rick McVey (Boss), Ben Mackel (Curley), Ashley Campos (Curley's Wife), Nicholas Piper (Slim), Sean Campos (Carlson), Ezra Colón (Whit), Jasper McGruder (Crooks), Apachee Blue Reedy (Old Dog); Barter Theatre; February 27–April 21, 2009

Four Places by Joel Drake Johnson; Director, Richard Rose; Set, Derek Smith; Costumes, Adrienne Webber; Wigs and Makeup, Ryan Fisher; Lighting, Cheri Prough DeVol; Sound, Bobby Beck; Stage Manager, Jessica Borda; Cast: Michael Poisson (Warren), Amy Baldwin (Ellen), Mary Lucy Bivins (Peggy), Hannah Ingram (Barb); Barter Stage II; March 7–April 11, 2009

Othello by William Shakespeare; Director, Richard Rose; Music, Peter Yonka; Fight Choreography, Mike Ostroski; Set, Derek Smith; Costumes, Kelly Jenkins; Lighting, Greg Potter; Sound, Bobby Beck; Stage Manager, Jessica Borda; Cast: Gwen Edwards (Bianca), Ben Mackel (Roderigo), Eugene Wolf (Iago), Rick McVey/Nicholas Piper (Brabantio), Jonathan Earl Peck (Othello), Sean Campos (Cassio), Nicholas Piper/Ryan Henderson (Ludovico), Mike Ostroski (Gratiano), Michael Poisson (Montano), Ashley Campos (Desdemona), Amy Baldwin (Emilia); Barter Stage II; April 15–May 16, 2009

Jimmie Rodgers: America's Blue Yodeler by Douglas Pote and Richard Rose; Vocal Arrangements, Eugene Wolf; Director, Mary Lucy Bivins; Music Director, Eugene Wolf and Tim Robertson; Set, Cheri Prough DeVol; Costumes, Amanda Aldridge; Wigs and Makeup, Ryan Fisher; Lighting, Cheri Prough DeVol; Sound, Bobby Beck; Stage Manager, Cindi A. Raebel; Assistant Stage Manager, Holley Housewright; Script Consultants, Nicholas Piper and Catherine Bush; Cast: Tom Angland (Jimmie Rodgers), David McCall (Ralph Peer/Aaron Rodgers/Jack/Announcer), Jasper McGruder (Hobo Bill), Ezra Colón (Railroad Bull/Uncle Buddy/Claude/Announcer/Nate Williamson/Fred Maisch), Carrie Smith (Mona/Elsie McWilliams/Girl in the Bar), Hannah Ingram (Carrie Rodgers/Eliza Rodgers), Roger Rasnake and Ed Snodderly (The Band), Barter Theatre; April 23–May 23, 2009

Six Dance Lessons in Six Weeks by Richard Alfieri; Director, Tricia Matthews; Choreography, Amanda Aldridge; Dance Captain, Sean Campos; Set, Cheri Prough DeVol; Costumes, Colleen Metzger; Lighting, Greg Potter; Sound, Bobby Beck; Stage Manager, Cindi A. Raebel; Cast: Mary Lucy Bivins (Lily), Sean Campos (Michael); Barter Stage II; May 21–July 26, 2009

The Wizard of Oz by L. Frank Baum; Music and Lyrics, Harold Arlen and E. Y. Harburg; Background Music, Herbert Stothart; Director, Richard Rose; Choreography, Amanda Aldridge; Music Director, Tim Robertson; Set, Richard

Finkelstein; Costumes, Amanda Aldridge; Wigs and Makeup, Ryan Fisher; Lighting, Lucas Benjaminh Krech; Sound, Bobby Beck; Dance Captain, Ashley Campos; Stage Manager, Jessica Borda; Assistant Stage Manager, Holley Housewright; Flying Effects, D2 Flying Effect; Cast: Gwen Edwards (Dorothy), Toto Harkins (Toto), Hannah Ingram (Aunt Emily Gale/Glinda), Michael Poisson (Uncle Henry Gale/Emerald City Guard), Amy Baldwin (Hunk/Scarecrow), Mike Ostroski (Hickory/Tinman), Rick McVey (Zeke/Cowardly Lion), Tricia Matthews (Miss Gultch/Wicked Witch), Eugene Wolf (Professor Marvel/Citizen/The Wizard of Oz), Ashley Campos (Twister/Nurse/Crow/Poppy/Ozian/Winkie/Jitterbug), Ben Mackel (Twister/Coroner/Crow/Poppy/Ozian/The Winkie General/Jitterbug), Ashley Harkins (Twister/Baby/Crow/Poppy/Ozian/Winkie/Jitterbug), Annalee Hunter (Twister/Baby/Crow/Poppy/Ozian/Winkie/Jitterbug), Eva Alom (Twister/Baby/Poppy/Ozian/Winkie/Jitterbug), Anita Ostrovsky (Twister/Baby/Poppy/Ozian/Winkie/Jitterbug), Ezra Colón (Mayor of Munchkinland/Ozian/Winkie/Jitterbug), Ryan Henderson (Barrister/Snow/Ozian/Monkey), Katie Becker (Nurse/Tree/Poppy/Ozian/Winkie), Liz Whittemore (Nurse/Tree/Poppy/Ozian/Winkie), Aria Brinkley (Lollipop Guild/Ozian/Monkey), Logan Fritz (Lollipop Guild/Ozian/Jitterbug), Morgan Merrill (Lollipop Guild/Ozian/Monkey), Matthew Torbett (Lollipop Guild/Ozian/Monkey), Robert Kitchens (Citizen/Tree/Snow/Ozian/Nikko), David McCall (Citizen/Snow/Ozian/Winkie/Jitterbug), Carrie Smith (Citizen/Snow/Ozian/Winkie); Barter Theatre; May 29–August 9, 2009

Amy Baldwin, Gwen Edwards, Rick McVey and Mike Ostroski in The Wizard of Oz *(photos by Leah Prater)*

Showtime at First Baptist by Ron Osborne; Director, Nicholas Piper; Set, Daniel Ettinger; Costumes, Colleen Metzger; Lighting, Lucas Benjaminh Krech; Wigs and Makeup, Ryan Fischer; Sound, Bobby Beck; Stage Manager, Jessica Borda; Cast: Mary Lucy Bivins (Edith), Evalyn Baron (Vera), Amy Baldwin (Mae Ellen), Hannah Ingram (Olene), Tricia Matthews (Lucille), Katie Becker (Annie);Barter Theatre; June 11–August 8, 2009

The Fantasticks by Tom Jones with Music by Harvey Schmidt; Director, Katy Brown; Musical Director, Tim Robertson; Set, Cheri Prough DeVol; Costumes, Michele Macadaeg; Lighting, Cheri Prough DeVol; Wigs and Makeup, Ryan Fischer; Sound, Bobby Beck; Fight Choreography, Sean Campos and Ezra Colón; Fight Captain, Sean Campos; Dance Captain, Ashley Campos; Stage Manager, Cindi A. Raebel; Assistant Stage Manager, Holley Housewright; Cast: Ashley Campos (The Mute), Sean Campos (El Gallo), Michael Poisson (Hucklebee), Rick McVey (Bellomy), Gwen Edwards (Luisa), Ben Mackel (Matt), Ezra Colón (Mortimer), Eugene Wolf (Henry); Barter Stage II; June 24–August 8, 2009

Berkeley Repertory Theatre

Berkeley, California
Forty-first Season
Artistic Director, Tony Taccone; Managing Director, Susie Medak

Yellowjackets by Itamar Moses; Director, Tony Taccone; Set, Annie Smart; Costumes, Meg Neville; Lighting, Alexander V. Nichols; Sound, Obadiah Eaves; Dramaturg, Madeleine Oldham; Stage Manager, Michael Suenkel; Assistant Stage Manager, Karen Szpaller; Casting Director, Amy Potozkin; Graffiti Art/Poster, Sam Fishman; Cast: Shoeresh Alaudini (Damian/Mr. Nelson), Jahmela Biggs (Tamika/Ms Robbins), Alex Curtis (Ryan/Mr Franks), Ben Freeman (Avi/Mr. Ivanov), Lance Gardner (James/Rashid), Amaya Alonso Hallifax (Alexa/Ms Alvarez), Kevin Hsieh (Sammy/Mr. Ling), Adrienne Papp (Gwen/Mom), Craig Piaget (Trevor/Mr. Terrence), Brian Rivera (Guillem/Mr. Behzad/Officer Sanchez), Erika Salazar (Sarine/Ms. Earl); World Premiere; Thrust Stage; August 29—October 12, 2008–extended through October 19, 2008

Joe Turner's Come and Gone by August Wilson; Director, Delroy Lindo; Set, Scott Bradley; Costumes, Reggie Ray; Lighting, William H. Grant III; Sound, Cliff Caruthers; Music Director, Dwight Andrews; Dramaturg, Douglas A. Jones, Jr; Stage Manager, Cynthia Cahill; Casting Director, Amy Potozkin; New York City Casting, Alan Filderman; Cast: Keanu Beausier (Reuben Mercer), Teagle F. Bougere (Herald Loomis), Kenya Brome (Martha Pentecost), Don Guillory (Jeremy Furlow), Dan Hiatt (Rutherford Selig), Inglish Amore Hills (Zonia Loomis), Barry Shabaka Henley (Seth Holly), Brent Jennings (Bynum Walker), Victor McElhaney (Reuben Mercer), Erica Peeples (Molly Cunningham), Tiffany Michelle Thompson (Mattie Campbell), Kim Staunton (Bertha Holly), Nia Renee Warren (Zonia Loomis); Roda Theatre; October 31–December 14, 2008

Teagle F. Bourgere in Joe Turner's Come and Gone

The Arabian Nights by Mary Zimmerman from The Book of the Thousand Nights and One Night; Director, Mary Zimmerman; Translator, Powys Mathers; Set, Daniel Ostling; Costumes, Mara Blumenfeld; Lighting, TJ Gerckens; Sound, Andre Pluess and The Lookingglass Ensemble; Stage Manager, Michael Suenkel; Casting, Stephanie Klapper and Amy Potozkin; Cast: Alana Arenas (Butcher, Sympathy the Learned, and others), Ryan Artzberger (King Shahryar), Barzin Akhavan (Harun al-Rashid and others), Ari Brand (Poor Man, Boy, and others), Noshir Dalal (Madman, Greengrocer, and others), Allen Gilmore (Scheherezade's Father, Ishak of Mosul, and others), Sofia Jean Gomez (Scheherezade), Melina Kalomas (Perfect Love and others), Ramiz Monsef (Clarinetist, Sage, and others), Jesse J. Perez (The Pastrycook, Robber, and others), Nicole Shalhoub (The Jester's Wife, The Other Woman, and others), Louis Tucci (Jafar, Sheik al-Fadl, and others), Pranidhi Varshney (Slave Girl and others), Stacey Yen (Dunyazade, Azizah, and others), Evan Zes (Sheik al-Islam, Abu al-Hasan, and others); Thrust

Stage; November 13, 2008–January 4, 2009–extended through January 18, 2009

In the Next Room (Or the Vibrator Play) by Sarah Ruhl; Director, Les Waters; Set, Annie Smart; Costumes, David Zinn; Lighting, Russell H. Champa; Sound, Bray Poor; Composer, Jonathan Bell; Dramaturg, Madeleine Oldham; Stage Manager, Michael Suenkel; Casting, Amy Potozkin and Janet Foster; Cast: Hannah Cabell (Catherine Givings), Maria Dizzia (Sabrina Daldry), Paul Niebanck (Dr. Givings), Melle Powers (Elizabeth), Stacy Ross (Annie), John Leonard Thompson (Mr. Daldry), Joaquín Torres (Leo Irving); World Premiere; Roda Theatre; January 30–March 15, 2009

Crime and Punishment by Fyodor Dostoevsky; Adapted by Marilyn Campbell and Curt Columbus; Director, Sharon Ott; Set, Christopher Barreca; Costumes, Lydia Tanji; Lights, Stephen Strawbridge; Sound, Cliff Caruthers; Stage Manager, Heath Belden; Casting, Amy Potozkin and Elissa Meyers; Cast: J.R. Horne (Porfiry, Marmelodov, and a Tradesman), Delia MacDougall (Sonia, Alyona, Mother, and Lizaveta), Tyler Pierce (Raskolnikov); Thrust Stage; Limited Season; February 27–March 29, 2009

Tyler Pierce in Crime and Punishment *(photos by Kevin Burne)*

The Lieutenant of Inishmore by Martin McDonagh; Director, Les Waters; Set, Antje Ellermann; Costumes, Anna R. Oliver; Lights, Alexander V. Nichols; Sound, Obadiah Eaves; Fight Director, Dave Maier; Dialect Coach, Lynne Soffer; Special Effects, Tolin FX; Stage Manager, Karen Szpaller; Casting, Karen Szpaller and New York Casting, Janet Foster; Cast: Michael Barrett Austin (Joey), Rowan Brooks (Brendan), Molly Camp (Mairead), James Carpenter (Donny), Blake Ellis (Padraic), Adam Farabee (Davey), Daniel Kreuger (James), Danny Wolohan (Christy), Roda Theatre; Limited Season; April 17– May 17, 2009–extended through May 24, 2009

You, Nero by Amy Freed; Director, Sharon Ott; Set, Erik Flatmo; Costumes, Paloma H. Young; Lighting, Peter Maradudin; Sound, Stephen LeGrand and Eric Drew Feldman; Stage Manager, Julie Haber; Casting, Amy Potozkin and Joanne DeNaut; Cast: Richard Doyle (Seneca, Zippo, and Patheticus), Donell Hill (Ensemble), Lori Larsen (Agrippina), Kasey Mahaffy (Fabiolo, Oxus, Octavia's Ghost, and Young Nero), Maggie Mason (Ensemble), Jeff McCarthy (Scribonius), Mike McShane (Burrus, Beppo, and Batheticus), Sarah Moser (Ensemble), Danny Scheie (Nero), Susannah Schulman (Poppaea); World Premiere; Thrust Stage; Presented in Association with South Coast Repertory; May 15–June 28, 2009

California Shakespeare Festival

Berkeley/Orinda, California
Thirty-fifth Season
Artistic Director, Jonathan Moscone; Managing Director, Debbie Chinn (2008), Susie Falk (2009)

Pericles by William Shakespeare; Director, Joel Sass; Set, Melpomene Katakalos; Costumes, Raquel M. Barreto; Lighting, Russel H. Champa; Sound, Jeff Mockus; Composer, Greg Brosofske; Dramaturg, Phillipa Kelly; Stage Manager, Scott Harrison; Cast: Shawn Hamilton (Gower/Lychorida/Diana/Others), Ron Campbell (Antiochus/Cleon/Fisherman/Knight/Others), Sarah Nealis (Antiochus' Daughter/Marina/Others), Christopher Kelly (Pericles/Pandar/Others), Alex Morf (Lysimachus/Thaliard/Fisherman/Knight/Leonine/Others), Danny Scheie (Helicanus/Simonides/Others), Domenique Lozano (Dionyza, Fisherman/Knight/ Cerimon/Others), Delia McDougall (Thasia/Bawd/Others), Kristoffer Barrera (Ensemble), Allison Brennan (Ensemble), Daniel Duque-Estrada (Ensemble), Mairin Lee (Ensemble); California Shakespeare Theater; May 28–June 22, 2008

An Ideal Husband by Oscar Wilde; Director, Jonathan Moscone; Set, Annie Smart; Costumes, Meg Neville; Lighting, Scott Zielinksi; Sound, Jeff Mockus; Dramaturg, Laura Hope; Stage Manager, Briana J. Fahey; Cast: Julie Eccles (Gertrude Chiltern), Delia MacDougall (Mrs. Marchmont), Nancy Carlin (Lady Basildon), Danny Scheie (Vicomte de Nanjac/Phipps), Ted Barker (Mason), L. Peter Callendar (Lord Caversham), Sarah Nealis (Mabel Chiltern), Joan Mankin (Lady Markby), Stacy Ross (Mrs. Cheveley), Michael Butler (Robert Chiltern), Elijah Alexander (Lord Goring), Kristoffer Barrera (Ensemble), Allison Brennan (Ensemble), Daniel Duque-Estrada (Ensemble), Tavis Kammet (Ensemble), Gina Seghi (Ensemble); July 2–July 27, 2008

Uncle Vanya by Anton Chekov; Adapter, Emily Mann; Director, Timothy Near; Set, Erik Flatmo; Costumes, Raquel M. Barreto; Lighting, York Kennedy; Sound, Jeff Mockus; Dramaturg, Laura Hope; Stage Manager, Les Reinhardt; Cast: James Carpenter (Alexander Serebryakov), Sarah Grace Wilson (Yelena), Annie Purcell (Sonya), Joann Mankin (Maria Voynitsky), Dan Hiatt (Vanya Voynitsky), Andy Murray (Mikhail Astrov), Howard Swain (Ilya Telegin), Barbara Oliver (Marina), T.Louis Weltz (Farmhand/Night Watchman); August 6–August 31, 2008

Twelfth Night by William Shakespeare; Director, Mark Rucker; Set, David Zinn; Costumes, Clint Ramos; Lighting, Tom Weaver; Sound, Andre Pluess; Dramaturg, Cathleen Sheehan; Stage Manager, Elizabeth Atkinson; Cast: Thomas Azar (Curio/ Ensemble), Raife Baker (Antonio), Catherine Castellanos (Maria), Dana Green (Olivia), Sharon Lockwood (Malvolio), Alex Morf (Viola/Sebastian), Andy Murray (Toby Belch), Dan Hiatt (Andrew Aguecheek), Peter Ruocco (Officer/Ensemble), Danny Scheie (Feste), Howard Swain (Sea Captain), Stephen Barker Turner (Count Orsino), Liam Vincent (Fabian), Brady M. Woolery (Officer/Ensemble); September 10–October 5, 2008

Romeo and Juliet by William Shakespeare; Director, Jonathan Moscone; Set, Neil Patel; Costumes, Raquel M. Barreto; Lighting, Russel H. Champa; Sound, Andre Pluess; Dramaturg, Philippa Kelly; Stage Manager, Briana J. Fahey; Cast: Julian Lopez-Morillas (Prince), Thomas Azar (Benvolio), Craig Marker (Tybalt), James Carpenter (Capulet), Julie Eccles (Lady Capulet), L. Peter Callender (Montague/Apothecary), Catherine Castellanos (Nurse/Lady Montague), Alex Morf (Romeo), Liam Vincent (Paris), Sarah Nealis (Juliet), Jud Williford (Mercutio/ Friar John), Dan Hiatt (Friar Lawrence), Matt Hooker (Ensemble), Patrick Lane (Ensemble), Marilet Martinez (Ensemble), Ashley Wickett (Ensemble); May 27– June 21, 2009

Center Theatre Group

Los Angeles, California
Forty-second Season
Artistic Director, Michael Ritchie; Managing Director, Charles Dillingham

Of Equal Measure by Tanya Barfield; Director, Leigh Silverman; Set, Richard Hoover and Sibyl Wickersheimer; Costumes, Rachel Myers; Lighting, Lap Chi Chu; Sound, Adam Phalen; Projections, Jason H. Thompson; Original Music, Kathryn Bostic; Dramaturg, Pier Carlo Talenti; Casting, Bonnie Grisan; Associate Producer, Neel Keller; Stage Manager, Elizabeth Atkinson; Stage Manager, Jennifer Brienen; Cast: Dennis Cockrum (Robert Lansing), JD Cullum (Joseph Tumulty), Joseph C. Phillips (David Leonard), Lawrence Pressman (President Woodrow Wilson), T. Ryder Smith (Mr. Plank), Christopher O'Neal Warren (Eugene Kingston), Michael T. Weiss (Edward Christianson), Michole Briana White (Jade Kingston), Ensemble: Scott Dawson, Michael Hyland; World Premiere; Kirk Douglas Theatre; June 29–July 27, 2008

The Drowsy Chaperone Music and Lyrics by Lisa Lambert and Greg Morrison; Book by Bob Martin and Don McKellar; by Special Arrangement with Paul Mack; Director and Choreography, Casey Nicholaw; Set, David Gallo; Costumes, Gregg Barnes; Lighting, Ken Billington and Brian Monahan; Sound, Acme Sound Partners; Casting, Telsey + Company; Hair, Josh Marquette; Makeup, Justen M. Brosnan; Orchestrations, Larry Blank; Dance and Incidental Music Arrangements, Glen Kelly; Musical Supervision and Vocal Arrangements, Phil Reno; Musical Director/Conductor, Robert Billig; Music Coordinator, John Miller; Production Supervisor, Brian Lynch and Chris Kluth; Stage Manager, Joshua Halperin; Tour Marketing/Publicity, Allied Live; Exclusive Tour Direction, The Booking Group; Associate Producers, Sonny Everett, Mariano Tolentino, Jr., Jeff Davis, Demo Bizar Ent.; General Management, The Charlotte Wilcox Company; Cast: Cliff

Stephanie J. Block, Allison Janney and Megan Hilty in 9 to 5
(photos by Craig Schwartz)

Bemis (Feldzieg), Andrea Chamberlain (Janet Van De Graaff), Jonathan Crombie (Man in Chair), Robert Dorfman (Underling), Georgia Engel (Mrs. Tottendale), Fran Jaye (Trix), Mark Ledbetter (Robert Martin), Marla Mindelle (Kitty), James Moye (Aldolpho), Nancy Opel (The Drowsy Chaperone), Chuck Rea (Super/Ensemble), Paul Riopelle (Gangster # 1), Peter Riopelle (Gangster # 2), Richard Vida (George), Ensemble: Kevin Crewell, Jen Taylor Farrell, Tiffany Haas, Jennifer Swiderski; Swings: Megan Nicole Arnoldy, Alicia Irving, Jody Madaras, Mason Roberts; National Tour; Ahmanson Theatre; July 8–July 20, 2008

The House of Blue Leaves by John Guare; Director, Nicholas Martin; Set, David Korins; Costumes, Gabriel Berry; Lighting, Donald Holder; Sound, Phillip G. Allen; Music and Lyrics, John Guare; Additional Music and Arrangements,

Michael Friedman; Fight Direction, Thomas Schall; Casting, Erika Sellin, CSA; Associate Producer, Neel Keller; Stage Manager, James T. McDermott; Stage Manager, Susie Walsh; Cast: Diedrich Bader (Billy Einhorn), Mia Barron (Corrinna Stroller), Kate Burton (Bananas Shaughnessy), Angela Goethals (The Little Nun), James B. Harnagel (The M.P.), James Immekus (Ronnie Shaughnessy), Jane Kaczmarek (Bunny Flingus), James Joseph O'Neil (The White Man), John Pankow (Artie Shaughnessy), Rusty Schwimmer (The Head Nun), Mary Kay Wulf (The Second Nun), Understudies: Zack Kraus, Rebecca Tilney, Virginia Louise Smith; Mark Taper Forum; August 30–October 19, 2008

9 to 5: The Musical Presented by Special Arrangement with Robert Greenblatt; Music and Lyrics by Dolly Parton; Book by Patricia Resnick; Based on the 20th Century Fox Picture; Director, Joe Mantello; Choreography, Andy Blankenbuehler; Musical Direction and Vocal/Song Arrangements, Stephen Oremus; Set, Scott Pask; Costumes, William Ivey Long; Lighting, Jules Fisher and Peggy Eisenhauer; Sound, John H. Shivers; Casting, Telsey + Company; Imaging, Peter Nigrini, Jules Fisher and Peggy Eisenhauer; Wigs/Hair, Paul Huntley; Technical Supervisor, Neil A. Mazzella; Production Supervisor, William Joseph Barnes; Associate Director, Dave Solomon; Associate Choreography, Rachel Bress; Makeup, Angelina Avallon; Orchestrator, Bruce Coughlin; Additional Orchestrations, Stephen Oremus and Alex Lacamoire; Dance Arrangements, Alex Lacamoire; Additional Musical Arrangements, Kevin Stites and Charles du Chateau; Associate Producer, Kelley Kirkpatrick; Stage Manager, Timothy R. Semon; Cast: Ioana Alfonso (Maria/Ensemble), Stephanie J. Block (Judy Bernly), Dan Cooney (Dick/Ensemble), Jeremy Davis (Bob Enright/Ensemble), Kathy Fitzgerald (Roz), Ann Harada (Kathy/Ensemble), Megan Hilty (Doralee Rhodes), Lisa Howard (Missy/Ensemble), Van Hughes (Josh/Ensemble), Allison Janney (Violet Newstead), Andy Karl (Joe), Marc Kudisch (Franklin Hart, Jr., Michael X. Martin (Tinsworthy/Ensemble), Karen Murphy (Margaret/Ensemble), Charlie Pollock (Dwayne/Ensemble), Tory Ross (Daphne/Ensemble), Maia Nkenge Wilson (Anita/Ensemble), Ensemble: Timothy George Anderson, Justin Bohon, Paul Castree, Autumn Guzzardi, Brendan King, Michael Mindlin, Jessica Lea Patty, Wayne Schroder, Brandi Wooten; Swings: Jennifer Balagna, Mark Myars; Understudies: Gaelen Gilliland, Kevin Kern; World Premiere; Ahmanson Theatre; September 3–October 19, 2008

The Civilians' This Beautiful City Written by Steven Cosson and Jim Lewis; Music and Lyrics by Michael Friedman; From Interviews conducted by Emily Ackerman, Marsha Stephanie Blake, Brad Heberlee, Stephen Plunkett, Alison Weller and the Authors; Director, Steven Cosson; Set, Neil Patel; Costumes, Alix Hester; Lighting, David Weiner; Sound, Ken Travis; Projection, Jason H. Thompson; Music Director, Erik James; Choreography, John Carrafa; Associate Producer, Kelley Kirkpatrick; Stage Manager, Hannah Cohen; Stage Manager, Jennifer Brienen; Cast: Emily Ackerman (Young Woman "God's Grace"/ T-Girl Christian, others), Marsha Stephanie Blake (Emmanuel Choir Member/Ben Reynolds/New Pastor at Emmanuel/others), Brad Heberlee (New Life Associate Pastor/Fairness and Equality Worker/Others), Brandon Miller (Alt Writer/ Military Religious Freedom Activist/ RHOP Leader/ others), Stephen Plunkett (TAG Pastor/Priest/Marcus Haggard/others), Alison Weller (Fairness and Equality Leader/RHOP Member/others), Musicians: Tom Corbett, Erik James, Mike Schadel, Brian Duke Song; Kirk Douglas Theatre; September 21–October 26, 2008

Spring Awakening Book and Lyrics by Steven Sater; Music by Duncan Sheik; Based on the Play by Frank Wedekind; Director, Michael Mayer; Choreography, Bill T. Jones; Music Supervisor, Kimberly Grigsby; Set, Christine Jones; Costumes, Susan Hilferty; Lighting, Kevin Adams; Sound, Brian Ronan; Orchestrations, Duncan Sheik; Vocal Arrangements, AnnMarie Milazzo; String Orchestrations, Simon Hale; Music Coordinator, Michael Keller; Casting, Jim Carnahan, C.S.A. and Carrie Gardner; Fight Direction, J. David Brimmer; Stage Manager, Eric Sprosty; Technical Supervision, Neil A. Mazzella; General Management, Abbie M. Strassler; Tour Marketing and Publicity, Georgiana Young; Music Director, Jared Stein; Resident Director, Beatrice Terry; Associate Choreography, JoAnn M. Hunter; Cast: Christy Altomare (Wendla), Blake Bashoff (Moritz), Steffi D (Ilse), Gabrielle Garza (Anna), Kimiko Glenn (Thea), Sarah Hunt (Martha), Anthony Lee Medina (Otto), Andy Mientus (Hanschen), Ben Moss (Ernst), Angela Reed (The Adult Women), Kyle Riabko (Melchior), Matt Shingledecker (Georg), Henry Stram

(The Adult Men), Ensemble: Julie Benko, Perry Sherman, Claire Sparks, Lucas A. Wells; Understudies: Todd Cerveris, Chase Davidson, Kate Fuglei; National Tour; Ahmanson Theatre; October 29–December 7, 2008

The School of Night by Peter Whelan; Director, Bill Alexander; Set, Simon Higlett; Costumes, Robert Perdziola; Lighting, Russell H. Champa; Sound, Cricket S. Myers; Music, Ilona Sekacz; Musical Direction, David O; Fight Direction, Steve Rankin; Dialect Coach, Joel Goldes; Commedia and Movement Direction, David Bridel; Casting, Erika Sellin, CSA; Associate Producer, Kelley Kirkpatrick; Stage Manager, David S. Franklin; Stage Manager, Michelle Blair; Cast: Michael Bakkensen (Thomas Kyd), Ian Bedford (Ingram Frizer), Tymberlee Chanel (Rosalinda Benoitti), Paula Christensen (Landlady/Ensemble), Mark H. Dold (Robyn Poley), Johnny Giacalone (Mostyn/Officer/Ensemble), Michael Kirby (Prison Jailer/Ensemble), Adrian LaTourelle (Thomas Walsingham), Henri Lubatti (Sir Walter Ralegh), Jon Monastero (Harlequin/Ensemble), Rob Nagle (Nicholas Skeres), Richard Robichaux (Steward/Ensemble), Alicia Roper (Audry Walsingham), John Sloan (Tom Stone), Nick Toren (Pantalone/Ensemble), Gregory Wooddell (Kit Marlowe); American Premiere; Mark Taper Forum; October 30–December 17, 2008

The Little Dog Laughed by Douglas Carter Beane; Director, Scott Ellis; Set, Allen Moyer; Costumes, Jeff Mahshie; Lighting, Donald Holder; Original Music and Sound, Lewis Flinn; Sound, Cricket S. Myers; Casting, Mele Nagler, CSA; Associate Producer, Neel Keller; Stage Manager, Gregory T. Livoti; Cast: Johnny Galecki (Alex), Brian Henderson (Mitchell), Zoe Lister-Jones (Ellen), Julie White (Diane), Kirk Douglas Theatre; November 16–December 21, 2008

Pippin Book by Roger O. Hirson; Music and Lyrics by Stephen Schwartz; Director and Choreography, Jeff Calhoun; Music Direction and Arrangements, Steven Landau; Set and Costumes, Tobin Ost; Lighting, Donald Holder; Sound, Phillip G. Allen; Illusions, Jim Steinmeyer; Hair and Wigs, Carol F. Doran; Associate Director, Coy Middlebrook; Associate Choreography, Richard J. Hinds; Casting, Bonnie Grisan and Erika Sellin; American Sign Language Masters, Linda Bove and Alan Champion; Associate Producer, Ann E. Wareham; Orchestrations, Tom Kitt; Stage Manager, David Sugarman; Stage Managers, Brian J. L'Ecuyer, Jennifer Brienen; Presented in Association with Deaf West Theatre; Cast: Michael Arden (Pippin), Jonah Blechman (Off-Stage Vocals/Swing/Magic Captain), Dan Callaway (Voice of Charles/Player/Soldier), Bryan Terrell Clark (Voice of Theo/Player/Noble), Nicolas Conway (Theo/Player), Rodrick Covington (Player/Voice of Torch Bearer/Voice of Noble/Courier #1/Voice of Couriers #2 and#3), James Royce Edwards (Lewis/Player), TL Forsberg (Player/Magician Assistant), Sara Gettelfinger (Fastrada/Player), Tyrone Giordano (Pippin), Harriet Harris (Berthe/Player), Rebecca Ann Johnson (Off-Stage Vocals/Swing), Troy Kotsur (Charles/Player), José F. Lopez, Jr. (Theo/Player), John McGinty (Player/Noble/Courier #2/Peasant), Anthony Natale (Player/Torch Bearer/Petitioner/Courier #3/ASL Captain), Aleks Pevec (Player/Voice of Petitioner/Visigoth Head/Voice of Peasant), Victoria Platt (Player/Magician Assistant), Ty Taylor (Leading Player), Nikki Tomlinson (Player/Magician Assistant), Melissa van der Schyff (Catherine/Player), Alexandria Wailes (Player/Magician Assistant/Visigoth Arm); Mark Taper Forum; January 15–March 15, 2009

Minsky's Book by Bob Martin; Music by Charles Strouse; Lyrics by Susan Birkenhead; Original Book by Evan Hunter; Director and Choreography, Casey Nicholaw; Music Director/ Vocal Arrangements, Phil Reno; Set, Anna Louizos; Costumes, Gregg Barnes; Lighting, Ken Billington; Sound, Acme Sound Partners; Hair, Josh Marquette; Casting, Telsey + Company; Associate Producer, Neel Keller; Orchestrations, Doug Besterman; Music Arrangements, Glen Kelly; Technical Supervisor, Peter Fulbright; Associate Choreography, Lee Wilkins; Associate Director, Casey Hushion; Stage Manager, Karen Moore; Stage Managers, Rachel S. McCutchen, Susie Walsh; Cast: Megan Nicole Arnoldy (Sunny), Roxane Barlow (Giggles/Ensemble), Jennifer Bowles (Curls), Kirsten Bracken (Flame), Kevin Cahoon (Buster), John Cariani (Jason Shimpkin), Rachel Dratch (Beula), Christopher Fitzgerald (Billy Minsky), Jennifer Frankel (Sylvie/Ensemble), Blake Hammond (Sergeant Crowley/Dr. Vinkle/Waiter/Ensemble), Philip Hoffman (Mr. Freitag/Judge/Ensemble), Stacey Todd Holt (Reporter/Ensemble), Beth Leavel

(Maisie), Katharine Leonard (Mary Sumner), Sabra Lewis (Flossie/Ensemble), Matt Loehr (Dr. Vankle/Ensemble), Ariel Reid (Bubbles/Ensemble), Jeffery Schecter (Reporter/Ensemble), Angie Schworer (Ginger/Ensemble), Sarrah Strimel (Borschtie/Ensemble), Gerry Vichi (Scratch), Paul Vogt (Boris), George Wendt (Randolph Sumner), Patrick Wetzel (Blind Man/Ensemble), Ensemble: Megan Nicole Arnoldy, Nathan Balser, Linda Griffin, Charlie Sutton; Swings: Jennifer Werner, Marc Kessler; World Premiere; Ahmanson Theatre; January 21–March 1, 2009

John Pankow in The House of Blue Leaves

Taking Over Written and Performed by Danny Hoch; Director, Tony Taccone; Set and Costumes, Annie Smart; Lighting and Projection, Alexander V. Nichols; Sound, Adam Phalen; Composer, Asa Taccone; Associate Producer, Kelley Kirkpatrick; Stage Manager, David S. Franklin; Kirk Douglas Theatre; January 21–February 22, 2009

Frost/Nixon by Peter Morgan; Director, Michael Grandage; Set and Costumes, Christopher Oram; Lighting, Neil Austin; Composer and Sound, Adam Cork; Video, Jon Driscoll; Hair and Wigs, Richard Mawbey; Casting, Daniel Swee, CSA; Tour Press Representative, Allied Live, LLC; Production Manager, Aurora Productions; Executive Producer, 101 Productions, Ltd.; Stage Manager, J.P. Elins; Exclusive Tour Direction, The Booking Group; Associate Director, Seth Sklar-Heyn; Cast: Meghan Andrews (Evonne Goolagong), Bob Ari (Bob Zelnick), Alan Cox (David Frost), Antony Hagopian (John Birt), Roxanna Hope (Caroline Cushing), Stacy Keach (Richard Nixon), Ted Koch (Jack Brennan), Stephen Rowe (Swifty Lazar/ Mike Wallace), Brian Sgambati (Jim Reston), Noel Velez (Manolo Sanchez), Ensemble: Peter Hilton, Tamara Lovatt-Smith, David Sitler; Understudy: Kelly McGrath; National Tour; Ahmanson Theatre; March 11-March 29, 2009

Lydia by Octavio Solis; Director, Juliette Carrillo; Set, Christopher Acebo; Costumes, Christal Weatherly; Lighting, Christopher Akerlind; Sound/Additional

Music and Arrangements, David Molina; Original Compositions, Chris Webb; Original Fight Choreography, Rick Sordelet; Associate Fight Director, Greg Derelian; Wigs and Hair, Carol F. Doran; Vocal and Dialect Coach, Natsuko Ohama; Associate Producer, Neel Keller; Stage Manager, Michelle Blair; Stage Manager, Joe Witt; Cast: Carlo Alban (Misha), Max Arciniega (Alvaro), Stephanie Beatriz (Lydia), Catalina Maynard (Rosa), Onahoua Rodriguez (Ceci), Tony Sancho (Rene), Daniel Zacapa (Claudio), Understudies: Alejandra Flores, Francisco Garcia, Rubén Garfias, Isabelle Ortega; Mark Taper Forum; April 2–May 17, 2009

Aint' Misbehavin,' The Fats Waller Musical Show Conceived by Richard Maltby, Jr. and Murray Horwitz; Created and Director, Richard Maltby Jr.; Choreography and Musical Staging, Arthur Faria; Supervising Music Director, William Foster McDaniel; Musical Adaptations, Orchestrations and Arrangements, Luther Henderson; Vocal and Music Concepts, Jeffery Gutcheon; Musical Arrangements, Jeffrey Gutcheon and William Elliott; Set, John Lee Beatty; Original Costume Design, Randy Barcelo; Costumes, Gail Baldoni; Lighting, Pat Collins; Sound, Tom Morse; Wigs, Gerard Kelly; Vocal Supervisor, Debra Byrd; Casting, Erika Sellin; Stage Manager, David S. Franklin; Associate Producer, Ann E. Wareham; Stage Manager, Matthew Silver; Cast: Eugene Barry- Hill (Eugene), Doug Eskew (Doug), Armelia McQueen (Armelia), Roz Ryan (Roz), Debra Walton (Debra), Understudies: Jacqueline René, Lance Roberts, Cynthia Thomas; Ahmanson Theatre; April 18–May 31, 2009

Bengal Tiger at the Baghdad Zoo by Rajiv Joseph; Director, Moisés Kaufman; Set, Derek McLane; Costumes, David Zinn; Lighting, David Lander; Sound, Cricket S. Myers; Music, Kathryn Bostic; Fight Director, Bobby C. King; Casting, Bonnie Grisan; Associate Producer, Neel Keller; Dramaturg, Pier Carlo Talenti; Stage Manager, Vanessa J. Noon; Cast: Glenn Davis (Tom), Brad Fleischer (Kev), Arian Moayed (Musa), Kevin Tighe (Tiger), Hrach Titizian (Uday), Sheila Vand (Hadia/Iraqi Teenager), Necar Zadegan (Iraqi Woman/Leper), World Premiere; Kirk Douglas Theatre; May 10–June 7, 2009

Oleanna by David Mamet; Director, Doug Hughes; Set, Neil Patel; Costumes, Catherine Zuber; Lighting, Donald Holder; Fight Direction, Rick Sordelet; Associate Producer, Ann E. Wareham; Stage Manager, Charles Means; Stage Manager, Marti McIntosh; Cast: Bill Pullman (John), Julia Stiles (Carol), Understudies: Blair Baker, Marty Lodge; Mark Taper Forum; May 28–July 12, 2009

Julia Stiles and Bill Pullman in Oleanna

Cincinnati Playhouse in the Park

Cincinnati, Ohio
Forty-ninth Season
Producing Artistic Director, Edward Stern; Executive Director, Buzz Ward

Emma Music, Lyrics and Book by Paul Gordon; Adapted from the novel by Jane Austen; Director, Robert Kelley; Music Director, Laura Bergquist; Choreography, Mary Beth Cavanaugh; Set, John Ezell; Costumes, Fumiko Bielefeldt; Lighting, Dennis Parichy; Sound, Michael Miceli; Casting Director, Rich Cole; PSM, Jenifer Morrow; ASM, Jamie Lynne Sullivan; Cast: Lianne Marie Dobbs (Emma), Christianne Tisdale (Mrs. Weston), Brian Herndon (Mr. Elton), Richert Easley (Mr. Woodhouse), Timothy Gulan (Mr. Knightley), Suzanne Grodner (Miss Bates), Sherry McCamley (Mrs. Bates/Housekeeper), Kurt Zischke (Mr. Weston), Dani Marcus (Harriet Smith), Travis Poelle (Frank Churchill), Julie Hanson (Jane Fairfax), Alex Organ (Mr. Robert Martin/Servant), Erin Maguire (Mrs. Elton/Mrs. Churchill), Ron Burrage (Butler/Minister), Kevin Barber, Jeremy Larson, Lauren Noll, Jolin Polasek (Servants), The Company (Citizens of Highbury), Laura Bergquist (Piano), Mark Kosmala (Cello), Loren Berzsenyi (Oboe/English Horn), Mari Thomas (Violin), Understudies: Julie Hanson (Emma), Travis Poelle (Mr. Knightley), Ron Burrage (Mr. Robert Martin/Mr. Woodhouse/Mr. Weston); Robert S. Marx Theatre; September 2–October 3, 2008

Durango by Julia Cho; Director, Wendy C. Goldberg; Set Kevin Judge; Costumes, Anne Kennedy; Lighting, Josh Epstein; Sound/Composer, Ryan Rumery; Fight Director, k. Jenny Jones; Casting Director, Rich Cole; Stage Manager, Andrea L. Shell; Cast: Thom Sesma (Boo-Seng Lee), Peter Kim (Isaac Lee), Andrew Cristi (Jimmy Lee), Roarke Walker (The Red Angel/Bob), Tony Campisi (Jerry/Ned); Thompson Shelterhouse Theatre; September 20–October 19, 2008

Love Song by John Kolvenbach; Director, Michael Evan Haney; Set Narelle Sissons; Costumes, Gordon DeVinney; Lighting, Justin Townsend; Sound/Composer, Fabian Obispo; Casting Director, Rich Cole; Stage Manager, Wendy J. Dorn; ASM, Jamie Lynne Sullivan; Cast: Joseph Parks (Beane), Gabra Zackman (Joan), Mark Boyett (Harry), Amy Tribbey (Molly), Jeremy Larson (Waiter); Robert S. Marx Theatre; October 21–November 21, 2008

I Love You, You're Perfect, Now Change Book and Lyrics by Joe DiPietro; Music by Jimmy Roberts; Director/Choreography, Dennis Courtney; Music Director/Piano, Michael Sebastian; Set, Brian C. Mehring; Costumes, David Kay Mickelsen; Lighting, Betsy Adams; Sound, Chuck Hatcher; Casting Director, Rich Cole; Production Stage Manager, Jenifer Morrow; Cast: Pamela Bob (Woman #1), Holly Davis (Woman #2), Michael Dean Morgan (Man #1), Bob Walton (Man #2), Mari Thomas (Violin); Thompson Shelterhouse Theatre; November 1–December 31, 2008

A Christmas Carol by Charles Dickens; Adapted by Howard Dallin; Director, Michael Evan Haney; Set. James Leonard Joy; Costumes, David Murin; Lighting, Kirk Bookman; Sound/Composer, David B. Smith; Lighting Contractor, Susan Terrano; Costume Coordinator, Cindy Witherspoon; Music Director, Rebecca N. Childs; Choreography, Dee Anne Bryll; Casting Director, Rich Cole; Stage Manager, Andrea L. Shell; ASM, Jamie Lynne Sullivan; Cast: Bruce Cromer (Ebenezer Scrooge), Wayne Pyle (Mr. Cupp/Percy/Guest at Fezziwig's), Ron Simons (Mr. Sosser//Topper/Man with Shoe Shine/Guest at Fezziwig's), Andy Prosky (Bob Cratchit/Schoolmaster Oxlip), Tony Roach (Fred), Gregory Procaccino (Jacob Marley/Old Joe), Dale Hodges (Ghost of Christmas Past/Rose/Mrs. Peake), Richard Lowenburg (Boy Scrooge/Guest at Fezziwig's/Bootblack/Streets), Maraia Reinhart (Fan/Guest at Fezziwig's/Streets), Keith Jochim (Mr. Fezziwig/Ghost of Christmas Present), Amy Warner (Mrs. Fezziwig/Patience/Streets), Andrew Ash (Dick Wilkins/Streets), Lauren Noll (Mary at Fezziwig's/Streets), Todd Lawson (Young and Mature Scrooge/Ghost of Christmas Future), Sabrina Veroczi (Belle/Catherine Margaret), Jeremy Larson (Rich Caroler/Constable/Streets/Undertaker), Regina Pugh (Mrs. Cratchit/Laundress at Fezziwig's), Eben Franckewitz (Peter Cratchit/Gregory/Apprentice at Fezziwig's), Katie Chase (Belinda Cratchit/Guest at Fezziwig's), Jo Ellen Pellman (Martha Cratchit/Guest at Fezziwig's), Owen

Gunderman (Tiny Tim), Beth Lach (Poor Caroler/Guest at Fezziwig's), Kevin Barber (Poor Caroler/Poulterer/Guest at Fezziwig's), Josh Odsess-Rubin (Guest at Fezziwig's/Man with Pipe/Streets), Methani Ryan (Ignorance/Matthew/Rich Son at Fezziwig's), Kendall Kerrington Young (Want/Guest at Fezziwig's/Streets), Landree Fleming (Guest at Fezziwig's/Mrs. Dilber/Streets), Jolin Polasek (Rich Caroler/Guest at Fezziwig's), Darius T. Brown (George/Charles/Apprentice at Fezziwig's), Julianne Fox (Guest at Fezziwig's/Streets); Robert S. Marx Theatre; December 4–December 30, 2008

Travels of Angelica Winner of the Mickey Kaplan New American Play Prize by Joseph McDonough; Director, Edward Stern; Set Joseph P. Tilford; Costumes/Projection Drawings, Susan Tsu; Lighting, Thomas C. Hase; Sound, Fitz Patton; Projections, John Boesche; Casting Director, Rich Cole; PSM, Jenifer Morrow; ASM, Jamie Lynne Sullivan; Cast: Erik Lochtefeld (Alexander Crumpler), Heather Wood (Lucia Crumpler), Sarah Dandridge (Emma), Jason Schuchman (Matthew), Joneal Joplin (Vincent Penny), Jo Twiss (Gabrielle Penny), Greg Thornton (Josiah Podge), World Premiere; Robert S. Marx Theatre; January 20–February 15, 2009

Blackbird by David Harrower; Director, Michael Evan Haney; Sets and Lighting, Kevin Rigdon; Costumes, Trish Rigdon; Fight Director, Drew Fracher; Casting Director, Rich Cole; Stage Manager, Andrea L. Shell; Cast: Joy Farmer-Clary (Una), John Ottavino (Ray), Thompson Shelterhouse Theatre; February 7–March 8, 2009

The Foreigner by Larry Shue; Director, Kenneth Albers; Set Paul Shortt; Costumes, Anne Murphy; Lighting, James Sale; Casting Director, Rich Cole; Dialect Coach, Charles J. Richie; Stage Manager, Whitney Frazier; Second Stage Manager, Jenifer Morrow; Cast: Tony DeBruno (S/Sgt. "Froggy" LeSeuer), John Scherer (Charlie Baker), Darrie Lawrence (Betty Meeks), Ted Deasy (Rev. David Marshall Lee), Nell Geisslinger (Catherine Simms), Remi Sandri (Owen Musser), Raymond McAnally (Ellard Simms), Andrew Ash, Beth Lach, Jeremy Larson, Lauren Noll, Jolin Polasek (Townspeople), Robert S. Marx Theatre; March 10–April 10, 2009

Last Train to Nibroc by Arlene Hutton; Director, Rob Ruggiero; Set Michael Schweikardt; Costumes, Alejo Vietti; Lighting, John Lasiter; Sound, Vincent Olivieri; Casting Director, Rich Cole; Dialect Coach, Ben Furey; Assistant Director, Nick Eilerman; Stage Manager, Joseph Millett; Cast: Timothy Kiefer (Raleigh), Dana Acheson (May); Thompson Shelterhouse Theatre; March 28–April 26, 2009

Dr. Jekyll and Mr. Hyde Adapted by Jeffrey Hatcher; Director, Edward Stern; Set, Robert Mark Morgan; Costumes, Elizabeth Covey; Lighting, Thomas C. Hase; Sound, Rusty Wandall; Casting Director, Rich Cole; PSM, Jenifer Morrow; ASM, Jamie Lynne Sullivan; Cast: Anthony Marble (Dr. Henry Jekyll), Anderson Matthews (Edward Hyde/Gabriel Utterson), Scott Schafer (Edward Hyde/Sir Danvers Carew/Richard Enfield/O.F. Sanderson/Inspector), Katie Fabel (Elizabeth Jelkes), Kyle Fabel (Edward Hyde/Dr. H.K. Lanyon/Police Doctor/Surgical Student), Bernadette Quigley (Edward Hyde/Poole/Surgical Student/Police Doctor), Other Roles (The Company); Robert S. Marx Theatre; April 21–May 22, 2009

Marry Me a Little Songs by Stephen Sondheim; Conceived and Developed by Craig Lucas and Norman René; Director/Choreography, Stafford Arima; Set Beowulf Boritt; Costumes, Gordon DeVinney; Lighting, Aaron Spivey; Music Director, Lynne Shankel; Casting Director, Rich Cole; Stage Manager, Andrea L. Shell; Cast: Benjamin Eakeley (Man), Sally Wilfert (Woman); Thompson Shelterhouse Theatre; May 9–June 14, 2009

City Theatre

Thirty-fourth Season
Philadelphia, Pennsylvania
Artistic Director, Tracy Brigden; Managing Director, Greg Quinlan

Without You by Anthony Rapp; Music and Lyrics, Jonathan Larson; Director, Steven Maler; Music Director, David Matos; Scenic Design, Tony Ferrieri; Costumes, Angela M. Vesco; Lighting, Andrew David Ostrowski; Sound, Dave Bjornson; Production Stage Manager, Patty Kelly; Cast: Anthony Rapp, Musicians: guitar, Davit Matos, bass, Daniel Tomko; drums, A.T. Vish; August 29–September 21, 2008

Long Story Short by Brendan Milburn and Valerie Vigoda; Director, Tracy Brigden; Music Director, Douglas Levine; Scenic Design, Neil Patel; Lighting, Andrew David Ostrowski; Costumes, C.T. Steele; Sound, Elizabeth Atkinson; Production Stage Manager, Patty Kelly; Cast: Ben Evans (Charles); World Premiere; October 23–November 16, 2008

The Brothers Size by Tarell Alvin McCraney; Director, Robert O'Hara; Scenic Design, Tony Ferrieri; Lighting, Christian DeAngelis; Costumes, Angela M. Vesco; Sound, Joe Pino; Production Stage Manager, Patty Kelly; Cast: Albert Jones (Ogun); Jared McNeill (Oshoosi); Joshua Elijah Reese (Elegba); November 13–December 21, 2008

Sister's Christmas Catechism by Maripat Donovan; dDrector, Marc Silva; Scenic Design, Catherine Evans, Costumes, Marc Silva; Production Stage Manager, Patty Kelly; Cast: Kimberly Richards (Sister); December 9–28, 2008

The Seafarer by Conor McPherson; Director, Tracy Brigden; Scenic Design, Narelle Sissons; Lighting, Andy Ostrowski; Costumes, Angela M. Vesco; Sound, Liz Atkinson; Production Stage Manager, Patty Kelly; Cast: Christopher Donahue (Sharky); Martin Giles (Ivan); Sam Redford (Nicky); Noble Shropshire (Richard) Mark Ulrich (Lockhart); January 22–February 15, 2009

Male Intellect: The 2nd Coming! Written and performed by Robert Dubac; January 29–March 15, 2009

Mary's Wedding by Stephen Massicotte; Director, Stuart Carden; Scenic Design, Tony Ferreri; Lighting, Andrew David Ostrowski; Costumes, Susan Tsu; Music, Andre Pluess; Sound, Andrew Pluess; Production Stage Manager, Patty Kelly; Cast: Robin Abramson (Mary); Braden Moran (Charlie); March 12–April 5, 2009

Human Error by Keith Reddin; Director, Tracy Brigden; Scenic Design, Luke Cantarella; Lighting, Jeff Croiter; Costumes, Ange Vesco; Sound, Eric Shim; Production Stage Manager, Patty Kelly; Cast: Tasha Lawrence (Miranda); Ray Anthony Thomas (Ron); April 2–May 10, 2009

Speak American by Eric Simonson; Director, Eric Simonson; Scenic Design, Tony Ferrieri; Lighting, Andrew David Ostrowski; Costumes, Michael Krass; Sound, Elizabeth Atkinson; Dialect, Don Wadsworth; Production Stage Manager, Patty Kelly; Cast: Nick Ducassi (Janusz Warczynski); Daina Michelle Griffith (Rebecca Eastman); Christopher McLinden (Yasen Dimitrov); Chase Newell (Jakub Nicolella); John Shepard (Ignak Wesnak); Mark Staley (Vlad Batyi); David Whalen (Tom O'Reilly); World Premiere; May 7–31, 2009

Cleveland Playhouse

Cleveland, Ohio
Ninety-third Season
Artistic Director, Michael Bloom; Associate Artistic Director, Seth Gordon; Managing Director, Kevin Moore

The Glass Menagerie by Tennessee Williams; Director, Michael Bloom; Set, Robert Mark Morgan; Costumes, Susan Tsu; Lighting, Michael Lincoln; Sound, James C. Swonger; Cast: Linda Purl (Amanda), Daniel Damon Joyce (Tom), Alison Lani (Laura), Sorin Brouwers (The Gentleman Caller); Drury Theatre; September 12–October 5, 2008

Noises Off by Michael Frayn; Director, David H. Bell; Set, James L. Joy; Costumes, David Kay Mickelsen; Lighting, Joseph Appelt; Voice/Text Coach, Don Wadsworth; Sound, James C. Swonger; Cast: Cassandra Bissell (Poppy Norton-Taylor), Donald Carrier (Frederick Fellowes), Timothy Gregory (Lloyd Dallas), Christopher Kelly (Garry Lejeune), Linda Kimbrough (Dotty Otley), Frank Kopyc (Selsdon Mowbray), Isabel Liss (Belinda Blair), Summer Naomi Smart (Brooke Ashton), Bob Turton (Tim Allgood); Bolton Theatre; a co-production with the Maltz Jupiter Theatre; October 3– October 26, 2008

Summer Naomi Smart, Frank Kopyc, Isabel Liss, Donald Carrier and Linda Kimbrough in Noises Off *(photo by Roger Mastroianni)*

A Raisin in the Sun by Lorraine Hansberry; Director, Lou Bellamy; Set, Vicki Smith; Costumes, Mathew J. LeFebvre; Lighting, Michelle Habeck; Assistant Director, Domenic Taylor; Sound, James C. Swonger; Cast: David Alan Anderson (Walter Lee), Scott Campbell (Moving Man), Aric Generette Floyd (Travis), Kyle Haden (George Murchison), Bakesta King (Beneatha), Erika LaVonn (Ruth), Adeoye Mabogunje (Joseph Asagai), Marvin Mallory (Moving Man), Patrick O'Brien (Karl Linder), Damron Russell Armstrong (Bobo), Franchelle Stewart Dorn (Lena); Drury Theatre; a co-production with Arizona Theatre Company and Penumbra Theatre Company; November 7–November 30, 2008

A Christmas Story by Philip Grecian, Based on the Motion Picture Written by Jean Shepherd, Leigh Brown and Bob Clark; Director, Seth Gordon; Set, Michael Ganio; Costumes, David Kay Mickelsen; Lighting, Richard Winkler; Sound, James C. Swonger; Cast: Olivia Doria (Esther Jane), Joey Stefanko (Flick), Lauren Cole (Helen), Elizabeth Ann Townsend (Mother), Wilbur Edwin Henry (Ralph), Kolin Morgenstern (Ralphie), Alex Bolton (Randy), Carole Monferdini (Miss Shields), Matthew Hemminger (Schwartz), Cameron McKendry (Scut Farkas), Charles Kartali (The Old Man); Bolton Theatre; November 28–December 21, 2008

Around the World in 80 Days by Mark Brown, Novel by Jules Verne; Director, Bart DeLorenzo; Set, Takeshi Kata; Costumes, Ann Closs-Farley; Lighting, Lap Chi Chu; Dialect Coach, Jerrold Scott; Sound, James C. Swonger; Cast: Joe Faust (Actor 1), Michael Webber (Actor 2), Brian Sills (Passepartout), Anna Khaja (Aouda), Keythe Farley (Phileas Fogg); Drury Theatre; January 9–February 1, 2009

Mahalia: A Gospel Musical by Tom Stolz; Director, Kent Gash; Set, Emily Beck; Costumes, Austin Sanderson; Lighting, William H. Grant III; Music Director, Jmichael; Sound, James C. Swonger; Cast: NaTasha Yvette Williams (Mahalia), Terry Burrell (Female Ensemble), C.E. Smith (Male Ensemble), Jmichael (Male Ensemble), Edward E. Ridley, Jr. (Organist); Bolton Theatre; January 30–February 22, 2009

Crime and Punishment by Marilyn Campbell and Curt Columbus, Novel by Fyodor Dostoevsky; Director, Anders Cato; Assistant Director, Jesse Freedman; Set, Lee Savage; Costumes, Olivera Gajic; Lighting, Jeff Davis; Sound, James C. Swonger; Cast: Patrick Husted (Porfiry), Lethia Nall (Sonia), Paul Anthony Stewart (Raskolnikov); Drury Theatre; February 27–March 22, 2009

The Lady With All the Answers by David Rambo; Director, Seth Gordon; Set, Tom Burch; Costumes, Charlotte Yetman; Lighting, Diane Ferry Williams; Sound, James C. Swonger; Cast: Mimi Kennedy (Eppie Lederer a.k.a. Ann Landers); Bolton Theatre; March 27–April 19, 2009

Heaven's My Destination by Lee Blessing, Novel by Thornton Wilder; Director, Michael Bloom; Set, Russell Parkman; Costumes, David Kay Mickelsen; Lighting, Justin Townsend; Sound, James C. Swonger; Composer, Josh Schmidt; Dialect Coach, Jerrold Scott; Cast: Katie Barrett (Actor E/Ensemble), Kailey Bell (Actor D/Ensemble), Diane Dorsey (Actor F/Ensemble), Michael Halling (George Brush), Christian Kohn (Actor B/Ensemble), Courtney Anne Nelson (Little Roberts Girl/Elizabeth/Rhoda), Justin Tatum (Actor A/Ensemble), John Woodson (Actor C/Ensemble); Drury Theatre; April 24–May 17, 2009

Katie Barrett, Michael Halling and Kailey Bell in Heaven's My Destination *(photo by Peter Jennings)*

Denver Center Theatre Company

Denver, Colorado
Thirtieth Season
Kent Thompson, Artistic Director; Charles Varin, General Manager; Edward Lapine, Production Manager

The Trip to Bountiful by Horton Foote; Director, Penny Metropulos; Set, Lisa M. Orzolek; Costumes, Deborah M. Dryden, Lighting, Don Darnutzer; Sound, Morgan A. McCauley; Dramaturg, Douglas Langworthy; Stage Managers, Lyle Raper, Christi B. Spann; Cast: Kathleen M. Brady (Carrie), Larry Bull (Ludie), Sara Kathryn Bakker (Jessie Mae), Julie Jesneck (Thelma), Jeffrey Roark (Houston Ticket Man/Hank), Rob Hille (Traveler), Mat Hostetler (Traveler), Leigh Miller (Traveler), Kathleen Wallace (Traveler), Christian Haines (Second Houston Ticket Man), Randy Moore (Roy), John Hutton (Sheriff); The Space Theatre; September 19– October 25, 2008

Noises Off by Michael Frayn; Director, Kent Thompson; Set, Vicki Smith; Costumes, Kevin Copenhaver; Lighting, Charles R. MacLeod; Sound, Craig Breitenbach; Fight Director, Geoffrey Kent; Vocal Coach, Michael Cobb; Stage Managers, Christopher C. Ewing, Mark D. Leslie, Kurt Van Raden; Cast: Kate Skinner (Dottie/Mrs. Clackett), David Ivers (Garry/Roger), Kate MacCluggage (Brooke/Vicki), Sam Gregory (Lloyd), Morgan Hallett (Poppy), Michael Keyloun (Tim), Brent Harris (Frederick/Philip), Megan Byrne (Belinda/Flavia), Philip Pleasants (Selsdon); The Stage Theatre; October 3–November 1, 2008

Glengarry Glen Ross by David Mamet; Director, Marco Barricelli; Set, Bill Forrester; Costumes, David Kay Mickelsen; Lighting, York Kennedy; Sound, Jason Ducat; Dramaturg, Douglas Langworthy; Vocal Coach, Sarah Felder; Stage Manager, A. Phoebe Sacks; Cast: Mike Hartman (Shelly), Vince Nappo (John), Lawrence Hecht (Dave), Michael Santo (George), Ian Merrill Peakes (Richard), James Michael Reilly (James), Chris Hietikko (Baylen); The Ricketson Theatre; October 10–November 22, 2008

The Miracle Worker by William Gibson; Director, Art Manke; Set, Tom Buderwitz; Costumes, Angela Balogh Calin; Lighting, Charles R. MacLeod; Sound, Morgan A. McCauley; Composer, Steven Cahill; Fight Director, Geoffrey Kent; Dramaturg, Douglas Langworthy; Voice Coach, Sarah Felder; Stage Manager, Christi B. Spann; Cast: Marcus Waterman (Anagnos), John Hutton (Arthur), Rachel Fowler (Kate), Jaliah Peters (Martha), Mykail Gholston (Percy), Daria LeGrand (Helen), Kate Hurster (Annie), Jeanne Paulsen (Aunt Ev), Leigh Miller (James), Wendelin Harston (Viney), Maggie Mirrione (Sarah); The Space Theatre; November 14–December 20, 2008

A Christmas Carol by Charles Dickens; Adapted by Richard Hellesen; Director, Bruce K. Sevy; Composer, David de Berry; Musical Director, Gregg Coffin; Choreography, Christine Rowan; Orchestrations, Thom Jenkins, Gregg Coffin; Dialect Coach, Kathryn G. Maes; Set, Vicki Smith; Costumes, Kevin Copenhaver; Lighting, Don Darnutzer; Sound, Craig Breitenbach; Stage Managers, Lyle Raper, Christopher C. Ewing, Kurt Van Raden; Cast: Philip Pleasants (Scrooge), Sam Gregory (Cratchit), John John Behlmann (Fred), David Ivers (Marley), Stephanie Cozart (Past), Bryce Baldwin (Child Ebenezer), Ellie Schwartz (Fan), Jeff Cribbs (Young Ebenezer), Chris Mixon (Fezziwig), Leslie O'Carroll (Mrs. Fezziwig), Nisi Sturgis (Belle), Larry Bull (Present), Leslie Alexander (Mrs. Cratchit), Alec Farmer (Tiny Tim), Andy Jobe (Yet to Come), Harvy Blanks, Kathleen M. Brady, Jenn Miller Cribbs, Ian Farmer, Christian Haines, Colin Harrington, Rob Hille, Mat Hostetler, Chris Maclean, Paul Morland, Christy Oberndorf , Melissa Ortiz, Jeffrey Roark, Christine Rowan, Max Schwartz, Mark Siegel, Christianna Sullins, Kathleen Wallace; The Stage Theatre; November 28–December 27, 2008

Inana by Michele Lowe; Director, Michael Pressman; Set, Vicki Smith; Costumes, David Kay Mickelsen: Lighting, Ann G. Wrightson; Sound, Morgan A. McCauley; Composer, Lindsay Jones; Dramaturg, Douglas Langworthy; Stage Manager, A. Phoebe Sacks; Cast: Piter Marek (Darius), Mahira Kakkar (Shali), David Ivers (Waiter/Dominic), Laith Nakli (Abdel-Hakim), Alok Tewari (Mohammed/Messenger), Reema Zaman (Mena /Hama), Nasser Faris (Emad), Commissioned World Premiere; The Ricketson Theatre; January 16–February 28, 2009

Chloe Nosan and Charlotte Booker in Dusty and the Big Bad World *(photos by Terry Shapiro)*

Dusty and the Big Bad World by Cusi Cram; Director, Kent Thompson; Set, William Bloodgood; Costumes, Bill Black; Lighting, Charles R. MacLeod; Sound, Jason Ducat; Dramaturg, Paul Walsh; Voice Coach, Kathryn G. Maes; Stage Managers, Christi B. Span, Mr. Erock; Cast: Kelly McAndrew (Jessica), Jeanine Serralles (Karen), Charlotte Booker (Marianne), Sam Gregory (Nathan), Chloe Nosan (Lizzie); World Premiere; The Space Theatre; January 23–February 28, 2009

Richard III by William Shakespeare; Director, Jesse Berger; Set, David M. Barber; Costumes, David Kay Mickelsen; Lighting, Don Darnutzer; Sound, Craig Breitenbach; Composer, Adam Wernick; Fight Director, Geoffrey Kent; Vocal Coach, Phil Thompson; Dramaturg, Scott Horstein; Stage Managers, Christopher C. Ewing, Kurt Van Raden; Cast: David Manis (Edward IV, Henry VI), Kurt Rhoads (Duke of Clarence), Andrew Long (Richard), Kathleen M. Brady (Duchess of York), Jeanne Paulsen (Margaret), Nisi Sturgis (Anne), Kathleen McCall (Queen Elizabeth), Sean Arbuckle (Woodville), Robert Jason Jackson (Hastings), John Hutton (Duke of Buckingham), Mike Hartman (Lord Stanley), Randy Moore (Mayor, Second Murderer, Earl of Oxford), Philip Pleasants (Bishop of Ely), Marcus Waterman (Brakenbury), Stephen Weitz (Catesby), Geoffrey Kent (Ratcliffe), Drew Cortese (Earle of Richmond, First Murderer), Benaiah Anderson (Brandon), Bryce Baldwin, Mateo Correa, Christian Haines, Rob Hille, Mat Hostetler, Kate Hurster, Chris Maclean, Leigh Miller, Matt Mueller, Melissa Ortiz; The Stage Theatre; January 30–February 28, 2009

Radio Golf by August Wilson, Director, Israel Hicks; Set, Michael Ganio; Costumes, David Kay Mickelsen; Lighting, Charles R. MacLeod; Sound, Jason Ducat; Stage Managers, Lyle Raper, Christi B. Spann; Cast: Terrence Riggins (Harmond), Darryl Alan Reed (Roosevelt), Kim Staunton (Mame), Harvy Blanks (Sterling), Charles Weldon (Elder Barlow); The Space Theatre; March 20–April 25, 2009

A Prayer for Owen Meany by John Irving; Adapted by Simon Bent; Director, Bruce K. Sevy; Set, William Bloodgood; Costumes, Bill Black; Lighting, Ann G. Wrightson; Sound, Craig Breitenbach; Composer/Arranger, Gregg Coffin; Fight Director, Geoffrey Kent; Dramaturg, Douglas Langworthy; Vocal Coach, Hilary Blair; Stage Managers, Christopher C. Ewing, Amy McCraney, Kurt Van Raden; Cast: David Ivers (John), Michael Wartella (Owen), Jeanne Paulsen (Harriet), Kathleen McCall (Tabitha), Kathleen M. Brady (Lydia/Samantha), James Michael Reilly (Dan), John Hutton (Rev. Merrill), Megan Byrne (Mrs. Merrill/Jarvit Mom), Mike Hartman (Mr. Meany/ Chickering), Gordana Rashovich (Mrs. Meany/Mrs. Lish), Cheryl Lynn Bowers (Barb/Jarvit Daughter), Sam Gregory (Rector Wiggins/Jarvit Son), Sean Lyons (Jarvit Son), Philip Pleasants (Mr. Fish/Dr. Dolder), Larry Paulsen (Chief Pike), Randy Moore (White), Doug Bynum, Kelli Crump, Rebecca Martin, Chris Mazza, M. Scott McLean, Kelli Crump, Jenna Panther, Dawn Scott, Joseph Yeargain; The Stage Theatre; March 27– April 25, 2009

SunSet and Margaritas by José Cruz González; Director, Nicholas C. Avila; Set and Costumes, Sara Ryung Clement; Lighting, Jane Spencer; Sound, Morgan A. McCauley; Dramaturgy, Douglas Langworthy; Stage Manager, A. Phoebe Sacks; Cast: Philip Hernandez (Gregorio), April Ortiz (Luz), Jamie Ann Romero (Bianca), Sol Castillo (Jojo), Sarah Nina Hayon (Gabby), Ricardo Gutierrez (Candelario), Bryant Mason (Sheriff Montoya), Romi Dias (Virgen de Guadalupe/La Soldadera/La Llorona/Olivia Serrano/Doña Rosita); Commissioned World Premiere; The Ricketson Theatre; April 3–May 16, 2009

Quilters by Molly Newman and Barbara Damashek; Composer and Lyricist, Barbara Damashek; Director, Penny Metropulos; Music Director and Re-orchestrator, Sterling Tinsley; Associate Music Director/ Conductor, Deborah Schmit-Lobis; Musical Stagers, Robert Davidson, Penny Metropulos; Set, William Bloodgood; Costumes, Constanza Romero; Lighting, Don Darnutzer; Sound, Craig Breitenbach; Dramaturg, Doug Langworthy; Stage Managers, – Christopher C. Ewing, Lyle Raper, Christi B. Spann; Cast: Victoria Adams-Zischke, Kathleen M. Brady, Susannah Flood, Kara Lindsay, Linda Mugleston, Christine Rowan, Jeff Skowron; The Stage Theatre; May 22–July 12, 2009

Susannah Flood, Kara Lindsay, Victoria Adams-Zischke, Linda Mugleston and Christine Rowan in Quilters

The 5th Avenue Theatre

Seattle, Washington

Twentieth Season

Producing Artistic Director, David Armstrong; Managing Director, Marilynn Sheldon

Shrek The Musical Music by Jeanine Tesori, Book and Lyrics by David Lindsay-Abaire, Based on DreamWorks Animation Motion Picture and the book by William Steig; Director, Jason Moore; Associate Director, Peter Lawrence; Set, Tim Hatley; Costumes, Tim Hatley; Lighting, Hugh Vanstone; Sound, Peter Hylenski; Dance Captain, Justin Greer; Choreography, Josh Prince; Dance Arrangements, Matthew Sklar; Music Director, Tim Weil; Orchestrations, Danny Troob; Associate Orchestrator, John Clancy; Music Coordinator, Michael Keller; Illusions Consultant, Marshall Magoon; Press Representative, Boneau/Bryan-Brown; General Management, Stuart Thompson Productions/James Triner; Production Manager, Aurora Productions; Marketing Director, Clint Bond, Jr.; Casting, Tara Rubin Casting, CSA; Hair and Wig Design, David Brian-Brown; Make-Up Design, Naomi Donne; Prosthetic Make-Up Design, Michael Marino; Puppet Design, Tim Hatley; Stage Managers, Rachel A. Wolff and Chad Lewis; Electronic Music Design, Andrew Barrett; Cast: Haven Burton (Gingy/Sugar Plum Fairy), Jennifer Cody (Cobbler's Elf/Duloc Greeter/Blind Mouse), Bobby Daye (Pig #2/

Bishop), Ryan Duncan (Pig #3/Pied Piper), Sarah Jane Everman (Ugly Duckling/Blind Mouse), Sutton Foster (Princess Fiona), Aymee Garcia (Mama Bear), Leah Greenhaus (Young Fiona/Flower Girl), Chester Gregory (Donkey), Lisa Ho (Baby Bear/Blind Mouse), Chis Hoch (Captain of the Guard/Big Bad Wolf), Danette Holden (Flutterbell/Magic Mirror Assistant), Brian D'Arcy James (Shrek), Kecia Lewis-Evans (Dragon), Jacob Ming-Trent (Papa Ogre/Pig #1), Marissa O'Donnell (Teen Fiona), Denny Paschall (Peter Pan), Greg Reuter (Guard/Gnome), Adam Riegler (Young Shrek), Noah Rivera (The White Rabbit), Christopher Sieber (Lord Farquaad), Jennifer Simard (Mother/Wicked Witch), Dennis Stowe (Barker/Papa Bear/Thelonius), John Tartaglia (Pinnochio/The Magic Mirror/Beggar), Keaton Whittaker (Young Fiona/Flower Girl), Swings: Justin Greer, Carolyn Ockert-Haythe, Heather Jane Rolff, David F.M. Vaughn; August 14–September 21, 2008

The Drowsy Chaperone Music and Lyrics by Lisa Lambert and Greg Morrison, Book by Bob Martin and Don Mckellar; Director, Casey Nicholaw; Set, David Gallo; Costumes, Gregg Barnes; Lighting, Ken Billington and Brian Monahan; Sound, Acme Sound Partners; Dance Captain, Jen Taylor Farrell; Assistant Dance Captain, Jody Madaras; Dance and Incidental Music Arrangements, Glen Kelly; Choreography, Casey Nicholaw; Music Director, Robert Billig; Musical Supervision and Vocal Arrangements, Phil Reno; Music Coordinator, John Miller; Orchestrations, Larry Blank; Associate Producers, Sonny Everett Mariano Tolentino, Jr., Jeff Davis, Demos Bizar Ent.; General Management, The Charlotte Wilcox Company; Exclusive Tour Direction, The Booking Group; Tour Marketing, Allied Live; Casting, Telsey + Company; Hair Design, Josh Marquetter; Make-Up Design, Justen M. Brossnan; Production Supervisor, Brian Lynch and Chris Kluth; Stage Manager, Brian J. L'Ecuyer; Cast: Jonathan Crombie (Man in Chair), Georgia Engel (Mrs. Tottendale), Noble Shropshire (Underling), Mark Ledbetter (Rober Martin), Richard Vida (George), Mason Roberts (Feldzief), Linda Griffin (Kitty), Paul Riopelle (Gangster #1), Peter Riopelle (Gangster #2), Dale Hensley (Aldolpho), Andrea Chamberlain (Janet Van De Graaff), Alicia Irving (The Drowsy Chaperone), Natasha Yvette Williams (Trix), Chuch Rea (Super), Swings: Megan Nicole Arnoldy, Jennifer Bowles, Jody Madaras; Ensemble: Kevin Crewell, Jen Taylor Farrell, Chuck Rea, Jennifer Swiderski; October 29–November 16, 2008

Seven Brides for Seven Brothers Music by Gene De Paul, Lyrics by Johnny Mercer, Book by Lawrence Kasha and David S. Landat, New Songs by Al Kasha and Joel Hirschhorn, Based on the MGM film and "The Sobbin' Women" by Stephen Vincent Benet; Director, Allison Narver; Set, Anna Louizos; Costumes, Jess Goldstein; Lighting, Tom Sturge; Assistant Lighting Design, Robert Aguilar; Sound, Ken Travis; Dance Captain, Karl Warden; Choreography, Patti Colombo; Music Director, Valerie Gebert; Fight Director, Geoffrey Alm; Production Assistant, Melissa T. Hamasaki; Hair and Make-Up, Mary Pyanowski; Technical Director, Mark Schmidt; Stage Managers, Bret Torbeck, Amy Gornet, Michael B. Paul; Production Supervisor, Andy Luft; Fight Captain, Wes Hart; Cast: Laura Griffith (Milly Bradon), Edward Watts (Adam Pontipee), Luke Longacre (Benjamin), Demian Boergadine (Caleb), Karl Warden (Daniel), Kyle Patrick Vaughn (Ephram), Wes Hart (Frank), Mo Brady (Gideon), Amanda Paulson (Dorcas), Brittany Jamieson (Ruth), Sara Christine Parish (Liza), Maya RS Perkins (Martha), Shanna Marie Palmer (Sarah), Meaghan Foy (Alice), Justing Ramsey (Jeb), David Alewine (Nathan), Christian Duhamel (Luke), Daniel Cruz (Matt), James Scheider (Joel), Ross Cornell (Zeke), Robertson Witmer (The Preacher), Neil Badders (Mr. Hoallum), Vickielee Wohlbach (Mrs. Hoallum), Eric Chappelle (Mr. Sander), Ann Evans (Mrs. Sander), Hanna Lagerway (Townsperson), Jeffrey Alewine (Townsperson), December 3–December 28, 2008

Memphis by David Bryan and Joe Dipierto; Director, Christopher Ashley; Directing Assistant, Adam Arian; Assistant to the Director, Mo Brady; Set, David Gallo; Associate Set Design, Steven C. Kemp; Costumes, Paul Tazewell and Sue Makkoo; Lighting, Howell Binkley; Moving Light Programmer, Matthew Bright; Assistant Lighting Design, Andrea Ruan; Associate Lighting Design, Mark T. Simpson; Sound, Ken Travis; Assistant Sound Design, Howell Binkley; Dace Captain, Jermaine R. Rembert and Charlie Williams; Choreography, Sergio Trujillo; Associate Choreographer, Edgar Godineaux; Music Director, Kenny Seymour; Music producer, Christopher Jahnke; Dialect Coach, Alyssa Keene; Dramaturg, Gabe Greene; Orchestrator, Daryl Waters; Dance Arrangements, August

Eriksmoen; Production Supervisor, Andrew G. Luft; Production Assistants, E. Sara Barnes and Melissa Y. Hamasaki; Hair and Make-Up, Charles G. LaPointe; Stage Managers, Arturo E. Porazzi, David M. Beris, and Monica A. Cuoco; Fight Captain, Brad Bass; Fight Director, Steve Rankin; Cast: Chad Kimball (Huey), Montego Glover (Felicia), J. Bernard Calloway (Delray), Melvin Abston (Delray), James Monroe Iglehart (Bobby), Derrick Baskin (Gator), Cass Morgan (Mama), Allen Fitzpatrick (Mr. Simmons), Anne Allgood (Clara), Kevin Covert (Buck/Gordon), John Eric Parker (Wailin' Joe), Ty Willis (Reverend Hobson), R. Hamilton Wright (Mr. Collins); Swings: Lauren Lim Jackson, Ty Willis; Ensemble: Anne Allgood, Brad Bass, Tracee Beazer, Josh Breckenridge, Kevin Covert, Dionne D. Figgins, Meaghan Foy, Lauren Lim Jackson, Cashae Monya, Jill Morrison, John Eric Parker, Maya RS Perkins, Jermaine R. Rembert, Daniel J. Watts, Charlie Williams, Ty Willis, R. Hamilton Wright; January 27–March 29, 2009

Hello Dolly! by Jerry Herman, Book by Michael Stewart, Based on "The Matchmaker" by Thornton Wilder; Director, David Armstrong; Set, Michael Anania; Costumes, James Schuette and Christine Tschirgi; Lighting, Tom Sturge and Robert Aguilar; Sound, Ken Traivs; Dance Captain, David Alewine; Choreography, David Armstrong; Associate Choreographer, Stephen Reed; Music Director, Joel Fram; Production Supervisor, Andy Luft; Production Assistant, Jessi Wasson; Production Runner, Michael Ledezma; Technical Director, Mark Schmidt; Hair and Make-Up, Mary Pyanowski; Stage Managers, Jeffrey K. Hanson, Lori Amondson, E. Sara Barnes; Cast: Jenifer Lewis (Mrs. Dolly Gallagher Levi), Julie Briskman (Ernestina), Matt Owen (Ambrose Kemper), Pat Cashman (Horace Vandergelder), Krystle Armstrong (Ermengarde), Greg McCormick Allen (Cornelius Hackl), Mo Brady (Barnaby Tucker), Tracee Beazer (Minnie Fay), Suzanne Bouchard (Irene Malloy), Cheryl Massey-Peters (Mrs. Rose), Richard Gray (Rudolph), Ty Willis (Judge), Ensemble: David Alewine, Neil Badders, Eric Brotherson, Gabriel Corey, Daniel Cruz, Jadd Davis, Bojohn Diciple, Michael Ericson, Brittany Jamieson, Brian Demar Jones, Corinna Lapid Munter, Kasey Nusbickel, Maya RS Perkins, James Schneider, Chelsi Schill, Karen Skrinde, Erricka S. Turner-Davis, Troy L. Wageman; Performance Interns: Kyle Clark, Myrna Conn, Heather Deardorff, Krista Gibbon, Makenzie Greenblatt, Daniel Osterman, Sarah Poppe, Justine Stillwell, Thaddeus Wilson; March 7–March 29, 2009

Sunday in the Park with George Music and Lyrics by Steven Sondheim, Book by James Lapine; Director, Sam Buntrock; Assistant to the Director, Mo Brady; Set, David Farley; Costumes, David Farley; Lighting, Ken Bilington; Associate Lighting Designer, Paul Toben; Assistant Lighting Designer, Kennith Elliot; Moving Light Programmer, Tim Rogers; Sound, Ken Travis; Dance Captain, Matt Owen; Choreography, Tara Wilkinson; Assistant Choreographer, Lou Castro; Music Director, Ian Eisendrath; Musical Stagings, Christopher Gattelli; Music Consultants, Caroline Humphris; Technical Director, Mark Schmidt; Production Supervisor, Andy Luft; Hair and Make-Up, Mary Pyanowski; Projection Design, Timothy Bird and The Creative Knifedge Network; Visual Engineer, Sam Hopkins; Team Leader AFX Animator, Nina Dunn; Production Assistant, Austin Garrison; Production Runner, Kate Jordan; Stage Managers, Amy Gornet, Jessica C. Bomball, and Bret Torbek; Stage Management Consultant, Rachel Zack; Cast: Hugh Panaro (George), Billie Wildrick (Dot), Carol Swarbrick (An Old Lady), Anne Allgood (Her Nurse), Amanda Paulson (Celeste #1), Krista Severeid (Celeste #2), Chad Jennings (Louis), Lauren Carlos (Louise), Keaton Whittaker (Louise), Susannah Mars (Frieda), Matt Owen (A Soldier), Richard Gray (Mr.), Anne Allgood (Mrs.), Nick DeSantis (Franz), Matt Owens (Bather), Chad Jennings (Bather), Lauren Carlos (Bather), Keaton Whittaker (Bather), Allen Fitzpatrick (Jules), Patti Cohenour (Yvonne), David Drummond (A Boatman), Hugh Panaro (George), Billie Wildrick (Marie), David Drummond (Dennis), Allen Fitzbatrick (Bob Greenburg), Patti Coheour (Naomi Eisen), Anne Allgood (Harriet Pawling), Chad Jennings (Billy Webster), Krista Severeid (A Photographer), Richard Gray (Charles Redmond), Matt Owen (Alex), Susannah Mars (Betty), Nick DeSantis (Lee Randolph), Carol Swarbrick (Blair Daniels), Amanda Paulson (Elaine), April 21–May 10, 2009

Grease by Jim Jacobs and Warren Casey, Additional Songs by Barry Gibb, John Farrar, Louis St. Louis, and Scott Simon; Director, Kathleen Marshall; Associate Director, David John O' Brien; Set, Derek McLane; Costumes, Martin Pakledinaz;

Lighting, Kenneth Posner; Sound, Brian Ronan; Dance Captain, Lisa Maitta and Brian Crum; Choreography, Kathleen Marshall; Associate Choreographer, Joyce Chittick; Music Director, Tom Whiddon; Orchestrations, Christopher Jahnke; Executive Producer, Max Finbow; Music Coordinator, Howard Joines, Press and Marketing, Amy Katz; General Management, Charlotte Wilcox Company; Casting, Jay Binder and Sara Schatz; Hair and Wig Design, Paul Huntley; Stage Manager, B.J. Foreman; Production Supervisor, Arthur Siccardi; Cast: Eric Schneider (Danny Zuko), Emily Padgett (Dandy Dumbrowski), David Ruffin (Kenickie), Nick Verina (Sonny La Tierri), Will Blum (Roger), Brian Crum (Doody), Allie Schulz (Betty Rizzo), Kelly Felthous (Marry), Bridie Carroll (Jan), Kate Morgan Chadwick (Frenchy), Erin Henry (Patty Simcox), Scot Patrick Allan (Eugene Florczyk), Roxie Lucas (Miss Lynch), Dominic Fortuna (Vince Fontaine), Dayla Perkins (Cha-Cha DiGregorio), Taylor Hicks (Teen Angel), Joseph Corella and Ruby Lewis ("Born to Hand Jive" Specialty Dancers), Brian Crum, Preston Ellis, Mark Raumaker, Mike Russo, Nick Verina (Vel-Doo-Rays), Jim Jacobs (Scientist), Brooke Stone (Sheila), Preston Ellis (Hero), Swings: Preston Ellis, Melissa Larsen, Lisa Maietta, Kevin Quillon, Mike Russo, Amber Stone; Ensemble: Joseph Corella, Preston Ellis, Melissa Larsen, Ruby Lewis, Dayla Perkins, Mark Raumaker, Matthew William Schmidt, Brooke Stone; May 12–May 30, 2009

Florida Stage

Manalapan, Florida
Twenty-second and Twenty-third Seasons
Artistic Director, Louis Tyrrell; Managing Director, Nancy Barnett

Dream a Little Dream: The Nearly True Story of the Mamas and the Papas by Denny Doherty and Paul Ledoux; Director, Michael Barnard; Scenic Design, Mark Pirolo; Lighting Design, Michael J. Eddy; Costume Design, Connie Furr-Solomon; Musical Direction, Christopher McGovern; Production Stage Manager, Suzanne Clement Jones; Assistant Stage Manager, Emily Swiderski; Casting, Rosen and Wojcik Casting; Cast: Stephen G. Anthony (Doherty), Kyle Harris (Denny Doherty), Christine Hope (Michelle Phillips), Shane Jacobsen (Zal and others), Liz Kimball (Jill and others), Michael Sample (John Phillips), Alisa Schiff (Cass Elliot), Eli Zoller (Scott McKenzie and others), Christopher McGovern (Piano), Christopher Kent (Guitar), Neel Shukla (Percussion), Rupert Ziawinski (Bass); Southeastern Premiere; June 26, 2008–August 31 2008

Dirty Business by William Mastrosimone; Director, Louis Tyrrell; Scenic Design, Victor A. Becker; Lighting Design, Richard Crowell; Costume Design, Suzette Pare; Sound Design, Matt Kelly; Production Stage Manager, James Danford; Casting, Rosen and Wojcik Casting; Cast: Elizabeth A. Davis (Judy), Jack Gwaltney (Frank), Dan Leonard (Joe), Gordon McConnell (Sam), James Lloyd Reynolds (Jack); World Premiere; October 22, 2008–November 30, 2008

Mezzulah, 1946 by Michele Lowe; Director, Louis Tyrrell; Scenic and Lighting Design, Richard Crowell; Costume Design, Erin Amico; Sound Design, Matt Kelly; Production Stage Manager, Suzanne Clement Jones; Casting, Rosen and Wojcik Casting; Musical Direction, Missy McArdle; Cast: Theo Allyn (Mezzulah Steiner), Scott Borish (Horace Steiner/Man #1), Kevin Cutts (Errol Hart/Man#3), James Denvil (Isaiah Benson), Anthony Giaimo (Charlie Steiner/Reverend), Deborah Hazlett (Mary Steiner), David Michael Holmes (Fist/Man #2), Blair Sams (Suzannah Hart), Erin Joy Schmidt (Elvira Glass/Mrs. Bates), Beth Wittig (Clementine Flynn/Sally Cauley); Southeastern Premiere; December 10, 2008–January 18, 2009

The Bridegroom of Blowing Rock by Catherine Trieschmann; Director, Cathey Crowell Sawyer; Scenic Design, Kent Goetz; Lighting Design, Suzanne M. Jones; Costume Design, Mark Pirolo; Sound Design, Matt Kelly; Production Stage Manager: James Danford; Casting, Rosen and Wojcik Casting; Cast: Donte Bonner (The Bridegroom), Susan Cato (Laura Farthing), Todd Allen Durkin (Pastor Burns), Lori Gardner (Maizey Hopewell), Lourelene Snedeker (Elsa

Farthing), Ricky Waugh (Jacob Farthing); World Premiere; January 28, 2009– March 9, 2009

CAGNEY! Book by Peter Colley; Music and Lyrics by Robert Creighton and Christopher McGovern; Additional songs by George M. Cohan; Director, Bill Castellino; Scenic Design, Mark Pirolo; Lighting Design, Jim Fulton; Costume Design, Erin Amico; Sound Design, Matt Kelly; Choreography, Jeff Shade; Production Stage Manager, Suzanne Clement Jones; Casting, Carol Hanzel; Musical Direction, Christopher McGovern; Cast: Robert Creighton (James Cagney), Darrin Baker (Jack Warner and others), Joel Newsome (Bob Hope and others), Brian Ogilvie (Bill Cagney and others), Tina Stafford (Jane and others), Ellen Zolezzi (Willie Cagney and others), Christopher McGovern (Piano), Julie Jacobs (Percussion), Glen Rovinelli (Woodwinds), Tom Stancampiano (Trumpet), Rupert Ziawinski (Bass), World Premiere; March 21–May 6

Tina Stafford, Brian Ogilvie, Robert Creighton, Ellen Zolezzi and Joel Newsome in Cagney! *(photo by Ken Jacques Photography)*

Yankee Tavern by Steven Dietz; Director, Michael Bigelow Dixon; Scenic Design, Richard Crowell; Lighting Design, Michael Jon Burris; Costume Design, Leslye Menshouse; Sound Design, Matt Kelly; Production Stage Manager, James Danford; Cast: Antonio Amadeo (Adam), Kim Morgan Dean (Janet), William McNulty (Ray), Mark Zeisler (Palmer); National New Play Network Rolling World Premiere; May 13–June 21

Ford's Theatre

Washington, DC
Fortieth Season (Reopening)
Artistic Director, Paul R. Tetreault; Special Projects Director, James R. Riley

A Christmas Carol by Charles Dickens; Director, Mark Ramont; Set, Court Watson (Original by G.W. Mercer), Costumes, Fabio Toblini; Lighting, Matthew Richards (Original by Pat Collins), Music, Mark Bennett; Sound, Ryan Rumery (Original by Michael Creason), Choreography, Karma Camp; Choral Director, George Fulginiti-Shaker; Dialect Coach, Leigh Wilson Smiley; Wig and Hair, Cookie Jordan; Stage Manager, Craig A. Horness; Assistant Stage Manager, Taryn Friend; Cast: Clinton Brandhagen (Nephew/Young Scrooge), Michael Bunce (First Solicitor), Stephen Carpenter (Second Solicitor), Michael John Casey (Bob

Cratchit), Emily Cochrane (Martha), Katie Culligan(Mrs. Fred's Sister), Elliot Dash (Fruit Vendor Bert/Ghost of Christmas Present), Michael Feldsher(Dick Wilkins/ Topper), Carols Gonzales (Clock Vendor/Ghost of Christmas Future), Michael Goodwin (Jacob Marley/Old Joe/Minister/Fezziwig Party Guest), Jewel Greenberg (Mrs. Fred/Beggar Woman), Claudia Miller (Mrs. Dilber/Mrs. Fezziwig/Mother at Doll Stand), Julia Proctor (Belle), Martin Rayner (Ebenezer Scrooge), Suzanne Richard (Doll Vendor/ Ghost of Christmas Past), Kimberly Schraf (Mrs. Cratchit), Harry A Winter (Mr. Fezziwig); Lansburgh Theatre; December 2–28, 2008

The Heavens Are Hung in Black by Stephen Still; Director, Stephen Rayne; Set, Takeshi Kata; Costumes, Wade Laboissonniere; Lighting, Pat Collins; Sound, Ryan Rumery; Video, Clint Allen; Wig and Makeup, Cookie Jordon; Stage Manager, Brand Prendergast; Assistant Stage Manager, Kate Killbane; Cast: David Selby (Abraham Lincoln), Benjamin Cook (Tad Lincoln), Jonathan Fielding (John Hay), Scott Westerman (Ward Lamon/ Marshal/Billy Brown), David Emerson Toney (Butler/ Dred Scott/ Old Black Soldier), Michael Goodwin (Walt Whitman), Stephen Carpenter (Union Major/Exeter), Norman Aronovic (John Brown/Canterbury), Robin Moseley (Mary Todd Lincoln), Hugh Nees (Edwin Stanton/Stephen Douglas), Edward James Hyland (William Seward/Jefferson Davis), Beth Hylton (Mrs. Winston/Young Woman), Chaney Tullos (Thomas Haley/Bedford), Benjamin Schiffbauer (Young Soldier), James Chatham (Willie Lincoln/Newsboy), Michael Kramer (Edwin Booth), Jonathan Watkins (Bates); Ford's Theatre; February 3–8, 2009

The Civil War Book and Lyrics by Frank Wildhorn, Gregory Boyd and Jack Murphy; Music, Frank Wildhorn; Director, Jeff Calhoun; Set, Tobin Ost; Costumes, Wade Laboissonniere; Lighting, Michael Gilliam; Sound, David Budries; Video, Aaron Rhyne; Wig and Makeup, Cookie Jordan; Stage Manager, Craig A. Horness; Assistant Stage Manager, Bradley C. Cooper; Ensemble: Sarah Darling, Elliot Dash, Eleasha Gamble, Darryl Reuben Hall, Sean Jeaness, Matthew John Kacergis, Kellee Knighten, Michael Lanning, Kingsley Leggs, Michael "Tuba" McKinsey, Aaron Reeder, Bart Shatto, Timothy Shew, Chris Sizemore, Stephen Gregory Smith, Bligh Voth, Michael Goodwin; Ford's Theatre; March 27–May 24, 2009

The Company of The Civil War *(photo by T. Charles Erickson)*

Geffen Playhouse

Los Angeles, California
Thirteenth Season
Producing Director, Gil Cates; Artistic Director, Randall Arney; Managing Director, Susan Barton and Ken Novice

Beethoven, As I Knew Him Music by Ludwig Van Beethoven, book by Hershey Felder; Director, Joel Zwick; Scenic/Projection Artist, Francois-Pierre Couture; Lighting, Richard Norwood; Sound, Erik Carstensen; Projection, Andrew Wilder, Christopher Ash; Production Management, Matt Marsden; Production Stage Management, GiGi Garcia; Cast: Hershey Felder (Ludwig van Beethoven/ Playwright); August 19–October 5, 2008

By the Waters of Babylon by Robert Schenkkan; Director, Richard Seyd; Scenic, Michael Ganio; Lighting, York Kennedy; Sound, Jon Gottlieb; Costume, Frances Kenny; Projection, Jason H. Thompson; Stage Manager, Mary Michelle Miner; Assistant Stage Manager, Elizabeth A. Brohm; Cast: Demian Bichir (Arturo), Shannon Cochran (Catherine); October 28 – December 7, 2008

Time Stands Still by Donald Margulies; Director, Daniel Sullivan; Scenic, John Lee Beatty; Costume, Rita Ryack; Lighting, Peter Kaczorowski; Sound, Jon Gottlieb; Stage Manager, James T. McDermott; Assistant Stage Manager, Jill Gold; Cast: Anna Gunn (Sarah), David Harbour (James), Alicia Silverstone (Mandy), Robin Thomas (Richard); February 3–March 15, 2009

The Seafarer by Conor McPherson; Director, Randall Arney; Set, Takeshi Kata; Costume, Janice Pytel; Lighting, Daniel Ionazzi; Sound, Richard Woodbury; PSM, James T. McDermott; ASM, Jennifer Brienen; Cast: Andrew Connolly (James "Sharky" Harkin, Tom Irwin (Mr. Lockhart), John Mahoney (Richard Harkin), Paul Vincent O'Connor (Ivan Curry), Matt Roth (Nicky Giblin); April 14–May 24, 2009

Farragut North by Beau Willimon; Director, Doug Hughes; Set, David Korins; Costume, Cathy Zuber; Lighting, Paul Gallo; Sound, David Van Tieghem, Walter Trarbach; Original Music by David Van Tieghem; Video Collages, Joshua White, Bec Stupak; Cast: Dan Bittner (Ben), Mia Barron (Ida Horowicz), Justin Huen (Frank and Waiter), Chris Noth (Paul Zara), Chris Pine (Stephen Bellamy), Olivia Thirlby (Molly), Isiah Whitlock, Jr. (Tom Duffy); June 16– July 26, 2009

Geva Theatre Center

Rochester, New York
Thirty-sixth Season
Artistic Director, Mark Cuddy; Managing Director, Greg Weber; Executive Director, Nan Hildebrandt

Menopause the Musical Book and Lyrics by Jeanie Linders; Director, Kathryn Conte; Choreography, Patty Bender; National Music Supervisor, Alan J. Plado; Production Lighting, Ryan A. Patridge Cast: Jeanne Croft (Iowa Housewife), Pammie O'Bannon (Earth Mother), Nancy Slusser (Soap Star), Fredena Williams (Professional Woman), Stage Manager, Kimberley J. First; Assistant Stage Manager, Janine Wochna; Geva Theatre Center Mainstage, July 7–August 10, 2008

Ella Book by Jeffrey Hatcher, Conceived by Rob Ruggiero and Dyke Garrison; Director, Rob Ruggiero; Musical Supervisor, Danny Holgate; Music Director, George Caldwell; Sets, Michael Schweikardt; Costumes, Alejo Vietti; Lighting, John Lasiter; Sound, Michael Miceli, Wigs, Charles LaPointe; Stage Manager, Kirsten Brannen; Assistant Stage Manager, Janine Wochna; Cast: Tina Fabrique (Ella Fitzgerald), Norman Granz (Harold Dixon), George Caldwell (Piano/ Conductor), Rodney Harper (Drums), Clifton Kellem (Bass), Thad Wilson (Trumpet), Joilet Harris (Standby Ella Fitzgerald), Geva Theatre Center Mainstage; September 9–October 12, 2008

Rooms: A Rock Romance Music and Lyrics by Paul Scott Goodman; Book by Paul Scott Goodman and Miriam Gordon; Director, Scott Schwartz; Music Direction, Arrangements and Orchestrations by Jesse Vargas; Sets, Adam Koch; Costumes, Alejo Vietti; Lighting, Herrick Goldman; Sound, Daniel Erdberg; Choreographed by Matt Williams; Dialect Advisor, Doug Honorof; Stage Manager, Janine Wochna. Cast: Natascia Diaz (Monica P. Miller), Doug Kreeger (Ian Wallace), Band: Jenny Cartney (Conductor/Keyboard), Phil Marshall (Guitar), Norm Tibbils (Guitar), Gary Terwilliger (Bass), Steve Curry (Drums). World Premiere. A Co-production with MetroStage; Geva Theatre Center Nextstage; September 19–October 26, 2008

Frost/Nixon by Peter Morgan; Director, Steven Woolf; Sets, Michael Schweikardt; Costumes, Elizabeth Cover; Lighting, Mary Jo Dondlinger; Sound, Rusty Wandall; Video Design, Eric Woolsey; Video Consultant, Bobby Miller; Stage Manager, Marianne Montgomery; Assistant Stage Managers, Kirsten Brannen and Janine Wochna; Casting Director, Rich Cole; Cast: David Anzuelo (Manolo Sanchez), Celeste Ciulla (Caroline Cushing), Margaret Folwell (Evonne Goolagong), Michael Frishman (Ollie), Jeremy Holm (Jack Brennan), Keith Jochim (Richard Nixon), Doug Kester (Studio Manager), Matt Landers (Swifty Lazar), H. Ted Limpert (Ensemble), Teri Madonna (Ensemble), Keith Merrill (John Birt), Michael Sheehan (Ensemble), Jeff Talbott (David Frost), David Christopher Wells (Bob Zelnick),Jim Wisniewski (Jim Reston), Co-production with Repertory Theatre of St Louis; Geva Theatre Center Mainstage; October 21–November 16, 2009

Triple Espresso by Bill Arnold, Michael Pearce Donley and Bob Stromberg; Director, William Partlan, Sets, Nayna Ramey; Costumes, Kathleen Egan; Lighting, Michael Klaers; Sound, John Markiewicz; Production Stage Manager, Maria Cruikshank; Stage Manager, Toni Elderkin; Cast: Duane Daniels (Bobby Bean), Christopher Hart (Buzz Maxwell), Dane Stauffer (Hugh Butternut), Geva Theatre Center Nextstage; November 6, 2008–January 11, 2009

A Christmas Story by Philip Grecian; Director, Mark Cuddy; Sets, Robert Koharchik; Costumes, B. Modern; Lighting, Kirk Bookman; Sound, Dan Roach; Dramaturg, Jean Gordon Ryon; Assistant Director, Melissa Rain Anderson; Stage Manager, Kirsten Brannen; Assistant Stage Managers, Janine Wochna and Marianne Montgomery; Casting Directors, Elissa Myers and Paul Fouquet, CSA; Cast: Alison Banks (Esther Jane), Eoin Dennis (Randy), Gavin Flood (Ralphie), Eric Michael Gillett (Ralph), Matthew Kemp (Flick), Selene Julia Klasner (Standby for Helen/Esther Jane), Rob Krakovski (The Old Man), Ben Lewandowski (Standby for Randy), Lanie MacEwan (Ralphie's Mom), Holden Maiorana (Scut Farkas), Brigitt Markusfeld (Miss Shields), Sage Melcher (Helen), Michael Motkowski (Schwartz), John Thomas Queenan III (Standby for Ralphie), Andrew York (Standby for Flick/Schwartz/Scut), Geva Theatre Center Mainstage, November 28–December 28, 2008

The House in Hydesville by Dan O'Brien; Director, Skip Greer; Sets, Patrick Clark; Costumes, B. Modern; Lighting, Matthew Reinert; Sound, Lindsay Jones; Dramaturg, Marge Betley; Stage Manager, Marianne Montgomery; Assistant Stage Manager, Janine Wochna; Casting, Elissa Myers and Paul Fouquet, CSA; Cast: Kristin Griffith (Margaret Fox), Lanie MacEwan (Leah Fox Fish), Garrett Neergaard (David Fox), Lauren Orkus (Cathie Fox), Annie Purcell (Maggie Fox), Michael Rudko (John Fox), Rachel Rusch (Lizzie Fish), World Premiere; Geva Theatre Center Mainstage; January 13–February 8, 2009

Sweeney Todd, The Demon Barber of Fleet Street Music and Lyrics by Stephen Sondheim; Book by Hugh Wheeler; Director, Mark Cuddy; Music Director, Don Kot; Sets, Adam Koch; Costumes, Devon Painter; Lighting, Robert Wierzel; Sound, Brian Jerome Peterson; Assistant Director, Jenny Lord; Stage Manager, Kirsten Brannen; Assistant Stage Manager; Janine Wochna; Casting, Elissa Myers and Paul Fouquet, CSA; Cast: Sharon Bayer (Ensemble), Leslie Becker (Beggar Woman), Daniel Bogart (Anthony), Ron DeStephano (Pirelli/ Ensemble), William Thomas Evans (Ensemble/ u/s Sweeney Todd), Sean Patrick Jernigan (Ensemble), Pegah Kadkhodaian (Ensemble/ u/s Beggar Woman), Beth Kirkpatrick (Ensemble/ u/s Mrs. Lovett), Jay Lusteck (Ensemble/ u/s

Beadle and Pirelli), Teri Madonna (Swing), Don Mayo (Jonas Fogg/ u/s Judge Turpin), Marissa McGowan (Johanna), Jason Mincer (Swing), Weston Wells Olson (Ensemble/u/s Anthony and Tobias), Roland Rusinek (Beadle Bamford), Kristie Dale Sanders (Mrs. Lovett), Hallie Silverston (Ensemble/ u/s Johanna), Stephen Tewksbury (Sweeney Todd), James Van Treuren (Judge Turpin), Christina Wagenet (Ensemble), Brad Weinstock (Tobias), Geva Theatre Center Mainstage; February 18–March 29, 2009

Evie's Waltz by Carter W. Lewis; Director, Tim Ocel; Sets, Jack Magaw; Costumes, Christina Selian; Lighting, Derek Madonia; Sound, Dan Roach; Dramaturg, Marge Betley; Stage Manager, Janine Wochna; Cast: Skip Greer (Clay), Annie Fitzpatrick (Gloria), Magan Wiles (Evie), Geva Theatre Center Nextstage; April 24– May 24. 2009

The Ladies Man by Charles Morey, translated and adapted from Tailleur pour Dames by Georges Feydeau; Director, Charles Morey; Sets, Bill Clarke; Costumes, Pamela Scofield; Lighting, Phil Monat; Sound, Joe Payne; Dramaturg, Richard J. Roberts; Stage Manager, Emily M; Arnold; Assistant Stage Manager, Janine Wochna; Production Assistant, Jenny Daniels; Casting Directors, Paul Fouquet, CSA and Lelia Shearer, CSA; Cast: John Guerrasio (Bassinet), Morgan Hallett (Marie), Jennifer Johansen (Suzanne Aubin), Michael Keyloun (Etienne), Kelly Mares (Yvonne Molineaux), Mark Mineart (Gustav Aubin), Max Robinson (Dr. Hercule Molineaux), Nance Williamson (Madame Aigreville), Geva Theatre Center Mainstage April 7–May 3

Fences by August Wilson; Director, Mark Cuddy; Sets, Shaun Motley; Costumes, Emilio Sosa; Lighting, Dawn Chiang; Sound, Ian Hildreth; Fight Consultant, Mark Mineart; Community Artistic Advisor, David Shakes; Stage Manager, Kirsten Brannen; Assistant Stage Manager, Janine Wochna; Casting, Elissa Myers and Paul Fouquet, CSA; Cast: Tony Todd (Troy Maxson), Wiley Moore (Jim Bono), Nora Cole (Rose), Jason Dirden (Lyons), Brian D. Coats (Gabriel), Jared McNeill (Cory), Samiah Dilbert/Brianna Randolph (Raynell), Geva Theatre Center Mainstage; May 19–June 21

Goodman Theatre

Chicago, Illinois
Eighty-fourth Season
Artistic Director, Robert Falls; Roche Schulfer, Executive Director

Turn of the Century by Marshall Brickman and Rick Elice; Director, Tommy Tune; Choreography, Noah Racey; Music Supervisor, Daryl Waters; Music Director, Michael Biagi; Sets, Walt Spangler; Costumes, Dona Granata; Lighting, Natasha Katz; Sound, Tom Morse; Orchestrations, Steve Orich; Vocal Arrangements, Daryl Waters and Michael Biagi; PSM, Joseph Drummond; SM, T. Paul Lynch; Cast: Jeff Daniels (Billy Clark), Rachel York (Dixie Wilson), Ron Orbach (Arif Hartoonian/ Max Dreyfus/Moses Baline), Rachel de Benedet (Phyllis Hartoonian/Lily Van Deusen), Kevin Gudahl (Harry Van Deusen), Rebecca Finnegan (Shirley/Lena Baline), Jonah Rawitz/Matthew Gold (Isreal Baline), Nicholas Belton, Jessica Leigh Brown, McKinley Carter, Sara Edwards, Adam Eses, Rebecca Finnegan, Lauren Haughton, Pat McRoberts, Jeff Parker, James Rank, Tommy Rapley, John Sanders, Aléna Watters, Kristen Beth Williams (Ensemble) Michael Parker Ayers, Molly A. Curry (Swings), World Premiere; Goodman Theatre-Albert; August 19– November 2, 2008

A Christmas Carol by Charles Dickens; Adapted by Tom Creamer; Director, William Brown; Sets, Todd Rosenthal; Lighting, Robert Christen; Costumes; Heidi Sue McMath; Sound, Cecil Averett; Musical Staging, Susan Hart; Composer/ Music Director, Andy Hansen; PSM, Alden Vasquez; YPS, Georgette Kelly; PSM, Alden Vasquez; SM, Jamie Wolfe; Cast: Larry Yando (Ebenezer Scrooge), William J. Norris (Mr. Ortle), Ann Joseph (Miss Crumb), Matt Schwader (Fred), Tim Gittings (Topper/Poulterer), Anish Jethmalani (Ghost of Jacob Marley),

Rachel York and Jeff Daniels in Turn of the Century

Steve Haggard (Ghost of Christmas Past/Undertaker), Penelope Walker (Ghost of Christmas Present), Brendan Marshall Rashid (Scrooge as a Young Man/Tree Seller /Ghost of Christmas Future), Ron Rains (Bob Cratchit), Karen Woditsch (Mrs. Cratchit), Matthew Heffernan (Peter Cratchit/ Scrooge as a Boy) Laney Kraus-Taddeo (Belinda Cratchit/Fan), Caroline Heffernan (Emily Cratchit/Want) Lucy Godinez (Martha Cratchit), Bret Tuomi (Mr. Fezziwig/ Chestnut Seller), Sharon Sachs (Mrs. Fezziwig/Philomena), Kevin Theis (Schoolmaster/ Percy/ Old Joe), Adam Poss (DickWilkins), Major Curda (Turkey Boy/ Ignorance), Ryan Cowhey (Tiny Tim), Monét Butler (Abby/Fred's Wife/Mrs. Dilber), Katie Jeep (Catherine), Justin Amolsch, (Horn/Mr. French), Gregory Hirte (Violin/Fiddle/ Mr. Spinet), Bethany Jorgensen (Violin/Adelle), Malcolm Ruhl (Accordian/Ruhl), Goodman Theatre-Albert; November 21–December 31, 2008

Ruined by Lynn Nottage; Director, Kate Whoriskey; Set, Derek McLane; Costumes, Paul Tazewell; Lighting, Peter Kaczorowski; Sound, Rob Milburn/ Michael Bodeen; Original Music, Dominic Kanza; Movement Director, Randy Duncan; Dramaturg, Tanya Palmer; PSM, Kimberly Osgood; Cast: Saidah Arrikah Ekulonah (Mama Nadi), Quincy Tyler Bernstine (Salima), Cherise Boothe (Josephine), Ali Amin Carter (Soldier #2), Chris Chalk (Jerome Kisembe), William Jackson Harper (Simon), Chiké Johnson (Fortune), Russell G. Jones (Christian), Simon Kashama (Soldier #1), Kevin Mambo (Commander Osembenga), Tom Mardirosian (Mr. Harari), Condola Phylea Rashad (Sophie), Rom Barkhordar; Understudies: Rom Barkordar, Lawrence Lacey, Patrese McClain, Taylar, Whitney White; World Premiere; Goodman Theatre-Owen; 2009 Pulitzer Prize winner Best Drama; November 8–April 19, 2008

Desire Under the Elms by Eugene O'Neill; Director, Robert Falls; Set, Walt Spangler; Costumes, Ana Kuzmanic; Lighting, Michael Philippi; Original Music/ Sound, Richard Woodbury; Dialect Coach, Linda Gates; Dramaturgy, Tanya Palmer/Neena Arndt; PSM, Joseph Drummond; SM, T. Paul Lynch; Cast: Brian Dennehy (Ephraim Cabot), Carla Gugino (Abbie Putnam), Boris McGiver (Peter Cabot), Pablo Schreiber (Eben Cabot), Daniel Stewart Sherman (Simeon Cabot), Understudies: Amy J. Carle, Michael Huftile, Brendan Marshall-Rashid, Craig Spidle; Goodman Theatre-Albert; January 17–March 1, 2009

Magnolia by Regina Taylor; Director, Anna D. Shapiro; Set, Todd Rosenthal; Lighting, James F. Ingalls; Costumes, Linda Cho; Sound, Richard Woodbury; Composer, Daryl Waters; Dramaturg, Tanya Palmer; PSM, Alden Vasquez; SM, Jamie Wolfe/Brett Presson; Cast: John Earl Jelks (Thomas), Tyla Abercrumbie (Maya),Tory O. Davis (Meshach), Roxanne Reese (Carlotta), Brandon J. Dirden (Cain), Ernest Perry, Jr. (Samuel), Annette O'Toole (Lily), John Judd (Beau), John

Carla Gugino and Brian Dennehy in Desire Under the Elms
(photos by Liz Lauren)

Hines (William), Caitlin Collins (Anna), Carrie Coon (Ariel), Cliff Chamberlain (Paul), Understudies: Victor Cole, Ethan Henry, Rachael Jenison, Michael Mahler, Kelly Owens, Hollis Resnick, La Donna Tittle, Mick Weber; World Premiere; Goodman Theatre-Albert; March 14–April 19, 2009

Ghostwritten by Naomi Iizuka; Director Lisa Pores; Set, Linda Buchanan; Costumes, Rachel Healy; Lighting, Keith Parham; Sound, Andre J. Pluess; Dramaturg, Neena Arndt; PSM, Kimberly Osgood; Cast: Arthur Acuna (Linh), Dieterich Gray (Chad/Not Chad), Kim Martin-Cotton (Susan), Lisa Tejero (Woman from Vietnam), Tiffany Villarin (Bea), Dan Waller (Martin), Understudies: Michael Bullaro, Steven Hadnagy, Cheryl Hamada, Yosh Hayashi, Christine Lin, Ginger Lee McDermott; World Premiere; Goodman Theatre-Owen; April 3–May 3, 2009

Rock 'n' Roll by Tom Stoppard; Director, Charles Newell; Set, John Culbert; Lighting, Christopher Akerlind; Costume, Ana Kuzmanic; Sound, Ray Nardelli/Joshua; Dialect Consultant Elizabeth Smith; Dramaturg, John Boller; PSM Joseph Drummond; SM, T. Paul Lynch/Mackenzie Brown; Cast: Greg Matthew Anderson (The Piper/Stephen), Mattie Hawkinson Esme (Younger/Alice), Timothy Edward Kane (Jan), Stephen Yoakam (Max) Mary Beth Fisher (Eleanor/Esme (Older), Johanna McKenzie Miller (Gillian/Magda/Deirdre), Thom Cox (Interrogator/Nigel), Kareem Bandealy (Ferdinand), John Hoogenakker (Milan), Amy J. Carle (Lenka), Susie McMonagle (Candida), Mick Weber (Policeman), Understudies: Janet Ulrich Brooks, Marika Engelhardt, Patrick Mulvey, Rebekah Ward-Hays; Goodman Theatre-Albert; May 2–June 7, 2009

The Crowd You're In With by Rebecca Gilman; Director, Wendy C. Goldberg; Set, Kevin Depinet; Costumes, Ana Kuzmanic; Lighting, Josh Epstein; Sound, Ray Nardelli/Joshua Horvath; Dramaturg, Tanya Palmer; PSM, Kimberly Osgood; Cast: Coburn Goss (Jasper), Kiff Vanden Heuvel (Dan), Janelle Snow (Melinda), Stephanie Childers (Windsong), Rob Riley (Tom), Linda Gehringer (Karen), Sean Cooper (Dwight), Understudies: Anabel Armour, William Dick, Mark D. Hines, Guy Masses, Justine C. Turner; Goodman Theatre-Owen; May 23–June 21, 2009

Boleros for the Disenchanted by Jose Rivera; Director, Henry Godinez; Set, Linda Buchanan; Lighting, Joseph Appelt; Costumes, Rachel Healy; Sound, Ray Nardelli/Joshua Horvath; Composer, Gustavo Leone; Dramaturg, Nina Arndt; PSM, Alden Vasquez; SM, Brett Presson; Cast: Liza Fernandez (Petra/Monica), Elizabeth Ledo (Young Flora/Eve), Sandra Marquez (Dona Milla/Older Flora), Joe Minoso (Young Eusebio/Oskar), René Rivera (Don Fermin/Older Eusebio), Felix Solis (Manuelo/Priest), Understudies: Isabel Quintero, Desmin Borges, Gustavo Mellado, Christina Nieves; Goodman Theatre-Albert; June 20–July 26, 2009

Goodspeed Musicals

East Haddam and Chester, Connecticut
Fourty-fifth Season
Executive Producer, Michael P. Price; Associate Producer, Bob Alwine; Line Producer, Donna Lynn Cooper Hilton; General Manager, Harriet Guin-Kittner

13 Music and Lyrics by Jason Robert Brown; Book by Dan Elish and Robert Horn; Director, Jeremy Sams; Choreography, Christopher Gatelli; Set & Costume, David Farley; Lighting, Brian MacDevitt; Sound, John Weston; Arrangements and Orchestrations, Jason Robert Brown; Music Director, Tom Kitt; Stage Manager, Rick Steiger; Technical Director, Lily Twining; Cast: Graham Phillips (Evan), Hudson Thames (Evan), Aaron Simon Gross (Archie), Allie Trimm (Patrice), Eric Nelson (Brett), Elizabeth Egan Gillies (Lucy), Ashton Smalling (Kendra), Kyle Crews (Malcolm), Alberto Calderon (Eddie), Eamon Foley (Steve/Richie), Joey LaVarco (Bill/Simon), Ariana Grande (Charlotte), Caitlin Gann (Molly), Taylor Bright (Cassie); Norma Terris Theatre; May 9–July 8, 2008

Half a Sixpence Music and Lyrics by David Heneker; Book by Beverly Cross; Director, Gordon Greenberg, Music Director, Michael O'Flaherty; Chroeography, Patti Colombo; Set, Rob Bissinger; Costumes, David C. Woolard; Lighting, Jeff Croiter; Sound, Jay Hilton; Hair & Wig, Mark Adam Rampmeyer; Orchestrations, Dan DeLange; Dance Arrangements, Gregory M. Brown; Assistant Music Director, F. Wade Russo; Production Manager, R. Glen Grusmark; Stage Manager, Bradley G. Spachman; Cast: Jon Peterson (Arthur Kipps), Danny Gardner (Sid), Cameron Henderson (Buggins), Wes Hart (Pearce), Kate Marilley (Flo), Elise Kinnon (Victoria), Caroline Massagee (Kate), James Judy (Shalford), Rod Roberts (Carshot), Sara Gettelfinger (Ann), Donna English (Mrs. Walsingham), Julia Osborne (Helen Walsingham), Jeff Skowron (Chitterlow), Cheryl McMahon (Mrs. Botting), Ensemble: Adriene Couvillion, Desiree Davar, Peter Leskowicz, Eric Shorey; Swings: Katie Warner Johnson, Colby Q. Lindeman; Goodspeed Opera House; July 11–September 19, 2008

Big River Music and Lyrics by Roger Miller; Book by William Hauptman; Director, Rob Ruggiero; Music Director, Michael O'Flaherty; Choreography, John MacInnis; Set, Michael Schweikardt; Costumes, Alejo Vietti; Lighting, John Lasiter; Sound, Jay Hilton; Hair & Wig , Mark Adam Rampmeyer; Orchestrations, Dan DeLange; Assistant Music Director, William J. Thomas; Dialect Coach, Gillian Lane-Plescia; Production Manager, R. Glen Grusmark; Stage Manager, Bradley G. Spachman; Cast: Will Reynolds (Huckleberry Finn), David M. Lutken (The Musician), Jim (Russell Joel Brown), Tom Sawyer (Jeremy Jordan), Mary Jo McConnell (Widow Douglas), Nancy Johnston (Miss Watson), Robin Haynes (Judge Thatcher), Danny Marr (Ben Rogers), Adam Shonkwiler (Joe Harper), Daniel Kwiatkowski (Dick Simon), Kenneth Cavett (Pap Finn), Ed Dixon (The King), John Bolton (The Duke), Marissa McGowan (Mary Jane Wilkes), Jill Kerley (Joanna Wilkes), Steve French (Counselor Robinson), A'Lisa D. Miles (Alice), Christine Lyons (Betsy), Tyrone Robinson (Ensemble), Swings: Barbara Brown, Kanova Latrice Johnson, Rob Morrison; Goodspeed Opera House; September 26–November 20, 2008

The Story of My Life Music and Lyrics by Neil Bartram; Book by Brian Hill; Director, Richard Maltby, Jr.; Set, Robert Brill; Costumes, Wade Laboissonniere, Sound, Carl Casella; Production , Dustin O'Neill; Orchestrations, Jonathan Tunick; Music Director, David Holcenberg; Associate Director, Lisa Shriver; Technical Director, Jason Grant; Stage Manager, Bess Marie Glorioso; Cast: Will Chase (Thomas Weaver), Malcolm Gets (Alvin Kelby), Norma Terris Theatre; October 10–November 2, 2008

Emmett Otter's Jug-Band Christmas Book by Timothy A. McDonald & Christopher Gattelli; Music and Lyrics by Paul Williams; Director & Choreography, Christopher Gattelli; Music Director, Larry Pressgrove; Set, Anna Louizos; Costumes, Gregg Barnes; Lighting, Brian MacDevitt; Orchestrations, Dan DeLange; Arrangements, Gregory M. Brown; Assistant Music Director, William J. Thomas; Sound, Jay Hilton; Production Manager, R. Glen Grusmark; Stage Manager, Bradley G. Spachman; Cast: Kate Wetherhead (Jane), Alan Campbell (Russ/Pa Otter), Daniel Reichard (Emmett Otter), Cass Morgan (Mrs. Alice Otter),

Robb Sapp (Wendell Porcupine), Lisa Howard (Mrs. Gretchen Fox), Kevin Covert (Mayor Harrison Fox), David Stephens (Yancy Woodchuck), Sheri Sanders (Madame Squirrel/Hetty Muskrat), Tyler Bunch (Doc Bullfrog/Catfish), Jeff Hiller (Will Possum/Charlie Muskrat), Madeleine Doherty (Mrs. Mink), James Silson (George Rabbit/Howard Snake), Anney McKilligan (Melissa Rabbit/Old Lady Possum), Leo Daignault (Chuck Stoat), Stephen Bienskie (Stan Weasel), Colin Hanlon (Fred Lizard), Daniel Torres (Harvey Beaver), Swings: Kristin Feeney, Matthew Furtado; Goodspeed Opera House; December 7–January 4, 2009

42nd Street Music by Harry Warren; Lyrics by Al Dubin; Book by Michael Stewart and Mark Bramble; Director, Ray Roderick; Choreography, Rick Conant; Set, Howard Jones; Costumes, David H. Lawrence; Lighting, Charlie Morrison; Sound, Jay Hilton; Hair & Wig, Mark Adam Rampmeyer; Orchestrations, Dan DeLange; Music Supervisor, Michael O'Flaherty; Music Director, William J. Thomas; Production Manager, R. Glen Grusmark; Stage Manager, Bradley G. Spachman; Cast: Tim Falter (Andy Lee), Dorothy Stanley (Maggie Jones), Dale Hensley (Bert Barry), Elise Kinnon (Phyllis Dale), Erin West (Lorraine Fleming), Jenifer Foote (Ann Reilly), Austin Miller (Billy Lawler), Kristen Martin (Peggy Sawyer), James Lloyd Reynolds (Julian Marsh), Laurie Wells (Dorothy Brock), Erick Devine (Abner Dillon), Jonathan Stewart (Pat Denning), Ensemble: Alissa Alter, Kelly Day, Brandon Davidson, Erin Denman, Joe Grandy, Chad Harlow, Ashley Peacock, Kristyn Pope, Colin Pritchard, Ernie Pruneda, Tara Jeanne Vallee; Goodspeed Opera House; April 17–July 4, 2009

Lucky Guy Book, Music and Lyrics by Willard Beckham; Director and Choreographer, Warren Carlyle; Musical Supervision and Orchestrations by Todd Ellison; Set, Walt Spangler; Costumes, William Ivey Long; Lighting, Ken Billington; Music Director, Antony Geralis; Sound, Jay Hilton; Stage Manager, Kim Vernance; Technical Director, Jason Grant; Associate Director/Choreographer, Parker Esse; Cast: Josh Grisetti (Billy Ray), Katie Adams (Chicky), Autumn Hurlbert (Wanda), Gary Beach, (Big Al), John Bolton (GC), Stacia Fernandez (Jeannie), The Lucky Guy Buckaroos: Stephen Carrasco, Robert H. Fowler, James Gray, Gavin Lodge; Norma Terris Theatre; May 14–June 14, 2009

Guthrie Theatre

Minneapolis, Minnesota
Forty-sixth Season
Director, Joe Dowling

Little House on the Prairie Music by Rachel Portman, Lyrics by Donna di Novelli, Book by Rachel Sheinkin, based on the "Little House" books by Laura Ingalls Wilder; Director, Francesca Zambello; Set, Adrianne Lobel; Costumes, Jess Goldstein; Lighting, Mark McCullough; Sound, Scott W. Edwards; Musical Supervisor/Conductor, Mary-Mitchell Campbell; Choreography, Michele Lynch; Orchestrations, Larry Hochman; Vocal and Dialect Coach, Lucinda Holshue; Dramatrug, Jo Holcomb; Associate Director/Associate Choreography, Tim Federle; Stage Manager, Michele Harms; Assistant Stage Manager, Justin Hossle; Assistant Director, Dina Rattan; Cast: Steve Blanchard (Charles "Pa" Ingalls), Melissa Gilbert (Caroline "Ma" Ingalls), Kara Lindsay (Laura Ingalls), Jenn Gambatese (Mary Ingalls), Maeve Moynihan (Carrie Ingalls), Sara Jean Ford (Nellie Oleson), Kevin Massey (Almanzo Wilder), Ensemble: Tori Adams, Mathias Anderson Lexy Armour, Rober O. Berdahl, Kurt Engh, Shawn Hamilton, Caroline Innerbichler, Noah Long, Ryan McCartan, Addi McDaniel, Mary Jo Mecca, Patricia Noonan, Prince Michael Okolie, James Ramlet, David L. Ruffin, Gayle Samuels, Amy Schroeder, Tony Vierling, Jordan Young; World Premiere, McGuire Proscenium Stage; July 26—October 5, 2008 A View from the Bridge by Arthur Miller; Director, Ethan McSweeny; Set, John Arnone; Costumes, Robert Perdziola; Lighting, Donald Holder; Sound, David Maddox; Fight Choreography, David Brimmer; Dramaturg, Carla Steen; Voice and Dialect Coach, Lucinda Holshue; Movement, Marcela Lorca; Stage Manager, Martha Kulig; Assistant Stage

Manager, Tiffany K. Orr; Assistant Director, Leah E. Cooper; Cast: John Carroll Lyn (Eddie Carbone), Amy Van Nostrand (Beatrice), Robyn Rikoon (Catherine), Bryce Pinkham (Rodolpho), Ron Menze (Marco), Richard S. Iglewski (Alfieri), Nathaniel Fuller (Alfieri), Michael Booth (First Immigration Officer), Mark Bradley (Mr. Lipari), J.C. Cutler (Tony), Hugh Kennedy (First Italian Immigrant), Joel Liestman (Second Immigration Officer), Tim McGee (Mike), Lee Mark Nelson (Louis), John Skelley (Second Italian Immigrant), Suzanne Warmanen (Mrs. Lipari); Wurtelle Thrust Stage; September 13—November 9, 2008

The Caretaker by Harold Pinter; Director, Benjamin McGovern; Set, Anna Lawrence; Costumes, Christine A. Richardson; Lighting, Tom Mays; Dramatrug, Michael Lupu; Dialect Coach, Mira Kehoe; Stage Manager, Elizabeth R. MacNally; Assistant Stage Manager, Meaghan Rosenberger; Cast: Steven Epp (Davies), Stephen Cartmell (Mick), Kris L. Nelson (Aston); Dowling Studio; October 11—November 2, 2008

Shadowlands by William Nicholson; Director, Joe Dowling; Set, Patrick Clark; Costumes, Decon Painter; Lighting, Marcus Dilliard; Sound, Scott W. Edwards; Music Consultant, Adam Wernick; Dramaturg, Jo Holcomb; Voice and Dialect Coach, Elisa Carlson; Movement, Marcela Lorca; Stage Manager, Chris A. Code; Assistant Stage manager, Timothy Markus; Assistant Director, Sarah Gioia; Cast: Simon Jones (C.S. Lewis), Charity Jones (Joy Davidman Gresham), Julian bailey (Dr. Maurice Oakley/Clerk/Doctor/Waiter in Hotel), Jennifer Blagen (Nurse/Woman in Tea Room/Witness), Bob Davis (Christopher Riley), Tucker Garborg (Douglas), Mykola Rieland (Douglas), Jonas Goslow (Alan Gregg/Waiter in Tea Room/Registrar/Priest), James A. Stephens (Major W. H. Lewis), Peter Thomson (Rev. "Harry" Harrington); McGuire Proscenium Stage; November 1—December 21, 2008

A Christmas Carol by Charles Dickens; Adapted by Barbara Field; Director, Gary Gisselman; Set, Neil Patel; Costumes, Jess Goldstein; Additional Costume Design, David Kay Michelsen; Lighting, Marcus Dilliard; Composer, Victor Zupanc; Musical Director, Anita Ruth; Sounds, Scott W. Edwards; Dramaturg, Michael Lupu; Voice and Dialect Coach, Elisa Carlson; Associate Director, Myron Johnson; Movement Coach, Myron Johnson; Stage Manager, Martha Kulig; Assistant Director, Robert Goudy; Assistant Stage Manager, Jason Clusman; Cast: Raye Birk (Ebenezer Scrooge), Michael Booth (Bob Cratchit), Laura Esping (Mrs. Dilber/Dorothea/Forrest), Nathaniel Fuller (Jacob Marley/Topper), Sally Windert (Mrs. Cratchit), Jon Andrew Hegge (Ghost of Christmas Yet to Come), Elizabeth Griffith (Petunia Fezziwig), Kathleen Humphry (Jane), Ann Michels (Ghost of Christmas Past/Mrs. Fred), Hugh Kennedy (Cecil/Young Scrooge/Squeeze), Michael Kissin (Fiddler/Krookings), Wayne A. Evenson (Mr. Fezziwig/Snarkers), Lee Mark Nelson (Fred), Bill McCallum (Ghost of Christmas Present), Sherwin F Resurreccion (Albert Hall/Edwards), Allyson Carey (Marigold Fezziwig), Richard Ooms (Mr. Squeeze/Blackings Foreman/Joe), John Skelley (Young Jacob Marley/Mr. Grub), Elizabeth Stahlmann (Belle/Ella), Vern Sutton (Blakely/Grasper/Elliott), Suzanne Warmanen (Mrs.Grigsby/Mrs. Fezziwig/Sophie); Wurtele Thrust Stage; November 18—December 31, 2008

A Delicate Balance by Edward Albee; Director, Gary Gisselman; Set, John Arnone; Costumes, David Kay Michelsen; Lighting, Don Darnutzer; Sound, Reid Rejsa; Dramaturg, Carla Steen; Voice and Dialect Coach, Lucinda Holshue; Stage Manager, Elizabeth R. MacNally; Assistant Director, Rob Goudy; Assistant Stage Manager, Justin Hossle; Cast: Margaret Daly (Agnes), Raye Birk (Tobias), Charity Jones (Julia), Stephen Yoakam (Harry), Angela Timberman (Edna), Candy Buckley (Claire); McGuire Proscenium Stage; January 16—March 1, 2009

The Two Gentlemen of Verona by William Shakespeare; Director, Joe Dowling; Set, Riccardo Hernandez; Costumes, Ann Hould-Ward; Lighting, Christopher Akerlind; Original Music and Lyrics, Keith Thomas; Sounds, Scott W. Edwards; Dramaturg, Michael Lupu; Voice and Dialect Coach, Andrew Wade; Movement, Joe Chvala and Marcela Lorca; Stage Manager, Chris A. Code; Assistant Director, Brian Balcom; Assistant Stage Manager, Michele Harms; Cast: Sam Bardwell (Velntine), Jonas Goslow (Proteus), Sun Mee Chomet (Julia), Valeri Mudek (Silvia), Jim Lichtscheidl (Lance), Randy Reyes (Speed), Sasha Andreev

(The Singer), Michal Booth (Pantino/Outlaw), Laura Esping (Lucetta), Nathaniel Fuller (Antonio/Outlaw), Hugh Kennedy (Outlaw), Kris L. Nelson (Eglamour), Lee Mark Nelson (Duke of Milan), Isabell Monk O'Connor (Host), John Skelley (Turio), Wyatt (Crab); Wurtele Thrust Stage; January 24—March 29, 2009

Happy Days by Samuel Beckett; Director, Rob Melrose; Set, Michael Locher; Costumes, Christine A. Richardson; Lighting, Frank Butler; Dramaturg, Michael Lupu; Stage Manager, Martha Kulig; Assistant Stage Manager, Meaghan Rosenberger; Cast: Sally Wingert (Winnie), Richard Ooms (Willie); Dowling Studio; February 14—March 8, 2009

Caroline, or Change Book and Lyrics by Tony Kushner, Music by Jeanine Tesori; Director, Marcela Lorca; Set, Richard Hoover; Costumes, Candice Donnelly; Choreography, Marcela Lorca; Lighting, Mary Louise Geiger; Sound, Scott W. Edwards; Dramaturg, Jo Holcomb; Voice and Dialect Coach, Lucinda Holshue; Stage Manager, Russell W. Johnson; Assistant Stage Manager, Jason Clusman; Assistant Stage Manager, Elizabeth R. MacNally; Assistant Director, Marcus Quiniones; Assistant Choreography, Marcus Quiniones; Cast: Great Oglesby (Caroline Thibodeaux), Noah Coon (Noah Gellman), Ryan McDowell Poehler (Noah Gellman), Jamecia Bennett (Washing Machine), T. Mychael Rambo (The Dryer), Felicia Boswell (The Radio), Lynnea Doublette (The Radio), Aurelia Williams (The Radio), Aimee K. Bryant (The Moon), Regina Marie Williams (Dotty Moffett), Julie Reiber (Rose), Nikki Renee Daniels (Emmie), Versell Ford IV (Jackie), Jackson M. Hurst (Jackie), Julius Andrews IV (Joe), Zadir King (Joe), Michelle Barber (Grandma Gellman), Bradley Greenwald (Stuart Gellman), Peter Thomson (Grandpa Gellman), Kenny Morris (Mr. Stopnick); Wurtele Thrust Stage; April 18—June 21, 2009

The Intelligent Homosexual's Guide to Capitalism and Socialism with a Key to the Scriptures by Tony Kushner; Director, Michael Greif; Set, Mark Wendland; Costumes, Clint Ramos; Lighting, Kevin Adams; Sound, Ken Travis; Music, Michael Friedman; Dramaturg, Jo Holcomb; Voice and Dialect Coach, Elisa Carlson; Stage Manager, Martha Kulig; Assistant Stage Manager, Chris A. Code; Assistant Stage Manager, Justin Hossle; Assistant Director, David Alpert; Cast: Michael Cristofer (Gus Marcantonio), Kathleen Chalfant (Benedicta Immacolata Marcantonio (Bennie), Stephen Spinella (Pier Luigi Marcantonio (Pill), Linda Emont (Maria Teresa Marcantonio (Empty), Ron Menzel (Vito Marcantonio (V, Vic, Vinnie), Michael Potts (Paul Pierce), Michael Esper (Eli Wolcott), Mark Benninghofen (Adam Buter), Charity Hones (Maeve Ludens), Sun Mee Chomet (Sooze Moon Marcantonio), Michelle O'Neill (Shelle O'Neill); World Premiere; McGuire Proscenium Stage; May 15—June 28, 2009

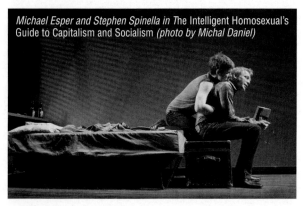

Michael Esper and Stephen Spinella in The Intelligent Homosexual's Guide to Capitalism and Socialism *(photo by Michal Daniel)*

Tiny Kushner by Tony Kushner; Director, Tony Taccone; Set, Annie Smart; Costumes, Anita Yavich; Lighting and Video, Alexander V. Nichols; Sound, Victor Zupanc; Dramaturg, Lauren Ignaut; Stage Manager, Michele Harms; Assistant Stage Manager, Meaghan Rosenberger; Cast: J.C. Cutler, Kate Eifrig, Jim Lichtscheidl, Valeri Mudek; World Premiere; Dowling Studio; May 16—June 13, 2009

Hartford Stage Company

Hartford, Connecticut
Forty-fourth Season
Artistic Director, Michael Wilson; Managing Director, Michael Stotts

Elaine Stritch at Liberty Music Director, Rob Bowman; Director, Jack O'Brien; Hair and Makeup, Bella Botier; Lighting, Cletus Karamon; Sound, Johnathan Tunick; PSM, Susie Cordon; ASM, Allison Sommers; Cast: Elaine Stritch (Herself), Clint Sharman (Trombone), Gary Seligson (Drums), Ronnie Buttacavoli (Trumpet), Jeff Levine (Bass), Les Scott (Reeds); June 24–June 29, 2008

Ella Music Direction and Arrangement by Danny Holgate, book by Jeffrey Hatcher; Director, Rob Ruggiero; Sets, Michael Schweikardt; Lighting, John Lasiter; Sound, Michael Miceli; Costumes, Alejo Vietti; PSM, Richard Costabile; Production Manager, Bryan T. Holcombe; ASM, Greg Hritz; Cast: Tina Fabrique (Ella), Harold Dixon (Norman), George Caldwell (Piano/Conductor), Rodney Harper (Drums), Clifton Kellem (Bass), Thad Wilson (Trumpet); July 8–July 27, 2008

Wishful Drinking Created and Performed by Carrie Fisher; Director, Tony Taccone; Scenic/Lighting/Projection, Alexander V. Nichols; Production Manager, Tom Aberger; Cast: Hershey Felder (George Gershwin/Playwright); August 6– August 17, 2008

A Midsummer Night's Dream by William Shakespeare; Composer, James Paul Prendergast; Director, Lisa Peterson; Sets, Rachel Hauck; Lighting, Stephen Strawbridge; Costumes, Ilona Somogyi; PSM, Susan R. White; Production Manager, Bryan T. Holcombe; ASM, Amber Dickerson; Cast: Johanna Day (Hippolyta/Titania), David Andrew Macdonald (Theseus/Oberon), Francis Jue (Philostrate/Puck), Everett Quinton (Egeus/Quince), Jake Lacy (Demetrius), Sanjit De Silva (Lysander), Christina Pumariega (Hermia), Susannah Flood (Helena), Lucas Caleb Rooney (Bottom), Steven Boyer (Flute), Nathan Johnson (Starveling), Kathy Deitch (Snout), Robert Patrick Sheire (Snug), Delaney Louise Jordan (Fairy Girl), Jordan Cyr (Fairy Boy); August 28–October 5, 2008

Resurrection by Daniel Beaty; Music Composed by Daniel Bernard Roumain; Director, Oz Scott; Sets, G.W. Mercier; Lighting, Jason Arnold; Sound, Michael Miceli; Costumes, Karen Perry; PSM, John Scutchins; ASM, Julien Winter Tremblay; Production Manager, Bryan T. Holcombe; Cast: Jeffery V. Thompson (60/The Bishop), Michael Genet (50/Mr. Rogers), Alvin Keith (40/Isaac), Che Ayende (30/Dre), Turron Kofi Alleyne (20/Twon), Thuliso Dingwall (10/Eric); October 16–November 16, 2008

A Christmas Carol by Charles Dickens; Adapted and Directed by Michael Wilson; Music Director, Ken Clark; Original Music and Sound, John Gromada; Sets, Tony Straiges; Lighting, Robert Wierzel; Costumes, Zack Brown; PSM, Martin Lechner; Production Manager, Bryan T. Holcombe; ASM, Julien Winter Tremblay; Dialect Coach, Gillian Lane-Plescia; Cast: Alan Rust (Ebenezer Scrooge), Bill Kux (Mrs. Dilber/Jacob Marley), Robert Hannon Davis (Bob Cratchit/Mr. Fezziwig), Curtis Billings (Fred/Scrooge at 30), Kyle Metzger (Lamplighter), Noble Shropshire (First Solicitor/Undertaker), Gustave Johnson (Second Solicitor), Johanna Morrison (Bettye Pidgeon/Spirit of Christmas Past), Deirdre Garrett (Rich Lady), Jeffery V. Thompson (Bert/Spirit of Christmas Present), Rob Cunliffe (Mr. Marvel), Kurt Peterson (Scrooge at 15), Natalie Brown (Mrs. Fezziwig/ Old Jo), Veronique Hurley (Nichola), Ellenkate Finley (Wendy), Amanda Karmelin (Fiddler), Daniel Toot (Dick Wilkins), Michelle Hendrick (Belle/Fred's Wife), Rebecka Jones (Mrs. Cratchit), Sarah Goosmann (Martha Cratchit), James DiMatteo (Mr. Topper), Brendan Fitzgerald (Time Cratchit), Andrew Shipman (Boy Scrooge), Alisha Kapur (Fan), Josie Kulp (Claire), Hollis Long (Belinda Cratchit), Miles Wilson-Toliver (Peter Cratchit), Zachary Cyr (Ignorance), Abbi Rice (Want), Michael Griffin (Turkey Boy), Rachel Dalton (Urchin); November 28–December 28, 2008

Dying City by Christopher Shinn; Director, Maxwell Williams; Sets, Wilson Chin; Lighting, Traci Klainer; Sound, Fitz Patton; Costumes, Alejo Vietti; PSM, Christina Lowe; Production Manager, Bryan T. Holcombe; Cast: Diane Davis (Kelly), Ryan King (Peter/Craig); January 8–February 8, 2009

To Kill A Mockingbird by Harper Lee; Adapted by Christopher Sergel; Music and Sound by John Gromada; Director, Michael Wilson; Sets, Jeff Cowie; Lighting, Rui Rita; Costumes, David C. Woolard; PSM, Lori Lundquist; Production Manager, Bryan T. Holcombe; ASM, Marisa Levy; Vocal and Dialect Coach, Robert H. Davis; Cast: Hallie Foote (Jean Louise Finch), Olivia Scott (Scout), Henry Hodges (Jem), Matthew Modine (Atticus), Pat Bowie (Calpurnia), Jennifer Harmon (Maudie Atkinson/Stephanie Crawford/Mrs. Dubose), Nafe Katter (Mr. Nathan Radley/Judge Taylor), Devon Adner (Boo Radley/Mr. Gilmer), Andrew Shipman (Dill), James DeMarse (Heck Tate/Walter Cunningham), Virginia Kull (Mayella Ewell), Mike Boland (Bob Ewell), Douglas Lyons (Tom Robinson), Daralyn Jay (Helen Robinson); February 19–April 4, 2009; extended to April 12, 2009

Noises Off by Michael Frayn; Music and Sound, David Stephen Baker; Director, Malcolm Morrison; Sets, Tony Straiges; Lighting, Rui Rita; Costumes, Ilona Somogyi; PSM, Cole P. Bonenberger; Production Manager, Bryan T. Holcombe; ASM, Julien Winter Tremblay; Cast: Johanna Morrison (Dotty Otley/Mrs. Clacket), Bill Kux (Lloyd Dallas), Noble Shropshire (Selsdon Mowbray/Burglar), Michael Bakkensen (Garry Lejeune/Roger Tramplemain), Liv Rooth (Brooke Ashton/Vicki), Andrea Cirie (Belinda Blair/Flavia Brent), David Andrew Macdonald (Frederick Fellowes/Philip Brent), Veronique Hurley (Poppy Norton-Taylor), Daniel Toot (Tim Allgood); April 23–May 17, 2009

Dividing the Estate by Horton Foote; Original Music and Sound, John Gromada; Director, Michael Wilson; Sets, Jeff Cowie; Lighting, Rui Rita; Costumes, David C. Woolard; PSM, Cole P. Bonenberger; Production Manager, Bryan T. Holcombe; ASM, Marisa Levy; Cast: Devon Abner (Son), Penny Fuller (Lucille), Lois Smith (Stella), Pat Bowie (Mildred), Arthur French (Doug), Gerald McRaney (Lewis), Keiana Richàrd (Cathleen), Maggie Lacey (Pauline), Hallie Foote (Mary Jo), Jenny Dare Paulin (Emily), Nicole Lowrance (Sissie), James DeMarse (Bob), Virginia Kull (Irene); May 28–July 5, 2009

Huntington Theatre Company

Boston, Massachusetts
Twenty-seventh Season
Artistic Director, Peter DuBois; Managing Director, Michael Maso

How Shakespeare Won the West by Richard Nelson; Director, Jonathan Moscone; Scenic Design, Antje Ellermann; Costume Design, Laurie Churba Kohn; Lighting Design, Japhy Weidman; Music and Sound Design, Rob Milburn and Michael Bodeen; Fight Direction, Thomas Schall; Production Stage Manager, Bethany Ford; Stage Manager, Leslie Sears; Cast: Ron Campbell (Abe/Barnum/Buffalo Bill/George Edgar Rice); Chris Henry Coffey (Hank Daley/Man in Buckskin); Nicholas Combs (Ensemble); Jon De Vries (George Demerest/3rd Miner/3rd Actor/Intolerant Man with Rope/Miner Who Loves Leather); Mary Beth Fisher (Alice Calhoun); Kelly Hutchinson (Ruth Oldfield/Laura Agnes); Jeremiah Kissel (Edward Oldfield/2nd Miner/2nd Actor); Curt Klump (Ensemble); Will Lebow (Thomas Jefferson Calhoun/Father on the Prairie); Erik Lochtefeld (Buck Buchanan); Sarah Nealis (Susan Calhoun); Susannah Schulman (Kate Denim/Kate Bateman/Mother on the Prairie); Joe Tapper (John Gough/1st Miner/1st Actor); World Premiere; Boston University Theatre; September 5–October 5, 2008

Adam Pascal Live* A cabaret performance with Adam Pascal (vocals); Larry Edoff (piano); and Joel Rosenblatt (drums); Virginia Wimberly Theatre at the Stanford Calderwood Pavilion at the Boston Center for the Arts; September 18–20th, 2008 *Part of the Huntington Presents series

Boleros for the Disenchanted by José Rivera; Director, Chay Yew; Scenic Design, Alexander Dodge; Costume Design, Anita Yavich; Lighting Design, Paul Whitaker; Music Composition and Sound Design, Fabian Obispo; Production Stage Manager, Lori M. Doyle; Stage Manager, Carola Morrone; Cast: Juan Javier Cardenas (Manuelo/Priest I, II); Flora Diaz (replacement Flora/Eve);

Maria-Christina Oliveras (Petra/Monica); Monica Raymund (Flora/Eve); Socorro Santiago (Dona Milla/Old Flora); Jaime Tirelli (Don Fermin/Old Eusebio); Elliot Villar (Eusebio/Oskar); Virginia Wimberly Theatre at the Stanford Calderwood Pavilion at the Boston Center for the Arts; October 10–November 15, 2008

Wishful Drinking* Created and performed by Carrie Fisher; Director, Tony Taccone; Scenic, Lighting, and Projection Design, Alexander V. Nichols; Production Stage Manager, Daniel Kells; Boston University Theatre, October 10–21, 2008 *Part of the Huntington Presents series

Tom Stoppard's Rock 'n' Roll Director, Carey Perloff; Scenic Design, Douglas W. Schmidt; Costume Design, Alex Jaeger; Lighting Design, Robert Wierzel; Sound Design, Jake Rodriguez; Production Stage Manger, Kimberly Mark Webb; Stage Manager, Jameson R. Croasdale; Cast: René Augesen (Eleanor/Esme (older); Bree Elrod (Gillian/Magda/Dierdre); Manoel Felciano (Jan); Rod Gnapp (Milan); Drew Hirshfield (The Piper/Policeman/Stephen); Delia MacDougall (Lenka); Robert Parsons (Interrogator/Nigel); Marcia Pizzo (Candida); Summer Serafin (Esme (younger)/Alice); Jack Willis (Max); Jud Williford (Ferdinand); Boston University Theatre; November 7 –December 7, 2008

The Corn is Green by Emlyn Williams. Director, Nicholas Martin; Scenic Design, James Noone; Costume Design, Robert Morgan; Lighting Design, France Aronson; Sound Design, Drew Levy; Assistant Director, Erick Herrscher; Production Stage Manager, Brandon Kahn; Stage Manager, Leslie Sears; Cast: Danny Bryck (John Owen); Kate Burton (Miss Moffat); Jared Craig (Idwal Morris); Mary Faber (Bessie Watty); Stephen Gabis (Old Tom) Will LeBow (The Squire); Dan Lovely (Robbart Robbatch); Patrick James Lynch (A Groom); Roderick McLachlan (John Goronwy Jones); Kathy McCafferty (Miss Ronberry); Michael Moran (Glyn Thomas); Kristine Nielsen (Mrs. Watty); Morgan Richie (Morgan Evans); Bobbie Steinbach (Sarah Pugh); Brian Vaughan (Will Hughes); Villagers: Lizzie Bassett, Andy Blaustein, Eliza Fichter, Daniel George, Abigail Gillian, Zachary LeClair, Farrell Parker, Raquel Sandler, Sophie Sinclair, Jordan Ben Sobel, Derek St. Pierre, Greg Stone; Boston University Theatre; January 9–February 8, 2009

Two Men of Florence by Richard N. Goodwin; Director, Edward Hall; Scenic and Costume Design, Francis O'Connor; Lighting Design, Ben Ormerod; Sound Design, Matt McKenzie; Composer, Simon Slater; Production Stage Manager, Gail P. Luna; Stage Manager, Carola Morrone; Cast: Diego Arciniegas (Bruno/Venetian Senator/Richelieu/Firenzuola/Simplico); Teddy Bourgeois (Ensemble); Dermot Crowley (Monsignor Giovanni Ciampoli); Joe Curnutte (Venetian Senator/Louis XIII/Nobleman/Lorenzo Bernini); Nat DeWolf (Venetian Senator/Grand Duke Cosimo II); Edward Hermann (Maffeo Barberini/Later Pope Urban VIII); Jeremiah Kissel (Niccolini); Andy Paris (Young Francesco Barberini); Joel Rainwater (Father Benedetto Castelli); Jay O. Sanders (Galileo Galilei); Molly Schreiber (Maria Celeste); Peter Van Wagner (Cardinal Bellarmine/Venetian Senator/Wackher/B. Landini); World Premiere; Boston University Theatre; March 6–April 5, 2009

The Miracle at Naples by David Grimm; Director, Peter DuBois; Scenic Design, Alexander Dodge; Costume Design, Anita Yavich; Lighting Design, Rui Rita; Sound Design, Ben Emerson; Production Stage Manager, Leslie Sears; Stage Manager, Amy Weissenstein; Cast: Paul Cereghino (Ensemble); Alma Cuervo (Francescina); Lucy DeVito (La Piccola); Sam Kikes (Ensemble); Dick Latessa (Don Bertolino Fortunato); Alfredo Narciso (Giancarlo); Rebecca Newman (Ensemble); Pedro Pascal (Tristano); Christina Pumariega (Flaminia); Gregory Wooddell (Matteo); World Premiere; Virginia Wimberly Theatre at the Stanford Calderwood Pavilion at the Boston Center for the Arts; April 3–May 9, 2009

Pirates! (or, Gilbert and Sullivan Plunder'd) Book and lyrics by William S. Gilbert; Music by Arthur Sullivan; Conceived by Gordon Greenberg, Nell Benjamin, and John McDaniel; Additional book and lyrics by Nell Benjamin; Music supervision and arrangements by John McDaniel; Director, Gordon Greenberg; Choreography, Denis Jones; Music Direction, F. Wade Russo; Scenic Design, Rob Bissinger; Costume Design, David C. Woolard; Lighting Design, Jeff Croiter; Sound Design, Drew Levy and Tony Smolenski IV; Orchestrations by Dan DeLange; Fight Direction, Michael Rossmy; Production Stage Manager, Gail P. Luna; Stage Manager, Carola Morone; Cast: Farah Alvin (Mabel); Krista

Buccellato (Cornelia); Anderson Davis (Frederic); Ed Dixon (Major-General); Wes Hart (Pirate); Cady Huffman (Ruth); Mel Johnson, Jr. (Sergeant); Steve Kazee (Pirate King); Sam Kiernan (Pirate/Policeman); Douglas Lyons (Pirate/Policeman); Chris Messina (Pirate/Policeman); Brittney A. Morello (Pippa); Julia Osborne (Edith); Joel Perez (Pirate); Michael Rossmy (Pirate); Caesar Samayoa (Samuel); Dave Schoonover (Pirate); Kristen Sergeant (Kate); Christopher Sergeeff (Pirate/Policeman); Erica Spyres (Isabel); Victor J. Wisehart (Pirate); Sarah Ziegler (Jane); Boston University Theatre, May 15–June 14, 2009

Indiana Repertory Theatre

Indianapolis, Indiana
Thirty-seventh Season
Artistic Director, Janet Allen; Managing Director, Steven Stolen

Sherlock Holmes: The Final Adventure by Sir Arthur Conan Doyle; Adapted by Steven Dietz; Director, Peter Amster; Sets, Russell Metheny; Costumes, Tracy Dorman; Lighting, Shannon McKinney; Sound, Joe Cerqua; Stage Manager, Nathan Garrison; Dialect Coach, Nancy Lipschultz; Cast: Jonathan Gillard Daly (Sherlock Holmes), Mark Goetzinger (Doctor Watson), Nigel Patterson (Professor Moriarty), Robert Neal (The King of Bohemia), Michele Graff (Irene Adler), Ryan Artzberger (James Larrabee), Diane Kondrat (Madge Larrabee), Robert K. Johansen (Sid Prince/Policeman/Postboy/Clergyman/Swiss Man); Mainstage; September 16–October 11, 2008

Macbeth by William Shakespeare; Director, Janet Allen; Sets, Gordon Strain; Costumes, Myron Elliott, Jr.; Lighting, Betsy Cooprider-Bernstein; Sound, Todd Mack Reischman; Stage Manager, Amy K. Denkmann; Cast: Milicent Wright (With/Muderer/Gentlewoman), Alexa Silvaggio (Witch/Murderer/Lady Macduff), Kristin Dulaney (Witch/Murderer), Frederick Marshall (Duncan/Porter/Seyton), David Stratton White (Malcolm), Evan McCullough (Donalbain/Young Soldier), Ben Tebbe (Lennox), John Robert Armstrong (Ross), Andrew Ahrens (Macbeth), Michael Shelton (Banquo), Jennifer Johansen (Lady Macbeth), Chris Hatch (Macduff), Taylor Kleyn (Fleance/Young Macduff); Upperstage; October 10–November 8, 2008

A Christmas Carol by Charles Dickens; Adapted by Tom Haas; Director, Priscilla Lindsay; Sets, Russell Metheny; Costumes, Murell Horton; Lighting, Michael Lincoln; Assistant Lighting, Besty Cooprider-Bernstein; Sound, Andrew Hopson; Stage Manager, Nathan Garrison; Choreography, David Hochoy; Musical Director, Christopher Ludwa; Cast: Charles Goad (Ebenezer Scrooge), Robert K. Johansen (Bob Cratchit/Schoolmaster/Undertaker), Jason Bradley (Fred Smackers), Kate Goetzinger (Felicity/Martha), Brian Noffke (Portly Gent/Young Marley/Broker 3), Lynne Perkins (Sister of Mercy/Charwoman/Mrs. Fezziwig), Constance Macy (Rose's Sister/Mrs. Cratchit), Mark Szewczyk (Belle's Husband/Waiter/Post Boy/Broker 1/ Poulter's Man), Mark Goetzinger (Marley's Ghost/Christmas Present/Old Joe/Solicitor), Alan Schmuckler (Christmas Past/Nutley/Coal Porter), Robert Neal (Fezziwig/Topper/Christmas Future/Doctor), Gwendolyn Whiteside (Belle/Maid/Fan), Lloyd Mulvey (Young Scrooge/Lamplighter/Broker 2), Allison Moody (Laundress/Plump Sister); Mainstage; November 15–December 28, 2008

This Wonderful Life by Steve Murray, conceived by Mark Setlock; Director, David Bradley; Sets, Jack McGaw; Costumes, Wendy Meaden; Lighting, Michael Lincoln; Sound, Todd Mack Reischman; Stage Manager, Amy K. Denkmann; Cast: Jerry Richardson (Narrator); Upperstage; November 25, 2008–January 4, 2009

To Kill a Mockingbird by Harper Lee; Adapted by Christopher Sergel; Director, Priscilla Lindsay; Sets, Robert M. Koharchik; Costumes, Linda Pisano; Lighting, Robert A. Shakespeare; Sound, Todd Mack Reischman; Stage Managers, Nathan Garrison, Tarin Hurstell; Cast: Tessa Buzzetti (Jean Louise Finch), Quentin Toetz (Jeremy Finch), Mark Goetzinger (Atticus Finch), Dwandra Nickole (Calpurnia), Lynne Perkins (Maudie Atkinson), Constance Macy (Stephanie Crawford),

Frederick Marshall (Mr. Dubose/Judge Taylor/Walter Cunningham), Robert Neal (Arthur Radley/Mr. Gilmer), Joseph J. Mervis (Charles Baker Harris), Charles Goad (Heck Tate), J. Blakemore (Revered Sykes), Nijay Johnson (Hattie Sykes), Melissa Fenton (Mayella Ewell), Robert K. Johansen (Bob Ewell), Johnathan Tremaine (Tom Robinson); Mainstage; January 23–February 21, 2009

Crime and Punishment by Fyodor Dostoevsky; Adapted by Marilyn Campbell and Curt Columbus; Director, John Green; Sets, Robert M. Koharchik; Costumes, Joel Ebarb; Lighting, Ryan Koharchik; Sound, Todd Mack Reischman; Stage Manager, Amy K. Denkmann; Cast: Andrew Ahrens (Raskolnikov), Peter Defaria (Porifry), Jenny McKnight (Sonia); Upperstage; February 10–March 8, 2009

The Ladies Man by Georges Feydeau; Adapted by Charles Morey; Director, Charles Morey; Sets, Bill Clarke; Costumes, Pamela Scofield; Lighting, Phil Monat; Sound, Joe Payne; Stage Manager, Nathan Garrison; Dialect Coach, Nancy Lipschultz; Cast: Michael Keyloun (Etienne), Morgan Hallett (Marie), Kelly Mares (Yvonne Molineaux), Max Robinson (Dr. Hercule Molineaux), John Guerrasio (Bassinet), Nance Williamson (Madame Aigreville), Jennifer Johansen (Suzanne Aubin), Mark Mineart (Gustav Aubin); Mainstage; March 3–22, 2009

Crowns by Regina Taylor; Adapted from the book by Michael Cunningham and Craig Marberry; Director, Patdro Harris; Sets, Felix E. Cochren; Costumes, Reggie Ray; Lighting, Jennifer Setlow; Sound, Jonathan Herter; Stage Manager, Amy K. Denkmann; Music Director, William Hubbard; Assistant Director, Connie Oates-Allen; Cast: Dennis W. Spears (Man), Shannon Antalan (Yolanda), Chandra Currelley (Mother Shaw), Crystal Fox (Jeanette), Roz White (Velma), Valerie Payton (Mabel), Terry Burrell (Wanda); Mainstage; April 7–May 2, 2009

Rabbit Hole by David Lindsay-Abaire; Director, James Still; Sets, Kate Sutton-Johnson; Costumes, Tracy Dorman; Lighting, Michael Lincoln; Sound, Michael Keck; Stage Manager, Tarin Hurstell; Cast: Lauren Lovett (Becca), Gwendolyn Whiteside (Izzy), Ryan Artzberger (Howie), Priscilla Lindsay (Nat), Drew Paramore (Jason); Upperstage; April 21–May 10, 2009

Interpreting William by James Still; Director, Lisa Rothe; Sets, Ann Sheffield; Costumes, Alex Jaeger; Lighting, Mary Louise Geiger; Sound, Todd Mack Reischman; Stage Manager, Nathan Garrison; Composer, Kim D. Sherman; Cast: David Alan Anderson (Bill), Tim Grimm (William Conner), Carmen Roman (Anna), Lena Hurt (Naomi), Delanna Studi (Mekinges/Liz), Robert Neal (John Conner/Stephen); World Premiere; Mainstage; May 12–31, 2009

Intiman Theatre

Seattle, Washington
Thirty-sixth Season
Artistic Director, Bartlett Sher; Interim Managing Director, Kevin Maifeld; Managing Director, Brian Coburn

The Diary of Anne Frank Dramatized by Frances Goodrich and Albert Hackett; Director, Sari Ketter; Sets, Nayna Ramey; Costumes, Frances Kenny; Lighting, Marcus Dilliard; Sound, Chris R. Walker; New York Casting, Janet Foster, C.S.A.; SM, Lisa Ann Chernoff; ASM, Jessi Wasson; Cast: Matthew Boston (Mr. Frank), Alban Dennis (Mr. Dussel), Lucy DeVito (Anne Frank), Lindsay Evans (Margot Frank), Jim Gall (Mr. Kraler), Carol Roscoe (Miep), Shellie Shulkin (Mrs. Van Daan), Amy Thone (Mrs. Frank), Conor Toms (Peter Van Daan), Michael Winters (Mr. Van Daan); March 21–May 17, 2008

Namaste Man by Andrew Weems; Director, Bartlett Sher; Sets and Costumes, Elizabeth Caitlin War; Lighting, Greg Sullivan; Sound, Peter John Still; Dramaturg, Mame Hunt; SM, Lisa Ann Chernoff; Cast: Andrew Weems; World Premiere; May 30–June 22, 2008

A Streetcar Named Desire by Tennessee Williams; Director, Sheila Daniels; Sets, Thomas Lynch; Costumes, Frances Kenny; Lighting and Projections, L.B. Morse; Composer, Jose J. Gonzales; Sound, Joseph Swartz; Fight Choreographer, Peter Dylan O'Connor; Dialect Coach, Lisa Norman; New York Casting, Janet Foster, C.S.A.; SM, Amy Poisson; ASM, Whitney Meredith Breite; Cast: Colin L. Byrne (Young Collector/Musician), Jose J. Gonzales (Pablo Gonzales/Musician), Timothy Hyland (Steve Hubbell), Charles Leggett (Doctor/Cop/Musician), Rebecca Meneses (Flower Seller/Prostitute/Musician), Angela Pierce (Blanche DuBois), Shelley Reynolds (Eunice Hubbell), Chelsey Rives (Stella Kowalski), Jonno Roberts (Stanley Kowalski), Khatt Taylor (Neighbor Woman/Nurse), Tim True (Mitch); July 3–August 2, 2008

The Little Dog Laughed by Douglas Carter Beane; Director, Fracaswell Hyman; Sets, Matthew Smucker; Costumes, Elizabeth Hope Clancy; Lighting, Greg Sullivan; Sound, Joseph Swartz; New York Casting, Janet Foster, C.S.A.; SM, Marianne C. Wunch; ASM, Jenna Kearns; Cast: Neal Bledsoe (Mitchell), Quinlan Corbett (Alex), Megan Hill (Ellen), Christa Scott-Reed (Diane); August 15–September 13, 2008

All the King's Men by Robert Penn Warren; Adapted by Adrian Hall; Director, Pam MacKinnon; Sets, Tony Cisek; Costumes, Deb Trout; Lighting, Colin K. Bills; Sound, Joseph Swartz; Music Director/Original Arrangements, Edd Key; Dialect Coach, Judith Shahn; New York Casting, Janet Foster, C.S.A.; SM, William Vann Carlton; ASM, Paulette Buse; Cast: Zaki Abdelhamid (Tom Stark/Ensemble), Philip Davidson (Judge Irwin/Ensemble), Amy Fleetwood (Lucy Stark/Ensemble), Mark Fullerton (Alex Michel/Byram B. White/Old Man/Ensemble), Alyssa Keene (Miss Dumonde/Nurse/Ensemble), Edd Key (Old Man/Ensemble), James Lapan (Sheriff/Theodore Murrell/Dr. Bland/Ensemble), Lori Larsen (Mother/Ensemble), Eddie Levi Lee (Tiny Duffy/Ensemble), Todd Licea (Adam Stanton/Ensemble), Deirdre Madigan (Sadie Burke/Ensemble), Leo Marks (Jack Burden), Marty Mukhalian (Slade/Mrs. Patton/Lily Littlepaugh/Ensemble), Peter Dylan O'Connor (Sugar-Boy/George/Ensemble), Michael Patten (Callahan/Dolph Pillsbury/Hugh Miller/Ensemble), Larry Paulsen (Ellis Burden/Editor/Mr. Patton/Ensemble), John Procaccino (Willie Stark), Betsy Schwartz (Anne Stanton/Ensemble); September 26–November 8, 2008

Black Nativity by Langston Hughes; Director, Jacqueline Moscou; Musical Direction and Arrangements, Pastor Patrinell Wright; Choreography, Kabby Mitchell III; Sets, Dana Perreault; Costumes, Doris Black; Lighting, Allen Lee Hughes; Sound, Joseph Swartz; Dramaturg, Elizabeth Heffron; SM, Antina Campbell; ASM, Parker Wolf; Cast: Rev. Mr. Joseph E. Connor (Narrator), Bojohn Diciple (Joseph), G. To'mas Jones (Narrator), Pamela Yasutake (Mary), Phyllis C. Yasutake (Narrator), Pastor Patrinell Wright (The Woman), The Total Experience Gospel Choir, The Black Nativity Choir, Timothy E. Davis (Piano), Walter Finch (Lead Guitar), Matthew D.L. Montgomery (Piano), Rick Pitts (Bass Guitar); November 29–December 27, 2008

Kansas City Repertory Theatre

Kansas City, Missouri
Fourty-fifth Season
Artistic Director, Eric Rosen
Managing Director, Cynthia Rider; Producing Director, Jerry Genochio

Clay by Matt Sax; Score, Matt Sax, Johnny Williams, John Schmidt; Director, Eric Rosen; Sets, Meghan Raham; Costumes, Emily Rebholz; Lighting, Jason Lyons; Orchestration/Sound, Joshua Horvath; PSM, Dennis Conners; Cast: Matt Sax; Copaken Stage; September 6–28, 2008

Radio Golf by August Wilson; Director, Lou Bellamy; Sets, Vicki Smith; Costumes, Mathew J. LeFebvre; Lighting, Michelle Habeck; Sound, John Story;

Assistant Director, Kyle Hatley; Casting, Harriet Bass; PSM, Mary R. Honour; ASMs, Beth Ellen Spencer, Brooke Redler; Cast: Julia Pace Mitchell (Mame Wilks), Kevyn Morrow (Harmond Wilks), Wiley Moore (Roosevelt Hicks), Abdul Salaam El Razzac (Elder Joseph Barlow), Stanley Wayne Mathis (Sterling Johnson); Spencer Theatre; Oct. 17–Nov. 9, 2008

A Christmas Carol by Charles Dickens; Adaptation, Barbara Field; Director, Linda Ade Brand; Sets, John Ezell; Costumes, Megan Turek; Lighting, Shane Rowse; Sound, John Story; Musical Director, Mark Ferrell, Choreography, Jennifer Martin; Assistant Director, Kyle Hatley; PSM, Beth Ellen Spencer; ASM, Brooke Redler; Cast: Robert Gibby Brand (Charles Dickens), Gary Neal Johnson (Ebenezer Scrooge), Walter Coppage (Bob Cratchit), Charles Fugate (Fred), Bruce Roach (Marley), Brad Shaw (Solicitor/Ghost of Christmas Future/Ensemble), Merle Moores (Solicitor/Grandma Fezziwig/Charwoman), Anthony Vaughn Merchant (Poulterer/Bobby/Ensemble), Andrea Agosto (Clovia/Poulterer's wife/Ensemble), Ruby Dibble (Ensemble), Kelsey Kallenberger (Ensemble), Ashley Beth Burnett (Saphronella/Maid/Ensemble), Elizabeth Ernst (Ensemble), Emily Levinson (Want/Ensemble), Brady Metcalf (Ensemble), Doogin Brown (Dick Wilkins/Young Man/Toy Vendor/Ensemble), Julane Havens (Fan/Martha/Ensemble), Brock Christian Lorenzen (Boy Scrooge/Ensemble), Jim Gall (Rat catcher/Ghost of Christmas Present), Bruce Roach (Marley), Kathleen Warfel (Ghost of Christmas Past), Zachary Hoar (Boy Scrooge/Ensemble), Grant Lorenzen (Tiny Tim), Whittaker Hoar (Tiny Tim), Grant Lorenzen (Tiny Tim/School boy), Brennan Hilleary (Ensemble), TJ Chasteen (Young Scrooge/Businessman/Ensemble), Vanessa Severo (Belle/Mrs. Fred), Jeanne Averill (Mrs. Cratchit/Ensemble), Aaron Caselman (Ensemble), Danny Cox (Mr. Fezziwig/Ensemble), Patrick DuLaney (Topper/Ensemble), Peggy Friesen (Mrs. Fezziwig/Harpist), Katie Hall (Belinda Cratchit/Ensemble), Sarah LaBarr (Auntie Fezziwig/Ensemble), Todd Carlton Lanker (Albert Hall/Ensemble), Ashlee LaPine (Giggly sister/Ensemble), Brock Christian Lorenzen (Boy Scrooge/Ensemble), Katherine McNamara (Belinda Cratchit/Ensemble), andi Meyer (Serious sister/Ensemble), Mark Robbins (Old Joe/Ensemble), Cheryl Weaver (Laundress/Ensemble), Jordan Lee Wooten (Peter Cratchit/Ensemble); Spencer Theatre; November 22–Dec. 27, 2008

The Glass Menagerie by Tennessee Williams; Director, David Cromer; Sets, Collette Pollard; Costumes, Janice Pytel; Lighting and Projection, Jeffrey Cady; Sound, Josh Schmidt; Assistant Director, Kyle Hatley; PSM, Mary R. Honour; Cast: Derek Hasenstab (Tom Wingfield), Annalee Jefferies (Amanda Wingfield), Susan Bennett (Laura Wingfield), Kyle Hatley (Jim O'Connor); Copaken Stage; January 9–February 15, 2009

Susan Bennett and Lee Fefferies in The Glass Menagerie
(photos by Don Ipock)

The Arabian Nights by Mary Zimmerman; Director, Mary Zimmerman; Sets, Daniel Ostling; Costumes, Mara Blumenfeld; Original Composition and Sound, Andre Pluess /The Lookingglass Ensemble; Lighting, T.J. Gerckens; Casting, Stephanie Klapper/Amy Potozkin; PSM, Cynthia Cahill; ASM, Beth Ellen Spencer; Cast: Ryan Artzberger (King Shahryar), Allen Gilmore (Scheherezade's Father/Ishak of Mosul/others), Sofia Jean Gomez (Scheherezade), Stacey Yen (Dunyazade/Azizah/others), Barzin Akhavan (Harun al-Rashid/others), Louis Tucci (Jafar/Sheik al-Fadl/others), Noshir Dalal (Madman, Greengrocer/others), Pranidhi Varshney (Slave girl/others), Melina Kalomas (Perfect Love/others), Evan Zes (Sheik al-Islam/Abu al-Hasan/others), Nicole Shalhoub (The Jester's Wife/The Other Woman/others), Alana Arenas (Butcher/Sympathy the Learned/others), Ramiz Monsef (Clarinetist/Sage/others), Ari Brand (Poor Man/Boy/others); Spencer Theatre; January 30–February 22, 2009

Winesburg, Ohio by Sherwood Anderson; Book and Lyrics, Eric Rosen; Music and additional lyrics, Andre Pluess, Ben Sussman; Director, Eric Rosen; Music Director, Molly Jessup; Sets, Jack Magaw; Costumes, Janice Pytel; Lighting, David Lander; Sound, Joshua Horvath; Orchestrations, Thomas Murray; Choreography, Jennifer Martin; Casting, Stephanie Klapper; Stage Manager, Mary R. Honour; Assistant Stage Manager, Brooke Redler; Cast: Jessalyn Kincaid (Young Elizabeth/others), James Judy (the Writer), Leslie Denniston (Elizabeth Willard), Gary Neal Johnson (Tom Willard/others), Geoff Packard (George Willard), Lesley Bevan (Kate Swift/others), Nancy Anderson (Alice Hindman/others), Seth Golay (Seth Richmond/others), Gary Holcombe (Wing Biddlebaum/others), Ashlee LaPine (Helen White/others), Bruce Roach (Joe Welling/others), John-Michael Zuerlein (Enoch Robinson/others), Jeff parker (Rev. Curtis Hartman/others), Musicians: Michalis Koutsoupides (Conductor/piano), Ryan Fisher (Guitar 1), Aaron Fry (Guitar 2), Rick Willoughby (Bass), Michael Winer (Violin); Spencer Theatre; March 13–April 5, 2009

The Borderland by Jim Grimsley; Director, Kyle Hatley; Sets, Meghan Raham; Costumes, A.W. Nadine Grant; Lighting, Victor En Yu Tan; Sound, Eric Sefton; Casting, Claire Simon, C.S.A.; PSM, Beth Ellen Spencer; Cast: Carla Noack (Helen Hammond), Matthew Rapport (Gordon Hammond), Angela Cristantello (Eleanor Rollins), Matthew Brumlow (Jake Rollins); Copaken Stage; April 3–26, 2009

A Flea in Her Ear by Georges Feydeau; Adaptation, David Ives; Director, Gary Griffin; Sets, Jack Magaw; Costumes, Mara Blumenfeld; Lighting, Jason Lyons; Sound, John Story; New York Casting, Stephanie Klapper; PSM, Mary R. Honour; ASM, Brooke Redler; Cast: Martin Buchanan (Etienne), Katie Kalahurka (Antoinette), Jonathan Root (Camille Chandebise), Mark Robbins (Dr. Finache), Anne L. Nathan (Lucienne Homenides), Carol Halstead (Raymonde Chandebise), John Scherer (Victor Chandebise/Poche), John Pasha (Romain Tournel), Thom Rivera (Carlos Homenides), Scott Cordes (Ferraillon), Lauren Lubow (Eugénie), Cheryl Weaver (Olympia), Allan Boardman (Baptiste), Michelangelo Milano (Rugby); Spencer Theatre; May 15–June 7, 2009

Anne L. Nathan and Carol Halstead in A Flea in Her Ear

La Jolla Playhouse

La Jolla, California
Thirty-ninth Season
Artistic Director, Christopher Ashley; Managing Director, Michael Rosenberg

33 Variations by Moises Kaufman; Music by Ludwig Van Beethoven; Director, Moises Kaufman; Set, Derek McLane; Costumes, Janice Pytel; Lighting, David Lander; Sound, Andre; Pluess; Choreography, Daniel Pelzig; Dramaturg, Mark Bly; LJP Dramaturg, Shirley Fishman; Wig Design, Charles LaPointe; Projection Design, Jeff Sugg; Casting, Telsey + Company; Stage Manager, Linda Marvel; Cast: Don Amendolia, Jayne Atkinson, Zach Grenier, Susan Kellermann, Ryan King, Laura Odeh, Erik Steele, Diane Walsh; April 8–May 4, 2008

The Night Watcher by Charlayne Woodward, Original Music by Karl Fredrik Lundeberg; Director, Robert Egan; Set, Myung Hee Cho and Ann Sheffield; Costumes, Myung Hee Cho and Ann Sheffield; Lighting, Stephen Sakowski; Sound, Karl Fredrik Lundeberg; Dramaturg, Shirley Fishman; Production Manager, Peter J. Davis; Stage Manager, Kelly Glasow; Cast: Charlayne Woodard; July 1–July 27, 2008

Memphis Book and Lyrics by Joe DiPietro, Music and Lyrics by David Bryan, Based on a Concept by George W. George; Director, Christopher Ashley; Set, David Gallo; Costumes, Paul Tazewell; Lighting Howell Binkley; Sound, Ken Travis; Choreography, Sergio Trujillo; Dance Arrangement, August Eriksmoen; Music Director, Kenny Seymour; Music Production, Christopher Jahnke; Orchestration, Daryl Waters; Preojection Design, Shawn Sagady and David Gallo; Wig Design, Charles G. LaPointe; Dialect Coach, Joel Goldes; Fight Director, Steve Rankin; Dramaturg, Gabriel Greene; Casting, Telsey + Company; Production Manager, Peter J. Davis; Stage Managers, Frank Hartenstein and Kelly A. Martindale; Cast: Brad Bass, Tracee Beazer, Josh Breckinridge, J. Bernard Calloway, Lorene Chesley, Kevin Covert, Dionne, D. Figgins, Allen Fitzpatrick, Montego Glover, Steve Gunderson, James Monroe Iglehart, Lauren Lim Jackson, Chad Kimball, Cashae Monya, Cass Morgan, Jill Morrison, Irungu Mutu, Jiehae Park, John Eric Parker, Jermaine R. Rembert, Pearl Rhein, Melanie Vaughan, Michael Benjamin Washington, Daniel J. Watts, Charlie Williams, Megan Yelaney; August 19–September 28, 2008

The Third Story by Charles Busch; Original Music by Lewis Flinn; Director, Carl Andress; Set, David Gallo; Costumes, Gregory Gale; Lighting, Christopher Akerlind; Sound, Walter Trarbach; Hair and Wig Design, Tom Watson; Dramaturg, Shirley Fishman; Voice and Dialect Coach, Eva Wielgat Barnes; Fight Director, Steve Rankin; Production Manager, Linda S. Cooper; Casting, Telsey + Company; Stage Manager, Lisa Porter; Cast: Charles Busch, Rebecca Lawrence, Scott Parkinson, Mary Beth Peil, Jennifer Van Dyck, Jonathan Walker; September 16–October 19, 2008

Tobacco Road Adapted by Jack Kirkland; Novel by Erskine Caldwell; Director, David Schweizer; Set, David Zinn; Costumes, David Zinn; Lighting, Christopher Akerlind; Sound and Composition, Sharokh Yadegari; Voice and Dialect Coach, Annie Hinton; Dramaturg, Gabriel Greene; Fight Master, George Yé; Production Manager, Peter J. Davis and Linda S. Cooper; Casting, Telsey + Company; Stage Manager, Anjee Nero; Cast: Lucy Ann Albert, Catherine Curtin, Kate Dalton, Mary Deaton, John Fleck, Joel J. Gelman, Jan Leslie Harding, Jess MacKinnon, Chris Reed, Sam Rosen, Josh Wade; September 30–October 26, 2008

Xanadu Book by Douglas Carter Beane; Music and Lyrics by Jeff Lynne and John Farrar, Based on the Universal Pictures Film Screenplay by Richard Danus and Marc Rubel; Director, Christopher Ashley; Set, David Gallo; Costumes, David Zinn; Lighting, Howell Binkley; Sound, Dan Moses Schreier; Choreography, Dan Knechtges; Music Director/Conductor, Jess Vargas; Music Supervisor/Arranger, Erick Stern; Music Coordination, John Miller; Projection Design, Zachary Borovay; Wig and Hair Design, Charles G. LaPointe; Dramaturg, Shirley Fishman; Stage Manager, Allen McMullen; Casting, Cindy Tolan; Cast: Talia Brinson, Joanna Glushak, Amy Goldberger, Larry Marshall, Vincent Rodriguez III, Jason

Michael Snow, Elizabeth Stanley, Kristopher L. Stock, Wayne Stribling, Jr., Julius Thomas III, Tiffany Topol, Max von Essen, Sharon Wilkins, J.B. Wing; November 11–December 21, 2008

Peter and the Starcatchers Book by Rick Elice, Music and Lyrics by Wayne Barker; Director, Roger Rees and Alex Timbers; Set, Neil Patel; Costumes, Paloma H. Young; Lighting, Jeff Croiter; Sound, Phil Allen; Choreography, Kelly Devine; Dramaturg, Ken Cerniglia and Gabriel Greene; Associate Producer, Dana I. Harrel; Associate Sound Designer, Ian Burch; Stage Manager, Clifford Schwartz; Assistant Stage Manager, Annette Ye; Cast: Adam Green, Carson Elrod, Andrew McGinn, David Rossmer, Christian Borle, Teddy Bergman, Celia Keenan-Bolger, John G. Preston, Irungu Mutu, Carlie Reuter, Jared Dager, Ron Choularton, Maggie Carney, Kevin Johnston, Johnny Wu; February 13–March 8, 2009

Maltz Jupiter Theatre

Jupiter, Florida
Sixth Season
Artistic Director, Andrew Kato; Managing Director, Tricia Trimble

Noises Off by Michael Frayn; Director, David H. Bell; Set, James Leonard Joy; Costumes, David Kay Mickelsen; Lighting, Joseph Appelt; Sound, James C. Swonger; Resident Sound Designer, Keith Kohrs; Voice/Text Coach, Don Wadsworth; Assistant Director, Scott Weinstein; Assistant Lighting Designer, Sara Hughly; Stage Manager, Andrew John Tucker; Assistant Stage Manager, Tara Weidenfeller; Associate Producer/Company Manager, Rachel Blacatnik; Production Manager, Molly Elizabeth McCarter; Technical Director, Bobby Brinson; Master Electrician, Jesse Sutten; Audio Engineer, Lane Starratt; Costume Shop Manager, Jenna Hoefert; Properties Mistress, Teresa J. Campani; Deck Chief, Nicholas Whipple; Wardrobe Mistress, Anna Hillbery; Deck Hand, Sima Bressler and Tyler Shaw; Cast: Linda Kimbrough (Dotty Otley/Mrs. Clackett), Timothy Gregory (Lloyd Dallas), Christopher Kelly (Garry Lejeune/Roger Tramplemain), Summer Naomi Smart (Brooke Ashton/Viki), Donald Carrier (Frederick Fellowes/Phillip Bent/Sheikh), Isabel Liss (Belinda Blair/Flavia Bent), Cassandra Bissell (Poppy Norton-Taylor), Bob Turton (Tim Allgood), Frank Kopyc (Selsdon Mowbray/Burglar); November 11–23, 2008

Sleuth by Anthony Shaffer; Director, Peter Flynn; Set/Costumes, Michael Bottari and Ronald Case; Lighting, Donald Edmund Thomas; Sound, Keith Kohrs; Fight Choreography, Lee Soroko; Stage Manager, Emily Swiderski; Assistant Stage Manager, Aprilrose Manza; Associate Producer/Company Manager, Rachel Blavatnik; Production Manager, Molly Elizabeth McCarter; Technical Director, Bobby Brinson; Master Electrician, Jesse Sutten; Audio Engineer, Lan Starratt; Costume Shop Manager, Jenna Hoefert; Properties Mistress, Teresa J. Campani; Deck Chief, Nicholas Whipple; Wardrobe Mistress, Anna Hillbery; Deck Hand, Sima Bressler; Wig and Makeup, Gerard Kelly; Cast: Mark Jacoby (Andrew Wyke), Jeremy Webb (Milo Tindle), Stanley Rushton (Inspector Doppler), Robin Mayfield (Detective Sergeant Tarrant), Liam McNutuley (Police Constable Higgs); December 2–14, 2008

Barnum Music by Cy Coleman, Lyrics by Michael Stewart, Book by Mark Bramble; Director, Gordon Greenberg; Choreography, Joshua Rhodes; Music Director, Helen Gregory; Set, Michael Schweikardt; Costumes, Alejo Vietti, Sound, Keith Kohrs; Wig/Hair, Michelle Hart; Circus Consultant, Pedro Reis; Assistant Director, Wes Grantom; Light Assistant, Richard Chamblin; Stage Manager, Andrew John Tucker; Assistant Stage Manager, Tara Weidenfeller; Associate Producer/Company Manager, Rachel Blavatnik; Production Manager, Molly Elizabeth McCarter: Technical Director, Bobby Brinson; Master Electrician, Jesse Sutten; Audio Engineer, Lane Starratt; Costume Shop Manager, Jenna Hoefert;

Properties Mistress, Teresa J. Campani; Deck Chief, Nicholas Whipple; Wardrobe Supervisor, Anna Hillbery; Spot Operator, Sima Bressler and Chris Cordova; Fly Man, Tyler Shaw; Deck Hand, Jared Slater and Dale Bassing; Dresser, Teresa J. Campani and BrAndy DeMil; Cast: Brad Oscar (P.T. Barnum), Misty Cotton (Chairy Barnum), Kevin Kraft (Ringmaster/Lyman/Scudder/Stratton/Goldschmidt/Concertmaster/Wilton/Morrissey/Bailey), Debra Walton (Joice Heth/Blues Singer), Nathaniel Braga (Tom Thumb), Renee Brna (Jenny Lind), Matt Baker (Dream Chiary), Amy Shure (Dream Jenny); January 6–25, 2009

Beehive by Larry Gallagher; Director and Choreography, Mark Martino; Music Director, Tom Frey; Set, Dan Kuchar; Costumes, Jose M. Rivera; Lighting, Donald Edmund Thomas; Projection, David Esler; Sound, Keith Kohrs; Wig, Gerard Kelly; Stage Manager, Emily Swinderski; Assistant Stage Manager, Aprilrose Manza; Associate Producer/Company Manager, Rachel Blavatnik; Production Manager, Molly Elizabeth McCarter; Technical Director, Bobby Brinson; Master Electrician, Jesse Sutten; Audio Engineer, Lane Starratt; Costume Shop Manager, Jenna Hoefert; Properties Mistress, Teresa J. Campani; Deck Chief, Nicholas Whipple; Wardrobe Supervisor, Anna Hillbery; Spot Operator, Sima Bressler and Chris Cordova; Dresser, Wendy Gathers; Cast: Bridget Beirne, Felcia Boswell, Lisa Estridge, Autumn Hurlbert, Anastacia McCleskey, Noel Molinelli; February 3–22, 2009

Evita Book and Lyrics by Tim Rice; music by Andrew Lloyd Webber; Director and Choreography, Marc Robin; Music Director, Helen Gregory; Orchestrations, Steven Bishop; Set, Robert Kovach; Costumes, M. Shan Jensen; Lighting, Donald Edmund Thomas; Sound, Keith Kohrs; Wigs, Gerard Kelly; Stage Manager, Andrew John Tucker; Assistant Stage Manager, Tara Weidenfeller; Associate Producer/Company Manager, Rachel Blavatnik; Production Manager, Molly Elizabeth McCarter; Technical Director, Bobby Brinson; Master Electrician, Jesse Sutten; Audio Engineer, Lane Starratt; Costume Shop Manager, Jenna Hoefert; Properties Mistress, Teresa J. Campani; Deck Chief, Nicholas Whipple; Assistant Costume Designer, Anna Hillbery; Spot Operator, Chris Corcova and Dale Bassing; Dresser, Brandy DeMil; Cast: Jodie Langel (Eva Peron), Rudy Martinez (Che), David Studwell (Juan Peron), Curt Dale Clark (Agustin Magaldi), Kelley McGillicuddy (Peron's Mistress), Ensemble: Mark Willis Borum, Sydney Carbo, Elizabeth Casalini, Desiree Davar, Alce Eacho, Tiffany Huet, Jay Johnson, Ken McMullen, Jo Patrick, Lisa Rumbaukas, Christopher Ryan, Nick Savarese, Michael Scirrotto, Patty Shukla, Sidney Erik Wright; Choir: Colleen Broom, Sarah Evans, Matthew Mellusi, Lauren Mulrooney, Valentina Pierce, Alina Pimentel, Aidan Renda, Emily Rynasko, Molli Sramowicz, Emily Sima, Elli Sweet; March 17–April 5, 2009

McCarter Theatre Center

Princeton, New Jersey
Forty-ninth Season
Artistic Director, Emily Mann; Managing Director, Timothy J. Shields

Herringbone book by Tom Cone; Music by Skip Kennon; Lyrics by Ellen Fitzhugh; Director, Roger Rees; Set, Eugene Lee; Costumes, William Ivey Long; Lighting, Kenneth Posner; Sound, Scott Lehrer and Leon Rothenberg; Musical Director, Dan Lipton; Choreography, Darren Lee; PSM, Cheryl Mintz; Cast: BD Wong (Herringbone), Musicians: Dan Lipton (Piano), Benjamin Campbell (Bass), Richard Huntley (Drums); Berlind Theatre; September 5–October 12, 2008

Talley's Folly by Lanford Wilson; Director, Marshall W. Mason; Set, John Lee Beatty; Costumes, Jennifer von Mayrhauser; Lighting, Phil Monat; Sound, Chuck London; PSM, Alison Cote; Cast: Richard Schiff (Matt Friedman), Margot White (Sally Talley); Matthews Theatre; October 12–November 2, 2008

A Christmas Carol by Charles Dickens; Adapted by David Thompson; Director, Michael Unger; Set, Ming Cho Lee; Costumes, Jess Goldstein; Lighting, Stephen Strawbridge; Sound, Brian Ronan; Original Music and Lyrics, Michael Starobin; Choreography, Rob Ashford; Musical Director, Charles Sundquist; Dialect Coach, Hazel Bowers; Supervising SM, Cheryl Mintz; SM, Hannah Woodward; Cast: Lisa Altomare (Mrs. Dilber), Dermot Crowley (Ebenezer Scrooge), Richard Gallagher (Young Scrooge/Mr. Bonds), Karron Graves (Fan/Mrs. Bonds), Stephen James King (Jacob Marley/Mr. Stocks), James Ludwig (Bob Cratchit), Janet Metz (Mrs. Cratchit), Ned Noyes (Fred/Undertaker), John O'Creagh (Mr. Fezziwig/Old Joe), Anne O'Sullivan (Mrs. Fezziwig/Mrs. Stocks/Laundress), Karen Pittman (Lily/Belle), Nikki E. Walker (Christmas Present); Matthews Theatre; December 7–28, 2008

Mrs. Warren's Profession by George Bernard Shaw; Director, Emily Mann; Set, Eugene Lee; Costumes, Jennifer von Mayrhauser; Lighting, Jeff Croiter; Sound, Karin Graybash; PSM, Alison Cote; Cast: Suzanne Bertish (Mrs. Warren), Robin Chadwick (Reverend Samuel Gardner), Edward Hibbert (Mr. Praed), Madeline Hutchins (Vivie Warren), Michael Izquierdo (Frank Gardner), Rocco Sisto (Sir George Crofts); Berlind Theatre; January 9–February 15, 2009

Eclipsed by Danai Gurira; Director, Liesl Tommy; Set, Carrie Ballenger; Costumes, Cynthia Abel Thom; Lighting, Paul Kilsdonk; Sound, Bill Kirby; Line Producer, Adam Immerwahr; Dramaturg, Carrie Hughes; PSM, Cheryl Mintz; Cast: Pascale Armand (Bessie), Nikiya Mathis (Maima), Keiana Richàrd (The Girl), Stacey Sargeant (Helena), April Yvette Thompson (Rita); The Room in the Berlind Theatre; January 29–February 8, 2009

Twelfth Night by William Shakespeare; Director, Rebecca Taichman; Set, Riccardo Hernandez; Costumes, Miranda Hoffman; Lighting, Christopher Akerlind; Original Music and Sound, Martin Desjardins; PSM, Alison Cote; SM, Lauren Kurinskas; Fight Director, Rick Sordelet; Choreography, Seán Curran; Cast: Rebecca Brooksher (Viola), Veanne Cox (Olivia), Stephen DeRosa (Feste), Rich Foucheux (Sir Toby Belch), Christopher Innvar (Orsino), Kevin Isola (Sebastian), Brent Langdon (Captain/Priest), Nancy Robinette (Maria), J. Fred Shiffman (Fabian), JaMario Stills (Antonio), Tom Story (Sir Andrew Aguecheek), Ted van Griethuysen (Malvolio), Ensemble: Janelle Abbott, Rich Dreher, Ben Graney, Jamal Green, Meda Miller, Valentina Fleer (Singer), Matthews Theatre; co-produced with The Shakespeare Theatre of Washington, D.C.; March 10–29, 2009

Rebecca Brooksher and Veanne Cox in Twelfth Night
(photo by T. Charles Erickson)

The Brother/Sister Plays: In the Red and Brown Water by Tarell Alvin McCraney; Director, Tina Landau; Set, James Schuette; Costumes, Karen Perry; Lighting, Jane Cox; Sound, Lindsay Jones; PSM, Cheryl Mintz; SM, Alison Cote; Cast: Barnaby Carpenter (O Li Roon/The Man from State), Samuel Ray Gates (Shango), Kimberly Hébert Gregory (Aunt Elegua), Brian Tyree Henry (The Egungun), Marc Damon Johnson (Ogun Size), Nikiya Mathis (Shun), Alano Miller (Elegba), Kianné Muschett (Oya), Heather Alicia Simms (Mama Moja/Nia/The Woman Who Reminds You), Berlind Theatre; co-produced with The Public Theatre; April 24–June 21, 2009

The Brother/Sister Plays, Part 2: The Brothers Size and Marcus; or The Secret of Sweet by Tarell Alvin McCraney; Director, Robert O'Hara; Set, James Schuette; Costumes, Karen Perry; Lighting, Jane Cox; Sound, Lindsay Jones; PSM, Cheryl Mintz; SM, Alison Cote; Cast: Barnaby Carpenter (O Li Roon), Samuel Ray Gates (Shua), Kimberly Hébert Gregory (Elegua/Shun), Brian Tyree Henry (The Egungun/Oshoosi Size/Terrell), Marc Damon Johnson (Ogun Size), Nikiya Mathis (Shaunta Iyun), Alano Miller (Elegba/Marcus), Kianné Muschett (Osha), Heather Alicia Simms (Oba), Berlind Theatre; co-produced with The Public Theatre; May 14–June 21, 2009

Marc Damon Johnson and Brian Tyree Henry in The Brothers Size
(photo by Richard Termine)

Media Theatre

Media, Pennsylvania
Sixteenth Season
Artistic Director, Jesse Cline; Executive Director, Patrick Ward

My Fair Lady Music and Lyrics by Alan Jay Lerner, book by Frederick Loewe; Director, Jesse Cline; Sets, Brenda Davis; Costumes, Mary Ann Swords-Greene; Lighting, Thom Weaver; Choreography, Kira Coviello; PSM, Blair Wasleben; Technical Director, Joe LeDuc; Cast: Elisa Matthews (Eliza Doolittle), Ian Kahn (Henry Higgins), Stephen Bonnell (Colonel Pickering), Bev Appleton (Alfred Doolittle), The Media Theatre; October 1–November 2, 2008

Oliver! Book, Music, and Lyrics by Lionel Bart; Director, Jesse Cline; Sets and Light Design, Kelly Michelle Leight; Costumes, Mary Ann Swords-Greene; PSM, Blair Walsleben; Technical Director, Joe LeDuc; Cast: Tovi Wayne (Oliver Twist), Bev Appleton (Fagin), Elisa Matthews (Nancy), Sean Thompson (Bill Sykes); The Media Theatre; December 3, 2008–January 4, 2009

Altar Boyz Music and Lyrics by Gary Adler and Michael Patrick Walker, book by Kevin Del Aguila; Director, Peter Reynolds; Sets, Adam Riggar; Lights, Kelly Michelle Leight; Costumes, Lauren Perigard; Choreography, Samuel Reyes; PSM,

Blair Walsleben; Technical Director, Joe LeDuc; Cast: Peter Drennen (Matthew), Michael Jennings Mahoney (Mark), Lee Markham (Luke), Adrian Gonzalez (Juan), Joey Contreras (Abraham); The Media Theatre; January 28–February 15, 2009

All Shook Up Book by Joe DiPietro; Director, Vincent Marini; Sets, Hiroshi Iwosaki; Lights, Joshua Schulman; Choreography, Gregory Daniels; Music Director, Samuel Heifetz; PSM, Blair Walsleben; Technical Director, Joe LeDuc; Artistic Input, Jesse Cline; Cast: Nicholas Cobey (Chad), Amanda Lea LaVergne (Natalie), Teddy Eck (Dean), Chanta C. Layton (Sylvia); The Media Theatre; March 11–April 5, 2009

Thoroughly Modern Millie Book by Richard Morris and Dick Scanlon; New Music by Jeanine Tesori; New Lyrics by Dick Scanlon; Director, Patricia Raine; Sets, Adam Riggar; Lights, Krista Billings; Costumes, Andrea Barrier; Choreography, Karen Cleighton; Technical Director, Joe LeDuc; Casting, Jesse Cline; Cast: Courtney Romano (Millie Dillmount), Shane Rhoades (Jimmy), April Woodall (Mrs. Meers), Scott Guthrie (Trevor); The Media Theatre; May 6–June 7, 2009

Merrimack Repertory Theatre

Lowell, Massachusetts
Thirtieth Season
Artistic Director; Charles Towers; Executive Director; Tom Parrish

The Fantasticks Book and Lyrics by Tom Jones; Music by Harvey Schmidt; Director, Jonathan Silverstein; Musical Director, John Bell; Set, Antje Ellermann; Costumes, Theresa Squire; Lighting, Josh Bradford; Stage Manager, Emily McMullen; Cast: David Villella (El Gallo), Piper Goodeve (Luisa), Nick Mannix (Matt), Dale Radunz (Hucklebee), Ira Denmark (Bellomy), Charles Hyman (Henry), Dane Knell (Mortimer), Christopher Sheenahn (Mute); October 16–November 9, 2008

David Villella, Ira Denmark, Nick Mannix, Piper Goodeve and Dale Radunz in The Fantasticks *(photos by Meghan Moore)*

Skylight by David Hare; Director; Charles Towers; Set, Bill Clarke; Costumes, Deb Newhall; Lighting, Dan Kotlowitz; Dialect Coach, Julie Nelson; Stage Manager, Emily McMullen; Cast: Amanda Fulks (Kyra), Joe Lanza (Edward), Chris McHale (Tom); November 20–December 14, 2008

Amanda Fulks and Chris McHale in Skylight

A View of the Harbor by Richard Dresser; Director; Charles Towers; Set, Richard Chambers; Costumes, Devon Painter; Lighting, Brian Lilienthal; Stage Manager, Emily McMullen; Cast: Kyle Fabel (Nick), Stephanie Fieger (Paige), Anderson Matthews (Daniel), Andrea Cirie (Kathryn); Regional Premiere; January 8–February 1, 2009

Tranced by Bob Clyman; Director; Kyle Fabel; Set, Campbell Baird; Costumes, Deb Newhall; Lighting, Brian Lilienthal; Composer; Shane Rettig; Stage Manager, Emily McMullen; Cast: Zainab Jah (Azmera), Mark Zeisler (Philip), Kimber Riddle (Beth), David Adkins (Logan); Regional Premiere; February 12–March 8, 2009

Bad Dates by Theresa Rebeck; Director; Adrianne Krstansky; Set, Susan Zeeman Rogers; Costumes, Deb Newhall; Lighting, Matthew Miller; Sound; Dave Wilson; Stage Manager, Emily McMullen; Cast: Elizabeth Aspenlieder (Haley Walker), Haviland Morris (Haley Walker); March 19–April 12, 2009

A Moon for the Misbegotten by Eugene O'Neill; Director; Edward Morgan; Set, Bill Clarke; Costumes, Jeni Schaefer; Lighting, Beverly Emmons; Sound; Michael Boso; Stage Manager, Emily McMullen; Cast: Kate Udall (Josie), Gordon Joseph Weiss (Phil Hogan), Michael Canavan (Jim Tyrone), Karl Baker Olson (Mike Hogan), John Kooi (Harder), Understudy: Jeremiah Kissel (Phil Hogan); April 23–May 17, 2009

Milwaukee Repertory Theater

Milwaukee, Wisconsin
Fifty-fifth Season
Artistic Director, Joseph Hanreddy; Managing Director, Timothy J. Shields

State of the Union by Howard Lindsay and Russel Crouse; Director, Michael Halberstam; Set, Keith Pitts; Costumes, Rachel Anne Healy; Lighting, Joel Moritz; Sound, Josh Schmidt; Literary Director, Kristin Crouch; Stage Manager, Whitney Frazier; Assistant Stage Manager, Amanda Weener; Assistant Director, Tina Myers; Cast: James Pickering (James Conover), Torrey Hanson (Spike Macmanus), Deborah Staples (Kay Thorndyke), Lee E. Ernst (Grant Matthews), Linda Stephens (Norah), Laura Gordon (Mary Matthews), Gerard Neugent (Perkins/Hopkins/Stevens), Aaron Shand (Bellboy/Ensemble), Daniel Mooney (Sam Parrish), Cassandra Stokes-Wylie (Jenny/Ensemble), Rose Pickering (Lulubelle Alexander), Peter Silbert (Judge Jefferson Davis Alexander), Linda Stephens (Mrs. Draper), Steve Pickering (Bill Hardy), Brian Rooney (Senator Lauterback/Wait Staff/Ensemble), Eric Bultman (Labor Leader/Ensemble), Jordan Laroya (Labor Leader/Ensemble), Joshua Innerst (Labor Leader/Ensemble), Samuel Hicks (Wait Staff/Ensemble), Dennis Kelly (Wait Staff/Ensemble), Heidi Wermuth (Ensemble); Quadracci Powerhouse Theater; September 16–October 12, 2008

Eurydice by Sarah Ruhl; Director, Jonathan Moscone; Set, Todd Rosenthal; Costumes, Katherine Roth; Lighting, Chris Akerlind; Sound Design and Original Composition, Jake Rodriguez; Chicago Casting, Claire Simon Casting; Choreography, Darci Brown Wutz; Literary Director, Kristin Crouch; Stage Manager, Mark S. Sahba; Assistant Stage Manager, Becky Merold; Assistant Director, Tina Myers; Cast: Lanise Antoine Shelley (Eurydice), William Dick (Her Father), Davis Duffield (Orpheus), Wayne T. Carr (A Nasty Interesting Man/Lord of the Underworld), Laurie Birmingham (Big Stone), Eric Hissom (Loud Stone), Jose Luis Sanchez (Little Stone); Quadracci Powerhouse Theater; October 28–November 23, 2008

The Blonde, The Brunette and the Vengeful Redhead by Robert Hewett; Director, Joseph Hanreddy; Set, Linda Buchanan; Costumes, Martha Hally; Lighting, Thomas C. Hase; Sound, Barry G. Funderburg; Literary Director, Kristin Crouch; Stage Manager, Whitney Frazier; Assistant Stage Manager, Becky Merold; Assistant Director, Tina Myers; Cast: Deborah Staples (Performer); Quadracci Powerhouse Theater; December 9, 2008–January 4, 2009

Trouble in Mind by Alice Childress; Director, Timothy Douglas; Set, Junghyun Georgia Lee; Costumes, Tracy Dorman; Lighting, Michael Gilliam; Sound, Ray Nardelli; Literary Director, Kristin Crouch; Stage Manager, Briana J. Fahey; Assistant Stage Manager, Laura F. Wendt; Assistant Director, Abigail Issac; Cast: Richard Halverson (Henry), Stephanie Berry (Wiletta Mayer), Wayne T. Carr (John Nevins), Rachel Leslie (Millie Davis), Ernest Perry, Jr. (Sheldon Forrester), Kelsey Brennan (Judy Sears), Lee E. Ernst (Al Manners), Jonathan Hicks (Eddie Fenton), James Pickering (Bill O'Wray); Quadracci Powerhouse Theater; January 20–February 15, 2009

Pride and Prejudice by Jane Austen; Adapted by Joseph Hanreddy and J.R. Sullivan; Director, J.R. Sullivan; Set, Michael Ganio; Costumes, Martha Hally; Lighting, Ann Wrightson; Sound, Barry G. Funderburg; Assistant Costume Designer, Rachel Laritz; Chicago Casting, Claire Simon Casting; Choreography, Isabella Kralj; Dialect, Sara Phillips; Literary Director, Kristin Crouch; Stage Manager, Richelle Harrington Calin; Assistant Stage Manager, Melissa Wanke; Stage Management Apprentice, Liz Eisenmenger; Assistant Director, Abigail Isaac; Cast: Lee Stark (Miss Elizabeth Bennet), Sarah Rutan (Miss Jane Bennet), Richelle Meiss (Miss Mary Bennet/Anne de Bourgh), Eva Balistrieri (Miss Catherine "Kitty" Bennet/Georgiana Darcy), Emily Vitrano (Miss Lydia Bennet), Jonathan Gillard Daly (Mr. Bennet), Laura Gordon (Mrs. Bennet), Jacque Troy (Lady Lucas/Mrs. Reynolds), Brian Rooney (Sir William Lucas), Elizabeth Ledo (Miss Charlotte Lucas), Gerard Neugent (Mr. Charles Bingley), Heidi Wermuth (Miss Caroline Bingley), Grant Goodman (Mr. Fitzwilliam Darcy), Brian Vaughn (Mr. Collins), James S. Rudy (Mr. Denny), Jason Bradley (Mr. Wickham), Rose Pickering

(Lady Catherine de Bourgh), Jordan Laroya (Colonel Fitzwilliam), Carey Cannon (Mrs. Gardiner), Peter Silbert (Mr. Gardiner), Andrea Dennison-Laufer (Servant/Laborer), Sam Hicks (Servant/Soldier/Laborer), Josh Innerst (Servant/Soldier/Laborer), Cassandra Stokes-Wylie (Servant/Laborer); Quadracci Powerhouse Theater; March 3–March 29, 2009

The Cherry Orchard by Anton Chekhov; a version by Tom Murphy; Director, Ben Barnes; Set, Todd Rosenthal; Costumes, Rachel Healy; Lighting, Thomas C. Hase; Sound, Barry G. Funderburg; Choreography, Ed Burgess; Chicago Casting, Claire Simon Casting; Literary Director, Kristin Crouch; Stage Manager, Amanda Weener; Assistant Stage Manager, Laura F. Wendt; Assistant Director, Abigail Isaac; Cast: Deborah Staples (Lyubov Andreyevna Ranyevskaya), Lee Stark (Anya), Erin Neal (Varya), Torrey Hanson (Leonid Gayev), Mark Corkins (Yermolay Lopakhin), Jürgen Hooper (Petya Trofimov), James Pickering (Boris Borisovich Simeonov-Pishchik), Laura Gordon (Charlotta Ivanovna), Gerard Neugent (Simon Panteleyevich Yepikhodov), Kathleen Romond (Dunyasha), Richard Halverson (Firs), Brian Vaughn (Yasha), Josh Innerst (Vagrant/Post Office Clerk), Brian Rooney (Vagrant), James S. Rudy (Vagrant), Aaron Shand (Vagrant), Jonathan Gillard Daly (Stationmaster), Andrea Dennison-Laufer (Ensemble), Sam Hicks (Ensemble), Jordan Laroya (Ensemble), Richelle Meiss (Ensemble), Rose Pickering (Ensemble), Cassandra Stokes-Wylie (Ensemble), Heidi Wermuth (Ensemble); Quadracci Powerhouse Theater; April 14–May 10, 2009

I Am My Own Wife by Doug Wright; Director, John Langs; Set, Brian Sidney Bembridge; Costumes, Holly Payne; Lighting, Noele Stollmack; Sound, Josh Schmidt; Dialect, Sara Phillips; Literary Director, Kristin Crouch; Stage Manager, Richelle Harrington Calin; Assistant Director, Abigail Isaac; Cast: Michael Gotch (Charlotte Von Mahlsdorf/John Marks/Doug Wright/Tante Luise/SS Officer/SS Commander/Young Lothar Berfelde/Herr Berfelde/Prison Guard/Minna Mahlich/Cultural Minister/Stasi Official/Alfred Kirschner/Young Homosexual Man/American Soldier and His Buddy/Customs Official/Stasi Agent/Nurse/Prison Official/German News Anchor/Politician Markus Kaufmann/Ulrike Liptsch/Josef Rudiger/Ziggy Fluss/First Neo-Nazi/Second Neo-Nazi/Brigitte Klensch/Karl Henning/Francois Garnier/Shirley Blacker/Daisuke Yamagishi/Mark Finley/Pradeep Gupta/Clive Twimbley/Dieter Jorgensen); Stiemke Theater; September 10–October 5, 2008

Guys on Ice Book and Lyrics by Fred Alley; Music by James Kaplan; Director and Choreography, Jeffrey Herbst; Musical Direction, James Kaplan; Set, James Maronek; Costumes, Neen Rock; Lighting, Jason Fassl; Sound, Dave Alley; Assistant Lighting Design, Matthew Carroll; Stage Manager, Kathi Karol Koenig; Tour Manager/Production Assistant, Cheryl L. Hanson; Cast: Steven M. Koehler (Lloyd), Doug Mancheski (Marvin), Lee Becker (Ernie the Moocher), Matthew Webb (Piano Player); Stiemke Theater; December 17, 2008–January 4, 2009

Mirandolina by Carlo Goldoni; Director, László Marton; Set and Lighting, Noele Stollmack; Costumes, Matthew LeFebvre; Sound, Barry G. Funderburg; Literary Director, Kristin Crouch; Fight Choreography, Lee E. Ernst; Stage Manager, Amanda Weener; Assistant Director, Tina Meyers; Cast: Brian Vaughn (Knight of Ripafratta), Torrey Hanson (Marquis of Forlipopoli), Steve Pickering (Count of Albafiorita), Deborah Staples (Mirandolina), Carey Cannon (Ortensia), Cristina Panfilio (Dejanira), Gerard Neugent (Fabrizio), Jordan Laroya (Knight's Servant); Stiemke Theater; January 28–February 22, 2009

I Just Stopped By to See the Man by Stephen Jeffreys; Director, Regge Life; Set, Debra Booth; Costumes, Rachel Laritz; Lighting, Jason Fassl; Sound, Regge Life; Literary Director, Kristin Crouch; Chicago Casting, Claire Simon Casting; Stage Manager, Mark S. Sahba; Assistant Director, Tina Myers; Cast: Cedric Young (Jesse), Lanise Antoine Shelley (Della), Erik Hellman (Karl); Stiemke Theater; April 8–May 3, 2009

Isn't It Romantic by David Hunter Koch; Director, David Hunter Koch; Musical Arrangements, William Knowles; Set, Susannah M. Barnes; Costumes, Alex Tecoma; Lighting, Aimee Hanyzewski; Cabaret Director, Sandy Ernst; Stage Manager, Kathi Karol Koenig; Cast: Jimi Ray Malary (Actor/Singer), William Knowles (Pianist), Don Linke (Bass), Scott Napoli (Drums); Stackner Cabaret; September 5–November 2, 2008

Greater Tuna by Jaston Williams, Joe Sears and Ed Howard; Director, J.R. Sullivan; Set, Susannah M. Barnes; Costumes, Alex Tecoma; Lighting, Jason Fassl; Sound, Ernie Brusubardis; Cabaret Director, Sandy Ernst; Stage Manager, Richelle Harrington Calin, Stage Management Intern, Holly Burnell; Cast: Lee. E. Ernst (Actor), Gerard Neugent (Actor); Stackner Cabaret; November 7–December 28, 2008

Dogpark: The Musical by Jahnna Beecham, Malcolm Hillgartner, Michael J. Hume; Director, Jahnna Beecham; Music Direction, Malcolm Hillgartner; Vocal Arrangements, Malcolm Hillgartner and Chip Duford; Choreography, Suzanne Seiber; Set, Susannah M. Barnes; Costumes, Holly Payne; Lighting, Aimee Hanyzewski; Sound, Malcolm Hillgartner; Cabaret Director, Sandy Ernst; Stage Manager, Mark S. Sahba, Stage Management Apprentice, Liz Eisenmenger; Cast: Lenny Banovez (Champ), Chip DuFord (Bogie), Jonathan Spivey (Itchy), Katherine Strohmaier (Daisy), Stackner Cabaret; January 9–March 1, 2009

Fire on the Bayou: A Mardi Gras Musical Extravaganza by Kevin Ramsey; Director, Kevin Ramsey; Music Direction, Jeremy Cohen and Eric Noden; Set, Jill Lynn Lyons; Costumes, Holly Payne; Lighting, Aimee Hanyzweski; Cabaret Director, Sandy Ernst; Stage Manager, Becky Merold; Donna Larsen, Stage Management Intern; Cast: Jeremy Cohen (Professor Short-hair), Jannie Jones (Queen Marie), Scott Napoli (Traps), Milton Craig Nealy (Spyboy Jambalaya), Eric Noden (Dr. Johnay); Stackner Cabaret; March 6–May 10, 2009

A Christmas Carol by Charles Dickens; Adapted by Joseph Hanreddy and Edward Morgan; Director, Judy Berdan; Set, Marjorie Bradley Kellogg; Costumes, Martha Hally; Lighting, Nancy Schertler; Sound, Barry G. Funderburg; Associate Lighting Designer, Aimee Hanyzewski; Music Director, Randal Swiggum; Music Arranger, John Tanner; Dance Choreography, Cate Deicher; Movement Choreography, Ed Burgess; Dialect, Gale Childs Daly; Children's Director, Shawn Gulyas; Wig and Hair Designer, Kevin C. McElroy; Make-Up Designer, Lara Leigh Dalbey; Production Stage Manager, Briana J. Fahey; Assistant Stage Managers, Amanda Weener and Laura F. Wendt; Stage Management Apprentice, Liz Eisenmener; Children's Stage Manager, Donna Larsen; Assistant Director, Abigail Isaac; Cast: James Pickering (Ebenezer Scrooge), Torrey Hanson (Bob Cratchit/Businessman), Michael Herold (Mr. Twyce/Mr. Oatway/Milkman/Mr. Topper/Businessman/Mourner), Michael Duncan (Mr. Grimgrind/Mr. Philpot/ Fezziwig Worker/Sailor Captain), Brian Gill (Fred/Fezziwig Worker/Businessman), Jenny Wanasek (Mrs. Dilber/Mrs. Oatway /Mrs. Fezziwig/Madeline), Peter Silbert (Mr. Scadger, the gravedigger/Ghost of Christmas Past/Barnaby), Steve Pickering (Reverend Waghorn/Ghost of Jacob Marley/Jacob Marley/Old Joe), Jonathan Smoots (Mr. Fezziwig/Ghost of Christmas Present), Laura Gordon (Mrs. Cratchit/ Mrs. Sidebottom/Cook at Fezziwigs), Elizabeth Ledo (Catherine, Fred's wife/Fan/ Mrs. Miggott), Paul Hurley (Young Scrooge/Lighthouse Man/Mourner), Katherine Strohmaier (Belle/Lucy, Catherine's sister/Mourner), Eric Bultman (Ghost of Christmas Future), Erikray Minturn (Dick Wilkins), Brian Rooney (Mr. Mudd), Diana Huey (Martha Cratchit), Thad Bruno (Peter Cratchit) Jacob Badovski (Tiny Tim), Connor Mills (Tiny Tim), Mary Elsa Henrichs (Belinda Crachit), Emily Zaffiro (Alice Crachet), Maia Thompson (Mary Crachit), Sam Skogstad (Percy Smudge), Jordan Horne (Boy Scrooge), Denzell Armon (Ignorance), Riley Luettgen (Want); Pabst Theater; November 28–December 28, 2008

The Old Globe

San Diego, California
Seventy-fourth Season
CEO/Executive Producer, Louis G. Spisto; Resident Artistic Director, Darko Tresnjak; Artistic Director Emeritus, Jack O'Brien; Founding Director, Craig Noel

Romeo and Juliet by William Shakespeare; Director, Richard Seer; Sets, Ralph Funicello; Costumes, Anna R. Oliver; Lighting, York Kennedy; Sound, Chris Walker; Stage Manager, Mary K. Klinger; Cast: Kandis Chappell (Lady Capulet), Joy Farmer-Clary (Ensemble/Rosaline), Ashley Clements (Ensemble), Vivia Font (Ensemble), Kimberly Parker Green (Ensemble), Sloan Grenz (Peter/Citizen), Graham Hamilton (Romeo), Wynn Harmon (Lord Capulet), Sam Henderson (Sampson/Friar John), Brian Huynh (Abram/Page to Paris), Charles Janasz (Lord Montague), John Keabler (Paris), Michael Kirby (Benvolio), Kern McFadden (Balthasar), Jonathan McMurtry (Escalus/Apothecary/Cousin Capulet), Owiso Odera (Mercutio), Deborah Taylor (Nurse), Tony Von Halle (Tybalt), Barbra Wengard (Lady Montague), James Winker (Friar Lawrence), Heather Wood (Juliet); Lowell Davies Festival Theatre; June 14–September 28, 2008

Anthony von Halle, Owiso Odera, Graham Hamilton, and Michael Kirby in Romeo and Juliet *(photos by Craig Schwartz)*

The Merry Wives of Windsor by William Shakespeare; Director, Paul Mullins, Sets, Ralph Funicello; Costumes, Denitsa D. Bliznakova; Lighting, York Kennedy; Sound, Chris Walker; Stage Manager, Mary K. Klinger; Cast: Celeste Ciulla (Mistress Page), Joy Farmer-Clary (Saloon Girl), Ashley Clements (Saloon Girl), Vivia Font (Saloon Girl), Sloan Grenz (Slender), Wynn Harmon (Doctor Caius), Sam Henderson (Nym), Eric Hoffman (Sir John Falstaff), Brian Huynh (Simple), Charles Janasz (Hugh Evans), John Keabler (Pistol), Michael Kirby (Bardolph), Katie MacNichol (Mistress Ford), Nathaniel McIntyre (Page), Jonathan McMurtry (Shallow), Owiso Odera (Fenton), Carolyn Ratteray (Anne Page), Deborah Taylor (Mistress Quickly), Bruce Turk (Ford), Tony Von Halle (Rugby), Barbra Wengerd (Hostess), Heather Wood (Saloon Girl); Lowell Davies Festival Theatre; June 14–September 28, 2008

All's Well That Ends Well by William Shakespeare; Director, Darko Tresnjak; Sets, Ralph Funicello; Costumes, Linda Cho; Lighting, York Kennedy; Sound, Chris Walker; Stage Manager, Mary K. Klinger; Cast: Kandis Chappell (Countess of Rossillion), Celeste Ciulla (Widow Capulet), Ashley Clements (French Lady/ Tourist 1), Vivia Font (Diana), Kimberly Parker Green (Helena), Sloan Grenz (Italian Soldier 2), Graham Hamilton (Bertram), Wynn Harmon (Attendant to the King of France/ Duke of Florence/Waiter), Eric Hoffmann (Lavatch/Merchant), Brian Huynh (Tourist 3), Charles Janasz (Lafew/Accordianist), John Keabler (French Lord 3/Italian Soldier 3), Michael Kirby (French Lord 4), Katie MacNichol (Mariana), Kern McFadden (Lord Dumaine the Younger), Nathaniel McIntyre (Lord Dumaine the Elder), Jonathan McMurtry (Reynaldo/Waiter), Carolyn Ratteray (French Lady/Merchant), Bruce Turk (Parolles), Tony Von Halle (Italian Soldier 1), Barbra Wengard (Isbel/Tourist 2), James Winker (King of France); Lowell Davies Festival Theatre; June 14–September 28, 2008

The Pleasure of His Company by Samuel Taylor and Cornelia Otis Skinner; Director, Darko Tresnjak; Sets, Alexander Dodge; Costums, Fabio Toblini; Lighting, York Kennedy; Sound, Paul Peterson; Stage Manager, Diana Moser; Cast: Patrick Page (Biddeford "Pogo" Poole), Jim Abele (Jim Dougherty), Erin Chambers (Jessica Poole), Ellen Karas (Katharine Dougherty), Ned Schmidtke (Mackenzie Savage), Sab Shimono (Toy), Matt Biedel (Roger Henderson); Old Globe Theatre; July 12–August 17, 2008

The Women by Clare Boothe Luce; Director, Darko Tresnjak; Sets, David Gordon; Lighting, Matt Richards; Costumes, Anna Oliver; Sound, Paul Peterson; Stage Manager, Bret Torbeck; Cast: Nancy Anderson (Miriam Aarons/Princess Tamara), Heather Ayers (Sylvia Fowler), Kate Baldwin (Mary Haines), Linda Gehringer (Mrs. Morehead), Mary Pat Green (1st Hairdresser/Head Saleswoman/Maggie/Lucy/Sadie), Jenn Harris (Olga/Miss Trimmerback/2nd Model/1st Cutie), Amy Hohn (Edith Potter), Aaryn Kopp (Jane/1st Model/Debutante), Amanda Kramer (Peggy Day), Kathleen McElfresh (Crystal Allen), Amanda Naughton (Nancy Blake), Aimee Nelson (Pedicurist/Fitter/Exercise Instructness/Helene/2nd Cutie), Blair Ross (2nd Hairdresser/2nd Saleswoman/Miss Watts/Nurse/Dowager), Kayla Solsbak (Little Mary) and Ruth Williamson (Countess de Lage); Old Globe Theatre; September 13–October 26, 2008

Dr. Seuss' How the Grinch Stole Christmas! Book and Lyrics by Timothy Mason; Music by Mel Marvin; Original Director, Jack O'Brien; Director, Ben Endsley Klein; Sets, John Lee Beatty; Lighting, Pat Collins; Costumes, Robert Morgan; Sound, Paul Peterson; Stage Managers: Leila Knox, Tracy Skoczelas; Cast: Kevin Bailey (Grinch), Martin Van Treuren (Old Max), Logan Lipton (Young Max), Melinda Gilb (Mama Who), Steve Gunderson (Papa Who), Eileen Bowman (Grandma Who), James Vasquez (Grandpa Seth Who), Skylar Starrs Siben and Issadora Tulalian (Cindy-Lou Who on alternate performances), Bibi Valderrama and Alison Norwood (Betty-Lou Who on alternate performances), Madison Simpson and Kayla Solsbak (Annie Who on alternate performances), Benjamin Shaffer and Dylan Mulvaney (Danny Who on alternate performances), Tommy Twomey and A.J. Foggiano (Boo Who on alternate performances), Adult Ensemble: Amy Biedel, Dennis Clark, Courtney Corey, Kurt Norby, Anise Ritchie and Jeffrey Rockwell; Children Ensemble: Hallie Bodenstab, Allison Ma, Charisma McKorn, Dallas Perry, Anna Strickland, Issabela Tulalian, Ashley Twomey, Sean Waters, Roma Watkins and Lucia Vecchio; Old Globe Theatre; November 15–December 28, 2008

Six Degrees of Separation by John Guare; Director, Trip Cullman; Sets, Andromache Chalfant; Costumes, Emily Rebholz; Lighting, Ben Stanton; Sound, Paul Peterson; Stage Manager, Diana Moser; Cast: Karen Ziemba (Ouisa), Thomas Jay Ryan (Flan), Donald Sage Mackay (Larkin), Keliher Walsh (Kitty), Tony Torn (Geoffrey), Samuel Stricklen (Paul), James Eckhouse (Dr. Fine), Joaquin Perez-Campbell (Rick/Hustler), Catherine Gowl (Elizabeth), Kevin Hoffmann (Ben), Sloan Grenz (Doug), Jordan McArthur (Woody), Andrew Dahl (Trent), Vivia Font (Tess), Steven Marzolf (Doorman/Policeman/Detective); Old Globe Theatre; January 10–February 15, 2009

Kingdom Book/lyrics by Aaron Jafferis; Music by Ian Williams; Director, Ron Daniels; Choreography, Tony Caligagan; Music Director, Cian McCarthy; Sets, Sean Fanning; Costumes, Charlotte Devaux; Lighting, Nate Parde; Sound, Paul Peterson; Stage Manager, Anjee Nero; Cast: Cedric Leiba, Jr. (Juan), Kyle Beltran (Andres), Miguel Jarquin-Moreland (Danny), Joey Auzenne (Hector), Amirah Vann (Marisa), Gerardo Rodriguez (Cano), Ensemble: Christian Amaraut, Joyelle Cabato, Bayardo De Murguia and Diahann McCrary; World Premiere; February 12 – 22, 2009 at The Lincoln High School Center for the Arts; February 12-15; Old Globe Theatre; February 19–22

Working Book by Stephen Schwartz and Nina Faso; Music and Lyrics by Susan Birkenhead, Craig Carnelia, Graciela Daniele, Micki Grant, Matt Landers, Lin-Manuel Miranda, Mary Rodgers, Stephen Schwartz and James Taylor; Director, Gordon Greenberg; Choreography, Joshua Rhodes; Musical Director/Conductor, Mark Hartman; Orchestrator, Alex Lacamoire; Sets, Beowulf Boritt; Costumes, Mattie Ullrich; Lighting, Jeff Croiter; Sound, Tony Smolenski IV; Projection Designer, Aaron Rhyne; Stage Manager, Dan Rosokoff; Cast: Adam Monley (Man

#1), Nehal Joshi (Man #2), Wayne Duvall (Man #3), Marie-France Arcilla (Woman #1), Danielle Lee Greaves (Woman #2), Donna Lynne Champlin (Woman #3); Old Globe Theatre; March 7–April 12, 2009

Cornelia by Mark V. Olsen; Director, Ethan McSweeny; Sets, John Lee Beatty; Costumes, Tracy Christensen; Lighting, Chris Akerlind; Sound, Paul Peterson; Stage Managers, Leila Knox and Anjee Nero; Cast: Melinda Page Hamilton (Cornelia), Robert Foxworth (George), Beth Grant (Ruby), Hollis McCarthy (Marie), T. Ryder Smith (Gerald); World Premiere; Old Globe Theatre; May 16–June 21, 2009

Sight Unseen by Donald Margulies; Director, Esther Emery; Sets, Nick Fouch; Costumes, Laurie Churba; Lighting, Chris Rynne; Sound, Paul Peterson; Stage Manager, Tracy Skoczelas; Cast: Tony Crane (Jonathan), Kelly McAndrew (Patricia), Ron Choularton (Nick), Katie Fabel (Grete); Globe's Arena Stage at SD Museum of Art's James S. Copley Auditorium; August 2–September 7, 2008

Back Back Back by Itamar Moses; Director, Davis McCallum; Sets, Lee Savage; Lighting, Russell Champa; Costumes, Christal Weatherly, Sound, Paul Peterson; Stage Manager, Tracy Skoczelas; Cast: Brendan Griffin (Kent), Nick Mills (Adam), Joaquin Perez-Campbell (Raul); World Premiere; Globe's Arena Stage at SD Museum of Art's James S. Copley Auditorium; September 19–October 26, 2008

Since Africa by Mia McCullough; Director, Seema Sueko; Sets, Nick Fouch; Lighting, Jason Bieber, Costumes, Charlotte Devaux; Sound, Paul Peterson; Stage Manager, Moira Gleason; Cast: Kristin Carpenter (The Nameless One/As Cast), Willie Carpenter, (Reggie Hudson), Ashley Clements (Eve MacIntyre), Linda Gehringer, (Diane MacIntyre), Warner Miller (Ater Dahl); Globe's Arena Stage at SD Museum of Art's James S. Copley Auditorium; January 24–March 8, 2009

Opus by Michael Hollinger; Director, Kyle Donnelly; Sets, Kate Edmunds; Lighting, York Kennedy; Costumes, Denitsa D. Bliznakova; Sound, Lindsay Jones; Stage Manager, Diana Moser; Cast: Jim Abele (Elliot), Jeffrey Bender (Alan), Mark H. Dold (Dorian), Corey Brill (Carl), Katie Sigismund (Grace); West Coast Premiere; Globe's Arena Stage at SD Museum of Art's James S. Copley Auditorium; March 21–April 26, 2009

The Price by Arthur Miller; Director, Richard Seer; Sets, Robin Roberts; Lighting, Chris Rynne; Costumes, Charlotte Devaux; Sound, Paul Peterson, Stage Manager, Diana Moser; Cast: Dominic Chianese (Gregory Solomon), Leisa Mather (Esther Franz), Andy Prosky (Victor Franz), James Sutorius (Walter Franz); Globe's Arena Stage at SD Museum of Art's James S. Copley Auditorium; May 9–June 14, 2009

James Sutorius, Andy Proskey, Leisa Mather and Dominic Chianese in The Price

Olney Theatre Center

Olney, Maryland
Seventieth Season
Artistic Director, Jim Petosa; Managing Director Amy Marshall

Doubt by John Patrick Shanley; Director, John Going; Sets, James Wolk; Costumes, Howard Vincent Kurtz; Lighting, Dennis Parichy; Sound, Jarett C. Pisani; Dialect Coach, Nancy Krebs; Stage Manager, Renee E. Yancey; Technical Director, Daniel P. Parker; Production Manager, Ryan Knapp; Coustumiere, Jeanne Bland; Company Manager, Eric C. Bailey; Cast: Brigid Cleary (Sister Aloysius Beauvier), James Denvil (Father Brendan Flynn), Patricia Hurley (Sister James), Deidra LaWan Starnes (Mrs. Miller); Mainstage; February 13–March 16, 2008

Bad Dates by Theresa Rebeck; Director, Lee Mikeska Gardner; Sets, Milagos Ponce de León; Costumes, Melanie Clark; Lighting, Andrew Griffin; Sound, Jarett C. Pisani; Stage Manager, William E. Cruttenden III; Technical Director, Daniel P. Parker; Production Manager, Ryan Knapp; Coustumiere, Jeanne Bland; Company Manager, Eric C. Bailey; Cast: Melissa Flaim (Haley Walker), Mulitz-Gudelsky Theatre Lab; March 19–April 20, 2008

1776 by Peter Stone, Music and Lyrics by Sherman Edwards; Director and Choreography, Stephen Nachame; Musical Director, Christophe Youstra; Sets, Robert Kovach; Costumes, Howard Vincent Kurtz; Lighting, Jeffrey Koger; Sound, Jarett C. Pisani; Wigs, Karlah Hamilton; Dialect Consultant, Lynn Watson; Stage Manager, Jess W. Speaker III; Technical Director, Daniel P. Parker; Production Manager, Ryan Knapp; Coustumiere, Jeanne Bland; Company Manager, Jenna Hendeson; Cast: Jessica Lauren Ball (Martha Jefferson), Don Edward Black (Stephen Hopkins), Paul Binotto (John Adams), Peter Boyer (Dr. Lyman Hall), Andrew Boza (Lewis Morris), Michael Bunce (Richard Henry Lee), John Dow (Rev. Jonathan Witherspoon), Byron Fenstermaker (Samuel Chase), James Garland (Leather Apron/Painter), Dave Joria (Charles Thomson), Don Kenefick (Dr. Josiah Bartlett), Scott Kenison (Joseph Hewes), Bill Largess (Caesar Rodney), Sam Ludwig (Courier), Joe Myering (Roger Sherman), Joe Peck (Robert Livingston), Rob Richardson (Thomas Jefferson), Carl Randolph (John Hancock), Ben Shovlin (Col. Thomas McKean), Thomas Adrian Simpson (John Dickinson), Chris Sizemore (Edward Rutledge), Jonathan Lee Taylor (Andrew McNair), Joseph Tanner (George Read), John Tweel (James Wilson), Harry A. Winter (Benjamin Franklin), Eileen Ward (Abigail Adams), Understudies and Swings: Peter Boyer (John Adams/John Hancock), James Garland (Edward Rutledge/Andrew McNair/Courier), H. Alan Hoffman (Male Swing), Dave Joria (Thomas Jefferson), Joe Myering (Benjamin Franklin), Joe Peck (John Dickinson), Ben Shovlin (Richard Henry Lee), Orchestra: Carolyn Alvarez (Piccolo/Flute/Clarinet), David Blackstone (Trombone/Keyboards), Brian Gibson (Percussion), Jason Sauders (Trumpet), Marcia Vogin (Violin), Christopher Youstra (Conductor/Piano/Accordion); Mainstage; April 9–May 18, 2008

Mousetrap by Agatha Christie; Director, John Going; Sets, James Wolk; Costumes, Liz Covey; Lighting, F. Mitchell Dana; Sound, Joe Payne, Jarett C. Pisani; Composer, James Prigmore; Wigs, Karlah Hamilton; Dialect Coach, Leigh Wilson Smiley; Stage Manager, Carey Stipe; Technical Director, Daniel P. Parker; Production Manager, Ryan N. Knapp; Costume Shop Manager, Jeanne Bland; Company Manager, Sean Cox; Cast: Scott Barrow (Giles Ralston through July 6), James Denvil (Giles Ralston after July 6), Julie-Ann Elliott (Mollie Ralston), Andrew Grusetskie (Detective Sergeant Trotter), Cornelia Hart (Mrs. Boyle), Paul Morella (Mr. Paravicini), Jeffries Thaiss (Christopher Wren), Harry A. Winter (Major Metcalf), MaryBeth Wise (Miss Casewell); Mainstage; June 11–July 20, 2008

Stuff Happens by David Hare; Director, Jeremy Skidmore; Sets, James Kronzer; Costumes, Debra Kim Sivigny; Lights, Dan Covey; Sound, Jarett C. Pisani; Dialect Coach, Jennifer Mendenhall; Stage Manager, Laura Smith; Technical Director, Daniel P. Parker; Production Manager, Ryan N. Knapp; Costume Shop Manager, Jeanne Bland; Company Manager, Sean Cox; Cast: Barry Abrams (Robin Cook/Paul Wolfowitz/Others), Jeff Allin (Jeremy Greenstock/John McCain/Donald Rumsfeld), Amir Arison (Prologue/Dominique de Villepin/Iraqi Exile/Others), Carlos Bustamante (Jacques Chirac/JD Levitte/Jonathan Powell/Others), Leo Erickson (Dick Cheney), Rick Foucheux (George W. Bush), Meghan Grady (Brit in New York/Others), Naomi Jacobson (Laura Bush/British Journalist/John Negoponte/Others), Daniel Ladmirault (General Amin/Richard Dearlove/Iraqi Spokesman/Jack Straw/Others), Daniel Lyons (Hans Blix/Alastair Campbell/Michael Gerson/George Tenet/Others), Stephen F. Schmidt (Tony Blair), Deidra LaWan Starnes (Condoleeza Rice), Frederick L. Strother, Jr. (Colin Powell); Mulitz-Gudelsky Theatre Lab; June 18–July 20, 2008

Rabbit Hole by David Lindsay-Abaire; Director, Mitchell Hébert; Sets, Marie-Noëlle Daigneault; Costumes, Kathleen Geldard; Lights, Charlie Morrison; Sound, Jarett C. Pisani; Stage Manager, Renee E. Yancey; Technical Director, Daniel P. Parker; Production Manager, Ryan N. Knapp; Costume Shop Manager, Jeanne Bland; Company Manager, Sean Cox; Cast: Megan Anderson (Izzy), Aaron Bliden (Jason), Deborah Hazlett (Becca), Kate Kiley (Nat), Paul Morella (Howie); Mainstage; August 6–September 7, 2008

The Underpants by Carl Sternheim; Adapted by Steve Martin; Director, John Going; Sets, James Wolk; Costumes, Liz Covey; Lights, Dennis Parichy; Sound, Jarett C. Pisani; Wigs, Nicole Paul; Dialect Coach, Nancy Krebs; Stage Manager, Jenna Henderson; Technical Director, Daniel P. Parker; Production Manager, Ryan N. Knapp; Costume Shop Manager, Jeanne Bland; Company Manager, Sean Cox; Cast: James Beneduce (Theo Maske), Vincent Clark (Klingelhoff), H. Alan Hoffman (Visitor), Allison McLemore (Louise Maske), Bruce Nelson (Benjamin Cohen), Joan Rosenfels (Gertrude Deuter), Jeffries Thaiss (Frank Versati); Mainstage; September 24–October 19, 2008

Peter Pan The Musical by J. M. Barrie, Music by Mark Charlap, Additional Music by Jule Styne, Lyrics by Carolyn Leigh, Additional Lyrics by Betty Comden and Adolph Green; Director, Eve Muson; Choreography, Boo Killebrew; Musical Director, Christopher Youstra; Sets, Tijana Bjelajac; Costumes, Pei Lee; Lights, Colin K. Bills; Sound, Jarett C. Pisani; Wigs, Karlah Hamilton; Assistant Director/Fight Choreography, Ryan Purcell; Projections, Brian; Stage Manager, Renee E. Yancey; Technical Director, Daniel P. Parker; Production Manager, Ryan N. Knapp; Costume Shop Manager, Jeanne Bland; Company Manager, Sean Cox; Cast: Aviad Bernstein (Michael), Ethan T. Bowen (Nana/Smee), Jace Casey (Michael), Steven Cupo (Cecco), David Frankenberger, Jr. (Slightly), Mitchell Hébert (Mr. Darling/Captain Hook), Patricia Hurley (Wendy/Older Wendy), Boo Killebrew (Liza/Tiger Lily/Jane), Sandra L. Murphy (Noodler), Joe Peck (Starkey), Matthew Schleigh (Curly), Kyle Schliefer (Nibs), Kevin Stockwell (Mullins), Dan Stowell (John), Daniel Townsend (Peter Pan), Dan Van Why (Tootles), Peggy Yates (Mrs. Darling/Jukes), Ensemble: Florrie Bagel, Elizabeth Fette, Jennifer Irons, Kara-Tameika Watkins; Understudies and Swings: Elizabeth Fette (Liza/Tiger Lily/Jane),

Paul Binotto, Harry A. Winter and Rob Richardson in 1776

David Frankenberger, Jr. (Nana/Smee), Dexter Hamlett (Male Swing), Jennifer Irons (Wendy/Older Wendy), Branda Lock (Female Swing), Joe Peck (Mr. Darling/Captain Hook), Matthew Schleigh (John), Kyle Schliefer (Peter Pan), Kara-Tameika Watkins (Mrs. Darling), Orchestra: Carolyn Alvores (Flute/Clarinet/Bass Clarinet), David Blackstone (Trombone), Kevin Gebo (Trumpet), Michale Ranelli (Percussion), Keith Tittermary (Keyboard), Christopher Youstra (Conductor/Piano/Accordion); Mainstage; November 19, 2008–January 11, 2009

Mitchell Hebert with Company of Peter Pan *(photos by Stan Barouh)*

Oregon Shakespeare Festival

Ashland, Oregon

Seventy-third Season

Artistic Director, Bill Rauch; Executive Director, Paul Nicholson

A Midsummer Night's Dream by William Shakespeare; Director, Mark Rucker; Sets, Walt Spangler; Costumes, Katherine Roth; Lighting, Robert Peterson; Composer/Sound, Todd Barton; Choreography/Co-composer, Ken Roht; Dramaturg, Martine Kei Green; Voice/Text, Andrew Wade; Movement/Fight, John Sipes; Assistant Fight, U. Jonathan Toppo; Music Asst/Vocal Coach, Kay Hilton; Stage Manager, D. Christian Bolender; Production Assistant, Emily Carr; FAIR Asst. Director, Corey Atkins; Cast: Michael Elich (Theseus), Shona Tucker (Hippolyta), Linda Alper (Egeus), Emily Sophia Knapp (Hermia), Tasso Feldman (Lysander), Christopher Michael Rivera (Demetrius), Kjerstine Anderson (Helena), Kevin Kenerly (Oberon), Christine Albright (Titania), John Tufts (Puck), Peter Quince (U. Jonathan Toppo), Ray Porter (Nick Bottom), Eileen DeSandre (Francis Flute), Josiah Phillips (Tom Snout), Jeffrey King (Snug), Richard Elmore (Robin Starveling), Jeany Park (Philostrate), Mark Bedard (Moth), Eddie Lopez (Cobweb), Neil Shah (Peaseblossom), Edgar Miguel Sanchez (Mustardseed), Collin Malcolm, Kevin Weatherby (Changling Child), Angus Bowmer Theatre; February 15-November 2, 2008

Fences by August Wilson; Director, Leah C. Gardiner; Sets, Scott Bradley; Costumes, Elizabeth Hope Clancy; Lighting, Dawn Chiang; Composer/Sound, Michael Keck; Dramaturg, Martine Kei Green; Voice/Text, Scott Kaiser; Movement/Fight, John Sipes; Asst. Fight, U. Jonathan Toppo; Stage Manager, Randall K. Lum; ASM, Mandy Younger; FAIR Asst. Director, Corey Atkins; Cast: Shona Tucker (Rose), Charles Robinson (Troy Maxson), Josiah Phillips (Jim Bono), Kevin Kenerly (Lyons), G. Valmont Thomas (Gabriel), Cameron Knight (Cory), Catiana Graham, Dominique Moore (Raynell); Angus Bowmer Theatre; February 16–July 6, 2008

The Clay Cart by draka; Translator, J.A.B. van Buitenen; Director, Bill Rauch; Sets, Christopher Acebo; Costumes, Deborah M. Dryden; Lighting, Christopher Akerlind; Composer/Sound, Andre Pluess; Choreography, Anjani Ambegaokar; Dramaturgs, Ketu H. Katrak, Dan Michon; Voice/Text, Andrew Wade; Movement/Fight, John Sipes; Asst. Fight, U. Jonathan Toppo; Stage Manager, Jeremy Eisen; Production Assistant, Mara Filler; Asst. Director, Terri McMahon; FAIR Asst. Director, Ross Matsuda; Cast: Michael J. Hume (Maitreya), Cristofer Jean (Ch rudatta), Dee Maaske (Mother of Samsth naka), Soneela Nankani (Samsth naka's Slave), Christine Albright (Radanik), James Edmondson (Vardham naka), Mariko Nakasone (Vansantasen 's Slave), Eileen DeSandre (Madanik), Jeffrey King (Masseur), Joshua Wolf Coleman (M thura), Anil Margsahayam (A Gambler), Juan Rivera LeBron (Dardura), Jasmine Risser, Kaj Pandey (Rohasena), Richard Howard (harvilaka), Jeany Park (Dh t), Tyrone Wilson (Libertine), Neil Shah (Aryaka), Robin Goodrin Nordli (Scrivener), Catherine E. Coulson (Bawd), Ryan Anderson (Town Crier), David Salsa (Coachman), Joseph Midyett (Coachman), and all cast members play ensemble roles. Tessa Brinckman, Ed Dunsavage, Terry Longshore (Musicians); Angus Bowmer Theatre; February 17–November 2, 2008

Miriam A. Laube and Cristofer Jean in The Clay Cart

The Further Adventures of Hedda Gabler by Jeff Whitty; Director, Bill Rauch; Sets, Christopher Acebo; Costumes, Shigeru Yaji; Lighting, Geoff Korf; Composer/Sound, Paul James Prendergast; Asst. Director, Gisela Cardenas; Choreography, Art Manke; Dramaturg, Lue Morgan Douthit; Voice/Text, David Carey; Movement/Fight, John Sipes; Stage Manager, Gwen Turos; Production Asst., Mara Filler; Cast: Robin Goodrin Nordli (Hedda Gabler), Christopher DuVal (Tesman), Kimberly Scott (Their Servant), Kate Mulligan (Their Neighbor), Gregory Linington (Lovborg), Anthony Heald (Patrick), Jonathan Haugen (Steven), Gwendolyn Mulamba (Woman in Pink); Angus Bowmer Theatre; April 15–November 1, 2008

A View From the Bridge by Arthur Miller; Director, Libby Appel; Sets, William Bloodgood; Costumes, Deborah M. Dryden; Lighting, Jane Cox; Composer/Sound, Irwin Appel; FAIR Asst. Director, Malika Oyetimein; Dramaturg, Gina Pisasale; Voice/Text, Ursula Meyer; Stage Manager, Jeremy Eisen; Production Asst., Elena Fast. Cast: Armando Durán (Eddie Carbone), Vilma Silva (Beatrice),

Stephanie Beatriz (Catherine), Juan Rivera LeBron (Rodolpho), David DeSantos (Marco), Tony DeBruno (Alfieri), Ensemble: Joseph Midyett, James J. Peck, Brent Hinkley, Tim Blough, B. Trevor Hill, David Salsa, Teresa Peterson, Samuel D. Dinkov, Jimmy Garcia, Tai Simmons, Mateo Peterson; Angus Bowmer Theatre; July 23–November 1, 2008

Welcome Home, Jenny Sutter by Julie Marie Myatt; Director, Jessica Thebus; Sets, Richard L. Hay; Costumes, Lynn Jeffries; Lighting, Allen Lee Hughes; Composer/Sound, Paul James Prendergast; Dramaturg, Lue Morgan Douthit; Voice/Text, Scott Kaiser; Movement/Fight, John Sipes; Stage Manager, Gwen Turos; Asst. Stage Manager, Amy Miranda Warner; Production Asst., Alena Fast; FAIR Assistant Director, Ross Matsuda; Cast: Gwendolyn Mulamba (Jenny Sutter), Kate Mulligan (Lou), David Kelly (Buddy), Gregory Linington (Donald), Cameron Knight (Hugo), K.T. Vogt (Cheryl); World Premiere; New Theatre; February 19–June 20, 2008

Coriolanus by William Shakespeare; Director, Laird Williamson; Sets, Richard L. Hay; Costumes, Deborah M. Dryden; Lighting, Robert Peterson; Composer/Sound, Todd Barton; Dramaturg, Alan Armstrong; Voice/Text, David Carey; Movement/Fight, John Sipes; Asst. Fight, U. Jonathan Toppo; Music Asst., Kay Hilton; Stage Manager, Jill Rendall; Production Asst., Alena Fast; Asst. Director, Michole Biancosino; Cast: U. Jonathan Toppo (First Citizen), Richard Elmore (Menenius), Danforth Comins (Caius Martius), James Jesse Peck (Lartius), Bill Geisslinger (Cominius), Demetra Pittman (Sicinius), Rex Young (Brutus), Michael Elich (Aufidius), Christopher Michael Rivera (Adrian), Robynn Rodriguez (Volumnia), Mahira Kakkar (Virgilia), Sarah Rutan (Valeria), Alexander Barnes, James Edson (Young Martius); New Theatre; March 26–November 2, 2008

Breakfast, Lunch and Dinner by Luis Alfaro; Director, Tracy Young; Sets, Robert Brill; Costume Designer, Nephelie Andonyadis; Lighting, Russell H. Champa; Sound, Jeremy J. Lee; Dramaturg, Lue Morgan Douthit; Voice/Text, Ursula Meyer; Stage Manager, Amy Miranda Warner; ASM, Melissa Wanke; Cast: G. Valmont Thomas (Al), René Millán (Officer Fernandez), Sandra Marquez (Minerva), Zilah Mendoza (Alice); New Theatre; Elizabethan Stage/Allen Pavilion; July 1–November 2, 2008

Othello by William Shakespeare; Director, Lisa Peterson; Set, Rachel Hauck; Costumes, Christopher Acebo; Lighting, Alexander V. Nichols; Composer/Sound, Paul James Prendergast; Assistant Director, Gisela Cardenas; Dramaturg, Jeff Rogers; Voice/Text, Scott Kaiser; Movement/Fight, John Sipes; Assistant Fight, U. Jonathan Toppo; Stage Manager, Randall K. Lum; Cast: Peter Macon (Othello), Dan Donohue (Iago), Sarah Rutan (Desdemona), Vilma Silva (Emilia), Danforth Comins (Cassio), Christopher DuVal (Roderigo), Tony DeBruno (Brabantio, Gratiano), Robert Vincent Frank (Duke, Ensemble), David DeSantos (Montano), Jonathan Haugen (Ludovico, Senator), Stephanie Beatriz (Bianca), Todd Bjurstrom (Gentleman 2, Herald), James Jesse Peck (Sailor, Gentleman), B. Trevor Hill (Gentleman), Daniel L. Haley (Ensemble), Edgar Miguel Sanchez (Ensemble), Arthur LaZalde (Ensemble), Jimmy Garcia (Ensemble), Chloe Brown (Clown); Elizabethan Stage/Allen Pavilion; June 3–October 10, 2008

Sarah Rutan and Peter Macon in Othello

Our Town by Thornton Wilder; Director, Chay Yew; Sets, Richard L. Hay; Costumes, Anita Yavich; Lighting, Robert Peterson; Composer/Sound, Todd Barton; Dramaturg, Judith Rosen; Voice/Text, Louis Colaianni; Movement/Fight, John Sipes; Assistant Fight, U. Jonathan Toppo; Stage Manager, Jill Rendall; ASM, Mandy Younger; FAIR Assistant Director, Rebecca Easton; Cast: Anthony Heald (Stage Manager), Todd Bjurstrom (George Gibbs), Mahira Kakkar (Emily Webb), Hassan El-Amin (Frank Gibbs), Richard Howard (Charles Webb), Demetra Pittman (Julia Gibbs), Kimberly Scott (Myrtle Webb), Rex Young (Howie Newsome), Catherine E. Coulson (Mrs. Soames), Jonathan Haugen (Constable Warren), Jeremy Peter Johnson (Sam Craig), Tyrone Wilson (Joe Stoddard), Ensemble: Bill Geisslinger, Daniel L. Haley, Dee Maaske, Robynn Rodriguez, Ryan Anderson, Mariko Nakasone, Anil Margsahayam; Rachel Kaiser (Rebecca Gibbs), Stanley Graham (Wally Webb), Alexander Barnes (Joe Crowell), Christopher Peterson (Si Crowell); Elizabethan Stage/Allen Pavilion; June 4–October 11, 2008

The Comedy of Errors by William Shakespeare; Director, Penny Metropulos; Sets, Michael Ganio; Costumes, Paul Tazewell; Lighting, Robert Peterson; Composer, Sterling Tinsley; Sound, Jeremy J. Lee; Dramaturg, Jeff Rogers; Voice/Text, Louis Colaianni; Movement/Fight, John Sipes; Assistant Fight, U. Jonathan Toppo, Choreography, Suzanne Seiber; Stage Manager, D. Christian Bolender; ASM, Melissa Wanke; FAIR Assistant Director, Rebecca Easton; Cast: Jeremy Peter Johnson (Antipholus of Syracuse), Mark Bedard (Antipholus of Ephesus), John Tufts (Dromio of Syracuse), Tasso Feldman (Dromio of Ephesus), Miriam A. Laube (Adriana); Emily Sophia Knapp (Luciana), Hassan El-Amin (Duke of Ephesus), Michael J. Hume (Egeon), David Kelly (Angelo), René Millán (First Merchant), Cristofer Jean (Second Merchant), Armando Durán (Dr. Pinch), Joshua Wolf Coleman (Jailor), Todd Bjurstrom (Nell), Linda Alper (Emilia), K.T. Vogt, Kjerstine Anderson, Mariko Nakasone, Soneela Nankani, Eddie Lopez, Anil Margsahayam (Ensemble), Elizabethan Stage/Allen Pavilion; June 5 –October 12, 2008

Paper Mill Playhouse

Millburn, New Jersey
Founded in 1934
Artistic Director, Mark S. Hoebee; Executive Director, Mark W. Jones

Rodger and Hammerstein's *Oklahoma*! Book and Lyrics by Oscar Hammerstein; Music by Richard Rodgers; Director, James Brennan; Music Director, Tom Helm; Choreographer, Peggy Hickey; Original Scenic & Costumes, Anthony Ward; Set Coordination & Additional Design, Michael Allen; Lighting, F. Mitchell Dana; Sound, Randy Hansen; Costume Coordination, Gail Baldoni; Hair and Wig, Mark Adam Rampmeyer; Production Stage Manager, Peter Hanson; Casting, Alison Franck; Cast: Louisa Flaningam (Aunt Eller), Adam Monley (Curly), Brynn O'Malley (Laurey), Joseph Kolinski (Ike Skidmore), Stephen Carrasco (Slim), Daniel Bogart (Cord Elam), Brian Sears (Will Parker), Andrew Varela (Jud Fry), Megan Sikora (Ado Annie), Jonathan Brody (Ali Hakim), Kiira Schmidt (Gertie Cummings), John Jellison (Andrew Carnes), Sabra Lewis (Dream Laurey), Kyle Vaughn (Dream Curly); Ensemble: Ashley Adamek, J. David Anderson, Daniel Bogart, Stephen Carrasco, Drew Kenneth Franklin, Cynthia Leigh Heim, Anne Horak, Ryan Jackson, Sam Kiernan, Kimberly Lemieux, Sabra Lewis, Lauren Marshall, Steve Schepis, Kiira Schmidt, Elizabeth Stacey, Samantha Sturm, Kyle Vaughn, Ryan Worsing; September 17–October 19, 2008

Disney High School Musical Book by David Simpatico; Director, Mark S. Hoebee; Choreographer, Denis Jones; Music Director, Bruce W. Coyle; Original Scenic Design, Kenneth Foy; Set Coordination, Stephen Cowles; Costumes, Wade Laboissonniere; Costume Coordination and Additional Design, Brian Hemesath; Lighting, Tom Sturge; Sound, Randy Hansen; Hair & Wig, Cookie Jordan; Production Stage Manager, Jess W. Speaker III; Casting, Alison Franck; Cast: Chase Peacock (Troy Bolton), Justin Keyes (Chad Danforth), Sean Samuels (Zeke

Baylor), Sydney Morton (Gabriella Montez), Krystal Joy Brown (Taylor McKessie), Joline Mujica (Martha Cox), Sam Kiernan (Kratnoff), Joseph Morales (Jack Scott), Christopher Messina (Ripper), Sean Ewing (Mongo), Bailey Hanks (Sharpay Evans), Logan Hart (Ryan Evans), Stephanie Pam Roberts (Kelsi Neilson), Dante Russo (James), Marissa Joy Ganz (Susan), Becca Tobin (Cathy), Spencer Kiely (Alan), Deanna Aguinaga (Cyndra), Patrick Boll (Coach Bolton / Karaoke MC), Donna English (Ms. Darbus/Ms. Tenny), Marissa Joy Ganz (Decathlon Moderator); Ensemble: Deanna Aguinaga, Adrian Arrieta, Kristy Cavanaugh, Brittany Conigatti, Beth Crandall, Charity Sharday de Loera, Dean de Luna, Sean Ewing, Zach Frank, Taylor Frey, Marissa Joy Ganz, Spencer Kiely, Sam Kiernan, Victoria Meade, Christopher Messina, Joline Mujica, Dennis Necsary, Krista Pioppi, Dante Russo, Becca Tobin; November 5–December 7, 2008

The Importance of Being Earnest by Oscar Wilde; Director, David Schweizer; Scenic Design, Alexander Dodge; Costumes, David Murin; Lighting, Matt Frey; Sound, Randy Hansen; Hair & Wig, Mark Adam Rampmeyer; Production Stage Manager, Charles M. Turner III; Casting, Alison Franck; Cast: Wayne Wilcox (John Worthing, J.P.), Jeffrey Carlson (Algernon Moncrieff), Keith Reddin (Rev. Canon Chasuble, D.D.), Chris Spencer Wells (Oscar Wilde / Lane / Merriman) Lynn Redgrave (Lady Bracknell), Annika Boras (Hon. Gwendolen Fairfax), Zoe Winters (Cecily Cardew), Cynthia Mace (Miss Prism), Justin Bellero, Matthew Capodicasa (Footmen); January 14–February 15, 2009

Master Class written by Terrence McNally; Director, Wendy C. Goldberg; Music Supervisor, Andrew Gerle; Scenic Design, Alexander Dodge; Costumes, Anne Kennedy; Hair & Wig, Charles LaPointe; Lighting, Josh Epstein; Sound, Randy Hansen; Production Stage Manager, Barbara Reo; Casting, Alison Franck; Cast: Barbara Walsh (Maria Callas), Andrew Gerle (Manny), Lauren Worsham (Sophie), Ryan King (Stagehand), Sarah Uriarte Berry (Sharon), Mike McGowan (Tony); March 4–April 5, 2009

1776 Book by Peter Stone; Music & Lyrics by Sherman Edwards; Director, Gordon Greenberg; Choreographer, Josh Rhodes; Music Director, Tom Helm; Set, Kevin Rupnik; Costumes, Alejo Vietti; Lighting, Jeff Croiter; Sound, Randy Hansen; Hair & Wig, Charles LaPointe; Production Stage Manager, Richard C. Rauscher; Casting, Alison Franck; Cast: Nick Wyman (John Hancock), Ian R. Gleason (Dr. Josiah Bartlett), Don Stephenson (John Adams), MacIntyre Dixon (Stephen Hopkins), Todd Horman (Roger Sherman), Matthew C. Thompson (Lewis Morris), Erick Buckley (Robert Livingston), Jeff Brooks (Rev. John Witherspoon), Conrad John Schuck (Benjamin Franklin), Robert Cucciloi (John Dickinson), Jamie LaVerdiere (James Wilson), James Coyle (Caesar Rodney), Kenneth Cavett (Col. Thomas McKean) Michael Rose (George Read), Ric Stoneback (Samual Chase), Aaron Ramey (Richard Henry Lee), Kevin Earley (Thomas Jefferson), Michael Scibilia (Joseph Hewes), James Barbour (Edward Rutledge), Tom Treadwell (Dr. Lyman Hall), Kevin Pariseau (Charles Thomson), John O'Creagh (Andrew McNair), Kerry O'Malley (Abigail Adams), Lauren Kennedy (Martha Jefferson), Griffin Matthews (Courier), Curly Glynn (Leather Apron/Painter); April 15–May 17, 2009

The Full Monty Music & Lyrics by David Yazbek; Book by Terrence McNally; Director, Mark S. Hoebee; Choreographer, Denis Jones; Music Director (June 10– June 21), Tom Helm; Music Director (June 24–July 12) Deana Muro; Sets, Rob Bissinger; Costumes, Randall E. Klein; Lighting, Charlie Morrison; Sound, Randy Hansen; Hair & Wig, Gerard Kelly; Casting, Alison Franck; PSM, Jess W. Speaker III; Cast: Jason Babinsky (Ethan Girard), Jenn Colella (Georgie Bukatinsky), Joe Coots (Dave Bukatinsky), Milton Craig Nealy (Noah "Horse" T. Simmons), Alex Maizus (Nathan Lukowski), Michele Ragusa (Vicki Nichols), Allen E. Read (Malcolm MacGregor), Luke Marcus Rosen (Nathan Lukowski), Michael Rupert (Harold Nichols), Elaine Stritch (Jeanette Burmeister), Kelly Sullivan (Pam Lukowski), Wayne Wilcox (Jerry Lukowski), Xander Chauncey (Buddy "Keno" Walsh), Jacqueline Colmer, Rheaume Crenshaw, Holly Davis, Mark Fisher, Jerome Lucas Harmann, Susan J. Jacks, Brian Ray Norris, Rob Richardson, Timothy Smith, Catharine Lena Stephani, Corey James Wright; June 10–July 12, 2009.

Elaine Stritch and Milton Craig Nealy in The Full Monty *(photo by Kevin Sprague)*

People's Light and Theatre Company

Malvern, Pennsylvania
Thirty-fourth Season
Artistic Director, Abigail Adams; Managing Director, Grace Grillet

The Persians by Ellen McLaughlin; Director, Jade King Carroll; Sets, James F. Pyne, Jr., Costumes, Marla J. Jurglanis; Lighting, Lily Fossner; Original Music and Soundscape, Daniel Kluger; Stage Manager, Kate McSorley; Dramaturg, Elizabeth Pool; Cast: Melanye Finister (Queen Atossa), Miriam Hyman (Herald), Stephen Novelli (Darius), Mark Hairston (Xerxes), Alda Cortese (Treasury), Kevin Bergen (Chariman), Peter DeLaurier (Admiral), Ceal Phelan (Justice), Mary Elizabeth Scallen (State), Rob Barnes (General), Jason Ma (Religion), Claire Inie-Richards (Attendant); Main Stage; September 24–October 19, 2008

Cinderella by Kathryn Petersen; Director, Pete Pryor; Sets, James F. Pyne, Jr., Costumes, Rosemarie E. McKelvey; Lighting, Paul Hackenmueller; Original Music/Lyrics, Michael Ogborn; Music Director, David Ames; Production Manager/Sound Designer, Charles T. Brastow; Stage Manager, Kate McSorley; Video Designer, Jorge Cousineau; Assistant Director/Choreography, Samantha Bellomo; Dramaturg, Elizabeth Pool; Cast: Mark Lazar (Hazel Opfinder), Tom Teti (Oliver Opfinder), Kim Carson (Ella Opfinder/Cinderella), Kimberly Rehfuss (Baroness Lucretia Loosestrife), Erin Weaver (Invasia Loosestrife), Susan McKey (Poisianna Loosestrife), Jeffrey Coon (Prince Aiden of Sargasso), Christopher Patrick Mullen (Barnaby, The Valet), Chris Faith (Big Gus), Elena Bossler (Sudsy Squirrel), Andrew Kane (Tom Cat), Maggie Fitzgerald (Flea); World Premiere; Main Stage; November 19, 2008–January 4, 2009

The Day of the Picnic by Russell Davis; Director, Abigail Adams; Sets, Matt Saunders, Costumes, Marla J. Jurglanis; Lighting, Dennis Parichy; Sound Designer, Christopher Colucci; Stage Manager, Patricia G. Sabato; Assistant Director/Choreography, Samantha Bellomo; Dramaturg, Dialect Coach, Lynne Innerst; Video Designer, Jorge Cousineau; Alexander Teacher/Coach, Jano Cohen; Elizabeth Pool; Cast: Carla Belver (Betsy Fullbright), Brenda Thomas (Denise Jones), Graham Smith (Dinko Tasovac/Elijah), Nalini Sharma (Udaya [Dawn]/Kumari Sastri/Mary Magdalene), Michael Rogers (Julius Njumbi), Alda Cortese (Cookie Brault/Deutero Isaiah); World Premiere; Main Stage; January 28–February 15, 2009

Chris Faith, Andrew Kane, Elena Bossler and Maggie Fitzgerald in Cinderella: A Musical Panto *(photo by Mark Garvin)*

A Tale of Two Cities by Dwayne Hartford; Based on the novel by Charles Dickens; Director, Ken Marini; Sets, James F. Pyne, Jr., Costumes, Marla J. Jurglanis; Lighting, Paul Hackenmueller; Multimedia Designer, Anton Marini; Production Manager/Sound Designer, Charles T. Brastow; Stage Manager, Kate McSorley; Dialect Coach, Lynne Innerst; Dramaturg, Sarah B. Mantell; Cast: Kevin Bergen (Sydney Carton), Michael Stewart Allen (Charles Darnay), Stephen Novelli (Doctor Manette), Julianna Zinkel (Lucie Manette), Peter DeLaurier (Defarge), Mary Elizabeth Scallen (Madame Defarge), Marcia Saunders (Miss Pross), Paul Meshejian (Marquis), Tom Teti (Mr. Lorry), Mark Lazar (Gaspard); East Coast Premiere; Main Stage; March 11–May 3, 2009

Eggs by Y York; Based on the novel by Jerry Spinelli; Director, Mark Lutwak; Sets, James F. Pyne, Jr., Costumes, Marla J. Jurglanis; Lighting, Dennis Parichy; Composer/Sound Designer, Christopher Colucci; Stage Manager, Patricia G. Sabato; Dramaturg, Elizabeth Pool; Cast: Claire Inie-Richards (Primrose), Nathaniel Brastow (David), Alda Cortese (Margaret), Kittson O'Neill (Madam Dufee), Brian Anthony Wilson (Refrigerator John); World Premiere; Steinbright Stage; April 23–May 24, 2009

Doubt by John Patrick Shanley; Director, David Bradley; Sets, Yoshi Tanokura, Costumes, Marla J. Jurglanis; Lighting, Dennis Parichy; Original Music/Soundscape, Michael Keck; Stage Manager, Kate McSorley; Dramaturg, Elizabeth Pool; Cast: Pete Pryor (Father Flynn), Ceal Phelan (Sister Aloysius), Elizabeth Webster-Duke (Sister James), Melanye Finister (Mrs. Muller); Main Stage; June 3–28, 2009

End Days by Deborah Zoe Laufer; Director, Jackson Gay; Sets, Adrian W. Jones, Costumes, Jessica Ford; Lighting, Dennis Parichy; Sound Design/Original Music, Broken Chord Collective; Stage Manager, Thomas E. Shotkin; Dramaturg, Elizabeth Pool; Cast: Susan McKey (Sylvia Stein), David Ingram (Arthur Stein), Claire Inie-Richards (Rachel Stein), Aubie Merrylees (Nelson Steinberg), Ross Beschler (Jesus/Stephen Hawking); Steinbright Stage; July 8–August 2, 2009

Philadelphia Theatre Company

Philadelphia, Pennsylvania
Thirty-fifth Season
Sara Garonzik, Producing Artistic Director; Diane Claussen, Managing Director

Unusual Acts of Devotion by Terrence McNally; Director, Leonard Foglia; Set, Santo Loquasto; Costumes, Jess Goldstein; Lighting, Brian Nason; Sound, Ryan Rumery; Casting, Telsey + Company; Production Dramaturg, Warren Hoffman; Stage Manager, Marti McIntosh; Production Manager, Michael Cristaldi; Director of Production, Bruce Charlick; Cast: Michael Aronov (Leo), Viola Harris (Mrs. Darnell), Faith Prince (Josie), Ana Reeder (Nadine), Richard Thomas (Chick); World premiere; Philadelphia Theatre Company's Suzanne Roberts Theatre; October 22–November 23, 2008

Judy Gold in 25 Questions for a Jewish Mother by Kate Moira Ryan with Judy Gold; Director, Karen Kohlhaas; Philadelphia Premiere; Philadelphia Theatre Company's Suzanne Roberts Theatre; December 11–22, 2008

Resurrection by Daniel Beaty; Director, Oz Scott; Music, Daniel Bernard Roumain; Set, G.W. Mercier; Costumes, Karen Perry; Lighting, Jason Arnold; Sound, Michael Miceli; Casting, Cindi Rush Casting; Production Dramaturg, Edward Sobel; Stage Manager, John Scutchins; Production Manager, Michael Cristaldi; Director of Production, Bruce Charlick; Cast: Turron Kofi Alleyne ('Twon), Che Ayende (Dre), Thuliso Dingwall (Eric), Alvin Keith (Isaac), Keith Randolph Smith (Mr. Rogers), Jeffrey V. Thompson (The Bishop); Philadelphia Theatre Company's Suzanne Roberts Theatre; January 23–February 22, 2009

At Home At The Zoo by Edward Albee; Director, Mary B. Robinson; Set, James Noone; Costumes, Millie Hiibel; Lighting, Michael Lincoln; Sound, Daniel A. Little; NY Casting, Alan Filderman; Philadelphia Casting, Lois Kitz; Stage Manager, Jon Goldman; Production Dramaturg, Jacqueline Goldfinger; Production Manger, Michael Cristaldi; Director of Production, Bruce Charlick; Cast: T. Scott Cunningham (Peter), Susan McKey (Ann), Andrew Polk (Jerry); Philadelphia premiere; Philadelphia Theatre Company's Suzanne Roberts Theatre; March 20–April 19, 2009

Grey Gardens Book by Doug Wright; Music by Scott Frankel; Lyrics by Michael Korie; Director, Lisa Peterson; Set and Costumes, David Zinn; Lighting, Matthew Richards; Sound, Ryan Rumery; Projection Design, Jorge Cousineau; Musical Director, Eric Ebbenga; Hair and Make-up Design, Jon Carter; Arranger, Doug Peck; Dialect Coach, Melani Julian; Philadelphia Casting, Lois Kitz; NY Casting, Alan Filderman; Production Dramaturg, Warren Hoffman; Stage Manager, Linda Harris; Production Manager, Michael Cristaldi; Director of Production, Bruce Charlick; Choreography, Stephen Terrell; Cast: Todd Almond (George Gould Strong), Greta Bradbury (Jacqueline "Jackie" Bouvier), Cole Burden (Joseph Patrick Kennedy/Jerry), Kim Carson ("Little" Edit Beale), Maggie Fitzgerald (Jacqueline "Jackie" Bouvier-Select Performances), Joy Franz (Edith Bouvier Beale), James Ijames (Brooks), John Jellison (J.V. "Major" Bouvier/Norman Vincent Peale), Anastasia Korbal (Lee Bouvier), Hollis Resnik ("Little" Edie/Edith Bouvier Beale); Philadelphia Premiere; Philadelphia Theatre Company's Suzanne Roberts Theatre; May 22–June 28, 2009

Hollis Resnik and Joy Franz in Grey Gardens *(photo by Mark Garvin)*

Pittsburgh Civic Light Opera

Pittsburgh, Pennsylvania
Sixty-second Season
Executive Producer, Van Kaplan

The Color Purple Based upon the novel written by Alice Walker and the Warner Bros./Amblin Entertainment Motion Picture; Tour Produced by AEG Live; Director, Gary Griffin; Choreographer, Donald Byrd; Music and Lyrics, Brenda Russell, Allee Willis, Stephen Bray; Sets, John Lee Beatty; Costumes, Paul Tazewell; Lighting, Brian MacDevitt; Sound, Jon Weston; Hair, Charles G. LaPointe; Production Managers, Arthur Siccardi, Curtis Cowley; Production Supervisor, Kristen Harris; Tour Marketing and Press, C Major Marketing; General Management, NLA/Amy Jacobs; Music Director, Sheilah Walker; Dance Music Arrangements, Daryl Waters; Additional Arrangements, Joseph Joubert; Music Coordinator, Seymour Red Press; Orchestrations, Jonathan Tunick; Music Supervisor & Incidental Music Arrangements, Kevin Stites; Cast: Jeannette Bayardelle (Celie), Felicia P. Fields (Sofia), Angela Robinson (Shug Avery), Rufus Bonds Jr. (Mister), Stu James (Harpo), Mariama Whyte (Nettie), Stephanie St. James (Squeak), Lynette Dupree (Church Lady Jarene, u/s Sofia), Kimberly Ann Harris (Church Lady Doris, u/s Sofia), Adam Wade (Ol' Mister), Bridgette Bentley (Church Soloist, u/s Sofia), Shani M. Borden (Swing, u/s Nettie), Brian Harlan Brooke (Swing, Dance Captain), Renee Monique Brown (Ensemble, u/s Shug), LaTrisa Coleman (Older Olivia, Assistant Dance Captain), Darius Crenshaw (Ensemble), Tiffany Daniels (Ensemble, u/s Squeak), Quentin Earl Darrington (Pa, Chief, u/s Mister, Ol' Mister), Alex De Castro (Young Celie, Young Olivia, Older Henrietta), Lesly Terrell Donald (Buster, Bobby, u/s Harpo), Aliyah D. Flowers (Swing, u/s Young Harpo), Andre Garner (Swing), Rhett George (Ensemble, u/s Harpo), Phyre Hawkins (Swing, u/s Celie), Dameka Hayes (Ensemble, u/s Squeak), Latonya Holmes (u/s Celie, u/s Nettie), Jenna Ford Jackson (Ensemble, u/s Shug), Chauncey Jenkins (Older Adam, Ensemble), Trent Armand Kendall (Preacher, u/s Ol' Mister), Kristopher Thompson-Bolden (Ensemble), Diamond White (Young Nettie, Young Henrietta), Anthony Williams II (Young Harpo, Young Adam); The Benedum Center; June 3–15, 2008

Peter Pan Based on the play by James M. Barrie; Director, Glenn Casale; Lyrics, Carolyn Leigh; Music, Mark Charlap; Additional Music, Jules Styne; Additional Lyrics, Betty Comden and Adolph Green; Associate Producing Director, Lori Berger; Production Technical Supervisor, John R. Edkins; Associate Artistic Director, Jason Coll; Lighting, John McLain; Flying Sequences, Paul Rubin; Sets, John Iacovelli; Costumes, Shigeru Yaji; Flight Choreography, Sean Boyd; Production Stage Manager, Daniel L. Bello; Production Manager, Sean West; Musical Direction, Vocal Arrangements, New Orchestrations, Craig Barna; Cast: Cathy Rigby (Peter Pan), Tom Hewitt (Mr. Darling/Captain Hook), Elisa Sagardia (Wendy Darling), Tiffany Helland (Liza, Tiger Lily), John Hickok (Gentleman Starkey/Fight Director), Barbara McCulloh (Mrs. Darling, Grown-Up Wendy/Mermaid), Michael Nostrand (Mr. Smee), Dianna Barger (2nd Twin, Jane), Brittany Bohn (Curly), Korey Buecheler (Tootles), Dane Wagner (Slightly), Benjamin Yahr (1st Twin), Brian Brazon (John Darling), Joseph Serafini (Michael Darling), Rehima Jordan (Nibs), Kim Arnett (Ensemble/Dance Captain), Zachary Berger (Nana, Bill Jukes, Crocodile, Ensemble), Callan Bergmann (Ensemble), Ward Billeisen (Cecco/Ensemble), Kyle Brown (Ensemble), Yurel Echezarreta (Ensemble), Ahmad Simmons (Ensemble), Cary Tedder (Ensemble); The Benedum Center; June 21–July 2, 2008

Mame by Jerome Lawrence; Music and Lyrics, Jerry Herman; Director, Richard Sabellico, Choreographer, Richard Stafford; Associate Producing Director, Lori Berger; Production Technical Supervisor, John R. Edkins; Associate Artistic Director, Jason Coll; Music Director, Tom Helm; Lighting, John McLain; Sets, Walt Spangler; Production Stage Manager, Daniel L. Bello; Production Manager, Sean West; Cast: Michele Lee (Mame Dennis), Ruth Williamson (Vera Charles), Donna Lynne Champlin (Agnes Gooch), John Hickok (Beauregard Jackson Pickett Burnside), Tim Brady (Dwight Babcock), Danny Cinski (Patrick Dennis,

age 10), Dana Steer (Ralph Devine/Patrick Dennis, age 19–29), Mary Stout (Dance Teacher, Madame Branislowski, Mother Burnside, Mrs. Upson), Paul Palmer (Mr. Upson), Patrick Boll (M. Lindsay Woolsey/Uncle Jeff), Barbara McCulloh (Sally Cato), Orville Mendoza (Ito), Nathan Steinhauer (Peter Dennis, u/s, Patrick Dennis, age 10), Zachary S. Berger (Leading man/Dancer/Ensemble), Callan Bergmann (Ensemble), Ward Billeisen (Ensemble), Ashley Blanchet (Pegeen Ryan, Ensemble), Kyle Brown (Doorman, Ensemble), Kaitlyn Davidson (Gloria Upson, Dancer, Dance Captain), Yurel Echezarreta (Gregor, Ensemble); Steffi Garrard (Ensemble), Alexa Glover (Ensemble), Tracy Groth (Ensemble), Tiffany Helland (Ensemble), Freddie Kimmel (Elevator Boy, Stage Manager, Junior Babcock, Ensemble), Scott Larsen (Messenger, Ensemble), Stephanie Maloney (Cousin Fan, Ensemble), Gabrielle McClinton (Art Model, Ensemble), Shina Ann Morris (Ensemble), Mary Michael Patterson (Ensemble), Justin Peebles (Ensemble), Ahmad Simmons (Ensemble), Cary Tedder (Ensemble) The Benedum Center; July 8–13, 2008

Smokey Joe's Café: The Songs of Leiber and Stoller by Jerry Leiber and Mike Stoller; Director and Chroreographer, Barry Ivan; Associate Producing Director, Lori Berger; Production Technical Supervisor, John R. Edkins; Associate Artistic Director, Jason Coll; Musical Director, Craig Barna; Lighting, John McLain; Sets, Tom Sturge; Production Stage Manager, Daniel L. Bello; production Manager, Sean West; Cast: Phillip Boykin, Terry Burrell, Renee Feder, Bob Gaynor, Deb Lyons, Kevyn Morrow, Clifton Oliver, Debra Walton, Harrison White; The Benedum Center; July 15–20, 2008

Annie Get Your Gun by Irving Berlin, Original Book by Herbert and Dorothy Fields, as revised by Peter Stone; Director, Charles Repole; Choreographer, John MacInnis; Associate Producing Director, Lori Berger; Production Technical Supervisor, John R. Edkins; Associate Artistic Director, Jason Coll; Musical Director, Tom Helm; Lighting, John McLain; Sets, Bruce Brockman; Costumes, Sharell Martin; Production Stage Manager, Daniel L. Bello; Production Manager, Sean West; Cast: Jenn Colella (Annie Oakley), Matthew Ashford (Frank Butler), Paula Leggett Chase (Dolly Tate), Joel Blum (Charlie Davenport), Patrick Boll (Buffalo Bill), Orville Mendoza (Sitting Bull), Savannah Wise (Winnie Tate), Andrew Cao (Tommy Keelor), Tim Brady (Wilson, Pawnee Bill), Michelle Coben (Jessie Oakley), Sidney Popielarcheck (Nellie Oakley), Ben Nadler (Little Jake), Zachary S. Berger (Ensemble/Messenger), Callan Bergmann (Ensemble/Messenger), Ward Billeisen (Ensemble, Mac, the Prop Man), Ashley Blanchet (Ensemble, Mrs. Sylvia Potter-Porter), Kyle Brown (Ensemble), Kaitlyn Davidson (Ensemble, Mrs. Schuyler Adams), Yurel Echezarreta (Ensemble), Steffi Garrard (Ensemble), Alexa Glover (Ensemble), Tracy Groth (Ensemble), Freddie Kimmel (Ensemble, Band Leader), Scott Larsen (Ensemble, Eagle Feather), Stephanie Maloney (Ensemble), Gabrielle McClinton (Ensemble), Shina Ann Morris (Ensemble, Dance Captain), Mary Michael Patterson (Ensemble), Justin Peebles (Ensemble, Running Deer), Lisa Rumbauskas (Ensemble), Ahmad Simmons (Ensemble), Cary Tedder (Ensemble); The Benedum Center; July 22–August 3, 2008

West Side Story Original Conception, Jerome Robbins; Book, Arthur Laurents; Music, Leonard Bernstein; Lyrics, Stephen Sondheim; Director, Van Kaplan; Choreographer, Mark Esposito; Associate Producing Director, Lori Berger; Production Technical Supervisor, John R. Edkins; Associate Artistic Director, Jason Coll; Musical Director, Tom Helm; Lighting Designer, John McLain; Scenery, Leo Meyers; Production Stage Manager, Daniel L. Bello; Production Manager, Sean West; Cast: Max Von Essen (Tony), Ali Ewoldt (Maria), Manoly Farrell (Anita), Wilson Mendieta (Bernardo), Spencer Howard (Riff/Fight Captain), Darren Biggart (A-Rab), Ward Billeisen (Snowboy), Andrew Cao (Chino), Allison Nock (Anybodys), Cary Tedder (Action), Mikey Winslow (Baby John), Amos Wolff (Big Deal), Gene A. Saraceni (Doc), Tim Brady (Lt. Schrank), Paul Palmer (Officer Krupke), Gary Kline (Gladhand), Zachary S. Berger (Luis), Callan Bergmann (Gee-Tar), Ashley Blanchet (Rosalia), Kyle Brown (Pepe), Kaitlyn Davidson (Velma), Jeff David (Diesel), Yurel Echezarreta (Anxious), Steffi Garrard (Clarice), Tracy Groth (Minnie), Freddie Kimmel (Mouthpiece), Scott Larsen (Toro), Gabrielle McClinton (Francisca), Shina Ann Morris (Consuela), Sydney Morton (Estella), Mary Michael Patterson (Pauline), Justin Peebles (Nibbles), Robert James Priore (Moose), Mahri Relin (Grazielle/Dance Captain), Lisa Rumbauskas (Margarita),

Ahmad Simmons (Indio), Kathryn Lin Terza (Teresita); The Benedum Center; August 5–17, 2008

I Love You, You're Perfect, Now Change by Joe DiPietro; Book and Lyrics, Joe DiPietro; Music, Jimmy Roberts; Associate Artistic Director, Jason Coll; Director, James Brennan; Stage Manager, Tim Brady; Costume Designer, Barbara Anderson; Musical Director, Deana Muro; Lighting Designer, Andrew David Ostrowski; Set Designer, Andrea Shockling; Associate Producing Director, Lori Berger; Cast: Joseph Domenic (Man One), Christine Laitta (Woman Two), Kristiann Menotiades (Woman One), Caitlin Elizabeth Reilly (Understudy), Mark Tinkey (Understudy), Ted Watts, Jr. (Man Two); The CLO Cabaret; October 9, 2008–February 1, 2009.

A Musical Christmas Carol by Charles Dickens; Stage Adaptation by David H. Bell; Director and Choreographer, Tim Gregory; Associate Producing Director, Lori Berger; Production Technical Supervisor, John R. Edkins; Sets, D Martyn Bookwalter; Lighting, Scott Nelson; Musical Director, Bruce Barnes; Musical Arrangements, Rob Bowman, McCrae Hardy; Stage Manager, Fredric H. Orner; Cast: Tom Atkins (Ebenezer Scrooge), Greggory Brandt (Caroler, Party Guest, Spirit at Window), Laura Lee Brautigam (Fran, Alice, Laundress), Christopher J. Cannon (Peter Cratchit, Young Scrooge's Schoolmate), Jeremy Czarniak (Fred, Businessman), Paul Domenic (Town Crier, Young Scrooge, Ghost of Christmas Yet to Come), Jodi Gage (Caroler, Party Guest, Spirit at Window), Brittany Graham (Caroler, Party Guest, Spirit at Window), Michael Greer (Goose Vendor, School Master, Toy Train Vendor, Topper), Tim Hartman (Charity Worker, Mr. Fezziwig, Ghost of Christmas Present, Businessman), Jeff Howell (Bob Cratchit), Christina McCann (Missy Watkins, Martha Cratchit), Scott P. Sambuco (Caroler, Party Guest, Spirit at Window, Young Scrooge's Schoolmate), Ryan Schmidt (Tom Watkins, Dick Wilkins, Undertaker), Joseph Serafini (Tiny Tim), Amanda Serra (Charity Worker, Ghost of Christmas Past/Peg), Amanda Slaughter (Belle/Bess), Jennifer Veltre Smith (Mrs. Cratchit), Derek Walton (Marley's Ghost, Young Marley, Businessman), Terry Wickline (Mrs. Dilber, Mrs. Fezziwig); The Benedum Center; December 5–21, 2008

My Way: "A Musical Tribute to Frank Sinatra" Conceived by David Grapes and Todd Olson; Book, Todd Olson; Original Production Director, David Grapes; Associate Producing Director, Lori Berger; Production Technical Supervisor, John R. Edkins; Set/Props Designer, Andrea Shockling; Lighting Designer, Andrew David Ostrowski; Costume Designer, Susan O'Neill; Production Stage Manager, Michael Greer; Music Director, Deana Muro; Choreographer, Gavan Pamer; Director, David Grapes; Cast: Joseph Domenic (Man #2), John Fedo (Man #1/Dance Captain), Karen M. Jeffreys (Woman #2), Kristiann Menotiades (Woman #1), Tim Brady (Understudy), Caitlin Elizabeth Reilly (Understudy); The CLO Cabaret; February 12–May 10, 2009

8-Track: The Sounds of the 70's Conceived and Directed, Rick Seeber; Choreography, Tonya Phillips Staples; Musical Arrangements, Michael Gribbin; Associate Producer, Patricia Williams; Production Sound Consultant, Mark Derryberry; Musical Supervisor, Rich Seeber; Associate Producing Director, Lori Berger; Production Technical Supervisor, John R. Edkins; Set/Props Designer, Andrea Shockling; Lighting Designer, Andrew David Ostrowski; Wardrobe Designer, Barbara Wolfe; Production Stage Manager, Tim Brady; Music Director, Deana Muro; Cast: Bradley Beahen (Baritone), Teddey Brown (Tenor), Kristiann Menotiades (Understudy/Assistant Stage Manager), Tess Primack (Alto), Jon-Michael Reese (Understudy), Tess Soltau (Soprano); The CLO Cabaret; May 21–September 27, 2009

Joseph and the Amazing Technicolor Dreamcoat Lyrics, Tim Rice; Music, Andrew Lloyd Webber; Director and Choreographer, Richard Stafford; Associate Producing Director, Lori Berger; Production Technical Supervisor, John R. Edkins; Musical Director, Craig Barna; Lighting Designer, John McLain; Set Designer, James Fouchard; Costume Designer, Susan Ruddie; Production Stage Manager, Daniel S. Rosokoff; Production Manager, Sean West; Cast: Shoshana Bean (Narrator), David Osmond (Joseph), Gene A. Saraceni (Jacob, Potiphar Guru), Peter Matthew Smith (Pharaoh, Levi), Callan Bergmann (Ensemble, Dan), Sae La Chin (Ensemble, Mrs. Potiphar), Kaitlyn Davidson (Ensemble), Lucas Fedele

(Ensemble, Issachar), Steffi Garrard (Ensemble), Michael Greer (Ensemble, Asher), Tracy Groth (Ensemble), Elisa Halma (Ensemble), Jamie Markovich (Ensemble), Gabrielle E. McClinton (Ensemble), Jarran Muse (Ensemble, Judah, Baker), Natalie Newman (Ensemble), Gavan Pamer (Ensemble, Reuben), Ahmad Simmons (Ensemble, Gad), Jason Sparks (Ensemble, Zebulun, Butler), Lauren Sprague (Ensemble), Jonathan Stahl (Ensemble, Napthatlie, Dance Captain), Kathryn Lin Terza (Ensemble), Cody Williams (Ensemble, Benjamin), Lee Zarrett (Ensemble, Simeon); The Benedum Center; May 26–June 7, 2009

Pittsburgh Public Theater

Pittsburgh, Pennsylvania
Thirty-fourth Season
Ted Pappas, Producing Artistic Director

The Chief by Rob Zellers and Gene Collier; Director, Ted Pappas; Sets and Costumes, Anne Mundell; Lighting, Phil Monat; Sound, Zach Moore; Stage Manager, Fred Noel; Cast: Tom Atkins (Arthur J. Rooney, Sr.); September 16–21, 2008

Radio Golf by August Wilson; Director, Ron OJ Parson; Sets, Jack Magaw; Costumes, Myrna Colley-Lee; Lighting, Brian Sidney Bembridge; Sound, Vincent Olivieri; Stage Manager, Fredric H. Orner; Cast: Tyla Abercrumbie (Mame Wilks), Morocco Omari (Harmond Wilks), Montae Russell (Sterling Johnson), E. Milton Wheeler (Roosevelt Hicks), Alfred H. Wilson (Elder Joseph Barlow); October 2–November 2, 2008

The Lady With All the Answers by David Rambo; Director, Ted Pappas; Sets, James Noone; Costumes, Ted Pappas; Lighting, Allen Hahn; Sound, Zach Moore; Stage Manager, Fred Noel; Cast: Helena Ruoti (Eppie Lederer "Ann Landers"); November 13–December 14, 2008

Helena Ruoti in The Lady With All the Answers *(photo by Ric Evans)*

Metamorphoses by Mary Zimmerman; Director, Ted Pappas; Sets, James Noone; Costumes, Susan Tsu; Lighting, Kirk Bookman; Sound, Zach Moore; Stage Manager, Ruth E. Kramer; Cast: J.T. Arbogast (Phaeton/others), Craig Baldwin (Orpheus/others), Ka-Ling Cheung (Myrrha/others), Tami Dixon (Therapist/others), Darren Eliker (Midas/others), Daina Michelle Griffith (Aphrodite/others), Lara Hillier (Alcyone/others), Daniel Krell (Erysichthon/others), Sipiwe Moyo (Eurydice/others), Bhavesh Patel (Vertumnus/others); January 15–February 15, 2009

The World Goes 'Round Music by John Kander, Lyrics by Fred Ebb; Conceived by Scott Ellis, Susan Stroman, David Thompson; Director, Marcia Milgrom Dodge; Music Director, Michael Rice; Sets, Narelle Sissons; Costumes, Martha Louise Bromelmeier; Lighting, Kirk Bookman; Sound, Zach Moore; Stage Manager, Zoya Kachadurian; Cast: Patrick Boyd, Rosena M. Hill, Tari Kelly, Michele Ragusa, Rob Sutton; March 5–April 5, 2009

A Moon for the Misbegotten by Eugene O'Neill; Director, Pamela Berlin; Sets, Allen Moyer; Costumes, Candice Donnelly; Lighting, Frances Aronson; Sound, Zach Moore; Stage Manager, Fredric H. Orner; Cast: Beth Wittig (Josie Hogan), Jason McCune (Mike Hogan), Tom Atkins (Phil Hogan), Victor Slezak (James Tyrone, Jr.), Daniel Krell (T. Stedman Harder); April 16–May 17, 2009

Harry's Friendly Service by Rob Zellers; Director, Ted Pappas; Sets, James Noone; Costumes, Martha Louise Bromelmeier; Lighting, Kirk Bookman; Sound, Zach Moore; Stage Manager, Fred Noel; Cast: Joel Ripka (john), Larry John Meyers (Skiddie), Edward James Hyland (Harry), Brooks Almy (Tina), Tressa Glover (Emily), Daryll Heysham (Sammy Carducci), Alex Coleman (Carmine Carducci); May 28–June 28, 2009

Edward James Hyland, Tressa Glover and Brooks Almy in Harry's Friendly Service *(photo by Michael Henninger)*

Playmaker's Repertory Company

Chapel Hill, North Carolina
Thirty-third Season
Producing Artistic Director, Joseph Haj; Managing Director, Hannah Grannemann

Pericles by William Shakespeare; Director, Joseph Haj; Set, Jan Chambers; Costumes, McKay Coble; Lighting, Justin Townsend; Stage Manager, Sarah Smiley; Cast, Prince T. Bowie (Cerimon/Ensemble), John Brummer (Ensemble), Jeffrey Blair Cornell (Antiochus/Simonides), Ray Dooley (Gower), Kahlil Gonzalez-Garcia (Ensemble), Joy Jones (Doinyza, Thaisa), Jimmy Kieffer (Ensemble), Derrick Ledbetter (Ensemble), Marianne Miller (Lychorida/Diana/Ensemble), Matthew Murphy (Lysimachus/Ensemble), Jason Powers (Thaliard/Boult/Ensemble), Scott Ripley (Pericles), Kenneth P. Strong (Helicanus/Cleon), Alice Whitley (Antiochus' daughter/Marina/Ensemble); Mainstage; September 24–October 12, 2008

Blue Door by Tanya Barfield; Director, Trezana Beverley; Sets, Marion Williams; Costumes, Jade Bettin; Lighting, Peter West; Sound, Michael Matthews; Stage Manager, Charles Bayang; Cast, Lelund Durond Thompson (Simon/Rex/Jesse), Sam Wellington (Lewis); Mainstage; October 22–November 9, 2008

Cummins and Scoullar's The Little Prince Adapted by Rick Cummins and John Scoullar; Director, Tom Quaintance; Sets and Costumes, McKay Coble; Lighting, Justin Townsend; Sound, Michèl Marrano; Stage Manager, Sarah Smiley; Cast, John Brummer (King/Merchant), Joy Jones (Snake/Conceited Man/Wall of Roses), Jimmy Kieffer (Businessman/Ensemble), Derrick Ledbetter (Little Prince), Marriane Miller (Rose/Wall of Roses), Matthew Murphy (Turkish Astronomer/Geographer), Flor De Liz Perez (Tippler/Wall of Roses), Jason Powers (Fox/Lamplighter), Scott Ripley (Aviator); Mainstage; November 26–December 14, 2008

Well by Lisa Kron; Director, Joseph Haj; Sets, Jan Chambers, McKay Coble; Costumes, Anne Porterfield; Lighting, Robert Peterson; Sound, Michael Matthews; Stage Manager, Sarah Smiley; Cast, Prince T. Bowie (Ensemble), Julie Fishell (Lisa Kron), Joy Jones (Ensemble), Jeffrey Meanza (Ensemble), Kim Ostrenko (Ensemble), Brenda Wehle (Ann Kron); Mainstage; January 24–March 1, 2009 (in repertory with The Glass Menagerie)

The Glass Menagerie by Tennessee Williams; Director, Libby Appel; Sets, McKay Coble, Jan Chambers; Costumes, Jan Chambers, Lighting, Robert Peterson, Sound, Michael Matthews, Stage Manager, Charles K. Bayang; Cast, Judith-Marie Bergan (Amanda), John Brummer (Gentleman Caller), Ray Dooley (Older Tom), Marianne Miller (Laura), John Tufts (Younger Tom); Mainstage; in repertory with Well; January 25–February 28, 2009 (in repertory with Well)

Pride and Prejudice Adapted by Jon Jory; Director, Timothy Douglas; Sets, Junghyun Georgia Lee; Costumes, Camille Assaf; Lighting, Marcus Doshi; Sound, Michael Matthews; Stage Manager, Charles Bayang; Cast, Noel Joseph Allain (Mr. Darcy), Alison Altman (Lydia Bennet), Jeffrey Blair Cornell (Mr. Bennet), Ray Dooley (Sir William Lucas/Collins/Mr. Gardiner), Julie Fishel (Mrs. Bennet), Kahlil Gonzalez-Garcia (Mr. Bingley/Servant), Joy Jones (Miss Bingley), Jimmy Kieffer (George Wickham/Ball Guest), Derrick Ledbetter (Colonel Fitxwilliam), Mereda Hart Mason (Mary Bennet), Marianne Miller (Jane Bennet), Julie Nelson (Lady Catherine/Mrs. Gardiner), Flor De Liz Perez (Kitty Bennet), Jason Powers (Ball Guest/Officer/Servant), Kristin Villanueva (Elizabeth Bennet), Alice Whitley (Charlotte Lucas); Mainstage; April 1–19, 2009

Kristin Villanueva , Mereda Hart Mason, Marianne Miller, Allison Altman, Flor De Liz Perez, Julie Fishell and Jeffrey Blair Cornell in Pride and Prejudice *(photo by Jon Gardiner)*

In The Continuum by Danai Gurira and Nikkole Salter; Director, Liesl Tommy; Sets and Costumes, Marion Williams; Lighting, Eric Ketchum; Sound, Michael Matthews; Stage Manager, Charles Bayang; Cast, Flor De Liz Perez (Nia/Others), DeWanda Wise (Abigail/Others); PRC [2] Second Stage, September 10–14, 2008

The Young Ladies of... by Taylor Mac; Director, Tracy Trevett; Sets, David Evan Morris; Lighting, Juliet Chia; Puppets, Basil Twist; Associate Production Manager, Natalie Robin; Cast, Taylor Mac; PRC [2] Second Stage; January 7–11, 2009

9 Parts of Desire by Heather Raffo; Director, Emily Ranii; Sets and Costumes, Marion Williams; Lighting, Ross Kolman; Sound, Michael Matthews; Stage Manager, Sarah Smiley; Cast, Elizabeth Huffman; PRC [2] Second Stage; April 22–26, 2009

Portland Stage Company

Portland, Maine
Thirty-fifth Season
Executive and Artistic Director: Anita Stewart; Managing Director: Camilla Barrantes

Julius Caesar by William Shakespeare; Director, Lucy Smith Conroy; Set, Anita Stewart; Costumes, Kris Hall; Lighting, Bryon Winn; Sound: Matt O'Hare; Stage Manager: Myles C. Hatch; Cast: Dan Domingues (Brutus), Mark Friedlander (Soothsayer), Tavia Gilbert (Cinna), J.P. Guimont (Caska), Kevin Kelly (Caesar /Strato), Natalie Rose Liberace (Calphurnia), Michael Sharon (Antony), Rebecca Watson (Cassius), Sally Wood (Portia/Octavius), Ensemble: Karen Ball, Rick Blake, Kristi DeVille, David Glendinning, Madeleine Paine, Denver Rey Whisman; Main Stage; September 23–October 19, 2008

Wait Until Dark by Frederick Knott; Director, Sam Buggeln; Set, Wilson Chin; Costumes, Chris Rumery; Lighting, Gregg Carville; Sound, Chris Fitze; Stage Manager, Shane Van Vliet; Cast: Demosthenes Chrysan (Sgt. Carlino), Zabryna Guevara (Susy Hendrix), James Herrera (Sam Hendrix), Bryant Richards (Mike Talman), John Wojda (Harry Roat, Jr.), Lynnea Harding and Lena Needelman (Gloria), Corey Gagne (Policeman), JP Guimont (Policeman); Main Stage; October 28– November 23, 2008

A Christmas Carol Based on the Tale by Charles Dickens; Adapted by Christopher Akerlind, Dawn McAndrews and Anita Stewart; Director and Set, Anita Stewart; Costumes, Jacqueline Firkins and Susan Thomas; Lighting, Bryon Winn; Composer, Peter John Still; Stage Manager, Myles C. Hatch; Cast: Maureen Butler (Mrs. Cratchit), Dan Domingues (Nephew Fred), Mark Honan (Bob Cratchit), John Little (Ebenezer Scrooge), Cristine McMurdo-Wallis (Ghosts), Daniel Noel (Jacob Marley) Sally Wood (Belle), Ensemble: Jane Ackermann, Rick Blake, Cecelia Botting, Spencer Cohen, Emma Dadmun, Hannah Daly, Nora Daly, Jenny DiPhilippo, Josie DiPhilippo, Alex Frank, Owen Freeman, David Glendinning, Cotey Green, August Halm-Perazone, Tim Hartel, Leo Hilton, Elinor Hilton, Charlotte Honan-Warnock, Louisa Mahoney, Madeleine Paine, Owen Pence, Bridget Ruff, Mary Savidge, Elizabeth Tarantino, Valerie Tarantino, Witt Tarantino; Main Stage; December 5– December 24, 2008

The SantaLand Diaries by David Sedaris; Director, Daniel Burson; Set, Anita Stewart; Costumes, Susan Thomas; Lights and Sound, Matthew Cost; Stage Manager, Marjorie Gallant; Cast: Dustin Tucker (David); Studio Theatre; November 28–December 21, 2008

Peer Gynt by Henrik Ibsen; Director and Set, Anita Stewart; Collaborators/Puppet Design, Figures of Speech; Costumes, Loyce Arthur; Lighting, Bryon Winn; Sound, Jill BC Du Boff; Dramaturg, Daniel Burson; Stage Manager, Shane Van Vliet; Cast: Noah Brody (Peer Gynt), Moira Driscoll (Aase/Lean One), J.P. Guimont (Aslak/Button Molder), Mark Honan (Solveig's Father/Troll King), Victoria Soyer (Ingrid/Woman in Green/Anitra), Dustin Tucker (Mads/Strange Passenger), Sally Wood (Solveig), Ensemble: Jane Ackerman, Mike Best, Cecelia Botting, Nora Daly, Cotey Green, August Halm-Perazone, Charlotte Honan-Warnock, Irene Lemay, Alison Matthews, Bill McCue, Owen Pence, Susan Reilly, Denver Rey Whisman; January 27–February 22, 2008

Out of Sterno by Deborah Zoe Laufer; Director, Casey Stangl; Set, Anita Stewart; Costumes, Chris Rumery; Lighting, Bryon Winn; Sound, Stephen Swift; Stage Manager, Myles C. Hatch; Cast: Patricia Buckley (Zena), Torsten Hillhouse (Hamel), Janice O'Rourke (Dotty), Phillip Taratula (Dan); World Premiere; Main Stage; March 3–March 22, 2009

The Passion of the Hausfrau by Bess Welden, Annette Jolles and Nicole Chaison; Director, Annette Jolles; Set and Projections, Anita Stewart; Lights, Matthew Cost; Composer/Sound, Hans Indigo Spencer; Projection Art, Nicole Chaison; Cast: Bess Welden (Hausfrau), World Premiere; Studio Theatre; March 19–April 11, 2009

Trying by Joanna McClelland Glass; Director, Paul Mullins; Set, Deb Booth; Costumes, Anita Stewart; Lighting, Michael Giannitti; Sound, Chris Fitze: Stage Manager, Shane Van Vliet; Main Cast: Sofia Jean Gomez (Sarah Schorr), Jonathan McMurtry (Judge Biddle); March 31–April 19, 2008

The Drawer Boy by Michael Healey; Director, Sally Wood; Set, Anita Stewart; Costumes, Anita Stewart; Lighting, Gregg Carville; Sound, Stephen Swift; Stage Manager, Myles C. Hatch; Cast: Larry Nicks (Morgan), Daniel Noel (Angus), Matthew Shawlin (Miles); Main Stage: April 28–May 24, 2008

FROM AWAY FESTIVAL: INTERNATIONAL PLAYWRIGHTS FESTIVAL

Just Vinyl by Alina Nelega; Directed by Andrew Harris; Cast: Mark Honan (Romeo), Sally Wood (Roberta), Tess Van Horn (Christina), Peter Brown (Michael), Moira Driscoll (Lili), Daniel Noel (Jimmy), Kristi DeVille (Fanny), Dustin Tucker (Andrew), Janice O'Rourke (Diane), J.P. Guimont (Pepe), Staged Reading; Main Stage; November 10, 2008

20TH ANNUAL LITTLE FESTIVAL OF THE UNEXPECTED

Last Gas by John Cariani; Director, Daniel Burson; Cast: Dave Mason (Nat), Peter Brown (Guy), John D. McNally (Dwight), Ian Carlsen (Troy), Moira Driscoll (C.T.), Abby Killeen (Lurene), Staged Reading; Studio Theatre; May 13 and 16, 2009

The Toymaker's War by Jennifer Fawcett; Director, Susan Schulman; Cast: Sally Wood (Sylvie), Ian Carlsen (Milan), Cecelia Botting (Lejla), Peter Brown (Peter), Staged Reading, Studio Theatre; May 14 and 16, 2009

The Real McGonagall by Willy Holtzman; Director, Ron Botting; Cast: Mark Honan (McGonagall), Staged Reading; Studio Theatre; May 15 and 16, 2009

J. P. Guimont, Moira Driscoll and Noah Brody in Peer Gynt (photo by Darren Setlow)

Repertory Theatre of St. Louis

St. Louis, Missouri
Forty-second Season
Artistic Director, Steven Woolf; Managing Director, Mark Bernstein

Frost Nixon by Peter Morgan; Director, Steven Woolf; Set, Michael Schweikardt; Costumes, Elizabeth Covey; Lighting, Mary Jo Dondlinger; Sound, Rusty Wandall; Video Design, Eric Woolsey; Video Consultant, Bobby Miller; Stage Manager, Glenn Dunn; Assistant Stage Manager, Shannon B. Sturgis; Cast: Keith Jochim (Richard Nixon), Michael Brightman (Ollie/others), Jim Wisniewski (Jim Reston), Steve Callahan (Studio Manager/others), Jeff Talbott (David Frost), Jeremy Holm (Jack Brennan), Kelley Ryan (Evonne Goolagong/others), Keith Merrill (John Birt), David Anzuelo (Manolo Sanchez), Matt Landers (Swifty Lazar), Jenny Mercein (Caroline Cushing), David Christopher Wells (Bob Zelnick); Virginia Jackson Browning Mainstage; September 3–September 28, 2008

Jane Austen's Emma-A New Musical Adapted from the novel by Jane Austen; Music, Lyrics and Book by Paul Gordon; Director, Robert Kelley; Musical Director, Laura Bergquist; Choreography, Mary Beth Cavanaugh; Orchestrator, Paul Gordon; Set, John Ezell; Costumes, Fumiko Bielefeldt; Lighting, Dennis Parichy; Sound, Michael Miceli; Stage Manager, T.R. Martin; Assistant Stage Manager, Tony Dearing; Cast: Lianne Marie Dobbs (Emma), Christianne Tisdale (Mrs. Weston), Kurt Zischke (Mr. Weston), Richert Easley (Mr. Woodhouse), Timothy Gulan (Mr. Knightley), Brian Herndon (Mr. Elton), Suzanne Grodner (Miss Bates), Donna Weinsting (Mrs. Bates/Housekeeper), Dani Marcus (Harriet Smith), Travis Poelle (Frank Churchill), Julie Hanson (Jane Fairfax), Alex Organ (Mr. Robert Martin/Servant), Erin Maguire (Mrs. Elton/Mrs. Churchill), Michael Brightman (Butler/Minister), Josie Adams (Servant), Courtney Leigh Halford (Servant), Sam Hay (Servant), Aaron Sitrick (Servant), The Company (Citizens of Highbury), Understudies: Julie Hanson (Emma), Travis Poelle (Mr. Knightley); Virginia Jackson Browning Mainstage; October 8–November 2, 2008

This Wonderful Life Written by Steve Murray; Conceived by Mark Setlock; Director, Martha Banta; Set, James Wolk; Costumes, Lou Bird; Lighting, Matt Frey; Sound, Jill BC Du Boff; Stage Manager, Glenn Dunn; Assistant Stage Manager, Shannon B. Sturgis; Cast: Mark Setlock; Virginia Jackson Browning Mainstage; November 26–December 28, 2008

Saint Joan by George Bernard Shaw; Director, Paul Mason Barnes; Set, Robert Mark Morgan; Costumes, Dorothy Marshall Englis; Lighting, Peter Sargent; Sound, Rusty Wandall; Stage Manager, T.R. Martin; Assistant Stage Manager, Tony Dearing; Cast: Jerry Vogel (Squire Robert de Baudricourt/Canon D'estivet/Promoter), Brian White (Steward to de Baudricourt/A Gentleman from the Vatican), Tarah Flanagan (Joan), Matt D'Amico (Bertrand de Poulengey/Brother Martin Ladvenu/Assessor), James Anthony (Archbishop of Rheims), Stephen Paul Johnson (Lord Chamberlain, Duc de la Tremouille/Canon Courcelles/Assessor), Greg Fink (Court Page), Keith Merrill (Gilles de Rais (Bluebeard)/Executioner), Jason Cannon (Captain La Hire/English Soldier), Bobby Steggert (Charles, the Dauphin), Kevin Orton (Jack Dunois, Bastard of Orleans), Ian Way (Page to Dunois), John Rensenhouse (Richard de Beauchamp, Earl of Warwick), Christopher Gerson (Chaplain John de Stogumber), Andrew Stroud (Page to Warwick), Tuck Milligan (Peter Cauchon/Bishop of Beauvais), Jonathan Gillard Daly (Brother John Lemaitre/Inquisitor), Jonathan Gillard Daly, Matt D'Amico, Jerry Vogel, Sam Hay, Tyler Beveridge, Greg Fink, Ian Way, Brian White (Pages/Monks/Soldiers/Courtiers); Virginia Jackson Browning Mainstage; January 7–February 1, 2009

The Miracle Worker by William Gibson; Director, Susan Gregg; Set, John Ezell; Costumes, James Scott; Lighting, Michael Philippi; Sound, Tom Mardikes; Stage Manager, Glenn Dunn; Assistant Stage Manager, Shannon B. Sturgis; Cast: Ashlee Marnae (Martha), Jarrett D. Harkless (Percy), Olivia Jane Prosser (Helen), Hannah Ryan (Helen), Krista Hoeppner (Kate), Matthew Carlson (James), Donna Weinsting (Aunt Ev), John Rensenhouse (Captain Keller), Jerry Vogel (Mr. Anagnos), Amy Landon (Annie), Monica Parks (Viney), Murray (Kellers' Dog); Virginia Jackson Browning Mainstage; February 11–March 8, 2009

Dr. Jekyll and Mr. Hyde Adapted by Jeffrey Hatcher; From the novella *Strange Case of Dr. Jekyll and Mr. Hyde* by Robert Louis Stevenson; Director, Edward Stern; Set, Robert Mark Morgan; Costumes, Elizabeth Covey; Lighting, Thomas C. Hase; Sound, Rusty Wandall; Stage Manager, Glenn Dunn; Assistant Stage Manager, Tony Dearing; Cast: Anthony Marble (Dr. Henry Jekyll), Anderson Matthews (Edward Hyde/Gabriel Utterson), Scott Schafer (Edward Hyde/Sir Danvers Carew/Richard Enfield/O.F. Sanderson/Inspector), Katie Fabel (Elizabeth Jelkes), Kyle Fabel (Edward Hyde/Dr. H.K. Lanyon/Police Doctor/Surgical Student), Bernadette Quigley (Edward Hyde/Poole/Surgical Student/Police Doctor) The Company (Other Roles); Virginia Jackson Browning Mainstage; March 18–April 12, 2009

Evie's Waltz by Carter W. Lewis; Director, Andrea Urice; Set, Bob Koharchik; Costumes, Dorothy Marshall Englis; Lighting, John Wylie; Sound, Rusty Wandall; Stage Manager, Shannon B. Sturgis; Cast: Ted Deasy (Clay), Annie Fitzpatrick (Gloria), Magan Wiles (Evie), World premiere; Emerson Studio Theatre; October 22–November 9, 2008

Blackbird by David Harrower; Director, Amy Saltz; Set, Luke Hegel-Cantarella; Costumes, Elizabeth Eisloeffel; Lighting, Mary Jo Dondlinger; Original Sound Design, J Hagenbuckle; Sound Design Adaptation, Rusty Wandall; Stage Manager, Champe Leary; Cast: Christopher Oden (Ray), Carmen Goodine (Una); Emerson Studio Theatre; January 21–February 8, 2009

Souvenir by Stephen Temperley; Director, Michael Evan Haney; Set, Brian C. Mehring; Costumes, Betsy Krausnick and Tracy Christenson; Lighting, John Wylie; Original Sound Design, Fitz Patton; Sound Design Adaptation, Rusty Wandall; Stage Manager, Champe Leary; Cast: Edwin Cahill (Cosme McMoon), Neva Rae Powers (Florence Foster Jenkins); Emerson Studio Theatre; March 11–March 29, 2009

The Lieutenant of Inishmore by Martin McDonagh; Director, Stuart Carden; Set, Gianni Downs; Costumes, Pei-Chi Su; Lighting, Jim French; Sound, Elizabeth Atkinson; Special Effects, Steve Tolin; Stage Manager, Champe Leary; Assistant Stage Manager, Kim Gifford; Cast: Matt DeCaro (Donny), Dan McCabe (Davey), David Whalen (Padraic), Keira Keeley (Mairead), Sean Meehan (James/Joey), Christopher McHale (Christy), Keith D. Gallagher (Brendan); The Grandel Theatre; September 17–October 12, 2008

The Little Dog Laughed by Douglas Carter Beane; Director, Rob Ruggiero; Set, Adrian W. Jones; Costumes, David Zyla; Lighting, Thomas Dunn; Sound, Zachary Williamson; Stage Manager, Champe Leary; Assistant Stage Manager, Kim Gifford; Cast: Erika Rolfsrud (Diane), Chad Allen (Mitchell), Mark Fisher (Alex), Lindsey Wochley (Ellen); The Grandel Theatre; November 5–November 30, 2008

Sean Meehan, David Whalen and Keith D. Gallagher in
The Lieutenant of Inishmore *(photos by Jerry Naunheim, Jr.)*

My Father's Dragon Book by Ruth Stiles Gannett; Adapted by Sarah Brandt; Music and Lyrics, Neal Richardson; Director, Bruce Longworth; Musical Director, Neal Richardson; Set and Costumes, Lou Bird; Stage Manager, Eric Barnes; Director of Education, Marsha Coplon; Artistic Supervisor, Jeffery Matthews; Cast: Briston Ashe (Cat/Tiger/Rhino/Lion/Dragon), Katie Consamus (Mom/Mouse/Tiger/Gorilla), Chauncy Thomas (Captain/Wild Boar), Amanda Williford (Jim/Elmer); World Premiere; Touring Company; October 20, 2008–April 4, 2009

Chauncy Thomas, Amanda Williford, Katie Consamus and Briston Ashe in My Father's Dragon

The Little Fir Tree by Brian Hohlfeld; Based on the Story by Hans Christian Andersen; Original Music by Neal Richardson; Director, Kat Singleton; Musical Director, Neal Richardson; Set and Costumes, Garth Dunbar; Stage Manager, Eric Barnes; Director of Education, Marsha Coplon; Artistic Supervisor, Jeffery Matthews; Cast: Briston Ashe (Narrator/The Boy), Katie Consamus (Narrator/Aunt Julia), Chauncy Thomas (Narrator/Father), Amanda Williford (Little Fir Tree); Touring Company; November 10–December 31, 2008

Robin Hood by Michael Erickson; Music by Neal Richardson; Director, Jeffery Matthews; Musical Director, Neal Richardson; Set, Scott Loebl; Costumes, Betsy Krausnick; Stage Manager, Eric Barnes; Director of Education, Marsha Coplon; Artistic Supervisor, Jeffery Matthews; Cast: Briston Ashe (Robin Hood), Katie Consamus (Henchman/Merry Man/King), Chauncy Thomas (Sheriff/Friar Tuck), Amanda Williford (Peasant Mother/Maid Marion); World Premiere; Touring Company; January 20–April 4, 2009

Seattle Repertory Theatre

Seattle, Washington
Forty-sixth Season
Producing Artistic Director, Jerry Manning; Managing Director, Benjamin Moore

The Night Watcher by Charlayne Woodard; Director, Dan Sullivan; Set, Tom Lynch; Costumes, Rose Pederson; Lighting, Geoff Korf; Sound, Obadiah Eaves; Projections, Peter Bjordahl; Stage Manager, Stina Lotti; Cast: Charlayne Woodard; Leo K. Theater; September 25–October 26, 2008

The Three Musketeers by Ken Ludwig; Adapted from the novel by Alexander Dumas; Director, Kyle Donnelly; Fight Direction, Rick Sordelet; Set, John Arnone; Costumes, Nan Cibula-Jenkins; Lighting, Nancy Schertler; Sound, Lindsay Jones; Composer, Wayne Barker; Choreography, Sonia Dawkins; Speech Coach, Judith Shahn; Stage Manager, Amy Poisson; Assistant Stage Manager, Tamesis Eve Batiste; Cast: Jim Abele (Cardinal Richelieu), Justin Alley (Ensemble), Geoffrey Alm (Father/Treville), Hans Altwies (Athos), Jeffrey M. Bender (Porthos), Cheyenne Casebier (Milady), Alban Dennis (Buckingham/King Louis), Montana von Fliss (Sabine), David Goldstein (Ensemble), Ellen Karas (Queen Anne), Kate Kraay (Ensemble), Shawn Law (Rochefort), Michael Rossmy (Basille), Ryan Shams (Aramis), Andrew William Smith (D'Artagnan), Jennifer Sue Johnson (Constance); Bagley Wright Theater; October 2 – November 8, 2008

Justin Alley, Shawn Law and Andrew William Smith in
The Three Musketeers *(photos by Chris Bennion)*

boom by Peter Sinn Nachtrieb; Director, Jerry Manning; Set, Jennifer Zeyl, Costumes, Harmony Arnold; Lighting, Robert Aguilar; Sound, Eric Chappelle; Stage Manager, Amy Poisson; Cast: Nick Garrison (Jules), Gretchen Krich (Barbara), Chelsey Rives (Jo); Leo K. Theater; November 13–December 20, 2008

You Can't Take It With You by Moss Hart and George S. Kaufman; Director, Warner Shook; Set, Michael Ganio; Costumes, Frances Kenny; Lighting, Mary Louise Geiger; Music and Music Direction, Michael Roth; Stage Manager, Stina Lotti; Assistant Stage Manager, Claire Zawa; Cast: Anne Allgood (Penny), Ian Bell (Henderson/G-man #2), Mark Chamberlin (Mr. Kirby), Frank Corrado, (Kolenkov), David Drummond (Head G-man), Curtis Eastwood (G-man #3), Bradford Farwell (Ed), Allen Galli (Mr. DePinna), Ben Hollandsworth (Tony), Elizabeth Huddle (Olga the Duchess), Elisa Karolina Hunt (Alice), Suzy Hunt (Gay Wellington), Kimberly King (Mrs. Kirby), Cecil Luellen (Donald), Khatt Taylor (Rheba), Annette Toutonghi (Essie), Michael Winters (Grandpa), R. Hamilton Wright (Paul Sycamore); Bagley Wright Theater; November 28, 2008–January 3, 2009

Ben Hollandsworth, Annette Toutonghi and Bradford Farwell in You Can't Take It With You

The Road to Mecca by Athol Fugard; Director, Leigh Silverman; Set, Rachel Hauck; Costumes, Rose Pederson; Lighting, Mary Louise Geiger; Sound, Eric Chappelle; Dialect, Judith Shahn; Stage Manager, Cristine Anne Reynolds; Assistant Stage Manager, Lori Amondson; Cast: Marya Sea Kaminski (Elsa), Dee Maaske (Miss Helen), Terry Edward Moore (Marius); Bagley Wright Theater; January 15–February 14, 2009

Betrayal by Harold Pinter; Director, Braden Abraham; Set, Etta Lilienthal; Costumes, Frances Kenny; Lighting and Projections, L.B. Morse; Music and Sound, Obadiah Eaves; Dialect, Deborah Hecht; Stage Manager, J.R. Welden; Cast: Cheyenne Casebier (Emma), Alex Podulke (Robert), David Christopher Wells (Jerry), John Farrage (The Waiter); Leo K. Theater; February 19–March 28, 2009

The Seafarer by Conor McPherson; Director, Wilson Milam; Set, Eugene Lee; Costumes, Deb Trout; Lighting, Geoff Korf; Sound, Matt Starritt; Dialect, Deborah Hecht; Fight Choreography, Geoffrey Alm; Stage Manager, Elisabeth Farwell; Assistant Stage Manager, Stina Lotti; Cast: Hans Altwies (Sharkey), Sean G. Griffin (Richard), Russell Hodgkinson (Ivan), Shawn Telford (Nicky), Frank Corrado (Mr. Lockhart); Bagley Wright Theater; February 26–March 28, 2009

Wishful Drinking by Carrie Fisher; Director, Tony Taccone; Set, Lighting, Projections, Alexander V. Nichols; Stage Manager, Daniel Kells; Assistant Stage Manager, Elizabeth Farwell; Cast: Carrie Fisher; Bagley Wright Theater; April 2–May 10, 2009

Breakin' Hearts and Takin' Names by Kevin Kling and Simone Perrin; Director, Braden Abraham; Set and Lighting, L.B. Morse; Costumes, Denise Damico; Sound, Matt Starritt; Stage Manager, Amy Poisson; Cast: Kevin Kling, Simone Perrin; World Premiere; Leo K. Theater; April 9–May 10, 2009

Shakespeare Theatre Company

Washington, DC
Twenty-third Season
Artistic Director, Michael Kahn; Managing Director, Chris Jennings

Romeo and Juliet by William Shakespeare; Director, David Muse; Set, Scott Bradley; Costumes, Jennifer Moeller; Lighting, Lap Chi Chu; Sound, The Broken Chord Collective; Stage Manager, Lurie Horns Pfeffer; Cast: Finn Wittrock (Romeo), James Davis (Juliet), Aubrey Deeker (Mercutio), Drew Eshelman (Nurse), Ted van Griethuysen (Friar Lawrence), Tyrone Mitchell (Paris), Dan Kremer (Capulet); Sidney Harman Hall; September 9–October 12, 2008

The Way of the World by William Congreve; Director, Michael Kahn; Set, Wilson Chin; Costumes, Jane Greenwood; Lighting, Charlie Morrison; Sound, Veronika Vorel; Stage Manager, M. William Shiner; Cast: Stacey Cabaj (Betty), Veanne Cox (Mrs. Millamant), Colleen Delany (Foible), Julie-Ann Elliott (Mincing), Stephen J. Hoochuk (Coachman), Christopher Innvar (Mirabell), Elizabeth Jernigan (Peg), Floyd King (Witwoud), Andrew Long (Fainall), Deanne Lorette (Mrs. Marwood), Doug Rees (Sir Wilful Witwoud), Nancy Robinette (Lady Wishfort), Todd Scofield (Waitwell), Jeffrey Scott (Footman), J. Fred Shiffman (Petulant), Peter Boyer (Ensemble); Lansburgh Theatre; September 30–November 16, 2008

Twelfth Night by William Shakespeare; Director, Rebecca Bayla Taichman; Set, Riccardo Hernandez; Costumes, Miranda Hoffman; Lighting, Christopher Akerlind; Sound, Martin Desjardins; Stage Manager, M. William Shiner; Cast: Samantha Soule (Viola), Veanne Cox (Olivia), Christopher Innvar (Orsino), Floyd King (Feste), Ted van Griethuysen (Malvolio), Tom Story (Sir Andrew Aguecheek), Rick Foucheux (Sir Toby Belch), Peter Katona (Sebastian), Nancy Robinette (Maria); Sidney Harman Hall; December 2–January 11, 2009

The Dog in the Manger by Lope de Vega; Director, Jonathan Munby; Set, Alexander Dodge; Costumes, Linda Cho; Lighting, Matthew Richards; Sound, Richard Martinez; Stage Manager, M.William Shiner; Cast: Wesley Broulik (Leonido), Leo Erickson (Camilo), Jonathan Hammond (Ricardo), Michael Hayden (Teodoro), Leigh Wade (Dorotea), Michelle Hurd (Diana), James Ricks (Fabio), John Livingstone Rolle (Count Federico), David Sabin (Octavio/Ludovico), Joel David Santner (Celio), Miriam Silverman (Marcela), Stacey Cabaj (Anarda), Amanda Thickpenny (Clara), David Turner (Tristan), Lansburgh Theatre; February 10–March 29, 2009

Ion by Euripides; Director, Ethan McSweeny; Set, Rachel Hauck; Costumes, Rachel Myer; Lighting, Tyler Micoleau; Sound, Michael Roth; Stage Manager, James Latus; Cast: Keith Eric Chappelle (Ion), Lisa Harrow (Creusa), Sam Tsoutsouvas (Xuthus), Floyd King (Old Servant), Tana Hicken (Pythia), Aubrey Deeker (Hermes), Colleen Delaney (Athene), Rebecca Baxter (Chorus), Lise Bruneau (Chorus), Kate Debelack (Chorus), Laiona Michelle (Chorus), Patricia Santomasso (Chorus); Sidney Harman Hall; March 10–April 12, 2009

Design for Living by Noel Coward; Director, Michael Kahn; Set, James Noone; Costumes, Robert Perdziola; Lighting, Mark McCullough; Sound, Martin Desjardins; Stage Manager, M. William Shiner; Cast: Gretchen Egolf (Gilda), Tom Story (Otto), Robert Sella (Leo), Kevin Hogan (Ernest), Catherine Flye (Miss Hodge), Todd Scofield (Mr. Birbeck), Sherri L. Edelen (Grace), Richard Thieriot (Henry), Rebecca Kaasa (Helen), Nathan Bennett (Matthew/Photographer); Lansburgh Theatre; May 12–June 28, 2009

King Lear by William Shakespeare; Director, Robert Falls; Set, Walt Spangler; Costumes, Ana Kuzmanic; Lighting, Michael Philippi; Sound, Richard Woodbury; Stage Manager, Lloyd Davis, Jr.; Cast: Stacy Keach (King Lear), Kim Martin-Cotton (Goneril), Kate Arrington (Regan), Laura Odeh (Cordelia), Andrew Long (Albany), Chris Genebach (Cornwall), Aubrey Deeker (France), Edward Gero (Gloucester), Joaquin Torres (Edgar), Jonno Roberts (Edmund), Steve Pickering (Kent), Howard Witt (Fool), Dieterich Gray (Oswald), Hugh Nees (Old Man), Gary Neal Johnson (Knight), Conrad Feininger (Medic), David Blixt (Captain); Sidney Harman Hall; June 16–July 26, 2009

Stacy Keach, Jonno Roberts, Laura Odeh and Kate Arrington in King Lear *(photo by Carol Rosegg)*

South Coast Repertory

Costa Mesa, California
Forty-fifth Season
David Emmes, Producing Artistic Director; Martin Benson, Artistic Director; Paula Tomei, Managing Director

An Italian Straw Hat Book and Lyrics by John Strand; Music by Dennis McCarthy; Director, Stefan Novinski; Musical Director, Dennis Castellano; Set, Donna Marquet; Costumes, Shigeru Yaji; Lighting, Lonnie Rafael Alcaraz; Sound, Drew Dalzell; Musical Staging, Christine Kellogg; Dramaturg, Megan Monaghan; Stage Manger, Jamie A. Tucker; Cast: Matthew Bartosch (Ensemble), Daniel Blinkoff (Fadley), Alan Blumenfeld (Felix/Beauperthuis), Richard Doyle (Noncort), Michelle Duffy (Anabelle/Baroness), Patrick Kerr (Uncle Fez/Viscount), Damon Kirsche (Emile/Nisnardi), Matthew Koehler (Bobby), Kasey Mahaffy (Tardiveau/ Farnsworth), Melissa van der Schyff (Virginia/Clara), Jake Wells (Ensemble), Erika Whalen (Helen); World Premiere; Segerstrom Stage; September 5–October 5, 2008

Dead Man's Cell Phone by Sarah Ruhl; Director, Bart DeLorenzo; Set, Keith E. Mitchell; Costumes, Angela Balogh Calin; Lighting, Lap-Chi Chu; Sound, John Zalewski; Stage Manager, Julie Haber; Cast: Andrew Borba (Dwight), Nike Doukas (Other Woman/Stranger), Shannon Holt (Hermia), Christina Pickles (Mrs. Gottlieb), Lenny Von Dohlen (Gordon), Margaret Welsh, (Jean); Julianne Argyros Stage; September 21–October 12, 2008

The Heiress by Ruth Goetz and Augustus Goetz; Director, Martin Benson; Set, Thomas Buderwitz; Costumes, Maggie Morgan; Lighting, Tom Ruzika; Sound/ Composer, Vincent Olivieri; Stage Manager, Chrissy Church; Cast: Tony Amendola (Dr. Austin Sloper), Karen Hensel (Mrs. Montgomery), Branden McDonald (Arthur Townsend), Lynn Milgrim (Lavinia Penniman), Rebecca Mozo (Marian Almond), Michael A. Newcomer (Morris Townsend), Jennifer Parsons (Maria), Kirsten Potter (Catherine Sloper), Amelia White (Elizabeth Almond); Segerstrom Stage; October 17–November 16, 2008

Tales of a Fourth Grade Nothing Based on the book by Judy Blume; Adapted for the stage by Bruce Mason; Director, Jessica Kubzansky; Set and Costumes, Angela Balogh Calin; Lighting, Jeremy Pivnick; Sound, John Zalewski; Stage Manager, Jennifer Ellen Butler; Cast: Larry Bates (Mr. Yarby/Sarah/Nurse/Jimmy Fargo/Mr. Vincent/Dr. Cone), Brenda Canela (Mrs. Yarby/Sheila Tubman/Dr. Brown/Jennie/Janet), Daniel Chaffin (Peter), Daniel T. Parker (Fudge), Jeanne Sakata (Mom/Mr. Denberg), Tom Shelton (Dad/Ralph/Viktor); Julianne Argyros Stage; November 7–23, 2008

A Christmas Carol by Charles Dickens; Adapted by Jerry Patch; Director, John-David Keller; Set, Thomas Buderwitz; Costumes, Dwight Richard Odle; Lighting, Donna and Tom Ruzika; Musical Arrangements/Composer, Dennis McCarthy; Sound, Drew Dalzell; Vocal Director, Dennis Castellano; Choreography, Sylvia C. Turner; Asst. Director, Hisa Takakuwa; Stage Manager, Jamie A. Tucker; Asst. Stage Manager, Chrissy Church; Cast: Christian Barillas , Daniel Blinkoff, Jennifer Chu, Richard Doyle, Karen Hensel, John-David Keller, Art Koustik, Timothy Landfield, Hal Landon Jr., Ann Marie Lee, Louis Lotorto, Jennifer Parsons, Tom Shelton; Ensemble: Matt Bartosch, Dan Behnke, Jill Maglione, Jake Wells; Kids: Mason Acevedo, Chris Bautista, Brianna Beach, Ellis Beardsley, Lucas Blankenhorn, Jordan Boggess, William Hopper, Christopher Huntley, Courtney Kato, Grace O'Brien, Jasmine O'Hea, Jamie Ostmann, Nick Slimmer, Bahaar Tadjbakhsh, Matthew Tanaka, Sanaz Toossi; 29th Annual Production; Segerstrom Stage; November 29–December 27, 2008

La Posada Mágica—The Magical Journey by Octavio Solis; Music by Marcos Loya; Director, Octavio Solis; Set, Christopher Acebo; Costumes, Shigeru Yaji; Lighting, Lonnie Rafael Alcaraz; Musical Director, Marcos Loya; Choreography, Gabriela Estrada; Assistant Director, Nicholas C. Avila; Stage Manager, Jennifer Ellen Butler; Cast: Denise Blasor (Consuelo/Widow), Danny Bolero (Papi/Jose Cruz), Sol Castillo (Refugio/Buzzard), David DeSantos (Eli/ Bones/Lauro), Gloria Garayua (Gracie), Miguel Najera (Horacio), Erica Ortega (Mariluz/Mom), Teresa Velarde (Caridad/Widow), Marcos Loya and Lorenzo Martinez (Musicians/Ensemble), 15th Annual Production; Julianne Argyros Stage; December 11–23, 2008

You, Nero by Amy Freed; Director, Sharon Ott; Set, Erik Flatmo; Costumes, Paloma H. Young; Lighting, Peter Maradudin; Music and Sound, Stephen LeGrand and Eric Drew Feldman; Dramaturg, John Glore; Stage Manager, Julie Haber; Cast: Richard Doyle (Zippo/Seneca/Patheticus), Caralyn Kozlowski (Poppaea/Inspiration), Hal Landon Jr., (Batheticus/Beppo/Burrus), Lori Larsen (Agrippina), Kasey Mahaffy (Manulius/Fabiolo/Octavia's Ghost/Young Nero), Danny Scheie (Nero), John Vickery (Scribonius), Ensemble: Angelle Buffet, Christopher Crawford, Marisa Hampton; Produced in Association with Berkeley Repertory Theatre; World Premiere; Julianne Argyros Stage; January 4–25, 2009

Richard Doyle, Lori Larsen and Hal Landon in You, Nero

Noises Off by Michael Frayn; Director, Art Manke; Set, John Iacovelli; Costumes, Angela Balogh Calin; Lighting, York Kennedy; Sound, Vincent Olivieri; Voice, David Nevell; Stage Manager, Jamie A. Tucker; Cast: Nancy Bell (Belinda Blair), Bill Brochtrup (Gary Lejeune), Kandis Chappell (Dotty Otley), Winslow Corbett (Poppy Norton-Taylor), Kaleo Griffith (Lloyd Dallas), Brian Hostenske (Tim Allgood), Timothy Landfield (Frederick Fellowes), Jennifer Lyon (Brooke Ashton), Nick Ullett (Selsdon Mowbray); Segerstrom Stage; February 6–March 8, 2009

A Year with Frog and Toad Music by Robert Reale; Book and Lyrics by Willie Reale; based on the books by Arnold Lobel; Director, Nick DeGruccio; Set. Fred Kinney; Costumes, Soojin Lee; Lighting, Steven Young; Muscial Director/Musical Arrangements, Deborah Wicks La Puma; Sound, Mark Johnson; Stage Manger, Amy Bristol Brownewell; Cast: Justin Michael Duval (Bird/Snail/Lizard/Father Frog/Mole), Emily Eiden (Bird/Mouse/Squirrel/Young Frog/Mole), Jim Holdridge (Toad), Alex Miller (Frog), Erika Whalen (Bird/Turtle/Squirrel/Mother Frog/Mole);Julianne Argyros Stage; February 13 – March 1, 2009

Goldfish by John Kolvenbach; Director, Loretta Greco; Set, Myung Hee Cho; Costumes, Alex Jaeger; Lighting, Lonnie Rafael Alcaraz; Sound, Michael Hooker; Dramaturg, John Glore; Stage Manager, Julie Haber; Cast: Tasso Feldman (Albert), Joan McMurtrey (Margaret), Conor O'Farrell (Leo), Kate Rylie (Lucy), World Premiere; Julianne Argyros Stage; March 15–April 5, 2009

Our Mother's Brief Affair by Richard Greenberg; Director, Pam MacKinnon; Set, Sibyl Wickersheimer; Costumes, Rachel Myers; Lighting, Lap-Chi Chu; Sound, Michael K. Hooker; Dramaturg, John Glore; Stage Manager, Kathryn Davies; Cast: Matthew Arkin (Lover/Father), Arye Gross (Seth); Marin Hinkle (Abby), Jenny O'Hara (Anna); World Premiere; Segerstrom Stage; April 3–May 3, 2009

Emilie—La Marquise Du Châtelet Defends her Life at the Petit Théâtre at Cirey Tonight by Lauren Gunderson; Director, David Emmes; Set, Cameron Anderson; Costumes, Nephelie andonyadis; Lighting, Lonnie Rafael Alcaraz; Music/Sound, Vincent Olivieri; Movement, Gabriela Estrada; Dramaturg, Kelly L. Miller, Stage Manager, Jennifer Ellen Bulter; Cast: Susan Denaker (Madam), Matthew Humphreys (Gentleman), Rebecca Mozo (Soubrette), Don Reilly (Voltaire), Natacha Roi (Emilie); World Premiere; Julianne Argyros Stage; April 19–May 10, 2009

Collected Stories by Donald Margulies; Director, Martin Benson; Set, Thomas Buderwitz; Costumes, Angela Balogh Calin; Lighting, Tom Ruzkia and Donna Ruzika; Sound, Mark Johnson; Stage Manager, Jamie A. Tucker; Cast: Kandis Chappell (Ruth Steiner), Melanie Lora (Lisa Morrison); Segerstrom Stage; May 15–June 14, 2009

The Brand New Kid A musical based on the children's book *The Brand New Kid* by Katie Couric; music by Michael Friedman; book by Melanie Marnich; lyrics by Michael Friedman and Melanie Marnich; Director, Shelley Butler; Set, Sibyl Wickersheimer; Costumes, Paloma H. Young; Lighting, Tom Ruzika; Musical Director, Doborah Wicks La Puma; Sound, Mark Johnson; Stage Manager, Kathryn Davies; Cast: Jennifer Chang (Carrie O'Toole/The Bird), Justin Michael Duval (Peter Barsinsky/Doodle the Poodle), Justin Figueroa (Ricky Jensen/The Tree), Brian Hostenske (Lazlo S. Gasky), Jennifer Parsons (Miss Kincaid/Mrs. Gasky/Cafeteria Lady), Erika Whalen (Ellie McSnelly); Julianne Argyros Stage; May 29–June 14, 2009

Steppenwolf Theatre Company

Chicago, Illinois
Thirty-eighth Season
Artistic Director, Martha Lavey; Executive Director, David Hawkanson

Kafka on The Shore by ensemble member Frank Galati; Director, ensemble member Frank Galati; based on the book by Haruki Murakami; Set, James Schuette; Costumes, Mara Blumenfeld; Lighting, James F. Ingalls; Sound and Music, Andre Pluess and Ben Sussman; Fight Choreography, Joe Dempsey; SM, Malcolm Ewen; ASM, Lauren V. Hickman; Cast: Francis Guinan and John Michael Hill with Christine Bunuan, Gerson Decanay, Mary Ann de la Cruz, Christopher Larkin, Aiko Nakasone, Andrew Pang, David Rhee, Lisa Tejero; Downstairs Theatre; Main Stage; September 18, 2008–November 16, 2008

Dublin Carol by Conor McPherson; Director, ensemble member Amy Morton; Set, Kevin Depinet; Costumes, Ana Kuzmanic; Lighting, Robert Christen; Sound, Rob Milburn and Michael Bodeen; SM, Michelle Medvin; Cast: Stephen Louis Grush, William Petersen, Nicole Wiesner; Upstairs Theatre; Main Stage; November 6, 2008–December 21, 2008

The Seafarer by Conor McPherson; Director, ensemble member Randall Arney; Set, Takeshi Kata; Costumes, Janice Pytel; Lighting, Daniel Lonazzi; Sound, Richard Woodbury; SM, Christine D. Freeburg; ASM, Rosie Marie Packer; Cast: Francis Guinan, Tom Irwin, John Mahoney and Alan Wilder with Randall Newsome; Downstairs Theatre; Main Stage; December 4, 2008–February 8, 2008 (extended through February 22, 2008)

John Mahoney, Alan Wilder, Francis Guinan, Randall Newsome and Tom Irwin in The Seafarer *(photos by Michael Brosilow)*

Art by Yasmina Reza; translated by Christopher Hampton; Director, Rick Snyder; Set, Antje Ellermann; Costumes, Ana Kuzmanic; Lighting, Bob Christen; Sound, Kevin O'Donnell; SM, Michelle Medvin; ASM, Jonathan Templeton; Cast: Ian Barford, K.Todd Freeman and Francis Guinan with Joe Dempsey and John Procaccino; Upstairs Theatre; Main Stage; February 5, 2009–June 7, 2009

The Tempest by William Shakespeare; Director/Ensemble Member Tina Landau; Set, Takeshi Kata; Costumes, James Schuette; Lighting, Jane Cox; Sound and Music, Josh Schmidt; Aerial Choreography, Sylvia Hernandez-DiStasi; Text and Verse Consultant, Rob Clare; SM, Malcolm Ewen; ASM, Christine D. Freeburg; Cast: Alana Arenas, K. Todd Freeman, Frank Galati, Jon Michael Hill, Tim Hopper, James Vincent Meredith, Yasen Peyankov, Lois Smith and Alan Wilder with Eric James Casady, Miles Fletcher, Stephen Louis Grush, Emma Rosenthal and Craig Spidle; Downstairs Theatre; Main Stage; March 26, 2009 – May 31, 2009

Up by Bridget Carpenter; Director/Ensemble Member, Anna D. Shapiro; Set, Dan Ostling; Costumes, Mara Blumenfeld; Lighting, Ann G. Wrightson; Sound, Richard Woodbury; Composition, David Singer; Dramaturg, Edward Sobel; Stage Manager, Laura D. Glenn; Assistant Stage Manager, Deb Styer; Cast: Ian Barford and Martha Lavey with Rachel Brosnahan, Jake Cohen, Tony Hernandez, Lauren Katz; Downstairs Theatre; Main Stage; June 18, 2009–August 23, 2009

The Glass Menagerie by Tennessee Williams; Director, ensemble member Yasen Peyankov; Set, Martin Andrew; Costumes, Natasha Vuchurovich Djukich; Lighting, Keith Parham; Sound and Music, Rob Milburn and Michael Bodeen; SM, Cassie Wolgamott; Cast: James T. Alfred, Shanésia Davis, Anthony Fleming III, Nambi E. Kelley; Downstairs Theatre; Steppenwolf for Young Adults; October 21, 2008–November 9, 2008

Of Mice and Men by John Steinbeck; Director, Michael Patrick Thornton; Set, Courtney O' Neill; Costumes, Branimira Ivanova; Lighting, Charles Cooper; Sound and Music, Miles Polaski; Fight Choreography, John Tovar; Stage Manager, Kathleen Petroziello; Cast: ensemble member Robert Breuler with Robert Belushi,

Frank Galati and Company of The Tempest

Emanueal Buckley, Ron Butts, Paul D'Addario, James D. Farruggio, Jessie Fisher, Richard Henzel, Keith Kupferer, Guy Massey; Downstairs Theatre; Steppenwolf for Young Adults; April 21, 2009–May 10, 2009

Pursued by Happiness by Keith Huff; Director, ensemble member Tim Hopper; Set, Kevin Depinet; Costumes, Debbie Baer; Lighting, Charles Cooper; Sound, Joseph Fosco; Dramaturg, Kimberly Senior; LSM, Jonathan Templeton; SM, Kathleen Petroziello and Cassie Wolgamott; Program Director, Edward Sobel; Program Assistant, Whitney Debo; Cast: Thomas Joseph Carroll, Kat McDonnell, Paul Noble, Barbara E. Robertson; Garage Theatre; First Look Repertory of New Work; July 23, 2008–August 10, 2008

Perfect Mendacity by Jason Wells; Director, David Cromer; Set, Kevin Depinet; Costumes, Debbie Baer; Lighting, Charles Cooper; Sound, Joseph Fosco; Dramaturg, Kimberly Senior; LSM, Jonathan Templeton; SM, Kathleen Petroziello and Cassie Wolgamott; Program Director, Edward Sobel; Program Assistant, Whitney Debo; Cast: Scott Aiello, Tim Curtis, Matt DeCaro, Aaron Todd Douglas, Liza Fernandez; Garage Theatre; First Look Repertory of New Work; July 24, 2008–August 10, 2008

Fair Use by Sarah Gubbins; Director, Meredith McDonough; Set, Kevin Depinet; Costumes, Debbie Baer; Lighting, Charles Cooper; Sound, Joseph Fosco; Dramaturg, Kimberly Senior; LSM, Jonathan Templeton; SM, Kathleen Petroziello and Cassie Wolgamott; Program Director, Edward Sobel; Program Assistant, Whitney Debo; Cast: Michele Graff, Brian King, Steven Marzolf, Kelli Simpkins, Halena Starr Kays; Garage Theatre; First Look Repertory of New Work; July 25, 2008–August 10, 2008

Tennessee Repertory Theatre

Nashville, Tennessee
Twenty-fourth Season
René D. Copeland, Producing Artistic Director

Sweeney Todd: The Demon Barber of Fleet Street Music and Lyrics by Stephen Sondheim, Book by Hugh Wheeler; Director, René D. Copeland; Musical Director, Timothy Fudge; Set, Gary C. Hoff; Costumes, Trish Clark; Lighting, Michael Barnett; Cast: Brook Bryant (Joanna), Matthew Carlton (Judge Turpin), Lane Davies (Sweeney Todd), Zachary Hess (Anthony Hope), Margueritte Lowell (Birdseller), Patrick Waller (Tobias Ragg), Samuel Whited (Beadle Bamford),

Martha Wilkinson (Mrs. Lovett), Holly Wooten (Lucy/Beggar Woman), Bobby Wyckoff (Adolfo Pirelli); Tennessee Repertory Theatre; October 4 – 18, 2008

Moonlight and Magnolias by Ron Hutchinson; Director, Martha Wilkinson; Set, Gary C. Hoff; Costumes, Trish Clark; Lighting, Michael Barnett; Cast: Evelyn Blythe (Mrs. Poppenguhl), Shane Bridges (David O. Selznick), Eric D. Pasto-Crosby (Victor Fleming), Peter Vann (Ben Hecht); Tennessee Repertory Theatre; November 8 – 22, 2008

The Santaland Diaries by David Sedaris, Adapted by Joe Mantello; Director, David Alford; Set, Gary C. Hoff; Costumes, Lane Fragomeli; Lighting, Barry Steele; Cast: Matt Chiorini (Crumpet); November 28 – December 20, 2008

Matt Chiorini in The Santaland Diaries *(photos by Harry Butler)*

Glengarry Glen Ross by David Mamet; Director, René D. Copeland; Set, Gary C. Hoff; Costumes, Trish Clark; Lighting, Phillip Franck; Cast: David Alford (Richard Roma), Kamal Bolden (Officer Baylen), David Compton (Dave Moss), Henry Haggard (George Aaronow), Eric D. Pasto-Crosby (Williamson), Brian Webb Russell (Shelly Levine), Christopher Strand (James Lingk); February 7–21, 2009

Rabbit Hole by David Lindsay-Abaire; Director, David Alford; Set, Gary C. Hoff; Costumes, Trish Clark; Lighting, Phillip Franck; Cast: Shane Bridges (Howie), Jamie Farmer (Izzy), Andy Kanies (Jason), Peggy Walton-Walker (Nat), Erin Whited (Becca); March 21 – April 4, 2009

Darwin in Malibu by Crispin Whittell; Director, René D. Copeland; Set, Gary C. Hoff; Costumes, Trish Clark, Lighting, Phillip Franck; Cast: Chip Arnold (Thomas Huxley), Henry Haggard (Charles Darwin), Kahle Reardon (Sarah), Samuel Whited (Samuel Wilberforce); May 2–16, 2009

Theatre Under The Stars

Houston, Texas
Forty-first Season
Artistic Director, Frank Young

Oprah Winfrey Presents The Color Purple National Tour; Hobby Center For The Performing Arts; September 16-28, 2008

Irving Berlin's White Christmas Director and Choreography, James A. Rocco; Lighting, Richard Winkler; Stage Manager, Roger Allan Raby; Musical Director/Conductor, Jeff Rizzo; Sound, Christopher K. Bond; Stage Manager, Debs Ramser; Set, Anna Louizos; Costumes, Carrie Robbins; Cast: Kevin Cooney (General Waverly), Michael Gruber (Bob Wallace), Tari Kelly (Judy Haynes), John Macinnis (Phil Davis), Carol Swarbrick (Martha Watson), Michael Tapley (Ralph Sheldrake), Jay Tribble (Ezekiel), Beverly Ward (Betty Haynes), Katie Leigh Allen (Ensemble), Brad Bass (Ensemble), Mallory Bechtel (Susan Waverly), Staci Bonura (Ensemble), Marnie Buckner (Ensemble), Sarah Burkett (Ensemble), Chris Canal (Ensemble), Kari Lee Cartwright (Ensemble), Marybelle Chaney (Ensemble/Rita), Laura Duggan (Ensemble/Mrs. Snoring Man), Tim Falter (Ensemble), Danny Gardner (Ensemble), Gabby Gillespie (Susan Waverly), Tyce Green (Ensemble), Storey Hinojosa (Ensemble), (Richard Keck (Ensemble), Robin Levine (Ensemble), Rachael Logue (Ensemble), Mark X. Laskowski (TV Announcer/Mr. Snoring Man/Mike Nulty/Regency Room Club Announcer), Brent Mcbeth (Ensemble), Jayme Mcdaniel (Ensemble/Dance Captain), Krissy Richmond (Ensemble/Rhoda), Jim Shaffer (Train Conductor), Trina Simon (Ensemble), Chris Tipps (Ensemble), Tony Vierling (Ensemble), Molly Marie Walsh (Ensemble), Zephyrus White (Ensemble); Hobby Center For The Performing Arts; December 4-17, 2008

Legally Blonde The Musical National Tour; Hobby Center For The Performing Arts; February 10-22, 2009

Les Misérables: Director, Fred Hanson; Sound, Christopher K. Bond; Stage Manager, Debs Ramser; Stage Manager, Roger Allan Raby; Music Director/Conductor, Robert Billig; Projection, Zachary Borovay; Associate Conductor, David Wolfson; Set, Matt Kinley; Lighting, John Demous; Hair and Wig, Cookie Jordan; Cast: Mallory Bechtel (Young Cosette/Young Eponine), Anderson Davis (Marius), Ed Dixon (Thenardier), Maddie Dyer (Young Cosette/Young Eponine), Rob Evan (Jean Valjean), Mary Gutzi (Mrs. Thenardier), Leah Horowitz (Cosette), Robert Hunt (Javert), Sam Linda (Gavroche), Andrea Rivette (Fantine), Sarah Shahinian (Eponine), Ed Watts (Enjolras), Cole Burden, (Ensemble/Grantiere), Sam Burkett (Ensemble), Sarah Burkett (Ensemble), Tiffany Chen (Ensemble), Christopher J. Deaton (Ensemble), Andrew Foote (Ensemble), Craig Foster (Ensemble), Tyce Green (Ensemble), Shawna Hamic (Ensemble), Jeremy Hays (Ensemble), Storey Hinojosa (Ensemble), Siri Howard (Ensemble), Devin Ilaw (Ensemble), Drew Jones (Ensemble), Margaret Kelly (Ensemble), C. Mingo Long (Ensemble), Betty Marie Muessig (Ensemble), Jason Ostrowski (Ensemble), Jack Paddison (Ensemble), Robyn Payne (Ensemble), Kevin Reed (Ensemble), Kyle Dean Reinford (Ensemble), Sydney Roberts (Ensemble), Jennifer Avery Semrick (Ensemble), Jen Sese (Ensemble), Alex Stone (Ensemble), Nina Sturtz (Ensemble), Chris Tipps (Ensemble), Anita Vasan (Ensemble), Kristopher Ward (Ensemble), David Weitzer (Ensemble); Hobby Center For The Performing Arts; March 24-April 5, 2009

Happy Days—A New Musical National Tour; Hobby Center For The Performing Arts; May 12-24, 2009

Cabaret Music and Lyrics, John Kander and Fred Ebb; Book, Joe Masteroff; Director, Bill Berry; Choreography, Bob Richard; Musical Director, Ian Eisendrath; Conductor, R.J. Tancioco; Set and Lighting, Tom Sturge; Costumes, Thomas G. Marquez; Sound, Christopher "Kit" Bond; Stage Manager, Roger Allan Raby; Stage Manager, Revecca L. Skupin; Assistant Stage Manager, Lynda Radisi; Cast: Leslie Kritzer (Sally Bowles), Leo Ash Evens (Emcee), Tyler Hanes (Cliff Bradshaw), Allen Fitzpatrick (Herr Schultz), Suzy Hunt (Fraulein Schneider), Angie Louise (Fraulein Kost), Mike Mcgowan (Ernst Ludwig), David Alewine (Rolf/Gorilla), Tommy Berklund (Max), Chris Canal (Ensemble), Emilee Dupré (Mausie), Tim Hausmann (Gunter/The Two Ladies), Storey Hinojosa (Ensemble), Tony Johnson (Bobby/German Sailor), Freddie Kimmel (Otto/Tenor Specialty), Carlynn Laurie (Gretl), Jeremy Leiner (Helmut/German Sailor), Johnathan Luna (Ensemble), Kate Marilley (Fritzi/The Two Ladies), Betty Marie Muessig (Ensemble), Jack Paddison (Ensemble), Maya Perkins (Frenchie/Dance Captain), Troy L. Wageman (Hanz/German Sailor), Kristin Warren (Hilde), Paige Wheat (Helga), Dana Winkle (Rosie); Hobby Center For The Performing Arts; June 16-28, 2009

Trinity Repertory Theatre

Providence, Rhode Island
Forty-fifth Season
Artistic Director, Curt Columbus; Executive Director, Michael Gennaro

The Dreams of Antigone by Curt Columbus and Trinity Rep's Resident Acting Company; Director, Brian McEleney; Set, Tristan Jeffers; Costumes, William Lane; Lighting, John Ambrosone; Sound, Peter Sasha Hurowitz; Stage Manager, Megan Schwarz; Cast: Stephen Berenson (Alcebaides), Angela Brazil (Ismene), Janice Duclos (Meletia), Mauro Hantman (Crito/Eteocles), Phyllis Kay (Eurydice), Barbara Meek (Agave), Aaron Rossini (Phaedrus/Polyneices), Anne Scurria (Xanthippe/Jocasta), Fred Sullivan, Jr. (Creon), Stephen Thorne (Haemon), Rachael Warren (Antigone), Joe Wilson, Jr. (Thersites/Oedipus); World Premiere; Dowling Theater; September 26–October 19, 2008

A Christmas Carol by Charles Dickens; Adapted by Adrian Hall and Richard Cumming, Original Music by Richard Cumming; Director, Liesl Tommy; Musical Direction by Doug Brandt; Set, Michael McGarty; Costumes, Ron Cesario; Lighting, Brian J. Lillienthal; Sound, Peter Sasha Hurowitz; Choreography by Christopher Windom; Ivy Cast: Mauro Hantman (Ebenezer Scrooge), Rachael Warren (Reader/Fan), Russ Salmon (Jacob Marley/Belle's Husband), Michael Propster (Bob Cratchit), Nick Newell (Fred/Young Scrooge), Robert Casey, Jr. (Solicitor/ Ghost of Christmas Present), Fred Sullivan, Jr. (Fezziwig/Solicitor/ Old Joe), Barbara Meek (Mrs. Partlet/ Mrs. Fezziwig), Anne Scurria (Ghost of Christmas Past/ Sister-in-Law/ Mrs. Dilber), Dean Robinson (Schoolmaster/Topper/ Undertaker's Man), Christopher Lysik (Young Scrooge), Austin Adams (Young Scrooge), Jeremy Roth-Rose (Young Marley/Ghost of Christmas Future), Teddy McNulty (Young Marley/ Ghost of Christmas Future), Sakari Monteiro (Young Fan/Hunger), Molly Coogan (Young Fan/Hunger), Patricia Lynn (Belle/Lucy), Paola Grande (Mrs. Cratchit), Christopher Lysik (Peter), Austin Adams (Peter), Phoebe Perelman (Martha), Ariel Dorsey (Martha), Julianna McGuirl (Belinda), Kateryne Nelson-Guerrero (Belinda), Max Theroux (Tiny Tim/Ignorance), Brady Curran (Tiny Tim/Ignorance), PSM, Megan Schwarz; Holly Cast: Joe Wilson, Jr. (Ebenezer Scrooge), Angela Williams (Reader/Fan), Jimmy King (Jacob Marley/Belle's Husband), Joe Short (Bob Cratchit), Craig Wesley Divino (Fred/Young Scrooge), Nate Dendy (Solicitor/ Ghost of Christmas Present), Richard Donelly (Fezziwig/Solicitor/ Old Joe), Phyllis Kay (Mrs. Partlet/ Mrs. Fezziwig), Parker Leventer (Ghost of Christmas Past/ Sister-in-Law/ Mrs. Dilber), Tom Gleadow (Schoolmaster/Topper/ Undertaker's Man), Nigel Richards (Young Scrooge),

Michael Albanese (Young Scrooge), Noah Pimentel (Young Marley/Ghost of Christmas Future), David O'Connell (Young Marley/Ghost of Christmas Future), Katherine Kerwin (Young Fan/Hunger), Sophia Diodati (Young Fan/Hunger), Craig Wesley Divino (Young Scrooge), Molly Schreiber (Belle/Lucy), D'Arcy Dersham (Mrs. Cratchit), Nigel Richards (Peter), Michael Albanese (Peter), Meghan Hurley (Martha), Daniela Zib (Martha), Emeline Herreid (Belinda), Dominique DeSimone (Belinda), Jack Feld (Tiny Tim/Ignorance), Liam Clancy (Tiny Tim/Ignorance), Holly SM, Michael Domue; Chace Theater; November 21–December 31, 2008

The Receptionist by Adam Bock; Director, Curt Columbus; Set, Eugene Lee; Costumes, William Lane; Lighting, Keith Parham; Sound, Peter Sasha Hurowitz; Stage Manager, Lloyd Davis, Jr.; Cast: Angela Brazil (Lorraine Taylor), Timothy Crowe (Edward Raymond), Janice Duclos (Beverly Wilkins), Timothy John Smith (Martin Dart); Dowling Theater; December 5–January 11, 2008

A Raisin in the Sun by Lorraine Hansberry; Director, Brian McEleney; Set, Michael McGarty; Costumes, William Lane; Lighting, John Ambrosone; Sound, Peter Sasha Hurowitz; Stage Manager, Buzz Cohen; Cast: Lynnette R. Freeman (Ruth Younger), Dustin Isom (Travis Younger), Nigel Richards (Travis Younger), Joe Wilson, Jr.(Walter Lee Younger), Angela K. Thomas (Beneatha Younger), Barbara Meek (Lena Younger), Jude Sandy (Joseph Asagai), Charlie Hudson III (George Murchison), Mauro Hantman (Karl Lindner), Johnny Lee Davenport (Bobo), Will Shaw (Moving Man); Chace Theater; January 30–March 8, 2009

The Secret Rapture by David Hare; Director, Curt Columbus; Set, James Schuette; Costumes, Ron Cesario; Lighting, Deb Sullivan; Sound, Peter Sasha Hurowitz; Stage Manager, Katie Ailinger; Dramaturgy by Deborah Salem Smith; Cast: Rachael Warren (Isobel Glass), Phyllis Kay (Marion French), Fred Sullivan, Jr. (Tom French), Anne Scurria (Katherine Glass), Stephen Thorne (Irwin Posner), Patricia Lynn (Rhonda Milne); Dowling Theater; February 20–March 29, 2009

The Importance of Being Earnest by Oscar Wilde; Director, Beth F. Milles; Set, Michael McGarty; Costumes, William Lane; Lighting, Russell Champa; Sound, Peter Sasha Hurowitz; Stage Manager, Jennifer Grutza; Cast: Mauro Hantman (John Worthing, J.P.), Karl Gregory (Algernon Moncrieff), Stephen Berenson (Rev. Canon Chasuble, D.D.), Patrick Mulryan (Merriman), Stephen Berenson (Lane), Janice Duclos (Lady Bracknell), Angela Brazil, (Gwendolen Fairfax), Rebecca Gibel (Cecily Cardew), Barbara Meek (Miss Prism); Chace Theater; April 10–May 10, 2009

Shapeshifter by Laura Schellhardt; Director, Laura Kepley; Set, Loy Arcenas; Costumes, William Lane; Lighting, Brian J. Lilienthal; Original Music and Sound, John Gromada; Stage Manager, Barbara Reo, Robin Grady; Cast: Miriam Silverman (Midge), Brian McEleney (Fierson), Anne Scurria (Maud), Rachael Warren (Mairie/Breeze/Feroc), Fred Sullivan (Mike), Joe Wilson, Jr. (Douglas), Stephen Thorne (Tom); World Premiere; Dowling Theater; May 1–May 31, 2009

Anne Scurria, Rachael Warren and Brian McEleney in Shapeshifter *(photo by Mark Turek)*

Wilma Theatre

Philadelphia, Pennsylvania
Thirtieth Season
Blanka Zizka, Co-Artistic Director; Jiri Zizka, Co-Artistic Director; James Haskins, Managing Director

Rock 'n' Roll by Tom Stoppard; Director, Blanka Zizka; Set and Projections, Matt Saunders, Costumes, Oana Botez-Ban; Lighting, Joshua L. Schulman; Sound, Andrea Sotzing; Hair and Makeup, Jon Carter; Dramaturg, Walter Bilderback; Production Manager, Eileen Harris; PSM, Patreshettarlini Adams; Technical Director, Clayton Tejada; Assistant Director, Carol Laratonda; ASM, Debby Lau; Cast: Mark Cairns (Milan/Policeman #2/Waiter), Barnaby Carpenter (Jan), David Chandler (Max), Julie Czarnecki (Candida), Ryan Farley (Ferdinand), Victoria Frings (Gillian/Magda/Deirdre), Mary McCool (Lenka), Jered McLenigan (The Piper/Policeman #1/Stephen), Kate Eastwood Norris (Eleanor/Adult Esme), Seth Reichgott (Interrogator/Nigel), Libby Woodbridge (Young Esme/Alice); September 17–October 26, 2008

Schmucks by Roy Smiles; Director, Jiri Zizka; Set, Bill Clarke, Costumes, Janus Stefanowicz; Lighting, Jerold R. Forsyth; Sound, Nick Rye; Movement Consultant, Jay Wojnarowski; Dramaturgs, Walter Bilderback and Richard Kotulski; Production Manager, Iain Campbell; PSM, Patreshettarlini Adams; Technical Director, Clayton Tejada; Assistant Director, Carol Laratonda; ASM, Debby Lau; Cast: Ian Alda (Joe Klein), Caitlin Clouthier (Mary Lenahan), Ron Crawford (Groucho Marx), Erik Jensen (Lenny Bruce); December 3, 2008–January 4, 2009

Scorched by Wajdi Mouawad; Translator, Linda Gaboriau; Director, Blanka Zizka; Set, Ola Maslik, Costumes, Oana Botez-Ban; Lighting, Thom Weaver; Sound, Jorge Cousineau; Composer, Amir ElSaffar; Fight Director, Michael Cosenza; Dramaturg, Walter; Production Manager, Iain Campbell; PSM, Patreshettarlini Adams; Technical Director, Clayton Tejada; Assistant Director, Sarah Bowden; ASM, Debby Lau; Cast: Jolly Abraham (Elhame/Sawda), Jacqueline Antaramian (Jihane/Nawal aged 40-45), Aadya Bedi (Nawal aged 14-19), Leila Buck (Janine), Janis Dardaris (Nazira/Nawal aged 60-65), Omar Koury (Antoine/Doctor/Abdessamad/Guide/School Janitor/Malak/Photographer/Chamseddine); February 25–March 29, 2009

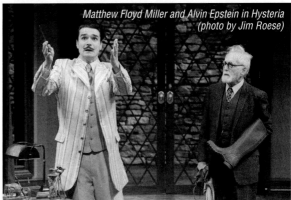

Matthew Floyd Miller and Alvin Epstein in Hysteria *(photo by Jim Roese)*

Hysteria by Terry Johnson; Director, Jiri Zizka; Set, Mimi Lien, Costumes, Janus Stefanowicz; Lighting, Jerold R. Forsyth; Sound, Nick Rye; Dramaturg, Walter Bilderback; Production Manager, Iain Campbell; PSM, Patreshettarlini Adams; Technical Director, Clayton Tejada; Assistant Director, Carol Laratonda; ASM, Debby Lau; Cast: Alvin Epstein (Sigmund Freud), Merwin Goldsmith (Yahuda), Mary McCool (Jessica), Matthew Floyd Miller (Salvador Dalí), Ensemble: Robert Ian Cutler, Will Harrell, Matteo LeCompte, Miranda Libkin, Kristen O'Rourke, Christine Perrotta, Ted Powell; May 13–June 14, 2009

Yale Repertory Theatre

New Haven, Connecticut
Forty-third Season
James Bundy, Artistic Director; Victoria Nolan, Managing Director

Passion Play by Sarah Ruhl; Director, Mark Wing-Davey; Sets, Allen Moyer; Associate Scenic Designer, Warren Karp; Costumes, Ilona Somogyi; Lighting, Stephen Strawbridge; Sound, Charles Coes; Dramaturg, Colin Mannex; Projections, Ruppert Bohle; Dialect Coach, Gillian Lane-Plescia; Fight Director, Rick Sordelet; Casting, Tara Rubin Casting; Production Stage Manager, James Mountcastle; Cast: Brendan Averett (Carpenter 1), Kathleen Chalfant (Queen Elizabeth/Hitler/Reagan), Austin Durant (Carpenter 2), Lauren Esposito (Ensemble), Dietrich Gray (Machinist/German Officer/Young Director), Brian Hastert (Ensemble), Slate Holmgren (Ensemble), Polly Noonan (Village Idiot/Violet), Barret O'Brien (Ensemble), Susan Pourfar (Mary 1), Keith Reddin (Director), Luke Robertson (Ensemble), Thomas Jay Ryan (Visiting Friar/Visiting Englishman/VA), Felix Solis (Pontius the Fish-Gutter), Joaquin Torres (John the Fisherman), Nicole Wiesner (Mary 2); University Theatre; September 19–October 11, 2008

Joaquin Torres and the Company of Passion Play

Happy Now? by Lucinda Coxon; Director, Liz Diamond; Sets, Sarah Pearline; Costumes, Heidi Hanson; Lighting, Matt Frey; Sound, David Budries; Dramaturg, Sarah Bishop-Stone; Speech and Dialect Coach, Pamela Prather; Fight Director, David DeBesse; Casting, Tara Rubin Casting; Production Stage Manager, Amanda Spooner; Cast: Kelly AuCoin (Johnny), Mary Bacon (Kitty), Will Connolly (Boy's Voice), Brian Keane (Carl), David Andrew Macdonald (Michael), Joan MacIntosh (June), Quentin Maré (Miles), Katharine Powell (Bea), Nondumiso Tembe (Girl's Voice); American Premiere; Yale Repertory Theatre; October 24–November 15, 2008

Rough Crossing by Tom Stoppard from an original play by Ferenc Molnár; Director, Mark Rucker; Choreography, Michelle Lynch; Music Director, Erika Schroth; Sets, Timothy R. Mackabee; Costumes, Luke Brown; Lighting, Jesse Belsky; Sound, Orchestral Arrangements, Phillip Owen; Dramaturgs, Walter Byongsok Chon, Miriam Felton-Dansky; Casting, Tara Rubin Casting; Production Stage Manager, Iris Dawn O'Brien; Cast: Sean Dugan (Adam), Ashlee Fife (Lady of the Chorus), Stephanie Fittro (Lady of the Chorus), Jenifer Foote (Lady of the Chorus), Shauna Hoskin (Lady of the Chorus), Patrick Kerr (Dvornichek), John G. Preston (Ivor), Reg Rogers (Turai), Susannah Schulman (Natasha), Greg Stuhr (Gal), Adina Verson (Lady of the Chorus), Adria Vitlar (Lady of the Chorus); University Theatre; November 28–December 20, 2008

Lydia by Octavio Solis; Director, Juliette Carrillo; Sets, Andrew Boyce; Costumes, Amanda Seymour; Lighting, Jesse Belsky; Sound, Additional Music and Arrangements, David Molina; Dramaturg, Matt Cornish; Vocal and Dialect Coach, Beth McGuire; Fight Director, Rick Sordelet; Casting, Tara Rubin Casting; Production Stage Manager, Donald Claxon; Cast: Carlo Albán (Misha), Christian Barillas (Alvaro), Stephanie Beatriz (Lydia), Catalina Maynard (Rosa), Onahoua Rodriguez (Ceci), Tony Sancho (Rene); East Coast Premiere; Yale Repertory Theatre; February 6–28, 2009

Notes from Underground by Fyodor Dostoevsky; Adapted by Bill Camp and Robert Woodruff based on a translation by Richard Pevear and Larissa Volokhonsky; Director, Robert Woodruff; Sets, David Zinn; Costumes, Moria Sine Clinton; Lighting, Mark Barton; Composer and Sound, Michaël Attias; Projections, Peter Nigrini; Associate Projection Designer, Daniel Vatsky; Dramaturg, Amy Boratko; Fight Director, Rick Sordelet; Vocal Coach, Walton Wilson; Casting, Tara Rubin Casting; Production Stage Manager, Kris Longley-Postema; Cast: Bill Camp (Man), Merritt Janson (Liza/Musician), Michaël Attias (Apollon/Musician); World Premiere; Yale Repertory Theatre; March 20–April 11, 2009

Death of a Salesman by Arthur Miller; Director, James Bundy; Composer, Dwight Andrews; Sets, Scott Dougan; Costumes, Katherine O'Neill; Lighting, Stephen Strawbridge; Sound, Sarah Pickett; Dramaturgs, Donesh Olyaie, Michael Walkup; Fight Director, Rick Sordelet; Vocal and Dialect Coach, Beth McGuire; Casting, Tara Rubin Casting; Production Stage Manager, Cynthia Cahill; Cast: Christina Maria Acosta (Miss Forsythe), Starla Benford (The Woman), La Tonya Borsay (Jenny), Thomas Jefferson Byrd (Ben), Austin Durant (Bernard), Charles S. Dutton (Willy Loman), Ato Essandon (Biff), Mark Sage Hamilton (Waiter), Stephen McKinley Henderson (Charley), Billy Eugene Jones (Happy), Stanley Wayne Mathis (Stanley), Howard W. Overshown (Howard), Tijuana T. Ricks (Letta), Kimberly Scott (Linda); Yale Repertory Theatre; April 24–May 23, 2009

Brian Keane and Mary Bacon in Happy Now? *(photos by Joan Marcus)*

THEATRICAL AWARDS

2008–2009

Top: *John Tartaglia presents the Theatre World Award to Wesley Taylor (photo by Jim Baldassare)*

Center: *Howard McGillin presents the Theatre World Award to Haydn Gwynne (background: Musical Director Henry Aronson) (photo by Jim Baldassare)*

Bottom: *Tovah Feldshuh and John Willis at the Theatre World Awards (photo by Raj Autencio)*

David Alvarez of Billy Elliot The Musical

Jennifer Grace of Our Town

Josh Grisetti of Enter Laughing The Musical

Haydn Gwynne of Billy Elliot The Musical

Chad L. Coleman of Joe Turner's Come and Gone

Marin Ireland of reasons to be pretty

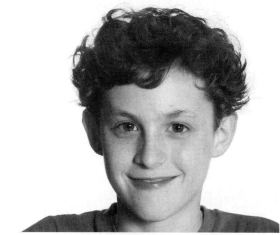

Trent Kowalik of Billy Elliot The Musical

Susan Louise O'Connor of Blithe Spirit

Colin Hanks of 33 Variations

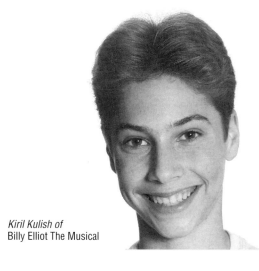

Kiril Kulish of
Billy Elliot The Musical

Condola Rashad of Ruined

Geoffrey Rush of Exit the King

Wesley Taylor of Rock of Ages

Josefina Scaglione of West Side Story

Special Award: *The Cast of* The Norman Conquests

Amelia Bullmore

Jessica Hynes

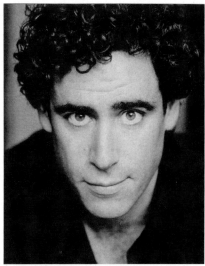
Stephen Mangan

Ben Miles

Paul Ritter

Amanda Root

65th Annual Theatre World Awards

(Photos by Raj Autencio, Jim Baldassare, and Walter McBride)

Tuesday, June 2, 2009, at Manhattan Theatre Club's Samuel J. Friedman Theatre

Originally dubbed *Promising Personalities* in 1944 by co-founders Daniel Blum, Norman MacDonald, and John Willis to coincide with the first release of *Theatre World*, the definitive pictorial and statistical record of the American theatre, the Theatre World Awards, as they are now known, are the oldest awards given for debut performances in New York City, as well as one of the oldest honors bestowed on New York actors.

Administered by the Theatre World Awards Board of Directors, a committee of current New York drama critics chooses six actors and six actresses for the Theatre World Award who have distinguished themselves in Broadway and Off-Broadway productions during the past theatre season. Occasionally, Special Theatre World Awards are also bestowed on performers, casts, or others who have made a particularly lasting impression on the New York theatre scene.

The Theatre World Award "Janus" statuette is an original bronze sculpture in primitive-modern style created by internationally recognized artist Harry Marinsky. It is adapted from the Roman myth of Janus, god of entrances, exits, and all beginnings, with one face appraising the past and the other anticipating the future. Originally cast and mounted on marble in the Del Chiaro Foundry in Pietrasanta, Italy, the awards are now cast by Sculpture House Casting of New York.

The Theatre World Award winners are selected by a committee of New York drama critics: David Cote (*Time Out New York* and NY1's *On Stage*), Peter Filichia (*Star-Ledger* and *TheaterMania.com*), Harry Haun (*Playbill*), Matthew Murray (*TalkinBroadway.com*), Frank Scheck (*New York Post*), Doug Watt (Critic Emeritus, *New York Daily News*), and Linda Winer (*Newsday*). The Theatre World Awards Board of Directors is: Kati Meister (Acting President), Erin Oestreich (Secretary), Scott Denny (Treasurer), Tom Lynch, and Barry Keating.

THE CEREMONY Writer and Host, Peter Filichia; Executive Producers, Scott Denny, Kati Meister, Erin Oestreich; Director, Barry Keating; Music Director/Accompanist, Henry Aronson; Associate Director, Jeremy Quinn; Production Manager, Mary K. Botosan; Production Stage Manager, Kimothy Cruse; Stage Manager, Alden Fulcomer; Assistant Stage Manager, Becca Wright; Production Assistants, Haley Hannah, Dana Li; Lighting Supervisor, Peter Hoerburger; Sound Supervisor, Brandon Wolcott; Reservation Coordinator, Betsy Krouner; Volunteer Coordinator, Shane Frampton-Wolters; Press Representative and Staff Photographer, Jim Baldassare; Program Layout and Design, Jeremy Quinn and Mary K. Botosan; Additional Staff Photographers, Raj Autencio, Bruce Glikas, Walter McBride and Michael Viade; Video Photographers, Richard Ridge and Bradshaw Smith; Presented on the set of the Manhattan Theatre Club production of *Accent on Youth*: scenic design by John Lee Beatty, lighting design by Brian MacDevitt, sound design by Obadiah Eaves.

Josefina Scaglione (JB)

WINNERS David Alvarez (*Billy Elliot The Musical*), Chad C. Coleman (*Joe Turner's Come and Gone*), Jennifer Grace (*Our Town*), Josh Grisetti (*Enter Laughing The Musical*), Haydn Gwynne (*Billy Elliot The Musical*), Colin Hanks (*33 Variations*), Marin Ireland (*reasons to be pretty*), Trent Kowalik (*Billy Elliot The Musical*), Kiril Kulish (*Billy Elliot The Musical*), Susan Louise O'Connor (*Blithe Spirit*), Condola Rashad (*Ruined*), Geoffrey Rush (*Exit the King*), Josefina Scaglione (*West Side Story*), Wesley Taylor (*Rock of Ages*)

SPECIAL AWARD The Cast of *The Norman Conquests*: Amelia Bullmore, Stephen Mangan, Ben Miles, Paul Ritter, Amanda Root

PRESENTERS Dylan Baker – *Eastern Standard* (1989); Craig Bierko – *The Music Man* (2000); Daniel Breaker – *Passing Strange* (2008); Kristen Chenoweth – *Steel Pier* (1997); Tovah Feldshuh – *Yentl* (1976); Jayne Houdyshell – *Well* (2006); Susan Kellermann – *Last Licks* (1980); Andrea Martin – *My Favorite Year* (1993); Howard McGillin – *The Mystery of Edwin Drood* (1986); Nellie McKay – *The Threepenny Opera* (2006); Loretta Ables Sayre – *South Pacific* (2008); John Tartaglia – *Avenue Q* (2004); Harriet Walter – *3 Birds Alighting on a Field* (1994)

Jennifer Grace receives her award from previous winner Dylan Baker (WM)

Marin Ireland receives her award from previous winner and friend, Jayne Houdyshell (JB)

Previous winner and presenter Nellie McKay entertains the crowd with an original song, "Feminists" before presenting to Susan Louise O'Connor (JB)

PERFORMANCES Ann Hampton Callaway – *Swing!* (2000); Nellie McKay – *The Threepenny Opera* (2006); Vivian Reed – *Bubbling Brown Sugar* (1976)

2009 THEATRE WORLD AWARD "JANUS" WRANGLER Olivia Ford, from the cast of *Joe Turner's Come and Gone*

VOLUNTEERS Tom Bernagozzi, Nikki Curmaci, Dan Debenport, Alece DeLuca, Taraneh Djangi, Oliver Gaag, Matt Greenstein, Sharon Hunter, Matthew Kernisky, Roxann Kraemer, Kelsey Maples, Michael Mele, Michael Messina, Kendra Mittermeyer, Barry Monush, Lauralee Reed, James Sheridan, Christina Stanton, David West, Stephen Wilde, Frank York

STAFF FOR MANHATTAN THEATRE CLUB Artistic Director, Lynne Meadow; Executive Producer, Barry Grove; General Manager, Florie Seery; Associate Artistic Director, Mandy Greenfield; Production Manager, Kurt Gardner; Associate Production Manager, Philip Naud; Assistant Production Manager, Kelsey Martinez; Properties Supervisor, Scott Laule; Assistant Properties Supervisor, Julia Sandy; Props Carpenter, Peter Grimes

Theatre World Awards co-founder John Willis and winner Geoffrey Rush (RA)

STAFF FOR ACCENT ON YOUTH Company Manager, Seth Shepsle; Production Stage Manager, Roy Harris; Stage Manager, Denise Yaney; Assistant Director, Rachel Slaven; Assistant Scenic Designer, Yoshinori Tanokura; Associate Lighting Designer, Peter Hoerburger; Associate Sound Designer, Brandon Wolcott; Lightboard Programmer, Marc Polimeni; Automation Operator, Vaughn Preston; Production Assistant, E. Bess Greer

BENEFACTOR ANGELS Alec Baldwin, David Fritz, Ben Hodges, John Mahoney, Kati Meister, Susan Stroman

BENEFACTOR STARS Christopher Goutman, Linda Hart, Cynthia Nixon, Leilani Jones Wilmore

BENEFACTORS Danny and Sandy Aiello, Karen Akers, John Allen, Elizabeth Ashley, Richard Backus, Dylan and Becky Ann Baker, Andre S. Bishop, Thomas Bernagozzi, Barbara and John Bunting, Barry and Judith Burke, Richard and Carolyn Chormann, Barbara Cook, Dona Crisman, David Cryer, Blythe Danner, Bambi Linn DeJesus, Leslie A. Denniston, Remmel T. Dickinson, Bradford Dillman, Paulette Dorr, Deanna Dunagan, Joan Eschert, Ed Evanko, Allen and Joan Hovis Eubank, Harvey Evans, Brian Farrell, Tovah Feldshuh, Bette-Lee Fox, Gail Gerber, Anita Gillette, Leigh and Stephanie Giroux, Marlene J. Gould, Tammy Grimes, John Halpern, Julie Harris, Rosemary Harris, Wayne and Lizbeth MacKay Hawley, Gloria K. Hodes, John and Merle Hook, Mark Jacoby, Ernestine Jackson, Elaine Joyce, Judy Kaye, Elliott Klein, Marian Klein, Judith Leeder, June Lockhart, Raymond & Suzanne Lowry, Daisy Maryles, John McMartin, Joanna Pettet, Kay Radtke, Ellen Richard, Cliff Robertson, Daphne Rubin-Vega, Susan Rueda, Betsy Sandler, Sheila A. Smith, Christina Stanton, Elisa Loti Stein, Mimy von Schreiner-Valenti, Russ Thacker, Priscilla and Richard Washburn, David and Nancy Wilson, Andrea Zuckerman

SPECIAL THANKS Raj Autencio, Leslie Baden, Barlow · Hartman Public Relations, Michelle Bergmann, Miriam Berman, Boneau/Bryan-Brown, Broadway Beat, Brian Blythe, Jim Byk, Philip Carrubba, Karen Carzo, Custom Glass Etching & Jack Vrtar, Helene Davis, Amanda Dekker, Jon Dimond, Brian Ferdman at TheaterMania.com, Irene Gandy, Leigh Giroux, Bruce Glikas, Allison Graham, Juliana Hannett, Hello Entertainment – David Garfinkle & Adam Silberman, Ben Hodges, Richard Hillman, Barbara Hoffman, Alana Karpoff, Amy Kass, Manhattan Theatre Club, Joe Machota, Kelsey Martinez, Tony Meisel, Michael Messina, Walter McBride, Lindsay Meck, Aaron Meier, Erin Moeller, Barry Monush, James Morgan, Christine Olver, O+M Company, Production Resource Group (Jeremiah Harris, Darren DeVerna, Stella Morelli & Connie Leahy), Aubrey Reuben, Jeffrey Richards, Diana Rissetto, Richard Ridge, Michael Riordan, Philip Rinaldi & Barbara Carroll, Elon Rutberg, Sculpture House Casting Inc. & Michael Perrotta, Matt Ross, Marisa Sechrest, Daniel Seth, Matt Shea, Bradshaw Smith, Susanne Tighe, Peter James Zielinski, the *Accent On Youth* production team, the entire staff of Manhattan Theatre Club, and the agents, management, and publicity teams of our winners and presenters. Very special thanks to Raúl Esparza.

Gift Bags Promotions supplied by Applause Theatre and Cinema Books/Hal Leonard Publications, The Araca Group, Monarch, TheaterMania.com, and *West Side Story*

Theatre World Awards After-Party generously sponsored by **Trattoria Dopo Teatro,** 125 West 44th Street between 6th Avenue and Broadway; Sound equipment generously provided by Jeremiah Harris/Production Resource Group.

The Theatre World Awards, Inc. is a 501 (c)(3) nonprofit organization, and our annual presentation is made possible by the generous contributions of previous winners and friends. For more information please visit the website at www.theatreworldawards.org.

Tax-deductible contributions can be sent via PayPay® to info@theatreworldawards.org, or checks and money orders sent to:

Theatre World Awards, Inc.
Box 246 Radio City Station
New York, NY 10101-0246

Chad L. Coleman receives his award from previous winner Loretta Ables Sayre (JB)

Theatre World Awards co-producer Scott Denny (RA)

Kristin Chenoweth (WM)

The Cast of The Norman Conquests meets the press (WM)

Andrea Martin presents to her Exit the King co-star, Geoffrey Rush (JB)

Colin Hanks receives his award from his 33 Variations co-star, Susan Kellermann (WM)

David Alvarez, Trent Kowalik, Kiril Kulish and presenter Tovah Feldshuh (WM)

Theatre World Editor in Chief Ben Hodges and former winner Joan Hovis-Eubank (1958), who traveled from her home in Thailand to attend the ceremony (RA)

Amelia Bullmore and Ben Miles (front) accept the Special Award for the cast of The Norman Conquests with (back) Amanda Root, Paul Ritter, Stephen Mangan and Jessica Hynes (JB)

Previous winner Vivian Reed thrills the crowd with her performance of "God Bless the Child" (JB)

Presenters Jayne Houdyshell and Howard McGillin meet the press (WM)

Wesley Taylor and his presenter John Tartaglia meet the press (WM)

Colin Hanks (WM)

Previous winner Harriet Walter before presenting the Special Theatre World Award to The Norman Conquests cast (WM)

Previous winner Craig Bierko before presenting to Josh Grisetti (JB)

The Billy Elliot boys: David Alvarez, Trent Kowalik and Kiril Kulish meet the press (WM)

Former winner Ann Hampton Callaway closes the awards ceremony with an improvisational composition featuring the highlights of the ceremony (JB)

Condola Rashad and her proud mother, Phylicia Rashad (WM)

Susan Louise O'Connor (WM)

Previous Theatre World Award Recipients

1944-45: Betty Comden (*On the Town*), Richard Davis (*Kiss Them For Me*), Richard Hart (*Dark of the Moon*), Judy Holliday (*Kiss Them for Me*), Charles Lang (*Down to Miami* and *The Overtons*), Bambi Linn (*Carousel*), John Lund (*The Hasty Heart*), Donald Murphy (*Signature* and *Common Ground*), Nancy Noland (*Common Ground*), Margaret Phillips (*The Late George Apley*), John Raitt (*Carousel*)

1945-46: Barbara Bel Geddes (*Deep Are the Roots*), Marlon Brando (*Truckline Café* and *Candida*), Bill Callahan (*Call Me Mister*), Wendell Corey (*The Wind is Ninety*), Paul Douglas (*Born Yesterday*), Mary James (*Apple of His Eye*), Burt Lancaster (*A Sound of Hunting*), Patricia Marshall (*The Day Before Spring*), Beatrice Pearson (*The Mermaids Singing*)

1946-47: Keith Andes (*The Chocolate Soldier*), Marion Bell (*Brigadoon*), Peter Cookson (*Message for Margaret*), Ann Crowley (*Carousel*), Ellen Hanley (*Barefoot Boy With Cheek*), John Jordan (*The Wanhope Building*), George Keane (*Brigadoon*), Dorothea MacFarland (*Oklahoma!*), James Mitchell (*Brigadoon*), Patricia Neal (*Another Part of the Forest*), David Wayne (*Finian's Rainbow*)

1947-48: Valerie Bettis (*Inside U.S.A.*), Edward Bryce (*The Cradle Will Rock*), Whitfield Connor (*Macbeth*), Mark Dawson (*High Button Shoes*), June Lockhart (*For Love or Money*), Estelle Loring (*Inside U.S.A.*), Peggy Maley (*Joy to the World*), Ralph Meeker (*Mister Roberts*), Meg Mundy (*The Happy Journey to Trenton and Camden* and *The Respectful Prostitute*), Douglass Watson (*Antony and Cleopatra*), James Whitmore (*Command Decision*), Patrice Wymore (*Hold It!*)

1948-49: Tod Andrews (*Summer and Smoke*), Doe Avedon (*The Young and Fair*), Jean Carson (*Bravo!*), Carol Channing (*Lend an Ear*), Richard Derr (*The Traitor*), Julie Harris (*Sundown Beach*), Mary McCarty (*Sleepy Hollow*), Allyn Ann McLerie (*Where's Charley?*), Cameron Mitchell (*Death of a Salesman*), Gene Nelson (*Lend an Ear*), Byron Palmer (*Where's Charley?*), Bob Scheerer (*Lend an Ear*)

1949-50: Nancy Andrews (*Touch and Go*), Phil Arthur (*With a Silk Thread*), Barbara Brady (*The Velvet Glove*), Lydia Clarke (*Detective Story*), Priscilla Gillette (*Regina*), Don Hanmer (*The Man*), Marcia Henderson (*Peter Pan*), Charlton Heston (*Design for a Stained Glass Window*), Rick Jason (*Now I Lay Me Down to Sleep*), Grace Kelly (*The Father*), Charles Nolte (*Design for a Stained Glass Window*), Roger Price (*Tickets, Please!*)

1950-51: Barbara Ashley (*Out of This World*), Isabel Bigley (*Guys and Dolls*), Martin Brooks (*Burning Bright*), Richard Burton (*The Lady's Not For Burning*), Pat Crowley (*Southern Exposure*), James Daly (*Major Barbara* and *Mary Rose*), Cloris Leachman (*A Story for a Sunday Evening*), Russell Nype (*Call Me Madam*), Jack Palance (*Darkness at Noon*), William Smithers (*Romeo and Juliet*), Maureen Stapleton (*The Rose Tattoo*), Marcia Van Dyke (*Marcia Van Dyke*), Eli Wallach (*The Rose Tattoo*)

1951-52: Tony Bavaar (*Paint Your Wagon*), Patricia Benoit (*Glad Tidings*), Peter Conlow (*Courtin' Time*), Virginia de Luce (*New Faces of 1952*), Ronny Graham (*New Faces of 1952*), Audrey Hepburn (*Gigi*), Diana Herbert (*The Number*), Conrad Janis (*The Brass Ring*), Dick Kallman (*Seventeen*), Charles Proctor (*Twilight Walk*), Eric Sinclair (*Much Ado About Nothing*), Kim Stanley (*The Chase*), Marian Winters (*I Am a Camera*), Helen Wood (*Seventeen*)

1952-53: Edie Adams (*Wonderful Town*), Rosemary Harris (*The Climate of Eden*), Eileen Heckart (*Picnic*), Peter Kelley (*Two's Company*), John Kerr (*Bernardine*), Richard Kiley (*Misalliance*), Gloria Marlowe (*In Any Language*), Penelope Munday (*The Climate of Eden*), Paul Newman (*Picnic*), Sheree North (*Hazel Flagg*), Geraldine Page (*Mid-Summer*), John Stewart (*Bernardine*), Ray Stricklyn (*The Climate of Eden*), Gwen Verdon (*Can-Can*)

1953-54: Orson Bean (*John Murray Anderson's Almanac*), Harry Belafonte (*John Murray Anderson's Almanac*), James Dean (*The Immoralist*), Joan Diener (*Kismet*), Ben Gazzara (*End as a Man*), Carol Haney (*The Pajama Game*), Jonathan

The Class of 1953: Paul Newman, Jay Greenberg, Theatre World founder Daniel Blum, Ray Stricklyn, Peter Kelley, Johnny Steward, Eileen Heckart, Edith Adams, Geraldine Page, Richard Kiley

Lucas (*The Golden Apple*), Kay Medford (*Lullaby*), Scott Merrill (*The Threepenny Opera*), Elizabeth Montgomery (*Late Love*), Leo Penn (*The Girl on the Via Flaminia*), Eva Marie Saint (*The Trip to Bountiful*)

1954-55: Julie Andrews (*The Boy Friend*), Jacqueline Brookes (*The Cretan Woman*), Shirl Conway (*Plain and Fancy*), Barbara Cook (*Plain and Fancy*), David Daniels (*Plain and Fancy*), Mary Fickett (*Tea and Sympathy*), Page Johnson (*In April Once*), Loretta Leversee (*Home is the Hero*), Jack Lord (*The Traveling Lady*), Dennis Patrick (*The Wayward Saint*), Anthony Perkins (*Tea and Sympathy*), Christopher Plummer (*The Dark is Light Enough*)

1955-56: Diane Cilento (*Tiger at the Gates*), Dick Davalos (*A View From the Bridge*), Anthony Franciosa (*A Hatful of Rain*), Andy Griffith (*No Time for Sergeants*), Laurence Harvey (*Island of Goats*), David Hedison (*A Month in the Country*), Earle Hyman (*Mister Johnson*), Susan Johnson (*The Most Happy Fella*), John Michael King (*My Fair Lady*), Jayne Mansfield (*Will Success Spoil Rock Hunter*), Sarah Marshall (*The Ponder Heart*), Gaby Rodgers (*Mister Johnson*), Susan Strasberg (*The Diary of Anne Frank*), Fritz Weaver (*The Chalk Garden*)

1956-57: Peggy Cass (*Auntie Mame*), Sydney Chaplin (*Bells Are Ringing*), Sylvia Daneel (*The Tunnel of Love*), Bradford Dillman (*Long Day's Journey Into Night*), Peter Donat (*The First Gentleman*), George Grizzard (*The Happiest Millionaire*), Carol Lynley (*The Potting Shed*), Peter Palmer (*Li'l Abner*), Jason Robards (*Long Day's Journey Into Night*), Cliff Robertson (*Orpheus Descending*), Pippa Scott (*Child of Fortune*), Inga Swenson (*The First Gentleman*)

1957-58: Anne Bancroft (*Two for the Seesaw*), Warren Berlinger (*Blue Denim*), Colleen Dewhurst (*Children of Darkness*), Richard Easton (*The Country Wife*), Tim Everett (*The Dark at the Top of the Stairs*), Eddie Hodges (*The Music Man*), Joan Hovis (*Love Me Little*), Carol Lawrence (*West Side Story*), Jacqueline McKeever (*Oh, Captain!*), Wynne Miller (*Li'l Abner*), Robert Morse (*Say, Darling*), George C. Scott (*Richard III*)

1958-59: Lou Antonio (*The Buffalo Skinner*), Ina Balin (*A Majority of One*), Richard Cross (*Maria Golovin*), Tammy Grimes (*Look After Lulu*), Larry Hagman (*God and Kate Murphy*), Dolores Hart (*The Pleasure of His Company*), Roger Mollien (French Theatre National Populaire), France Nuyen (*The World of Suzie Wong*), Susan Oliver (*Patate*), Ben Piazza (*Kataki*), Paul Roebling (*A Desert Incident*), William Shatner (*The World of Suzie Wong*), Pat Suzuki (*Flower Drum Song*), Rip Torn (*Sweet Bird of Youth*)

1959-60: Warren Beatty (*A Loss of Roses*), Eileen Brennan (*Little Mary Sunshine*), Carol Burnett (*Once Upon a Mattress*), Patty Duke (*The Miracle Worker*), Jane Fonda (*There Was a Little Girl*), Anita Gillette (*Russell Patterson's Sketchbook*), Elisa Loti (*Come Share My House*), Donald Madden (*Julius Caesar*), George Maharis (*The Zoo Story*), John McMartin (*Little Mary Sunshine*), Lauri Peters (*The Sound of Music*), Dick Van Dyke (*The Boys Against the Girls*)

1960-61: Joyce Bulifant (*Whisper to Me*), Dennis Cooney (*Every Other Evil*), Sandy Dennis (*Face of a Hero*), Nancy Dussault (*Do Re Mi*), Robert Goulet (*Camelot*), Joan Hackett (*Call Me By My Rightful Name*), June Harding (*Cry of the Raindrop*), Ron Husmann (*Tenderloin*), James MacArthur (*Invitation to a March*), Bruce Yarnell (*The Happiest Girl in the World*)

1961-62: Elizabeth Ashley (*Take Her, She's Mine*), Keith Baxter (*A Man for All Seasons*), Peter Fonda (*Blood, Sweat and Stanley Poole*), Don Galloway (*Bring Me a Warm Body*), Sean Garrison (*Half-Past Wednesday*), Barbara Harris (*Oh, Dad, Poor Dad, Mamma's Hung You in the Closet and I'm Feeling So Sad*), James Earl Jones (*Moon on a Rainbow Shawl*), Janet Margolin (*Daughter of Silence*), Karen Morrow (*Sing, Muse!*), Robert Redford (*Sunday in New York*), John Stride (*Romeo and Juliet*), Brenda Vaccaro (*Everybody Loves Opal*)

1962-63: Alan Arkin (*Enter Laughing*), Stuart Damon (*The Boys from Syracuse*), Melinda Dillon (*Who's Afraid of Virginia Woolf?*), Robert Drivas (*Mrs. Dally Has a Lover*), Bob Gentry (*Angels of Anadarko*), Dorothy Loudon (*Nowhere to Go But Up*), Brandon Maggart (*Put It in Writing*), Julienne Marie (*The Boys from Syracuse*), Liza Minnelli (*Best Foot Forward*), Estelle Parsons (*Mrs. Dally Has a Lover*), Diana Sands (*Tiger Tiger Burning Bright*), Swen Swenson (*Little Me*)

1963-64: Alan Alda (*Fair Game for Lover*), Gloria Bleezarde (*Never Live Over a Pretzel Factory*), Imelda De Martin (*The Amorous Flea*), Claude Giraud (*Phédre*), Ketty Lester (*Cabin in the Sky*), Barbara Loden (*After the Fall*), Lawrence Pressman (*Never Live Over a Pretzel Factory*), Gilbert Price (*Jerico-Jim Crow*), Philip Proctor (*The Amorous Flea*), John Tracy (*Telemachus Clay*), Jennifer West (*Dutchman*)

1964-65: Carolyn Coates (*The Trojan Women*), Joyce Jillson (*The Roar of the Greasepaint – The Smell of the Crowd*), Linda Lavin (*Wet Paint*), Luba Lisa (*I Had a Ball*), Michael O'Sullivan (*Tartuffe*), Joanna Pettet (*Poor Richard*), Beah Richards (*The Amen Corner*), Jaime Sanchez (*Conerico Was Here to Stay* and *The Toilet*), Victor Spinetti (*Oh, What a Lovely War*), Nicolas Surovy (*Helen*), Robert Walker (*I Knock at the Door* and *Pictures in the Hallway*), Clarence Williams III (*Slow Dancing on the Killing Ground*)

The Class of 1961: Nancy Dussault, June Harding, Joyce Bulifant, Robert Goulet, Richard Burton, Theatre World founder Daniel Blum, Dennis Cooney, Bruce Yarnell

1965-66: Zoe Caldwell (*Slapstick Tragedy*), David Carradine (*The Royal Hunt of the Sun*), John Cullum (*On a Clear Day You Can See Forever*), John Davidson (*Oklahoma!*), Faye Dunaway (*Hogan's Ghost*), Gloria Foster (*Medea*), Robert Hooks (*Where's Daddy?* and *Day of Absence*), Jerry Lanning (*Mame*), Richard Mulligan (*Mating Dance* and *Hogan's Ghost*), April Shawhan (*3 Bags Full*), Sandra Smith (*Any Wednesday*), Leslie Ann Warren (*Drat! The Cat!*)

1966-67: Bonnie Bedelia (*My Sweet Charlie*), Richard Benjamin (*The Star-Spangled Girl*), Dustin Hoffman (*Eh?*), Terry Kiser (*Fortune and Men's Eyes*), Reva Rose (*You're A Good Man, Charlie Brown*), Robert Salvio (*Hamp*), Sheila Smith (*Mame*), Connie Stevens (*The Star-Spangled Girl*), Pamela Tiffin (*Dinner at Eight*), Leslie Uggams (*Hallelujah, Baby!*), Jon Voight (*That Summer – That Fall*), Christopher Walken (*The Rose Tattoo*)

1967-68: David Birney (*Summertree*), Pamela Burrell (*Arms and the Man*), Jordan Christopher (*Black Comedy*), Jack Crowder – a.k.a. Thalmus Rasulala (*Hello, Dolly!*), Sandy Duncan (*Ceremony of Innocence*), Julie Gregg (*The Happy Time*), Stephen Joyce (*Stephen D.*), Bernadette Peters (*George M*), Alice Playten (*Henry, Sweet Henry*), Michael Rupert (*The Happy Time*), Brenda Smiley (*Scuba Duba*), Russ Thacker (*Your Own Thing*)

1968-69: Jane Alexander (*The Great White Hope*), David Cryer (*Come Summer*), Blythe Danner (*The Miser*), Ed Evanko (*Canterbury Tales*), Ken Howard (*1776*), Lauren Jones (*Does a Tiger Wear a Necktie?*), Ron Leibman (*We Bombed in New Haven*), Marian Mercer (*Promises, Promises*), Jill O'Hara (*Promises, Promises*), Ron O'Neal (*No Place to Be Somebody*), Al Pacino (*Does a Tiger Wear a Necktie?*), Marlene Warfield (*The Great White Hope*)

1969-70: Susan Browning (*Company*), Donny Burks (*Billy Noname*), Catherine Burns (*Dear Janet Rosenberg, Dear Mr. Kooning*), Len Cariou (*Henry V* and *Applause*), Bonnie Franklin (*Applause*), David Holliday (*Coco*), Katharine Houghton (*A Scent of Flowers*), Melba Moore (*Purlie*), David Rounds (*Child's Play*), Lewis J. Stadlen (*Minnie's Boys*), Kristoffer Tabori (*How Much, How Much*), Fredricka Weber (*The Last Sweet Days of Isaac*)

1970-71: Clifton Davis (*Do It Again*), Michael Douglas (*Pinkville*), Julie Garfield (*Uncle Vanya*), Martha Henry (*The Playboy of the Western World, Scenes From American Life,* and *Antigone*), James Naughton (*Long Days Journey Into Night*), Tricia O'Neil (*Two by Two*), Kipp Osborne (*Butterflies Are Free*), Roger Rathburn (*No, No, Nanette*), Ayn Ruymen (*The Gingerbread Lady*), Jennifer Salt (*Father's Day*), Joan Van Ark (*School for Wives*), Walter Willison (*Two by Two*)

1971-72: Jonelle Allen (*Two Gentlemen of Verona*), Maureen Anderman (*Moonchildren*), William Atherton (*Suggs*), Richard Backus (*Promenade, All!*), Adrienne Barbeau (*Grease*), Cara Duff-MacCormick (*Moonchildren*), Robert Foxworth (*The Crucible*), Elaine Joyce (*Sugar*), Jess Richards (*On The Town*), Ben Vereen (*Jesus Christ Superstar*), Beatrice Winde (*Ain't Supposed to Die a Natural Death*), James Woods (*Moonchildren*)

1972-73: D'Jamin Bartlett (*A Little Night Music*), Patricia Elliott (*A Little Night Music*), James Farentino (*A Streetcar Named Desire*), Brian Farrell (*The Last of Mrs. Lincoln*), Victor Garber (*Ghosts*), Kelly Garrett (*Mother Earth*), Mari Gorman (*The Hot I Baltimore*), Laurence Guittard (*A Little Night Music*), Trish Hawkins (*The Hot I Baltimore*), Monte Markham (*Irene*), John Rubinstein (*Pippin*), Jennifer Warren (*6 Rms Riv Vu*), Alexander H. Cohen (Special Award)

1973-74: Mark Baker (*Candide*), Maureen Brennan (*Candide*), Ralph Carter (*Raisin*), Thom Christopher (*Noel Coward in Two Keys*), John Driver (*Over Here*), Conchata Ferrell (*The Sea Horse*), Ernestine Jackson (*Raisin*), Michael Moriarty (*Find Your Way Home*), Joe Morton (*Raisin*), Ann Reinking (*Over Here*), Janie Sell (*Over Here*), Mary Woronov (*Boom Boom Room*), Sammy Cahn (Special Award)

1974-75: Peter Burnell (*In Praise of Love*), Zan Charisse (*Gypsy*), Lola Falana (*Dr. Jazz*), Peter Firth (*Equus*), Dorian Harewood (*Don't Call Back*), Joel Higgins (*Shenandoah*), Marcia McClain (*Where's Charley?*), Linda Miller (*Black Picture Show*), Marti Rolph (*Good News*), John Sheridan (*Gypsy*), Scott Stevensen (*Good News*), Donna Theodore (*Shenandoah*), Equity Library Theatre (Special Award)

1976 Winner Vivian Reed

1975-76: Danny Aiello (*Lamppost Reunion*), Christine Andreas (*My Fair Lady*), Dixie Carter (*Jesse and the Bandit Queen*), Tovah Feldshuh (*Yentl*), Chip Garnett (*Bubbling Brown Sugar*), Richard Kelton (*Who's Afraid of Virginia Woolf?*), Vivian Reed (*Bubbling Brown Sugar*), Charles Repole (*Very Good Eddie*), Virginia Seidel (*Very Good Eddie*), Daniel Seltzer (*Knock Knock*), John V. Shea (*Yentl*), Meryl Streep (*27 Wagons Full of Cotton*), The Cast of *A Chorus Line* (Special Award)

1976-77: Trazana Beverley *(for colored girls…)*, Michael Cristofer (*The Cherry Orchard*), Joe Fields (*The Basic Training of Pavlo Hummel*), Joanna Gleason (*I Love My Wife*), Cecilia Hart (*Dirty Linen*), John Heard (*G.R. Point*), Gloria Hodes (*The Club*), Juliette Koka (*Piaf…A Remembrance*), Andrea McArdle (*Annie*), Ken Page (*Guys and Dolls*), Jonathan Pryce (*Comedians*), Chick Vennera (*Jockeys*), Eva LeGallienne (Special Award)

1977-78: Vasili Bogazianos (*P.S. Your Cat Is Dead*), Nell Carter (*Ain't Misbehavin'*), Carlin Glynn (*The Best Little Whorehouse in Texas*), Christopher Goutman (*The Promise*), William Hurt (*Ulysses in Traction, Lulu,* and *The Fifth of July*), Judy Kaye (*On the 20th Century*), Florence Lacy (*Hello, Dolly!*), Armelia McQueen (*Ain't Misbehavin'*), Gordana Rashovich (*Fefu and Her Friends*), Bo Rucker (*Native Son*), Richard Seer (*Da*), Colin Stinton (*The Water Engine*), Joseph Papp (Special Award)

1978-79: Philip Anglim (*The Elephant Man*), Lucie Arnaz (*They're Playing Our Song*), Gregory Hines (*Eubie!*), Ken Jennings (*Sweeney Todd*), Michael Jeter (*G.R. Point*), Laurie Kennedy (*Man and Superman*), Susan Kingsley (*Getting Out*), Christine Lahti (*The Woods*), Edward James Olmos (*Zoot Suit*), Kathleen Quinlan (*Taken in Marriage*), Sarah Rice (*Sweeney Todd*), Max Wright (*Once in a Lifetime*), Marshall W. Mason (Special Award)

1979-80: Maxwell Caulfield (*Class Enemy*), Leslie Denniston (*Happy New Year*), Boyd Gaines (*A Month in the Country*), Richard Gere (*Bent*), Harry Groener (*Oklahoma!*), Stephen James (*The 1940's Radio Hour*), Susan Kellermann (*Last Licks*), Dinah Manoff (*I Ought to Be in Pictures*), Lonny Price (*Class Enemy*), Marianne Tatum (*Barnum*), Anne Twomey (*Nuts*), Dianne Wiest (*The Art of Dining*), Mickey Rooney (*Sugar Babies* – Special Award)

1980-81: Brian Backer (*The Floating Light Bulb*), Lisa Banes (*Look Back in Anger*), Meg Bussert (*The Music Man*), Michael Allen Davis (*Broadway Follies*), Giancarlo Esposito (*Zooman and the Sign*), Daniel Gerroll (*Slab Boys*), Phyllis Hyman (*Sophisticated Ladies*), Cynthia Nixon (*The Philadelphia Story*), Amanda Plummer (*A Taste of Honey*), Adam Redfield (*A Life*), Wanda Richert (*42nd Street*), Rex Smith (*The Pirates of Penzance*), Elizabeth Taylor (*The Little Foxes* – Special Award)

1981-82: Karen Akers (*Nine*), Laurie Beechman (*Joseph and the Amazing Technicolor Dreamcoat*), Danny Glover (*Master Harold…and the Boys*), David Alan Grier (*The First*), Jennifer Holliday (*Dreamgirls*), Anthony Heald (*Misalliance*), Lizbeth Mackay (*Crimes of the Heart*), Peter MacNicol (*Crimes of the Heart*), Elizabeth McGovern (*My Sister in This House*), Ann Morrison (*Merrily We Roll Along*), Michael O'Keefe (*Mass Appeal*), James Widdoes *(Is There Life After High School?)*, Manhattan Theatre Club (Special Award)

1982-83: Karen Allen (*Monday After the Miracle*), Suzanne Bertish (*Skirmishes*), Matthew Broderick (*Brighton Beach Memoirs*), Kate Burton *(Winners)*, Joanne Camp (*Geniuses*), Harvey Fierstein (*Torch Song Trilogy*), Peter Gallagher (*A Doll's Life*), John Malkovich (*True West*), Anne Pitoniak (*'Night Mother*), James Russo (*Extremities*), Brian Tarantina (*Angels Fall*), Linda Thorson (*Streaming*), Natalia Makarova (*On Your Toes* – Special Award)

1983-84: Martine Allard (*The Tap Dance Kid*), Joan Allen (*And a Nightingale Sang*), Kathy Whitton Baker (*Fool For Love*), Mark Capri (*On Approval*), Laura Dean (*Doonesbury*), Stephen Geoffreys (*The Human Comedy*), Todd Graff (*Baby*), Glenne Headly (*The Philanthropist*), J.J. Johnston (*American Buffalo*), Bonnie Koloc (*The Human Comedy*), Calvin Levels (*Open Admissions*), Robert Westenberg (*Zorba*), Ron Moody (*Oliver* – Special Award)

1984-85: Kevin Anderson (*Orphans*), Richard Chaves (*Tracers*), Patti Cohenour (*La Boheme* and *Big River*), Charles S. Dutton (*Ma Rainey's Black Bottom*), Nancy Giles (*Mayor*), Whoopi Goldberg (*Whoopi Goldberg*), Leilani Jones (*Grind*), John Mahoney (*Orphans*), Laurie Metcalf (*Balm in Gilead*), Barry Miller (*Biloxi Blues*), John Turturro (*Danny and the Deep Blue Sea*), Amelia White (*The Accrington Pals*), Lucille Lortel (Special Award)

1957 Winner Jason Robards presents to 1983 Winner Matthew

1985 Winner John Mahoney

1985-86: Suzy Amis (*Fresh Horses*), Alec Baldwin (*Loot*), Aled Davies (*Orchards*), Faye Grant (*Singin' in the Rain*), Julie Hagerty (*The House of Blue Leaves*), Ed Harris (*Precious Sons*), Mark Jacoby (*Sweet Charity*), Donna Kane (*Dames at Sea*), Cleo Laine (*The Mystery of Edwin Drood*), Howard McGillin (*The Mystery of Edwin Drood*), Marisa Tomei (*Daughters*), Joe Urla (*Principia Scriptoriae*), Ensemble Studio Theatre (Special Award)

1986-87: Annette Bening (*Coastal Disturbances*), Timothy Daly (*Coastal Disturbances*), Lindsay Duncan (*Les Liaisons Dangereuses*), Frank Ferrante (*Groucho: A Life in Revue*), Robert Lindsay (*Me and My Girl*), Amy Madigan (*The Lucky Spot*), Michael Maguire (*Les Misérables*), Demi Moore (*The Early Girl*), Molly Ringwald (*Lily Dale*), Frances Ruffelle (*Les Misérables*), Courtney B. Vance (*Fences*), Colm Wilkinson (*Les Misérables*), Robert DeNiro (Special Award)

1987-88: Yvonne Bryceland (*The Road to Mecca*), Philip Casnoff (*Chess*), Danielle Ferland (*Into the Woods*), Melissa Gilbert (*A Shayna Maidel*), Linda Hart (*Anything Goes*), Linzi Hateley (*Carrie*), Brian Kerwin (*Emily*), Brian Mitchell (*Mail*), Mary Murfitt (*Oil City Symphony*), Aidan Quinn (*A Streetcar Named Desire*), Eric Roberts (*Burn This*), B.D. Wong (*M. Butterfly*), Tisa Chang and Martin E. Segal (Special Awards)

1988-89: Dylan Baker (*Eastern Standard*), Joan Cusack (*Road* and *Brilliant Traces*), Loren Dean (*Amulets Against the Dragon Forces*), Peter Frechette (*Eastern Standard*), Sally Mayes (*Welcome to the Club*), Sharon McNight (*Starmites*), Jennie Moreau (*Eleemosynary*), Paul Provenza (*Only Kidding*), Kyra Sedgwick (*Ah, Wilderness!*), Howard Spiegel (*Only Kidding*), Eric Stoltz (*Our Town*), Joanne Whalley-Kilmer (*What the Butler Saw*); Pauline Collins of *Shirley Valentine* (Special Award), Mikhail Baryshnikov (Special Award)

1989-90: Denise Burse (*Ground People*), Erma Campbell (*Ground People*), Rocky Carroll (*The Piano Lesson*), Megan Gallagher (*A Few Good Men*), Tommy Hollis (*The Piano Lesson*), Robert Lambert (*Gypsy*), Kathleen Rowe McAllen (*Aspects of Love*), Michael McKean (*Accomplice*), Crista Moore (*Gypsy*), Mary-Louise Parker (*Prelude to a Kiss*), Daniel von Bargen (*Mastergate*), Jason Workman (*Jason Workman*), Stewart Granger (*The Circle* – Special Award), Kathleen Turner (*Cat on a Hot Tin Roof* – Special Award)

1990-91: Jane Adams (*I Hate Hamlet*), Gillian Anderson (*Absent Friends*), Adam Arkin (*I Hate Hamlet*), Brenda Blethyn (*Absent Friends*), Marcus Chong (*Stand-up Tragedy*), Paul Hipp (*Buddy*), LaChanze (*Once on This Island*), Kenny Neal (*Mule Bone*), Kevin Ramsey (*Oh, Kay!*), Francis Ruivivar (*Shogun*), Lea Salonga (*Miss Saigon*), Chandra Wilson (*The Good Times Are Killing Me*); Tracey Ullman (*The Big Love* and *Taming of the Shrew*), Ellen Stewart (Special Award)

1991-92: Talia Balsam (*Jake's Women*), Lindsay Crouse (*The Homecoming*), Griffin Dunne (*Search and Destroy*), Laurence Fishburne (*Two Trains Running*), Mel Harris (*Empty Hearts*), Jonathan Kaplan (*Falsettos* and *Rags*), Jessica Lange (*A Streetcar Named Desire*), Laura Linney (*Sight Unseen*), Spiro Malas (*The Most Happy Fella*), Mark Rosenthal (*Marvin's Room*), Helen Shaver (*Jake's Women*), Al White (*Two Trains Running*), The Cast of *Dancing at Lughnasa* (Special Award), Plays for Living (Special Award)

1992-93: Brent Carver (*Kiss of the Spider Woman*), Michael Cerveris (*The Who's Tommy*), Marcia Gay Harden (*Angels in America: Millennium Approaches*), Stephanie Lawrence (*Blood Brothers*), Andrea Martin (*My Favorite Year*), Liam Neeson (*Anna Christie*), Stephen Rea (*Someone Who'll Watch Over Me*), Natasha Richardson (*Anna Christie*), Martin Short (*The Goodbye Girl*), Dina Spybey (*Five Women Wearing the Same Dress*), Stephen Spinella (*Angels in America: Millennium Approaches*), Jennifer Tilly (*One Shoe Off*), John Leguizamo and Rosetta LeNoire (Special Awards)

1993-94: Marcus D'Amico (*An Inspector Calls*), Jarrod Emick (*Damn Yankees*), Arabella Field (*Snowing at Delphi* and *4 Dogs and a Bone*), Aden Gillett (*An Inspector Calls*), Sherry Glaser (*Family Secrets*), Michael Hayden (*Carousel*), Margaret Illman (*The Red Shoes*), Audra McDonald (*Carousel*), Burke Moses (*Beauty and the Beast*), Anna Deavere Smith (*Twilight: Los Angeles, 1992*), Jere Shea (*Passion*), Harriet Walter (*3Birds Alighting on a Field*)

1994-95: Gretha Boston (*Show Boat*), Billy Crudup (*Arcadia*), Ralph Fiennes (*Hamlet*), Beverly D'Angelo (*Simpatico*), Calista Flockhart (*The Glass Menagerie*), Kevin Kilner (*The Glass Menagerie*), Anthony LaPaglia (*The Rose Tattoo*), Julie Johnson (*Das Barbecü*), Helen Mirren (*A Month in the Country*), Jude Law (*Indiscretions*), Rufus Sewell (*Translations*), Vanessa Williams (*Kiss of the Spider Woman*), Brooke Shields (Special Award)

1995-96: Jordan Baker (*Suddenly Last Summer*), Joohee Choi (*The King and I*), Karen Kay Cody (*Master Class*), Viola Davis (*Seven Guitars*), Kate Forbes (*The School for Scandal*), Michael McGrath (*Swinging on a Star*), Alfred Molina (*Molly Sweeney*), Timothy Olyphant (*The Monogamist*), Adam Pascal (*Rent*), Lou Diamond Phillips (*The King and I*), Daphne Rubin-Vega (*Rent*), Brett Tabisel (*Big*), The Cast of *An Ideal Husband* (Special Award)

1996-97: Terry Beaver (*The Last Night of Ballyhoo*), Helen Carey (*London Assurance*), Kristin Chenoweth (*Steel Pier*), Jason Danieley (*Candide*), Linda Eder (*Jekyll & Hyde*), Allison Janney (*Present Laughter*), Daniel McDonald (*Steel Pier*), Janet McTeer (*A Doll's House*), Mark Ruffalo (*This Is Our Youth*), Fiona Shaw (*The Waste Land*), Antony Sher (*Stanley*), Alan Tudyk (*Bunny Bunny*), The Cast of *Skylight* (Special Award)

1991 Winner Adam Arkin and his father 1963 Winner Alan Arkin

1993 Winners Natasha Richardson and Liam Neeson

1997-98: Max Casella (*The Lion King*), Margaret Colin (*Jackie*), Ruaidhri Conroy (*The Cripple of Inishmaan*), Alan Cumming (*Cabaret*), Lea Delaria (*On the Town*), Edie Falco (*Side Man*), Enid Graham (*Honour*), Anna Kendrick (*High Society*), Ednita Nazario (*The Capeman*), Douglas Sills (*The Scarlet Pimpernel*), Steven Sutcliffe (*Ragtime*), Sam Trammel (*Ah, Wilderness!*), Eddie Izzard (Special Award), The Cast of *The Beauty Queen of Leenane* (Special Award)

1998-99: Jillian Armenante (*The Cider House Rules*), James Black (*Not About Nightingales*), Brendan Coyle (*The Weir*), Anna Friel (*Closer*), Rupert Graves (*Closer*), Lynda Gravátt (*The Old Settler*), Nicole Kidman (*The Blue Room*), Ciáran Hinds (*Closer*), Ute Lemper (*Chicago*), Clarke Peters (*The Iceman Cometh*), Toby Stephens (*Ring Round the Moon*), Sandra Oh (*Stop Kiss*), Jerry Herman (Special Award)

1999-2000: Craig Bierko (*The Music Man*), Everett Bradley (*Swing!*), Gabriel Byrne (*A Moon for the Misbegotten*), Ann Hampton Callaway (*Swing!*), Toni Collette (*The Wild Party*), Henry Czerny (*Arms and the Man*), Stephen Dillane (*The Real Thing*), Jennifer Ehle (*The Real Thing*), Philip Seymour Hoffman (*True West*), Hayley Mills (*Suite in Two Keys*), Cigdem Onat (*The Time of the Cuckoo*), Claudia Shear (*Dirty Blonde*), Barry Humphries (*Dame Edna: The Royal Tour* – Special Award)

2000-2001: Juliette Binoche (*Betrayal*), Macaulay Culkin (*Madame Melville*), Janie Dee (*Comic Potential*), Raúl Esparza (*The Rocky Horror Show*), Kathleen Freeman (*The Full Monty*), Deven May (*Bat Boy*), Reba McEntire (*Annie Get Your Gun*), Chris Noth (*The Best Man*), Joshua Park (*The Adventures of Tom Sawyer*), Rosie Perez (*References to Salvador Dali Make Me Hot*), Joely Richardson (*Madame Melville*), John Ritter (*The Dinner Party*), The Cast of *Stones in His Pocket* – Seán Campion & Conleth Hill (Special Awards)

2001-2002: Justin Bohon (*Oklahoma!*), Simon Callow (*The Mystery of Charles Dickens*), Mos Def (*Topdog/Underdog*), Emma Fielding (*Private Lives*), Adam Godley (*Private Lives*), Martin Jarvis (*By Jeeves*), Spencer Kayden (*Urinetown*), Gretchen Mol (*The Shape of Things*), Anna Paquin (*The Glory of Living*), Louise Pitre (*Mamma Mia!*), David Warner (*Major Barbara*), Rachel Weisz (*The Shape of Things*)

2002-2003: Antonio Banderas (*Nine*), Tammy Blanchard (*Gypsy*), Thomas Jefferson Byrd (*Ma Rainey's Black Bottom*), Jonathan Cake (*Medea*), Victoria Hamilton (*A Day in the Death of Joe Egg*), Clare Higgins (*Vincent in Brixton*), Jackie Hoffman (*Hairspray*), Mary Stuart Masterson (*Nine*), John Selya (*Movin' Out*), Daniel Sunjata (*Take Me Out*), Jochum ten Haaf (*Vincent in Brixton*), Marissa Jaret Winokur (*Hairspray*), Peter Filichia and Ben Hodges (Special Awards)

2003-2004: Shannon Cochran (*Bug*), Stephanie D'Abruzzo (*Avenue Q*), Mitchel David Federan (*The Boy From Oz*), Alexander Gemignani (*Assassins*), Hugh Jackman (*The Boy From Oz*), Isabel Keating (*The Boy From Oz*), Sanaa Lathan (*A Raisin in the Sun*), Jefferson Mays (*I Am My Own Wife*), Euan Morton (*Taboo*), Anika Noni Rose (*Caroline, or Change*), John Tartaglia (*Avenue Q*), Jennifer Westfeldt (*Wonderful Town*), Sarah Jones (*Bridge and Tunnel* – Special Award)

2004-2005: Christina Applegate (*Sweet Charity*), Ashlie Atkinson (*Fat Pig*), Hank Azaria (*Spamalot*), Gordon Clapp (*Glengarry Glen Ross*), Conor Donovan (*Privilege*), Dan Fogler (*The 25th Annual Putnam County Spelling Bee*), Heather Goldenhersh (*Doubt*), Carla Gugino (*After the Fall*), Jenn Harris (*Modern Orthodox*), Cheyenne Jackson (*All Shook Up*), Celia Keenan-Bolger (*The 25th Annual Putnam County Spelling Bee*), Tyler Maynard (*Altar Boyz*)

2005-2006: Harry Connick Jr. (*The Pajama Game*), Felicia P. Fields (*The Color Purple*), Maria Friedman (*The Woman in White*), Richard Griffiths (*The History Boys*), Mamie Gummer (*Mr. Marmalade*), Jayne Houdyshell (*Well*), Bob Martin (*The Drowsy Chaperone*), Ian McDiarmid (*Faith Healer*), Nellie McKay (*The Threepenny Opera*), David Wilmot (*The Lieutenant of Inishmore*), Elisabeth Withers-Mendes (*The Color Purple*), John Lloyd Young (*Jersey Boys*)

2006–2007: Eve Best (*A Moon for the Misbegotten*), Mary Birdsong (*Martin Short: Fame Becomes Me*), Erin Davie (*Grey Gardens*), Xanthe Elbrick (*Coram Boy*), Fantasia (*The Color Purple*), Johnny Galecki (*The Little Dog Laughed*), Jonathan Groff (*Spring Awakening*), Gavin Lee (*Mary Poppins*), Lin-Manuel Miranda (*In the Heights*), Bill Nighy (*The Vertical Hour*), Stark Sands (*Journey's End*), Nilaja Sun (*No Child…*), The Actors Fund (Special Award)

2007–2008: de'Adre Aziza (*Passing Strange*), Cassie Beck (*The Drunken City*), Daniel Breaker (*Passing Strange*), Ben Daniels (*Les Liaisons Dangereuses*), Deanna Dunagan (*August: Osage County*), Hoon Lee (*Yellow Face*), Alli Mauzey (*Cry-Baby*), Jenna Russell (*Sunday in the Park with George*), Mark Rylance (*Boeing-Boeing*), Loretta Ables Sayre (*South Pacific*), Jimmi Simpson (*The Farnsworth Invention*), Paulo Szot (*South Pacific*)

1997 Winner Alison Janney

Major New York Theatrical Awards

AMERICAN THEATRE WING'S ANTOINETTE PERRY "TONY" AWARDS

Sunday, June 7, 2009 at Radio City Music Hall; 63rd annual; Host: Neil Patrick Harris. Presented for distinguished achievement in the Broadway theatre. The 2008–2009 Tony Awards Nominating Committee (appointed by the Tony Awards Administration Committee) included: Joe Benincasa (Executive Director, The Actors Fund), Robert Callely (Theatre Executive), Ben Cameron (Program Director for the Arts, The Doris Duke Charitable Foundation), Thomas Cott (Producer/Marketing Director), Jacqueline Z. Davis (Executive Director, The New York Public Library for the Performing Arts at Lincoln Center), John Dias (Producer/Dramaturg/Educator), Michael D. Dinwiddie (Associate Professor, Gallatin School of Individualized Study at NYU), Teresa Eyring (Executive Director, Theatre Communications Group), Sue Frost (Producer), Elena K. Holy (Producing Artistic Director, The Present Company), Betty Jacobs (Script Consultant/Theatre Historian), Geoffrey Johnson (Retired Casting Director), Michael Kantor (Director, Producer, Writer), Robert Kimball (Author, Theatre Historian), Howard Marren (Composer), Laurence Maslon (Associate Arts Professor, Graduate Acting Program (Tisch School for the Arts at NYU), Jon Nakagawa (Director, Contemporary Programming, Lincoln Center for the Performing Arts), Phyllis Newman (Actor), Alice Playten (Actor), Theresa Rebeck (Playwright), Roger Rees (Actor, Director, Playwright, Lecturer, Administrator), Donald Saddler (Choreographer), Steven Suskin (Theatre Author), Tamara Tunie (Actor, Producer), William Tynan (Actor, Journalist), Tom Viola (Executive Director, Broadway Cares/Equity Fights AIDS), Kimberlee Wertz (Music Contractor), Doug Wright (Playwright), Andrew Zerman (Casting Director)

Best Play: *God of Carnage* by Yasmina Reza; Producers: Robert Fox, David Pugh & Dafydd Rogers, Stuart Thompson, Scott Rudin, Jon B. Platt, The Weinstein Company, The Shubert Organization

Nominees: *Dividing the Estate* by Horton Foote; Producers: Lincoln Center Theater, Bernard Gersten, André Bishop, Primary Stages; *reasons to be pretty* by Neil LaBute; Producers: Jeffrey Richards, Jerry Frankel, MCC Theater, Gary Goddard Entertainment, Ted Snowdon, Doug Nevin/Erica Lynn Schwartz, Ronald Frankel/Bat-Barry Productions, Kathleen Seidel, Kelpie Arts, LLC, Jam Theatricals, Rachel Helson/Heather Provost; *33 Variations* by: Moisés Kaufman; Producers: David Binder, Ruth Hendel, Barbara Whitman, Goldberg/Mills, Latitude Link, Arielle Tepper Madover, Bill Resnick, Eric Schnall, Jayne Baron Sherman, Wills/True Love Productions, Tectonic Theater Project, Greg Reiner, Dominick Balletta, Jeffrey LaHoste

Best Musical: *Billy Elliot The Musical* Producers: Universal Pictures Stage Productions, Working Title Films, Old Vic Productions, Weinstein Live Entertainment

Nominees: *Next to Normal* Producers: David Stone, James L. Nederlander, Barbara Whitman, Patrick Catullo, Second Stage Theatre, Carole Rothman, Ellen Richard; *Rock of Ages* Producers: Matthew Weaver, Carl Levin, Jeff Davis, Barry Habib, Scott Prisand, Relativity Media, Corner Store Fund, Janet Billig Rich, Hillary Weaver, Toni Habib, Paula Davis, Simon and Stefany Bergson/Jennifer Maloney, Charles Rolecek, Susanne Brook, Israel Wolfson, Sara Katz/Jayson Raitt, Max Gottlieb/John Butler, David Kaufman/Jay Franks, Mike Wittlin, Prospect Pictures, Laura Smith/Bill Bodnar, Happy Walters, Michele Caro, The Araca Group; *Shrek The Musical* Producers: Dreamworks Theatricals, Neal Street Productions

Best Book of a Musical: *Billy Elliot The Musical* by Lee Hall

Nominees: *Next to Normal* by Brian Yorkey; *Shrek The Musical* by David Lindsay-Abaire; *[title of show]* by Hunter Bell

Best Original Score (music and/or lyrics): *Next to Normal* Music by Tom Kitt, Lyrics by Brian Yorkey

Nominees: *Billy Elliot, The Musical* Music by Elton John, Lyrics by Lee Hall; *9 to 5: The Musical* Music & Lyrics by Dolly Parton; *Shrek The Musical* Music by Jeanine Tesori, Lyrics by David Lindsay-Abaire

Best Revival of a Play: *The Norman Conquests* by Alan Ayckbourn; Producers: Sonia Friedman Productions, Steven Baruch, Marc Routh, Richard Frankel, Tom Viertel, Dede Harris, Tulchin/Bartner/Lauren Doll, Jamie deRoy, Eric Falkenstein, Harriet Newman Leve, Probo Productions, Douglas G. Smith, Michael Filerman/Jennifer Manocherian, Richard Winkler, Dan Frishwasser, Pam Laudenslager/Remmel T. Dickinson, Jane Dubin/True Love Productions, Barbara Manocherian/Jennifer Isaacson, The Old Vic Theatre Company

Nominees: *Joe Turner's Come and Gone* Producers: Lincoln Center Theater, André Bishop, Bernard Gersten; *Mary Stuart* New Version: Peter Oswald; Producers: Arielle Tepper Madover, Debra Black, Neal Street Productions/Matthew Byam Shaw, Scott Delman, Barbara Whitman, Jean Doumanian/Ruth Hendel, David Binder/CarlWend Productions/Spring Sirkin, Daryl Roth/James L. Nederlander/Chase Mishkin, The Donmar Warehouse; *Waiting for Godot* Producers: Roundabout Theatre Company, Todd Haimes, Harold Wolpert, Julia C. Levy, Elizabeth Ireland McCann

Best Revival of a Musical: *Hair* Producers: The Public Theater, Oskar Eustis, Andrew D. Hamingson, Jeffrey Richards, Jerry Frankel, Gary Goddard Entertainment, Kathleen K. Johnson, Nederlander Productions, Inc., Fran Kirmser Productions/Jed Bernstein, Marc Frankel, Broadway Across America, Barbara Manocherian/WenCarLar Productions, JK Productions/Terry Schnuck, Andy Sandberg, Jam Theatricals, The Weinstein Company/Norton Herrick, Jujamcyn Theaters, Joey Parnes, Elizabeth Ireland McCann

Nominees: *Guys and Dolls* Producers: Howard Panter and Ambassador Theatre Group, Tulchin/Bartner, Bill Kenwright, Northwater Entertainment, Darren Bagert, Tom Gregory, Nederlander Presentations, Inc., David Mirvish, Michael Jenkins/Dallas Summer Musicals, Independent Presenters Network, Olympus Theatricals, Sonia Friedman Productions; *Pal Joey* Producers: Roundabout Theatre Company, Todd Haimes, Harold Wolpert, Julia C. Levy, Marc Platt; *West Side Story* Producers: Kevin McCollum, James L. Nederlander, Jeffrey Seller, Terry Allen Kramer, Sander Jacobs, Roy Furman/Jill Furman Willis, Freddy DeMann, Robyn Goodman/Walt Grossman, Hal Luftig, Roy Miller, The Weinstein Company, Broadway Across America

Best Special Theatrical Event: *Liza's at The Palace...* Producers: John Scher and Metropolitan Talent Presents, LLC; Jubilee Time Productions, LLC

Nominees: *Slava's Snowshow* Producers: David J. Foster, Jared Geller, Joseph Gordon-Levitt, Judith Marinoff Cohn, John Pinckard; *Soul of Shaolin* Producers: Nederlander Worldwide Productions, LLC; Eastern Shanghai International Culture Film & Television Group; China on Broadway; *You're Welcome America. A Final Night with George W. Bush* Producers: Jeffrey Richards, Jerry Frankel, Steve Traxler, Home Box Office Inc., Gary Sanchez Productions, Bat-Barry Productions, Ken Davenport, Ergo Entertainment, Ronald Frankel, Jon B. Platt, James D. Stern, The Weinstein Company, Tara Smith/b. Swibel, Dede Harris/Sharon Karmazin, Arny Granat

Best Performance by a Leading Actor in a Play: Geoffrey Rush, *Exit the King*

Nominees: Jeff Daniels, *God of Carnage*; Raúl Esparza, *Speed-the-Plow*; James Gandolfini, *God of Carnage*; Thomas Sadoski, *reasons to be pretty*

Best Performance by a Leading Actress in a Play: Marcia Gay Harden, *God of Carnage*

Nominees: Hope Davis, *God of Carnage*; Jane Fonda, *33 Variations*; Janet McTeer, *Mary Stuart*; Harriet Walter, *Mary Stuart*

Best Performance by a Leading Actor in a Musical: David Alvarez/Trent Kowalik/Kiril Kulish, *Billy Elliot The Musical*

Nominees: Gavin Creel, *Hair*; Brian d'Arcy James, *Shrek The Musical*; Constantine Maroulis, *Rock of Ages*; J. Robert Spencer, *Next to Normal*

Best Performance by a Leading Actress in a Musical: Alice Ripley, *Next to Normal*

Nominees: Stockard Channing, *Pal Joey*; Sutton Foster, *Shrek The Musical*; Allison Janney, *9 to 5: The Musical*; Josefina Scaglione, *West Side Story*

Best Performance by a Featured Actor in a Play: Roger Robinson, *Joe Turner's Come and Gone*

Nominees: John Glover, *Waiting for Godot*; Zach Grenier, *33 Variations*; Stephen Mangan, *The Norman Conquests*; Paul Ritter, *The Norman Conquests*

Best Performance by a Featured Actress in a Play: Angela Lansbury, *Blithe Spirit*

Nominees: Hallie Foote, *Dividing the Estate*; Jessica Hynes, *The Norman Conquests*; Marin Ireland, *reasons to be pretty*; Amanda Root, *The Norman Conquests*

Best Performance by a Featured Actor in a Musical: Gregory Jbara, *Billy Elliot The Musical*

Nominees: David Bologna, *Billy Elliot The Musical*; Marc Kudisch, *9 to 5: The Musical*; Christopher Sieber, *Shrek The Musical*; Will Swenson, *Hair*

Best Performance by a Featured Actress in a Musical: Karen Olivo, *West Side Story*

Nominees: Jennifer Damiano, *Next to Normal*; Haydn Gwynne, *Billy Elliot The Musical*; Martha Plimpton, *Pal Joey*; Carole Shelley, *Billy Elliot The Musical*

Best Scenic Design of a Play: Derek McLane, *33 Variations*

Nominees: Dale Ferguson, *Exit the King*; Rob Howell, *The Norman Conquests*; Michael Yeargan, *Joe Turner's Come and Gone*

Best Scenic Design of a Musical: Ian MacNeil, *Billy Elliot The Musical*

Nominees: Robert Brill, *Guys and Dolls*; Scott Pask, *Pal Joey*; Mark Wendland, *Next to Normal*

Best Costume Design of a Play: Anthony Ward, *Mary Stuart*

Nominees: Dale Ferguson, *Exit the King*; Jane Greenwood, *Waiting for Godot*; Martin Pakledinaz, *Blithe Spirit*

Best Costume Design of a Musical: Tim Hatley, *Shrek The Musical*

Nominees: Gregory Gale, *Rock of Ages*; Nicky Gillibrand, *Billy Elliot The Musical*; Michael McDonald, *Hair*

Best Lighting Design of a Play: Brian MacDevitt, *Joe Turner's Come and Gone*

Nominees: David Hersey, *Equus*; David Lander, *33 Variations*; Hugh Vanstone, *Mary Stuart*

Best Lighting Design of a Musical: Rick Fisher, *Billy Elliot The Musical*

Nominees: Kevin Adams, *Hair*; Kevin Adams, *Next to Normal*; Howell Binkley, *West Side Story*

Best Sound Design of a Play: Gregory Clarke, *Equus*

Nominees: Paul Arditti, *Mary Stuart*; Russell Goldsmith, *Exit the King*; Scott Lehrer and Leon Rothenberg, *Joe Turner's Come and Gone*

Best Sound Design of a Musical: Paul Arditti, *Billy Elliot The Musical*

Nominees: Acme Sound Partners, *Hair*; Peter Hylenski, *Rock of Ages*; Brian Ronan, *Next to Normal*

Best Direction of a Play: Matthew Warchus, *God of Carnage*

Nominees: Phyllida Lloyd, *Mary Stuart*; Bartlett Sher, *Joe Turner's Come and Gone*; Matthew Warchus, *The Norman Conquests*

Best Direction of a Musical: Stephen Daldry, *Billy Elliot The Musical*

Nominees: Michael Greif, *Next to Normal*; Kristin Hanggi, *Rock of Ages*; Diane Paulus, *Hair*

Best Choreography: Peter Darling, *Billy Elliot The Musical*

Nominees: Karole Armitage, *Hair*; Andy Blankenbuehler, *9 to 5: The Musical*; Randy Skinner, *Irving Berlin's White Christmas*

Best Orchestrations: (tie) Martin Koch, *Billy Elliot The Musical*; Michael Starobin and Tom Kitt, *Next to Normal*

Nominees: Larry Blank, *Irving Berlin's White Christmas*; Danny Troob and John Clancy, *Shrek The Musical*

Special Tony Award for Lifetime Achievement in the Theatre: Jerry Herman

Regional Theatre Tony Award: Signature Theatre of Arlington Virginia

Isabelle Stevenson Award for Service (new)**:** Phyllis Newman

Tony Honor for Excellence in the Theatre: Shirley Herz

PAST TONY AWARD-WINNING PRODUCTIONS Awards listed are Best Play followed by Best Musical, and, as awards for Best Revival and the subcategories of Best Revival of a Play and Best Revival of a Musical were instituted, they are listed respectively.

1947: No award given for musical or play **1948:** *Mister Roberts* (play) **1949:** *Death of a Salesman*; *Kiss Me, Kate* (musical) **1950:** *The Cocktail Party*; *South Pacific* **1951:** *The Rose Tattoo*; *Guys and Dolls* **1952:** *The Fourposter*; *The King and I* **1953:** *The Crucible*; *Wonderful Town* **1954:** *The Teahouse of the August Moon*; *Kismet* **1955:** *The Desperate Hours*; *The Pajama Game* **1956:** *The Diary of Anne Frank*; *Damn Yankees* **1957:** *Long Day's Journey into Night*; *My Fair Lady* **1958:** *Sunrise at Campobello*; *The Music Man* **1959:** *J.B.*; *Redhead* **1960:** *The Miracle Worker*, *Fiorello!* & *The Sound of Music* (tie) **1961:** *Becket*; *Bye Bye Birdie* **1962:** *A Man for All Seasons*; *How to Succeed in Business Without Really Trying* **1963:** *Who's Afraid of Virginia Woolf?*, *A Funny Thing Happened on the Way to the Forum* **1964:** *Luther*, *Hello, Dolly!* **1965:** *The Subject Was Roses*; *Fiddler on the Roof* **1966:** *The Persecution and Assassination of Marat as Performed by the Inmates of the Asylum of Charenton Under the Direction of the Marquis de Sade*; *Man of La Mancha* **1967:** *The Homecoming*; *Cabaret* **1968:** *Rosencrantz and Guildenstern Are Dead*; *Hallelujah Baby!* **1969:** *The Great White Hope*; *1776* **1970:** *Borstal Boy*; *Applause* **1971:** *Sleuth*; *Company* **1972:** *Sticks and Bones*; *Two Gentlemen of Verona* **1973:** *That Championship Season*; *A Little Night Music* **1974:** *The River Niger*; *Raisin* **1975:** *Equus*; *The Wiz* **1976:** *Travesties*; *A Chorus Line* **1977:** *The Shadow Box*; *Annie* **1978:** *Da*; *Ain't Misbehavin'*; *Dracula* (innovative musical revival) **1979:** *The Elephant Man*; *Sweeney Todd* **1980:** *Children of a Lesser God*; *Evita*; *Morning's at Seven* (best revival) **1981:** *Amadeus*; *42nd Street*; *The Pirates of Penzance* **1982:** *The Life and Adventures of Nicholas Nickelby*; *Nine*; *Othello* **1983:** *Torch Song Trilogy*; *Cats*; *On Your Toes* **1984:** *The Real Thing*; *La Cage aux Folles*; *Death of a Salesman* **1985:** *Biloxi Blues*; *Big River*; *A Day in the Death of Joe Egg* **1986:** *I'm Not Rappaport*; *The Mystery of Edwin Drood*; *Sweet Charity* **1987:** *Fences*; *Les Misérables*; *All My Sons* **1988:** *M. Butterfly*; *The Phantom of the Opera*; *Anything Goes* **1989:** *The Heidi Chronicles*; *Jerome Robbins' Broadway*; *Our Town* **1990:** *The Grapes of Wrath*; *City of Angels*; *Gypsy* **1991:** *Lost in Yonkers*; *The Will Rogers' Follies*; *Fiddler on the Roof* **1992:** *Dancing at Lughnasa*; *Crazy for You*; *Guys and Dolls* **1993:** *Angels in America: Millenium Approaches*; *Kiss of the Spider Woman*; *Anna Christie* **1994:** *Angels in America: Perestroika*; *Passion*; *An Inspector Calls* (play revival); *Carousel* (musical revival) **1995:** *Love! Valour! Compassion!*; *Sunset Boulevard*; *The Heiress*; *Show Boat* **1996:** *Master Class*; *Rent*; *A Delicate Balance*; *King and I* **1997:** *Last Night of Ballyhoo*; *Titanic*; *A Doll's House*; *Chicago* **1998:** *Art*; *The Lion King*; *View from the Bridge*; *Cabaret* **1999:** *Side Man*; *Fosse*; *Death of a Salesman*; *Annie Get Your Gun* **2000:** *Copenhagen*; *Contact*; *The Real Thing*; *Kiss Me, Kate* **2001:** *Proof*; *The Producers*; *One Flew Over the Cuckoo's Nest*; *42nd Street* **2002:** Edward Albee's *The Goat, or Who Is Sylvia?*; *Thoroughly Modern Millie*; *Private Lives*; *Into the Woods* **2003:** *Take Me Out*; *Hairspray*; *Long Day's Journey Into Night*; *Nine* **2004:** *I Am My Own Wife*; *Avenue Q*; *Henry IV*; *Assassins* **2005:** *Doubt*; *Monty Python's Spamalot*; *Glengarry Glen Ross*; *La Cage aux Folles* **2006:** *The History Boys*; *Jersey Boys*; *Awake and Sing!*; *The Pajama Game* **2007:** *The Coast of Utopia*; *Spring Awakening*; *Journey's End*; *Company* **2008:** *August: Osage County*; *In the Heights*; *Boeing-Boeing*; *South Pacific*

DRAMA DESK AWARDS

Sunday, May 17, 2009 at LaGuardia Concert Hall-Lincoln Center; 54th annual; Host: Harvey Fierstein. Originally known as the Vernon Rice Awards until 1964 (named after the former *New York Post* theatre critic); Presented for outstanding achievement in the 2008–2009 season for Broadway, Off-Broadway, and Off-Off Broadway productions, voted on by an association of New York drama reporters, editors, and critics; Board of Directors: William Wolf (President), Leslie Hoban Blake (Vice President), Charles Wright (Treasurer and 2nd Vice President), Richard Ridge (Secretary), Robert Cashill, Isa Goldberg, David Kaufman, Ellis Nassour, Sam Norkin, Barbara Siegel; Nominating Committee: Barbara Siegel – Chairperson (*TheaterMania.com* and *TalkinBroadway.com*), Dan Bacalzo (*TheatreMania.com*), Christopher Byrne (*Gay City News*), Patrick Christiano (*TheaterLife.com* and *Dan's Papers*), Jason Clark (*Entertainment Weekly* and *TheatreOnline.com*) Gerald Raymond (*Back Stage* and *The Advocate*), and Richard Ridge (*Broadway Beat TV*); Executive Producer, Robert R. Blume; Producer, Lauren Class Schneider; Director of Ceremony, Jeff Kalpak; Special Event Director, Randie Levine-Miller; Presenters: Lauren Ambrose, Stockard Channing, John Cullum, André De Shields, Jim Dale, Jason Danieley, Raúl Esparza, Jane Fonda, Victor Garber, Cheyenne Jackson, Carson Kressley, John Lithgow, Marin Mazzie, Audra McDonald, Rex Reed, Michael Rupert, and Tom Wopat.

Outstanding Play: *Ruined* by Lynn Nottage

Nominees: *Body Awareness* by Annie Baker; *Becky Shaw* by Gina Gionfriddo; *reasons to be pretty* by Neil LaBute; *Fifty Words* by Michael Weller; *Lady* by Craig Wright

Outstanding Musical: *Billy Elliot The Musical*

Nominees: *9 to 5: The Musical*; *Fela! A New Musical*; *Liza's at the Palace…*; *Shrek The Musical*; *The Story of My Life*

Outstanding Revival of a Play: *The Norman Conquests*

Nominees: *Blithe Spirit*; *Exit the King*; *Mary Stuart*; *The Cripple of Inishmaan*; *Waiting for Godot*

Outstanding Revival of a Musical: *Hair*

Nominees: *Enter Laughing The Musical*; *Pal Joey*; *West Side Story*

Outstanding Actor in a Play: Geoffrey Rush, *Exit the King*

Nominees: Simon Russell Beale, *The Winter's Tale*; Reed Birney, *Blasted*; Raúl Esparza, *Speed-The-Plow*; Bill Irwin, *Waiting for Godot*; Daniel Radcliffe, *Equus*; Thomas Sadoski, *reasons to be pretty*

Outstanding Actress in a Play: Janet McTeer, *Mary Stuart*

Nominees: Saidah Arrika Ekulona, *Ruined*; Jane Fonda, *33 Variations*; Marcia Gay Harden, *God of Carnage*; Elizabeth Marvel, *Fifty Words*; Jan Maxwell, *Scenes From an Execution*

Outstanding Actor in a Musical: Brian d'Arcy James, *Shrek The Musical*

Nominees: James Barbour, *A Tale of Two Cities*; Daniel Breaker, *Shrek The Musical*; Josh Grisetti, *Enter Laughing The Musical*; Sahr Ngaujah, *Fela! A New Musical*; Will Swenson, *Hair*

Outstanding Actress in a Musical: Allison Janney, *9 to 5: The Musical*

Nominees: Stephanie J. Block, *9 to 5: The Musical*; Stockard Channing, *Pal Joey*; Sutton Foster, *Shrek The Musical*; Megan Hilty, *9 to 5: The Musical*; Karen Murphy, *My Vaudeville Man!*

Outstanding Featured Actor in a Play: Pablo Schreiber, *reasons to be pretty* (Off-Broadway production)

Nominees: Brian d'Arcy James, *Port Authority*; Jeremy Davidson, *Back Back Back*; Peter Friedman, *Body Awareness*; Ethan Hawke, *The Winter's Tale*; Jeremy Shamos, *Animals Out of Paper*

Outstanding Featured Actress in a Play: Angela Lansbury, *Blithe Spirit*

Nominees: Rebecca Hall, *The Cherry Orchard*; Zoe Kazan, *The Seagull*; Andrea Martin, *Exit the King*; Carey Mulligan, *The Seagull*; Condola Rashad, *Ruined*

Outstanding Featured Actor in a Musical: Gregory Jbara, *Billy Elliot The Musical*

Nominees: Hunter Foster, *Happiness*; Demond Green, *The Toxic Avenger*; Marc Kudisch, *9 to 5: The Musical*; Bryce Ryness, *Hair*; Christopher Sieber, *Shrek The Musical*

Outstanding Featured Actress in a Musical: Haydn Gwynne, *Billy Elliot The Musical*

Nominees: Farah Alvin, *The Marvelous Wonderettes*; Christina Bianco, *Forbidden Broadway Goes to Rehab*; Karen Olivo, *West Side Story*; Nancy Opel, *The Toxic Avenger*; Martha Plimpton, *Pal Joey*

Outstanding Director of a Play: Matthew Warchus, *The Norman Conquests*

Nominees: Sarah Benson, *Blasted*; Michael Blakemore, *Blithe Spirit*; Garry Hynes, *The Cripple of Inishmaan*; Terry Kinney, *reasons to be pretty*; Kate Whoriskey, *Ruined*

Outstanding Director of a Musical: Stephen Daldry, *Billy Elliot The Musical*

Nominees: Walter Bobbie, *Irving Berlin's White Christmas*; Joe Mantello, *9 to 5: The Musical*; Jason Moore, *Shrek The Musical*; Diane Paulus, *Hair*; Stuart Ross, *Enter Laughing The Musical*

Outstanding Choreography: Peter Darling, *Billy Elliot The Musical*

Nominees: Karole Armitage, *Hair*; Andy Blankenbuehler, *9 to 5: The Musical*; Bill T. Jones, *Fela! A New Musical*; Randy Skinner, *Irving Berlin's White Christmas*; Lynne Taylor-Corbett and Shonn Wiley, *My Vaudeville Man!*

Outstanding Music: Elton John, *Billy Elliot The Musical*

Nominees: Neil Bartram, *The Story of My Life*; Zina Goldrich, *Dear Edwina*; Dolly Parton, *9 to 5: The Musical*; Stephen Sondheim, *Road Show*; Jeanine Tesori, *Shrek The Musical*

Outstanding Lyrics: Stephen Sondheim, *Road Show*

Nominees: Neil Bartram, *The Story of My Life*; Jason Robert Brown, *13*; Marcy Heisler, *Dear Edwina*; David Lindsay-Abaire, *Shrek The Musical*; Dolly Parton, *9 to 5: The Musical*

Outstanding Book of a Musical: Lee Hall, *Billy Elliot The Musical*

Nominees: Steven Cosson and Jim Lewis, *This Beautiful City*; Joe DiPietro, *The Toxic Avenger*; Brian Hill, *The Story of My Life*; David Lindsay-Abaire, *Shrek The Musical*; Patricia Resnick, *9 to 5: The Musical*

Outstanding Orchestrations: Martin Koch, *Billy Elliot The Musical*

Nominees: Larry Blank, *Irving Berlin's White Christmas*; Bruce Coughlin, Stephen Oremus, Alex Lacamoire, *9 to 5: The Musical*; Aaron Johnson and Antibalas, *Fela! A New Musical*; Edward B. Kessel, *A Tale of Two Cities*; Danny Troob and John Clancy, *Shrek The Musical*

Outstanding Music in a Play: Dominic Kanza, *Ruined*

Nominees: Mark Bennett, *The Cherry Orchard*; Mark Bennett, *The Winter's Tale*; DJ Rekha, *Rafta, Rafta…*; Richard Woodbury, *Desire Under the Elms*; Gary Yershon, *The Norman Conquests*

Outstanding Set Design of a Play: David Korins, *Why Torture is Wrong, and the People Who Love Them*

Nominees: Dale Ferguson, *Exit the King*; Rob Howell, *The Norman Conquests*; Derek McLane, *33 Variations*; Neil Patel, *Fifty Words*; Walt Spangler, *Desire Under the Elms*

Outstanding Set Design of a Musical: Tim Hatley, *Shrek The Musical*

Nominees: Anna Louizos, *Irving Berlin's White Christmas*; Thomas Lynch, *Happiness*; Scott Pask, *9 to 5: The Musical*; Scott Pask, *Hair*; Basil Twist, *Arias With a Twist*

Outstanding Costume Design of a Musical: Tim Hatley, *Shrek The Musical*

Nominees: Rob Howell, *The Norman Conquests*; William Ivey Long, *9 to 5: The Musical*; Michael McDonald, *Hair*; Martin Pakledinaz, *Blithe Spirit*; Carrie Robbins, *Irving Berlin's White Christmas*

Outstanding Lighting Design of a Play: David Hersey, *Equus*

Nominees: Marcus Doshi, *Hamlet* (Theatre for a New Audience); Ben Kato, *Washing Machine*; R. Lee Kennedy, *Bury the Dead*; Paul Pyant, *The Winter's Tale*; Hugh Vanstone, *Mary Stuart*

Outstanding Lighting Design of a Musical: Rick Fisher, *Billy Elliot The Musical*

Nominees: Kevin Adams, *Hair*; Jules Fisher and Kenneth Posner, *9 to 5: The Musical*; Jason Lyons, *Clay*; Sinéad McKenna, *Improbable Frequency*; Richard Pilbrow, *A Tale of Two Cities*

Outstanding Sound Design: Paul Arditti, *Billy Elliot The Musical*

Nominees: Acme Sound Partners, *Irving Berlin's White Christmas*; Gregory Clarke, *Equus*; John Gromada, *Shipwrecked! An Entertainment*; André J. Pluess, *33 Variations*; John H. Shivers, *9 to 5: The Musical*

Outstanding Solo Performance: Lorenzo Pisoni, *Humor Abuse*

Nominees: Mike Birbiglia, *Sleepwalk With Me*; Frank Blocker, *Southern Gothic Novel*; Michael Laurence, *Krapp, 39*; Matt Sax, *Clay*; Campbell Scott, *The Atheist*

Unique Theatrical Experience: *Celebrity Autobiography: In Their Own Words*

Nominees: *Absinthe* (2008 Edition); *Arias With a Twist*; *Désir*; *Soul of Shaolin*; *Surrender*

Outstanding Ensemble Performances: *The Cripple of Inishmaan* (Atlantic Theater Company); *The Norman Conquests* (Broadway revival)

Special Awards: Liza Minnelli (for her enduring career of sustained excellence and her performance in *Liza's at the Palace…*); *Forbidden Broadway* (for being an unparalleled New York institution for nearly three decades cherished for its satire and celebration of Broadway); Atlantic Theater Company and Artistic Director Neil Pepe (for exceptional craftsmanship, dedication to excellence, and productions that engage, inspire, and enlighten); TADA! Youth Theater (for providing and invaluable contribution to the future of the theater)

PAST DRAMA DESK AWARD-WINNING PRODUCTIONS From 1954–1974, non-competitive awards were presented to various artists: performers, playwrights, choreographers, composers, designers, directors, theatre companies and occasionally to specific productions. In 1975 the awards became competitive, and citations for Outstanding New Play (P) – or in some instances Outstanding New American Play (AP) and Outstanding New Foreign Play (FP), Outstanding Musical (M), Musical Revue (MR), Outstanding Revival, (R) –and later, Outstanding Play Revival (RP) and Outstanding Musical Revival (RM)– were instituted and presented as the season demanded. If year or a specific category within a year is missing, no production awards were presented in that year or specific category.

1955: *The Way of the World*; *A Thieve's Carnival*; *Twelfth Night*; *The Merchant of Venice* **1956:** *The Iceman Cometh* **1963:** *The Coach with Six Insides*; *The Boys from Syracuse* **1964:** *In White America*; *The Streets of New York* **1970:** *Borstal Boy* (P); *The Effect of Gamma Rays on Man-in-the-Moon Marigolds* (AP); *Company* (M) **1975:** *Same Time, Next Year* (AP), *Equus* (FP); **1976:** *Streamers* (P); *The Royal Family* (R) **1977:** *A Texas Trilogy* (AP); *The Comedians* (FP); *Annie* (M) **1978:** *Da* (P); *Ain't Misbehavin'* (M) **1979:** *The Elephant Man* (P); *Sweeney Todd, The Demon Barber of Fleet Street* (M) **1980:** *Children of a Lesser God* (P); *Evita* (M) **1981:** *Amadeus* (P); *Lena Horne: The Lady and Her Music* (M) **1982:** *"Master Harold"…and the boys* (P); *Nine* (M); *Entertaining Mr. Sloane* (R) **1983:** *Torch Song Trilogy* (P); *Little Shop of Horrors* (M); *On Your Toes* (R) **1984:** *The Real Thing* (P); *Sunday in the Park with George* (M); *Death of a Salesman* (R) **1985:** *As Is* (P); *A Day in the Death of Joe Egg* (R) **1986:** *A Lie of the Mind* (P); *The Mystery of Edwin Drood* (M); *Lemon Sky* (R) **1987:** *Fences* (P);

Les Misérables (M) **1988:** *M. Butterfly* (P); *Into the Woods* (M); *Anything Goes* (R) **1989:** *The Heidi Chronicles* (P); *Jerome Robbins' Broadway* (M); *Our Town* (R) **1990:** *The Piano Lesson* (P); *City of Angels* (M); *Gypsy* (R) **1991:** *Lost in Yonkers* (P); *The Secret Garden* (M); *And the World Goes Round* (MR); *A Little Night Music* (R) **1992:** *Lips Together, Teeth Apart* (P); *Crazy for You* (M); *Guys and Dolls* (R) **1993:** *Jeffrey* (P); *Kiss of the Spider Woman* (M); *Anna Christie* (R) **1994:** *Angels in America: Perestroika* (P); *Passion* (M); *Howard Crabtree's Whoop-Dee-Doo* (MR); *An Inspector Calls* (RP); *She Loves Me* (RM) **1995:** *Love! Valour! Compassion!* (P); *Showboat* (M); *The Heiress* (R) **1996:** *Master Class* (P); *Rent* (M); *A Delicate Balance* (RP); *The King and I* (RM) **1997:** *How I Learned to Drive* (P), *The Life* (M); *Howard Crabtree's When Pigs Fly* (MR); *A Doll's House* (RP); *Chicago* (RM) **1998:** *The Beauty Queen of Leenane* (P); *Ragtime* (M); *A View from the Bridge* (RP); *1776* (RM) **1999:** *Wit* (P); *Parade* (M); *Fosse* (MR); (tie) *Death of a Salesman* and *The Iceman Cometh* (RP); *You're a Good Man, Charlie Brown* (RM) **2000:** *Copenhagen* (P); *Contact* (M); *The Real Thing* (RP); *Kiss Me, Kate* (RM) **2001:** *Proof* (P); *The Producers* (M); *Forbidden Broadway 2001: A Spoof Odyssey* (MR); *The Best Man* (RP); *42ⁿᵈ Street* (RM) **2002:** (tie) *The Goat, or Who Is Sylvia?* and *Metamorphoses* (P); *Private Lives* (RP); *Into the Woods* (RM) **2003:** *Take Me Out* (P); *Hairspray* (M); *Long Day's Journey Into Night* (RP); *Nine* (RM) **2004:** *I Am My Own Wife* (P); *Wicked* (M); *Henry IV* (RP); *Assassins* (RM) **2005:** *Doubt* (P); *Monty Python's Spamalot* (M); *Forbidden Broadway: Special Victims Unit* (MR); *Twelve Angry Men* (RP); *La Cage aux Folles* (RM) **2006:** *The History Boys* (P); *The Drowsy Chaperone* (M); *Awake and Sing!* (RP); *Sweeney Todd, The Demon Barber of Fleet Street* (RM) **2007:** *The Coast of Utopia* (P); *Spring Awakening* (M); *Journey's End* (RP); *Company* (RM) **2008:** *August: Osage County* (P); *Passing Strange* (M); *Forbidden Broadway: Rude Awakening* (MR); *Boeing-Boeing* (RP); *South Pacific* (RM)

VILLAGE VOICE OBIE AWARDS

Monday, May 18, 2009 at Webster Hall; 54th annual; Hosts: Martha Plimpton and Daniel Breaker. Presented for outstanding achievement in the 2008–2009 season; Judges: Michael Feingold (Committee Chair and *Village Voice* chief theatre critic), Alexis Soloski (*Village Voice* theatre critic), Eric Grode (*New York Sun*), Andy Probst (*AmericanTheatreWeb.com*), Eisa Davis (actor-playwright), Ty Jones (actor-playwright), Moisés Kaufman (playwright-director), Chay Yew (playwright); produced by Eileen Phelan; publicity by Gail Parenteau.

Best New American Play: ($1,000): *Ruined* by Lynn Nottage (Manhattan Theatre Club)

Performance: Francois Battiste, *The Good Negro* (Public Theater); Quincy Tyler Bernstine, *Ruined* (Manhattan Theatre Club); Kevin T. Carroll, sustained excellence of performance; Saidah Arrika Ekulona, *Ruined* (Manhattan Theatre Club); Jonathan Groff, *Prayer for My Enemy* & *The Singing Forest* (Public Theater); Birgit Huppuch, *Telephone* (Foundry Theatre); Russell Gebert Jones, *Ruined* (Manhattan Theatre Club); Aaron Monaghan, *The Cripple of Inishmaan* (Atlantic Theater Company); Sahr Ngaujah, *Fela! A New Musical*; Lorenzo Pisoni, *Humor Abuse* (Manhattan Theatre Club); James Sugg, *Chekhov Lizardbrain* (Pig Iron Theatre Company); John Douglass Thompson, *Othello* (Theatre for a New Audience);

Music and Lyrics: Stephen Sondheim, *Road Show* (Public Theater)

Direction: David Cromer, *Our Town* (Barrow Street Theatre); Katie Mitchell, *The Waves* (National Theatre of Great Britain/Lincoln Center Theater "New Visions" series); Ken Rus Schmoll, *Telephone* (Foundry Theatre)

Design: Toni-Leslie James, sustained excellence of costume design with special reference to *Wig Out!* (Vineyard Theatre); David Korins, sustained excellence of set design with special reference to *Why Torture is Wrong, and the People Who Love Them* (Public Theater)

Special Citations: Sarah Benson (director) and Louisa Thompson (set designer), *Blasted* (Soho Rep); David Esbjornson (director) and Christian Camargo, *Hamlet* (Theatre for a New Audience)

Ross Wetzsteon Memorial Award ($2,000): HERE Arts Center

Lifetime Achievement: Earle Hyman

Obie Theater Grants ($10,000 divided among winners): The Chocolate Factory, Classical Theatre of Harlem, and Lark Play Development Center

PAST OBIE AWARD-WINNING BEST NEW PLAYS If year is missing, no award was given that season; multiple plays were awarded in some seasons.

1956: *Absalom, Absalom* **1957:** *A House Remembered* **1959:** *The Quare Fellow* **1961:** *The Blacks* **1962:** *Who'll Save the Plowboy?* **1964:** *Play* **1965:** *The Old Glory* **1966:** *The Journey of the Fifth Horse* **1970:** *The Effect of Gamma Rays on Man-in-the-Moon Marigolds* **1971:** *The House of Blue Leaves* **1973:** *The Hot L Baltimore* **1974:** *Short Eyes* **1975:** *The First Breeze of Summer* **1976:** *American Buffalo, Sexual Perversity in Chicago* **1977:** *Curse of the Starving Class* **1978:** *Shaggy Dog Animation* **1979:** *Josephine* **1981:** *FOB* **1982:** *Metamorphosis in Miniature; Mr. Dead and Mrs. Free* **1983:** *Painting Churches; Andrea Rescued; Edmond* **1984:** *Fool for Love* **1985:** *The Conduct of Life* **1987:** *The Cure; Film Is Evil, Radio Is Good* **1988:** *Abingdon Square* **1990:** *Prelude to a Kiss; Imperceptible Mutabilities in the Third* Kingdom; *Bad Benny, Crowbar, Terminal Hip* **1991:** *The Fever* **1992:** *Sight Unseen; Sally's Rape; The Baltimore Waltz* **1994:** *Twilight: Los Angeles, 1992* **1995:** *Cryptogram* **1996:** *Adrienne Kennedy* **1997:** *One Flea Spare* **1998:** *Pearls for Pigs and Benita Canova* **2001:** *The Syringa Tree* **2004:** *Small Tragedy*

OUTER CRITICS CIRCLE AWARDS

Thursday, May 21, 2009 at Sardi's Restaurant; 59th annual. Presented for outstanding achievement for Broadway and Off-Broadway productions during the 2008–2009 season. Winners are voted on by theatre critics of out-of-town periodicals and media. Executive Committee: Simon Saltzman (President), Mario Fratti (Vice President), Rosalind Friedman (Recording Secretary), Louis A. Rachow (Treasurer), Patrick Hoffman (Corresponding Secretary), Aubrey Reuben, Glenn M. Loney, Thomás Gentile (Members-at-Large), Marjorie Gunner (President Emerita); Presenters: Tyne Daly, Donna Murphy, the cast of *The Norman Conquests.*

Outstanding New Broadway Play: *God of Carnage*

Nominees: *Irena's Vow; reasons to be pretty; 33 Variations*

Outstanding New Broadway Musical: *Billy Elliot The Musical*

Nominees: *Rock of Ages; Shrek The Musical; A Tale of Two Cities*

Outstanding New Off-Broadway Play: *Ruined*

Nominees: *Becky Shaw; Farragut North; Shipwrecked! An Entertainment; Why Torture is Wrong, and the People Who Love Them*

Outstanding New Off-Broadway Musical: *The Toxic Avenger*

Nominees: *Happiness; Rooms: A Rock Romance; What's That Smell? The Music of Jacob Sterling*

Outstanding New Score (Broadway or Off-Broadway)**:** *Billy Elliot The Musical*

Nominees: *Happiness; Rooms: A Rock Romance; Shrek The Musical*

Outstanding Revival of a Play: *The Norman Conquests*

Nominees: *Blithe Spirit; The Cripple of Inishmaan; Joe Turner's Come and Gone; Waiting for Godot*

Outstanding Revival of a Musical: *Hair*

Nominees: *Enter Laughing The Musical; Pal Joey; West Side Story*

Outstanding Director of a Play: Matthew Warchus, *The Norman Conquests*

Nominees: Garry Hynes, *The Cripple of Inishmaan;* Anthony Page, *Waiting for Godot;* Bartlett Sher, *Joe Turner's Come and Gone;* Moisés Kaufman, *33 Variations*

Outstanding Director of a Musical: Stephen Daldry, *Billy Elliot The Musical*

Nominees: Arthur Laurents, *West Side Story;* Jason Moore, *Shrek The Musical;* Diane Paulus, *Hair;* Susan Stroman, *Happiness*

Outstanding Choreography: Peter Darling, *Billy Elliot The Musical*

Nominees: Karole Armitage, *Hair;* Andy Blankenbuehler, *9 to 5: The Musical;* Josh Prince, *Shrek The Musical;* Susan Stroman, *Happiness*

Outstanding Actor in a Play: Geoffrey Rush, *Exit the King*

Nominees: Raúl Esparza, *Speed-the-Plow;* Bill Irwin, *Waiting for Godot;* Nathan Lane, *Waiting for Godot;* Thomas Sadoski, *reasons to be pretty*

Outstanding Actress in a Play: Marcia Gay Harden, *God of Carnage*

Nominees: Saidah Arrika Ekulona, *Ruined;* Carla Gugino, *Desire Under the Elms;* Janet McTeer, *Mary Stuart;* Harriet Walter, *Mary Stuart*

Outstanding Actor in a Musical: Brian d'Arcy James, *Shrek The Musical*

Nominees: James Barbour, *A Tale of Two Cities;* Matt Cavenaugh, *West Side Story;* Josh Grisetti, *Enter Laughing The Musical;* David Pittu, *What's That Smell? The Music of Jacob Sterling*

Outstanding Actress in a Musical: (tie) Sutton Foster, *Shrek The Musical;* Josefina Scaglione, *West Side Story*

Nominees: Megan Hilty, *9 to 5: The Musical;* Leslie Kritzer, *Rooms: A Rock Romance;* Nancy Opel, *The Toxic Avenger*

Outstanding Featured Actor in a Play: David Pearse, *The Cripple of Inishmaan*

Nominees: Zach Grenier, *33 Variations;* John Benjamin Hickey, *Mary Stuart;* Russell G. Jones, *Ruined;* Patrick Page, *A Man for All Seasons*

Outstanding Featured Actress in a Play: Angela Lansbury, *Blithe Spirit*

Nominees: Andrea Martin, *Exit the King;* Kristine Nielsen, *Why Torture is Wrong, and the People Who Love Them;* Susan Louise O'Connor, *Blithe Spirit;* Condola Rashad, *Ruined*

Outstanding Featured Actor in a Musical: Gregory Jbara, *Billy Elliot The Musical*

Nominees: Daniel Breaker, *Shrek The Musical;* Aaron Simon Gross, *13;* Christopher Sieber, *Shrek The Musical;* Wesley Taylor, *Rock of Ages*

Outstanding Featured Actress in a Musical: Haydn Gwynne, *Billy Elliot The Musical*

Nominees: Kathy Fitzgerald, *9 to 5: The Musical;* Karen Olivo, *West Side Story;* Martha Plimpton, *Pal Joey;* Carole Shelley, *Billy Elliot The Musical*

Outstanding Scenic Design (Play or Musical): Tim Hatley, *Shrek The Musical*

Nominees: Santo Loquasto, *Waiting for Godot;* Derek McLane, *33 Variations;* Ian MacNeil, *Billy Elliot The Musical;* Walt Spangler, *Desire Under the Elms*

Outstanding Costume Design (Play or Musical): Tim Hatley, *Shrek The Musical*

Nominees: Nicky Gillibrand, *Billy Elliot The Musical;* John Napier, *Equus;* Martin Pakledinaz, *Blithe Spirit;* Catherine Zuber, *Joe Turner's Come and Gone*

Outstanding Lighting Design (Play or Musical): Rick Fisher, *Billy Elliot the Musical*

Nominees: Kevin Adams, *Hair;* David Hersey, *Equus;* Peter Kaczorowski, *Ruined;* David Lander, *33 Variations*

Outstanding Solo Performance: Lorenzo Pisoni, *Humor Abuse*

Nominees: Mike Birbiglia, *Sleepwalk With Me;* Mike Burstyn, *Lansky;* Mike Daisey, *If You See Something, Say Something;* Matt Sax, *Clay*

Outstanding Ensemble Performance: The Cast of *The Norman Conquests*: Amelia Bullmore, Jessica Hynes, Stephen Mangan, Ben Miles, Paul Ritter, Amanda Root

John Gassner Playwriting Award: Gina Gionfriddo, *Becky Shaw*

Nominees: Annie Baker, *Body Awareness*; Beau Willimon, *Farragut North*

Special Achievement Award: David Alvarez, Trent Kowalik, and Kiril Kulish for their performances in *Billy Elliot The Musical*

PAST OUTER CRITICS CIRCLE AWARD-WINNING PRODUCTIONS

Awards listed are for Best Play and Best Musical; as other categories were cited, they are indicated as such: (R) Best Revival; (RP) Best Play Revival; (RM) Best Musical Revival; (BP) Best Productions; (OP) Best Off-Broadway Play; (OM) Best Off-Broadway Musical. Beginning with 1990, shows listed are: Best (New) Play, Best (New) Musical, Best Play Revival, Best Musical Revival, Best Off-Broadway Play, Best New Off-Broadway Musical. In 1999, the awards were qualified as "Outstanding" instead of "Best"; if year is missing, no production awards were presented.

1950: *The Cocktail Party*; *The Consul* **1951:** *Billy Budd*; *Guys and Dolls* **1952:** *Point of No Return*; no musical award **1953:** no play award; *Wonderful Town* **1954:** *The Caine Mutiny Court-Martial*; *Kismet* **1955:** *Inherit the Wind*; *Three for Tonight* **1956:** *The Diary of Anne Frank*; *My Fair Lady* **1957:** *Long Day's Journey Into Night*; *My Fair Lady* **1958:** *Look Homeward, Angel*; *The Music Man* **1959:** *The Visit*; no musical award **1960:** *The Miracle Worker*, *Bye Bye Birdie* **1962:** *Anything Goes* (R) **1964:** *The Trojan Women* (R-classic); *The Lower Depths* (R-modern) **1965:** (BP) – *Oh What a Lovely War*, *Tartuffe* **1966:** (BP) – *Wait a Minim!*, *Mame* **1967:** (BP) – *America Hurrah*; *Cabaret*; *You Know I Can't Hear You When the Water's Running*; *You're A Good Man, Charlie Brown* **1968:** (BP) – *Rosencrantz and Guildenstern are Dead*; *The Price*; *George M!*; *Your Own Thing* **1969:** *Dames at Sea* (OM) **1970:** *Child's Play*, *Company*; *The White House Murder Case* (OP); *The Last Sweet Days of Isaac* (OM) **1971:** (BP) – *A Midsummer Night's Dream*; *Follies*; *No, No, Nanette* **1972:** *Sticks and Bones* and *That Championship Season*; no musical award **1974:** *A Moon for the Misbegotten* and *Noel Coward in Two Keys*; *Candide* **1975:** *Equus*; no musical award **1977:** *for colored girls…*; *Annie* **1978:** *Da*; no musical award **1979:** *The Elephant Man*; *Sweeney Todd, the Demon Barber of Fleet Street* **1980:** *Children of a Lesser God*; *Barnum* **1981:** *Amadeus*; *The Pirates of Penzance* (R); *March of the Falsettos* (OM) **1982:** *"Master Harold"…and the Boys*; *Nine*; *A Soldier's Play* (OP) **1983:** *Brighton Beach Memoirs*; *Cats*; *You Can't Take It With You* (RP); *On Your Toes* (RM); *Extremities* (OP); *Little Shop of Horrors* (OM) **1984:** *The Real Thing*; *La Cage aux Folles*; *Death of a Salesman* (R); *Painting Churches* (OP); *A… My Name is Alice* (Revue) **1985:** *Biloxi Blues*; *Sunday in the Park With George*; *Joe Egg* (R); *The Foreigner* (OP); *Kuni-Leml* (OM) **1986:** *I'm Not Rappaport*; *The Mystery of Edwin Drood*; *Loot* (R); *A Lie of the Mind* (OP); *Nunsense* (OM) **1987:** *Fences*; *Les Les Misérables*; *All My Sons* (R); *The Common Pursuit* (OP); *Stardust* (OM) **1988:** *M. Butterfly*; *The Phantom of the Opera*; *Anything Goes* (R); *Driving Miss Daisey* (OP); *Oil City Symphony* and *Romance, Romance* (OM) **1989:** *The Heidi Chronicles*; *Jerome Robbins' Broadway* **1990:** *The Grapes of Wrath*; *City of Angels*; *Cat on a Hot Tin Roof*; *Gypsy*; *Prelude to a Kiss*; *Closer Than Ever* **1991:** *Lost in Yonkers*; *Miss Saigon*; *Fiddler on the Roof* (R); *The Sum of Us*; *Falsettoland*; *And The World Goes Round* (Revue) **1992:** *Dancing at Lughnasa*; *Crazy for You*; *The Visit*; *Guys and Dolls*; *Marvin's Room*; *Song of Singapore* **1993:** *The Sisters Rosensweig*; *The Who's Tommy*; *Anna Christie*; *Carnival*; *Jeffrey*; *Ruthless!* **1994:** *Angels in America*; *Kiss of the Spider Woman*; *An Inspector Calls*; *She Loves Me*; *Three Tall Women*; *Annie Warbucks* **1995:** *Love! Valour! Compassion!*; *Sunset Boulevard*; *The Heiress*; *Show Boat*; *Camping with Henry and Tom*; *Jelly Roll* **1996:** *Master Class*; *Victor/Victoria*; *Inherit the Wind*; *The King and I*; *Molly Sweeney* and *Picasso at the Lapin Agile*; *Rent* **1997:** *The Last Night at Ballyhoo*; *The Life*; *A Doll's House*; *Chicago*; *How I Learned to Drive*; *Howard Crabtree's When Pigs Fly* **1998:** *The Beauty Queen of Leenane*; *Ragtime*; *A View From the Bridge*; *Cabaret*; *Never the Sinner* and *Gross Indecency: The Three Trials of Oscar Wilde*; *Hedwig and the Angry Inch* **1999:** *Not About Nightingales*; *Fosse*; *The Iceman Cometh*; *Annie Get Your Gun*

and *Peter Pan* and *You're A Good Man, Charlie Brown*; *Wit*; *A New Brain* **2000:** *Copenhagen*; *Contact*; *A Moon for the Misbegotten*; *Kiss Me, Kate*; *Dinner With Friends*; *The Wild Party* **2001:** *Proof*; *The Producers*; *The Best Man* and *One Flew Over the Cuckoo's Nest*; *42nd Street*; *Jitney*; *Bat Boy: The Musical* **2002:** *The Goat, or Who Is Sylvia?*; *Urinetown the Musical* and *The Dazzle*; *Morning's at Seven*; *Oklahoma!*; *tick, tick…BOOM!* **2003:** *Take Me Out*; *Hairspray*; *A Day in the Death of Joe Egg*; *Nine*; *The Exonerated*; *A Man of No Importance* **2004:** *I Am My Own Wife*; *Wicked*; *Henry IV*; *Wonderful Town*; *Intimate Apparel*; *Johnny Guitar* and *The Thing About Men* **2005:** *Doubt*; *Monty Python's Spamalot*; *Twelve Angry Men*; *La Cage aux Folles*; *Fat Pig* and *Going to St. Ives*; *Altar Boyz* **2006:** *The History Boys*; *Jersey Boys*; *Awake and Sing!*; *Sweeney Todd, the Demon Barber of Fleet Street*; *Stuff Happens*; *Grey Gardens* **2007:** *The Coast of Utopia*; *Spring Awakening*; *Journey's End*; *Company*; *Indian Blood*; *In the Heights* **2008:** *August: Osage County*; *Xanadu* and *Young Frankenstein*; *The Homecoming*; *South Pacific*; *Dividing the Estate*; *Adding Machine*

LUCILLE LORTEL AWARDS

Monday, May 3, 2009 at the Broadway Ballroom of the Marriott Marquis; 24th annual; Host: Kristen Johnston. Presented by the League of Off-Broadway Theatres and Producers for outstanding achievement Off-Broadway. The 2008–2009 awards voting committee consisted of Terry Berliner (SDC), John Clinton Eisner (Lark Theatre Company), Kurt Everhart (*nyconstage.org*), Peter Filichia (*TheatreMania.com*), Jerry Fiske (Fellowship for the Performing Arts), George Forbes (Off-Broadway League), Liz Frankel (The Public Theater), Susan Gallin (Susan Gallin Productions), Eleanor Goldhar (Guggenheim Foundation), Melanie Herman (MH Productions), Linda Herring (Tribeca Performing Arts Center), Walt Kiskaddeon (Actors' Equity Association), Renee Lasher (SDC), Russell Lehrer (Actors' Equity Association), Niclas Nagler (Off-Broadway League), Barbara Pasternack (Theatreworks USA), Richard Price (Theatre Development Fund), Mark Rossler (New York Foundation for the Arts), David Savran (The Graduate Center – CUNY), and Barbara Toy (American Theatre Wing).

Outstanding Play: *Ruined* by Lynn Nottage (Manhattan Theatre Club and Goodman Theatre)

Nominees: *Animals Out of Paper* by Rajiv Joseph (Second Stage); *Becky Shaw* by Gina Gionfriddo (Second Stage), *The Good Negro* by Tracey Scott Wilson (The Public Theater and Dallas Theater Center); *The Sound and the Fury (April Seventh, 1928)* by William Faulkner, created by Elevator Repair Service (New York Theatre Workshop and Elevator Repair Service)

Outstanding Musical: *Fela! A New Musical* Book by Jim Lewis and Bill T. Jones, music and lyrics by Fela Anikulapo, additional music by Aaron Johnson and Jordan McLean, additional lyrics by Jim Lewis (Produced by Ruth and Stephen Hendel and Roy Gabay)

Nominees: *My Vaudeville Man!* Book and lyrics by Jeff Hochhauser, music and lyrics by Bob Johnston (York Theatre Company and Melanie Herman); *Road Show* Music and lyrics by Stephen Sondheim, book by John Weidman (The Public Theatre); *Saved* Music and lyrics by Michael Friedman, book and lyrics by John Dempsey and Rinne Groff (Playwrights Horizon and Elephant Eye Theatrical); *This Beautiful City* Music and lyrics by Michael Friedman, lyrics by Steve Cosson and Jim Lewis, created by The Civilians (Vineyard Theatre)

Outstanding Revival: *Our Town* (Produced by Scott Morfee, Jean Doumanian, Tom Wirtshafter, Ted Snowdon, Eagle Productions, Dena Hammerstein/Pam Pariseau, The Weinstein Company, Burnt Umber Productions)

Nominees: *Enter Laughing The Musical* (York Theatre Company); *Othello* (Theatre for a New Audience); *The Cripple of Inishmaan* (Atlantic Theater Company); *The Glass Cage* (Mint Theatre)

Outstanding Solo Show: *Humor Abuse* Created and performed by Lorenzo Pisoni, co-created and directed by Erica Schmidt (Manhattan Theatre Club)

Nominees: *Sleepwalk With Me* Written and performed by Mike Birbiglia (Produced by Eli Gonda, Ryan Scott Warren, Marc Turtletaub, Peter Saraf, and Nathan Lane)

Outstanding Director: David Cromer, *Our Town*

Nominees: Arin Arbus, *Othello*; Garry Hynes, *The Cripple of Inishmaan*; Kate Whoriskey, *Ruined*; Robert Woodruff, *Chair*

Outstanding Choreography: Bill T. Jones, *Fela! A New Musical*

Nominees: Martha Clarke, *Garden of Earthly Delights*; Janet Miller, *The Marvelous Wonderettes*; Lynne Taylor-Corbett and Shonn Wiley, *My Vaudeville Man!*; Sergio Trujillo, *Saved*

Outstanding Lead Actor: John Douglas Thompson, *Othello* (Theatre for a New Audience)

Nominees: Ned Eisenberg, *Othello*; Josh Grisetti, *Enter Laughing The Musical*; Brian d'Arcy James, *Port Authority*; Sahr Ngaujah, *Fela! A New Musical*

Outstanding Lead Actress: Saidah Arrika Ekulona, *Ruined* (Manhattan Theatre Club and Goodman Theatre)

Nominees: Ellyn Burstyn, *Little Flower of East Orange*; Carmen M. Herlihy, *crooked*; Kellie Overbey, *The Savannah Disputation*; Annie Parisse, *Becky Shaw*

Outstanding Featured Actor: Aaron Monaghan, *The Cripple of Inishmaan* (Atlantic Theater Company)

Nominees: Utkarsh Ambudkar, *Animals Out of Paper*; Francois Battiste, *The Good Negro*; John McMartin, *Saturn Returns*; Thomas Sadoski, *Becky Shaw*

Outstanding Featured Actress: Kerry Condon, *The Cripple of Inishmaan* (Atlantic Theater Company)

Nominees: Annika Boras, *Chair*; Lisa Emery, *Distracted*; Mamie Gummer, *Uncle Vanya*; Juliet Rylance, *Othello*

Outstanding Scenic Design: Roger Hanna, *The Glass Cage* (Mint Theatre)

Nominees: Beowulf Boritt, *Animals Out of Paper*; Marina Draghici, *Fela! A New Musical*; James Schuette, *Wig Out!*; David Zinn, *Chair*

Outstanding Costume Design: Marina Draghici, *Fela! A New Musical*

Nominees: Ann Hould-Ward, *Road Show*; Toni-Leslie James, *Wig Out!*; Karen Perry, *The First Breeze of Summer*; Theresa Squire, *Rafta, Rafta...*

Outstanding Lighting Design: Christopher Akerlind, *Garden of Earthly Delights*

Nominees: Mark Barton, *Chair*; Lap Chi Chu, *The Good Negro*; Marcus Doshi, *Othello*; Jason Lyons, *Mourning Becomes Electra*

Outstanding Sound Design: John Gromada, *Shipwrecked! An Entertainment* (Primary Stages)

Nominees: Quentin Chiappetta, *Irena's Vow*; Robert Kaplowitz, *Wig Out!*; Jane Shaw, *The Widowing of Mrs. Holroyd*; Matt Tierney, *The Sound and the Fury (April Seventh, 1928)*

Outstanding Body of Work: The Lark Play Development Center

Edith Olivier Award for Sustained Excellence: Ira Weitzman

PAST LUCILLE LORTEL-AWARD WINNING PRODUCTIONS Awards listed are Outstanding Play and Outstanding Musical, respectively, since inception.

1986: *Woza Africa!*; no musical award **1987:** *The Common Pursuit*; no musical award **1988:** no play or musical award **1989:** *The Cocktail Hour*; no musical award **1990:** no play or musical award **1991:** *Aristocrats*; *Falsettoland* **1992:** *Lips Together, Teeth Apart*; *And the World Goes 'Round* **1993:** *The Destiny of Me*; *Forbidden Broadway* **1994:** *Three Tall Women*; *Wings* **1995:** *Camping with Henry & Tom*; *Jelly Roll!* **1996:** *Molly Sweeney*; *Floyd Collins* **1997:** *How I Learned to Drive*; *Violet* **1998:** (tie) *Gross Indecency* and *The Beauty Queen of Leenane*; no musical award **1999:** *Wit*; no musical award **2000:** *Dinner With*

Friends; *James Joyce's The Dead* **2001:** *Proof*; *Bat Boy: The Musical* **2002:** *Metamorphoses*; *Urinetown* **2003:** *Take Me Out*; *Avenue Q* **2004:** *Bug*; *Caroline or Change* **2005:** *Doubt*; *The 25th Annual Putnam County Spelling Bee* **2006:** *The Lieutenant of Inishmore*; *The Seven* **2007:** *Stuff Happens*; (tie) *In the Heights* and *Spring Awakening* **2008:** *Betrayed*; *Adding Machine*

NEW YORK DRAMA CRITICS' CIRCLE AWARD

Monday, May 11, 2009 at the Algonquin Hotel; 74th annual. Presented by members of the press in the New York area. New York Drama Critics' Circle Committee: Adam Feldman – President (*Time Out New York*), Hilton Als (*The New Yorker*), Melissa Rose Bernardo (*Entertainment Weekly*), David Cote (*Time Out New York*), Joe Dziemianowicz – Treasurer (*The Daily News*), Michael Feingold (*The Village Voice*), Robert Feldberg (*The Bergen Record*), Elysa Gardner (*USA Today*), John Heilpern (*The New York Observer*), Michael Kuchwara (*Associate Press*), David Rooney (*Variety*), Frank Scheck (*New York Post*), David Sheward (*Back Stage*), John Simon (*Bloomberg News*), Alexis Soloski (*The Village Voice*), Terry Teachout (*The Wall Street Journal*), Elizabeth Vincentelli (*New York Post*), Linda Winer (*Newsday*), Richard Zoglin (*Time*); Vice President (non-voting): Eric Grode (*The New York Sun*)

Best Play: *Ruined* by Lynn Nottage

Best Foreign Play: *Black Watch* by Gregory Burke

Best Musical: *Billy Elliot The Musical* by Elton John and Lee Hall

Special Citations: Angela Lansbury, for her contribution to the American Theatre; Gerard Alessandrini for *Forbidden Broadway*; Matthew Warchus and the Cast of *The Norman Conquests*

PAST DRAMA CRITICS' CIRLCE AWARD-WINNING PRODUCTIONS
From 1936 to 1962, the New York Drama Critics' Circle presented awards for Best American Play, Best Foreign Play, and Best Musical, although some years no awards were given in specific categories. For entries below during those years, the first entry (unless otherwise indicated) is for Best American Play, (F) for Best Foreign Play, and (M) for Best Musical. For listings from 1962 to the present, the first listing (unless otherwise indicated) is for Best Play, and proceeding listings are as follow (depending on which awards were cited): (A) Best American Play; (F) Best Foreign Play; (M) Best Musical. Special Citations, periodically presented, are indicated as (SC).

1936: *Winterset* **1937:** *High Tor* **1938:** *Of Mice and Men*, *Shadow and Substance* (F) **1939:** *The White Steed* (F) **1940:** *The Time of Your Life* **1941:** *Watch on the Rhine*, *The Corn Is Green* (F) **1942:** *Blithe Spirit* (F) **1943:** *The Patriots* **1944:** *Jacobowsky and the Colonel* (F) **1945:** *The Glass Menagerie* **1946:** *Carousel* (M) **1947:** *All My Sons*, *No Exit* (F), *Brigadoon* (M) **1948:** *A Streetcar Named Desire*, *The Winslow Boy* (F) **1949:** *Death of a Salesman*, *The Madwoman of Chaillot* (F), *South Pacific* (M) **1950:** *The Member of the Wedding*, *The Cocktail Party* (F), *The Consul* (M) **1951:** *Darkness at Noon*, *The Lady's Not for Burning* (F), *Guys and Dolls* (M) **1952:** *I Am a Camera*, *Venus Observed* (F), *Pal Joey* (M), *Don Juan in Hell* (SC) **1953:** *Picnic*, *The Love of Four Colonels* (F), *Wonderful Town* (M) **1954:** *Teahouse of the August Moon*, *Ondine* (F), *The Golden Apple* (M) **1955:** *Cat on a Hot Tin Roof*, *Witness for the Prosecution* (F), *The Saint of Bleecker Street* (M) **1956:** *The Diary of Anne Frank*, *Tiger at the Gates* (F), *My Fair Lady* (M) **1957:** *Long Day's Journey into Night*, *The Waltz of the Toreadors* (F), *The Most Happy Fella* (M) **1958:** *Look Homeward Angel*, *Look Back in Anger* (F), *The Music Man* (M) **1959:** *A Raisin in the Sun*, *The Visit* (F), *La Plume de Ma Tante* (M) **1960:** *Toys in the Attic*, *Five Finger Exercise* (F), *Fiorello!* (M) **1961:** *All the Way Home*, *A Taste of Honey* (F), *Carnival* (M) **1962:** *Night of the Iguana*, *A Man for All Seasons* (F), *How to Succeed in Business Without Really Trying* (M) **1963:** *Who's Afraid of Virginia Woolf?*, *Beyond the Fringe* (SC) **1964:** *Luther*, *Hello Dolly!* (M), *The Trojan Women* (SC) **1965:** *The Subject Was Roses*, *Fiddler on the Roof* (M) **1966:** *Marat/Sade*, *Man of La Mancha* (M), *Mark Twain Tonight - Hal Holbrook* (SC) **1967:** *The Homecoming*, *Cabaret* (M)

1968: *Rosencrantz and Guildenstern Are Dead*, *Your Own Thing* (M) **1969:** *The Great White Hope*, *1776* (M) **1970:** *Borstal Boy*, *The Effect of Gamma Rays on Man-in-the-Moon Marigolds* (A), *Company* (M) **1971:** *Home*, *The House of Blue Leaves* (A), *Follies* (M), **1972:** *That Championship Season*, *The Screens* (F), *Two Gentlemen of Verona* (M), *Sticks and Bones* (SC), *Old Times* (SC) **1973:** *The Changing Room*, *The Hot L Baltimore* (A), *A Little Night Music* (M) **1974:** *The Contractor*, *Short Eyes* (A), *Candide* (M) **1975:** *Equus*, *The Taking of Miss Janie* (A), *A Chorus Line* (M) **1976:** *Travesties*, *Streamers* (A), *Pacific Overtures* (M) **1977:** *Otherwise Engaged*, *American Buffalo* (A), *Annie* (M) **1978:** *Da*, *Ain't Misbehavin'* (M) **1979:** *The Elephant Man*, *Sweeney Todd* (M) **1980:** *Talley's Folly*, *Betrayal* (F), *Evita* (M), Peter Brook's *Le Centre International de Créations Théâtricales* at La MaMa ETC (SC) **1981:** *A Lesson from Aloes*, *Crimes of the Heart* (A), *Lena Horne: The Lady and Her Music* (SC), *The Pirate of Penzance* at New York Shakespeare Festival (SC) **1982:** *The Life and Adventures of Nicholas Nickleby*, *A Soldier's Play* (A) **1983:** *Brighton Beach Memoirs*, *Plenty* (A), *Little Shop of Horrors* (M), Young Playwrights Festival (SC) **1984:** *The Real Thing*, *Glengarry Glen Ross* (F), *Sunday in the Park with George* (M), Samuel Beckett (SC) **1985:** *Ma Rainey's Black Bottom* **1986:** *A Lie of the Mind*, *Benefactors* (A), *The Search for Signs of Intelligent Life in the Universe* (SC) **1987:** *Fences*, *Les Liaisons Dangereuses* (F), *Les Misérables* (M) **1988:** *Joe Turner's Come and Gone*, *The Road to Mecca* (F), *Into the Woods* (M) **1989:** *The Heidi Chronicles*, *Aristocrats* (F), *Bill Irwin: Largely New York* (SC) **1990:** *The Piano Lesson*, *Privates on Parade* (F), *City of Angels* (M) **1991:** *Six Degrees of Separation*, *Our Country's Good* (F), *The Will Rogers Follies* (M) Eileen Atkins - *A Room of One's Own* (SC) **1992:** *Dancing at Lughnasa*, *Two Trains Running* (A) **1993:** *Angels in America: Millenium Approaches*, *Someone Who'll Watch Over Me* (F), *Kiss of the Spider Woman* (M) **1994:** *Three Tall Women*, *Twilight: Los Angeles, 1992* - Anna Deavere Smith (SC) **1995:** *Arcadia*, *Love! Valour! Compassion!* (A), Signature Theatre Company's Horton Foote Season (SC) **1996:** *Seven Guitars*, *Molly Sweeny* (F), *Rent* (M), New York City Center's *Encores!* (SC) **1997:** *How I Learned to Drive*, *Skylight* (F), *Violet* (M), *Chicago* - Broadway revival (SC) **1998:** *Art*, *Pride's Crossing* (A), *Lion King* (M), *Cabaret* – Broadway revival (SC) **1999:** *Wit*, *Closer* (F), *Parade* (M), David Hare (SC) **2000:** *Jitney*, *James Joyce's The Dead* (M), *Copenhagen* (F) **2001:** *The Invention of Love*, *The Producers* (M), *Proof* (A) **2002:** *Edward Albee's The Goat, or Who is Sylvia?*, *Elaine Stritch: At Liberty* (SC) **2003:** *Take Me Out*, *Talking Heads* (F), *Hairspray* (M) **2004:** *Intimate Apparel*, Barbara Cook (SC) **2005:** *Doubt*, *The Pillowman* (F) **2006:** *The History Boys*, *The Drowsy Chaperone* (M), John Doyle, Sarah Travis and the Cast of *Sweeney Todd* (SC), Christine Ebersole (SC) **2007:** *The Coast of Utopia*, *Radio Golf* (A), *Spring Awakening* (M), *Journey's End* (SC) **2008:** *August: Osage County*, *Passing Strange* (M)

DRAMA LEAGUE AWARDS

Friday, May 15, 2009; Broadway Ballroom at The Marriott Marquis; 75th annual. Co-Hosted by Jeremy Irons and Cynthia Nixon; Presented for distinguished achievement in the New York theater; winners are selected by members of the League; Honorary Co-Chairs: Jane Alexander, Matt Cavenaugh, Raul Esparza, Tovah Feldshuh, Jane Fonda, Lauren Graham, Allison Janney, Constantine Maroulis, David Hyde Pierce and Geoffrey Rush; Presenters: Jane Fonda, Sutton Foster, Patrick Wilson, Carla Gugino, John Lithgow, Stephen Daldry, Harold Prince, Tyne Daly, Irv Welzer.

Play: *God of Carnage*

Musical: *Billy Elliot The Musical*

Revival of a Play: *Blithe Spirit*

Revival of a Musical: *Hair*

Performance: Geoffrey Rush

Julia Hansen Award for Excellence in Directing: Arthur Laurents

Achievement in Musical Theatre: Elton John

Unique Contribution to Theater: Angela Lansbury

75th Anniversary Leadership Award: Herbert Blodgett

PULITZER PRIZE AWARD WINNERS FOR DRAMA

Established in 1917; Administered by the Pulitzer Prize Board, Columbia University; Lee C. Bollinger, President. Winner is chosen by a jury, composed of three to four critics, one academic and one playwright, however the board has final authority over choice. Presented for an outstanding drama or musical presented in New York or regional theater. The award goes to the playwright but production of the play as well as the script, is taken into account.

2009 Winner: *Ruined* by Lynn Nottage

PAST PULITZER PRIZE WINNERS If year is missing, no award was presented that year.

1918: *Why Marry?* by Jesse Lynch Williams **1920:** *Beyond the Horizon* by Eugene O'Neill **1921:** *Miss Lulu Bett* by Zona Gale **1922:** *Anna Christie* by Eugene O'Neill **1923:** *Icebound* by Owen Davis **1924:** *Hell-Bent for Heaven* by Hatcher Hughes **1925:** *They Knew What They Wanted* by Sidney Howard **1926:** *Craig's Wife* by George Kelly **1927:** *In Abraham's Bosom* by Paul Green **1928:** *Strange Interlude* by Eugene O'Neill **1929:** *Street Scene* by Elmer Rice **1930:** *The Green Pastures* by Marc Connelly **1931:** *Alison's House* by Susan Glaspell **1932:** *Of Thee I Sing* by George S. Kaufman, Morrie Ryskind, Ira and George Gershwin **1933:** *Both Your Houses* by Maxwell Anderson **1934:** *Men in White* by Sidney Kingsley **1935:** *The Old Maid* by Zoe Atkins **1936:** *Idiot's Delight* by Robert E. Sherwood **1937:** *You Can't Take It with You* by Moss Hart and George S. Kaufman **1938:** *Our Town* by Thornton Wilder **1939:** *Abe Lincoln in Illinois* by Robert E. Sherwood **1940:** *The Time of Your Life* by William Saroyan **1941:** *There Shall Be No Night* by Robert E. Sherwood **1943:** *The Skin of Our Teeth* by Thornton Wilder **1945:** *Harvey* by Mary Chase **1946:** *State of the Union* by Howard Lindsay and Russel Crouse **1948:** *A Streetcar Named Desire* by Tennessee Williams **1949:** *Death of a Salesman* by Arthur Miller **1950:** *South Pacific* by Richard Rodgers, Oscar Hammerstein II, and Joshua Logan **1952:** *The Shrike* by Joseph Kramm **1953:** *Picnic* by William Inge **1954:** *The Teahouse of the August Moon* by John Patrick **1955:** *Cat on a Hot Tin Roof* by Tennessee Williams **1956:** *The Diary of Anne Frank* by Frances Goodrich and Albert Hackett **1957:** *Long Day's Journey Into Night* by Eugene O'Neill **1958:** *Look Homeward, Angel* by Ketti Frings **1959:** *J.B.* by Archibald MacLeish **1960:** *Fiorello!* by Jerome Weidman, George Abbott, Sheldon Harnick, and Jerry Bock **1961:** *All the Way Home* by Tad Mosel **1962:** *How to Succeed in Business Without Really Trying* by Abe Burrows, Willie Gilbert, Jack Weinstock, and Frank Loesser **1965:** *The Subject Was Roses* by Frank D. Gilroy **1967:** *A Delicate Balance* by Edward Albee **1969:** *The Great White Hope* by Howard Sackler **1970:** *No Place to Be Somebody* by Charles Gordone **1971:** *The Effect of Gamma Rays on Man-in-the-Moon Marigolds* by Paul Zindel **1973:** *That Championship Season* by Jason Miller **1975:** *Seascape* by Edward Albee **1976:** *A Chorus Line* by Michael Bennett, James Kirkwood, Nicholas Dante, Marvin Hamlisch, and Edward Kleban **1977:** *The Shadow Box* by Michael Cristofer **1978:** *The Gin Game* by D.L. Coburn **1979:** *Buried Child* by Sam Shepard **1980:** *Talley's Folly* by Lanford Wilson **1981:** *Crimes of the Heart* by Beth Henley **1982:** *A Soldier's Play* by Charles Fuller **1983:** *'night, Mother* by Marsha Norman **1984:** *Glengarry Glen Ross* by David Mamet **1985:** *Sunday in the Park with George* by James Lapine and Stephen Sondheim **1987:** *Fences* by August Wilson **1988:** *Driving Miss Daisy* by Alfred Uhry **1989:** *The Heidi Chronicles* by Wendy Wasserstein **1990:** *The Piano Lesson* by August Wilson **1991:** *Lost in Yonkers* by Neil Simon **1992:** *The Kentucky Cycle* by Robert Schenkkan **1993:** *Angels in America: Millenium Approaches* by Tony Kushner **1994:** *Three Tall Women* by Edward Albee **1995:** *Young Man from Atlanta* by Horton Foote **1996:** *Rent* by Jonathan Larson **1998:** *How I Learned to Drive* by Paula Vogel **1999:** *Wit* by Margaret Edson **2000:** *Dinner with Friends* by Donald Margulies **2001:** *Proof* by David Auburn **2002:** *Topdog/Underdog* by Suzan Lori-Parks **2003:** *Anna in the Tropics* by Nilo Cruz **2004:** *I Am My Own Wife* by Doug Wright **2005:** *Doubt* by John Patrick Shanley **2007:** *Rabbit Hole* by David Lindsay-Abaire **2008:** *August: Osage County* by Tracy Letts

Regional and Other Theatrical Awards

ACCLAIM AWARDS

May 18, 2009; Jarson-Kaplan Theater at the Aronoff Center for the Arts; April 4, 2009; 4th annual; Presented by The Cincinnati Enquirer and the League of Cincinnati Theatres and hosted by the Cincinnati Arts Association for outstanding work in Cincinnati/Northern Kentucky theatre. The non-competitive awards recognize the work of local artists as well as guest artists, and support a variety of initiatives for area theatre artists and educators.

Outstanding Play: *Love Song* by John Kolvenback (Cincinnati Playhouse in the Park)

Outstanding Musical: *Two Gentlemen of Verona* (CCM – University of Cincinnati College – Conservatory of Music)

Outstanding Revival: *Amadeus* (Cincinnati Shakespeare Company)

Outstanding Independent Production: *A Little Night Music* (New Stage Collective)

Outstanding New Play: *The Travels of Angelica* by Joseph McDonough (Cincinnati Playhouse in the Park)

Outstanding Orchestrations: David Kreppel, *Don't Make Me Pull This Show Over: Dispatches from the Frontlines of Parenting* ((Ensemble Theatre of Cincinnati)

Outstanding Direction: Aubrey Berg, *Good News* (CCM); Ken Jones, *Working* (Northern Kentucky University); Jeremy Dublin, *Twelfth Night* (Cincinnati Shakespeare Company); Mark Hardy, *The Women* (Northern Kentucky University); Andrew Palermo, *Two Gentlemen of Verona* (CCM)

Outstanding Musical Director/Arranger/Accompanist: Steve Goers, *Good News* (CCM); Alan Patrick Kenny, *A Little Night Music* (New Stage Collective); Roger Grodsky, *Two Gentlemen of Verona* (CCM); Jarney Strawn, *Jesus Christ Superstar* (Commonwealth Theatre Company)

Outstanding Choreography: Patti James, *Good News* (CCM); Jane Green & Ruby Streate, *Once on This Island* (Northern Kentucky University); Andrew Palermo, *Two Gentlemen of Verona* (CCM)

Outstanding Equity Lead Performances: Adrian Sparks, *The Seafarer* (Ensemble Theatre of Cincinnati); Joy Farmer-Clay, *Blackbird* (Cincinnati Playhouse in the Park)

(CCM); Joseph Parks, *Love Song* (Cincinnati Playhouse in the Park); Thom Sesma, *Durango* (Cincinnati Playhouse in the Park)

Outstanding Equity Supporting Performance: Kate Wilford, *Death of a Salesman* (New Edgecliff Theatre)

Outstanding Non-Equity Performances: Brooke Rucidio, *Peter Pan* (Covedale Center for the Performing Arts); Lesley Hitch, *Guys and Dolls* (Covedale Center for the Performing Arts)

Outstanding Supporting Performances: Raymond McAnally, *The Foreigner* (Cincinnati Playhouse in the Park); Heather Wood, *Travels of Angelica* (Ensemble Theatre of Cincinnati)

Outstanding Featured Actor in a Musical: Joe Moeller, *Good News* (CCM)

Outstanding Supporting Actress: Lisa Mindelle, *Bat Boy: The Musical* (CCM)

Outstanding Performances: Nick Rose, *Timon of Athens* (Cincinnati Shakespeare Company), Lauren Sprague, *Two Gentlemen of Verona* (CCM); Bruce Croner, *Amadeus* (Cincinnati Shakespeare Company)

Outstanding Ensemble: *Two Gentlemen of Verona* (CCM)

Outstanding Ensemble Vocal Performance: Charlie Clark, A. Beth Harris,

Jessica Hendy, Allen Kendall, Kate Wilford for *Don't Make Me Pull This Show Over: Dispatches from the Frontlines of Parenting*. (Ensemble Theatre of Cincinnati)

Outstanding Collegiate Principal Ensemble: Hannah Dowdy, Katie Kershaw, Samantha Wright, Julie Wacksman, Lauren Helton in *The Women* (Northern Kentucky University); Michael Carr, Kendall Karg, Britany Middleton, Alison Vodnoy, *On the Verge, or the Geography of Yearning* (CCM)

Outstanding Solo Performance and Script: Alison Vodnoy, *In Rehearsal* (Cincinnati Fringe Festival)

Outstanding Set Design: Paul Shortt, *The Foreigner* (Cincinnati Playhouse in the Park); Kevin Judge, *Durango* (Cincinnati Playhouse in the Park); Lyle Benjamin & Dan Dermody (non-Equity), *Jitney* (Queen City Off-Broadway)

Outstanding Costume Design: Reba Senske, *Two Gentlemen of Verona* (CCM)

Outstanding Lighting Design: Thomas Hase, *Dr. Jekyll and Mr. Hyde* (Cincinnati Playhouse in the Park)

Outstanding Equity Design: Brian Mehring (design) and Shannon Rae Lutz (properties), *Gem of the Ocean* (Ensemble Theatre of Cincinnati)

Outstanding Design: Joseph P. Tilford (sets), Thomas C. Hase (lighting), Susan Tsu (illustrator), John Boesche (projections), *Travels of Angelica* (Ensemble Theatre of Cincinnati);

Enquirer/Fifth Third Bank Theater Educator Award ($2,500): Emily Himonidis, St. Henry District High School (Erlanger, Kentucky); Second place ($1,000): John Whapman, Sycamore High School (Cincinnati)

Trailblazer Award: Richard Hess, College-Conservatory of Music, University of Cincinnati

Acclaim MVPs: Cathy Springfield, Xavier Players (Xavier University); Jim Stump, President of League of Cincinnati Theatres

Special Recognition: Doug Borntrager (Know Theatre), Christopher Guthrie (Cincinnati Shakespeare Company), Michael Haney (Cincinnati Playhouse in the Park), Kelly Mengelkoch (Cincinnati Shakespeare Company), Ensemble Theatre of Cincinnati 2008–2009 Intern Company

AMERICAN THEATRE CRITICS ASSOCIATION AWARDS
Steinberg New Play Award and Citations

April 4, 2009; Ceremony at the Humana Festival at Actors Theatre Louisville; founded in 1977. The Harold and Mimi Steinberg/ATCA Awards honor new plays that had their world premieres in the previous year in professional productions outside New York City. From 1977–1984 ACTA gave only one play a citation. After 1985, three citations were awarded. Currently the new play award comes with a $25,000 prize and the two other citations are awarded a $7,500 prize.

2009 New Play Award: *Song of Extinction* by E.M. (Ellen) Lewis (premiered at Moving Arts, Hollywood, CA); **Citations:** *Great Falls* by Lee Blessing (premiered Actors Theatre of Louisville); *Superior Donuts* by Tracy Letts (premiered at Steppenwolf Theater)

Past Recipients (after 1986, first entry is the principal citation): **1977:** *And the Soul Shall Dance* by Wakako Yamauchi **1978:** *Getting Out* by Marsha Norman **1979:** *Loose Ends* by Michael Weller **1980:** *Custer* by Robert E. Ingham **1981:** *Chekhov in Yalta* by John Driver and Jeffrey Haddow **1982:** *Talking With* by Jane Martin **1983:** *Closely Related* by Bruce MacDonald **1984:** *Wasted* by Fred Gamel **1985:** (no principal citation) *Scheherazade* by Marisha Chamberlain, *The Shaper* by John Steppling, *A Shayna Maidel* by Barbara Lebow **1986:** *Fences* by August Wilson; *Fugue* by Lenora Thuna; *Hunting Cockroaches* by Januscz Glowacki **1987:** *A Walk in the Woods* by Lee Blessing; *The Film Society* by John Robin Baitz; *Back to the World* by Stephen Mack Jones **1988:** *Heathen Valley* by Romulus Linney; *The Voice of the Prairie* by John Olive; *The Deal* by Matthew

Witten **1989:** *The Piano Lesson* by August Wilson; *Generations* by Dennis Clontz; *The Downside* by Richard Dresser **1990:** *2* by Romulus Linney; *Pick Up Ax* by Anthony Clarvoe; *Marvin's Room* by Scott McPherson **1991:** *Two Trains Running* by August Wilson; *Sincerity Forever* by Mac Wellman; *The Ohio State Murders* by Adrienne Kennedy **1992:** *Could I Have This Dance* by Doug Haverty; *American Enterprise* by Jeffrey Sweet; *Miss Evers' Boys* by David Feldshuh **1993:** *Children of Paradise: Shooting a Dream* by Steven Epp, Felicity Jones, Dominique Serrand, and Paul Walsh; *Black Elk Speaks* by Christopher Sergel; *Hurricane* by Anne Galjour **1994:** *Keely and Du* by Jane Martin **1995:** *The Nanjing Race* by Reggie Cheong-Leen; *Rush Limbaugh in Night School* by Charlie Varon; *The Waiting Room* by Lisa Loomer **1996:** *Amazing Grace* by Michael Cristofer; *Jungle Rot* by Seth Greenland; *Seven Guitars* by August Wilson **1997:** *Jack and Jill* by Jane Martin; *The Last Night of Ballyhoo* by Alfred Uhry; *The Ride Down Mount Morgan* by Arthur Miller **1998:** *The Cider House Rules, Part II* by Peter Parnell; *Jitney* by August Wilson; *The Old Settler* by John Henry Redwood **1999:** *Book of Days* by Lanford Wilson; *Dinner With Friends* by Donald Margulies; *Expecting Isabel* by Lisa Loomer **2000:** *Oo-Bla-Dee* by Regina Taylor; *Compleat Female Stage Beauty* by Jeffrey Hatcher; *Syncopation* by Allan Knee **2001:** *Anton in Show Business* by Jane Martin; *Big Love* by Charles L. Mee; *King Hedley II* by August Wilson **2002:** *The Carpetbagger's Children* by Horton Foote; *The Action Against Sol Schumann* by Jeffrey Sweet; *Joe and Betty* by Murray Mednick **2003:** *Anna in the Tropics* by Nilo Cruz; *Recent Tragic Events* by Craig Wright; *Resurrection Blues* by Arthur Miller **2004:** *Intimate Apparel* by Lynn Nottage; *Gem of the Ocean* by August Wilson; *The Love Song of J. Robert Oppenheimer* by Carson Kreitzer **2005:** *The Singing Forest* by Craig Lucas; *After Ashley* by Gina Gionfriddo; *The Clean House* by Sarah Ruhl; *Madagascar* by J.T. Rogers **2006:** *A Body of Water* by Lee Blessing; *Red Light Winter* by Adam Rapp; *Radio Golf* by August Wilson **2007:** *Hunter Gatherers* by Peter Sinn Nachtrieb; *Opus* by Michael Hollinger; *Guest Artist* by Jeff Daniels **2008:** *33 Variations* by Moises Kaufman; *End Days* by Deborah Zoe Laufer; *Dead Man's Cell Phone* by Sarah Ruhl

M. Elizabeth Osborn Award

April 4, 2009; Ceremony at the Humana Festival at Actors Theatre Louisville; established in 1993. Presented by the American Theatre Critics Association in memory of Theatre Communications Group and American Theatre play editor M. Elizabeth Osborn to an emerging playwright who has not received other major national awards, has not had a significant New York production, and whose work has not been staged widely in regional theatres; $1,000 prize and recognition in the *Best Plays Theater Yearbook* edited by Jeffrey Eric Jenkins.

2009 Winner: Yusseff El Guindi for *Our Enemies: Lively Scenes of Love and Combat* (premiered at Silk Road Theatre Project in Chicago)

Past Recipients: 1994: *Hurricane* by Anne Galjour **1995:** *Rush Limbaugh in Night School* by Charlie Varon **1996:** *Beast on the Moon* by Richard Kalinoski **1997:** *Thunder Knocking On the Door* by Keith Glover **1998:** *The Glory of Living* by Rebecca Gilman **1999:** *Lamarck* by Dan O'Brien **2000:** *Marked Tree* by Coby Goss **2001:** *Waiting to Be Invited* by S.M. Shephard-Massat **2002:** *Chagrin Falls* by Mia McCullough **2003:** *The Dinosaur Within* by John Walch **2004:** *The Intelligent Design of Jenny Chow* by Rolin Jones **2005:** *Madagascar* by J.T. Rogers **2006:** *American Fiesta* by Steven Tomlinson **2007** *Vestibular Sense* by Ken LaZebnik **2008:** *Gee's Bend* by Elyzabeth Wilder

THE ASCAP FOUNDATION AWARDS

December 10, 2008; Allen Room at Rose Hall; 13th annual. The ASCAP Foundation provides Awards to emerging composers and songwriters and recognition to honor the achievements of established composers and songwriters in 2008.

Champion Award: Judy Collins

Harold Adamson Lyric Award: Christopher Dimond (Musical Theatre); Dustin James (Country)

Robert Allen Award: Shwa Losben

Harold Arlen Award: Cinco Paul (Musical Theater); Sascha Peres (Film & TV)

Louis Armstrong Scholarship: Dean Saghafi-Ezaz

Louis Armstrong Jazz Scholarship Honoring Duke Ellington: Mark Einhorn, Colin Gordon

Louis Armstrong Scholarship Honoring W.C. Handy: Felicia Bennett, Tyrell Brown

Louis Armstrong Scholarship at the University of New Orleans: Adam R. Bock

Charlotte V. Bergen Scholarship: Peng-Peng Gong

Irving Berlin Summer Camp Scholarship: Ilana Rainero-de Haan

Leonard Bernstein Composer Fellowship: Jeff Stanek

Boosey & Hawkes Young Composer Award Honoring Aaron Copland: Christopher Castro

Leon Brettler Award: Mike Willis

Irving Burgie Scholarship: William Wells

Irving Caesar Scholarship: Matija Budisin, Daniel Lofaso, Michael Lofaso, Jose Serrano, Elvis Vanterpool-Krajnak

Sammy Cahn Award: Cinco Paul

Cherry Lane Foundation/Music Alive! Scholarship in honor of Quincy Jones: Gregory Watkins

Cy Coleman Award: Molly Gachignard

Eunice & Hal David Instructor-in-Residence Award: Pat Bass

Fran Morgenstern Davis Scholarship: Josh Freilich, Carla Jablonski

John Denver Music Scholarships supported by Music Alive!/Cherry Lane Foundation: James Cowan, Corey Hawkins

Jamie deRoy & Friends Award: Johnny Rodgers

Louis Dreyfus Warner/Chappell City College Scholarship Honoring George & Ira Gershwin: Ziv Shalev

Max Dreyfus Scholarship: Felice Kuan

Fellowship for Composition & Film Scoring: Gavin Keese

Ira Gershwin Scholarship: Dwight Rivera

Leo Kaplan Award: John Supko

Steve Kaplan TV & Film Studies Scholarship: Patrick Murray

Leiber & Stoller Music Scholarship: Alin Melik-Adamyan, Erik Muench

Livingston & Evans Music Scholarship: Ryan Garrett

Frederick Loewe Scholarship: Mark Evans

Henry Mancini Music Scholarship: Ernest Adzentoivich

Michael Masser Scholarship: Mellisa Andrea Batallès, Simon Wiskowski, Noah Yaghoubian

Morton Gould Young Composer Awards: Timothy Andres, Emily Bear, Yuri Boguinia, Ryan Brown, Paul Dooley, Sean Friar, Judd Greenstein, Eric Guinivan, Trevor Gureckis, Andrew Hsu, Evan Johnson, Elizabeth A. Kelly, Martin Kennedy, Angel Lam, Jane Lange, Wei-Chieh Lin, Javier Jimmy Lopez, Paula Matthusen, Missy Mazzoli, Eric Nathan, Douglas Pew, Thomas Reeves, Chris Rogerson, Natasha Sinha, Kenneth David Stewart, Conrad Tao, Siddarth Viswanathan, Zachary Wadsworth, Daniel Wohl, Cynthia Wong

Rudolf Nissim Prize: Jack Jarrett

Rudy Perez Songwriting Scholarship: Raquel Borges

Joan & Irwin Robinson Scholarship: Kevin Dalias

David Rose Scholarship: Jeff Kryka

Vanguard Award: Gonzalo Rubalcaba

Young Jazz Composer Awards sponsored by the Gibson Foundation: Roy Assaf, Sharel Cassity, Michael Dease, Jesse Elder, Quamon Fowler, Ross Garren, Tyler Gilmore, Nicholas Grondin, Alex Heitlinger, Bryson Kern, Pascal Le Boeuf, Remy Le Boeuf, Ben Markley, Linda Oh, Rick Parker, Joshua Richman, Sherisse Rogers, Kendrick Scott, Jaleel Shaw, Stephen Smith, Omar Thomas

AUDELCO AWARDS - THE "VIVS"

November 17, 2008; Harlem Stages/Aaron Davis Hall – Marion Anderson Theatre; 36th annual. Presented for excellence in Black Theatre for the 2007–2008 season by the Audience Development Committee, created by Vivian Robinson. Co-Chairs: Maurice Hines and Melba Moore.

Outstanding Dramatic Production of the Year: *The First Breeze of Summer* (Signature Theatre Company)

Outstanding Lead Actor: Ty Jones, *Emancipation* (Classical Theatre of Harlem)

Outstanding Lead Actress: Leslie Uggams, *The First Breeze of Summer* (Signature Theatre Company)

Outstanding Supporting Actor: (tie) Victor Dickerson, *Queens of Heart* (Theatre for the New City); John Earl Jelks, *The First Breeze of Summer* (Signature Theatre Company)

Outstanding Supporting Actress: Yaya DaCosta, *The First Breeze of Summer* (Signature Theatre Company)

Outstanding Musical Production of the Year: *Fela! A New Musical* (37 Arts/Handel-Gabay Productions)

Outstanding Performance in a Musical/Female: Vickilyn Reynolds, *Hattie…What I Need You to Know!*

Outstanding Performance in a Musical/Male: Sahr Ngaujab, *Fela! A New Musical* (37 Arts/Handel-Gabay Productions)

Outstanding Director/Dramatic Production: (tie) Ruben Santiago-Hudson, *The First Breeze of Summer* (Signature Theatre Company); Eric Coleman, *Josh: Black Babe Ruth Satchel Requiem for Racism* (New Federal Theatre)

Outstanding Ensemble Performance: Kenneth D. Alston, Ramone Diggs, Phumizile Sojola, *Three Mo' Tenors* (Little Shubert Theatre)

Outstanding Solo Performance: Petronia Paley, *On the Way to Timbuktu* (Ensemble Studio Theatre)

Outstanding Musical Director: Aaron Johnson, *Fela! A New Musical* (37 Arts/Handel-Gabay Productions)

Outstanding Set Design: Michael Carnahan, *The First Breeze of Summer* (Signature Theatre Company)

Outstanding Costume Design: Karen Perry, *The First Breeze of Summer* (Signature Theatre Company)

Outstanding Lighting Design: Marcus Doshi, *The First Breeze of Summer* (Signature Theatre Company)

Outstanding Sound Design: Robert Kaplowitz, *Fela! A New Musical* (37 Arts/Handel-Gabay Productions)

Outstanding Playwright: Leslie Lee, *The First Breeze of Summer* (Signature Theatre Company)

BARRYMORE AWARDS

October 6, 2008; Crystal Tea Room at the Wannamaker Building; 14th annual. Presented by the Theatre Alliance of Greater Philadelphia for excellence in theatre in the greater Philadelphia area for the 2007-2008 season.

Outstanding Production of a Play: *Six Characters in Search of an Author* (The People's Light & Theatre Company)

Outstanding Production of a Musical: *Les Misérables* (Walnut Street Theatre)

Outstanding Direction of a Play: Dan Kern, *Skylight* (Lantern Theater Company)

Outstanding Direction of a Musical: Terrence J. Nolen, *Assassins* (Arden Theatre Company)

Outstanding Musical Direction: Eric Ebbenga, *Assassins* (Arden Theatre Company)

Outstanding Leading Actor in a Play: Jeb Kreager, *Frozen* (InterAct Theatre Company)

Outstanding Leading Actress in a Play: Geneviève Perrier, *Skylight* (Lantern Theater Company)

Outstanding Leading Actor in a Musical: Hugh Panaro, *Les Misérables* (Walnut Street Theatre)

Outstanding Leading Actress in a Musical: Kim Carson, *Hedwig and the Angry Inch* (Azuka Theatre)

Outstanding Supporting Actor in a Play: Triney Sandoval, *Eurydice* (The Wilma Theater)

Outstanding Supporting Actress in a Play: Lee Ann Etzold, *The Happiness Lecture* (Philadelphia Theatre Company)

Outstanding Supporting Actor in a Musical: Scott Greer, *Assassins* (Arden Theatre Company)

Outstanding Supporting Actress in a Musical: Christina DeCicco, *Les Misérables* (Walnut Street Theatre)

Outstanding Set Design: Beowulf Boritt, *Art* (Delaware Theatre Company)

Outstanding Lighting Design: Joshua Schulman, *Art* (Delaware Theatre Company)

Outstanding Costume Design: Richard St. Clair, *Sleeping Beauty* (Arden Theatre Company)

Outstanding Sound Design: Christopher Colucci, *Suburban Love Songs* (1812 Productions)

Outstanding Original Music: Toby Twining, *Eurydice* (The Wilma Theater)

Outstanding Choreography/Movement: Karen Getz, *Suburban Love Songs* (1812 Productions)

Outstanding New Play: *Wittenberg* by David Davalos (Arden Theatre Company)

Outstanding Ensemble in a Play: *Suburban Love Songs* (1812 Productions)

Outstanding Ensemble in a Musical: *The World Goes 'Round* (11th Hour Theatre Company)

F. Otto Haas Award for Emerging Philadelphia Theatre Artist: Matt Pfeiffer

Excellence in Theatre Education/Community Service Prize: PASSPORT Theater Residency Program at the Philadelphia Theatre Company

Lifetime Achievement Honoree: Dolly Beechman Schnall

Ted & Stevie Wolf Award for New Approaches to Collaborations: Arden Theatre Company & Christ Church (*Our Town in Old City*)

BAY AREA THEATRE CRITICS CIRCLE AWARDS

Founded in 1977. Presented by members of the print and electronic media for outstanding achievement in theatre in the San Francisco Bay Area for the 2008 calendar year.

Theatres Over 300 Seats - Drama

Entire Production: *Uncle Vanya* (California Shakespeare Theater)

Principal Performance, Female: Pamela Reed, *Curse of the Starving Class* (American Conservatory Theater)

Principal Performance, Male: Dan Hiatt, *Uncle Vanya* (California Shakespeare Theater)

Supporting Performance, Female: Phoebe Moyer, *The Foreigner* (San Jose Repertory Theatre)

Supporting Performance, Male: Andy Murray, *Uncle Vanya* (California Shakespeare Theater)

Director: Timothy Near, *Uncle Vanya* (California Shakespeare Theater)

Set Design: Loy Arcenas, *Curse of the Starving Class* (American Conservatory Theater)

Costume Design: (tie) Anna R. Oliver, *Dr. Jekyll and Mr. Hyde* (San Jose Repertory Theatre); Beaver Bauer, *The Government Inspector* (American Conservatory Theater)

Lighting Design: Japhy Weideman, *Curse of the Starving Class* (American Conservatory Theater)

Sound Design: Jeff Mockus, *Uncle Vanya* (California Shakespeare Theater)

Specialties (Fight choreographer, video, music directors, original score): Marcus Shelby (musical director/original score), *Sonny's Blues* (Word for Word in association with Lorraine Hansberry Theatre)

Original Script: Itamar Moses, *Yellowjackets* (Berkeley Repertory Theatre)

Solo Performance: Nilaja Sun, *No Child…* (Berkeley Repertory Theatre)

Ensemble: *Sonny's Blues* (Word for Word in association with Lorraine Hansberry Theatre)

Theatres Over 300 Seats - Musicals

Entire Production: *Caroline, of Change* (TheatreWorks)

Principal Performance, Female: Beth Glover, *Grey Gardens* (TheatreWorks)

Principal Performance, Male: Shane Partlow, *The Will Rogers Follies* (Diablo Light Opera)

Supporting Performance, Female: Allison Blackwell, *Caroline, of Change* (TheatreWorks)

Supporting Performance, Male: (tie) Julian Hornik, *Caroline, of Change* (TheatreWorks); Paul Myrvold, *Grey Gardens* (TheatreWorks)

Director: Robert Kelley, *Caroline, of Change* (TheatreWorks)

Music Director: William Liberatore, *Caroline, of Change* (TheatreWorks)

Set Design: J.B. Wilson, *Caroline, of Change* and *Grey Gardens* (TheatreWorks)

Costume Design: Fumiko Bielefeldt, *Caroline, of Change* (TheatreWorks)

Lighting Design: Pamela Grey, *Grey Gardens* (TheatreWorks)

Sound Design: no award presented this season in this category

Original Script: no award presented this season in this category

Specialties (Fight choreographer, video, music directors, original score): Sheri Stockdale (choreographer), *The Will Rogers Follies* (Diablo Light Opera)

Solo Performance: Mark Nadler, *Russian on the Side* (Produced by Joe Watson at Marines Memorial Theatre)

Ensemble: *Caroline, of Change* (TheatreWorks), *Merrily We Roll Along* (TheatreWorks)

Touring Production: *The Drowsy Chaperone* (Best of Broadway)

Theatres 100 – 300 Seats - Drama

Entire Production: *The Best Man* (Marin Theatre Company)

Principal Performance, Female: Susie Damilano, *Bug* (SF Playhouse)

Principal Performance, Male: Andy Murray, *The Seafarer* (Marin Theatre Company)

Supporting Performance, Female: (tie) Christine Macomber, *The Cocktail Hour* (Ross Valley Players); Velina Brown, *Abraham Lincoln's Big Gay Dance Party* (SF Playhouse)

Supporting Performance, Male: (tie) Julian Lopez-Morillas, *The Seafarer* (Marin Theatre Company); Warren David Keith, *The Devil's Disciple* (Aurora Theatre Company)

Director: Mary Ann Rodgers, *The Cocktail Hour* (Ross Valley Players)

Set Design: J.B. Wilson, *The Seafarer* (Marin Theatre Company)

Costume Design: Anna R. Oliver, *The Devil's Disciple* (Aurora Theatre Company)

Lighting Design: Jon Tracy, *Bug* (SF Playhouse)

Sound Design: Cliff Caruthers, *Bug* (SF Playhouse)

Specialties (Fight choreographer, video, music directors, original score): Chris Houston (music composer), *Abraham Lincoln's Big Gay Dance Party* (SF Playhouse)

Original Script: Aaron Loeb, *Abraham Lincoln's Big Gay Dance Party* (SF Playhouse)

Solo Performance: no award presented this season in this category

Ensemble: *The Best Man* (Aurora Theatre Company)

Theatres 100 – 300 Seats - Musicals

Entire Production: *The Musical of Musicals (The Musical!)* (Center Repertory Company of Walnut Creek)

Principal Performance, Female: Lauren English, *Cabaret* (SF Playhouse)

Principal Performance, Male: Mike Farrell, *The Musical of Musicals (The Musical!)* (Center Repertory Company of Walnut Creek)

Supporting Performance, Female: Karen Grassle, *Cabaret* (SF Playhouse)

Supporting Performance, Male: Louis Parnell, *Cabaret* (SF Playhouse)

Director: Mindy Cooper, *The Musical of Musicals (The Musical!)* (Center Repertory Company of Walnut Creek)

Musical Director: Brandon Adams, *The Musical of Musicals (The Musical!)* (Center Repertory Company of Walnut Creek)

Set Design: Robert Broadfoot, *The Musical of Musicals (The Musical!)*

Costume Design: Cassandra Carpenter, *The Musical of Musicals (The Musical!)*

Lighting Design: Kurt Landisman, *The Musical of Musicals (The Musical!)*

Sound Design: Will McCandless, *Jacques Brel Is Alive and Well and Living in Paris* (Marin Theatre Company)

Specialties (Fight choreographer, video, music directors, original score): Stephanie Temple (choreography), *Zanna, Don't!* (New Conservatory Theatre Center)

Original Script: no award presented this season in this category

Solo Performance: no award presented this season in this category

Ensemble: *Zanna, Don't!* (New Conservatory Theatre Center)

Theatres Under 99 Seats - Drama

Entire Production: *Victims of Duty* (Cutting Ball Theater)

Performance, Female: Joyce Henderson, *Ladies of the Camellias* (Off Broadway West Theatre Company)

Performance, Male: Liam Vincent, *Dead Mother or Shirley Not All in Vain* (Thick Description)

Director: Joyce Henderson, *The Taming of the Shrew* (Off Broadway West Theatre Company)

Original Script: Susan Jackson, *Blessing Her Hearst* (part of the Marin Fringe Fall 2008 Program One at Dominican University)

Solo Performance: Andrew Nance, *I Am My Own Wife* (New Conservatory Theatre Center)

Ensemble: *Ladies of the Camellias* (Off Broadway West Theatre Company)

Theatres Under 99 Seats - Musicals

Entire Production: *In This House* (Playhouse West)

Performance, Female: Lynda DiVito, *In This House* (Playhouse West)

Performance, Male: Sean Owens, *Vera Wilde* (Shotgun Players)

Director: Lois Grandi, *In This House* (Playhouse West)

Musical Director: (tie) Dave Dobrusky, *In This House* (Playhouse West); Tim Hanson, *Thrill Me* (New Conservatory Theatre Center – Walker Theatre)

Specialties (Fight choreographer, video, music directors, original score): (tie) Chris Jeffries (original score) and Lisa Clark (set designer), *Vera Wilde* (Shotgun Players)

Ensemble: *Vera Wilde* (Shotgun Players)

Special Awards

Paine Knickerbocker Award: Robert Cole (Cal Performances)

Barbara Bladen Porter Award: Dan Hiatt

Gene Price Award: Debbie Chin (Executive Director, California Shakespeare Theater); Charles Zukow (Bay Area publicist)

BISTRO AWARDS

April 28, 2009; Gotham Comedy Club; 24th annual. Presented by *Back Stage* for outstanding achievement in the cabaret field; Winners selected by a committee consisting of Elizabeth Ahlfors (*Cabaret Scenes*), David Finkle (*Back Stage's* "Bistro Bits" columnist), Rob Lester (*Cabaret Scenes* & *TalkinBroadway.com*), Erv Raible (Executive/Artistic Director of the Cabaret Conference – Yale University), Roy Sander (former "Bistro Bits" columnist) and Sherry Eaker (*Back Stage* Editor at Large); Produced by Sherry Eaker; Originally created by the late *Back Stage* cabaret critic Bob Harrington.

Outstanding Vocalists: Euan Morton (Metropolitan Room) and Susan Winter (Metropolitan Room)

Outstanding Jazz Vocalist: Laurel Massé (Birdland and Metropolitan Room)

Outstanding Debut: Deb Berman (Metropolitan Room)

Ira Eaker Special Achievement Award: Kim Smith (Don't Tell Mama, Joe's Pub, Duo Theatre)

Outstanding Major Engagement: Amanda McBroom (Metropolitan Room)

BMI Award for Outstanding Songwriter/Entertainer: Julie Gold (The Duplex)

ASCAP Award for Outstanding CD: Carol Hall, *Hallways: The Songs of Carol Hall*

Outstanding Vocal Group: Uptown Express (Metropolitan Room)

Outstanding Duo: Alison Fraser & Mary Testa, *Together Again: The Songs of Rusty Magee* (Laurie Beechman Theatre at the West Bank Café)

Outstanding Theme Show: *Tapestry Rewoven – A Jazz Re-imagining of the Carole King Classic*, conceived and performed by Karen Kohler, directed by John-Richard Thompson, musical direction by Doug Oberhamer, arrangements by Tom Nazziola, Doug Oberhamer, and Karen Kohler (Zipper Factory Theatre)

Outstanding Tribute Show: Liz McCartney, *Rosemary & Time: A Musical Tribute to the Life of Rosemary Clooney* ((Laurie Beechman Theatre at the West Bank Café)

Outstanding Revue: *Nashville* co-starring Daryl Glenn and Jo Lynn Burks, music direction and arrangements by Jo Lynn Burks, directed and choreographed by Vince DeGeorge (Metropolitan Room)

Outstanding Lounge Entertainer: Brian Nash (The Duplex)

Outstanding Burlesque/Vaudeville Act: Narcisster (Joe's Pub)

Outstanding Series: Opening Doors Theatre Company's Closing Notice Series; Susanne Adams, Artistic and Managing Director; Hector Coris, Associate Artistic and Marketing Director (The Duplex)

Outstanding Director: Lennie Watts

Outstanding Technical Director: Lisa Moss (The Duplex)

Special Awards: Robert Kimball (for preserving, documenting and celebrating the Great American Songbook); Joseph Macchia (for his *Cabaret Cares* benefit series)

Enduring Artistry Award: Liza Minnelli

Bob Harrington Lifetime Achievement Award: Charles Aznavour

BROADWAY.COM AUDIENCE AWARDS

May 22, 2009; 10th annual. The Broadway.com Audience Awards give real theatergoers a chance to honor their favorite Broadway and Off-Broadway shows and performers.

New Broadway Musical: *Billy Elliot The Musical*

New Broadway Play: *God of Carnage*

Broadway Musical Revival: *Hair*

Broadway Play Revival: *Equus*

New Off-Broadway Musical: *Saved the Musical*

New Off-Broadway Play: *reasons to be pretty*

Leading Actor in a Broadway Musical: Gavin Creel, *Hair*

Leading Actress in a Broadway Musical: Alice Ripley, *Next to Normal*

Leading Actor in a Broadway Play: Daniel Radcliffe, *Equus*

Leading Actress in a Broadway Play: Jane Fonda, *33 Variations*

Featured Actor in a Broadway Musical: Aaron Tveit, *Next to Normal*

Featured Actress in a Broadway Musical: Karen Olivo, *West Side Story*

Featured Actor in a Broadway Play: Patrick Wilson, *All My Sons*

Featured Actress in a Broadway Play: Angela Lansbury, *Blithe Spirit*

Diva Performance: Sutton Foster, *Shrek The Musical*

Solo Performance: Lorenzo Pisoni, *Humor Abuse*

Onstage Pair: Gavin Creel and Will Swenson, *Hair*

Ensemble Cast: *[title of show]*: Hunter Bell, Jeff Bowen, Susan Blackwell, Heidi Blickenstaff

Breakthrough Performance (Male): Daniel Radcliffe, *Equus*

Breakthrough Performance (Female): Kerry Ellis, *Wicked*

Replacement (Male): Hunter Parrish, *Spring Awakening*

Replacement (Female): Laura Osnes, *South Pacific*

New Broadway Song: "Get Out and Stay Out," *9 to 5: The Musical*

Long-Running Broadway Show: *Wicked*

Long-Running Off-Broadway Show: *Altar Boyz*

CARBONELL AWARDS

April 6, 2009; Broward Center for the Performing Arts – Amaturo Theatre; 33rd annual. Presented for outstanding achievement in South Florida theater during the 2008 calendar year.

Regional Awards

Best New Work: *Dirty Business* by William Mastrosimone (Florida Stage)

Best Ensemble: *Two Sisters and a Piano* (The Promethean Theatre)

Best Production of a Play: *The Seafarer* (Mosaic Theatre Company)

Best Director of a Play: Richard Jay Simon, *The Seafarer* (Mosaic Theatre Company)

Best Actor in a Play: Gregg Weiner, *The Seafarer* (Mosaic Theatre Company)

Best Actress in a Play: Elizabeth Dimon, *Souvenir* (Palm Beach Dramaworks)

Best Supporting Actor in a Play: Dennis Creghan, *The Seafarer* (Mosaic Theatre Company)

Best Supporting Actress in a Play: Kim Morgan Dean, *A Body of Water* (Mosaic Theatre Company)

Best Production of a Musical: *Adding Machine* (GableStage)

Best Director of a Musical: Joseph Adler, *Adding Machine* (GableStage)

Best Actor in a Musical: Oscar Cheda, *Adding Machine* (GableStage)

Actress in a Musical: Maribeth Graham, *Adding Machine* (GableStage)

Best Supporting Actor in a Musical: Jim Ballard, *Adding Machine* (GableStage)

Best Supporting Actress in a Musical: Stacy Schwartz, *Adding Machine* (GableStage)

Best Musical Direction: Eric Alsford, *Adding Machine* (GableStage)

Best Choreography: Ron DeJesus, *The Full Monty* (Maltz Jupiter Theatre)

Best Scenic Design: Sean McClelland, *The Seafarer* (Mosaic Theatre Company)

Best Lighting Design: Sevim Abaza, *4.48 Psychosis* (The Naked Stage)

Best Costume Design: Erin Amico, *Souvenir* (Palm Beach Dramaworks)

Best Sound Design: Marty Mets, *4.48 Psychosis* (The Naked Stage)

George Abbott Award for Outstanding Achievement in the Arts: David Arisco, Artistic Director of Actors' Playhouse at the Miracle Theater

Stock–Roadshow Awards

Best Production: *Sweeney Todd, The Demon Barber of Fleet Street* (Broadway Across America at the Adrienne Arsht Center for the Performing Arts of Miami-Dade County

Best Actor: Jim Brochu, *Zero Hour* (Broward Stage Door Theatre)

Best Actress: Judy Kaye, *Sweeney Todd, The Demon Barber of Fleet Street* (Broadway Across America at the Adrienne Arsht Center for the Performing Arts of Miami-Dade County

Best Supporting Actor: Julian Gamble, *Twelve Angry Men* (Broadway Across America at the Broward Center for the Performing Arts)

Best Supporting Actress: Nancy Opel, *The Drowsy Chaperone* (Broadway Across America at the Broward Center for the Performing Arts)

CONNECTICUT CRITICS' CIRCLE AWARDS

June 15, 2009; 19th annual. Presented for outstanding achievement in Connecticut theater, selected by statewide reviews, feature writers, columnists, and broadcasters, for 2008–2009 season.

Outstanding Production of a Play: *Dividing the Estate* by Horton Foote (Hartford Stage)

Outstanding Production of a Musical: *Big River* by Roger Miller (Goodspeed Musicals)

Outstanding Actress in a Play: Andrea Maulella, *Tryst* (Westport Country Playhouse)

Outstanding Actor in a Play: Colman Domingo, *Coming Home* (Long Wharf Theater)

Outstanding Actress in a Musical: Kristen Martin, *42nd Street* (Goodspeed Musicals)

Outstanding Actor in a Musical: Russell Joel Brown, *Big River* (Goodspeed Musicals)

Outstanding Direction of a Play: Michael Wilson, *Dividing the Estate* (Hartford Stage)

Outstanding Direction of a Musical: (tie) Semina De Laurentis, *The Producers* (Seven Angels Theater); Rob Ruggiero, *Big River* (Goodspeed Musicals)

Outstanding Choreography: Rick Conant, *42nd Street* (Goodspeed Musicals)

Outstanding Set Design: Michael Schweikardt, *Big River* (Goodspeed Musicals)

Outstanding Lighting Design: Robert Wiertzel, *Of Mice and Men* (Westport Country Playhouse)

Outstanding Costume Design: Ilona Somogyi, *Passion Play* (Yale Repertory Theater)

Outstanding Sound Design: David Levy, *Around the World in 80 Days* (Westport Country Playhouse)

Outstanding Ensemble Performance: Donnetta Lavinia Grays, Lizan Mitchell, Portia, Anthony Mark Stockard *No Child...* (TheaterWorks)

Outstanding Touring Production: *Marilyn: Forever Blonde* (Ivoryton Playhouse)

Outstanding Debut Awards: Donnetta Lavinia Grays, *No Child...* (TheaterWorks); Olivia Scott, *To Kill a Mockingbird* (Hartford Stage)

Tom Killen Memorial Award: Rob Ruggiero

Special Achievement Award: Elizabeth Helitzer and Mark Parenti, *Around the World in 80 Days* (Westport Country Playhouse)

CRAIG NOEL AWARDS

January 26, 2009; Museum of Contemporary Art; 7th annual. Presented by the San Diego Theatre Critics Circle for outstanding achievement in the greater San Diego theatre in the 2008 calendar year.

New Play: *In This Corner* by Steven Drukman (The Old Globe)

New Musical: *Memphis* (La Jolla Playhouse)

Dramatic Production: *Fences* (Cygnet Theatre)

Musical Production: (tie) *Dreamgirls* (Sand Diego Musical Theatre); *Xanadu* (La Jolla Playhouse)

Direction of a Play: Delicia Turner Sonnenberg, *Fences* (Cygnet Theatre)

Direction of a Musical: (tie) Sean Murray, *A Little Night Music* (Cygnet's Old Town Theatre); *Les Misérables* (Moonlight Stage Productions)

Choreography: Bill T. Jones, *The Seven* (La Jolla Playhouse)

Orchestrations: Larry Hochman, *Dancing in the Dark* (The Old Globe)

Lead Performance in a Play, Female: (tie) Sylvia M'Lafi Thompson, *Fences* (Cygnet Theatre); Amanda Sitton, *Golden Boy* (New Village Arts)

Lead Performance in a Play, Male: (tie) Antonio T.J. Johnson, *Fences* (Cygnet Theatre); Tom Andrew (body of work for *Terra Nova*, *It's a Wonderful Life: A Radio Play*, and *Night Sky*)

Featured Performance in a Play, Female: (tie) Jo Anne Glover, *The Receptionist* (Cygnet Theatre); Rachael VanWormer, *Bash* (Ion Theatre) & *Corpus Christi* (Diversionary Theatre)

Featured Performance in a Play, Male: (tie) Manny Fernandes, *Golden Boy* (New Village Arts); Bobby Plasencia, *Water & Power* (San Diego Repertory Theatre

Lead Performance in a Musical, Female: Deborah Smith, *The Light in the Piazza* (Lamb's Player's Theatre)

Lead Performance in a Musical, Male: Chad Kimball, *Memphis* (La Jolla Playhouse)

Featured Performance in a Musical, Female: Lillias White, *The Princess and the Black-Eyed Pea* (San Diego Repertory Theatre)

Featured Performance in a Musical, Male: (tie) Tony Houck, *Scrooge in Rouge* (Diversionary Theatre); Patrick Page, *Dancing in the Dark* (The Old Globe); Tonex, *Dreamgirls* (San Diego Musical Theatre) & *The Princess and the Black-Eyed Pea* (San Diego Repertory Theatre)

Ensemble: *Fences* (Cygnet Theatre)

Solo Performance: Linda Libby, *Request Programme* (Ion Theatre)

Touring Production: *Spring Awakening* (Broadway San Diego)

Set Design: Derek McLane, *33 Variations* (LaJolla Playhouse)

Lighting Design: David Lander, *33 Variations* (LaJolla Playhouse)

Costume Design: (tie) Jennifer Brawn Gittings, *Scrooge in Rouge* (Diversionary Theatre); Anna Oliver, *The Women* (The Old Globe)

Sound Design: Tim Boyce, *A Streetcar Named Desire* (Ion Theatre)

Lifetime Achievement: Jonathan McMurty (actor); Arthur Wagner (UCSD Department of Theatre & Dance)

Special Achievement: Steve Karo, for restoration effort of the Balboa Theatre

47DRAMATIST GUILD AWARDS

Established in 2000, these awards are presented by the Dramatists Guild of America to outstanding writers at the Dramatists Guild Annual Benefit and Awards Gala. **2009 Winners:**

Elizabeth Hull-Kate Warriner Award (to the playwright whose work deals with social, political or religious mores of the time): *New Jerusalem* by David Ives

Frederick Loewe Award for Dramatic Composition: Tom Kitt for *Next to Normal*

Flora Roberts Award: Polly Pen

Lifetime Achievement: Lanford Wilson

ED KLEBAN AWARD

June 1, 2009; BMI; 19th annual. Presented by New Dramatists in honor of Edward Kleban; award is given annually to both a librettist and a lyricist ($100,000 to each recipient payable over two years); Board of Directors: Andre Bishop, Sheldon Harnick, Richard Maltby Jr., Francis Neuwirth (Treasurer), Alan J. Stein (Secretary), John Weidman, Maury Yeston (President). Judges: Sheldon Harnick, Thomas Z. Shepard and Sherman Yellen.

2009 Winners: Beth Falcone (lyricist); Kait Kerrigan (librettist)

ELLIOT NORTON AWARDS

May 11, 2009; Sanders Theatre at Harvard University; 27th annual. Presented for outstanding contribution to the theater in Boston from April 2008 to March 2009; selected by a Boston Theater Critics Association selection committee comprising of Terry Byrne, Carolyn Clay, Iris Fanger, Louise Kennedy, Joyce Kullhawik, Sandy MacDonald, Robert Nesti, Ed Siegel and Caldwell Titcomb.

Visiting Production: *Wishful Drinking* Written and performed by Carrie Fisher (Hunting Theatre Company)

Outstanding Production, Large Company: *Endgame* (American Repertory Theatre)

Outstanding Production, Midsized Company: *Speech & Debate*, Lyric Stage Company

Outstanding Production, Small Company: *Awake and Sing!* (Sandra Feinstein-Gamm Theatre)

Outstanding Production, Fringe Company: *Look Back in Anger* (Orfeo Group)

Outstanding Musical Production: *Show Boat* (North Shore Music Theatre)

Outstanding Solo Performance: Elizabeth Aspenlieder, *Bad Dates* (Merrimack Repertory Theatre)

Outstanding New Script: *The Oil Thief* by Joyce Van Dyke (Boston Playwrights' Theatre)

Outstanding Director, Large Company: Nicholas Martin, *She Loves Me* and *The Corn Is Green* (Huntington Theatre Company)

Outstanding Director, Midsized Company: Scott Edmiston, *The History Boys* and *The Light in the Piazza* (SpeakEasy Stage Company) and *Cat on a Hot Tin Roof* (Lyric Stage Company of Boston)

Outstanding Director, Small/Fringe Company: Summer L. Williams, *Voyeurs de Venus* (Company One)

Outstanding Actor, Large Company: Fred Sullivan Jr., *As You Like It* (Free Shakespeare, presented by Citi Performing Arts Center) and *Blithe Spirit* (Trinity Repertory Company)

Outstanding Actor, Small/Midsized Company: Will Lyman, *Exits and Entrances* (New Repertory Theatre) and *The Oil Thief* (Boston Playwrights' Theatre)

Outstanding Actress: Large Company: Kate Burton, *The Corn Is Green* (Huntington Theatre Company)

Outstanding Actress, Small/Midsized Company: Marianna Bassham, *Blackbird* (SpeakEasy Stage Company)

Outstanding Ensemble: *The Seafarer* (SpeakEasy Stage Company)

Outstanding Design, Large Company: Francis O'Connor (set and costumes), *Two Men of Florence* (Huntington Theatre Company)

Outstanding Design, Small/Midsize Company: Janie E. Howland (set design), *Eurydice* (New Repertory Theatre) and *The History Boys* (SpeakEasy Stage Company)

Norton Prize for Sustained Excellence: Rick Lombardo, Artistic Director of the New Repertory Theatre

Theatre Hero Award: Joyce Kulhawik

Special Citation: Howard Gotlieb Archival Research Center (Boston University)

Special Award: Paul Benedict (posthumous), accepted by Al Pacino

THE EQUITY AWARDS

St. Clair Bayfield Award Established in 1973 in memory of Equity member St. Clair Bayfield, the Award honors the best performance by an actor in a Shakespearean play in the New York metropolitan area. **2008 Winner:** Stark Sand, *The Tempest* (Classic Stage Company)

Joe A. Callaway Award Established by Equity member Joe A. Callaway in 1989 to encourage participation in the classics and non-profit theatre. **2008 Winners:** Kathryn Meisle and Everett Quinton, *Women Beware Women* (Red Bull Theatre Company)

Clarence Derwent Awards 65th annual; Presented to honor the most promising female and male performers on the New York metropolitan scene. **2009 Winners:** Quincy Tyler Bernstein, *Ruined* (Manhattan Theatre Club); Aaron Tveit, *Next to Normal* (Broadway)

Lucy Jordan Award Established in 1992 to honor the legacy of Lucy Finney Jordan, a former ballerina and chorus "gypsy" who, for many years, was the "face" of Actors' Equity in the Western Region as the Union's Outside Field Rep. The award is given to those who demonstrate a lifetime commitment to the theatre and especially, helping other theatre artists. **2008 Winner:** Christopher Comte (Seattle, Washington)

Rosetta LeNoire Award Established in 1988, the award was named in honor of the actress Rosetta LeNoire, who was also the first recipient, not only because of her body of work in the theatre - and her work with the then titled Actors' Equity Association's Ethnic Minorities Committee - but also for founding the AMAS Repertory Theatre Company. **2008 Winners:** Bethune Theatredanse

Paul Robeson Award Established in 1974 to recognize a person who best exemplified the principles by which Mr. Robeson lived. It was created by donations from members of the acting profession. **2008 Winner:** Sidney Poitier

Richard Seff Award Established in 2003, this annual award is given to a male and female character actor who is 50 years old or older and who has been a member of the Actors' Equity for 25 years or longer, for the best performance in a featured or unfeatured supporting role in a Broadway or Off-Broadway production. **2008 Winners:** Lynn Cohen, *Chasing Manet* (Primary Stages); Roger Robinson, *Joe Turner's Come and Gone* (Lincoln Center Theater on Broadway)

Roger Sturtevant Musical Theatre Award 5th annual; established in 2005 in memory of Roger Sturtevant, a beloved box office treasurer and part-time casting director. This award is presented to Equity Membership Candidates who have demonstrated outstanding abilities in the musical theatre field. **2009 Winners:** Kalyn Hemphill and Aaron Reeder

Patrick Quinn Award 2nd annual; Established in memory of beloved actor, humanitarian, and former AEA President, Patrick Quinn who passed away in September, 2006; presented to a person who has worked tirelessly for the betterment of actors. **2008 Winner:** Alan Eisenberg, former AEA Executive Director

ACCA Award 3rd annual; Presented to an outstanding Broadway chorus. **2008 Winner:** *In the Heights*

Alan Eisenberg Award 2nd annual; created by former AEA Executive Director, this award is presented to an outstanding graduating senior of the University of Michigan Musical Theatre program, Mr. Eisenberg's alma mater. **2008 Winner:** Garen McRoberts

FRED EBB AWARD

December 1, 2008; American Airlines Theatre Penthouse Lounge; 4th annual. The Fred Ebb Award recognizes excellence in musical theatre songwriting, by a lyricist, composer, or songwriting team that has not yet achieved significant commercial success. The award is meant to encourage and support aspiring songwriters to create new works for the musical theatre. The selection panel includes Mitchell S. Bernard, Sheldon Harnick, David Loud, Marin Mazzie, Tim Pinckney, and Arthur Whitelaw. The prize includes a $50,000 award.

2008 Winner: Adam Gwon

Past Recipients: 2005: John Bucchino **2006:** Robert L. Freedman and Steven Lutvak **2007:** Peter Mills

GEORGE FREEDLEY MEMORIAL AWARD

Established in 1968 to honor the late George Freedley, theatre historian, critic, author, and first curator of the New York Public Library Theatre Collection, this award honors a work about live theatre published in or distributed in the United States during the previous year. Presented by authors, publishers and members of the Theatre Library Association. Due to a change in schedule, the winner for 2007 was announced on October 10, 2008.

2007 Winner: Felicia Hardison Londré for *The Enchanted Years of the Stage: Kansas City at the Crossroads of American Theater, 1870-1930*

GEORGE JEAN NATHAN AWARD

With his preamble "it is my object and desire to encourage and assist in developing the art of drama criticism and the stimulation of intelligent playgoing," the late George Jean Nathan provided in his will for a prize known as the George Jean Nathan Award for Dramatic Criticism. The prize consists of the annual net income of half of Mr. Nathan's estate, which "shall be paid to the American who has written the best piece of drama criticism during the theatrical year (July 1 to June 30), whether it is an article, an essay, treatise or book. The award now amounts to $10,000 and in addition, the winner receives a trophy symbolic of, and attesting to, the award. **2008–2009 Winner:** Randy Gener, Senior Editor of *American Theatre*

GLAAD MEDIA AWARDS

New York: March 28, 2009 at the Marriott Marquis; Los Angeles: April 18, 2009 at the Nokia Theatre; 20th annual. Presented by the Gay and Lesbian Alliance Against Defamation for fair, accurate and inclusive representations of gay individuals in the media as a means of eliminating homophobia and discrimination based on gender identity and sexual orientation.

2009 Winners in Theater: New York Theater – Broadway & Off-Broadway: *Wig Out!* by Tarell Alvin McCraney; Outstanding New York Theater – Off-Off-Broadway: *Arias with a Twist* by Joey Arias and Basil Twist; Los Angeles Theater: *Secrets of the Trade* by Jonathan Tolins

GRAMMY AWARDS

February 8, 2009; Staples Center, Los Angeles; 51st annual. Presented by the Recording Academy for excellence in the recording industry for albums released October 1, 2007–September 30, 2008. 2008 Winners in selected categories:

Best Musical Show Album: *In the Heights* (Kurt Deutsch, Alex Lacamoire, Andrés Levin, Lin-Manuel Miranda, Joel Moss & Bill Sherman, producers; Lin-Manuel Miranda, composer/lyricist; Original Broadway Cast starring Lin-Manuel Miranda; released by Razor & Tie Entertainment/Ghostlight Records)

Nominees: *Gypsy* (Time Life); *The Little Mermaid* (Walt Disney Records); *South Pacific* (Masterworks Broadway); *Young Frankenstein* (Decca Broadway)

Best Compilation Soundtrack for Motion Picture, Television, or Other Visual Media: *Juno* (Fox Music/Rhino)

Nominees: *American Gangster* (Def Jam); *August Rush* (Columbia/Sony Music Soundtrax); *Mamma Mia!* (Decca Records); *Sweeney Todd, the Demon Barber of Fleet Street* (Nonesuch Records)

Best Song Written for Motion Picture, Television, or Other Visual Media: "Down to Earth from *Wall-E* (written by Peter Gabriel and Thomas Newman; produced by Walt Disney Records/Pixar)

Nominees: "Ever Ever After" from *Enchanted* (written by Alan Menken & Stephen Schwartz; performed by Carrie Underwood; produced by Walt Disney Records); "Say" from *The Bucket List* (written and performed by John Mayer; produced by Aware/Columbia); "That's How You Know" from *Enchanted* (written by Alan Menken & Stephen Schwartz; performed by Amy Adams; produced by Walt Disney Records); "Walk Hard" from *Walk Hard: The Dewey Cox Story* (written by Judd Apatow, Marshall Crenshaw, Jake Kasdan & John C. Reilly; performed by John C. Reilly; produced by Columbia)

HELEN HAYES AWARDS

April 13, 2009; The Warner Theatre; 25th annual. Presented by the Washington Theatre Awards Society in recognition of excellence in Washington, D.C. for the 2008–2009 season; written by Renee Calarco; directed by Jerry Whiddon; co-produced and designed by Daniel MacLean Wagner; musical direction by George Hummel; co-produced by Linda Levy Grossman.

Outstanding Resident Play: (tie) *Blackbird* (The Studio Theatre); *Twelfth Night* (Shakespeare Theatre Company and McCarter Theatre Center)

Outstanding Resident Musical: *Les Misérables* (Signature Theatre)

Outstanding Lead Actress, Resident Musical: (tie) Natascia Diaz, *ROOMS a Rock Romance* (MetroStage and Geva Theatre Center); Chita Rivera, *The Visit* (Signature Theatre)

Outstanding Lead Actor, Resident Musical: David Margulies, *The Happy Time* (Signature Theatre)

Outstanding Lead Actress, Resident Play: (tie) Lisa Joyce, *Blackbird* (The Studio Theatre); Deidra LaWan Starnes, *Intimate Apparel* (African Continuum Theatre Company)

Outstanding Lead Actor, Resident Play: Ted van Griethuysen, *Major Barbara* (Shakespeare Theatre Company)

Outstanding Supporting Actress, Resident Musical: (tie) Sherri L. Edelen, *Les Misérables* (Signature Theatre); Angelina Kelly, *Ace: The New Musical Adventure* (Signature Theatre)

Outstanding Supporting Actor, Resident Musical: Christopher Bloch, *Les Misérables* (Signature Theatre)

Outstanding Supporting Actress, Resident Play: Helen Carey, *Major Barbara* (Shakespeare Theatre Company)

Outstanding Supporting Actor, Resident Play: Floyd King, *Twelfth Night* (Shakespeare Theatre Company and McCarter Theatre Center)

Outstanding Director, Resident Play: Paata Tsikurishvili, *Romeo and Juliet* (Synetic Theater)

Outstanding Director, Resident Musical: Eric Schaeffer, *Les Misérables* (Signature Theatre)

Outstanding Set Design, Resident Production: Daniel Conway, *Stunning* (Woolly Mammoth Theatre Company)

Outstanding Costume Design, Play or Musical: Catherine Zuber, *Love's Labour's Lost* (The Shakespeare Theatre Company)

Outstanding Costume Design, Resident Production: Marianne Custer, *Alice* (Round House Theatre)

Outstanding Lighting Design, Resident Production: Chris Lee, *Kiss of the Spider Woman* (Signature Theatre)

Outstanding Sound Design, Resident Production: Matthew M. Nielson, *1984* (Catalyst Theatre Company)

Outstanding Musical Direction, Resident Production: Jon Kalbfleisch, *Les Misérables* (Signature Theatre)

Outstanding Choreography: Irina Tsikurishvili, *Carmen* (Synetic Theater)

Outstanding Ensemble, Resident Musical: *Les Misérables* (Signature Theatre)

Outstanding Ensemble, Resident Play: *Romeo and Juliet* (Synetic Theater)

Outstanding Non-Resident Production: *Next to Normal* (Arena Stage)

Outstanding Lead Actress, Non-Resident: (tie) Alice Ripley, *Next to Normal* (Arena Stage); Nilaja Sun, *No Child…* (Woolly Mammoth Theatre Company)

Outstanding Lead Actor, Non-Resident: Stacy Keach, *Frost/Nixon* (Kennedy Center)

Outstanding Supporting Performer, Non-Resident: Aaron Tveit, *Next to Normal* (Arena Stage)

Charles MacArthur Award for Outstanding New Play or Musical: Stefanie Zadravec, *Honey Brown* (Theater J)

John Aniello Award for Outstanding Emerging Theatre Company: Constellation Theatre Company

HENRY HEWES DESIGN AWARDS

December 12, 2008; Sardi's Restaurant; 44th annual. Sponsored by the American Theatre Wing, these awards are presented for outstanding design originating in the U.S. for the 2007–2008 theatre season. The award (formerly known as the Maharam Theatre Design Award up until 1999) is named after the former theatre critic for the *Saturday Review* who passed away July 20, 2006. The awards are selected by a committee comprising of Jeffrey Eric Jenkins (chair), Dan Bacalzo, David Barbour, David Cote, Tish Dace, Glenda Frank, Mario Fratti, and Joan Ungaro.

Scenic Design: Mark Wendland, *Next to Normal* (Second Stage), *Richard III* (Classic Stage Company), and *Unconditional* (LAByrinth Theater Company)

Lighting Design: Donald Holder, *Cyrano de Bergerac* (Broadway), *Les Liaisons Dangereuses* (Broadway: Roundabout Theatre), and *South Pacific* (Broadway: Lincoln Center Theater)

Costume Design: Katrina Lindsay, *Les Liaisons Dangereuses* (Broadway: Roundabout Theatre)

Notable Effects: Jim Findlay and Jeff Sugg (projections), *The Slug Bearers of Kayrol Island* (Vineyard Theatre)

IRNE AWARDS

April 6, 2009; Boston Center for the Arts. Founded in 1997 by Beverly Creasey and Larry Stark. Presented by The Independent Reviewers of New England for extraordinary theatre in the Boston area during the 2008 calendar year.

Large Theatre

Best New Play: *Boleros for the Disenchanted* by Jose Rivera (Huntington Theatre Company)

Best Musical: *She Loves Me* (Huntington Theatre Company)

Best Play: *A Delicate Balance* (Merrimack Repertory Company)

Best Set Design: Bill Clarke, *A Delicate Balance* (Merrimack Repertory Company)

Best Lighting Design: John Ambrosone, *Blithe Spirit* (Trinity Repertory Theatre) and *A Delicate Balance* (Merrimack Repertory Company)

Best Costume Design: Florence Klotz, *Show Boat* (North Shore Music Theatre)

Best Sound Design: John A. Stone, *Show Boat* (North Shore Music Theatre)

Best Choreography: Michael Lichtefeld, *Bye Bye Birdie* and *42nd Street* (North Shore Music Theatre)

Best Solo Performance: Anna Deavere Smith, *Let Me Down Easy* (American Repertory Theatre)

Best Ensemble: *Show Boat* (North Shore Music Theatre)

Best Actress, Drama or Comedy: Amanda Fulks, *Skylight* (Merrimack Repertory Company)

Best Actor, Drama or Comedy: Jack Davidson, *A Delicate Balance* (Merrimack Repertory Company)

Best Supporting Actress, Drama or Comedy: Penny Fuller, *A Delicate Balance* (Merrimack Repertory Company)

Best Supporting Actor, Drama or Comedy: Ross Bickell, *A Delicate Balance* (Merrimack Repertory Company)

Best Actress, Musical: Bianca Marroquin, *Bye Bye Birdie* (North Shore Music Theatre) and *Chicago* (Broadway Across America – National Tour)

Best Actor, Musical: Eric Kunze, *Joseph and the Amazing Technicolor Dreamcoat* (Reagle Players) and *Whistle Down the Wind* (Citi Performing Arts Center – National Tour)

Best Supporting Actress, Musical: Sharon Wilkins, *Show Boat* (North Shore Music Theatre)

Best Supporting Actor, Musical: Phillip Boykin, *Show Boat* (North Shore Music Theatre)

Best Music Director: Brian Cimmet, *Show Boat* (North Shore Music Theatre)

Best Director, Musical: Nicholas Martin, *She Loves Me* (Huntington Theatre Company)

Best Director, Drama or Comedy: Charles Towers, *A Delicate Balance* (Merrimack Repertory Company)

Best Visiting Production: *The Devil's Music* (Cape Playhouse)

Small Theatre

Best New Play: *According to Tip* by Dick Flavin (New Repertory Theatre)

Best Musical: *The Light in the Piazza* (SpeakEasy Stage Company)

Best Drama or Comedy: *The History Boys* (SpeakEasy Stage Company)

Best Set Design: Susan Zeeman Rogers, *The Light in the Piazza* (SpeakEasy Stage Company)

Best Lighting Design: Karen Perlow, *The Light in the Piazza* (SpeakEasy Stage Company)

Best Costume Design: Stacey Stephens, *Crazy for You* (Fiddlehead Theatre)

Best Sound Design: Benjamin Emerson, *The Seafarer* (SpeakEasy Stage Company)

Best Choreography: Wendy Hall, *Crazy for You* (Fiddlehead Theatre)

Best Solo Performance: Ken Howard, *According to Tip* (New Repertory Theatre)

Best Ensemble: *The History Boys* (SpeakEasy Stage Company)

Best Actress, Drama or Comedy: Michelle Dowd, *Seascape* (Zeitgeist Stage Company)

Best Actor, Drama or Comedy: Diego Arciniegas, *Faith Healer* (Publick Theatre)

Best Supporting Actress, Drama or Comedy: Sonia Maslovskaya, *A Shayna Maidel* (Hovey Players)

Supporting Actor, Drama or Comedy: Karl Baker Olson, *The History Boys* (SpeakEasy Stage Company) and *The Lieutenant of Inishmore* (New Repertory Theatre)

Best Actress, Musical: Amelia Broome, *The Light in the Piazza* (SpeakEasy Stage Company)

Best Actor, Musical: David Costa, *Crazy for You* (Fiddlehead Theatre)

Best Supporting Actress, Musical: Erica Spyres, *The Light in the Piazza* (SpeakEasy Stage Company)

Best Supporting Actor, Musical: Mason Sand, *Assassins* (Company One)

Best Music Director: Jose Delgado, *The Light in the Piazza* (SpeakEasy Stage Company)

Best Director, Musical: Scott Edmiston, *The Light in the Piazza* (SpeakEasy Stage Company)

Best Director, Drama or Comedy: Akiba Abaka, *In the Continuum* (Up You Mighty Race)

Best Promising Performance by a Child Actor: Jimmy Larkin, *Falsettos* (Turtle Lane Playhouse)

Best Visiting Production: *Camp Logan* (African American Theatre Festival-Our Place Theatre)

Special Recognition

Kenneth A. MacDonald Award for Theater Excellence: Joe Antoun of Centastage

ITBA AWARDS

Inaugural Year; Founded by Ken Davenport, the Independent Theater Bloggers Association was created to provide structure to the quickly growing theatrical blogosphere, and give the new media voices a chance to recognize excellence for Broadway, Off-Broadway, and Off-Off Broadway productions. 2009 Members included: Bill Brown (creatingtheater.com), Linda Buchwald (pataphysicalscience.blogspot.com), Donald Butchko (me2ism.blogspot.com), Chris Caggiano (ccagiano.typepad.com), Zack Calhoon (zackcalhoon.blogspot.com), JodiSchoen-brun Carter (off-stage-right.com), Corine Cohen (corinescorner.com), Kevin Daly (theatreaficianado.blogspot.com), Ken Davenport (theproducersperspective.com), Ryan J. Davis (ryanjdavis.blogspot.com), Jeremy Dobrish (JeremysGreenRoom.com), Donell James Foreman (thedjf.blogspot.com), Michael Gilboe (broadwaybullet.com), Diana Glazer (lezbehonest.tumblr.com), Byrne Harrison (stagebuzz.com), Leonard Jacobs (clydefitch.com), Patrick Lee (justshowstogoyou.com), James Marino (broadwaystars.com), Tulis McCall (ushernonsense.com), Jesse North (stagerush.blogspot.com), Aaron Riccio (thatsoundscool.blogspot.com), Sarah Roberts (sarahbsadventures.blogspot.com), Michael Roderick (oneproducerinthecity.typepad.com), Adam Rothenberg (adaumbellesguest.com), David Spencer (ailsesay.com), Ethan Stanislawski (tynansanger.com), Gil Varod (BroadwayAbridged.com), Kim Weild (kimweild.com)

Best Broadway Play: *reasons to be pretty* by Neil LaBute

Best Broadway Musical: *Billy Elliot The Musical* by Elton John and Lee Hall

Best Broadway Revival of a Play: *The Norman Conquests* by Alan Ayckbourn

Best Revival of a Musical: *Hair* by Galt MacDermot, James Rado, and Gerome Ragni

Best Off-Broadway Play: *Ruined* by Lynn Nottage

Best Off-Broadway Musical: *Fela! A New Musical* by Fela Anikulapo Kuti, Jim Lewis, and Bill T. Jones

Best Off-Broadway Revival (Musical or Play): *Our Town* by Thornton Wilder

Best Off-Off Broadway Play: *Universal Robots* by Mac Rogers

Best Off-Off Broadway Unique Theatrical Experience: *Suspicious Package* by Gyda Arber & Aaron Baker

Citation for Excellence in Off-Off Broadway Theatre: Flux Theatre Ensemble

JONATHAN LARSON PERFORMING ARTS FOUNDATION AWARDS

Jonathan Larson's dream was to infuse musical theatre with a contemporary, joyful urban vitality. After 12 years of struggle as a classic "starving artist," his dream came true with the phenomenal success of *Rent*. To celebrate his creative spirit and honor his memory, Jonathan's family and friends created the Jonathan Larson Performing Arts Foundation. The mission of the Foundation is to provide financial support and encouragement to a new generation of musical theatre composers, lyricists and bookwriters, as well as nonprofit theatre companies that develop and produce their work.

2009 Recipients: Mark Allen, Dave Malloy, Thomas Mizer, and Curtis Moore, Ryan Scott Oliver

JOSEPH JEFFERSON AWARDS

Equity Wing Awards

October 20, 2008; North Shore Center for Performing Arts, Skokie, Illinois; 40th annual. Presented for achievement in Chicago Equity theater from August 1, 2007–July 31, 2008; given by the Jefferson Awards Committee. Beginning this year, the Jeff Awards honored the work of Large and Midsize theatres in separate categories for productions and technical elements.

Production – Play – Large: *The Comedy of Errors* (Chicago Shakespeare Theater)

Production – Play – Midsize: *A Steady Rain* (Chicago Dramatists)

Production – Musical – Large: *Les Misérables* (Marriott Theatre)

Production – Musical – Midsize: *The Hunchback of Notre Dame* (Bailiwick Repertory Theatre)

Production – Revue: *Ella* (Northlight Theatre)

Ensemble: *Funk It Up About Nothin'* (Chicago Shakespeare Theater)

Director – Play: Barbara Gaines, *The Comedy of Errors* (Chicago Shakespeare Theater)

Director – Musical: (tie) Jim Corti, *Sweet Charity* (Drury Lane Oakbrook); Dominic Missimi, *Les Misérables* (Marriott Theatre)

Director – Revue: Rob Ruggiero, *Ella* (Northlight Theatre)

New Work: *A Steady Rain* by Keith Huff (Chicago Dramatists)

New Adaptation: Ron West, *The Comedy of Errors* (Chicago Shakespeare Theater)

Solo Performance: Nilaja Sun, *No Child…* (Lookingglass Theatre Company)

Actress in a Principal Role – Play: Lois Smith, *The Trip to Bountiful* (Goodman Theatre)

Actor in a Principal Role – Play: Randy Steinmeyer, *A Steady Rain* by Keith Huff (Chicago Dramatists)

Actress in a Supporting Role – Play: Hallie Foote, *The Trip to Bountiful* (Goodman Theatre)

Actor in a Supporting Role – Play: Mark Ulrich, *Juno and the Paycock* (The Artistic Home)

Actress in a Principal Role – Musical: Summer Naomi Smart, *Sweet Charity* (Drury Lane Oakbrook)

Actor in a Principal Role – Musical: John Cudia, *Les Misérables* (Marriott Theatre)

Actress in a Supporting Role – Musical: Jessie Mueller, *Carousel* (Court Theatre and Long Wharf Theatre)

Actor in a Supporting Role – Musical: Richard Todd Adams, *Les Misérables* (Marriott Theatre)

Actress in a Revue: E. Faye Butler, *Ella* (Northlight Theatre)

Actor in a Revue: James Rank, *The American Dream Songbook* (Next Theatre Company)

Scenic Design – Large: E. David Cosier, *The Trip to Bountiful* (Goodman Theatre)

Scenic Design – Midsize: Kevin Depinet, *Cadillac* (Chicago Dramatists)

Costume Design – Large: Ana Kuzmanic, *The Comedy of Errors* (Chicago Shakespeare Theater)

Costume Design – Midsize: Bill Morey, *Nine* (Porchlight Music Theatre Chicago)

Lighting Design – Large: J.R. Lederle, *The Turn of the Screw* (Writers' Theatre)

Lighting Design – Midsize: Mike Durst, *Requiem for a Heavyweight* (Shattered Globe Theatre)

Sound Design – Large: Barry G. Funderburg, *Carter's Way* (Steppenwolf Theatre)

Sound Design – Midsize: Jack Arky, *Because We Have No Words* (Piven Theatre)

Choreography: Mitzi Hamilton, *Sweet Charity* (Drury Lane Oakbrook)

Original Incidental Music: David Pavkovic, *Nelson Algren: For Keeps and A Single Day* (Lookingglass Theatre Company/Museum of Contemporary Art)

Musical Direction: Doug Peck, *Carousel* (Court Theatre and Long Wharf Theatre)

Fight Choreography: Nick Sandys, *Requiem for a Heavyweight* (Shattered Globe Theatre)

Artistic Specialization: John Musial–Videography, *Nelson Algren: For Keeps and A Single Day* (Lookingglass Theatre Company/Museum of Contemporary Art)

Special Award for Outstanding Achievement: Eileen Boevers, founder of the Apple Tree Theatre

Non-Equity Awards

June 8, 2009; Park West; 36th annual. Formerly called the Citations, the Non-Equity Awards are for outstanding achievement in professional productions which played at Chicago theaters not operating under union contracts from April 1, 2008–March 31, 2009; given by the Jefferson Awards Committee.

Production – Play: *Our Town* (The Hypocrites)

Production – Musical or Revue: *Evita* (Theo Ubique Theatre Company/Michael James)

Ensemble: *In Arabia We'd All Be Kings* (Steep Theatre Company)

Director – Play: David Cromer, *Our Town* (The Hypocrites)

Director – Musical or Revue: Fred Anzevino, *Evita* (Theo Ubique Theatre Company/Michael James)

New Work: Ken Prestininzi, *Beholder* (Trap Door Theatre)

New Adaptation: Katie McLean, *The Mark of Zorro* (Lifeline Theatre)

Actress in a Principal Role – Play: Laura Coover, *Blue Surge* (Eclipse Theatre Company)

Actor in a Principal Role – Play: Esteban Andres Cruz, *Jesus Hopped the 'A' Train* (Raven Theatre)

Actress in a Supporting Role – Play: Mary Redmon, *Enchanted April* (Circle Theatre)

Actor in a Supporting Role – Play: Nathaniel Swift, *Blue Surge* (Eclipse Theatre Company)

Actress in a Principal Role – Musical or Revue: Maggie Portman, *Evita* (Theo Ubique Theatre Company/Michael James)

Actor in a Principal Role – Musical: Chris Damiano, *Evita* (Theo Ubique Theatre Company/Michael James)

Actress in a Supporting Role – Musical or Revue: Amanda Hartley, *The Robber Bridegroom* (Griffin Theatre Company)

Actor in a Supporting Role – Musical or Revue: Chris Damiano, *Jacques Brel's Lonesome Losers of the Night* (Theo Ubique Theatre Company/Michael James)

Solo Performance: Janet Ulrich Brooks, *Golda's Balcony* (Pegasus Players)

Scenic Design: (tie) Alan Donahue, *Mariette in Ecstasy* (Lifeline Theatre); Bob Knuth, *Enchanted April* (Circle Theatre)

Costume Design: Suzanne Mann, *Hay Fever* (Circle Theatre)

Lighting Design: Jared B. Moore, *Touch* (New Leaf Theatre)

Sound Design: (tie) Victoria Delorio, *The Mark of Zorro* (Lifeline Theatre); Joshua Horvath, *Rose and the Rime* (The House Theatre of Chicago)

Choreography: Brenda Didier, *Evita* (Theo Ubique Theatre Company/Michael James)

Original Incidental Music: Kevin O'Donnell, *Rose and the Rime* (The House Theatre of Chicago)

Musical Direction: Ryan Brewster, *Evita* (Theo Ubique Theatre Company/Michael James)

Artistic Specialization: Geoff Coates–Fight Choreography, *The Mark of Zorro* (Lifeline Theatre)

Special Award for Outstanding Achievement: Arlene Crewsdon, founder of Pegasus Players

KENNEDY CENTER

Honors 31st annual; December 7, 2008 (broadcast on CBS December 30, 2008); for distinguished achievement by individuals who have made significant contributions to American culture through the arts: Morgan Freeman, George Jones, Barbra Streisand, Twyla Tharp, Pete Townshend & Roger Daltrey

Mark Twain Prize 11th annual; November 10, 2008 (Broadcast on PBS February 4, 2009); for American humor: George Carlin (posthumously – the announcement was made June 18, 2008, and Carlin passed away June 22)

KEVIN KLINE AWARDS

March 30, 2009; Roberts Orpheum Theatre; 4th annual; Host: Lee Roy Reams. Presented for outstanding achievement in professional theatre in the Greater St. Louis area for the 2006 calendar year; produced by The Professional Theatre Awards Council (Steve Isom, Executive Director); Winners were selected by a floating pool of 45 judges.

Outstanding Production of a Play: *The Little Dog Laughed* (Repertory Theatre of St. Louis)

Outstanding Director of a Play: Rob Ruggiero, *The Little Dog Laughed* (Repertory Theatre of St. Louis)

Outstanding Production of a Musical: *Sarafina!* (The Black Rep)

Outstanding Director of a Musical: Rob Ruggiero, *Ella* (Repertory Theatre of St. Louis)

Outstanding Lead Actress in a Play: Erika Rolfsrud, *The Little Dog Laughed* (Repertory Theatre of St. Louis)

Outstanding Lead Actor in a Play: David Whalen, *The Lieutenant of Inishmore* (Repertory Theatre of St. Louis)

Outstanding Lead Actress in a Musical: Tina Fabrique, *Ella* (Repertory Theatre of St. Louis)

Outstanding Lead Actor in a Musical: (tie) Jeffrey D. Pruett, *Pippin* (Stray Dog Theatre); Lewis J. Stadlen, *The Producers* (The Muny)

Outstanding Supporting Actress in a Play: Colleen Backer, *Morning's at Seven* (Stray Dog Theatre)

Outstanding Supporting Actor in a Play: John Pierson, *The Late Henry Moss* (St. Louis Actors' Studio)

Outstanding Supporting Actress in a Musical: Colleen Backer, *Smoke on the Mountain* (Mustard Seed Theatre)

Outstanding Supporting Actor in a Musical: Christopher Hickey, *Smoke on the Mountain* (Mustard Seed Theatre)

Outstanding Musical Direction: Danny Holgate, *Ella* (Repertory Theatre of St. Louis)

Outstanding Choreography: Keith Tyrone, *Serafina!* (The Black Rep)

Outstanding Costumes Design: Lou Bird, *Thoroughly Modern Millie* (Stages St. Louis)

Outstanding Lighting Design: Thomas Dunn, *The Little Dog Laughed* (Repertory Theatre of St. Louis)

Outstanding Set Design: Adrian W. Jones, *The Little Dog Laughed* (Repertory Theatre of St. Louis)

Outstanding Sound Design: Tori Meyer, *Grace and Glorie* (Insight Theatre Company)

Outstanding Ensemble in a Play: *Grace and Glorie* (Insight Theatre Company)

Outstanding Ensemble in a Musical: *Serafina!* (The Black Rep)

Production for Young Audiences: *Me & Richard 3* (Shakespeare Festival St. Louis)

Outstanding New Play or Musical: Carter W. Lewis, *Evie's Waltz* (Repertory Theatre of St. Louis)

LOS ANGELES DRAMA CRITICS CIRCLE

March 17, 2009; El Portal Theatre; 40th annual; Hosts: Vicki Lewis and Wenzel Jones. Presented for excellence in theatre in the Los Angeles and Orange County during the 2008 calendar year.

Productions: *Anything* (Elephant Theatre Company at the Lillian Theatre); *Gem of the Ocean* (Fountain Theatre); *Louis & Keely Live at the Sahara* (Sacred Fools Theater Company at Sacred Fools and at the Matrix Theatre)

T.H. McCulloh Award for Best Revival: *Of Mice and Men* (Theatre Banshee)

Direction: Jeremy Aldridge, *Louis & Keely Live at the Sahara* (Sacred Fools Theater Company at Sacred Fools and at the Matrix Theatre); Ben Bradley, *Gem of the Ocean* (Fountain Theatre); David Fofi, *Anything* (Elephant Theatre Company at the Lillian Theatre)

Writing: Athol Fugard, *Victory* (Fountain Theatre)

Adaptation: Sean T. Cawelti with Miles Taber and the Rogues, *The Tragical Comedy or Comical Tragedy of Mr. Punch* (Rogue Artists Ensemble at Bootleg Theater)

Musical Direction: Dennis Kaye, *Louis & Keely Live at the Sahara* (Sacred Fools Theater Company at Sacred Fools and at the Matrix Theatre)

Musical Score: Michael Friedman, *Bloody Bloody Andrew Jackson* (Center Theatre Group–Kirk Douglas Theatre); Dolly Parton, *9 to 5: The Musical*, (Center Theatre Group–Ahmanson Theatre)

Choreography: Andy Blankenbuehler, *9 to 5: The Musical* (Center Theatre Group–Ahmanson Theatre); Lee Martino, *Kiss of the Spider Woman* (Havok Theatre Company at Bootleg Theatre)

Lead Performance: Sean Branney, *Of Mice and Men* (Theatre Banshee); Jake Broder, *Louis & Keely Live at the Sahara* (Sacred Fools Theater Company at Sacred Fools and at the Matrix Theatre); Ellen Geer, *Long Day's Journey Into Night* (Theatricum Botanicum); John Glover, *Secrets of the Trade* (the Black Dahlia Theatre); Louis Jacobs, *Anything* (Elephant Theatre Company at the Lillian Theatre); Judy Kaye, *Sweeney Todd, The Demon Barber of Fleet Street* (Center Theatre Group–Ahmanson Theatre)

Featured Performance: JD Cullum, *Don Juan* (A Noise Within); Beth Kennedy, *As U2 Like It* (Troubadour Theater Company at the Falcon Theatre); Sharon Lawrence, *Orson's Shadow* (Pasadena Playhouse); Adolphus Ward, *Gem of the Ocean* (Fountain Theatre)

Ensemble Performance: *Assassins* (West Coast Ensemble at The El Centro Theatre)

Solo Performance: Nilaja Sun, *No Child…* (Center Theatre Group–Kirk Douglas Theatre)

Set Design: Laura Fine Hawkes, *Snake in the Grass* (Salem K Theatre Company at The Matrix Theatre)

Lighting Design: Steven Young, *Thrill Me: The Leopold & Loeb Story* (Havok Theatre Company at the Hudson Backstage Theatre)

Costume Design: Shigeru Yaji, *An Italian Straw Hat: A Vaudeville* (South Coast Repertory)

Sound Design: Ken Rich, *The Common Air* (SoulArt and Elephant C.A.F.E at Theatre Asylum)

CGI/Video Design: Brian White, *The Tragical Comedy or Comical Tragedy of Mr. Punch* (Rogue Artists Ensemble at Bootleg Theater)

Puppet and Mask Design: Joyce Hutter & Patrick Rubio, *The Tragical Comedy or Comical Tragedy of Mr. Punch* (Rogue Artists Ensemble at Bootleg Theater)

Margaret Harford Award (for Sustained Excellence in Theatre):

Fight Choreography: Ned Mochel, *On An Average Day* (VS. Theatre Company at the Elephant Theatre Lab)

Ted Schmitt Award (for outstanding world premiere play in Los Angeles): *Song of Extinction* by E.M. Lewis

Polly Warfield Award (for outstanding single season by a small to mid-sized theatre): Sacred Fools Theater Company

Angstrom Award (for career achievement in lighting design): Lisa D. Katz

Margaret Harford Award (for sustained excellence in theater): Los Angeles Women's Shakespeare Company

Joel Hirschhorn Award (for outstanding achievement in musical theatre): Nick DeGruccio

MAC AWARDS

May 18, 2009; B.B. King's; 23rd annual. Presented by the Manhattan Association of Cabarets and Clubs to honor achievements in cabaret, comedy, jazz, and live entertainment in the previous year.

Female Vocalist: Terese Genecco, *Swingin in the City* & *Last Call* (Metropolitan Room, Iridium, Rrazz Room, Peppermill, The M Bar, Angelica's)

Male Vocalist: Marcus Simeone, *The Heart* (Metropolitan Room)

Major Artist: Klea Blackhurst & Billy Stritch, *Dreaming of a Song: The Music of Hoagy Carmichael* (Metropolitan Room)

Celebrity Artist: Marilyn Maye, *Love on the Rocks* (Metropolitan Room)

New York Debut–Female: Cait Doyle, *Hot Mess in Manhattan* (The Duplex, Don't Tell Mama)

New York Debut–Male: Ben Cherry, *I Hate New York…a love story* (Metropolitan Room)

Musical Comedy Performer/Duo/Group: Shawn Ryan, *Shawn Ryan Live* (Laurie Beechman Theatre)

Vocal Duo or Group: Karen Oberlin & Miles Phillips, *The Pleasure of Your Company* (Metropolitan Room)

Revue/Special Production: *Nashville* by Daryl Glenn & Jo Lyn Burks (Metropolitan Room)

Variety Production/Recurring Series: Joseph Macchia, *Cabaret Cares* at the Laurie Beechman Theatre

Open Mic: Jim Caruso's Cast Party (Birdland)

Piano Bar/Restaurant Singing Entertainer–Female: Anne Steele (Don't Tell Mama, Brandy's)

Piano Bar/Restaurant Singing Entertainer–Male: Eric Pickering (Don't Tell Mama)

Piano Bar/Restaurant Instrumentalist: Tracy Stark (Don't Tell Mama)

Musical Director: Tracy Stark for Karen Black at the Metropolitan Room, Gurland & Farley at the Laurie Beechman, Karen Oberlin & Miles Phillips at the Metropolitan Room

Director: Lennie Watts for the 2008 MAC Awards, Uptown Express, and Judy Kreston at the Metropolitan Room

Technical Director: Jean-Pierre Perreaux for Baby Jane Dexter, Annie Ross & Marilyn Maye at the Metropolitan Room

Jazz Female Vocalist: Laurie Krauz (Enzo's, Metropolitan Room, Laurie Beechman Theatre, The Kitano)

Jazz Male Vocalist: Jack Donahue (Birdland)

Jazz Duo/Singer/Instrumentalist: Daryl Sherman (Cocktail Terrace-Waldorf Astoria, Dizzy's Coca Cola, Enzo's, Shanghai Jazz)

Stand-up Comic–Female: Maureen Langan (Don't Tell Mama)

Stand-up Comic–Male: Rick Younger (Broadway Comedy Club, Laurie Beechman Theatre)

Major Stand-up Comic–Female: Jackie Hoffman

Major Stand-up Comic–Male: Mario Cantone

Comedy/Improv Duo or Group: Chicago City Limits

Recording: *Right Here, Right Now* – Karen Mason

Jazz Recording: *Charmed Life: Shaynee Rainbolt Sings Russell Garcia* – Shaynee Rainbolt

Song: "Come Home" by Mark Janas & Peter Napolitano

Special Musical Material: Carol Hall, *This Is My Birthday*

2009 Board of Directors Awards: Joey Reynolds and Myra Chanin of the *Joey Reynolds Show*; Eva Swann and Vocal Ease

Hanson Award: Will Trice

Time Out New York Special Achievement Award: Poor Baby Bree

Lifetime Achievement Award: Polly Bergen

MARGO JONES CITIZEN OF THE THEATER MEDAL

Presented by the Ohio State University Libraries and College of the Arts to a citizen of the theater who has made a lifetime commitment to the theater in the United States and has demonstrated an understanding and affirmation of the craft of playwriting. The Medal Committee is comprised of Deborah Robison for the family of Jerome Lawrence, Janet Waldo Lee and Lucy Lee for the family of Robert E. Lee, Alan Woods, Mary Taratino, and Nena Couch (from the Jerome Lawrence Institute).

2009 Winner: Bill Rauch (Oregon Shakespeare Festival)

Past Recipients: 1961: Lucille Lortel **1962:** Michael Ellis **1963:** Judith Rutherford Marechal; George Savage (university award) **1964:** Richard Barr; Edward Albee; and Clinton Wilder; Richard A. Duprey (university award) **1965:** Wynn Handman; Marston Balch (university award) **1966:** Jon Jory; Arthur Ballet (university award) **1967:** Paul Baker; George C. White (workshop award) **1968:** Davey Marlin-Jones; Ellen Stewart (workshop award) **1969:** Adrian Hall; Edward Parone and Gordon Davidson (workshop award) **1970:** Joseph Papp **1971:** Zelda Fichandler **1972:** Jules Irving **1973:** Douglas Turner Ward **1974:** Paul Weidner **1975:** Robert Kalfin **1976:** Gordon Davidson **1977:** Marshall W. Mason **1978:** Jon Jory **1979:** Ellen Stewart **1980:** John Clark Donahue **1981:** Lynne Meadow **1982:** Andre Bishop **1983:** Bill Bushnell **1984:** Gregory Mosher **1985:** John Lion **1986:** Lloyd Richards **1987:** Gerald Chapman **1988:** no award **1989:** Margaret Goheen **1990:** Richard Coe **1991:** Otis L. Guernsey Jr. **1992:** Abbot Van Nostrand **1993:** Henry Hewes **1994:** Jane Alexander **1995:** Robert Whitehead **1996:** Al Hirschfield **1997:** George C. White **1998:** James Houghton **1999:** George Keathley **2000:** Eileen Heckart **2001:** Mel Gussow **2002:** Emilie S. Kilgore **2003-2004:** Christopher Durang and Marsha Norman **2005-2006:** Jerome Lawrence and Robert E. Lee **2007-2008:** David Emmes and Martin Benson

MUSICAL THEATER HALL OF FAME

This organization was established at New York University on November 10, 1993. Inductees: Harold Arlen, Irving Berlin, Leonard Bernstein, Eubie Blake, Abe Burrows, George M. Cohan, Betty Comden, Dorothy Fields, George Gershwin, Ira Gershwin, Adolph Green, Oscar Hammerstein II, E.Y. Harburg, Larry Hart, Jerome Kern, Burton Lane, Alan Jay Lerner, Frank Loesser, Frederick Loewe, Mary Martin, Ethel Merman, Cole Porter, Jerome Robbins, Richard Rodgers, Harold Rome.

NATIONAL ARTS CLUB AWARDS
Joseph Kesselring Fellowship and Honors

National Arts Club member Joseph Otto Kesselring was born in New York in 1902. He was an actor, author, producer, and playwright. Mr. Kesselring died in 1967, leaving his estate in a trust, which terminated in 1978 when the life beneficiary died. A bequest was made to the National Arts Club "on condition that said bequest be used to establish a fund to be known as the Joseph Kesselring Fund, the income and principal of which shall be used to give financial aid to playwrights, on such a basis of selection and to such as the National Arts Club may, in its sole discretion, determine." A committee appointed by the president and the governors of the National Arts Club administers the Kesselring Prizes. It approves monetary prizes annually to playwrights nominated by qualified production companies whose dramatic work has demonstrated the highest possible merit and promise and is deserving of greater recognition, but who as yet has not received prominent national notice or acclaim in the theater. The winners are chosen by a panel of judges who are independent of the Club. In addition to a cash prize, the first-prize winner also receives a staged reading of a work of his or her choice. In the fall of 2007, the Club redefined the award to consist of the Kesselring Fellowship, and created a new category called the Kesselring Honors.

2009 Fellowship Winners: Rajiv Joseph and David Adjmi

2009 Honors: Jenny Schwartz and Tarrel Alvin McCraney

Previous Fellowship Recipients: 1980: Susan Charlotte **1981:** Cheryl Hawkins **1982:** No Award **1983:** Lynn Alvarez **1984:** Philip Kan Gotanda **1985:** Bill Elverman **1986:** Marlane Meyer **1987:** Paul Schmidt **1988:** Diane Ney **1989:** Jo Carson **1990:** Elizabeth Egloff, Mel Shapiro **1991:** Tony Kushner **1992:** Marion Isaac McClinton **1993:** Anna Deavere Smith **1994:** Nicky Silver **1995:** Amy Freed, Doug Wright **1996:** Naomi Wallace **1997:** No Award **1998:** Kira Obolensky **1999:** Heather McDonald **2000:** David Auburn **2001:** David Lindsay-Abaire **2002:** Melissa James Gibson **2003:** Bridget Carpenter **2004:** Tracey Scott Wilson **2005:** Deb Margolin **2006:** Mark Schultz **2007:** Jordan

Harrison

Previous Honors Recipients (if year is missing none were presented): **1980:** Carol Lashof **1981:** William Hathaway **1983:** Constance Congdon **1985:** Laura Harrington **1986:** John Leicht **1987:** Januzsz Glowacki **1988:** Jose Rivera, Frank Hogan **1989:** Keith Reddin **1990:** Howard Korder **1991:** Quincy Long, Scott McPherson **1992:** José Rivera **1993:** Han Ong **1996:** Nilo Cruz **1997:** Kira Obolensky, Edwin Sanchez **1998:** Erik Ehn **1999:** Steven Dietz **2000:** Jessica Hagedorn **2001:** Dael Orlandersmith **2002:** Lydia Diamond **2003:** Lynn Nottage **2004:** John Borello **2005:** Tanya Barfield **2006:** Bruce Norris **2007:** Will Eno, Rinne Groff, Marcus Gardley

Medals of Honor

Presented by the National Arts Club for outstanding service in the arts.

2008–2009 Winners: Jeff Koonz (artist); Joyce Carol Oats (author); Norman Jewison (film director)

NATIONAL MEDALS OF THE ARTS

November 17, 2008; East Room at the White House. Presented to individuals who and organizations that have made outstanding contributions to the excellence, growth, support, and availability of the arts in the United States, selected by the President of the United States from nominees presented by the National Endowment of the Arts. **2008 Winners**: Olivia de Havilland (actress, Paris, France); Fisk Jubilee Singers (choral ensemble, Nashville, TN); Ford's Theatre Society, (theater and museum, Washington, DC);Hank Jones (jazz musician, NEA Jazz Master-1989), New York, NY; Stan Lee (comic book writer/producer, Los Angeles, CA); José Limón Dance Foundation (modern dance company and institute, New York, NY);Jesús Moroles (sculptor, Rockport, TX); The Presser Foundation (music patron, Haverford, PA); Richard and Robert Sherman (songwriting team, Los Angeles and London); **2008 Citizen Medals:** Dana Gioia (Chairman, National Endowment for the Arts); Bruce Cole (Chairman, National Endowment for the Humanities), Adair Margo (Chair, President's Committee on the Arts and Humanities), Anne-Imelda M. Radice & Robert S. Martin (current and former Director of the Institute for Museum and Library Services)

NEW DRAMATISTS LIFETIME ACHIEVEMENT AWARD

May 19, 2009; Marriott Marquis; 60th annual. Presented to an individual who has made an outstanding artistic contribution to the American theater. **2009 Winner:** Horton Foote (posthumous)

NEW YORK INNOVATIVE THEATRE AWARDS

September 22, 2008; Haft Auditorium at F.I.T; 4th annual. Presented to honor individuals and organizations who have achieved artistic excellence in Off-Off-Broadway theatre for the 2007-2008 season. The New York IT Awards committee recognizes the unique and essential role Off-Off-Broadway plays in contributing to American and global culture, and believes that publicly recognizing excellence in independent theatre will expand audience awareness and appreciation of the full New York theatre experience. Staff: Jason Bowcutt, Shay Gines, Nick Micozzi, Executive Directors; Awards Committee: Paul Adams (Emerging Artists Theatre), Dan Bacalzo (*TheatreMania.com*), Christopher Borg (Actor/Director), Jason Bowcutt (IT Awards), Tim Errickson (Boomerang Theatre Company), Thecla Farrell (Castillo Theatre), Constance Congdon (Playwright), Shay Gines (New York IT Awards), Ben Hodges (*Theatre World*), Leonard Jacobs (*Back Stage*), Ron Lasko (Spin Cycle P.R.), Blake Lawrence, Bob Lee, Nick Micozzi (IT Awards), Risa Shoup, (chashama), Nicky Paraiso (La MaMa E.T.C.), Jeff Riebe (The January

Initiative), Akia Squiterri (Rising Sun Performance Company).

Outstanding Ensemble: *Fight Girl Battle World* (Vampire Cowboys Theatre Company): Elena Chang, Noshir Dalal, Jon Hoche, Kelley Rae O'Donnell, Melissa Paladino, Maureen Sebastian, Andrea Marie Smith, Paco Tolson, Temar Underwood

Outstanding Solo Performance: Andrea Caban, *You Got Questions? I Got Answers!* (Coyote Rep Theatre Company)

Outstanding Actor in a Featured Role: Rob Sheridan, *The Two Lives of Napoleon Beazley* (Incumbo Theater Company)

Outstanding Actress in a Featured Role: Megan Byrne, *No End of Blame* (Potomac Theatre Project)

Outstanding Actor in a Lead Role: Cameron J. Oro, *The Accidental Patriot* (The Stolen Chair Theatre Company)

Outstanding Actress in a Lead Role: Stephanie Barton-Farcus, *Elizabeth Rex* (Nicu's Spoon)

Outstanding Choreography/Movement: Qui Nguyen, *Fight Girl Battle World* (Vampire Cowboys Theatre Company)

Outstanding Director: Edward Elefterioun, *The Night of Nosferatu* (Rabbit Hole Ensemble)

Outstanding Set Design: Sean Breault, *Art of Memory* (Company SoGoNo)

Outstanding Costume Design: Jessica Wegener, *Fight Girl Battle World* (Vampire Cowboys Theatre Company)

Outstanding Lighting Design: Kevin Hardy, *The Night of Nosferatu* (Rabbit Hole Ensemble)

Outstanding Sound Design: Dan Bianchi, *The Island of Dr. Moreau* (RADIOTHEATRE)

Outstanding Original Music: Dan Bianchi, *The Island of Dr. Moreau* (RADIOTHEATRE)

Outstanding Original Full-Length Script: Bekah Brunstetter, *You May Go Now* (Babel Theatre Project)

Outstanding Original Short Script: Aliza Shane, *The Three Sillies* (Looking Glass Theatre)

Outstanding Performance Art Production: *Removable Parts* (HERE Arts Center)

Outstanding Production of a Musical: *Yank! A New Musical* (The Gallery Players)

Outstanding Production of a Play: *Burn, Crave, Hold: The James Wild Project* (blessed unrest)

Artistic Achievement Award: Judith Malina

Stewardship Award: The New York Theatre Experience (Martin & Rochelle Denton)

Caffe Cino Fellowship Award ($1,000 grant): Boomerang Theatre Company

OTTO RENÉ CASTILLO AWARDS

May 17, 2009; Castillo Theatre All Stars Project; 11th annual. Presented to artists for and theatres from around the world in recognition for contributions to Political Theatre. The Otto Award is named for the Guatemalan poet and revolutionary Otto Rene Castillo, who was murdered by that country's military junta in 1968. **2009 Winners:** Los Angeles Poverty Department; Roadside Theater (Norton, Virginia); Ntozake Shange (playwright); Street Spirits Theatre Company (Prince George, British Columbia Canada); Teatro Visión (San Jose, California)

OVATION AWARDS

November 17, 2008; Harriet & Charles Luckman Fine Arts Complex at Cal State; 19th annual; Host: Neil Patrick Harris. Established in 1989, the L.A. Stage Alliance Ovation Awards are Southern California's premiere awards for excellence in theatre. Winners were selected by a 190 member voting pool of theatre professionals working in the Los Angeles theatre community for productions that played September 1, 2007–August 21, 2008.

Playwrighting for an Original Play: *The Quality of Life* by Jane Anderson (Geffen Playhouse)

Book/Lyrics/Music for an Original Musical: *It's Only Life* conceived by John Bucchino and Daisy Prince, music and lyrics by John Bucchino (Rubicon Theatre Company)

Ray Stricklyn Memorial Award for Solo Performance: Nilaja Sun, *No Child...* (Center Theatre Group–Kirk Douglas Theatre)

Ensemble Performance: Stan Chandler, David Engel, Larry Raben, Darcie Roberts, *The Andrews Brothers* (Music Theatre West)

Director of a Play: Matt Shakman, *Secrets of the Trade* (Black Dahlia Theatre)

Director of a Musical: (tie) Nick DeGruccio, *Jekyll & Hyde* (Cabrillo Music Theatre); Larry Raben, *Singin' in the Rain* (Cabrillo Muisc Theatre)

Choreographer: Bradley Rapier, *City Kid – The Musical* (City Kid Productions LLC)

Musical Direction: Alby Potts, *Singin' in the Rain* (Cabrillo Music Theatre)

Touring Production: *Avenue Q* (Center Theatre Group–Ahmanson Theatre)

Play–Intimate Theatre: *The Quality of Life* by Jane Anderson (Geffen Playhouse)

Play–Large Theatre: *R. Buckminster Fuller: The History (and Mystery) of the Universe* by D.W. Jacobs (Rubicon Theatre Company)

Musical–Intimate Theatre (Franklin R. Levy Memorial Award): *Louis & Keely: Live at the Sahara* (Sacred Fools Theatre Company)

Musical–Large Theatre: *Miss Saigon* (Civic Light Opera of South Bay Cities)

Set Design–Intimate Theatre: Desma Murphy, *And Neither Have I Wings to Fly* (Road Theatre Company)

Set Design–Large Theatre: Thomas S. Giamario, *Bus Stop* (Rubicon Theatre Company)

Costume Design–Intimate Theatre: Scott A. Lane, *Pest Control the Musical* (Open at the Top Productions)

Costume Design–Large Theatre: Paul Tazewell, *Ray Charles Live! – A New Musical* (Pasadena Plahouse)

Lighting Design–Intimate Theatre: Jeremy Pivnick, *Crime and Punishment* (Actors Co-op/Crossley Theatre)

Lighting Design–Large Theatre: (tie) Darrell Clark, *Miss Saigon* (Civic Light Opera of South Bay Cities); Steven Young, *Jekyll & Hyde* (Cabrillo Music Theatre)

Sound Design–Intimate Theatre: Ken Rich, *The Common Air* (Elephant Stageworks)

Sound Design–Large Theatre: John Feinstein, *Miss Saigon* (Civic Light Opera of South Bay Cities)

Lead Actor in a Play: (tie) Joe Spano, *R. Buckminster Fuller: The History (and Mystery) of the Universe* (Rubicon Theatre Company); John Glover, *Secrets of the Trade* (Black Dahlia Theatre)

Lead Actress in a Play: Laurie Metcalf, *The Quality of Life* (Geffen Playhouse)

Lead Actor in a Musical: Robert J. Townsend, *Jekyll & Hyde* (Cabrillo Music Theatre)

Lead Actress in a Musical: Jennifer Paz, *Miss Saigon* (Civic Light Opera of South Bay Cities)

Featured Actor in a Play: Barry Lynch, *Of Mice and Men* (Theatre Banshee)

Featured Actress in a Play: J. Nicole Brooks, *As Much As You Can* (Hendel Productions West/Celebration Theatre)

Featured Actor in a Musical: Randy Rogel, *Singin' in the Rain* (Cabrillo Music Theatre)

Featured Actress in a Musical: Gwen Stewart, *All Shook Up* (Musical Theatre West)

PITTSBURGH CIVIC LIGHT OPERA'S RICHARD RODGERS AWARD

May 9, 2009; Omni William Penn Hotel, Pittsburgh; founded in 1988. Recognizes the lifetime contributions of outstanding talents in musical theatre; Presented by The Pittsburgh Civic Light Opera in conjunction with the families of Richard Rodgers and Oscar Hammerstein II. **2009 Recipient:** Stephen Schwartz

Past Recipients: 1988: Mary Martin **1989:** Dame Julie Andrews **1991:** Harold Prince **1992:** Sir Cameron Mackintosh **1993:** Stephen Sondheim **1996:** Lord Andrew Lloyd Webber **2000:** Gwen Verdon **2002:** Bernadette Peters **2007:** Shirley Jones **2008:** Rob Marshall and Kathleen Marshall

PRINCESS GRACE AWARDS

October 15, 2008; Cipriani on 42nd Street, New York; 24th annual. Presented by the Princess Grace Foundation – USA for excellence in theatre, dance, and film across the United States. **2008 Awards:**

Statue Awards: Rose Bond (media artist) and Alexander T. Hammond (designer and art director); *Awards in Theatre and Playwrighting:* Arin Arbus, Los Angeles (Grace LeVine Theater Award: Directing Fellowship at Theatre for a New Audience); Jaime Castañeda, San Antonio, TX (Gant Gaither Theater Award: Directing Apprenticeship at American Theater Company); Ben Gunderson, Moorhead, MN (Robert and Gloria Houseman Theater Award: Acting Scholarship at North Carolina School of the Arts); Patrick Kennelly, Evanston IL (Pierre Cardin Theater Award: Directing Scholarship at UCLA); Arnulfo Maldonado, Eagle Pass, TX (Fabergé Theater Award: Costume Design Fellowship at Diverse City Theater); Kaneza Schaal, Freestone, CA (Acting Apprenticeship at The Wooster Group); Kara Lee Corthon, Cumberland, MD (Playwrighting Fellowship at New Dramatists); Maureen C. Huskey, Denver, CO (Directing Honoraria at California Institute of the Arts); Thomas Pasculli, Newton, NJ (Acting Honoraria at Double Edge Theatre Productions, Inc); Ashley Sparks, Stuarts Draft, VA (Directing Honoraria at ArtSpot Productions); Damon E. Williams, Havertown, PA (Acting Honoraria at Temple University); *Special Project Awards for Theater:* Rosemary Newcott and Chi Wang Yang; *Works in Progress Award:* Nancy Bannon (dance), Sheila Callaghan (playwrighting), Maureen Tow (theater)

RICHARD RODGERS AWARDS

For staged readings of musicals in nonprofit theaters, administered by the American Academy of Arts and Letters and selected by a jury including Stephen Sondheim (chairman), Lynn Ahrens, John Guare, Sheldon Harnick, David Ives, Richard Maltby Jr., and Lin-Manuel Miranda.

2009 Winners: *Cheer Wars* by Karlan Judd and Gordon Leary; *Rosa Parks* by Scott Ethier and Jeff Hughes

ROBERT WHITEHEAD AWARD

March 10, 2009; Sardi's Restaurant; Founded in 1993. Presented for outstanding achievement in commercial theatre producing, bestowed on a graduate of the fourteen-week Commercial Theater Institute Program who has demonstrated a quality of production exemplified by the late producer, Robert Whitehead. The Commercial Theater Institute (Jed Bernstein, Director) is the nation's only formal program that professionally trains commercial theatre producers. It is a joint project of the League of American Theatres and Producers, Inc., and Theatre Development Fund. **2009 Winner:** Dori Bernstein

Previous Recipients: **1993:** Susan Quint Gallin; Benjamin Mordecai **1994:** Dennis Grimaldi **1995:** Kevin McCollum **1996:** Randall L. Wreghitt **1997:** Marc Routh **1998:** Liz Oliver **1999:** Eric Krebs **2000:** Anne Strickland Squadron **2001–2003:** No Award **2004:** David Binder **2005–2007:** No Award **2008:** Nick Scandalios

SOCIETY OF STAGE DIRECTORS AND CHOREOGRAPHERS (SSDC) AWARDS

Mr. Abbot Award Lifetime achievement honor presented exclusively for directors and choreographers annually. **2009 Recipient:** Donald Saddler

Joe A. Callaway Awards Also known as the "Joey," this award, created in 1989, is issued for excellence in the craft of direction and/or choreography for Off and Off-Off-Broadway. **2008 Winners:** Giovanna Sardelli (Director), *Animals Out of Paper* (Second Stage); Lynne Taylor-Corbett (Choreographer), *Wanda's World* (AMAS Musical Theatre)

STEINBERG DISTINGUISHED PLAYWRIGHT AWARD

October 21, 2008; Loft & Garden at Rockefeller Center; Inaugural Year (to be presented biennially, alternating with the Steinberg Emerging Playwright Award). Created by the Harold and Mimi Steinberg Charitable Trust This, this new award honors an American playwright whose body of work has made significant contributions to the American theater. Nominating and Selection Committee: André Bishop (Artistic Director, Lincoln Center Theater), David Emmes (Producing Artistic Director, South Coast Repertory), Oskar Eustis (Artistic Director, The Public Theater), Polly K. Carl (Producing Artistic Director, Playwrights Center), Martha Lavey (Artistic Director, Steppenwolf Theatre Company), Eduardo Machado (playwright/Artistic Director, INTAR Theatre), and Marc Masterson (Artistic Director, Actors Theatre of Louisville). The winner receives 'The Mimi,' a statue designed by David Rockwell, and a $200,000 cash prize, making it the largest award ever created to honor and encourage artistic achievement in the American Theatre.

2009 Recipient: Tony Kushner

SUSAN SMITH BLACKBURN PRIZE

February 25, 2009; London; 31st annual; Presenter: Sigourney Weaver. Presented to women who have written works of outstanding quality for the English-speaking theater. The Prize is administered in Houston, London, and New York by a board of directors who choose six judges each year. 2008–2009 Judges: Sigourney Weaver, Edward Albee, Peter Gill, Jenny Jules, Emily Mann, Genista McIntosh. The winner receives a $20,000 cash prize and a signed and numbered print by artist Willem de Kooning. The Special Commendation winner receives a $5,000 cash prize, and finalists each receive $1,000.

2009 Winner: Chloë Moss, *This Wide Night* (England)

Special Commendation: Lucinda Cox, *Happy Now?* (England)

Finalists: Anupama Chandrasekhar, *Free Outgoing* (India); Ann Marie Healy, *What Once We Felt* (U.S.); Michele Lowe, *Inana* (U.S.); Elizabeth Meriwether, *Oliver!* (U.S.); Lynn Nottage, *Ruined* (U.S.); Kaite O'Reilly, *The Almond and the Seahorse* (Wales); Amy Rosenthal, *On The Rocks* (England); Esther Wilson, *Ten Tiny Toes* (England)

THEATRE DEVELOPMENT FUND AWARDS

Fred and Adele Astaire Awards

June 1, 2009; Haft Auditorium at F.I.T.; Established in 1982; Host: Alan Cumming. Originally known as the Astaire Awards these awards were founded by the Anglo-American Contemporary Dance Foundation and have been administered by Theatre Development Fund since 1991. These awards recognize outstanding achievement in dance on Broadway and in film. The awards had been on a three year hiatus until this season. 2009 Nominating Committee: Anna Kisselgoff (former *New York Times* Chief Dance Critic), Wendy Perron (*Dance Magazine* Editor-in-Chief), Sylviane Gold (*Dance Magazine*), Linda Winer (*Newsday*), Damian Woetzel (former principal dancer, New York City Ballet); Chairman Emeritus, Doug Watt; Honorary Chairs, Ava Astaire McKenzie & Richard McKenzie; Producers, Ron Glucksman and Patricia Watt; Presenters: Liza Minnelli, Tony Danza, Bebe Neuwirth, Geoffrey Rush

Best Broadway Choreographer: Peter Darling, *Billy Elliot The Musical*

Best Film Choreographer: Longines Fernandes, *Slumdog Millionaire*

Best Female Dancer: Pia Glenn, *You're Welcome America. A Final Night with George W. Bush*

Best Male Dancer: David Alvarez, Trent Kowalik, and Kiril Kulish, *Billy Elliot The Musical*

Douglas Watt Lifetime Achievement Award: Stanley Donen

Irene Sharaff Awards

March 27, 2009; Hudson Theatre; 15th annual. Founded in 1993, this award has become an occasion for the costume design community to come together to honor its own and pays tribute to the art of costume design. Named after the revered costume designer, the awards are decided upon by the TDF Costume Collection Advisory Committee (Gregory A. Poplyk–Chairman, Gregg Barnes, Suzy Benzinger, Dean Brown, Linda Fisher, Lana Fritz, Rodney Gordon, Desmond Heeley, Allen Lee Hughes, Holly Hynes, Carolyn Kostopoulous, Kitty Leech, Anna Louizos, Mimi Maxmen, David Murin, Sally Ann Parsons, Robert Perdziola, Carrie Robbins, Tony Walton, Patrick Wiley, David Zinn).

Lifetime Achievement Award: William Ivey Long

Young Master Award: Clint Ramos

Artisan Award: Sally Ann Parsons

The Robert L.B. Tobin Award: Bob Crowley

Memorial Tribute: Irene Sharaff

THE THEATER HALL OF FAME

January 26, 2009; Gershwin Theatre North Rotunda; 38th annual; Host: Dana Ivey. The Theater of Hall of Fame was created in 1971 to honor those who have made outstanding contributions to the American theater in a career spanning at least twenty-five years, with at least five major credits; Producer, Terry Hodge; Honorary Chair, Dame Celia Lipton Farris; Presenters: Stephen Sondheim, Jack O'Brien, Frank Rich, Terrence McNally, Ann Reinking

2009 Inductees (for the year 2008): Alan Ayckbourn, Emanuel Azenberg, Patricia Birch, Roscoe Lee Brown, Richard Easton, Marvin Hamlisch, Nathan Lane, Jonathan Tunick

Previous Inductees: George Abbott, Maude Adams, Viola Adams, Stella Adler, Edward Albee, Theoni V. Aldredge, Ira Aldridge, Jane Alexander, Mary Alice, Winthrop Ames, Judith Anderson, Maxwell Anderson, Robert Anderson, Julie Andrews, Margaret Anglin, Jean Anouilh, Harold Arlen, George Arliss, Boris Aronson, Adele Astaire, Fred Astaire, Eileen Atkins, Brooks Atkinson, Lauren Bacall, Pearl Bailey, George Balanchine, William Ball, Anne Bancroft, Tallulah Bankhead, Richard Barr, Philip Barry, Ethel Barrymore, John Barrymore, Lionel Barrymore, Howard Bay, Nora Bayes, John Lee Beatty, Julian Beck, Samuel Beckett, Brian Bedford, S.N. Behrman, Barbara Bel Geddes, Norman Bel Geddes, David Belasco, Michael Bennett, Richard Bennett, Robert Russell Bennett, Eric Bentley, Irving Berlin, Sarah Bernhardt, Leonard Bernstein, Earl Blackwell, Kermit Bloomgarden, Jerry Bock, Ray Bolger, Edwin Booth, Junius Brutus Booth, Shirley Booth, Philip Bosco, Dion Boucicault, Alice Brady, Bertolt Brecht, Fannie Brice, Peter Brook, John Mason Brown, Robert Brustein, Billie Burke, Abe Burrows, Richard Burton, Mrs. Patrick Campbell, Zoe Caldwell, Eddie Cantor, Len Cariou, Morris Carnovsky, Mrs. Leslie Carter, Gower Champion, Frank Chanfrau, Carol Channing, Stockard Channing, Ruth Chatterton, Paddy Chayefsky, Anton Chekhov, Ina Claire, Bobby Clark, Harold Clurman, Lee. J. Cobb, Richard L. Coe, George M. Cohan, Alexander H. Cohen, Jack Cole, Cy Coleman, Constance Collier, Alvin Colt, Betty Comden, Marc Connelly, Barbara Cook, Thomas Abthorpe Cooper, Katherine Cornell, Noel Coward, Jane Cowl, Lotta Crabtree, Cheryl Crawford, Hume Cronyn, Rachel Crothers, Russel Crouse, John Cullum, Charlotte Cushman, Jean Dalrymple, Augustin Daly, Graciela Daniele, E.L. Davenport, Gordon Davidson, Ossie Davis, Owen Davis, Ruby Dee, Alfred De Liagre Jr., Agnes DeMille, Colleen Dewhurst, Howard Dietz, Dudley Digges, Melvyn Douglas, Eddie Dowling, Alfred Drake, Marie Dressler, John Drew, Mrs. John Drew, William Dunlap, Mildred Dunnock, Charles Durning, Eleanora Duse, Jeanne Eagles, Fred Ebb, Ben Edwards, Florence Eldridge, Lehman Engel, Maurice Evans, Abe Feder, Jose Ferber, Cy Feuer, Zelda Fichandler, Dorothy Fields, Herbert Fields, Lewis Fields, W.C. Fields, Harvey Fierstein, Jules Fisher, Minnie Maddern Fiske, Clyde Fitch, Geraldine Fitzgerald, Henry Fonda, Lynn Fontanne, Horton Foote, Edwin Forrest, Bob Fosse, Brian Friel, Rudolf Friml, Charles Frohman, Daniel Frohman, Robert Fryer, Athol Fugard, John Gassner, Larry Gelbart, Peter Gennaro, Grace George, George Gershwin, Ira Gershwin, Bernard Gersten, William Gibson, John Gielgud, W.S. Gilbert, Jack Gilford, William Gillette, Charles Gilpin, Lillian Gish, Susan Glaspell, John Golden, Max Gordon, Ruth Gordon, Adolph Green, Paul Green, Charlotte Greenwood, Jane Greenwood, Joel Grey, Tammy Grimes, George Grizzard, John Guare, Otis L. Guernsey Jr., A.R. Gurney, Mel Gussow, Tyrone Guthrie, Uta Hagen, Sir Peter Hall, Lewis Hallam, T. Edward Hambleton, Oscar Hammerstein II, Walter Hampden, Otto Harbach, E.Y. Harburg, Sheldon Harnick, Edward Harrigan, Jed Harris, Julie Harris, Rosemary Harris, Sam H. Harris, Rex Harrison, Kitty Carlisle Hart, Lorenz Hart, Moss Hart, Tony Hart, June Havoc, Helen Hayes, Leland Hayward, George Hearn, Ben Hecht, Eileen Heckart, Theresa Helburn, Lillian Hellman, Katharine Hepburn, Victor Herbert, Jerry Herman, James A. Herne, Henry Hewes, Gregory Hines, Al Hirschfeld, Raymond Hitchcock, Hal Holbrook, Celeste Holm, Hanya Holm, Arthur Hopkins, De Wolf Hopper, John Houseman, Eugene Howard, Leslie Howard, Sidney Howard, Willie Howard, Barnard Hughes, Henry Hull, Josephine Hull, Walter Huston, Earle Hyman, Henrik Ibsen, William Inge, Dana Ivey, Bernard B. Jacobs, Elise Janis, Joseph Jefferson, Al Jolson, James Earl Jones, Margo Jones, Robert Edmond Jones, Tom Jones, Jon Jory, Raul Julia, Madeline Kahn, John Kander, Garson Kanin, George S. Kaufman, Danny Kaye, Elia Kazan, Gene Kelly, George Kelly, Fanny Kemble, Jerome Kern, Walter Kerr, Michael Kidd, Richard Kiley, Willa Kim, Sidney Kingsley, Kevin Kline, Florence Klotz, Joseph Wood Krutch, Bert Lahr, Burton Lane, Frank Langella, Lawrence Langner, Lillie Langtry, Angela Lansbury, Charles Laughton, Arthur Laurents, Gertrude Lawrence, Jerome Lawrence, Eva Le Gallienne, Canada Lee, Eugene Lee, Ming Cho Lee, Robert E. Lee, Lotte Lenya, Alan Jay Lerner, Sam Levene, Robert Lewis, Beatrice Lillie, Howard Lindsay, John Lithgow, Frank Loesser, Frederick Loewe, Joshua

Logan, William Ivey Long, Santo Loquasto, Pauline Lord, Lucille Lortel, Dorothy Loudon, Alfred Lunt, Patti LuPone, Charles MacArthur, Steele MacKaye, Judith Malina, David Mamet, Rouben Mamoulian, Richard Mansfield, Robert B. Mantell, Frederic March, Nancy Marchand, Julia Marlowe, Ernest H. Martin, Mary Martin, Raymond Massey, Elizabeth Ireland McCann, Ian McKellen, Siobhan McKenna, Terrence McNally, Sanford Meisner, Helen Menken, Burgess Meredith, Ethel Merman, David Merrick, Jo Mielziner, Arthur Miller, Marilyn Miller, Liza Minnelli, Helena Modjeska, Ferenc Molnar, Lola Montez, Victor Moore, Robert Morse, Zero Mostel, Anna Cora Mowatt, Paul Muni, Brian Murray, Tharon Musser, George Jean Nathan, Mildred Natwick, Alla Nazimova, Patricia Neal, James M. Nederlander, Mike Nichols, Elliot Norton, Jack O'Brien, Sean O'Casey, Clifford Odets, Donald Oenslager, Laurence Olivier, Eugene O'Neill, Jerry Orbach, Geraldine Page, Joseph Papp, Estelle Parsons, Osgood Perkins, Bernadette Peters, Molly Picon, Harold Pinter, Luigi Pirandello, Christopher Plummer, Cole Porter, Robert Preston, Harold Prince, Jose Quintero, Ellis Rabb, John Raitt, Tony Randall, Michael Redgrave, Ada Rehan, Elmer Rice, Lloyd Richards, Ralph Richardson, Chita Rivera, Jason Robards, Jerome Robbins, Paul Robeson, Richard Rodgers, Will Rogers, Sigmund Romberg, Harold Rome, Billy Rose, Lillian Russell, Donald Saddler, Gene Saks, Diana Sands, William Saroyan, Joseph Schildkraut, Harvey Schmidt, Alan Schneider, Gerald Shoenfeld, Arthur Schwartz, Maurice Schwartz, George C. Scott, Marian Seldes, Peter Shaffer, Irene Sharaff, George Bernard Shaw, Sam Shepard, Robert F. Sherwood, J.J. Shubert, Lee Shubert, Herman Shumlin, Neil Simon, Lee Simonson, Edmund Simpson, Otis Skinner, Lois Smith, Maggie Smith, Oliver Smith, Stephen Sondheim, E.H. Sothern, Kim Stanley, Jean Stapleton, Maureen Stapleton, Joseph Stein, Frances Sternhagen, Roger L. Stevens, Isabelle Stevenson, Ellen Stewart, Dorothy Stickney, Fred Stone, Peter Stone, Tom Stoppard, Lee Strasburg, August Strindberg, Elaine Stritch, Charles Strouse, Jule Styne, Margaret Sullivan, Arthur Sullivan, Jessica Tandy, Laurette Taylor, Ellen Terry, Sada Thompson, Cleon Throckmorton, Tommy Tune, Gwen Verdon, Robin Wagner, Nancy Walker, Eli Wallach, James Wallack, Lester Wallack, Tony Walton, Douglas Turner Ward, David Warfield, Wendy Wasserstein, Ethel Waters, Clifton Webb, Joseph Weber, Margaret Webster, Kurt Weill, Orson Welles, Mae West, Robert Whitehead, Richard Wilbur, Oscar Wilde, Thorton Wilder, Bert Williams, Tennessee Williams, August Wilson, Elizabeth Wilson, Lanford Wilson, P.G. Wodehouse, Peggy Wood, Alexander Woollcott, Irene Worth, Teresa Wright, Ed Wynn, Vincent Youmans, Stark Young, Florenz Ziegfeld, Patricia Zipprodt

Founders Award

Established in 1993 in honor of Earl Blackwell, James M. Nederlander, Gerald Oestreicher, and Arnold Weissberger. The Theater Hall of Fame Founders Award is voted by the Hall's board of directors and is presented to an individual for his of her outstanding contribution to the theater. There was no award presented this season.

Past Recipients: (if year is missing, no award was presented) **1993:** James M. Nederlander **1994:** Kitty Carlisle Hart **1995:** Harvey Sabinson **1996:** Henry Hewes **1997:** Otis L. Guernsey Jr. **1998:** Edward Colton **2000:** Gerard Oestreicher; Arnold Weissberger **2001:** Tom Dillon **2003:** Price Berkley **2004:** No Award **2005:** Donald Seawell **2007:** Roy Somlyo

TOURING BROADWAY AWARDS

May 4, 2009; Hilton New York; 7th annual; Host: Seth Rudetsky. Presented by the Broadway League for excellence in touring Broadway in the 2008 season; Winners selected by League presenters representing over 240 markets; Presenters: Liza Minnelli and Jerry Zaks

Best New Touring Musical: *Legally Blonde The Musical* by Heather Hach, Nell Benjamin and Laurence O'Keefe (Produced by Hal Luftig, Fox Theatricals, Dori Berinstein, James L. Nederlander, Independent Presenters Network, Roy Furman, Broadway Asia, Barbara Whitman, Wolkenberg/Freitag, Hendel/Nocciolino, Stern/Meyer, Asnes/Zotovich, Bartner/Jenkins, and Warren Trepp)

Bets Touring Play: *Frost/Nixon* by Peter Morgan (Produced by Arielle Tepper Madover, Independent Presenters Network, Broadway Across America, Fox Theatricals, Mary Lu Roffe, Robert G. Bartner, Debra Black, Lauren Doll, Ruth Hendel, Barbara Whitman, The Donmar Warehouse)

Best Design of a Touring Production: *Legally Blonde The Musical* (Sets, David Rockwell; Costumes, Gregg Barnes; Lighting, Ken Posner and Paul Miller)

Best Score of a Touring Production: *Spring Awakening* Music by Duncan Sheik; Lyrics by Steven Sater

Best Direction of a Touring Production: Michael Mayer, *Spring Awakening*

Best Choreography of a Touring Production: Jerry Mitchell, *Legally Blonde The Musical*

Best Long-Running Touring Musical: *Wicked* (Produced by Marc Platt, Universal Pictures, The Araca Group, Jon B. Platt and David Stone)

Touring Broadway Achievement Award: Bill Miller

Touring Broadway Audience Choice Award: *Wicked*

UNITED STATES INSTITUTE FOR THEATRE TECHNOLOGY (USITT) AWARDS

Presented at the 49th annual USITT Conference and Stage Expo, March 18–21, 2009 at the Duke Energy Convention Center in Cincinnati, Ohio.

USITT Award First presented in 1967, this award recognizes a lifetime contribution in the performing arts community in any capacity. Recipients of this award do not need to be members of the Institute nor must they have any connection to USITT. **2009 Winner:** Oscar Brockett (Kennedy Center American College Theatre Festival)

Thomas DeGaetani Award First presented in 1983, this award honors an outstanding lifetime contribution to the performing arts community by an individual living and/or working in the area where the Annual Conference & Stage Expo is Held. **2009 Recipient:** Paul Vincent

Joel E. Rubin Founder's Award First Presented in 1970, this award is presented to a USITT member in recognition of outstanding and continued service to the Institute. **2009 Recipient:** Arnold Aronson

Distinguished Achievement Awards First presented in 1998, this award recognizes achievement by designers and technicians with established careers in the areas of scenic design, lighting design, technical direction, costume design, theatre architecture, theatrical consulting, production management, sound design, arts management, and costume direction. The recipient, who does not have to be a member of USITT. **2009 Recipients:** Architecture: Barton Myers, FAIA; Costume Design & Technology: Lenna Kaleva; Lighting Design: Jules Fisher; Management: Robert Rody; Scenic Design: Franco Colavecchia; Sound Design: Jack Mann; Technical Production: Ben Sammler

International Health & Safety Award First presented in 1985, this award is recognizes outstanding contribution towards health and safety in the performing arts. It is only given in those years where there is important activity in the area of the Conference and Expo, and can be presented to an individual for career-long dedication as well as for specific initiatives. (No recipient in 2009)

Golden Pen Award First presented in 1986, this award is presented to an author of an outstanding major, recent publication in the field of design and production for the performing arts. **2009 Recipient:** Deborah Nadoolman Landis for *Dressed: A Century of Hollywood Costume Design*

Herbert D. Greggs Awards First presented in 1979 and 1998, respectively, the Herbert D. Greggs Award (highest honor) and the Herbert D. Greggs Merit Award promote innovative, in-depth writing about theatre design and technology in *TD&T*. **2009 Greggs Award Recipient:** Annie O. Cleveland and M. Barrett Cleveland for "Fort Worth for Entertainment: Billy Rose's Casa Mañana (1936–

1939)" Winter 2008. **2009 Greggs Merit Award:** C. Thomas Ault for "Color in 16th and 17th Century of Italian Stage Design" Summer 2008

Architecture Awards Created in 1994 and sponsored by the USITT Architecture Commission, these awards honors excellence in the design of theatre projects. Honor Awards (the highest designation) and Merit Awards are evaluated by a panel of distinguished jurors for creative image, contextual resonance, community contribution, explorations in new technologies, and functional operations. **2009 Honor Awards:** Norwegian National Opera and Ballet (Oslo, Norway) designed by Snohetta AS; The Martin Woldson Theater at the Fox (Spokane, Washington), designed by NAC Architecture; **2009 Merit Awards:** California State University Fullerton Performing Arts Center (Fullerton, California) designed by Pfeiffer Partners Architects; Charles R. Walgreen Jr. Drama Center & Arthur Miller Theatre (Ann Arbor, Michigan), designed by Kuwabara Payne McKenna Blumberg Architects; Mesa Arts Center (Mesa, Arizona), designed by BOORA Architects

Special Citations Special Citations recognize outstanding achievement in any area of the performing arts by an individual or an organization. The initial Special Citation was presented in 1963. (No recipients in 2009)

International Travel Awards for Individual/Professionals and Students Established in 2004 to provide USITT members with funding for international travel for advanced research and education in theatre related fields. The student award was established in 2003 to assist USITT student members. **2009 Student Travel Award Recipient:** Leigh Spencer Brown, University of Tennessee (no Individual/Professional award presented in 2009)

Rising Star Award Established by LDI and *LiveDesign* magazine in 2005, this award is given annually to a young professional at the beginning of his or her career; recipients must be in the first four years of professional (non-academic) work following the completion of his or her highest degree. **2009 Recipient:** Sean Savoie (lighting designer)

Tech Expo Winners The Theatre Technology Exhibition, popularly known as Tech Expo, is mounted in alternate years at USITT's Annual Conference. Projects that demonstrate developments and creative solutions in all technical areas are juried by a distinguished panel of theatrical technicians. Prizes are awarded to the most inventive exhibitions; all entries that are accepted appear in the *Tech Expo Catalog*. **2009 Winners:** Tom Korder and Steven Ferrier: Pneumatic Folding Screens; Gregory Bell: A Split Hook for Captain Hook; Mary Copenhagen: Masks Made Using Cotton Organdy

YD & T Awards These awards are presented to young designers and technicians for recognition at the beginning of their careers, and made possible by gifts to USITT. **2009 Recipients:**

KM Fabrics Technical Production Award: Mary Weber

Robert E. Cohen Sound Achievement Award: Corinne Carrillo

USITT Barbizon Lighting Award: Catherine Girardi

USITT Rose Brand Scene Design Award: Arnold Bueso

USITT Zelma H. Weisfeld Costume Design & Technology Award: A.W. Nadine Grant

USITT Kryolan Corporation Makeup Design Award: Ming-Yen Ho

USITT Frederick A. Buerki Golden Hammer Scenic Technology Award: John McCullough

USITT Clear-Com Stage Management Award: E.J. Wilson

USITT W. Oren Parker Scene Design Award: Ryan Wineinger

USITT Stage Technology Lighting Design Award: Andy Baker

WILLIAM INGE THEATRE FESTIVAL AWARDS

April 22–25, 2009; 28th annual. The Inge Festival brings some of the world's most beloved playwrights to America's heartland in Independence, Missouri. During the four-day festival, honorees are chosen for distinguished achievement in American theater. Also, the festival selects a winner of the Otis Guernsey New Voices Playwriting Award, which recognizes contemporary playwrights whose voices are helping shape the American theater of today. It is named for the late Otis L. Guernsey Jr., beloved theater writer and editor who was a frequent guest at the William Inge Theatre Festival and a champion of exciting new plays.

2007 Honorees: Tom Jones and Harvey Schmidt

17th Annual Otis Guernsey New Voices in Playwrighting Award: Carlos Murillo

Previous Festival Honorees: 1982: William Inge Celebration; **1983:** Jerome Lawrence **1984:** William Gibson **1985:** Robert Anderson **1986:** John Patrick **1987:** Garson Kanin **1988:** Sidney Kingsley (in Independence), Robert E. Lee (on the road) **1989:** Horton Foote **1990:** Betty Comden & Adolph Green **1991:** Edward Albee **1992**: Peter Shaffer **1993:** Wendy Wasserstein **1994:** Terrence McNally **1995:** Arthur Miller **1996:** August Wilson **1997:** Neil Simon **1998**: Stephen Sondheim **1999:** John Guare **2000:** A.R. Gurney **2001:** Lanford Wilson **2002:** John Kander & Fred Ebb **2003:** Romulus Linney **2004:** Arthur Laurents **2005:** Tina Howe **2006:** 25th Anniversary retrospective **2007:** Jerry Bock & Sheldon Harnick **2008:** Christopher Durang

Previous New Voices Recipients: 1993: Jason Milligan **1994:** Catherine Butterfield **1995:** Mary Hanes **1996:** Brian Burgess Cross **1997:** Joe DiPietro **1998:** David Ives **1999:** David Hirson **2000:** James Still **2001:** Mark St. Germain **2002:** Dana Yeaton **2003:** Theresa Rebeck **2004:** Mary Portser **2005:** Lynne Kaufman **2006:** Melanie Marnich **2007:** JT Rogers **2008:** Adam Bock

LONGEST-RUNNING SHOWS

Top: *Idina Menzel and Kristin Chenoweth in* Wicked *(2004)*
(photo by Joan Marcus)

Center: *Michael Tucker, Cleavon Little, and Judd Hirsch in*
I'm Not Rappaport *(1986) (photo by Martha Swope)*

Bottom: *Kathy Bates, Jane Galloway, and Susan Merson in*
Vanities *(1975) (photo by Nathaniel Tileston)*

The original cast of Rent *(1996)*
(photo by Joan Marcus/Carol Rosegg)

The original cast of Hair *(1968) (photo by Dagmar)*

Anthony Perkins and Ralph Seymour in Equus *(1975) (photo by Van Williams)*

William Daniels and the cast of 1776 *(1969) (photo by Harry Nigro)*

Vivian Blaine and cast in Guys and Dolls *(1951) (photo by Alix Jeffry)*

Tom Ewell and Vanessa Brown in The Seven Year Itch *(1952) (photo by Talbot-Giles)*

Ilene Graff, James Naughton, Lenny Baker, and Joanna Gleason in I Love My Wife *(1977) (photo by Martha Swope)*

Michael McGuire, Paul Sorvino, Richard A. Dysart, Charles Durning, and Walter McGinn in That Championship Season *(1972) (photo by George E. Joseph)*

Longest-Running Shows on Broadway

The Phantom of the Opera*
8,875 performances
Opened January 26, 1988

Cats
7,485 performances
Opened October 7, 1982
Closed September 10, 2000

Les Misérables
6,680 performances
Opened March 12, 1987
Closed May 18, 2003

A Chorus Line
6,137 performances
Opened July 25, 1975
Closed April 28, 1990

Oh! Calcutta (revival)
5,959 performances
Opened September 24, 1976
Closed August 6, 1989

Beauty and the Beast
5,464 performances
Opened April 18, 1994
Closed July 29, 2007

Chicago* (revival)
5,204 performances
Opened November 19, 1996

Rent
5,124 performances
Opened April 29, 1996
Closed September 7, 2008

The Lion King*
4,789 performances
Opened November 13, 1997

Miss Saigon
4,097 performances
Opened April 11, 1991
Closed January 28, 2001

42nd Street
3,486 performances
Opened August 25, 1980
Closed January 8, 1989

Grease
3,388 performances
Opened February 14, 1972
Closed April 13, 1980

Fiddler on the Roof
3,242 performances
Opened September 22, 1964
Closed July 2, 1972

Life With Father
3,224 performances
Opened November 8, 1939
Closed July 12, 1947

Tobacco Road
3,182 performances
Opened December 4, 1933
Closed May 31, 1941

Mamma Mia!*
3,152 performances
Opened October 12, 2001

Hello, Dolly!
2,844 performances
Opened January 16, 1964
Closed December 27, 1970

My Fair Lady
2,717 performances
Opened March 15, 1956
Closed September 29, 1962

Hairspray
2,641 performances
Opened August 15, 2002
Closed January 4, 2009

The Producers
2,502 performances
Opened April 19, 2001
Closed April 22, 2007

Avenue Q*
2,414 performances
Opened July 31, 2003

Cabaret (1998 revival)
2,378 performances
Opened March 19, 1998
Closed January 4, 2004

Annie
2,377 performances
Opened April 21,1977
Closed January 22, 1983

Man of La Mancha
2,328 performances
Opened November 22, 1965
Closed June 26, 1971

Abie's Irish Rose
2,327 performances
Opened May 23, 1922
Closed October 21, 1927

Wicked*
2,310 performances
Opened October 30, 2003

Oklahoma!
2,212 performances
Opened March 31, 1943
Closed May 29, 1948

Smokey Joe's Café
2,036 performances
Opened March 2, 1995
Closed January 16, 2000

Pippin
1,944 performances
Opened October 23, 1972
Closed June 12, 1977

South Pacific
1,925 performances
Opened April 7, 1949
Closed January 16, 1954

The Magic Show
1,920 performances
Opened May 28, 1974
Closed December 31, 1978

Aida
1,852 performances
Opened March 23, 2000
Closed September 5, 2004

Gemini
1,819 performances
Opened May 21, 1977
Closed September 6, 1981

Deathtrap
1,793 performances
Opened February 26, 1978
Closed June 13, 1982

Harvey
1,775 performances
Opened November 1, 1944
Closed January 15, 1949

Dancin'
1,774 performances
Opened March 27, 1978
Closed June 27, 1982

La Cage Aux Folles
1,761 performances
Opened August 21, 1983
Closed November 15, 1987

Hair
1,750 performances
Opened April 29, 1968
Closed July 1, 1972

The Wiz
1,672 performances
Opened January 5, 1975
Closed January 29, 1979

Born Yesterday
1,642 performances
Opened February 4, 1946
Closed December 31, 1949

The Best Little Whorehouse in Texas
1,639 performances
Opened June 19, 1978
Closed March 27, 1982

Crazy for You
1,622 performances
Opened February 19, 1992
Closed January 7, 1996

Ain't Misbehavin'
1,604 performances
Opened May 9, 1978
Closed February 21, 1982

Monty Python's Spamalot
1,574 performances
Opened March 17, 2005
Closed January 11, 2009

Mary, Mary
1,572 performances
Opened March 8, 1961
Closed December 12, 1964

Evita
1,567 performances
Opened September 25, 1979
Closed June 26, 1983

The Voice of the Turtle
1,557 performances
Opened December 8, 1943
Closed January 3, 1948

Jekyll & Hyde
1,543 performances
Opened April 28, 1997
Closed January 7, 2001

Barefoot in the Park
1,530 performances
Opened October 23, 1963
Closed June 25, 1967

Brighton Beach Memoirs
1,530 performances
Opened March 27, 1983
Closed May 11, 1986

42nd Street (revival)
1,524 performances
Opened May 2, 2001
Closed January 2, 2005

Dreamgirls
1,522 performances
Opened December 20, 1981
Closed August 11, 1985

Mame
1,508 performances
Opened May 24, 1966
Closed January 3, 1970

Grease (1994 revival)
1,505 performances
Opened May 11, 1994
Closed January 25, 1998

Jersey Boys*
1,467 performances
Opened November 6, 2006

Same Time, Next Year
1,453 performances
Opened March 14, 1975
Closed September 3, 1978

Arsenic and Old Lace
1,444 performances
Opened January 10, 1941
Closed June 17, 1944

The Sound of Music
1,443 performances
Opened November 16, 1959
Closed June 15, 1963

Me and My Girl
1,420 performances
Opened August 10, 1986
Closed December 31, 1989

**How to Succeed in Business
Without Really Trying**
1,417 performances
Opened October 14, 1961
Closed March 6, 1965

Hellzapoppin'
1,404 performances
Opened September 22, 1938
Closed December 17, 1941

The Music Man
1,375 performances
Opened December 19, 1957
Closed April 15, 1961

Funny Girl
1,348 performances
Opened March 26, 1964
Closed July 15, 1967

Mummenschanz
1,326 performances
Opened March 30, 1977
Closed April 20, 1980

Movin' Out
1,303 performances
Opened October 24, 2002
Closed December 11, 2005

Angel Street
1,295 performances
Opened December 5, 1941
Closed December 30, 1944

Lightnin'
1,291 performances
Opened August 26, 1918
Closed August 27, 1921

Promises, Promises
1,281 performances
Opened December 1, 1968
Closed January 1, 1972

The King and I
1,246 performances
Opened March 29, 1951
Closed March 20, 1954

Cactus Flower
1,234 performances
Opened December 8, 1965
Closed November 23, 1968

Sleuth
1,222 performances
Opened November 12, 1970
Closed October 13, 1973

Torch Song Trilogy
1,222 performances
Opened June 10, 1982
Closed May 19, 1985

1776
1,217 performances
Opened March 16, 1969
Closed February 13, 1972

Equus
1,209 performances
Opened October 24, 1974
Closed October 7, 1977

Sugar Babies
1,208 performances
Opened October 8, 1979
Closed August 28, 1982

Guys and Dolls
1,200 performances
Opened November 24, 1950
Closed November 28, 1953

Amadeus
1,181 performances
Opened December 17, 1980
Closed October 16, 1983

Cabaret
1,165 performances
Opened November 20, 1966
Closed September 6, 1969

Mister Roberts
1,157 performances
Opened February 18, 1948
Closed January 6, 1951

Annie Get Your Gun
1,147 performances
Opened May 16, 1946
Closed February 12, 1949

Guys and Dolls (1992 revival)
1,144 performances
Opened April 14, 1992
Closed January 8, 1995

The Seven Year Itch
1,141 performances
Opened November 20, 1952
Closed August 13, 1955

**The 25th Annual Putnam
County Spelling Bee**
1,136 performances
Opened May 2, 2005
Closed January 20, 2008

**Bring in 'da Noise,
Bring in 'da Funk**
1,130 performances
Opened April 25, 1996
Closed January 19, 1999

Butterflies Are Free
1,128 performances
Opened October 21, 1969
Closed July 2, 1972

Pins and Needles
1,108 performances
Opened November 27, 1937
Closed June 22, 1940

Plaza Suite
1,097 performances
Opened February 14, 1968
Closed October 3, 1970

Fosse
1,093 performances
Opened January 14, 1999
Closed August 25, 2001

They're Playing Our Song
1,082 performances
Opened February 11, 1979
Closed September 6, 1981

Grand Hotel (musical)
1,077 performances
Opened November 12, 1989
Closed April 25, 1992

Kiss Me, Kate
1,070 performances
Opened December 30, 1948
Closed July 25, 1951

Don't Bother Me, I Can't Cope
1,065 performances
Opened April 19, 1972
Closed October 27, 1974

The Pajama Game
1,063 performances
Opened May 13, 1954
Closed November 24, 1956

Mary Poppins*
1,061 performances
Opened November 16, 2006

Shenandoah
1,050 performances
Opened January 7, 1975
Closed August 7, 1977

Annie Get Your Gun (1999 revival)
1,046 performances
Opened March 4, 1999
Closed September 1, 2001

**The Teahouse of the August
Moon**
1,027 performances
Opened October 15, 1953
Closed March 24, 1956

Damn Yankees
1,019 performances
Opened May 5, 1955
Closed October 12, 1957

Contact
1,010 performances
Opened March 30, 2000
Closed September 1, 2002

Never Too Late
1,007 performances
Opened November 26, 1962
Closed April 24, 1965

Big River
1,005 performances
Opened April 25, 1985
Closed September 20, 1987

The Will Rogers Follies
983 performances
Opened May 1, 1991
Closed September 5, 1993

Any Wednesday
982 performances
Opened February 18, 1964
Closed June 26, 1966

Sunset Boulevard
977 performances
Opened November 17, 1994
Closed March 22, 1997

Urinetown the Musical
965 performances
Opened September 20, 2001
Closed January 18, 2004

**A Funny Thing Happened
on the Way to the Forum**
964 performances
Opened May 8, 1962
Closed August 29, 1964

The Odd Couple
964 performances
Opened March 10, 1965
Closed July 2, 1967

Anna Lucasta
957 performances
Opened August 30, 1944
Closed November 30, 1946

Kiss and Tell
956 performances
Opened March 17, 1943
Closed June 23, 1945

Show Boat (1994 revival)
949 performances
Opened October 2, 1994
Closed January 5, 1997

Dracula (1977 revival)
925 performances
Opened October 20, 1977
Closed January 6, 1980

Bells Are Ringing
924 performances
Opened November 29, 1956
Closed March 7, 1959

The Moon Is Blue
924 performances
Opened March 8, 1951
Closed May 30, 1953

Beatlemania
920 performances
Opened May 31, 1977
Closed October 17, 1979

Proof
917 performances
Opened October 24, 2000
Closed January 5, 2003

The Elephant Man
916 performances
Opened April 19, 1979
Closed June 28, 1981

The Color Purple
910 performances
Opened December 1, 2005
Closed February 24, 2008

Kiss of the Spider Woman
906 performances
Opened May 3, 1993
Closed July 1, 1995

Thoroughly Modern Millie
904 performances
Opened April 18, 2002
Closed June 20, 2004

Luv
901 performances
Opened November 11, 1964
Closed January 7, 1967

The Who's Tommy
900 performances
Opened April 22, 1993
Closed June 17, 1995

Chicago
898 performances
Opened June 3, 1975
Closed August 27, 1977

Applause
896 performances
Opened March 30, 1970
Closed July 27, 1972

Can-Can
892 performances
Opened May 7, 1953
Closed June 25, 1955

Carousel
890 performances
Opened April 19, 1945
Closed May 24, 1947

I'm Not Rappaport
890 performances
Opened November 19, 1985
Closed January 17, 1988

Hats Off to Ice
889 performances
Opened June 22, 1944
Closed April 2, 1946

Fanny
888 performances
Opened November 4, 1954
Closed December 16, 1956

Children of a Lesser God
887 performances
Opened March 30, 1980
Closed May 16, 1982

Follow the Girls
882 performances
Opened April 8, 1944
Closed May 18, 1946

Kiss Me, Kate (revival)
881 performances
Opened November 18, 1999
Closed December 30, 2001

City of Angels
878 performances
Opened December 11, 1989
Closed January 19, 1992

Camelot
873 performances
Opened December 3, 1960
Closed January 5, 1963

I Love My Wife
872 performances
Opened April 17, 1977
Closed May 20, 1979

The Bat
867 performances
Opened August 23, 1920
Unknown closing date

My Sister Eileen
864 performances
Opened December 26, 1940
Closed January 16, 1943

No, No, Nanette (revival)
861 performances
Opened January 19, 1971
Closed February 3, 1973

Ragtime
861 performances
Opened January 18, 1998
Closed January 16, 2000

Song of Norway
860 performances
Opened August 21, 1944
Closed September 7, 1946

Spring Awakening
859 performances
Opened December 10, 2006
Closed January 18, 2009

Chapter Two
857 performances
Opened December 4, 1977
Closed December 9, 1979

A Streetcar Named Desire
855 performances
Opened December 3, 1947
Closed December 17, 1949

Barnum
854 performances
Opened April 30, 1980
Closed May 16, 1982

Comedy in Music
849 performances
Opened October 2, 1953
Closed January 21, 1956

Raisin
847 performances
Opened October 18, 1973
Closed December 7, 1975

Blood Brothers
839 performances
Opened April 25, 1993
Closed April 30, 1995

You Can't Take It With You
837 performances
Opened December 14, 1936
Unknown closing date

La Plume de Ma Tante
835 performances
Opened November 11, 1958
Closed December 17, 1960

Three Men on a Horse
835 performances
Opened January 30, 1935
Closed January 9, 1937

The Subject Was Roses
832 performances
Opened May 25, 1964
Closed May 21, 1966

Black and Blue
824 performances
Opened January 26, 1989
Closed January 20, 1991

The King and I (1996 revival)
807 performances
Opened April 11, 1996
Closed February 22, 1998

Inherit the Wind
806 performances
Opened April 21, 1955
Closed June 22, 1957

Anything Goes (1987 revival)
804 performances
Opened October 19, 1987
Closed September 3, 1989

Titanic
804 performances
Opened April 23, 1997
Closed March 21, 1999

No Time for Sergeants
796 performances
Opened October 20, 1955
Closed September 14, 1957

Fiorello!
795 performances
Opened November 23, 1959
Closed October 28, 1961

Where's Charley?
792 performances
Opened October 11, 1948
Closed September 9, 1950

The Ladder
789 performances
Opened October 22, 1926
Unknown closing date

Fiddler on the Roof (2004 revival)
781 performances
Opened February 26, 2004
Closed January 8, 2006

Forty Carats
780 performances
Opened December 26, 1968
Closed November 7, 1970

Lost in Yonkers
780 performances
Opened February 21, 1991
Closed January 3, 1993

The Prisoner of Second Avenue
780 performances
Opened November 11, 1971
Closed September 29, 1973

M. Butterfly
777 performances
Opened March 20, 1988
Closed January 27, 1990

The Tale of the Allergist's Wife
777 performances
Opened November 2, 2000
Closed September 15, 2002

Oliver!
774 performances
Opened January 6, 1963
Closed November 14, 1964

The Pirates of Penzance (1981 revival)
772 performances
Opened January 8, 1981
Closed November 28, 1982

The Full Monty
770 performances
Opened October 26, 2000
Closed September 1, 2002

Woman of the Year
770 performances
Opened March 29, 1981
Closed March 13, 1983

My One and Only
767 performances
Opened May 1, 1983
Closed March 3, 1985

Sophisticated Ladies
767 performances
Opened March 1, 1981
Closed January 2, 1983

Bubbling Brown Sugar
766 performances
Opened March 2, 1976
Closed December 31, 1977

Into the Woods
765 performances
Opened November 5, 1987
Closed September 3, 1989

State of the Union
765 performances
Opened November 14, 1945
Closed September 13, 1947

Starlight Express
761 performances
Opened March 15, 1987
Closed January 8, 1989

The First Year
760 performances
Opened October 20, 1920
Unknown closing date

A Chorus Line (revival)
759 performances
Opened October 5, 2006
Closed August 17, 2008

Broadway Bound
756 performances
Opened December 4, 1986
Closed September 25, 1988

You Know I Can't Hear You When the Water's Running
755 performances
Opened March 13, 1967
Closed January 4, 1969

Two for the Seesaw
750 performances
Opened January 16, 1958
Closed October 31, 1959

Joseph and the Amazing Technicolor Dreamcoat
747 performances
Opened January 27, 1982
Closed September 4, 1983

Death of a Salesman
742 performances
Opened February 10, 1949
Closed November 18, 1950

for colored girls who have considered suicide/when the rainbow is enuf
742 performances
Opened September 15, 1976
Closed July 16, 1978

Sons o' Fun
742 performances
Opened December 1, 1941
Closed August 29, 1943

Candide (1974 revival)
740 performances
Opened March 10, 1974
Closed January 4, 1976

Gentlemen Prefer Blondes
740 performances
Opened December 8, 1949
Closed September 15, 1951

The Man Who Came to Dinner
739 performances
Opened October 16, 1939
Closed July 12, 1941

Nine
739 performances
Opened May 9, 1982
Closed February 4, 1984

Call Me Mister
734 performances
Opened April 18, 1946
Closed January 10, 1948

Victor/Victoria
734 performances
Opened October 25, 1995
Closed July 27, 1997

West Side Story
732 performances
Opened September 26, 1957
Closed June 27, 1959

High Button Shoes
727 performances
Opened October 9, 1947
Closed July 2, 1949

Finian's Rainbow
725 performances
Opened January 10, 1947
Closed October 2, 1948

Claudia
722 performances
Opened February 12, 1941
Closed January 9, 1943

The Gold Diggers
720 performances
Opened September 30, 1919
Unknown closing date

Jesus Christ Superstar
720 performances
Opened October 12, 1971
Closed June 30, 1973

Carnival!
719 performances
Opened April 13, 1961
Closed January 5, 1963

The Diary of Anne Frank
717 performances
Opened October 5, 1955
Closed June 22, 1955

**A Funny Thing Happened
on the Way to the Forum** (revival)
715 performances
Opened April 18, 1996
Closed January 4, 1998

I Remember Mama
714 performances
Opened October 19, 1944
Closed June 29, 1946

Tea and Sympathy
712 performances
Opened September 30, 1953
Closed June 18, 1955

Junior Miss
710 performances
Opened November 18, 1941
Closed July 24, 1943

Footloose
708 performances
Opened October 22, 1998
Closed July 2, 2000

Last of the Red Hot Lovers
706 performances
Opened December 28, 1969
Closed September 4, 1971

The Secret Garden
706 performances
Opened April 25, 1991
Closed January 3, 1993

Company
705 performances
Opened April 26, 1970
Closed January 1, 1972

Seventh Heaven
704 performances
Opened October 30, 1922
Unknown closing date

Gypsy
702 performances
Opened May 21, 1959
Closed March 25, 1961

The Miracle Worker
700 performances
Opened October 19, 1959
Closed July 1, 1961

That Championship Season
700 performances
Opened September 14, 1972
Closed April 21, 1974

The Music Man (2000 revival)
698 performances
Opened April 27, 2000
Closed December 30, 2001

Da
697 performances
Opened May 1, 1978
Closed January 1, 1980

Cat on a Hot Tin Roof
694 performances
Opened March 24, 1955
Closed November 17, 1956

Li'l Abner
693 performances
Opened November 15, 1956
Closed July 12, 1958

The Children's Hour
691 performances
Opened November 20, 1934
Unknown closing date

Purlie
688 performances
Opened March 15, 1970
Closed November 6, 1971

Dead End
687 performances
Opened October 28, 1935
Closed June 12, 1937

The Lion and the Mouse
686 performances
Opened November 20, 1905
Unknown closing date

White Cargo
686 performances
Opened November 5, 1923
Unknown closing date

Dear Ruth
683 performances
Opened December 13, 1944
Closed July 27, 1946

East Is West
680 performances
Opened December 25, 1918
Unknown closing date

Come Blow Your Horn
677 performances
Opened February 22, 1961
Closed October 6, 1962

The Most Happy Fella
676 performances
Opened May 3, 1956
Closed December 14, 1957

The Drowsy Chaperone
672 performances
Opened May 1, 2006
Closed December 30, 2007

Defending the Caveman
671 performances
Opened March 26, 1995
Closed June 22, 1997

The Doughgirls
671 performances
Opened December 30, 1942
Closed July 29, 1944

The Impossible Years
670 performances
Opened October 13, 1965
Closed May 27, 1967

Irene
670 performances
Opened November 18, 1919
Unknown closing date

Boy Meets Girl
669 performances
Opened November 27, 1935
Unknown closing date

The Tap Dance Kid
669 performances
Opened December 21, 1983
Closed August 11, 1985

Beyond the Fringe
667 performances
Opened October 27, 1962
Closed May 30, 1964

Who's Afraid of Virginia Woolf?
664 performances
Opened October 13, 1962
Closed May 16, 1964

Blithe Spirit
657 performances
Opened November 5, 1941
Closed June 5, 1943

A Trip to Chinatown
657 performances
Opened November 9, 1891
Unknown closing date

The Women
657 performances
Opened December 26, 1936
Unknown closing date

Bloomer Girl
654 performances
Opened October 5, 1944
Closed April 27, 1946

The Fifth Season
654 performances
Opened January 23, 1953
Closed October 23, 1954

Rain
648 performances
Opened September 1, 1924
Unknown closing date

Witness for the Prosecution
645 performances
Opened December 16, 1954
Closed June 30, 1956

Call Me Madam
644 performances
Opened October 12, 1950
Closed May 3, 1952

Janie
642 performances
Opened September 10, 1942
Closed January 16, 1944

The Green Pastures
640 performances
Opened February 26, 1930
Closed August 29, 1931

Auntie Mame
639 performances
Opened October 31, 1956
Closed June 28, 1958

A Man for All Seasons
637 performances
Opened November 22, 1961
Closed June 1, 1963

Jerome Robbins' Broadway
634 performances
Opened February 26, 1989
Closed September 1, 1990

The Fourposter
632 performances
Opened October 24, 1951
Closed May 2, 1953

Dirty Rotten Scoundrels
627 performances
Opened March 3, 2005
Closed September 3, 2006

The Music Master
627 performances
Opened September 26, 1904
Unknown closing date

Two Gentlemen of Verona
(musical)
627 performances
Opened December 1, 1971
Closed May 20, 1973

The Tenth Man
623 performances
Opened November 5, 1959
Closed May 13, 1961

The Heidi Chronicles
621 performances
Opened March 9, 1989
Closed September 1, 1990

Is Zat So?
618 performances
Opened January 5, 1925
Closed July 1926

August: Osage County*
616 performances
Opened December 4, 2007

Anniversary Waltz
615 performances
Opened April 7, 1954
Closed September 24, 1955

The Happy Time (play)
614 performances
Opened January 24, 1950
Closed July 14, 1951

Separate Rooms
613 performances
Opened March 23, 1940
Closed September 6, 1941

Affairs of State
610 performances
Opened September 25, 1950
Closed March 8, 1952

Oh! Calcutta!
610 performances
Opened June 17, 1969
Closed August 12, 1972

Star and Garter
609 performances
Opened June 24, 1942
Closed December 4, 1943

The Mystery of Edwin Drood
608 performances
Opened December 2, 1985
Closed May 16, 1987

The Student Prince
608 performances
Opened December 2, 1924
Unknown closing date

Sweet Charity
608 performances
Opened January 29, 1966
Closed July 15, 1967

Bye Bye Birdie
607 performances
Opened April 14, 1960
Closed October 7, 1961

Riverdance on Broadway
605 performances
Opened March 16, 2000
Closed August 26, 2001

Irene (revival)
604 performances
Opened March 13, 1973
Closed September 8, 1974

Sunday in the Park With George
604 performances
Opened May 2, 1984
Closed October 13, 1985

Adonis
603 performances
Opened circa. 1884
Unknown closing date

Broadway
603 performances
Opened September 16, 1926
Unknown closing date

Peg o' My Heart
603 performances
Opened December 20, 1912
Unknown closing date

Master Class
601 performances
Opened November 5, 1995
Closed June 29, 1997

Street Scene (play)
601 performances
Opened January 10, 1929
Unknown closing date

Flower Drum Song
600 performances
Opened December 1, 1958
Closed May 7, 1960

Kiki
600 performances
Opened November 29, 1921
Unknown closing date

A Little Night Music
600 performances
Opened February 25, 1973
Closed August 3, 1974

Art
600 performances
Opened March 1, 1998
Closed August 8, 1999

Agnes of God
599 performances
Opened March 30, 1982
Closed September 4, 1983

Don't Drink the Water
598 performances
Opened November 17, 1966
Closed April 20, 1968

Wish You Were Here
598 performances
Opened June 25, 1952
Closed November 28, 1958

Sarafina!
597 performances
Opened January 28, 1988
Closed July 2, 1989

A Society Circus
596 performances
Opened December 13, 1905
Closed November 24, 1906

Legally Blonde
595 performances
Opened April 29, 2007
Closed October 19, 2008

Absurd Person Singular
592 performances
Opened October 8, 1974
Closed March 6, 1976

A Day in Hollywood/A Night in the Ukraine
588 performances
Opened May 1, 1980
Closed September 27, 1981

The Me Nobody Knows
586 performances
Opened December 18, 1970
Closed November 21, 1971

The Two Mrs. Carrolls
585 performances
Opened August 3, 1943
Closed February 3, 1945

Kismet (musical)
583 performances
Opened December 3, 1953
Closed April 23, 1955

Gypsy (1989 revival)
582 performances
Opened November 16, 1989
Closed July 28, 1991

Brigadoon
581 performances
Opened March 13, 1947
Closed July 31, 1948

Detective Story
581 performances
Opened March 23, 1949
Closed August 12, 1950

The Little Mermaid*
581 performances
Opened January 10, 2008

No Strings
580 performances
Opened March 14, 1962
Closed August 3, 1963

Brother Rat
577 performances
Opened December 16, 1936
Unknown closing date

Blossom Time
576 performances
Opened September 29, 1921
Unknown closing date

Pump Boys and Dinettes
573 performances
Opened February 4, 1982
Closed June 18, 1983

Show Boat
572 performances
Opened December 27, 1927
Closed May 4, 1929

The Show-Off
571 performances
Opened February 5, 1924
Unknown closing date

Sally
570 performances
Opened December 21, 1920
Closed April 22, 1922

Jelly's Last Jam
569 performances
Opened April 26, 1992
Closed September 5, 1993

Golden Boy (musical)
568 performances
Opened October 20, 1964
Closed March 5, 1966

One Touch of Venus
567 performances
Opened October 7, 1943
Closed February 10, 1945

The Real Thing
566 performances
Opened January 5, 1984
Closed May 12, 1985

Happy Birthday
564 performances
Opened October 31, 1946
Closed March 13, 1948

Look Homeward, Angel
564 performances
Opened November 28, 1957
Closed April 4, 1959

Morning's at Seven (revival)
564 performances
Opened April 10, 1980
Closed August 16, 1981

The Glass Menagerie
561 performances
Opened March 31, 1945
Closed August 3, 1946

I Do! I Do!
560 performances
Opened December 5, 1966
Closed June 15, 1968

Wonderful Town
559 performances
Opened February 25, 1953
Closed July 3, 1954

The Last Night of Ballyhoo
557 performances
Opened February 27, 1997
Closed June 28, 1998

Rose Marie
557 performances
Opened September 2, 1924
Unknown closing date

Strictly Dishonorable
557 performances
Opened September 18, 1929
Unknown closing date

Sweeney Todd, the Demon Barber of Fleet Street
557 performances
Opened March 1, 1979
Closed June 29, 1980

The Great White Hope
556 performances
Opened October 3, 1968
Closed January 31, 1970

A Majority of One
556 performances
Opened February 16, 1959
Closed June 25, 1960

The Sisters Rosensweig
556 performances
Opened March 18, 1993
Closed July 16, 1994

Sunrise at Campobello
556 performances
Opened January 30, 1958
Closed May 30, 1959

Toys in the Attic
556 performances
Opened February 25, 1960
Closed April 8, 1961

Jamaica
555 performances
Opened October 31, 1957
Closed April 11, 1959

**Stop the World—
I Want to Get Off**
555 performances
Opened October 3, 1962
Closed February 1, 1964

Grease (2007 revival)
554 performances
Opened August 19, 2007
Closed January 4, 2009

Florodora
553 performances
Opened November 10, 1900
Closed January 25, 1902

Noises Off
553 performances
Opened December 11, 1983
Closed April 6, 1985

Ziegfeld Follies (1943)
553 performances
Opened April 1, 1943
Closed July 22, 1944

Dial "M" for Murder
552 performances
Opened October 29, 1952
Closed February 27, 1954

Good News
551 performances
Opened September 6, 1927
Unknown closing date

Peter Pan (revival)
551 performances
Opened September 6, 1979
Closed January 4, 1981

How to Succeed in Business without Really Trying (revival)
548 performances
Opened March 23, 1995
Closed July 14, 1996

Let's Face It
547 performances
Opened October 29, 1941
Closed March 20, 1943

Milk and Honey
543 performances
Opened October 10, 1961
Closed January 26, 1963

Within the Law
541 performances
Opened September 11, 1912
Unknown closing date

Pal Joey (revival)
540 performances
Opened January 3, 1952
Closed April 18, 1953

The Sound of Music (revival)
540 performances
Opened March 12, 1998
Closed June 20, 1999

What Makes Sammy Run?
540 performances
Opened February 27, 1964
Closed June 12, 1965

The Sunshine Boys
538 performances
Opened December 20, 1972
Closed April 21, 1974

What a Life
538 performances
Opened April 13, 1938
Closed July 8, 1939

Crimes of the Heart
535 performances
Opened November 4, 1981
Closed February 13, 1983

Damn Yankees (revival)
533 performances
Opened March 3, 1994
Closed August 6, 1995

The Unsinkable Molly Brown
532 performances
Opened November 3, 1960
Closed February 10, 1962

The Red Mill (revival)
531 performances
Opened October 16, 1945
Closed January 18, 1947

Rumors
531 performances
Opened November 17, 1988
Closed February 24, 1990

A Raisin in the Sun
530 performances
Opened March 11, 1959
Closed June 25, 1960

Godspell
527 performances
Opened June 22, 1976
Closed September 4, 1977

Fences
526 performances
Opened March 26, 1987
Closed June 26, 1988

The Solid Gold Cadillac
526 performances
Opened November 5, 1953
Closed February 12, 1955

Doubt
525 performances
Opened March 9, 2005
Closed July 2, 2006

Biloxi Blues
524 performances
Opened March 28, 1985
Closed June 28, 1986

Irma La Douce
524 performances
Opened September 29, 1960
Closed December 31, 1961

The Boomerang
522 performances
Opened August 10, 1915
Unknown closing date

Follies
521 performances
Opened April 4, 1971
Closed July 1, 1972

Rosalinda
521 performances
Opened October 28, 1942
Closed January 22, 1944

The Best Man
520 performances
Opened March 31, 1960
Closed July 8, 1961

Chauve-Souris
520 performances
Opened February 4, 1922
Unknown closing date

Blackbirds of 1928
518 performances
Opened May 9, 1928
Unknown closing date

The Gin Game
517 performances
Opened October 6, 1977
Closed December 31, 1978

Side Man
517 performances
Opened June 25, 1988
Closed October 31, 1999

Sunny
517 performances
Opened September 22, 1925
Closed December 11, 1926

Victoria Regina
517 performances
Opened December 26, 1935
Unknown closing date

The 39 Steps*
515 performances
Opened January 15, 2008

In the Heights*
512 Performances
Opened March 9, 2008

Xanadu
512 Performances
Opened July 10, 2007
Closed September 28, 2008

Curtains
511 Performances
Opened March 22, 2007
Closed June 29, 2008

Fifth of July
511 performances
Opened November 5, 1980
Closed January 24, 1982

Half a Sixpence
511 performances
Opened April 25, 1965
Closed July 16, 1966

The Vagabond King
511 performances
Opened September 21, 1925
Closed December 4, 1926

The New Moon
509 performances
Opened September 19, 1928
Closed December 14, 1929

The World of Suzie Wong
508 performances
Opened October 14, 1958
Closed January 2, 1960

The Rothschilds
507 performances
Opened October 19, 1970
Closed January 1, 1972

On Your Toes (revival)
505 performances
Opened March 6, 1983
Closed May 20, 1984

Sugar
505 performances
Opened April 9, 1972
Closed June 23, 1973

The Light in the Piazza
504 performances
Opened March 17, 2005
Closed July 2, 2006

Shuffle Along
504 performances
Opened May 23, 1921
Closed July 15, 1922

Up in Central Park
504 performances
Opened January 27, 1945
Closed January 13, 1946

Carmen Jones
503 performances
Opened December 2, 1943
Closed February 10, 1945

Saturday Night Fever
502 performances
Opened October 21, 1999
Closed December 30, 2000

The Member of the Wedding
501 performances
Opened January 5, 1950
Closed March 17, 1951

Panama Hattie
501 performances
Opened October 30, 1940
Closed January 13, 1942

Personal Appearance
501 performances
Opened October 17, 1934
Unknown closing date

Bird in Hand
500 performances
Opened April 4, 1929
Unknown closing date

Room Service
500 performances
Opened May 19, 1937
Unknown closing date

Sailor, Beware!
500 performances
Opened September 28, 1933
Unknown closing date

Tomorrow the World
500 performances
Opened April 14, 1943
Closed June 17, 1944

* Production is still running as
of May 31, 2009; count includes
performances up to and including
that date.

*Larry Kert and Carol Lawrence
in* West Side Story *(1957)
(photo by Fred Fehl)*

*Harold Lang,
Vivienne Segal,
and Jack Waldron
in* Pal Joey *(1952)
(photo by John
Bennewitz)*

Longest-Running Shows Off-Broadway

The Fantasticks
17,162 performances
Opened May 3, 1960
Closed January 13, 2002

Blue Man Group*
9,440 performances
Opened November 17, 1991

Perfect Crime*
9,034 performances
Opened April 18, 1987

Stomp*
6,432 performances
Opened February 27, 1994

Tony 'n' Tina's Wedding*
5,798 performances
Opened May 1, 1987

I Love You, You're Perfect, Now Change
5,003 performances
Opened August 1, 1996
Closed July 29, 2008

Nunsense
3,672 performances
Opened December 12, 1985
Closed October 16, 1994

Naked Boys Singing*
2,794 performances
Opened July 22, 1999

The Threepenny Opera
2,611 performances
Opened September 20, 1955
Closed December 17, 1961

De La Guarda
2,475 performances
Opened June 16, 1998
Closed September 12, 2004

Forbidden Broadway 1982–87
2,332 performances
Opened January 15, 1982
Closed August 30, 1987

Little Shop of Horrors
2,209 performances
Opened July 27, 1982
Closed November 1, 1987

Godspell
2,124 performances
Opened May 17, 1971
Closed June 13, 1976

Vampire Lesbians of Sodom
2,024 performances
Opened June 19, 1985
Closed May 27, 1990

Jacques Brel is Alive and Well and Living in Paris
1,847 performances
Opened January 22, 1968
Closed July 2, 1972

Forever Plaid
1,811 performances
Opened May 20, 1990
Closed June 12, 1994

Vanities
1,785 performances
Opened March 22, 1976
Closed August 3, 1980

The Donkey Show
1,717 performances
Opened August 18, 1999
Closed July 16, 2005

Menopause the Musical
1,712 performances
Opened April 4, 2002
Closed May 14, 2006

You're A Good Man, Charlie Brown
1,597 performances
Opened March 7, 1967
Closed February 14, 1971

The Blacks
1,408 performances
Opened May 4, 1961
Closed September 27, 1964

The Vagina Monologues
1,381 performances
Opened October 3, 1999
Closed January 26, 2003

One Mo' Time
1,372 performances
Opened October 22, 1979
Closed 1982–83 season

Grandma Sylvia's Funeral
1,360 performances
Opened October 9, 1994
Closed June 20, 1998

Altar Boyz*
1,776 performances
Opened March 1, 2005

Let My People Come
1,327 performances
Opened January 8, 1974
Closed July 5, 1976

Late Nite Catechism
1,268 performances
Opened October 4, 1995
Closed May 18, 2003

Driving Miss Daisy
1,195 performances
Opened April 15, 1987
Closed June 3, 1990

The Hot L Baltimore
1,166 performances
Opened September 8, 1973
Closed January 4, 1976

I'm Getting My Act Together and Taking It on the Road
1,165 performances
Opened May 16, 1987
Closed March 15, 1981

Little Mary Sunshine
1,143 performances
Opened November 18, 1959
Closed September 2, 1962

Steel Magnolias
1,126 performances
Opened November 17, 1987
Closed February 25, 1990

El Grande de Coca-Cola
1,114 performances
Opened February 13, 1973
Closed April 13, 1975

The Proposition
1,109 performances
Opened March 24, 1971
Closed April 14, 1974

Our Sinatra
1,096 performances
Opened December 8, 1999
Closed July 28, 2002

Beau Jest
1,069 performances
Opened October 10, 1991
Closed May 1, 1994

The Fantasticks* (revival)
1,055 performances
Opened August 23, 2006

Jewtopia
1,052 performances
Opened October 21, 2004
Closed April 29, 2007

Tamara
1,036 performances
Opened November 9, 1989
Closed July 15, 1990

One Flew Over the Cuckoo's Nest (revival)
1,025 performances
Opened March 23, 1971
Closed September 16, 1973

Slava's Snow Show
1,004 Performances
Opened September 8, 2004
Closed January 14, 2007

The Boys in the Band
1,000 performances
Opened April 14, 1968
Closed September 29, 1985

Fool For Love
1,000 performances
Opened November 27, 1983
Closed September 29, 1985

Forbidden Broadway: 20th Anniversary Celebration
994 performances
Opened March 20, 2002
Closed July 4, 2004

Other People's Money
990 performances
Opened February 7, 1989
Closed July 4, 1991

Cloud 9
971 performances
Opened May 18, 1981
Closed September 4, 1983

Secrets Every Smart Traveler Should Know
953 performances
Opened October 30, 1997
Closed February 21, 2000

Sister Mary Ignatius Explains It All for You & The Actor's Nightmare
947 performances
Opened October 21, 1981
Closed January 29, 1984

The Gazillion Bubble Show*
944 performances
Opened February 15, 2007

Your Own Thing
933 performances
Opened January 13, 1968
Closed April 5, 1970

Curley McDimple
931 performances
Opened November 22, 1967
Closed January 25, 1970

Leave It to Jane (revival)
928 performances
Opened May 29, 1959
Closed 1961–62 season

The Mad Show
871 performances
Opened January 9, 1966
Closed September 10, 1967

Hedwig and the Angry Inch
857 performances
Opened February 14, 1998
Closed April 9, 2000

Forbidden Broadway
Strikes Back
850 performances
Opened October 17, 1996
Closed September 20, 1998

When Pigs Fly
840 performances
Opened August 14, 1996
Closed August 15, 1998

Scrambled Feet
831 performances
Opened June 11, 1979
Closed June 7, 1981

The Effect of Gamma Rays on
Man-in-the-Moon Marigolds
819 performances
Opened April 7, 1970
Closed June 1, 1973

Forbidden Broadway SVU
816 performances
Opened December 16, 2004
Closed April 15, 2007

Over the River and
Through the Woods
800 performances
Opened October 5, 1998
Closed September 3, 2000

A View From the Bridge (revival)
780 performances
Opened November 9, 1965
Closed December 11, 1966

The Boy Friend (revival)
763 performances
Opened January 25, 1958
Closed 1961–62 season

True West
762 performances
Opened December 23, 1980
Closed January 11, 1981

Forbidden Broadway
Cleans Up Its Act!
754 performances
Opened November 17, 1998
Closed August 30, 2000

Isn't It Romantic
733 performances
Opened December 15, 1983
Closed September 1, 1985

Dime a Dozen
728 performances
Opened June 13, 1962
Closed 1963–64 season

The Pocket Watch
725 performances
Opened November 14, 1966
Closed June 18, 1967

The Connection
722 performances
Opened June 9, 1959
Closed June 4, 1961

The Passion of Dracula
714 performances
Opened September 28, 1977
Closed July 14, 1979

Love, Janis
713 performances
Opened April 22, 2001
Closed January 5, 2003

Adaptation & Next
707 performances
Opened February 10, 1969
Closed October 18, 1970

Oh! Calcutta!
704 performances
Opened June 17, 1969
Closed August 12, 1972

Scuba Duba
692 performances
Opened November 11, 1967
Closed June 8, 1969

The Foreigner
686 performances
Opened November 2, 1984
Closed June 8, 1986

The Knack
685 performances
Opened January 14, 1964
Closed January 9, 1966

My Mother's Italian, My Father's
Jewish
& I'm in Therapy
684 performances
Opened December 8, 2006
Closed August 24, 2008

Fully Committed
675 performances
Opened December 14, 1999
Closed May 27, 2001

The Club
674 performances
Opened October 14, 1976
Closed May 21, 1978

The Balcony
672 performances
Opened March 3, 1960
Closed December 21, 1961

Penn & Teller
666 performances
Opened July 30, 1985
Closed January 19, 1992

Dinner With Friends
654 performances
Opened November 4, 1999
Closed May 27, 2000

Fuerza Bruta: Look Up*
637 performances
Opened October 24, 2007

America Hurrah
634 performances
Opened November 7, 1966
Closed May 5, 1968

Cookin'
632 Performances
Opened July 7, 2004
Closed August 7, 2005

Oil City Symphony
626 performances
Opened November 5, 1987
Closed May 7, 1989

The Countess
618 performances
Opened September 28, 1999
Closed December 30, 2000

The Exonerated
608 performances
Opened October 10, 2002
Closed March 7, 2004

The Dining Room
607 performances
Opened February 11, 1982
Closed July 17, 1983

Hogan's Goat
607 performances
Opened March 6, 1965
Closed April 23, 1967

Drumstruck
607 performances
Opened June 16, 2005
Closed November 16, 2006

Beehive
600 performances
Opened March 30, 1986
Closed August 23, 1987

Criss Angel Mindfreak
600 performances
Opened November 20, 2001
Closed January 5, 2003

The Trojan Women
600 performances
Opened December 23, 1963
Closed May 30, 1965

The Syringa Tree
586 performances
Opened September 14, 2000
Closed June 2, 2002

The Musical of Musicals
(The Musical!)
583 Performances
Opened December 16, 2003
Closed November 13, 2005

Krapp's Last Tape
& The Zoo Story
582 performances
Opened August 29, 1960
Closed May 21, 1961

Three Tall Women
582 performances
Opened April 13, 1994
Closed August 26, 1995

**The Dumbwaiter
& The Collection
578 performances**
Opened January 21, 1962
Closed April 12, 1964

**Forbidden Broadway 1990
576 performances**
Opened January 23, 1990
Closed June 9, 1991

**Dames at Sea
575 performances**
Opened April 22, 1969
Closed May 10, 1970

The Crucible (revival)
571 performances
Opened 1957
Closed 1958

The Iceman Cometh (revival)
565 performances
Opened May 8, 1956
Closed February 23, 1958

**Forbidden Broadway 2001: A
Spoof Odyssey
552 performances**
Opened December 6, 2000
Closed February 6, 2002

The Hostage (revival)
545 performances
Opened October 16, 1972
Closed October 8, 1973

**Wit
545 performances**
Opened October 6, 1998
Closed April 9, 2000

**What's a Nice Country Like You
Doing in a State Like This?
543 performances**
Opened July 31, 1985
Closed February 9, 1987

**Forbidden Broadway 1988
534 performances**
Opened September 15, 1988
Closed December 24, 1989

**Gross Indecency: The Three
Trials of Oscar Wilde
534 performances**
Opened September 5, 1997
Closed September 13, 1998

**Frankie and Johnny
in the Claire de Lune
533 performances**
Opened December 4, 1987
Closed March 12, 1989

**Six Characters in Search
of an Author** (revival)
529 performances
Opened March 8, 1963
Closed June 28, 1964

**All in the Timing
526 performances**
Opened November 24, 1993
Closed February 13, 1994

**Oleanna
513 performances**
Opened October 3, 1992
Closed January 16, 1994

**Making Porn
511 performances**
Opened June 12, 1996
Closed September 14, 1997

**The Dirtiest Show in Town
509 performances**
Opened June 26, 1970
Closed September 17, 1971

**Happy Ending
& Day of Absence
504 performances**
Opened June 13, 1965
Closed January 29, 1967

**Greater Tuna
501 performances**
Opened October 21, 1982
Closed December 31, 1983

**A Shayna Maidel
501 performances**
Opened October 29, 1987
Closed January 8, 1989

The Boys From Syracuse (revival)
500 performances
Opened April 15, 1963
Closed June 28, 1964

* Production is still running as
of May 31, 2009; count includes
performances up to and including
that date.

*Reuben Greene, Cliff Gorman, and Kenneth Nelson in
The Boys in the Band (1968) (photo by Friedman-Abeles)*

*Jennifer Simard, Melissa Weil, Jordan Leeds, and Robert Roznowski
– the original cast of I Love You, You're Perfect, Now Change (1996)
(photo by Carol Rosegg)*

Michael West and David Pevsner in When Pigs Fly *(1996) (photo by Gerry Goodstein)*

Larry Shue and Anthony Heald in The Foreigner *(1984) (photo by Van Williams)*

David Christmas and Bernadette Peters in Dames at Sea *(1968) (photo by Lee Owens)*

Donna English and Jared Bradshaw in Forbidden Broadway: SVU *(2006) (photo by Carol Rosegg)*

OBITUARIES

EDIE ADAMS

BEA ARTHUR

BETSY BLAIR

DORIS COLE ABRAHAMS, 88, Bronx, New York-born producer, died Feb. 17, 2009, in Manhattan, New York, of heart failure. Beginning her career producing in London, England, her credits with the Oscar Lewenstein production company include *Billy Liar*, *Luther*, with Albert Finney, and *Semi-Detached*, with Laurence Olivier. Opening her own production company, Albion Productions, in the 1960s, her additional West End credits earned while there were Tom Stoppard's *Enter a Free Man* and *Travesties*, and *Wild Oats*, the cast for which included Jeremy Irons. Stateside and teaming with Kermit Bloomgarden, her Broadway credits include Peter Shaffer's *Equus* (Tony Award), and *Travesties* in 1975. Survivors include her daughter, Carole Abrahams.

EDIE ADAMS (Elizabeth Edith Enke), 81, Kingston, Pennsylvania-born screen, stage, and television actress-singer, died in Los Angeles, California, of pneumonia and cancer on Oct. 15, 2008. A 1953 Theatre World Award winner for her role in *Wonderful Town*, her other Broadway credits include *Li'l Abner*, for which she won a 1957 Best Featured Actress in a Musical Tony Award. Following her film debut in the 1960 Academy Award winner *The Apartment*, she was seen in such films as *Lover Come Back*, *Under the Yum Yum Tree*, *It's a Mad Mad Mad Mad World*, *Love with the Proper Stranger*, *The Best Man*, *Made in Paris*, *The Oscar*, *The Honey Pot*, and *Up in Smoke*. Her first husband was comedian Ernie Kovacs, who left her widowed in 1962. Her daughter from her marriage to Kovacs, Mia, was killed in a car crash in 1982. Her son from her second marriage survives her.

BRUCE ADLER 63, Manhattan, New York-born actor, died July 25, 2008, in Davie, Florida, of liver cancer. Making his Off-Broadway in 1957 in *It's a Funny World*, his other Off-Broadway credits include *Hard to be a Jew*, *Big Winner*, *The Golden Land*, *The Stranger's Return*, *The Rise of David Levinsky*, and *On Second Avenue*. His Broadway credits include *A Teaspoon Every 4 Hours*, *Oklahoma!* (1979), *Oh, Brother!*, *Sunday in the Park with George*, *Broadway*, *Those Were The Days* (Tony nomination), *Crazy for You* (Tony nomination), *Du Barry Was a Lady* (Encores). His film credits include the singing narrator in *Aladdin*, and he was the veteran of many regional theatre credits. He was also a veteran of the U.S. Army. His wife, Amy London; son, Jake; and two stepchildren survive him.

FRANK ALETTER, 83, College Point, Long Island-born actor, died May 13, 2009, in Tarzana, California, of cancer. His Broadway credits include *Bells Are Ringing*, *Mister Roberts*, *Wish You Were Here*, and *Time Limit!* His film roles include *Tora! Tora! Tora!* Best known for his work in television, his starring roles in that medium include *Bringing Up Buddy*, *It's About Time*, *The Cara Williams Show*, and *Nancy*. His roles as a supporting actor in television number over 100, including *Perry Mason*, *The Lucy Show*, *MASH*, *Kojak*, *All in the Family*, *Fantasy Island*, *Murder, She Wrote*, and *Dallas*. He was a veteran of the U.S. Army in W.W. II and for many years served on the board of directors of the Screen Actors Guild. His first marriage, to actress and former Miss America Lee Meriwether ended in divorce. He is survived by his second wife, Estella, daughters Kyle Oldham

and Lesley Aletter, stepdaughters, Alix and Julia Hodes, and granddaughter, Ryan Oldham.

ROBERT ANDERSON (Robert Woodruff Anderson), 91, New York, New York-born playwright, died Feb. 9, 2009, in New York, New York, of pneumonia, and had been suffering from Alzheimer's disease for several years. Best known for his Broadway play *Tea and Sympathy*, which starred Deborah Kerr and John Kerr (who reprised their roles in the film), his other Broadway credits include contributing sketches to *Dance Me a Song*, *All Summer Long*, Silent *Night, Holy Night* starring Henry Fonda and Barbara Bel Geddes), *I Never Sang for My Father* (with Hal Holbrook, Lillian Gish, and Alan Webb), and *Solitaire/Double Solitaire*. His screenplays include *Until They Sail*, The *Sand Pebbles* with Steve McQueen (1966), and *The Nun's Story* with Audrey Hepburn. His novels include *After* (1973), and *Getting Up and Going Home* (1978), and he also had many television credits. He was a veteran of the U.S. Army in W.W. II, and taught playwriting for the American Theatre Wing. His stepson, Nevin Terence Busch, and his stepdaughter, Mary-Kelly Busch, survive him.

ROSE ARRICK, actress/teacher, died Nov. 21, 2008, in New York, New York, of a heart attack. Her Broadway credits include *The Heroine*, *The Ninety Day Mistress*, *Unlikely Heroes*, *Bad Habits*, *A View From the Bridge*, *All My Sons*, *What's Wrong With This Picture?*, and *The Tale of the Allergist's Wife*. Off-Broadway credits include *The Lady Akane*, and *After the Fall*. She was also a longtime teacher at HB Studios in New York, and her many television and film roles in those media include *Law & Order: Special Victims Unit*, *Being Claudine*, *Ishtar*, *Those Lips, Those Eyes*, and *A New Leaf*. Her daughter, Sophie Arrick Lewis; grandchildren, Emma and Ben Bowers; sister, Joan Picower Seltzer; nieces, Jenny Picower and Eve Berk; and grandniece, Emily Berk, survive her.

BEA ARTHUR (Bernice Frankel), 86, New York, New York-born actress, died Apr. 25, 2009, in Los Angeles, California, of cancer. Making her Broadway debut in *Seventh Heaven*, her other Broadway credits include *Nature's Way*, *Fiddler on the Roof*, *Mame* (Tony Award), *The Floating Light Bulb*, and *Bea Arthur on Broadway*. Her Off-Broadway credits include *The Threepenny Opera*, *Shoestring Revue*, *Ulysses in Nighttown*, and *The Gay Divorcé*. She was best known for her groundbreaking title role in the television show *Maude* (1972-1978), for which she won an Emmy Award, and which was a spinoff from *All in the Family*. She was also well-known for the role of Dorothy Zbornak on *The Golden Girls* (1985-1992), for which she won her second Emmy Award. Her other television roles include those on *Amanda's*, *Curb Your Enthusiasm*, and *Malcolm in the Middle*. Her numerous film roles include *That Kind of Woman*, *Lovers and Other Strangers*, *The History of the World: Part I* and *For Better or Worse*. In 2001-2002, she toured the country in a one-woman show of songs and stories entitled *...And Then There's Bea*. She was chairwoman of the Art Attack Foundation, a nonprofit performing arts scholarship organization. She was inducted into the Television Academy Hall of

SYDNEY CHAPLIN

KEITH CHARLES

MARILYN COOPER

Fame. Her second marriage was to Tony-winning Broadway director Gene Saks, ended in divorce. She is survived by her two sons by her marriage to Saks, Matthew and Daniel, and granddaughters, Kyra and Violet.

CLIVE BARNES (Clive Alexander Barnes), 81, London, England-born theatre critic, died Nov. 19, 2008, in Manhattan, New York, of complications from cancer. He began his career writing for several publications including *The Daily Express*, then *The Spectator* and *The Times* in London, and he was eventually hired as the full-time dance critic for *The New York Times*, a position he held until 1977. He subsequently held the position of chief theatre critic at *The Times* for nearly ten years, from 1967-1977. In 1978 he became a dual dance-theatre critic at the *New York Post*, where he remained for the next thirty years, publishing his last review on Oct. 31, 2008. He wrote the column *Attitudes* for *Dance* magazine since 1989 and additionally contributed to *Ballet* and *The Stage* magazines. He was a veteran of the Royal Air Force. His publication *Ballet in Britain Since the War* was published in 1953. His books authored or contributed to, include *Frederick Ashton and His Ballets*, *Dance Scene USA*, and *Nureyev*. His wife, Valerie Taylor Barnes; son, Christopher, of London; daughter, Maya Johansen, of Woodstock, New York; and two grandchildren survive him.

PAUL BENEDICT, 70, Silver City, New Mexico-born screen, stage, and television actor/director; perhaps best known for playing neighbor Harry Bentley on the long-running sitcom *The Jeffersons*, from 1975-1983, and then again from 1983-1985, was found dead at his Martha's Vineyard, Massachusetts, home on Dec. 1, 2008. He began his career in the 1960s in Boston in the Theatre Company, with Robert De Niro, Dustin Hoffman, and Al Pacino, and went on to perform onstage with Off-Broadway credits including *Live Like Pigs*, *The Infantry*, *Little Murders*, *The Local Stigmatic*, *The White House Murder Case*, *The Cherry Orchard*, and *It's Only a Play*. His directing credits Off-Broadway include *Frankie and Johnny in the Clair de Lune*, *The Kathy & Mo Show: Parallel Lives*, and *Bad Habits*. He made his Broadway debut in 1968 in *Leda Had a Little Swan*, followed by *Bad Habits*, *Any Given Day*, *The Play's the Thing*, *Hughie* (1996), and *The Music Man* (2000). His film credits include *Cold Turkey*, *Taking Off*, *They Might Be Giants*, *Jeremiah Johnson*, *Up the Sandbox*, *This Is Spinal Tap*, *The Front Page* (1974), *Mandingo*, *Smile*, *The Goodbye Girl*, *The Man with Two Brains*, *Cocktail*, *The Chair*, *The Freshman* (1990), *The Addams Family*, *Waiting for Guffman*, *A Mighty Wind*, and *After the Sunset*. He was beloved by millions of children for appearing as Benedict the Mad Painter on television in *Sesame Street*. His characteristic oversized jaw and angular features were attributed to the pituitary disorder acromegaly, but he used them to his advantage. Survivors include his brother and three sisters.

BETSY BLAIR (Elizabeth Winifred Boger), 85, Cliffside Park, New Jersey-born actress, died Mar. 13, 2009, in London, England, from cancer. Her Broadway credits include her 1940 debut in *Panama Hattie*, followed by *The Beautiful People*, *The Glass Menagerie*, *King Richard II*, and *Face of a Hero*. In the 1970s she received a bachelor's degree in speech therapy and worked for a time simultaneously both as a speech therapist and an actress. Her film credits include *The Guilt of Janet Ames*, *Another Part of the Forest*, *The Snake Pit*, *Kind Lady*, *Marty* (Best Supporting Actress Academy Award nomination), and following her move to Europe, *Il Grido*, *Lies My Father Told Me*, *I Delfini*, *Calle Mayor*, *Othello*, and *All Night Long*. She was married to performer Gene Kelly from 1941-1957, and her 2003 memoir was entitled *The Memory of All That: Love and Politics in New York, Hollywood, and Paris* (Alfred A. Knopf). She was blacklisted in the 1950s while married to Kelly. Her second marriage was to Czech-born film director Karel Reisz, from 1963 until his death. Her daughter, Kerry Kelly Novick, three stepsons, Matthew, Toby, and Barney Reisz; eight grandchildren; and four great-granchildren survive her.

ERIC BLAU (Milton Eric Blau), 87, Bridgeport, Connecticut-born writer, died Feb. 17, 2009, in Manhattan, New York, of pneumonia following a stroke. Creator of *Jacque Brel Is Alive and Well and Living in Paris*, opened at the Village Gate in 1968, and, running for four years, became one of the longest-running shows in Off-Broadway history. It has been performed in thousands of venues all over the world. One of his first works incorporating Brel songs was *O Oysters!* Following the success of *Jacques Brel...*, he published poetry and several novels. He was a veteran of the U.S. Army Signal Corps in W.W. II. His wife, Elly Stone; son, Matthew, of Brattleboro, Vermont; son, John, of Forest Hills, New York; son, Peter, of Brooklyn, New York; and great-granddaughter, survive him.

AUGUSTO BOAL, 78, Rio de Janeiro, Brazil-born director, died May 2, 2009, in Rio de Janeiro, Brazil, of respiratory failure, following a battle with leukemia. A creator of innovative theatre in an interactive and political vein that became known under the umbrella term Theatre of the Oppressed and eventually had factions in over forty countries, his many productions include *Of Mice and Men*. Variations entitled Invisible Theater and Forum Theatre followed. His many books include *Theatre of the Oppressed*, published in 1974, *Hamlet and the Baker's Son: My Life in Theatre and Politics* and *Games for Actors and Non-Actors*. He is survived by his wife, Cecilia, and two sons, Julian and Fabian.

STEFAN BRECHT (Stefan Sebastian Brecht), 84, Berlin, Germany-born theatre historian, died Apr. 13, 2009 in Manhattan, New York, of a heart attack, following a battle with Lewy body dementia. A major chronicler of avant-garde theatre, his publications include the series *The Original Theater of the City of New York: From the Mid-Sixties to the Mid-Seventies*, as well as the individual volumes *Queer Theatre*, *The Theatre of Visions: Robert Wilson*, and *Peter Schumann's Bread and Puppet Theatre*. His short volume of poetry was entitled *Stefan Brecht: Poems*. He earned his Phd in philosophy from Harvard University, and was a veteran of the U.S. Army. He is survived by his wife, clothing designer Rena Gill; daughter, Sarah, of Sligo, Ireland; and Sebastian, of Manhattan; son, Michael Böhm, of

IRENE DAILEY

MEL FERRER

NINA FOCH

Bremen, Germany; half-sister, Hanne Hiob, of Munich; and three grandchildren.

DONNY(IE) BURKS (Donald Robert Burks), 68, Martinsville, Virginia-born basketball player/actor/musician/producer, died Sunday, Jan. 3, 2009, of heart failure. An All American athlete and the first African-American captain of St. John's basketball team in 1963, he turned down offers from NBA basketball teams to become an actor. A 1970 Theatre World Award winner for the title role in *Billy Noname* Off-Broadway, he made his Broadway debut in *Hair* in 1970, followed by *Truckload*, *The American Clock*, and *The Tap Dance Kid*. His film credits include *Cotton Comes to Harlem*, *Shaft*, *William Craft*, *Bang the Drum Slowly*, and *Without a Trace*. His television credits include *Muggable Mary*, *The Today Show*, and *The Joe Franklin Show*, as well as many as a voiceover artist. He also produced *The Talk of the Town*, a musical that ran in the Algonquin Hotel's Oak Room about the Algonquin Round Table scene. His son, Nicholas Lagerfelt; aunts, Algie Lampkins, Yuanita (Nelo) Lampkins, and May Lampkins; cousins, Delores (Jean) Bunn, Curtis Lampkins, Beverly Lampkins, Rachel Lampkins, Ronald Lampkins, Penny Bunn, Terence Bunn, Michael Raye, Sky Raye, and Sierra Brown survive him.

BERTRAND CASTELLI, 78, Salon de Provence, Bouches du Rhone, France-born writer/producer/painter, died Aug. 1, 2008, off of the coast of the Caribbean in the Yucatán Peninsula in Mexico, where he was artist in residence at the Maroma Resort and Spa in Riviera Maya, after being struck by a boat. The original executive producer of *Hair* (1968), he was responsible for director Tom O'Horgan being hired, as well as for other crucial artistic decisions in the revolutionary musical vehicle. An international bon vivant, he had several simultaneous careers, and was a highly regarded painter in his last years. His daughters, Pandora Castelli, and Josephine, of Manhattan; granddaughter; and two stepsons, Michael and Winston Dutton of Santa Barbara, California, survive him.

SYDNEY CHAPLIN (Sydney Earle Chaplin), 82, Los Angeles, California-born actor, died Mar. 3, 2009, in Rancho Mirage, California, following a stroke. A 1957 Theatre World Award winner as well as a Best Featured Actor in a Musical Tony Award winner for his role in *Bells Are Ringing*, his other Broadway credits include *Goodbye, Charlie*, *Subways are for Sleeping*, *In the Counting House*, and *Funny Girl* (Tony nomination). He appeared in his father's films *Limelight* and *A Countess from Hong Kong*, and additionally in the films *Land of the Pharaohs*, *Abdulla the Great*, and *Pillars of the Sky*. He was a veteran of W.W. II, and in later life, he owned Chaplin's restaurant in Palm Springs, California, for nearly a decade. The son of legendary screen actor Charlie Chaplin and his second wife, Lita Grey, Sydney Chaplin's first two marriages ended in divorce. His wife, Margaret Beebe Chaplin; son by his first marriage, Stephan; granddaughter; half-sister, actress Geraldine Chaplin, among eight other half-siblings that Charlie Chaplin had with wife Oona O'Neill Chaplin.

KEITH CHARLES, 74, actor, died Jul. 1, 2008, from lung cancer. His Broadway credits include *Celebration*, *Applause* (with Lauren Bacall), *Happy Birthday, Wanda June*, and *Threepenny Opera*. His Off-Broadway credits include *The Fantasticks*, *The Death of a Well-Loved Boy* (1967), and *Night and Her Stars*. His many television and film credits include *Law & Order*, *Kate and Allie*, *Newhart*, *Remington Steele*, *Dallas*, *Barnaby Jones*, *As the World Turns*, *Ryan's Hope*, *Guiding Light*, *The Edge of Night*, *The Secret Storm*, *Search For Tomorrow*, *Love of Life*, and *One Life to Live*. His wife, Nancy Ford, survives him.

MARILYN COOPER, 74, Bronx, NY-born actress, died Apr. 23, 2009, in Englewood, New Jersey. A Tony winner for her role in *Woman of the Year* (with Lauren Bacall), her other Broadway credits include her debut in *Mr. Wonderful*, *West Side Story*, *Brigadoon*, *Gypsy*, *Hallelujah, Baby! Golden Rainbow*, *Two by Two*, *Odd Couple*, and *Broadway Bound*.

IRENE DAILEY, 88, New York, New York-born actress, who won a 1979 Emmy for her role as Liz Matthews on the daytime serial *Another World*, died of colon cancer on Sept. 24, 2008, in Guerneville, California. First gaining acclaim in London, she performed there to rave reviews in *Tomorrow—With Pictures*. Making her Broadway debut in 1943 in *Nine Girls*, her other Broadway credits include *Nine Girls*, *Truckline Café*, *Idiot's Delight*, *Miss Lonelyhearts*, *Andorra*, *The Subject Was Roses*, and *You Know I Can't Hear You When the Water's Running*. Her Off-Broadway credits include *Good Woman of Setzuan*, *Rooms*, *The Loves of Cass McGuire*, and *Edith Stein*. She was seen in the films *No Way to Treat a Lady*, *Daring Game*, *Five Easy Pieces*, *The Grissom Gang*, *The Amityville Horror* (1979), and *Stacking*. She played her role on *Another World* from 1974-1986, and then again from 1988-1994, and spent a year as well on *The Edge of Night* on television in 1969. Her many other television credits include *Ben Casey*, *Dr. Kildare*, *The Twilight Zone*, and *The Defenders*. Her brother, actor/dancer, Dan Dailey, died in 1978. There are no reported survivors.

LUTHER DAVIS (Luther Berryhill Davis), 91, Brooklyn, New York-born writer, died July 29, 2008, in West Palm Beach, Florida, from natural causes. A 1954 Tony Award winner for his book of *Kismet*, his other Broadway credits include *Crazy with the Heat* (contributor), *Kiss Them for Me*, *Leonard Sillman's New Faces of 1952*, *Timbuktu!* (Tony nomination), and *Grand Hotel* (Tony nomination). His screenplays include *The Hucksters*, *Lady in a Cage*, and *A Lion in the Streets*. He was a veteran of the U.S. Army, rising to the rank of major. His wife, Jennifer Bassey Davis, and two daughters, Rory Bolander of Los Angeles, California, and Noel Davis, of Orange County, California, survive him.

NATHAN DAVIS, 91, Chicago, Illinois-born actor, died Oct. 15, 2008, in Chicago, Illinois, of emphysema and Parkinson's disease. Beginning his career in earnest around age sixty, he racked up numerous credits at the Steppenwolf Theatre, following the theatre's production of *The Grapes of Wrath* from Chicago

HORTON FOOTE

DODY GOODMAN

A. LARRY HAINES

to London, La Jolla, and then on to Broadway. He played the supporting role of Gaston in Steve Martin's *Picasso at the Lapin Agile* in 1994 at the Westwood Playhouse and at Steppenwolf. His film credits include *Holes*, *Stony Island*, *Code of Silence*, and *Thief*. His numerous television credits include those on *Frasier* and *Cheers*. He was a veteran of W.W. II. His wife of sixty-seven years, Metta; son, Richard; daughter Jo Ellen Davis Friedman; seven grandchildren; and five great-grandchildren survive him.

MEL FERRER (Melchor Ferrer), 90, Elberon, New Jersey-born screen, stage, and television actor, died in Santa Barbara, California, near his Carpinteria, California, ranch on June 2, 2008, following a period of failing health. His Broadway credits include *You Never Know*, *Kind Lady*, *Strange Fruit*, and *Ondine*, and directed José Ferrer in a 1946 revival of *Cyrano de Bergerac*, before embarking upon a notable film career. He starred in such notable films as *Lili* and *War and Peace* (1956; opposite his then-wife Audrey Hepburn), *Lost Boundaries*, *Born to Be Bad*, *The Brave Bulls*, *Scaramouche* (1952), *Rancho Notorious*, *Knights of the Round Table*, *The Sun Also Rises*, *The World the Flesh and the Devil*, *Blood and Roses*, *The Longest Day*, *The Fall of the Roman Empire*, *Sex and the Single Girl*, *El Greco* (also producer), *Brannigan*, *The Norsemen*, and *Lili Marleen*. He directed Hepburn in *Green Mansions* and produced her film *Wait Until Dark*, among other behind-the-scenes credits. He also appeared numerous times on television, and had a recurring role on the evening soap opera *Falcon Crest* in the 1980s. His fifth wife, Lisa; six children; nine grandchildren; and one great-grandchild survive him.

NINA FOCH (Nina Consuela Maud Fock), 84, Leyden, The Netherlands-born actress, died Dec. 5, 2008, in Los Angeles, California, from complications of the blood disorder myelodysplasia. Her Broadway credits include her debut in 1947 in *John Loves Mary*, followed by *Twelfth Night*, *A Phoenix Too Frequent*, *King Lear*, *Measure for Measure*, *The Taming of the Shrew*, and *A Second String*. Her Broadway directing credits include *Ways and Means*, as part of *Tonight at 8:30p.m.*, in 1967. Following her 1944 feature debut in *The Return of the Vampire*, she was seen in such films as *She's a Soldier Too*, *Cry of the Werewolf*, *A Song to Remember*, *Escape in the Fog*, *My Name is Julia Ross*, *Johnny O'Clock*, *The Dark Past*, *Johnny Allegro*, *An American in Paris*, *Young Man with Ideas*, *Scaramouche* (1952), *Sombrero*, *You're Never Too Young*, *The Ten Commandments* (1956), *Three Brave Men*, *Cash McCall*, *Spartacus*, *Such Good Friends*, *Mahogany*, *Skin Deep*, *Sliver*, *It's My Party*, *Hush*, *Pumpkin*, and *How to Deal*. She also had numerous television credits, including those on *The Chevrolet Tele-Theater*, *NCIS*, *Studio One*, *That Girl*, and *Route 66*. Affiliated for four decades with the University of Southern California's film school, she also taught at the American Film Institute's film studies center in the 1970s. Her son, Dirk De Brito from her second marriage and three grandchildren survive her.

HORTON FOOTE (Albert Horton Foote Jr.), 92, Wharton, Texas-born playwright, died Mar. 4, 2009, in Hartford, Connecticut, in his sleep, following a brief illness.

He had been in Connecticut with his family finalizing *The Orphans' Home Cycle*, his nine-play event that will be co-produced by Hartford Stage and New York's Signature Theatre in fall 2009. His Broadway credits as an actor include *The Coggerers*, and as a writer, *Only the Heart*, *Six O'Clock Theatre*, *Two's Company*, *The Trip to Bountiful*, *The Travelling Lady*, *The Young Man from Atlanta* (1995 Pulitzer Prize for Drama, Tony nomination), and *Dividing the Estate* (2008 Drama Desk Award, 2009 Tony nomination). He also received a 2006 Drama Desk Career Achievement Award for his body of work. Off-Broadway credits include *Lily Dale*, *The Widow Claire*, *Talking Pictures*, *Night Seasons* (also directed), *Laura Dennis*, *The Last of the Thorntons*, *The Carpetbagger's Children*, and *The Day Emily Married*. He directed his daughter Daisy B. Foote's play *When they Speak of Rita*, Off-Broadway. A Best Original Screenplay Academy Award winner for *Tender Mercies*, he won his first Oscar for his adaptation of Harper Lee's *To Kill a Mockingbird* (ranked 25th of the 100 greatest films of all time by the American Film Institute). His other screenplays include *Baby the Rain Must Fall*. The writer of more than fifty plays during his six-decade career, he began his career as an apprentice at the Pasadena Playhouse in California from 1933-35, and had roles in summer stock on Martha's Vineyard, Massachusetts, before forming the American Actors Company in New York with a group of artists that included choreographers Agnes DeMille and Jerome Robbins. *Wharton Dance* was his first play. He also wrote teleplays for television including those on *Playhouse 90*, *U.S. Steel Hour*, *Studio One*, and *Philco Television Playhouse*. His other awards and honors include the William Inge Lifetime Achievement Award (1989), the Ian McLellan Hunter Memorial Award for Lifetime Achievement from the Writers Guild of America (1999), and the National Medal of Arts from President Bill Clinton in 2000. He is survived by daughters, actress Hallie and playwright Daisy; sons Horton Jr., who also acted and directed, and Walter, a lawyer; and two grandchildren. His wife Lillian and frequent collaborator died in 1992. On Thursday, Mar. 5, 2009, Broadway theatres dimmed their lights in his honor, for one minute at 8:00p.m.

GEORGE FURTH (George Schweinfurth), 75, Chicago, Illinois-born actor/writer, died Aug. 11, 2008, in Santa Monica, California, from complications of a lung infection. A Tony Award winner for his book of the Stephen Sondheim musical *Company*, his other Broadway credits include *A Cook for Mr. General*, *Hot Spot*, *Company*, *Twigs*, *Sondheim: A Musical Tribute*, *The Act*, *The Supporting Cast*, *Merrily We Roll Along*, *Precious Stone*, and *Getting Away With Murder*. His films include *The Best Man*, *A Very Special Favor*, *The Boston Strangler*, *Butch Cassidy and the Sundance Kid*, *Myra Breckinridge*, *Blazing Saddles*, *Shampoo*, *Norman … is That You?*, *Oh, God!*, *Hooper*, *The Man with Two Brains*, and *Bulworth*. There are no reported survivors.

ESTELLE GETTY (Estelle Scher), 84, New York, New York-born actress, best known for her Emmy Award-winning role of Sophia Petrillo on the sitcom *The*

EILEEN HERLIE

JENNIFER HILARY

PAT HINGLE

Golden Girls, died on July 22, 2008, in Hollywood, California, following a long battle with Lewy Body dementia. Making her Off-Broadway debut in 1971 in *The Divorce of Judy and Jane*, her other Off-Broadway credits include *Widows and Children First*, *Table Settings*, *Demolition of Hannah Fay*, *Never Too Old*, *A Box of Tears*, *Hidden Corners*, *I Don't Know Why I'm Screaming*, *Under the Bridge There's a Lonely Place*, *Light Up the Sky*, *Pocketful of Posies*, and *Fits and Starts*, before making her Broadway debut in 1982 in *Torch Song Trilogy*. She was also seen in such films as *Tootsie*, *Mask*, *Mannequin*, *Stop! Or My Mom Will Shoot*, and *Stuart Little*. Her two sons, a brother, and a sister survive her.

WILLIAM GIBSON, 94, Bronx, New York-born writer, died on Nov. 25, 2008, in Stockbridge, Massachusetts. A 1960 Best Play Tony Award winner for *The Miracle Worker*, his other Broadway credits include *Two for the Seesaw* (Tony nomination), *Golden Boy* (Tony nomination), *A Cry for Players*, *Seesaw*, *Golda*, *Monday After the Miracle*, *Raggedy Ann*, and *Golda's Balcony* (a reworking of *Golda*, starring Tony-nominated Tovah Feldshuh). He earned an Oscar nomination for adapting his play *The Miracle Worker* to the screen, and additionally helped adapt his novel *The Cobweb* and his play *Golda's Balcony* to the screen. Sons, Thomas, of Stockbridge, Massachusetts, and Daniel, of Cambridge, Massachusetts, survive him.

STEVEN GILBORN (Steven Neil Gilborn), 72, New Rochelle, NY-born actor, died Jan. 2, 2009, at his home in North Chatham, New York, of cancer. Perhaps best known for his role as Ellen DeGeneres's father on the sitcom *Ellen*, his Broadway credits include his 1973 debut in *Creeps*, followed by *Basic Training of Pavlo Hummel*, *Tartuffe*, and *Teibele and Her Demon*. Off-Broadway credits include *Rosmersholm*, *Henry V*, *Measure for Measure*, *Ashes*, *The Dybbuk*, *Museum*, *Shadow of a Gunman*, *It's Hard to Be a Jew*, *Isn't It Romantic*, *Principia Scriptoriae*, *Panache*, and *Festival of One Acts*. His regional theatre credits include *The Tempest* and *Much Ado About Nothing* at the Folger Theatre, and *Awake and Sing!* at the McCarter Theatre in Princeton, New Jersey. His numerous television credits include those on *The Wonder Years*, *Law & Order*, *The West Wing*, and *NYPD Blue*. His film credits include *The Brady Bunch Movie* and *Nurse Betty*, and he additionally taught at the University of California, Berkeley, the Massachusetts Institute of Technology, and Columbia University. His wife, Karen Halverson; two daughters, Lailia Giborn of Washington and Marya Gilborn of Manhattan; two brothers, Jeffrey of Cranston, Rhode Island, and Craig of Mount Tabor, Vermont; and four grandchildren survive him.

DODY GOODMAN (Dolores Goodman), 93, Columbus, Ohio-born performer, perhaps best known for her many Emmy-nominated appearances on *The Jack Paar Show*, died of natural causes on June 22, 2008, in Englewood, New Jersey. She had been living at the Actors Fund Home prior to her death. First professionally dancing in the ballet company of Radio City Music Hall, her Broadway debut was in 1941 in *Viva O'Brien*, *Wine, Women and Song*, *Something for the Boys*, *One*

Touch of Venus, *Laffing Room Only*, *Miss Liberty*, *Call Me Madam*, *My Darlin' Aida*, *Wonderful Town*, *A Rainy Day in Newark*, *My Daughter, Your Son*, *The Front Page*, *Lorelei*, and *Grease*. Her Off-Broadway credits include *Shoestring Revue*, *Shoestring '57*, *Parade*, *New Cole Porter Revue*, *Ah Wilderness!*, *Selling Off*, and *Nunsense*, She was seen in such motion pictures as *Bedtime Story* (1964), *Grease*, *Max Duggan Returns*, *Splash*, and *Cool as Ice*. Her television credits in addition to *The Jack Paar Show* include *Mary Hartman, Mary Hartman*, *Diff'rent Strokes*, *Search for Tomorrow*, and *One Life to Live*. Several nieces and nephews survive her.

SIMON GRAY (Simon James Holliday Gray), 71, Hayling Island, England-born writer, died Aug. 7, 2008, in London, England, after suffering from cancer. His Broadway credits include *Wise Child*, *Butley* (Tony nomination), and *Otherwise Engaged* (Tony nomination, Drama Desk Award). His Off-Broadway his credits include *The Common Pursuit* (also director, Drama Desk nomination), *The Rear Column*, *Quartermaine's Terms*, and *The Holy Terror* (also director). His other plays include *Molly* and *Cell Mates*. With credits including forty plays, television plays, and screenplays, among his five novels were *The Smoking Diaries*, *The Year of Jouncer*, and *The Last Cigarette*. He also lectured at what is now Queen Mary College, University of London. He is survived by his wife, Victoria Rothschild, the youngest daughter of the third Baron Rothschild and fellow lecturer at college; daughter, Beryl Kevern; and son, Benjamin, both from his first marriage to Beryl Kevern.

A. LARRY HAINES, 89, Mt. Vernon, Kentucky-born actor, died July 17, 2008, in Delray Beach, Florida. His Broadway credits include his debut in 1962 in *A Thousand Clowns*, followed by *Generation* (Best Featured Actor in a Play Tony nomination), *Promises, Promises*, (Best Featured Actor in a Musical Tony nomination), *Last of the Red Hot Lovers*, *Twigs*, *No Hard Feelings*, and *Tribute*. Perhaps best known for playing Stu on the daytime drama *Search for Tomorrow* for thirty-five years, he won three Daytime Emmy Awards for his role on the program. He also appeared on *Another World* and *Loving*, and appeared elsewhere on television on *Maude* and *Kojak*, among other programs. He was a radio actor in the pioneering days of the medium, appearing on *The Inner Sanctum*. His wife, Jean Perlman Haines, and daughter, Debora, survive him.

EILEEN HERLIE (Eileen Isobel Herlihy), 90, Glasgow, Scotland-born screen, stage, and television actress, died on Oct. 8, 2008, in New York, New York, of pneumonia. Her Broadway credits include *The Matchmaker* (with Ruth Gordon), *Makropoulos Secret*, *Epitaph for George Dillon* (1958, and 1959 revival), *Take Me Along* (1960 Best Actress in a Musical Tony nomination), *All-American*, *Photo Finish*, *Hamlet*, *Halfway Up the Tree*, *Emperor Henry IV*, and *Crown Matrimonial*. She played Gertrude opposite Laurence Olivier in the 1948 Oscar-winning *Hamlet*, and her other films include *The Great Gilbert and Sullivan*, *Freud*, *The Seagull* (1968), and *For Better, for Worse*. She is perhaps best known for the

VAN JOHNSON

DAVID JONES

MILTON KATSELAS

thirty-two years she played the role of Myrtle Fargate on the long-running daytime drama *All My Children*, first appearing in 1976, with Emmy nominations as best supporting actress in 1984, 1985, and 1986. She gave her last performance less than five months before she died. Her brother, Alfred Herlihy of Glasgow, Scotland, survives her.

MICHAEL HIGGINS (Michael Patrick Higgins), 88, Brooklyn, New York-born actor, died Nov. 5, 2008, in New York, New York, of heart failure. His Broadway credits include *Antigone, Our Lan', Romeo and Juliet, The Carefree Tree, The Lark, Uncle Vanya, The Iceman Cometh, Equus,* and *Mixed Couples.* Off-Broadway credits include *The Carefree Tree, Easter, For the Time Being, The Crucible* (Obie Award), *Diff'rent, The Long Voyage Home, A Pair of Pairs, King Lear, Macbeth, Life is a Dream, The Queen and the Rebels, Medea, L'Ete (Summer), Reunion* (Obie Award), *A Tale Told, Richard II, The Seagull, Levitation, Love's Labour's Lost,* and *In This Fallen City.* His film credits include *The Stepford Wives* (1975), *The Seduction of Joe Tynan,* and *Fort Apache, the Bronx.* He was a veteran of the U.S. Army in W.W. II, and was awarded both the Bronze Star and the Purple Heart for his combat service. His daughter, Deidre Higgins; wife, the former Elizabeth Lee Goodwin; two sons, Sean and Christopher; two brothers, Hugh and Thomas; two sisters, Marie Higgins and Anna Karlya; and four grandchildren survive him.

JENNIFER HILARY (Jennifer Mary Hilary), 65, Frimley, Surrey, England-born actress, died Aug. 6, 2008, in London, England. Her Broadway credits include *The Rehearsal, Ivanov,* and *Avanti.* She additionally appeared in over thirty television shows and films, with British credits including *Midsomer Murders, Slipstream, Tales of the Unexpected, Z Cars, The Idol, The Heroes of Telemark,* and *Becket.* She accrued numerous British regional theatre credits, including those at Birmingham Repertory and Liverpool Playhouse.

PAT HINGLE (Martin Patterson Hingle), 84, Miami, Florida-born actor, died Jan. 3, 2009, in Carolina Beach, North Carolina, of myelodysplasia, a blood disorder. His Broadway debut was in 1953 in *End as a Man,* followed by *Festival, Cat on a Hot Tin Roof, Girls of Summer, The Dark at the Top of the Stairs* (Tony nomination), *J.B., Deadly Game, Strange Interlude* (1963), *Blues For Mr. Charlie, A Girl Could Get Lucky, The Glass Menagerie* (1965), *Johnny No Trump, The Price, Child's Play, The Selling of the President, That Championship Season, A Lady from the Sea, A Life,* and *1776.* His regional credits include *Troilus and Cressida* and *Macbeth* at the American Shakespeare Festival in Stratford, Connecticut. His multitudinous film credits include *On the Waterfront, No Down Payment, Splendor in the Grass, The Strange One, The Grifters, Citizen Cohn, Batman,* and *Batman Returns.* His television credits include *Murder, She Wrote, In the Heat of the Night,* and *Cheers.* He was a veteran of the U.S. Navy in W.W. II. He is survived by his wife, Julia; son, Bill Hingle; daughters Jody Smith and Molly Mantione; two stepchildren, Katherine Joy and Gregory Swanson; two sisters, Jamie Petty and Joyce France; and eleven grandchildren.

VAN JOHNSON (Charles Van Dell Johnson), 92, Newport, Rhode Island-born actor, died Dec. 12, 2008, in Nyack, New York, of natural causes. His Broadway credits include *New Faces of 1936, Too Many Girls, Pal Joey, Come on Strong, On a Clear Day You Can See Forever, Mating Dance, La Cage aux Folles,* and *Show Boat.* One of the most enduring presences in the history of cinema, following his 1940 debut in *Too Many Girls,* he starred in such 1940s hits as *A Guy Named Joe* and *Thirty Seconds Over Tokyo,* as well as appeared during his career in *Dr. Gillespie's Assistant, The Human Comedy, Two Girls and a Sailor, The White Cliffs of Dover, Thrill of a Romance, Week-End at the Waldorf, Easy to Wed, No Leave No Love, Till the Clouds Roll By, The Romance of Rosy Ridge, State of the Union, Command Decision, Mother is a Freshman, In the Good Old Summertime, Battleground, The Big Hangover, Duchess of Idaho, Three Guys Named Mike, Go for Broke!, It's a Big Country, When in Rome, Plymouth Adventure, Easy to Love, Siege at Red River, The Caine Mutiny, Brigadoon, The Last Time I Saw Paris, The End of the Affair* (1955), *The Bottom of the Bottle, Miracle in the Rain, Kelly and Me, Wives and Lovers, Divorce American Style, Where Angels Go Trouble Follows!, Yours Mine and Ours, The Kidnapping of the President,* and *The Purple Rose of Cairo.* His numerous television credits include *Batman* and *Murder, She Wrote.* His daughter, Schuyler, survives him.

DAVID JONES (David Hugh Jones), director, died Sept. 18, 2008, in Rockport, Maryland, of a heart attack. His Broadway credits include *No Man's Land, Taking Sides,* and *The Caretaker.* As an associate director under Peter Hall of the Royal Shakespeare Company, he is credited with single-handedly resurrecting the reputation of Gorky, the early twentieth century Russian playwright. He directed Gorky's *Enemies, The Lower Depths, Summerfolk,* and *The Zykovs,* all at the Royal Shakespeare Company's Adwych Theatre, in the 1970s. In the 1990s he directed Gorky's *Barbarians* there. His directing film credits include *84 Charing Cross Road, Betrayal, Jacknife,* and *The Confession.* His television credits include *Law & Order: Special Victims Unit, The Practice,* and *Chicago Hope.* He additionally taught at the Yale School of Drama. Survivors include his companion, Joyce Tenneson; sister, Gwyneth Jones, of Somerset, England; and two sons, Jesse, of Brooklyn, New York, and Joseph, of Tucson, Arizona.

PETER KAPATAN, 51, actor, died June 4, 2008, in New York, New York. His Broadway credits include *Got Tu Go Disco, Joseph and the Amazing Technicolor Dreamcoat, Sunset Boulevard, Titanic,* and *The Wedding Singer.* Off-Broadway credits include *Olympus on My Mind* and *The Wild Party.* National tours include *Camelot* (with Richard Burton), *Aida,* and *The Scarlet Pimpernel.* His parents, Peter and Helen Kapatan; brother, Nicholas Kapetan, all of Fairfield, Connecticut; sisters, Melissa (Kapetan) Russow of Milford, Connecticut, and Christine Kapetan of Topanga, California; and several nieces and nephews survive him.

EARTHA KITT

JONATHAN MOORE

PAUL NEWMAN

PETER KASS (Peter Meyer Kass), 85, Brooklyn, New York-born actor/director/ teacher, died Aug. 4, 2008, in Manhattan, New York, of heart failure. His Broadway credits as an actor include *The Innocent Voyage*, *Jacobowsky and the Colonel*, *No Exit*, *Skipper Next to God*, *The Country Girl*, and as a director, *Night Music*, *The Sign in Sidney Brustein's Window*, *Postmark Zero*, and *Nathan Weinstein, Mystic, Connecticut*. A veteran of the U.S. Army in W.W. II, he also taught with stints at Boston University and New York University. His Off-Broadway credits as a writer include *Monopoly*, and as a director, two plays written by his son, Sam Henry Kass: *Side Street Scenes* and *Family Snapshots*. His wife, the former Nance Robbins; two sons, Robbie Kass and Sam, both of Santa Monica, California; and five grandchildren survive him.

MILTON KATSELAS (Milton George Katsalas), 75, Pittsburgh, Pennsylvania-born director and acting teacher, died Oct. 24, 2008, in Los Angeles, California, of heart failure. A former assistant to Elia Kazan on *Tea and Sympathy*, he directed the landmark Edward Albee play, *Zoo Story*, Off-Broadway, in 1960. His Broadway credits as an actor include *The Lark*, followed by directing credits including *The Garden of Sweets*, *On an Open Roof*, *The Rose Tatoo*, *Butterflies are Free*, (Tony Nomination for best director of a play), *Camino Real*, and *Private Lives*. Founding the Beverly Hills Playhouse acting school in 1978, he mentored actors including Alec Baldwin, James Cromwell, Burt Reynolds, John Glover, George Clooney, Kate Hudson, and Tyne Daly. His film credits as director are *Butterflies are Free*, *40 Carats*, *Report to the Commissioner*, and *When You Comin' Back Red Ryder?* He also founded the Beverly Hills Playhouse acting school. His two brothers, Tasso, of Pittsburgh, Pennsylvania, and Chris, of Evergreen, Colorado, and sister, Sophia Katsafanas, survive him.

EARTHA KITT (Eartha May Kitt), 81, North, South Carolina-born singer-actress, known for her sensual way of performing songs like "C'est Si Bon," "Love for Sale," and "Santa Baby," died Dec. 25, 2008, in New York, New York, of colon cancer. Beginning her professional career by accepting a dare from a friend that resulted in her winning a position with the Katherine Dunham Dance Company, Her Broadway credits include *Carib Song*, *Bal Negre*, *Leonard Sillman's New Faces 1952*, *Mrs. Patterson*, *Shinbone Alley*, *Jolly's Progress*, *Timbuktu!* (Tony nomination), *The Wild Party* (Tony nomination, Drama Desk Award nomination), and *Nine*. She was also seen in such movies as *The Mark of the Hawk*, *St. Louis Blues*, *Anna Lucasta* (1959), *Uncle Tom's Cabin*, *Friday Foster*, *Erik the Viking*, *Ernest Scared Stupid*, *Boomerang* (1992), *Fatal Instinct*, *Harriet the Spy*, *Holes*, and *And then Came Love*. Her television credits include *I Spy* in 1965 (Emmy nomination), and notable appearances on *Batman*. She garnered a Grammy nomination for her album, *Back in Business*, in 1994, and won two Daytime Emmy Awards as outstanding performer in an animated program for her role as the scheming empress–wanabe Yzma in *The Emperor's New School*. She became an advocate for homeless children for UNICEF, and published three autobiographies.

Her daughter, Kitt Shapiro, and two grandchildren, survive her.

ALVIN KLEIN, 73, Brownsville, Brooklyn, New York-born theatre critic, died Feb. 28, 2009, in New York, New York, of a heart attack. Covering the New Jersey, Connecticut, Long Island, and Westchester County sections of *The New York Times* from the late 1970s until September 2004, he wrote nearly 3,500 reviews and features. Beginning his career at New York public radio at WNYC in 1966, he went on to become the station's opening night theatre critic until the late 1980s. He was a past president of the Drama Desk organization and a member of the awards committee of the Lucille Lortel Foundation. His son, Gideon, of Las Vegas, Nevada; daughter, Alexandra Klein Rafaeli, of Manhattan; and two grandchildren survive him.

PEARL LANG (Pearl Lack), 87, Chicago, Illinois-born dancer/choreographer, died Feb. 24, 2009, in Manhattan, New York, of a heart attack while recuperating from hip surgery. Her Broadway credits include *One Touch of Venus*, *Carousel*, *Finian's Rainbow*, *Touch and Go*, *Peer Gynt*, and *Sholom Aleichem*. A major player in the Martha Graham Dance Company until 1952 and where she created such dances as *Diversion of Angels*, her other roles performed with the Graham company include roles in *El Penitente*, *Appalachian Spring*, *Letter to the World*, and *Clytemnestra*. Founding her own company, the Pearl Lang Dance Theater, in 1952, she choreographed for the Dutch National Ballet, Boston Ballet, and the Batsheva Dance Company of Israel, among other credits. She was also a teacher at Yale, the Juillard School, and the Neighborhood Playhouse, as well as at the Martha Graham School of Contemporary Dance. Her husband, actor Joseph Wiseman; two nieces; and a nephew survive her.

HUGH LEONARD (John Joseph Byrne, aka John Keyes Byrne, aka Jack), 82, Dublin, Ireland-born writer, died Feb. 12, 2009, in Dublin, Ireland, of multiple ailments. A 1978 Tony Award winner for his play *Da*, his other Broadway credits include *The au Pair Man* (Tony nomination), and *A Life* (Tony nomination). His other thirty or so plays include *Stephen D*, *The Poker Session*, *Summer*, and *The Patrick Pearse Motel*. He adapted Dickens' *Great Expectations* and *A Tale of Two Cities* for British television, was a longtime columnist for *The Sunday Independent* and contributor to *The New York Times*, and his books include *Home Before Night*, *Out After Dark*, and *Rover and Other Cats*. His daughter, Danielle Byrne, and wife, Katherine, survive him.

STUART LITTLE (Stuart West Little), 86, Hartford, Connecticut-born theatre writer, died July 27, 2008, in Caanan, Connecticut, of congestive heart failure. Beginning his career with *The New York Herald Tribune* in 1946, he rose to assistant editor and then to writing a theatre news column for the paper from 1958-1966. He then turned to writing books on theatre in the 1970s, one co-written with theatre producer Arthur Cantor was entitled *The Playmakers* (Norton, 1970), another in 1972 entitled *Off-Broadway: The Prophetic Theater* (Coward,

HAROLD PINTER

ROBERT PROSKY

NATASHA RICHARSON

McCann, & Geoghegan), and finally, in 1974, *Enter Joseph Papp: In Search of a New American Theater* (Coward, McCann, & Geoghegan). From 1986-2001 he edited the quarterly newsletter of the Theatre Development Fund. He was a veteran of W.W. II in the Office of Strategic Services, where he wrote psychological profiles of high-ranking Nazis. His wife, Anastazia Lillie Marie Raben-Levetzau; son, Christopher Little, of Norfolk, Connecticut; two daughters, Caroline Larken of Pewsey Wiltshire, England, and Suzanne Little of New York, New York; brother, Edward H. Little of East Haddam, Connecticut; sister, Virginia L. Miller, of Bloomfield, Connecticut; three grandchildren; and four great-grandchildren, survive him.

KERMIT LOVE (Kermit Ernest Hollingshead Love), 91, Spring Lake, New Jersey-born costumer, died June 21, 2008, in Poughkeepsie, New York, of congestive heart failure. His Broadway credits include *Naughty Naughty '00* (1937 & 1946), *The Fireman's Flame*, *Old Acquaintance*, *One Touch of Venus*, *Suds in Your Eyes*, *Dark Hammock*, and *Ballet Theatre*, before going on to become one of the most renowned costumers in ballet. His collaborations include those with George Balenchine for more than forty years including on *Fancy Free*, Agnes de Mille, Robert Joffrey, Jerome Robbins, and Twyla Tharp. Some of his more notable performances include *Don Quixote*, *L'Enfant et les Sortiléges*, *Rodeo*, and *The Nutcracker*. But he is perhaps best remembered for his costume designs of Big Bird and Mr. Snuffleupagus on television's *Sesame Street*. He also played the character himself of Willy the Hot Dog Man on the show. His partner, Christopher Lyall, survives him.

ANNA MANAHAN, 84, Waterford, Ireland-born actress, died Mar. 8, 2009, in Waterford, Ireland, of multiple organ failure. Her Broadway credits include *Lovers* (Tony nomination) in 1968, before winning a Best Performance By a Supporting Actress in a Play Tony Award in 1998 for her role as Mag Folan in *The Beauty Queen of Leenane*. She had originated the role at the Druid Theatre in Galway in 1996, before continuing with it to London, Sydney, and New York. She was a familiar presence on Irish television, with roles including those on *Fair City*, *The Riordans*, *The Irish RM*, and *Leave It To Mrs. O'Brien*. Her film roles include those in *Hear My Song* and *A Man of No Importance*. She appeared in stage plays by some of Ireland's most celebrated writers, including J.M. Synge, Oscar Wilde, Sean O'Casey, George Bernard Shaw, and Brian Friel. Beginning her training at the Gaiety Theatre in Dublin, Ireland, she later became a member of an acting company that included Hilton Edwards and Micheal MacLiammoir. She was awarded a Freedom of the City Award in 2002 from Waterford, Ireland, and was grand marshal for the city's St. Patrick's Day Parade in 2005. Her brothers, Val and Joe, survive her.

JOHN McGLINN (John Alexander McGlinn III), 55, Bryn Mawr, Pennsylvania-born restorer of musicals, died Feb. 14, 2009, in Manhattan, New York, of an apparent heart attack. In addition to supervising a complete overhaul of *Show Boat*, a partly restored version of which appeared on Broadway in 1983, he produced an album of George Gershwin songs with the soprano Kiri Te Kanawa, and a companion album of Gershwin overtures, performed in period style. He also supervised the recording of restored versions of *Anything Goes*, *No, No, Nanette*, *Annie Get Your Gun*, *Brigadoon*, and *Kiss Me, Kate*, in addition to restoring the original orchestrations and previously lost dance music to the 1954 Broadway version of *Peter Pan*. He is survived by his brother, Evan, of Mineral Point, Wisconsin; and two sisters, Lee Lawrence, of Reno, Nevada, and Lorin Reiter, of Denver, Colorado.

RICHARD MONETTE (Richard Jean Monette), 64, Montreal, Canada-born actor/ artistic director/producer, died Sept. 9, 2008, in London, Ontario, of pulmonary artery blockage. His affiliation with the Stratford Shakespeare Festival, widely considered the most important theatre in Canada, began in 1965, and the period during which he served as artistic director became the theatre's most successful time artistically and fiscally. Beginning his career as an actor, he appeared on Broadway in *Soldiers*, followed by *Hosanna*. He appeared in the original London cast of *Oh! Calcutta!* Before becoming a permanent fixture at the festival, including roles such as Caliban, Hamlet, Romeo, Edmund, Prince Hal, Henry V, Antonio, and Mercutio. Under Monette's leadership, the Stratford Shakespeare Festival started an acting conservatory, established a program for developing new plays, built a fourth stage, and created an endowment of fifty million for the festival coffers. The Stratford Shakespeare Festival published his memoir, *This Rough Magic: The Making of an Artistic Director*, in 2008. His brother, Mark, survives him.

JONATHAN MOORE, 85, New Orleans, Louisiana-born actor, died. His Broadway credits include *Dylan*, *1776*, *Checking Out*, *Amadeus*, and *Wild Honey*. He made his Off-Broadway debut in *After the Angels*, followed by *Berkeley Square*, *The Biko Inquest*, and *Sullivan and Gilbert*.

TAD MOSEL (George Ault Mosel Jr.), 86, New Rochelle, New York-born actor/ writer, died Aug. 24, 2008, in Concord, New Hampshire, of cancer. A Pulitzer Prize winner and Tony nominee for his play *All The Way Home*, based on James Agee's novel *A Death in the Family*, the play ran 333 performances from 1960-1961. His screenplays include *Dear Heart* starring Glenn Ford and Geraldine Page and *Up the Down Staircase* starring Sandy Dennis. His numerous television credits include *The Adams Chronicles* (Emmy nomination), *That's Where the Town's Going*, *Goodyear Television Playhouse*, *Studio One*, and *Playhouse 90*. He was a veteran of the U.S. Army in W.W. II, and co-wrote the 1978 biography *Leading Lady: The World and Theatre of Katherine Cornell*.

DANIEL NAGRIN, 91, New York, New York-born dancer/choreographer/teacher, died Dec. 29, 2008, in Tempe, Arizona. His Broadway credits as a dancer include *Tis of Thee*, *Of V We Sing*, *Up in Central Park*, *Show Boat*, *Lend an Ear*, *Annie Get Your Gun*, *Touch and Go*, *Bless You All*, and *Plain and Fancy* (1955 Donaldson

GERALD "GERRY" SCHOENFELD

RON SILVER

DR. BARBARA ANN TEER

Award), and as assistant to Helen Tamaris, *By the Beautiful Sea*. Making his professional debut with the company of Anna Sokolow, followed by work with Sue Ramos, he also worked with Helen Tamaris, who became his first wife. His best-known solos include *Strange Hero* and *Spanish Dance*, From 1960-1965, he and Tamaris ran the Tamiris-Nagrin Dance Company. He formed his own company, Workgroup, in 1970. A prolific teacher who toured throughout the world at colleges and festivals, he was a professor of dance from 1982 to 1992 at the Arizona State University. He received a 1993 fellowship awarded to master teachers and mentors by the National Endowment of the Arts. In France he was honored in 2007 with a yearlong festival called Dances of Resistance. A fifteen-hour retrospective of his work can be seen at the New York Public Library for the Performing Arts at Lincoln Center, and he authored four books on the medium. His wife, Phyllis Steele Nagrin, survives him.

GLADYS NEDERLANDER (Gladys Rackmil), 83, producer, died Jul. 21, 2008. A two-time Tony nominee as a producer for *The Goodbye Girl* in 1993 and the 1980 production of *West Side Story*, her other Broadway credits include *Legend*, *Caesar and Cleopatra*, *Platinum*, *The Madwoman of Central Park West*, *West Side Story*, *Perfectly Frank*, *Death and the Maiden*, *Solitary Confinement*, and *The Goodbye Girl*. The wife of Robert Nederlander and one of the family of Nederlanders that constitute one of the most influential theatrical producing family owners/producing organizations of the twentieth century, she was also an associate producer of the film *Death and the Maiden*. She was also nominated for a Cable ACE Award for producing A&E's *The Parallax Garden*, among other television credits that include *A Case of Libel*, *Intimate Strangers*, *Sahara*, *When Will I Be Loved*, and *Orpheus Descending*.

PAUL NEWMAN (Paul Leonard Newman), 83, Cleveland, Ohio-born actor, died Sept. 26, 2008, at his home in Westport, Connecticut, following a long bout with lung cancer. A Theatre World Award winner for his Broadway debut in *Picnic* in 1953, his other Broadway credits include *The Desperate Hours*, *Sweet Bird of Youth*, *Baby Want a Kiss*, and *Our Town* (Tony nomination). He became one of the most enduring and admired of all film stars, earning nine Oscar nominations for his work, winning the Academy Award for Best Actor in 1986 for his performance in *The Color of Money*. Following his 1954 film debut in *The Silver Chalice*, he appeared in *Somebody Up There Likes Me*, *The Rack*, *Until They Sail*, *The Helen Morgan Story*, *The Left-Handed Gun*, *The Long Hot Summer*, *Cat on a Hot Tin Roof* (his first Oscar nomination), *Rally 'Round the Flag Boys!*, *The Young Philadelphians*, *From the Terrace*, *Exodus*, *The Hustler* (Oscar nomination), *Paris Blues*, *Sweet Bird of Youth* (repeating his stage role), *Adventures of a Young Man*, *Hud* (Oscar nomination), *A New Kind of Love*, *The Prize*, *What a Way to Go!*, *The Outrage*, *Lady L*, *Harper*, *Torn Curtain*, *Hombre*, *Cool Hand Luke* (Oscar nomination), *The Secret War of Harry Frigg*, *Winning*, *Butch Cassidy and the Sundance Kid*, *King: A Filmed Record ... Montgomery to Memphis*, *WUSA* (also

coproducer), *Sometimes a Great Notion* (which he also directed and coexecutive produced), *Pocket Money*, *The Life and Times of Judge Roy Bean*, *The Mackintosh Man*, *The Sting*, *The Towering Inferno*, *The Drowning Pool*, *Buffalo Bill and the Indians*, *Silent Movie*, *Slap Shot*, *Quintet*, *When Time Ran Out ...*, *Fort Apache–The Bronx*, *Absence of Malice*, *The Verdict*, *Harry and Son* (which he also directed, produced, and wrote), *Hello Actors Studio*, *Fat Man and Little Boy*, *Blaze*, *Mr. & Mrs. Bridge*, *The Hudsucker Proxy*, *Nobody's Fool* (Oscar nomination), *Twilight*, *Message in a Bottle*, *Where the Money Is*, *Road to Perdition* (Oscar nomination), *Cars* (voice), and *The Price of Sugar* (narrator). He also directed-produced *Rachel, Rachel* (earning an Oscar nomination for producer), *The Effect of Gamma Rays on Man-in-the-Moon Marigolds*, and *The Glass Menagerie* (1987). On television he was awarded an Emmy for his performance in *Empire Falls*, which he also executive produced. He received a special Academy Award in 1986, honoring his career, and a Jean Hersholt Humanitarian Award in 1994, for his many charitable contributions, including the Scott Newman Center devoted to anti-drug education, and several Hole in the Wall Gang camps, designed for children with life-threatening diseases. He was also the founder of Newman's Own food products. His wife of fifty years, actress and frequent costar Joanne Woodward; two daughters from his first marriage; his three daughters with Woodward; two grandchildren; and his brother, survive him.

TOM O'HORGAN, 84, Chicago, Illinois-born director, died Jan. 13, 2009, in Venice, Florida, of natural causes, following a battle with Alzheimer's disease. A pioneer of experimental theatre in the 1960s performing at such early Off-Off-Broadway venues as Caffé Cino, Judson Memorial Church, and LaMaMa, E.T.C., he gained wide recognition by taking over the direction of the groundbreaking *Hair* when the show moved from Off-Broadway at The Public Theater for its historic run. His Broadway credits include *Hair* (Tony nominee, and 1977 revival), *Lenny* (1971 Drama Desk Award), *Jesus Christ Superstar* (and 1977 revival; all of the preceding four were running simultaneously in 1971, in their original productions), *Inner City*, *Dude*, *The Leaf People*, *I Won't Dance*, *The Three Musketeers*, and *Senator Joe* (never officially opened). His Off-Broadway credits include *To the Water Tower*, *When the Owl Screams*, *The Wrecking Ball*, *6 From La Mama*, *Tom Paine* (1968 Drama Desk Vernon Rice Award), *Futz!* (Drama Desk Award), *Birdbath*, and *Masked Man*. In 1968 he was named theatrical director of the year by *Newsweek* magazine.

THARON MUSSER (Tharon Myrene Musser), 84, Roanoke, Virginia-born theatrical lighting designer, died Apr. 19, 2009, in Newtown, Connecticut. She had been suffering from Alzheimer's disease. One of the most prolific, influential, and innovative lighting designers in theatre history, she collaborated with some of the most legendary theatrical artists of the twentieth century, including Stephen Sondheim, Jerry Herman, John Kander and Fred Ebb, and Michael Bennett. She was a three-time Tony Award winner for her work on *Follies*, *A Chorus Line*, and

Dreamgirls. Her other Broadway credits include *Long Day's Journey Into Night, Li'l Abner, Shinbone Alley, Monique, Makropoulos Secret, The Chairs and The Lesson, The Infernal Machine, The Entertainer, The Firstborn, The Shadow of a Gunman, J.B., The Rivalry, The Beaux Strategem, Once Upon a Mattress, The Great God Brown* (and 1972 revival), *Only in America, Five Finger Exercise, Peer Gynt, The Long Dream, The Tumbler, The Garden of Sweets, Giants, Sons of Giants, Calculated Risk, Nowhere to Go But Up, Andorra, Mother Courage and Her Children, Here's Love, Marathon '33, Any Wednesday, The Seagull, The Crucible, Golden Boy, Alfie!, Kelly, All in Good Time, Flora The Red Menace, Minor Miracle, Malcolm, The Great Indoors, The Lion in Winter, Mame, A Delicate Balance, Breakfast at Tiffany's, Hallelujah, Baby!, The Imaginary Invalid, A Touch of the Poet, Tonight at 8:30, The Birthday Party, After the Rain, The Promise, Everything in the Garden, Lovers, Maggie Flynn, The Fig Leaves Are Falling, A Way of Life, The Gingham Dog, Blood Red Roses, Applause* (Tony nomination), *The Boy Friend, The Trial of the Catonsville Nine, On the Town, The Prisoner of Second Avenue, Night Watch, The Creation of the World and Other Business, Don Juan, The Sunshine Boys, A Little Night Music* (Tony nominee), *Sondheim: A Musical Tribute, The Good Doctor* (Tony nomination), *Candide, Scapino, Mack & Mabel, God's Favorite, Good News, The Wiz, Same Time, Next Year, Me and Bessie, Pacific Overtures* (Tony nomination), *1600 Pennsylvania Avenue, California Suite, The Act* (Tony nomination), *Chapter Two, Tribute, Ballroom* (Tony nomination), *They're Playing Out Song* (Tony nomination), *Whose Life Is It Anyway?* (and 1980 revival), *The 1940's Radio Hour, Romantic Comedy, Last Licks, Children of a Lesser God* (Tony nomination), *I Ought to Be in Pictures, The Roast, 42nd Street* (Tony nomination), *Fools, The Moony Shapiro Songbook, Dreamgirls, Special Occasions, Merlin, Brighton Beach Memoirs, Private Lives, The Real Thing* (Tony nomination), *Open Admissions, Biloxi Blues, The Odd Couple, Jerry's Girls, Broadway Bound, A Month of Sundays, Teddy & Alice, Rumors, Welcome to the Club, Artist Descending a Staircase* (Tony nomination), *Lost in Yonkers, The Secret Garden* (Tony nomination), *Jake's Women, The Goodbye Girl, Laughter on the 23rd Floor, Uncle Vanya, The Lonesome West* and *A Chorus Line* (2006 revival). Bringing the new technology to Broadway of a computerized lighting design in 1975 with *A Chorus Line,* she forever changed the way theatre lighting worked. And leading a fight within the United Scenic Artists union, she helped to establish theatre design as a separate field. Prior, scenic designers had handled sets, costumes, and lights. Her work extended also to dance, Off-Broadway, repertory theatre in Dallas, Miami, Boston, England, Europe, and South America. Her early work included that at the José Limon Dance Company. In addition, she worked with the American Shakespeare Festival in Stratford, Connecticut, for thirteen seasons. She is survived by her life partner, lighting designer Marilyn Rennagel. On Tuesday, Apr. 21, Broadway theatres dimmed their lights at 8:00p.m. for one minute in her honor.

GENE PERSSON (Eugene Clair Persson), 74, Long Beach, California-born producer, died June 6, 2008, in Manhattan, New York, of a heart attack. A former child actor in Hollywood, he appeared as a young man as a child of Ma and Pa Kettle, and in the television shows *The Walter Winchell File* and *Dragnet.* Off-Broadway he produced *You're a Good Man Charlie* Brown in 1967, which opened at Theatre 80 and ran almost four years, and subsequently had two Broadway revivals (the latter winning a Drama Desk Award for best revival of a musical and a Tony nomination for the same), and was twice adapted for television. Other Off-Broadway credits include *Journey to the Day, Rooms, Big Man/Duet For Three, Album, The Freak,* and *Snoopy.* His other Broadway credits include *The Trial of Lee Harvey Oswald, The Sudden & Accidental Re-Education of Horse Johnson, The Watering Place,* and *Rainbow Jones. The Toilet* and *The Slave,* two racially charged plays by LeRoi Jones, who later became known as Amiri Baraka. In Los Angeles, California, he produced the controversial *Dutchman,* which he also made into a film. His first wife was actress Shirley Knight. His wife, Ruby Persson; three children, Lukas Persson, Markus Persson, and Kaitlin Hopkins, all of New York, New York, survive him.

HAROLD PINTER, 78, Hackney, London, England-born writer, who became one of the most influential playwrights of the twentieth century with such cryptic works as *The Caretaker* and *The Birthday Party,* died on Dec. 24, 2008, following

a five-year battle with cancer of the esophagus. His Broadway credits include *The Caretaker* (1961 Tony nomination and 1986 and 2003 revivals), *The Homecoming* (1967 Tony Award for Best Play, and 1991 and 2007 revivals), *The Birthday Party, The Man in the Glass Booth* (Tony nomination), *Old Times* (Tony nomination), *No Man's Land* (Tony nomination), *Betrayal* (1980 & 2000), and directing credits including *The Man in the Glass Booth, The Innocents,* and *Butley,* and *Otherwise Engaged,* both by writer Simon Gray. His Off-Broadway credits as a writer include *The Pinter Plays, Play/The Lover, The Caretaker, The New Pinter Plays, Tea Party/ The Basement, The Local Stigmatic, Landscape/Silence, The Homecoming, The Caretaker, Old Times, Other Places, The Birthday Party, Mountain Language, Moonlight, Ashes to Ashes,* and *Celebration and The Room* (Lucille Lortel Award nomination). His other plays include *A Kind of Alaska, Moonlight, Ashes to Ashes,* and *Celebration.* His screenplays include *The Servant, The Pumpkin Eater, The Quilter Memorandum, Accident, The Go-Between, The Last Tycoon, The French Lieutenant's Woman, Betrayal* (adapted from his play), *Turtle Diary, The Handmaid's Tale, The Comfort of Strangers,* and *Sleuth* (2007). As an actor he could be seen in such movies as *Mansfield Park, The Tailor of Panama,* and *Mojo.* Awarded the Nobel Prize in Literature in 2005, he was the recipient of a 1999 Lucille Lortel Award for outstanding lifetime achievement. His novels include *The Dwarfs.* His first wife was actress Vivien Merchant, a fellow company member in the Hampstead Theatre Club in London, England. He is survived by his second wife, Lady Antonia Fraser, son, Daniel, stepchildren, Benjamin, Damian, Orlando, Rebecca, Flora, and Natasha.

MARY PRINTZ (Mary Selina Horn), 85, Grosse Point, Michigan-born and Hampton, Virginia-reared telephone answering service maven, and the inspiration for the 1956 musical *Bells Are Ringing,* died Feb. 21, 2009, in Tappan, New York, of congestive heart failure, a result of post-polio syndrome. Answering the number at her Belles Celebrity Answering Service, Plaza 2-2232, for many years, Ms. Printz's clients include Candice Bergen, Noel Coward, Shirley MacLaine, Robert Redford, Burt Reynolds, Spencer Tracy, Tennessee Williams, and Adolph Green, one of the creators of *Bells Are Ringing,* who was inspired by her to create the musical. At its height, the service employed nearly two-dozen employees to handle nearly 600 clients. Ms. Printz operated the service until her death. The original production starred Judy Holliday, who won a Tony Award, and ran for three years. It was revived in 2001 with Faith Prince. Her husband; two sons, William Horn Printz and Joe Printz; and a granddaughter survive her.

ROBERT PROSKY (Robert Joseph Prosky), 77, Philadelphia, Pennsylvania-born screen, stage, and television character actor died on Dec. 8, 2008, in Washington, DC, of complications from a heart procedure. His Broadway credits include *Moonchildren, A View from the Bridge, Glengarry Glen Ross* (Drama Desk Award for outstanding ensemble work, Tony nomination), *A Walk in the Woods* (Tony nomination), *Twelve Angry Men,* and *Democracy.* His Off-Broadway credits include *Pale Horse, Pale Rider, Camping with Henry and Tom,* and *The Golem.* He was also the veteran of hundreds of stage and screen roles, honing his crafts in many roles at Arena Stage in Washington, DC. He was seen in such movies as *Hanky Panky, The Lords of Discipline, Christine, The Natural, Outrageous Fortune, Broadcast News, Things Change, Green Card, Rudy, Mrs. Doubtfire, Dead Man Walking,* and *Dudley Do-Right.* On television he was best known for his role as Sgt. Jablonski on *Hill Street Blues.* His wife, the former Ida Hove, and sons; John, Andrew, and Stefan; and three grandchildren survive him.

NATASHA RICHARDSON, 45, London, England-born actress, died Mar. 18, 2009, of a brain hemorrhage, or epidural hematoma, following a fall on a beginner's ski slope at the Mont Tremblant resort in Quebec, north of Montreal, Canada. A 1993 Theatre World Award winner for her performance in the title role of *Anna Christie,* in which she starred with her future husband, Liam Neeson, she also received a 1998 Tony Award for Best Actress in a Musical for her role as Sally Bowles in the revival of *Cabaret.* Her numerous film roles include those in *Gothic, A Month in the Country, Patty Hearst, Fat Man and Little Boy, The Handmaid's Tale, The Comfort of Strangers, The Favour, The Watch and the Very Big Fish, Past Midnight, Widow's Peak, Nell, The Parent Trap, Blow Dry, Chelsea Walls, Waking Up in Reno, Maid in Manhattan, Asylum, The White Countess, Evening,* and *Wild Child.* Her television credits include *In the Secret State, Ghosts, Suddenly, Last*

Summer, and *Zelda*. Her husband, actor Liam Neeson; two sons, Micheal, and Daniel; mother, actress Vanessa Redgrave; aunt, actress Lynn Redgrave; uncle, Corin Redgrave; sister, actress Joely Richardson; and cousin, actress Jemma Redgrave, survive her. On Thursday, Mar. 19, 2009, Broadway theatres dimmed their lights in her honor, at 8:00p.m. for one minute, and theatres the West End of London followed suit on Friday, Mar. 20, 2009.

DOROTHY SARNOFF, 94, Brooklyn, New York-born actress/singer, died Dec. 20, 2008, in Manhattan, New York. She began her career as an opera singer, singing with the NBC Symphony Orchestra and the St. Louis Municipal Orchestra, before performing principle roles with the Philadelphia opera company. She then joined the New Opera Company in New York, and her eventual Broadway credits include *Rosalinda*, *La Tosca*, *Faust*, *Magdalena*, *The King and I*, and *My Darlin' Aida*. She was perhaps best known for Speech Dynamics, her image consulting company, with clients including Jimmy Carter, Menachem Begin, Bob Dole, and Danielle Steel. Her *Speech Can Change Your Life*, in 1970, became a best seller, followed by her other publications *Make the Most of Your Best* and *Never be Nervous Again*.

GERALD "GERRY" SCHOENFELD, 84, New York, New York-born theatre producer, died Nov. 25, 2008, in Manhattan, New York, of a heart attack. Responsible for bringing *A Chorus Line*, *Cats*, and *The Phantom of the Opera*, among scores of other productions to the stage, he was also an integral part of the revitalization effort of 42nd Street. He shared the role of head of the Shubert Organization with Bernard Jacobs for twenty-four years, Mr. Schoenfeld, whose title was president, ran the largest theater-owning enterprise in the United States, one that dates to the turn of the twentieth century. The Shubert Organization, which owns and operates seventeen Broadway theaters, also includes one Off-Broadway theatre, as well as the Shubert Theatre in Boston, Massachusetts, and the Forrest Theatre in Philadelphia, Pennsylvania. It manages the National Theater in Washington, DC. The Shubert Foundation controls the Shubert Organization, and Mr. Schoenfeld was primarily responsible for maintaining the theatres, while Mr. Jacobs was primarily responsible for booking the shows in the theatres, and Mr. Schoenfeld assumed some of Mr. Jacobs' duties following his death in 1996. In short, Gerald Schoenfeld was widely considered to have been the person most responsible for the revitalization of midtown New York City in the 1970s and 1980s, with an influence that will last much beyond. His Broadway credits as a producer proper include *Liza*, *The Night That Made America Famous*, *Sherlock Holmes*, *Truckload*, *Very Good Eddie*, *Godspell*, *Sly Fox*, *Your Arms Too Short to Box With God*, *The Gin Game* (1977), *The Merchant*, *Dancin'*, *Elliot Feld Ballet*, *The Mighty Gents*, *Ain't Misbehavin'* (and 1988 revival), *Zoot Suit*, *King Richard III*, *Devour the Snow*, *Last Licks*, *Children of a Lesser God*, *Division Street*, *Amadeus*, *Piaf*, *Rose*, *The Life and Adventures of Nicholas Nickleby*, *Dreamgirls*, *'Master Harold'…and the boys*, *Cats*, *Good*, *Angels Fall*, *Marcel Marceau on Broadway*, *'night Mother*, *All's Well That Ends Well*, *The Real Thing*, *Glengarry Glen Ross*, *The Human Comedy*, *A Moon for the Misbegotten*, *Sunday in the Park with George*, *The Wiz*, *Whoopi Goldberg*, *Harrigan 'n' Hart*, *Joe Egg*, *As Is*, *The Odd Couple*, *Song and Dance*, *Big Deal*, *Social Security*, *The Petition*, *Long Day's Journey Into Night*, *The Life and Adventures of Nicholas Nickleby*, *Stepping Out*, *Safe Sex*, *Barbara Cook: A Concert for the Theatre*, *Pygmalion*, *Les Liaisons Dangereuses*, *Roza*, *Chess*, *Jerome Robbins' Broadway*, *Lend Me a Tenor*, *The Heidi Chronicles*, *The Secret Rapture*, *A Few Good Men*, *Tru*, *City of Angels*, *The Grapes of Wrath*, *Lettice and Lovage*, *Once on This Island*, *The Most Happy Fella*, *A Streetcar Named Desire* (1992), *Someone Who'll Watch Over Me*, *Wonderful Tennessee*, *Joseph and the Amazing Technicolor Dreamcoat* (1993), *An Inspector Calls*, *Passion*, *Indiscretions*, *Skylight*, *The Judas Kiss*, *The Blue Room*, *Closer*, *Amy's View*, *The Ride Down Mt. Morgan*, *Dirty Blonde*, *Amour*, *Spamalot*, *Children and Art*, *Three Days of Rain*, *Faith Healer*, *The Vertical Hour*, *The Year of Magical Thinking*, *Inherit the Wind* (2007), *Coram Boy*, *Deuce*, *Passing Strange*, *Thurgood*, and *Equus*. He played a small part in Woody Allen's film *Broadway Danny Rose*, in 1982. A veteran of the U.S. Army in W.W. II, he is survived by his wife of fifty-eight years, Pat; brother, Irving; daughter, Carrie Schoenfeld-Guglielmi; and two grandchildren. On Tuesday, Nov. 25, 2009, Broadway theatres dimmed their lights in his honor, at 8:00p.m. for one minute.

PAUL SILLS (Paul Silverberg), 80, Chicago, Illinois-born director/teacher/theatre founder, died June 2, 2008, in Baileys Harbor, Wisconsin, of complications of pneumonia. His early work was as co-founder of The Playwrights Theatre Club, where the company included Mike Nichols and Ed Asner. He next co-founded The Compass players with playwright and producer David Shepherd in 1955, and it became known for launching the careers of actors including Mike Nichols, Elaine May, and Barbara Harris. In 1959, he co-founded Second City, which is now the stuff of legend, having served as the training ground there for early talents such as Alan Arkin and Avery Schreiber, and would go on to boast John Belushi and Dan Aykroyd, among many others. He served in the position until the mid-1960s. He started the Story Theatre in 1968, which specialized in adaptations of folk tales and other literary material. His *Paul Sills' Story Theatre* was an early success at the Mark Taper Forum in Los Angeles, in 1970, went on to Broadway with a cast including Valerie Harper and Paul Sand, and won Sills a Drama Desk Award as outstanding director. In 1988, he co-founded the New Actors Workshop in Manhattan, New York, with Mike Nichols and George Morrison. A veteran of W.W. II, he is survived by his wife, Carol; children, David, Rachel, Polly, Aretha Amelia, and Neva; Brother, William; four grandchildren; and two great-grandchildren.

RON SILVER (Ronald Arthur Silver), 62, Manhattan, New York-born actor/activist, died Mar. 15, 2009, at his home in Manhattan, of esophageal cancer. A 1988 Tony Award winner as best actor for his role in *Speed-the-Plow*, his other Broadway credits include *Hurlyburly* and *Social Security*. His Off-Broadway credits include *Friends*, *Hunting Cockroaches*, and *And*. His numerous television credits include recurring roles on *Rhoda*, *Chicago Hope*, *The West Wing*, and *Veronica's Closet*, as well as television movies including *Kissinger and Nixon* (1995) and *When Billie Beat Bobby*. His numerous film credits include *Garbo Talks*, *Enemies: A Love Story*, *Reversal of Fortune*, *Blue Steel*, and *Ali*. As an activist he was co-founder of the Creative Coalition, a group that advocates for First Amendment rights, public education, and arts support, and served on the committees for the Council on Foreign Relations. He is survived by his son, Adam, of Los Angeles, California; daughter, Alexandra, of Manhattan; brother, Mitchell, of Newton, Massachusetts; brother, Keith, of Stamford, Connecticut; and parents, of Manhattan. On Mar. 18, 2009, Broadway theatres dimmed their lights in his honor, at 8:00p.m. for one minute.

LEE SOLTERS, 89, Brooklyn-born press agent, died May 18, 2009, in West Hollywood, California. At its peak, his firm employed forty people, and represented over 300 productions, including the original productions of *Guys and Dolls*, *Funny Girl*, *The King and I*, *My Fair Lady*, and *Camelot*. He represented clients including Barbra Streisand, Michael Jackson, Carol Channing, Yul Brynner, Cary Grant, Mae West, and Dolly Parton. He also handled musical acts, including The Eagles and Led Zeppelin. He is survived by his daughter, Susan Reynolds; son, Larry; two grandchildren; and a great-grandson.

ROY SOMLYO, 83, Detroit, Michigan-born theatre producer/general manager, died Jan. 27, 2009, in Manhattan, New York, of cancer. During a fifty year period, he brought more than 100 shows to London, tour, or on Broadway, where his credits include *Goodbye*, *My Fancy*, *Caesar and Cleopatra*, *The Devil's Disciple*, *Fanny*, *The Matchmaker*, *Patate*, *Cue for Passion*, *Epitaph for George Dillon*, *Triple Play*, *Gypsy*, *An Evening With Yves Montand* (1959 and 1961), *A Distant Bell*, *The Cool World*, *An Evening With Mike Nichols and Elaine May*, *Beyond the Fringe*, *The School for Scandal*, *An Evening with Maurice Chevalier*, *Lorenzo*, *Ages of Man*, *Karmon Israeli Dancers*, *Man and Boy*, *Rugatino*, *Hamlet*, *Comedy in Music Opus 2*, *Baker Street*, *Maurice Chevalier at 77*, *Ken Murray's Hollywood*, *The Devils*, *Ivanov*, *A Time for Singing*, *At the Drop of Another Hat*, *The Homecoming*, *Black Comedy/White Lies*, *Little Murders*, *The Unknown Soldier and His Wife*, *Marlene Dietrich* (1967 & 1968), *Halfway Up the Tree*, *Dear World*, *Home*, *Fun City*, *6 Rms Riv Vu*, *Good Evening*, *Ulysses in Nighttown*, *Who's Who in Hell*, *We Interrupt This Program*, *Comedians*, *Anna Christie*, *I Remember Mama*, *A Day in Hollywood/A Night in the Ukraine*, *84 Charing Cross Road*, *Edmund Kean*, *La Tragedie de Carmen*, *Kipling*, *Uptown…It's Hot!*, *Sherlock's Last Case*, *Checkmates*, and *Gypsy Passion*. He also was managing producer of the annual Tony Awards telecast for over ten years (from 1987-1998), in addition to producing the television programs *Night of 100 Stars* and *Your Money or Your Wife*. A four-time Emmy winner for outstanding variety, music, or comedy specials, he received three of them for his Tony Awards telecasts, and the fourth for *Night of 100 Stars*. Spending much of his career as general manager of associate producer for Alexander H. Cohen, he was also a veteran of W.W. II. He was awarded the 2007 Theater Hall of Fame Founders Award. His wife, the former Nancy Rifici; daughter, Lauren McGowan; son, David; two sisters, Caroline Miller and Emily Somlyo; and four grandchildren survive him.

MILAN STITT (Milan William Stitt), 68, Detroit, Michigan-born playwright, died Mar. 18, 2009, in Manhattan, New York, of liver cancer. Best known for his only Broadway play, *The Runner Stumbles*, he also was founder and director of play development program at Circle Repertory Theatre, mentoring future luminaries such as Albert Innaurato and David Mamet. He also served as director of Circle Rep from 19940-1996. Following his tenure at Circle Rep, he was professor of dramatic writing at Carnegie Mellon University, and had previously taught at Yale, Princeton, the University of Michigan, and New York University. His other works include the plays *Back in the Race*, and his television work included *Ephraim McDowell's Kentucky Ride*. *The Runner Stumbles* was made into a film starring Dick Van Dyke and Kathleen Quinlan. A sister survives him.

RONALD TAVEL, 72, Brooklyn, New York-born playwright, died Apr. 27, 2009, in Bangkok, Thailand, of a heart attack. A progenitor of avant-garde theatre, his early works include *Shower* and *The Life of Juanita Castro*, based on screenplays he had written for Andy Warhol films. He staged many one-act plays based on scripts for Warhol, including *The Life of Lady Godiva*, *Kitchenette*, and *Indira Gandhi's Daring Device*. He eventually wrote and appeared in over twenty Warhol films, including *Harlot*, *Screen Test No. 2*, *The Hunchback of Notre Dame*, and *The Chelsea Girls*. Other theatre works, totaling over forty-one, include *Gorilla Queen*. He was an Obie winner for *Boy on the Straight-Back Chair*, and *Bigfoot*. He is survived by his brother, Harvey Tavel.

DR. BARBARA ANN TEER, 71, East St. Louis, Illinois-born actress/teacher/theatre founder, died July 20, 2009, in Harlem, New York, of natural causes. Her Broadway credits include *Kwamina* and *Where's Daddy* before giving up her commercial career to help revitalize Harlem, primarily by founding the National Black Theatre there. Her Off-Broadway credits include *Raisin' Hell in the Son*, *Home Movies/Softly Consider the Nearness* (Vernon Rice Drama Desk Award), *Happy Ending/Day of Absence*, *Who's Got His Own*, *The Experiment*, and as a director, *Five on the Black Hand Side*. But as executive director of the National Black Theater, Ms. Teer traveled the globe, producing theatre in such countries as Guyana, Haiti, South Africa, and Trinidad. She also arranged for the purchase of the home of the National Black Theatre's home at 125th St. and 5th Ave. She was awarded honorary doctorates from the University of Rochester and Southern Illinois University. She additionally wrote and directed for a troupe that performed at Lincoln Center and on *Soul* on television. She is survived by her daughter, Sade Lythcott; and son, Michael Lythcott, both of Manhattan.

DALE WASSERMAN, 94, Rhinelander, Wisconsin-born writer, best known for writing the book of the classic musical *Man of La Mancha* (1966 Tony Award for best musical, with revivals in 1972, 1977, 1992, and 2002, and which he also adapted into a film), died Dec. 21, 2008, in Paradise Valley, Arizona, of congestive heart failure. A production stage manager and lighting designer for *The Azuma Kabuki Dancers and Musicians* on Broadway in 1963, his Broadway writing credits proper that followed include *Livin' the Life* and *One Flew Over the Cuckoo's Nest*. His other film credits are *The Vikings*, *Quick Before it Melts*, *Mister Buddwing*, and *A Walk with Love and Death*. He was a founding member and trustee of the Eugene O'Neill Theatre Center. He won a Writers Guild of America Award for *The Lincoln Murder Case* on television, among credits. His wife, Martha Nelly Garza, survives him.

JAMES WHITMORE, 87, White Plains, New York-born actor, died Feb. 6, 2009, in Malibu, California, of lung cancer. A 1948 Theatre World Award winner as well as a Tony winner for his role in a *Command Decision*, his other Broadway credits include *Winesburg, Ohio*, *Inquest*, *Will Rogers' USA*, *Bully*, and *Almost Eagle*. A veteran of the Actors Studio and the American Theatre Wing, he eventually taught an acting workshop after moving to Hollywood in the 1950s. He was best known for his one-man shows, including *Will Rogers' U.S.A.*, in which he toured for thirty years, *Give 'em Hell Harry!* as Harry Truman, and as Theodore Roosevelt in *Bully*. He received a best supporting actor Oscar nomination in 1949 for *Battleground*, and another in 1975 for best actor in the film version of *Give 'em Hell, Harry!* His other film credits include *The Asphalt Jungle*, *Them!*, *Kiss Me Kate*, *Battle Cry*, *Oklahoma!*, *Planet of the Apes*, *Tora! Tora! Tora!*, *The Serpent's Egg*, *Nuts*, *The Shawshank Redemption*, and *The Majestic*. His television credits include a long run as the commercial spokesperson for Miracle-Gro garden products (he was an avid flower and vegetable gardner), and notable appearances in *The Twilight Zone*, and *Bonanza*. He won a 2000 Emmy Award for a role on *The Practice*, and had another nomination for *Mister Sterling*. He starred in three television series: *The Law and Mr. Jones*, *My Friend Tony*, and *Temperatures Rising*. He was also a veteran of W.W. II. He was married to actress Audra Lindley from 1972-1979, and is survived by his wife, Noreen; sons, Steve, James Jr. and Dan; eight grandchildren; and five great-grandchildren.

SUSAN "SUE" WILLIS, 83, Seneca County, Ohio-born actress, died May 14, 2009, in New York, New York. Her Broadway credits include *Dylan*, *Cabaret*, *Oliver!*, *Gypsy*, *Follies*, and *Take Me Along*. Her Off-Broadway credits include *Children of the Sun* and *The Madwoman of Chaillot*. National tours include *Fiddler on the Roof*, *Mame*, *Picnic*, *Zorba*, and *The Merchant of Venice*. Her regional and summer stock credits include those at the Great Lakes Theatre Festival, the San Diego Shakespeare Festival, the Old Globe Theatre, and the Cleveland Playhouse. Her motion picture roles include those in *Mystic River*, *The Majestic*, *What About Bob?*, *She-Devil*, and *The Faculty*. Her television credits include those on *All My Children*, *Law & Order*, *Third Watch*, *Law & Order: SVU*, *Million Dollar Mysteries*, and *Sex in the City*. She had toured recently in a cabaret act with pianist Rod Derefinko entited *My First 50 Years in the Theatre*, and with the late Elizabeth Council, toured the nation with *Plays for Living*. She also worked extensively in Fire Island Pines theatre, and served as a council member of the Episcopal Actors Guild. She is survived by her cousin, Albert Allman, of Tiffin, New York.

ALLEN ZWERDLING, 86, Brooklyn, New York-born former founder and editor of *Back Stage*, died Jan. 12, 2009, at his home in Rosendale, New York, of natural causes. First an employee of *Show Business*, he then co-founded *Back Stage* with Ira Eaker, in 1960, which they owned until it was sold to *Billboard Publications* in 1986. He was briefly a producer of the American Players Theater in Zurich, Switzerland, and was also a director of the Kansas City Resident Theater, before beginning his career as an editor in 1948. Considered the industry standard in casting calls and other information for actors, the circulation of *Back Stage* grew to its current figure of over 30,000, plus another 20,000 online members. He was a veteran of Special Forces in W.W. II. He is survived by his two daughters, Sherry Zwerdling of Key West, Florida, and Jan Heyes of Topanga Canyon, California; son, Gary Zwerdling, of Rosendale; and a grandson.

Index

John Willis (Editor Emeritus) was editor in chief of both *Theatre World* and its companion series *Screen World* for forty-three years. *Theatre World* and *Screen World* are the oldest definitive pictorial and statistical records of each American theatrical and foreign and domestic film season, and are referenced daily by industry professionals, students, and historians worldwide.

Mr. Willis has also served as editor of *Dance World*, *Opera World*, and *A Pictorial History of the American Theatre 1860–1985*. Previously, he served as assistant to *Theatre World* founder Daniel Blum on *Great Stars of the American Stage*, *Great Stars of Film*, *A Pictorial History of the Talkies*, *A Pictorial History of Television*, and *A Pictorial Treasury of Opera in America*.

For over forty years he presided over the presentation of the annual Theatre World Awards, incorporated in 1997 as a 501 (c)(3) nonprofit organization. Begun in 1945 and presented by past winners, they are the oldest awards given to actors for a Broadway or Off-Broadway debut role.

On behalf of *Theatre World*, Mr. Willis received a 2001 Tony Honor for Excellence in the Theatre, the 2003 Broadway Theater Institute Lifetime Achievement Award, a 1994 Special Drama Desk Award, and in 1993, the first Outstanding Special Lucille Lortel Award. On behalf of *Screen World*, he received the prestigious 1998 National Board of Review Wiliam K. Everson Award for Film History. He has also received a Professional Excellence Award from his alma mater, Milligan College.

He has served on the nominating committees of the Tony Awards and the New York University Musical Hall of Fame, and has served on the national board of directors for the Clarence Brown Theatre at the University of Tennessee in Knoxville, TN, as well as the past board of directors of the National Board of Review. In addition, Mr. Willis is retired from the New York public school system.

In 1993, the auditorium in which he had performed as a high school student was renovated and christened the John Willis Performing Arts Center at Morristown-Hamblen High School East, in Morristown, TN. And in 2007, a classroom in the new Milligan College theatre complex was named in his honor.

Ben Hodges (Editor in Chief) served as an editorial assistant for seven years on the 2001 Special Tony Honor Award-winning *Theatre World*, becoming the associate editor to John Willis in 1998 and editor in chief in 2007. *Theatre World*–at sixty-five–is the most complete annual pictorial and statistical record of the American theatre, including Broadway, Off-Broadway, Off-Off-Broadway, and regional theatre productions, and is referenced daily by students, historians, and industry professionals worldwide.

Also an assistant for seven years to John Willis for the prestigious Theatre World Awards given for Broadway and Off-Broadway debut performances, Ben was elected to the Theatre World Awards board of directors in 2002 and served as executive producer for the annual ceremony from 2002-2007. In 2003 he was presented with a Special Theatre World Award in recognition of his ongoing stewardship of the event. He also served as executive producer for the 2005 LAMBDA Literary Foundation "Lammy" Awards, given for excellence in LGBT publishing.

The Commercial Theater Institute Guide to Producing Plays and Musicals, which Hodges co-edited with late Commercial Theater Institute director Frederic B. Vogel, was released by Applause Theatre and Cinema Books in 2007, and with contributions by twenty-eight Broadway producers, general managers, attorneys, and publicists, is in its second printing and has become the definitive resource in its field. It has also been adopted as a course book by North Carolina School for the Arts, among other colleges and universities.

Forbidden Acts, the first collected anthology of gay and lesbian plays from the span of the twentieth century, edited and with an introduction by Hodges, was published by Applause Theatre and Cinema Books in 2003 and became a finalist for the 2003 LAMBDA Literary Award for Drama, and is in its second printing. It has been adopted as a course book by New York University, Cornell University, Salisbury University, University of Las Vegas, and University of Louisville, among other colleges and universities.

His *Out Plays: Landmark Gay and Lesbian Plays from the Twentieth Century*, edited and with an introduction by Hodges, featuring a foreword by Harvey Fierstein and a new introduction to *The Boys in the Band* by Mart Crowley, was

released by Alyson Books in spring 2008. With *Out Plays*, Hodges becomes the most prolific single anthologist of published gay and lesbian American plays. His *The American Theatre Wing Presents The Play That Changed My Life: America's Foremost Playwrights on the Plays That Influenced Them*, with essays by scores of America's foremost American playwrights including David Auburn, Christopher Durang, Lynn Nottage, and John Patrick Shanley, is due from Applause Theatre and Cinema Books in fall 2009.

As an actor, director, and/or producer, Ben has appeared in New York with The Barrow Group Theater Company, Origin Theater Company, Daedalus Theater Company, Monday Morning Productions, the Strawberry One-Act Festival, Coyote Girls Productions, Jet Productions, New York Actors' Alliance, and Outcast Productions. Additionally, he has appeared in numerous productions presented by theatre companies that he founded, including the Tuesday Group and Visionary Works. On film, he can be seen in *Macbeth: The Comedy*.

In 2001, Ben became director of development and then served as executive director for Fat Chance Productions Inc. and the Ground Floor Theatre, a New York-based nonprofit theatre and film production company. *Prey for Rock and Roll* was developed by Fat Chance from their stage production (the first legit production to play CBGBs) into a critically acclaimed feature film starring Gina Gershon and *The Sopranos'* Emmy winner Drea de Matteo. *Prey for Rock and Roll* debuted at the Sundance Film Festival in 2003 and won Best Feature at the 2003 Santa Cruz Film Festival. Additionally, Fat Chance produced the American premiere of award-winning Irish playwright Enda Walsh's *Misterman* Off-Broadway, and a host of readings, workshops, and productions in their Ground Floor Theatre, their mission statement being to present new works by new artists.

In 2003, frustrated with the increasingly daunting economic prospects involved in producing theatre on a small scale in New York, Ben organized NOOBA, the New Off-Off Broadway Association, an advocacy group dedicated to representing the concerns of expressly Off-Off-Broadway producers in the public forum and in negotiations with other local professional arts organizations; their chief objective the reformation of the Actors' Equity Basic Showcase Code.

He also serves on the New York Innovative Theatre Awards Committee, selecting outstanding individuals for recognition Off-Off-Broadway, and as vice-president of Summer Stage New York, a professional summer theatre program in Fayetteville, New York, and as executive producer of the annual Fire Island Pines Literary Weekend.

In 2005 Ben founded and served for two years as executive director of The Learning Theatre Inc., a 501(c)(3) nonprofit organization incorporating theatre into the development and lives of learning disabled and autistic children. He currently serves on the board of directors.

In support of his projects and publications, Ben has appeared on nationwide radio on *The Joey Reynolds Show*, *The Michael Dresser Show*, *Stage and Screen with Mark Gordon*, and on television on New York 1 and *Philly Live* in Philadelphia, PA–the only live televised LGBT call-in show in the United States. Reviews and articles on Ben, his projects, or publications have appeared in *The New York Times*, *The New Yorker*, *GQ*, *Elle*, *Genre*, *Back Stage*, *Time Out New York*, *Playbill*, *Next*, *New York Blade*, *Library Journal*, *The Advocate*, *Chicago Free Press*, *Philadelphia Gay News*, *Houston Voice*, *Stage Directions*, *Between the Lines*, *The Flint Journal*, and *Citizen Tribune*, as well as the web sites CurtainUp.com and in Peter Filichia's Diary on Theatermania.com. He has made guest appearances in support of his publications at the Good Beans Café in Flint, Michigan, at the Common Language Bookstore in Ann Arbor, Michigan, at A Different Light in both Los Angeles and San Francisco, The Open Book in Sacramento, and at Giovanni's Room in Philadelphia, as well as at the DR2 Theatre D-2 Lounge in New York City.

He holds a BFA in Theatre Acting and Directing from Otterbein College in Westerville, Ohio, is an alumnus of the Commercial Theater Institute, and is a candidate for a 2013 Juris Doctor degree from Seton Hall University School of Law in Newark, New Jersey. He lives in New York City. For more information or to schedule speaking engagements, please visit benhodges.com, or e-mail benjaminhodges@gmail.com.

Carol Delawder Dawson (Associate Regional Editor) is a thirty-year veteran drama teacher in public and private schools in New Hampshire, Maine, and Tennessee. She is a graduate of The Ohio State University with a bachelor's degree in theatre education and a graduate of The University of Tennessee with a master's degree in theatre education. She is a Northwestern University Theater & Speech Fellow Award winner. She remains active in developing theatre curriculum for secondary schools in New England.

Scott Denny (Associate Editor) Scott Denny is and actor and singer who has worked professionally for over twenty years. Originally from Terre Haute, Indiana, he attended Western Kentucky University in Bowling Green, Kentucky and holds a degree in performing arts. His professional theatrical credits include Richard Henry Lee in the national tour of *1776*, Uncle Wes in the Las Vegas and national touring production of *Footloose*, and the assistant company manager and swing on the first national tour of Susan Stroman's production of *The Music Man*. Regionally he has appeared in *Evita, The Wizard of Oz*, and *The King and I* at Houston's Theatre Under the Stars, *The Mikado* starring Eric Idle at Houston Grand Opera, and in the regional premieres of *Silver Dollar* and *Paper Moon* at Stage One in Wichita, Kansas. His summer stock and dinner theatre credits include *Me and My Girl, Gypsy, She Loves Me, The Best Little Whorehouse in Texas*, among several others. In New York he has appeared Off-Off-Broadway in *Election Day The Musical, Like You Like It, Vanity Fair*, and in several readings and workshops. He screen credits include the independent films *Red Hook, Clear Blue Tuesday*, and the upcoming *Redefining Normal*. Scott served as assistant editor on *Theatre World* Volume 60, and has been an associate editor on Volumes 61-64. In the fall of 2006 Scott was nominated to the Board of Directors of the Theatre World Awards where he now serves as the Treasurer. He served as an associate producer for the 2006 Theatre World Awards, and as co-producer of the 2007, 2008, and 2009 Awards. Scott also works as a production assistant for the Macy's Thanksgiving Day Parade and Macy's Annual Events. Since 2003 Scott has also worked as an outside group sales manager specializing in incentive groups for Cruise Everything, a travel agency located in Fort Myers, Florida. He coordinated the entertainment and sales for three cruises with two of QVC's most known and loved personalities, the Quacker Factory host Jeanne Bice, and Jenniefer Kirk of Kirks Folly Jewelry.

Amanda Flynn (Assistant Editor) was an original member of the Los Angeles cast of *Wicked* as an understudy to Glinda. She was also a part of the Las Vegas cast of *Mamma Mia* where she understudied the role of Sophie. She has been seen regionally at the McCarter Theatre, Fulton Opera House, Bard Summerscape Festival, Carousel Dinner Theatre, and the Stage Door Theatre. She also appeared in a national print ad for Redbook Magazine, and was a top 25 contestant on the reality TV show *Legally Blonde: The Search for the Next Elle Woods*. She is a former teacher for *Dancin' USA*, a dance educational company based in Texas, and continues to teach workshops and master classes for students wanting to pursue a career in the performing arts. She studied vocal performance at Baylor University, and is a member of AEA and AFTRA. www.amandaflynn.com.

Shay Gines (Contributing Off-Off Broadway Editor) graduated from the Actors Training Program at the University of Utah. Since then she has done everything from spackling walls at the Pasadena Playhouse and running follow-spot for the Pioneer Theatre Company to serving as the Artist in Residence for Touchstone Theatre. She has performed in theatres of all sizes from thirty seats to 1,000 across the country, from Los Angeles, California, to New York, New York. She is an award-winning producer whose Off and Off-Off-Broadway shows include: *Home Again Home Again Jiggity Jig, What the F**k?!, Hamlet*, and *Muse of Fire*. She was a founding member and the producing director for Esperance Theatre Company, served for five years as an associate director for Emerging Artists Theatre Company, and is a founding director for the New York Innovative Theatre Foundation.

Robert Rokicki (Assistant Editor) is a composer, lyricist, and performer. He is a graduate of the University of Michigan (BFA Musical Theatre, BA English) and a member of Dramatists Guild, Actor's Equity, and an alumus of the Tony Award-winning BMI workshop. His musical, *LOVE, NY* (co-written with Mike Ruby), received the 2009 American Harmony award and was presented at New World Stages (New York), Curtain Call (Connecticut), and Oklahoma University. His work has been featured at such places as Lincoln Center, the Knitting Factory, and Upright LA Cabaret. Other credits: *Martha & Me (*sold-out run at New York Fringe Festival); won the Young Playwrights Competition at Denver Center for the Performing Arts. Broadway performers have sung his songs throughout New York and benefits across the country. As an actor: *Evita 25th Annicersary Tour*, directed by Hal Prince & Larry Fuller, *South Pacific* concert at Carnegie Hall, many Off-Broadway and regional credits (Carbonell Award Nomination). www.robertrokicki.com.

Nicole Estvanik Taylor (Contributing Regional Editor) is the managing editor of *American Theatre* magazine, published by Theatre Communications Group, and her byline appears frequently in its pages. She has also written about the arts for *TheatreForum* and the Creative Capital Foundation. She was born into a family whose home phone number doubled as the box office for a community theatre troupe, which accounts for the role of theatre in her life; her taste for magazine work came later, during a stint as an *Atlantic Monthly* intern and a post-college editorial gig at her alma mater's quarterly publication, *Boston College Magazine*. She is a graduate of the Columbia Publishing Course and has also worked as a freelance copy editor on several books.